7e

Marketing Essentials

CARL McDANIEL
Department of Marketing
University of Texas at Arlington

CHARLES W. LAMB
M.J. Neeley School of Business
Texas Christian University

JOSEPH F. HAIR, JR.
Department of Marketing
Kennesaw State University

Australia • Brazil • Japan • Korea • Mexico • Singapore • Spain • United Kingdom • United States

Marketing Essentials, 7e

McDaniel, Lamb, Hair

Vice President of Editorial, Business: Jack W. Calhoun

Editor-in-Chief: Melissa S. Acuña

Acquisitions Editor: Michael Roche

Developmental Editor: Dana Freeman, B-Books Ltd.

Editorial Assistant: Kayti Purkiss

Marketing Manager: Keri L. Witman

Sr. Content Project Manager: Tamborah Moore

Print Buyer: Arethea Thomas

Media Editor: John Rich

Sr. Art Director: Stacy Shirley

Sr. Marketing Communications Manager: Jim Overly

Production and Composition Service: MPS Limited, a Macmillan Company

Internal Designer: Joe Devine, Red Hangar Design

Cover Design: Patti Hudepohl

Photo Credits:
B/W Image: Getty Images/Hisham Ibrahim
Cover Image: iStock Images/billyfoto

Sr. Rights Acquisitions Specialist/Text: Mardell Glinski Schultz

Text Permissions Researcher: Sue C. Howard

Sr. Rights Acquisitions Specialist/Images: Deanna Ettinger

Photo Researcher: Terri Miller/E-Visual Communications, Inc.

Library of Congress Control Number: 2010935812

International Edition:

ISBN-13: 978-1-111-22192-8

ISBN-10: 1-111-22192-8

Cengage Learning International Offices

Asia
www.cengageasia.com
tel: (65) 6410 1200

Australia/New Zealand
www.cengage.com.au
tel: (61) 3 9685 4111

Brazil
www.cengage.com.br
tel: (55) 11 3665 9900

India
www.cengage.co.in
tel: (91) 11 4364 1111

Latin America
www.cengage.com.mx
tel: (52) 55 1500 6000

UK/Europe/Middle East/Africa
www.cengage.co.uk
tel: (44) 0 1264 332 424

Represented in Canada by Nelson Education, Ltd.
tel: (416) 752 9100/(800) 668 0671
www.nelson.com

Cengage Learning is a leading provider of customized learning solutions with office locations around the globe, including Singapore, the United Kingdom, Australia, Mexico, Brazil, and Japan. Locate your local office at: **cengage.com/global.**

For product information: **www.cengage.com/international**
Visit your local office: **www.cengage.com/global**
Visit our corporate website: **www.cengage.com**

Printed in Canada
1 2 3 4 5 6 7 14 13 12 11 10

BRIEF CONTENTS

CONTENTS

PART 1
The World of Marketing 1

PART 2
Analyzing Marketing Opportunities 187

6 CONSUMER DECISION MAKING 188

7 BUSINESS MARKETING 230

PART 3
Product and Distribution Decisions 331

4

PREFACE

ABOUT THIS EDITION

Your students experience marketing through billboards, television commercials, and even in the cereal aisle at the grocery store. *Marketing Essentials, 7e,* with its engaging presentation of concepts will give students the ability to recognize how much marketing principles play a role in their day-to-day lives. With coverage of current marketing practices and exciting new features McDaniel, Lamb, and Hair's *Marketing Essentials 7e* will have your students saying, "Now that's marketing."

SO WHAT'S NEW?

If you are already familiar with *Marketing Essentials*, you may be asking, "So what's new?" The answer is quite a bit.

New Content

In addition to the dozens of new examples in each chapter, we have added new topical content and revised and updated existing material throughout the book. A series of end-of-chapter Marketing Plan exercises—and the Marketing Plan Worksheets on their companion Web site—are designed to encourage students to apply the marketing principles and strategies they've just learned. At the completion of each exercise, students are one step closer to building a complete strategic marketing plan for a company of their choosing.

New Student Engagement

Regular study and practice throughout a course leads to better outcomes for both students and professors. Marketing classes have historically relied on intermittent and fewer assessments (a few case studies, mid-term and final exams, or a semester-long project or simulation) as the major method for assessing students. Because of this, students often focused their energies on courses that required frequent homework and sometimes relied on cramming for exams, or were left wondering if they were progressing appropriately in the course. Likewise, instructors have had fewer points in the course to ensure that students understand the material. To help in this regard, we have developed a series of interactive exercises to keep students engaged and prepare them for class discussion. These homework exercises use the most appropriate media (video or simulation for instance) and every question is automatically graded with immediate feedback, which provides review guidelines that link back to the text so students can come to class better prepared. Instructors can view dashboard reports to measure student performance and progress in the course. Please contact your Cengage representative for more information.

PART 1 We have retained the proven format of Chapter 1 (An Overview of Marketing) and the Career Appendix that introduces students to various aspects of a career in marketing, like types of marketing jobs, pay scales, preparation for interviewing, and what to expect the first year on the job. Chapter 2 (Strategic Planning for Competitive Advantage) reintegrates the BCG portfolio matrix and culminates with a Marketing Plan Appendix on E-motion software, a real company based in Massachusetts. The thorough—and real—marketing plan helps students better understand the level of detail needed in plotting out a marketing strategy. Based on feedback, we've divided our old chapter on social responsibility and the marketing environment into two new chapters: Chapter 3 (Ethics and Social Responsibility) and Chapter 4 (The Marketing Environment). Chapter 3 covers the concept of civil society and the role ethics play in keeping it functioning smoothly. The chapter explores in depth the concepts of morality and business ethics, ethical decision making, and the cultural differences that affect the understanding and application of ethics. Chapter 3 concludes with a detailed discussion of corporate social responsibility and cause-related marketing. Chapter 4 offers detailed updates on demographic groups and has new material related to global innovation as a technological factor in the marketing environment. Chapter 5 (Developing a Global Vision) has been greatly revised to reflect constant changes in the global marketplace. There is new material on job outsourcing and the growing protectionist trend of blocking foreign investment. Chapter 5 also covers doing business in India and China, and a new section updates the status of the European Union and how the U.S. interacts with the EU as a trading partner.

PART 2 Chapter 6 (Consumer Decision Making) has been streamlined to keep the material focused. New examples keep the discussion relevant for today. Chapter 7 (Business Marketing) has new statistics on business marketing on the Internet and discussion of trends related to reintermediation. In Chapter 8 (Segmenting and Targeting Markets) we've thoroughly updated all the sections on age, gender, and ethnic segmentation with the latest data and information on trends in behavior. The section on perceptual mapping has been updated with new graphics. Chapter 9 (Decision Support Systems and Marketing Research) has a new expanded example to illustrate the research process. The sections on mystery shopping and ethnographic research have been updated and expanded. The section on blogging has been reframed to include the larger category of consumer-generated media and how marketers make use of such media in their research efforts. A new section examines how companies are using behavioral targeting combined with marketing research to increase advertising response and sales.

PART 3 Chapter 10 (Product Concepts) has been refreshed with new examples, and Chapter 11 (Developing and Managing Products) has a completely updated section on the importance of innovation and revised material on the marketing implications of the diffusion process. Chapter 12 (Marketing Channels and Supply Chain Management) covers the logistics function in the supply chain and identifies the ways companies assess the performance of the their supply chains. Chapter 13 (Retailing) covers new trends like pop-up shops and store-in-a-store that are becoming more prevalent and includes new information on the impact of location decisions on stores. The chapter also includes updated retailing statistics.

PART 4 Chapter 14 (Marketing Communications and Advertising) has been thoroughly revised and reorganized to reflect the format followed in Chapter 2 on marketing strategy. The communication process is described in detail, a quick introduction to the promotional mix follows before a more thorough discussion of promotional goals, AIDA, and integrated marketing communication is given. The chapter also includes information on the factors affecting the promotional mix as well as new examples throughout to keep the chapter content relevant for today's students. Examples throughout the chapter help Marketing students stay abreast of a wide variety of alternative media, including social media marketing. Current statistics on the impact of advertising and Internet advertising keep the chapter up to date. Chapter 16 (Pricing Concepts) includes a revised section on pricing power. The chapter also includes new sections on targeting technology used in conjunction with yield management systems and on guaranteed price matching. Revised legislation on resale price maintenance and predatory bidding is covered, illustrating the dynamic impact of the legal environment on pricing decisions. This chapter also covers the latest cases in price fixing.

New Annotated Marketing Plan

Our new marketing plan appendix after Chapter 2 includes annotations that tie each part of the plan to the material throughout the book Students will see the correlation between the chapters in the book and the elements of a professional marketing plan for a real company.

New "Anatomy of" Feature

For several chapters in the Seventh Edition of *Marketing Essentials*, we have created a unique graphic that illustrates a particular chapter concept. Each "Anatomy of" is set on a full page and uses photography to show how the elements of a concept connect. The Seventh Edition includes anatomies of a multinational company, buying decision, packaging design, product life cycle, store layout, integrated marketing campaign, and more. Anatomies help students visualize the connection between marketing concepts and their real-world application.

New "By the Numbers" Feature

Each chapter concludes with a quick numeric recap of some interesting statistics from the chapter. By the Numbers keeps marketing alive for students and acts as an engaging and visual conclusion to the chapter.

CLASSIC FEATURES HAVE BEEN UPDATED AND ENHANCED

Marketing and You Surveys

Today's students demand their courses be relevant, and to help you make that connection, we have added a short survey to each chapter opener. Adapted from material in the *Marketing Scales Handbook*, these short polls are an engaging way to introduce students to a new concept. Even though this is their first marketing course, Marketing & You polls show them that they already have experience with marketing. Scoring instruc-

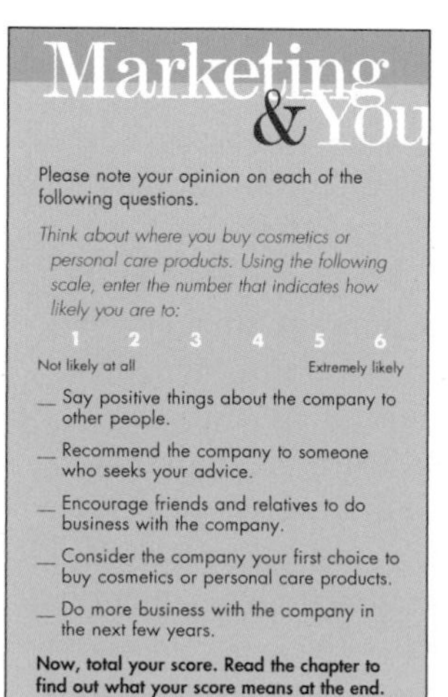

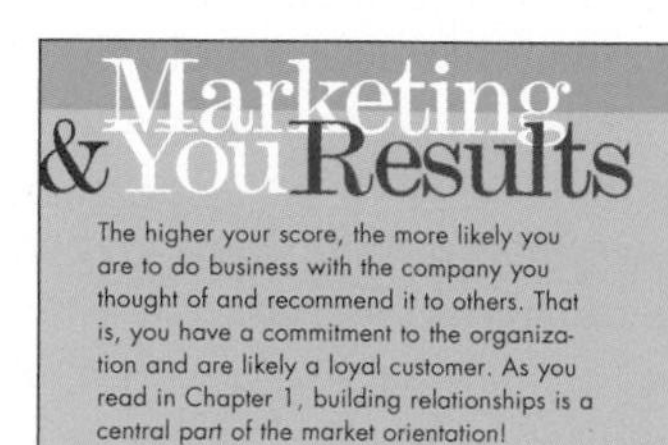

AVAILABILITY OF RESOURCES MAY DIFFER BY REGION. Check with your local Cengage Learning representative for details.

tions are given, and general results provided. Marketing & You is not meant to be used in a scientific context; it is just an interesting and fun way to introduce the chapter material.

Visual Learning Outcome Summaries

Through our years of teaching, we know that not all students learn the material the same way. Some can read books and understand the concepts just from their verbal presentation. Other students need to rewrite the material in their own words in order to understand it completely. Still others learn best from diagrams and exhibits. Student focus groups have confirmed this experience in a more quantitative way.

For this reason, we have retained our visual **Review Learning Outcomes**, which are designed to give students a picture of the content, to help them recall the material. For example, Learning Outcome 4 in Chapter 5 discusses the various ways of entering the global marketing place. The detailed discussion, of everything from exporting to direct investment, ends with the following review:

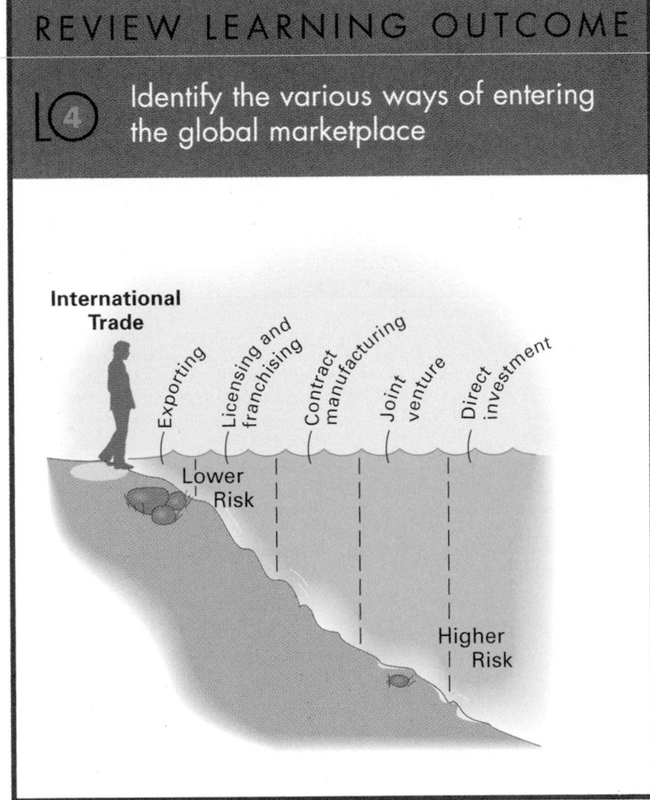

These reviews are not meant to repeat every nuance of the chapter content. Rather, they are meant to provide visual cues that prompt the student to recall the salient points in the chapter.

Global Perspectives Boxes

Today most businesses compete not only locally and nationally, but globally as well. Companies that may have never given a thought to exporting now face competition abroad. Thinking globally should be a part of every manager's tactical and strategic planning. Accordingly, we address this topic in detail early in Chapter 5. Global marketing is fully integrated throughout the book, cases, and videos, as well.

Our **Global Perspectives** boxes provide expanded global examples of the marketing issues facing companies on several continents. Each box concludes with thought-provoking questions carefully prepared to stimulate class discussion. You'll read about how U.S. ethical practices compare around the globe, how McDonald's is moving into Russia, how luxury retailers are becoming global giants, and more.

GLOBAL Perspectives GLOBAL

The Challenges of Global Marketing Research

Karl Feld, Research Manager at D3 Systems Incorporated, a Vienna, Virginia, marketing research firm, explains how global research can create unique problems not found in the United States. The story is told in his words.

Imagine you're driving a vehicle of unknown manufacture with dials you can't read down a muddy or dusty dirt track with no name to find a house with no number to make sure your contractor's employee interviewed the right respondent in a language you don't speak. You've been doing this for days, maybe even weeks. There's no running water, no electricity, no telephones, no mail service, and possibly no food other than what you've brought with you. Welcome to collecting research data from most of the world's people.

Questionnaire design in multicultural, multilingual research must use both the proper language and cultural context to elicit the desired responses. Context applies both to the language in the survey and the way it is administered, which is often more important than the questionnaire design itself. People in some cultures better relate to conversational interviewing styles than fixed questionnaire order. Some cultures require sensitive questions to be in a different order than others. In some places, people will only talk in particular settings. In research that I conducted in Bosnia-Herzegovina, for example, questionnaires had to be administered in a neutral location not affiliated with any local ethnic group.

Similarly, research in Arabic, Muslim countries which involve women generally must be conducted under the watchful eyes of the responsible male family leader, as social custom requires women not meet with outsiders without male presence. In Russia, it used to be extremely difficult to get face-to-face interviews inside people's homes. Public places were preferred. In Japan, it is only in private places like the home that face-to-face interviews will capture meaningful data.

In my experience in yesterday's Russia and Moldova, and in today's China, respondents asked questions of substance often will refuse to provide meaningful answers without approval from another authority. This is especially the case when interviewing professionals. Appropriate lag time, or preapproval, needs to be factored into timelines and interviewing environment to allow for this phenomenon.

I was also involved in a research study completed in South Africa. The study's sample frame was to draw from all adults in South Africa. Given that many South African villages lack building addresses, roads, and convenient grid layouts, sampling had to be designed using satellite maps to select dwelling units using an interval formula. A similar problem exists in Mexico, where streets are unidentified and houses unnumbered, compounded by walls and servants who keep strangers out. In Saudi Arabia, there is no officially recognized census of population and there are no elections and therefore no voter registration records or maps of population centers.[21]

Do you think that conducting research in developing countries is worth the effort? Do you think that doing marketing research in Western Europe is the same as the United States?

Ethics in Marketing Boxes

In this edition we continue our emphasis on ethics. The **Ethics in Marketing** boxes, complete with questions focusing on ethical decision making, have all been revised. This feature offers provocative examples of how ethics comes into play in many marketing decisions. Is it ethical to advertise prescription drugs direct to consumers? Is it right for companies to use teens as buzz agents for their products? Are organic claims about products misleading? Are multiple distribution channels unethical? Students will consider these and many other hotly debated, ethical questions.

ETHICS in Marketing ETHICS

Willbros Petroleum's Bribery Problem in Nigeria

As national economies become increasingly globalized, Western businesspeople are struggling with how to deal with local business corruption. Bribes, kickbacks, and under-the-table payments to both local channel partners and government officials are considered to be just "part of the cost of doing business" in many emerging nations. Though American law clearly makes such practices illegal, U.S. firms wanting to do business in places such as China, Russia, and Eastern Europe are increasingly finding they must develop tactics to address corrupt practices if they expect to succeed when developing these marketplaces.

Though many different types of corrupt activities are taking place, bribery is particularly problematic for American businesses doing business in foreign markets. For example, though Houston-based company Willbros had been working in Nigeria for nearly a half century, it was recently caught up in a bribery scandal that resulted project. The Willbros top management team was later blackmailed for an additional $1.5 million in payments in order to maintain the contract.

Willbros acknowledged as part of a plea for reduced punishment that members of its leadership team owned portions of some of Willbros' Nigerian customers and suppliers, and may have received illegal payments related to deals made with these companies and government officials. The results were predictable: The company was prosecuted by the U.S. Securities and Exchange Commission, and its leaders scrambled to cooperate with investigators in an attempt to avoid jail time. Yet, while Willbros was made an example of what can happen to U.S. businesses that participate in shady deals overseas, the problem of bribery remains one that continues to vex American companies wanting to expand their operations to new markets.

When attempting to increase business by entering

Customer Experience Boxes

At its very best, marketing is about creating an excellent experience for the consumer. In each chapter of this edition we have a new feature box that showcases a very current example of the **Customer Experience** in action in light of that chapter's topic. For example, has the customer experience at Starbucks—an integral part of that company's brand and a huge factor in customer loyalty—been watered down in recent years? How does Zappos' great customer service help reduce cognitive dissonance? Did the recent presidential race tap into modern marketing principles—that is, did Obama's campaign managers use ground-level tactics on everything from segmentation and database management to analytics, social networking, and online communities to garner the best customer experience?

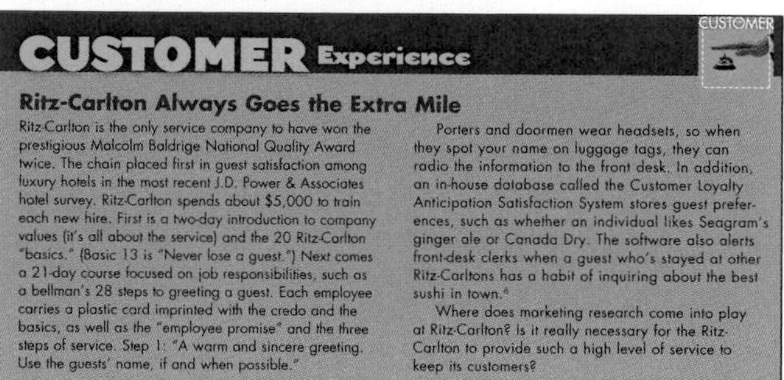
CUSTOMER Experience

Ritz-Carlton Always Goes the Extra Mile

Ritz-Carlton is the only service company to have won the prestigious Malcolm Baldrige National Quality Award twice. The chain placed first in guest satisfaction among luxury hotels in the most recent J.D. Power & Associates hotel survey. Ritz-Carlton spends about $5,000 to train each new hire. First is a two-day introduction to company values (it's all about the service) and the 20 Ritz-Carlton "basics." (Basic 13 is "Never lose a guest.") Next comes a 21-day course focused on job responsibilities, such as a bellman's 28 steps to greeting a guest. Each employee carries a plastic card imprinted with the credo and the basics, as well as the "employee promise" and the three steps of service. Step 1: "A warm and sincere greeting. Use the guests' name, if and when possible."

Porters and doormen wear headsets, so when they spot your name on luggage tags, they can radio the information to the front desk. In addition, an in-house database called the Customer Loyalty Anticipation Satisfaction System stores guest preferences, such as whether an individual likes Seagram's ginger ale or Canada Dry. The software also alerts front-desk clerks when a guest who's stayed at other Ritz-Carltons has a habit of inquiring about the best sushi in town.[4]

Where does marketing research come into play at Ritz-Carlton? Is it really necessary for the Ritz-Carlton to provide such a high level of service to keep its customers?

Review and Applications

To help students focus their study time, we continue to group end-of-chapter discussions and writing questions with their related learning outcome summary. Questions are numbered according to the learning outcome to which they correspond. For example, the summary point for Chapter 8, Learning Outcome 4 has three related questions. They are numbered 4.1, 4.2, and 4.3. This organization helps students identify questions pertinent to the learning outcome they are studying, allowing each chapter to function as a series of content blocks that can be read over multiple study sessions.

LO 4

Describe the bases commonly used to segment consumer markets. Five bases are commonly used for segmenting consumer markets. Geographic segmentation is based on region, size, density, and climate characteristics. Demographic segmentation is based on age, gender, income level, ethnicity, and family life-cycle characteristics. Psychographic segmentation includes personality, motives, and lifestyle characteristics. Benefits sought is a type of segmentation that identifies customers according to the benefits they seek in a product. Finally, usage segmentation divides a market by the amount of product purchased or consumed.

4.1 Choose magazine ads for five different consumer products. For each ad, write a description of what you think the demographic characteristics of the targeted market are.

4.2 Investigate how Delta Air Lines (**www.delta.com**) uses its Web site to cater to its market segments.

4.3 Is it possible to identify a single market for two distinctly different products? For example, how substantial is the market composed of consumers who use Apple *and* who drive Volkswagens? Can you think of other product combinations that would interest a single market? (Do not use products that are complementary, like a bike and a bike helmet. Think of products, like the iPod and the car, that are very different.) Complete the following sentences and describe the market for each set of products you pair together.

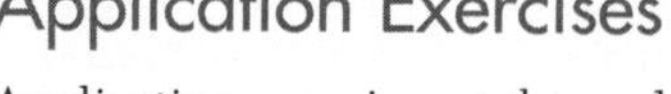

Application Exercises

Application exercises at the end of each chapter give students the opportunity to work with marketing concepts in various real-world contexts. We incorporate activities (rather than questions) to help students appreciate the width and depth of the marketing industry. These exercises come from instructors around the country who have contributed their teaching ideas to our unique supplement, **Great Ideas in Teaching Marketing**, since the First Edition. Each exercise selected was a winner in the "Best of the Great Ideas in Teaching Marketing," as voted by a panel of 35 faculty judges. You can be sure that these applications will be successful whether used as classroom activities or team project assignments.

Some examples are researching the complete supply chain for a specified product; creating an advertising campaign for a product, using the rules from the Hasbro game Taboo; role playing a televised interview after a marketing crisis; and much more.

EXERCISES

APPLICATION EXERCISE

As you now know from reading the chapter, an important part of the strategy-making process involves scanning the environment for changes that affect your marketing efforts. This exercise is designed to introduce you to the business press and to help you make the connection between the concepts you learn in the classroom and real-world marketing activities.

Activities

1. Find a current article of substance in the business press (*The Wall Street Journal, The Financial Times, Fortune, BusinessWeek, Inc.*, etc.) that discusses topics you have covered in this course. Although this is only Chapter 2, you will be surprised by the amount of terminology you have already learned. If you are having trouble finding an article, read through the table of contents at the beginning of the book to familiarize yourself with the names of concepts that will be presented later in the course. Read your article carefully, making notes about relevant content.
2. Write a one-paragraph summary of the key points in your article; then, write a list of the terms or concepts critical to understanding the article. Provide definitions of those terms. If you are unfamiliar with a term or concept that is central to the article, do some research in your textbook or see your professor during office hours. Relate these key points to the concepts in your text by citing page numbers.
3. Explain the environments that are relevant to the situation presented in the article. (Chapter 4 contains a full list of environmental factors.)

Ethics Exercise

The business press has reported on numerous scandals and trials in recent years. Although some might say that these occurrences are the work of a few bad apples spoiling the bunch, it is clear that ethical decision making plays a very important role in a company's success and prosperity. An **Ethics Exercise** appears at the end of every chapter. A brief scenario presents students with a situation in which the right thing to do may or may not be crystal clear. Use these exercises to show students the limitations to a code of ethics and to reinforce the importance of not simply

AVAILABILITY OF RESOURCES MAY DIFFER BY REGION. Check with your local Cengage Learning representative for details.

consulting existing rules of conduct, but also of developing an ethical personality.

ETHICS EXERCISE

Jane Barksdale has designed a line of clothing targeted toward Hispanic Americans. The items are sold only by catalog and on the Internet. She thinks that she can increase sales by claiming in ads that the firm is owned by a Hispanic American and all the employees are Hispanic Americans. She is not Hispanic American nor are most of the employees. She needs a high level of sales to pay her bank loan and remain in business.

Questions

1. Should Jane claim that she is Hispanic American? Explain your response.
2. Does the Federal Trade Commission address this issue? Go to **www.ftc.gov** and search for guidelines for small business advertising or e-commerce. What does Jane risk in making false claims in her ads?

Case Studies

One of the most powerful illustrations of how marketing concepts operate in the real world is the case study. Twelve chapters have entrepreneurship cases, highlighting the challenges facing entrepreneurs in the 21st century. These cases focus on a wide variety of companies and products. Your students will find these cases an exciting and challenging aspect of each chapter.

Company Clips

The Seventh Edition retains our unique set of videos on companies your students and you will recognize, as well as the related summaries and discussion questions at the end of each chapter. Company Clips segments average 8 minutes in length, which is enough time to cover core marketing issues facing Method, *ReadyMade* magazine, Sephora, Vans, Kodak, and Acid + All. Segments are rich enough to allow you to teach through the video, integrating lecture and video to create a richer learning experience. Tips on how to do this are included in the Instructor Manual with Video Guide.

OUR PEDAGOGY IS DESIGNED WITH YOUR STUDENTS IN MIND

All of our content is anchored by the cornerstone of our text, our fully **Integrated Learning System (ILS)**. The text and all major supplements are organized around the learning outcomes that appear at the beginning of each chapter, so *Marketing Essentials* is both easy to teach from and to learn from.

Just like the content in the textbook, material in the Instructor Manual, Test Bank, and PowerPoint presentation is all clearly organized by learning outcome number. In addition, we consider multiple learning styles in the organization of our text pedagogy.

Our Text Pedagogy Excites and Reinforces Learning

Pedagogical features are meant to reinforce learning, but that doesn't mean that they have to be boring. We have created teaching tools within the text itself that will excite student interest as well as teach. Not one of our features is casually included: Each has been designed and written to meet a specific learning need, level, or style.

- Terms: Key terms appear in boldface in the text, with definitions in the margins, making it easy for students to check their understanding of key definitions. A complete, alphabetical list of key terms appears at the end of each chapter as a study checklist, with page citations for easy reference.
- Review and Applications: The end of each chapter contains a section titled Review and Applications, a summary that distills the main points of the chapter. Chapter summaries are organized around the learning outcomes so that students can quickly check their understanding of chapter concepts. Discussion questions and activities are under the learning outcome to which they pertain.
- 

Writing Questions: To help students improve their writing skills, we have included writing exercises in the review section at the end of each chapter. These exercises are marked with the icon shown here. The writing questions are designed to be brief, so that students can accomplish writing assignments in a short time and instructors' grading time is minimized.
- 

Team Activities: The ability to work collaboratively is a key to success in today's business world. End-of-chapter team activities, identified by the icon shown here, give students opportunities to learn to work together by engaging in consensus building and problem solving.
- 

Online Activities: Understanding how to use the Internet for professional (and academic) purposes is critical in today's business environment. End-of-chapter activities accompanied by this icon give the students the opportunity to hone their skills in this area.
- Application Exercise: These activities are based on winning teaching ideas from the "Best of the Great Ideas in Teaching Marketing" contest held

in conjunction with the publication of the Eighth Edition of *Marketing*. Developed by professors across the country, these exercises allow students to explore the principles of marketing in greater detail through engaging and enjoyable activities.

- Ethics Exercise: Short ethical dilemmas help students practice doing the right thing. Questions following each scenario prompt students to make an ethical decision and explain the rationale behind it.
- Case Studies: All chapters contain a case study with questions that help students work through problems facing real small businesses today.
- Company Clips: All chapters contain a summary of the Company Clip video with related viewing and discussion questions.

All components of our comprehensive support package have been developed to help you prepare lectures and tests as quickly and easily as possible. We provide a wealth of information and activities beyond the text to supplement your lectures, as well as teaching aids in a variety of formats to fit your own teaching style.

WE INTEGRATE TECHNOLOGY IN A MEANINGFUL WAY

From the beginning, we have integrated new technologies into our Integrated Learning System in a meaningful way. The Seventh Edition continues this tradition by adding new and exciting content to our technology materials. We have also enhanced and refined popular media supplements to bring concepts alive in the classroom.

We Offer a Companion Web Site

McDaniel, Lamb, and Hair's Web site at **www.cengage.com/international** contains the key supplements that support the textbook: Instructor's Manual, Test Bank, and the PowerPoint presentation without embedded video. For students, the companion Web site offers crossword puzzles of key terms, interactive quizzes, and career exercises with electronic resources to help them investigate careers in the various marketing fields.

INNOVATIVE AND VALUABLE INSTRUCTOR SUPPLEMENTS

Video Package

Available on DVD and online in the Coursemate, WebTutor, and CengageNOW web-based platforms, the video package to accompany *Marketing Essentials, 7e,* continues to showcase the nuts and bolts of marketing at modern companies. The rich Company Clip videos will help reinforce what your students have learned by showing people who are doing marketing every day—and not according to thematic units.

New to this edition is an additional series of video cases that feature companies with inventive marketing solutions. Each video is embedded with assessment questions and simulation exercises that will challenge your students's comprehension of key concepts.

A Value-Added Instructor Manual Like No Other

Our Instructor's Manual is the core of our **Integrated Learning System**. For the Seventh Edition of *Marketing Essentials*, we have made our popular Instructor's Manual even more valuable for new and experienced instructors alike. Here is a list of the features that will reduce class preparation time:

- Suggested syllabi for 12- and 16-week terms.
- A pedagogy grid for each chapter briefly laying out (1) all the options the professor has in the chapter, and (2) the key points addressed by the features in each chapter. The features included on the grid are the boxed features, Application Exercise, Ethics Exercise, Case Study, and Company Clip.
- Three suggested lesson plans for each chapter: a lecture lesson plan, a small-group-work lesson plan, and a video lesson plan.

We have retained the proven features like the chapter outline, lists of support material, additional class activities, and solutions for all Review and Applications, and Case Studies in the book. There are also teaching tips for setting up each of the Application Exercises. Our manual is truly "one-stop shopping" for instructors teaching any size marketing course.

Certified Test Bank and Windows Testing Software

The Test Bank of the Seventh Edition has been reviewed by a panel of marketing faculty across the country who helped identify questions that may cause problems in their implementation. Faculty reviewers have helped us cull any troublesome questions. You can be sure that, no matter which questions you select for quizzes, tests, and exams, they are of the best quality. The Test Bank is organized around the learning outcomes to help you prepare on a class-by-class basis, and all questions are tagged with relevant AACSB standards to help you monitor trends in student performance necessary for accreditation. The Test Bank is available in Windows

AVAILABILITY OF RESOURCES MAY DIFFER BY REGION. Check with your local Cengage Learning representative for details.

software formats (ExamView testing software) and on the Instructor's companion Web site at www.cengage.com/international.

With ExamView, you can choose to prepare tests that cover all learning outcomes or that emphasize only those you feel are most important. This updated Test Bank is one of the most comprehensive on the market, with over 3,500 true/false, multiple-choice, scenario, and essay questions. Our testing database, combined with the ease of ExamView, takes the pain out of exam preparation.

WebTutor™ Tool Box

Preloaded with content and available via a free access code when packaged with this text, WebTutor™ ToolBox pairs a range of supplemental content with sophisticated course management functionality. You can assign materials (including online quizzes) and have the results flow automatically to your grade book. WebTutor™ ToolBox is ready to use as soon as you log on—or you can customize its preloaded content by uploading images and other resources, adding Web links, or creating your own practice materials. Students only have access to student resources on the Web site, www.cengage.com/international. Instructors can enter an access code for password-protected Instructor Resources.

Other Outstanding Supplements

- **Handbook for New Instructors: Getting Started with Great Ideas:** This helpful supplement was specifically designed for instructors preparing to teach their first course in principles of marketing. We have bolstered our helpful hints on everything from developing a course outline to grading, with winning general teachings from our "Best of the Great Ideas in Teaching Marketing" contest. To give you a complete resource for teaching ideas, we have included all of the winning entries, nearly one hundred in all, at the end of the Handbook in the Instructor Manual. You'll find great teaching ideas for every chapter, plus a wealth of general tips. If you're new, let professors from around the country help you get started teaching principles of marketing!
- **Great Ideas in Teaching Marketing:** We have begun collecting Great Ideas on our instructor's resource page on the McDaniel, Lamb, and Hair Web site. In this way, we can accept submissions year-round. Great Ideas in Teaching Marketing will still be published with each new edition of *Marketing* as part of the **Handbook for New Instructors**. You can also review all current great ideas by chapter at **www.cengage.com/international.**

INNOVATIVE AND VALUABLE STUDENT SUPPLEMENTS

Marketing Essentials, 7e, provides an excellent vehicle for learning the fundamentals. For students to gain a true understanding of marketing, however, it's best if they can apply the principles they are learning in the classroom. And it's best if they have study aids that address their particular learning style. Our student supplements meet the needs of a variety of learning styles, from visual to auditory, from hands-on to abstract conceptualization.

CourseMate

Interested in a simple way to complement your text and course content with study and practice materials? Cengage Learning's Marketing CourseMate brings course concepts to life with interactive learning, study, and exam preparation tools that support the printed textbook. Watch student comprehension soar as your class works with the printed textbook and the textbook-specific Web site.

Marketing CourseMate goes beyond the book to deliver what you need: it includes an interactive eBook as well as interactive teaching and learning tools, such as quizzes, flash cards, homework videos cases, simulations, and more. Engagement Tracker monitors student engagement in the course.

CengageNOW (for WebCT®, and Blackboard®)

Ensure that your students have the understanding of Marketing procedures and concepts they need with CengageNOW. This integrated, online course management and learning system combines the best of current technology to save time in planning and managing your course and assignments. With CengageNOW, you can reinforce comprehension with customized student learning paths and efficiently test and automatically grade assignments.

WebTutor ™ (for WebCT® and Blackboard®)

Online learning is growing at a rapid pace. Whether you are looking to offer courses at a distance or in a Web-enhanced classroom, South-Western, a part of Cengage Learning, offers you a solution with WebTutor. WebTutor provides instructors with text-specific content that interacts with the two leading systems of higher education course management: WebCT and Blackboard.

WebTutor is a turnkey solution for instructors who want to begin using technology like Blackboard or WebCT but do not have Web-ready content available or do not want to be burdened with developing their own content. By incorporating WebTutor into your course plan, everyone in your class becomes a front-row student.

So much more than just an online study guide, WebTutor offers unmatched depth of content and rich communication tools, such as practice quizzes, concept reviews, animated figures, discussion forums, video clips, and more. WebTutor's chat and email software makes it easy to set up virtual office hours, which encourages a collaborative learning environment and facilitates communication between you and your students.

Business & Company Resource Center (BCRC)

Available as an optional resource, BCRC puts a complete business library at your students's fingertips. BCRC is a premier online business research tool that allows students to seamlessly search thousands of periodicals, journals, references, financial information sources, market share reports, company histories, and much more. View a guided tour of the Business & Company Resource Center at **gale .com/BusinessRC**.

Marketing Essentials, 7th Edition Web Site

Our text's Web site (**www.cengage.com/international**) is filled with useful Instructor tools and key resources in electronic format: Test Bank, PowerPoint collections, Instructor's Manual, and more.

MEET THE AUTHORS

Carl McDaniel

Carl McDaniel is a professor of marketing from the University of Texas–Arlington, where he currently holds courses for the executive MBA program on campus and in China. He was the chairman of the marketing department at UTA for 32 years. McDaniel's career spanned more than than 40 years during which he the recipient of several awards for outstanding teaching. McDaniel has also been a district sales manager for Southwestern Bell Telephone Company and served as a board member of the North Texas Higher Education Authority, a billion-dollar financial institution.

In addition to *Marketing*, McDaniel has written and coauthored over 50 textbooks in marketing and business. McDaniel's research has appeared in such publications as the *Journal of Marketing, Journal of Business Research, Journal of the Academy of Marketing Science*, and *California Management Review*.

McDaniel is a member of the American Marketing Association, the Academy of Marketing Science, and the Society for Marketing Advances. In addition to his academic experience, McDaniel has business experience as the co-owner of a marketing research firm. Recently, McDaniel served as senior consultant to the International Trade Çentre (ITC), Geneva, Switzerland. The ITC's mission is to help developing nations increase their exports. He has a bachelor's degree from the University of Arkansas and his master's degree and doctorate from Arizona State University.

Charles W. Lamb

Charles W. Lamb is the M.J. Neeley Professor of Marketing, M.J. Neeley School of Business, Texas Christian University. He served as chair of the department of marketing from 1982 to 1988 and again from 1997 to 2003. He is currently chair of the Department of Information Systems and Supply Chain Management and is a former president of the Academy of Marketing Science and the Southwestern Marketing Association.

Lamb has authored and coauthored more than a dozen books and anthologies on marketing topics and over 150 articles that have appeared in academic journals and conference proceedings.

In 1997, he was awarded the prestigious Chancellor's Award for Distinguished Research and Creative Activity at TCU. This is the highest honor that the university bestows on its faculty. Other key honors he has received include the M.J. Neeley School of Business Research Award and selection as a Distinguished Fellow of the Academy of Marketing Science and a Fellow of the Southwestern Marketing Association.

Lamb earned an associate degree from Sinclair Community College, a bachelor's degree from Miami University, an MBA from Wright State University, and a doctorate from Kent State University. He previously served as assistant and associate professor of marketing at Texas A&M University.

Joseph F. Hair

Joseph Hair is Professor of Marketing at Kennesaw State University. He previously held the Alvin C. Copeland Endowed Chair of Franchising and was Director, Entrepreneurship Institute, Louisiana State University. Hair also held the Phil B. Hardin Chair of Marketing at the University of Mississippi. He has taught graduate and undergraduate marketing and marketing research courses.

Hair has authored 40 books, monographs, and cases, and over 70 articles in scholarly journals. He has also participated on many university committees and has chaired numerous departmental task forces. He serves on the editorial review boards of several journals.

He is a member of the American Marketing Association, Academy of Marketing Science, Southern Marketing Association, and Southwestern Marketing Association. He was the 2004 recipient of the Academy of Marketing Science Excellence in Teaching Award and recognized in 2007 as Innovative Marketer of the Year by the Marketing Management Association.

AVAILABILITY OF RESOURCES MAY DIFFER BY REGION. Check with your local Cengage Learning representative for details.

Hair holds a bachelor's degree in economics, a master's degree in marketing, and a doctorate in marketing, all from the University of Florida. He also serves as a marketing consultant to businesses in a variety of industries, ranging from food and retail, to financial services, health care, electronics, and the U.S. Departments of Agriculture and Interior.

ACKNOWLEDGMENTS

This book could not have been written and published without the generous expert assistance of many people. First, we wish to thank Julie Baker and Stacy Landreth Grau, Texas Christian University, and Chad Autry, Oklahoma City University, for their contributions to several chapters. We must also thank Julia Knispel and David Ferrell for contributing all of the new Case Studies.

We also wish to thank each of the following persons for their work on the best supplement package that is available today. Our gratitude goes out to Dr. Laurie A. Babin, University of Louisiana at Monroe, as well as Thomas and Betty Pritchett of Kennesaw State University for revising our comprehensive Test Bank and for writing the quizzes that appear in other parts of the package; Dr. Amit J. Shah of Frostburg State University, Maryland for updating the instructor manual and Powerpoint slides; Eric Brengle for designing the fantastic PowerPoint templates; and Deborah Baker for executing the revision beautifully.

Our deepest gratitude goes to the team at Cengage Learning that has made this text a market leader. Jamie Bryant and Dana Freeman, our developmental editors at B-books, are world-class in their abilities and dedication. Tamborah Moore, our production editor, helped make this text a reality. A special thanks goes to Mike Roche, our editor at Cengage, for his suggestions and support.

Finally, we are particularly indebted to our reviewers and to faculty who have contributed to this edition and throughout the years:

Keith Absher
University of North Alabama

Roshan (Bob) D. Ahuja
Xavier University

M. Wayne Alexander
Minnesota State University Moorhead

Jackie Anderson
Davenport University School of Business

Joseph Anderson
Northern Arizona University

Linda Anglin
Minnesota State University Mankato

Christopher Anicich
California State University, Fullerton

Barry Ashmen
Bucks County Community College

Stephen Baglione
Saint Leo University

Kathleen M. Bailey
Loyola University of New Orleans

Gregory J. Baleja
Alma College

Andrew Banasiewicz
Louisiana State University

Barry L. Bayus
University of North Carolina–Chapel Hill

Fred Beasley
Northern Kentucky University

John L. Beisel
Pittsburgh State University

Christine A. Bell
Albright College

Ken Bell
Ellsworth Community College

Thomas S. Bennett
Gaston Community College

Marcel L. Berard
Community College of Rhode Island

Deirdre Bird
Providence College

Robert J. Blake
Concordia University

David M. Blanchette
Rhode Island College

L. Michelle Bobbitt
Bradley University

James C. Boespflug
Arapahoe Community College

Larry Borgen
Normandale Community College

William H. Brannen
Creighton University

David Brennan
Webster University

Rich Brown
Freed-Hardeman University

William G. Browne
Oregon State University

Pat LeMay Burr
University of Incarnate Word

Richard M. Burr
Trinity University

Victoria Bush
University of Mississippi

Deborah Chiviges Calhoun
College of Notre Dame of Maryland

Joseph E. Cantrell
DeAnza College

Shery Carder
Lake City Community College

G. L. Carr
University of Alaska, Anchorage

Stephen B. Castleberry
University of Minnesota, Duluth

Ed Cerny
University of South Carolina

Meg Clark
Cincinnati State Technical and Community College

Irvine Clarke III
James Madison University

Barbara Coleman
Augusta College

Robert A. Compton
Valley Forge Military College

Brian I. Connett
California State University, Northridge

John Alan Davis
Mohave Community College

Debra Decelles
State University of New York College–Brockport

Ronald Decker
University of Wisconsin, Eau Claire

William M. Diamond
SUNY–Albany

Gary M. Donnelly
Casper College

John T. Drea
Western Illinois University

Debbie Easterling
University of Maryland–Eastern Shore

Jacqueline K. Eastman
Valdosta State University

Kevin M. Elliott
Minnesota State University Mankato

G. Scott Erickson
Ithaca College

Karen A. Evans
Herkimer County Community College

Theresa B. Flaherty
Old Dominion University

P. J. Forrest
Mississippi College

Raymond Frost
Central Connecticut State University

John Gardner
State University of New York College–Brockport

S. J. Garner
Eastern Kentucky University

Leonard R. Geiser
Goshen College

Cornelia J. Glenn
Owensboro Community College

James H. Glenn
Owensboro Community College

Lynn R. Godwin
University of St. Thomas

Daniel J. Goebel
University of Southern Mississippi

Jana G. Goodrich
The Pennsylvania State University

Darrell Goudge
University of Central Oklahoma

Reginald A. Graham
Eastern Montana College

Gordon T. Gray
Oklahoma City University

Donna H. Green
Wayne State University

Mark Green
Simpson College

Dwayne D. Gremler
University of Idaho

Alice Griswold
Clarke College

Barbara Gross
California State University at Northridge

Richard A. Halberg
Houghton College

Randall S. Hansen
Stetson University

David M. Hardesty
University of Miami

Martha Hardesty
St. Catherine University

Dorothy R. Harpool
Wichita State University

Hari S. Hariharan
University of Wisconsin, Madison

L. Jean Harrison-Walker
University of Houston–Clear Lake

Michael Hartford
Morehead State University

James W. Harvey
George Mason University

Timothy S. Hatten
Black Hills State University

Paula J. Haynes
University of Tennessee at Chattanooga

James E. Hazeltine
Northeastern Illinois University

Charlane Bomrad Held
Onondaga Community College

Tom Hickey
Oswego State University of New York

Patricia M. Hopkins
California State Polytechnic

Mark B. Houston
University of Missouri

Kristen B. Hovsepian
Ashland University

Amy R. Hubbert
University of Nebraska at Omaha

R. Vish Iyer
University of Northern Colorado

Anita Jackson
Central Connecticut State University

Anupam Jaju
George Mason University

Bruce H. Johnson
Gustavus Adolphus College

Russell W. Jones
University of Central Oklahoma

Mathew Joseph
University of South Alabama

Vaughn Judd
Auburn University–Montgomery

Jacqueline J. Kacen
University Illinois

Ira S. Kalb
University of Southern California

William J. Kehoe
University of Virginia

J. Steven Kelly
DePaul University

Philip R. Kemp
De Paul University

Raymond F. Keyes
Boston College

Sylvia Keyes
Bridgewater State College

G. Dean Kortge
Central Michigan University

John R. Kuzma
Minnesota State University, Mankato

Bernard P. Lake
Kirkwood Community College

Thomas J. Lang
University of Miami

J. Ford Laumer, Jr.
Auburn University

Kenneth R. Lawrence
New Jersey Institute of Technology

Richard M. Lei
Northern Arizona University

Ron Lennon
Barry University

Judith J. Leonard
Eastern Kentucky University

J. Gordon Long
Georgia College

Sandra L. Lueder
Sacred Heart University

Michael Luthy
Bellarmine College

James L. Macke
Cincinnati State Technical and Community College

Charles S. Madden
Baylor University

Deanna R. D. Mader
Marshall University

Fred H. Mader
Marshall University

Larry Maes
Davenport University

Shirine Mafi
Otterbein College

Jack K. Mandel
Nassau Community College

Karl Mann
Tennessee Tech University

Phylis M. Mansfield
The Pennsylvania State University—Erie/Behrend

Cathy L. Martin
Northeast Louisiana University

Gregory S. Martin
University of West Florida

Irving Mason
Herkimer County Community College

Lee H. McCain
Seminole Community College

Michael McCall
Ithaca College

Nancy Ryan McClure
University of Central Oklahoma

Kim McKeage
University of Maine

Bronna McNeely
Midwestern State University

Sanjay S. Mehta
Sam Houston State University

Taylor W. Meloan
University of Southern California

Ronald E. Michaels
University of Central Florida

Charles E. Michaels, Jr.
University of South Florida

Mark A. Mitchell
Coastal Carolina University

William C. Moncrief
Texas Christian University

Michael C. Murphy
Langston University

Elwin Myers
Texas A&M University

Suzanne Altobello Nasco
Southern Illinois University

Murugappan Natesan
University of Alberta

N. Chinna Natesan
Southwest Texas State University

Roy E. Nicely
Valdosta State College

Carolyn Y. Nicholson
Stetson University

Chuck Nielson
Louisiana State University

Robert O'Keefe
DePaul University

Patrick A. Okonkwo
Central Michigan University

Brian Olson
Johnson County Community College

Anil M. Pandya
Northeastern Illinois University

Michael M. Pearson
Loyola University, New Orleans

John Perrachione
Truman State University

Monica Perry
California State University, Fullerton

Constantine G. Petrides
Borough of Manhattan Community College

Julie M. Pharr
Tennessee Technological University

Chris Pullig
University of Virginia

William Rech
Bucks County Community College

Allan C. Reddy
Valdosta State University

Joseph Reihing
State University of New York, Nassau

Jamie M. Ressler
Palm Beach Atlantic University

Sandra Robertson
Thomas Nelson Community College

John Ronchetto
University of San Diego

Dick Rose (deceased)
University of Phoenix

Al Rosenbloom
Dominican University

Barbara-Jean Ross
Louisiana State University

Lawrence Ross
Florida Southern College

Anthony Rossi
State University of New York College–Brockport

Carl Saxby
University of Southern Indiana

Jan Napoleon Saykiewicz
Duquesne University

Deborah Reed Scarfino
William Jewel College

Jeffrey Schmidt
University of Illinois

Peter A. Schneider
Seton Hall University

James A. Seaman
Nyack College

Trina Sego
Boise State University

Donald R. Self
Auburn University–Montgomery

Matthew D. Shank
Northern Kentucky University

John Shapiro
Northeastern State University

David L. Sherrell
University of Memphis

Peggy O. Shields
University of Southern Indiana

Mandeep Singh
Western Illinois University

Lois J. Smith
University of Wisconsin–Whitewater

Mark T. Spence
Southern Connecticut State College

James V. Spiers
Arizona State University

Thomas Stevenson
University of North Carolina–Charlotte

Karen L. Stewart
Richard Stockton College

James E. Stoddard
University of New Hampshire

Judy Strauss
University of Nevada, Reno

Randy Stuart
Kennesaw State University

Robin Stuart
Marketing Consultant

Susan Sunderline
State University of New York College–Brockport

Albert J. Taylor
Austin Peay State University

Janice E. Taylor
Miami University of Ohio

Ronald D. Taylor
Mississippi State University

James L. Thomas
Jacksonville State University

Kay Blythe Tracy
Gettysburg College

Gregory P. Turner
College of Charleston

Richard Turshen
Pace University

Sandra T. Vernon
Fayetteville Technical Community College

Franck Vingeron
California State University at Northridge

Charles R. Vitaska
Metro State College, Denver

James Ward
Arizona State University

Beth A. Walker
Arizona State University

Jim Wenthe
Georgia College and State University

Stacia Wert-Gray
University of Central Oklahoma

Janice K. Williams
University of Central Oklahoma

Laura A. Williams
San Diego State University

Elizabeth J. Wilson
Boston College

Robert D. Winsor
Loyola Marymount University

Leon Winer
Pace University

Arch G. Woodside
Boston College

Barbara Ross-Wooldridge
University of Tampa

Linda Berns Wright
Mississippi State University

William R. Wynd
Eastern Washington University

Merv H. Yeagle
University of Maryland

To Michelle and Mimi Olson.
—Carl McDaniel

To my wife, Julie Baker, and our daughters, Christine Stock, Jennifer McPhaul, and Kara Baker.
—Charles W. Lamb

To my newest joy in life, my grandsons Joseph F. Hair, IV (Joss) and Declan John Hair.
—Joseph F. Hair, Jr.

The World of Marketing

PART 1

WHAT'S INSIDE

CHAPTER 1

An Overview of Marketing

©ISTOCKPHOTO.COM/CHRIS SCHMIDT

LEARNING OUTCOMES

- LO 1 Define the term *marketing*
- LO 2 Describe four marketing management philosophies
- LO 3 Discuss the differences between sales and market orientations
- LO 4 Describe several reasons for studying marketing

WHAT IS MARKETING?

What does the term *marketing* mean to you? Many people think it means the same as personal selling. Others think marketing is the same as personal selling and advertising. Still others believe marketing has something to do with making products available in stores, arranging displays, and maintaining inventories of products for future sales. Actually, marketing includes all of these activities and more.

Marketing has two facets. First, it is a philosophy, an attitude, a perspective, or a management orientation that stresses customer satisfaction. Second, marketing is activities and processes used to implement this philosophy.

The American Marketing Association's definition of marketing focuses on the second facet. **Marketing** is the activity, set of institutions, and processes for creating, communicating, delivering, and exchanging offerings that have value for customers, clients, partners, and society at large.[1]

Marketing involves more than just activities performed by a group of people in a defined area or department. In the often-quoted words of David Packard, cofounder of Hewlett-Packard, "Marketing is too important to be left only to the marketing department." Marketing entails processes that focus on delivering value and benefits to customers, not just selling goods, services, and/or ideas. It uses communication, distribution, and pricing strategies to provide customers and other stakeholders with the goods, services, ideas, values, and benefits they desire when and where they want them. It involves building long-term, mutually rewarding relationships when these benefit all parties concerned. Marketing also entails an understanding that organizations have many connected stakeholder "partners," including employees, suppliers, stockholders, distributors, and society at large.

> *Marketing is too important to be left only to the marketing department.*

Research shows that companies that reward employees with incentives and recognition on a consistent basis are those that perform best.[2] Home Depot CEO Frank Blake rejects the notion that you should pay employees as little as you can and get as much work out of them as possible.[3] The motto of Wegmans Food Markets, the Rochester-based grocery chain that has been ranked by *Fortune* magazine as the best company to work for in America, states, "Employees first, customers second." The rationale is that if employees are happy, customers will be too.[4]

One desired outcome of marketing is an **exchange**; people giving up something to receive something they would rather have. Normally, we think of money as the medium of exchange. We "give up" money to "get" the goods and services we want. Exchange does not require money, however. Two persons may barter or trade such items as baseball cards or oil paintings. An exchange can take place only if the following five conditions exist:

1. There must be at least two parties.
2. Each party has something that might be of value to the other party.

Marketing & You

Please note your opinion on each of the following questions.

Think about where you buy cosmetics or personal care products. Using the following scale, enter the number that indicates how likely you are to:

1	2	3	4	5	6
Not likely at all					Extremely likely

__ Say positive things about the company to other people.

__ Recommend the company to someone who seeks your advice.

__ Encourage friends and relatives to do business with the company.

__ Consider the company your first choice to buy cosmetics or personal care products.

__ Do more business with the company in the next few years.

Now, total your score. Read the chapter to find out what your score means at the end.

marketing
The activity, set of institutions, and processes for creating, communicating, delivering, and exchanging offerings that have value for customers, clients, partners, and society at large.

exchange
People giving up something to receive something they would rather have.

production orientation
A philosophy that focuses on the internal capabilities of the firm rather than on the desires and needs of the marketplace.

sales orientation
The idea that people will buy more goods and services if aggressive sales techniques are used and that high sales result in high profits.

3. Each party is capable of communication and delivery.
4. Each party is free to accept or reject the exchange offer.
5. Each party believes it is appropriate or desirable to deal with the other party.[5]

Exchange will not necessarily take place even if all these conditions exist. They are, however, necessary for exchange to be possible. For example, you may place an advertisement in your local newspaper stating that your used automobile is for sale at a certain price. Several people may call you to ask about the car, some may test-drive it, and one or more may even make you an offer. All five conditions are necessary for an exchange to exist. But unless you reach an agreement with a buyer and actually sell the car, an exchange will not take place. Notice that marketing can occur even if an exchange does not occur. In the example just discussed, you would have engaged in marketing even if no one bought your used automobile.

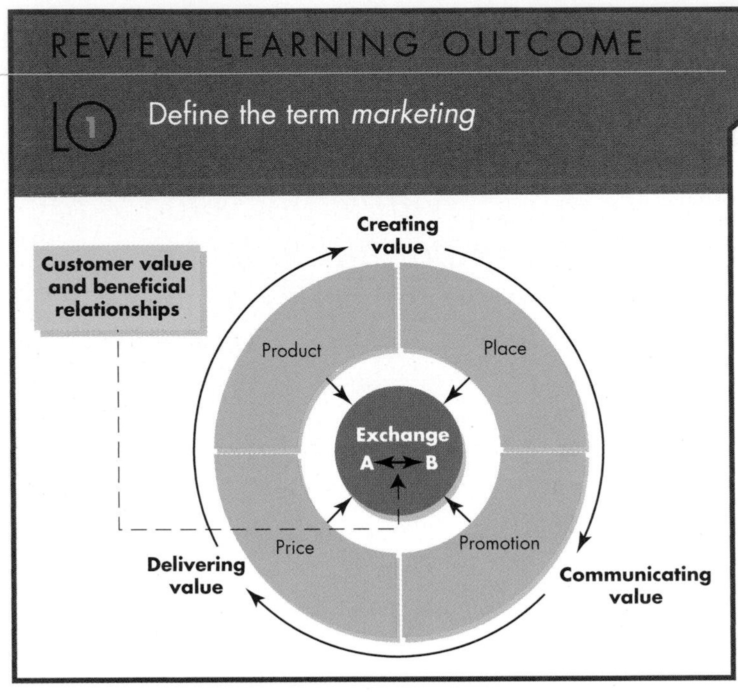

MARKETING MANAGEMENT PHILOSOPHIES

Four competing philosophies strongly influence an organization's marketing processes. These philosophies are commonly referred to as production, sales, market, and societal marketing orientations.

Production Orientation

A **production orientation** is a philosophy that focuses on the internal capabilities of the firm rather than on the desires and needs of the marketplace. A production orientation means that management assesses its resources and asks these questions: "What can we do best?" "What can our engineers design?" "What is easy to produce, given our equipment?" In the case of a service organization, managers ask, "What services are most convenient for the firm to offer?" and "Where do our talents lie?" Some have referred to this orientation as a *Field of Dreams* orientation, from the movie's well-known line, "If we build it, they will come." The furniture industry is infamous for its disregard of customers and for its slow cycle times. This has always been a production-oriented industry.

There is nothing wrong with assessing a firm's capabilities; in fact, such assessments are major considerations in strategic marketing planning (see Chapter 2). A production orientation falls short because it does not consider whether the goods and services that the firm produces most efficiently also meet the needs of the marketplace. Sometimes what a firm can best produce is exactly what the market wants. For example, the research and development department of 3M's commercial tape division developed and patented the adhesive component of Post-It Notes a year before a commercial application was identified. In other situations, as when competition is weak or demand exceeds supply, a production-oriented firm can survive and even prosper. More often, however, firms that succeed in competitive markets have a clear understanding that they must first determine what customers want and then produce it, rather than focusing on what company management thinks should be produced.

© R.ALCORN/THOMSON

Sales Orientation

A **sales orientation** is based on the ideas that people will buy more goods and services if aggressive sales techniques are used and that high sales result in high profits. Not only are sales to the final buyer emphasized, but intermediaries are also encouraged to push manufacturers' products more aggressively. To sales-oriented firms, marketing means selling things and collecting money.

The fundamental problem with a sales orientation, as with a production orientation, is a lack of understanding of the needs and wants of the marketplace. Sales-oriented companies often find that, despite the quality of their sales force, they cannot convince people to buy goods or services that are neither wanted nor needed.

Some sales-oriented firms simply fail to understand what is important to their customers. Many so-called dot-com businesses that came into existence in the late 1990s are no longer around because they focused on the technology rather than the customer.

Market Orientation

The **marketing concept** is a simple and intuitively appealing philosophy that articulates a market orientation. It states that the social and economic justification for an organization's existence is the satisfaction of customer wants and needs while meeting organizational objectives. It is based on an understanding that a sale does not depend on an aggressive sales force, but rather on a customer's decision to purchase a product. What a business thinks it produces is not of primary importance to its success. Instead, what customers think they are buying—the perceived value—defines a business. The marketing concept includes the following:

© CARL D. WALSH/AURORA PHOTOS

1. Focusing on customer wants and needs so that the organization can distinguish its product(s) from competitors' offerings
2. Integrating all the organization's activities, including production, to satisfy these wants
3. Achieving long-term goals for the organization by satisfying customer wants and needs legally and responsibly

The recipe for success is to consistently deliver a unique experience that your competitors cannot match and that satisfies the intentions and preferences of your target buyers.[6] This requires a thorough understanding of your customers and distinctive capabilities that enable your company to execute plans on the basis of this customer understanding, and delivering the desired experience using and integrating all of the resources of the firm.[7]

Firms that adopt and implement the marketing concept are said to be market oriented. Achieving a **market orientation** involves obtaining information about customers, competitors, and markets; examining the information from a total business perspective; determining how to deliver superior customer value; and implementing actions to provide value to customers.

What are the names of some firms known for delivering superior customer value and satisfaction? The third annual National Retail Federation/American Express Customer Service Survey listed L.L. Bean, Zappos.com, Amazon.com, Overstock.com, and Blair as the top five U.S. retailers for customer service.[8] *BusinessWeek* listed USAA, L.L. Bean, Fairmont Hotels, Lexus, and Trader Joe's as its best-in-class Customer Service Champs.[9]

Understanding your competitive arena and competitors' strengths and weaknesses is a critical component of a market orientation. This includes assessing what existing or potential competitors might be intending to do tomorrow as well as what they are doing today. Western Union failed to define its competitive arena as telecommunications, concentrating instead on telegraph services, and was eventually outflanked by fax technology. Had Western Union been a market-oriented company, its management might have better understood the changes taking place, seen the competitive threat, and developed strategies to counter the threat.

marketing concept
The idea that the social and economic justification for an organization's existence is the satisfaction of customer wants and needs while meeting organizational objectives.

market orientation
A philosophy that assumes that a sale does not depend on an aggressive sales force but rather on a customer's decision to purchase a product. It is synonymous with the marketing concept.

Societal Marketing Orientation

The **societal marketing orientation** extends the marketing concept by acknowledging that some products that customers want may not really be in their best interests or the best interests of society as a whole. This philosophy states that an organization exists not only to satisfy customer wants and needs and to meet organizational objectives, but also to preserve or enhance individuals' and society's long-term best interests. Marketing products and containers that are less toxic than normal, are more durable, contain reusable materials, or are made of recyclable materials is consistent with a societal marketing orientation. The American Marketing Association's definition of marketing recognizes the importance of a societal marketing orientation by including "society at large" as one of the constituencies for which marketing seeks to provide value.

© AP IMAGES/PRNEWSFOTO/PEPSI-COLA COMPANY

Although the societal marketing concept has been discussed for over 30 years, it did not receive widespread support until the early 2000s. Concerns such as climate change, the depleting ozone layer, fuel shortages, pollution, and raised health concerns have caused consumers and legislators to be more aware of the need for companies and consumers to adopt measures that conserve resources and cause less damage to the environment.

Studies reporting consumers' attitudes toward, and intentions to buy, more environmentally friendly products show widely varying results. One study that helps explain some of this contradiction found that 44 percent of consumers were "theoretically" interested in buying environmentally friendly products, but the proportion doing so was much less.[10] The three top reasons customers gave for not following through by purchasing and using these more environmentally friendly products were doubts about effectiveness, expense, and lack of availability at convenient outlets.[11] Another study generally confirmed the notion that many consumers have favorable attitudes regarding environmentally friendly products but are not willing to accept trade-offs. Specifically, 50 to 75 percent of consumers reported that environmental issues are important, but they are not willing to make trade-offs for higher costs or lower performance. Only 5 to 10 percent are willing to accept trade-offs to buy environmentally friendly products.[12]

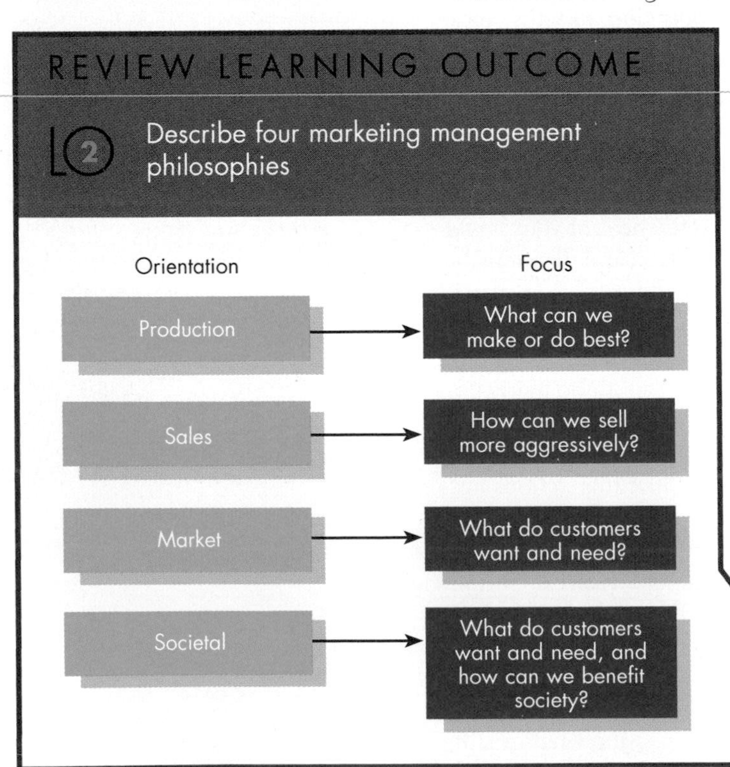

Some believe that many consumers want to "go green" but don't know where to start.[13] One study found that while half of its respondents thought a company's environmental record was important, only 7 percent could name an environmentally friendly product they had purchased.[14]

Many marketers have made substantial commitments to either produce products using more environmentally friendly processes or making more environmentally friendly products. Coca-Cola has committed to spending $44 million to build the world's largest plastic-bottle-to-bottle recycling plant.[15] The company has also set a goal of returning to communities and nature an equivalent amount of water as used in its beverages and their production.[16] Home Depot, UPS, and Wal-Mart are also among the business leaders in the so-called "eco-friendly" movement.[17]

What will the future bring? The current trends are that more customers are becoming concerned about the environment each year, more customers are trying to buy environmentally friendly products and support more environmentally friendly companies, and more companies are joining the movement by developing processes and products that do less damage to the environment than in the past. The number of "green" products released in the U.S. more than doubled from 2005 to 2007, and even more were introduced in 2008.[18] Adopting a societal marketing orientation and clearly communicating this decision and the actions that support it helps firms differentiate themselves from competitors and strengthens their positioning.

DIFFERENCES BETWEEN SALES AND MARKET ORIENTATIONS

The differences between sales and market orientations are substantial. The two orientations can be compared in terms of five characteristics: the organization's focus, the firm's business, those to whom the product is directed, the firm's primary goal, and the tools used to achieve those goals.

The Organization's Focus

Personnel in sales-oriented firms tend to be "inward looking," focusing on selling what the organization makes rather than making what the market wants. Many of the historic sources of competitive advantage—technology, innovation, economies of scale—allowed companies to focus their efforts internally and prosper. Today, many successful firms derive their competitive advantage from an external, market-oriented focus. A market orientation has helped companies such as the Royal Bank of Canada and Southwest Airlines outperform their competitors. These companies put customers at the center of their business in ways most companies do poorly or not at all.

A sales orientation has led to the demise of many firms including Streamline.com, the Digital Entertainment Network, and Urban Box Office. As one technology industry analyst put it, "No one has ever gone to a Web site because they heard there was great Java running."[19]

Southwest Airlines was recently named one of *BusinessWeek* "Customer Service Champs," and has ranked in as one of "America's Top Ten" most admired corporations by *Fortune* magazine for 11 consecutive years.

COURTESY OF SOUTHWEST AIRLINES

Customer Value Customer value is the relationship between benefits and the sacrifice necessary to obtain those benefits. Customer value is not simply a matter of high quality. A high-quality product that is available only at a high price will not be perceived as a good value, nor will bare-bones service or low-quality goods selling for a low price. Instead, customers value goods and services that are of the quality they expect and that are sold at prices they are willing to pay. Value can be used to sell a Mercedes-Benz as well as a Tyson frozen chicken dinner.

Lower-income consumers are price sensitive, but they will pay for products if they deliver a benefit that is worth the money.[20] The Global Perspectives box in this chapter illustrates that point.

The automobile industry provides another illustration of the importance of creating customer value. To penetrate the fiercely competitive luxury automobile market, Lexus adopted a customer-driven approach, with particular emphasis on service. Lexus stresses product quality with a standard of zero defects in manufacturing. The service quality goal is to treat each customer as one would treat a guest in one's home, to pursue the

societal marketing orientation
The idea that an organization exists not only to satisfy customer wants and needs and to meet organizational objectives, but also to preserve or enhance individuals' and society's long-term best interests.

customer value
The relationship between benefits and the sacrifice necessary to obtain those benefits.

GLOBAL Perspectives

P&G in Mexico

In the early 2000s the Mexican market share for Downy fabric softener was low and stagnant. Proctor & Gamble (P&G) wasn't sure what could be done about it, since the assumption was that people who didn't have modern washing machines didn't use softener. Not wanting to compromise the Downy brand by dropping the price too much, P&G decided to try to come up with something specific to the needs of the lower-income consumer.

One of the things P&G people noticed was the problem of water. Millions of rural women still lug buckets back from wells or communal pumps. In the cities, many have running water for only a few hours a day. Most homes do not have fully automatic washing machines; even fewer have dryers. All this makes doing the laundry a seriously draining chore.

At the same time, lower-income Mexican women take laundry very, very seriously. They cannot afford to buy many new clothes, but they take great pride in ensuring that their family is dressed well. Sending your children to school in clean, ironed clothing is a visible sign of being a good mother. P&G found that Mexican women spend more time on laundry than on the rest of their housework combined. More than 90 percent use softener, even women who do some or all of their laundry by hand.

"By spending time with women, we learned that the softening process is really demanding," recalls Antonio Hidalgo, P&G brand manager for Downy Single Rinse at the time of its debut in March 2004. A typical load of laundry went through the following six-step process: wash; rinse; rinse; add softener; rinse; rinse. No problem if all this is just a matter of pressing a button every once in a while. But it's no joke if you are doing the wash by hand or have to walk half a mile to get water. Even semiautomatic machines require that water be added and extracted manually. And if you get the timing wrong, the water supply might run out in the middle. "The big aha!" says a P&G executive, was discovering how valuable water was to lower-income Mexicans. "And we only got that by experiencing how they live their life."

Putting it all together, P&G knew that Mexican women liked to use softener; they had high standards for performance; and doing the laundry was arduous and time consuming, and required large amounts of water.

Having identified a problem (making laundry easier and less water-intensive), P&G turned to its labs for an answer. Their solution: Downy Single Rinse (DSR). Instead of a six-step process, DSR reduced it to three—wash, add softener, rinse—saving enormous time, effort, and water. The product was launched in 2004 and became an immediate hit.[21]

What lessons can other consumer goods manufacturers learn from P&G's experience? Explain why value is more important than price in marketing to lower-income households.

perfect person-to-person relationship, and to strive to improve continually. This pursuit has enabled Lexus to establish a clear, high-quality image and capture a significant share of the luxury car market.

Marketers interested in customer value:

- *Offer products that perform:* This is the bare minimum requirement. The example discussed in the Global Perspectives box in this chapter illustrates the importance of listening to customers to determine the performance characteristics that are most important to them.
- *Earn trust:* A stable base of loyal customers enhances a firm's ability to grow and prosper. About 80 percent of Starbucks' revenues come from customers who visit the store an average of 18 times per month.[22]
- *Avoid unrealistic pricing:* E-marketers are leveraging Internet technology to redefine how prices are set and negotiated. With lower costs, e-marketers can often offer lower prices than their brick-and-mortar counterparts. The enormous popularity of auction sites such as eBay and Amazon.com and the customer-bid model used by Priceline illustrates that online customers are interested in bargain prices. Many are not willing to pay a premium for the convenience of examining the merchandise and

taking it home with them. Others will gladly pay a premium for an experience that is not only functionally rewarding, but emotionally rewarding as well. Executives at Starwood Hotels and Resorts' "W" chain believe that they are able to make an emotional connection when customers walk through the door of their hotel room and see the bed with clean-looking, sumptuous linens and other amenities.[23]

- *Give the buyer facts*: Today's sophisticated consumer wants informative advertising and knowledgeable salespeople. It is becoming very difficult for business marketers to differentiate themselves from competitors. Rather than trying to sell products, salespeople need to find out what the customer needs, which is usually a combination of products, services, and thought leadership.[24] In other words, salespeople need to start with the needs of the customer and work toward the solution.
- ***Offer organization-wide commitment in service and after-sales support***: According to Gartner Research vice president Michael Maoz, organizations should incorporate customer service as a wide-ranging business strategy in order to keep up with customer expectations. "In the past, customer service was a department, the place that you called for specific redress of a grievance or information about your bill. Right now, rather than a function in that department, it is an enterprise strategy. That transition has profound implications on how we design all our processes across all our different communications channels."[25]
- *Co-Creation:* Some companies and products allow customers to help create their own experience. For example, TiVo allows people to watch chosen TV shows on their own schedules.

Customer Satisfaction **customer satisfaction** is the customer's evaluation of a good or service in terms of whether that good or service has met the customer's needs and expectations. Failure to meet needs and expectations results in dissatisfaction with the good or service. Some companies, in their passion to drive down costs, have damaged their relationships with customers. Dell Computers, Home Depot, and Northwest Airlines are examples of companies where executives lost track of the delicate balance between efficiency and service.[26] Each has realized change is needed and has implemented improvements. Firms that have a reputation for delivering high levels of customer satisfaction do things differently from their competitors. Top management is obsessed with customer satisfaction, and employees throughout the organization understand the link between their job and satisfied customers. The culture of the organization is to focus on delighting customers rather than on selling products.

Nordstrom's impeccable reputation for customer service comes not from its executives or its marketing team, but from the customers themselves. The retail giant is willing to take risks, do unusual and often expensive favors for shoppers, and reportedly even accept returns on items not purchased there. Still, they keep improving. The company recently installed a new database enabling salespeople to assist customers in locating items in inventory somewhere in the chain, but not in a particular store. Customers can then purchase these items online.[27]

customer satisfaction
Customers' evaluation of a good or service in terms of whether it has met their needs and expectations.

Building Relationships Attracting new customers to a business is only the beginning. The best companies view new-customer attraction as the launching point for developing and enhancing a long-term relationship. Companies can expand market share in three ways: attracting new customers, increasing business with existing customers, and retaining current customers. Building relationships with existing customers directly addresses two of the three possibilities and indirectly addresses the other.

The Customer Experience box in this chapter provides more information about providing customers with rewarding experiences that lead to long-term relationships.

CUSTOMER Experience

The Essence of Marketing

When one strips away all of the functions, plans, and strategies of marketing and asks the simple question, "What is this all about?" the answer is the customer experience. Think about it—whether you buy something a second or third time or become loyal to a brand depends on the experience that you had while purchasing and consuming the product or service. Most products need to be sold to a customer more than once in order for the company to start making money. Coca-Cola, for example, would have real problems if people bought just one can of Coke and then never purchased a Coke again.

A theme that you will find running throughout this text is the critical importance of providing a good customer experience. In each chapter you will find a box entitled, "Customer Experience" that links the chapter material to the customer experience. Quality is the key driver that can make the customer experience a good one. When we speak of quality we aren't simply referring to product quality or service quality. We are talking about having the highest-quality personnel operations, financial operations, sales activities, and anything else with which the organization is involved. General Electric is the pioneer of a concept called "Six Sigma." A company that adheres to Six Sigma will have only 3.4 defects per 1 million opportunities to experience failure! Thus, purchasers almost never receive a defective product, which is the beginning of a good customer experience.

A good customer experience can lead to customer satisfaction, which, in turn, can lead to loyalty. Satisfaction and loyalty are related but different. Customers are satisfied when their needs and expectations are met. Customers are loyal when they buy again due to rational and emotional ties to the product or service. While satisfaction is necessary for loyalty, it is not sufficient for true loyalty.

You would think that all companies would strive to create a great customer experience. However, a recent study showed that this is not the case. A study of executives conducted nationwide found that 80 percent strongly agree that customer strategies are more important to a company's success than ever before, but many companies fail to design and deliver those strategies and, as such, lose customer commitment and loyalty.[28]

Why do you think that some companies don't have policies to maximize the customer experience? Why is there not a perfect one-to-one relationship between satisfaction and loyalty? That is, if you are satisfied, why might you not be loyal?

relationship marketing
A strategy that focuses on keeping and improving relationships with current customers.

Relationship marketing is a strategy that focuses on keeping and improving relationships with current customers. It assumes that many consumers and business customers prefer to have an ongoing relationship with one organization than to switch continually among providers in their search for value. USAA is a good example of a company focused on building long-term relationships with customers. In 2007, a *BusinessWeek*/J.D. Powers & Associates survey ranked USAA as the top provider of customer service among U.S. firms.[29] Customer retention was a core value of the company long before customer loyalty became a popular business concept. USAA believes so strongly in the importance of customer retention that managers' and executives' bonuses are based, in part, on this dimension.

Most successful relationship marketing strategies depend on customer-oriented personnel, effective training programs, employees with authority to make decisions and solve problems, and teamwork.

Customer-Oriented Personnel For an organization to be focused on building relationships with customers, employees' attitudes and actions must be customer oriented. An employee may be the only contact a particular customer has with the firm. In that customer's eyes, the employee is the firm. Any person, department, or division that is not customer-oriented weakens the positive image of the entire organization. For example, a potential customer who is greeted discourteously may well assume that the employee's attitude represents the whole firm.

Isadore Sharp, founder, chair, and CEO of the Four Seasons hotel chain, says that "personal service is not something you can dictate as a policy. It comes from the culture. How you treat your employees is how you expect them to treat the customer."[30]

Some companies, such as Coca-Cola, Delta Air Lines, Hershey Company, Kellogg's, Nautilus, and Sears, have appointed chief customer officers (CCOs). These customer advocates provide an executive voice for customers and report directly to the CEO. Their responsibilities include ensuring that the company maintains a customer-centric culture and that all company employees remain focused on delivering customer value.

The Role of Training Leading marketers recognize the role of employee training in customer service and relationship building. Sales staff at The Container Store receive over 240 hours of training and generous benefits compared to an industry average of 8 hours training and modest benefits.

Empowerment In addition to training, many market-oriented firms are giving employees more authority to solve customer problems on the spot. The term used to describe this delegation of authority is **empowerment**. Employees develop ownership attitudes when they are treated like part-owners of the business and are expected to act the part. These employees manage themselves, are more likely to work hard, account for their own performance and the company's, and take prudent risks to build a stronger business and sustain the company's success. FedEx customer service representatives are trained and empowered to resolve customer problems. Although the average FedEx transaction costs only $16, the customer service representatives are empowered to spend up to $100 to resolve a customer problem.

Employees at Ritz-Carlton hotels are encouraged to take whatever steps they feel are necessary to ensure that guests enjoy their visits. Any employee can spend up to $2,000—without seeking permission from management—to solve a problem for guests. One Ritz-Carlton chef in Bali had special eggs and milk imported from Singapore and personally delivered by plane so that he could cook for a young guest with food allergies.[31]

© R.ALCORN/THOMSON

Empowerment gives customers the feeling that their concerns are being addressed and gives employees the feeling that their expertise matters. The result is greater satisfaction for both customers and employees.

Teamwork Many organizations that are frequently noted for delivering superior customer value and providing high levels of customer satisfaction, such as Southwest Airlines and Walt Disney World, assign employees to teams and teach them team-building skills. **Teamwork** entails collaborative efforts of people to accomplish common objectives. Job performance, company performance, product value, and customer satisfaction all improve when people in the same department or work group begin supporting and assisting each other and emphasize cooperation instead of competition. Performance is also enhanced when cross-functional teams align their jobs with customer needs. For example, if a team of telecommunications service representatives is working to improve interaction with customers, back-office people such as computer technicians or training personnel can become part of the team with the ultimate goal of delivering superior customer value and satisfaction.

The Firm's Business

A sales-oriented firm defines its business (or mission) in terms of goods and services. A market-oriented firm defines its business in terms of the benefits its customers seek. People who spend their money, time, and energy expect to receive benefits, not just goods and services. This distinction has enormous implications. As a senior executive of the Coca-Cola Co. noted, Coke is in the hydration business.[32]

empowerment
Delegation of authority to solve customers' problems quickly—usually by the first person that the customer notifies regarding a problem.

teamwork
Collaborative efforts of people to accomplish common objectives.

Because of the limited way it defines its business, a sales-oriented firm often misses opportunities to serve customers whose wants can be met through a wide range of product offerings instead of specific products. For example, in 1989, 220-year-old Britannica had estimated revenues of $650 million and a worldwide sales force of 7,500. Just five years later, after three consecutive years of losses, the sales force had collapsed to as few as 280 representatives. How did this respected company sink so low? Britannica managers saw that competitors were beginning to use CD-ROMs to store huge masses of information, but chose to ignore the new computer technology, as well as an offer to team up with Microsoft.

It's not hard to see why parents would rather give their children an encyclopedia on a compact disc instead of a printed one. The CD-ROM versions were either given away or sold by other publishers for under $400. A full 32-volume set of *Encyclopaedia Britannica* weighs about 120 pounds, costs a minimum of $1,500, and takes up four and one-half feet of shelf space. If Britannica had defined its business as providing information instead of publishing books, it might not have suffered such a precipitous fall.

Adopting a "better late than never" philosophy, Britannica has made its complete 32-volume set available free on the Internet. The company no longer sells door-to-door and hopes to return to profitability by selling advertising on its Web site.

Answering the question, "What is this firm's business?" in terms of the benefits customers seek, instead of goods and services, offers at least three important advantages:

- It ensures that the firm keeps focusing on customers and avoids becoming preoccupied with goods, services, or the organization's internal needs.
- It encourages innovation and creativity by reminding people that there are many ways to satisfy customer wants.
- It stimulates an awareness of changes in customer desires and preferences so that product offerings are more likely to remain relevant.

Having a market orientation and focusing on customer wants do not mean that customers will always receive everything they want. It is not possible, for example, to profitably manufacture and market automobile tires that will last for 100,000 miles for $25. Furthermore, customers' preferences must be mediated by sound professional judgment as to how to deliver the benefits they seek. As Henry Ford once said, "If I had listened to the marketplace, I would have built a faster, cheaper horse."[33] Consumers have a limited set of experiences. They are unlikely to request anything beyond those experiences because they are not aware of benefits they may gain from other potential offerings. For example, before the Internet, many people thought that shopping for some products was boring and time consuming, but could not express their need for electronic shopping.

Those to Whom the Product is Directed

A sales-oriented organization targets its products at "everybody" or "the average customer." A market-oriented organization aims at specific groups of people. The fallacy of developing products directed at the average user is that relatively few average users

IMAGE COURTESY OF THE ADVERTISING ARCHIVES

actually exist. Typically, populations are characterized by diversity. An average is simply a midpoint in some set of characteristics. Because most potential customers are not "average," they are not likely to be attracted to an average product marketed to the average customer. Consider the market for shampoo as one simple example. There are shampoos for oily hair, dry hair, and dandruff. Some shampoos remove the gray or color hair. Special shampoos are marketed for infants and elderly people. There is even shampoo for people with average or normal hair (whatever that is), but this is a fairly small portion of the total market for shampoo.

A market-oriented organization recognizes that different customer groups want different features or benefits. It may therefore need to develop different goods, services, and promotional appeals. A market-oriented organization carefully analyzes the market and divides it into groups of people who are fairly similar in terms of selected characteristics. Then the organization develops marketing programs that will bring about mutually satisfying exchanges with one or more of those groups.

Paying attention to the customer isn't exactly a new concept. Back in the 1920s, General Motors began designing cars for every lifestyle and pocketbook. This was a breakthrough for an industry that had been largely driven by production needs ever since Henry Ford promised any color as long as it was black. Chapter 8 thoroughly explores the topic of analyzing markets and selecting those that appear to be most promising to the firm.

The Firm's Primary Goal

A sales-oriented organization seeks to achieve profitability through sales volume and tries to convince potential customers to buy, even if the seller knows that the customer and product are mismatched. Sales-oriented organizations place a higher premium on making a sale than on developing a long-term relationship with a customer. In contrast, the ultimate goal of most market-oriented organizations is to make a profit by creating customer value, providing customer satisfaction, and building long-term relationships with customers. The exception is so-called nonprofit organizations that exist to achieve goals other than profits. Nonprofit organizations can and should adopt a market orientation.

Tools the Organization Uses to Achieve Its Goals

Sales-oriented organizations seek to generate sales volume through intensive promotional activities, mainly personal selling and advertising. In contrast, market-oriented organizations recognize that promotion decisions are only one of four basic marketing mix decisions that have to be made: product decisions, place (or distribution) decisions, promotion decisions, and pricing decisions. A market-oriented organization recognizes that each of these four components is important. Furthermore, market-oriented organizations recognize that marketing is not just a responsibility of the marketing department. Interfunctional coordination means that skills and resources throughout the organization are needed to create, communicate, and deliver superior customer service and value.

A Word of Caution

This comparison of sales and market orientations is not meant to belittle the role of promotion, especially personal selling, in the marketing mix. Promotion is the means by which organizations communicate with present and prospective customers about the merits and characteristics of their organization and products. Effective promotion is an essential part of effective marketing. Salespeople who work for market-oriented organizations are generally perceived by their customers to be problem solvers and important links to supply sources and new products. Chapter 15 examines the nature of personal selling in more detail.

REVIEW LEARNING OUTCOME

LO3 Discuss the differences between sales and market orientations

	What is the organization's focus?	What business are you in?	To whom is the product directed?	What is your primary goal?	How do you seek to achieve your goal?
Sales Orientation	Inward, on the organization's needs	Selling goods and services	Everybody	Profit through maximum sales volume	Primarily through intensive promotion
Market Orientation	Outward, on the wants and preferences of customers	Satisfying customer wants and needs and delivering superior value	Specific groups of people	Profit through customer satisfaction	Through coordinated marketing and interfunctional activities

WHY STUDY MARKETING?

Now that you understand the meaning of the term *marketing*, why it is important to adopt a marketing orientation, how organizations implement this philosophy, and how one-to-one marketing is evolving, you may be asking, "What's in it for me?" or "Why should I study marketing?" These are important questions, whether you are majoring in a business field other than marketing (such as accounting, finance, or management information systems) or a nonbusiness field (such as journalism, economics, or agriculture). There are several important reasons to study marketing: Marketing plays an important role in society, marketing is important to businesses, marketing offers outstanding career opportunities, and marketing affects your life every day.

Marketing Plays an Important Role in Society

The total population of the United States exceeds 300 million people.[34] Think about how many transactions are needed each day to feed, clothe, and shelter a population of this size. The number is huge. And yet it all works quite well, partly because the well-developed U.S. economic system efficiently distributes the output of farms and factories. A typical U.S. family, for example, consumes 2.5 tons of food a year. Marketing makes food available when we want it, in desired quantities, at accessible locations, and in sanitary and convenient packages and forms (such as instant and frozen foods).

Marketing Is Important to Business

The fundamental objectives of most businesses are survival, profits, and growth. Marketing contributes directly to achieving these objectives. Marketing includes the following activities, which are vital to business organizations: assessing the wants and satisfactions of present and potential customers, designing and managing product offerings, determining prices and pricing policies, developing distribution strategies, and communicating with present and potential customers.

All businesspeople, regardless of specialization or area of responsibility, need to be familiar with the terminology and fundamentals of accounting, finance, management, and marketing. People in all business areas need to be able to communicate with specialists in other areas. Furthermore, marketing is not just a job done by people in a marketing department. Marketing is a part of the job of everyone in the organization. Therefore, a basic understanding of marketing is important to all businesspeople.

Marketing Offers Outstanding Career Opportunities

Between a fourth and a third of the entire civilian workforce in the United States performs marketing activities. Marketing offers great career opportunities in such areas as professional selling, marketing research, advertising, retail buying, distribution management, product management, product development, and wholesaling. Marketing career opportunities also exist in a variety of nonbusiness organizations, including hospitals, museums, universities, the armed forces, and various government and social service agencies.

As the global marketplace becomes more challenging, companies all over the world and of all sizes have to become better marketers. For a comprehensive look at career opportunities in marketing and a variety of other useful information about careers, read the Career Appendix at the end of this chapter and visit our Web site at **www.cengage.com/international.**

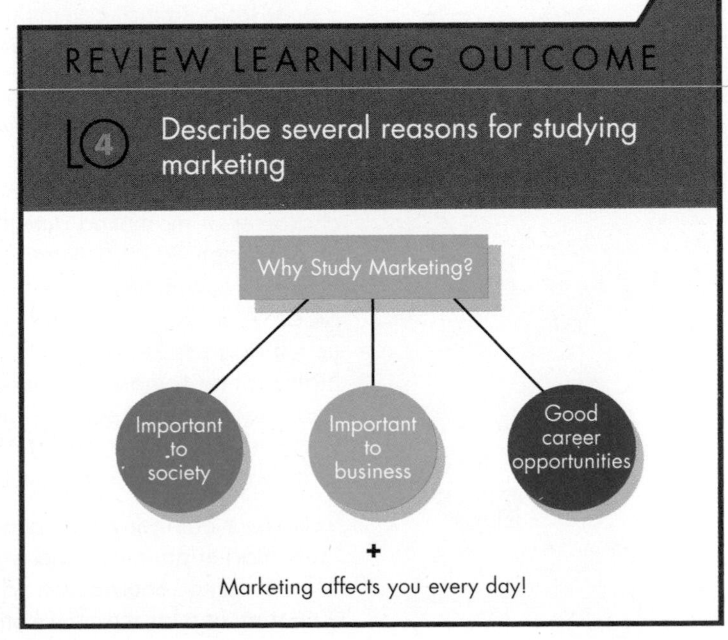

Marketing Affects Your Life Every Day

Marketing plays a major role in your everyday life. You participate in the marketing process as a consumer of goods and services. About half of every dollar you spend pays for marketing costs, such as marketing research, product development, packaging, transportation, storage, advertising, and sales expenses. By developing a better understanding of marketing, you will become a better-informed consumer. You will better understand the buying process and be able to negotiate more effectively with sellers. Moreover, you will be better prepared to demand satisfaction when the goods and services you buy do not meet the standards promised by the manufacturer or the marketer.

Number of competing marketing philosophies (or orientations) that influence an organization's marketing processes ▶ **4**

240 ◀ Number of training hours/year for The Container Store sales staff

Number of sales staff training hours/year retail industry average ▶ **8**

16 ◀ The dollar cost of the average FedEx transaction

The dollar amount FedEx customer service reps are empowered to spend to resolve a customer problem ▶ **100**

2.5 ◀ Tons of food a typical U.S. family consumes each year

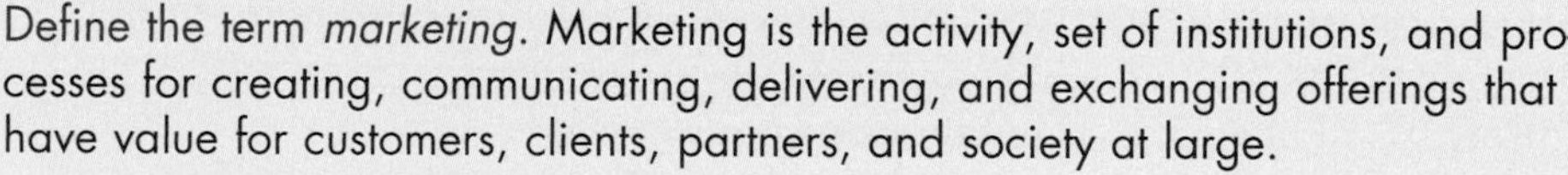

REVIEW AND APPLICATIONS

Define the term *marketing*. Marketing is the activity, set of institutions, and processes for creating, communicating, delivering, and exchanging offerings that have value for customers, clients, partners, and society at large.

1.1 What is the AMA? What does it do? How do its services benefit marketers? **www.marketingpower.com**

Describe four marketing management philosophies. The role of marketing and the character of marketing activities within an organization are strongly influenced by its philosophy and orientation. A production-oriented organization focuses on the internal capabilities of the firm rather than on the desires and needs of the marketplace. A sales orientation is based on the beliefs that people will buy more products if aggressive sales techniques are used and that high sales volumes produce high profits. A market-oriented organization focuses on satisfying customer wants and needs while meeting organizational objectives. A societal marketing orientation goes beyond a market orientation to include the preservation or enhancement of individuals' and society's long-term best interests.

2.1 Your company president has decided to restructure the firm to make it more market oriented. She is going to announce the changes at an upcoming meeting. She has asked you to prepare a short speech outlining the general reasons for the new company orientation.

2.2 Donald E. Petersen, former chairman of the board of Ford Motor Company, remarked, "If we aren't customer driven, our cars won't be either." Explain how this statement reflects the marketing concept.

2.3 Give an example of a company that might be successfully following a production orientation. Why might a firm in this industry be successful following such an orientation?

Discuss the differences between sales and market orientations. First, sales-oriented firms focus on their own needs; market-oriented firms focus on customers' needs and preferences. Second, sales-oriented companies consider themselves to be deliverers of goods and services, whereas market-oriented companies view themselves as satisfiers of customers. Third, sales-oriented firms direct their products to everyone; market-oriented firms aim at specific segments of the population. Fourth, although the primary goal of both types of firms is profit, sales-oriented businesses pursue maximum sales volume through intensive promotion, whereas market-oriented businesses pursue customer satisfaction through coordinated activities.

3.1 A friend of yours agrees with the adage "People don't know what they want—they only want what they know." Write your friend a letter expressing the extent to which you think marketers shape consumer wants.

3.2 Your local supermarket's slogan is "It's your store." However, when you asked one of the stock people to help you find a bag of chips, he told you it was not his job and that you should look a littler harder. On your way out, you noticed a sign with an address for complaints. Draft a letter explaining why the supermarket's slogan will never be credible unless the employees carry it out.

3.3 How does Philip Morris handle the sensitive issues associated with marketing tobacco? What kind of information does its Web site at **www.philipmorris.com/** provide about smoking and its negative effects on health? How do you think Philip Morris is able to justify such marketing tactics? After checking around the site, do you think that approach makes the company more or less trustworthy?

Describe several reasons for studying marketing. First, marketing affects the allocation of goods and services that influence a nation's economy and standard of living. Second, an understanding of marketing is crucial to understanding most businesses. Third, career opportunities in marketing are diverse, profitable, and expected to increase significantly during the coming decade. Fourth, understanding marketing makes consumers more informed.

4.1 Write a letter to a friend or family member explaining why you think that a course in marketing will help you in your career in some field other than marketing.

KEY TERMS

customer satisfaction	9	marketing	3	relationship marketing	10
customer value	7	marketing concept	5	sales orientation	4
empowerment	11	market orientation	5	societal marketing orientation	6
exchange	3	production orientation	4	teamwork	11

EXERCISES

APPLICATION EXERCISE

Understanding the differences among the various marketing management philosophies is the starting point for understanding the fundamentals of marketing.[35] From reading the chapter, you may be convinced that the market orientation is the most appealing philosophy and the one best suited to creating a competitive advantage. Not all companies, however, use the market orientation. And even companies that follow it may not execute well in all areas.

Activities

1. Visit your local grocery store and go through the cereal, snack-food, and dental hygiene aisles. Go up and down each aisle slowly, noticing how many different products are available and how they are organized on the shelves.
2. Count the varieties of product in each product category. For example, how many different kinds of cereal are on the shelves? How many different sizes? Do the same for snack food and toothpaste.
3. Now try to find a type of product in the grocery store that does not exhibit such variety. There may not be many. Why do you think there are enough kinds of cereals to fill an entire aisle (and then some), but only a few different types of, say, peanut butter? Can this difference be explained in terms of marketing management philosophy (peanut butter manufacturers do not follow the marketing concept) or by something else entirely?
4. Have you ever wanted to see a particular kind of cereal or snack food on the shelf? Think of product varietals (like grapefruit-flavored toothpaste or peanut butter-covered popcorn) that you have never seen on the shelf but would be interested in trying if someone would make it. Write a letter or send an e-mail to an appropriate company, suggesting that it add your concept to its current product line.

ETHICS EXERCISE

In today's business environment, ethics are extremely important. In recent years, there have been numerous scandals and trials that stem from a lack of ethical judgment. For this reason, we are including an ethical exercise in every chapter. A brief scenario will present you with a situation in which the right thing to do may or may not be crystal clear, and you will need to decide the ethical way out of the dilemma.

Rani Pharmaceuticals is the maker of several popular drugs used to treat high blood pressure and arthritis. Over time, the company has developed a positive relationship with many of the patients who use its medications through a quarterly newsletter that offers all the latest information on new medical research findings and general health and fitness articles. The company has just been acquired by a group of investors who also own Soothing Waters Hot Tubs and Spas. The marketing director for Soothing Waters would like to use Rani's mailing list for a direct-mail promotion.

Questions

1. What should Rani Pharmaceuticals do?
2. Do you think it is ethical to use customer information across multiple divisions of the same company? Explain.
3. To which marketing management philosophy do you think the marketing director for Soothing Waters subscribes? Explain.

MARKETING PLAN EXERCISE

You can use many of the basic concepts of marketing introduced in this book to get the career you want by marketing yourself to a prospective employer. This exercise and the Career Appendix at the end of this chapter can help you plan that particular marketing campaign. Build a marketing plan for yourself in a one-page document or table with these elements:

1. *What is your mission?* Are you looking for part-time or temporary experience to enhance your résumé, a career stepping-stone, or a full-time, long-term career choice? (This mission will help you set the stage for the rest of your plan.)
2. *What are your strengths and weaknesses?* Make an honest self-assessment, because these issues often come up during job interviews. What about opportunities and threats in the marketplace? Who are your competitors? Do you have a competitive advantage? List any special leadership skills, international travel, computer experience, team projects, communications efforts, and other attributes. (Any competitive advantages you possess should be noted in the cover letter of your résumé and in your job interview.)
3. *What are your objectives?* Do you need to find a job within the next thirty days, or are you more flexible? Are there specific job activities that you would like to perform? (These job activities could be stated in the objectives portion of your résumé. Be sure the objectives are very specific: general objectives are of little use to you or an employer.)
4. *What is your target market?* Are you looking only for jobs with big, established organizations or small entrepreneurial firms? Are you looking at companies in a particular industry? Do you have any geographic preferences? When you figure out your target, compile a list of firms that meet your requirements and describe them. (The more you know about your target-market potential employers, the more prepared you will be in an interview.)
5. You are the product. *How can you best present yourself?* Think of your own packaging with regard to dress, appearance, mannerisms, and speech.
6. What about place? *Are you willing to travel or relocate?* Or do you need an employer close to home? How will you travel to the employer? Is telecommuting an option?
7. *How will you promote yourself?* A carefully constructed cover letter, résumé, business card, and personal Web site can all help communicate your skills to a potential employer.
8. Think carefully about pricing issues, including salary, commission, bonuses, overtime, flexible time, insurance, and other benefits. *What is a fair price for you?* What is a normal price for a company of that size in that industry to offer?
9. And finally, *how will you implement your plan?* That is, what is your plan for applying to companies? How will you contact them for potential interviews? How will you prepare your wardrobe and work on your interviewing skills? When job offers come in, how will you evaluate them? If job offers don't come in, can you find out why and control for these aspects?

The Appendix at the end of this chapter introduces various aspects of a career in marketing, such as types of marketing jobs, pay scales, preparation for interviewing, and what to expect the first year on the job.

CASE STUDY: NETFLIX READY FOR PRIMETIME

Shocked at the $40 fee he incurred for a late return of *Apollo 13,* Netflix founder Reed Hastings decided that in the age of the Internet, there had to be a better way to rent videos for home viewing. Thus, in 1997, he started an Internet-based, DVD rental service that offered direct-to-home deliveries with no late fees. A mere decade and 4 million subscribers later, Netflix has taken on established video rental companies such as Blockbuster, Hollywood Video, and Wal-Mart and emerged as the leader in innovation and customer service.

In addition to betting that the Internet would be the future of the video rental market, Hastings made a few other key predictions that helped him develop a company with almost $700 million in revenue in under ten years. He watched as moviegoers fled public theaters for the comfort of home theater systems, and he observed those same consumers embracing the features, capacity, and high-quality format of the DVD. Realizing that the Internet could allow those same convenience seekers 24-hour browsing and selection access to an unprecedented volume of movie titles in a single digital catalog, Hastings shrewdly designed a service that outperforms traditional, store-based video rentals.

Netflix allows consumers to choose from a variety of subscription plans. The most popular plan offers three DVDs for $17.99 per month. Once a subscriber builds a list of favorite movies and TV shows from a selection of over 60,000 titles, Netflix mails out the three titles at the top of the list, along with return-addressed prestamped envelopes. After viewing the DVDs, the customer simply mails them back to Netflix in the supplied packaging. When the titles are scanned in at one of the distribution warehouses, the customer is simultaneously sent the next selections on the favorites list.

With 34 strategically placed distribution centers, Netflix can deliver 92 percent of its movies within one day of being ordered. That outstanding delivery service is just the tip of the iceberg. Netflix's Web site takes personalization to new levels through its high-powered recommendation software, called Cinematch. Cinematch uses over a million lines of code and over half a billion customer-supplied ratings to suggest rental choices upon request.

Amazingly, over 60 percent of the titles added to users' favorites lists come from Cinematch recommendations, and over a million ratings are sent to Netflix every day. Just how effective is Cinematch? Netflix uses fewer than 50 customer service reps to support its entire customer base! Of those, 10 are authorized to make direct callbacks to customers with complaints to find out how the problem could have been prevented in the first place. It's that kind of attention to customers that forced retail giant Wal-Mart to give up and turn over its entire customer list to Netflix.

Netflix even added two key features to its service in response to customer requests. The first is the ability to generate multiple favorites lists for a single account, allowing families to build multiple wish lists that can differ as much as *Steel Magnolias* and *Old School.* The second is the addition of a community feature called "Friends." Friends enables users to share the titles, ratings, and preferences for recently viewed shows with those they invite to be part of their network.

Always looking to the future, Hastings wants to diversify Netflix by adding high-definition DVD rentals to its current service, selling previously rented DVDs in the rapidly growing used-DVD market, and developing an on-demand video download service. Though it's impossible to tell exactly what blockbuster service Netflix will deliver next, it's a safe bet its customers will applaud.[36]

Questions

1. Describe the elements of the exchange process as they occur between Netflix and its customers.
2. Which marketing management philosophy does Netflix subscribe to?
3. How does Netflix's approach to relationship marketing increase customer satisfaction?

COMPANY CLIPS

METHOD—LIVE CLEAN

Method, the innovative branding concept in household cleaning, was conceived by roommates Eric Ryan and Adam Lowry during their drive to a ski lodge. Eric had been thinking of ways to introduce design to the home care industry (i.e., cleaning products) and began talking about his vision to Adam. A chemical engineer from Stanford University with a degree in environmental science, Adam was the perfect sounding board. He soon realized that he could use his expertise to create naturally derived, biodegradable formulas for the beautiful products Eric had in mind.

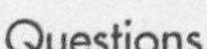

Questions

1. Is method best described as having a market orientation or a societal-marketing orientation?
2. How does method implement the marketing concept?

Marketing & You Results

The higher your score, the more likely you are to do business with the company you thought of and recommend it to others. That is, you have a commitment to the organization and are likely a loyal customer. As you read in Chapter 1, building relationships is a central part of the market orientation!

Career Appendix

One of the most important decisions in your life is choosing a career. Not only will your career choice affect your income and lifestyle, but it also will have a major impact on your happiness and self-fulfillment.

You can use many of the basic concepts of marketing introduced in this book to get the career you want by marketing yourself. The purpose of marketing is to create exchanges that satisfy individual as well as organizational objectives, and a career is certainly an exchange situation for both you and an organization. The purpose of this appendix is to help you market yourself to prospective employers by providing some helpful tools and information.

AVAILABLE CAREERS

Marketing careers have a bright outlook into the next decade. The U.S. Bureau of Labor Statistics estimates that employment in marketing fields will grow between 21 and 35 percent through 2012. Many of these increases will be in the areas of sales, public relations, retailing, advertising, marketing research, product management, and marketing management.

- ***Sales:*** There are more opportunities in sales than in any other area of marketing. Sales positions vary greatly among companies. Some selling positions focus more on providing information; others emphasize locating potential customers, making presentations to committees, and closing the sale. Because compensation is often in the form of salary plus commission, there are few limits on the amount of money a person can make and therefore great potential. Sales positions can be found in many organizations, including manufacturing, wholesaling, retailing, insurance, real estate, financial services, and many other service businesses.
- ***Public relations:*** Public relations firms help create an image or a message for an individual or organization and communicate it effectively to a desired audience. All types of firms, profit and nonprofit organizations, individuals, and even countries employ public relations specialists. Communication skills, both written and oral, are critical for success in public relations.
- ***Retailing:*** Retail careers require many skills. Retail personnel may manage a sales force or other personnel, select and order merchandise, and be responsible for promotional activities, inventory control, store security, and accounting. Large retail stores have a variety of positions, including store or department manager, buyer, display designer, and catalog manager.
- ***Advertising:*** Many organizations employ advertising specialists. Advertising agencies are the largest employers; however, manufacturers, retailers, banks, radio and television stations, hospitals, and insurance agencies all have advertising departments. Creativity, artistic talent, and communication skills are a few of the attributes needed for a successful career in advertising. Account executives serve as a liaison between the advertising agency and the client. Account executives must have a good knowledge of business practices and possess excellent sales skills.
- ***Marketing management:*** Marketing managers develop the firm's detailed marketing strategy. With the help of subordinates, including market research managers and product development managers, they determine the demand for products and services offered by the firm and its competitors. In addition, they identify potential markets—for example, business firms, wholesalers, retailers, government, or the general public. Marketing managers develop pricing strategy with an eye toward maximizing the firm's share of the market and its profits while ensuring that the firm's customers are satisfied. In collaboration with sales, product development, and other managers, they monitor trends that indicate the need for new products and services and oversee product development. Marketing managers work with advertising and promotion managers to promote the firm's products and services and to attract potential users.
- ***Marketing research:*** The most rapid growth in marketing careers is in marketing research. Marketing research firms, advertising agencies, universities, private firms, nonprofit organizations, and governments provide growing opportunities in marketing research. Researchers conduct industry research, advertising research, pricing and packaging research, new-product testing, and test marketing. Researchers are involved in one or more stages of the research process, depending on the size of the organization conducting the research. Marketing research requires knowledge of

EXHIBIT 1

The FAB Matrix

Need of Employer This job requires . . .	Feature of Job Applicant I have . . .	Advantage of Feature This feature means that . . .	Benefit to Employer You will . . .
• Frequent sales presentations to individuals and groups.	• Taken 10 classes that required presentations.	• I require limited or no training in making presentations.	• Save on the cost of training and have an employee with the ability and confidence to be productive early.
• Knowledge of personal computers, software, and applications.	• Taken a personal computer course and used Lotus in most upper-level classes.	• I can already use Word, Excel, dBase, SAS, SPSS, and other software.	• Save time and money on training.
• A person with management potential.	• Been president of a student marketing group and social fraternity president for two years.	• I have experience leading people.	• Save time because I am capable of stepping into a leadership position as needed.

statistics, data processing and analysis, psychology, and communication.

- ***Product management:*** Product managers coordinate all or most of the activities required to market a product. Thus, they need a general knowledge of all aspects of marketing. Product managers are responsible for the successes and failures of a product and are compensated well for this responsibility. Most product managers have previous sales experience and skills in communication. The position of product manager is a major step in the career path of top-level marketing executives.

Starting in a marketing job is also one of the *best routes to the top* of any organization. More CEOs come from sales and marketing backgrounds than from any other field. As examples, Lee Iacocca (Chrysler), Phil Lippincott (Scott Paper), John Akers (IBM), John Sparks (Whirlpool), and Bruno Bich (Bic Pen) came up through sales and marketing. Typically, a college graduate enters the marketing field in a sales position, then moves to sales supervisor, and next sales manager at the district, regional, and national levels. Individuals who prefer to advance through the ranks of marketing management can usually make a career move into product or brand management or another marketing headquarters job after serving for a couple of years in the initial sales position.

Probably the most difficult part of job hunting is deciding exactly what type of work you would like. Many students have had no working experience other than summer jobs, so they are not sure what career to pursue. Too often, college students and their parents rush toward occupational fields that seem to offer the highest monetary payoff or are currently "hot," instead of looking at the long run over a 40- to 50-year working life. One straightforward approach to deciding what type of job to undertake is to do a "self-analysis." This involves honestly asking yourself what your skills, abilities, and interests really are and then identifying occupational fields that match up well with your personality profile. Some students prefer to take various vocational aptitude tests to help identify their interests and abilities. Your college's placement office or psychology department can inform you about the availability of these tests. You may find it useful to develop a FAB (feature–advantage–benefit) matrix that shows what your skills are, why they offer an advantage, and how they would benefit an employer. Exhibit 1 shows an example.

YOUR FIRST MARKETING ASSIGNMENT

Marketing yourself to a prospective employer will usually be your first big marketing assignment. With your services (as represented by your qualifications, education, training, and personal characteristics) as the product, you must convince prospective employers that they should buy your services over those of many other candidates for the job. All the steps of the marketing and sales process apply: identifying opportunities, developing yourself as a product, prospecting for potential employers, planning your approach to them, approaching with a résumé and cover letter, making your sales presentation and demonstrating your qualifications in a personal interview, dealing with objections or giving reasons why the employer should hire you over other candidates, attempting to close the sale by enthusiastically asking for the job and employing appropriate closing techniques, and following up by thanking the prospective employer for the interview and reinforcing a positive impression.

Prospecting for a Potential Employer

After you have determined what you're selling (your skills, abilities, interests, and so forth) and identified the type of job you think you would like, you might begin your personal selling process by looking at the *College Placement Annual* at your college placement office. The *College Placement Annual* provides a variety of information about prospective employers and lists the organizations according to the types of jobs they have available—for example, advertising, banking, marketing research, and sales. Another very important source is an online search on the Internet. Other sources of information about prospective employers include directories such as those published by Dun and Bradstreet, Standard & Poor's, and trade associations; the annual American Marketing Association membership directory (company listings); the Yellow Pages of telephone books in cities where you would like to live and work; and classified sections of *The Wall Street Journal* or city newspapers. Before contacting a particular company, look up its annual report and stock evaluation (from *Value Line* or various other sources) in your college library to learn as much as possible about the company and its prospects for the future. You might also obtain a list of articles on the company from the *Business Periodicals Index* (*BPI*).

College Placement Office

Use your college placement office to find out which companies are going to be interviewing on campus on what dates; then sign up for interviews with those companies that seem to best match your job skills and requirements. Usually, the college placement office has books, pamphlets, or files that will give you leads on other prospective employers that may not be interviewing on campus that term.

Job-Hunting Expenses

Although campus interviews are convenient, students seldom get a job without follow-up interviews with more senior managers—usually at company headquarters. These additional interviews generally take a full day and may involve long-distance trips. You should be forewarned that job hunting can be expensive. Printing your résumé, typing cover letters, buying envelopes and stamps, making long-distance telephone calls, incurring travel expenses, and buying new clothing will require a sizable outlay of money. Even though most companies eventually reimburse you for expenses incurred on a company visit, they seldom pay in advance. Reimbursement can take several weeks, so you may encounter some cash-flow problems over the short run.

The Internet

The Internet is the fastest-growing medium for job searching today. Many companies are using the Internet to assist them in their recruiting efforts. Some companies are even conducting initial interviews online via videoconferencing. Just as some companies post jobs on a bulletin board, companies can list job opportunities on job posting Web sites. Some of the more popular job search Web sites are listed in Exhibit 2. These sites also contain information about résumé writing and interviewing, as well as tips that you can use to secure the job that you want.

EXHIBIT 2

Helpful Internet Addresses for Job Searches/Résumé Writing

The Monster board	**http://www.monster.com**
JobWeb	**http://www.jobweb.org**
Career Builder	**http://www.careerbuilder.com**
Proven Resumes.com	**http://www.provenresumes.com**
WSJ Career Journal	**http://www.careerjournal.com**

Employment Agencies

Although many employment agencies receive fees from employers for providing good job candidates, others charge job seekers huge fees (sometimes thousands of dollars) for helping them find jobs. Therefore, make sure you fully understand the fee arrangement before signing up with an employment agency. Some employment agencies may not be worth your time and/or money because they use a programmed approach to helping you write your résumé and cover letter and prospect for potential employers. Potential employers have seen these "canned" formats and approaches so many times that your personal advertisement (your résumé and cover letter) will be almost indistinguishable from others.

The Hidden Job Market

It has been estimated that nearly 90 percent of available jobs are never advertised and never reach employment agency files, so creative resourcefulness often pays off in finding the best jobs. Consider every reasonable source for leads. Sometimes your professors, deans, or college administrators can give you names and contact persons at companies that have hired recent graduates.

Do not be bashful about letting other people know that you are looking for work. Classmates, friends, and business associates of your family may be of help not only directly but also indirectly, acting as extra pairs of eyes and ears alert to job opportunities for you.

Planning Your Approach (The Preapproach)

After conducting your self-analysis and identifying potential employers looking for people with your abilities and interests, you need to prepare your résumé (or personal advertisement). Your résumé should focus on your achievements to date, your educational background, your work experience, and your special abilities and interests. Some students make the mistake of merely listing their assigned responsibilities on different jobs without indicating what they accomplished on the job. If you achieved something on the job, say it—for example, "Helped computerize office files," "Increased sales in my territory by 10 percent," "Received a 15 percent raise after three months on the job," or "Promoted to assistant store manager after four months." When looking for a job, remember that employers are looking for a track record of achievement, so you must distinguish yourself from those who may have had the same assigned job responsibilities as you did but performed poorly. If your work experience is minimal, consider a "skills" résumé, in which you emphasize your particular abilities, such as organizing, programming, or leadership skills, and give supporting evidence whenever you can. Examples of various types of résumés can be found in the *College Placement Annual* and in various other job-hunting publications. (Ask your college business reference librarian to direct you.) Exhibit 2 lists some Web sites where you can learn about résumé formats.

Remember that there is no one correct format for your résumé. A little tasteful creativity can help differentiate your résumé from countless look-alike résumés. If you are a young college graduate, your résumé will usually be only one page long, but do not worry about going to a second page if you have something important to present. One student so blindly followed the one-page résumé rule that he left out having served in the military—service that is usually viewed very positively by prospective employers, especially if it involved significant leadership responsibilities or work experience.

If you know what job you want, you may want to put your job objective near the top of your résumé. If you are not sure what job you want or want to send out the same résumé for several different jobs, then you can describe your job objective in your cover letter. A key element in the cover letter is convincing the prospective employer to grant you an interview. Thus, you must talk in terms of the employer's interests, not just your own. You are answering the question: "Why should we hire you?" You may need to send a letter with your résumé enclosed to a hundred or more companies to obtain five to ten interviews, so do not be discouraged if you get replies from only a few companies or are told by many companies that they have no job opportunities at present. You will probably need only a few interviews and just one job offer to get your career started.

Review some of the publications and sources mentioned in the previous section on prospecting (e.g., *College Placement Annual*, Dun and Bradstreet directories, and annual reports) to learn as much as you can about your prospective employer so that you can tailor your cover letter. Remember, the employer is thinking in terms of the company's needs, not yours. For one example of a résumé, see Exhibit 3. A cover letter is illustrated in Exhibit 4.

EXHIBIT 3

Sample Résumé

RACHEL E. SANFORD
2935 Mountain View Road
Ellington, PA 19401
(216) 567-0000

JOB OBJECTIVE	Sales representative for a consumer-products company
EDUCATION	Graduated *cum laude* with BS in Marketing Management (June 2006), University of Southern Pennsylvania. Career-related courses included Selling and Sales Management, Public Speaking, Business Writing, Public Relations, Marketing Research, Computer Programming, and Multivariate Data Analysis.
ACTIVITIES AND HONORS	President, Student Marketing Association; Vice president, Chi Omega Sorority; Captain, women's varsity tennis team; sportswriter for the *Campus View* student newspaper. Named to Who's Who among American College Students, 2004–2005. On Dean's List all four years. Overall grade point average = 3.65.
WORK EXPERIENCE	
Summer 2005	*Sales representative*, Peabody Manufacturing Company. Sold women's blouses to boutiques and small department stores in southeastern Pennsylvania. Exceeded assigned sales quota by 20 percent; named "outstanding" summer employee for 2005.
Summer 2004	*Buyer*, Hamm's Department Stores, Inc., Midway, Pa. Developed purchase plan, initiated purchase orders, monitored and controlled expenditures for nearly $2 million worth of women's clothing. Made monthly progress reports (written and oral) to Hamm's Executive Committee. Received 15 percent bonus as #2 buyer in the six stores of the Hamm's chain in special "Back to School" purchasing competition.
Summer 2003	*Retail clerk*, Hamm's Department Stores, Inc., Midway, Pa. After 3 months, received 10 percent pay raise and promotion to evening salesclerk supervisor over seven part-time salesclerks. Devised new inventory control system for handbags and accessories that cut costs over $50,000 annually.
Summer 2002	*Cosmetics salesperson*, Heavenly Charm, Inc., Midway, Pa. Sold $63,000 worth of Heavenly Charm cosmetics door to door. Named #1 salesperson in the sales region. Offered full-time job as sales supervisor.
INTERESTS	Tennis, golf, public speaking, short story writing, and reading biographies.

EXHIBIT 4

Sample Cover Letter

Rachel E. Sanford
2935 Mountain View Road
Ellington, PA 19401

Mr. Samuel Abramson
District Sales Manager
Hixson Appliance Company
Philadelphia, PA 19103

Dear Mr. Abramson:

Hixson has been a familiar name to me ever since I was barely able to see over my mother's kitchen counter. Virtually every appliance we had was a Hixson, so I know firsthand what fine quality products you sell. My career interest is in sales, and there is no company that I would rather work with than Hixson Appliance.

I will be graduating this June from Southern Pennsylvania University with a BS in marketing management, and I would like you to consider me for a job as a sales representative with your company. As you can see in my enclosed résumé, I have successfully worked in sales jobs during three of the last four summers. My college course electives (e.g., public speaking, business writing, and public relations) have been carefully selected with my career objective in mind. Even my extracurricular activities in sports and campus organizations have helped prepare me for working with a variety of people and competitive challenges.

Will you please grant me an interview so that I can convince you that I'm someone you should hire for your sales team? I'll call you next Thursday afternoon to arrange an appointment at your convenience.

Look forward to meeting you soon.

Sincerely,

Rachel E. Sanford

Enclosure

Making Your Approach

Prospective employers can be approached by mail, telephone, the Internet, or personal contact. Personal contact is best, but this usually requires that you know someone with influence who can arrange an interview for you. Of course, a few enterprising students have devised elaborate and sometimes successful schemes to get job interviews. For example, we know of one young man who simply went to the headquarters of the company he wanted to work for and asked to see the president. Told that the president of the company could not see him, the student said that he was willing to wait until the president had time. This audacious individual went back three different days until the president finally agreed to see him, perhaps mainly out of curiosity about what sort of young man would be so outrageous in his job search.

Fortunately for this young man, he had a lot to offer and was able to communicate this to the president, so he was hired. This unorthodox approach shows how far people have gone to impress potential employers, and if you feel comfortable doing it, then go ahead. A personal contact within the company certainly can win you some special attention and enable you to avoid competing head-on with the large number of other candidates looking for a job. Most students, however, start their approach in the traditional way by mailing their résumé and cover letter to the recruiting department of the company. More recently, students have begun to e-mail their résumés, and some companies are requiring this as a means of screening out applicants who are not computer literate. Unless your résumé matches a particular need at that time, it will probably be filed away for possible future reference or merely discarded. To try to get around the system, some students send their letter by express mail or mailgram or address it to a key executive, with "Personal" written on the envelope. These students believe that bypassing the company's personnel office will increase the likelihood that their cover letter and résumé will be read by someone with authority to hire. Other students send their résumé on a CD or DVD, and one student in Louisiana sent a King Cake to the recipient of the résumé, while another sent a packet of Louisiana spices. Using gimmicks, no matter how creative, to get a job interview will offend some executives and thus cause you to be rejected from consideration for a job. But you can probably also be sure that a few executives will admire your efforts and grant you an interview.

Only you know how comfortable you feel with different approaches to obtaining a job interview. We advise you not to use an approach that is out of character for you and thus will make you feel awkward and embarrassed.

Making Your Sales Presentation

Your personal sales presentation will come during the interview with the prospective employer's recruiters or interviewers. Like any presentation, it requires thorough preparation and an effective follow-up, as well as a solid performance during the interview itself.

Pre-Interview Considerations

Preparing for the interview is crucial. You will already have gathered information on the company, as suggested in the preceding sections; you should review it now. Exhibit 5 shows a pre-interview checklist that can help you prepare. In addition, the self-assessment test in Exhibit 6 can help you determine if you're ready for the interview.

Keep the following in mind in preparing for your interview:

- Find out the exact place and time of the interview.
- Be certain you know the interviewer's name and how to pronounce it if it looks difficult.
- Do some research on the company with which you are interviewing—talk to people and read the company literature to know what its products or services are, where its offices are located, what its growth has been, and how its prospects look for the future.
- Think of two or three good questions that you would like to ask during your interview.
- Plan to arrive at the designated place for your interview a little early so that you will not feel rushed and worried about being on time.
- Plan to dress in a manner appropriate to the job for which you are interviewing.

A guide for the interview conversation itself is to prepare nine positive thoughts before you go in for the interview:

- Three reasons why you selected the employer to interview
- Three reasons you particularly like the employer
- Three assets you have that should interest the employer

EXHIBIT 5

Before the Interview

- **Practice**
  - ✓ Questions you may be asked
  - ✓ Questions you want to ask about the position and organization
  - ✓ Role-playing an interview
- **Self-assessment**
  - ✓ Goals
  - ✓ Skills, abilities, accomplishments
  - ✓ Work values (important factors you look for in a job)
  - ✓ Experiences
  - ✓ Personality
- **Research**
  - ✓ Obtain company literature
  - ✓ Write or visit the organization
  - ✓ Talk to people familiar with the organization
- **Obtain references**
- **Plan ahead**
  - ✓ Attire to be worn to the interview
  - ✓ Directions to the interview site
  - ✓ Time of arrival (get there with at least 5–10 minutes to spare)

EXHIBIT 6

Self-Assessment Test

How assertive are you (or will you be) as you interview for a position? Listed below are questions that will help you to evaluate yourself: answer yes or no to the questions, being honest with yourself. If you have five or fewer yes answers, you still have some work to do. A good score is seven or more yes answers.

Yes No

___ ___ Have you made an effort to research the company before the interview?

___ ___ Have you prepared several questions that you want to ask?

___ ___ If an interviewer asks a personal question unrelated to the job, will you be able to tactfully call this to his attention?

___ ___ If an interviewer gives you a hypothetical job-related problem, do you have confidence in your ability to respond in a timely and succinct manner?

___ ___ If the interviewer seems distracted or uninterested during your interview, will you be able to steer the interview back on track and gain her attention?

___ ___ When you meet the interviewer, will you be the first to introduce yourself and begin the conversation?

___ ___ If the interviewer continually interrupts when you are responding to questions or giving information about yourself, can you politely handle this?

___ ___ If the interviewer never gives you the opportunity to talk about yourself and you have only five minutes remaining in the interview, have you thought about phrases or ways to redirect the interview and regain control of the process?

___ ___ When the interviewer is beginning to close the interview, are you prepared to ask questions about how you stand, what the determining factors are for candidate selection, and by what date you will have an answer?

Try to make a positive impression on everyone you encounter in the company, even while waiting in the lobby for your interview. Sometimes managers will ask their receptionists and secretaries for an opinion of you, and your friendliness, courtesy, professional demeanor, personal habits, and the like will all be used to judge you. Even the magazines you choose to read while waiting can be a positive or negative factor. For instance, it will probably be less impressive if you leaf through a popular magazine like *People* or *Sports Illustrated* than if you read something more professional such as *BusinessWeek* or *The Wall Street Journal*.

During the Interview

During the interview, do not be merely a passive respondent to the interviewer's questions. Being graciously assertive by asking reasonable questions of your own will indicate to the interviewer that you are alert, energetic, and sincerely interested in the job. The personal interview is your opportunity to persuade the prospective employer that you should be hired. To use a show business analogy, you will be onstage for only a short time (during the personal interview), so try to present an honest but positive image of yourself. Perhaps it will help you to be alert and

EXHIBIT 7

Some Questions Frequently Asked During a Job Interview

- Of the jobs you've had to date, which one did you like best? Why?
- Why do you want to work for our company?
- Tell me what you know about our company.
- Do any of your relatives or friends work for our company? If so, in what jobs?
- Tell me about yourself, your strengths, weaknesses, career goals, and so forth.
- Is any member of your family a professional marketer? If so, what area of marketing?
- Why do you want to start your career in marketing?
- Persuade me that we should hire you.
- What extracurricular activities did you participate in at college? What leadership positions did you have in any of these activities?
- What benefits have you derived from participation in extracurricular activities that will help you in your career?
- Where do you see yourself within our company in five years? In ten years? Twenty years?
- What is your ultimate career goal?
- What do you consider your greatest achievement to date?
- What is your biggest failure to date?
- What is (was) your favorite subject in school? Why?
- Are you willing to travel and possibly relocate?
- How would the people who know you describe you?
- How would you describe yourself?
- What do you like most about marketing?
- What do you like least about marketing?
- If we hire you, how soon could you start work?
- What is the minimum we would have to offer you to come with us?
- What goals have you set for yourself? How are you planning to achieve them?
- Who or what has had the greatest influence on the development of your career interests?
- What factors did you consider in choosing your major?
- Why are you interested in our organization?
- What can you tell me about yourself?
- What two or three things are most important to you in a position?
- What kind of work do you want to do?
- What can you tell me about a project you initiated?
- What are your expectations of your future employer?
- What is your GPA? How do you feel about it? Does it reflect your ability?
- How do you resolve conflicts?
- What do you feel are your strengths? Your weaknesses? How do you evaluate yourself?
- What work experience has been the most valuable to you and why?
- What was the most useful criticism you ever received, and who was it from?
- Can you give an example of a problem you have solved and the process you used?
- Can you describe the project or situation that best demonstrates your analytical skills?
- What has been your greatest challenge?

EXHIBIT 7

Some Questions Frequently Asked During a Job Interview (continued)

- Can you describe a situation where you had a conflict with another individual and explain how you dealt with it?
- What are the biggest problems you encountered in college? How did you handle them? What did you learn from them?
- What are your team-player qualities? Give examples.
- Can you describe your leadership style?
- What interests or concerns you about the position or the company?
- In a particular leadership role you had, what was the greatest challenge?
- What idea have you developed and implemented that was particularly creative or innovative?
- What characteristics do you think are important for this position?
- How have your educational and work experiences prepared you for this position?
- Can you take me through a project where you demonstrated skills?
- How do you think you have changed personally since you started college?
- Can you tell me about a team project that you are particularly proud of and discuss your contribution?
- How do you motivate people?
- Why did you choose the extracurricular activities you did? What did you gain? What did you contribute?
- What types of situations put you under pressure, and how do you deal with the pressure?
- Can you tell me about a difficult decision you have made?
- Can you give an example of a situation in which you failed and explain how you handled it?
- Can you tell me about a situation when you had to persuade another person of your point of view?
- What frustrates you the most?
- Knowing what you know now about your college experience, would you make the same decisions?
- What can you contribute to this company?
- How would you react to having your credibility questioned?
- What characteristics are important in a good manager? How have you displayed one of these characteristics?
- What challenges are you looking for in a position?
- What two or three accomplishments have given you the most satisfaction?
- Can you describe a leadership role of yours and tell why you committed your time to it?
- How are you conducting your job search, and how will you make your decision?
- What is the most important lesson you have learned in or out of school?
- Can you describe a situation where you had to work with someone who was difficult? How was the person difficult, and how did you handle it?
- We are looking at a lot of great candidates; why are you the best person for this position?
- How would your friends describe you? Your professors?
- What else should I know about you?

enthusiastic if you imagine that you are being interviewed on television. Exhibit 7 lists a number of questions that are frequently asked during interviews.

Sometimes prospective employers will ask you to demonstrate certain abilities by having you write a timed essay about some part of your life, sell something (such as a desk calculator) to the interviewer, or respond to hostile questions. Be calm and confident during any such unorthodox interviewing approaches and you will make a good impression. Remember, most employers want you to perform well because they are looking for the best people they can find in a given time frame for the money they have to offer.

If you are given intelligence, aptitude, or psychological tests, you should try to be honest so that you do not create unrealistic expectations that you will not be able to fulfill. It is just as important that you do not create a false impression and begin with a company that is not right for you as it is to secure employment in the first place. Many experts say that it is not very difficult to "cheat" on aptitude or psychological tests if you are able to "play the role" and provide the answers that you know the company wants to read. Usually, the so-called safe approach in most personality and preference (interest) tests is to not take extreme positions on anything that is not clearly associated with the job you are applying for. For sales jobs, it is probably safe to come across as highly extroverted and interested in group activities, but it may not be safe to appear to be overly interested in literature, music, art, or any solitary activity. In addition, the "right" answers tend to indicate a conservative, goal-oriented, money-motivated, and gregarious personality.

Dealing with Objections Sometimes interviewers will bluntly ask, "Why should we hire you?" This requires that you think in terms of the employer's needs and present in concise form all your major "selling points." Also, sometimes the interviewer may bring up reasons why you are not the ideal candidate. For example, he or she may say: (1) "We're really looking for someone with a little more experience"; (2) "We'd like to get someone with a more technical educational background"; or (3) "We need someone to start work within two weeks." These kinds of statements are similar to objections or requests for additional information. In other words, the interviewer is saying, "Convince me that I shouldn't rule you out for this reason." To overcome such objections, you might respond to each, respectively, along the following lines:

(1) "I've had over a year's experience working with two different companies during my summer vacations, and I've worked part-time with a third company all during college. I'm a fast learner, and I've adapted well to each of the three companies, so I feel that my working experience is equivalent to that of someone who has had three or four years' experience with the same company."

(2) "Although I didn't choose to earn a technical undergraduate degree, I've taken several technical courses in college, including basic engineering courses, chemistry, physics, and two years of math. I'm very confident that I can quickly learn whatever is necessary technically to do the job, and my real strength is that my education has been a blend of technical and managerial courses."

(3) "Well, I do have one more term of school, so I couldn't start full-time work in two weeks, but perhaps we could work out an arrangement in which I could work part-time—maybe Friday, Saturday, and Sunday or on weekends until I graduate."

Good "salespeople" do not allow an objection to block a sale. Providing reasonable solutions or alternative perspectives can often overcome objections or, at least, allow room for further negotiation toward a compromise solution.

How to Act during the Interview The following can help you behave appropriately during the interview:

- Think positive. Be enthusiastic, interested, knowledgeable, and confident.
- Take few notes. It is acceptable to take notes during the interview, but limit them to things that are essential to remember. You want to focus more on listening and observing rather than writing.
- Relate to the interviewer. Build positive rapport with the interviewer. Listen and observe; relate yourself to the employer or position.
- Watch your body language. Be aware of nervousness (fidgeting, shaking leg, tapping, etc.). Project confidence (eye contact, firm handshake, upright posture).
- Be aware of the questions the employer asks. Answer with information relevant to the position. Provide a direct answer; avoid being long-winded.
- Think about the questions you ask. They should indicate that you know something about the job. Avoid questions that could easily be answered elsewhere (through research). Obtain information you need to know to be satisfied with the job (interviewing is a two-way process). Salary and benefit questions should be asked after the job is offered.
- Achieve effective closure. Ask when the employer expects to make a decision. Restate your interest and ability to perform the job. Show confidence and enthusiasm (smile, end with a firm handshake). Obtain the employer's business card, if possible (it may be useful when writing a thank-you letter).

Interview Questions Too many employment applicants spend all their time preparing for the questions employers will ask them. Too often, they fail to ask vital questions that would help them learn if a job is right for them. Failing to ask important questions during the interview often leads to jobs that offer neither interest nor challenge. Too often, uninformed applicants accept positions hoping that they will develop into something more meaningful and rewarding later. Exhibit 8 suggests questions that you may want to ask.

Closing the Sale

Although it is not likely that a prospective employer will offer you a job immediately after the job interview, you should nevertheless let the interviewer know that you definitely want the job and are confident that you will do an excellent job for the employer. You will need to use your best judgment on how to best do this.

In each stage of the personal selling process, you should be looking for feedback from the interviewer's body language and voice inflections or tone.

Following Up the Interview

Within a few days after any job interview, whether you want the job or not, it is business courtesy to write thank-you letters to interviewers. In these letters you can reinforce the positive impression you made in the interview and again express your keen interest in working for the company. If you do not hear from the company within a few weeks, it may be appropriate to write another letter expressing your continuing interest in the job and asking for a decision so that you can consider other options if necessary. As a possible reason for this follow-up letter, you might mention an additional personal achievement since the interview, give a more detailed answer to one of the interviewer's questions, or perhaps send a newspaper or magazine article of interest. A neat, well-written, courteous follow-up letter gives you a chance not only to make a stronger impression on the interviewer but also to exhibit positive qualities such as initiative, energy,

EXHIBIT 8

Sample Interview Questions to Be Asked by Job Candidates

- Where is the organization going? What plans or projects are being developed to maintain or increase its market share? Have many new product lines been decided upon recently? Is the sales growth in the new product line sustainable?
- Who are the people with whom I will be working? May I speak with some of them?
- May I have a copy of the job description?
- What might be a typical first assignment?
- Do you have a performance appraisal system? How is it structured? How frequently will I be evaluated?
- What is the potential for promotion in the organization? In promotions, are employees ever transferred between functional fields? What is the average time to get to _______ level in the career path? Is your policy to promote from within, or are many senior jobs filled by experienced people from outside? Do you have a job posting system?
- What type of training will I receive? When does the training program begin? Is it possible to move through your program faster? About how many individuals go through your internship program?
- What is the normal routine of a (an) _______ like? Can I progress at my own pace, or is it structured? Do employees normally work overtime?
- How much travel is normally expected? Is a car provided to traveling personnel?
- How much freedom is given to new people? How much discipline is required? How much input does the new person have? How much decision-making authority is given to new personnel?
- How frequently do you relocate employees? Is it possible to transfer from one division to another?
- What is the housing market for a single person in _______ (city)? Is public transportation adequate?
- How much contact with and exposure to management is there?
- How soon should I expect to report to work?

sensitivity to others' feelings, and awareness of business protocol.

Many applicants fail to write a thank-you letter after an interview, yet many employers say that the deciding factor between several similar job candidates is often the thank-you note. The thank-you letter should be typewritten. If the interviewer is a very technology-driven person, a thank-you e-mail may also be appropriate. However, the personal touch of a typewritten and hand-signed letter leaves a better impression.

Be sure to write a follow-up letter in all of the following situations:

- After two or three weeks of no reply.
- When a job has been refused. Express your regret that no job is available and ask if you might be considered in the future. Also, ask how you could improve yourself to better fit what the company is looking for.
- After an interview. Express your thanks for the interviewer's time and courtesy. Answer any unanswered questions and clarify any misconceptions.
- To accept a job (even if previously done in person or on the phone). State your acceptance. Reiterate the agreement, the time for beginning work, and the like. Do not start asking for favors.
- To refuse a job offer. Graciously decline the offer. Be warm and interested and indicate that you appreciate the offer.

Follow-up letters are also appropriate after you have received replies to both solicited and unsolicited letters of inquiry. Always make certain that your letters possess the attitude, quality, and skill of a professional.

ON THE JOB

Working Conditions

Advertising, marketing, promotions, public relations, and sales managers work in offices close to those of top managers. Long hours, including evenings and weekends, are common. About 44 percent of advertising, marketing, and public relations managers work more than 40 hours per week. Substantial travel may also be involved. For example, attendance at meetings sponsored by associations or industries is often mandatory. Sales managers travel to local, regional, and national offices and to various dealers and distributors. Advertising and promotions managers may travel to meet with clients or representatives of communications media. At times, public relations managers travel to meet with special interest groups or government officials. Job transfers between headquarters and regional offices are common, particularly among sales managers.

Moving Up the Ladder

Most advertising, marketing, promotions, public relations, and sales management positions are filled by promoting experienced staff or related professional personnel. For example, many managers are former sales representatives, purchasing agents, buyers, or product, advertising, promotions, or public relations specialists. In small firms, where the number of positions is limited, advancement to a management position usually comes slowly. In large firms, promotion may occur more quickly.

Although experience, ability, and leadership are emphasized for promotion, advancement can be accelerated by participation in management training programs conducted by many large firms. Many firms also provide their employees with continuing education opportunities, either in-house or at local colleges and universities, and encourage employee participation in seminars and conferences, often provided by professional societies. In collaboration with colleges and universities, numerous marketing and related associations sponsor national or local management training programs. Staying abreast of what is happening in your industry and getting involved in related industry associations can be important for your career advancement.

YOUR EARLY WORKING CAREER

Even though you want to choose a company that you will stay with throughout your working life, it is realistic to recognize that you will probably work for three, four, or more companies during your career. If you are not fully satisfied with your job or company during the first few years of your full-time working life, remember that you are building experience and knowledge that will increase your marketability for future job opportunities. Keep a positive outlook and do the best you can in all job assignments—and your chance for new opportunities will come. Do not be too discouraged by mistakes that you may make in your career; nearly every successful person has made and continues to make many mistakes. View these mistakes largely as learning experiences, and they will not be too traumatic or damaging to your confidence.

Good luck in your marketing career!

© MICHAEL THOMAS/GETTY IMAGES

CHAPTER 2

Strategic Planning for Competitive Advantage

LEARNING OUTCOMES

- LO1 Understand the importance of strategic marketing and know a basic outline for a marketing plan
- LO2 Develop an appropriate business mission statement
- LO3 Describe the components of a situation analysis
- LO4 Explain the criteria for stating good marketing objectives
- LO5 Identify sources of competitive advantage
- LO6 Identify strategic alternatives
- LO7 Discuss target market strategies
- LO8 Describe the elements of the marketing mix
- LO9 Explain why implementation, evaluation, and control of the marketing plan are necessary
- LO10 Identify several techniques that help make strategic planning effective

THE NATURE OF STRATEGIC PLANNING

Strategic planning is the managerial process of creating and maintaining a fit between the organization's objectives and resources and the evolving market opportunities. The goal of strategic planning is long-run profitability and growth. Thus, strategic decisions require long-term commitments of resources.

A strategic error can threaten a firm's survival. On the other hand, a good strategic plan can help protect and grow the firm's resources. For instance, if the March of Dimes had decided to focus on fighting polio, the organization would no longer exist. Most of us view polio as a conquered disease. The March of Dimes survived by making the strategic decision to switch to fighting birth defects.

Strategic marketing management addresses two questions: What is the organization's main activity at a particular time? How will it reach its goals? Here are some examples of strategic decisions:

- General Electric Company has initiated an effort called "Ecomagination," which will shift its focus to being an environmentally conscious company that is working to solve some of the planet's most critical environmental issues. This effort represents a complete transformation in strategy for GE that is changing the way it develops products, sells to customers, and enters emerging markets.[1]
- Toys"R"Us has suffered as younger and younger children abandon traditional toys for electronic entertainment and because parents tend to buy toys during weekly trips to one-stop shops like Wal-Mart. The company responded by expanding its infant line, Babies"R"Us, and is using it to lure parents of older children into their toy selections.[2]
- McDonald's decision to offer more healthful foods by focusing on fresh fruits and vegetables with its new line of premium salads.[3]
- SC Johnson's introduction of Shout Color Catchers, a laundry sheet for the washer that collects loose dyes and prevents clothes from bleeding color onto other laundry items.

All these decisions have affected or will affect each organization's long-run course, its allocation of resources, and ultimately its financial success. In contrast, an operating decision, such as changing the package design for Post's cornflakes or altering the sweetness of a Kraft salad dressing, probably won't have a big impact on the long-run profitability of the company.

Marketing & You

What do you think about planning? Enter your answers on the lines provided.

Describes my style

1 2 3 4 5 6 7

Not at all — Perfectly

__ I start my work without spending too much time on planning.*

__ I list the steps necessary for completing a task before starting it.

__ I think about strategies I will fall back on if problems arise.

__ Because so many aspects of my work are unpredictable, planning is not useful.*

__ I keep good records of the projects I'm working on.

__ I set personal goals for myself.

__ Each week I make a plan for what I need to do.

__ I do not waste time thinking about what I should do.*

__ I am careful to work on the highest-priority tasks first.

__ Planning is a waste of time.*

__ Planning is an excuse for not working.*

__ I don't need to develop a strategy for completing my assignments.*

Now, total your score, reversing your score for items with asterisks—that is, if you put a 2, put a 6, and vice versa. Read the chapter, and see what your score means at the end.

strategic planning
The managerial process of creating and maintaining a fit between the organization's objectives and resources and evolving market opportunities.

planning
The process of anticipating future events and determining strategies to achieve organizational objectives in the future.

marketing planning
Designing activities relating to marketing objectives and the changing marketing environment.

marketing plan
A written document that acts as a guidebook of marketing activities for the marketing manager.

How do companies go about strategic marketing planning? How do employees know how to implement the long-term goals of the firm? The answer is a marketing plan.

What is a Marketing Plan?

Planning is the process of anticipating future events and determining strategies to achieve organizational objectives in the future. **Marketing planning** involves designing activities relating to marketing objectives and the changing marketing environment. Marketing planning is the basis for all marketing strategies and decisions. Issues such as product lines, distribution channels, marketing communications, and pricing are all delineated in the **marketing plan**. The marketing plan is a written document that acts as a guidebook of marketing activities for the marketing manager. In this chapter, you will learn the importance of writing a marketing plan and the types of information contained in a marketing plan.

Why Write a Marketing Plan? By specifying objectives and defining the actions required to attain them, you can provide in a marketing plan the basis by which actual and expected performance can be compared. Marketing can be one of the most expensive and complicated business activities, but it is also one of the most important. The written marketing plan provides clearly stated activities that help employees and managers understand and work toward common goals.

Writing a marketing plan allows you to examine the marketing environment in conjunction with the inner workings of the business. Once the marketing plan is written, it serves as a reference point for the success of future activities. Finally, the marketing plan allows the marketing manager to enter the marketplace with an awareness of possibilities and problems.

EXHIBIT 2.1

Elements of a Marketing Plan

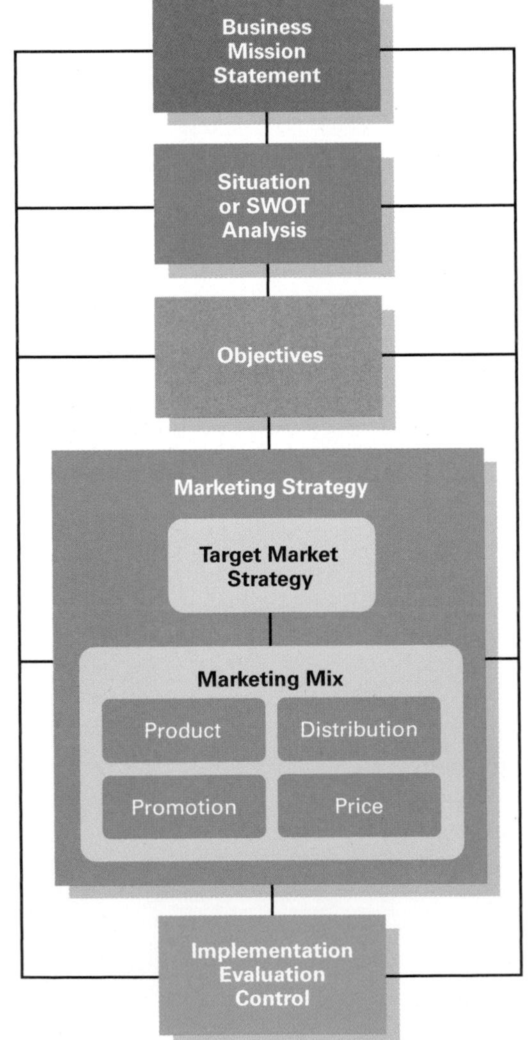

Marketing Plan Elements Marketing plans can be presented in many different ways. Most businesses need a written marketing plan because a marketing plan is large and can be complex. Details about tasks and activity assignments may be lost if communicated orally. Regardless of the way a marketing plan is presented, some elements are common to all marketing plans. These include defining the business mission, performing a situation analysis, defining objectives, delineating a target market, and establishing components of the marketing mix. Exhibit 2.1 shows these elements, which are also described further below. Other elements that may be included in a plan are budgets, implementation timetables, required marketing research efforts, or elements of advanced strategic planning. A marketing planning outline and an example of a marketing plan appear in the appendices to this chapter.

Selecting which alternative to pursue depends on the overall company philosophy and culture. The choice also depends on the tool used to make the decision. Companies generally have one of two philosophies about when they expect profits. They either pursue profits right away or first seek to increase market share and then pursue profits. In the long run, market share and profitability are compatible goals. Many companies have long followed this credo: Build market share, and profits will surely follow. Michelin, the tire producer, consistently sacrifices short-term profits to achieve market share. On the other hand, IBM stresses profitability and stock valuation over market share, quality, and customer service. As you can see, the same strategic alternative may be viewed entirely differently by different firms.

A number of tools exist to help managers select a strategic alternative. The most common of these tools are in matrix form. The portfolio matrix is described here in more detail.

Writing the Marketing Plan

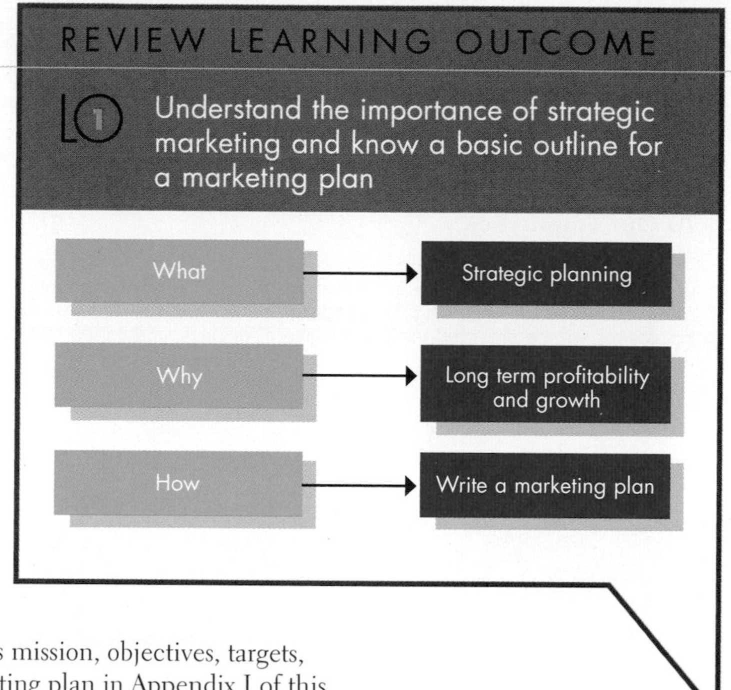

The creation and implementation of a complete marketing plan will allow the organization to achieve marketing objectives and succeed. However, the marketing plan is only as good as the information it contains and the effort, creativity, and thought that went into its creation. Having a good marketing information system and a wealth of competitive intelligence (covered in Chapter 9) is critical to a thorough and accurate situation analysis. The role of managerial intuition is also important in the creation and selection of marketing strategies. Managers must weigh any information against its accuracy and their own judgment when making a marketing decision.

Note that the overall structure of the marketing plan (Exhibit 2.1) should not be viewed as a series of sequential planning steps. Many of the marketing plan elements are decided on simultaneously and in conjunction with one another. Further, every marketing plan has a different content, depending on the organization, its mission, objectives, targets, and marketing mix components. The example of a marketing plan in Appendix I of this chapter should not be regarded as the only correct format for a marketing plan. Many organizations have their own distinctive format or terminology for creating a marketing plan. Every marketing plan should be unique to the firm for which it was created. Remember, however, that although the format and order of presentation should be flexible, the same types of questions and topic areas should be covered in any marketing plan. As you can see by the extent of the marketing planning outline and the example of the e-motion software marketing plan in Appendix II, creating a complete marketing plan is not a simple or quick effort.

DEFINING THE BUSINESS MISSION

© DAVID YOUNG WOLF/PHOTOEDIT

The foundation of any marketing plan is the firm's **mission statement**, which answers the question, "What business are we in?" The way a firm defines its business mission profoundly affects the firm's long-run resource allocation, profitability, and survival. The mission statement is based on a careful analysis of benefits sought by present and potential customers and an analysis of existing and anticipated environmental conditions. The firm's mission statement establishes boundaries for all subsequent decisions, objectives, and strategies. The Southwest Airlines mission statement is shown in Exhibit 2.2.

A mission statement should focus on the market or markets the organization is attempting to serve rather than on the good or service offered. Otherwise, a new technology may quickly make the good or service obsolete and the mission statement irrelevant to company functions. Business mission statements that are stated too narrowly suffer from **marketing myopia**—defining a business in terms of goods and services rather than in terms of the benefits customers seek. In this context, *myopia* means narrow, short-term thinking. For example, Frito-Lay defines its mission as being in the snack-food business rather than in the corn chip business. The mission of sports teams is not just to play games but to serve the interests of the fans.

mission statement
A statement of the firm's business based on a careful analysis of benefits sought by present and potential customers and an analysis of existing and anticipated environmental conditions.

marketing myopia
Defining a business in terms of goods and services rather than in terms of the benefits that customers seek.

EXHIBIT 2.2

Southwest Airlines Mission Statement

The mission of Southwest Airlines is dedication to the highest quality of Customer Service delivered with a sense of warmth, friendliness, individual pride, and Company Spirit.

To Our Employees

We are committed to provide our Employees a stable work environment with equal opportunity for learning and personal growth. Creativity and innovation are encouraged for improving the effectiveness of Southwest Airlines. Above all, Employees will be provided the same concern, respect, and caring attitude within the organization that they are expected to share externally with every Southwest Customer.

Source: http://www.southwestairlines.com/about_swa/mission

Alternatively, business missions may be stated too broadly. "To provide products of superior quality and value that improve the lives of the world's consumers" is probably too broad a mission statement for any firm except Procter & Gamble. Care must be taken when stating what business a firm is in. For example, the mission of Ben & Jerry's centers on three important aspects of its ice cream business: (1) Product: "To make, distribute, and sell the finest quality all natural ice cream and related products in a wide variety of innovative flavors made from Vermont Dairy products"; (2) Economic: "To operate the company on a sound financial basis of profitable growth, increasing value for our shareholders, and creating career opportunities and financial rewards for our employees"; and (3) Social: "To operate the company in a way that actively recognizes the central role that business plays in the structure of society by initiating innovative ways to improve the quality of life of a broad community—local, national, and international."[4] By correctly stating the business mission in terms of the benefits that customers seek, the foundation for the marketing plan is set. Many companies are focusing on designing more appropriate mission statements because these statements are frequently displayed on the company's Web sites.

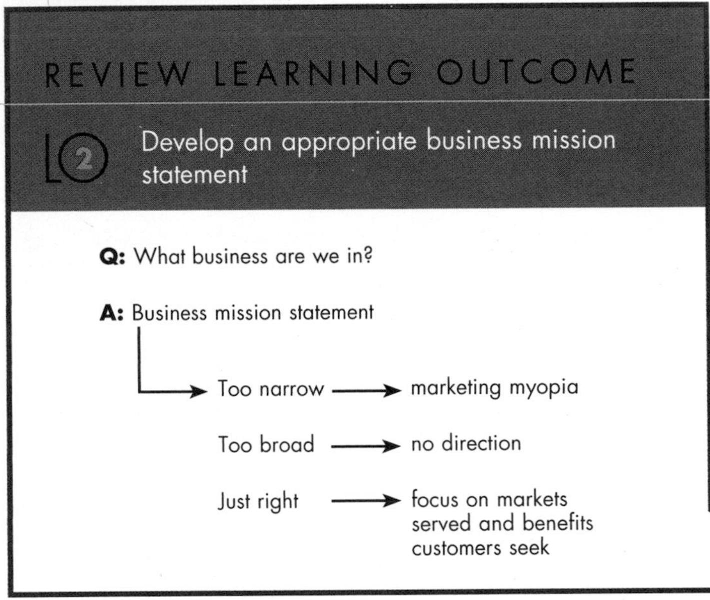

The organization may need to define a mission statement and objectives for a **strategic business unit (SBU)**, which is a subgroup of a single business or a collection of related businesses within the larger organization. A properly defined SBU should have a distinct mission and specific target market, control over its resources, its own competitors, and plans independent of the other SBUs in the organization. Thus, a large firm such as Kraft Foods may have marketing plans for each of its SBUs, which include breakfast foods, desserts, pet foods, and beverages.

strategic business unit (SBU)
A subgroup of a single business or a collection of related businesses within the larger organization.

SWOT analysis
Identifying internal strengths (S) and weaknesses (W) and also examining external opportunities (O) and threats (T).

LO3

CONDUCTING A SITUATION ANALYSIS

Marketers must understand the current and potential environment that the product or service will be marketed in. A situation analysis is sometimes referred to as a **SWOT analysis**; that is, the firm should identify its internal strengths (S) and weaknesses (W) and also examine external opportunities (O) and threats (T).

When examining internal strengths and weaknesses, the marketing manager should focus on organizational resources such as production costs, marketing skills, financial resources, company or brand image, employee capabilities, and available technology. For example, a potential weakness for AirTran Airways (formerly ValuJet) is the age of its airplane fleet, which could project an image of danger or low quality. Other weaknesses include high labor turnover rates and limited flights. A potential strength is the airline's low operating costs, which translate into lower prices for consumers. Another issue to consider in this section of the marketing plan is the historical background of the firm—its sales and profit history.

When examining external opportunities and threats, marketing managers must analyze aspects of the marketing environment. This process is called **environmental scanning**—the collection and interpretation of information about forces, events, and relationships in the external environment that may affect the future of the organization or the implementation of the marketing plan. Environmental scanning helps identify market opportunities and threats and provides guidelines for the design of marketing strategy. The six most often studied macroenvironmental forces are social, demographic, economic, technological, political and legal, and competitive. These forces are examined in detail in Chapter 3. Rising gas prices and a weakening dollar have created a complex, but possibly advantageous, environment for McDonald's. While increased gas costs may discourage some consumers from visiting its drive-through windows, the fast-food giant hopes that its widespread availability, its inexpensive prices, and its new gourmet-style coffee offerings will attract consumers trying to save money by downgrading from Starbucks and other pricy venues. McDonald's marketers are even taking advantage of gas price increases by running commercials in which teenagers decide not to fill their empty gas tank and buy $1 double cheeseburgers to fill their stomachs instead.[5]

REVIEW LEARNING OUTCOME

LO3 Describe the components of a situation analysis

INTERNAL

Strengths
- production costs
- marketing skills
- financial resources
- image
- technology

Weaknesses

EXTERNAL

Opportunities
- social
- demographic
- economic
- technological
- political/legal
- competitive

Threats

LO4 SETTING MARKETING PLAN OBJECTIVES

Before the details of a marketing plan can be developed, objectives for the plan must be stated. Without objectives, there is no basis for measuring the success of marketing plan activities.

A **marketing objective** is a statement of what is to be accomplished through marketing activities. To be useful, stated objectives should meet several criteria:

© AP IMAGES/PAUL SAKUMA

McDonald's marketers are taking advantage of gas price increases by running commercials in which teenagers decide not to fill their empty gas tank and buy $1 double cheeseburgers to fill their stomachs instead.

- *Realistic:* Managers should develop objectives that have a chance of being met. For example, it may be unrealistic for start-up firms or new products to command dominant market share, given other competitors in the marketplace.
- *Measurable:* Managers need to be able to quantitatively measure whether or not an objective has been met. For example, it would be difficult to determine success for an objective that states "To increase sales of cat food." If the company sells 1 percent more cat food, does that mean the objective was met? Instead, a specific number should be stated, "To increase sales of Purina brand cat food from $300 million to $345 million."
- *Time-specific:* By what time should the objective be met? "To increase sales of Purina brand cat food between January 1, 2010 and December 31, 2010."
- *Compared to a benchmark:* If the objective is to increase sales by 15 percent, it is important to know the baseline against which the objective will be measured. Will it be current sales? Last year's sales? For example, "To increase sales of Purina brand cat food by 15 percent over 2010 sales of $300 million."

environmental scanning
Collection and interpretation of information about forces, events, and relationships in the external environment that may affect the future of the organization or the implementation of the marketing plan.

marketing objective
A statement of what is to be accomplished through marketing activities.

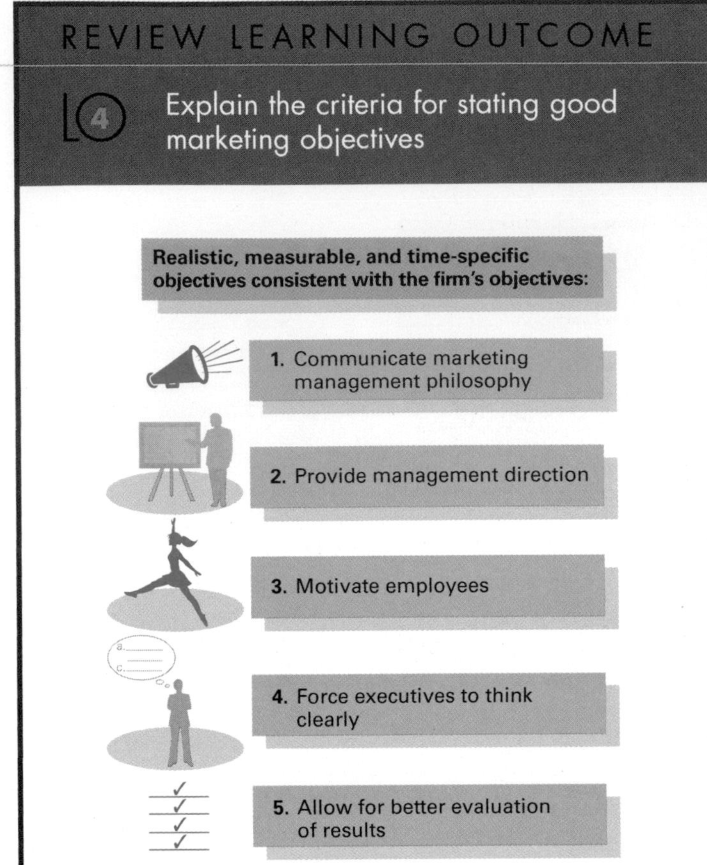

Objectives must also be consistent with and indicate the priorities of the organization. Specifically, objectives flow from the business mission statement to the rest of the marketing plan. Exhibit 2.3 shows some well-stated and some poorly stated objectives. Notice how well they do or do not meet the aforementioned criteria.

Carefully specified objectives serve several functions. First, they communicate marketing management philosophies and provide direction for lower-level marketing managers so that marketing efforts are integrated and pointed in a consistent direction. Objectives also serve as motivators by creating something for employees to strive for. When objectives are attainable and challenging, they motivate those charged with achieving the objectives. Additionally, the process of writing specific objectives forces executives to clarify their thinking. Finally, objectives form a basis for control; the effectiveness of a plan can be gauged in light of the stated objectives.

COMPETITIVE ADVANTAGE

Performing a SWOT analysis allows firms to identify their competitive advantage. A **competitive advantage** is a set of unique features of a company and its products that are perceived by the target market as significant and superior to the competition. It is the factor or factors that cause customers to patronize a firm and not the competition. There are three types of competitive advantages: cost, product/service differentiation, and niche strategies.

Cost Competitive Advantage

Cost leadership can result from obtaining inexpensive raw materials, creating an efficient scale of plant operations, designing products for ease of manufacture, controlling overhead costs, and avoiding marginal customers. DuPont, for example, has an exceptional cost competitive advantage in the production of titanium dioxide. Technicians created a production process using low-cost feedstock, giving DuPont a 20 percent cost advantage over its competitors. The cheaper feedstock technology is complex and can be duplicated only by investing about $100 million and several years of testing time.

competitive advantage
The set of unique features of a company and its products that are perceived by the target market as significant and superior to the competition.

EXHIBIT 2.3

Examples of Marketing Objectives

Poorly Stated Objectives	Well-Stated Objectives
Our objective is to maximize profits.	Our objective is to achieve a 10 percent return on investment from January 1, 2009 until December 31, 2009, with a payback on new investments of no longer than December 31, 2013.
Our objective is to better serve customers.	Our objective is to obtain customer satisfaction ratings of 90 percent on the 2009 annual customer satisfaction survey, and to retain 85 percent of our 2009 customers as repeat purchasers in 2010.
Our objective is to be the best that we can be.	Our objective is to increase market share from 30 percent in 2009 to 40 percent in 2010 by increasing promotional expenditures by 14 percent over 2009 levels from January 1, 2010 to December 31, 2010.

© iSTOCKPHOTO.COM/JASMINE AWAD

Having a **cost competitive advantage** means being the low-cost competitor in an industry while maintaining satisfactory profit margins.

A cost competitive advantage enables a firm to deliver superior customer value. Wal-Mart, the world's leading low-cost general merchandise store, offers good value to customers because it focuses on providing a large selection of merchandise at low prices and good customer service. Wal-Mart is able to keep its prices down because it has strong buying power in its relationships with suppliers. Costs can be reduced in a variety of ways.

- *Experience curves:* **Experience curves** tell us that costs decline at a predictable rate as experience with a product increases. The experience curve effect encompasses a broad range of manufacturing, marketing, and administrative costs. Experience curves reflect learning by doing, technological advances, and economies of scale. Firms like Boeing use historical experience curves as a basis for predicting and setting prices. Experience curves allow management to forecast costs and set prices based on anticipated costs as opposed to current costs.
- *Efficient labor:* Labor costs can be an important component of total costs in low-skill, labor-intensive industries such as product assembly and apparel manufacturing. Many U.S. manufacturers such as Nike, Levi Strauss, and Liz Claiborne have gone offshore to achieve cheaper manufacturing costs. Many American companies are also outsourcing activities such as data entry and other labor-intensive jobs.
- *No-frills goods and services:* Marketers can lower costs by removing frills and options from a product or service. Southwest Airlines, for example, offers low fares but no seat assignments or meals. Low costs give Southwest a higher load factor and greater economies of scale, which, in turn, mean lower prices for consumers.
- *Government subsidies:* Governments may provide grants and interest-free loans to target industries. Such government assistance enabled Japanese semiconductor manufacturers to become global leaders.
- *Product design:* Cutting-edge design technology can help offset high labor costs. BMW is a world leader in designing cars for ease of manufacture and assembly. Reverse engineering—the process of disassembling a product piece by piece to learn its components and obtain clues as to the manufacturing process—can also mean savings. Reverse engineering a low-cost competitor's product can save research and design costs. Japanese engineers have reverse engineered many products, such as computer chips coming out of Silicon Valley.
- *Reengineering:* Reengineering entails fundamental rethinking and redesign of business processes to achieve dramatic improvements in critical measures of performance. It often involves reorganizing from functional departments such as sales, engineering, and production to cross-disciplinary teams.
- *Production innovations:* Production innovations such as new technology and simplified production techniques help lower the average cost of production. Technologies such as computer-aided design and computer-aided manufacturing (CAD/CAM) and increasingly sophisticated robots help companies like Boeing, Ford, and General Electric reduce their manufacturing costs.
- *New methods of service delivery:* Medical expenses have been substantially lowered by the use of outpatient surgery and walk-in clinics. Airlines, such as Delta, are lowering reservation and ticketing costs by encouraging passengers to use the Internet to book flights and by providing self-check-in kiosks at the airport.

Product/Service Differentiation Competitive Advantage

Because cost competitive advantages are subject to continual erosion, product/service differentiation tends to provide a longer lasting competitive advantage. The durability of this strategy tends to make it more attractive to many top managers. A **product/service differentiation competitive advantage** exists when a firm provides something

© PURESTOCK/JUPITERIMAGES

cost competitive advantage
Being the low-cost competitor in an industry while maintaining satisfactory profit margins.

experience curves
Curves that show costs declining at a predictable rate as experience with a product increases.

product/service differentiation competitive advantage
The provision of something that is unique and valuable to buyers beyond simply offering a lower price than the competition's.

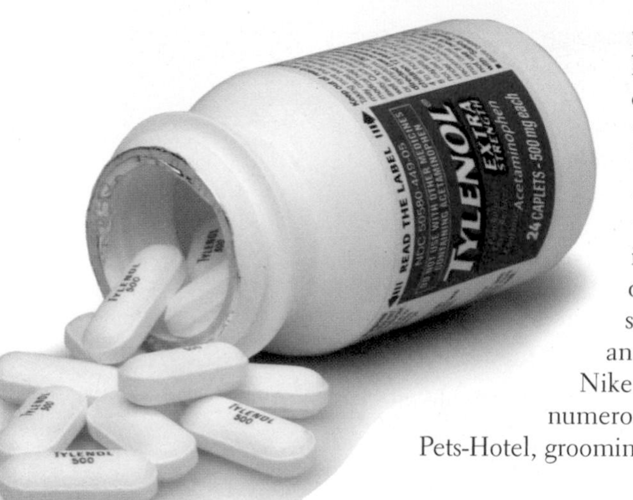

© DANIEL HURST/EDITORIAL/ALAMY

unique that is valuable to buyers beyond simply offering a low price. Examples include brand names (Lexus), a strong dealer network (Caterpillar Tractor for construction work), product reliability (Maytag appliances), image (Neiman Marcus in retailing), or service (FedEx). A great example of a company that has a strong product/service competitive advantage is Nike. Nike's advantage is built around one simple idea—product innovation. The company's goal is to think of something that nobody has thought of before or improve something that already exists. Nike Air, ACG, Nike Swift, and Nike Shox are examples of innovative shoes introduced by Nike.[6] Another example is PetSmart. Not only does PetSmart offer numerous products for all types of pets; it also offers services such as Pets-Hotel, grooming, and training.

Niche Competitive Advantage

A **niche competitive advantage** seeks to target and effectively serve a single segment of the market (see Chapter 8). For small companies with limited resources that potentially face giant competitors, niche targeting may be the only viable option. A market segment that has good growth potential but is not crucial to the success of major competitors is a good candidate for developing a niche strategy.

niche competitive advantage
The advantage achieved when a firm seeks to target and effectively serve a small segment of the market.

sustainable competitive advantage
An advantage that cannot be copied by the competition.

Many companies using a niche strategy serve only a limited geographic market. Buddy Freddy's is a very successful restaurant chain, but is found only in Florida. Migros is the dominant grocery chain in Switzerland. It has no stores outside that small country.

Block Drug Company uses niche targeting by focusing its product line on tooth products. It markets Polident to clean false teeth, Poligrip to hold false teeth, and Sensodyne toothpaste for persons with sensitive teeth. The Orvis Company manufactures and sells everything that anyone might ever need for fly-fishing. Orvis is a very successful niche marketer.

Building Sustainable Competitive Advantage

The key to having a competitive advantage is the ability to sustain that advantage. A **sustainable competitive advantage** is one that cannot be copied by the competition. Nike, discussed earlier, is a good example of a company that has a sustainable competitive advantage. Others include Rolex (high-quality watches), Nordstrom department stores (service), and Southwest Airlines (low price). In contrast, when Datril was introduced into the pain-reliever market, it was touted as being exactly like Tylenol, only cheaper. Tylenol responded by lowering its price, thus destroying Datril's competitive advantage and ability to remain on the market. In this case, low price was not a sustainable competitive advantage. Without a competitive advantage, target customers don't perceive any reason to patronize an organization instead of its competitors.

The notion of competitive advantage means that a successful firm will stake out a position unique in some manner from its rivals. Imitation of competitors indicates a lack of competitive advantage and almost ensures mediocre performance. Moreover, competitors rarely stand still, so it is not surprising that imitation causes managers to feel trapped in a seemingly endless game of catch-up. They are regularly surprised by the new accomplishments of their rivals.

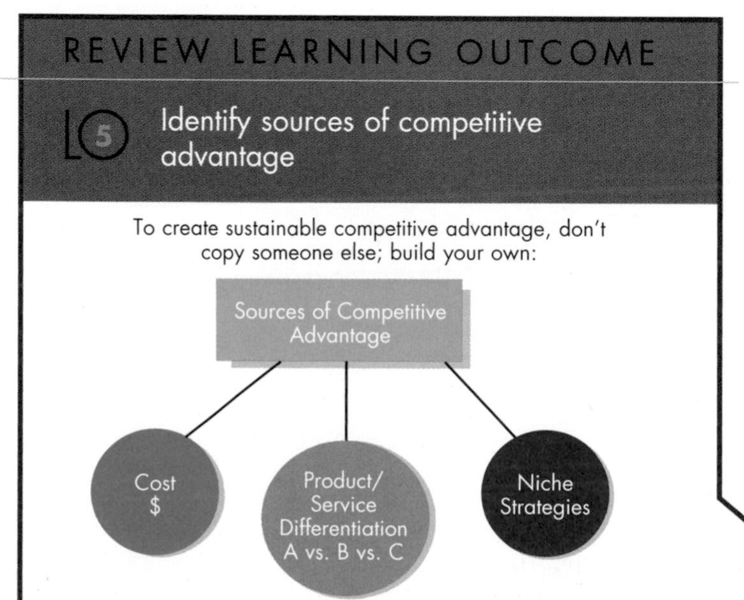

CUSTOMER Experience

Retail Entertainment

Bass Pro Shops was named the "Outdoor Retailer of the Year" in 2007 by the *Sporting Goods Business* magazine. This honor is due, in part, to the fact that the company understands how to offer the customer a quality experience by entertaining them while they shop. This experiential aspect of Bass Pro Shops provides them with a strong competitive advantage.

They operate almost 50 stores throughout the United States, about 30 of which are designed to showcase the characteristics of the area where they are located. These stores bring in elements of a natural-history museum, an art gallery, and an aquarium. Taxidermy mounts on the walls are animals native to the each area, and stores have an indoor water feature that contains indigenous fish species. For example, a Florida store features the hull of a sunken ship, while a Massachusetts store has a 30-foot-long blue whale on display.

In some of the aquariums, professional fishermen and store staff hold demonstrations that show customers how to use artificial bait. Classes are offered at the stores, ranging from fly-casting, Dutch-oven cooking, archery hunting, and GPS navigation. Most stores also offer full service restaurants on site. The Las Vegas store is connected to a casino and cabin-themed resort.

The design details of the stores are a unique feature that enhances the customer experience. Bass Pro has their own shop that builds the pine and cedar log buildings, and 55 artisans that include coppersmiths, blacksmiths, carvers, and painters who hand-make the lighting fixtures, wood carvings, and iron work that is used throughout the store. Artists paint large murals on the walls and ceilings that incorporate mounted animals.

Stores receive up to 3 million visitors every year. In fact, Bass Pro Shops have assumed the status of a tourist destination. Some people spend their vacations driving from store to store.[7]

How might the concept of retail entertainment be applied to other types of retail stores or shopping areas/malls? Either think of examples you have experienced or create a new idea for using this concept.

Companies need to build their own competitive advantages rather than copy a competitor. The sources of tomorrow's competitive advantages are the skills and assets of the organization. Assets include patents, copyrights, locations, equipment, and technology that are superior to those of the competition. Skills are functions such as customer service that the firm performs better than its competitors. Netflix, for example, created and remains dominant in the market for renting movies by mail. Marketing managers should continually focus the firm's skills and assets on sustaining and creating competitive advantages.

Remember, a sustainable competitive advantage is a function of the speed with which competitors can imitate a leading company's strategy and plans. Imitation requires a competitor to identify the leader's competitive advantage, determine how it is achieved, and then learn how to duplicate it.

STRATEGIC DIRECTIONS

The end result of the SWOT analysis and identification of a competitive advantage is to evaluate the strategic direction of the firm. Selecting a strategic alternative is the next step in marketing planning.

Strategic Alternatives

To discover a marketing opportunity, management must know how to identify the alternatives. One method for developing alternatives is Ansoff's strategic opportunity matrix (see Exhibit 2.4), which matches products with markets. Firms can explore these four options:

market penetration
A marketing strategy that tries to increase market share among existing customers.

market development
A marketing strategy that entails attracting new customers to existing products.

product development
A marketing strategy that entails the creation of new products for current customers.

diversification
A strategy of increasing sales by introducing new products into new markets.

- *Market penetration:* A firm using the **market penetration** alternative would try to increase market share among existing customers. If Kraft Foods started a major campaign for Maxwell House coffee, with aggressive advertising and cents-off coupons to existing customers, it would be following a penetration strategy. McDonald's sold the most Happy Meals in history with a promotion that included Ty's Teeny Beanie Babies. Customer databases, discussed in Chapter 9, helped managers implement this strategy.
- *Market development:* **Market development** means attracting new customers to existing products. Ideally, new uses for old products stimulate additional sales among existing customers while also bringing in new buyers. McDonald's, for example, has opened restaurants in Russia, China, and Italy and is eagerly expanding into Eastern European countries. Sara Lee is entering the market for meals on the go by introducing Hillshire Farm Salad Entrees, kits that contain meat and other ingredients that the company already makes, to be added to lettuce.[8] In the nonprofit area, the growing emphasis on continuing education and executive development by colleges and universities is a market development strategy.
- *Product development:* A **product development** strategy entails the creation of new products for present markets. McDonalds introduced yogurt parfaits, entrée salads, and fruit to offer their current customers more healthy options. Managers following the product development strategy can rely on their extensive knowledge of the target audience. They usually have a good feel for what customers like and dislike about current products and what existing needs are not being met. In addition, managers can rely on established distribution channels.
- *Diversification:* **Diversification** is a strategy of increasing sales by introducing new products into new markets. For example, Ralph Lauren developed a new brand of clothing called Rugby to appeal to young people from 14 to 29.[9] Sony practiced a diversification strategy when it acquired Columbia Pictures; although motion pictures are not a new product in the marketplace, they were a new product for Sony. Coca-Cola manufactures and markets water-treatment and water-conditioning equipment, which has been a very challenging task for the traditional soft drink company. A diversification strategy can be risky when a firm is entering unfamiliar markets. On the other hand, it can be very profitable when a firm is entering markets with little or no competition.

Selecting a Strategic Alternative

Portfolio Matrix Recall that large organizations engaged in strategic planning may create strategic business units. Each SBU has its own rate of return on investment, growth potential, and associated risk. Management must find a balance among the SBUs that yields the overall organization's desired growth and profits with an acceptable level of risk. Some SBUs generate large amounts of cash, and others need cash to foster growth. The challenge is to balance the organization's "portfolio" of SBUs for the best long-term performance.

To determine the future cash contributions and cash requirements expected for each SBU, managers can use the Boston Consulting Group

EXHIBIT 2.4
Ansoff's Strategic Opportunity Matrix

	Present Product	New Product
Present Market	**Market penetration:** McDonald's sells more Happy Meals with Disney movie promotions.	**Product development:** McDonald's introduces premium salads and McWater.
New Market	**Market development:** McDonald's opens restaurants in China.	**Diversification:** McDonald's introduces line of children's clothing.

(BCG) portfolio matrix. The **portfolio matrix** classifies each SBU by its present or forecast growth and market share. The underlying assumption is that market share and profitability are strongly linked. The measure of market share used in the portfolio approach is *relative market share*, the ratio between the company's share and the share of the largest competitor. For example, if firm A has a 50 percent share and the competitor has 5 percent, the ratio is 10 to 1. If firm A has a 10 percent market share and the largest competitor has 20 percent, the ratio is 0.5 to 1.

Exhibit 2.5 is a hypothetical portfolio matrix for a large computer manufacturer. The size of the circle in each cell of the matrix represents dollar sales of the SBU relative to dollar sales of the company's other SBUs. The following categories are used in the matrix:

EXHIBIT 2.5

Portfolio Matrix for a Large Computer Manufacturer

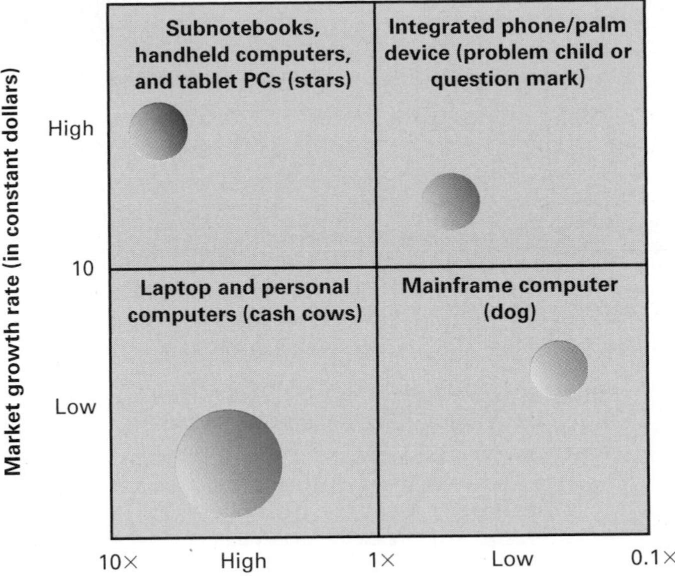

Note: The size of the circle represents the dollar sales relative to sales of other SBUs on the matrix—for example, 10x means sales are ten times greater than those of the next largest competitor.

- *Stars:* A **star** is a market leader and growing fast. For example, computer manufacturers have identified notebook and handheld models as stars. Star SBUs usually have large profits but need a lot of cash to finance rapid growth. The best marketing tactic is to protect existing market share by reinvesting earnings in product improvement, better distribution, more promotion, and production efficiency. Management must strive to capture most of the new users as they enter the market.
- *Cash cows:* A **cash cow** is an SBU that usually generates more cash than it needs to maintain its market share. It is in a low-growth market, but the product has a dominant market share. Personal computers and laptops are categorized as cash cows in Exhibit 2.5. The basic strategy for a cash cow is to maintain market dominance by being the price leader and making technological improvements in the product. Managers should resist pressure to extend the basic line unless they can dramatically increase demand. Instead, they should allocate excess cash to the product categories where growth prospects are the greatest. For instance, the Clorox Company owns Kingsford charcoal; the Glad brand of products; Fresh Step, Scoop Away, and other pet litters; Brita water filtration systems; and K. C. Masterpiece barbecue sauce, among others. Traditionally, the company's cash cow has been Clorox bleach, which owns the lion's share of a low-growth market. The Clorox Company has been highly successful in stretching the Clorox line to include scented chlorine bleach as well as Clorox 2, chlorine-free bleach for colored clothing. Another example is Heinz, which has two cash cows: ketchup and Weight Watchers frozen dinners.
- *Problem children:* A **problem child**, also called a **question mark**, shows rapid growth but poor profit margins. It has a low market share in a high-growth industry. Problem children need a great deal of cash. Without cash support, they eventually become dogs. The strategy options are to invest heavily to gain better market share, acquire competitors to get the necessary market share, or drop the SBU. Sometimes a firm can reposition the products of the SBU to move them into the star category. Zima brand beer, targeted at Generation X, was a problem child for Adolph Coors Company. The company ultimately withdrew its heavy marketing investment in Zima and positioned it as a niche product.
- *Dogs:* A **dog** has low growth potential and a small market share. Most dogs eventually leave the marketplace. In the computer manufacturer example, the mainframe computer has become a dog. Other examples include Warner-Lambert's Reef mouthwash and Campbell's Red Kettle soups. Frito-Lay has produced several dogs, including Stuffers cheese-filled snacks, Rumbles granola nuggets, and Toppels cheese-topped crackers—a trio irreverently known as Stumbles, Tumbles, and Twofers. The strategy options for dogs are to harvest or divest.

portfolio matrix
A tool for allocating resources among products or strategic business units on the basis of relative market share and market growth rate.

star
In the portfolio matrix, a business unit that is a fast-growing market leader.

cash cow
In the portfolio matrix, a business unit that usually generates more cash than it needs to maintain its market share.

problem child (question mark)
In the portfolio matrix, a business unit that shows rapid growth but poor profit margins.

dog
In the portfolio matrix, a business unit that has low growth potential and a small market share.

marketing strategy
The activities of selecting and describing one or more target markets and developing and maintaining a marketing mix that will produce mutually satisfying exchanges with target markets.

market opportunity analysis (MOA)
The description and estimation of the size and sales potential of market segments that are of interest to the firm and the assessment of key competitors in these market segments.

After classifying the company's SBUs in the matrix, the next step is to allocate future resources for each. The four basic strategies are to:

- *Build:* If an organization has an SBU that it believes has the potential to be a star (probably a problem child at present), building would be an appropriate goal. The organization may decide to give up short-term profits and use its financial resources to achieve this goal. Procter & Gamble built Pringles from a money loser into a record profit maker.
- *Hold:* If an SBU is a very successful cash cow, a key goal would surely be to hold or preserve market share so that the organization can take advantage of the very positive cash flow. Bisquick has been a prosperous cash cow for General Mills for over two decades.
- *Harvest:* This strategy is appropriate for all SBUs except those classified as stars. The basic goal is to increase the short-term cash return without too much concern for the long-run impact. It is especially worthwhile when more cash is needed from a cash cow with long-run prospects that are unfavorable because of low market growth rate. For instance, Lever Brothers has been harvesting Lifebuoy soap for a number of years with little promotional backing.
- *Divest:* Getting rid of SBUs with low shares of low-growth markets is often appropriate. Problem children and dogs are most suitable for this strategy. Procter & Gamble dropped Cincaprin, a coated aspirin, because of its low growth potential.

REVIEW LEARNING OUTCOME

LO 6 Identify strategic alternatives

Market development = ↑ customers
Market penetration = ↑ share
Product development = ↑ products
Diversification = ↑ New Products + ↑ New Markets

LO 7

DESCRIBING THE TARGET MARKET

Marketing strategy involves the activities of selecting and describing one or more target markets and developing and maintaining a marketing mix that will produce mutually satisfying exchanges with target markets.

Target Market Strategy

A market segment is a group of individuals or organizations that share one or more characteristics. They therefore may have relatively similar product needs. For example, parents of newborn babies need products such as formula, diapers, and special foods. The target market strategy identifies the market segment or segments on which to focus. This process begins with a **market opportunity analysis (MOA)**—the description and estimation of the size and sales potential of market segments that are of interest to the firm and the assessment of key competitors in these market segments. After the firm describes the market segments, it may target one or more of them. There are three general strategies for selecting target markets. Target market(s) can be selected by appealing to the entire market with one marketing mix, concentrating on one segment, or appealing to multiple market segments using multiple marketing mixes. The characteristics, advantages, and disadvantages of each strategic option are examined in Chapter 8. Target markets could be smokers who are concerned about white teeth (the target of Topol toothpaste), people concerned about sugar and calories in their soft drinks (Diet Pepsi), or college students needing inexpensive about-town transportation (Yamaha Razz scooter).

Any market segment that is targeted must be fully described. Demographics, psychographics, and buyer behavior should be assessed. Buyer behavior is covered in Chapters 6 and 7. If segments are differentiated by ethnicity, multicultural aspects of the marketing mix should be examined. If the target market is international, it is especially important to describe differences in culture, economic and technological development, and political structure that may affect the marketing plan. Global marketing is covered in more detail in Chapter 5.

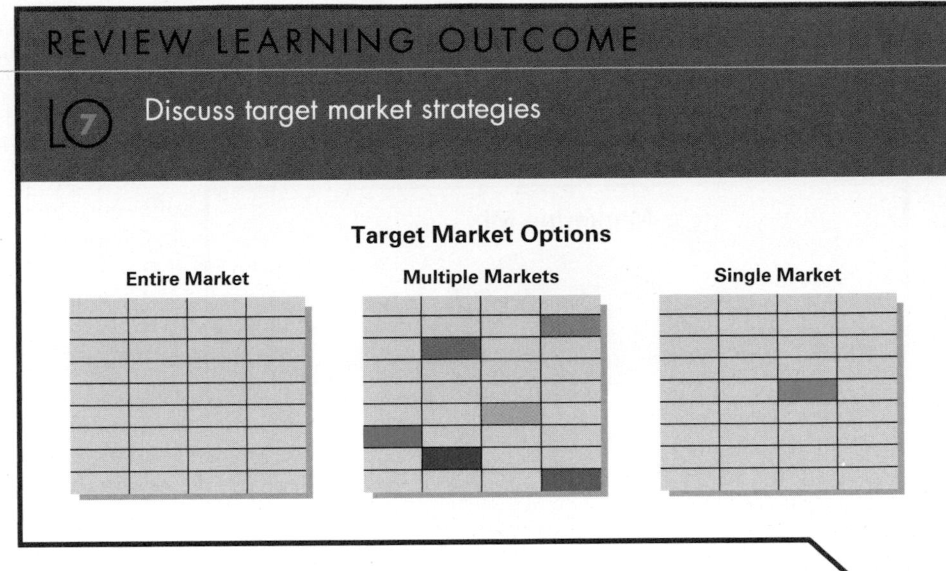

THE MARKETING MIX

The term **marketing mix** refers to a unique blend of product, place (distribution), promotion, and pricing strategies (often referred to as the **four Ps**) designed to produce mutually satisfying exchanges with a target market. The marketing manager can control each component of the marketing mix, but the strategies for all four components must be blended to achieve optimal results. Any marketing mix is only as good as its weakest component. For example, the first pump toothpastes were distributed over cosmetic counters and failed. Not until pump toothpastes were distributed the same way as tube toothpastes did the products succeed. The best promotion and the lowest price cannot save a poor product. Similarly, excellent products with poor placement, pricing, or promotion will likely fail.

Successful marketing mixes have been carefully designed to satisfy target markets. At first glance, McDonald's and Wendy's may appear to have roughly identical marketing mixes because they are both in the fast-food hamburger business. However, McDonald's has been most successful at targeting parents with young children for lunchtime meals, whereas Wendy's targets the adult crowd for lunches and dinner. McDonald's has playgrounds, Ronald McDonald the clown, and children's Happy Meals. Wendy's has salad bars, carpeted restaurants, and no playgrounds.

Variations in marketing mixes do not occur by chance. Astute marketing managers devise marketing strategies to gain advantages over competitors and best serve the needs and wants of a particular target market segment. By manipulating elements of the marketing mix, marketing managers can fine-tune the customer offering and achieve competitive success.

> *"Strategic planning should be an ongoing process."*

Product Strategies

Typically, the marketing mix starts with the product "P." The heart of the marketing mix, the starting point, is the product offering and product strategy. It is hard to design a place strategy, decide on a promotion campaign, or set a price without knowing the product to be marketed.

The product includes not only the physical unit but also its package, warranty, after-sale service, brand name, company image, value, and many other factors. A Godiva chocolate has many product elements: the chocolate itself, a fancy gold wrapper, a customer satisfaction guarantee, and the prestige of the Godiva brand name. We

marketing mix
A unique blend of product, place, promotion, and pricing strategies designed to produce mutually satisfying exchanges with a target market.

four Ps
Product, place, promotion, and price, which together make up the marketing mix.

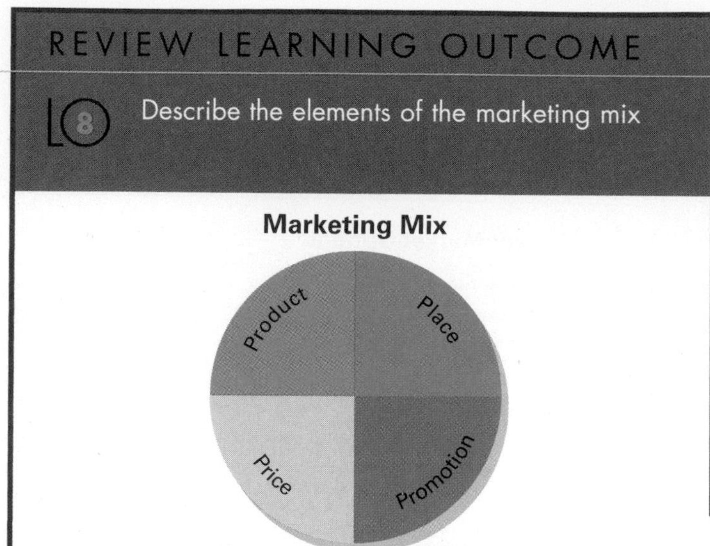

buy things not only for what they do (benefits) but also for what they mean to us (status, quality, or reputation).

Products can be tangible goods such as computers, ideas like those offered by a consultant, or services such as medical care. Products should also offer customer value. Product decisions are covered in Chapters10 and 11.

Place (Distribution) Strategies

Place, or distribution, strategies are concerned with making products available when and where customers want them. Would you rather buy a kiwi fruit at the 24-hour grocery store within walking distance or fly to Australia to pick your own? A part of this place "P" is physical distribution, which involves all the business activities concerned with storing and transporting raw materials or finished products. The goal is to make sure products arrive in usable condition at designated places when needed. Place strategies are covered in Chapter 12.

© COURTESY OF THE BEEF CHECKOFF PROGRAM

Promotion Strategies

Promotion includes advertising, public relations, sales promotion, and personal selling. Promotion's role in the marketing mix is to bring about mutually satisfying exchanges with target markets by informing, educating, persuading, and reminding them of the benefits of an organization or a product. A good promotion strategy, like using the Dilbert character in a national promotion strategy for Office Depot, can dramatically increase sales. Each element of the promotion "P" is coordinated and managed with the others to create a promotional blend or mix. These integrated marketing communications activities are described in Chapters 14 and 15.

implementation
The process that turns a marketing plan into action assignments and ensures that these assignments are executed in a way that accomplishes the plan's objectives.

Pricing Strategies

Price is what a buyer must give up to obtain a product. It is often the most flexible of the four marketing mix elements—the quickest element to change. Marketers can raise or lower prices more frequently and easily than they can change other marketing mix variables. Price is an important competitive weapon and is very important to the organization because price multiplied by the number of units sold equals total revenue for the firm. Pricing decisions are covered in Chapter 16.

FOLLOWING UP ON THE MARKETING PLAN

Implementation

Implementation is the process that turns a marketing plan into action assignments and ensures that these assignments are executed in a way that accomplishes the

ETHICS in Marketing

Surrogate Ads

Indian law prohibits companies from advertising tobacco and liquor. However, companies that sell these products are among the largest advertisers in the country. They accomplish this by using what are known as "surrogate advertisements," which instead of featuring cigarettes and alcoholic beverages, focus on unrelated, cheap-to-make products that they also produce. Surrogate products include CDs, playing cards, and bottled water that all have the same brand name as the companies' spirits and smokes. These ads have been blamed for luring India's young people (10–14 years old) to take up smoking. One study showed that current use of tobacco was five times lower among students who had not watched surrogate promotions. The companies say that they buy ads for the actual products advertised and deny that they use surrogate advertising.

India's Health Minister has asked the Information and Broadcasting Ministry to take action against the companies that are showing surrogate ads. The government has asked that broadcasters stop airing ads from tobacco and liquor companies for products with brand names that are the same as their tobacco and liquor brands, regardless of the product being advertised. If broadcasters comply, they could experience an estimated $50 million loss of advertising revenue, and even more if the government extends the ban on surrogate ads to other forms of media.

Government actions against surrogate ads are causing the liquor and tobacco companies to use sponsorships of sporting events, concerts, and other entertainment venues as an alternative to promoting their products. For example, the chairman of the UB Group, which markets Kingfisher beer and Royal Challenge whiskey, bought a professional cricket team. The team was named the "Royal Challengers" and the colors and logos of the team are the same as those of the whiskey brand. Bacardi Martini India sells a line of music CDs with the brand name Bacardi Blast, which is also the branding used for high-profile events.[10] Is it ethical for India's tobacco and liquor companies to use surrogate advertising to get their brand names in front of customers? Take a stand and defend your answer.

plan's objectives. Implementation activities may involve detailed job assignments, activity descriptions, timelines, budgets, and lots of communication. Although implementation is essentially "doing what you said you were going to do," many organizations repeatedly experience failures in strategy implementation. Brilliant marketing plans are doomed to fail if they are not properly implemented. These detailed communications may or may not be part of the written marketing plan. If they are not part of the plan, they should be specified elsewhere as soon as the plan has been communicated.

Evaluation and Control

After a marketing plan is implemented, it should be evaluated. **Evaluation** entails gauging the extent to which marketing objectives have been achieved during the specified time. Four common reasons for failing to achieve a marketing objective are unrealistic marketing objectives, inappropriate marketing strategies in the plan, poor implementation, and changes in the environment after the objective was specified and the strategy was implemented.

Once a plan is chosen and implemented, its effectiveness must be monitored. **Control** provides the mechanisms for evaluating marketing results in light of the plan's objectives and for correcting actions that do not help the organization reach those objectives within budget guidelines. Firms need to establish formal and informal control programs to make the entire operation more efficient.

evaluation
Gauging the extent to which the marketing objectives have been achieved during the specified time period.

control
Provides the mechanisms for evaluating marketing results in light of the plan's objectives and for correcting actions that do not help the organization reach those objectives within budget guidelines.

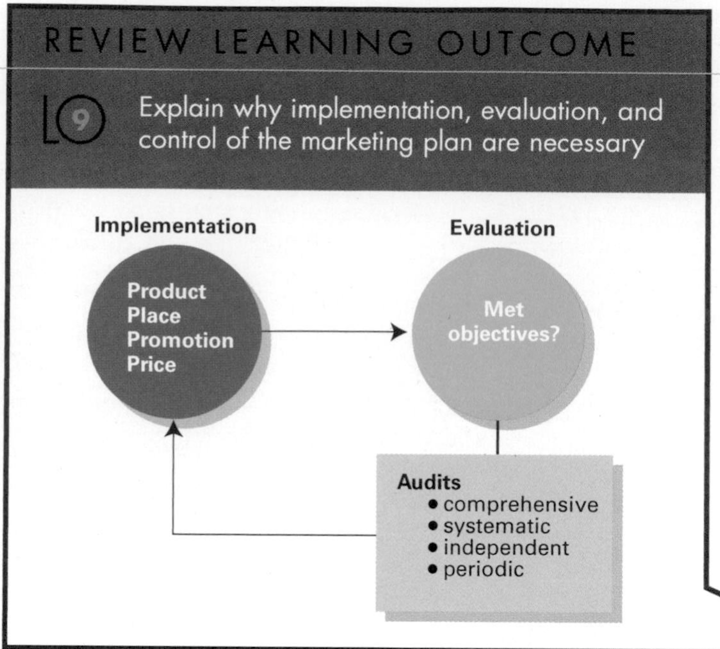

Perhaps the broadest control device available to marketing managers is the **marketing audit**—a thorough, systematic, periodic evaluation of the objectives, strategies, structure, and performance of the marketing organization. A marketing audit helps management allocate marketing resources efficiently. It has four characteristics:

- *Comprehensive:* The marketing audit covers all the major marketing issues facing an organization and not just trouble spots.
- *Systematic:* The marketing audit takes place in an orderly sequence and covers the organization's marketing environment, internal marketing system, and specific marketing activities. The diagnosis is followed by an action plan with both short-run and long-run proposals for improving overall marketing effectiveness.
- *Independent:* The marketing audit is normally conducted by an inside or outside party who is independent enough to have top management's confidence and to be objective.
- *Periodic:* The marketing audit should be carried out on a regular schedule instead of only in a crisis. Whether it seems successful or is in deep trouble, any organization can benefit greatly from such an audit.

marketing audit
A thorough, systematic, periodic evaluation of the objectives, strategies, structure, and performance of the marketing organization.

Although the main purpose of the marketing audit is to develop a full profile of the organization's marketing effort and to provide a basis for developing and revising the marketing plan, it is also an excellent way to improve communication and raise the level of marketing consciousness within the organization. It is a useful vehicle for selling the philosophy and techniques of strategic marketing to other members of the organization.

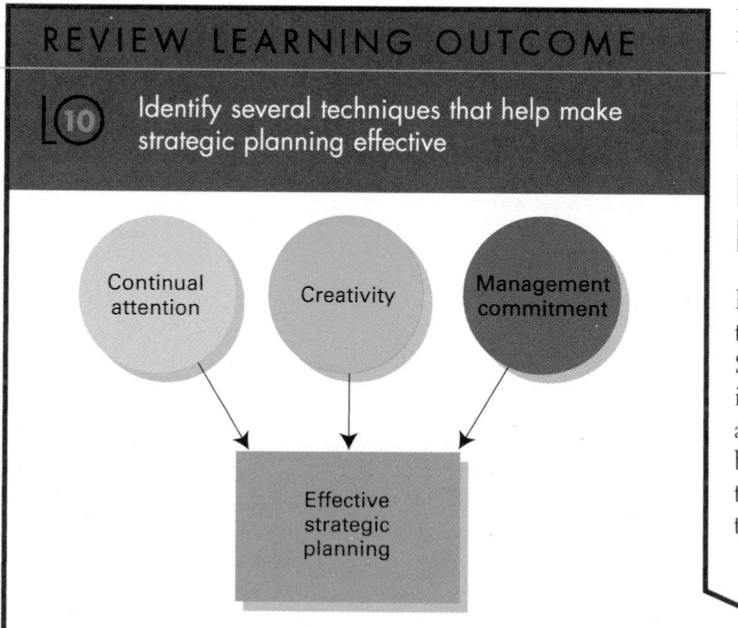

LO 10

EFFECTIVE STRATEGIC PLANNING

Effective strategic planning requires continual attention, creativity, and management commitment. Strategic planning should not be an annual exercise in which managers go through the motions and forget about strategic planning until the next year. It should be an ongoing process because the environment is continually changing and the firm's resources and capabilities are continually evolving.

Sound strategic planning is based on creativity. Managers should challenge assumptions about the firm and the environment and establish new strategies. For example, major oil companies developed the concept of the gasoline service station in an age when cars needed frequent and rather elaborate servicing. They held on to the full-service approach, but independents were quick to respond to new realities and moved to lower-cost self-service and convenience-store operations. The majors took several decades to catch up.

Perhaps the most critical element in successful strategic planning is top management's support and participation. For example, Michael Anthony, CEO of Brookstone, Inc., and the Brookstone buying team earn hundreds of thousands of frequent-flyer miles searching the world for manufacturers and inventors of unique products that can be carried in its retail stores, catalogs, and Internet site. Anthony has codeveloped some of these products and has also been active in remodeling efforts for Brookstone's 250 permanent and seasonal stores.

3 ◀ Types of competitive advantages

4 ◀ Elements of the marketing mix; quadrants in the Boston Consulting Group (BCG) portfolio matrix

Macroenvironmental forces affecting marketing ▶ **6**

3 million
▲ Visitors to Bass Pro Shops each year

Debut of the Boston Consulting Group (BCG) portfolio matrix ▶ **1996**

REVIEW AND APPLICATIONS

Understand the importance of strategic marketing and know a basic outline for a marketing plan. Strategic marketing planning is the basis for all marketing strategies and decisions. The marketing plan is a written document that acts as a guidebook of marketing activities for the marketing manager. A marketing plan provides the basis by which actual and expected performance can be compared.

Although there is no set formula or a single correct outline, a marketing plan should include basic elements such as stating the business mission, setting objectives, performing a situation analysis of internal and external environmental forces, selecting target market(s), delineating a marketing mix (product, place, promotion, and price), and establishing ways to implement, evaluate, and control the plan.

1.1 Your cousin wants to start his own business, but he has decided not to write a marketing plan because he thinks that preparing one would take too long. He says he doesn't need a formal proposal because he has already received funding from your uncle. Explain why it is important for him to write a plan anyway.

1.2 After graduation, you decide to take a position as the marketing manager for a small snack-food manufacturer. The company, Shur Snak, is growing, and this is the first time that the company has ever employed a marketing manager. Consequently, there is no marketing plan in place for you to follow. Outline a basic marketing plan for your boss to give her an idea of the direction you want to take the company.

1.3 How are Coke and Pepsi using their Web sites, **www.coca-cola.com** and **www.pepsi.com**, to promote their newest product offerings? Do you see hints of any future strategies the companies might implement? Where?

Develop an appropriate business mission statement. The mission statement is based on a careful analysis of benefits sought by present and potential customers and an analysis of existing and anticipated environmental conditions. The firm's mission statement establishes boundaries for all subsequent decisions, objectives, and strategies. A mission statement should focus on the market or markets the organization is attempting to serve rather than on the good or service offered.

2.1 Thinking back to question 1.2, write a business mission statement for Shur Snak. What elements should you include? Evaluate the mission statement you wrote against some of those you can find online.

Describe the components of a situation analysis. In the situation (or SWOT) analysis, the firm should identify its internal strengths (S) and weaknesses (W) and also examine external opportunities (O) and threats (T). When examining external opportunities and threats, marketing managers must analyze aspects of the marketing environment in a process called environmental scanning. The six most often studied macroenvironmental forces are social, demographic, economic, technological, political and legal, and competitive.

3.1 Competition in the private courier sector is fierce. UPS and FedEx dominate, but other companies, such as DHL and even the United States Postal Service (USPS), still have a decent chunk of the express package delivery market. Perform a mini-situation analysis on one of the companies listed below by stating one strength, one weakness, one opportunity, and one threat. You may want to consult the following Web sites as you build your grid:

UPS	**www.ups.com**	DHL	**www.dhl-usa.com**
FedEx	**www.fedex.com**	USPS	**www.usps.com**

Explain the criteria for stating good marketing objectives. Objectives should be realistic, measurable, and time specific. Objectives must also be consistent and indicate the priorities of the organization.

4.1 Building on the Shur Snak example, imagine that your boss has stated that the marketing objective of the company is to do the best job of satisfying the needs and wants of the customer. Explain that although this objective is admirable, it does not meet the criteria for good objectives. What are these criteria? What is a specific example of a better objective for Shur Snak?

LO 5

Identify sources of competitive advantage. A competitive advantage is a set of unique features of a company and its products that are perceived by the target market as significant and superior to the competition. There are three types of competitive advantages: cost, product/service differentiation, and niche strategies. Sources of cost competitive advantages include experience curves, efficient labor, no-frills goods and services, government subsidies, product design, reengineering, product innovations, and new methods of service delivery. A product/service differentiation competitive advantage exists when a firm provides something unique that is valuable to buyers beyond just low price. Niche competitive advantages come from targeting unique segments with specific needs and wants. The goal of all these sources of competitive advantage is to be sustainable.

5.1 Break into small groups and discuss examples (at least two per person) of the last few products you have purchased. What specific strategies were used to achieve competitive advantage? Is that competitive advantage sustainable against the competitors?

Identify strategic alternatives. The strategic opportunity matrix can be used to help management develop strategic alternatives. The four options are market penetration, product development, market development, and diversification. In selecting a strategic alternative, managers may use a portfolio matrix, which classifies strategic business units as stars, cash cows, problem children, or dogs, depending on their present or projected growth and market share.

6.1 Based on your SWOT analysis, decide what the strategic growth options are for the company you chose in question 3.1.

Discuss target market strategies. The target market strategy identifies which market segment or segments to focus on. This process begins with a market opportunity analysis (MOA), which describes and estimates the size and sales potential of market segments that are of interest to the firm. In addition, an assessment of key competitors in these market segments is performed. After the market segments are described, one or more may be targeted by the firm. The three strategies for selecting target markets are appealing to the entire market with one marketing mix, concentrating on one segment, or appealing to multiple market segments using multiple marketing mixes.

7.1 You are given the task of deciding the marketing strategy for a transportation company. How do the marketing mix elements change when the target market is (a) low-income workers without personal transportation, (b) corporate international business travelers, or (c) companies with urgent documents or perishable materials to be delivered to customers?

Describe the elements of the marketing mix. The marketing mix (or four Ps) is a blend of product, place, promotion, and pricing strategies designed to produce mutually satisfying exchanges with a target market. The starting point of the marketing mix is the product offering. Products can be tangible goods, ideas, or services. Place (distribution) strategies are concerned with making products available when and where customers want them. Promotion includes advertising, public relations, sales promotion, and personal selling. Price is what a buyer must give up to obtain a product and is often the easiest to change of the four marketing mix elements.

8.1 Choose three or four other students and make up a team. Create a marketing plan to increase enrollment in your school. Describe the four marketing mix elements that make up the plan.

Explain why implementation, evaluation, and control of the marketing plan are necessary. Before a marketing plan can work, it must be implemented; that is, people must perform the actions in the plan. The plan should also be evaluated to see if it has achieved its objectives. Poor implementation can be a major factor in a plan's failure. Control provides the mechanisms for evaluating marketing results in light of the plan's objectives and for correcting actions that do not help the organization reach those objectives within budget guidelines.

9.1 Have your school enrollment marketing plan team (from question 8.1) develop a plan to implement, evaluate, and control the marketing strategy.

Identify several techniques that help make strategic planning effective. First, management must realize that strategic planning is an ongoing process and not a once-a-year exercise. Second, good strategic planning involves a high level of creativity. The last requirement is top management's support and cooperation.

10.1 What techniques can make your school enrollment marketing plan more effective?

KEY TERMS

EXERCISES

APPLICATION EXERCISE

As you now know from reading the chapter, an important part of the strategy-making process involves scanning the environment for changes that affect your marketing efforts. This exercise is designed to introduce you to the business press and to help you make the connection between the concepts you learn in the classroom and real-world marketing activities.

Activities

1. Find a current article of substance in the business press (*The Wall Street Journal, The Financial Times, Fortune, BusinessWeek, Inc.*, etc.) that discusses topics you have covered in this course. Although this is only Chapter 2, you will be surprised by the amount of terminology you have already learned. If you are having trouble finding an article, read through the table of contents at the beginning of the book to familiarize yourself with the names of concepts that will be presented later in the course. Read your article carefully, making notes about relevant content.
2. Write a one-paragraph summary of the key points in your article; then, write a list of the terms or concepts critical to understanding the article. Provide definitions of those terms. If you are unfamiliar with a term or concept that is central to the article, do some research in your textbook or see your professor during office hours. Relate these key points to the concepts in your text by citing page numbers.
3. Explain the environments that are relevant to the situation presented in the article. (Chapter 4 contains a full list of environmental factors.)

ETHICS EXERCISE

Abercrombie & Fitch, a retail clothing chain based in New Albany, Ohio, launched a line of thong underwear for preteen girls. Words like "eye candy" and "wink wink" were printed on the front of the skimpy underwear that some argued would fit girls aged 5 to 10. Abercrombie is known for its provocative ads and sexually oriented catalogs. Supporters of the strategy claim that producing thong-style underwear for 10- to 16-year-olds is a good move; critics think that the line is tasteless and that marketing it to young girls is contemptuous.

Questions

1. Is marketing adult-styled undergarments to a younger audience unethical? Why or why not?

2. Would Abercrombie have been in the spotlight had the sexy words been omitted from the product? Explain your answer.

MARKETING PLAN EXERCISE

Throughout the rest of this book, these end-of-chapter marketing plan exercises will help you build a strategic marketing plan for a company of your choosing. The company you choose should be one that interests you, such as the manufacturer of your favorite product, a local business where you would like to work, or even a business you would like to start yourself to satisfy an unmet need or want. Once you've completed the marketing plan exercise for each chapter in Part 1 of this textbook, you can complete the Part 1 Marketing Planning Worksheet on your companion Web site at **www.cengage.com/international**. Use the following exercises to guide you through the first part of your strategic marketing plan:

Questions

1. Describe your chosen company. How long has it been in business, or when will it start business? Who are the key players? Is the company small or large? Does it offer a good or service?

2. Write the mission statement of your company, keeping in mind the benefits offered to customers rather than the product or service sold. If you are starting the online arm of a traditional store, should you make any changes to the company's overall mission statement?

3. List at least three specific, measurable objectives for your company. Be sure these objectives relate to the mission statement and include a time frame.

4. Begin a SWOT analysis by determining the primary strength of your company by asking, "What is the key differential or competitive advantage of my firm?" What are other keys to the potential success of your company? What other strengths can your firm capitalize on?

5. Continue the SWOT analysis by taking an honest look at the weaknesses of your firm. How can you overcome them?

CASE STUDY: CIRQUE DU SOLEIL: THE FIRE WITHIN

A 27-foot-long bronze clown shoe is the only indication that there is something other-worldly within the concrete walls of the large, rather nondescript building. Located in Montreal, the building is home to what many feel is the most successful entertainment company in the world—Cirque du Soleil.

The company's massive headquarters houses practice rooms the size of airplane hangars where cast members work on their routines. More than 300 seamstresses, engineers, and makeup artists sew, design, and build custom materials for exotic shows with stage lives of 10 to 12 years. In fact, the production staff often invents materials, such as the special waterproof makeup required for the production of *O*, a show performed mostly in a 1.5 million-gallon pool of water that was also specially designed and engineered by Cirque employees. Another key in-house resource is Cirque's team of 32 talent scouts and casting staff that recruits and cultivates performers from all over the world. The department maintains a database of 20,000 names, any of whom could be called at any time to join the members of Cirque's cast, who number 2,700 and speak 27 languages.

Shows with exotic names like *Mystère, La Nouba, O, Dralion, Varekai,* and *Zumanity* communicate through style and tone that they are intended to do more than just amuse. Cirque designs productions with distinct personalities that are meant to evoke awe, wonder, inspiration, and reflection. As one cast member put it, "The goal of a Cirque performer is not just to perform a quadruple somersault, but to treat it as some manifestation of a spiritual, inner life. Like in dance, the goal is . . . to have a language, a conversation, with the audience."

Incredibly, every one of the 15 shows that Cirque has produced over its 20-year history has returned a profit. In contrast, 90 percent of the high-budget Broadway shows that strive to reach the same target market fail to break even. Cirque's statistics, however, are eye-popping. *Mystère,* which opened at the Treasure Island hotel and casino in Las Vegas in 1993 and still runs today, cost $45 million to produce and has returned over $430 million; *O,* which opened at the Bellagio hotel and casino in 1998, cost $92 million to produce and has already returned over $480 million. Though the company splits about half of its profits with its hotel and casino partners, those same partners sometimes absorb up to 75 percent of Cirque's production costs.

At the helm of this incredible business machine is the dynamic duo of Franco Dragone and Daniel Lamarre. Dragone, a Belgian, is the creative force behind most of the company's ten current productions, and Lamarre, a former television executive, presides over show and new venture development. Together, they have transformed a one-tour, one-residence circus company into an entertainment powerhouse with five simultaneous world tours; four permanent facilities in Las Vegas—Treasure Island, the Bellagio, New York–New York, and the MGM Grand—all of which are part of the Mirage family of casinos; another permanent theater at Disney World; and a series of shows on the cable television channel Bravo that has already won an Emmy.

Lamarre claims that his business is successful because he and his staff "let the creative people run it." He guides the company with an invisible hand, making sure that business policies do not interfere with the creative process; it is Dragone and his team of creative and production personnel, not a predetermined budget, that defines the content, style, and material requirements for each project. Because of their sound planning, Cirque du Soleil can claim that it is one of the world's elite businesses, as well as one of the world's elite entertainment companies.[11]

Questions

1. Based on what you have read in the case, outline a rudimentary SWOT analysis for Cirque du Soleil.

2. List and describe at least three keys to Cirque du Soleil's competitive advantage.

3. Explain how Cirque du Soleil implements, evaluates, and controls the elements of its marketing plan.

COMPANY CLIPS

© NKP MEDIA, INC./CENGAGE

METHOD—HEALTHY HOME

Cash-strapped start-up companies generally do not spend a great deal of time and money on planning. Founders are so busy with the rudiments of business—finding customers and creating, manufacturing, and delivering the product—that they may even forget important things, like invoicing. Eric Lowry reinforces this notion in the opening of the second method video segment. Nonetheless, strategic planning is an important part of successful marketing. Listen closely to the segment, which introduces method's CEO, Alastair Dorward, and gauge for yourself how much planning you think this innovative start-up did before launching its brand.

Questions

1. Based on what you heard in the video, does method have a marketing plan?
2. Explain the elements that make up method's competitive advantage. Is it sustainable?
3. What are the elements in method's marketing mix?
4. What are method's target market strategies and how does it use them in its operations?

Marketing & You Results

The higher your score, the greater importance you place on planning. You also develop plans more often and devote more energy to the planning process. High scores also indicate a motivation to work "smart" and efficiently. If your score was low, you are less inclined to spend energy planning and, as a result, may have lower performance.

Marketing Plan Outline

Appendix I

I BUSINESS MISSION

II SITUATION ANALYSIS (SWOT ANALYSIS)

- A. Internal Strengths and Weaknesses
- B. External Opportunities and Threats

III OBJECTIVES

IV MARKETING STRATEGY

- A. Target Market Strategy
- B. Marketing Mix
  1. Product
  2. Place/Distribution
  3. Promotion
  4. Price

V IMPLEMENTATION, EVALUATION, AND CONTROL

As you read in Chapter 2, there is more than one correct format for a marketing plan. Many organizations have their own distinctive format or terminology for creating a marketing plan, and every marketing plan should be unique to the firm for which it was created. The format and order of presentation, therefore, must be flexible.

This appendix presents only one way to organize a marketing plan. The outline is meant to give you a more detailed look at what you need to include, topics you need to cover, and the types of questions you must answer in any marketing plan. But, depending on the product or service for which you are drafting a plan, this set of questions may only be the starting point for more industry-specific issues you need to address.

An actual marketing plan from e-motion software follows this outline. The e-motion marketing plan includes annotations that tie each part of the plan to the material throughout the book. You'll see the correlation between chapter concepts and the elements of a professional marketing plan for a real company.

If you are assigned a marketing plan as a course requirement, this appendix can help you organize your work. In addition, worksheets that guide you through the process of marketing planning are available on your textbook's companion site. The worksheets can be completed electronically or printed out and filled in by hand.

I BUSINESS MISSION

- What is the mission of the firm? What business is it in? How well is its mission understood throughout the organization? Five years from now, what business does it wish to be in?
- Does the firm define its business in terms of benefits its customers want rather than in terms of goods and services?

II SITUATION ANALYSIS (SWOT ANALYSIS)

- Has one or more competitive advantages been identified in the SWOT analysis?
- Are these advantages sustainable against the competition?

A. Internal Strengths and Weaknesses

- What is the history of the firm, including sales, profits, and organizational philosophies?
- What is the nature of the firm and its current situation?
- What are the firm's resources (financial, human, time, experience, asset, skill)?
- What policies inhibit the achievement of the firm's objectives with respect to organization, resource allocation, operations, hiring, training, and so on?

B. External Opportunities and Threats

- *Social:* What major social and lifestyle trends will have an impact on the firm? What action has the firm been taking in response to these trends?
- *Demographics:* What impact will forecasted trends in the size, age, profile, and distribution of population have on the firm? How will the changing nature of the family, the increase in the proportion of women in the workforce, and changes in the ethnic composition of the population affect the firm? What action has the firm taken in response to these developments and trends? Has the firm reevaluated its traditional products and expanded the range of specialized offerings to respond to these changes?
- *Economic:* What major trends in taxation and income sources will have an impact on the firm? What action has the firm taken in response to these trends?
- *Political, Legal, and Financial:* What laws are now being proposed at international, federal, state, and local levels that could affect marketing strategy and tactics? What recent changes in regulations and court decisions affect the firm? What political changes are taking place at each government level? What action has the firm taken in response to these legal and political changes?
- *Competition:* Which organizations are competing with the firm directly by offering a similar product? Which organizations are competing with the firm indirectly by securing its prime prospects' time, money, energy, or commitment? What new competitive trends seem likely to emerge? How effective is the competition? What benefits do competitors offer that the firm does not? Is it appropriate for the firm to compete?
- *Technological:* What major technological changes are occurring that affect the firm?
- *Ecological:* What is the outlook for the cost and availability of natural resources and energy needed by the firm? Are the firm's products, services, and operations environmentally friendly?

III OBJECTIVES

- Is the firm's mission statement able to be translated into operational terms regarding the firm's objectives?
- What are the stated objectives of the organization? Are they formally written down? Do they lead logically to clearly stated marketing objectives? Are objectives based on sales, profits, or customers?
- Are the organization's marketing objectives stated in hierarchical order? Are they specific so that progress toward achievement can be measured? Are the objectives reasonable in light of the organization's resources? Are the objectives ambiguous? Do the objectives specify a time frame?
- Is the firm's main objective to maximize customer satisfaction or to get as many customers as possible?

IV MARKETING STRATEGY

A. Target Market Strategy

- Are the members of each market homogeneous or heterogeneous with respect to geographic, sociodemographic, and behavioral characteristics?
- What are the size, growth rate, and national and regional trends in each of the organization's market segments?
- Is the size of each market segment sufficiently large or important to warrant a unique marketing mix?
- Are market segments measurable and accessible to distribution and communication efforts?
- Which are the high- or low-opportunity segments?
- What are the evolving needs and satisfactions being sought by target markets?
- What benefits does the organization offer to each segment? How do these benefits compare with benefits offered by competitors?
- Is the firm positioning itself with a unique product? Is the product needed?
- How much of the firm's business is repeat versus new business? What percentage of the public can be classified as nonusers, light users, or heavy users?
- How do current target markets rate the firm and its competitors with respect to reputation, quality, and price? What is the firm's image with the specific market segments it seeks to serve?

- Does the firm try to direct its products only to specific groups of people or to everybody?
- Who buys the firm's products? How does a potential customer find out about the organization? When and how does a person become a customer?
- What are the major objections given by potential customers as to why they do not buy the firm's products?
- How do customers find out about and decide to purchase the product? When and where?
- Should the firm seek to expand, contract, or change the emphasis of its selected target markets? If so, in which target markets, and how vigorously?
- Could the firm more usefully withdraw from some areas where there are alternative suppliers and use its resources to serve new, unserved customer groups?
- What publics other than target markets (financial, media, government, citizen, local, general, and internal) represent opportunities or problems for the firm?

B. Marketing Mix

- Does the firm seek to achieve its objective chiefly through coordinated use of marketing activities (product, place, promotion, and pricing) or only through intensive promotion?
- Are the objectives and roles of each element of the marketing mix clearly specified?

1. Product

- What are the major product/service offerings of the firm? Do they complement each other, or is there unnecessary duplication?
- What are the features and benefits of each product offering?
- Where are the firm and each major product in the life cycle?
- What are the pressures among various target markets to increase or decrease the range and quality of products?
- What are the major weaknesses in each product area? What are the major complaints? What goes wrong most often?
- Is the product name easy to pronounce? Spell? Recall? Is it descriptive, and does it communicate the benefits the product offers? Does the name distinguish the firm or product from all others?
- What warranties are offered with the product? Are there other ways to guarantee customer satisfaction?
- Does the product offer good customer value?
- How is customer service handled? How is service quality assessed?

2. Place/Distribution

- Should the firm try to deliver its offerings directly to customers, or can it better deliver selected offerings by involving other organizations? What channel(s) should be used in distributing product offerings?
- What physical distribution facilities should be used? Where should they be located? What should be their major characteristics?
- Are members of the target market willing and able to travel some distance to buy the product?
- How good is access to facilities? Can access be improved? Which facilities need priority attention in these areas?
- How are facility locations chosen? Is the site accessible to the target markets? Is it visible to the target markets?
- What are the location and atmosphere of retail establishments? Do these retailers satisfy customers?
- When are products made available to users (season of year, day of week, time of day)? Are these times most appropriate?

3. Promotion

- How does a typical customer find out about the firm's products?
- Does the message the firm delivers gain the attention of the intended target audience? Does it address the wants and needs of the target market, and does it suggest benefits or a means for satisfying these wants? Is the message appropriately positioned?
- Does the promotion effort effectively inform, persuade, educate, and remind customers about the firm's products?

- Does the firm establish budgets and measure effectiveness of promotional efforts?
  a. Advertising
     - Which media are currently being used? Has the firm chosen the types of media that will best reach its target markets?
     - Are the types of media used the most cost-effective, and do they contribute positively to the firm's image?
     - Are the dates and times the ads will appear the most appropriate? Has the firm prepared several versions of its advertisements?
     - Does the organization use an outside advertising agency? What functions does the ad agency perform for the organization?
     - What system is used to handle consumer inquiries resulting from advertising and promotions? What follow-up is done?
  b. Public Relations
     - Is there a well-conceived public relations and publicity program? Does the program have the ability to respond to bad publicity?
     - How is public relations normally handled by the firm? By whom? Have those responsible nurtured working relationships with media outlets?
     - Is the firm using all available public relations avenues? Is an effort made to understand each of the publicity outlet's needs and to provide each with story types that will appeal to its audience in readily usable forms?
     - What does the annual report say about the firm and its products? Who is being effectively reached by this vehicle? Does the benefit of the publication justify the cost?
  c. Personal Selling
     - How much of a typical salesperson's time is spent soliciting new customers as compared to serving existing customers?
     - How does the sales force determine which prospect will be called on and by whom? How is the frequency of contacts determined?
     - How is the sales force compensated? Are there incentives for encouraging more business?
     - How is the sales force organized and managed?
     - Has the sales force prepared an approach tailored to each prospect?
     - Has the firm matched sales personnel with the target market characteristics?
     - Is there appropriate follow-up to the initial personal selling effort? Are customers made to feel appreciated?
     - Can database or direct marketing be used to replace or supplement the sales force?
  d. Sales Promotion
     - What is the specific purpose of each sales promotion activity? Why is it offered? What does it try to achieve?
     - What categories of sales promotion are being used? Is sales promotion directed to the trade, the final consumer, or both?
     - Is the effort directed at all the firm's key publics or restricted to only potential customers?

4. Price

- What levels of pricing and specific prices should be used?
- What mechanisms does the firm have to ensure that the prices charged are acceptable to customers?
- How price sensitive are customers?
- If a price change is put into effect, how will the number of customers change? Will total revenue increase or decrease?
- Which method is used for establishing a price: going rate, demand oriented, or cost based?
- What discounts are offered, and with what rationale?

- Has the firm considered the psychological dimensions of price?
- Have price increases kept pace with cost increases, inflation, or competitive levels?
- How are price promotions used?
- Do interested prospects have opportunities to sample products at an introductory price?
- What methods of payment are accepted? Is it in the firm's best interest to use these various payment methods?

V IMPLEMENTATION, EVALUATION, AND CONTROL

- Is the marketing organization structured appropriately to implement the marketing plan?
- What specific activities must take place? Who is responsible for these activities?
- What is the implementation timetable?
- What other marketing research is necessary?
- What will be the financial impact of this plan on a one-year projected income statement? How does projected income compare with expected revenue if the plan is not implemented?
- What are the performance standards?
- What monitoring procedures (audits) will take place and when?
- Does the firm seem to be trying to do too much or not enough?
- Are the core marketing strategies for achieving objectives sound? Are the objectives being met, and are the objectives appropriate?
- Are enough resources (or too many resources) budgeted to accomplish the marketing objectives?

The E-Motion Software Marketing Plan

Appendix II

e-motionsoftware
we keep the business of business moving

I COMPANY DESCRIPTION

Scott Keohane and a partner founded e-motion software in 2003 and established its worldwide headquarters in Austin, Texas. They envisioned software solutions that conformed to a particular business, not the other way around, with products designed to (1) improve operating efficiency, (2) empower users, (3) enhance security, (4) improve ROI, and (5) streamline business processes. [Chapter 1: Market Orientation—focusing upon customer needs and integrating all activities to readily provide customer satisfaction, while achieving long-term company goals.] Ultimately, however, Keohane's partner did not want to remain with the company. Keohane converted the partner's shares into a note, according to the partnership agreement the two had in place.

The origins of the company were based in Keohane's 10 years of entrepreneurial endeavors, with 4 years of this time spent as an independent consultant in the Oracle applications marketplace. Oracle is the world's largest enterprise software company. According to Oracle's Web site, the company's business is information—how to manage it, use it, share it, and protect it. Commercial enterprise information management software systems, such as those offered by Oracle, promised seamless integration of all information flowing through a company.

In a global marketplace in which external company collaborations are driving business efforts and internal cross-functional integration is critical for timely decision making, enterprise systems could help position companies in a highly competitive environment. [Chapter 7: Business Marketing—E-motion software operates as a business marketer since it provides good and services to organizations for purposes other than personal consumption.] Enterprise systems, such as the Oracle E-Business Suite, provided a simplified, unifying corporate technology platform. This type of platform enabled companies to utilize high-quality internal and external information both strategically and tactically. There were numerous product families in the E-Business Suite (e.g., advanced procurement, contracts, performance management, customer data/relationship management, financial, human resource management, logistics, manufacturing, marketing, order management, projects, sales, service, and supply chain management). [Chapter 9: E-Business is one product line in Oracle's product mix width. There are numerous product items in this product line.]

As an independent consultant, Keohane was continually asked to customize existing Oracle technology or create one-off applications to meet common requirements. The need for third-party products that would withstand upgrades to the underlying Oracle architecture was identified and e-motion software was formed. The overall business concept was to utilize the Oracle E-Business Suite as the underlying framework for customization to fit a particular customer's needs. Soon after incorporation, e-motion software became a member of the Oracle Partner Network. By joining the Oracle Partner Network, e-motion software gained access to Oracle Software Licenses, technical training, marketing funds, and co-marketing opportunities. [Chapter 7: Strategic Partnership—E-motion software partnered with Oracle so as to improve the offerings to its customers.]

II BUSINESS MISSION

[Chapter 2: The foundation of any marketing plan is the firm's mission statement.]

E-motion software is committed to the Oracle E-Business Suite of Applications and will provide a level of support that is unmatched in the industry. The company's goals are to make Oracle Applications more reliable, to enhance the Applications' functionality, and to make the Suite's use more efficient. [Chapter 2: What business is e-motion software in?] The company's products offer an attractive alternative to in-house development and support. E-motion software customers will be utilizing functional products that are self-funding. That is, the savings achieved through a more efficient workforce and security enhances will far exceed the cost of the company's products. The company's commitment extends from the methods used to build e-motion software products to the company's simple installation procedures to the post-installation service. E-motion software products run on multiple server platforms, require no customization, and are fully compatible with existing hardware and software warranties. [Chapter 2: E-motion software is focused on markets served and benefits sought by its customers.]

III SITUATION ANALYSIS

[Chapter 2: Marketers must understand the current and potential environment before defining marketing tactics.]

Industry Analysis

[Chapter 2: Environmental scanning is the collection and interpretation of information about forces, events, and relationships in the external environment that may affect the future of the organization or the implementation of the marketing plan.]

Trends The Enterprise Resource Planning (ERP) community has undergone a radical change since the turn of the century. Historically, applications were designed for the professional user or technology expert. Today's marketplace, however, has shifted from the professional user to employee users. That is, employees in all functional areas have access to and utilize information from the ERP application. Thus, ERP providers have shifted to developing applications intended for individual employee use instead of releasing bigger applications designed for the professional user. These self-service, employee-based applications have fundamentally changed the way ERP applications are sold, implemented, and administered. Professional users are no longer the keepers of the data, manually entering and updating data from forms and memos. They have now become administrators in charge of ensuring data integrity. The promise of turning departments, such as HR and benefits, from manual intensive data entry shops to proactive reporting shops has shifted the marketplace to self-service suite applications. This emerging trend has prompted the development of self-service applications that enable employees to utilize systems within their individual realms of expertise, yet systems that are integrated across the firm.

Competitors E-motion software represents a new voice within the Oracle community. The company is creating a new niche in the marketplace and, as such, competition comes from a variety of sources. There are currently no head-to-head competitors. Competition can be split into three very distinct groups: Oracle, consulting firms, and in-house development centers.

Apart from being the company that created the ERP industry, *Oracle* has resources that dwarf every other company in the ERP marketplace. The availability of capital and the size of the development group infer that Oracle can simply reallocate a small development team to work on competing products. Oracle has, however, repeatedly released products that were little more than advanced betas, resulting in weeks of downtime for companies implementing the new products. By building applications that require no customization to Oracle code, e-motion software can confidently assure its customers that its products will work.

Consulting firms could advise the client to include the cost of custom application development into the total cost of the consulting engagement. This is standard protocol for competing consultancies and would effectively stop e-motion software from entering into a client site. Most consultancies, however, do not have a support and development center to handle ongoing system management. E-motion software will compete directly with consultancies by providing superior service at an affordable price.

The *In-House Development Center* (IHDC) poses a tricky problem for e-motion software. If a company has an IHDC, it is usually a trusted source that knows the company, its standards, and its software. Additionally, the IHDC is usually considered a "no-cost" center since salaries are already included in the company's budget. Thus, program development and implementation is considered just another project with no additional cost. On the positive side, information technology (IT) budgets were slashed and IT departments scaled down over the past few years. While IT spending has begun to trend upward again, the creation of IHDC units has lagged this spending trend. E-motion software plans to capitalize on this lag in IHDC unit development and upward spending trend.

Customer Profile The marketplace has moved from professional users to employee users. Basically, professional users are now babysitters, ensuring that employees do not enter incorrect information into the system. This poses quite a quandary. Professional users must maintain the integrity of the system while releasing control of it at the same time. This often forces the professional user to become a reactive unit, rushing to fix things when they break down. Employee users do not generally know the idiosyncrasies of the ERP system, of which there are many. Thus to maintain system integrity and ensure data reliability, professional users are often double-checking employee's data entry and also answering help desk calls regarding how to use the system. This is not, however, what a self-service ERP solution is designed to deliver. E-motion software proposes to enter the self-service arena with a broad range of products designed to regain the efficiencies promised by self-service applications.

Technology The costs of developing and maintaining an ERP solution require that the underlying technology be relevant for several years after product purchase and installation. The rapid emergence of Internet-based transactions (e.g., banking, loan applications, etc.) brought self-service applications to the forefront of business opportunity. Initially, Oracle attempted to use a mix of PL/SQL and DHTML code in the self-service offerings. This mix, however, did not provide the best-looking applications, had little functionality, and were difficult to implement. Oracle then switched to using Java Server Pages (JSP) as its self-service foundation, with PL/SQL and HTML as the accessory languages. Products with the JSP foundation were well received in the marketplace. E-motion software plans to adhere to Oracle's decision to use JSP, especially since JSP offers e-motion software some key benefits: (1) JSP is robust and flexible allowing all applications to use the same coding techniques, (2) JSP is recyclable which means that e-motion software can leverage existing code across new applications, (3) JSP is accessible since Java is one of the most well-known programming languages, (4) JSP is portable, allowing e-motion software to easily enter other ERP markets, and (5) the use of JSP means that e-motion software will always comply with Oracle approved practices.

SWOT Analysis

The strengths, weaknesses, opportunities, and threats (SWOT) analysis provides a snapshot of e-motion software's internal strengths and weaknesses and external opportunities and threats. [Chapter 2: Performing a SWOT analysis allows firms to identify their competitive advantage.]

Strengths [Chapter 2: Strengths are *internal* to the firm.]

- Founder—Scott Keohane is not only extremely knowledgeable about the third-party marketplace; he is also personally and financially dedicated to making the business a success.
- Active and committed advisory council
- Reliable products and product support
- Member of Oracle Partner Network

Weaknesses [Chapter 2: Weaknesses are *internal* to the firm.]

- A one-person company that has to supplement the company with independent consulting services
- Not enough time dedicated to company development
- While considerable anecdotal information, the company is lacking in marketing research.
- Financial resources

Opportunities [Chapter 2: Opportunities are *external* to the firm.]

- Changing marketplace that coincides with e-motion software's product development
- The move toward employee users instead of professional users
- Growth market
- Technological changes
- Refocus on IT applications
- Persistent threat of security breaches
- Growing focus on cross-functional interactions in the business press

- New entries into the workforce (e.g., recent college graduates) are trained to use computers in decision making and thus expect companies to have data programs in place.

Threats [Chapter 2: Threats are *external* to the firm.]

- Competitors—all three groups of competitors likely have deeper pockets than e-motion software
- Offerings can be duplicated by knowledgeable experts.
- Limited market access across the United States
- Economies of scale in larger companies such as Oracle
- IT departments do not have unlimited budgets.

IV MARKETING OBJECTIVE

The marketing objective is to establish the company as an expert in the third-party marketplace. [Chapter 2: The marketing objective statement provides a look at what the company seeks to accomplish. It is consistent with the priorities of the organization.] The third-party product market for functions that are specifically designed for integration with Oracle Applications is in its infancy. E-motion software has to establish itself as a leader in this new marketplace. To accomplish this objective, customers must see that e-motion software products are safe and secure and that they do not affect existing Oracle functionality or their Oracle warranty.

Objective Metric: Three major Oracle clients by the end of 2005 [Chapter 2: Stated objectives must be measurable and time specific.]

To accomplish this marketing objective, e-motion software must obtain three major Oracle clients by the end of 2005. These clients will serve as reference sites for the company. These clients will enable e-motion software to demonstrate the gains achieved by using e-motion software products. As such, the clients need to be vocal and create viral marketing within the industry.

Objective Metric: One client in each region of the United States by the end of 2006 [Chapter 2: Stated objectives must be measurable and time specific.]

Given the close-knit nature of Oracle clients through organizations such as the Oracle Application User's Group (OAUG), e-motion software needs to gain clients within each of the major geographic areas in the United States: Northeast, Mid-Atlantic, Southeast, Midwest, Northwest, and West Coast.

V MARKETING STRATEGY

Target Market Strategy

E-motion software's sales plan is based on the company's understanding of the marketplace and on how it will resolve inefficiencies with the use of the Oracle E-Business Suite of Applications. From his consulting experience in helping potential clients install and maintain their individualized suite of applications, Keohane has considerable understanding of users' needs. To obtain clients, e-motion software, will rely on continuing relationships with prospective clients, maintaining ongoing relationships with other consulting firms with an ongoing relationship, and reaching new clients via marketing and sales initiatives.

Geographically, e-motion software will direct its marketing and sales efforts within the contiguous United States. [Chapter 8: Geographic segmentation refers to segmenting markets by region of a country or the world, market size, market density, or climate.] Though global operations are potential clients, the current size of e-motion software suggests that the U.S. marketplace is more viable at this time. [Chapter 8: Accessibility—the firm must be able to reach members of the targeted segment.] Within this marketplace, e-motion software will focus upon companies that have between 500 and 10,000 employees. These are the small to midsize companies that utilize the Oracle E-Business Suite of Applications. Companies of this size are unlikely to have their own development staffs in place or have the desire to develop and/or support homegrown applications. [Chapter 8: Responsiveness—the targeted market must respond to the marketing mix offered by the company.] Within these small to midsize companies, the individual target customer varies by the product offering. For example, a database administrator will be targeted for the company's system administrator products, and the IT director will be targeted for the functional line of product offerings.

Marketing Mix

[Chapter 2: Marketing mix (the four Ps) refers to the unique blend of product, place (distribution), promotion, and pricing strategies.]

Product [Chapter 6: E-motion software provides a business service to its customers.]

E-motion software develops applications specifically for the Oracle E-Business Suite. For clients of Oracle Applications who desire greater efficiency and an increase in ROI on their installed ERP systems, e-motion software will offer a line of products designed specifically to improve performance of the existing Oracle Application installation. Clients that have in-house development staff will be able to lower the total cost of ownership of a product by having e-motion software upgrade their Oracle installation. [Chapter 7: The buying center includes all persons in an organization who become involved in the purchase decision. In-house development staff will play a critical role in the buying process.] Clients without in-house staff, however, are more likely to benefit from e-motion software installations because they will now be able to perform a greater number of tasks that are not offered by Oracle. [Chapter 7: In this instance, the members of the buying center are different than a company with an in-house development staff.]

As a product-based company, e-motion software cannot ignore the importance of product marketing. The three product attributes that will drive the business are level of service, usability, and clear return on purchase price. [Chapter 7: Quality, service, and price are important evaluative criteria in a purchase decision involving software products.] The reluctance of some customers to install relatively new third-party products into their ERP systems is an obstacle to overcome via product marketing. [Chapter 7: This is often a new buy for the customer.] The company has to deliver on the promise of the products—that promise being that "E-motion software products make the business process of our customers more efficient, while easily understanding the upgrades to the underlying Oracle Application." E-motion must remain focused on this promise during both the product development and the product delivery process. [Chapter 7: Keeping current customers satisfied is just as important as attracting new ones.]

E-motion software's product line consists of functions that respond to inefficiencies identified from years of experience with Oracle ERP systems. Because the product portfolio is built expressly for the Oracle Applications E-Business Suite, the products are updated continually to maintain compatibility as well as to take advantage of new technologies and capabilities released by Oracle. [Chapter 10: Quality and functional modifications keep e-motion software's products up-to-date with ongoing technological changes.] All products enjoy the following characteristics: tight integration with Oracle, intuitive design, compatible architecture, and streamlined interfaces. Product offerings are iPraise, Responsibility Management, Password Reset, and Global Directory. [Chapter 10: E-motion software's product mix width is composed of one product—enterprise software. This product line is comprised of four product items.]

iPraise. [Chapter 10: iPraise is an individual brand.] The employee appraisal system developed by e-motion software is the most dynamic appraisal system available to Oracle customers. Combining e-motion software's commitment to streamlined application interfaces with the vast functionality available to Oracle E-Business Suite customers, iPraise represents the next generation of appraisal systems. The system is flexible, allowing it to be configured to meet the specific needs of the organization. Using the appraisal configuration engine, the customer can choose to include or omit several aspects of the appraisal process and even determine in which order they are to be constructed. Thus, iPraise is a complete solution for Oracle customers. Customers can opt to integrate other modules of Oracle that have been configured previously with the E-Business Suite. Installing iPraise is fast and easy.

Responsibility Management. [Chapter 10: Responsibility Management is an individual brand.] Responsibility Management solves one of the most important questions faced by all Oracle system administrators: "Who has access to which data?" Using Responsibility Management, a system administrator or database administrator can quickly, easily, and accurately identify who has access to which data in real-time. Responsibility Management can inform the administrator of the following:

- Employees with particular responsibility
- Employees without a single responsibility
- User names that are not attached to any employee
- User names that are attached to more than one employee
- User accounts that are expiring in *x* number of days
- User accounts created in *x* days prior
- All users that have been given *y* responsibilities in *x* days prior

Results are displayed in a simple table that can be arranged and sorted. The table can also be exported to Excel for further investigation.

In addition to the query capabilities, Responsibility Management enables the system administrator to make changes to the user account, such as

- End-date a responsibility
- User account expiration update for a particular responsibility
- Bulk assignment of responsibilities (by organization, job, location, etc.)
- Bulk end-dating of responsibilities (by organization, job, location, etc.)

Overall, Responsibility Management enables system administrators to enforce security policies by providing a simple, easy-to-use function to identify who has what responsibility. Each day that a person has access not identified with his or her position is unnecessary and insecure.

Password Reset. [Chapter 10: Password Reset is an individual brand.] Forgotten passwords are the single largest end-user issue. Every day, help desks are bombarded with calls from end-users who have forgotten their passwords.

The standard Oracle log-in link does not provide a solution for this problem; thus, end-users are forced to call the help desk to reset the password. E-motion software's Password Reset function is the solution.

Password Reset is modeled after the standard password reset functionality available on most Web sites. Even if the user is using Password Reset for the first time, all the components will seem familiar and the user will know where to go next without receiving complex instructions or training. Password Reset functions as a part of the Oracle Applications. There are not outside Web sites to access or other applications to open. The user simply clicks on a link from the login page, enters the required information, and the password is reset. The user can then login immediately with the new password. Password Reset validates a user's identity by going directly to the Oracle database and running queries against it. This tight integration ensures reliability.

Global Directory. [Chapter 10: Global Directory is an individual brand.] Most companies utilize a separate system for their corporate directory. This requires entering and maintaining all employee information in Oracle and then reentering that information into a separate system. Worse yet, they print the company directory from a separate system. Not only is this extremely inefficient, but there is a greater chance for error. In today's fast-changing world, employee information can change on a weekly basis. As a result, the "other" system is often neglected and its data are unreliable. Global Directory solves this issue by "going to source" and gathering data directly from the Oracle database; thus, Global Directory has up-to-the-minute validity. Global Directory allows users to query the database for a wide variety of information. The results can be customized to give your employees the depth of knowledge they require.

Global Directory functions as a part of the Oracle Applications. There are no outside Web sites to access or other applications to open. Using the export function, users can transfer results into Excel, XML, or CSV, making it possible to utilize the information for such items as contact lists, distribution forms, and mailing labels.

Place/Distribution E-motion software is now headquartered in Bedford, Massachusetts. However, home office location has little to do with the actual distribution of e-motion software's products since the products are installed and implemented at the client company. E-motion software will perform its own marketing channel functions (e.g., transactional, logistical, and facilitating) and does not foresee the need for any intermediaries in this process. [Chapter 12: Channel members facilitate the exchange between buyer and seller. E-motion software is the only channel member engaged in getting its product to the customer. Thus, it uses a direct channel.] However, e-motion software is a strong supporter of industry groups, such as the Oracle Applications User Group, and related industry events. Such support allows the company to become recognized as a vendor among Oracle Applications clients.

E-motion software does offer a partner program for companies that wish to resell or refer e-motion software products to Oracle ERP clients. The program is segmented into two separate categories. The Alliance Partner Referral Program is tailored for businesses that have customer relationships with companies in specific industries or with businesses or IT needs that e-motion software programs can uniquely address. An Alliance Partner will identify e-motion software customers and refer them to e-motion software for a revenue share of the revenue from the referred account. As part of the program, Alliance Partner members receive all the training and materials needed to promote e-motion software solutions to their client base. The Alliance Solution Provider Program is designed for qualified Oracle-focused consultancies with a strong track record for providing top-notch service to their clients. Partner program members are trained and certified by e-motion software. Once certified, implementation partners can then configure and implement e-motion software products with unparalleled service and support. [Chapter 12: This is a form of a strategic channel alliance for e-motion software.]

Promotion [Chapter 14: E-motion software strives for integrated marketing communications.]

As a third party purveyor of products for Oracle, it is important for e-motion software to convey, clearly and succinctly, its "reason for being." Company material will have the heading: "e-motion software: we keep the business of business moving." [Chapter 13: This is the company's unique selling proposition.] We will emphasize the Oracle connection with the following statement on documents, as appropriate: "Oracle clients around the country are realizing true gains in productivity and efficiency by taking every day tasks and putting them in *motion*."

E-motion software will adhere to mainstream thinking regarding the promotion of third-party products for ERP solutions. [Chapter 14: As a complex buying decision, personal selling and strong print are effective methods for reaching potential customers.]

- A cohesive, easy-to-maneuver, and user-friendly Web site (www.e-motionsoftware.com) [Chapter 13: Company Web sites can be used to introduce new products, promote existing products, obtain consumer feedback, post news releases, etc.]
- Recorded demos on the company Web site (requires users to register for a demo user account) [Chapter 16: Registration is important for customer relationship management.]

Product Pricing Sheet

	License Price	Software Update & Support	Licensing Metric	Minimum
Application Infrastructure:				
Password Reset	$15,000	$2,700/year	Enterprise	N/A
Responsibility Management	$6	18 percent/year	User	2,000
User Application:				
iPraise	$10	18 percent/year	User	2,000
Corporate Information:				
Global Directory	$2	18 percent/year	User	2,000

- Press releases as a member of the Certified Oracle Partner Network [Chapter 15: Public relations is an important element of the promotional mix. Press releases can place positive information in the news media to attract attention to e-motion software.]
- Demonstrations presented at trade shows and events [Chapter 15: Trade promotions push a product through the distribution channel and are popular among business marketers. Trade shows and events are an important aspect of sales promotions.]
- Word-of-mouth and reference sites [Chapter 15: Referrals are a good source for leads in the personal selling process.]
- The Internet via Google AdWords campaigns to drive potential clients to the company Web site [Chapter 14: The Internet has changed the advertising industry. Popular Internet sites sell advertising space to marketers, and search engine advertising is a popular approach.]
- Product datasheets that provide pertinent product data, features, and benefits of installation (available on the company Web site or via hard copy) [Chapter 14: Product information is critical in the sales process.]

Importantly, e-motion software is a company that relies heavily on direct selling to reach potential customers. [Chapter 15: Producers of most business goods rely more heavily on personal selling than advertising. Informative personal selling is common for installations such as those offered by e-motion software.] This promotional method requires a large amount of cold calling. [Chapter 15: Personal selling is important when product has high value and is technically complex. Relationship selling, or consultative selling, builds long-term relationships with clients.] E-motion software purchases the names of potential customers from marketing services that collect such information from customers of Oracle ERP products. [Chapter 15: Generating leads is the first step in the selling process.]

Price E-motion software prices its products to sufficiently cover the costs associated with development, sales, and support and to provide cash flow for future growth and development. [Chapter 16: As a new company, e-motion software is very concerned about covering its costs and having money left over for investment into the business. While not stated exactly, it appears that the company has a profit-oriented pricing objective.] The table above provides the company's standard price list. These list prices can vary, however, as there is a trickle-down effect in the industry. Essentially, pricing starts with Oracle, trickles through the consulting firm, and then down to e-motion products.

Prices are based on industry standards for classification. [Chapter 16: Status quo pricing is when a company meets the competition or going rate pricing. It appears that e-motion software is using status quo logic in its price setting.] For example, Password Reset, as an enterprise system product, has a total purchase price of $15,000, with a $2,700 software update and support fee. [Chapter 16: Two-part pricing is when the company charges two separate amounts for the product. In this instance, the buyer pays the $15,000 for the enterprise system product and then pays another $2,700 for the update and fee.] Responsibility Management, iPraise, and Global Directory are priced on a per employee (user) basis with a minimum purchase per number of employees. For example, Global Directory is $2 per employee with a minimum purchase of 2,000 employees. Thus, the least amount a company could purchase this product for is $4,000. The 18 percent annual maintenance fee is the industry standard. [Chapter 16: This shows the two-part, status quo pricing.]

Five-Year Financial Projection Plan

	2006	2007	2008	2009	2010
Revenues:					
iPraise	$50,000	$100,000	$600,000	$2,250,000	$5,500,000
Responsibility Mgt	$60,000	$80,000	$160,000	$420,000	$700,000
Password Reset	$225,000	$180,000	$180,000	$150,000	$75,000
Global Directory	$45,000	$75,000	$180,000	$300,000	465,000
Cost of Goods Sold	0	0	0	0	0
General & Administrative	$350,000	$765,000	$1,600,000	$2,165,000	$2,600,000

VI IMPLEMENTATION, EVALUATION, AND CONTROL

Marketing Research

The company needs to keep abreast of two distinct segments in the marketplace: its client needs and Oracle's direction. E-motion software needs to understand its clients and their ongoing needs. [Chapter 9: E-motion software captures customer data, storing and integrating it into a customer database.] This includes meeting current needs and forecasting future needs as the Oracle Application Suite continues to evolve. E-motion software must also maintain up-to-date and accurate intelligence on both current Oracle offerings and planned initiatives. [Chapter 8: Ongoing marketing research will help the company keep abreast of what is happening in the marketplace.] By doing this, it will be able to introduce products that complement new Oracle functions and will be less likely to offer products that compete for functions that are included at no charge in an Oracle license. Additionally, this will present opportunities to introduce products that complement new Oracle functionality.

Organizational Structure and Plan

As a start-up company, e-motion software currently has only one member on its staff, Scott Keohane. As e-motion software matures into a stable, profitable organization, the need for employees will grow. The first foreseeable employee need is in the area of sales. The plan is to hire a salesperson in early 2006 to allow Mr. Keohane can continue his consulting on a regular basis, while at the same time ensuring a steady supply of funds for continued development efforts. To obtain the financial flexibility it needs to manage its cash flow successfully, the company has made contractors a significant component of its workforce. Contractors are used in the following areas: application development, database administration, and marketing. Current contractors have been associated with e-motion software almost since the company's inception and are largely credited with its early successes.

To provide a management resource from which Keohane can receive regular advice and guidance, e-motion software has assembled a nonvoting, nonbinding advisory council to assist in decision making, overall strategy, and execution. The advisory council is composed of four outside members who have made a commitment to provide their expertise and experience, free of charge, to e-motion software. Advisory members interact quarterly via teleconference.

Financial Projections

[Chapter 2: Evaluation and control are important mechanisms for monitoring the effectiveness of the marketing plan. Financial objectives are a common measure of success/failure.]

The financial objective is to be financially solvent within the first two years of operation.

Objective Metric: Sales of $250,000 by the end of 2005
Sales of $2 million by the end of 2007
Gross margin higher than 80 percent
Positive cash flow yearly

[Chapter 2: Stated objectives must be measurable and time specific.]

The five-year financial projection plan (in U.S. dollars) for e-motion software can be reviewed in the table above.

Implementation Timetable

[Chapter 2: Implementation is the process that turns a marketing plan into action assignments and ensures that these assignments are executed appropriately.]

2005

- The company plans to have three major Oracle clients by the end of 2005.

2006

- The company plans to have secured at least one client in each region of the United States by the end of 2006. This would mean at least one customer in the Northeast, the Mid-Atlantic, the Southeast, the Midwest, the Northwest, and the West Coast.
- Keohane plans to hire one full-time salesperson.

VII SUMMARY

E-motion software continually monitors activities with current and potential clients. As a consultant in the industry, Keohane is always on the lookout for potential clients. He has set quarterly and yearly sales targets, and actual sales will be compared to these quarterly plans. Additionally, Keohane will continue in his efforts to enlist at least one client in each of the major geographic regions of the United States. However, it may take a qualified salesperson to devote the time necessary to acquire new customers. Additionally, by not being restricted to Keohane's current consultancies, a dedicated salesperson could more readily identify potential e-motion software clients by not being restricted to current consultancies that Keohane is involved with. Of major concern is that the current financial strategy of supporting the new business by personal funds from consulting may prove to be too onerous for Keohane.

Ultimately, the goal is to "make it big." The hope is that, over the next five years, the small products that e-motion software has developed will hopefully generate cash sufficient to build a larger module that one of the larger ERP companies (e.g., Oracle) will want to acquire.

CHAPTER

3

Ethics and Social Responsibility

©ROGER L. WOLLENBERG/UPI /LANDOV

MR. PARSONS
MR. O'NEAL
MR. FINNEGAN
MR. MOZILO

LEARNING OUTCOMES

- LO 1 Explain the determinants of a civil society
- LO 2 Explain the concept of ethical behavior
- LO 3 Describe ethical behavior in business
- LO 4 Discuss corporate social responsibility
- LO 5 Describe the arguments for and against social responsibility
- LO 6 Explain cause-related marketing

John Mackey, CEO of the Whole Foods Market, went online using the screen name "rahodeb" (a scramble of Deborah, his wife's name) and attacked competitor Wild Oats Markets on Yahoo! He said the smaller company was "mediocre with a terrible track record." William Swanson, Chairman and CEO of Raytheon, wrote a book titled *Swanson's Unwritten Rules of Management.* It was later discovered the book contained passages that exactly mirrored a 1944 book by an engineering professor. David Edmondson, former CEO of RadioShack, claimed to have degrees in theology and psychology, but completed only two semesters of course work.[1] And the list could go on.

The activities of these top managers were clearly wrong. Yet for several thousand years, religious teaching and secular ethics have sought to encourage socially beneficial behavior. The literature of virtually every religious tradition, as well as Eastern and Western philosophy, are full of examples, rules, and guidance regarding what constitutes right and wrong.

LO 1

DETERMINANTS OF A CIVIL SOCIETY[2]

Have you ever stopped and thought about the social glue that binds society together? That is, what factors are in place that keep people and organizations from running amuck and doing harm, and what factors create order in a society like ours as opposed to chaos. The six modes of social control are listed below:

1. *Ethics:* The first is ethical rules and guidelines along with customs and traditions that provide principles of right action.
2. *Laws:* Often rules and guidelines are codified into law. Laws created by governments are then enforced by governmental authority. Thus, the dictum, "Thou shall not steal," is part of formal law throughout the land. Law, however, is not a perfect mechanism for ensuring good corporate and employee behavior. This is because laws often address the lowest common denominator of socially acceptable behavior. In other words, just because something is not illegal doesn't mean that it is right. For example, an individual goes to Barnes and Noble every day and spends the afternoon reading books and magazines in the store. The store has big comfortable chairs and the clerks never bother him or ask him to leave. He even takes his own lunch if he plans to spend the day there. He does this at least 20 days per month. The bookstore allows this practice and it is not against the law. It is, however, not ethical. If everyone who bought books followed this individual's behavior, Barnes and Noble would soon be bankrupt!
3. *Formal and Informal Groups:* Businesses, professional organizations (such as the American Marketing Association), clubs (e.g., Shriners or Ducks Unlimited), and professional associations (e.g., American Medical Association) all have codes of conduct. These codes prescribe acceptable and desired behaviors of their members.

Marketing & You

Using the following scale, enter the numbers that reflect your opinions.

1 2 3 4 5 6 7 8 9

Completely disagree — Completely agree

__ The ethics and social responsibility of a firm are essential to its long-term profitability.

__ Business ethics and social responsibility are critical to the survival of a business enterprise.

__ The overall effectiveness of a business can be determined to a great extent by the degree to which it is ethical and socially responsible.

__ Good ethics is often good business.

__ Business has a social responsibility beyond making a profit.

__ Corporate planning and goal-setting sessions should include discussions of ethics and social responsibility.

__ Social responsibility and profitability can be compatible.

Now, total your score. Find out what it means after you read the chapter.

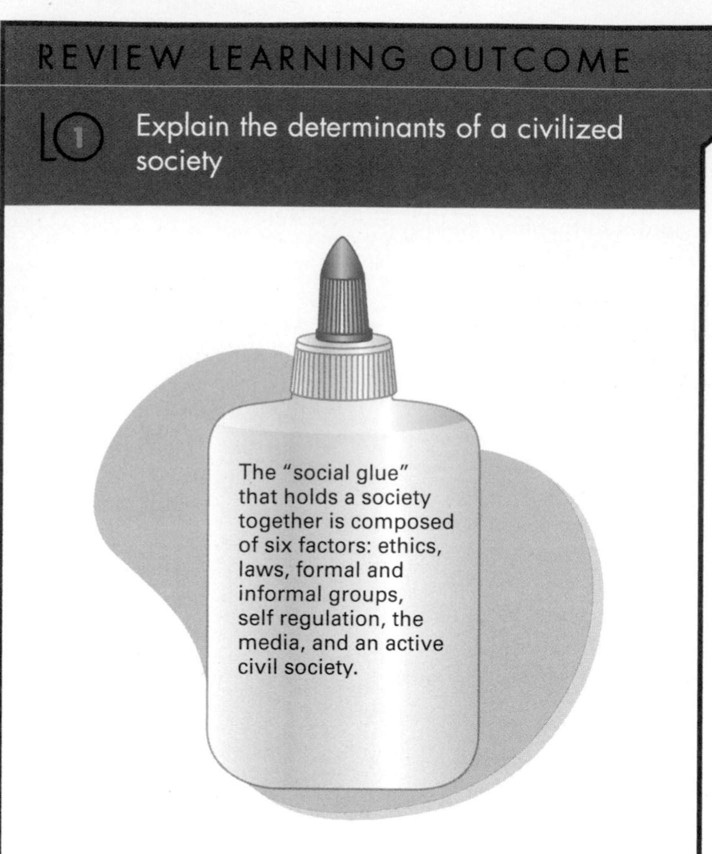

4. *Self regulation*: Self regulation involves the voluntary acceptance of standards established by nongovernmental entities such as the American Association of Advertising Agencies (AAAA) or the American Manufacturers Association. The AAAA has a self-regulation arm that deals with deceptive advertising. Other associations have regulations relating to child labor, environmental issues, conservation, and a host of other issues.

5. *The Media:* In an open, democratic society, the media play a key role in informing the public about actions of individuals and organizations. These stories sometimes praise, such as the media coverage of Wal-Mart's efforts to help people and reopen stores after Hurricane Katrina. Or, they shine the spotlight on unscrupulous behavior, such as those of Enron and Worldcom. Business firms dislike negative publicity, which can lead to lost sales, damage to corporate reputations, government actions, and legal liability. Conversely, favorable publicity stimulates sales and builds the firm's reputation.
   An example of investigative reporting comes from *Smart Money* magazine. When millions of Americans have problems with a product or service, they often call the Better Business Bureau (BBB). *Smart Money* raises the question, "Is the BBB too cozy with the firms it monitors?" For example, a woman in Shreveport, Louisiana, had a problem with Cingular (now AT&T) over her cell phone. The BBB has an online complaint form, which is about ten pages long, that the Shreveport resident carefully filled out. What she didn't know was that the BBB had been asking for extra information from unhappy cell phone customers, then giving or selling the data to some of the firms themselves.[3] Cingular, in fact, paid the BBB $50,000 for its customer-driven intelligence. Rick Weirick, product development officer of the BBB's national council, said that the fee was just to defray costs.[4]

6. *An Active Civil Society:* An informed and engaged society can help shape and mold individual and corporate behavior. The last state in the union to get a Wal-Mart store was Vermont. Citizen campaigns against the big-box retailer were deciding factors in management's decision to avoid the state. When pro football player Michael Vick was convicted of dog fighting, a grass roots campaign sprang up to boycott Nike. Vick had an endorsement contract with the shoe manufacturer.

All six factors above individually and in combination are critical to achieving a socially coherent, vibrant, civilized society. These six factors (the social glue) are more important today than ever before due to the increasing complexity of the global economy and the melding of customs and traditions within societies.

THE CONCEPT OF ETHICAL BEHAVIOR

It has been said that ethics is something everyone likes to talk about but nobody knows exactly what it is. Others have noted that defining ethics is like trying to "nail Jell-O to the wall." You begin to think that you've got it, but that's when it starts slipping out between your fingers.

> *Ethics is something everyone likes to talk about but nobody knows exactly what it is.*

Ethics refers to the moral principles or values that generally govern the conduct of an individual or a group. Ethics also can be viewed as the standard of behavior by which conduct is judged. As noted above, standards that are legal may not always be ethical, and vice versa. Laws are the values and standards enforceable by the courts. Ethics, then, consists of personal moral principles. For example, there is no legal statute that makes it a crime for someone to "cut in line." If someone doesn't want to wait in line and cuts to the front, it often makes others very angry. We sneer at drivers who sneak along the side of the road to get around a line of traffic as we sit and wait our turn.

If you have ever resented a line-cutter, then you understand ethics and have applied ethical standards in life. Waiting your turn in line is an expectation society has. "Waiting your turn" is not an ordinance, a statute, or even a federal regulation. "Waiting your turn" is an age-old principle developed because it was fair to proceed with first-in-time, first to be served. "Waiting your turn" exists because when there are large groups waiting for the same road, theater tickets, or fast food at noon in a busy downtown area, we found that lines ensured order and that waiting your turn was a just way of allocating the limited space and time allotted for the movie tickets, the traffic, or the food. "Waiting your turn" is an expected but unwritten behavior that plays a critical role in an orderly society.[5]

© COMSTOCK IMAGES/JUPITERIMAGES

So it is with ethics. Ethics consists of those unwritten rules we have developed for our interactions with each other. These unwritten rules govern us when we are sharing resources or honoring contracts. "Waiting your turn" is a higher standard than the laws that are passed to maintain order. Those laws apply when physical force or threats are used to push to the front of the line. Assault, battery, and threats are forms of criminal conduct for which the offender can be prosecuted. But the law does not apply to the stealthy line-cutter who simply sneaks to the front, perhaps using a friend and a conversation as a decoy for edging into the front. No laws are broken, but the notions of fairness and justice are offended by one individual putting himself above others and taking advantage of others' time and position.

When you say to yourself, "That's unjust!" or "That's unfair!" you have just defined ethics for yourself. Ethics is not just about standards of behavior; ethics is about honesty, justice, and fairness. This is true for both personal and business behavior.

Ethical questions range from practical, narrowly defined issues, such as a business person's obligation to be honest with his customers, to broader social and philosophical questions, such as a company's responsibility to preserve the environment and protect employee rights. Many ethical conflicts develop from conflicts between the differing interests of company owners and their workers, customers, and surrounding community. Managers must balance the ideal against the practical—the need to produce a reasonable profit for the company's shareholders with honesty in business practices, and larger environmental and social issues.

Ethical Theories

People usually base their individual choice of ethical theory on their life experiences. The following are some of the ethical theories that apply to marketing.[6]

Deontology The **deontological theory** states that people should adhere to their obligations and duties when analyzing an ethical dilemma. This means that a person will follow his or her obligations to another individual or society because upholding one's duty is what is considered ethically correct. For instance, a deontologist will always keep his promises to a friend and will follow the law. A person who follows this theory will produce very consistent decisions because they will be based on the individual's set duties. Note that this theory is not necessarily concerned with the welfare of others. Say, for example, a salesperson has decided that it's his ethical duty (and very practical!) to always be on time to meetings with clients. Today he is running late. How is he supposed to drive? Is the deontologist supposed to speed, breaking the law to uphold his

ethics
The moral principles or values that generally govern the conduct of an individual.

deontological ethical theory
A theory that states that people should adhere to their obligations and duties when analyzing an ethical dilemma.

utilitarian ethical theory
A theory that holds that the choice that yields the greatest benefit to the most people is the choice that is ethically correct.

casuist ethical theory
A theory that compares a current ethical dilemma with examples of similar ethical dilemmas and their outcomes.

duty to society, or is the deontologist supposed to arrive at his meeting late, breaking his duty to be on time? This scenario of conflicting obligations does not lead us to a clear, ethically correct resolution, nor does it protect the welfare of others from the deontologist's decision.

Utilitarianism The **utilitarian ethical theory** is founded on the ability to predict the consequences of an action. To a utilitarian, the choice that yields the greatest benefit to the most people is the choice that is ethically correct. One benefit of this ethical theory is that the utilitarian can compare similar predicted solutions and use a point system to determine which choice is more beneficial for more people. This point system provides a logical and rational argument for each decision and allows a person to use it on a case-by-case context.

There are two types of utilitarianism: act utilitarianism and rule utilitarianism. *Act utilitarianism* adheres exactly to the definition of utilitarianism as described in the above section. In act utilitarianism, a person performs the acts that benefit the most people, regardless of personal feelings or the societal constraints such as laws. *Rule utilitarianism*, however, takes into account the law and is concerned with fairness. A rule utilitarian seeks to benefit the most people but through the fairest and most just means available. Therefore, added benefits of rule utilitarianism are that it values justice and doing good at the same time.

As is true of all ethical theories, however, both act and rule utilitarianism contain numerous flaws. Inherent in both are the flaws associated with predicting the future. Although people can use their life experiences to attempt to predict outcomes, no human being can be certain that his predictions will be true. This uncertainty can lead to unexpected results, making the utilitarian look unethical as time passes because his choice did not benefit the most people as he predicted.

Another assumption that a utilitarian must make is that he has the ability to compare the various types of consequences against each other on a similar scale. However, comparing material gains such as money against intangible gains such as happiness is impossible because their qualities differ so greatly.

Casuist The **casuist ethical theory** compares a current ethical dilemma with examples of similar ethical dilemmas and their outcomes. This allows one to determine the severity of the situation and to create the best possible solution according to others' experiences. Usually, one will find examples that represent the extremes of the situation so that a compromise can be reached that will hopefully include the wisdom gained from the previous situations.

One drawback to this ethical theory is that there may not be a set of similar examples for a given ethical dilemma. Perhaps that which is controversial and ethically questionable is new and unexpected. Along the same line of thinking, this theory assumes that the results of the current ethical dilemma will be similar to results in the examples. This may not be necessarily true and would greatly hinder the effectiveness of applying this ethical theory.

Aristotle and Plato taught that solving ethical dilemmas requires training, that individuals solve ethical dilemmas when they develop and nurture a set of virtues.

REVIEW LEARNING OUTCOME

Explain the concept of ethical behavior

Ethical conflicts for business owners, managers, customers, workers, and the communities can sometimes be resolved through the reliance on ethical theories such as deontology, utilitarianism, casuist, moral relativism, and virtue ethics.

Moral Relativists[7] **Moral relativists** believe in time-and-place ethics; that is, ethical truths depend on the individuals and groups holding them. Arson is not always wrong in their book. If you live in a neighborhood in which drug dealers are operating a crystal meth lab or crack house, arson is ethically justified. If you are a parent and your child is starving, stealing a loaf of bread is ethically correct. The proper resolution to ethical dilemmas is based upon weighing the competing factors at the moment and then

EXHIBIT 3.1

Standards for Being Virtuous

Virtue Standard	Definition	Virtue Standard	Definition
Ability	being dependable and competent	Humility	giving proper credit
Acceptance	making the best of a bad situation	Humor	bringing relief; making the world better
Amiability	fostering agreeable social contexts	Independence	getting things done despite bureaucracy
Articulateness	ability to make and defend one's case	Integrity	being a model of trustworthiness
Attentiveness	listening and understanding	Justice	treating others fairly
Autonomy	having a personal identity	Loyalty	working for the well-being of an organization
Caring	worrying about the well-being of others despite power	Pride	being admired by others
Charisma	inspiring others	Prudence	minimizing company and personal losses
Compassion	sympathetic	Responsibility	doing what it takes to do the right thing
Coolheadedness	retaining control and reasonableness in heated situations	Saintliness	approaching the ideal in behavior
Courage	doing the right thing despite the cost	Shame (capable of)	regaining acceptance after wrong behavior
Determination	seeing a task through to completion	Spirit	appreciating a larger picture in situations
Fairness	giving others their due; creating harmony	Toughness	maintaining one's position
Generosity	sharing, enhancing others' well-being	Trust	dependable
Graciousness	establishing a congenial environment	Trustworthiness	fulfilling one's responsibilities
Gratitude	giving proper credit	Wittiness	lightening the conversation when warranted
Heroism	doing the right thing despite the consequences	Zeal	getting the job done right; enthusiasm
Honesty	telling the truth; not lying		

Source: From Robert C. Solomon, *A Better Way to Think About Business: How Personal Integrity Leads to Corporate Success* (New York: Oxford University Press, 2003), 18. Used by permission of Oxford University Press, Inc.

making a determination to take the lesser of the evils as the resolution. Moral relativists do not believe in absolute rules. Their beliefs center on the pressure of the moment and whether the pressure justifies the action taken.

Virtue Ethics[8] Aristotle and Plato taught that solving ethical dilemmas requires training, that individuals solve ethical dilemmas when they develop and nurture a set of virtues. A **virtue** is a character trait valued as being good. Aristotle taught the importance of cultivating virtue in his students and then had them solve ethical dilemmas using those virtues once they had become an integral part of their being through their virtue training.

Some modern philosophers have embraced this notion of virtue and have developed lists of what constitutes a virtuous business person. Exhibit 3.1 reveals a list of virtuous standards.

moral relativists
Persons who believe that ethical truths depend on the individuals and groups holding them.

virtue
A character trait valued as being good.

morals
The rules people develop as a result of cultural values and norms.

LO 3

ETHICAL BEHAVIOR IN BUSINESS

Depending upon which, if any, ethical theory a businessperson has accepted and uses in his or her daily conduct, the action taken may vary. For example, faced with bribing a foreign official to get a critically needed contract or shutting down a factory and laying off a thousand workers, a person following a deontology strategy would not pay the bribe. Why? A deontologist always follows the law. However, a moral relativist will probably pay the bribe.

While the boundaries of what is legal and what is not are often fairly clear (e.g., don't run a red light, don't steal money from a bank, and don't kill someone), the boundaries of ethical decision making are predicated on which ethical theory one is following. The law typically relies on juries to determine if an act is legal or illegal. Society determines whether an action is ethical or unethical. Sometimes society decides that a person acted unethically—recall the O.J. Simpson murder trial—but a jury may decide that no illegal act was committed. The jury in Simpson's most recent trial for armed robbery and kidnapping found him guilty (and obviously unethical). In a business-related case, a jury recently found Richard Scrushy, charged with a $1.4 billion fraud at HealthSouth Corporation, innocent on all counts. On the other hand, Bernard Ebbers, former CEO of WorldCom, was found guilty of securities fraud and filing false documents and was sentenced to 25 years in prison.

Morals are the rules people develop as a result of cultural values and norms. Culture is a socializing force that dictates what is right and wrong. Moral standards may also reflect the laws and regulations that affect social and economic behavior. Thus, morals can be considered a foundation of ethical behavior.

Morals are usually characterized as good or bad. "Good" and "bad" have different connotations, including "effective" and "ineffective." A good salesperson makes or exceeds the assigned quota. If the salesperson sells a new stereo or television set to a disadvantaged consumer—knowing full well that the person can't keep up the monthly payments—is the salesperson still a good one? What if the sale enables the salesperson to exceed his or her quota?

"Good" and "bad" can also refer to "conforming" and "deviant" behaviors. A doctor who runs large ads offering discounts on open-heart surgery would be considered bad, or unprofessional, in the sense of not conforming to the norms of the medical profession. "Bad" and "good" are also used to express the distinction between criminal and law-abiding behavior. And finally, different religions define "good" and "bad" in markedly different ways. A Muslim who eats pork would be considered bad, as would a fundamentalist Christian who drinks whiskey.

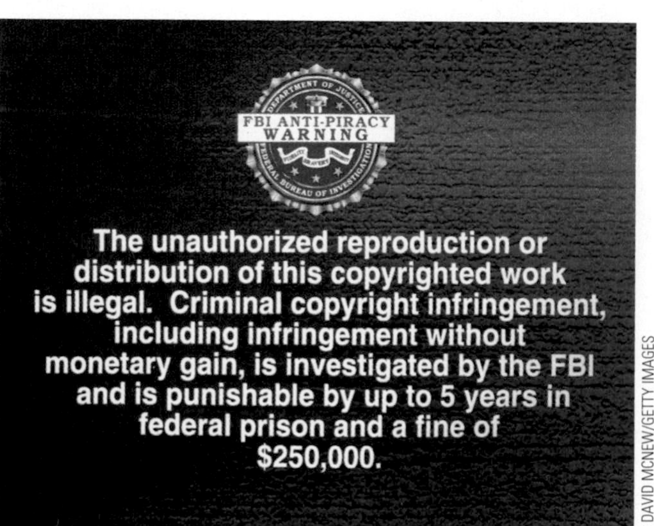

© DAVID MCNEW/GETTY IMAGES

Morality and Business Ethics

Today's business ethics actually consist of a subset of major life values learned since birth. The values businesspeople use to make decisions have been acquired through family, educational, and religious institutions.

Ethical values are situation specific and time oriented. Nevertheless, everyone must have an ethical base that applies to conduct in the business world and in personal life. One approach to developing a personal set of ethics is to examine the consequences of a particular act. Who is helped or hurt? How long lasting are the consequences? What actions produce the greatest good for the greatest number of people? A second approach stresses the importance of rules. Rules come in the form of customs, laws, professional standards, and common sense. Consider these examples of rules:

- Always treat others as you would like to be treated.
- Copying copyrighted computer software is against the law.
- It is wrong to lie, bribe, or exploit.

Another approach emphasizes the development of moral character within individuals. Ethical development can be thought of as having three levels[9]:

- *Preconventional morality*, the most basic level, is childlike. It is calculating, self-centered, and even selfish, based on what will be immediately punished or rewarded. Fortunately, most businesspeople have progressed beyond the self-centered and manipulative actions of preconventional morality.
- *Conventional morality* moves from an egocentric viewpoint toward the expectations of society. Loyalty and obedience to the organization (or society) become paramount. At the level of conventional morality, a marketing decision maker would be concerned only with whether the proposed action is legal and how it will be viewed by others. This type of morality could be likened to the adage "When in Rome, do as the Romans do."
- *Postconventional morality* represents the morality of the mature adult. At this level, people are less concerned about how others might see them and more concerned about how they see and judge themselves over the long run. A marketing decision maker who has attained a postconventional level of morality might ask, "Even though it is legal and will increase company profits, is it right in the long run? Might it do more harm than good in the end?"

EXHIBIT 3.2

Unethical Practices Marketing Managers May Have to Deal With

- Entertainment and gift giving
- False or misleading advertising
- Misrepresentation of goods, services, or company capabilities
- Lying to customers in order to get the sale
- Manipulation of data (falsifying or misusing statistics or information)
- Misleading product or service warranties
- Unfair manipulation of customers
- Exploitation of children or disadvantaged groups
- Stereotypical portrayals of women, minority groups, or senior citizens
- Invasion of customer privacy
- Sexually oriented advertising appeals
- Product or service deception
- Unsafe products or services
- Price deception
- Price discrimination
- Unfair or inaccurate statements about competitors
- Smaller amounts of product in the same-size packages

Ethical Decision Making

How do businesspeople make ethical decisions? There is no cut-and-dried answer. Some of the ethical issues managers face are shown in Exhibit 3.2. Studies show that the following factors tend to influence ethical decision making and judgments[10]:

- *Extent of ethical problems within the organization:* Marketing professionals who perceive fewer ethical problems in their organizations tend to disapprove more strongly of "unethical" or questionable practices than those who perceive more ethical problems. Apparently, the healthier the ethical environment, the more likely that marketers will take a strong stand against questionable practices.
- *Top-management actions on ethics:* Top managers can influence the behavior of marketing professionals by encouraging ethical behavior and discouraging unethical behavior. Research found that 13 percent of large-company top executives thought that having strong ethical traits was the most important leadership trait of CEOs. That is down from 20 percent in 2003.[11] The most important trait to the majority of respondents was the ability to inspire others (37 percent).[12] Other research found three ethics-related actions by managers have the greatest impact on employee ethics. These are setting a good example, keeping promises and commitments, and supporting others in adhering to ethics standards.[13]
- *Potential magnitude of the consequences:* The greater the harm done to victims, the more likely that marketing professionals will recognize a problem as unethical.
- *Social consensus:* The greater the degree of agreement among managerial peers that an action is harmful, the more likely that marketers will recognize a problem as unethical.

code of ethics
A guideline to help marketing managers and other employees make better decisions.

- *Probability of a harmful outcome:* The greater the likelihood that an action will result in a harmful outcome, the more likely that marketers will recognize a problem as unethical.
- *Length of time between the decision and the onset of consequences:* The shorter the length of time between the action and the onset of negative consequences, the more likely that marketers will perceive a problem as unethical.
- *Number of people to be affected:* The greater the number of persons affected by a negative outcome, the more likely that marketers will recognize a problem as unethical.

In order to comply with new human rights policies, police in Northern Ireland will not be issued with controversial Taser stun guns in the immediate future.

© AP IMAGES/PAMPC PA

As you can see, many factors determine the nature of ethical decision making. An example is Taser International Inc., the world's largest maker of stun guns. Management talks tough when the subject turns to people who've sued the company for injuries or deaths allegedly inflicted by electric shock from its weapons. The word has gotten out: Taser doesn't settle. Taser general counsel Doug Klint said, "Anyone who sues us is in for a fight." Taser's stun gun, sold mainly to police departments, fires two insulated conductive wires with barbs at the end as far as 35 feet, delivering a 50,000-volt jolt that temporarily paralyzes the target. Taser's refusal to settle personal-injury or wrongful-death claims has resulted in fewer lawsuits being filed, Klint said. While about 50 suits are still pending, Taser has seen a "significant decline" in the rate of new litigation. "There was a lot of controversy in 2005, a lot of concerns about the safety of the product, but I think after 52 consecutive wins in court, we've laid the concerns to rest," Chief executive officer Rick Smith said in an interview. When asked whether the company considers settling, he said, "We like to litigate every one that we can."[14] Lawyers for alleged Taser victims say the company overstates its legal scoreboard to discourage lawsuits and boost its stock price. "They're trying to deter other litigants while making themselves look good to investors," said Las Vegas attorney E. Brent Bryson, who represents plaintiffs in two cases over Taser-related deaths.[15]

Ethical Guidelines and Training

Many organizations have become more interested in ethical issues. One sign of this interest is the increase in the number of large companies that appoint ethics officers—from virtually none a few years ago to almost 33 percent of large corporations now. More and more companies are providing ethics resources for their employees. Today over 70 percent of employees in the United States can seek advice on ethics questions via telephone, e-mail, Web, or in-person. (See **www.ethics.org** for more information.) In addition, many companies of various sizes have developed a **code of ethics** as a guideline to help marketing managers and other employees make better decisions. Some of the most highly praised codes of ethics are those of Intel, IBM, Starbucks, and Costco.

Creating ethics guidelines has several advantages:

- The guidelines help employees identify what their firm recognizes as acceptable business practices.
- A code of ethics can be an effective internal control on behavior, which is more desirable than external controls like government regulation.
- A written code helps employees avoid confusion when determining whether their decisions are ethical.
- The process of formulating the code of ethics facilitates discussion among employees about what is right and wrong and ultimately leads to better decisions.

An example of a basic code of ethics is shown in Exhibit 3.3.

EXHIBIT 3.3

General Mills Code of Ethics

Times may change, but our values have endured. Honesty. Integrity. Trust. Our values are the source of our strength. They remain the heart of who we are and what we do.

For more than 130 years — since John S. Pillsbury and Cadwallader C. Washburn first began building their competing businesses along the Mississippi River — we have held our company and ourselves to the highest standards of ethical conduct and personal integrity.

We set very high expectations for ourselves — and for the integrity of our company. We will not compromise those standards.

- We strive for the highest quality in our products, services, and relationships.
- We set and maintain the highest standards for all aspects of our work.
- We advance and grow our businesses honestly and ethically, taking no shortcuts that might compromise our high standards.
- We comply with local laws in every nation where we operate. We recognize and respect the cultures, customs, and practices of our consumers and customers in nations around the world.
- We steer clear of conflicts of interest, and work to avoid even the perception of conflict.
- We deliver on our promises.
- We are ever mindful of the trust our consumers, customers, partners, and employees place in General Mills. We will never knowingly or willfully undermine that trust.

Source: General Mills

Businesses, however, must be careful not to make their code of ethics too vague or too detailed. Codes that are too vague give little or no guidance to employees in their day-to-day activities. Codes that are too detailed encourage employees to substitute rules for judgment. For instance, if employees are involved in questionable behavior, they may use the absence of a written rule as a reason to continue behaving that way, even though their conscience may be saying no. The checklist in Exhibit 3.4 is an example of a simple but helpful set of ethical guidelines. Following the checklist will not guarantee the "rightness" of a decision, but it will improve the chances that the decision will be ethical. Although many companies have issued policies on ethical behavior, marketing managers must still put the policies into effect. They must address the classic "matter of degree" issue. For example, marketing researchers must often resort to deception to obtain unbiased answers to their research questions. Asking for a few minutes of a respondent's time is dishonest if the researcher knows the interview

EXHIBIT 3.4

Ethics Checklist

- Does the decision benefit one person or group but hurt or not benefit other individuals or groups? In other words, is my decision fair to all concerned?
- Would individuals or groups, particularly customers, be upset if they knew about my decision?
- Has important information been overlooked because my decision was made without input from other knowledgeable individuals or groups?
- Does my decision presume that my company is an exception to a common practice in this industry and that I therefore have the authority to break a rule?
- Would my decision offend or upset qualified job applicants?
- Will my decision create conflict between individuals or groups within the company?
- Will I have to pull rank or use coercion to implement my decision?
- Would I prefer to avoid the consequences of my decision?
- Did I avoid truthfully answering any of the above questions by telling myself that the risks of getting caught are low or that I could get away with the potentially unethical behavior?

will last 45 minutes. Not only must management post a code of ethics, but it must also give examples of what is ethical and unethical for each item in the code. Moreover, top management must stress to all employees the importance of adhering to the company's code of ethics. Without a detailed code of ethics and top management's support, creating ethical guidelines becomes an empty exercise.

Ethics Training Ethics training is a good way to help employees put good ethics into practice. Because of the numerous corporate scandals in the past decade, such as Enron, Tyco, Worldcom, Hewlett-Packard, and Adelphia Communications Corporation, more and more companies are offering ethics training to their employees. Today, about 70 percent of all large employers (over 500 employees) provide ethics training.[16] Simply giving employees a long list of "dos and don'ts" is a start, but doesn't really help navigate the gray areas. What is needed then is a more contextual approach to ethics training.

Lockheed Martin is one firm that has moved to contextual ethics training. Recently, Manny Zulueta met with seven colleagues to watch a DVD. In one scene, a worker complained to his manager's boss after the manager yelled at her workers. The manager apologized, but the worker soon felt that the manager was retaliating by giving him lousy assignments, nitpicking his work, and reprimanding him for arriving late. Mr. Zulueta, Lockheed Martin's senior vice president of shared services, then led what he says was a "nuanced" discussion about the ethical issues involved in that scene. Zuelueta's colleagues rightly noted that they needed more information—they needed to put the scene in context—to discern whether the manager's actions were retaliatory.[17] Understanding the context of an ethical problem helps employees navigate the gray areas.

Do ethics training programs work? While there are exceptions depending on the quality of the program, the general answer is yes.[18] In addition to Lockheed Martin, another company that does a good job with ethics training is the accounting and consulting firm Ernst & Young (E&Y). Michael Hamilton, chief learning and development officer for the Americas, said undeniable ethics is the foundation of why people hire the firm. To help provide employees with an ethical foundation, E&Y implemented a formal ethics curriculum, including a mandatory two-hour Web-based course titled "Living Our Core Values." The first 45 minutes of the course set forth the ethical foundation and values for the firm. The remaining bulk of the learning is experiential, applying E&Y standards or the firm's collective wisdom regarding those values to real-life situations.

"We put employees in situations and ask them to take the firm's values and ethics to solve problems at the firm itself," Hamilton said. "It's the only way you can give them that experience. You can talk at them all day, but when it comes to making tough calls and essentially interpreting between the lines, you have to let people have an emotional connection that says, 'This is what I feel, in my heart, is right, based on the firm's values.' You can't expect people to exercise the right answers unless you give them a chance to apply them to real-life situations."[19]

The Most Ethical Companies Each year, *Ethisphere* magazine (targeted toward top management and focused on ethical leadership) examines over 5,000 companies in 30 separate industries seeking the world's most ethical companies. It then lists the top 100. The magazine uses a rigorous format to identify true ethical leadership. A few of the selected winners are shown in Exhibit 3.5.

Forcing Ethical Standards on Others A company such as Wal-Mart has a huge amount of power over its suppliers. As the world's largest seller of toys, Wal-Mart ordered its suppliers to meet a new set of children's-product safety requirements by the fall of 2008 that goes far beyond existing government regulations. The standards include strict limits for lead and a broad array of other heavy metals and chemicals that have been linked to various medical and developmental problems in children.

EXHIBIT 3.5

Selected Winners of the World's Most Ethical Companies Award

ALCOA

Perry Minis, Director of Global Ethics & Compliance

Perry Minis is the Director of Global Ethics & Compliance for Alcoa, a metals and mining company with over 120,000 employees in 44 countries. Minnis, who started with Alcoa in finance 39 years ago, runs the Global Ethics & Compliance department to track metrics and determine if the company has a positive impact on the community. According to Minnis, "Our management has a very strong focus on safety. Alcoa is considered to be one of the safest corporations in the world." The company's Ethics and Compliance Council, which includes the CEO, vice presidents, and department directors, was formed in order to notify all executives of the latest in operations. The Council presents findings to the Board on a quarterly basis.

Minnis notes that Alcoa's Code of Conduct has been condensed to apply to specific roles and translated into different languages in order to make it an effective tool for all employees. The Code is also provided to suppliers, so they understand Alcoa's expectations and policies. "If a vendor's values or policies differ drastically from Alcoa, chances are they won't be doing business with us," emphasizes Minnis. He continues, "The most important thing is our values. We have a set of values and policies that is consistent across the company, and we train all employees to adhere to and uphold those values."

EATON

Sandy Cutler, CEO

Sandy Cutler, CEO of Eaton Corporation, spoke in great detail about the basic beliefs that make Eaton a value-based company. These core values have allowed Eaton to maintain a strong foundation and sense of stability during recent internal changes and mergers. Rather than approaching ethics as a compliance issue, Cutler believes, "It's about doing business right through internal philosophies and customer commitments. We'll lose business before we will compromise our values."

Eaton employs 61,000 people in 125 countries, and almost all of their products are targeted at helping people and companies to effectively use energy. For example, Eaton developed a technology with the EPA for UPS that allowed the shipping company to save 70 percent in fuel economy. Additionally, Eaton developed a hybrid electric bus technology for possible use during the Beijing Olympics.

Eaton places high value on contributions in the workplace and community, believing they are key components for doing business right. "People will work where the company and the community involvement values reflect their own," insists Cutler. Every employee at Eaton has the opportunity to raise questions if they believe their personal morals are at risk. If a company is committed to doing business ethically, "you can cut the top off and the bottom would keep working," maintains Cutler.

JOHN DEERE

James R. Jenkins, Senior Vice President and General Counsel

In business for 170 years, John Deere prides itself on enabling "human flourishing." With core values of integrity, quality, innovation, and commitment, the company provides advanced products and services for agriculture, forestry, construction, and landscaping, as well as manufacturing engines for use in heavy equipment. James R. Jenkins, Senior VP and General Counsel for Deere & Company, said, "John Deere fully recognizes the need to conduct business with integrity. Our broad approach to citizenship, coupled with market leadership, helps us improve the world while growing a business."

Deere believes in creating and distributing service in ways that respect the earth's limited resources while providing commitment to helping find policy solutions that benefit the environment. "We believe that effective policy to address global climate change must include development and support of renewable energy sources including agricultural, forestry, wind, and bio-technologies, as well as processing and distribution improvements," says Jenkins.

With a passionate commitment to doing what is right and operating ethically, John Deere makes their conduct guidelines transparent to employees, customers, and suppliers. Acting out of principled, long-term self-interest, Deere contributes to the greater good by supporting the quality of life in their communities, protecting the environment, and preserving precious resources. According to Jenkins, "We believe that exceptional performance will not be sustainable if it is at the expense of our values."

Source: Ethisphere.com (August 28, 2007).

The initiative also encourages suppliers to mark children's products with "traceability information," including the factory in which the goods were made. About 80 percent of the toys sold in the United States, including those marketed by U.S.-based toy makers, are manufactured in China.

Wal-Mart's action, and similar moves by rivals such as Target Corp. and Toys"R"Us Inc., follow the discovery of high lead levels in children's products, the recall of about 25 million toys in 2007, and toy-related deaths. The new Wal-Mart standards are estimated to increase toy manufacturing costs by 5 to 7 percent.[20]

Wal-Mart also has implemented strict new quality, environmental, and safety standards for its Chinese suppliers. It also began requiring specific levels of energy efficiency for its Chinese suppliers in 2009. Wal-Mart feels that the new standards will

Foreign Corrupt Practices Act
A law that prohibits U.S. corporations from making illegal payments to public officials of foreign governments to obtain business rights or to enhance their business dealings in those countries.

help because in some factories up to 20 percent of the goods produced were rejected as not up to quality standards. This resulted in a lot of waste. Wal-Mart hopes to eliminate customer returns due to defective merchandise by 2012.[21]

The ultimate question many ask is, "Does being ethical pay?" We explore this issue in the "Customer Experience" box below.

Cultural Differences in Ethics

Studies suggest that ethical beliefs vary only a little from culture to culture. Certain practices, however, such as the use of illegal payments and bribes, are far more acceptable in some places than in others. Some countries have a dual standard concerning illegal payments. For example, German businesspeople typically treat bribes as tax-deductible business expenses. In Russia, bribes and connections in the government are essential for doing business. For instance, bribing a public official is the fastest method for accomplishing bureaucratic tasks such as registering a business. What we call bribery is a natural way of doing business in some other cultures. Do these widespread practices suggest that global marketers should adopt a "When in Rome, do as the Romans do" mentality?

Yet another example of cultural differences is the Japanese reluctance to enforce their antitrust laws. Everyday business practices, from retail pricing to business structuring, ignore antitrust regulations against restraint of trade, monopolies, and price discrimination. Not surprisingly, the Japanese are tolerant of scandals involving antitrust violations, favoritism, price fixing, bribery, and other activities considered unethical in the United States.

Concern about U.S. corporations' use of illegal payments and bribes in international business dealings led to passage of the **Foreign Corrupt Practices Act**. This act prohibits U.S. corporations from making illegal payments to public officials of foreign governments to obtain business rights or to enhance their business dealings in those countries. The act has been criticized for putting U.S. businesses at a competitive disadvantage. Many contend that bribery is an unpleasant but necessary part of international business.

CUSTOMER Experience

Will Consumers Pay More for an Ethical Company's Products?

In a perfect world, consumers would pay more for good companies' products than unethical companies' products if the product were relatively homogenous. But does this really happen? To find out, researchers conducted a series of experiments. They showed consumers the same products—coffee and T-shirts—but told one group the items had been made using high ethical standards and another group that low standards had been used. A control group got no information. In all of the tests, consumers were willing to pay a slight premium for the ethically made goods. But they went much further in the other direction: they would buy unethically made products only at a steep discount. What's more, consumer attitudes played a big part in shaping those results. People with high standards for corporate behavior rewarded the ethical companies with bigger premiums and punished the unethical ones with bigger discounts.[22]

Other research has found that there is a positive relationship between a firm's ethical ideals and practices and profitability. High ethical standards tended to inspire and motivate employees. It also gave them a feeling of well-being. Strong corporate ethics tend to build a high level of internal trust that enables the firm to retain good employees. This, in turn, can lower costs and lead to higher profits.[23]

Do you think that high ethical standards pay off for businesses? Why or why not? Are you willing to pay more for essentially the same product if it is sold by a company with high ethical standards? Why or why not?

Ethical Dilemmas Related to Developing Countries

For companies, the benefits of seeking international growth are several. A company that cannot grow further in its domestic market may reap increased sales and economies of scale not only by exporting its product but also by producing it abroad. A company may also wish to diversify its political and economic risks by spreading its operations across several nations.

Expanding into developing countries offers multinational companies the benefits of low-cost labor and natural resources. But many multinational firms have been criticized for exploiting developing countries. Although the firms' business practices may be legal, many business ethicists argue that they are unethical. The problem is compounded by the intense competition among developing countries for industrial development. Ethical standards are often overlooked by governments hungry for jobs or tax revenues.

In the face of the rising number of smokers in their country, the Malaysian government has banned the advertising of tobacco products. However, many firms in the tobacco industry skirt the law by sponsoring sports and entertainment events, such as this motorsport event, or by advertising their brands without referring to cigarettes.

Take the tobacco industry, for instance. With tobacco sales decreasing and regulations stiffening in the United States and Western Europe, tobacco companies have come to believe that their future lies elsewhere: in China, Asia, Africa, Eastern Europe, and Russia. Despite the known health risks of their product, the large tobacco companies are pushing their way into markets that typically have few marketing or health-labeling controls. In Hungary, Marlboro cigarettes are sometimes handed out to young fans at pop concerts. In the last 10 years, cigarette advertising on Japanese television has soared from 40th to 2nd place in air time and value; it appears even during children's shows.

Interestingly, at a time when smoking is being discouraged in the United States, U.S. trade representatives are talking to developing countries like China and Thailand about lowering their tariffs on foreign cigarettes. Japan, Taiwan, and South Korea have already given in to the threats. Entering these developing countries, the tobacco companies and trade representatives insist, will help U.S. tobacco manufacturers make up for losses in their home market. Worldwide, tobacco causes nearly 5 million deaths per year. It is expected to rise to 10 million by 2020.[24] Is it ethical for tobacco executives to promote and export this product?

REVIEW LEARNING OUTCOME

LO 3 Describe the role of ethics and ethical decisions in business

MORALITY

Preconventional	Conventional	Postconventional
What's in it for me?	Everyone else is doing it!	Is this good in the long run?
Will I get caught?	When in Rome . . .	

ETHICAL CLIMATE

TOP-MANAGEMENT'S ETHICS

MAGNITUDE OF CONSEQUENCES

SOCIAL CONSENSUS

PROBABILITY OF HARM

LENGTH OF TIME BETWEEN DECISION AND IMPACT

NUMBER OF PEOPLE AFFECTED

ETHICAL TRAINING

corporate social responsibility
Business's concern for society's welfare.

sustainability
The idea that socially responsible companies will outperform their peers by focusing on the world's social problems and viewing them as opportunities to build profits and help the world at the same time.

Environmental issues are another example. As U.S. environmental laws and regulations gain strength, many companies are moving their operations to developing countries, where it is often less expensive to operate. These countries generally enforce minimal or no clean-air and waste-disposal regulations. For example, an increasing number of U.S. companies have located manufacturing plants called *maquiladoras* in Mexico, along the U.S.–Mexican border. Many blame the *maquiladoras* for "not putting back into the border area what they have been taking out," referring to the region's inadequate sewers and water-treatment plants.

Because Mexico has been eager to attract foreign employers, *maquiladoras* pay little in taxes, which would normally go toward improving the country's infrastructure. Cuidad Juárez, a populous and polluted *maquiladora* city bordering El Paso, Texas, generates millions of gallons of sewage a day and has no sewage system at all.

CORPORATE SOCIAL RESPONSIBILITY

Corporate social responsibility is a business's concern for society's welfare. This concern is demonstrated by managers who consider both the long-range best interests of the company and the company's relationship to the society within which it operates. The newest theory in social responsibility is called sustainability. This refers to the idea

EXHIBIT 3.6

Stakeholders in a Typical Corporation

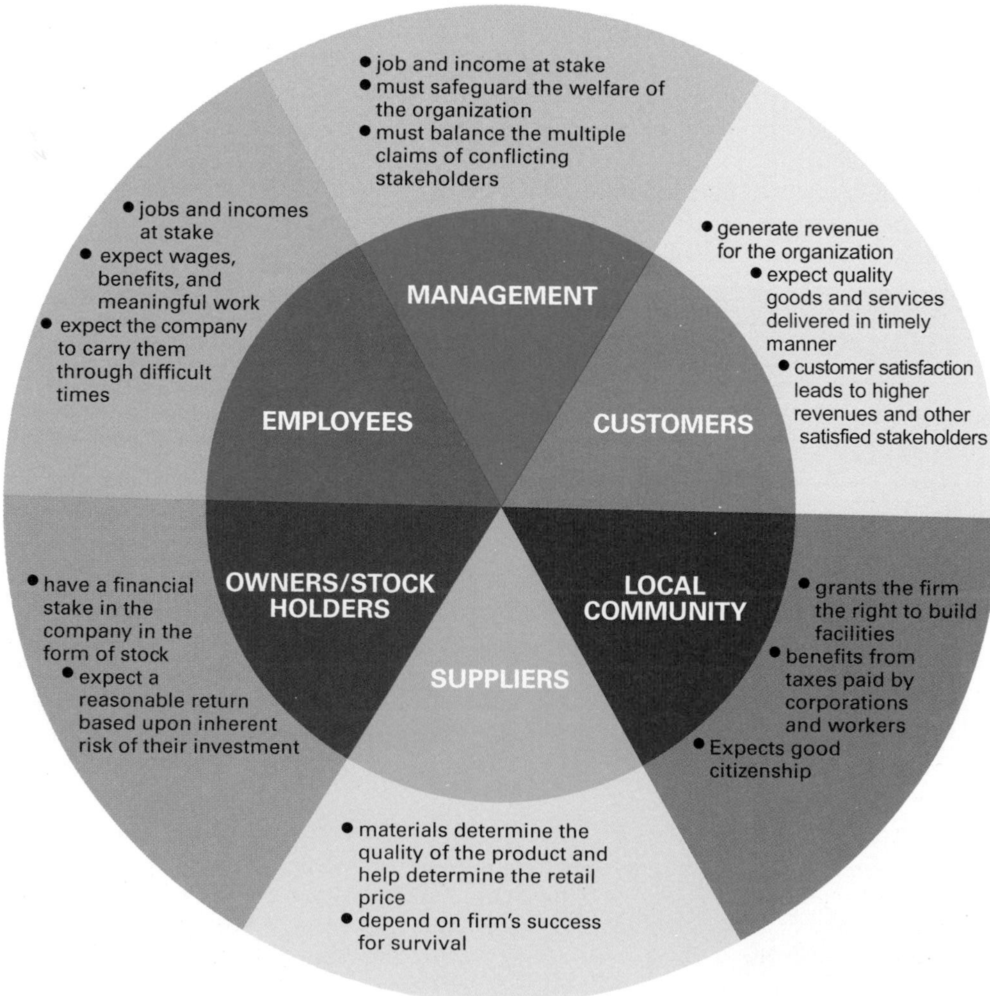

that socially responsible companies will outperform their peers by focusing on the world's social problems and viewing them as opportunities to build profits and help the world at the same time. It is also the notion that companies cannot thrive for long (i.e., lack sustainability) in a world where billions of people are suffering and are desperately poor. Thus, it is in business's interest to find ways to attack society's ills. Only business organizations have the talent, creativity, and executive ability to do the job.

REVIEW LEARNING OUTCOME

LO 4 Discuss corporate social responsibility

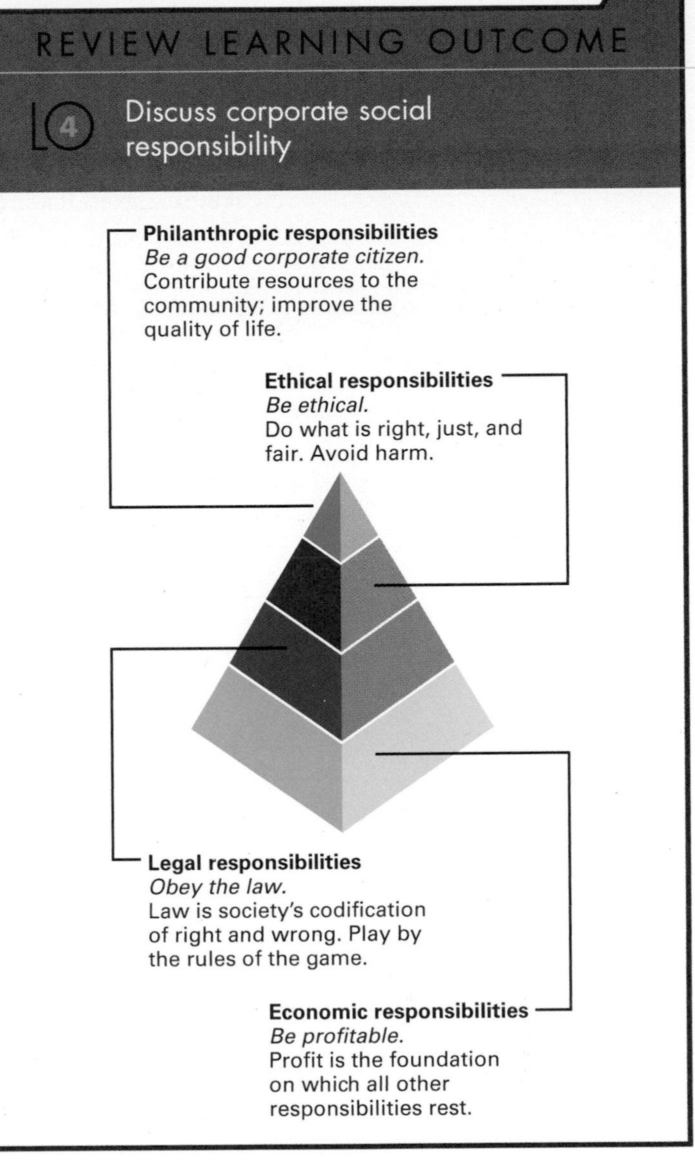

Stakeholders and Social Responsibility

A second approach to social responsibility is known as the **stakeholder theory**. This says that social responsibility is paying attention to the interest of every affected stakeholder in every aspect of a firm's operation.[25] The stakeholders in a typical corporation are shown in Exhibit 3.6.

- *Employees* have their jobs and incomes at stake. If the firm moves or closes, employees often face a severe hardship. In return for their labor, employees expect wages, benefits, and meaningful work. In return for their loyalty, workers expect the company to carry them through difficult times.
- *Management* plays a special role, as they also have a stake in the corporation. Part of their stake is like that of the employees. On the other hand, management must safeguard the welfare of the organization. Sometimes this means balancing the multiple claims of conflicting stakeholders. For example, stockholders want higher return and perhaps lower costs by moving factories overseas. This naturally conflicts with employees, the local community, and perhaps suppliers.
- *Customers* generate the revenue for the organization. In exchange, they expect high-quality goods and services delivered in a timely manner. Customer satisfaction leads to higher revenues and the ability to enhance the satisfaction of other stakeholders.
- *The local community*, through its government, grants the firm the right to build facilities. In turn, it benefits directly from local taxes paid by the corporation and indirectly by property and sales taxes paid by the workers. The firm is expected to be a good citizen by paying a fair wage, not polluting the environment, and so forth.
- *Suppliers* are vital to the success of the firm. If a critical part, for example, is not available for an assembly line, then production grinds to a halt. The materials supplied determine the quality of the product produced and create a cost floor, which helps determine the retail price. In turn, the firm is the customer of the supplier and is therefore vital to the success and survival of the supplier. Small firms who sold most of their production to Wal-Mart and were subsequently dropped by Wal-Mart have sometimes gone bankrupt.
- *Owners* have a financial stake in the form of stock in a corporation. They expect a reasonable return based upon the amount of inherent risk on their investment. Often managers and employees have a portion of their retirement funds in company stock. In the case of Enron's bankruptcy, many workers lost their entire retirement savings.

stakeholder theory
A theory that holds that social responsibility is paying attention to the interest of every affected stakeholder in every aspect of a firm's operation.

pyramid of corporate social responsibility
A model that suggests corporate social responsibility is composed of economic, legal, ethical, and philanthropic responsibilities and that the firm's economic performance supports the entire structure.

One theorist suggests that total corporate social responsibility has four components: economic, legal, ethical, and philanthropic. The **pyramid of corporate social responsibility** portrays economic performance as the foundation for the other three responsibilities. At the same time that it pursues profits (economic responsibility), however, a business is expected to obey the law (legal responsibility); to do what is right, just, and fair (ethical responsibilities); and to be a good corporate citizen (philanthropic responsibility). These four components are distinct but together constitute the whole. Still, if the company doesn't make a profit, then the other three responsibilities are moot.

LO5

ARGUMENTS AGAINST AND FOR CORPORATE SOCIAL RESPONSIBILITY (CSR)

Today very few managers are against social responsibility initiatives. The debate, instead, is the degree and kinds of social responsibility that an organization should pursue.

Arguments Against CSR

Skeptics say business should focus on making a profit and leave social and environmental problems to nonprofit organizations (like the World Wildlife Federation or the Sierra Club) and government. The late economist Milton Friedman believed that the free market, not companies, should decide what is best for the world. He asked, "If businesspeople do have a social responsibility other than making maximum profits for stockholders, how are they to know what it is?"[26] Friedman argued that when business executives spend more money than they need to—to purchase delivery vehicles with hybrid engines or to pay higher wages in developing countries, or even to donate company funds to charity—they are spending shareholders' money to further their own agendas. It is better to pay dividends and let the shareholders give the money away, if they choose.

Another argument is that businesses are created to produce goods and services, and not to handle welfare activities. They don't have the expertise to make social decisions. And if managers take time and monies to pursue social responsibilities, it will take away from the primary goals of the firm.

A final argument is that being socially responsible might damage the company in the global marketplace. That is, cleaning up the environment, ensuring product safety, and donating money and time for social causes all raise costs. This will be reflected in the final prices of the goods and services a company sells. In countries that don't emphasize social responsibility, a company will have lower costs because it doesn't engage in activities related to social responsibility. If the American company competes with the foreign competitor in the global marketplace, it will be at an economic disadvantage.

Arguments For Social Responsibility

The most basic argument for social responsibility is that it is simply the right thing to do. Some societal problems have been brought about by corporations such as pollution and poverty-level wages; it is the responsibility of business to right these wrongs. Another position is that business has the resources, so business should be given the chance to solve social problems. For example, business can provide a fair work environment, safe products, and informative advertising.

Another, more pragmatic, reason for being socially responsible is that, if business isn't responsible, then government will create new regulations and perhaps levy fines against corporations. For example, Valero Energy was recently fined $4.25 million for pollution at three of its refineries and was required to spend an additional $232 million on new pollution controls.[27] To the extent that business polices itself with self-disciplined standards and guidelines, government intervention can be avoided.

A final argument for social responsibility is that it can be a profitable undertaking. Smart companies, they say, can prosper and build shareholder value by tackling global problems. For General Electric, selling more wind power and energy-efficient locomotives is a no-brainer. When it comes to philanthropy, or supply chain audits designed to keep GE from being linked to sweatshops, or decisions about granting domestic-partner benefits, the business case usually comes down to GE's reputation and its desire to attract and engage great people. Some years back, for example, GE decided not to sell low-end ultrasound machines in China (and to put warning labels on the high-end machines it did sell) because it did not want the machines to be used for gender screening that could lead to abortions. The potential harm to GE's image was too great to take the risk.

But applying that kind of cost-benefit analysis to decisions with moral dimensions is a tricky business. Although GE operates in more than 100 countries, it has decided not to do business in Myanmar because the government there is a notorious violator of human rights and has been spotlighted by human-rights groups—and because the business upside is limited. GE has judged that it has more to lose than gain by being there.

Wal-Mart has experienced its share of criticism for not paying a living wage, putting small independent firms out of business, and using too much energy. However, Wal-Mart has aggressively become proactive toward the environment and hopes to make money by "being green." Lee Scott, Wal-Mart's CEO, vows to use 100 percent renewable energy, drastically reduce waste through recycling, and sell "sustainable" products that are more environmentally friendly. Cutting energy use is saving money, and consumers appreciate Wal-Mart's forays into organic cotton products and coffee certified to have earned farm workers a decent wage.

© ED ZURGA/BLOOMBERG VIA GETTY IMAGES

Switching stores to more efficient light bulbs and adding skylights for natural light has trimmed Wal-Mart's electricity bill by 17 percent since 2002. Using less packaging on house-brand toys will save $2.4 million annually in shipping costs. Even Wal-Mart's push to slash America's electricity use—and thus greenhouse gas emissions—by selling 100 million compact fluorescent bulbs a year has a bottom-line benefit. Customers will save $3 billion and the expectation is that these savings will come back in terms of purchases at Wal-Mart.[28]

Some other companies that profit from being socially responsible are shown in Exhibit 3.7. One recent study found that, for large companies, a one percent increase in the firm's social responsibility ratings led to a $17 million increase in profits.[29]

Growth of Social Responsibility

Social responsibility of businesses is growing around the world. A recent study of social responsibility, in selected countries, asked the following: "Does your company consider social responsibility factors when making business decisions?" The percentage of firms that said "yes" were Brazil, 62 percent; Canada, 54 percent; Australia, 52 percent; America, 47 percent; India, 38 percent; China, 35 percent; Mexico, 26 percent.[30]

Another survey pointed out that 47 percent of American firms was simply not adequate. Seventy-five percent felt that United States companies needed to do more in the area of social responsibility.[31]

The UN Global Compact One way that U.S. firms can do more is join the UN's Global Compact. The United Nations Global Compact, the world's largest global corporate citizenship initiative, has seen its ranks swell over the past few years. In 2001—the first full year after its launch—just 67 companies joined, agreeing to abide by ten principles covering, among other things, human rights, labor practices, and the environment. The ten principles are shown in Exhibit 3.8. In 2008, there were more than 5,600 participants in 120 countries around the world.[32]

EXHIBIT 3.7

Doing Well by Doing Good

Automobiles

Toyota: The maker of the top-selling Prius hybrid leads in developing efficient gas-electric vehicles.

Renault: Integrates sustainability throughout organization; has fuel-efficient cars and factories.

Volkswagen: A market leader in small cars and clean diesel technologies.

Computers & Peripherals

Hewlett-Packard: Despite board turmoil, the company rates high on ecological standards and digital technology for the poor.

Toshiba: At the forefront of developing eco-efficient products, such as fuel cells for notebook PC batteries.

Dell: Among the first U.S. PC makers to take hardware back from consumers and recycle it for free.

Retail

Marks & Spencer: Buys local product to cut transit costs and fuel use; good wages and benefits help retain staff.

Home Retail Group: High overall corporate responsibility standards have led to strong consumer and staff loyalty.

Aeon: Environmental accounting has saved $5.6 million; good employee policies in China and SE Asia.

Household Durables

Philips Electronics: Top innovator of energy-saving appliances, lighting, and medical gear and goods for the developing world.

Sony: Is ahead on green issues and ensuring quality, safety, and labor standards of global suppliers.

Matsushita Electric: State-of-the-art green products; eliminated 96 percent of the most toxic substances in its global operations.

Pharmaceuticals

Roche: Committed to improving access to medicine in poor nations; invests in drug research for Third World.

Novo Nordisk: Spearheads efforts in diseases like leprosy and bird flu and is a leading player in lower-cost generics.

Glaxo-SmithKline: One of few pharmas to devote R&D to malaria and TB; first to offer AIDS drugs at cost.

Utilities

FPL: Largest U.S. solar generator; has 40 percent of wind-power capacity; strong shareholder relations.

Source: "Who's Doing Well by Doing Good," *BusinessWeek*, January 29, 2007, 53. Reprinted from the January 29, 2007, issue of *BusinessWeek* by special permission, copyright © 2007 by The McGraw-Hill Companies, Inc.

Firms are realizing that corporate social responsibility isn't easy or quick. It doesn't work without long-term strategy and effort, and coordination throughout the enterprise. It doesn't always come cheap, either. And the payoff, both to society and the business itself, isn't always immediate. Businesses say they want to be responsible citizens, but that's often not their only reason for taking action. In a recent survey, the United Nations Global Compact asked members why they had joined. "Networking opportunities" was the second-most-popular reason; "Addressing humanitarian concerns" was third. The first was to "Increase trust in company."[33]

Proactive Social Responsibility Two companies that are frequently lauded for their social responsibility are food giant H. J. Heinz and Chiquita, the banana grower. Heinz has been a leader in social responsibility from its inception. For Chiquita, its awakening came later.

H. J. Heinz[34]

Founded in 1869, H. J. Heinz Co. was socially responsible long before corporate social responsibility became a banner corporations were advised to adopt. In fact, founder Henry Heinz was one of the first advocates of pure food and corporate transparency. "Our history is captured by the pure food products label," says Ted Smyth, SVP and chief administrative officer for Heinz. "Realizing horseradish was being sold with ingredients like sawdust to fill it out, Henry Heinz used a clear bottle so the consumer could see it wasn't adulterated. It was a great success and brilliant marketing."

EXHIBIT 3.8

The Principles of the UN Global Compact

Human Rights

- Principle 1: Businesses should support and respect the protection of internationally proclaimed human rights; and
- Principle 2: make sure that they are not complicit in human rights abuses.

Labor Standards

- Principle 3: Businesses should uphold the freedom of association and the effective recognition of the right to collective bargaining;
- Principle 4: the elimination of all forms of forced and compulsory labor;
- Principle 5: the effective abolition of child labor; and
- Principle 6: the elimination of discrimination in respect of employment and occupation.

Environment

- Principle 7: Businesses should support a precautionary approach to environmental challenges;
- Principle 8: undertake initiatives to promote greater environmental responsibility; and
- Principle 9: encourage the development and diffusion of environmentally friendly technologies.

Anti-Corruption

- Principle 10: Businesses should work against corruption in all its forms, including extortion and bribery.

Source: www.unglobalcompact.org/AboutTheGC/TheTenPrinciples/index.html, accessed January 21, 2009.

These days, consumers are concerned with not only the quality, but also the nutritional content of foods. More than 70 percent of Heinz products can be classified in the health category, and incremental health improvements are planned. Ingredients such as trans fat, salt, and sugar are being removed. Organic varieties are available, and many foods are being fortified with vitamins and minerals. "We operate in fundamentally healthy categories," says Andrew Towle, VP of global marketing. "Removing ingredients of concern is a technical challenge. We cannot go backward in taste."

Established in 1951, The Heinz Co. Foundation (HCF) is funded by the company to promote health, nutrition, and well-being in communities where Heinz operates. Indeed, social responsibility is undeniably part of Heinz's DNA, yet many are unaware of it because social responsibility is standard practice. In 2002, HCF began its micronutrient program, supported by Dr. Stanley Zlotkin, creator of Sprinkles, an iron-supplement multivitamin powder. The company has used existing packaging and distribution channels to deliver the supplements to more than 1.2 million children in 15 countries. "Sixty packets can cure one child of anemia for a year," says HCF director Tammy Aupperle. "We hope to reach 10 million by 2010." In 2003, Heinz and Helen Keller International, which fights causes and consequences of blindness and malnutrition, partnered in Indonesia. They distributed more than 44 million supplement packets, benefiting more than 400,000 people. The model will be replicated in India and China.

IMAGE COURTESY OF THE ADVERTISING ARCHIVES

A few additional Heinz initiatives are

- *Nutrient program:* Nutritional supplement packets have been distributed to more than 1.2 million children in Indonesia, Guyana, Mongolia, Pakistan, Haiti, Ghana, and other countries.
- *Health and wellness initiatives:* A Global Health & Wellness Task Force is addressing ingredients of concern (sodium, sugar, and others), adding more goodness to products, and adding functional benefits for consumers.

GLOBAL Perspectives

What Good Works Can Do

In 1967, the year after Botswana gained its independence from Britain, a huge diamond deposit was discovered in a remote area called Orapa, about 400 kilometers, or 250 miles, from the capital city of Gaborone. The company that found the source was DeBeers, then, as now, the dominant seller of "rough stones" in the world. Four years and $33 million later, the mine was ready for production.

In the early years of its nationhood, Botswana was one of the poorest countries in the world, with a per capita income of about $80 a year. Today, it is among the most prosperous countries in Africa, with a real middle class and a per capita income approaching $6,000 a year. By contrast, the average citizen in Angola earns about $2,500 a year, while in the Democratic Republic of the Congo, it is a little more than $1,500, according to the World Bank.

There is no question that the discovery of the diamonds was the most important catalyst in Botswana's economic growth. Prior to the discovery, Botswana had an agricultural economy. By the early 1980s, diamond, manganese, and copper mines controlled by DeBeers accounted for fully 50 percent of the country's gross domestic product. Though the Botswana economy has since diversified, DeBeers' operations still account for around one-third of the Botswana gross domestic product. There is also no question, though, that Botswana was greatly aided by something else: DeBeers' own sense of corporate responsibility.

From the start, it entered into a 50–50 diamond mining venture with the government; about a decade ago, it also sold the government a 15 percent stake in the company. It has also built hospitals and schools in Botswana, worked to help the country deal with HIV and AIDS, assisted the government in building roads and infrastructure, and been involved in a hundred other things that have helped make Botswana an African success story. Most of the executives in the government-company venture are black Africans who have been trained by DeBeers. In 2008, the company closed its diamond sorting facility in London and opened the largest, most technologically advanced diamond sorting complex in the world in Gaborone. It employs 600 people.

"We think our approach is a competitive advantage," said Gareth Penny, the cherubic, 45-year-old South African who has been the company chief executive since 2006. It is hard to disagree. Botswana's citizens need roads, but so does DeBeers, to transport its diamonds. DeBeers needs a healthy workforce, so its emphasis on HIV awareness and treatment is clearly in its self-interest. A more prosperous Botswana helps DeBeers in every way imaginable, not least by providing a stable environment in which it can do business. "The country can now attract banks and service industries—and avoid the natural resource curse," Penny said.[36]

Do you think that DeBeers was simply acting in its own self-interest and social responsibility played no part? What else might DeBeers do in Botswana to demonstrate its social responsibility?

- *Sustainable agriculture:* Agricultural practices include hybrid seeds, water conservation and reuse, recycling waste, minimal pesticide use, and partnership with Chinese government and farmers.
- *Eco-friendly packaging:* New packaging includes reduced steel, recycled paper trays and cartons, non-bleached cartons, and reduced resin use.

Heinz is a firm that truly cares about its stakeholders.

Chiquita Cleans Up Its Act[35]

"For decades the $3.9-billion-a-year fruit giant was synonymous with the notion of the greedy multinational. Farmworkers toiled long hours in dangerous conditions, agrochemical runoff contaminated water, and tropical forests were cleared for expansion," says J. Gary Taylor, coauthor of *Smart Alliance*, a book about Chiquita.

Enter Rainforest Alliance, which had previously worked with timber companies in Indonesia to lessen the impact of logging. In 1992 the Alliance sent banana companies a list of environmental and worker-rights standards required to gain its certification. During the next two years, Dave McLaughlin, Chiquita CEO, says Chiquita spent $40,000 to overhaul the Costa Rican farms, phase out toxic pesticides, and build new warehouses to store chemicals. McLaughlin began monitoring water quality and providing workers with better safety equipment. The farms also started recycling programs.

Today all 110 of Chiquita's company-owned farms and the vast majority of its independent farms are certified by the Rainforest Alliance. Things are getting better for its Latin American employees, who can now join unions. Four recent initiatives are

- ☛ One hundred percent of the plastic bags and twine used on Chiquita farms is recycled.
- ☛ Pesticide use has been cut by 26 percent, and workers are provided with better protective gear.
- ☛ Working conditions have been improved by new Chiquita-built housing and schools for employees' families.
- ☛ Buffer zones along farm borders help prevent chemical runoff and erosion.

Chiquita is an example of a multinational firm that has taken its social responsibility very seriously. Perhaps one of the greatest impacts a firm has had on any country is DeBeers, the diamond company. The story unfolds in the Global Perspectives box.

The Cost of Ignoring Social Responsibilities[37]

In today's environment, a firm that disregards its stakeholders and its social responsibilities does so at its own peril. In the case of AOL, it didn't treat its customers (key stakeholders) as they should have been treated. A deluge of AOL customers complained that they tried to close their accounts only to be thwarted in their attempts or to discover they were still being billed for services that they thought had been canceled. Although it had long been one of the Internet's best-known companies, AOL didn't set up an online cancellation system. All cancellation requests had to be made by fax, mail, or telephone. Subscribers who phoned AOL to cancel their service sometimes were greeted by aggressive customer service representatives who were paid bonuses of up to $3,000 if they found a way to retain the business. Customers complained that AOL's incentive system created an obstructive culture that made service cancellations difficult. "Consumers who called were put on hold or transferred repeatedly until they hung up in disgust," says Connecticut Attorney General Richard Blumenthal, who described AOL's practices as "outlandish and underhanded."

These customer complaints led to a $3 million settlement with 48 states and the District of Columbia. As part of the resolution, AOL agreed to make it easier for its remaining customers to leave and to maintain an online channel for processing cancellations.

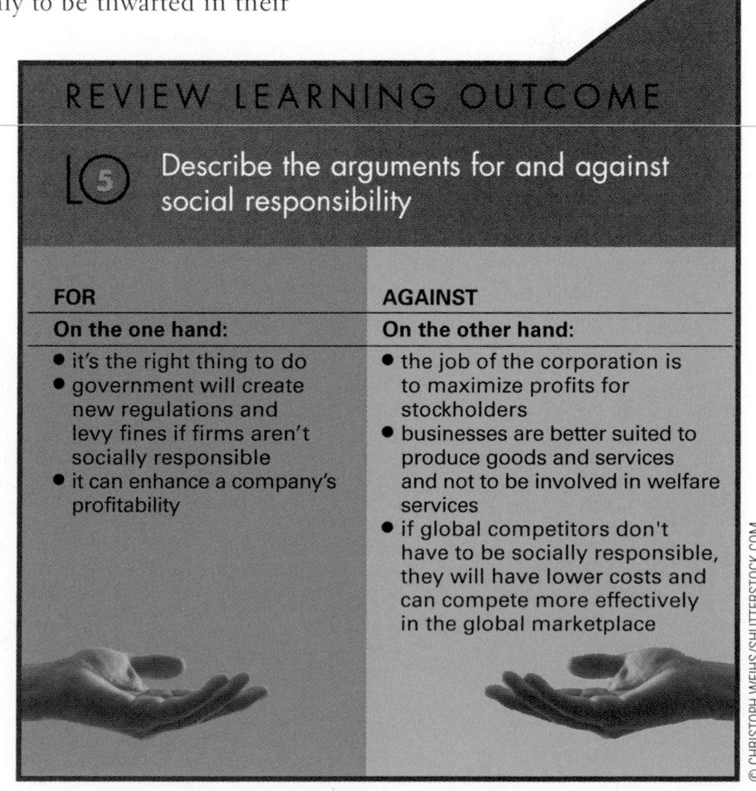

cause-related marketing
The cooperative marketing efforts between a "for-profit" firm and a "nonprofit organization."

Green Marketing

An outgrowth of the social responsibility movement is green marketing. **Green marketing** is the development and marketing of products designed to minimize negative effects on the physical environment or to improve the environment.[38] Not only can a company aid the environment through green marketing, but it can often help its bottom line as well. Environmentally aware consumers tend to earn more and are willing to pay more for green products.[39] The problem, however, is that only a very small percentage of customers make their buying decisions primarily of the environmental qualities of the product.[40] Also, it may not be readily apparent how one product is better for the environment than another. Thus, the marketer may have to educate the consumer about the green product. To make the sale, the green marketer may even use a traditional non-green benefit. For example, General Electric energy-efficient CFL flood lights are good for the environment. The promotion theme is "Long life for hard to reach places." GE is selling convenience because the floodlight doesn't need replacing as often.[41]

Some green products have practical consumer benefits that are readily apparent to consumers. A few examples are: energy efficient washing machines and other appliances (cut electric bills), heat-reflective windows (cut air conditioning costs), and organic foods (no pesticides poisoning the food or planet). Each Dole organic banana has a sticker with a number. If you enter that number at **doleorganic.com,** a Google Earth application will show you the exact place where the fruit was grown.[42]

One company that has done an excellent job of going green is Waste Management, which disposes waste for 22 million customers. The company produces more renewable energy each year than the entire North American solar industry. Its Wheelabrator division combusts waste to create electricity. Waste Management has also had 33 working landfills certified as wildlife habitat preserves. The firm hopes to have 100 certified by the Wildlife Habitat Council before 2020.[43]

LO6

CAUSE-RELATED MARKETING

A sometimes controversial subset of social responsibility is **cause-related marketing.** Sometimes referred to as simply "cause marketing," it is the cooperative efforts of a "for-profit" firm and a "nonprofit organization" for mutual benefit. Cause-related marketing is sometimes used as any marketing effort for social or other charitable causes. Cause marketing differs from corporate giving (philanthropy) as the latter generally involves a specific donation that is tax deductible, while cause marketing is a marketing relationship not based on a straight donation.

Cause-related marketing is very popular and is estimated to generate about $7 billion a year in revenue.[44] It creates good public relations for the firm and will often stimulate sales of the brand. Yet, the huge growth of cause-related marketing can lead to a case of consumer cause fatigue. A 2007 nationwide survey found that 36 percent said they bought a product in the previous 12 months after learning of its maker's commitment to social issues, down from 43 percent in 2004. Only 14 percent said they intentionally paid more for a product that supports a cause, down from 28 percent. And just 30 percent said they told a family member or friend about a product or company committed to a social issue, compared with 43 percent in 2004.[45]

Examples of cause-related marketing abound. Starwood Hotels has announced that for every Westin Heavenly Bed, Sheraton Sweet Sleeper Bed, and Four Points by Sheraton Four Comfort Bed sold through Starwood retail channels, the firm will donate $50 to the Special Olympics. Avaya recently publicized that it will donate $5 to the American Cancer Society for each pink desk phone faceplate it sells. The money is to be used to raise breast cancer awareness. Starbucks donates 5 cents of every sale of Ethos Water to help children around the world get access to clean drinking water. American Express launched a campaign to restore the Statue of Liberty and Ellis Island. The company contributes 1 cent per card transaction and $1 for every new card issued. American Express collected $1.7 million for the restoration effort.[46]

Cause-Related Marketing Controversy

Few causes have been more saturated with marketing than breast cancer awareness. Consumers can buy everything from food to toilet paper with labels that feature a pink ribbon. This generally signifies that for each product sold money is donated to breast cancer awareness. Yoplait ran a campaign that donated 10 cents to the Canadian Breast Cancer Foundation every time a consumer mailed back one of its yogurt carton lids. Aside from the fact that someone would have to eat three cartons of yogurt a day for more than three months just to raise $20, and that consumers spent more on postage than they raised with each lid, Yoplait left it to the fine print to state it was capping donations at $80,000—keeping the rest as profit.[47]

The Gap has been criticized for The Gap (Product) Red campaign. Thanks to the Gap and others, more than $25 million has been raised to fight HIV/AIDS, tuberculosis, and malaria. The Gap has stated that "50 percent of (Product) Red products" are being directed to the cause. Yet the promotional expenditures for the (Product) Red campaign were $100 million![48]

The Susan G. Komen Breast Cancer Foundation is on the receiving end of much cause-related marketing. The Foundation recently put out an information piece titled, "Five Questions to Ask before Participating in a Cause-Related Marketing Program." The questions are

1. Is this company committed? Read the product packaging and promotional materials or display and visit the company Web site to make sure the company is credible and committed to the cause.
2. How is the program structured? Transparency is key. Is the company clearly stating how the money is raised and how much will be going to charity? For example, if it's a donation per purchase, ask how much of purchase price goes to charity—is it 2 percent or 10 percent—or some other amount? If there is a minimum contribution guaranteed by the company, what is the amount? Is there a maximum donation that will be made by the company?
3. Who does the program benefit? Does it support a well-managed, reputable nonprofit or fund? Again, the Komen Foundation recommends that consumers read Web sites. The Komen

REVIEW LEARNING OUTCOME

LO6 Explain cause-related marketing

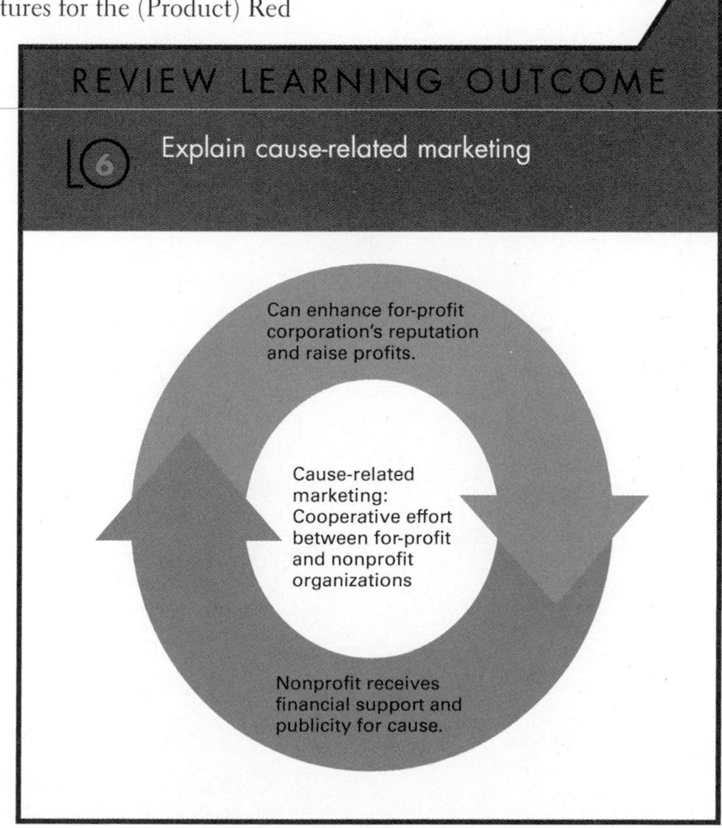

Foundation makes it very clear on its site what it is, how it structures programs, and how the monies are used. The Better Business Bureau's Wise Giving Alliance is one resource for information on nonprofit organizations.

4. How will the organization that benefits use my money? It should be abundantly clear where the monies go. What organization will they support? Will the dollars generated go to research, education, community programs, or all of the above? The Komen Foundation is very specific about their programs, activities, and grants awarded to support their mission to eradicate breast cancer as a life-threatening disease. Visit **ww5.komen.org** to view the Komen Foundation's most recent Annual Report.

5. Is the program meaningful to me? Is the program supporting a cause you believe in or have been touched by? Based on the details of the program and the potential for dollars to be raised, does the program make sense to you? Selecting the right program is a personal choice based on your interests, your passions, and a cause that is important to you.[49]

13 ◄ percent of today's large-company top executives who report that having strong ethical traits is the most important leadership trait of CEOs

20 ◄ percent of large-company top executives in 2003 who reported that having strong ethical traits was the most important leadership trait of CEOs

37 ◄ percent of large-company top executives who report that the most important trait of CEOs is the ability to inspire others

$2.4 million ◄ shipping costs saved annually by Wal-Mart by using less packaging on house-brand toys

70 ◄ percent of large employers offer ethics training

17 ◄ percent Wal-Mart trimmed off electricity bill by switching to efficient light bulbs and adding skylights

REVIEW AND APPLICATIONS

Explain the determinants of a civil society. The "social glue" that holds a society together is composed of six factors. They are ethics, laws, formal and informal groups, self-regulation, the media, and an active civil society. All of these are necessary for a coherent, vibrant, and civil society. These six factors are more important in countries than ever before because of the increasing complexity of the global economy and the melding of customs and traditions within societies.

1.1 Explain how each of the six factors contributes to a civil society.

1.2 Why is a free and uncontrolled media important in a country?

1.3 Can customs and laws sometimes conflict, especially when a society experiences an influx of immigrants?

Explain the concept of ethical behavior. Ethics are the moral principles or values that generally govern the conduct of an individual or a group. Ethics can also be viewed as the standard of behavior by which conduct is judged. Ethical conflicts sometimes arise between businesses, customers, workers, and the surrounding community. Conflicts can sometimes be resolved through the reliance on ethical theories. Ethical theories that are applicable to marketing include deontology, utilitarianism, casuist, moral relativism, and virtue ethics.

2.1 It is sometimes said that ethics hold a person to higher standards than laws. Explain.

2.2 Moral relativists are basically time and place ethicists. Explain what this means.

2.3 Explain the differences between utilitarianism, casuist, and deontology theories.

Describe ethical behavior in business. The law typically relies on juries to determine whether an act is legal or illegal. Society determines whether an action is ethical or unethical. Morals are the rules that people develop as a result of cultural values and norms. More and more companies are using ethics training to help put good ethics into practice. Ethical beliefs vary a little from culture to culture. However, some ethical practices vary significantly from one culture to the next.

3.1 Explain the difference between ethics and morals and describe the relationship between the two.

3.2 What are the differences between preconventional morality, conventional morality, and postconventional morality? Give an example of each.

3.3 Give several examples of how ethical practices can vary from one culture to the next.

Discuss corporate social responsibility. Responsibility in business refers to a firm's concern for the way its decisions affect society. A second theory says that the corporation should always pay attention to the interests of its stakeholders. These are management, customers, the local community, owners/stockholders, suppliers, and employees. Social responsibility has four components: economic, legal, ethical, and philanthropic. These are intertwined, yet the most fundamental is earning a profit. If a firm does not earn a profit, the other three responsibilities are moot. Most businesspeople believe they should do more than pursue profits. Although a company must consider its economic needs first, it must also operate within the law, do what is ethical and fair, and be a good corporate citizen. The concept of sustainability is that socially responsible companies will outperform their peers by focusing on the world's social problems and viewing them as an opportunity to earn profits and help the world at the same time.

4.1 Describe at least three situations in which you would not purchase the products of a firm even though it is very socially responsible.

4.2 A firm's only responsibility to society is to earn a fair profit. Comment.

4.3 Is sustainability a viable concept for America's businesses?

4.4 Illustrate how there can be conflicts between the needs and desires of various stakeholders.

Describe the arguments for and against social responsibility. Today, virtually all managers endorse social responsibility of corporations. It is, instead, a matter of what types of responsibility and the degree of responsibility. The arguments against social responsibility are: The job of the corporation is to maximize profits for stockholders; businesses are better suited to produce goods and services and not to be involved in welfare services; if global competitors aren't socially responsible it could hurt the domestic competitor. The arguments for social responsibility are: It's the right thing to do; government will create new regulations and levy fines if firms aren't socially responsible; social responsibility can enhance a company's profitability.

5.1 Explain the relationship between the global economy and social responsibility.

5.2 Defend the proposition that the only responsibility of the firm is to make money for the stockholders.

5.3 Explain how a firm can earn additional profits by being socially responsible.

Explain cause-related marketing. Cause-related marketing is the cooperative effort between a for-profit firm and a nonprofit organization. It is different from philanthropy, which is a specific, tax deductible donation. Cause-related marketing is very popular because it can enhance the reputation of the corporation and also make additional profit for the company. Sometimes companies have abused cause-related marketing and received much greater benefits than the nonprofit that has supposedly been helped. These cases are a small minority.

6.1 Why are more firms jumping on the cause-related marketing bandwagon?

6.2 Explain the controversy surrounding some cause-related marketing.

6.3 What are some questions that consumers should consider before participating in a cause-related campaign?

KEY TERMS

Term	Page
casuist ethical theory	76
cause-related marketing	94
code of ethics	80
corporate social responsibility	86
deontological ethical theory	75
ethics	75
Foreign Corrupt Practices Act	84
moral relativists	76
morals	78
pyramid of corporate social responsibility	88
stakeholder theory	87
sustainability	86
utilitarian ethical theory	76
virtue	77

EXERCISES

APPLICATION EXERCISE

Many companies today are concerned with social responsibility. They may pursue philanthropic activities and/or strive to be ethical. Your goal for this assignment is to evaluate how firms are being socially responsible. Limit your answers to one page, and provide a printout of the Web site you visited.

Activities

1. Choose a company and find that company's Web site on the Internet. Once you get to the Web site, look for information that tells you about the firm's efforts to be socially responsible. Look for things like news releases, company information, information about community programs, and so on? Look in your textbook and your notes to help you define what might be considered

socially responsible activities. Describe what you find and explain why you think the company is involved with the activities you describe.

2. Do the activities described on the Web site seem consistent with the company's products? Why or why not? (For example, a shoe company may sponsor a race that raises money to help prevent a disease. People who participate in the race may use that company's running shoes, and therefore, the race would be consistent with the company's products.)
3. Evaluate how effective you think the information you find is in terms of how it is presented, what impact it might have and whether it will help to sell the company's products. Be sure to support any claims you make.
4. Does the information you collected during this activity improve your evaluation of the company? Would it influence your decision to buy the company's product? Why or why not?

ETHICS EXERCISE

Jane Barksdale has designed a line of clothing targeted toward Hispanic Americans. The items are sold only by catalog and on the Internet. She thinks that she can increase sales by claiming in ads that the firm is owned by a Hispanic American and all the employees are Hispanic Americans. She is not Hispanic American nor are most of the employees. She needs a high level of sales to pay her bank loan and remain in business.

Questions

1. Should Jane claim that she is Hispanic American? Explain your response.
2. Does the Federal Trade Commission address this issue? Go to **www.ftc.gov** and search for guidelines for small business advertising or e-commerce. What does Jane risk in making false claims in her ads?

MARKETING PLAN EXERCISE

These end-of-chapter marketing plan exercises are designed to help you use what you learned in the chapter to build a strategic marketing plan for a company of your choosing. Once you've completed the marketing plan exercise for each chapter in Part 1 of this textbook, you can complete the Part 1 Marketing Planning Worksheet on your companion Web site at **www.cengage.com/international.**

In the first part of this exercise (Chapter 2), you described your chosen company, wrote its mission statement and set its marketing objectives. Use the following exercises to guide you through the next part of your strategic marketing plan:

1. Identify any ethical issues that could impact your chosen firm. What steps should be taken to handle these issues?
2. How should your company integrate corporate social responsibility into its marketing plan?
3. In addition to suggestions for philanthropic responsibilities, write up a brief code of ethics for your firm. To see other codes of ethics, go to **www.iit.edu/libraries/csep/codes/coe.html.**

CASE STUDY: ROCKSTAR GAMES: CAUGHT IN THEIR OWN VICE?

In Oakland, California, police arrest a gang of teens who now face charges for five homicides, several carjackings, and a slew of armed robberies. Roughly 2,000 miles away in Tennessee, stepbrothers Joshua and William Buckner, ages

14 and 16, are arrested and plead guilty to reckless homicide, aggravated assault, and reckless endangerment for fatally shooting one motorist and critically wounding a second.

The tie that binds these seemingly unrelated crimes is a video game—Rockstar Games' *Grand Theft Auto: Vice City.* When questioned about their crimes, both sets of perpetrators cited boredom and a desire to emulate the action of the main character in *Vice City* as the cause of their violent behavior.

In *Vice City,* players assume the role of Tommy Vercetti, an ex-con who loses cocaine and money in a botched drug deal. To recoup his losses, he must accomplish various missions in an attempt to ascend the hierarchy of *Vice City*'s underworld. The game awards points to players for mass shootings, graphic rapes, liaisons with prostitutes, car thefts, and drug sales. The violence is extreme and often grotesque. In one mission, players controlling Vercetti can earn points for raping a woman in the back of a stolen car and then deciding whether to kick her to death, cut her to pieces with a machete, or fatally shoot her.

Its graphic violence and sexually explicit material have earned *Vice City* an M rating from the Entertainment Software Rating Board, which indicates to consumers that the game is intended only for gamers aged 17 or older. Younger gamers, however, are playing the game in large numbers, and critics, parents, and politicians are horrified to find that children are being exposed to a game that glorifies such behavior. Racism rears its head in the game too, as Vercetti at one point is instructed by a narrator to "shoot the Haitians."

The backlash against Rockstar Games has been significant. Haitian and Cuban groups have filed suit against the company in Florida, where state legislators have proposed a bill that would increase the fines levied against retailers who rent or sell M-rated video games to minors. The lawmakers note that several small towns and cities have already passed such legislation.

In New York, Rockstar's racial insensitivity aroused the ire of the state attorney general, New York City Mayor Michael Bloomberg, and the Anti-Defamation League. Their pressure persuaded Rockstar to remove the racially offensive line from all future copies of the game. Other than that, Rockstar has officially declined to comment on any other inquiries. The Interactive Entertainment Merchants Association, an industry group including giant retailers such as Wal-Mart and Blockbuster, Inc., has reacted by adopting procedures intended to stop the sale of mature and adult video games to minors.

Despite the negative reactions, the game has gained mass-market acceptance. *Vice City* alone accounted for nearly half of Rockstar's $1.04 billion in revenue in 2003—a year when revenue for all M-rated video games actually declined from $910 million to $833 million. Rockstar currently dominates the adult segment of the market with the ten M-rated games it produces. Players of the game say its plot lines are pure fantasy, and the chief operating officer of Rockstar Games, Terry Donovan, defends his company by claiming that if the popular HBO television series *The Sopranos* was a video game, it would be *Grand Theft Auto.*

His customers, he asserts, are young male professionals who are willing to spend serious money on intense simulation-type games that provide primal stress release. Donovan and many others believe that the M rating is enough to alert parents to the games' adult content and that legislation from the government infringes on freedom of speech. At the moment, the popular counterargument is that like drugs, alcohol, and pornography, the games represent a threat to the psychological development of young people and should be controlled as such.[50]

Questions

1. Describe the technological, social, and political forces acting on the video game industry.
2. How is Rockstar responding to its environmental conditions? Do you agree with Rockstar's approach? Why or why not?

3. Do you think Rockstar Games' chief operating officer, Terry Donovan, displays adequate concern for corporate social responsibility? Explain.

COMPANY CLIPS

METHOD—PEOPLE AGAINST DIRTY

Method's first "lab" was the kitchen of founders Eric Ryan and Adam Lowry, two friends whose goal was to evolve the household cleaner from a toxic object that hid under the sink to an all-natural, biodegradable, and stylish countertop accessory. This video segment shows method through yet another lens, that of corporate social responsibility (CSR) and sustainability. Chemical engineer Adam Lowry outlines the chemical aspects of traditional cleaning products and describes how method's products are healthier. As you watch the video, keep in mind the various marketing orientations you learned in Chapter 1.

Questions

1. Does method have a societal marketing orientation, or is it just a market-oriented company that integrates a number of environmental practices into its operations? Explain.
2. How is method practicing sustainability?
3. Discuss the changing social factors that have made it possible for method to be so successful.

Marketing & You Results

The higher your score, the more important you think ethics and socially responsible behavior are to achieving corporate objectives. A high score also suggests that you are an ethical idealist, or someone who sees right and wrong as absolute, rather than an ethical relativist, or someone who sees right and wrong as situation dependent.

CHAPTER 4

The Marketing Environment

LEARNING OUTCOMES

- LO 1 Discuss the external environment of marketing, and explain how it affects a firm
- LO 2 Describe the social factors that affect marketing
- LO 3 Explain the importance to marketing managers of current demographic trends
- LO 4 Explain the importance to marketing managers of multiculturalism and growing ethnic markets
- LO 5 Identify consumer and marketer reactions to the state of the economy
- LO 6 Identify the impact of technology on a firm
- LO 7 Discuss the political and legal environment of marketing
- LO 8 Explain the basics of foreign and domestic competition

THE EXTERNAL MARKETING ENVIRONMENT

If there is one constant in the external environment (outside the firm) where firms work and compete, it is that things are constantly changing. If the organization doesn't understand or fails to react to the changing world around it, it will soon be a follower rather than a leader. In the worst-case scenario, the firm disappears from the marketplace. Applebee's was, at one time, a hot, trendy restaurant chain. Now, the company faces falling profits and unhappy stockholders. What happened? Applebee's didn't adapt quickly enough to the changing environment. High gasoline prices resulted in many customers staying at home. More importantly, it didn't change quickly enough when competitors copied it. Newer eateries offer slick interiors in contrast with Applebee's busy walls full of photos and sports memorabilia. Menus at many newer generation restaurants stress the freshness or naturalness of the food. Applebee's still focused on the fried and breaded items.[1]

Perhaps the most important decisions a marketing manager must make relate to the creation of the marketing mix. Recall from Chapters 1 and 2 that a marketing mix is the unique combination of product, place (distribution), promotion, and price strategies. The marketing mix is, of course, under the firm's control and is designed to appeal to a specific group of potential buyers. A **target market** is a defined group that managers feel is most likely to buy a firm's product.

As the Applebee's example shows, managers must alter the marketing mix because of changes in the environment in which consumers live, work, and make purchasing decisions. Also, as markets mature, some new consumers become part of the target market; others drop out. Those who remain may have different tastes, needs, incomes, lifestyles, and buying habits than the original target consumers.

Although managers can control the marketing mix, they cannot control elements in the external environment that continually mold and reshape the target market. Review Learning Outcome 1 shows the controllable and uncontrollable variables that affect the target market, whether it consists of consumers or business purchasers. The uncontrollable elements in the center of the diagram continually evolve and create changes in the target market. In contrast, managers can shape and reshape the marketing mix, depicted on the left side of the diagram, to influence the target market. That is, managers react to changes in the external environment and attempt to create a more effective marketing mix.

Marketing & You

Using the following scale, enter the numbers that reflect your opinions.

1 2 3 4 5 6 7

Strongly disagree — Strongly agree

___ I need more hours in the day to get my work done.

___ I *don't* have to overextend myself to find the time to get my work done.

___ I feel like I'm always "fighting fires."

___ I seldom have to take shortcuts to get my work done on time.

___ I never have enough time to think ahead.

___ I feel like I have a lot of time on my hands.

___ I feel like no matter how hard I work, I'll never get caught up.

Total your score. Read the chapter and find out what your score means at the end.

Source: From Scale #119, *Marketing Scales Handbook*, G. Bruner, K. James, H. Hensel, eds., Vol. III. © by American Marketing Association.

Understanding the External Environment

Unless marketing managers understand the external environment, the firm cannot intelligently plan for the future. Thus, many organizations assemble a team of specialists to continually collect and evaluate environmental information, a process called *environmental scanning*. The goal in gathering the environmental data is to identify future market opportunities and threats.

Does environmental scanning really make a difference? The Aberdeen Group is a Boston-based research firm. It found that firms that used feedback, from the external environment, to create and modify their marketing mix had an average 26 percent increase in return on their marketing investment over the previous year.[2]

target market
A defined group most likely to buy a firm's product.

Philips Electronics is a firm that is proactive in trying to keep a step ahead of the latest environmental trends. The firm's new strategic plan focuses on "sense and simplicity."

Companies that used environmental scanning less efficiently had only a 4 percent return. Those firms that didn't use scanning at all tended to be laggards in the marketplace. In summary, using environmental scanning to understand the ever-changing marketplace and then adapting the marketing mix accordingly are critical to long-term success of the organization.

Philips Electronics is a firm that is proactive in trying to keep a step ahead of the latest environmental trends. The firm's new strategic plan focuses on "sense and simplicity." The idea is to give consumers what they want in the way of electronic products in the health, lifestyle, and technology areas. Because Philips is dominated by engineers, it decided that if it was really going to create products that are simple to use and consumer-oriented, it needed help. The company created a four-person advisory group of opinion leaders from around the globe. The group consists of Sara Berman, a British fashion designer; Dr. Peggy Fritzsche, a California radiology professor; Gary Chang, a leading Chinese architect; and John Maeda, an MIT graphic designer. They meet several days each month in places like Paris, Rome, or New York to help Philips understand how the environment of business is changing. Their goal is to help Philips create intuitive, easy-to-use products that meet specific needs. Andrea Ragnatti, chief marketing officer for Philips, notes that it took the firm quite a while to adopt the marketing concept. She notes, "In the past we just developed the technology and hoped someone would buy it. Now we are starting from the point of discovering what exactly consumers want a product to do."[3]

Philips Electronics does a good job of understanding the ever-changing external environment. Some of the key areas that firms should monitor in the external environment are

- *Understanding current customers.* That is, how they buy, where they buy, what they buy, and when they buy.
- *Understanding what drives consumer decisions.* Successful firms know why customers buy. One study showed that

REVIEW LEARNING OUTCOME

LO1 Discuss the external environment of marketing, and explain how it affects a firm

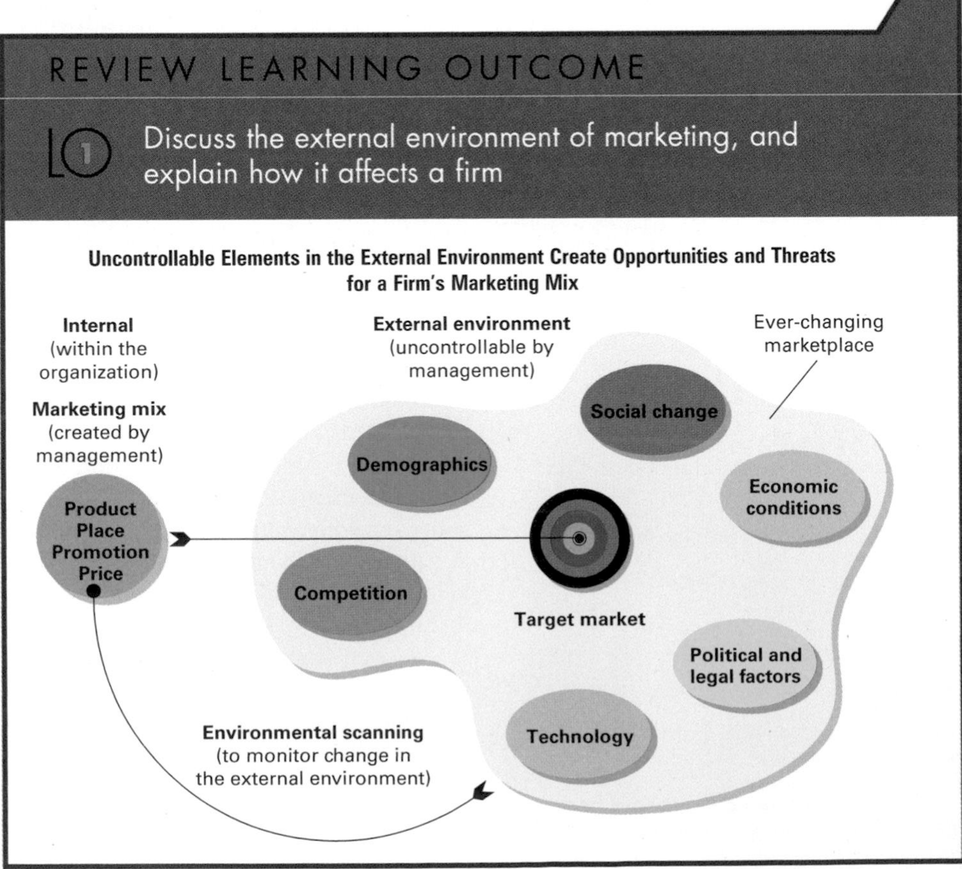

grocery shoppers patronize 3.6 stores regularly. Why? Because distinct stores filled distinct roles in a consumer's shopping portfolio. They went to Costco for bulk items; Trader Joe's (a local chain) to find interesting and unique items; and Wal-Mart for one-stop shopping for a variety of basic goods. The local chain was losing business to niche stores to buy high-margin items like meat, seafood, and produce. Intelligence data showed that the local chain could recapture about half of these consumers by stocking more variety in organic, international foods, and signature products.[4]

- *Identify the most valuable customers and understand their needs.* Often 20 percent of a firm's customers produce 80 percent of the firm's revenue. An organization must understand what drives that loyalty and then take steps to ensure that those drivers are maintained and enhanced.
- *Understand the competition.* Successful firms know their competitors and attempt to forecast their future moves. Competitors offer both threats to a firm's market share and profitability but also may offer opportunities to our firm to capture competitors' business. During the economic downturn of 2007–2009, T.J. Maxx, the off-price retailer, noted that competitors were taking 60 to 90 days to pay their vendors. T.J. Maxx had the cash and decided to pay within 30 days. This caused the big-name fashion brands to flock to the retailer. Now, TJX, which owns T.J. Maxx, Marshalls, and HomeGoods, has a better assortment of well-known brands to sell in its stores. For the first time, T.J. Maxx is selling items like True Religion jeans for $99 (regularly $160) and Bottega Veneta sweaters for $149 (normally $750). Sales, market share, and profit are up for TJX.[5]

Environmental Management

No one business is large or powerful enough to create major change in the external environment. Thus, marketing managers are basically adapters rather than agents of change. For example, despite the huge size of firms like General Electric, Wal-Mart, Apple, and Caterpillar, they don't control social change, demographics, or other factors in the external environment.

However, just because a firm cannot fully control the external environment, it doesn't mean that it is helpless. Sometimes a firm can influence external events. For example, extensive lobbying by FedEx has enabled it to acquire virtually all of the Japanese routes that it has sought. Japan had originally opposed new cargo routes for FedEx. The favorable decision was based on months of lobbying by FedEx at the White House, at several agencies, and in Congress for help in overcoming Japanese resistance. When a company implements strategies that attempt to shape the external environment within which it operates, it is engaging in **environmental management**.

The factors within the external environment that are important to marketing managers can be classified as social, demographic, economic, technological, political and legal, and competitive.

SOCIAL FACTORS

Social change is perhaps the most difficult external variable for marketing managers to forecast, influence, or integrate into marketing plans. Social factors include our attitudes, values, and lifestyles. Social factors influence the products people buy, the prices paid for products, the effectiveness of specific promotions, and how, where, and when people expect to purchase products.

American Values

A *value* is a strongly held and enduring belief. During the United States' first 200 years, four basic values strongly influenced attitudes and lifestyles:

- *Self-sufficiency:* Every person should stand on his or her own two feet.

environmental management
When a company implements strategies that attempt to shape the external environment within which it operates.

component lifestyles
The practice of choosing goods and services that meet one's diverse needs and interests rather than conforming to a single, traditional lifestyle.

- *Upward mobility:* Success would come to anyone who got an education, worked hard, and played by the rules.
- *Work ethic:* Hard work, dedication to family, and frugality were moral and right.
- *Conformity:* No one should expect to be treated differently from everybody else.

These core values still hold for a majority of Americans today. A person's values are key determinants of what is important and not important, what actions to take or not to take, and how one behaves in social situations.

People typically form values through interaction with family, friends, and other influencers such as teachers, religious leaders, and politicians. The changing environment can also play a key role in shaping one's values. For example, people born during the 1980s and 1990s tend to be more comfortable with technology and its importance in the home than persons born in the 1960s.

Values influence our buying habits. Today's consumers are demanding, inquisitive, and discriminating. No longer willing to tolerate products that break down, they are insisting on high-quality goods that save time, energy, and often calories. U.S. consumers rank the characteristics of product quality as (1) reliability, (2) durability, (3) easy maintenance, (4) ease of use, (5) a trusted brand name, and (6) a low price. Shoppers are also concerned about nutrition and want to know what's in their food, and many have environmental concerns.

Personality Traits Vary by Region[6]

Certain regional stereotypes have existed for a long time and have become clichés: the stressed and hurried New Yorker and the cool, laid-back Californian. New research, based upon 600,000 interviews, has looked at geography and personality. Even after controlling for variables such as race, income, and education levels, a state's dominant personality turns out to be strongly linked to certain outcomes. Amiable states, like Minnesota, tend to be lower in crime. Dutiful states—an eclectic bunch that includes New Mexico, North Carolina, and Utah—produce a disproportionate share of mathematicians. States that rank high in openness to new ideas are quite creative, as measured by per-capita patent production. But they're also high-crime and a bit aloof. As for high-anxiety states, that group includes not just New York and New Jersey, but also states stressed by poverty, such as West Virginia and Mississippi. As a group, these states tend to have higher rates of heart disease and lower life expectancy.

The most conscientious states were mostly in America's heartland, but also included Florida, Georgia, and North Carolina. The states highest on "openness" were along the West Coast but also included Maine. "Extraversion" was strongest in the Upper Midwest along with Georgia, Florida, and Maine. The linking of geography and personalities raises intriguing chicken-and-egg-type questions. Do states tend to nurture specific personalities because of their histories, cultures, even climates? Or do Americans, seeking kindred spirits, migrate to the states where they feel at home? Maybe both forces are at work—but in what balance? As of yet, we don't know the answer.

The Growth of Component Lifestyles

People in the United States today are piecing together **component lifestyles**. A lifestyle is a mode of living; it is the way people decide to live their lives. In other words, they are choosing products and services that meet diverse needs and interests rather than conforming to traditional stereotypes.

In the past, a person's profession—for instance, banker—defined his or her lifestyle. Today, a person can be a banker and also a gourmet, fitness enthusiast, dedicated single parent, and Internet guru. Each of these lifestyles is associated with different goods and services and represents a target audience. For example, for the gourmet, marketers offer cooking utensils, wines, and exotic foods through magazines such as *Bon Appétit* and *Gourmet*. The fitness enthusiast buys Adidas equipment and special jogging outfits and reads *Runner* magazine. Component lifestyles increase the complexity of consumers' buying habits. The banker may own a BMW but change the oil himself or herself. He or she may buy fast food for lunch but French wine for dinner, own sophisticated photographic equipment and a low-priced home stereo, and shop for socks at Kmart or Wal-Mart and suits or dresses at Brooks Brothers. The unique lifestyles of every consumer can require a different marketing mix.

The Changing Role of Families and Working Women

Component lifestyles have evolved because consumers can choose from a growing number of goods and services, and most have the money to exercise more options. The growth of dual-income families has resulted in increased purchasing power. Approximately 63 percent of all females between 16 and 65 years old are now in the workforce. Today, more than 10 million women-owned businesses in the United States, employing 18.2 million persons, generate \$3.6 trillion in revenues.[7] The phenomenon of working women has probably had a greater effect on marketing than any other social change.

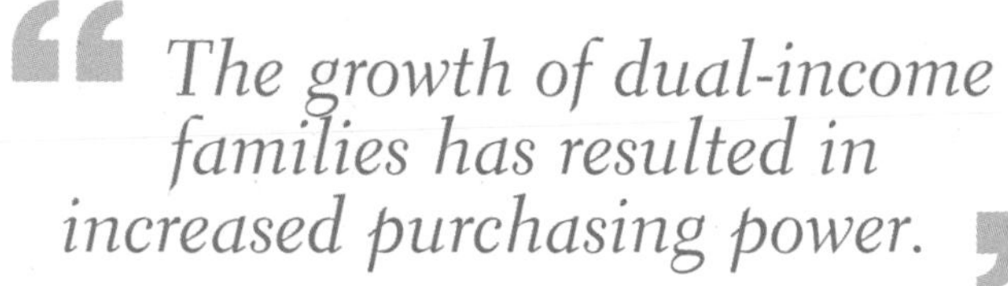

As women's earnings grow, so do their levels of expertise, experience, and authority. Working-age women are not the same group businesses targeted 30 years ago. They expect different things in life—from their jobs, from their spouses, and from the products and services they buy. Home improvement centers, such as Home Depot or Lowe's, know that women shoppers are vital to their success. Yet, women feel that these retailers offer an unnecessarily complex shopping process. A recent study found that women want a stress-free experience and want to feel that Lowe's and Home Depot appreciate their business. Ninety-seven percent of the women interviewed said that having one person capable of answering all of their questions was one of the most important services a home improvement retailer could provide.[8]

Single women now account for 27 percent of all first-time home buyers and 21 percent of the homebuyers overall. This is more than double the rate of 20 years ago.[9] Part of this is due to the fact that women are earning more than ever before. In big cities, such as New York, Boston, Chicago, and Dallas, women under 30 years old are earning more than their male counterparts.[10]

Single and married women are making purchase decisions and buying more products and services that were traditionally dominated by males. This has not been lost on savvy marketers, as the Customer Experience box explains.

In a timely ad—featuring a woman of color serving in the military and supporting a family—Wal-Mart has appealed to a growing demographic and one that is likely to appreciate the low prices Wal-Mart offers.

IMAGE COURTESY OF THE ADVERTISING ARCHIVES

There Is Never Enough Time

Research shows that the large percentage of people who say they never have enough time to do all that they need to do keeps inching up. It is estimated that over 80 percent of the working population is worried about having too little time.[11] With the economic downturn of 2007–2009, many stay-at-home moms are going back to work to help make ends meet. These time-constrained mothers find that they have even fewer quality hours to spend with their families.[12]

Over 31 percent of college-educated male workers are regularly working 50 or more hours a week, up from 22 percent in 1980. About 40 percent of American adults get less than seven hours of sleep on weekdays, up from 34 percent in 2001. Almost 60 percent of meals are rushed, and 34 percent of lunches are eaten on the run.[13] To manage their scarce time, about 74 percent of working adults engage in multitasking—doing

CUSTOMER Experience

Harley-Davidson Navigates Down New Roads

Harley-Davidson Inc., based in Milwaukee, Wisconsin, is the largest motorcycle manufacturer in the United States and leads the pack in heavyweight motorcycle sales. With more than 9,000 full-time employees and more than 1,500 dealers worldwide, the century-old company sells more than $6.1 billion in motorcycles and accessories annually. A leather jacket, a weathered tan, and a rough smattering of whiskers have long been the hallmarks of a Harley-Davidson rider—but no longer. The company says the number of female Harley-Davidson owners has tripled in the past 20 years; female buyers now account for 12 percent of new Harley-Davidson purchases, up from 4 percent in 1990. For years, Harley-Davidson primarily had tailored both its product design and its marketing to a target market of 35- to 55-year-old males. Now, Harley-Davidson wants more women to move from the back of the bike onto the driver's seat. Says Leslie Prevish, Harley-Davidson's women's outreach manager: "We have marketed to women for decades and have an advertisement in our archives from 1920 that encourages women to ride, [but] we've boosted our efforts in the last five years as we've increased our overall marketing efforts to grow the sport."

The challenge for Harley-Davidson is to maintain its tough, road-tested brand identity while finding new ways to connect with female consumers—and to continue to play to its strengths rather than indulging in female stereotypes. "Women riders are diverse, so some like the black and chrome, while others prefer purples and pinks," Prevish says. "Our materials and initiatives appeal to a common personality trait of strong, independent women who enjoy taking on a challenge and feeling of adventure."

The company started by making its product more accessible to females, modifying motorcycles to fit women's smaller frames and offering an instructional manual and courses to teach women how to handle their bikes. Rider's Edge New Rider courses have become an important marketing vehicle with which Harley-Davidson can encourage women to enter the sport. "While there are some shifts in [the] emphasis of the brand as we continue to increase relevance for the women's market, we remain true to the brand," says Ken Ostermann, general manager of outreach marketing at Harley-Davidson. A financial analyst for Harley-Davidson adds, "I don't think we're going to see any pink [Harley-Davidson motorcycles] on the road.... There is a market that they're going after that is, 'I want to be free, I want to be independent, I want to be my own person,' and that person can be a guy or a girl," he says. "They don't have to add bigger mirrors so women can do their cosmetics.... They want to sell Harleys to women, and they want to sell them to women who want to ride a Harley.[15]

Do you think that targeting women will alienate its core male market? Why? Should Harley produce a motorcycle directed only to the female market?

REVIEW LEARNING OUTCOME

LO 2 Describe the social factors that affect marketing

Social Factors: Values; Time pressure; Component lifestyles; Changing role of women

more than one thing at a time.[14] They're talking on their cell phones while rushing to work or school, answering e-mails during conference calls, waking up at 4 A.M., and generally multitasking day and night.

"With Americans now spending a record-breaking 60 percent of their waking hours at work, the days of stopping by your neighbor's front porch in the afternoon to discuss current events over an iced tea are over," said Stephanie Molnar, CEO of WorkPlace Media. "These days, time-starved consumers are more likely to stop by a colleague's cubicle on their way out for an iced coffee than socialize with neighbors back at home, where household chores and family responsibilities take precedence over casual conversation."[16] On an average day (which includes all 7 days of the week), 83 percent of women and 66 percent of men spent some time doing household activities, such as housework, cooking, lawn care, or financial and other household management.[17] Recent research has found that

- With rising pump prices and busy schedules, consumers are highly likely to consolidate shopping trips, making purchases on their drive to or from work, or during their lunch break. Almost three-fourths of at-work consumers indicate they regularly or occasionally dine out or purchase groceries and beverages during the workday.
- At-work consumers research products online before purchasing, with almost half of them (47.2 percent) reporting having researched electronics online in the last 90 days during the workday before making a purchase in a store.
- Word-of-mouth is highly influential on purchases made by at-work consumers, with 95.6 percent indicating they regularly or occasionally give advice to their peers about products and services, and 92.9 percent indicating they also *seek* advice from peers before making purchases.
- Because the workplace is full of conversation among peers, it presents the perfect environment to create buzz for product introductions and new store openings. While taking a break from work, at-work consumers are likely to socialize with co-workers as 67.8 percent indicate they do so. 42.2 percent also indicate they communicate with friends and family during the workday.[18]

DEMOGRAPHIC FACTORS

Another uncontrollable variable in the external environment—also extremely important to marketing managers—is **demography**, the study of people's vital statistics, such as their age, race and ethnicity, and location. Demographics are significant because the basis for any market is people. Demographic characteristics are strongly related to consumer buyer behavior in the marketplace.

Population[19]

The most basic statistic of all is population because people are directly or indirectly the basis of all markets. The U.S. population is now slightly above 300 million. But it is the 400 million milestone, which the United States will reach in about 30 to 35 years, that has demographers and economists really talking. Those additional 100 million people, many of them immigrants, will replace aging baby boomers in the workforce, fill the Social Security coffers, and, in all likelihood, keep the economy vital and life interesting. But they also will further crowd cities and highways, put new strains on natural resources, end the majority status of whites, and probably widen the gulf between society's haves and have-nots.

With about 86 people per square mile nationwide now, the United States would seem to have plenty of room for more. Even after the next 100 million people are added, the United States still will have one-sixth the density of Germany, whose population is expected to stop growing within a few years. But those averages hide disparities that could prove worrying. Even as it grows, the population is increasingly concentrating in just a dozen or so states, such as Florida, Texas, North Carolina, and Colorado. North Dakota is losing population, Ohio is adding a mere 20,000 people a year, and heartland states like Kansas and Nebraska average fewer than 14 households per square mile. The economic downturn of 2007–2009 has resulted in more people staying put. The housing slump has made it harder to sell a home, so homeowners who would like to relocate will find it more difficult to do so.[20]

More than half the population lives within 50 miles of the coasts. In the next decade, an additional 25 million people—half the total population increase—will join them there. That concentration of population is likely to result in megacities of

demography
The study of people's vital statistics, such as their age, race and ethnicity, and location.

25 million or more as people head to them for jobs. Economists predict that market forces eventually will shift some of the U.S. population back to interior states where housing is cheaper, land is more abundant, social services are less stressed, and labor is cheaper for businesses.

We turn our attention now to a closer look at age groups, their impact, and the opportunities they present for marketers. The cohorts have been given the names of tweens, Generation Y, Generation X, and baby boomers. You will find that each cohort group has its own needs, values, and consumption patterns.

© RUBBERBALL/JUPITERIMAGES

Tweens
Ages 9–14
Pop. 20 million
Spend over $21 billion/year
Heavy buying influence on parents
Biggest growth area: cell phone usage

Tweens

They watch cable channels designed just for them, they cruise the Net with ease, they know what they want—and often get it. They are America's tweens (today's pre- and early adolescents, ages 9 to 14), a population of more than 20 million. With attitudes, access to information, sophistication well beyond their years, and purchasing power to match, these young consumers spend over $21 billion annually. If one adds in the amount parents spend on tweens, the total spending is estimated as high as $300 billion.[21]

Tweens' styles don't reflect those of their parents. They want their own look. And parents spend about $230 per tween on back-to-school clothes to give them just that.[22] In fact, there is now a clothing line just for the girl tween called "It Chick." It Chick clothing includes sparkly tank tops, dressier tops with satin-bow detailing, and cool, retro roller-skate T-shirts. Denim skorts, leggings, and gauchos are also part of the collection. Abercrombie stores, the tween version of Abercrombie & Fitch, features loud, thumping music; blowup posters of young girls and boys; and clothing just for preteens. Clothes are not the only product area that has caught the eye of "tween marketers." Cell phone usage by tweens will be the industry's biggest growth area through 2011. This will be a financial windfall for the carriers because tweens like text messaging.[23]

Tweens overwhelmingly (92 percent) recognize television commercials for what they are—"just advertising." About three-quarters regard billboards and radio spots as paid advertising, and about half recognize promotional mediums such as product placements on television shows.[24]

What is really important to tweens? Research found the following (in order of importance): being happy, getting along with family, getting good grades, being healthy, the school he or she goes to, and being good with money. Parents of tweens had generally the same rankings, except they were much more likely than their tweens to mention "getting lots of sleep" and "eating right."[25]

Tweens are not the youngest market that is growing in importance. Pre-tweens, ages 6 to 9, are moving beyond Chuck E. Cheese. For example, every treatment chair at Peaches & Cream Spa is filled. Feet are buffed, nails meticulously polished, and shoulders massaged with hot stones as the sound of female voices fills the room with intense discussion on the issues du jour—which, at the moment, includes speculation on who among them owns the most My Little Pony toys. The clients are all pre-tweens. They are attending a "princess spa birthday party."[26]

© RUBBERBALL/JUPITERIMAGES

Teens
Ages 13–19
Pop. 25 million
Spend $195 billion/year
Two-thirds go to a mall once/week.
90 percent engage in on-demand media/entertainment.

Teens

There are approximately 25 million teens in the United States, and they spend about $195 billion annually. They spend approximately 72 hours per week tuned in electronically. This includes TV, Internet, music, video games, cell phones, and text messages. Many teens participate in online social networks such as MySpace, which has 70 million unique visitors each month. Fully 68 percent of teens have created profiles on MySpace, Zanga, or Facebook.[27]

The average teen may spend 11.5 hours a week online, but not everything is more appealing to teens in an online format. When asked a series of "would you rather" questions, teens chose reality over virtual reality in many aspects of their lives. Given the choice, teens would rather have real friends (91 percent) than online friends (9 percent), date someone from school (87 percent) than someone from the Internet (13 percent), and shop in a store (82 percent) than shop online (18 percent). Even though teens prefer real stores, they do shop online (58 percent). On average, teens who make a purchase online are spending $46 per month, and 26 percent of teens are spending $50 or more. Clothes and music are the two most popular online purchases, followed by books and electronics.[28]

Recently Kohl's launched a new line of plaid skirts and printed T-shirts, but they aren't available in its 1,000 retail stores. Instead, it's selling them on Stardoll .com, a virtual community for teens and tweens where they can use "Stardollars"—purchased online at a nominal sum—to buy apparel for their online characters. Old-line retailers, including Sears, JCPenney, and Nordstrom, are enticing teens to try virtual versions of their clothes, hoping that they will buy the real thing later on. In a recent experiment, JCPenney determined that 1.5 million avatars (an icon, picture, or 3-D model or representation of a computer user in a shared virtual reality) wore its clothing in one virtual world. In the same virtual community, 5 million JCPenney outfits were tried on.[29]

For teens, shopping has become a social sport online or at the mall. Over 62 percent say that they love to shop. They patronize the big box retailers, such as Best Buy, and luxury brands, with little room for retailers in between. Teens love Armani, Gucci, and Coach. They also go to Taco Bell and drink Coke.

A few more interesting facts about teens:

- The average teen or tween earns about $30.00 per week. A substantial portion of their budget (43 percent) is spent on fashion.
- Teens are multicultural. Four in 10 children ages 5 to 9 (40 percent) are nonwhite or Hispanic, as are 38 percent of those ages 15 to 17.
- Music and entertainment are (still) critical to everyday life. Eight in 10 teens (80 percent) listen to music during their free time.
- Entertainment has to be on-demand for teens. More than 90 percent engage in on-demand media consumption.
- Life revolves around the mall. More than two-thirds of teens go to the mall at least once a week, both to shop and socialize.
- It's not all about new media. The average teen reader spends 43 minutes per day reading.[30]

Generation Y

Those designated by demographics as **Generation Y** were born between 1979 and 1994. They are about 73 million strong, more than three times as large as Generation X. And though Generation Y is much smaller than the baby boom, which lasted nearly 20 years and produced 78 million children, its members are plentiful enough to put their own footprints on society. Most Gen Yers are the children of baby boomers and hence are also referred to as "echo boomers," or the "millennial generation."

They already spend nearly $200 billion annually and over their lifetimes will likely spend about $10 trillion. Some have already started their careers and are making major purchasing decisions such as cars and homes; at the very least, they are buying lots of computers, MP3 players, cell phones, DVDs, and sneakers.

Researchers have found Gen Yers to be

- *Impatient:* Gen Y has grown up in a world that's always been automated, and they've had access to computers, CD-ROMs, the Internet, DVD players, chat rooms, instant messaging, and the like, for as long as they can remember, so it's no surprise that they expect things to be done *now*.

Generation Y
People born between 1979 and 1994.

Generation X
People born between 1965 and 1978.

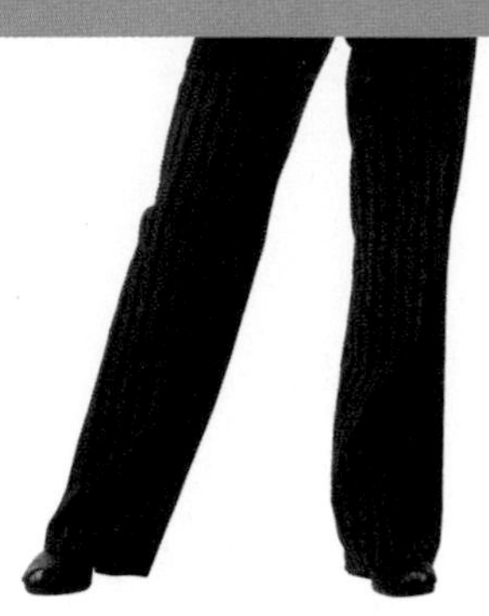

© RUBBERBALL/JUPITERIMAGES

- *Family-oriented:* Unlike Gen X before them, overall Gen Yers had relatively stable childhoods. They also grew up in a very family-focused time when even big companies strived to become more family- and kid-friendly. It's the generation that inspired spin-off stores like babyGap and the makeover of Las Vegas into a family vacation destination.
- *Inquisitive:* Knowing more than their parents about computers and technology has always been a source of pride for the echo boomers. It's led to a natural inquisitiveness that many still possess. They want to know why things happen, how things work, and what they can do next.
- *Opinionated:* From the time they were children, Gen Yers have been encouraged by their parents, teachers, and other authority figures to share their opinions. That's translated to a group who feel that their opinions are always needed and welcomed.
- *Diverse:* This is the most ethnically diverse generation the nation has ever seen, and many don't identify themselves as being only one race. Consequently, they're much more accepting overall of people who are different from themselves.
- *Time managers:* Their entire lives have been scheduled—from playgroups to soccer camp to Little League. So, it's no surprise that they've picked up a knack for planning along the way.
- *"Street Smart"*: The term isn't used in the literal sense, but simply means that these young people have seen a lot. With the Internet and 24-hour cable TV news exposing them to recounts of violence, war, and sexuality at a young age, they're not easily shocked. They're much more aware of the world around them than earlier generations were.[31]
- *Connected*: Fifty-four percent use social networking sites like MySpace or Facebook; 44 percent have created profiles featuring photos, hobbies, and interests.[32]

Gen Yers care about the environment. They will often seek out "green" products. They also look to brands for information about the environment. In the case of Honest Tea, many applauded the brand's decision to go to plastic after it was explained via its packaging that less fuel is used to ship plastic than the heavier glass bottles. The favorite green brands of Gen Yers are Whole Foods, Trader Joe's, Toyota, Honda, and Google.[33]

Generation X

Generation X—people born between 1965 and 1978—consists of 40 million consumers. It was the first generation of latchkey children—products of dual-career households or, in roughly half of the cases, of divorced or separated parents. Gen Xers have been bombarded by multiple media since their cradle days; thus, they are savvy and cynical consumers.

Gen Xers, now in their 30s and 40s, are reaching the age where they are sending their kids off to college. Gen Xers tend to be more protective and involved with their kids than were the baby boomer generation. They highly value the importance of education. Sixty-three percent say they began planning for their kids' college education in elementary school or earlier.[34]

Although Gen Xers are buying homes and spending money to decorate and renovate them, most companies still ignore them, focusing instead on the larger demographic groups—baby boomers and Gen Y. However, some furniture retailers, such as Williams-Sonoma's Pottery Barn and Crate & Barrel, target Gen Xers who want to mix and match different styles. Ethan Allen is now attracting Gen Xers with its new TV ads. Williams-Sonoma also appeals to more Gen Xers with West Elm, its newer furniture concept, which offers edgier designs and lower prices than those found at Pottery Barn.

Gen Xers are avid buyers of the latest clothes, technology, and recreational products. Now that they have advanced in the corporate world, they are demanding certain values from the retailers that they patronize. Gen Xers want frankness, client service, reliability, and authenticity. If retailers aren't true to their word, they quickly lose their Gen X customer.[35]

Gen Xers are careful shoppers when it comes to home furnishings. Some 31 percent of Gen Xers polled said they checked at least four stores before buying, and 65 percent held no loyalty to any retail brand (only 13 percent did) while 41 percent said they'd shop at any store "that had a good deal." Asked what furniture brands come immediately to mind, the largest bloc of respondents (35 percent) said "none," and 70 percent cited brand as the least important factor in buying.[36]

Researchers have found that a male Gen X traveler is more likely than a boomer to pick a hotel with a sports bar. But the pub must be genuine and the workout room cutting edge. So, Holiday Inn Select is adding Sporting News Grill restaurants and Fitness by Nautilus workcut centers to its offerings. In-room amenities will include Wolfgang Puck coffee, Moen showerheads, and Garden Botanika bath products.

A study of over 5,000 Gen Xers in 17 countries determined that their favorite brands were Google (88 percent), Sony (76 percent), Nokia (69 percent), and BMW (66 percent).[37] Why does tailoring the merchandise to particular age groups matter? One reason is that each generation enters a life stage with its own tastes and biases, and tailoring products to what customers value is key to sales.

Baby Boomers—America's Mass Market

When Vespa motor scooters came puttering back into the U.S. market in 2000 after a 15-year absence, managers at the Italian company figured their biggest customers would be twentysomethings looking for a cheap way to get around. But executives at Piaggio, Vespa's parent company, noticed something odd as they scootered back and forth to their Manhattan offices: The most enthusiastic sidewalk gawkers were often aging baby boomers who remembered the candy-colored bikes from their youth. It turns out that boomers have lost none of their affection for Vespa. Better yet, now they can afford to buy top-of-the-line models with all the trimmings. Much to the company's surprise, consumers age 50 and older now buy a quarter of the scooters Vespa sells in the United States. In fact, the average U.S. head of household is now nearly 50 years old (49.5 years).[38] More than 80 percent of the growth in the number of households between 2008 and 2013 will be among those headed by people 55 and older.[39] The oldest region of the country is New England, and the youngest is the West Coast. Diversity drives a lower average age of a region.

There are 77 million **baby boomers** (persons born between 1946 and 1964), making them the largest demographic segment in the population today. The oldest have already turned 60. With average life expectancy at an all-time high of 77.4 years, more and more Americans over 50 consider middle age a new start on life. Fewer than 20 percent say they expect to stop work altogether as they age. Of those who plan to keep working at least part-time, 67 percent said they'll do so to stay mentally active, and 57 percent said to stay physically active. People now in their 50s may well work longer than any previous generation.[40] The economic downturn of 2007–2009 has resulted in baby boomers' savings and housing values declining very rapidly. As a result, boomers are postponing retirement. It is estimated that boomers lost over $2 trillion in the 2008 stock market meltdown.[41] Only 23 percent of persons over 55 years old have more than $250,000 in savings and investment.[42]

Many marketers believe that consumers' brand preferences are locked in by age 40. That might have been true for previous generations, but today's over-50 crowd is just as likely, and in some cases more likely, as everyone else to try different brands within a product category. According to Yankelovich, Inc., 33 percent of consumers older than 50 agree that it's "risky" to buy an unfamiliar brand. That's less than the 36 percent of respondents aged 16 to 34 and only a little more than the 30 percent of people aged 35 to 49 who agree with that notion.[43] In some categories such as cosmetics and electronics, older consumers are even more willing to brand-hop than younger ones.

Baby Boomers
Born between 1946–1964
Pop. 77 million
Fewer than 20 percent expect to stop working.
Heavily rely on word-of-mouth promotion
Account for 60 percent spent on consumer goods

baby boomers
People born between 1946 and 1964.

Procter & Gamble's Cover Girl brand, which depends on women older than 55 for about 20 percent of its sales, has just launched its first line of makeup aimed at older women. The name of the product, Advanced Radiance Age-Defying makeup, hints that advancing age can be pretty. And although ads still show a stunningly gorgeous face, that face belongs to an older woman—55-year-old former supermodel Christie Brinkley.

Baby boomers are not a monolithic group. A recent lifestyle study divided this huge market into four segments:

- *"Looking for balance" boomers:* About one-quarter of boomers (27 percent) fall into this very active and busy segment. They represent an excellent market for companies that can offer them time-saving products and services. Though money is important, saving time is equally important to this segment. Companies engaged in travel-related businesses and food-service businesses will find key opportunities here.
- *"Confident and living well" boomers:* Confident and living well boomers represent 23 percent of all boomers. They have the highest incomes of all the segments and relish the chance to be the first to purchase a new product or service. They are technologically oriented and care about what is stylish and trendy. They are the most active boomers, and travel is one of their favorite interests. Marketers offering luxury goods and services will find prime boomer prospects here.
- *"At ease" boomers:* At ease boomers represent 31 percent of all boomers. They are at peace with themselves and do not worry about the future, job security, or financial security. They express the least interest in luxury goods and services and don't travel much. They are the most home-centric and family-oriented segment of the boomers. Marketers of traditional household products and services will find this group of boomers most receptive to their offerings. New products and innovations are least likely to appeal to this group. Established and trusted brand names will resonate most strongly with this boomer segment.
- *"Overwhelmed" boomers:* As the smallest segment of the boomer population, overwhelmed boomers represent less than 20 percent of boomers. This group has the lowest income of all the segments. They worry about the future and their financial security. This segment is also the least active, and health is a big concern for them. They are also the least social boomers, spending little time with family and friends. These boomers are also far less accepting of technology and are well below average on using electronic, digital, and tech products.[44]

Baby boomers, because of the sheer size of the market segment, account for 60 percent of all shopping dollars spent on consumer packaged goods.[45] Baby boomers are also heavily involved in word-of-mouth promotion. When fellow boomers ask them for advice on products and services, 89 percent of them deliver it. And they are likely to seek such a recommendation approximately 90 times per year. Moreover, 93 percent of baby boomers trust their friends for information.[46] Nevertheless, marketers spend countless hours trying to create promotional messages that will resonate with boomers. Here are a few examples:

- *Connecting with boomers' sense of themselves as trailblazers.* At every stage of their lives, boomers have challenged the status quo. Brands that convey a totally new benefit will appeal to boomers' inherent desire to break from the norm. American Express's Ameriprise financial services division expresses it well: "You changed everything that came before you. That was you then … that's still you now."
- *Focusing on their lives, not their ages.* Boomers don't need to be reminded of how old they are getting. Rather than stressing their age, Centrum Silver uses advertising to reflect older consumers' passion to continue doing the things they love.

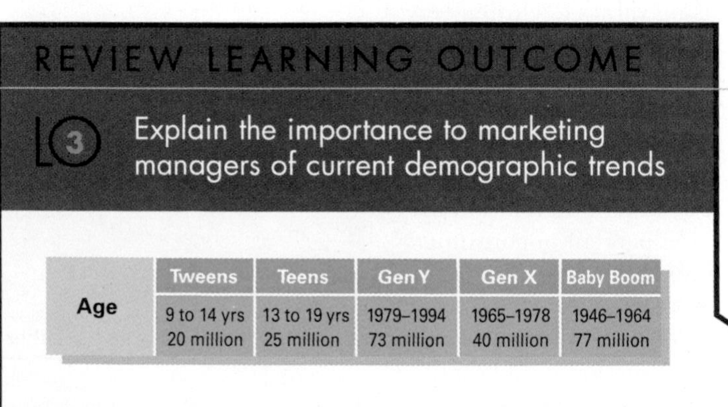

	Tweens	Teens	Gen Y	Gen X	Baby Boom
Age	9 to 14 yrs 20 million	13 to 19 yrs 25 million	1979–1994 73 million	1965–1978 40 million	1946–1964 77 million

- *Linking the brand with a major life event.* Bayer Aspirin's "Do More" effort builds an emotional bond by telling the story of someone who "had a heart attack and lived"; that's why the person is committed to Bayer.
- *Knowing that boomers are jaded students of ads.* Boomers are idealists, but they grew up with TV ads and are skeptical of empty promises. The Dove campaign that shows real-looking women instead of models is not just relatable; it preempts boomers' suspicions about exaggerated beauty claims.[47]

IMAGE COURTESY OF THE ADVERTISING ARCHIVES

Rocawear apparel was launched by hip-hop artist Jay-Z. The company's marketing strategy is designed to show the target customer that the brand is "not merely on the pulse" but "creates the pulse"—an appeal to a "street savvy," "urban" customer interested in a hip lifestyle brand.

LO4

GROWING ETHNIC MARKETS

The minority population of the United States in 2008 reached 101 million. About one in three U.S. residents is a minority. To put this into perspective, there are more minorities here today than there were people in the United States in 1910. In fact, the minority population in the United States is larger than the total population of all but 11 countries.[48] Whites will comprise less than half of the U.S. population by 2042.[49]

The Asian population will continue to increase because of immigration and higher birthrates, and the non-Hispanic black population will increase mostly because of higher birthrates. In 2050 the share of the black population will have increased by one percentage point to 14 percent; Asians will rise to about 9 percent from 5 percent today.[50] But it is the Hispanic population that is driving minority growth. The total U.S. population is projected to grow to 439 million by 2050, and most of that growth will come from Hispanics (see Exhibit 4.1). By 2050 about one in three U.S. residents will be Hispanic. While immigration continues to be a driver of the growing Hispanic population, for the past several years most of the growth has come from births.[51]

Four states and the District of Columbia (68 percent) are majority-minority. The states are Hawaii (75 percent), New Mexico (57 percent), California (57 percent), and Texas (52 percent).[52] Counties around Denver, Las Vegas, and Orlando will all have majority-minorities by 2010.

In 2009, Hispanics wielded more than $1 trillion in spending power, an increase of 345 percent since 1990. In that same year, African Americans' spending topped $921 billion, and Asian Americans' spending power soared over 400 percent since 1990, to $526 billion—far outpacing total U.S. growth in buying power.[53]

Companies across the United States have recognized that diversity can result in bottom-line benefits. More than ever, diversity is emerging as a priority goal for visionary leaders who embrace the incontestable fact that the United States is becoming a truly multicultural society. Smart marketers increasingly are reaching out and tapping these growing markets. Recently, Pepsi attributed one percentage point of its 7.4 percent revenue growth, or about $250 million, to new products inspired by diversity efforts. Those products included guacamole-flavored Doritos chips and Gatorade Xtremo, aimed at Hispanics, and Mountain Dew Code Red, which tends to appeal to African Americans.[54]

EXHIBIT 4.1

U.S. Population by Race

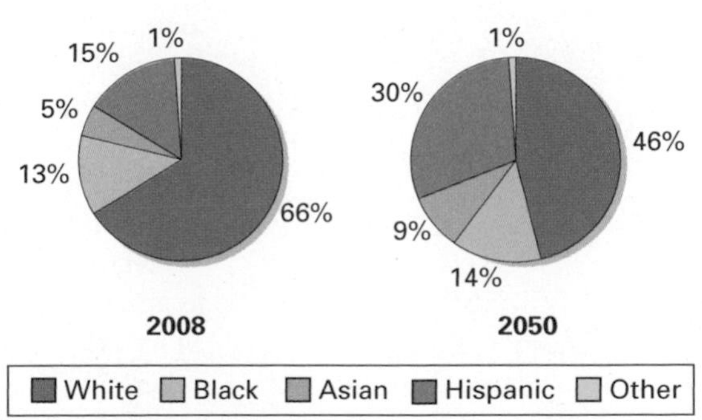

Source: U.S. Census Bureau.

Marketing to Hispanic Americans

The term *Hispanic* encompasses people of many different backgrounds. Nearly 60 percent of Hispanic Americans are of Mexican descent. The next largest group, Puerto Ricans, makes up just under 10 percent of Hispanics. Other groups, including Central Americans, Dominicans, South Americans, and Cubans, each account for less than 5 percent of all Hispanics.

The diversity of the Hispanic population and the language differences create many challenges for those trying to target this market. Hispanics, especially recent immigrants, often prefer products from their native country. Therefore, many retailers along the southern U.S. border import goods from Mexico. In New York City, more than 6,000 *bodegas* (grocery stores) sell such items as plantains, chorizo (pork sausage), and religious candles to Puerto Rican Americans. The *bodegas* also serve as neighborhood social centers. Fresh produce is usually very important to Hispanics because of the tradition of shopping every day at open-air produce markets in their native country.

In general, Hispanics tend to be very brand loyal, but they often are not aware of many mainstream U.S. brands. Instead, many Hispanics are loyal to the brands found in their homeland. If these are not available, Hispanics will choose brands that reflect their native values and culture. This preference for brands from home has helped Mexico's Jarritos become one of the fastest-growing soft drinks in the United States. Yet until recently it was *una marca desapareciendo*—a dying brand. Despite having name recognition in its homeland that rivaled that of Coca-Cola, the 55-year-old soda was losing ground to imported U.S. rivals. So parent company Novamex boldly crossed the border. In the past few years, it has moved onto the competition's turf with marketing that speaks to Mexican Americans' thirst for the good old days. Today, Jarritos's 11 flavors are sold in more than 50,000 U.S. outlets.[55]

Wal-Mart has been the largest retailer in Mexico since 2000. But until recently, it has taken a low-key approach to targeting Hispanics in the United States. Now the world's largest retailer is stepping up efforts to attract America's fastest-growing immigrant group. In 2004, Wal-Mart began printing its monthly ad circulars in English and Spanish. It also launched its own Hispanic magazine, called *Viviendo* (Living), which it distributes free at 1,300 stores heavily shopped by Hispanics. The glossy quarterly magazine features profiles of Latino leaders and celebrities next to ads highlighting Wal-Mart's expanding line of products and services geared toward Hispanics.

In another move, Wal-Mart recently teamed up with Sprint to offer a new prepaid wireless service expressly targeted to Hispanics. Wal-Mart is also stocking a line of bathroom and tabletop accessories from New York restaurateur and cookbook author Zarela Martinez, whose designs are inspired by Mexican folk art and culture. And Wal-Mart's three-year-old financial-services department offers cut-rate fees on money wire transfers, a big lure for immigrants who support family back home.[56]

Sprint recently teamed up with Juanes, a popular Columbian rocker. Sprint will sponsor concerts and provide the technological backdrop for mobile music and video, and a series of "mobisodes" featuring an exclusive behind-the-scenes look at the recording of his music video. Purchases of a Sprint Power Vision phone get a virtual backstage pass.[57] The campaign features in-store promotions in major Hispanic markets.

About 68 percent of U.S. Hispanics have home Internet access, and 42 percent shop online.[58] Hispanics who use the Internet are, on average, much younger than the general online population. Sixty-three percent of Hispanics who have Internet access use the Web to look for information, rather than to play games or hang out in chat rooms, versus 52 percent of the general population.[59] Kraft Foods has realized that the Net is a good way to connect with Hispanics. The company launched **www.comidakraft.com**, where Hispanics can share or post their recipes online, through what's called the Recipe Connection. The Recipe Connection page encourages Hispanic consumers to submit a favorite recipe containing at least one Kraft food product, "perhaps one that has been passed down in your family or an original creation from your own kitchen." Many of the recipes later appear in the magazine, *comida y familia*, a Spanish-language recipe index published by Kraft.

Marketers have found that simply having TV programs in Spanish is not sufficient to attract the target market. It must also be meaningful to their culture. Previously, MTV en Español was just that—traditional MTV in Spanish. The program today is called MTV Tr3s, which is bilingual (subtitles appear in Spanish when English is spoken) and features shows like *Quiero Mis Quinces*, about *quinceañera* (15th birthday) parties, and *Pimpeando*, about car culture.

Marketing to African Americans

Many firms are creating new and different products for the African American market. Often entrepreneurial African Americans are the first to realize unique product opportunities. For example, when Yla Eason couldn't find an African American superhero doll to buy for her son, she founded Olmec Corporation. Now this New York–based toy manufacturer is a $2 million company, marketing more than 60 kinds of African American and Hispanic dolls. Eason has a distribution partnership with Hasbro.

Several companies owned by African Americans—such as Soft Sheen, M&M Johnson, and ProLine—target the African American market for health and beauty aids. Huge corporations like Revlon, Gillette, and Alberto-Culver have either divisions or major product lines for this market as well. Alberto-Culver's hair-care line for this segment includes 75 products. In fact, hair-care items are the largest single category in the African American health and beauty aid industry. Maybelline with its Shades of You product line has the largest share (28 percent) of the African American health and beauty aid market.

Allstate has been targeting black consumers for several decades. Each year it spends more of its advertising budget to reach the African American market. Allstate offers *The Black Enterprise African American Travel Guide* and gives away Allstate-branded hand fans, extolling Allstate's aid to black families, at churches with predominantly black congregations. The African American twist Allstate adds to its "You're in good hands . . ." tagline is the connotation, "Only Allstate respects you enough to give you the insurance experience you truly deserve."[60]

There are few differences between African American and non-African American households when it comes to shopping at grocery, mass merchandisers (JCPenney, Sears), and warehouse club stores. A much larger proportion of African American consumers shop at convenience-oriented formats such as drug, dollar, and convenience/gas stores. Nearly half (46 percent) of African American households shop at beauty supply stores—almost three times the rate for non–African American households. Automotive supply stores and electronic stores follow beauty stores as the most popular alternative channels for African American consumers.[61]

African American consumers create a wide range of possibilities for marketers in various industries:

- *Food and Beverage:* 3.9 million black consumers spend $150 or more per week on groceries.
- *Health and Fitness:* 7.6 million African Americans said they exercise regularly at home, which opens up possibilities for marketers of exercise equipment.
- *Clothing:* African American men and women represent 22 percent and 26 percent of all suit-buyers, respectively.[62]

Black media continue to offer advertisers access to African American consumers, who nevertheless also share many of the mainstream media preferences of other American viewers and readers:

- Television is a top source of media consumption, with 4 in 10 households containing 4 or more televisions.
- Spending on magazines is 6 percent more than the national average.
- Radio and newspapers are less popular than the average.
- Internet use was 41 percent in 2008; by 2012, penetration in the African American community is expected to reach 62 percent.[63]

The promotional dollars spent on African Americans continue to rise, as does the number of black media choices. BET, the black cable TV network, has over 80 million viewers. The 40-year-old *Essence* magazine reaches one-third of all black females ages 18 to 49. But radio holds a special appeal. African Americans spend considerable time with radio (an astounding 4 hours a day versus 2.8 hours for other groups), and urban audiences have an intensely personal relationship with the medium. ABC Radio Network's Tom Joyner reaches an audience of more than 8 million in 115 markets, and Doug Banks is heard by 1.5 million listeners in 36 markets. Pepsi used radio to raise the level of Mountain Dew awareness and its market share in urban markets. Artists like Busta Rhymes personify the image of Mountain Dew and create the lyrics and the vibe that sells the product.

Coca-Cola recently used the TV program *American Idol* to target black consumers. The new ads, titled "Timeline," feature a series of milestones in black history complemented by images that illustrate the progression of the Coca-Cola contour bottle over time. "'Timeline' pays respect to the many incredible contributions that African Americans have made to culture, science, and community," said Anne Sempowski Ward, assistant vice president, African American Marketing, Coca-Cola North America. "This special salute honors the past and inspires optimism for the future, and reminds people that Coca-Cola was there to celebrate these landmark achievements."[64]

The election of President Obama has given hope and motivation to several generations of African Americans. Young people are realizing that hard work and good education can create opportunities once thought not possible. Recent research shows that more African Americans than ever before are achieving the American dream. In 2009, there were 2.4 million African Americans earning more than $75,000 annually.[65] Some of the characteristics of this group are

- Affluent African Americans most often read the newspapers *The New York Times* and *The Wall Street Journal,* as well as the magazines *BusinessWeek, Newsweek, Jet,* and *The Economist.*
- 50 percent go out for fine dining, and more than 25 percent go to clubs/bars at least once a week.
- More than 20 percent go clothes shopping at least once a week. Men focus their fashion spending on career wear, casual wear, and shoes, while women spend on purses and shoes.
- 75 percent shop in higher-end, specialty department stores, and 66 percent shop in traditional department stores. Outlets and "last chance" stores also are popular destinations, suggesting that even affluent shoppers look for bargains.
- More than 10 percent travel on business at least once a week and about one quarter shop during business travel.
- More than 70 percent have a passport and have used it on international travel in the past year. About one-third travel internationally at least three times a year and one-tenth travel internationally at least every other month.
- While more than 60 percent have gym or fitness center memberships and one-third have home gyms, nearly 40 percent wish they were doing more to stay fit.[66]

Marketing to Asian Americans

Asian Americans, who represent only 4.2 percent of the U.S. population, have the highest average family income of all groups. At $66,500, it exceeds the average U.S. household income by more than $10,000. Forty-eight percent of all Asian Americans have at least a bachelor's degree.[67]

Because Asian Americans are younger, better educated, and have higher incomes than average, they are sometimes called a "marketer's dream." Not only is their purchasing power expected to grow, but as a group, Asian Americans are more comfortable with technology than the general population is. They are far more likely to use automated teller machines, and many more of them own the latest electronic gear, such as the iPhone. Of those Asian Americans who use the Internet, 52 percent bank online.[68]

A number of products have been developed specifically for the Asian American market. For example, Kayla Beverly Hills salon draws Asian American consumers because the firm offers cosmetics formulated for them. Anheuser-Busch's agricultural products division targets the Asian American market with eight varieties of California-grown rice, each with a different label, to cover a range of nationalities and tastes.

Cultural diversity within the Asian American market complicates promotional efforts. Some of the major cultural differences among key groups of Asian Americans are the following:

☛ CHINESE

Largest Asian American segment
Four distinct geographic areas in Chinese category: Taiwan, Hong Kong, People's Republic of China, and Southeast Asia
Two major dialects: Mandarin and Cantonese
May be cautious in personal and business dealings
Tend to be price-conscious
Embrace idea of planning for long term
Strong emphasis on family and education

☛ FILIPINO

Second-largest Asian American segment
High rate of U.S. acculturation due to English competency
Heritage/cultural values that are similar to Hispanic culture
Strong sense of family and community preservation
Highly religious (predominately Roman Catholic)

☛ ASIAN INDIAN

Third-largest Asian American segment
Speak many different languages, and come from a variety of Indian cultural and religious backgrounds
National heritage, culture, and values very important
Extreme emphasis on education
Highly price-/value-conscious
Very loyal to strong brands
Respond best to advertising in English, with Indian national cultural values woven in seamlessly

☛ VIETNAMESE

Fourth-largest Asian American segment
Large number of immigrants were refugees
Quality-conscious and value seekers
Strong political beliefs
Extremely strong tendency for cultural and community preservation
Strong emphasis on family and education

☛ KOREAN

Fifth-largest Asian American segment
Most homogeneous of top Asian subgroups, with the majority of Korean Americans coming from similar socioeconomic backgrounds in Korea
Most likely of all Asian American segments to have immigrated as complete family units
May be more emotional in decision making
Prefer name brands to lower prices
Strong emphasis on family and education

☛ JAPANESE

Sixth-largest Asian American segment
Highest percentage of U.S.-born individuals of any Asian American segment (due to waves of immigration dating back to the mid-1800s)

A critical mass of Japanese temporary residents in the United States, to establish a subculture; includes students, temporary workers and trainees, and expatriate business families

Tend to value group consensus over individual opinion

Value name brands over price

Strong emphasis on family and education[69]

Although Asian Americans embrace the values of the larger U.S. population, they also hold on to the cultural values of their particular subgroup. Consider language. Many Asian Americans, particularly Koreans and Chinese, speak their native tongue at home. Filipinos are far less likely to do so. Cultural values are also apparent in the ways different groups make big-ticket purchases. In Japanese American homes, the husband alone makes the decision on such purchases nearly half the time; the wife decides only about 6 percent of the time. In Filipino families, however, wives make these decisions a little more often than their husbands do, although by far the most decisions are made by husbands and wives jointly or with the input of other family members.[70]

Asian Americans like to shop at stores owned and managed by other Asian Americans. Small businesses such as flower shops, grocery stores, and appliance stores are often best equipped to offer the products that Asian Americans want. For example, at first glance the Ha Nam supermarket in Los Angeles's Koreatown might be any other grocery store. But next to the Kraft American singles and the State Fair corn dogs are jars of whole cabbage kimchi. A snack bar in another part of the store cooks up aromatic mung cakes, and an entire aisle is devoted to dried seafood.

One American food product held in high esteem in Asia is Hormel's canned meat product, Spam (no, not what you receive in your e-mail inbox). In South Korea, wedding couples are said to have a long and prosperous life if they receive a wedding pack of Spam. In Hawaii, Spam is sold at McDonald's restaurants, and travel agents send tours packed with Hawaiian residents on annual pilgrimages to the Spam Museum in Austin, Minnesota.[71]

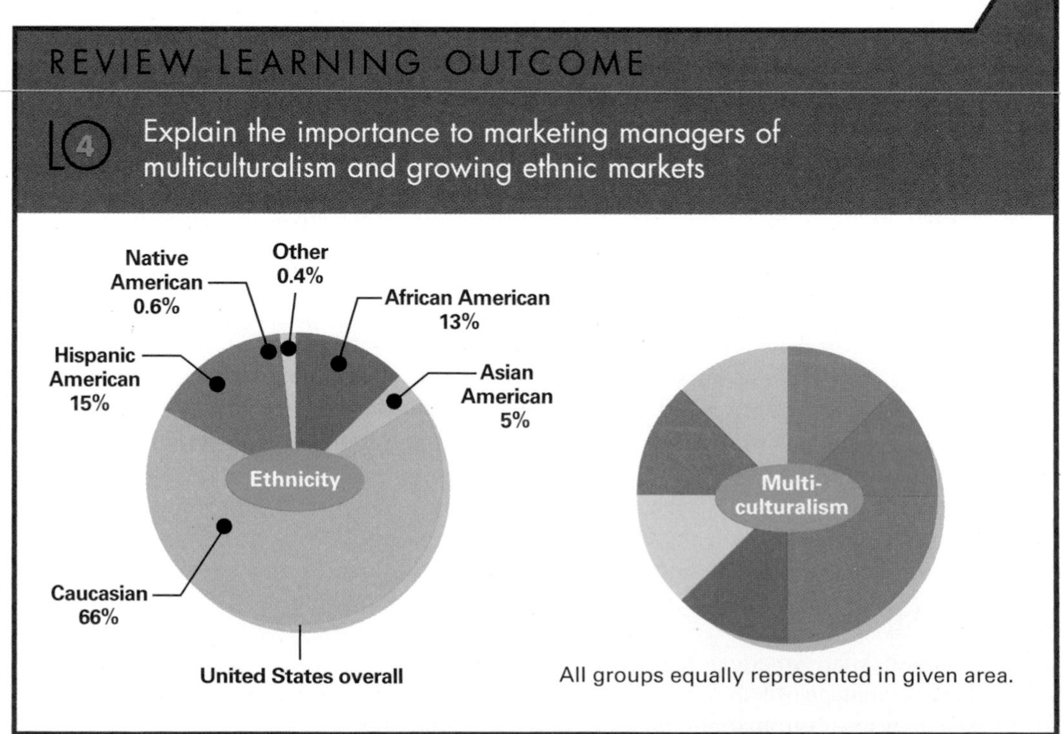

Ethnic and Cultural Diversity

Multiculturalism occurs when all major ethnic groups in an area—such as a city, county, or census tract—are roughly equally represented. Because of its current demographic transition, the trend in the United States is toward greater multiculturalism.

San Francisco County is the most diverse county in the nation. The proportions of major ethnic groups are closer to being equal there than anywhere else. People of many ancestries have long been attracted to the area. Elsewhere, however, a careful examination of the statistics from the latest U.S. Census Bureau reveals that the nation's minority groups, especially Hispanics and Asians, are heavily clustered in selected regions and markets. Rather than witnessing the formation of a homogeneous national melting pot, we are seeing the creation of numerous mini-melting pots, while the rest of America remains much less diverse.

In a broad swath of the country, the minority presence is still quite limited. America's racial and ethnic patterns have taken on distinctly regional dimensions. Hispanics dominate large portions of counties in a span of states stretching from California to Texas. Blacks are strongly represented in counties of the South as well as selected urban areas in the Northeast and Midwest. The Asian presence is relatively small and highly concentrated in a few scattered counties, largely in the West. And Native Americans are concentrated in select pockets in Oklahoma, the Southeast, the upper Midwest, and the West. Multiethnic counties are most prominent in California and the Southwest, with mixes of Asians and Hispanics, or Hispanics and Native Americans.

ECONOMIC FACTORS

In addition to social and demographic factors, marketing managers must understand and react to the economic environment. The three economic areas of greatest concern to most marketers are consumers' incomes, inflation, and recession.

Consumers' Incomes

As disposable (or after-tax) incomes rise, more families and individuals can afford the "good life." In recent years, however, U.S. incomes have risen at a rather slow pace. After adjustment for inflation, the median household income in the United States in 2008 was projected to be approximately $49,000. This means half of all U.S. households earned less and the other half earned more.[72]

Education is the primary determinant of a person's earning potential. For example, only 1 percent of those with only a high school education earn over $100,000 annually. By comparison, 13 percent of college-educated workers earn six figures or more.[73] Along with "willingness to buy," or "ability to buy," income is a key determinant of target markets. A marketer who knows where the money is knows where the markets are. If you are seeking a new store location for Dollar General, a retail chain that caters to lower-income consumers, you would probably concentrate on the South and Midwest because most households with annual incomes of less than $45,000 are concentrated in these areas.

The U.S. Census Bureau normally deals in very big numbers; for example, the richest 1 percent of the households (719,910 of them) have an average annual income of $364,657.[74] Sometimes, however, the Census Bureau puts the U.S. economy under a microscope. Here are a few key findings from the most current census:

- In ranking larger American cities, the Census Bureau found San Jose, California, and Plano, Texas, had the highest median incomes, at around $71,000, while Miami and Cleveland had the lowest, with median incomes below $25,000.

multiculturalism
When all major ethnic groups in an area—such as a city, county, or census tract—are roughly equally represented.

purchasing power
A comparison of income versus the relative cost of a set standard of goods and services in different geographic areas.

inflation
A measure of the decrease in the value of money, expressed as the percentage reduction in value since the previous year.

- Cleveland also had the highest poverty rate for big cities at 32.4 percent, followed closely by Detroit, two cities suffering from the downturn in the American automobile industry and manufacturing.
- Camden, New Jersey, a city struggling with crime, had a poverty rate of 44 percent, the highest number among small to midsize cities—but so, too, did College Station, Texas, home of Texas A&M University.
- Among counties with populations of more than 250,000, the three where the households had the highest median incomes were in suburban Washington, D.C.—Loudoun and Fairfax counties in Virginia and Howard County in Maryland.
- The ratio of single men to single women between ages 15 and 44 was highest in Nevada (120.2 per 100 women), North Dakota (120.1) and Alaska (118.9). It was lowest in the District of Columbia (93.4).[75]

Purchasing Power

Rising incomes don't necessarily mean a higher standard of living. Increased standards of living are a function of purchasing power. **Purchasing power** is measured by comparing income to the relative cost of a set standard of goods and services in different geographic areas, usually referred to as the cost of living. Another way to think of purchasing power is income minus the cost of living (i.e., expenses). In general, a cost of living index takes into account housing, food and groceries, transportation, utilities, health care, and miscellaneous expenses such as clothing, services, and entertainment. Homefair's salary calculator uses these metrics when it figures that the cost of living in New York City is almost three times the cost of living in Youngstown, Ohio. This means that a worker living in New York must earn nearly $279,500 to have the same standard of living as someone making $100,000 in Youngstown.

When income is high relative to the cost of living, people have more discretionary income. That means they have more money to spend on nonessential items (in other words, on wants rather than needs). This information is important to marketers for obvious reasons. Consumers with high purchasing power can afford to spend more money without jeopardizing their budget for necessities, like food, housing, and utilities. They also have the ability to purchase higher-priced necessities, for example, a more expensive car, a home in a more expensive neighborhood, or a designer handbag versus a purse from a discount store.

Inflation

Inflation is a measure of the decrease in the value of money, generally expressed as the percentage reduction in value since the previous year, which is the rate of inflation. Thus, in simple terms, an inflation rate of 5 percent means you will need 5 percent more units of money than you would have needed last year to buy the same basket of products. If inflation is 5 percent, you can expect that, on average, prices have risen by about 5 percent since the previous year. Of course, if pay raises are matching the rate of inflation, then employees will be no worse off in terms of the immediate purchasing power of their salaries.

In times of low inflation, businesses seeking to increase their profit margins can do so only by increasing their efficiency. If they significantly increase prices, no one will purchase their goods or services.

From November 2006 until November 2008, prices rose 7.8 percent. Wages and benefits did not rise as much as prices; therefore, real purchasing power fell.[76] In more inflationary times, marketers use a number of pricing strategies to cope. But in general, marketers must be aware that inflation causes consumers to either build up or diminish their brand loyalty. In one research session, a consumer panelist noted, "I used to use just Betty Crocker mixes, but now I think of either Betty Crocker or

Duncan Hines, depending on which is on sale." Another participant said, "Pennies count now, and so I look at the whole shelf, and I read the ingredients. I don't really understand, but I can tell if it's exactly the same. So now I use this cheaper brand, and honestly, it works just as well." Inflation pressures consumers to make more economical purchases. Nevertheless, most consumers try hard to maintain their standard of living.

In creating marketing strategies to cope with inflation, managers must realize that, regardless of what happens to the seller's cost, the buyer is not going to pay more for a product than the subjective value he or she places on it. No matter how compelling the justification might be for a 10 percent price increase, marketers must always examine its impact on demand. Many marketers try to hold prices level for as long as is practical.

Recession

A **recession** is a period of economic activity characterized by negative growth. More precisely, a recession is defined as when the gross domestic product falls for two consecutive quarters. Gross domestic product is the total market value of all final goods and services produced during a period of time. Final goods are the end product of the production process, such as a car. If one counted the value of the engine, brakes, and seats (intermediate goods), plus the value of the car, then they would be double counting. The official beginning of the 2007–2009 recession was December 2007.[77] While the causes of the recession are very complex, it began with the collapse of inflated housing prices. Those high prices led people to take out mortgages they couldn't afford from banks that should have known the money would not be repaid. By 2008, the recession had spread around the globe.

The declining stock market, growing unemployment, and collapsing home prices have taken a toll on consumer confidence. As mentioned above, many consumers are shifting to store brands that, on average, cost 46 percent less than manufacturers' brands.[78] Kimberly-Clark has noticed a big decline in its potty-training pants as young parents leave their children in diapers longer. Diapers are cheaper than training pants. Procter & Gamble has seen its bargain-priced Gain detergent rise rapidly in sales. More consumers are using coupons than ever before.

recession
A period of economic activity characterized by negative growth, which reduces demand for goods and services.

Like Gain, some brands that help the consumer save money do very well in a recession. McCormick spices have shown an uptick in sales recently. This is because people are eating out less and cooking more at home. Similarly, snack foods such as

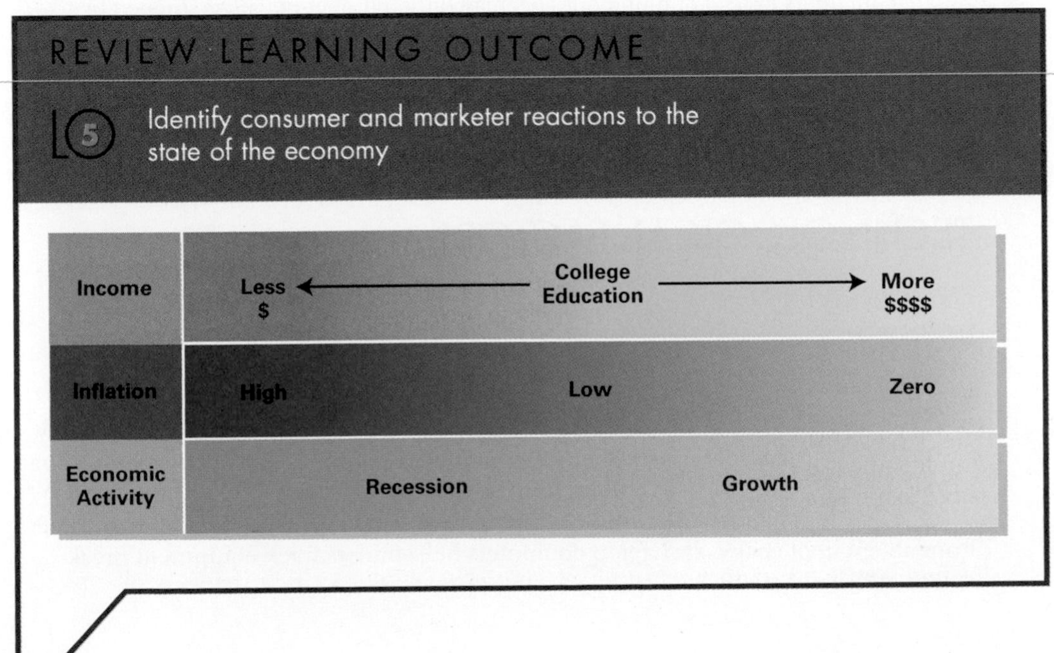

EXHIBIT 4.2

What Consumers Are Now Doing to Save Money

Opting to do it themselves (lawn care, house cleaning)	68 percent
Turning the thermostat down or up	65 percent
Eating out less often	59 percent
Buying fewer new clothes	59 percent
Fixing items that are broken versus replacing them	56 percent
Cutting back on drinking alcohol and smoking	50 percent
Choosing less expensive restaurants	42 percent
Purchasing cheaper brands	36 percent
Engaging in leisure activities closer to home	31 percent

Source: Yankelovich.

nuts and potato chips are doing well in the down economy. In most recessions, movies and theaters don't experience a downturn in a recession. Consumers find escapism for a relatively small amount of money. Also, beer and wine sales tend to hold up quite well, but consumers don't trade up to higher-price brands. Because people tend to hang on to durable goods longer in a recession, there is a greater demand for repair services, remodeling services, and do-it-yourself products.[79] Other things that consumers are doing to save money are shown in Exhibit 4.2.

Retailers and manufacturers redouble their efforts to cut costs during a recession. They often try to lower prices to attract new customers and hold existing ones, but also often cut costs simply to survive. George Falzon, the owner of a jewelry store, has been hit by high metal prices and the recession. That left him with lots of pricey display bridal jewelry sitting around. So Mr. Falzon began stocking his store with different types of displays: faux pieces which are crafted of plated silver, with cubic zirconium centers. He readily tells customers that the display pieces are replicas. Since most bridal jewelry is special-ordered anyway, customers generally don't mind, he says. The real pieces take about a week to arrive. Having lower-cost replicas serve as display pieces is saving Mr. Falzon about $75,000 in inventory at any given time. That means he can spend less than he did before and offer four times as many styles of engagement rings and wedding bands.[80]

Costco, the deep discounter, has to hold prices in line. It gets about 75 percent of its profits from annual membership fees. If prices get too high, members simply won't renew their memberships. After Procter & Gamble announced a 6 percent price hike on Bounty paper towels and Charmin toilet paper, Costco bought hundreds of truckloads at the old price and put them into a warehouse, saving customers precious pennies per roll. It has even looked into growing its own pumpkins to help preserve the $5.99 price tag on its store-baked pies.

Costco has even gotten vendors to redesign product packages to fit more items on a pallet, the wooden platforms it uses to ship and display its goods. Putting cashews into square containers instead of round ones decreased the number of pallets shipped by 24,000 in 2008, cutting the number of trucks by 600. By reshaping everything from laundry detergent buckets to milk jugs, Costco has needed 200,000 fewer pallets overall.[81]

TECHNOLOGICAL FACTORS

Sometimes new technology is an effective weapon against inflation and recession. New machines that reduce production costs can be one of a firm's most valuable assets. The power of a personal-computer microchip doubles about every 18 months. Our ability, as a nation, to maintain and build wealth depends in large part on the speed and effectiveness with which we invent and adopt machines that lift productivity. For example, coal mining is typically thought of as unskilled, backbreaking labor. But visit the Twentymile Mine near Oak Creek, Colorado, and you will find workers with push-button controls who walk along massive machines that shear 30-inch slices from an 850-foot coal wall. Laptop computers help miners track equipment breakdowns and water quality.

Research

The United States excels at both basic and applied research. **Basic research** (or *pure research*) attempts to expand the frontiers of knowledge but is not aimed at a specific, pragmatic problem. Basic research aims to confirm an existing theory or to learn more about a concept or phenomenon. For example, basic research might focus on high-energy physics. **Applied research**, in contrast, attempts to develop new or improved products. The United States has dramatically improved its track record in applied research. For example, the United States leads the world in applying basic research to aircraft design and propulsion systems.

Rather than invention for the sake of invention, many firms are turning to the marketing concept to guide their research. To give its scientists guidance, Dow first interviews customers to find out their wants and needs. A wish list of products and/or technical characteristics helps the scientists create inventions with market value. Dow recently created a fiber called XLA after learning that apparel makers wanted a "soft stretch" fiber with a natural feel. Dow thinks that the product might deliver sales of $300 million within ten years.

Although developing new technology internally is a key to creating and maintaining a long-term competitive advantage, external technology is also important to managers for two reasons. First, by acquiring the technology, the firm may be able to operate more efficiently or create a better product. Second, a new technology may render your existing products obsolete.

An example of operating more efficiently by using external technology is UPS. Not so long ago, UPS drivers worked off maps, 3 × 5 note cards, and their own memory to figure out the best way to run their routes. That changed when UPS began to implement a $600 million route optimization system—think MapQuest on steroids—that each evening maps out the next day's schedule for the majority of its 56,000 drivers. So sophisticated is the software that it designs each route to minimize the number of left turns, thus reducing the time and gas that drivers waste idling at stoplights. The latest wrinkle: a new feature that, with the aid of global positioning system technology, warns drivers with a beep if they pull into the wrong driveway. It also enables UPS to send a driver more quickly after you call in a pickup because dispatchers know exactly which driver is closest. UPS now offers package-flow technology to launch a service that allows customers to reroute a package in transit to a different address.[82]

basic research
Pure research that aims to confirm an existing theory or to learn more about a concept or phenomenon.

applied research
An attempt to develop new or improved products.

Global Innovation

Microsoft spent $80 million to open an Advanced Technology Center outside Beijing, China. With nearly 500 engineers, PhD students, and visiting professors, it is one of Microsoft's most important facilities for developing graphics, handwriting-recognition, and voice-synthesizing technologies. The technology center illustrates how innovation is increasingly becoming a global process conducted at worldwide research and development operations. Like Microsoft, IBM has facilities around the world including major labs in China, Israel, Switzerland, Japan, and India.

General Electric has become a leader in wind energy technology by tapping into a global network. The technology for GE's new wind turbines comes from the following countries:

- *United States:* The main research center in Niskayuna, New York, handles basic research, while other centers in New York, Pennsylvania, South Carolina, California, and Virginia tackle other design and engineering aspects.

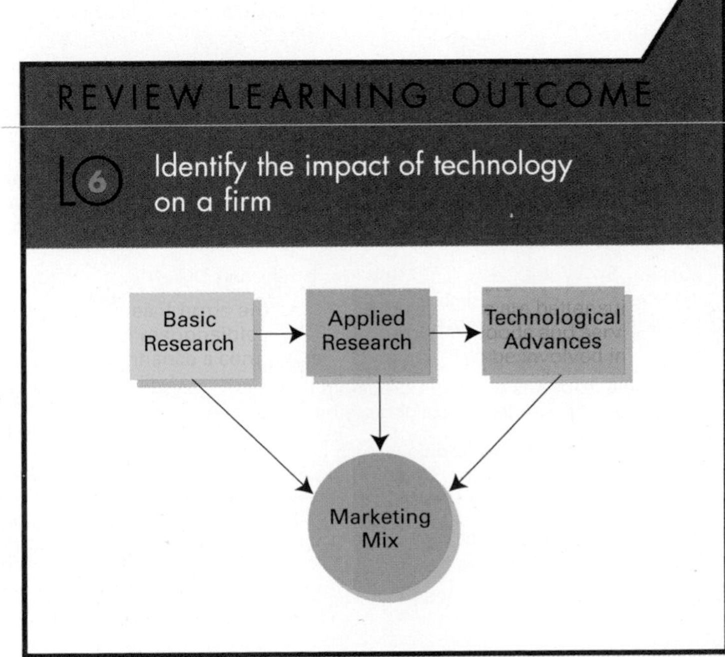

- *Canada:* Engineers at GE Consumer & Industrial in Peterborough, Ontario, provided the manufacturing technology for the generator.
- *India:* Researchers at Bangalore have crafted a series of analytical models and turbine system design tools that affect the entire turbine.
- *China:* Researchers in Shanghai are in charge of the turbine simulator to test new products and conduct high-end tests for variable-speed power electronics.
- *Germany:* The lead experts on the gearbox work at GE Wind operations in Salzbergen. Researchers in Munich design sensors and monitor advanced controls.[83]

Innovation Carries to the Bottom Line

Innovation pays off big for creative organizations. One study found that the most innovative firms have an average profit margin growth of 3 percent higher than the typical firm.[84] Other research has found higher stock market returns among firms that spend heavily on research and development.[85] Each year, respected business journals pay tribute to the most innovative companies around the globe. *BusinessWeek's* rankings are shown in Exhibit 4.3.

EXHIBIT 4.3

The World's Most Innovative Companies

Ranking 1—Apple: Apple is a master of product and store design. Now that it's invading the cell-phone market, will it continue its winning streak?

Ranking 2—Google: It didn't invent search advertising, but lifted it to its current heights. Google's famously chaotic innovation process has plunged it into everything from radio ads to online office software.

Ranking 3—Toyota Motor: Toyota's dominance in hybrids could lead to the first plug-in electric auto. Now the No. 1 carmaker, its continuous improvement process is copied worldwide.

Ranking 4—General Electric: CEO Jeff Immelt's push for "imagination breakthroughs," or growth opportunities of $50 million to $100 million, are increasingly leading GE into emerging markets and "green" technology.

Ranking 5—Microsoft: To some, Microsoft is more fast follower than leading innovator. Still, the software giant's massive R&D budget generates creations that help ensure the popularity of Windows and Office.

Ranking 6—Procter & Gamble: After years of scouting for new products outside its walls, P&G has mapped the innovation strengths of global regions. CEO A.G. Lafley is pushing for more disruptive new ideas.

Ranking 7—3M: The legendary Post-it Note is just one of 3M's many creations, which include everything from dental fillings to roofing shingles. Next on its list: diagnostic tests for infectious diseases.

Ranking 8—Walt Disney: CEO Bob Iger is refueling Disney's creative culture. Moves such as putting ABC shows on iTunes and acquiring Pixar helped move Disney up.

Ranking 9—IBM: The tech services behemoth held an online brainstorm with 150,000 people to dream up new ideas. It hosts annual symposia with outsiders to collaborate on forecasting.

Ranking 10—Sony: This traditional tech hardware maker is devoting more resources to software. To turn its PlayStation 3 console from living-room box into virtual gateway, it created a 3-D online world.

Ranking 11—Wal-Mart Stores: Wal-Mart is struggling with growth, but its "green" actions, such as using its leverage as the world's largest retailer to cut suppliers' packaging waste, helped it make the top 20.

Ranking 12—Honda Motor: Headed by a former R&D chief, Honda has been known for its fuel-efficient cars. But its environmental approach isn't limited to autos. Next up: solar panels and a fuel-sipping jet.

Ranking 13—Nokia: To build sales in emerging markets, managers spend time in the homes of local customers. This has led to features for illiterate users such as an icon-driven handset directory.

Ranking 14—Starbucks: The coffee chain's 50-person R&D group created eight new flavors in one year. It also started its own music label and partnered with outsiders to publish books and produce movies.

Ranking 15—Target: Target stands out from its discount rivals by selling designer-inspired products. Innovative marketing, such as buying all the ads in one issue of *The New Yorker*, has also set it apart.

Ranking 16—BMW: BMW is flat, flexible, and fast-reacting. Employees are urged to "break the rules" to cut costs or push through winning ideas, such as the Z4 coupe, which higher-ups initially nixed.

Ranking 17—Samsung Electronics: Samsung stays ahead with intensive investment in new facilities and production systems. These days, it's focusing on the convergence of technologies and phone features.

Ranking 18—Virgin Group: Most of its businesses, such as credit card or mobile virtual networks, are collaborative; Virgin supplies the branding and customer service while partners put up much of the cash.

Ranking 19—Intel: The world's largest chipmaker, Intel is making a big headway in selling to the health-care market. It recently previewed its most powerful chip to date and is planning a $2.5 billion plant in China.

Ranking 20—Amazon: The online retailer is now innovating its business model, turning its backroom operations into a digital utility that rents out computer power and warehouse space to other firms.

Source: Reprinted from the May 14, 2007, issue of *BusinessWeek* by special permission, copyright © 2007 by The McGraw-Hill Companies, Inc.

ETHICS in Marketing

Maybe Technology Can Save the Planet: But Should It?

Recently, a private company proposed "fertilizing" parts of the ocean with iron, in hopes of encouraging carbon-absorbing blooms of plankton. Meanwhile, researchers elsewhere are talking about injecting chemicals into the atmosphere, launching sun-reflecting mirrors into stationary orbit above the Earth, or taking other steps to reset the thermostat of a warming planet. This technology might be useful, even lifesaving. But it would inevitably produce environmental effects impossible to predict and impossible to undo. So a growing number of experts say it is time for broad discussion of how and by whom it should be used, or if it should be tried at all.

Similar questions are being raised about nanotechnology, robotics, and other powerful emerging technologies. There are even those who suggest humanity should collectively decide to turn away from some new technologies as inherently dangerous. "The complexity of newly engineered systems, coupled with their potential impact on lives, the environment, etc., raise a set of ethical issues that engineers had not been thinking about," said William Wulf, a computer scientist.

When scientists and engineers discuss geoengineering, it is obvious they are talking about technologies with the potential to change the planet. But the issue of engineering ethics applies as well to technologies whose planet-altering potential may not emerge until it is too late. Ronald Arkin, a computer scientist that advises the U.S. Army on robotic weapons, says robotics researchers should consider not just how to make robots more capable, but also who must bear responsibility for their actions and how much human operators should remain "in the loop," particularly with machines to aid soldiers on the battlefield or the disabled in their homes. Paul Thompson, a philosopher at Michigan State and former secretary of the International Society for Environmental Ethics, said many scientists were trained to limit themselves to questions answerable in the real world, in the belief that "scientists and engineers should not be involved in these kinds of ethical questions."[86]

New technology involves many "unknown unknowns." These factors will not become obvious until the technology is put into widespread use. Should government step in and block new technology with many "unknown unknowns?" If you were going to block one technology, which one mentioned above would it be? Why?

While innovation can raise productivity and make the world a better place to live, is applying new technology always the right thing to do? We explore this issue in the Ethics in Marketing box above.

POLITICAL AND LEGAL FACTORS

Business needs government regulation to protect innovators of new technology, the interests of society in general, one business from another, and consumers. In turn, government needs business because the marketplace generates taxes that support public efforts to educate our youth, pave our roads, protect our shores, and so on. The private sector also serves as a counterweight to government. The decentralization of power inherent in a private-enterprise system supplies the limitation on government essential for the survival of a democracy.

Every aspect of the marketing mix is subject to laws and restrictions. It is the duty of marketing managers or their legal assistants to understand these laws and conform to them because failure to comply with regulations can have major consequences for a firm. Sometimes just sensing trends and taking corrective action before a government agency acts can help avoid regulation. The tobacco industry failed to do this. As a result, Joe Camel and the Marlboro Man are fading into the sunset in the United States along with other strategies used to promote tobacco products.

The challenge is not simply to keep the marketing department out of trouble, however, but to help it implement creative new programs to accomplish marketing objectives. It is all too easy for a marketing manager or sometimes a lawyer to say "no" to a marketing innovation that actually entails little risk. For example, an overly cautious lawyer could hold up sales of a desirable new product by warning that the package design could prompt a copyright infringement suit. Thus, it is important to have a thorough understanding of the laws established by the federal government, state governments, and regulatory agencies to govern marketing-related issues.

Federal Legislation

Federal laws that affect marketing fall into several categories. First, the Sherman Act, the Clayton Act, the Federal Trade Commission Act, the Celler-Kefauver Antimerger Act, and the Hart-Scott-Rodino Act were passed to regulate the competitive environment. Second, the Robinson-Patman Act was designed to regulate pricing practices. Third, the Wheeler-Lea Act was created to control false advertising. The Lanham Act protects trademarks. These key pieces of legislation are summarized in Exhibit 4.4. The primary federal laws that protect consumers are shown in Exhibit 4.5.

EXHIBIT 4.4

Primary U.S. Laws That Affect Marketing

Legislation	Impact On Marketing
Sherman Act of 1890	Makes trusts and conspiracies in restraint of trade illegal; makes monopolies and attempts to monopolize a misdemeanor.
Clayton Act of 1914	Outlaws discrimination in prices to different buyers; prohibits tying contracts (which require the buyer of one product to also buy another item in the line); makes illegal the combining of two or more competing corporations by pooling ownership of stock.
Federal Trade Commission Act of 1914	Created the Federal Trade Commission to deal with antitrust matters; outlaws unfair methods of competition.
Robinson-Patman Act of 1936	Prohibits charging different prices to different buyers of merchandise of like grade and quantity; requires sellers to make any supplementary services or allowances available to all purchasers on a proportionately equal basis.
Wheeler-Lea Amendments to FTC Act of 1938	Broadens the Federal Trade Commission's power to prohibit practices that might injure the public without affecting competition; outlaws false and deceptive advertising.
Lanham Act of 1946	Establishes protection for trademarks.
Celler-Kefauver Antimerger Act of 1950	Strengthens the Clayton Act to prevent corporate acquisitions that reduce competition.
Hart-Scott-Rodino Act of 1976	Requires large companies to notify the government of their intent to merge.

EXHIBIT 4.5

Primary U.S. Laws Protecting Consumers

Legislation	Impact On Marketing
Federal Food and Drug Act of 1906	Prohibits adulteration and misbranding of foods and drugs involved in interstate commerce; strengthened by the Food, Drug, and Cosmetic Act (1938) and the Kefauver-Harris Drug Amendment (1962).
Federal Hazardous Substances Act of 1960	Requires warning labels on hazardous household chemicals.
Kefauver-Harris Drug Amendment of 1962	Requires that manufacturers conduct tests to prove drug effectiveness and safety.
Consumer Credit Protection Act of 1968	Requires that lenders fully disclose true interest rates and all other charges to credit customers for loans and installment purchases.
Child Protection and Toy Safety Act of 1969	Prevents marketing of products so dangerous that adequate safety warnings cannot be given.
Public Health Smoking Act of 1970	Prohibits cigarette advertising on TV and radio and revises the health hazard warning on cigarette packages.
Poison Prevention Labeling Act of 1970	Requires safety packaging for products that may be harmful to children.
National Environmental Policy Act of 1970	Established the Environmental Protection Agency to deal with various types of pollution and organizations that create pollution.
Public Health Cigarette Smoking Act of 1971	Prohibits tobacco advertising on radio and television.
Consumer Product Safety Act of 1972	Created the Consumer Product Safety Commission, which has authority to specify safety standards for most products.
Child Protection Act of 1990	Regulates the number of minutes of advertising on children's television.
Children's Online Privacy Protection Act of 1998	Empowers the FTC to set rules regarding how and when marketers must obtain parental permission before asking children marketing research questions.
Aviation Security Act of 2001	Requires airlines to take extra security measures to protect passengers, including the installation of stronger cockpit doors, improved baggage screening, and increased security training for airport personnel.
Homeland Security Act of 2002	Protects consumers against terrorist acts. Created the Department of Homeland Security.
Do Not Call Law of 2003	Protects consumers against unwanted telemarketing calls.
CAN-SPAM Act of 2003	Protects consumers against unwanted e-mail, or spam.

State Laws

Legislation that affects marketing varies state by state. Oregon, for example, limits utility advertising to 0.5 percent of the company's net income. California has forced industry to improve consumer products and has enacted legislation to lower the energy consumption of refrigerators, freezers, and air conditioners. Several states, including New Mexico and Kansas, are considering levying a tax on all in-state commercial advertising.

Many states and cities are attempting to fight obesity by regulating fast-food chains and other restaurants. California has passed a law banning trans fats in restaurants and bakeries. New York City chain restaurants must now display calorie counts on menus. Boston has now banned trans fats in restaurants. And the list goes on.

Consumer Product Safety Commission (CPSC)
A federal agency established to protect the health and safety of consumers in and around their homes.

Federal Trade Commission (FTC)
A federal agency empowered to prevent persons or corporations from using unfair methods of competition in commerce.

Food and Drug Administration (FDA)
A federal agency charged with enforcing regulations against selling and distributing adulterated, misbranded, or hazardous food and drug products.

Regulatory Agencies

Although some state regulatory bodies actively pursue violators of their marketing statutes, federal regulators generally have the greatest clout. The Consumer Product Safety Commission, the Federal Trade Commission, and the Food and Drug Administration are the three federal agencies most directly and actively involved in marketing affairs. These agencies, plus others, are discussed throughout the book, but a brief introduction is in order at this point.

The sole purpose of the **Consumer Product Safety Commission (CPSC)** is to protect the health and safety of consumers in and around their homes. The CPSC has the power to set mandatory safety standards for almost all products that consumers use (about 15,000 items). The CPSC consists of a five-member committee and about 400 staff members, including technicians, lawyers, and administrative help. The commission can fine offending firms up to $500,000 and sentence their officers to up to a year in prison. It can also ban dangerous products from the marketplace. The CPSC oversees about 400 recalls per year. The CPSC operates under rules that prohibit staff from publicizing information about product complaints until the manufacturer OK's the release. Besides handing over a lot of control to companies, this process routinely delays public disclosure of hazards. It has also been suggested that the CPSC is extremely underfunded.[87]

The **Federal Trade Commission (FTC)** also consists of five members, each holding office for seven years. The FTC is empowered to prevent persons or corporations from using unfair methods of competition in commerce. It is authorized to investigate the practices of business combinations and to conduct hearings on antitrust matters and deceptive advertising. The FTC has a vast array of regulatory powers (see Exhibit 4.6). Nevertheless, it is not invincible. For example, the FTC had proposed to ban all advertising to children under age 8, to ban all advertising of the sugared products that are most likely to cause tooth decay to children under age 12, and to require the food industry to pay for dental health and nutritional advertisements. Business reacted by lobbying to reduce the FTC's power. The two-year lobbying effort resulted in passage of the FTC Improvement Act of 1980. The major provisions of the act are as follows:

- It bans the use of unfairness as a standard for industry-wide rules against advertising. All the proposals concerning children's advertising were therefore suspended, because they were based almost entirely on the unfairness standard.
- It requires oversight hearings on the FTC every six months. This congressional review is designed to keep the commission accountable. Moreover, it keeps Congress aware of one of the many regulatory agencies it has created and is responsible for monitoring.

Businesses rarely band together to create change in the legal environment as they did to pass the FTC Improvement Act. Generally, marketing managers react only to legislation, regulation, and edicts. It is usually less costly to stay attuned to the regulatory environment than to fight the government. If marketers had toned down their hard-hitting advertisements to children, they might have avoided an FTC inquiry altogether. The FTC also regulates advertising on the Internet as well as Internet abuses of consumer privacy. The **Food and Drug Administration (FDA)**, another powerful agency, is charged with enforcing regulations against selling and distributing adulterated, misbranded, or hazardous food and drug products. In the last decade it took a very aggressive stance against tobacco products and is now paying attention to the fast-food industry.

The Battle Over Consumer Privacy

The popularity of the Internet for direct marketing, for collecting consumer data, and as a repository for sensitive consumer data has alarmed privacy-minded consumers. So

EXHIBIT 4.6

Powers of the Federal Trade Commission

Remedy	Procedure
Cease-and-Desist Order	A final order is issued to cease an illegal practice—and is often challenged in the courts.
Consent Decree	A business consents to stop the questionable practice without admitting its illegality.
Affirmative Disclosure	An advertiser is required to provide additional information about products in advertisements.
Corrective Advertising	An advertiser is required to correct the past effects of misleading advertising. (For example, 25 percent of a firm's media budget must be spent on FTC-approved advertisements or FTC-specified advertising.)
Restitution	Refunds are required to be given to consumers misled by deceptive advertising. According to a 1975 court-of-appeals decision, this remedy cannot be used except for practices carried out after the issuance of a cease-and-desist order.
Counteradvertising	The FTC proposed that the Federal Communications Commission permit advertisements in broadcast media to counteract advertising claims (also that free time be provided under certain conditions).

many online users have complained about "spam," the Internet's equivalent of junk mail, that the U.S. Congress passed the CAN-SPAM Act in an attempt to regulate it. The act, which took effect on January 1, 2004, does not totally ban spam, but it does prohibit commercial e-mailers from using a false address and presenting false or misleading information. It also requires commercial e-mailers to provide a way for recipients to "opt out" of receiving further e-mail from the sender. A person opting out cannot be required to pay a fee or provide any other personally identifying information other than an email address.[88]

Another problem is that Web surfers, including children who are using the Internet, are routinely asked to divulge personal information in order to access certain screens or purchase goods or services online. Internet users who once felt fairly anonymous when using the Web are now disturbed by the amount of information marketers collect on them and their children as they visit various sites in cyberspace.

Most consumers are unaware of how technology is used to collect personal data or how the personal information is used and distributed after it is collected. The government actively sells huge amounts of personal information to list compilers. State motor vehicle bureaus sell names and addresses of individuals who get driver's licenses. Hospitals sell the names of women who just gave birth on their premises. Consumer credit databases, developed and maintained by large providers such as Equifax Marketing Services and TransUnion, are often used by credit card marketers to prescreen targets for solicitations.

Although privacy policies for companies in the United States are largely voluntary and there are almost no regulations on the collection and use of personal data, collecting consumer data outside the United States is a different matter. Database marketers venturing into new data territories must carefully navigate foreign privacy laws. The European Union's *European Data Protection Directive*, for instance, states that any business that trades with a European organization must comply with the EU's rules for handling information about individuals or risk prosecution. This directive prohibits the export of personal data to countries not doing enough to protect privacy, in particular, the United States.

More than 50 nations have, or are developing, privacy legislation. Europe has the strictest legislation regarding the collection and use of consumer data, and other countries look to that legislation when formulating their policies. Australia, for instance, recently introduced legislation that would require private companies

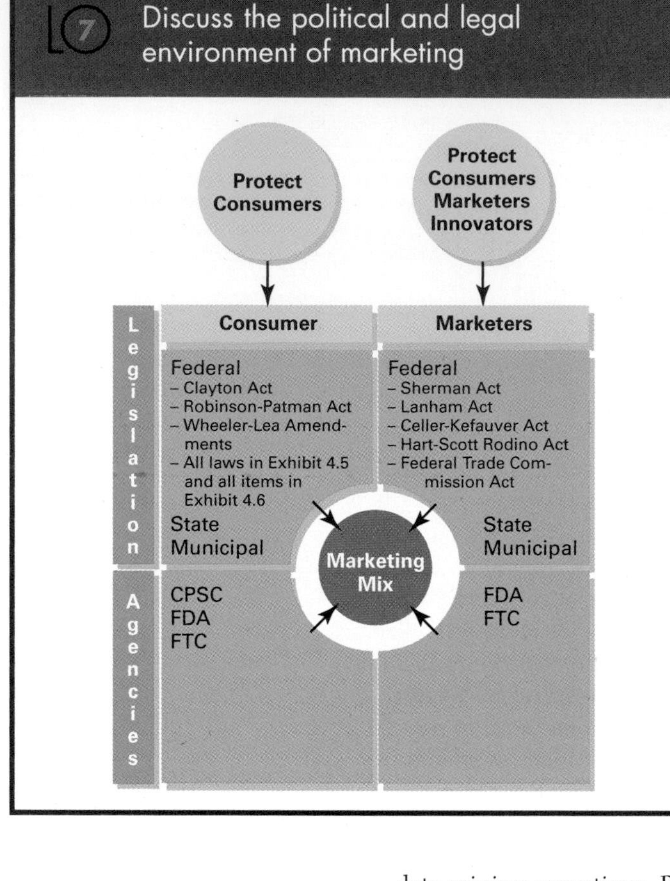

to follow a set of guidelines regarding the collection, storage, use, and transfer of personal information about individuals. Common privacy rules include obtaining data fairly and lawfully, using the information only for the original purpose specified, making sure it is accurate and up-to-date, and destroying data after the purpose for collection is completed. The EU requires that consumers be presented with an opt-out provision at the point of data collection.

Despite cries from consumer and advocacy groups for privacy legislation, to date Congress has failed to act. So far, only the states have enacted meaningful protections, with California in the lead. Now, more than 30 states have adopted laws that require notification if a customer's personal information has been improperly exposed. In 2007, The TJX Companies, which owns Marshalls, T.J. Maxx, HomeGoods, and A.J. Wright, reported that customers' credit and debit card information, along with some driver's license data, had been lifted from its computer system. When asked how many people were affected, a spokesperson for TJX replied, "substantially less than millions."[89] Others put the number of persons exposed at 45 million.[90]

Identity Theft People are right to be concerned about their personal information. Identity theft costs $55 billion per year. One company that has come under fire is ChoicePoint. Since spinning off from the credit bureau Equifax in 1997, it has been buying up databases and data-mining operations. Businesses, individuals, and even the FBI now rely on its storehouse. But its customers have also included Nigerian scammers who apparently used the data to steal people's identities.

In 1998, Congress passed the Identity Theft and Assumption Deterrence Act. This law prohibits knowingly transferring or using another person's identification with the intent to commit an unlawful activity, such as theft of funds. Guilty parties face up to 15 years in prison.

Governmental Actions Three other key laws (one a state law) have been passed to protect consumers from identity theft. The federal laws are:

- *Gramm-Leach-Bliley Act (Financial Services Modernization Act):* This act is aimed at financial companies. It requires those corporations to tell their customers how they use their personal information and to have policies that prevent fraudulent access to it. Partial compliance has been required since 2001.
- *Health Insurance Portability and Accountability Act:* This law is aimed at the healthcare industry. It limits disclosure of individuals' medical information and imposes penalties on organizations that violate privacy rules. Compliance has been required for large companies since 2003.

The state law is

- *California's Notice of Security Breach Law:* If any company or agency that has collected personal information about a California resident discovers that non-encrypted information has been taken by an unauthorized person, the company or agency must tell the resident. Compliance has been required since 2003. (Some 30 other states are considering similar laws.)

COMPETITIVE FACTORS

The competitive environment encompasses the number of competitors a firm must face, the relative size of the competitors, and the degree of interdependence within the industry. Management has little control over the competitive environment confronting a firm.

Competition for Market Share and Profits

As U.S. population growth slows, global competition increases, costs rise, and available resources tighten, firms find that they must work harder to maintain their profits and market share regardless of the form of the competitive market. Take, for example, something as basic as facial tissues. Both Kimberly-Clark and Procter & Gamble go head-to-head in this $1 billion market. Kimberly-Clark is marketing its new, 3-ply tissue as the company's biggest innovation for Kleenex Facial Tissues in four decades. The new Kleenex Facial Tissue with Lotion is softer and 17 percent stronger than its predecessor, the company claims. For P&G, it is the addition of shea butter, a moisturizer, to its Puffs Plus line of lotion tissues, plus new box designs for three of its primary Puffs products. Lotion tissues make up about 20 percent of the facial tissue category and have grown 7 percent between 2006 and 2008.[91]

Kimberly-Clark could use a boost for its Kleenex brand, which saw sales decline 5.9 percent to $495 million in 2008. P&G, meanwhile, saw its Puffs product grow 3.2 percent to $258 million, thanks in large part to its Puffs Plus tissues with lotion, aloe, and vitamin E. Puffs Plus grew 14.7 percent to $136 million.[92] The tissue battle is one of millions that goes on every day in the American marketplace.

American aircraft manufacturer Boeing still faces competition from European company Airbus, even though Airbus recently lost its edge in that $50 billion market. Airbus has been beset with problems, while Boeing's new 787 Dreamliner gave the company a much needed lift. Marketers tout the Dreamliner's features, which include large windows, mood lighting, electronic shades, wider seats and aisles, and a state-of-the-art climate control system, as providing a unique flying experience. By 2007, Boeing had sold over 500 Dreamliners, whereas the huge Airbus A350 lagged far behind. Both Boeing and Airbus have experienced delivery problems. Boeing's difficulties have been due to parts availability and a machinist strike. Airbus has experienced management and logistics problems.

Global Competition

Boeing is a very savvy international competitor conducting business throughout the world. Many foreign competitors also consider the United States to be a ripe target market. Thus, a U.S. marketing manager can no longer focus only on domestic competitors. In automobiles, textiles, watches, televisions, steel, and many other areas, foreign competition has been strong. In the past, foreign firms penetrated U.S. markets by concentrating on price, but today the emphasis has switched to product quality. Nestlé, Sony, Rolls-Royce, and Sandoz Pharmaceuticals are noted for quality, not cheap prices.

For a century, vacuuming has been synonymous with one brand, whose iconic status is such that the British and French still refer to "hoovering the carpet."

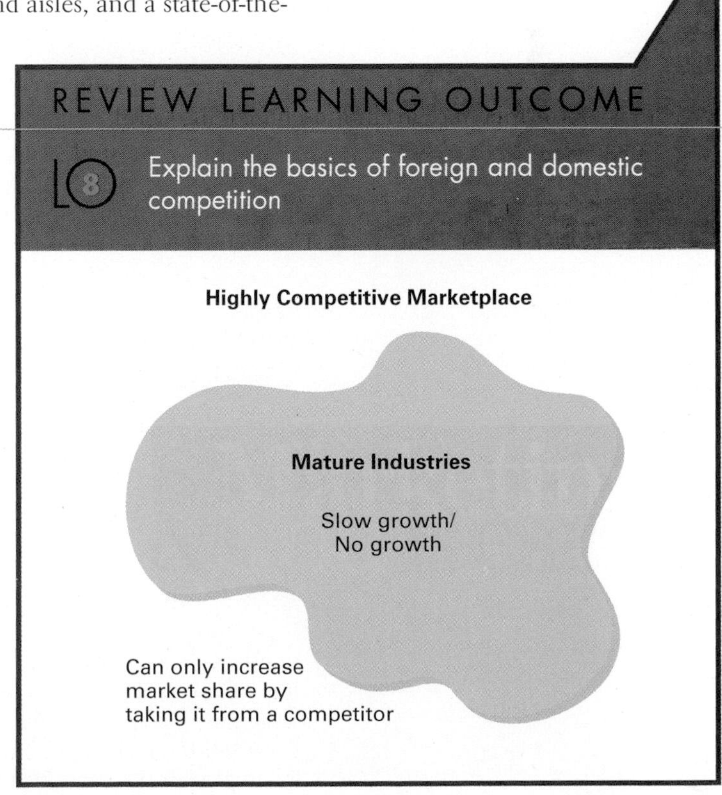

But two years after launching his bagless cleaners in the United States, English inventor James Dyson's company now makes America's best-selling vacuum. Dyson has captured 21 percent of the U.S. market, leaving Canton, Ohio–based Hoover with 16 percent. Dyson's clean sweep is all the more surprising given that his product goes for $399 to $550 while an average vacuum costs $150.[93]

Not all global competitors that enter the U.S. market are successful at taking market share from American firms. In 2004, DHL entered the U.S. market determined to take market share from UPS and FedEx. DHL entered the market by purchasing Airborne, a package delivery service with a weak ground network. When DHL came into the market, it began with a mutlimillion-dollar promotion campaign. The campaign brought DHL a rush of business that it wasn't prepared to handle. As a result, DHL developed a reputation for poor service. To save money, DHL closed one of its two U.S. hubs in 2005 and shifted all traffic to its Wilmington, Ohio, hub. The transition was not smooth, resulting in long delays causing customers to defect to rivals. In late fall 2008, DHL announced that it was stopping domestic deliveries and cutting 9,500 jobs.[94]

Global competition is discussed in much more detail in Chapter 5.

6 ◄ components of the external marketing environment

percent of adult Americans who get less than 7 hours of sleep each night ► **40**

maximum fine the CPSC can issue for violations ▼ **$500,000**

$21 ◄ billion spent by tweens in 2008

56,000 ◄ drivers at UPS

REVIEW AND APPLICATIONS

Discuss the external environment of marketing and explain how it affects a firm. The external marketing environment consists of social, demographic, economic, technological, political and legal, and competitive variables. Marketers generally cannot control the elements of the external environment. Instead, they must understand how the external environment is changing and the impact of that change on the target market. Then marketing managers can create a marketing mix to effectively meet the needs of target customers.

1.1 What is the purpose of environmental scanning? Give an example.

1.2 Form six teams and make each one responsible for one of the uncontrollable elements in the marketing environment. Your boss, the company president, has asked each team to provide one-year and five-year forecasts of the major trends the firm will face. The firm is in the telecommunications equipment industry. It has no plans to become a telecommunications service provider like, for example, Verizon and AT&T. Each team should use the library, the Internet, and other data sources to make its forecasts. Each team member should examine a minimum of one data source. The team members should then pool their data and prepare a recommendation. A spokesperson for each team should present the findings to the class.

Describe the social factors that affect marketing. Within the external environment, social factors are perhaps the most difficult for marketers to anticipate. Several major social trends are currently shaping marketing strategies. First, people of all ages have a broader range of interests, defying traditional consumer profiles. Second, changing gender roles are bringing more women into the workforce and increasing the number of men who shop. Third, an increase in the number of dual-career families has created demand for time-saving goods and services.

2.1 Every country has a set of core values and beliefs. These values may vary somewhat from region to region of the nation. Identify five core values for your area of the country. Clip magazine advertisements that reflect these values and bring them to class.

2.2 Give an example of component lifestyles based on someone you know.

Explain the importance to marketing managers of current demographic trends. Today, several basic demographic patterns are influencing marketing mixes. Because the U.S. population is growing at a slower rate, marketers can no longer rely on profits from generally expanding markets. Marketers are also faced with increasingly experienced consumers among the younger generations such as tweens and teens. And because the population is also growing older, marketers are offering more products that appeal to middle-aged and older consumers.

3.1 Baby boomers in America are aging. Describe how this might affect the marketing mix for the following:

a. Bally's Health Clubs

b. McDonald's

c. Whirlpool Corporation

d. The state of Florida

e. Target stores

3.2 You have been asked to address a local Chamber of Commerce on the subject of "Generation Y." Prepare an outline for your talk.

3.3 How should Ford Motor Company market differently to Generation Y, Generation X, and baby boomers?

Explain the importance to marketing managers of multiculturalism and growing ethnic markets. Multiculturalism occurs when all major ethnic groups in an area are roughly equally represented. Growing multiculturalism makes the marketer's task more challenging. America is not a melting pot but numerous mini-melting pots. Hispanics are the fastest-growing segment of the population followed by African Americans. Many companies are now creating departments and product lines to effectively target multicultural market segments. Companies have quickly found that ethnic markets are not homogeneous.

4.1 Go to the library and look up a minority market such as the Hispanic market. Write a memo to your boss that details the many submarkets within this segment.

4.2 Using the library and the Internet, find examples of large companies directing marketing mixes to each major ethnic group.

Identify consumer and marketer reactions to the state of the economy. In recent years, U.S. incomes have risen at a slow pace. At the same time, the financial power of women has increased, and they are making the purchasing decisions for many products in traditionally male-dominated areas. During a time of inflation, marketers generally attempt to maintain level pricing to avoid losing customer brand loyalty. During times of recession, many marketers maintain or reduce prices to counter the effects of decreased demand; they also concentrate on increasing production efficiency and improving customer service.

5.1 Explain how consumers' buying habits may change during a recessionary period.

5.2 Periods of inflation require firms to alter their marketing mix. Suppose a recent economic forecast predicts that inflation will be almost 10 percent during the next 18 months. Your company manufactures hand tools for the home gardener. Write a memo to the company president explaining how the firm may have to alter its marketing mix.

Identify the impact of technology on a firm. Monitoring new technology is essential to keeping up with competitors in today's marketing environment. The United States excels in basic research and, in recent years, has dramatically improved its track record in applied research. Without innovation, U.S. companies can't compete in global markets. Innovation is increasingly becoming a global process.

6.1 Give three examples of how technology has benefited marketers. Also, give several examples of firms that have been hurt because they did not keep up with technological changes.

Discuss the political and legal environment of marketing. All marketing activities are subject to state and federal laws and the rulings of regulatory agencies. Marketers are responsible for remaining aware of and abiding by such regulations. Some key federal laws that affect marketing are the Sherman Act, Clayton Act, Federal Trade Commission Act, Robinson-Patman Act, Wheeler-Lea Amendments to the FTC Act, Lanham Act, Celler-Kefauver Antimerger Act, and Hart-Scott-Rodino Act. Many laws, including privacy laws, have been passed to protect the consumer as well. The Consumer Product Safety Commission, the Federal Trade Commission, and the Food and Drug Administration are the three federal agencies most involved in regulating marketing activities.

7.1 The Federal Trade Commission and other governmental agencies have been both praised and criticized for their regulation of marketing activities.

To what degree do you think the government should regulate marketing? Explain your position.

7.2 Can you think of any other areas where consumer protection laws are needed?

7.3 What topics are currently receiving attention in FDA News (**www.fdanews.com**)? What effect has the attention had on market share?

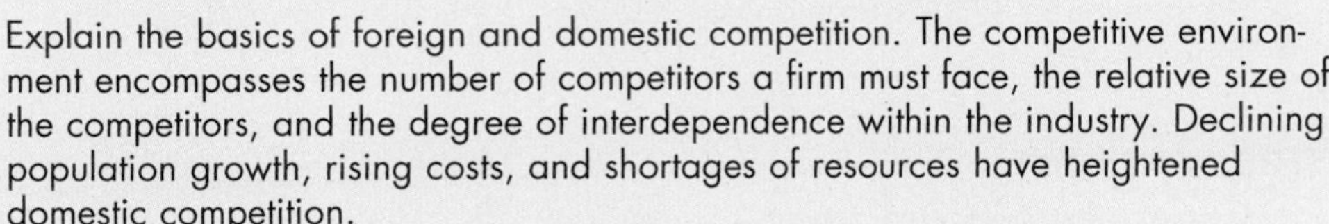

Explain the basics of foreign and domestic competition. The competitive environment encompasses the number of competitors a firm must face, the relative size of the competitors, and the degree of interdependence within the industry. Declining population growth, rising costs, and shortages of resources have heightened domestic competition.

8.1 Explain how the nature of competition is changing in America.

8.2 Might there be times when a company becomes too competitive? If so, what could be the consequences?

KEY TERMS

EXERCISES

APPLICATION EXERCISE

Demographic factors play a large role in shaping the external marketing environment. One of those demographic factors is culture. The importance of cultural understanding cannot be overstated, especially in today's global marketplace and our own multicultural country. In general, Americans tend to be ethnocentric; that is, they are quick to prejudge other cultural norms as wrong (or of less significance) because they differ from American practices.

One way to be exposed to another culture is to examine the foods typical of that culture. In this exercise, you will need to work in a team to create a guide to ethnic dining in your city or area. The finished guide will be descriptive in nature; it is not meant to be a rating guide.

Activities

1. Identify ethnic dining categories for inclusion in your guide. Once you have identified categories for your area, make a list of restaurants for each category.

2. You will need to create a data collection form so that the same information is collected from each restaurant. For example, you will want to include the name, address, and phone number for each restaurant. Think of other information that would be helpful.

3. Divide up the restaurant list your team generated in Activity 1 so that each team member is responsible for collecting information from a certain number of restaurants. Consider dividing the list geographically so that each team member can visit an assortment of ethnic restaurants. If your budget allows, eat at a few of the restaurants in addition to collecting the information. After you have all the information, meet to review and compare your findings.
4. Was there a meal or type of food that you particularly liked? Disliked? Which type of ethnic restaurant seemed most foreign to you? Why do you think that was?

ETHICS EXERCISE

Gary Caplan has developed a new "energy drink" designed to burn calories while sleeping, which he intends to market to grossly overweight consumers. According the Centers for Disease Control and Prevention, 20 percent of Americans are obese. Gary's mother, a doctor, argues that it's unethical to target the obese—that they are as vulnerable a target market as much as the elderly and children.

Questions

1. Is Gary targeting a "vulnerable" market?
2. Does the AMA Statement of Ethics address this issue? Go to **www.marketingpower.com** and review the statement. Then write a brief paragraph on what it contains that relates to Gary Caplan's marketing decision.

MARKETING PLAN EXERCISE

These end-of-chapter marketing plan exercises are designed to help you use what you learned in the chapter to build a strategic marketing plan for a company of your choosing. Once you've completed the marketing plan exercise for each chapter in Part 1 of this textbook, you can complete the Part 1 Marketing Planning Worksheet on your companion Web site at **www.cengage.com/international.** Now continue building your strategic marketing plan that you started in Chapter 2 by completing the following exercises:

1. Describe how your company will handle privacy concerns.
2. Scan the marketing environment. Identify opportunities and threats to your chosen company in areas such as technology, the economy, the political and legal environment, and competition. Is your competition foreign, domestic, or both? Also identify opportunities and threats based on possible market targets, including social factors, demographic factors, and multicultural issues.
3. Complete your company's SWOT analysis by identifying opportunities and threats in the external marketing environment by performing environmental scanning:
    a. List the demographic, ethnic, and social trends that could impact your firm, by investigating data from the U.S. Census Bureau at **www.census.gov.**
    b. Determine which economic factors could influence the strategies of your firm by visiting the U.S. Economic and Statistics Administration at **www.esa.doc.gov** or the Bureau of Economic Analysis at **www.bea.doc.gov.**
    c. Explore **www.lawguru.com** and report on at least three political and legal factors that could influence your marketing decisions.

d. Investigate the Web sites of federal government agencies that regulate your firm and industry and list at least six laws that regulate your business offering. The Federal Trade Commission is at **www.ftc.gov.** The Federal Communications Commission is at **www.fcc.gov.** The Food and Drug Administration is at **www.fda.gov.** The Consumer Product Safety Commission is at **www.cpsc.gov.** The Better Business Bureau is at **www.bbb.org.** The Internal Revenue Service is at **www.irs.gov.**

e. Identify your key competitors. A simple "yellow pages" listing of firms in the same business category can start your search. For online competitors, try **www.bizrate.com.**

f. Competition often comes from companies that are working on the same exact market as yours. That is especially true on the Internet. After you search for your direct competition, look for and think about what other companies are positioned to execute a similar business strategy for your target market. Determine if there are any players who might be able to develop technology more quickly or reach your target customers more effectively than you.

CASE STUDY: STARBUCKS

SELLING COFFEE IN THE LAND OF TEA

Starbucks has been doing business in China since 1999 when they opened their first coffee shop in Beijing. Today, hundreds of Starbucks stores sell coffee in the land of tea, including one at the Great Wall. It has become one of the most popular brands among the country's 20- to 40-year-old upwardly mobile Chinese, or "Chuppies," as they're called, but so far China accounts for only about 10 percent of Starbucks' global sales. Nevertheless, Chairman Howard Schultz believes the country will someday be the company's largest market outside North America. "The market response," he says, "has exceeded our expectations."

This may seem surprising when you consider the fact that the majority of China's one billion-plus population are tea drinkers who didn't know what coffee was until Nestlé introduced a powdered version on store shelves in the 1980s. But Starbucks is betting that it can win the new generation over by marketing its signature product as an emblem of modern China's new sophistication.

"Coffee represents the change," says Wang Jinlong, president of Starbucks Greater China. "The disposable income is concentrated on the young people, and this is the place they want to come." Success in China could depend on how well Starbucks markets itself to what Wang calls the "little emperors." China's one-child law has spawned a generation that isn't interested in collective goals, he says. Instead, they embrace the Western belief in individuality that Starbucks embodies.

After surveying Chinese consumers, Starbucks compiled a list of the top reasons they go to cafés. Surprisingly, the number one reason was "to gather with family and friends," while "to drink coffee" lagged behind at number six. Living spaces are generally small and cramped there, making places to congregate important to the Chinese.

Da Wei Sun, manager of outlets in Beijing, believes that Starbucks found success in China because it took this idea of a place to gather and gave people in the cities a "third space" beyond work and home, making it cool to have a latte and hang out. Starbucks offers more food on the Chinese menu, including duck sandwiches, moon pies, and green-tea cheesecake, than in other countries, and more seating as well. Only 20 percent of North American customers eat and drink inside the store after ordering, but the number is close to 90 percent in China.

China remains a communist country, so a change in its one-party dictatorship could potentially affect business overnight. Schultz says the key to establishing stores there is to first find local partners who understand the changing political and business landscapes. Starbucks initially entered China by authorizing local developers to use its brand and setting up joint ventures with partners.

Industry analyst Pei Liang advised that for long-term success in the country, Starbucks would need to acquire controlling stakes in its joint ventures. This, Pei explained, would strengthen management's control and put it in position to reap more of the profits as the market grew. "Licensing or holding a minority stake is an effective tool when first stepping into a new market because it involves a small investment," says Pei. "But Starbucks, the brand's owner, receives only royalty fees from the licensee."

In late 2006, Starbucks announced that it was buying out its partner in China and taking control of 60 stores. The market had changed after Beijing entered the World Trade Organization in 2001, making it easier for foreign companies to navigate alone. "Buying out one's partner is becoming more common," says industry consultant Kent D. Kedl. "Starbucks probably feels they *sic* know better how China works now so they *sic* can go it on their own."

Chairman Howard Schultz says that Starbucks will concentrate most of its future expansion efforts in China, and Kedl predicts it will see continued success there: "It's not just a drink in China. It's a destination. It's a place to be seen and a place to show how modern one is." And with China's economy continuing to grow in double digits, the number of Chuppies willing to pay $3.63 for a Mocha Frappuccino Grande is likely to grow, too.

Source: "Starbucks Targets Growing China Market," *AsiaPulse News*, 6/13/2006; Janet Adamy, "Starbucks' Task China? Winning Over Tea Drinkers," *The Seattle Times*, 11/30/2006; Jeffrey S. Harrison, "Exporting a North American Concept to Asia", *Cornell Hotel & Restaurant Quarterly*, May 2005; Craig Harris, "Starbucks Sees China as Key to Its International Growth," *Seattle Post-Intelligencer*, 10/7/2006; Dexter Roberts, "Starbucks Caffeinates Its China Growth Plan," *Business Week Online*, 10/26/2006.

Questions

1. Many of the same environmental factors, such as cultural factors, that operate in the domestic market also exist internationally. Discuss the key cultural factors Starbucks had to consider as it expanded into China.
2. Discuss the key political and legal factors Starbucks had to consider in the Chinese marketplace. What are the risks of entering a country with these factors? What changes have occurred in China's political and legal structure to the advantage of foreign companies?
3. What demographic factors were important for Starbucks to understand in China? What were the demographics they decided to target?
4. What was the initial global-market strategy Starbucks employed to enter China? Discuss the advantages and disadvantages to this early strategy. How has their strategy changed since then and why?

COMPANY CLIPS

METHOD—ENTERING A CROWDED MARKET

Companies large and small, new and old are all participants in the market, and as such, they are all subject to the forces that act on each entity in the marketplace. The same is true of method. As you've already seen in the company clips from Chapters 2 and 3, method has been attentive to the customer, analyzed the competition, focused on social change, and identified economic factors that have affected how it does and will do business. Review the company clips from Chapters 2 and 3 to hear founders Adam Lowry and Eric Ryan and CEO Alastair Dorward describe several factors in the external environment that have influenced how method entered the market and the success the company has experienced.

© NKP MEDIA, INC./CENGAGE

Questions

1. Method's founders and CEO repeatedly reference the role of competition and consumers in their assessments of their external environment. Is there a hierarchy to the environmental factors discussed in this chapter? Explain.
2. Should other companies imitate the emphasis method gives to certain factors in its external environment? Why or why not?
3. Does method's assessment of its external environment seem to be lacking anything? What?

Marketing & You Results

A high score means you have a strong perception of time limitations for work-related task completion. Research indicates that when you perceive yourself to be working under time pressure your creativity is negatively affected. As you read in Chapter 4, time is an important social factor in the external environment that affects marketing. Understanding your own perceptions and reaction to time constraints will be helpful in planning to meet the needs of the time-constrained consumer. Your challenge as a busy marketer will be to continue thinking creatively on their behalf.

© JOHN WILKES/SUPERSTOCK

CHAPTER 5

Developing a Global Vision

LEARNING OUTCOMES

- LO 1 Discuss the importance of global marketing
- LO 2 Discuss the impact of multinational firms on the world economy
- LO 3 Describe the external environment facing global marketers
- LO 4 Identify the various ways of entering the global marketplace
- LO 5 List the basic elements involved in developing a global marketing mix
- LO 6 Discover how the Internet is affecting global marketing

REWARDS OF GLOBAL MARKETING

Today, global revolutions are under way in many areas of our lives such as management, politics, communications, and technology. The word *global* has assumed a new meaning, referring to a boundless mobility and competition in social, business, and intellectual arenas. No longer just an option, **global marketing**—marketing that targets markets throughout the world—has become imperative for business.

U.S. managers must develop a global vision not only to recognize and react to international marketing opportunities but also to remain competitive at home. Often a U.S. firm's toughest domestic competition comes from foreign companies. Moreover, a global vision enables a manager to understand that customer and distribution networks operate worldwide, blurring geographic and political barriers and making them increasingly irrelevant to business decisions. In summary, having a **global vision** means recognizing and reacting to international marketing opportunities, using effective global marketing strategies, and being aware of threats from foreign competitors in all markets.

Over the past two decades, global trade has climbed from $200 billion a year to over $11 trillion. Countries and companies that were never considered major players in global marketing are now important, and some of them show great skill.

Today, marketers face many challenges to their customary practices. Product development costs are rising, the life of products is getting shorter, and new technology is spreading around the world faster than ever. But marketing winners relish the pace of change instead of fearing it.

An example of a young company with a global vision that has capitalized on new technology is Ashtech in Sunnyvale, California. Ashtech makes equipment to capture and convert satellite signals from the U.S. government's Global Positioning System. Ashtech's chief engineer and his team of ten torture and test everything built by Ashtech—expensive black boxes of chips and circuits that use satellite signals to tell surveyors, farmers, mining machine operators, and others where they are with great accuracy. Over half of Ashtech's output is exported. Its biggest customer is Japan.

Adopting a global vision can be very lucrative for a company. Gillette, for example, gets about two-thirds of its revenue from its international division. H. J. Heinz, the ketchup company, gets over half of its revenue from international sales. Although Cheetos and Ruffles haven't done very well in Japan, the potato chip has been quite successful. PepsiCo's (owner of Frito-Lay) overseas snack business brings in more than $3.25 billion annually. The William Wrigley Jr. Company, makers of Wrigley's Spearmint, Juicy Fruit, Altoids, Life Savers, and other products, has global annual sales of over $4.7 billion.[1]

Another company with a global vision is Pillsbury. The Pillsbury Doughboy is used in India to sell a product that the company had just about abandoned in America: flour. Pillsbury (owned by General Mills) has many higher-margin products

Marketing & You

How would you describe your interest in other cultures? Enter your answers on the lines provided.

1	2	3	4	5	6	7
Strongly disagree			Neither disagree nor agree			Strongly agree

___ I would like to have opportunities to meet people from other countries.

___ I am very interested in trying food from different countries.

___ We should have a respect for traditions, cultures, and ways of life of other nations.

___ I would like to learn more about other countries.

___ I have a strong desire for overseas travel.

___ I would like to know more about foreign cultures and customs.

___ I have a strong desire to meet and interact with people from foreign countries.

Now, total your score. Read the chapter, and find out what your score means at the end.

Source: From Scale #98, *Marketing Scales Handbook*, G. Bruner, K. James, H. Hensel, eds., Vol. III. © by American Marketing Association.

global marketing
Marketing that targets markets throughout the world.

global vision
Recognizing and reacting to international marketing opportunities, using effective global marketing strategies, and being aware of threats from foreign competitors in all markets.

such as microwave pizzas in other parts of the world, but it discovered that in this tradition-bound market, it needed to push the basics.

Even so, selling packaged flour in India has been almost revolutionary, because most Indian housewives still buy raw wheat in bulk, clean it by hand, store it in huge metal hampers, and, every week, carry some to a neighborhood mill, or *chakki*, where it is ground between two stones.

To help reach those housewives, the Doughboy himself has gotten a makeover. In TV advertising, he presses his palms together and bows in the traditional Indian greeting. He speaks six regional languages.

Global marketing is not a one-way street, whereby only U.S. companies sell their wares and services throughout the world. Foreign competition in the domestic market used to be relatively rare but now is found in almost every industry. In fact, in many industries U.S. businesses have lost significant market share to imported products. In electronics, cameras, automobiles, fine china, tractors, leather goods, and a host of other consumer and industrial products, U.S. companies have struggled at home to maintain their market shares against foreign competitors. In 2007, Toyota became the number one automobile company in the American market.

Importance of Global Marketing to the United States

Many countries depend more on international commerce than the United States does. For example, France, Britain, and Germany all derive more than 19 percent of their gross domestic product (GDP) from world trade, compared to about 12 percent for the United States. Nevertheless, the impact of international business on the U.S. economy is still impressive:

- The United States exports about a fifth of its industrial production.
- One in every five jobs in the United States is directly or indirectly supported by exports.[2]
- Every U.S. state has realized net employment gains directly attributed to foreign trade.[3]
- U.S. businesses export over $800 billion in goods to foreign countries every year, and almost a third of U.S. corporate profits comes from international trade and foreign investment.
- Exports account for 25 percent of U.S. economic growth.
- The United States is the world's leading exporter of farm products, selling more than $60 billion in agricultural exports to foreign countries each year.
- Chemicals, office machinery and computers, automobiles, aircraft, and electrical and industrial machinery make up almost half of all nonagricultural exports.
- About half of U.S. merchandise imports are raw materials, capital goods, and industrial products used by U.S. manufacturers to make goods in the United States.[4] America is the world's largest importer.
- America exports over $1.6 trillion in goods and services each year.[5]

These statistics might seem to imply that practically every business in the United States is selling its wares throughout the world, but nothing could be further from the truth. About 85 percent of all U.S. exports of manufactured goods are shipped by 250 companies; less than 10 percent of all manufacturing businesses, or around 25,000 companies, export their goods on a regular basis. Most small and medium-size firms are essentially nonparticipants in global trade and marketing. Only the very large multinational companies have seriously attempted to compete worldwide. Fortunately, more of the smaller companies are now aggressively pursuing international markets.

The Fear of Trade and Globalization

© AP IMAGES/EYEPRESS

The protests during meetings of the World Trade Organization, the World Bank, and the International Monetary Fund (the three organizations are discussed later in the chapter) show that many people fear world trade and globalization. What do they fear? The negatives of global trade are as follows:

- Millions of Americans have lost jobs due to imports, production shifts abroad, or outsourcing of tech jobs. Most find new jobs—that often pay less.
- Millions of others fear losing their jobs, especially at those companies operating under competitive pressure.
- Employers often threaten to outsource jobs if workers do not accept pay cuts.
- Service and white-collar jobs are increasingly vulnerable to operations moving offshore.

Jobs Outsourcing The notion of jobs outsourcing (sending U.S. jobs abroad) has been highly controversial for the past several years. Many executives say that it is about corporate growth, efficiency, productivity, and revenue growth. Most companies see cost savings as a key driver in outsourcing. While India, because of its educated, English-speaking population, has always been a popular country for receiving offshoring work, other countries are gaining as well.

While many corporations are excited about the advantages of offshoring, politicians, unions, and workers are not. Alan Blinder, former Federal Reserve vice-chairman, says as many as 40 million jobs may be shipped out of the country in the next decade or two.[6] That is more than double the total of workers employed in manufacturing today. Dr. Blinder notes that new communications technology allows services to be delivered electronically from afar. His list of "highly offshorable jobs" are

Occupation	Number of U.S. Workers[7]
Computer programmers	389,090
Data entry keyers	296,700
Actuaries	15,770
Film and video editors	15,200
Mathematicians	2,930
Medical transcriptionists	90,380
Interpreters and translators	21,930
Economists	12,490
Graphic designers	178,530
Bookkeeping, accounting, and auditing clerks	1,815,340
Microbiologists	15,250
Financial analysts	180,910

Source: Reprinted with permission of *The Wall Street Journal* from David Wessel and Bob Davis, "Job Prospects: Pain From Free Trade Spurs Second Thoughts," *Wall Street Journal*, March 28, 2007, p. A1. Copyright © 2007 Dow Jones & Company, Inc. All Rights Reserved Worldwide.

Other economists strongly disagree with Dr. Blinder. Dr. Jagdish Bhagwati, Colombia University, says, "He's dead wrong. I have no doubt that we are creating far more jobs than we are losing."[8]

The Loss of Skill, Technology, and Manufacturing Facilities Wages in China are rising 10 to 15 percent a year, and shipping costs have risen dramatically around the globe. The cost of sending a 40-foot shipping container from Shanghai to San Diego has soared 150 percent to $5,500 since 2000. Also, the value of the U.S. dollar has fallen dramatically against the Chinese yuan and the euro during the same period.

This makes imports into the U.S. more expensive. All of these factors make the possibility of manufacturing in the United States more attractive than in the past.[9]

The problem is that many American factories and supplier networks withered away during the period of globalization. An American inventor has created a long-lasting, fast-charging battery for notebook computers that may revolutionize the industry. The company, Boston-Power, would like to make the batteries in the Unites States. However, there are no battery factories left! Yet in China there are more than 200 battery manufacturers with plenty of workers and laboratories.[10]

Rising costs in China are eroding the 40 to 50 percent cost advantage it once had. Yet, the migration of manufacturing back to America may be a long and slow process. Even companies such as Donso, a Pennsylvania manufacturer of oil rig parts and gear boxes, is flooded with orders after years of losing business to China. But the firm is reluctant to spend $30 million to build a new foundry because of what has happened in the past. Many goods, such as toys, small appliances, and clothing, will probably never be produced in huge quantities in America because they are very labor-intensive. While there is no doubt that some manufacturers will return to the states as China's cost advantage slips further, perhaps America's best opportunity is in keeping new technologies from ever leaving the country. It is important for the United States to remain in the forefront of innovation in areas such as nanotechnology, solid state lighting, and renewable energy. It should be economically feasible to produce the goods resulting from the technology in the Unites States.

Benefits of Globalization

Traditional economic theory says that globalization relies on competition to drive down prices and increase product and service quality. Business goes to the countries that operate most efficiently and/or have the technology to produce what is needed.

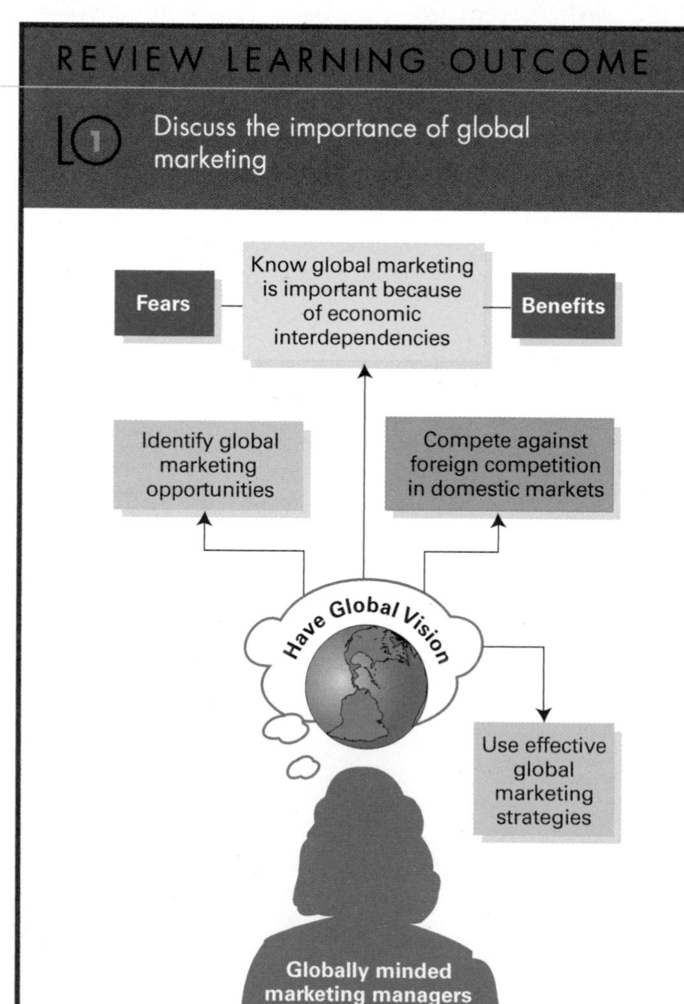

In summary, globalization expands economic freedom, spurs competition, and raises the productivity and living standards of people in countries that open themselves to the global marketplace. For less developed countries, globalization also offers access to foreign capital, global export markets, and advanced technology while breaking the monopoly of inefficient and protected domestic producers. Faster growth, in turn, reduces poverty, encourages democratization, and promotes higher labor and environmental standards. Though government officials may face more difficult choices as a result of globalization, their citizens enjoy greater individual freedom. In this sense, globalization acts as a check on governmental power by making it more difficult for governments to abuse the freedom and property of their citizens.

Globalization deserves credit for helping lift many millions out of poverty and for improving standards of living of low-wage families. In developing countries around the world, globalization has created a vibrant middle class that has elevated the standards of living for hundreds of millions of people. That's particularly true in China, where the incomes of low-skilled workers have consistently risen. The poor in countries like Vietnam and elsewhere in Southeast Asia have also benefited greatly since those countries have opened their economies. In many developing countries around the world, life expectancies and health care have improved, as have educational opportunities.[11]

MULTINATIONAL FIRMS

The United States has a number of large companies that are global marketers. Many of them have been very successful. A company that is heavily engaged in international trade, beyond exporting and importing, is called a **multinational corporation**. Multinational corporations move resources, goods, services, and skills across national boundaries without regard to the country in which the headquarters is located. Many U.S.-based multinationals earn a large percentage of their total revenue abroad, as shown in Exhibit 5.1. ExxonMobil earns a huge 72 percent of its revenue outside the United States. In contrast, America's largest firm, Wal-Mart, has 24 percent of its sales outside the country.

Are multinationals good for the United States? Certainly not everyone agrees on this topic, but researchers estimate that multinationals pay workers 6 percent more on average than domestic companies.[12] In addition, multinationals tend to be better managed and less aggressive about cutting jobs than comparable domestic firms.[13] This may be because American multinationals tend to keep research and development and headquarters in the United States.

Yet multinationals are not without their critics. Even though they are less aggressive about cutting jobs, they have removed over two million jobs in the United States while adding jobs overseas.[14] Also, some multinationals have shifted income to low-tax countries, which has reduced corporate income tax payments in America. The multinationals claim that this was necessary because the United States has a very complicated tax structure with one of the highest corporate income tax rates among industrialized nations.

multinational corporation
A company that is heavily engaged in international trade, beyond exporting and importing.

Multinationals often develop their global business in stages. In the first stage, companies operate in one country and sell into others. Second-stage multinationals set up foreign subsidiaries to handle sales in one country. In the third stage, they operate an entire line of business in another country. The fourth stage has evolved primarily due to the Internet and involves mostly high-tech companies. For these firms, the executive suite is virtual. Their top executives and core corporate functions are in different countries, wherever the firms can gain a competitive edge through the availability of talent or capital, low costs, or proximity to their most important customers.

A good example of a fourth-stage company is Trend Micro, an Internet antivirus software company. Its top executives, engineers, and support staff are spread around the world so that they can respond quickly to new virus threats—which can start anywhere and spread like wildfire. The main virus response center is in the Philippines, where 250 ever-vigilant engineers work evening and midnight shifts as needed. Six other labs are scattered from Munich to Tokyo.

Trend Micro's financial headquarters is in Tokyo, where it went public; product development is in PhD-rich Taiwan; and most of its sales are in Silicon Valley—inside the giant American market. When companies fragment this way, they are no longer limited to the strengths, or hobbled by the weaknesses, of their native lands.

Such fourth-stage multinationals are being created around the world. They include business-intelligence-software maker Business Objects, with headquarters in France and San

EXHIBIT 5.1

America's Largest Firms That Earn At Least Thirty Percent of Their Revenue Abroad

	Revenue in Billions	Percent Foreign
ExxonMobil	$372.8	72.2
Hewlett-Packard	104.3	66.6
Dow Chemical	53.5	65.9
Chevron	210.8	65.7
Intl. Business Machines	98.8	63.0
Procter & Gamble	76.5	58.2
American Intl. Group	110.1	57.8
Ford Motor	172.5	53.1
United Technologies	54.8	51.0
General Electric	176.7	49.0
Johnson & Johnson	61.1	46.9
General Motors	182.3	44.2
Boeing	66.4	40.7
Dell	61.1	38.9
Microsoft	51.1	38.7
ConocoPhillips	178.6	31.4

Source: "As the World Turns," *Fortune*, May 5, 2008, 225.

capital-intensive
Using more capital than labor in the production process.

Jose, California; Wipro, a tech-services supplier with headquarters in India and Santa Clara, California; and computer-peripherals maker Logitech International, with headquarters in Switzerland and Fremont, California.

A multinational company may have several worldwide headquarters, depending on where certain markets or technologies are. Britain's APV, a maker of food-processing equipment, has a different headquarters for each of its worldwide businesses. ABB Asea Brown Boveri, the European electrical engineering giant based in Zurich, Switzerland, groups its thousands of products and services into 50 or so business areas. Each is run by a leadership team that crafts global business strategy, sets product development priorities, and decides where to make its products. None of the teams work out of the Zurich headquarters; instead, they are scattered around the world. Leadership for power transformers is based in Germany, electric drives in Finland, and process automation in the United States.

The role of multinational corporations in developing nations is a subject of controversy. Multinationals' ability to tap financial, physical, and human resources from all over the world and combine them economically and profitably can be of benefit to any country. They also often possess and can transfer the most up-to-date technology. Critics, however, claim that often the wrong kind of technology is transferred to developing nations. Usually, it is **capital-intensive** (requiring a greater expenditure for equipment than for labor) and thus does not substantially increase employment. A "modern sector" then emerges in the nation, employing a small proportion of the labor force at relatively high productivity and income levels and with increasingly capital-intensive technologies. In addition, multinationals sometimes support reactionary and oppressive regimes if it is in their best interests to do so. Other critics say that the firms take more wealth out of developing nations than they bring in, thus widening the gap between rich and poor nations. The petroleum industry in particular has been heavily criticized in the past for its actions in some developing countries.

To counter such criticism, more and more multinationals are taking a proactive role in being good global citizens. Sometimes companies are spurred to action by government regulation, and in other cases multinationals are attempting to protect their good brand name.

Blocking Foreign Investment

A new backlash against multinational corporations is that governments from China to Canada are placing restrictions on foreign purchases of factories, land, and companies in their countries. This has a major impact on U.S. multinationals because they serve foreign markets primarily through sales in their foreign affiliates and not through exports from the United States. The foreign affiliates manufacture and sell goods locally and rely on local labor and distribution to reach nearby customers.

These new barriers to ownership are partially due to a backlash against globalization. Perhaps more important is the view that the United States is erecting barriers to foreign investment. In 2006, a Dubai-owned company tried to buy operations at five American ports, and the year before, the state-owned Chinese oil company Cnooc Ltd. tried to buy California-based oil giant Unocal Corp. Both deals were ultimately voided amid uproar. This prompted Congress to pass legislation to subject foreign investment in the United States, or CFIUS, to review by an interagency council that screens foreign purchases of U.S. assets with national-security implications.[15]

Now China's new regulations let government officials block a local purchase by a multinational if it is a danger to "economic security." Russia has considered blocking foreign ownership in 39 "strategic sectors" of its economy. If more countries begin to block foreign investment by multinationals, it will definitely have a noticeable impact on global trade.

Global Marketing Standardization

Traditionally, marketing-oriented multinational corporations have operated somewhat differently in each country. They use a strategy of providing different product features, packaging, advertising, and so on. However, Ted Levitt, a former Harvard professor, described a trend toward what he referred to as "global marketing," with a slightly different meaning.[16]

He contended that communication and technology have made the world smaller so that almost all consumers everywhere want all the things they have heard about, seen, or experienced. Thus, he saw the emergence of global markets for standardized consumer products on a huge scale, as opposed to segmented foreign markets with different products. In this book, global marketing is defined as individuals and organizations using a global vision to effectively market goods and services across national boundaries. To make the distinction, we can refer to Levitt's notion as **global marketing standardization.**

Global marketing standardization presumes that the markets throughout the world are becoming more alike. Firms practicing global marketing standardization produce "globally standardized products" to be sold the same way all over the world. Uniform production should enable companies to lower production and marketing costs and increase profits. Levitt cited Coca-Cola, Colgate-Palmolive, and McDonald's as successful global marketers. His critics point out, however, that the success of these three companies is really based on variation, not on offering the same product everywhere. McDonald's, for example, changes its salad dressings and provides self-serve espresso for French tastes. It sells bulgogi burgers in South Korea and falafel burgers in Egypt. It also offers different products to suit tastes in Germany (where it offers beer) and Japan (where it offers sake). Further, the fact that Coca-Cola and Colgate-Palmolive sell some of their products in more than 160 countries does not signify that they have adopted a high degree of standardization for all their products globally. Only three Coca-Cola brands are standardized, and one of them, Sprite, has a different formulation in Japan. Some Colgate-Palmolive products are marketed in just a few countries. Axion paste dishwashing detergent, for example, was formulated for developing countries, and La Croix Plus detergent was custom made for the French market. Colgate toothpaste is marketed the same way globally, although its advanced Gum Protection Formula is used in only 27 nations.

> *"Ted Levitt, a former Harvard professor, contended that communication and technology have made the world smaller so that almost all consumers everywhere want all the things they have heard about, seen, or experienced."*

Nevertheless, some multinational corporations are moving toward a degree of global marketing standardization. 3M markets some of its industrial tapes the same way around the globe. Procter & Gamble calls its new philosophy "global planning." The idea is to determine which product modifications are necessary from country to country while trying to minimize those modifications. P&G has at least four products that are marketed similarly in most parts of the world: Camay soap, Crest toothpaste, Head and Shoulders shampoo, and Pampers diapers. However, the smell of Camay, the flavor of Crest, and the formula of Head and Shoulders, as well as the advertising, vary from country to country.

global marketing standardization
Production of uniform products that can be sold the same way all over the world.

One of the latest attempts at global marketing standardization is Levi's with its button-fly 501 jeans. It has retooled its factories so that the 501 will have the same fit in all 110 countries where it sells jeans. It also launched its first global marketing campaign in which print and television ads contained the same theme, content, and slogan, "Live Unbuttoned," the world over. In some cases, the actors were changed to resemble the populace in the country where the ad was being presented.

Levi Strauss says the fabric on the jeans is designed to mold to the wearer's body, regardless of body shape, which will help to account for differences in body type. The company also says it will continue to tailor the sizes offered to different parts of the world.[17]

A scene from one of Levi's 501 "Live Unbuttoned" global television ads. The "unbuttoned" campaign went global to reach a new generation of jeans consumers around the world.

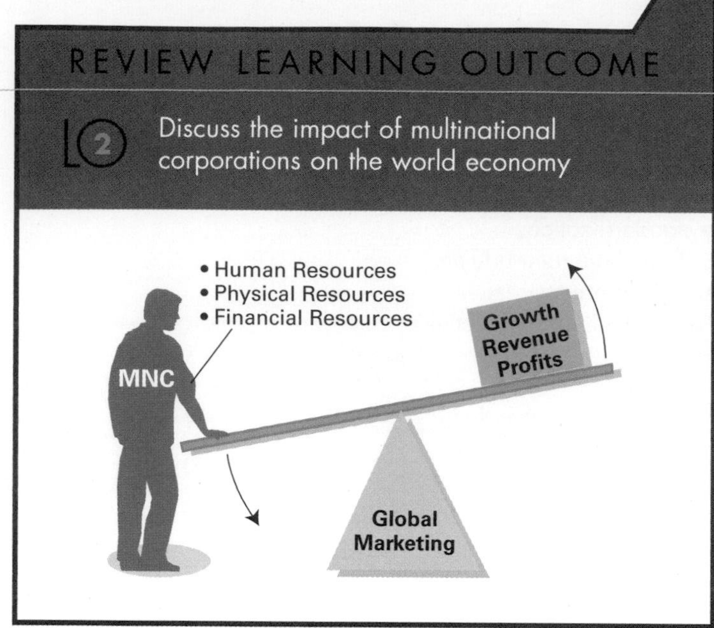

Levi Strauss has long played the localization game just like most other companies. It has had creative teams in different regions that tinkered with the fit of its 501 jeans to cater to local tastes and fads. A 501 jean bought in New York sometimes had a different fit and look than one bought in Hong Kong. And because the Levi's brand has stood for different things in different places, the marketing message has varied by location. In Europe, where the company ran separate ad campaigns, Levi Strauss is considered premium denim, and its five-pocket 501s are more expensive there. But in America, a Levi's 501 jean is considered more of a staple, and ads have consistently alluded to Levi Strauss's American roots.[18]

Why is Levi's pursuing global marketing standardization? Because it is cheaper to have a single promotional campaign and to produce, sell, and market one kind of jeans than dozens of varieties of the same product.

EXTERNAL ENVIRONMENT FACING GLOBAL MARKETERS

A global marketer or a firm considering global marketing must consider the external environment. Many of the same environmental factors that operate in the domestic market also exist internationally. These factors include culture, economic and technological development, political structure and actions, demographic makeup, and natural resources.

Culture

Central to any society is the common set of values shared by its citizens that determines what is socially acceptable. Culture underlies the family, the educational system, religion, and the social class system. The network of social organizations generates overlapping roles and status positions. These values and roles have a tremendous effect on people's preferences and thus on marketers' options. A company that does not understand a country's culture is doomed to failure in that country. Cultural blunders lead to misunderstandings and often perceptions of rudeness or even incompetence. For example, when people in India shake hands, they sometimes do so rather limply. This isn't a sign of weakness or disinterest; instead, a soft handshake conveys respect. Avoiding eye contact is also a sign of deference in India.

© BETTMANN/CORBIS

A U.S. luggage manufacturer found out that culture also affects thinking and perception. The company designed a new Middle East advertising campaign around the image of its luggage being carried on a magic flying carpet. Many of the participants in a group in a marketing research study thought they were seeing advertising for Samsonite *carpets*. Green Giant learned that it could not use its Jolly Green Giant in parts of Asia where wearing a green hat signifies that a man has an unfaithful wife. Procter & Gamble research showed that Italians devote 21 hours a week to household chores other than cooking—Americans spend just 4 hours. They wash kitchen and bathroom floors at least four times a week, compared to the U.S. consumer's once-a-week cleansing. Despite those hours and hours of labor, Italians aren't necessarily a perfect market for convenience products. They want products that are tough cleaners, not timesavers. For example, dishwasher makers targeting the Italian market have had to fight the perception that machines don't get dishes as clean as hand-washing. When Unilever's Cif brand cleaning spray flopped, company research found that Italian women needed convincing that a spray could be strong enough, especially on kitchen grease. The company spent 18 months reformulating the product, testing its power against grease. It changed the focus of advertising from convenience to cleaning ability. And when it was learned that the women felt they needed different cleaners for different tasks, new varieties were created. Containers were also made 50 percent larger because Italians clean so frequently.

P&G's Swiffer Wet mop bombed as a cleaner, but research found that Italian women were using it to polish after mopping, so the firm created a Swiffer with beeswax, which it sells only in Italy. Another variety, the Swiffer duster, is sold in many countries but is especially popular in Italy, selling five million boxes in its first eight months—twice the company's forecasts. "It was a real shift of mind-set on how to market products like these," said Alessandra Bellini, head of marketing for Unilever's home and personal-care products. "If you present a product as quick and easy, women may feel like a cheat. . . . It took us a while to understand that Italians didn't want that."[19]

The Japanese culture is one that has always been signified by hard work, devotion to the company, and lifetime employment. Yet this tradition seems to be changing among many young people. Those workers under 40 are shunning choice promotions and even foregoing raises in favor of routine jobs with little responsibility. Japanese recruitment agencies report that young people are looking to change jobs not to get ahead, but to leave positions that are too demanding.

With management posts increasingly harder to fill, Sanyo Electric Company recently started holding compulsory career-training retreats for workers turning 30. At the retreats, executives give pep talks "to remind them their best years are still ahead," says Jun Nakamura, Sanyo's head of human resources. "We want to tell this generation that though it's been tough, they shouldn't give up yet."[20]

The French have a strong dislike for outdoor advertising. A survey found 58 percent of the French don't care for billboards. As one police chief outside Paris noted, "We have a culture that doesn't like commerce that goes back to the Middle Ages."[21] Because of the prominence of outdoor ads, they are a target for anticapitalist sentiment. Every last Friday of each month Alex Baret, a 31-year-old musician, rides a train to central Paris. When he arrives, he pulls out a can of spray paint and defaces a billboard with *Harcelement Publicitaire*, or in English, "Harassment by Advertising."[22]

In India, two-thirds of the population still depends upon farming to earn a living. Owning land is an important component of the culture. Recently, Indian farmers blocked construction of a new factory being built by Tata Motors. The factory was to produce the Nano car, expected to be priced around $2,240.[23] Farmers' unwillingness to give up their land has resulted in Tata looking elsewhere to construct the plant.

Language is another important aspect of culture that can create problems for marketers. Marketers must take care in translating product names, slogans, instructions, and promotional messages so as not to convey the wrong meaning. For example, Mitsubishi Motors had to rename its Pajero model in Spanish-speaking countries because the term describes a sexual activity. Toyota Motors' MR2 model dropped the number two in France because the combination sounds like a French swearword. Coca-Cola had difficulty finding a suitable translation for its name into Mandarin. The transliteration of the syllables of Coca-Cola in Chinese characters could have resulted in Chinese people thinking it read "bite the wax tadpole" or other nonsensical phrases.

Each country has its own customs and traditions that determine business practices and influence negotiations with foreign customers. In many countries, personal relationships are more important than financial considerations. For instance, skipping social engagements in Mexico may lead to lost sales. Negotiations in Japan often include long evenings of dining, drinking, and entertaining, and only after a close personal relationship has been formed do business negotiations begin. The Japanese go through a very elaborate ritual when exchanging business cards. An American businesswoman was unaware of this important cultural tradition. She came into a meeting and tossed some of her business cards across the table at a group of stunned Japanese executives. One of them turned his back on her and walked out. The deal never went through.

Making successful sales presentations abroad requires a thorough understanding of the country's culture. Germans, for example, don't like risk and need strong reassurance. A successful presentation to a German client will emphasize three points: the bottom-line benefits of the product or service, that there will be strong service support, and that the product is guaranteed. In southern Europe, it is an insult to show a price list. Without negotiating, you will not close the sale. The English want plenty of documentation for product claims and are less likely to simply accept the word of the sales representative. Scandinavian and Dutch companies are more likely to approach business transactions as Americans do than are companies in any other country.

Never try to do business in Europe in August. Why not? You'll find that everyone has gone on vacation. Today, all European countries have laws requiring companies to provide employees with vacations of at least four weeks (the standard in Belgium, Britain, Germany, and Italy, among others) to five weeks (as in Austria, Denmark, France, and Sweden). But most workers get more vacation time because of collective agreements negotiated by unions or other compensation arrangements.

Economic and Technological Development

A second major factor in the external environment facing the global marketer is the level of economic development in the countries where it operates. In general, complex and sophisticated industries are found in developed countries, and more basic industries are found in less developed nations. Average family incomes are higher in more developed countries than in the less developed countries. Larger incomes mean greater purchasing power and demand not only for consumer goods and services but also for the machinery and workers required to produce consumer goods.

© AP IMAGES/NG HAN GUAN

Haier Group is one of China's fastest-growing companies and one of the world's top brands. In fact, for the third consecutive year, Haier Group was named one of the world's 100-most-recognizable brands in a global name-brand list.

According to the World Bank, the combined gross national income (GNI) of the 234 nations for which data are available is approximately $34 trillion. Divide that up among the world's 6.8 billion inhabitants, and you get just $5,230 for every man, woman, and child on Earth. The United States accounts for almost a third of the income earned worldwide, or $12.3 trillion—more than any other single country. If America's GNI were divided equally among its 297 million residents, each American would receive $41,400—6.6 times the world average. Even so, Americans are still not the richest people on the planet. That title goes to the residents of Luxembourg, where the per capita GNI is $56,230.[24]

The most expensive place in the world to live is Moscow (34 percent more expensive than New York, America's most expensive city). Other more expensive places, relative to New York, are London (26 percent), Seoul (22 percent), Tokyo (22 percent), and Hong Kong (19 percent).[25] A daily newspaper in Moscow costs $6.30. At the other end of the spectrum is Asunción in Paraguay, which is the least expensive city. It costs about half as much as it does to live in New York.

Doing Business in China and India[26]

The two countries of growing interest to many multinationals are India and China because of their huge economic potential. They have some of the highest growth rates in the world and are emerging as megamarkets. Take cell phones. The number of users in China exceeds 450 million, and the estimated figure for India is 150 million—a number that is growing by six million new subscribers a month.

China and India present different but complementary strengths that multinationals can use. China is much stronger than India in mass manufacturing and logistics; in contrast, India is much stronger than China in software and information-technology services.

Outside the United States, IBM relies on China as the primary source for its hardware business and has decided to relocate its global procurement headquarters to Shenzhen. Complementing these moves, IBM has made its Indian operations one of its most important global hubs for the delivery of information technology services to clients worldwide. Nearly one-sixth of IBM's global workforce is now based in India.

China and India have the world's two largest populations, two of the world's largest geographical areas, greater linguistic and sociocultural diversity than any other country, and among the highest levels of income disparity in the world—some people are extremely poor whereas others are very rich.

Given this scale and variety, there is no "average Chinese customer" or "average Indian customer." In each country, even the middle of the income pyramid consists of more than 300 million people encompassing significant diversity in incomes, geographic climates, cultural habits, and even language and religious beliefs. Because of this diversity, market success in China and India is rarely possible without finely segmenting the local market in each country and developing a strategy tailored to the needs of the targeted segments.

Haier Group, China's leading appliance maker, has proved to be particularly adept at fine market segmentation. The company's line of washing machines for the Chinese market includes a washing machine for rural peasants that can clean not only clothes but also sweet potatoes and peanuts. Haier also sells a tiny washing machine designed to clean a single change of clothes, which has proved to be a hit with the busy urban customers in Shanghai.

Political Structure and Actions

Political structure is the third important variable facing global marketers. Government policies run the gamut from no private ownership and minimal individual freedom to little central government and maximum personal freedom. As rights of private property increase, government-owned industries and centralized planning tend to decrease. But a political environment is rarely at one extreme or the other. India, for instance, is a republic with elements of socialism, monopoly capitalism, and competitive capitalism in its political ideology.

Some of the world's biggest corporations are facing intense pressure from China to allow state-approved unions to form in their Chinese facilities, though many companies fear that admitting the unions will give their Chinese employees the power to disrupt their operations and will significantly increase the cost of doing business.

Union officials are aiming at the China operations of the 500 biggest global corporations, which would mean millions of new union members, saying they intend to combat worker exploitations. "As the economy and society develops, China needs to improve workers' legal rights and interests, which is a demand of a civilized society," says Wang Ying, an official at the All-China Federation of Trade Unions in Beijing.[27] Wal-Mart, which for years has fought hard against unions in the United States and elsewhere, now has unions operating in nearly all of its 108 stores in China. "We have a good relationship working with the union," said Jonathan Dong, a Wal-Mart spokesman in China. "The union provides a complement to what we do."[28]

A recent World Bank study found that the least amount of business regulation fosters the strongest economies.[29] The least regulated and most efficient economies are concentrated among countries with well-established common-law traditions, including Australia, Canada, New Zealand, the United Kingdom, and the United States. On a par with the best performers are Singapore and Hong Kong; not far behind are

European Union (EU)
A free trade zone encompassing 27 European countries.

Mercosur
The largest Latin American trade agreement; includes Argentina, Bolivia, Brazil, Chile, Colombia, Ecuador, Paraguay, Peru, Uruguay, and Venezuela.

Uruguay Round
An agreement to dramatically lower trade barriers worldwide; created the World Trade Organization.

Denmark, Norway, and Sweden, social democracies that recently streamlined their business regulation.

The World Bank also found that the poorest countries, which need new businesses and entrepreneurship the most, were the most difficult countries in which to start a new business. Heavy regulation and red tape prevent both economic and job growth. The more roadblocks there are, the more opportunities for underpaid government officials to get kickbacks. But there are also other problems. The World Bank report noted that trade unions prevented Peru from reducing mandatory severance payments, while notaries in Croatia for years have stalled its efforts to simplify procedures to start businesses. It takes 153 days to start a business in Mozambique, for example, but 2 days in Canada. Enforcing a contract in Indonesia can cost more than the contract's actual value; doing the same in South Korea costs just 5.4 percent of a contract's value.[30]

AMR Research Inc., a Boston consulting firm, says it surveyed supply-chain managers at big U.S. firms in 2008 about how they would rank the risks they face doing business globally. About 30 percent of them rated "country risk"—geopolitical problems or natural disasters—as their most significant.[31] The managers' worries are not far-fetched.

Energy companies have been among the first to feel the new nationalism. Nationalism is pride in one's country and its sovereignty. It makes legitimate the principle of national self-determination. Since oil prices started rising in 2004, Russia, Venezuela, Bolivia, and Ecuador have nationalized (taken over by the government) foreign-owned oil assets, the first big wave of nationalization since the 1970s. After Venezuela's state-owned oil firm doubled its ownership of heavy-oil projects along the Orinoco River in 2007, ConocoPhillips pulled out, taking a $4.5 billion charge.[32] Exxon Mobil Corp. left as well and is suing Venezuela for compensation.

Legal Considerations

Closely related to and often intertwined with the political environment are legal considerations. In France, nationalistic sentiments led to a law that requires pop music stations to play at least 40 percent of their songs in French (even though French teenagers love American and English rock and roll).

Many legal structures are designed to either encourage or limit trade. Here are some examples:

- *Tariff: a tax levied on the goods entering a country.* The United States maintains tariffs as high as 27 percent on Canadian softwood lumber. U.S. lumber producers and environmentalists have alleged that Canada's provincial governments subsidize the softwood industry by charging below-market rates to cut trees and not enforcing environmental laws. Because a tariff is a tax, it will either reduce the profits of the firms paying the tariff or raise prices to buyers or both. Normally, a tariff raises prices of the imported goods and makes it easier for domestic firms to compete. U.S. shrimpers lobbied for tariffs against foreign pond-raised shrimp, which were enacted.
- *Quota: a limit on the amount of a specific product that can enter a country.* The United States has strict quotas for imported textiles, sugar, and many dairy products. Several U.S. companies have sought quotas as a means of protection from foreign competition. For example, Harley-Davidson convinced the U.S. government to place quotas on large motorcycles imported to the United States. These quotas gave the company the opportunity to improve its quality and compete with Japanese motorcycles.
- *Boycott: the exclusion of all products from certain countries or companies.* Governments use boycotts to exclude companies from countries with which they have a political dispute. Several Arab nations boycotted Coca-Cola because it maintained distributors in Israel.
- *Exchange control: a law compelling a company earning foreign exchange from its exports to sell it to a control agency, usually a central bank.* A company wishing

to buy goods abroad must first obtain foreign currency exchange from the control agency. Generally, exchange controls limit the importation of luxuries. For instance, Avon Products drastically cut back new production lines and products in the Philippines because exchange controls prevented the company from converting pesos to dollars to ship back to the home office. The pesos had to be used in the Philippines. China restricts the amount of foreign currency each Chinese company is allowed to keep from its exports. Therefore, Chinese companies must usually get the government's approval to release funds before they can buy products from foreign companies.

- *Market grouping (also known as a common trade alliance): occurs when several countries agree to work together to form a common trade area that enhances trade opportunities.* The best-known market grouping is the **European Union (EU)**, which will be discussed in more detail later. The EU, which was known as the European Community before 1994, has been evolving for more than four decades, yet until recently, many trade barriers existed among its member nations.
- *Trade agreement: an agreement to stimulate international trade.* Not all government efforts are meant to stifle imports or investment by foreign corporations. The Uruguay Round of trade negotiations is an example of an effort to encourage trade, as was the grant of most favored nation (MFN) status to China. The largest Latin American trade agreement is **Mercosur,** which includes Argentina, Bolivia, Brazil, Chile, Colombia, Ecuador, Paraguay, Peru, Uruguay, and Venezuela. The elimination of most tariffs among the trading partners has resulted in trade revenues of over $16 billion annually. The economic boom created by Mercosur will undoubtedly cause other nations to seek trade agreements on their own or to enter Mercosur. The European Union hopes to have a free trade pact with Mercosur in the future.

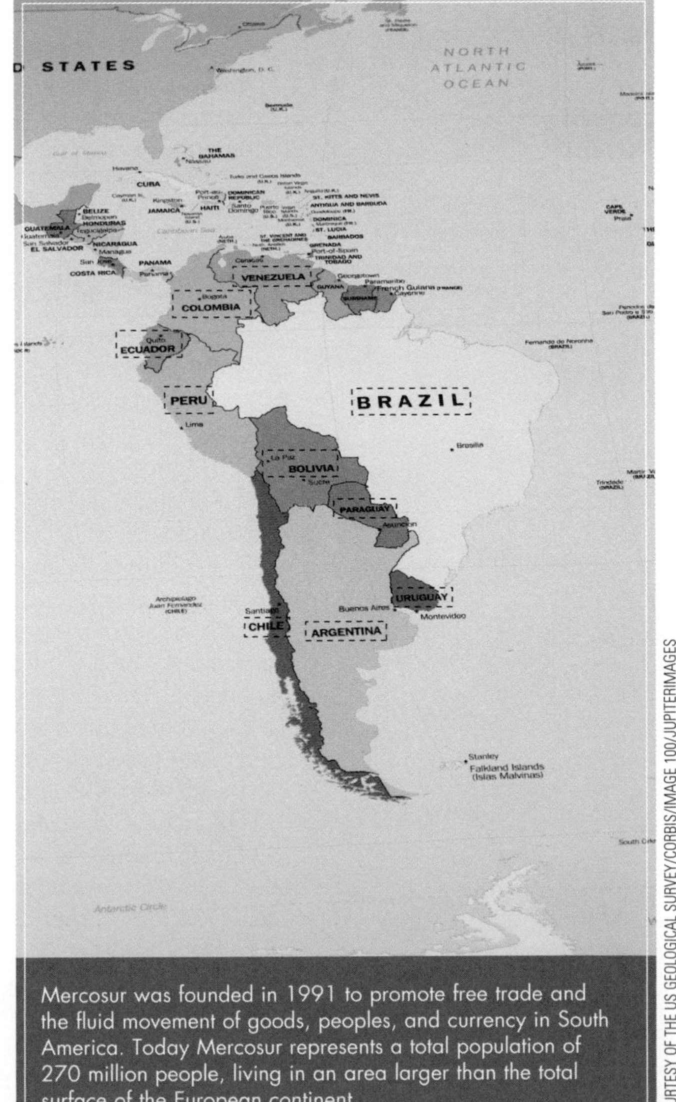

Mercosur was founded in 1991 to promote free trade and the fluid movement of goods, peoples, and currency in South America. Today Mercosur represents a total population of 270 million people, living in an area larger than the total surface of the European continent.

Uruguay Round, the Failed Doha Round, and Bilateral Agreements

The **Uruguay Round** is an agreement that has dramatically lowered trade barriers worldwide. Adopted in 1994, the agreement has been signed by 151 nations. It is the most ambitious global trade agreement ever negotiated. The agreement has reduced tariffs by one-third worldwide—a move that has raised global income by $235 billion annually. Perhaps most notable is the recognition of new global realities. For the first time, an agreement covers services, intellectual property rights, and trade-related investment measures such as exchange controls.

The Uruguay Round made several major changes in world trading practices:

- *Entertainment, pharmaceuticals, integrated circuits, and software:* The rules protect patents, copyrights, and trademarks for 20 years. Computer programs receive 50 years of protection and semiconductor chips receive 10 years of protection. But many developing nations were given a decade to phase in patent protection for drugs. France, which limits the number of U.S. movies and TV shows that can be shown, refused to liberalize market access for the U.S. entertainment industry.
- *Financial, legal, and accounting services:* Services came under international trading rules for the first time, creating a vast opportunity for these competitive U.S. industries. Now it is easier for managers and key personnel to be admitted to a country. Licensing standards for professionals, such as doctors, cannot discriminate

World Trade Organization (WTO)
A trade organization that replaced the old General Agreement on Tariffs and Trade (GATT).

General Agreement on Tariffs and Trade (GATT)
A trade agreement that contained loopholes that enabled countries to avoid trade-barrier reduction agreements.

North American Free Trade Agreement (NAFTA)
An agreement between Canada, the United States, and Mexico that created the world's largest free trade zone.

against foreign applicants. That is, foreign applicants cannot be held to higher standards than domestic practitioners.

- *Agriculture:* Europe is gradually reducing farm subsidies, opening new opportunities for such U.S. farm exports as wheat and corn. Japan and Korea are beginning to import rice. But U.S. growers of sugar and citrus fruit have had their subsidies trimmed.
- *Textiles and apparel:* Strict quotas limiting imports from developing countries are being phased out, causing further job losses in the U.S. clothing trade. But retailers and consumers are the big winners, because past quotas have added $15 billion a year to clothing prices.
- *A new trade organization:* The **World Trade Organization (WTO)** replaced the old **General Agreement on Tariffs and Trade (GATT),** which was created in 1948. The old GATT contained extensive loopholes that enabled countries to avoid the trade-barrier reduction agreements—a situation similar to obeying the law only if you want to! Today, all WTO members must fully comply with all agreements under the Uruguay Round. The WTO also has an effective dispute settlement procedure with strict time limits to resolve disputes.

The latest round of WTO trade talks began in Doha, Qatar, in 2001. For the most part, the periodic meetings of WTO members under the Doha Round have been very contentious. After seven years, the Doha Round collapsed in the summer of 2008. China and India were to lower their tariffs on industrial goods, in exchange for European and American tariff and subsidy cuts on farm products.

China and India, however, demanded a "safeguard" clause that would allow them to raise tariffs on key crops such as cotton, sugar, and rice if there were a sudden surge in imports. The two sides couldn't agree, however, on where to set the threshold for any import surge that would trigger the clause. The United States wanted to set the trigger at a 40 percent jump. China and India wanted the trigger set much lower, at a 10 percent increase.[33]

The demise of the Doha Round was the first multilateral (many nations) free trade act failure since World War II. The cost of the failure is estimated at over $100 billion annually. Moreover, trade is the engine of growth for countries around the globe. In 1990, trade represented about 40 percent of world GDP, according to the World Bank. By 2004, trade exceeded 55 percent of world GDP, and the global economy had expanded by 50 percent. The five fastest-growing countries from 1990 to 2004 were Albania, Bosnia and Herzegovina, China, Ireland, and Vietnam, and all of them had annual double-digit increases in trade. Meanwhile, the countries that traded the least—Iran, many African countries—have stagnated.[34]

The failure of Doha has resulted in many countries, such as China, India, and other Asian and African countries, seeking bilateral trade agreements. A bilateral agreement is simply a pact between two nations. America already has bilateral agreements with Australia, Bahrain, Chile, Israel, Jordan, Singapore, and Morocco. The U.S. has pending bilateral agreements with Panama, Columbia, and South Korea. Trade between Korea and the United States is already over $80 billion annually.[35] If all three pending agreements pass, U.S. exports will increase $1.1 billion to Columbia, $5.25 billion to Panama, and $10.3 billion to South Korea.[36]

The trend toward globalization has resulted in the creation of additional agreements and organizations: the North American Free Trade Agreement, the Central America Free Trade Agreement, the European Union, the World Bank, and the International Monetary Fund.

North American Free Trade Agreement

At the time it was instituted, the **North American Free Trade Agreement (NAFTA)** created the world's largest free trade zone. Ratified by the U.S. Congress in 1993, the agreement includes Canada, the United States, and Mexico, with a combined population of 360 million and economy of $6 trillion.

Canada, the largest U.S. trading partner, entered a free trade agreement with the United States in 1988. Thus, many of the new long-run opportunities for U.S. business under NAFTA have been in Mexico, America's third-largest trading partner. Tariffs on Mexican exports to the United States averaged just 4 percent before the treaty was signed, and most goods entered the United States duty-free. Therefore, the main impact of NAFTA was to open the Mexican market to U.S. companies. When the treaty went into effect, tariffs on about half the items traded across the Rio Grande disappeared. The pact removed a web of Mexican licensing requirements, quotas, and tariffs that limited transactions in U.S. goods and services. For instance, the pact allowed U.S. and Canadian financial-services companies to own subsidiaries in Mexico for the first time in 50 years.

In August 2007, the three member countries met in Canada to "tweak" NAFTA, but not make substantial changes. For example, the members agreed to further remove trade barriers on hogs, steel, consumer electronics, and chemicals. They also directed the North American Steel Trade Committee, which represents the three governments, to focus on subsidized steel from China. Most Canadians (73 percent) and Americans (77 percent) feel that NAFTA has played a key role in North American prosperity.[37] The survey was not conducted in Mexico.

The real question is whether NAFTA can continue to deliver rising prosperity in all three countries. America has certainly benefited from cheaper imports and more investment opportunities abroad. Over the years, Mexico has also made huge economic gains due to NAFTA. Exports to Mexico have more than tripled since 1993—but at $161 billion they still account for only 1.1 percent of the economy. Total U.S. exports have more than doubled over the same period, to more than $1.6 trillion a year, so the boost from NAFTA is small. Though imports from Mexico have risen nearly fivefold since 1993—potentially threatening some U.S. businesses—they amounted to only $240 billion in 2008, or less than 1.7 percent of the $14 trillion U.S. economy.[38] And for all the fears of factories being shipped south, the total U.S. investment in Mexican factories and offices adds up to only $75 billion. Mexico received just $21 billion in foreign direct investment in 2007, while the United States attracted $190 billion.[39]

According to the U.S. Trade Respresentative (USTR), employment in America has grown 24 percent since NAFTA took effect, and real wages have risen 19.3 percent, compared with only 11 percent in the 14 years prior. The USTR also reports that, due to NAFTA, the value of U.S. farm and food exports to Mexico and Canada grew 165 percent, compared with 65 percent worldwide.[40]

President Obama has talked about renegotiating NAFTA. He cites the number of jobs lost to Mexico since NAFTA took effect. It is true that jobs in the textile, auto parts, and electronics production have migrated to Mexico. Yet far more jobs have been lost to China than Mexico. Investment in automation and information technology has led to massive reductions in factory workers everywhere—including China and Mexico. Moreover, the growth of the Mexican economy under NAFTA has created export opportunities and jobs (different jobs from pre-NAFTA) in America. For example, General Electric recently sold $350 million in turbines built in Houston, over 100 locomotives made in Erie, Pennsylvania, and numerous aircraft engines to Mexico.[41]

President Obama also wants NAFTA to adopt tougher labor and environmental standards and enforcement. Mexico doesn't guarantee workers' rights to form independent unions or to bargain collectively. At press time, NAFTA had not been reopened.

Central America Free Trade Agreement

The newest free trade agreement is the **Central America Free Trade Agreement (CAFTA)** instituted in 2005. Besides the United States, the agreement includes Costa Rica, the Dominican Republic, El Salvador, Guatemala, Honduras, and Nicaragua. Between 2005 and 2007 trade between the United States and CAFTA countries grew 18 percent. U.S. exports to CAFTA nations were $23 billion in 2007, up 33 percent since 2005. U.S. imports from CAFTA were $19 billion, up 4 percent since 2005.[42] As the statistics indicate, CAFTA has been an unqualified success. It has created new

Central America Free Trade Agreement (CAFTA)
A trade agreement, instituted in 2005, that includes Costa Rica, the Dominican Republic, El Salvador, Guatemala, Honduras, Nicaragua, and the United States.

commercial opportunities for its members, promoted regional stability, and is an impetus for economic development for an important group of U.S. neighbors.

European Union

The EU is one of the world's most important free trade zones and now encompasses most of Europe. More than a free trade zone, it is also a political and economic community. As a free trade zone it guarantees the freedom of movement of people, goods, services, and capital between member states. It also maintains a common trade policy with outside nations and a regional development policy. The EU represents member nations in the WTO. Recently, the EU also began venturing into foreign policy as well, such as Iran's refining of uranium.

The European Union currently has 27 member states: Austria, Belgium, Bulgaria, Cyprus, the Czech Republic, Denmark, Estonia, Finland, France, Germany, Greece, Hungary, Ireland, Italy, Latvia, Lithuania, Luxembourg, Malta, the Netherlands, Poland, Portugal, Romania, Slovakia, Slovenia, Spain, Sweden, and the United Kingdom (see Exhibit 5.2). There are currently three official candidate countries, Croatia, the Republic of Macedonia, and Turkey. In addition, the western Balkan countries of Albania, Bosnia and Herzegovina, Montenegro, and Serbia are officially recognized as potential candidates.[43]

To join the EU, a country must meet the Copenhagen criteria, defined at the 1993 Copenhagen European Council. These require a stable democracy that respects human rights and the rule of law; a functioning market economy capable of competition within the EU; and the acceptance of the obligations of membership, including EU law. Evaluation of a country's fulfillment of the criteria rests with the European Council.[44]

EXHIBIT 5.2

The European Union

Source: © European Community.

Governance The government of the EU consists of a number of institutions, primarily the Commission, Council, and Parliament. The European Commission is the EU's executive branch and is responsible for the day-to-day running of the EU. It is currently composed of 27 commissioners, one from each member state. The Council of the European Union (also known as the Council of Ministers) forms part of the EU's legislative branch, the other being the Parliament. It is composed of the national ministers responsible for the specific area of the EU law being addressed. For example, European legislation regarding agriculture would be treated by a Council composed of the national ministers for agriculture. The body's presidency rotates between the member states every six months.

The other half of the legislative branch is the European Parliament, which is the only directly elected institution. The 785 Members of the European Parliament are directly elected by European citizens every five years (the last full election was in 2009). Although the elections are in national constituencies, the members are seated in the meeting room according to political groups rather than nationality. The institution has near-equal legislative powers with the Council in community matters and has the power to reject or censure the Commission.[45]

The European Union Commission and the courts have not always been kind to U.S. multinationals. First, the EU court blocked a merger between two U.S. companies—General Electric and Honeywell. In late 2007, it concluded that Microsoft used its dominance in desktop computer software to muscle into server software and media players. The EU courts said that Microsoft blocked competition and fined the company $613 million.[46] Before acquiring DoubleClick (a company that tracks Web surfing), Google asked the European Commission to first approve the proposed merger.

The Importance of the EU to the United States The European Union is the largest economy in the world. It has a gross domestic product of about $18 trillion, compared with about $11.5 trillion for the Unites States. Unemployment, although higher than in the United States, is at its lowest level in at least 15 years. In 2006, labor productivity matched that of the United States, again for the first time in many years.[47]

The EU is also a huge market, with a population of nearly 500 million. The United States and the EU have the largest bilateral trade and investment relationship in world history. Together, they account for more than half of the global economy, while bilateral trade accounts for 7 percent of the world total. U.S. and EU companies have invested an estimated $2 trillion in each other's economies, employing directly and indirectly as many as 14 million workers. Nearly every U.S. state is involved with exporting to, importing from, or working for European firms. California, which has an economy tied closely to Asia, has roughly 1 million workers connected to European investment or trade.[48]

Some economists have called the EU the "United States of Europe." It is an attractive market, with purchasing power almost equal to that of the United States. But the EU will probably never be a United States of Europe. For one thing, even if a united Europe achieves standardized regulations, marketers will not be able to produce a single Europroduct for a generic Euroconsumer. With more than 15 different languages and individual national customs, Europe will always be far more diverse than the United States. Thus, product differences will continue to be necessary. It will be a long time, for instance, before the French begin drinking the instant coffee that Britons enjoy. Preferences for washing machines also differ: British homemakers want front-loaders, and the French want top-loaders; Germans like lots of settings and high spin speeds; Italians like lower speeds. Even European companies that think they understand Euroconsumers often have difficulties producing "the right product." Atag Holdings NV, a diversified Dutch company whose main business is kitchen appliances, was confident it could cater to both the "potato" and "spaghetti" belts—marketers' terms for consumer preferences in northern and southern Europe. But Atag quickly discovered that preferences vary much more than that. For example, on its ovens, burner shape and size, knob and clock placement, temperature range, and

World Bank
An international bank that offers low-interest loans, advice, and information to developing nations.

International Monetary Fund (IMF)
An international organization that acts as a lender of last resort, providing loans to troubled nations, and also works to promote trade through financial cooperation.

colors vary greatly from country to country. Although Atag's kitchenware unit has lifted foreign sales to 25 percent of its total from 4 percent in the mid-1990s, it now believes that its range of designs and speed in delivering them, rather than the magic bullet of a Europroduct, will keep it competitive.

An entirely different type of problem facing global marketers is the possibility of a protectionist movement by the EU against outsiders. For example, European automakers have proposed holding Japanese imports at roughly their current 10 percent market share. The Irish, Danes, and Dutch don't make cars and have unrestricted home markets; they would be unhappy about limited imports of Toyotas and Nissans. But France has a strict quota on Japanese cars to protect Renault and Peugeot. These local carmakers could be hurt if the quota is raised at all.

The World Bank and International Monetary Fund

Two international financial organizations are instrumental in fostering global trade. The **World Bank** offers low-interest loans to developing nations. Originally, the purpose of the loans was to help these nations build infrastructure such as roads, power plants, schools, drainage projects, and hospitals. Now the World Bank offers loans to help developing nations relieve their debt burdens. To receive the loans, countries must pledge to lower trade barriers and aid private enterprise. In addition to making loans, the World Bank is a major source of advice and information for developing nations. The United States has granted the organization $60 million to create knowledge databases on nutrition, birth control, software engineering, creating quality products, and basic accounting systems.

A survey, funded by the World Bank, of 2,500 global opinion leaders showed that improving the economic conditions of the world's poorest people should be the World Bank's top priority. Today, there are 1.4 billion people in the developing world—that is 1 in 4 people—still living on less than $1.25 per day. Between 2007 and 2009, the World Bank funneled $3.5 billion to the International Development Association.[49] That program provides money for development projects in the world's most impoverished countries, mostly in Africa. The World Bank also cancelled the debts of 19 of their poorest borrowers.

The **International Monetary Fund (IMF)** was founded in 1945, one year after the creation of the World Bank, to promote trade through financial cooperation and eliminate trade barriers in the process. The IMF makes short-term loans to member nations that are unable to meet their budgetary expenses. It operates as a lender of last resort for troubled nations. In exchange for these emergency loans, IMF lenders frequently extract significant commitments from the borrowing nations to address the problems that led to the crises. These steps may include curtailing imports or even devaluing the currency.

Demographic Makeup

The three most densely populated nations in the world are China, India, and Indonesia. But that fact alone is not particularly useful to marketers. They also need to know whether the population is mostly urban or rural, because marketers may not have easy access to rural consumers. In Belgium about 90 percent of the population lives in an urban setting, whereas in Kenya almost 80 percent of the population lives in a rural setting. Belgium is thus the more attractive market. Just as important as population is personal income within a country.

Another key demographic consideration is age. There is a wide gap between the older populations of the industrialized countries and the vast working-age populations of developing countries. This gap has enormous implications for economies, businesses, and the competitiveness of individual countries. It means that while Europe and Japan struggle with pension schemes and the rising cost of health care, countries like China, Brazil, and Mexico can reap the fruits of what's known as a demographic dividend: falling labor costs, a healthier and more educated population, and the entry of millions of women into the workforce.

The demographic dividend is a gift of falling birthrates, and it causes a temporary bulge in the number of working-age people. Population experts have estimated that one-third of East Asia's economic miracle can be attributed to a beneficial age structure. But the miracle occurred only because the governments had policies in place to educate their people, create jobs, and improve health.

REVIEW LEARNING OUTCOME

LO 3 Describe the external environment facing global marketers

Natural Resources
• dependence
• independence

Cultural
• values
• language
• customs
• traditions

Demography
• urban v. rural
• young v. old
• purchasing power

Global Marketing Mix

Economic Development

Political Structure
• tariffs
• quotas
• boycotts
• exchange controls
• market groupings
• trade agreements

Technological Development

Natural Resources

A final factor in the external environment that has become more evident in the past decade is the shortage of natural resources. For example, petroleum shortages have created huge amounts of wealth for oil-producing countries such as Norway, Saudi Arabia, and the United Arab Emirates. Both consumer and industrial markets have blossomed in these countries. Other countries—such as Indonesia, Mexico, and Venezuela—were able to borrow heavily against oil reserves in order to develop more rapidly. On the other hand, industrial countries like Japan, the United States, and much of western Europe experienced an enormous transfer of wealth to the petroleum-rich nations. The high price of oil has created inflationary pressures in petroleum-importing nations. It also created major problems for airlines and other petroleum-dependent industries.

Petroleum is not the only natural resource that affects international marketing. Warm climate and lack of water mean that many of Africa's countries will remain importers of foodstuffs. The United States, on the other hand, must rely on Africa for many precious metals. Japan depends heavily on the United States for timber and logs. A Minnesota company manufactures and sells a million pairs of disposable chopsticks to Japan each year. The list could go on, but the point is clear. Vast differences in natural resources create international dependencies, huge shifts of wealth, inflation and recession, export opportunities for countries with abundant resources, and even a stimulus for military intervention.

GLOBAL MARKETING BY THE INDIVIDUAL FIRM

A company should consider entering the global marketplace only after its management has a solid grasp of the global environment. Some relevant questions are

- "What are our options in selling abroad?"
- "How difficult is global marketing?" and
- "What are the potential risks and returns?"

Concrete answers to these questions would probably encourage the many U.S. firms not selling overseas to venture into the international arena. Foreign sales can be an important source of profits.

Companies decide to "go global" for a number of reasons. Perhaps the most important is to earn additional profits. Managers may feel that international sales will result in higher profit margins or more added-on profits. A second stimulus is that a firm may have a unique product or technological advantage not available to other international

EXHIBIT 5.3

Risk Levels for Five Methods of Entering the Global Marketplace

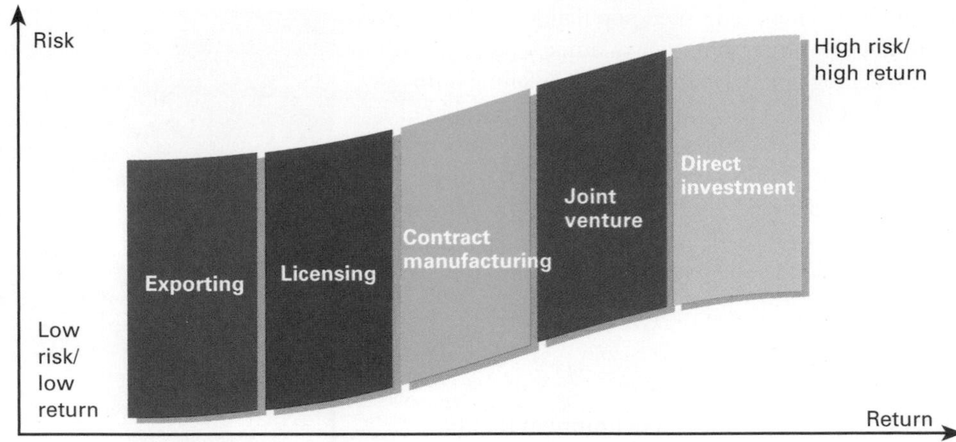

exporting
Selling domestically produced products to buyers in another country.

competitors. Such advantages should result in major business successes abroad. In other situations, management may have exclusive market information about foreign customers, marketplaces, or market situations. While exclusivity can provide an initial motivation for international marketing, managers must realize that competitors can be expected to catch up with the firm's information advantage. Finally, saturated domestic markets, excess capacity, and potential for economies of scale can also be motivators to "go global." Economies of scale mean that average per-unit production costs fall as output is increased.

Many firms form multinational partnerships—called strategic alliances—to assist them in penetrating global markets; strategic alliances are examined in Chapter 7. Five other methods of entering the global marketplace are, in order of risk, exporting, licensing and franchising, contract manufacturing, the joint venture, and direct investment (see Exhibit 5.3).

Exporting

When a company decides to enter the global market, exporting is usually the least complicated and least risky alternative. **Exporting** is selling domestically produced products to buyers in another country. A company can sell directly to foreign importers or buyers. Exporting is not limited to huge corporations such as General Motors or 3M. Indeed, small companies account for 96 percent of all U.S. exporters, but only 30 percent of the export volume.[50] The United States is the world's largest exporter.

The U.S. Commercial Service within the Department of Commerce promotes itself as "Your Global Business Partner." It offers trade specialists in more than a hundred U.S. cities and 150 overseas offices to help beginning exporters, and helps those already engaged in global marketing increase their business. The primary services offered by the U.S. Commercial Service are marketing research, locating qualified buyers and partners, trade events, and global business consulting. These services are explained in more detail in Exhibit 5.4.

The federal government has created a Web site, **www.export.gov**, that brings together all of the resources across the U.S. government to assist American firms that wish to go global. The site directs you to the U.S. Commercial Service for things like marketing research and trade leads, the Export-Import Bank for loan information, and the U.S. Department of Agriculture for agricultural export assistance. In all, **www.export.gov** brings together nineteen federal agencies that offer some form of export assistance. The Export-Import Bank helps in the export of U.S. goods and services. It doesn't compete directly with private banks, but provides export financing that fills gaps in trade financings. That is, the Export-Import Bank assumes credit and country risks that the private sector is unable or unwilling to accept. About 85 percent of the Export-Import Bank's financing is to small businesses.[51] For those interested

EXHIBIT 5.4

Assistance Provided by the U.S. Commercial Service to Exporters

COUNSELING AND ADVOCACY

- **Advocacy:** Get a competitive edge with U.S. Commercial Service advocacy. U.S. diplomats and other officials help your company when unanticipated problems arise—resolve payment issues, settle disputes, win contracts, and overcome regulatory hurdles. Support can include government-to-government meetings by U.S. Commercial Service officers and ambassadors with high-level foreign government officials, in addition to direct intervention with international companies.
- **Counseling:** Increase your export sales and enter new international markets with U.S. Commercial Service export counseling. Trade specialists in more than 100 U.S. cities and 80 countries provide in-depth export consulting and customized business solutions. Our trade specialists near you work with our team of experts overseas in getting you the information and advice that you need to succeed.
- **Platinum Key Service:** Get long-term, comprehensive, customized support to achieve your business goals. The Platinum Key Service is solution oriented and custom-tailored to your needs. Identify markets, launch products, develop major project opportunities, resolve market entry questions, and receive assistance on regulatory matters. Our in-country trade specialists will work closely with you to identify needs, provide progress reports, and ensure timely resolution.

MARKET RESEARCH

- **Market Research Library:** Accurate, up-to-date information lets you target the best international markets. Our single comprehensive market research includes overviews on doing business in more than 120 countries and profiles of 110 industry sectors. You can also get updates on new regulations, currency fluctuations, business trends, and government-financed projects. Much of this research is available at no charge.
- **Customized Market Research:** Receive specific intelligence on the export prospects for your product or service in a potential market.
- **Business Facilitation Service:** Get low-cost logistical and administrative support when you're on international business travel. Our Business Facilitation Service offers flexible solutions to let you do business when you're away from home.

FINDING INTERNATIONAL PARTNERS

- **International Partner Search:** Find qualified international buyers, partners, or agents without traveling overseas. U.S. Commercial Service specialists will deliver detailed company information on up to five prescreened international companies that have expressed an interest in your company's products and services.
- **Gold Key Matching Service:** Save time and money by letting the U.S. Commercial Service help you find a buyer, partner, agent, or distributor. The Gold Key Service provides you with one-on-one appointments with prescreened potential agents, distributors, sales representatives, association and government contracts, licensing or joint venture partners, and other strategic business partners in your targeted export market.
- **Commercial News USA:** Promote your products and services to more than 400,000 international buyers in 145 countries. Commercial News USA is a product catalog distributed by U.S. embassies and consulates worldwide and has a proven track record of high response rates and solid sales results.
- **Trade Leads:** View announcements from qualified international companies looking to source U.S. products and services and advertise government tender projects through our trade leads database. All of our trade leads are prescreened by our U.S. embassy or consulate staff overseas and are provided as a free service for U.S. exporters.
- **International Company Profile:** Prevent costly mistakes with quick, low-cost credit checks or due-diligence reports on international companies. Before you do business with a prospective agent, distributor, or partner, the International Company Profile will give you the background information you need to evaluate the company.

TRADE EVENTS AND RELATED SERVICES

- **U.S. Pavilions at Certified Trade Fairs:** Exhibit at U.S. Pavilions certified by the U.S. Commercial Service and increase your chances of finding new business. Certified U.S. Pavilions offer one-on-one business matching, business counseling from trade specialists, and special exhibit services designed to help U.S. exporters maximize returns from trade shows and make more international sales.
- **Trade Fair Certification:** Exhibiting at a trade show abroad can lead to tremendous export opportunities for U.S. companies. This is why the Trade Fair Certification Program was created: to help companies like yours make important exhibiting decisions and free you of many of the concerns you may have about exhibiting outside the United States.
- **International Buyer Program:** Find new international business partners at U.S. trade shows with the International Buyer Program. The IBP recruits more than 125,000 foreign buyers and distributors to 32 top U.S. trade shows per year. U.S. Commercial Service trade specialists arrange meetings for U.S. exporters and international delegates and provide export counseling at the show's International Business Center.
- **Trade Missions:** Meet face-to-face with prescreened international business contacts in promising markets with U.S. Commercial Service trade missions. Trade missions save you time and money by allowing you to maximize contact with qualified distributors, sales representatives, or partners in one to four countries.
- **Virtual Trade Missions:** If your schedule or travel budget limits your ability to travel overseas, consider Virtual Trade Missions. An interactive two-hour videoconference lets you meet virtually. Planning an International Trade Mission? Every year, the U.S. Commercial Service supports dozens of trade missions organized by state economic organizations, elected officials, chambers of commerce, and industry associations through our Certified Trade Mission program.

EXHIBIT 5.4

Assistance Provided by the U.S. Commercial Service to Exporters (continued)

- **Catalog Events:** Looking for an affordable, low-risk way to promote your products and services in promising markets throughout the world? Increase your company's international sales potential by showcasing your products and services with the International Catalog Exhibition Program.
- **Trade Specialists:** U.S. Commercial Service trade specialists located in international markets will translate your company profile into the local language, display your marketing materials, collect sales leads from interested local buyers, and then assist you as you follow up with the local contacts.

Source: U.S. Commercial Services.

buyer for export
An intermediary in the global market that assumes all ownership risks and sells globally for its own account.

export broker
An intermediary who plays the traditional broker's role by bringing buyer and seller together.

export agent
An intermediary who acts like a manufacturer's agent for the exporter. The export agent lives in the foreign market.

licensing
The legal process whereby a licensor agrees to let another firm use its manufacturing process, trademarks, patents, trade secrets, or other proprietary knowledge.

in international business, a nongovernmental Web site that offers links to hundreds of useful sites is available from the International Federation of International Trade Associations (**http://fita.org**).

Instead of selling directly to foreign buyers, a company may decide to sell to intermediaries located in its domestic market. The most common intermediary is the export merchant, also known as a **buyer for export**, which is usually treated like a domestic customer by the domestic manufacturer. The buyer for export assumes all risks and sells internationally for its own account. The domestic firm is involved only to the extent that its products are bought in foreign markets.

A second type of intermediary is the **export broker**, who plays the traditional broker's role by bringing buyer and seller together. The manufacturer still retains title and assumes all the risks. Export brokers operate primarily in agricultural products and raw materials.

Export agents, a third type of intermediary, are foreign sales agents-distributors who live in the foreign country and perform the same functions as domestic manufacturers' agents, helping with international financing, shipping, and so on. The U.S. Department of Commerce has an agent-distributor service that helps about 5,000 U.S. companies a year find an agent or distributor in virtually any country of the world. A second category of agents resides in the manufacturer's country but represents foreign buyers. This type of agent acts as a hired purchasing agent for foreign customers operating in the exporter's home market.

Licensing and Franchising

Another effective way for a firm to move into the global arena with relatively little risk is to sell a license to manufacture its product to someone in a foreign country. **Licensing** is the legal process whereby a licensor allows another firm to use its manufacturing process, trademarks, patents, trade secrets, or other proprietary knowledge. The licensee, in turn, pays the licensor a royalty or fee agreed on by both parties.

Because licensing has many advantages, U.S. companies have eagerly embraced the concept, sometimes in unusual ways. Caterpillar, the producer of heavy machinery, has licensed Wolverine World Wide to make "CAT" brand shoes and boots. Europeans have latched onto CAT gear as the new symbol of American outdoor culture. CAT is one of Europe's hottest brands, which translates into almost $1 billion in licensing revenues.

A licensor must make sure it can exercise sufficient control over the licensee's activities to ensure proper quality, pricing, distribution, and so on. Licensing may also create a new competitor in the long run, if the licensee decides to void the license agreement. International law is often ineffective in stopping such actions. Two common ways of maintaining effective control over licensees are shipping one or more critical components from the United States or locally registering patents and trademarks to the U.S. firm, not to the licensee. Garment companies maintain control by delivering only so many labels per day; they also supply their own fabric, collect the scraps, and do accurate unit counts.

Entertainment characters and properties, such as Celine Dion, Antonio Banderas, and SpongeBob SquarePants, account for 24 percent of worldwide retail sales of licensed goods. Total license sales now run over $187 billion annually.[52] Corporate trademark/brand properties and fashion labels each account for 21 percent of the total. The United States and Canada account for 65 percent of all global licensing sales.[53]

Franchising is a form of licensing that has grown rapidly in recent years. More than 400 U.S. franchisors operate more than 40,000 outlets in foreign countries, bringing in sales of over $9 billion.[54] Over half of the international franchises are for fast-food restaurants and business services. Franchisors cannot always offer the same product or the same method of distribution in countries around the globe. Domino's Pizza, for example, found that in Japan it had to modify its delivery procedures because addresses there often aren't sequential but instead are determined by a building's age. On Aruba, it soon found that using motorcycles to deliver pizzas was too dangerous because of the island's strong winds. (Small trucks solved the problem.) In the Philippines, locations of stores at times were chosen using feng shui, a Chinese art that positions buildings according to spiritual flow. And because many Icelanders stay up all hours, Domino's stores there must be open much longer than elsewhere. When the company went into Italy, many Italians found its pizza "too American—the sauce being too bold, the toppings too heavy," a company spokesman recalls.[55]

Contract Manufacturing

Firms that do not want to become involved in licensing or to become heavily involved in global marketing may engage in **contract manufacturing,** which is private-label manufacturing by a foreign company. The foreign company produces a certain volume of products to specification, with the domestic firm's brand name on the goods. The domestic company usually handles the marketing. Thus, the domestic firm can broaden its global marketing base without investing in overseas plants and equipment. After establishing a solid base, the domestic firm may switch to a joint venture or direct investment.

Recently, particularly in China, contract manufacturers have been making overruns and selling the excess production directly to either consumers or retailers. New Balance, for example, found that a contract manufacturer was producing extra running shoes and selling them to unauthorized retailers. The retailers were selling the knockoff New Balance shoes for $20, while authorized retailers were trying to sell the same shoe for $60. Recently, New Balance changed its relationship with its suppliers. It cut the number of factories it uses in China to six and monitors them more closely. It has also begun using high-tech shoe labels to better spot counterfeits and keep control of its own production. Yet this still didn't solve all of New Balance's problems. One contract manufacturer, Horace Chang, produced a shoe called "the classic," a low-tech shoe without midsole engineering that defines a high-performance shoe. Unhappy with Mr. Chang because of "overproduction," New Balance terminated the contract and asked for molds, specifications, signs, labels, packages, wrappers, and ads. They were not returned. He continued to sell in Taiwan, Hong Kong, Italy, and Germany. In addition, Mr. Chang launched a competing brand called "Henkees." A long court battle in China was to no avail. Finally, an American international arbitrator awarded New Balance $9.9 million.[56] To date, the firm hasn't collected a penny. Yet New Balance still uses contract manufacturing in China because the market is too important to pass up.

Today there are three terms used to describe brand theft:

- *Counterfeit*—a product that bears a trademark that its maker had no authority to use. The U.S. military has recently had a rash of problems from counterfeit microchips (tiny electric circuits) being installed in fighter jets, helicopters, and even on long-range radar on board the aircraft carrier USS *Ronald Reagan*. Although no deaths have occurred from the fake chips, numerous malfunctions have occurred. Tiny businesses in rural China heat up circuit boards from old computers and then strip out the chips. They are then sold to firms like Jinlong Electronics that purportedly sells military quality chips. This means chips that are more durable and can withstand temperature extremes. Instead, the old computer chips are sanded to remove the old markings and restamped "military" with a new date. The Defense Supply Center, a major Pentagon electronics parts buyer, has begun to require suppliers to

contract manufacturing
Private-label manufacturing by a foreign company.

joint venture
When a domestic firm buys part of a foreign company or joins with a foreign company to create a new entity.

document that microchips conform to quality standards and can be traced to the manufacturing source.[57]

- *Knockoff*—a broad term encompassing both counterfeits and items that look like branded products, though they don't actually bear forged trademarks.
- *Third shift*—an unauthorized product made by an unauthorized or authorized contractor. Thus, a contract manufacturer may use two production shifts to produce authorized product and a third shift to produce goods to be sold through an unauthorized channel. The contract manufacturer gets all of the revenue from production.

In addition to problems with third shifts and counterfeiting, cultural differences can sometimes create difficulties in contract manufacturing agreements. The Ethics in Marketing box describes one such conflict.

Joint Venture

Joint ventures are somewhat similar to licensing agreements. In an international **joint venture**, the domestic firm buys part of a foreign company or joins with a foreign

ETHICS in Marketing

Sometimes Expectations Get Lost in Translation

In the mid-1990s, a U.S. firm engaged in contract manufacturing with a Chinese motorcycle producer to make small motorcycles to export to Latin America and Africa. Since the mid-1980s, the Chinese manufacturer had been producing about 450,000 motorcycles per year, all for its domestic market, under a licensing agreement with a Japanese auto company. But the performance of the motorcycles was poor. To ensure higher quality for this new partnership's motorcycles, the U.S. partner insisted on the use of Japanese imports for key engine components, in place of the inferior Chinese-made parts the manufacturer had been using. Both parties agreed that the U.S. partner would send an observer for the purpose of quality control, including confirmation that the Japanese components were being installed in the bikes.

This system worked well for five years. Nearly 250,000 high-quality motorcycles were profitably produced and sold. Customers were pleased with the quality and service. At the beginning of the sixth year, the observer representing the U.S. partner quit. The American executives chose not to replace him, assuming that after five years of high-quality production, the Chinese would continue using the Japanese parts for the export motorcycles. This decision was made without consulting the Chinese.

A few months later, the U.S. company began to receive complaints from customers about the quality of the motorcycles. The problem was the same everywhere: The engine would run well for the first 200 miles or so, then it would begin to smoke and eventually the engine would seize up, rendering the bike inoperable. It was quickly determined that the Chinese manufacturer had substituted poorly made Chinese parts for the specified higher-quality Japanese-made components. Efforts to resolve the problem caused greater friction. Confronted with several thousand motorcycles that would require replacement parts as well as major servicing in 15 countries, the U.S. partner calculated that $400,000 would be needed just to begin to deal with the problem. Both parties then agreed that they would meet in Shanghai later that year to negotiate how to share these costs. Prior to the meeting in Shanghai, the Chinese sent a fax demanding that the Americans provide comprehensive documentation for every customer complaint.

The Americans were further distressed to learn that before any negotiations could occur, they would have to verbally present their findings on each motorcycle. The presentations were scheduled over a four-day period. On the second day, after presentations had been made for only about 200 of the motorcycles, the U.S. side decided that they had had all they could take. The two Americans stormed out of the room.[58]

Were the Chinese being unethical by substituting poorly made Chinese parts after the observer quit? The Chinese viewed the disappearance of the observer with no explanation as a breach in the relationship. Thus, they weren't bound by the terms of the original agreement. The Chinese decided to cut costs to maximize their profits. Was it unethical for the Chinese to require the Americans to verbally explain the problems with each motorcycle? Why?

company to create a new entity. A joint venture is a quick and relatively inexpensive way to go global and to gain needed expertise. For example, Robert Mondavi Wineries entered into a joint venture with Baron Philippe de Rothschild, owner of Bordeaux's First Growth chateau, Mouton-Rothschild. They created a wine in California called Opus One. It was immediately established as the American vanguard of quality and price. Mondavi has entered other joint ventures with the Frescobaldi family in Tuscany and with Errazuriz in Chile.

Joint ventures can be very risky. Many fail; others fall victim to a takeover, in which one partner buys out the other. Sometimes joint venture partners simply can't agree on management strategies and policies. Though joint ventures are very popular in the auto industry, many have not worked out. Joint venture factories—General Motors/Toyota, Suzuki/GM, Mazda/Ford, DaimlerChrysler/Mitsubishi—have not been particular successes. GM has a 50–50 joint venture with the Shanghai Automotive Corporation, owned by the Shanghai city government. The joint venture, founded in 1997, makes Buicks, Cadillacs, and Chevrolets. It has created hundreds of millions of dollars profit for GM. Now, the Chinese company, using the technology and the money earned from selling joint-venture cars, is becoming a serious competitor to GM; the Chinese Roewe is said to be bigger and more luxurious than the American Buick. The chairman of Shanghai Automotive says, "We now want to build a global Chinese brand."[59]

Similarly, Paris-based Danone is fighting with the Hangzhou Wahaha Group over the terms of its joint-venture. The Wahaha brand of soft drinks, juices, and teas are better known to many in China than Coca-Cola. Wahaha is China's largest soft drink producer. It entered into a joint venture with Danone to speed expansion of the Wahaha brand back in 1996. Today, Wahaha controls many factories outside the joint venture, which Danone claims is costing it $25 million per month. At press time, the two sides were locked in a bitter court battle.[60]

direct foreign investment Active ownership of a foreign company or of overseas manufacturing or marketing facilities.

Direct Investment

Active ownership of a foreign company or of overseas manufacturing or marketing facilities is **direct foreign investment**. Direct foreign investment by U.S. firms is currently about $2,100 billion. Direct investors have either a controlling interest or a large minority interest in the firm. Thus, they have the greatest potential reward and the greatest potential risk. Because of the problems discussed above with contract manufacturing and joint ventures in China, multinationals are going it alone. Today, nearly five times as much foreign direct investment comes into China in the form of stand-alone efforts as comes in for joint ventures.[61]

Wal-Mart is the world's largest global retailer with sales of over $375 billion annually. The company operates more than 4,100 facilities in the United States and more than 3,100 additional facilities in Argentina, Brazil, Canada, China, Costa Rica, El Salvador, Guatemala, Honduras, Japan, Mexico, Nicaragua, Puerto Rico, and the United Kingdom. Wal-Mart has established a joint venture with Bharti Enterprises to launch wholesale cash-and-carry in India. Wal-Mart employs more than 2 million associates worldwide, including more than 1.4 million in the United States. Wal-Mart is not only one of the largest private employers in the United States, but the largest in Mexico and one of the largest in Canada as well.[62]

Many U.S. companies practice direct investment by building manufacturing or marketing facilities in foreign countries, like the Chinese Wal-Mart Supercenter pictured here.

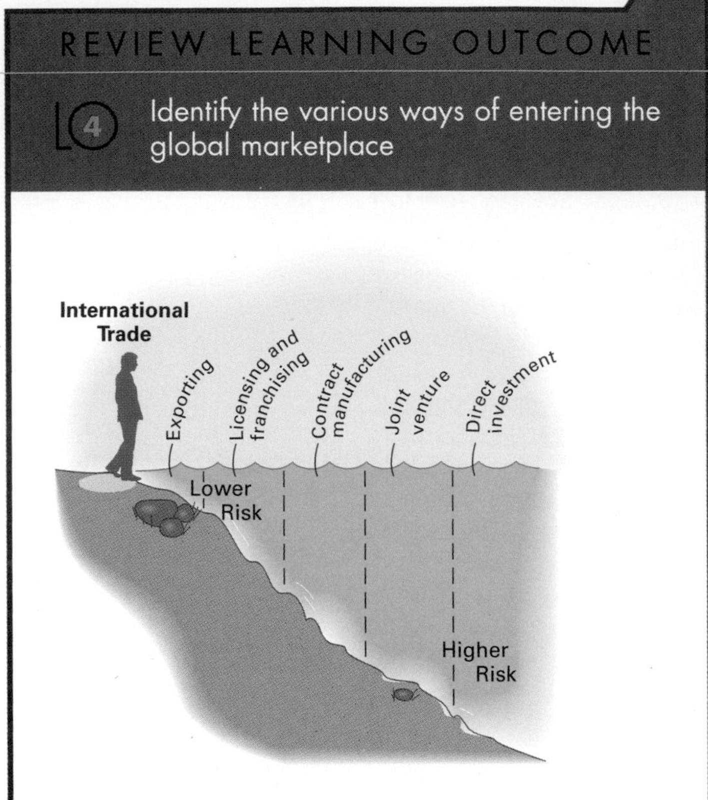

The company has, on occasion, stumbled in its quest for growth. Wal-Mart had difficulty with local labor laws and discounters undercutting it in Germany. It pulled out after losing $1 billion. Wal-Mart also pulled out of Korea and has struggled in Japan. The company operates 394 stores in Japan under the Seiyu brand name. In 2009, Wal-Mart announced a shift in its global focus to emerging markets including Mexico, China, and Brazil. More than half of its global direct investment will be in emerging countries.[63]

A firm may make a direct foreign investment by acquiring an interest in an existing company, such as Wal-Mart did in Japan, or by building new facilities. It might do so because it has trouble transferring some resource to a foreign operation or getting that resource locally. One important resource is personnel, especially managers. If the local labor market is tight, the firm may buy an entire foreign firm and retain all its employees instead of paying higher salaries than competitors. For example, when Wal-Mart decided to enter China, it purchased the general merchandise chain Trust-Mart for about $1 billion.

In most cases, Wal-Mart has built stores from scratch in the global marketplace rather than buying an existing chain. Overcoming the culture of the chain Wal-Mart bought in Germany was too difficult and was one reason they pulled out of the market. A large part of the difficulty Wal-Mart has experienced with the Seiyu chain it bought in Japan was culturally related.

Toyota, the world's largest auto manufacturer, traditionally makes direct investment in new plants and equipment. In India, Toyota has a very small market share but the firm plans to quickly change that by building a new manufacturing facility in 2010. The problem, however, was a lack of skilled workers. So Toyota made an unusual investment: It opened a school. The first class will graduate the same year that the new plant opens. In addition to technical training, students learn discipline, confidence, and continuous improvement. Competition to enter Toyota's school is tough. When it opened in 2007, the school had over 5,000 applications for 64 slots.[64]

The United States is a popular place for direct investment by foreign companies. In 2008, the value of foreign-owned businesses in the United States was more than $650 billion. For example, in 2007 Taiwan-based Aur bought U.S. computer maker Gateway. Two years earlier, China's Lenovo Group purchased the PC operations of IBM.

THE GLOBAL MARKETING MIX

To succeed, firms seeking to enter into foreign trade must still adhere to the principles of the marketing mix. Information gathered on foreign markets through research is the basis for the four Ps of global marketing strategy: product, place (distribution), promotion, and price. Marketing managers who understand the advantages and disadvantages of different ways of entering the global market and the effect of the external environment on the firm's marketing mix have a better chance of reaching their goals.

The first step in creating a marketing mix is developing a thorough understanding of the global target market. Often this knowledge can be obtained through the same types of marketing research used in the domestic market (see Chapter 9). However, global marketing research is conducted in vastly different environments. Conducting a survey can be difficult in developing countries, where Internet ownership is growing but is not always common and mail delivery is slow or sporadic. Drawing samples based on known population parameters is often difficult because of the lack of data. In some cities in South America, Mexico, Africa, and Asia, street maps are unavailable, streets are unidentified, and houses are unnumbered. Moreover, the questions a marketer can ask may differ in other cultures. In some cultures, people tend to be more private than in the United States and will not respond to personal questions on surveys. For instance, in France, questions about one's age and income are considered especially rude.

© STEVE STOCK/ALAMY
© LENSCAP/ALAMY

Product and Promotion

With the proper information, a good marketing mix can be developed. One important decision is whether to alter the product and the promotion for the global marketplace. Other options are to radically change the product or to moderately adjust either the promotional message or the product to suit local conditions.

One Product, One Message

The strategy of global marketing standardization, which was discussed earlier, means developing a single product for all markets and promoting it the same way all over the world. For instance, Procter & Gamble uses the same product and promotional themes for Head and Shoulders in China as it does in the United States. The advertising draws attention to a person's dandruff problem, which stands out in a nation of black-haired people. Head and Shoulders is now the best-selling shampoo in China despite costing over 300 percent more than local brands. Buoyed by its success with Head and Shoulders, P&G is using the same product and same promotion strategy with Tide detergent in China. It also used another common promotion tactic that has been successful in the United States. The company spent half a million dollars to reach agreements with local washing machine manufacturers, which now include a free box of Tide with every new washer.

Other multinational firms are also applying uniform branding around the world on products such as Dove, Perrier, L'Oréal, and Hellmann's. Starbucks faced a big obstacle in China. Coffee was traditionally so unpopular in China's tea-drinking culture until recently that many Starbucks didn't brew regular drip coffee until someone ordered it. Starbucks faced a dilemma: Should they change their offerings to have more local appeal, or attempt to change Chinese tastes? Starbucks bet that a new generation of Chinese, with growing spending power and a desire for high status brands would try coffee. Coffee represents change from the old way of doing things. Once people enter a Chinese Starbucks, the education process begins. The chain stacks cream and sugar counters with brochures titled "Coffee Brewing Wisdom" and others that answer questions like "What is espresso?" Workers float through stores passing out small cups of pumpkin-spice latte and other drinks. Good-for-you messages about coffee are sometimes part of the pitch. The process seems to be working. One of your authors recently visited a number of Starbucks in several cities and observed many young upscale Chinese in every one! China is now Starbucks' fourth-largest global market, following Canada, Japan, and the United Kingdom. Despite recent store closings in the United States, Starbucks plans to add 60 stores in China. The firm already has 660 stores in China.[65]

In a recent survey, 13,000 consumers in 20 countries were asked about brand preferences across several product categories. In developing countries, local products were often viewed less favorably than global brands. Exhibit 5.5 reveals that Western brands fair quite well in the countries surveyed. The top cola brand in every country was either Pepsi or Coke.[66]

Global media—especially satellite and cable TV networks like CNN International, MTV Networks, and British Sky Broadcasting—make it possible to beam advertising

EXHIBIT 5.5

Emerging Markets Like American Brands

Top Brands in Various Countries			
Argentina		**Saudi Arabia**	
Car:	Ford	Fast food:	McDonald's
Fast food:	McDonald's	Iced tea:	Lipton
Makeup:	Avon	Mobile phone:	Nokia
Mobile phone:	Sony	Packaged cheese:	Kraft
Motorcycle:	Honda	Salty snacks:	Lay's
TV:	Philips	TV:	Sony
Top cola brand:	Coca-Cola	Top cola brand:	Pepsi
China		**South Africa**	
Beer:	Budweiser	Car:	Toyota
Coffee (ready to drink):	Nestea	Designer clothing store:	Levi's
Fast food:	KFC	Fast food:	KFC
Mobile phone:	Panasonic	Lipstick:	Revlon
Soap:	Safeguard	Mobile phone:	Nokia
TV:	Sony	TV:	LG
Top cola brand:	Coca-Cola	Top cola brand:	Coca-Cola
Egypt		**Thailand**	
Designer clothing store:	Nike	Beer:	Heineken
Fuel:	Mobil	Car:	Toyota
Hotel:	Hilton, Sheraton	Convenience store:	7-Eleven
Makeup:	Avon	Moisturizer:	Nivea
Shampoo:	Pert Plus	Whiskey/Scotch:	Johnnie Walker
TV:	Toshiba	TV:	Sony
Top cola brand:	Pepsi	Top cola brand:	Pepsi
India		**Turkey**	
Conditioner:	Garnier	Car:	BMW
Fast food:	McDonald's	Cognac:	Rémy Martin
Motor oil:	Castrol	Designer clothing store:	DKNY, Gucci
MP3 player:	Sony	Fast food:	McDonald's
Coffee (ready to drink):	Nescafé	Hotel:	Hilton
TV:	LG	Iced tea:	Lipton
Top cola brand:	Pepsi	Top cola brand:	Coca-Cola
Romania			
Car:	Mercedes	Shampoo:	Head and Shoulders
Fast food:	McDonald's	Whiskey/Scotch:	Jack Daniels
Lipstick:	Avon	Top cola brand:	Coca-Cola
MP3 player:	Sony		

Source: Synovate, Chicago (2007). Used by permission of Aegis Group, plc.

to audiences unreachable a few years ago. Eighteen-year-olds in Paris often have more in common with 18-year-olds in New York than with their own parents. Almost all of MTV's advertisers run unified, English-language campaigns in the nations the firm reaches. The audiences buy the same products, go to the same movies, listen to the same music, and sip the same colas. Global advertising works on that simple premise. Although teens throughout the world prefer movies above all other forms of television programming, they are closely followed by music videos, stand-up comedy, and then sports.

Global marketing standardization can sometimes backfire. Unchanged products may fail simply because of cultural factors. The game *Trivial Pursuit* failed in Japan. It seems that getting the answers wrong can be seen as a loss of face. Any type of war game tends to do very poorly in Germany, even though Germany is by far the world's biggest game-playing nation. A successful game in Germany has plenty of details and thick rulebooks.

Sometimes the desire for absolute standardization must give way to practical considerations and local market dynamics. For example, because of the feminine connotations of the word *diet*, the European version of Diet Coke is Coca-Cola Light. In France, its country of origin, the leading brand of yogurt is called Danone, whereas in the United States, it goes by its anglicized name, Dannon. Even if the brand name differs by market—as with Lay's potato chips, which are Sabritas in Mexico—a strong visual relationship may be created by uniform application of the brandmark and graphic elements on packaging.

Product Invention

In the context of global marketing, product invention can be taken to mean either creating a new product for a market or drastically changing an existing product. Campbell's Soup invented a watercress and duck gizzard soup that is now selling well in China. It is also considering a cream of snake soup. Frito-Lay's most popular potato chip in Thailand is shrimp flavored. Popular ice cream flavors in Japan include pickled orchid, eel, fish, sea slug, whale meat, soft-shelled turtle, and cedar chips. McDonald's was struggling in Japan until it added a shrimp burger to the menu. Pepsi has found success in Japan with "limited edition" drinks that create buzz on YouTube and other sites. The most successful has been "Ice Cucumber," where bloggers are debating whether it tastes more like melon or cucumber. Another popular "limited edition" drink was a cinnamon-based beverage called "Pepsi Red."[67]

Whirlpool has launched what it bills as the world's cheapest automatic washer, with an eye on low-income consumers who thought they could never afford one. Whirlpool invested $30 million over 18 months to develop the washing machine in Brazil. But the Ideale (the machine's brand name) is a global project because it is also being manufactured in China and India. The washer was launched first in Brazil and China (where its Chinese name means Super Hand-Washing Washer). It followed in India a few months later. Soon it will be marketed in other developing countries. The target retail price: $150 to $200. Just about a quarter of Brazilian households have an automatic washing machine, and penetration is only about 8 percent in China and 4.5 percent in India.[68]

Consumers in different countries use products differently. For example, in many countries, clothing is worn much longer between washings than in the United States, so a more durable fabric must be produced and marketed. For Peru, Goodyear developed a tire that contains a higher percentage of natural rubber and has better treads than tires manufactured elsewhere in order to handle the tough Peruvian driving conditions. Rubbermaid has sold millions of open-top wastebaskets in America; Europeans, picky about garbage peeking out of bins, want bins with tight lids that snap into place.

McDonald's was once vilified for pushing its American-created fast food on the world. Now it is taking a different approach and selling more than ever in the global marketplace. The Customer Experience box explains why.

CUSTOMER Experience

Big Macs Take on a Local Flavor

The next time you're in Brazil, say, or Italy or Portugal, and feeling like a taste of Americana, stop off at a local McDonald's restaurant and order a Big Tasty burger. As the name suggests, it's a giant sandwich consisting of a 5.5-ounce beef patty slathered in smoky barbecue sauce. Once you include the square-chopped lettuce, tomatoes, and three slices of cheese, it all adds up to a whopping 840 calories. Just don't try looking for the Big Tasty in the United States, McDonald's home territory. It's not on sale there. In fact, there's precious little about the burger that's American at all, other than the fact that it's sold by McDonald's. It was dreamed up in a test kitchen in Germany and then tweaked, trialed, and launched in Sweden.

McDonald's worldwide operations are now far bigger than its U.S. domestic business, and they are growing substantially faster. And as the world has become the principal revenue engine for the company, it has turned this iconic American brand upside down, transforming the way it does business. These days, new ideas can—and frequently do—come from anywhere.

Walk out of London's Cannon Street Station and turn right, leaving St. Paul's Cathedral behind you, and you'll come across a restaurant with three giant, green swivel armchairs in the window that look like the modernist Egg chair created by the late Danish designer Arne Jacobsen. Inside, lime-green slats partition off several seating zones. The pillars are orange. Funky murals hang on the walls and, between them, green- and red-striped wallpaper. It's 4,000 miles from here to Chicago, but light-years removed from the tired, red-and-white vinyl seats and Formica tabletops that have long served as McDonald's standard décor. If it wasn't for the golden arches over the door, you might not realize at first glance that it was a McDonald's restaurant at all. In fact, the furnishings come from a catalog of different décor types that a team of McDonald's designers in Paris has worked up with the help of an architect named Philippe Avanzi, based in Grenoble, France.

It's not just the décor that varies. McDonald's in Britain in 2008 added freshly ground fair-trade coffee to its menu, along with organic milk. It boasts that its eggs are free range. Naturally the Brits serve up McDonald's classics such as Big Macs, Happy Meals, and Double Cheeseburgers. But you can also order porridge for breakfast and a range of other items customized for British tastes, including a variant of a French chicken sandwich—with salsa dressing.

Such variation has become the norm, belying McDonald's image as a big American corporation that serves standard fare around the world. In India, where eating beef is a religious taboo, the Big Mac equivalent is the Maharaja Mac, made from chicken, and there's a plethora of vegetarian dishes on the menu. And even some of the classics are now tweaked from market to market. In Germany, less coriander is used in SouthWest salads, while Britain puts less salt on its Chicken McNuggets.[69]

Do you think that McDonald's made the right move in letting global managers design their own stores and products? What if a manager wanted to change the McDonald's logo? The Big Tasty burger hasn't been introduced in America. Why do you think this is true? Hint: Seventy percent of McDonald's customers in the United States come from the drive-through.

Product Adaptation

Another alternative for global marketers is to slightly alter a basic product to meet local conditions. Sometimes it is as simple as changing the package size. In India, Unilever sells single-use sachets of Sunsilk shampoo for 2 to 4 cents. Unilever's Rexona brand deodorant sticks sell for 16 cents and up. They are big hits in India, the Philippines, Bolivia, and Peru—where Unilever has grabbed 60 percent of the deodorant market. A nickel-size Vaseline package and a tube containing enough Close Up toothpaste for 20 brushings sell for about 8 cents each. In Nigeria, Unilever sells 3-inch-square packets of margarine that don't need refrigeration.

Sometimes power sources and/or voltage must be changed on electronic products. It may be necessary, for example, to change the size and shape of the electrical plug. In other cases, the change may be a bit more radical. In India, people often lack reliable access to electricity or can't afford batteries. So, Freeplay Energy Group of London created a radio that is charged by cranking a handle.

One of the world's best at product adaptation is the Korean firm LG Electronics. Kimchi, made from fermented cabbage seasoned with garlic and chili, is served with most meals in Korea, but when it's stored inside a normal refrigerator, its pungent odor taints nearby foods. LG Electronics introduced the kimchi refrigerator, a product specifically designed to address the odor problem. Featuring a dedicated compartment that isolates smelly kimchi from other foods, the fridge gradually became a must-have in Korean homes.

To meet the needs of Indian consumers, LG rolled out refrigerators with larger vegetable- and water-storage compartments, surge-resistant power supplies, and brightly colored finishes that reflect local preferences (red in the south, green in Kashmir). In Iran, LG offers a microwave oven with a preset button for reheating shish kebabs—a favorite dish. Saudi Arabians like LG's Primian refrigerator, which includes a special compartment for storing dates; the fruit, a Middle Eastern staple, spoils easily. For Saudis and other oil-rich consumers, LG has introduced a gold-plated 71-inch flat-screen television that sells for $80,000.

Chinese don't like sweet cookies and Kraft's Oreos were not selling well. Not only were Oreos too sweet; the Chinese also thought the package was too expensive at 79 cents. The company developed 20 prototypes of reduced-sugar Oreos and tested them with Chinese consumers before arriving at a formula that tasted right. Kraft also introduced packages containing fewer Oreos for just 29 cents.

Although Oreos were selling better, Kraft was still not satisfied. China's cookie-wafer segment was growing faster than traditional biscuit-like cookies. Kraft decided to remake the Oreo itself. The new Chinese Oreo consisted of four layers of crispy wafer filled with vanilla and chocolate cream, coated in chocolate.[70]

Promotion Adaptation

Another global marketing strategy is to maintain the same basic product but alter the promotional strategy. Bicycles are mainly pleasure vehicles in the United States. In many parts of the world, however, they are a family's main mode of transportation. Thus, promotion in these countries should stress durability and efficiency. In contrast, U.S. advertising may emphasize escaping and having fun.

Harley-Davidson decided that its American promotion theme, "One steady constant in an increasingly screwed-up world," wouldn't appeal to the Japanese market. The Japanese ads combine American images with traditional Japanese ones: American riders passing a geisha in a rickshaw, Japanese ponies nibbling at a Harley motorcycle. Waiting lists for Harleys in Japan are now six months long.

Kit Kat bars are a hit the world over, but Nestlé didn't have much luck selling them in Japan until it figured out how to crack the teen market. In Japan, the product's name is pronounced "kitto katsu," which roughly translates to "I hope you win." Fueling a rumor that Kit Kats bring success at crucial school exams, Nestlé rolled out packages combining the candy with other good-luck charms. Now 90 percent of Japanese schoolkids say they've heard of Kit Kat bars, and Kit Kat sales have soared 28 percent.[71]

Personal selling is part of promotion, and nowhere has adaption been taken so far as has Lexus in Japan. In the luxury car market in Japan, Lexus is overshadowed by BMW and Mercedes-Benz. To rectify that, Lexus hired a Japanese etiquette school that specialized in teaching the art of beautifying daily behavior. Now, when a Lexus salesperson opens a car door in a Lexus showroom for a potential customer, he or she points with all five fingers to the handle, right hand followed by left. Then, the salesperson gracefully opens the door with both hands, in the same way Japanese samurais in the 14th century would have opened a sliding screen door.

At Lexus showrooms, sales consultants lean 5 to 10 degrees forward and assume a warrior's "waiting position" when a customer is looking at a car. When serving customers coffee or tea, employees must kneel on the floor with both feet together and both knees on the ground. The coffee cup must never make a noise when it is placed on the

© AP IMAGES/PRNEWSFOTO/SC JOHNSON

SC Johnson's motorcycle distribution project in Nigeria has a twofold goal—to increase sales with smaller retailers, while at the same time developing skills and growing incomes for local entrepreneurs.

table. All salespeople use a mirror to practice the "Lexus Face," a closed-mouth smile said to put customers at ease.[72]

Language barriers, translation problems, and cultural differences have generated numerous headaches for international marketing managers. Consider these examples:

- A toothpaste claiming to give users white teeth was especially inappropriate in many areas of Southeast Asia, where the well-to-do chew betel nuts and black teeth are a sign of higher social status.
- Procter & Gamble's Japanese advertising for Camay soap nearly devastated the product. In one commercial, a man meeting a woman for the first time immediately compared her skin to that of a fine porcelain doll. Although the ad had worked in other Asian countries, the man came across as rude and disrespectful in Japan.
- A teenager careening down a store aisle on a grocery cart in a Coca-Cola ad was perceived as too rebellious in Singapore.

Place (Distribution)

Solving promotional and product problems does not guarantee global marketing success. The product still has to get adequate distribution. For example, Europeans don't play sports as much as Americans do, so they don't visit sporting-goods stores as often. Realizing this, Reebok started selling its shoes in about 800 traditional shoe stores in France. In one year, the company doubled its French sales. Harley-Davidson had to open two company-owned stores in Japan to get distribution for its Harley clothing and clothing accessories.

The Japanese distribution system is considered the most complicated in the world. Imported goods wind their way through layers of agents, wholesalers, and retailers. For example, a bottle of 96 aspirins costs about $20 because the bottle passes through at least six wholesalers, each of whom increases the selling price. As a result, the Japanese consumer pays the world's most exorbitant prices. These distribution channels seem to be based on historical and traditional patterns of socially arranged trade-offs, which Japanese officials claim are very hard for the government to change. Today, however, the system seems to be changing because of pressure from Japanese consumers, who are putting more emphasis on low prices in their purchasing decisions. The retailer who can cut distribution costs and therefore the retail price gets the sale. For example, Kojima, a Japanese electronics superstore chain like the U.S. chains RadioShack and Best Buy, had to bypass General Electric's Japanese distribution partner Toshiba to import its merchandise at a good price. Toshiba's distribution system required refrigerators to pass through too many hands before they reached the retailer. Kojima went directly to GE headquarters in the United States and persuaded the company to sell it refrigerators, which were then shipped directly to Kojima. It is now selling GE refrigerators for about $800—half the price of a typical Japanese model.

Innovative distribution systems can create a competitive advantage for savvy companies. Every day, dozens of flights touch down at Kenya's Nairobi Airport, unloading tourists. But when some of those same KLM and Kenya Airlines aircraft take off for the late-night trip home, they're carrying far more than weary travelers returning from African safaris. Their planes are crammed with an average 25 tons apiece of fresh beans, bok choy, okra, and other produce that was harvested and packaged just the day before. It's all bound for eager—and growing—markets in Brussels, London, Paris, and other European cities.

Those flights are integral parts of an innovative supply chain. Vegpro Kenya, one of the nation's top produce exporters, operates seven farms within a two-hour drive of the airport. Every morning, trucks full of just-picked vegetables—30 varieties in all—dash to the airport. There, inside Vegpro's 27,000-square-foot air-conditioned cargo bay, more than 1,000 workers wash and sort the vegetables before they are rushed onto planes, ensuring that there's no break in the "cool chain" before the produce arrives in European stores the next day.

To combat distribution problems, companies are using creative strategies. Colgate-Palmolive has introduced villagers in India to the concept of brushing teeth by rolling into villages with video vans that show half-hour infomercials on the benefits of toothpaste. The company received more than half of its revenue in that nation from rural areas until 2006. The rural market has been virtually invisible, due to a lack of distribution. Unilever's Indian subsidiary, Hindustan Lever, sells its cosmetics, toothpastes, and detergents door-to-door. It now has over a million direct-sales consultants.

In many developing nations, channels of distribution and the physical infrastructure are inadequate. In China, the main modes of transport are truck and train. But in a fragmented trucking industry with few major companies, multinationals have difficulty determining which companies are reliable. A lack of refrigerated trucks has meant that poultry giant Tyson Foods can distribute in only a handful of Chinese cities.[73] In the rail system, theft is a major problem.

If China is bad, India is worse. Most Indian roads are simple two-lane affairs, maintained badly if at all. Shipping goods by rail costs twice as much on average as in developed countries and three times as much as in China. At India's ports, shipments often languish for days waiting for customs clearance and loading berths; goods typically take 6 to 12 weeks to reach the United States, compared with 2 to 3 weeks for goods from China.[74] UPS uses 37 minivans in Mumbai's very congested streets. Buildings in Mumbai often lack street numbers, so delivery personnel ask passersby for directions. During seasonal monsoons in July and August, workers at UPS depots shrink-wrap packages in plastic to keep them dry, and UPS rolls out its biggest trucks to navigate flooded streets that might swallow a minivan. On the city's industrial outskirts, India's ubiquitous three-wheeled auto rickshaws swarm like bees into any gaps that open up between lumbering trucks and buses. Vehicles might share a thoroughfare with milkmen on bicycles and a street merchant pushing a cartload of bananas.[75]

In traffic-choked cities from Manila to Montevideo, McDonald's deploys fleets of motor scooters to get hot food to customers. All told, McDonald's delivers in some 25 cities, with a half-dozen more in 2008. In 2007 the company launched deliveries in Taipei, with 1,000 drivers, and expanded Shanghai to citywide service. It is now testing the concept in Beirut and Riyadh. In Egypt, where the setup was pioneered in 1995, deliveries now account for 27 percent of all McDonald's revenue—up to 80 percent at some restaurants. Today, almost all of McDonald's 35 restaurants in and around Cairo deliver, while only a couple have drive-through windows.[76]

American companies importing goods to the United States are facing other problems. Logistics has been a growing challenge for U.S. companies seeking to cut costs by shifting more production to countries where manufacturing is cheaper. Now, however, the rising costs for shipping goods are adding to their profit pressures. The surge in global trade in recent years has added to strains and charges for all forms of transport. As a result, some manufacturers are developing costly buffer stocks—which can mean setting up days' or weeks' worth of extra components—to avoid shutting down production lines and failing to make timely deliveries. Others are shifting to more expensive but more reliable modes of transport, like airfreight, which is faster and less prone to delays than ocean shipping. Some companies are turning to new information technology to keep supply chains flowing and are hiring experts to help determine the best U.S. ports to use each week.

Pricing

Once marketing managers have determined a global product and promotion strategy, they can select the remainder of the marketing mix. Pricing presents some unique problems in the global sphere. Exporters must not only cover their production costs but also consider transportation costs, insurance, taxes, and tariffs. When deciding on a final

floating exchange rates
Prices of different currencies move up and down based on the demand for and the supply of each currency.

dumping
The sale of an exported product at a price lower than that charged for the same or a like product in the "home" market of the exporter.

price, marketers must also determine what customers are willing to spend on a particular product. Marketers also need to ensure that their foreign buyers will pay the price. Because developing nations lack mass purchasing power, selling to them often poses special pricing problems. Sometimes a product can be simplified in order to lower the price. The firm must not assume that low-income countries are willing to accept lower quality, however. Although the nomads of the Sahara are very poor, they still buy expensive fabrics to make their clothing. Their survival in harsh conditions and extreme temperatures requires this expense. Additionally, certain expensive luxury items can be sold almost anywhere. L'Oréal was unsuccessful selling cheap shampoo in India, so the company targets the rising class. It now sells a $17 Paris face powder and a $25 Vichy sunscreen. Both products are very popular.

Exchange Rates

The exchange rate is the price of one country's currency in terms of another country's currency. If a country's currency *appreciates*, less of that currency is needed to buy another country's currency. If a country's currency *depreciates*, more of that currency will be needed to buy another country's currency.

How do appreciation and depreciation affect the prices of a country's goods? If, say, the U.S. dollar depreciates relative to the Japanese yen, U.S. residents have to pay more dollars to buy Japanese goods. To illustrate, suppose the dollar price of a yen is $0.012 and that a Toyota is priced at 2 million yen. At this exchange rate, a U.S. resident pays $24,000 for a Toyota ($0.012 x 2 million yen = $24,000). If the dollar depreciates to $0.018 to one yen, then the U.S. resident will have to pay $36,000 for a Toyota.

As the dollar depreciates, the prices of Japanese goods rise for U.S. residents, so they buy fewer Japanese goods—thus, U.S. imports may decline. At the same time, as the dollar depreciates relative to the yen, the yen appreciates relative to the dollar. This means prices of U.S. goods fall for the Japanese, so they buy more U.S. goods—and U.S. exports rise.

Currency markets primarily operate under a system of **floating exchange rates**. Prices of different currencies "float" up and down based on the demand for and the supply of each currency. Global currency traders create the supply of and demand for a particular country's currency based on that country's investment, trade potential, and economic strength.

Dumping

Dumping is the sale of an exported product at a price lower than that charged for the same or a like product in the "home" market of the exporter. This practice is regarded as a form of price discrimination that can potentially harm the importing nation's competing industries. Dumping may occur as a result of exporter business strategies that include (1) trying to increase an overseas market share, (2) temporarily distributing products in overseas markets to offset slack demand in the home market, (3) lowering unit costs by exploiting large-scale production, and (4) attempting to maintain stable prices during periods of exchange rate fluctuations.

Historically, the dumping of goods has presented serious problems in international trade. As a result, dumping has led to significant disagreements among countries and diverse views about its harmfulness. Some trade economists view dumping as harmful only when it involves the use of "predatory" practices that intentionally try to eliminate competition and gain monopoly power in a market. They believe that predatory dumping rarely occurs and that antidumping rules are a protectionist tool whose cost to consumers and import-using industries exceeds the benefits to the industries receiving protection.

Recently, the U.S. accused Vietnam of dumping textile products on the U.S. market. The U.S. imports about $4 billion worth of garments from Vietnam each year.[77] To date, the dumping claim has not been resolved.

Countertrade

Global trade does not always involve cash. Countertrade is a fast-growing way to conduct global business. In **countertrade,** all or part of the payment for goods or services is in the form of other goods or services. Countertrade is thus a form of barter (swapping goods for goods), an age-old practice whose origins have been traced back to cave dwellers. The U.S. Department of Commerce says that roughly 30 percent of all global trade is countertrade. In fact, both India and China have made billion-dollar government purchasing lists, with most of the goods to be paid for by countertrade. Recently, the Malaysian government bought 20 diesel-powered locomotives and paid for them with palm oil.

REVIEW LEARNING OUTCOME

List the basic elements involved in developing a global marketing mix

Global Marketing Mix

PRODUCT + PROMOTION	PLACE (Distribution)	PRICE
One Product, One Message	Channel Choice	Dumping
Product Invention	Channel Structure	Countertrade
Product Adaptation	Country Infrastructure	Exchange Rates
Message Adaptation		Purchasing Power

One common type of countertrade is straight barter. For example, PepsiCo sends Pepsi syrup to Russian bottling plants and in payment gets Stolichnaya vodka, which is then marketed in the West. Another form of countertrade is the compensation agreement. Typically, a company provides technology and equipment for a plant in a developing nation and agrees to take full or partial payment in goods produced by that plant. For example, General Tire Company supplied equipment and know-how for a Romanian truck tire plant. In turn, General Tire sold the tires it received from the plant in the United States under the Victoria brand name. Pierre Cardin gives technical advice to China in exchange for silk and cashmere. In these cases, both sides benefit even though they don't use cash.

countertrade
A form of trade in which all or part of the payment for goods or services is in the form of other goods or services.

THE IMPACT OF THE INTERNET

In many respects "going global" is easier than it has ever been before. Opening an e-commerce site on the Internet immediately puts a company in the international marketplace. Sophisticated language translation software can make any site accessible to persons around the world. Global shippers such as UPS, FedEx, and DHL help solve international e-commerce distribution complexities. E4X, Inc. offers software to ease currency conversions. Sites that use E4X's software can post prices in U.S. dollars, then ask their customers what currency they wish to use for payment. If the answer is a currency other than dollars, E4X takes over the transaction and translates the price into any of 22 currencies, collects the payment from the customer, and pays the site in dollars, just as though it were any other transaction. Customers never realize they're dealing with a third party.

REVIEW LEARNING OUTCOME

Discover how the Internet is affecting global marketing

Nevertheless, the promise of "borderless commerce" and the global "Internet economy" are still being restrained by the old brick-and-mortar rules, regulations, and habits. For example, Lands' End is not allowed to mention its unconditional refund policy on its e-commerce site in Germany because German retailers, which normally do not allow returns after 14 days, sued and won a court ruling blocking mention of it. Credit cards may be the currency of the Internet, but not everyone uses them. Whereas Americans spend an average of $6,500 per year by credit card, Japanese spend less than $2,000. Many Japanese don't even have a credit card. So how do they pay for e-commerce purchases? 7-Eleven Japan, with over 8,000 convenience stores, has come to the rescue. eS-Books, the Japanese Web site partner of Yahoo! Japan, lets shoppers buy books and videos on the Internet, then specify to which 7-Eleven the merchandise is to be shipped. The buyer goes to that specific store and pays cash for the e-purchase.

Like the Japanese, Scandinavians are reluctant to use credit cards, and the French have an *horreur* of revealing the private information that Net retailers often request. French Web sites tend to be decidedly French. For example, FNAC, the largest French video, book, and music retailer, offers a daily "cultural newspaper" at its site. A trendy Web site in France will have a black background, while bright colors and a geometrical layout give a site a German feel. Dutch surfers are keen on video downloads, and Scandinavians seem to have a soft spot for images of nature.

6 ◀ number of regional Indian languages spoken in Pillsbury Doughboy advertisements

portion of industrial production exported by the U.S. ▶ **1/5**

160 ◀ number of countries in which Coca-Cola sells its products

weeks of vacation time legally required in France ▶ **5**

450 million
▲ number of cell phone users in China

number of days it takes to start a business in Mozambique ▶ **153**

2 ◀ number of days it takes to start a business in Canada

$6 trillion
▲ combined economy of Canada, Mexico, and the U.S.

percentage of U.S. exports generated by small companies ▶ **96**

400 ◀ number of U.S. franchises with overseas locations

ANATOMY OF a Multinational Company: Starbucks

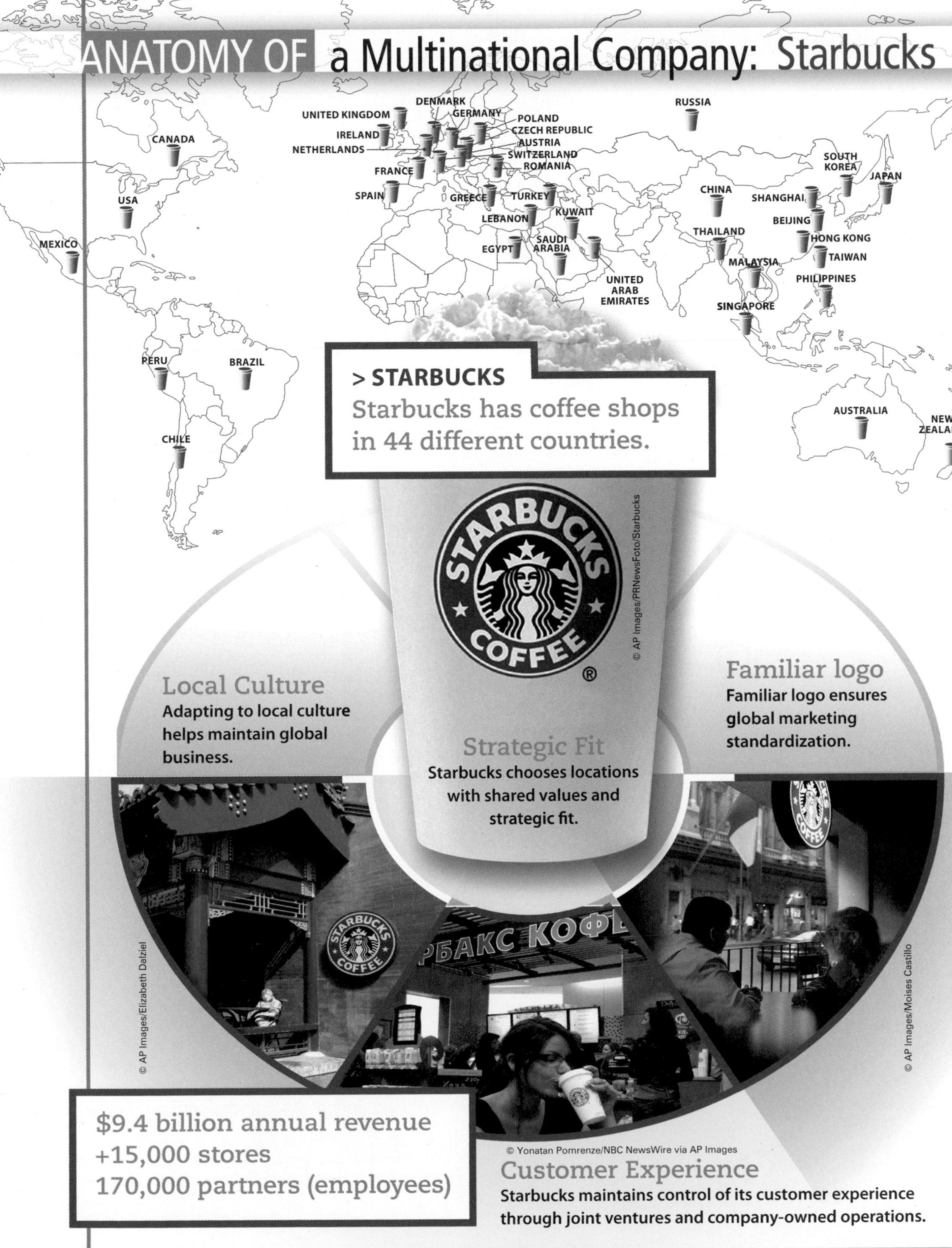

© AP Images/PRNewsFoto/Starbucks

© AP Images/Elizabeth Dalziel

© AP Images/Moises Castillo

© Yonatan Pomrenze/NBC NewsWire via AP Images

REVIEW AND APPLICATIONS

Discuss the importance of global marketing. Businesspeople who adopt a global vision are better able to identify global marketing opportunities, understand the nature of global networks, create effective global marketing strategies, and compete against foreign competition in domestic markets.

1.1 What is meant by "having a global vision"? Why is it important?

1.2 Isolationists have suggested that America would be much better off economically and politically if we just "built a wall" around the country and didn't deal with outsiders. Do you agree? Why or why not?

1.3 Discuss jobs outsourcing. Is it beneficial to U.S. firms?

Discuss the impact of multinational firms on the world economy. Multinational corporations are international traders that regularly operate across national borders. Because of their vast size and financial, technological, and material resources, multinational corporations have a great influence on the world economy. They have the ability to overcome trade problems, save on labor costs, and tap new technology. However, some countries are beginning to block foreign investment by multinationals.

2.1 Rubbermaid, the U.S. manufacturer of kitchen products and other household items, is considering moving to global marketing standardization. What are the pros and cons of this strategy?

2.2 Do you believe that multinationals are beneficial or harmful to developing nations? Why? What could foreign governments do to make them more beneficial?

Describe the external environment facing global marketers. Global marketers face the same environmental factors as they do domestically: culture, economic, and technological development; political structure and actions; demography; and natural resources. Cultural considerations include societal values, attitudes, and beliefs; language; and customary business practices. A country's economic and technological status depends on its stage of industrial development, which, in turn, affects average family incomes. The political structure is shaped by political ideology and policies such as tariffs, quotas, boycotts, exchange controls, trade agreements, and market groupings. Demographic variables include the size of a population and its age and geographic distribution.

3.1 Many marketers now believe that teenagers in the developed countries are becoming "global consumers." That is, they all want and buy the same goods and services. Do you think this is true? If so, what has caused the phenomenon?

3.2 Renault and Peugeot dominate the French market but have no presence in the U.S. market. Why do you think that this is true?

3.3 Suppose that your state senator has asked you to contribute a brief article to her constituents' newsletter that answers the question, "Will there ever be a United States of Europe?" Write a draft of your article, and include reasons why or why not.

3.4 Divide into six teams. Each team will be responsible for one of the following industries: entertainment; pharmaceuticals; computers and software;

financial, legal, or accounting services; agriculture; and textiles and apparel. Interview one or more executives in each of these industries to determine how the WTO, NAFTA, and CAFTA have affected and will affect their organizations. If a local firm cannot be contacted in your industry, use the library and the Internet to prepare your report.

3.5 What are the major barriers to international trade? Explain how government policies may be used to either restrict or stimulate global marketing.

Identify the various ways of entering the global marketplace. Firms use the following strategies to enter global markets, in descending order of risk and profit: direct investment, joint venture, contract manufacturing, licensing and franchising, and exporting.

4.1 Candartel, an upscale manufacturer of lamps and lampshades in America, has decided to "go global." Top management is having trouble deciding how to develop the market. What are some market entry options for the firm?

4.2 Explain how the U.S. Commercial Service can help companies wanting to enter the international market.

4.3 What are some of the advantages and potential disadvantages of entering a joint venture?

4.4 Why is direct investment considered risky?

List the basic elements involved in developing a global marketing mix. A firm's major consideration is how much it will adjust the four Ps—product, promotion, place (distribution), and price—within each country. One strategy is to use one product and one promotion message worldwide. A second strategy is to create new products for global markets. A third strategy is to keep the product basically the same but alter the promotional message. A fourth strategy is to slightly alter the product to meet local conditions.

5.1 The sale of cigarettes in many developed countries either has peaked or is declining. However, the developing markets represent major growth markets. Should U.S. tobacco companies capitalize on this opportunity?

5.2 Describe at least three situations where an American company might want to keep the product the same but alter the promotion. Also, give three examples where the product must be altered.

5.3 Explain how exchange rates can affect a firm's global sales.

Discover how the Internet is affecting global marketing. Simply opening a Web site can open the door for international sales. International carriers, like UPS, can help solve logistics problems. Language translation software can help an e-commerce business become multilingual. Yet cultural differences and old-line rules, regulations, and taxes hinder rapid development of e-commerce in many countries.

6.1 Describe how "going global" via the Internet presents opportunities and challenges.

6.2 Give several examples of how culture may hinder "going global" via the Internet.

KEY TERMS

buyer for export 164
capital-intensive 148
Central America Free Trade Agreement (CAFTA) 157
contract manufacturing 165
countertrade 177
direct foreign investment 167
dumping 176
export agent 164
export broker 164
exporting 162
European Union (EU) 155
floating exchange rates 176
General Agreement on Tariffs and Trade (GATT) 156
global marketing 143
global marketing standardization 149
global vision 143
International Monetary Fund (IMF) 160
joint venture 166
licensing 164
Mercosur 155
multinational corporation 147
North American Free Trade Agreement (NAFTA) 156
Uruguay Round 155
World Bank 160
World Trade Organization (WTO) 156

EXERCISES

APPLICATION EXERCISE

To be effective as a marketer, it is important to know geography. How will you be able to decide whether to expand into a new territory (domestic or foreign) if you don't know where it is and something about its culture, currency, and economy? If you can't place the European countries on a blank map, or if you can't label the lower 48 states without a list to help you, you're not alone. In one study, students incorrectly located over 50 percent of European countries and over 25 percent of the states in the Unites States. To help you brush up on your geography, we've compiled some tools that you may find useful.

Activities

1. To review domestic geography, go to **www.50states.com/tools/usamap.htm** and print the blank map of the United States. Label the map. For a challenge, add the state capitals to the map.
2. Once you have successfully labeled the U.S. map, you may be ready to try labeling a world map. If so, go to **www.clickandlearn.com** and view the free, printable, blackline maps. Under the category of The World and Continents, choose the blackline detail map. This shows country outlines, whereas the basic blackline outline map shows only the continents. You will notice that there are also blackline maps for each continent, so if taking on the entire world is too daunting, start with more manageable blocks.
3. To be a global marketer, it is not enough to know where countries are located. You will need to know about the culture, the main exports, the currency, and even the main imports. Select a half-dozen or so countries with which you are unfamiliar, and research basic geographic information about them.

ETHICS EXERCISE

Moore Electronics sells automated lighting for airport runways. The government of an Eastern European country has offered Moore a contract to provide equipment for the 15 major airports in the country. The official in charge of awarding the contract, however, is demanding a 5 percent kickback. He told Moore to build this into the contract price so that there would be no cost to Moore. Without the kickback, Moore loses the contract. Such kickbacks are considered a normal way of doing business in this country.

Questions

1. What should Moore do?
2. Review the Foreign Corrupt Practices Act online at **www.usdoj.gov/criminal/fraud/fcpa/.** Write a brief paragraph on what this statute contains that relates to Moore's dilemma. Some American executives think this law causes American corporations to suffer a competitive disadvantage. Do you agree? Why or why not?

MARKETING PLAN EXERCISE

These end-of-chapter marketing plan exercises are designed to help you use what you learned in the chapter to build a strategic marketing plan for a company of your choosing. Once you've completed the marketing plan exercise for each chapter in Part 1 of this textbook, you can complete the Part 1 Marketing Planning Worksheet on your companion Web site at **www.cengage.com/international.** Now continue building your strategic marketing plan that you started in Chapter 2 by completing the following exercises:

1. Assume your company is or will be marketing globally. How should your company enter the global marketplace? How will international issues affect your firm?
2. If you choose an Internet presence, your product or service will be visible to a global community. Assess the international marketplace for your particular offering. A listing of international chambers of commerce is at **www.worldchambers.com** and the CIA World Factbook is at **www.cia.gov/cia/publications/factbook/index.html.**

CASE STUDY: MTV: ROCKING THE WORLD ONE NATION AT A TIME

To most people, MTV is as American as apple pie, baseball, and freedom of speech. It is a cultural icon to every American who grew up in the 1980s or 1990s, and it is easily one of the most palpable influence on the behavior of the demographic it targets with its programming. A closer look at MTV's business, however, reveals that its true significance is its ability to translate its formula for success into the many languages of the world. The network now owns 33 distinct channels that broadcast shows in 18 languages to 1.8 billion viewers in over 160 countries.

MTV Networks International, a subsidiary of MTV that actually dwarfs its parent, took its first steps on foreign soil with MTV Europe in 1987 and soon thereafter became Europe's largest television network. With a blueprint for success in hand, the large subsidiary turned its attention to the global youth market, which today includes over 2.5 billion people between the ages of 10 and 34. As it watched demand for television sets and paid programming services explode in rapidly developing markets, such as China, Latin America, and India, MTV was poised to capitalize.

Large and diverse markets, however, are difficult to understand and expensive to penetrate. Initially, MTV simply tried to export a standardized version of its American programming, but it quickly discovered that teens from around the world—while they do enjoy American music—are mostly interested in what's happening in their own regions. MTV responded by undertaking the costly and complex task of producing localized content for specific markets. Now, veejay selection, programming, and service offerings are all unique in any given market.

Digital television and interactive services are very popular in Europe, so MTV UK developed a service that allows viewers to obtain information on CDs, check concert dates, and vote for their favorite performers during the MTV European Music Awards directly from their TV sets. In Asia, a virtual animated veejay named LiLi can interact with viewers in five different languages. Controlled by an actor behind the image, LiLi can also interview guests and provide popular culture tips. Brazilian viewers, who also tend to be huge soccer fans, enjoy *Rockgol*, an MTV-produced soccer championship that has been opposed by Brazilian record industry executives and musicians.

MTV Japan, a joint venture between MTV Networks and local investment firm H&Q Asia Pacific, operates in the world's second largest music market and one of the world's most advanced mobile telecommunications markets. Identifying those two trends, MTV Japan developed a service that lets subscribers use their mobile phones to download entertainment news and new music or vote for their favorite veejay.

The development cycle is long for such detailed international projects, but MTV Networks International president Bill Roedy is a patient man. He spent ten years working with Chinese officials for the right to air MTV programming for just six hours a day. The payoff? Forty cable providers now carry MTV Mandarin into 60 million Chinese homes. Roedy is also sensitive to foreign leaders' fears that their culture will be "Americanized" by MTV. Before his networks enter markets with extreme cultural differences, such as Israel, Singapore, Cuba, or China, Roedy meets with key political figures to allay their fears. "We've had very little resistance once we explain that we're not in the business of exporting American culture," he notes.[78]

Questions

1. Identity the key environmental challenges MTV has faced in its effort to expand globally, and discuss how MTV has overcome them.
2. What is MTV's global market entry strategy? Discuss whether you agree with MTV's approach, and identify its advantages and disadvantages.
3. Discuss MTV's global product strategy.

COMPANY CLIPS

© NKP MEDIA, INC./CENGAGE

METHOD—GLOBAL BEGINNINGS

In the twenty-first century, start-ups can become global businesses much faster than in anytime in history. So, while new companies are forging their way domestically, they may also experience an added layer of challenges from trying to enter global markets at the same time. In this final video segment on method, founder Eric Ryan and CEO Alastair Dorward describe their company's perspective on global expansion and which foreign markets represent good opportunities for method.

Questions

1. Is method a multinational company? Explain.
2. Which environmental factors facing all global marketers is method confronting as it begins to expand into foreign markets?
3. Outline method's global marketing mix.
4. What is innovative about how method envisions moving into foreign markets? Would method's strategy for global expansion work for other companies or industries? Which ones? Explain.

Marketing & You Results

This questionnaire measures cultural openness. The higher your score, the more interested you are in learning about other cultures and interacting with people from other countries. People with high cultural openness tend to be less ethnocentric and more open to buying imported products than people with low cultural openness. As you read in Chapter 5, cultural openness is an important aspect of developing a global vision.

WHAT'S INSIDE

CHAPTER 6

Consumer Decision Making

© iSTOCKPHOTOS.COM/PAUL PIEBINGA

LEARNING OUTCOMES

LO 1 Explain why marketing managers should understand consumer behavior

LO 2 Analyze the components of the consumer decision-making process

LO 3 Explain the consumer's postpurchase evaluation process

LO 4 Identify the types of consumer buying decisions and discuss the significance of consumer involvement

LO 5 Identify and understand the cultural factors that affect consumer buying decisions

LO 6 Identify and understand the social factors that affect consumer buying decisions

LO 7 Identify and understand the individual factors that affect consumer buying decisions

LO 8 Identify and understand the psychological factors that affect consumer buying decisions

THE IMPORTANCE OF UNDERSTANDING CONSUMER BEHAVIOR

Consumers' product and service preferences are constantly changing. Marketing managers must understand these desires in order to create a proper marketing mix for a well-defined market. So it is critical that marketing managers have a thorough knowledge of consumer behavior. **Consumer behavior** describes how consumers make purchase decisions and how they use and dispose of the purchased goods or services. The study of consumer behavior also includes the factors that influence purchase decisions and product use.

Understanding how consumers make purchase decisions can help marketing managers in several ways. For example, if a manager knows through research that gas mileage is the most important attribute for a certain target market, the manufacturer can redesign a car to meet that criterion. If the firm cannot change the design in the short run, it can use promotion in an effort to change consumers' decision-making criteria, for example, by promoting style, durability, and cargo capacity.

REVIEW LEARNING OUTCOME

LO 1 Explain why marketing managers should understand consumer behavior

Consumer behavior = HOW → consumers make purchase decisions; consumers use and dispose of products

What is your buying behavior?
Using the scales below, enter your answers.

1 2 3 4 5
Very often — Sometimes — Never

__ I have felt others would be horrified if they knew of my spending habits.

__ I've bought things even though I couldn't afford them.

__ I've written a check when I knew I didn't have enough money in the bank to cover it.

__ I've bought myself something in order to make myself feel better.

__ I've felt anxious or nervous on days I didn't go shopping.

__ I've made only the minimum payments on my credit cards.

1 2 3 4 5
Strongly agree — Strongly disagree

__ If I have any money left at the end of the pay period, I just have to spend it.

__ Having more money would solve my problems.

__ I have bought something, arrived home, and didn't know why I had bought it.

Now, total your score. Read the chapter to find out what your score means at the end.

Source: From Scale #98, *Marketing Scales Handbook*, G. Bruner, K. James, H. Hensel, eds., Vol. III. © by American Marketing Association.

THE CONSUMER DECISION-MAKING PROCESS

When buying products, particularly new or expensive items, consumers generally follow the **consumer decision-making process** shown in Exhibit 6.1: (1) need recognition, (2) information search, (3) evaluation of alternatives, (4) purchase, and (5) postpurchase behavior. These five steps represent a general process that can be used as a guide for studying how consumers make decisions. It is important to note, though, that consumers' decisions do not always proceed in order through all of these steps. In fact, the consumer may end the process at any time or may not even make a purchase. The section on the types of consumer buying decisions later in the chapter discusses why a consumer's progression through these steps may vary. We begin, however, by examining the basic purchase process in greater detail.

consumer behavior
Processes a consumer uses to make purchase decisions, as well as to use and dispose of purchased goods or services; also includes factors that influence purchase decisions and product use.

consumer decision-making process
A five-step process used by consumers when buying goods or services.

EXHIBIT 6.1

Consumer Decision-Making Process

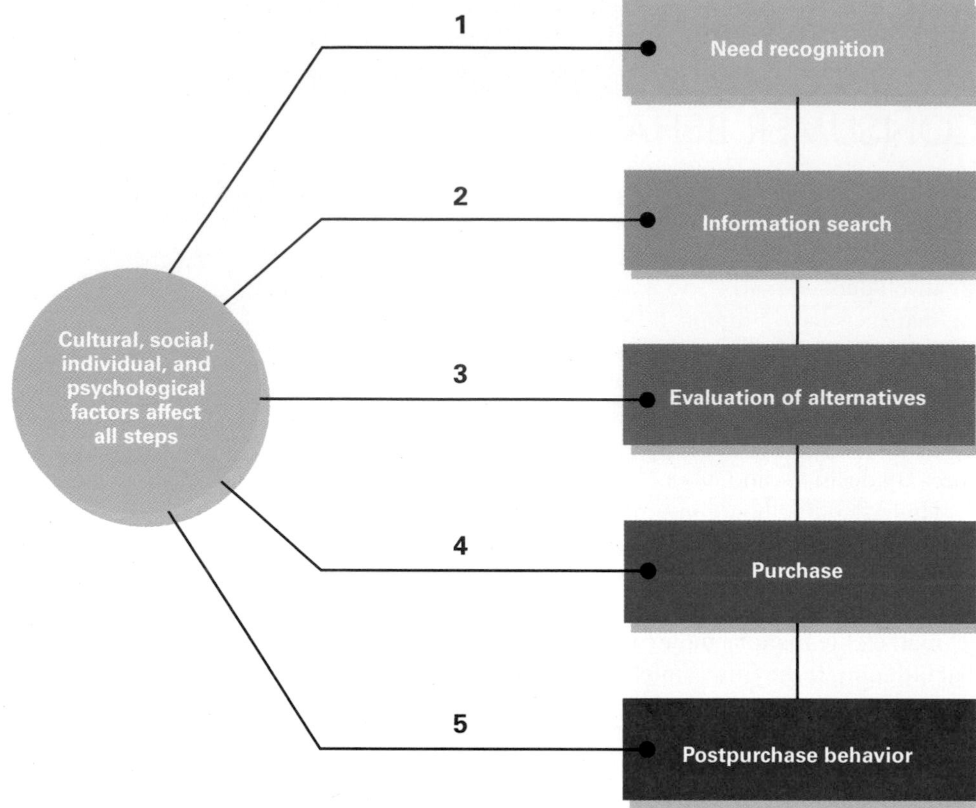

need recognition
Result of an imbalance between actual and desired states.

want
The way a consumer goes about addressing a need.

stimulus
Any unit of input affecting one or more of the five senses: sight, smell, taste, touch, hearing.

Need Recognition

The first stage in the consumer decision-making process is need recognition. **Need recognition** occurs when consumers are faced with an imbalance between actual and desired states that arouses and activates the consumer decision-making process. A **want** is the way that a consumer goes about addressing a need. For example, have you ever gotten blisters from an old running shoe? Or maybe you have seen a TV commercial for a new sports car and wanted to buy it. Need recognition is triggered when a consumer is exposed to either an internal or an external **stimulus**. *Internal stimuli* are occurrences you experience, such as hunger or thirst. For example, you may hear your stomach growl and then realize that you are hungry. *External stimuli* are influences from an outside source such as someone's recommendation of a new restaurant, the color of an automobile, the design of a package, a brand name mentioned by a friend, or an advertisement on television or radio.

A marketing manager's objective is to get consumers to recognize an imbalance between their present status and their preferred state. Advertising and sales promotion often provide this stimulus. Surveying buyer preferences provides marketers with information about consumer wants and needs that can be used to tailor products and services. Marketing managers can create wants on the part of the consumer. For example, when college students move in to their own apartment or dorm room, they often need to furnish it and want new furniture rather than hand-me-downs from their parents. A want can be for a specific product, or it can be for a certain attribute or feature of a product. In this example, the college students not only need home furnishings, but also want items that reflect their personal sense of style. Similarly, consumers may want ready-to-eat meals, drive-through dry-cleaning service, and Internet shopping to fill their need for convenience.

Another way marketers create new products and services to meet wants is by observing trends in the marketplace. IKEA, the home furnishing giant, watches the home decor trends and then creates affordable, trendy furniture. For example, marketers at IKEA realized that Generation Y consumers prefer furniture that is stylish, easy to clean, multifunctional, and portable. As a result, IKEA uses "bold orange, pink and green colors." The wood boasts a lacquered finish that can be wiped clean and doesn't need polish. IKEA also offers a space-saving, multifunction desk that can be converted into a dining table; it has wheels so that it can be easily moved.

Consumers recognize unfulfilled needs in various ways. The two most common occur when a current product isn't performing properly and when the consumer is about to run out of something that is generally kept on hand. Consumers may also recognize unfulfilled wants if they become aware of a product that seems superior to the one currently used. Such wants are usually created by advertising and other promotional activities. For example, aware of the popularity of MP3s and consumers' desire to take their music with them, car stereo manufacturers such as SonicBlue and Kenwood have added MP3 interfaces. Other companies, including Apple, Microsoft, RCA, and Creative Technology, are hoping to fulfill consumer desires for smaller audio and video players, referred to as portable media centers. The newest devices have wireless Internet connection capabilities providing access to downloadable movies and TV as well as music and video games. But Apple continues to lead the field with its iPod Shuffle and Nano and extensive downloadable music and TV programs.

Marketers selling their products in global markets must carefully observe the needs and wants of consumers in various regions. Unilever hit on an unrecognized need of European consumers when it introduced Persil Tablets, premeasured laundry detergent in tablet form. Though the tablets are more expensive than regular detergents, Unilever found that European consumers considered laundry a chore and wanted the process to be as simple and uncomplicated as possible. Unilever launched the tablets as a less messy and more convenient alternative. The laundry tablets were an immediate success in the United Kingdom and enabled Unilever's Persil brand to beat out rival Procter & Gamble's best-selling Ariel powder detergent.[1]

Unlike nonmarketing-controlled information, which is neutral, marketing-controlled information is biased toward a specific product. This ad from Stonyfield Farm might be doing double duty—attempting to build bias for hormone-free Stonyfield products and against its possibly growth-hormone-using competitors' products.

Information Search

After recognizing a need or want, consumers search for information about the various alternatives available to satisfy it. For example, as gasoline prices increase, many people are searching for information on vehicles that use alternatives to gasoline, such as Honda's hybrid models. An information search can occur internally, externally, or both. In an **internal information search**, the person recalls information stored in the memory. This stored information stems largely from previous experience with a product. For example, while traveling with your family, you encounter a hotel where you stayed during spring break earlier that year. By searching your memory, you can probably remember whether the hotel had clean rooms and friendly service.

In contrast, an **external information search** seeks information in the outside environment. There are two basic types of external information sources: nonmarketing controlled and marketing controlled. A **nonmarketing-controlled information source** is not associated with marketers promoting a product. These information sources include personal experiences (trying or observing a new product); personal sources (family, friends, acquaintances, and coworkers who may recommend a product or service); and public sources, such as Underwriters Laboratories, *Consumer Reports*, and other rating organizations that comment on products and services. For example, if you are in the mood to go to the movies, you may search your memory for past experiences at various cinemas when determining which one to go to (personal experience). To choose which movie you will see, you may rely on the recommendation of a friend or family member (personal sources). Alternatively, you may read the critical reviews in the newspaper or online (public sources). Marketers gather information on how these information sources

internal information search
The process of recalling past information stored in the memory.

external information search
The process of seeking information in the outside environment.

nonmarketing-controlled information source
A product information source that is not associated with advertising or promotion.

marketing-controlled information source
A product information source that originates with marketers promoting the product.

work and use it to attract customers. For example, car manufacturers know that younger customers are likely to get information from friends and family, so they try to develop enthusiasm for their products via word of mouth.

Living in the digital age has changed the way consumers get nonmarketing-controlled information. It can be from blogs, bulletin boards, activist Web sites, Web forums, and/or consumer opinion sites like **www.consumerreview.com**, **www.triadvisor.com**, or **www.epinions.com**. The average American spends at least six hours per week online, according to many estimates. Nearly 94 percent of U.S. consumers regularly or occasionally research products online before making an offline purchase and nearly half of those consumers then share the information and advice they gleaned online with other consumers, according to Worthington, Ohio-based market research firm BIGresearch.[2]

The latest research has examined how consumers use information picked up on the Internet. For example, in Web forums the information seeker has normally never met the information provider or ever interacted with the person before. Researchers found that an information provider's response speed, the extent to which the provider's previous responses within the forum had been positively evaluated by others, and the breadth of the provider's previous responses across different but related topics affected the information seeker's judgment about the value of the information. So, for example, if other information seekers had found the provider trustworthy, then the current seeker tended to believe the information.[3]

A **marketing-controlled information source** is biased toward a specific product because it originates with marketers promoting that product. Marketing-controlled information sources include mass-media advertising (radio, newspaper, television, and magazine advertising), sales promotion (contests, displays, premiums, and so forth), salespeople, product labels and packaging, and the Internet. Many consumers, however, are wary of the information they receive from marketing-controlled sources, believing that most marketing campaigns stress the product's positive attributes and ignore its faults. These sentiments tend to be stronger among better educated and higher-income consumers. Some marketing-controlled information sources can shift out of marketers' control, however, when there is bad news to report. Toy maker Mattel Inc. has made headlines for its recall of toys with lead paint contamination or powerful magnets that can cause illness or even death in children who ingest them. Newspaper stories across the country, in this instance a nonmarketing-controlled information source, recounted the many toy recalls Mattel has had to make in the past. Mattel then used marketing-controlled information sources to try to combat the negative publicity. Damage control for Mattel took the form of full-page ads in *The New York Times* and *The Wall Street Journal*, as well as video coverage on its own and Yahoo's Web sites, with an apology and assurances of future safety of its products from Bob Eckert, Mattel's chairman and CEO.

The extent to which an individual conducts an external search depends on his or her perceived risk, knowledge, prior experience, and level of interest in the good or service. Generally, as the perceived risk of the purchase increases, the consumer enlarges the search and considers more alternative brands. For example, suppose that you want to purchase a surround sound system for your home stereo. The decision is relatively risky because of the expense and technical nature of the stereo system, so you are motivated to search for information about models, prices, options, compatibility with existing entertainment products, and capabilities. You may decide to compare attributes of many speaker systems because the value of the time expended finding the "right" stereo will be less than the cost of buying the wrong system.

A consumer's knowledge about the product or service will also affect the extent of an external information search. A consumer who is knowledgeable and well informed about a potential purchase is less likely to search for additional information. In addition, the more knowledgeable consumers are, the more efficiently they will conduct the search process, thereby requiring less time to search. For example, many consumers know that AirTran and other discount airlines have much lower fares, so they generally use the discounters and do not even check fares at other airlines.

The extent of a consumer's external search is also affected by confidence in one's decision-making ability. A confident consumer not only has sufficient stored information about the product, but also feels self-assured about making the right decision. People lacking this confidence will continue an information search even when they know a great deal about the product. Consumers with prior experience in buying a certain product will have less perceived risk than inexperienced consumers. Therefore, they will spend less time searching and limit the number of products that they consider.

A third factor influencing the external information search is product experience. Consumers who have had a positive prior experience with a product are more likely to limit their search to items related to the positive experience. For example, when flying, consumers are likely to choose airlines with which they have had positive experiences, such as consistent on-time arrivals. They will avoid airlines with which they had a negative experience, such as lost luggage.

Finally, the extent of the search is positively related to the amount of interest a consumer has in a product. A consumer who is more interested in a product will spend more time searching for information and alternatives. For example, suppose you are a dedicated runner who reads jogging and fitness magazines and catalogs. In searching for a new pair of running shoes, you may enjoy reading about the new brands available and spend more time and effort than other buyers in deciding on the right shoe.

The consumer's information search should yield a group of brands, sometimes called the buyer's **evoked set** (or **consideration set**), which are the consumer's most preferred alternatives. From this set, the buyer will further evaluate the alternatives and make a choice. Consumers do not consider all brands available in a product category, but they do seriously consider a much smaller set. For example, from the many brands of pizza available, consumers are likely to consider only the alternatives that fit their price range, location, take-out/delivery needs, and taste preferences. Having too many choices can, in fact, confuse consumers and cause them to delay the decision to buy or, in some instances, cause them not to buy at all.

Evaluation of Alternatives and Purchase

After getting information and constructing an evoked set of alternative products, the consumer is ready to make a decision. A consumer will use the information stored in memory and obtained from outside sources to develop a set of criteria. Recent research has shown that exposure to certain cues in your everyday environment can affect decision criteria and purchase. For example, when NASA landed the Pathfinder spacecraft on Mars, it captured media attention worldwide. The candy maker Mars also noted a rather unusual increase in sales. Although the Mars Bar takes its name from the company's founder and not the planet, consumers apparently responded to news about the planet Mars by purchasing more Mars Bars. In a recent lab experiment, participants who used an orange (green) pen chose more orange (green) products. Thus, conceptual cues or primers (the pen color) influenced product evaluations and purchase likelihood.[4]

The environment, internal information, and external information help consumers evaluate and compare alternatives. One way to begin narrowing the number of choices in the evoked set is to pick a product attribute and then exclude all products in the set that don't have that attribute. For example, assume Jane and Jill, both college sophomores, are looking for their first apartment. They need a two-bedroom apartment, reasonably priced, and located near campus. They want the apartment to have a swimming pool, washer and dryer, and covered parking. Jane and Jill begin their search with all apartments in the area and then systematically eliminate possibilities that lack the features they need. Hence, if there are 50 alternatives in the area, they may reduce their list to just 10 apartments that possess all of the desired attributes.

Another way to narrow the number of choices is to use cutoffs. Cutoffs are either minimum or maximum levels of an attribute that an alternative must pass to be considered. Suppose Jane and Jill set a maximum of $1,000 to spend on combined rent. Then all apartments with rent higher than $1,000 will be eliminated, further reducing the list of apartments from ten to eight. A final way to narrow the choices is to rank the attributes under consideration in order of importance and evaluate the products based on how well each performs on the most important attributes. To reach a final decision on one of the

evoked set (consideration set)
A group of brands, resulting from an information search, from which a buyer can choose.

brand extensions
A well-known and respected brand name from one product category is extended into other product categories.

remaining eight apartments, Jane and Jill may decide proximity to campus is the most important attribute. As a result, they will choose to rent the apartment closest to campus.

If new brands are added to an evoked set, the consumer's evaluation of the existing brands in that set changes. As a result, certain brands in the original set may become more desirable. Suppose Jane and Jill find two apartments located equal distance from campus, one priced at $800 and the other at $750. Faced with this choice, they may decide that the $800 apartment is too expensive given that a comparable apartment is cheaper. If they add a $900 apartment to the list, however, then they may perceive the $800 apartment as more reasonable and decide to rent it.

The purchase decision process described above is a piecemeal process. That is, the evaluation is made by examining alternative advantages and disadvantages along important product attributes. A different way consumers can evaluate a product is according to a categorization process. The evaluation of an alternative depends upon the particular category to which it is assigned. Categories can be very general (motorized forms of transportation), or they can be very specific (Harley-Davidson motorcycles). Typically, these categories are associated with some degree of liking or disliking. To the extent that the product can be assigned membership to a particular category, it will receive an evaluation similar to that attached to the category. If you go to the grocery store and see a new organic food on the shelf, you may evaluate it on your liking and opinions of organic food.

So, when consumers rely on a categorization process, a product's evaluation depends on the particular category to which it is perceived as belonging. Given this, companies need to understand whether consumers are using categories that evoke the desired evaluations. Indeed, how a product is categorized can strongly influence consumer demand. For example, what products come to mind when you think about the "morning beverages" category? To the soft drink industry's dismay, far too few of us include sodas in this category. Several attempts have been made at getting soft drinks on the breakfast table, but with little success.

Brand extensions, in which a well-known and respected brand name from one product category is extended into other product categories, is one way companies employ categorization to their advantage. Brand extensions are a common business practice. Disney took a name built on cartoon characters and amusement parks and extended it to the cruise line industry. Kimberly-Clark, the maker of Huggies, the best-selling brand of disposable diapers in the United States, has extended the Huggies name to disposable washcloths and liquid soap for babies, and Huggies toiletries. Coca-Cola has Coke, Diet Coke, Coke Zero, Cherry Coke, Diet Cherry Coke, Caffeine-free Coke, and the list goes on.[5]

To Buy or Not to Buy Ultimately, the consumer has to decide whether to buy or not buy. Specifically, consumers must decide

1. Whether to buy
2. When to buy

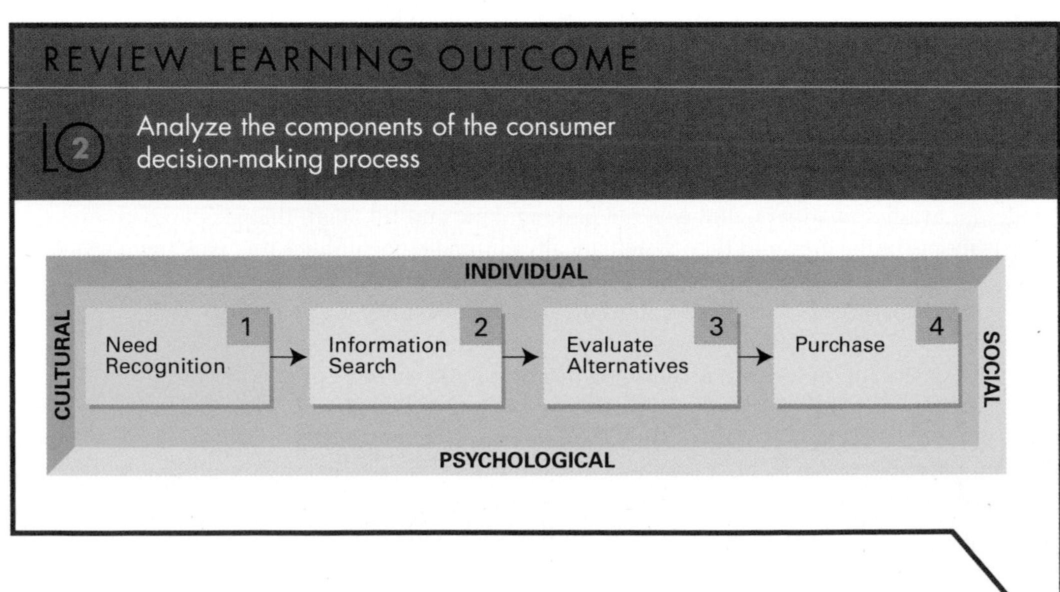

3. What to buy (product type and brand)
4. Where to buy (type of retailer, specific retailer, online or in-store)
5. How to pay

When a person is buying an expensive or complex item, it is often a *fully planned purchase* based upon a lot of information. People rarely buy a new home simply on impulse. Often consumers will make a *partially planned purchase* where they know the product category they want to buy (shirts, pants, reading lamp, car floor mats) but wait until they get to the store to choose a specific style or brand. Finally, there is the *unplanned purchase* where people buy on impulse. Research has found that up to 68 percent of the items bought during major shopping trips and 54 percent on smaller shopping trips are unplanned.[6]

POSTPURCHASE BEHAVIOR

When buying products, consumers expect certain outcomes from the purchase. How well these expectations are met determines whether the consumer is satisfied or dissatisfied with the purchase. For example, if a person bids on a used car stereo from eBay and wins, he may have fairly low expectations regarding performance. If the stereo's performance turns out to be of superior quality, then the person's satisfaction will be high because his expectations were exceeded. Conversely, if the person bid on a new car stereo expecting superior quality and performance, but the stereo broke within one month, he would be very dissatisfied because his expectations were not met. Price often influences the level of expectations for a product or service.

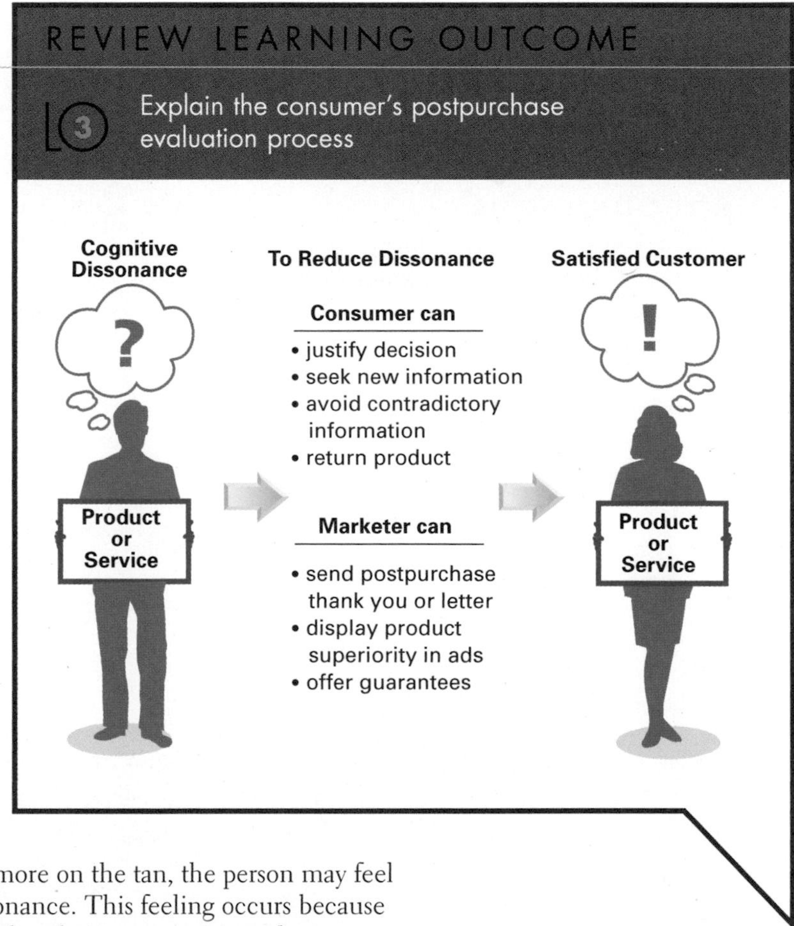

For the marketer, an important element of any postpurchase evaluation is reducing any lingering doubts that the decision was sound. When people recognize inconsistency between their values or opinions and their behavior, they tend to feel an inner tension called **cognitive dissonance**. For example, suppose a person who normally tans in a tanning bed decides to try a new "airbrush" tanning method, called a "Hollywood" or "mystic" tanning. Mystic tanning costs $30 to $50, significantly more than "fake tanner" or a tanning bed. Prior to spending more on the tan, the person may feel inner tension or anxiety, which is a feeling of dissonance. This feeling occurs because she knows the product has some disadvantages, such as being expensive, and some advantages, such as being free of harmful ultraviolet rays. In this case, the disadvantage of higher cost battles the advantage of no harmful UV rays.

Consumers try to reduce dissonance by justifying their decision. They may seek new information that reinforces positive ideas about the purchase, avoid information that contradicts their decision, or revoke the original decision by returning the product. To ensure satisfaction, thereby reducing dissonance, consumers using the "mystic tanning" mentioned above may ask several friends about their experiences, do online research, and talk with the tanning booth representative to obtain additional information about the

cognitive dissonance
Inner tension that a consumer experiences after recognizing an inconsistency between behavior and values or opinions.

procedure. In some instances, people deliberately seek contrary information in order to refute it and reduce dissonance. Dissatisfied customers sometimes rely on word of mouth to reduce cognitive dissonance, by letting friends and family know they are displeased.

Marketing managers can help reduce dissonance through effective communication with purchasers. For example, a customer service manager may slip a note inside the package congratulating the buyer on making a wise decision. Postpurchase letters sent by manufacturers and dissonance-reducing statements in instruction booklets may help customers feel at ease with their purchase. Advertising that displays the product's superiority over competing brands or guarantees can also help relieve the possible dissonance of someone who has already bought the product. In the tanning example, the tanning salon may offer a 100 percent money-back guarantee. The **mystictan.com** Web site explains the procedure and even shows endorsements from various celebrities. Because the company offers this additional information and communicates effectively with its customers, its customers are more likely to understand the procedure and the expected results; hence, it is likely that the outcome will meet or exceed their expectations rather than being disappointing.

One factor that can raise or lower dissonance is service during and after the sale. The Customer Experience box explains how Zappos.com provides great customer service.

CUSTOMER Experience

CUSTOMER

At Zappos.com Service Is Always On

Zappos.com is an online retailer known originally for footwear, but also offering clothing, handbags, and accessories. Founded in 1999 and renowned for its unparalleled customer service, Zappos offers nearly 1,200 brands and about 2.7 million products, and had $1 billion in gross sales in 2008.

While Zappos is familiar to shoppers because of its wide selection of brands, styles, and sizes, the Henderson, Nevada-based company strives to position itself as the absolute online service leader. Shoppers love the company for its free shipping and returns, 365-day return policy and 24-7 customer service. But that's just the beginning of Zappos' corporate culture of service: The company and its 1,600 employees—half of whom work in its headquarters and call center, the other half in its Shepherdsville, Kentucky, warehouse—embrace ten core concepts, the first of which is to "Deliver WOW through service." Other concepts range from being open and honest and driving change to having fun. "Customer service is everything to us, and the reason we can stay focused and successful is that it's ingrained into our culture, and our brand is our culture," says Aaron Magness, who works in business development for Zappos.

Zappos' service-oriented culture starts in the hiring process. According to Magness, while half of the initial interview is dedicated to finding out if potential hires have the right technical skills for the job, the other half is about making sure they're a good cultural fit. "Getting customers excited about the service they had at Zappos has to come naturally," he says. "You can't teach it; you have to hire for it."

Once hired, all new employees, regardless of position, are required to complete a four-week customer loyalty training program in the call center to learn the history of the company, get immersed in its culture, and make sure they're a good fit. To ensure that's the case, CEO Tony Hsieh steps in during the second week of training and offers $2,000 to anyone who wants to quit. Magness says that only about 1 percent of the trainees actually take the offer.

Once Zappos wins over shoppers (roughly 75 percent of its orders are placed by repeat customers), the company works to keep them engaged through various online and social media outlets, including inviting customers to submit online reviews. It also maintains an active presence on Facebook and Twitter. "We want to let our customers speak for themselves on our site. If someone wants to say 'I really didn't like this shirt,' we want other customers to know. We're not afraid to hear good reviews and bad reviews," Magness says.

On Twitter, Hsieh has about 12,000 followers who read his posts on topics ranging from free shoe giveaways and feedback requests to where he's having dinner. According to Magness, not only does this ability to relate to the company help create a stronger relationship with shoppers, but also it provides the company with valuable consumer insight.[7]

How does Zappos' great customer service help reduce cognitive dissonance? Can a company put too much emphasis on customer service? Have you ever had poor customer service from an online vendor? If so, what did it do to your level of dissonance?

TYPES OF CONSUMER BUYING DECISIONS AND CONSUMER INVOLVEMENT

All consumer buying decisions generally fall along a continuum of three broad categories: routine response behavior, limited decision making, and extensive decision making (see Exhibit 6.2). Goods and services in these three categories can best be described in terms of five factors: level of consumer involvement, length of time to make a decision, cost of the good or service, degree of information search, and the number of alternatives considered. The level of consumer involvement is perhaps the most significant determinant in classifying buying decisions. **Involvement** is the amount of time and effort a buyer invests in the search, evaluation, and decision processes of consumer behavior.

Frequently purchased, low-cost goods and services are generally associated with **routine response behavior.** These goods and services can also be called low-involvement products because consumers spend little time on search and decision before making the purchase. Usually, buyers are familiar with several different brands in the product category but stick with one brand. For example, a person may routinely buy Tropicana orange juice. Consumers engaged in routine response behavior normally don't experience need recognition until they are exposed to advertising or see the product displayed on a store shelf. Consumers buy first and evaluate later, whereas the reverse is true for extensive decision making. A consumer who has previously purchased a whitening toothpaste and was satisfied with it will probably walk to the toothpaste aisle and select that same brand without spending 20 minutes examining all other alternatives.

Limited decision making typically occurs when a consumer has previous product experience but is unfamiliar with the current brands available. Limited decision making is also associated with lower levels of involvement (although higher than routine decisions) because consumers do expend moderate effort in searching for information or in considering various alternatives. But what happens if the consumer's usual brand of whitening toothpaste is sold out? Assuming that toothpaste is needed, the consumer will be forced to choose another brand. Before making a final decision, the consumer will likely evaluate several other brands based on their active ingredients, their promotional claims, and the consumer's prior experiences.

Consumers practice **extensive decision making** when buying an unfamiliar, expensive product or an infrequently bought item. This process is the most complex type of consumer buying decision and is associated with high involvement on the part of the consumer. This process resembles the model outlined in Exhibit 6.1. These consumers want to make the right decision, so they want to know as much as they can about the product category and available brands. People usually experience the most cognitive dissonance when buying high-involvement products. Buyers use several criteria for evaluating their options and spend much time seeking information. Buying a home or a car, for example, requires extensive decision making.

The type of decision making that consumers use to purchase a product does not necessarily remain constant. For instance, if a routinely purchased product no longer satisfies, consumers may practice

involvement
The amount of time and effort a buyer invests in the search, evaluation, and decision processes of consumer behavior.

routine response behavior
The type of decision making exhibited by consumers buying frequently purchased, low-cost goods and services; requires little search and decision time.

limited decision making
The type of decision making that requires a moderate amount of time for gathering information and deliberating about an unfamiliar brand in a familiar product category.

extensive decision making
The most complex type of consumer decision making, used when buying an unfamiliar, expensive product or an infrequently bought item; requires use of several criteria for evaluating options and much time for seeking information.

EXHIBIT 6.2

Continuum of Consumer Buying Decisions

	Routine	Limited	Extensive
Involvement	low	low to moderate	high
Time	short	short to moderate	long
Cost	low	low to moderate	high
Information Search	internal only	mostly internal	internal and external
Number of Alternatives	one	few	many

limited or extensive decision making to switch to another brand. And people who first use extensive decision making may then use limited or routine decision making for future purchases. For example, when a family gets a new puppy, they will spend a lot of time and energy trying out different toys to determine which one the dog prefers. Once the new owners learn that the dog prefers a bone to a ball, however, the purchase no longer requires extensive evaluation and will become routine.

Factors Determining the Level of Consumer Involvement

The level of involvement in the purchase depends on the following five factors:

Luxury cars are a sign of higher social class status.

- *Previous experience:* When consumers have had previous experience with a good or service, the level of involvement typically decreases. After repeated product trials, consumers learn to make quick choices. Because consumers are familiar with the product and know whether it will satisfy their needs, they become less involved in the purchase. For example, a consumer purchasing cereal has many brands to choose from—just think of any grocery store cereal aisle. If the consumer always buys the same brand because it satisfies his hunger, then he has a low level of involvement. When a consumer purchases cereal for the first time, however, it likely will be a much more involved purchase.
- *Interest:* Involvement is directly related to consumer interests, as in cars, music, movies, bicycling, or electronics. Naturally, these areas of interest vary from one individual to another. A person highly involved in bike racing will be very interested in the type of bike she owns and will spend quite a bit of time evaluating different bikes. If a person wants a bike only for recreation, however, he may be fairly uninvolved in the purchase and just look for a bike from the most convenient location.
- *Perceived risk of negative consequences:* As the perceived risk in purchasing a product increases, so does a consumer's level of involvement. The types of risks that concern consumers include financial risk, social risk, and psychological risk. First, financial risk is exposure to loss of wealth or purchasing power. Because high risk is associated with high-priced purchases, consumers tend to become extremely involved. Therefore, price and involvement are usually directly related: As price increases, so does the level of involvement. For example, someone who is purchasing a new car for the first time (higher perceived risk) will spend a lot of time and effort making this purchase. Second, consumers take social risks when they buy products that can affect people's social opinions of them (for example, driving an old, beat-up car or wearing unstylish clothes). Third, buyers undergo psychological risk if they feel that making the wrong decision might cause some concern or anxiety. For example, some consumers feel guilty about eating foods that are not healthy, such as regular ice cream rather than fat-free frozen yogurt.
- *Situation:* The circumstances of a purchase may temporarily transform a low-involvement decision into a high-involvement one. High involvement comes into play when the consumer perceives risk in a specific situation. For example, an individual might routinely buy low-priced brands of liquor and wine. When the boss visits, however, the consumer might make a high-involvement decision and buy more prestigious brands.
- *Social visibility:* Involvement also increases as the social visibility of a product increases. Products often on social display include clothing (especially designer labels), jewelry, cars, and furniture. All these items make a statement about the purchaser and, therefore, carry a social risk.

Marketing Implications of Involvement

Marketing strategy varies according to the level of involvement associated with the product. For high-involvement product purchases, marketing managers have several responsibilities. First, promotion to the target market should be extensive and informative. A good ad gives consumers the information they need for making the purchase decision, as well as specifying the benefits and unique advantages of owning the product. For example, a recent two-page ad for Toyota's Camry Hybrid provides extensive information on the personal and planet-wide benefits of choosing their vehicle. Photos of a wide-eyed young girl and a globe are meant to appeal to the customer's care for the future, while captions on interior photos of the car and its engine note the vehicle's unique technology that "drives just like a regular car," benefits that might appeal to the consumer's need for performance.[8] Another ad featured in earlier pages of the same magazine shows the Camry Hybrid being driven along a country road, surrounded by green pastures and grazing horses. The ad is meant to appeal to the consumer who cares that the vehicle is built in the United States and that Toyota is committed to America, its air, its communities, and its future.

For low-involvement product purchases, consumers may not recognize their wants until they are in the store. Therefore, in-store promotion is an important tool when promoting low-involvement products. Marketing managers focus on package design so the product will be eye-catching and easily recognized on the shelf. Examples of products that take this approach are Campbell's soups, Tide detergent, Velveeta cheese, and Heinz ketchup. In-store displays also stimulate sales of low-involvement products. A good display can explain the product's purpose and prompt recognition of a want. Displays of health and beauty aid items in supermarkets have been known to increase sales many times above normal. Coupons, cents-off deals, and two-for-one offers also effectively promote low-involvement items.

Linking a product to a higher-involvement issue is another tactic that marketing managers can use to increase the sales or positive publicity of a low-involvement product. For example, in response to government and consumer concerns about childhood obesity, food manufacturers that advertise to children, such as Kellogg's, Hershey, McDonald's, and General Mills, have pledged to devote at least half of their marketing to the promotion of healthy dietary choices and lifestyles. In Kellogg's case, nearly $206 million in advertising dollars is at stake.[9]

REVIEW LEARNING OUTCOME

LO 4 Identify the types of consumer buying decisions and discuss the significance of consumer involvement

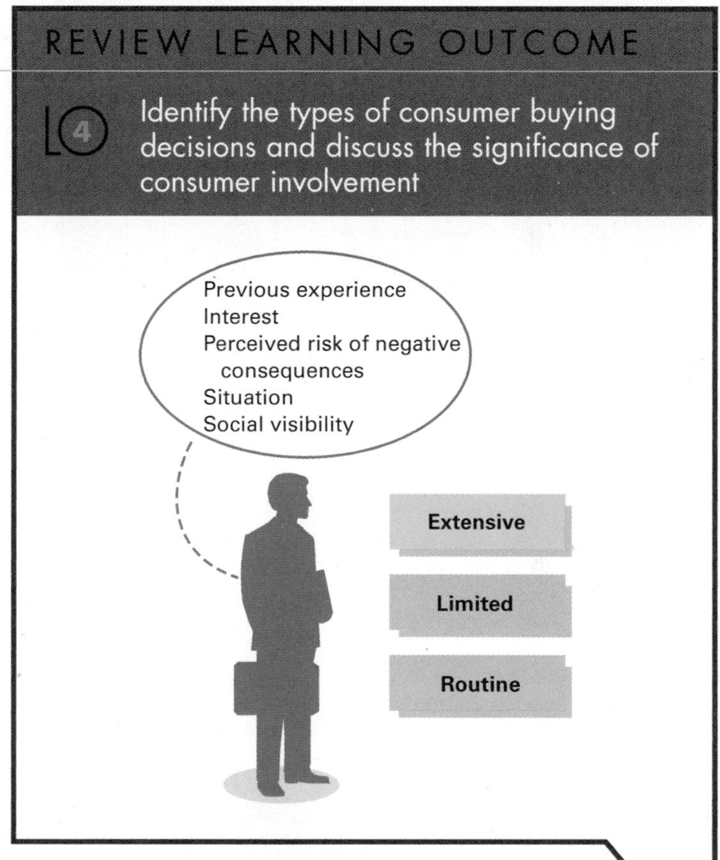

FACTORS INFLUENCING CONSUMER BUYING DECISIONS

The consumer decision-making process does not occur in a vacuum. On the contrary, underlying cultural, social, individual, and psychological factors strongly influence the decision process. These factors have an effect from the time a consumer perceives a stimulus through postpurchase behavior. Cultural factors, which include culture and values, subculture, and social class, exert a broad influence over consumer decision making. Social factors sum up the social interactions between a consumer and influential groups of people, such as reference groups, opinion leaders, and family members.

EXHIBIT 6.3

Factors That Affect the Consumer Decision-Making Process

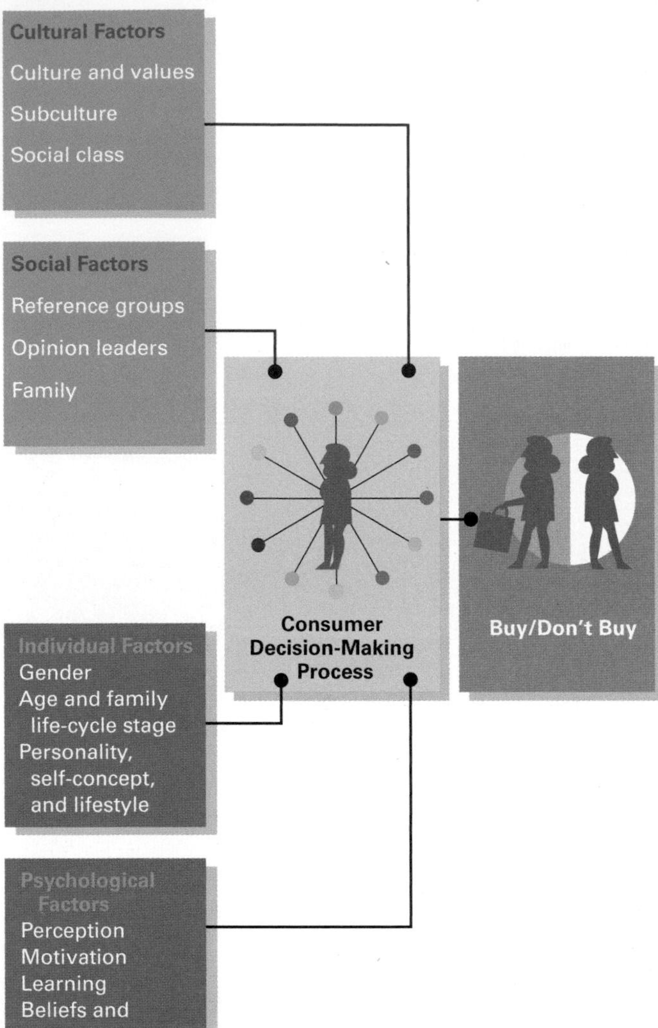

Individual factors, which include gender, age, family life-cycle stage, personality, self-concept, and lifestyle, are unique to each individual and play a major role in the type of products and services consumers want. Psychological factors determine how consumers perceive and interact with their environments and influence the ultimate decisions consumers make. They include perception, motivation, learning, beliefs, and attitudes. Exhibit 6.3 summarizes these influences.

LO5

CULTURAL INFLUENCES ON CONSUMER BUYING DECISIONS

Of all the factors that affect consumer decision making, cultural factors exert the broadest and deepest influence. Marketers must understand the way people's culture and its accompanying values, as well as their subculture and social class, influence their buying behavior.

Culture and Values

Culture is the essential character of a society that distinguishes it from other societal groups. The underlying elements of every culture are the values, language, myths, customs, rituals, and laws that shape the behavior of the people, as well as the material artifacts, or products, of that behavior as they are transmitted from one generation to the next. Exhibit 6.4 lists some defining components of American culture.

Culture is pervasive. Cultural values and influences are the ocean in which individuals swim, and yet most are completely unaware that it is there. What people eat, how they dress, what they think and feel, and what language they speak are all dimensions of culture. It encompasses all the things consumers do without conscious choice because their culture's values, customs, and rituals are ingrained in their daily habits.

Culture is functional. Human interaction creates values and prescribes acceptable behavior for each culture. By

EXHIBIT 6.4

Components of American Culture

COMPONENT	EXAMPLES
Values	Success through hard work; Emphasis on personal freedom
Language	English as the dominant language
Myths	George Washington never told a lie. Abraham Lincoln walked a mile to return a penny.
Customs	Bathing daily; Shaking hands when greeting new people; Standard gratuity of 15 to 20 percent at restaurants
Rituals	Thanksgiving Day dinner; Singing the "Star Spangled Banner" before baseball games; Going to religious services on the appropriate day
Laws	Child labor laws; Sherman Anti-Trust Act guarantees competition
Material artifacts	Diamond engagement rings; Cell phones

Source: Adapted from *Consumer Behavior* by William D. Wells and David Prensky. Copyright © 1996 by John Wiley & Sons, Inc. Reprinted by permission of John Wiley & Sons, Inc. All Rights Reserved.

establishing common expectations, culture gives order to society. Sometimes these expectations are enacted into laws. For example, drivers in our culture must stop at a red light. Other times these expectations are taken for granted. For example, grocery stores and hospitals are open 24 hours, whereas banks are open only during bankers' hours.

Culture is learned. Consumers are not born knowing the values and norms of their society. Instead, they must learn what is acceptable from family and friends. Children learn the values that will govern their behavior from parents, teachers, and peers. As members of our society, they learn to shake hands when they greet someone, to drive on the right-hand side of the road, and to eat pizza and drink Coca-Cola.

Culture is dynamic. It adapts to changing needs and an evolving environment. The rapid growth of technology in today's world has accelerated the rate of cultural change. Television has changed entertainment patterns and family communication and has heightened public awareness of political and other news events. Automation has increased the amount of leisure time we have and, in some ways, has changed the traditional work ethic. Cultural norms will continue to evolve because of our need for social patterns that solve problems.

Modern Manners explores the ways in which new technologies, such as cell phones, have changed American culture.

In the United States, rapidly increasing diversity is causing major shifts in culture. For example, the growth of the Hispanic community is influencing American food, music, clothing, and entertainment. Additionally, African American culture has been embraced by the mainstream. Indeed, African American women make up one of the fastest-growing segments of the American population. The projected growth rate of this segment is 8 percent, compared to 4 percent for the total U.S. population. Additionally, one in two married black women is the primary decision maker in buying a house, versus one in four married white women. Traditionally, marketers have not taken advantage of the opportunity to market to African American women. Now, however, many companies are taking note of this rapidly growing segment of the population. For example, Kraft's Honey Bunches of Oats cereal developed an advertising campaign that focused on black women. Research showed that African American women do not like to eat cereal when others are around, so the print ad shows a black woman eating a bowl of cereal alone with the caption "Take a breather. This moment is yours. Just you and your bowl of Honey Bunches of Oats."[10]

The most defining element of a culture is its **values**—the enduring beliefs shared by a society that a specific mode of conduct is personally or socially preferable to another mode of conduct. People's value systems have a great effect on their consumer behavior. Consumers with similar value systems tend to react alike to prices and other marketing-related inducements. Values also correspond to consumption patterns. For example, Americans place a high value on convenience. This value has created lucrative markets for products such as breakfast bars, energy bars, and nutrition bars that allow consumers to eat on the go. Values can also influence consumers' TV viewing habits or the magazines they read. For instance, people who strongly object to violence avoid crime shows, and those who oppose pornography do not buy *Hustler*. Core American values—those considered central to the American way of life—are presented in Exhibit 6.5.

Values represent what is most important in people's lives. Therefore, marketers watch carefully for shifts in consumers' values over time. For example, millions of Americans have an interest in spirituality, as evidenced by the soaring sales of books with religious or spiritual themes and the popularity of television shows with similar themes. Similarly, after the September 11 terrorist attacks, when many people were fearful and concerned about self-protection, gun sales soared as did the sale of drugs to cure anthrax.

culture
The set of values, norms, attitudes, and other meaningful symbols that shape human behavior, and the artifacts, or products, of that behavior as they are transmitted from one generation to the next.

value
The enduring belief that a specific mode of conduct is personally or socially preferable to another mode of conduct.

EXHIBIT 6.5

Core American Values

Success	Americans admire hard work, entrepreneurship, achievement, and success. Those achieving success in American society are rewarded with money, status, and prestige. For example, Bill Gates, once a nerdy computer buff, built Microsoft Corporation into an internationally known giant. Gates is now one of the richest people in the world.
Materialism	Americans value owning tangible goods. American society encourages consumption, ownership, and possession. Americans judge others based on their material possessions; for example, the type of car they own, where they live, and what type of clothes they wear.
Freedom	The American culture was founded on the principle of religious and political freedom. The U.S. Constitution and the Bill of Rights assure American citizens the right to life, liberty, and the pursuit of happiness. These freedoms are fundamental to the legal system and the moral fiber of American culture. The Internet, for example, is built on the principle of the right to free speech. Lawmakers who have attempted to limit the material available on the Internet have met with tough opposition from proponents of free speech. Spam has become such a major problem in recent years, however, that individuals are becoming more receptive to laws restricting spam even if they limit spammers' free speech.
Progress	Technological advances, as well as advances in medicine, science, health, and the quality of products and services, are important to Americans. Each year, for example, more than 20,000 new or improved consumer products are introduced on America's supermarket shelves.*
Youth	Americans are obsessed with youth and spend a good deal of time on products and procedures that make them feel and look younger. Americans spend millions each year on health and beauty aids, health clubs, and healthy foods. Media and advertising encourage the quest for youth by using young, attractive, slim models, such as those in ads from fashion designer Calvin Klein.
Capitalism	Americans believe in a free enterprise system characterized by competition and the chance for monetary success. Capitalism creates choices, quality, and value for Americans. Laws prohibit monopolistic control of a market and regulate free trade. Americans encourage small business success, such as that found by Apple Computer, Wal-Mart, and McDonald's, all of which started as small enterprises with a better idea that toppled the competition.

*Data obtained from the Food Marketing Institute Web site at **http://www.fmi.org,** 2004.

Source: *Consumer Behavior* by William D. Wells and David Prensky.

subculture
A homogeneous group of people who share elements of the overall culture as well as unique elements of their own group.

James Stengel, global marketing director for Procter & Gamble, had this to say about the changes he's seen in today's consumers, "The biggest thing going on with U.S. consumers is that they want to trust something. They want to be understood, they want to be respected, [and] they want to be listened to. They don't want to be talked to. It's trust in the largest sense of the word. People really do care what's behind the brand, what's behind the business. They care about the values of a brand and the values of a company. We can never forget that. We can never be complacent about that."[11]

Understanding Cultural Differences

As more companies expand their operations globally, the need to understand the cultures of foreign countries becomes more important. A firm has little chance of selling products in a culture it does not understand. Like people, products have cultural values and rules that influence their perception and use. Culture, therefore, must be understood before the behavior of individuals within the cultural context can be understood. Colors, for example, may have different meanings in global markets than they do at home. In China, white is the color of mourning, and brides wear red. In the United States, black is for mourning, and brides wear white.

Language is another important aspect of culture that global marketers must deal with. When translating product names, slogans, and promotional messages into foreign languages, they must be careful not to convey the wrong message. General Motors discovered too late that Nova (the name of an economical car) literally means "doesn't go" in Spanish; Coors encouraged its English-speaking customers to "Turn it loose," but the phrase in Spanish means "Suffer from diarrhea."

Though marketers expanding into global markets generally adapt their products and business formats to the local culture, some fear that increasing globalization, as well as the proliferation of the Internet, will result in a homogeneous world culture in the future. U.S. companies in particular, they fear, are Americanizing the world by exporting bastions of American culture, such as McDonald's fast-food restaurants, Starbucks coffeehouses, Microsoft software, and American movies and entertainment.

One of the world's fastest growing countries is China. Perhaps the most important aspect of a multinational firm's success in selling in any country is understanding the culture. The Global Perspectives box illustrates one firm's attempt at modifying its products based upon culture.

PepsiCo vies with Coca-Cola Co. in the world's fastest-growing soft-drinks arena—China. China's expanding market is the biggest after the United States and Mexico for the competing drinks giants. Which marketing elements do you think will give Pepsi an advantage over Coca-Cola or vice versa?

Subculture

A culture can be divided into subcultures on the basis of demographic characteristics, geographic regions, national and ethnic background, political beliefs, and religious beliefs. A **subculture** is a homogeneous group of people who share elements of the overall culture as well as cultural elements unique to their own group. Within subcultures, people's attitudes, values, and purchase decisions are even more similar than they are within the broader culture. Subcultural differences may result in considerable variation within a culture in what, how, when, and where people buy goods and services.

In the United States alone, countless subcultures can be identified. Many are concentrated geographically. People belonging to the Mormon religion, for example, are clustered mainly in Utah; Cajuns are located in the bayou regions of southern Louisiana. Many Hispanics live in states bordering Mexico, whereas the majority of Chinese, Japanese, and Korean Americans are found on the West Coast. Other subcultures are geographically dispersed. Computer hackers, people who are hearing or visually impaired, Harley-Davidson bikers, military families, university

GLOBAL Perspectives

Fisher-Price's Global Game Plan is Based upon Understanding Local Cultures

Between 2006 and 2008, the average gross domestic product per capita in China has passed $2,000, and now is close to $2,500. That core of perhaps 250 million Chinese consumers—especially in coastal cities—actually earns closer to $10,000 a year on average. Given modest living expenses, they are left with considerable disposable income. They are eager to spend this income.

Fisher-Price wants to capture a piece of that disposable income. In developing a line of talking toys aimed at children in China, engineers at Fisher-Price had to struggle to perfect the Mandarin "Sh" sound, which involves a soft hiss that was difficult to encode on sound-data chips embedded in the toys. Developers finally solved the problem of recording the phrase "It's learning time!" in Mandarin, but new challenges are ahead. The company will soon be examining the LCD screens on learning toys to determine whether Chinese characters can be displayed clearly.

Fisher-Price is pursuing other developing markets as well, including Brazil, Russia, and Poland. Each presents its own cultural challenges. For example, the company ran into trouble with a reading toy called "Storybook Rhymes" that featured a traditional Turkish poem paired with an illustration of a pig. "We realized this wasn't appropriate for a Muslim country," says Kelly Chapman, who heads product design, referring to cultural restrictions on pork. In development, the company replaced the pig with pictures of cats.[12]

Why is culture so important to multinational firms? Can you think of a product or service sold in the global marketplace where culture doesn't matter?

social class
A group of people in a society who are considered nearly equal in status or community esteem, who regularly socialize among themselves both formally and informally, and who share behavioral norms.

professors, and gays may be found throughout the country. Yet they have identifiable attitudes, values, and needs that distinguish them from the larger culture.

Once marketers identify subcultures, they can design special marketing programs to serve their needs. According to the U.S. Census Bureau, the Hispanic population is the largest and fastest-growing subculture, increasing four times as fast as the general population. To tap into this large and growing segment, marketers have been forming partnerships with broadcasters that have an established Latino audience. The Univision Radio network covers approximately 73 percent of the U.S. Hispanic population and has over 10 million listeners weekly. State Farm has partnered with Julie Stav, the leading financial expert to the Latino community, to sponsor evening broadcasts of her hugely successful Spanish-language radio show. When Sweden-based furniture manufacturer IKEA found that it wasn't capturing the large Latino demographic in U.S. cities, it started advertising in Spanish. It also launched a series of commercials featuring Latina soap opera stars on Telemundo—the second-largest U.S. Spanish-language broadcaster. IKEA saw immediate results with more Latinos in their stores.[13]

Social Class

The United States, like other societies, has a social class system. A **social class** is a group of people who are considered nearly equal in status or community esteem, who regularly socialize among themselves both formally and informally, and who share behavioral norms.

A number of techniques have been used to measure social class, and a number of criteria have been used to define it. One view of contemporary U.S. status structure is shown in Exhibit 6.6.

As you can see from Exhibit 6.6, the upper and upper-middle classes comprise the small segment of affluent and wealthy Americans. In terms of consumer buying patterns, the affluent are more likely to own their own home and purchase new cars and trucks and are less likely to smoke. The very rich flex their financial muscles by spending more on vacation homes, vacations and cruises, and housekeeping and gardening services. The most affluent consumers are more likely to attend art auctions and galleries, dance performances, operas, the theater, museums, concerts, and sporting events. Marketers often pay attention to the superwealthy. For example, the Mercedes-Benz Maybach 62, touted as the "world's most luxurious car," is aimed at this group. Priced at $375,000, the car features electronic doors, reclining seats with footrests, a workstation with media capability, a champagne cooler, and lots more. Similarly, New York-based designer Calvin Stewart sells A.P.O. jeans featuring fully customized denim embellished with diamond, gold, and platinum details—starting at $1,000 a pair.

An ad such as this one for Avon featuring an admired celebrity like Salma Hayek, entices consumers who aspire to a certain lifestyle (or think they deserve it) to use the product being used by the celebrity.

IMAGE COURTESY OF THE ADVERTISING ARCHIVES

The majority of Americans today define themselves as middle class, regardless of their actual income or educational attainment. This phenomenon most likely occurs because working-class Americans tend to aspire to the middle-class lifestyle while some of those who do achieve affluence may downwardly aspire to respectable middle-class status as a matter of

EXHIBIT 6.6

U.S. Social Classes

Upper Classes		
Capitalist class	1 percent	People whose investment decisions shape the national economy; income mostly from assets, earned or inherited; university connections
Upper-middle class	14 percent	Upper-level managers, professionals, owners of medium-sized businesses; well-to-do, stay-at-home homemakers who decline occupational work by choice; college educated; family income well above national average
Middle Classes		
Middle class	33 percent	Middle-level white-collar, top-level blue-collar; education past high school typical; income somewhat above national average; loss of manufacturing jobs has reduced the population of this class
Working class	32 percent	Middle-level blue-collar, lower-level white-collar; income below national average; largely working in skilled or semiskilled service jobs
Lower Classes		
Working poor	11–12 percent	Low-paid service workers and operatives; some high school education; below mainstream in living standard; crime and hunger are daily threats
Underclass	8–9 percent	People who are not regularly employed and who depend primarily on the welfare system for sustenance; little schooling; living standard below poverty line

Source: Adapted from Richard P. Coleman, "The Continuing Significance of Social Class to Marketing," *Journal of Consumer Research*, December 1983, 267; Dennis Gilbert and Joseph A. Kahl, *The American Class Structure: A Synthesis* (Homewood, IL: Dorsey Press, 1982), ch. 11, accessed online at **http://en.wikipedia.org/wiki/social_structure_of_the_united_states**, May 2008.

principle. Attaining goals and achieving status and prestige are important to middle-class consumers. People falling into the middle class live in the gap between the haves and the have-nots. They aspire to the lifestyle of the more affluent, but are constrained by the economic realities and cautious attitudes they share with the working class.

A recent poll asked whether the United States is split into "haves" and "have-nots"; 48 percent said it is and 48 percent said it isn't. (The rest declined to choose.) The researchers also asked people to say which class they belong to, if they had to pick. While a large percentage said they're "haves" (45 percent), that's down from the 52 percent who did so in 2001 and down even more from the 59 percent saying so in 1988. The rest said they fit in neither group or refused to pick. More women than men situated themselves among the have-nots (37 percent vs. 30 percent). Even 32 percent of middle-income consumers said that they were have-nots, meaning that they perceived their standard of living as inadequate for their purchasing power.[14]

The working class is a distinct subset of the middle class. Interest in organized labor is one of the most common attributes among the working class. This group often rates job security as the most important reason for taking a job. The working-class person depends heavily on relatives and the community for economic and emotional support. The emphasis on family ties is one sign of the group's intensely local view of the world. They like the local news far more than do middle-class audiences who favor national and world coverage. They are also more likely to vacation closer to home.

Lifestyle distinctions between the social classes are greater than the distinctions within a given class. The most significant difference between the classes occurs between the middle and lower classes, where there is a major shift in lifestyles. Members of the lower class typically have incomes at or below the poverty level. This social class has the highest unemployment rate, and many individuals or families are subsidized through the welfare system. Many are illiterate, with little formal education. Compared to more affluent consumers, lower-class consumers have poorer diets and typically purchase very different types of foods when they shop.

EXHIBIT 6.7

Social Class and Education

Educational Profile	Median Household Income
Those with less than a 9th grade education	$ 17,261
Those with a 9th–12th grade education (no diploma)	$ 21,737
High school graduates	$ 35,744
College graduates, BA	$ 64,406
College graduates, MA	$ 74,476
Professional degree holders	$ 100,000

Source: U.S. Census, available at http://www.pbs.org/peoplelikeus/resources/stats.html, May 2005.

Social class is typically measured as a combination of occupation, income, education, wealth, and other variables. For instance, affluent upper-class consumers are more likely to be salaried executives or self-employed professionals with at least an undergraduate degree. Working-class or middle-class consumers are more likely to be hourly service workers or blue-collar employees with only a high school education. Educational attainment, however, seems to be the most reliable indicator of a person's social and economic status (see Exhibit 6.7). Those with college degrees or graduate degrees are more likely to fall into the upper classes, while those people with some college experience fall closest to traditional concepts of the middle class.

Marketers are interested in social class for two main reasons. First, social class often indicates which medium to use for advertising. Suppose an insurance company seeks to sell its policies to middle-class families. It might advertise during the local evening news because middle-class families tend to watch more television than other classes do. If the company wants to sell more policies to upscale individuals, it might place a print ad in a business publication like *The Wall Street Journal*. The Internet, long the domain of more educated and affluent families, is becoming an increasingly important advertising outlet for advertisers hoping to reach blue-collar workers and homemakers. As the middle class rapidly adopts the medium, marketers have to do more research to find out which Web sites will reach their audience.

REVIEW LEARNING OUTCOME

LO 5 Identify and understand the cultural factors that affect consumer buying decisions

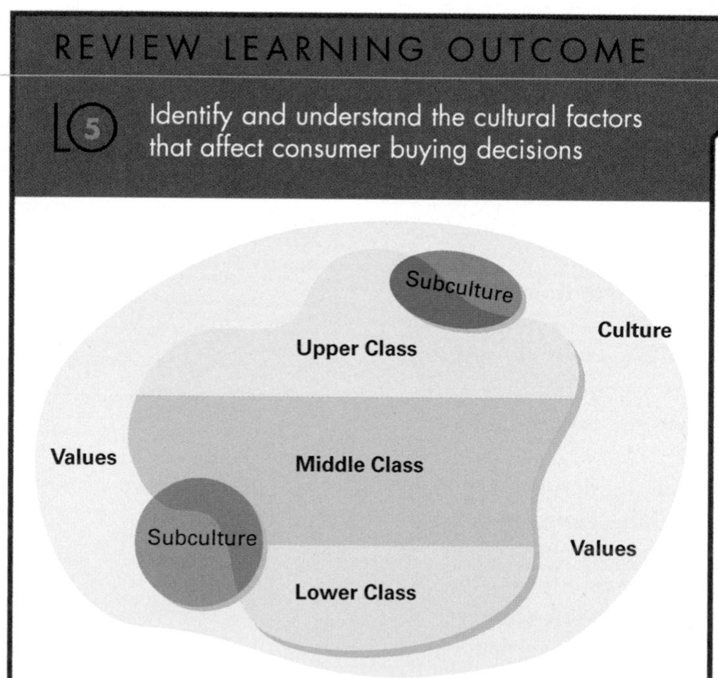

Second, knowing what products appeal to which social classes can help marketers determine where to best distribute their products. Affluent Americans, a fifth of the U.S. population, were responsible for nearly half of all new car and truck sales and over half of hotel stays and vacation homes. This same group spent nearly twice as much as less-affluent Americans on restaurant fare, alcohol, sporting events, plays, and club memberships.[15]

For the first time in a long while, however, industry analysts are seeing shares of discount chains faring better than their full-priced and upscale counterparts. These days, analysts say, the big-box and discount retailers' greatest challenge has been courting consumers who fall in the middle-income level. The result is a fiercely competitive retail environment where discount retailers have focused less on their core, low-income consumers, who are most impacted by rising housing and gas costs. Overall, however, shares of discount chains are faring better during this particular penny-pinching economy than their full-priced and upscale counterparts, because discount retailers have focused on getting current customers to purchase a wider array of products in the store, rather than trying to attract new shoppers.[16]

SOCIAL INFLUENCES ON CONSUMER BUYING DECISIONS

Many consumers seek out the opinions of others to reduce their search and evaluation effort or uncertainty, especially as the perceived risk of the decision increases. Consumers may also seek out others' opinions for guidance on new products or services, products with image-related attributes, or products where attribute information is lacking or uninformative. Specifically, consumers interact socially with reference groups, opinion leaders, and family members to obtain product information and decision approval.

Reference Groups

All the formal and informal groups that influence the buying behavior of an individual are that person's **reference groups**. Consumers may use products or brands to identify with or become a member of a group. They learn from observing how members of their reference groups consume, and they use the same criteria to make their own consumer decisions.

Reference groups can be categorized very broadly as either direct or indirect (see Exhibit 6.8). Direct reference groups are face-to-face membership groups that touch people's lives directly. They can be either primary or secondary. **Primary membership groups** include all groups with which people interact regularly in an informal, face-to-face manner, such as family, friends, and coworkers. In contrast, people associate with **secondary membership groups** less consistently and more formally. These groups might include clubs, professional groups, and religious groups.

Consumers also are influenced by many indirect, nonmembership reference groups they do not belong to. **Aspirational reference groups** are those a person would like to join. To join an aspirational group, a person must at least conform to the norms of that group. (**Norms** are the values and attitudes deemed acceptable by the group.) Thus, a person who wants to be elected to public office may begin to dress more conservatively, as other politicians do. He or she may go to many of the restaurants and social engagements that city and business leaders attend and try to play a role that is acceptable to voters and other influential people. Similarly, teenagers today may dye their hair and

reference group
A group in society that influences an individual's purchasing behavior.

primary membership group
A reference group with which people interact regularly in an informal, face-to-face manner, such as family, friends, or fellow employees.

secondary membership group
A reference group with which people associate less consistently and more formally than a primary membership group, such as a club, professional group, or religious group.

aspirational reference group
A group that someone would like to join.

norm
A value or attitude deemed acceptable by a group.

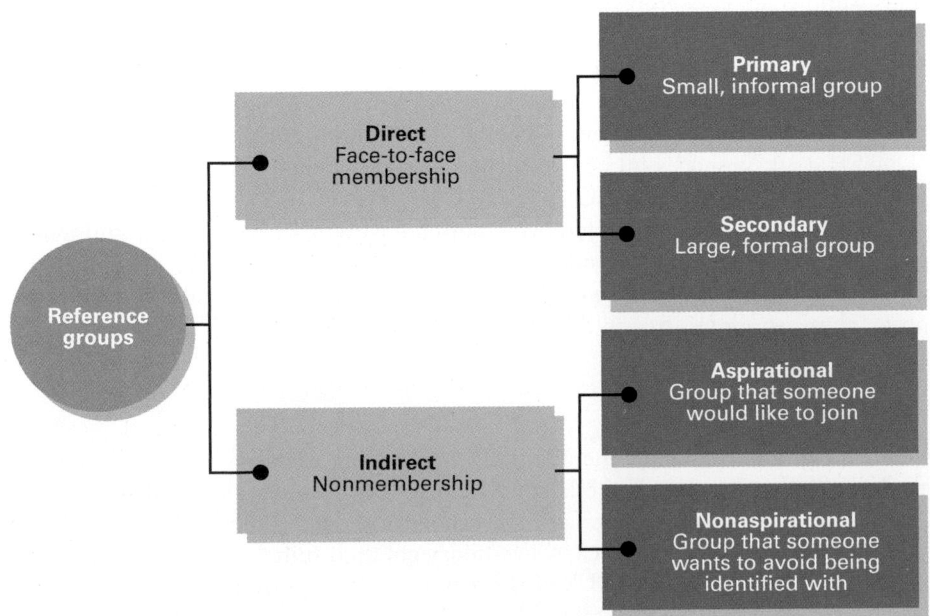

EXHIBIT 6.8

Types of Reference Groups

nonaspirational reference group
A group with which an individual does not want to associate.

opinion leader
An individual who influences the opinions of others.

experiment with body piercing and tattoos. Athletes are an aspirational group for several market segments. To appeal to the younger market, Coca-Cola signed basketball star LeBron James to be the spokesperson for its Sprite and POWERade brands, and Nike signed a sneaker deal with him reportedly worth $90 million. Coca-Cola and Nike assumed James would encourage consumers to drink Coke brands and buy Nike shoes because they would like to identify with James.

Nonaspirational reference groups, or dissociative groups, influence our behavior when we try to maintain distance from them. A consumer may avoid buying some types of clothing or car, going to certain restaurants or stores, or even buying a home in a certain neighborhood in order to avoid being associated with a particular group.

The activities, values, and goals of reference groups directly influence consumer behavior. For marketers, reference groups have three important implications: (1) they serve as information sources and influence perceptions, (2) they affect an individual's aspiration levels, and (3) their norms either constrain or stimulate consumer behavior. For example, research firms devoted to uncovering what's cool in the teen market have identified a couple of influential groups among today's teens based on their interests in clothes, music, and activities. Tracking these groups reveals how products become cool and how groups influence the adoption of cool products by other groups. A trend or fad often starts with teens who have the most innovative tastes. These teens are on the cutting edge of fashion and music, and they wear their attitude all over their bodies in the form of tattoos, body piercing, studded jewelry, or colored tresses. Certain fads embraced by these "Edgers" will spark an interest in the small group of teens researchers call "Influencers," who project the look other teens covet. Influencers also create their own trends in music and clothing choices. Once a fad is embraced and adopted by Influencers, the look becomes cool and desirable. The remaining groups that compose the majority of the teen population will not embrace a fad until it gets its seal of approval from the Influencers.

Understanding the effect of reference groups on a product is important for marketers as they track the life cycle of their products. Retailer Abercrombie & Fitch noticed it was beginning to lose its target audience of college students when its stores began attracting large numbers of high school students trying to be more like college students. To solve the problem, A&F created its Hollister store chain specifically for high school students. The retailer also opened a chain called Abercrombie for a target market of boys and girls, ages seven to fourteen. Another A&F chain, Ruehl, offers Greenwich Village–inspired clothing for the post-college-age market.

Marketers and researchers can now gauge teen opinions, test new product ideas, and even get help creating marketing buzz by tapping into the ever-expanding online teen communities. For example, Piczo, an online community with 28 million registered users worldwide, has a group of influential "insiders" who will advise brands on how to best leverage the site. "Piczo Insiders" exchange opinions and offer feedback on marketing campaigns that are running on the Piczo site. These teens will collaborate online with marketers and are responsive to any research activity or project that they think will improve the Piczo user experience. The Insiders recently contributed real-life stories to "Don't Hide It," a successful new campaign for the National Society for the Prevention of Cruelty to Children (NSPCC).

Research has shown that reference groups are particularly powerful in influencing purchases of fragrances, wine, snack food, candy, clothing, and sodas.[17] People with well-formed networks of somewhat overlapping reference groups and those with strong personal values are less susceptible to reference group influences.[18]

Opinion Leaders

Reference groups frequently include individuals known as group leaders, or **opinion leaders**—those who influence others. Obviously, it is important for marketing managers to persuade such people to purchase their goods or services. Many products and services that are integral parts of Americans' lives today got their initial boost from opinion leaders. For example, DVDs and SUVs (sport-utility vehicles) were purchased by opinion leaders well ahead of the general public.

Opinion leaders are often the first to try new products and services out of pure curiosity. They are typically self-indulgent and status-seeking, making them more likely to explore unproven but intriguing products and services.[19] Technology companies have found that teenagers, because of their willingness to experiment, are key opinion leaders for the success of new technologies.

Opinion leadership is a casual, face-to-face phenomenon and is usually inconspicuous, so locating opinion leaders can be a challenge. Thus, marketers often try to create opinion leaders. They may use high school cheerleaders to model new fall fashions or civic leaders to promote insurance, new cars, and other merchandise. On a national level, companies sometimes use movie stars, sports figures, and other celebrities to promote products, hoping they are appropriate opinion leaders. The effectiveness of celebrity endorsements varies, though, depending largely on how credible and attractive the spokesperson is and how familiar people are with him or her. Endorsements are most likely to succeed if a reasonable association between the spokesperson and the product can be established.

The activities, values, and goals of reference groups directly influence consumer behavior. Consumers may use the Neutrogena brand—and participate in skin cancer prevention behavior as she does—because they aspire to be like actress Jennifer Garner.

© AP IMAGES/PRNEWSFOTO/NEUTROGENA

Celebrities and sports figures aren't the only people marketers consider opinion leaders, however. Managers at BMW are rethinking who the U.S. opinion leaders are for their brand. Historically, the automaker targeted car enthusiasts. Today, the company is looking at the "idea class," a group composed of roughly 1.5 million architects, professionals, innovators, and entrepreneurs who are more interested in design, authenticity, and independent thinking. Over a five-year period, BMW has increased U.S. sales by 62 percent, but still has less than a 2 percent share of the U.S. market.[20]

Respected organizations such as the American Heart Association and the American Cancer Society may also serve as opinion leaders. Marketers may seek endorsements from them as well as from schools, churches, cities, the military, and fraternal organizations as a form of group opinion leadership. Salespeople often ask to use opinion leaders' names as a means of achieving greater personal influence in a sales presentation.

How Blogs Are Defining Today's Opinion Leaders Increasingly, marketers are looking to Web logs, or blogs, as they're commonly called, to find opinion leaders. A new blog is created every second of every day according to Technorati, a blog-monitoring site, so it's getting harder to separate the true opinion leaders from intermediate Web users who are just looking to share random thoughts or vacation photos with family and friends. As of this printing, Technorati monitors 35.3 million blogs, Feedster monitors 80 million, and Nielsen BuzzMetrics boasts coverage of more than 25 million blogs.[21] The fashion industry used to dismiss bloggers as irrelevant and small-time, effectively limiting their access to hot events during semi-annual fashion week shows. Now, however, fashion bloggers have the attention of the fashion establishment because many are claiming bigger followings than traditional media. Still, not all fashion blogs are equal. Bloggers from FashionTribes.com and Bagtrends.com received tickets to some fall 2006 shows, but shopology.com and Coutorture.com were denied access because their audiences were too small.[22]

EXHIBIT 6.9

Tweens and Teens Weigh in on Advertising Tactics

Ad Tactic	Like		Dislike	
	8–12 yrs	13–18 yrs	8–12 yrs	13–18 yrs
Famous person uses product	39%	21%	12%	22%
Person in a movie uses product	33%	20%	12%	19%
Cartoon or TV show about product	31%	13%	25%	34%
Popular kids given free product	24%	12%	43%	44%
Product advertised on cell phones	5%	4%	41%	55%
Product mentioned in online chats	5%	4%	37%	45%
Product written about on a blog site	14%	10%	24%	32%

Source: Adapted from "Today's Youth Look to Advertising as Much as Their Friends When Making Purchase Decisions", *PR Newswire*, August 21, 2006.

One way marketers are identifying true opinion leaders is by looking to teen blogs to identify the social trends that are shaping consumer behavior. During the research phase of development for its teen-targeted RED Blogs service, AOL discovered that over 50 percent of teens do not mind sharing their feelings in public forums. This is especially evident at social networking sites like MySpace, Facebook, and Xanga, where teens and twentysomethings post extensive personal profiles, photo collections, links to user groups they belong to, and detailed descriptions of their social events.

Raised with MTV, 500-channel cable services, a rapidly maturing Internet, and ever-expanding cell phone capabilities, teens have unprecedented access to the world around them. Furthermore, they are no longer passive observers of the culture their parents have created. They can follow their favorite bands, actors, or athletes via their Web sites and blogs and expect to interact with them instead of just admiring them from afar. With their unprecedented ability to network and communicate with each other, young people rely on each others' opinions more than marketing messages when making purchase decisions. And blogs are becoming a key way that teens communicate their opinions (see Exhibit 6.9). Consequently, today's marketers are reading teen blogs, developing products that meet the very specific needs that teens express there, and learning unique and creative ways to put key influencers in charge of marketing their brands for them.

socialization process
How cultural values and norms are passed down to children.

Family

The family is the most important social institution for many consumers, strongly influencing values, attitudes, self-concept—and buying behavior. For example, a family that strongly values good health will have a grocery list distinctly different from that of a family that views every dinner as a gourmet event. Moreover, the family is responsible for the **socialization process**, the passing down of cultural values and norms to children. Children learn by observing their parents' consumption patterns, and so they will tend to shop in a similar pattern.

Decision-making roles among family members tend to vary significantly, depending on the type of item purchased. Family members assume a variety of roles in the purchase process. *Initiators* suggest, initiate, or plant the seed for the purchase process. The initiator can be any member of the family. For example, Sister might initiate the product search by asking for a new bicycle as a birthday present. *Influencers* are those members of the family whose opinions are valued. In our example, Mom might function as a price-range watchdog, an influencer whose main role is to veto or approve price ranges. Brother may give his opinion on certain makes of bicycles. The *decision maker* is the family member who actually makes the decision to buy or not to buy. For example, Dad or Mom is likely to choose the final brand and model of bicycle to buy after seeking further information from Sister about cosmetic features such as color, and then imposing additional criteria of his or her own, such as durability and safety. The *purchaser* (probably Dad or Mom) is the one who actually exchanges money for the product. Finally, the *consumer* is the actual user—Sister, in the case of the bicycle.

Marketers should consider family purchase situations along with the distribution of consumer and decision-maker roles among family members. Ordinary marketing views the individual as both decision maker and consumer. Family marketing adds several other possibilities: Sometimes more than one family member or all family members are involved in the decision; sometimes only children are involved in the decision; sometimes more than one consumer is involved; sometimes the decision maker and the consumer are different people. Exhibit 6.10 represents the patterns of family purchasing relationships that are possible.

In most households when parental joint decisions are being made, spouses consider their partner's needs and perceptions to maintain decision fairness and harmony.[23] This tends to minimize family conflict. Research also shows that in harmonious households the spouse that has "won" a previous decision is less likely to use strong influence in a subsequent decision.[24] This balancing factor is key in maintaining long-term family harmony.

Children can have great influence over the purchase decisions of their parents. In many families, with both parents working and short on time, children are encouraged to participate. In addition, children in single-parent households become more involved in family decisions at an earlier age. Children are especially influential in decisions about food and eating out. Exactly how much of an influence kids have varies depending on factors such as age, race, socioeconomic status, and region. For example, *Restaurants & Institutions'* New American Diner study shows that children age 5 or younger frequently influence restaurant visits, while children ages 6 to 18 have only occasional influence. Females, Generation Xers, Asian American diners, and Midwesterners are most likely to say children influence which restaurants they visit.[25] Children influence purchase decisions for many more products and services than food. Even though they are usually not the actual purchasers of such items, children often participate in decisions about toys, clothes, vacations, recreation, automobiles, and many other products. And if those children happen to be teenagers? American teens have a total income of $80 billion of their own, and parents spend an additional $110 billion each year on them. Recent data shows that while teens make up only 7 percent of the U.S. population, they actually contribute to 11 percent of U.S. spending.[26]

Traditionally, children learn about consumption from their parents. In today's technologically overloaded world, that trend is reversing. Teenagers and adult children often contribute information and influence the purchase of parents' technology products.[27] Often they even help with installation and show the parents how to use the product!

EXHIBIT 6.10

Relationships among Purchasers and Consumers in the Family

		Purchase Decision Maker		
		Parent(s) Only	Child/Children Only	Some or All Family Members
Consumer	Parent(s)	golf clubs cosmetics wine	Mother's Day card	Christmas gifts minivan
	Child/ Children	diapers breakfast cereal	candy small toys	bicycle
	Some Family Members	videos long-distance phone service	children's movies	computers sports events
	All Family Members	clothing life insurance	fast-food restaurant	swim club membership vacations

Source: Reprinted with permission from "Pulling the Family's Strings" by Robert Boutillier in *American Demographics*.

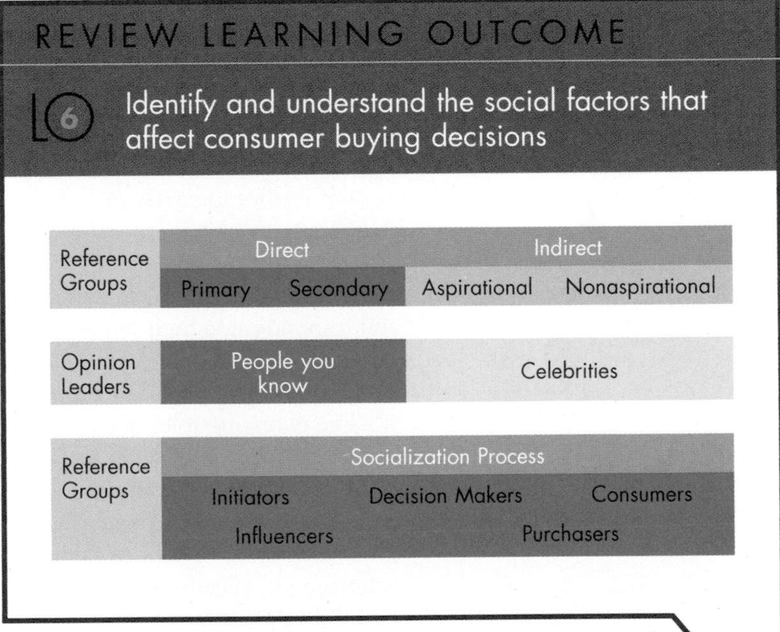

INDIVIDUAL INFLUENCES ON CONSUMER BUYING DECISIONS

A person's buying decisions are also influenced by personal characteristics that are unique to each individual, such as gender; age and life-cycle stage; and personality, self-concept, and lifestyle. Individual characteristics are generally stable over the course of one's life. For instance, most people do not change their gender, and the act of changing personality or lifestyle requires a complete reorientation of one's life. In the case of age and life-cycle stage, these changes occur gradually over time.

Gender

Physiological differences between men and women result in different needs, such as health and beauty products. Just as important are the distinct cultural, social, and economic roles played by men and women and the effects that these have on their decision-making processes. For example, many networks have programming targeted to women, while Spike TV calls itself the "first network for men." Two magazines are geared to men who like to shop: *Details* is an upscale fashion magazine for affluent men in their 20s and 30s; *Complex* is a magazine for younger men whose fashions range from hip-hop and skateboarding to mainstream style.

Trends in gender marketing are influenced by the changing roles of men and women in society. For example, men used to rely on the women in their lives to shop for them. Today, however, more men are shopping for themselves. The number of men shopping online was up to 57 percent in 2007 from 38 percent in 2006. Census Bureau figures show that in March 2003, the latest year for which Census statistics are available, there were 299,000 married-family households in which the husband was at home with at least one child under six. This figure was up 29 percent from 1993.[28] Men who have begun staying at home with their young children have noticed how few baby items, such as diaper bags, are made with a man's use in mind. One man went so far as to create his own product line, at **dadgear.com.** The first year the products hit the market, revenue was slightly higher than $40,000; projected revenue for 2006 was $800,000 to $1 million.[29] Whether because of the advent of online shopping or retailers wising up to the way men like to shop, today more men are comfortable shopping for themselves. A study commissioned by *GQ* found that 84 percent of men said they purchase their own clothes, compared with 65 percent four years ago.[30]

Men's roles aren't the only ones that are changing. Women around the world are working and earning more, and many industries are attracting new customers by marketing to women. For example, nearly 40 percent, or 50 million, of American Airlines' customers are women. If AA raises that number by 2 percent, it will make another $94 million in revenue each year. Acknowledging that, American has launched an online community resource especially for women travelers at **www.aa.com/women.** Wyndham Hotels and Resorts developed a program called Women On Their Way to enhance the experience of their female guests. American and Wyndham believe that by listening and responding to their female customers' insights, the travel experience for all of their customers will improve. These special programs are also designed to foster women travelers' belief that their business is valued.

The changing roles of women are also forcing companies that have traditionally targeted women to develop new strategies. One reason is because women's decision making tends to be multi-minded and integrative, meaning that they consider and move back and forth among many criteria, as opposed to being single-minded and focused. They tend to view shopping as a learning process, educating themselves on the available options and typically adding criteria as they learn more. It is not unusual for a woman to shift back to an earlier stage of the decision process as she learns something that may cause her even to change categories. For example, a woman may have decided to buy an SUV because her friends all love theirs and she likes the looks of the new models. Once on the showroom floor, however, she may see a new minivan that offers great storage and fuel mileage. Suddenly, she's including minivans in her consideration set and has added two new criteria to the qualifying list.

Age and Family Life-Cycle Stage

The age and family life-cycle stage of a consumer can have a significant impact on consumer behavior. How old a consumer is generally indicates what products he or she may be interested in purchasing. Consumer tastes in food, clothing, cars, furniture, and recreation are often age related. The table in Exhibit 6.11 uses data compiled by the Bureau of Labor Statistics to show the differences in spending on certain items by Americans by age.

Related to a person's age is his or her place in the family life cycle. As Chapter 8 explains in more detail, the *family life cycle* is an orderly series of stages through which consumers' attitudes and behavioral tendencies evolve through maturity, experience, and changing income and status. Marketers often define their target markets in terms of family life cycle, such as "young singles," "young married with children," and "middle-aged married without children." For instance, young singles spend more than average on alcoholic beverages, education, and entertainment. New parents typically increase their spending on health care, clothing, housing, and food and decrease their spending on alcohol, education, and transportation. Households with older children spend more on food, entertainment, personal care products, and education, as well as cars and gasoline. After their children leave home, spending by older couples on vehicles, women's clothing, health care, and long-distance calls typically increases. For instance, the presence of children in the home is the most significant determinant of the type of vehicle that's driven off the new-car lot. Parents are the ultimate need-driven car consumers, requiring larger cars and trucks to haul their children and all their belongings. It comes as no surprise then that for all households with children, SUVs rank either first or second among new-vehicle purchases, followed by minivans.

EXHIBIT 6.11

Average Annual Expenditures by Age

Item	Age					
	<25	25–34	35–44	45–54	55–64	>65
Food at home	$2,265	$3,210	$4,125	$4,003	$3,457	$2,905
Food away from home	1,876	2,790	3,268	3,178	2,784	1,610
Household furnishings and equipment	925	2,034	2,198	1,933	1,944	1,235
Apparel and services	1,477	2,106	2,335	2,191	1,888	1,040
Vehicle purchases	2,273	3,930	4,183	3,223	3,348	1,977
Entertainment	1,448	2,462	3,551	3,163	2,730	1,966
Personal care products and services	337	512	662	686	632	528

Source: Bureau of Labor Statistics, 2005, by the U.S. Census Bureau.

Marketers should also be aware of the many nontraditional life-cycle paths that are common today and provide insights into the needs and wants of such consumers as divorced parents, lifelong singles, and childless couples. Three decades ago, married couples with children under the age of 18 accounted for about half of U.S. households. Today, such families make up only 23 percent of all households, while people living alone or with nonfamily members represent more than 30 percent. Furthermore, according to the U.S. Census Bureau, the number of single-mother households grew by 25 percent over the last decade. The shift toward more single-parent households is part of a broader societal change that has put more women on the career track. Although many marketers continue to be wary of targeting nontraditional families, Charles Schwab targeted single mothers in an advertising campaign featuring Sarah Ferguson, the Duchess of York and a divorced mom. The idea was to appeal to single mothers' heightened awareness of the need for financial self-sufficiency.

Life Events Another way to look at the life cycle is to look at major events in one's life over time. Life-changing events can occur at any time. A few examples are: death of a spouse, moving to a different place, birth or adoption of a child, retirement, getting fired, divorce, and marriage. Typically, such events are quite stressful and consumers often take steps to minimize that stress. Many times such life-changing events will mean new consumption patterns.[31] A recently divorced person may try to improve his or her appearance by joining a health club and dieting. A person moving to a different

personality
A way of organizing and grouping the consistencies of an individual's reactions to situations.

self-concept
How consumers perceive themselves in terms of attitudes, perceptions, beliefs, and self-evaluations.

ideal self-image
The way an individual would like to be.

real self-image
The way an individual actually perceives himself or herself.

lifestyle
A mode of living as identified by a person's activities, interests, and opinions.

city will need a new dentist, grocery store, auto service center, and doctor, to name a few shops and service providers. Marketers realize that life-events often mean a chance to gain a new customer. The Welcome Wagon offers a number of free gifts and services for area newcomers. Lowe's sends out a discount coupon to those moving to a new community. And when you put your home on the market, very quickly you start getting flyers from moving companies promising a great price on moving your household goods.

Personality, Self-Concept, and Lifestyle

Each consumer has a unique personality. **Personality** is a broad concept that can be thought of as a way of organizing and grouping how an individual typically reacts to situations. Thus, personality combines psychological makeup and environmental forces. It includes people's underlying dispositions, especially their most dominant characteristics. Although personality is one of the least useful concepts in the study of consumer behavior, some marketers believe that personality influences the types and brands of products purchased. For instance, the type of car, clothes, or jewelry a consumer buys may reflect one or more personality traits.

Self-concept, or self-perception, is how consumers perceive themselves. Self-concept includes attitudes, perceptions, beliefs, and self-evaluations. Although self-concept may change, the change is often gradual. Through self-concept, people define their identity, which in turn provides for consistent and coherent behavior.

Self-concept combines the **ideal self-image** (the way an individual would like to be) and the **real self-image** (how an individual actually perceives himself or herself). Generally, we try to raise our real self-image toward our ideal (or at least narrow the gap). Consumers seldom buy products that jeopardize their self-image. For example, someone who sees herself as a trendsetter wouldn't buy clothing that doesn't project a contemporary image.

Human behavior depends largely on self-concept. Because consumers want to protect their identity as individuals, the products they buy, the stores they patronize, and the credit cards they carry support their self-image. No other product quite reflects a person's self-image as much as the car he or she drives. For example, many young consumers do not like family sedans like the Honda Accord or Toyota Camry and say they would buy one for their mom, but not for themselves. Likewise, younger parents may avoid purchasing minivans because they do not want to sacrifice the youthful image they have of themselves just because they have new responsibilities. To combat decreasing sales, marketers of the Nissan Quest minivan decided to reposition it as something other than a "mom mobile" or "soccer mom car." They chose the ad copy "Passion built it. Passion will fill it up," followed by "What if we made a minivan that changed the way people think of minivans?"

By influencing the degree to which consumers perceive a good or service to be self-relevant, marketers can affect consumers' motivation to learn about, shop for, and buy a certain brand. Marketers also consider self-concept important because it helps explain the relationship between individuals' perceptions of themselves and their consumer behavior.

Personality and self-concept are reflected in lifestyle. A **lifestyle** is a mode of living, as identified by a person's activities, interests, and opinions. Psychographics is the analytical technique used to examine consumer lifestyles and to categorize consumers. Unlike personality characteristics, which are hard to describe and measure, lifestyle characteristics are useful in segmenting and targeting consumers. Lifestyle and psychographic analysis explicitly addresses the way consumers outwardly express their inner selves in their social and cultural environment.

Many companies now use psychographics to better understand their market segments. For many years, marketers selling products to mothers conveniently assumed that all moms were fairly homogeneous and concerned about the same things—the health and well-being of their children—and that they could all be reached with a similar message. But recent lifestyle research has shown that there are traditional, blended, and nontraditional moms, and companies like Procter & Gamble and Pillsbury are using strategies to reach these different types of mothers. Psychographics is also effective with other market segments.

An example of a lifestyle segment are those people who are snackers. Snacking can be part of a healthy diet or it can be loaded with junk food. Thus, there are healthy and unhealthy snackers. Today, 21 percent of all meals are snacks.[32] A few findings on snacks and snackers are:

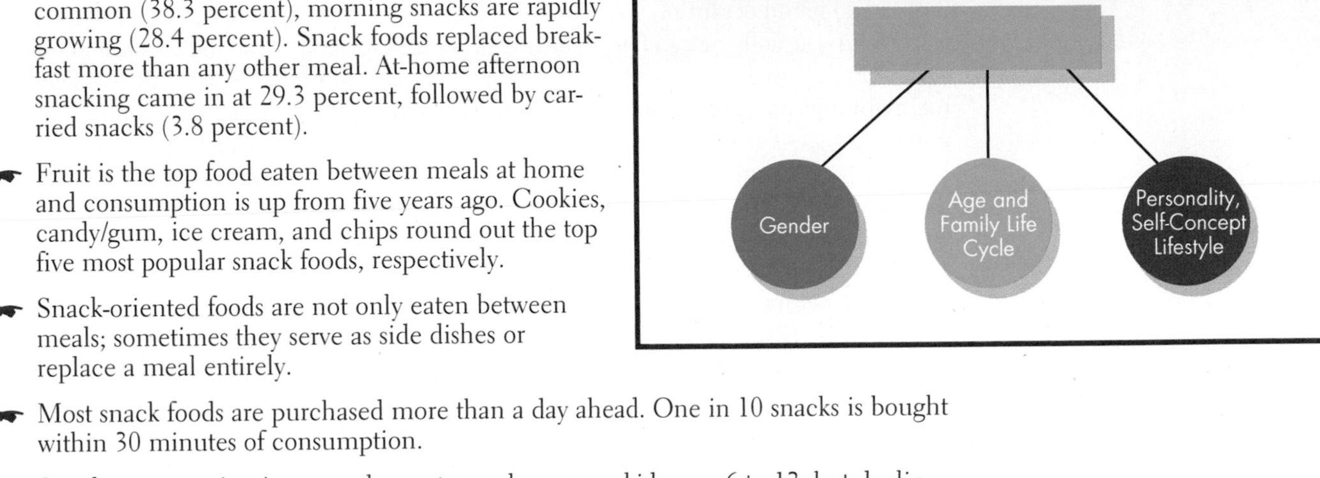

- While late-night refrigerator trips are still the most common (38.3 percent), morning snacks are rapidly growing (28.4 percent). Snack foods replaced breakfast more than any other meal. At-home afternoon snacking came in at 29.3 percent, followed by carried snacks (3.8 percent).
- Fruit is the top food eaten between meals at home and consumption is up from five years ago. Cookies, candy/gum, ice cream, and chips round out the top five most popular snack foods, respectively.
- Snack-oriented foods are not only eaten between meals; sometimes they serve as side dishes or replace a meal entirely.
- Most snack foods are purchased more than a day ahead. One in 10 snacks is bought within 30 minutes of consumption.
- Snack consumption is currently most popular among kids ages 6 to 12, but declining among children 2 to 5, adults ages 18 to 34, and those over 55.[33]

Psychographics and lifestyle segmentation are discussed in more detail in Chapter 8.

LO 8

PSYCHOLOGICAL INFLUENCES ON CONSUMER BUYING DECISIONS

An individual's buying decisions are further influenced by psychological factors: perception, motivation, learning, and beliefs and attitudes. These factors are what consumers use to interact with their world. They are the tools consumers use to recognize their feelings, gather and analyze information, formulate thoughts and opinions, and take action. Unlike the other three influences on consumer behavior, psychological influences can be affected by a person's environment because they are applied on specific occasions. For example, you will perceive different stimuli and process these stimuli in different ways depending on whether you are sitting in class concentrating on the instructor, sitting outside of class talking to friends, or sitting in your dorm room watching television.

Perception

The world is full of stimuli. A stimulus is any unit of input affecting one or more of the five senses: sight, smell, taste, touch, and hearing. The process by which we select, organize, and interpret these stimuli into a meaningful and coherent picture is called **perception**. In essence, perception is how we see the world around us and how we recognize that we need some help in making a purchasing decision.

People cannot perceive every stimulus in their environment. Therefore, they use **selective exposure** to decide which stimuli to notice and which to ignore. A typical

perception
The process by which people select, organize, and interpret stimuli into a meaningful and coherent picture.

selective exposure
The process whereby a consumer notices certain stimuli and ignores others.

selective distortion
A process whereby a consumer changes or distorts information that conflicts with his or her feelings or beliefs.

selective retention
A process whereby a consumer remembers only that information that supports his or her personal beliefs.

consumer is exposed to more than 2,500 advertising messages a day, but notices only between 11 and 20.

The familiarity of an object, contrast, movement, intensity (such as increased volume), and smell are cues that influence perception. Consumers use these cues to identify and define products and brands. The shape of a product's packaging, such as Coca-Cola's signature contour bottle, for instance, can influence perception. Color is another cue, and it plays a key role in consumers' perceptions. Packaged foods manufacturers use color to trigger unconscious associations for grocery shoppers who typically make their shopping decisions in the blink of an eye. When Pepsi departed from its usual blue can for a red can in a marketing campaign for the 2008 Olympics in China, they risked brand confusion with Coke products. One Pepsi drinker in China said, "This is so weird. I usually just go for the blue can; it's easy to spot. . . the red can just doesn't look right." Pepsi officials say they coordinated the can with the color of China's flag to highlight their sponsorship of Team China. Pepsi had used national colors on promotional packages before, such as yellow and green cans to sponsor Brazilian teams.[34]

Ampacet, a world leader in color additives for plastics, reported in 2007 that nature-inspired colors and organic values were becoming more popular as the economy and global focus shifted from the tech-boom to bio- or eco-boom. Ecological consequences and concerns have resulted in marketing initiatives such as "going green." Packaging colors like natural greens, earthy browns, and strong yellows are in, as well as metallics such as steely silver, carbon black, gold, and copper. Color researchers speculate that technological overload has led to resurgence in the appreciation of simplistic luxury. Color names for fabrics and makeup reflect that trend with names such as Grounded, Champagne Chic, and Serene Blue.[35]

What is perceived by consumers may also depend on the stimuli's vividness or shock value. Graphic warnings of the hazards associated with a product's use are perceived more readily and remembered more accurately than less vivid warnings or warnings that are written in text. "Sexier" ads excel at attracting the attention of younger consumers. Companies like Calvin Klein and Guess use sensuous ads intended to create a fantasy or mood to capture the attention of the target audience. Fragrance advertisements often make promises of the "outcome" of wearing their product, often the promise of a role transformation on the part of the wearer. David Rubin, brand development director for Axe deodorant, says Axe's theme from the very start has been "giving guys an edge in the mating game."[36]

Two other concepts closely related to selective exposure are selective distortion and selective retention. **Selective distortion** occurs when consumers change or distort information that conflicts with their feelings or beliefs. For example, suppose a college student buys a SonicBlue Rio MP3 player. After the purchase, if the student gets new information about an alternative brand, such as an Apple iPod, he or she may distort the information to make it more consistent with the prior view that the SonicBlue Rio is just as good as the iPod, if not better. Business travelers who fly often may distort or discount information about airline crashes because they must use air travel constantly in their jobs.

Selective retention is remembering only information that supports personal feelings or beliefs. The consumer forgets all information that may be inconsistent. After reading a pamphlet that contradicts one's political beliefs, for instance, a person may forget many of the points outlined in it. Similarly, consumers may see a news report on suspected illegal practices by their favorite retail store, but soon forget the reason the store was featured on the news.

Which stimuli will be perceived often depends on the individual. People can be exposed to the same stimuli under identical conditions but perceive them very differently. For example, two people viewing a TV commercial may have different interpretations of the advertising message. One person may be thoroughly engrossed by the message and become highly motivated to buy the product. Thirty seconds after the ad ends, the second person may not be able to recall the content of the message or even the product advertised.

Marketing Implications of Perception Marketers must recognize the importance of cues, or signals, in consumers' perception of products. Marketing managers first identify the important attributes, such as price or quality, that the targeted consumers want in a product and then design signals to communicate these attributes. For example, consumers will pay more for candy in expensive-looking foil packages. But shiny labels on wine bottles signify less expensive wines; dull labels indicate more expensive wines. Marketers also often use price as a signal to consumers that the product is of higher quality than competing products. Gibson Guitar Corporation briefly cut prices on many of its guitars to compete with Japanese rivals Yamaha and Ibanez, but found that it sold more guitars when it charged more for them. Consumers perceived that the higher price indicated a better quality instrument.[37]

Of course, brand names send signals to consumers. The brand names of Close-Up toothpaste, DieHard batteries, and Caress moisturizing soap, for example, identify important product qualities. Names chosen for search engines and sites on the Internet, such as Yahoo!, Amazon.com, and Excite, are intended to convey excitement, intensity, and vastness. Companies may even change their names to send a message to consumers. As today's utility companies increasingly enter unregulated markets, many are shaking their stodgy "Power & Light & Electric" names in favor of those that let consumers know they are not just about electricity anymore, such as Reliant Resources, Entergy, and Cinergy.

Consumers also associate quality and reliability with certain brand names. Companies watch their brand identity closely, in large part because a strong link has been established between perceived brand value and customer loyalty. Brand names that consistently enjoy high perceived value from consumers include Kodak, Disney, National Geographic, Mercedes-Benz, and Fisher-Price. Naming a product after a place can also add perceived value by association. Brand names using the words Santa Fe, Dakota, or Texas convey a sense of openness, freedom, and youth, but products named after other locations might conjure up images of pollution and crime.

Marketing managers are also interested in the *threshold level of perception:* the minimum difference in a stimulus that the consumer will notice. This concept is sometimes referred to as the "just-noticeable difference." For example, how much would Apple have to drop the price of its iPod Shuffle before consumers recognized it as a bargain—$25? $50? or more? One study found that the just-noticeable difference in a stimulus is about a 20 percent change. For example, consumers will likely notice a 20 percent price decrease more quickly than a 15 percent decrease. This marketing principle can be applied to other marketing variables as well, such as package size or loudness of a broadcast advertisement.[38]

© LEIGH PRATHER/SHUTTERSTOCK.COM

> "Consumers will likely notice a 20 percent price decrease more quickly than a 15 percent decrease."

Besides changing such stimuli as price, package size, and volume, marketers can change the product or attempt to reposition its image. But marketers must be careful when adding features. How many new services will discounter Target Stores need to add before consumers perceive it as a full-service department store? How many sporty features will General Motors have to add to a basic two-door sedan before consumers start perceiving it as a sports car?

Marketing managers who intend to do business in global markets should be aware of how foreign consumers perceive their products. For instance, in Japan, product labels are often written in English or French, even though they may not translate into anything meaningful. Many Japanese associate foreign words on product labels with the exotic, the expensive, and high quality.

Marketers have often been suspected of sending advertising messages subconsciously to consumers in what is known as *subliminal perception*. The controversy began when a researcher claimed to have increased popcorn and Coca-Cola sales at a movie theater after flashing "Eat popcorn" and "Drink Coca-Cola" on the screen every five seconds for 1/300th of a second, although the audience did not consciously recognize the messages. Almost immediately consumer protection groups became concerned that advertisers were brainwashing consumers, and this practice was pronounced illegal in California and Canada. Although the researcher later admitted to making up the data

motive
A driving force that causes a person to take action to satisfy specific needs.

Maslow's hierarchy of needs
A method of classifying human needs and motivations into five categories in ascending order of importance: physiological, safety, social, esteem, and self-actualization.

and scientists have been unable to replicate the study since, consumers are still wary of hidden messages that advertisers may be sending.

Motivation

By studying motivation, marketers can analyze the major forces influencing consumers to buy or not buy products. When you buy a product, you usually do so to fulfill some kind of need. These needs become motives when aroused sufficiently. For instance, suppose this morning you were so hungry before class that you needed to eat something. In response to that need, you stopped at McDonald's for an Egg McMuffin. In other words, you were motivated by hunger to stop at McDonald's. **Motives** are the driving forces that cause a person to take action to satisfy specific needs.

Why are people driven by particular needs at particular times? One popular theory is **Maslow's hierarchy of needs**, shown in Exhibit 6.12, which arranges needs in ascending order of importance: physiological, safety, social, esteem, and self-actualization. As a person fulfills one need, a higher-level need becomes more important.

The most basic human needs are *physiological*—that is, the needs for food, water, and shelter. Because they are essential to survival, these needs must be satisfied first. Ads showing a juicy hamburger or a runner gulping down Gatorade after a marathon are examples of appeals to satisfy the physiological needs of hunger and thirst.

Safety needs include security and freedom from pain and discomfort. Marketers sometimes appeal to consumers' fears and anxieties about safety to sell their products. For example, aware of the aging population's health fears, the retail medical imaging centers Heart Check America and HealthScreen America advertise that they offer consumers a full body scan for early detection of health problems such as coronary disease and cancer. On the other hand, some companies or industries advertise to allay consumer fears. For example, in the wake of the September 11 terrorist attacks, the airline industry found itself having to conduct an image campaign to reassure consumers about the safety of air travel.

After physiological and safety needs have been fulfilled, *social needs*—especially love and a sense of belonging—become the focus. Love includes acceptance by one's peers, as well as sex and romantic love. Marketing managers probably appeal more to this need than to any other. Ads for clothes, cosmetics, and vacation packages suggest that buying the product can bring love. The need to belong is also a favorite of marketers, especially those marketing products to teens.

Teens consider the iPod to be not only their favorite brand but also as defining their generation. Other such brands include American Eagle Outfitters, Axe, Baby Phat, Facebook, Google, Hollister, MTV, MySpace, Vans, and YouTube. The VP of Research at MTV says marketers need to understand a new dynamic in the "millennial generation" consumer. The relationship this generation has with their parents is completely different from previous generations'. Parents can be a best friend. Brands that become too focused on "influential" teens can miss that parents can be the biggest influencer on this age group, especially when it comes to big-ticket items.[39]

Love is acceptance without regard to one's contribution. Esteem is

EXHIBIT 6.12

Maslow's Hierarchy of Needs

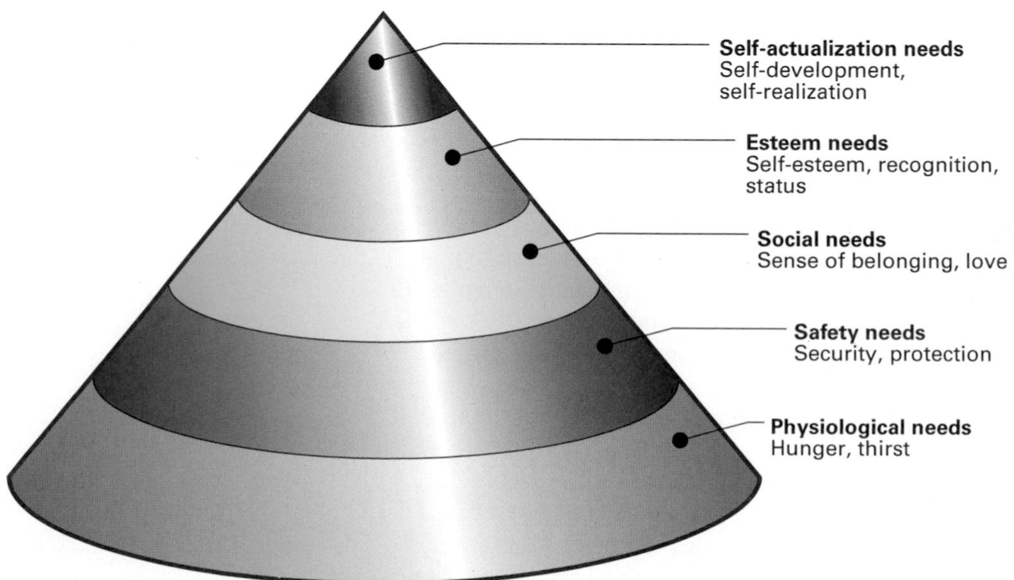

acceptance based on one's contribution to the group. *Self-esteem needs* include self-respect and a sense of accomplishment. Esteem needs also include prestige, fame, and recognition of one's accomplishments. Montblanc pens, Mercedes-Benz automobiles, and Neiman Marcus stores all appeal to esteem needs. Most high-end spas and health clubs appeal to consumers' self-esteem needs. Like exclusive country clubs, clubs such as Chicago's East Bank Club are designed to make members feel proud of their commitment to fitness while also giving them a sense of social accomplishment. In fact, the clubs can be so effective that even during an economic recession, patrons will not give up their membership because to do so would be a public admission of financial problems.

Asian consumers, in particular, are strongly motivated by status and appearance. Asians tend to be conscious of their place in a group, institution, or society as a whole. The importance of gaining social recognition turns Asians into some of the most image-conscious consumers in the world. Status-conscious Asians will not hesitate to spend freely on premium brands, such as BMW, Mercedes-Benz, and the best Scotch whiskey and French cognac. Indeed, marketers of luxury products such as Gucci, Louis Vuitton, and Prada find that demand for their products is so strong among image-conscious consumers that their sales are generally unaffected by economic downturns. In some cases, companies have been able to make up for sluggish European and U.S. sales by raising prices and volume in Asia.

The highest human need is *self-actualization*. It refers to finding self-fulfillment and self-expression, reaching the point in life at which "people are what they feel they should be." Maslow felt that very few people ever attain this level. Even so, advertisements may focus on this type of need. For example, American Express ads convey the message that acquiring its card is one of the highest attainments in life. Microsoft appealed to consumers' needs for self-actualization when it chose "Your Potential. Our Passion" as the Windows XP slogan; similarly, the U.S. Army changed its slogan from "Be all that you can be" to "Army of One," and the U.S. Navy adopted a slogan urging young people to "Accelerate Your Life."

Learning

Almost all consumer behavior results from **learning**, which is the process that creates changes in behavior through experience and practice. It is not possible to observe learning directly, but we can infer when it has occurred by a person's actions. For example, suppose you see an advertisement for a new and improved cold medicine. If you go to the store that day and buy that remedy, we infer that you have learned something about the cold medicine.

There are two types of learning: experiential and conceptual. *Experiential learning* occurs when an experience changes your behavior. For example, if the new cold medicine does not relieve your symptoms, you may not buy that brand again. *Conceptual learning*, which is not acquired through direct experience, is the second type of learning. Assume, for example, that you are standing at a soft drink machine and notice a new diet flavor with an artificial sweetener. Because someone has told you that diet beverages leave an aftertaste, you choose a different drink. You have learned that you would not like this new diet drink without ever trying it.

Reinforcement and repetition boost learning. Reinforcement can be positive or negative. If you see a vendor selling frozen yogurt (stimulus), buy it (response), and find the yogurt to be quite refreshing (reward), your behavior has been positively reinforced. On the other hand, if you buy a new flavor of yogurt and it does not taste good (negative reinforcement), you will not buy that flavor of yogurt again (response). Without positive or negative reinforcement, a person will not be motivated to repeat the behavior pattern or to avoid it. Thus, if a new brand evokes neutral feelings, some marketing activity, such as a price change or an increase in promotion, may be required to induce further consumption. Learning theory is helpful in reminding marketers that concrete and timely actions are what reinforce desired consumer behavior.

learning
A process that creates changes in behavior, immediate or expected, through experience and practice.

Repetition is a key strategy in promotional campaigns because it can lead to increased learning. Most marketers use repetitious advertising so that consumers will learn what their

stimulus generalization
A form of learning that occurs when one response is extended to a second stimulus similar to the first.

stimulus discrimination
A learned ability to differentiate among similar products.

belief
An organized pattern of knowledge that an individual holds as true about his or her world.

attitude
A learned tendency to respond consistently toward a given object.

unique advantage is over the competition. Generally, to heighten learning, advertising messages should be spread out over time rather than clustered together.

A related learning concept useful to marketing managers is stimulus generalization. In theory, **stimulus generalization** occurs when one response is extended to a second stimulus similar to the first. Marketers often use a successful, well-known brand name for a family of products because it gives consumers familiarity with and knowledge about each product in the family. Such brand-name families spur the introduction of new products and facilitate the sale of existing items. Jell-O frozen pudding pops rely on the familiarity of Jell-O gelatin; Clorox bathroom cleaner relies on familiarity with Clorox bleach; and Dove shampoo relies on familiarity with Dove soap. Microsoft entered the video game industry, hoping that the Microsoft brand would guarantee sales for the Xbox. Initial response to the Xbox was strong based on Microsoft's reputation. Since then, Microsoft has worked hard to be successful in an industry dominated by other brand giants Sony and Nintendo. The latest generation Xbox 360 Elite has jaw-dropping high-definition graphics, unmatched online play, and compelling digital entertainment; it plays music and movies stored in an array of devices, including MP3 players, and displays photos from digital cameras. Branding is examined in more detail in Chapter 10.

Another form of stimulus generalization occurs when retailers or wholesalers design their packages to resemble well-known manufacturers' brands. Such imitation often confuses consumers, who buy the imitation thinking it's the original. U.S. manufacturers in foreign markets have sometimes found little, if any, brand protection. BMW and DaimlerChrysler recently sued Chinese car manufacturers for creating near-exact replicas of their cars. Cosmetics giant L'Oreal, maker of Gucci and other luxury brands, is threatening legal action against eBay unless the auction site cracks down on sales of counterfeit L'Oreal products on its site. DVD piracy is rampant in China; so much so that special DVD-counterfeit-sniffing dogs have become a common sight in international airports. After the terrorist attacks of September 11 and subsequent stepped-up security regulations, authentication technologies have been used successfully in identifying fake passports, currency, and credit cards. Those same technologies—and others, such as embedded microchips, holographic symbols, and tamperproof packaging—are now being used in everyday products such as clothing, footwear, computers, cell phones, video games, jewelry, software, pharmaceuticals, and medical devices, making it easier for importers and retailers to spot fakes.[40]

The opposite of stimulus generalization is **stimulus discrimination**, which means learning to differentiate among similar products. Consumers may perceive one product as more rewarding or stimulating. For example, some consumers prefer Coca-Cola and others prefer Pepsi. Many insist they can taste a difference between the two brands.

With some types of products—such as aspirin, gasoline, bleach, and paper towels—marketers rely on promotion to point out brand differences that consumers would otherwise not recognize. This process, called *product differentiation*, is discussed in more detail in Chapter 8. Usually, product differentiation is based on superficial differences. For example, Bayer tells consumers that it's the aspirin "doctors recommend most."

Beliefs and Attitudes

Beliefs and attitudes are closely linked to values. A **belief** is an organized pattern of knowledge that an individual holds as true about his or her world. A consumer may believe that Sony's camcorder makes the best home videos, tolerates hard use, and is reasonably priced. These beliefs may be based on knowledge, faith, or hearsay. Consumers tend to develop a set of beliefs about a product's attributes and then, through these beliefs, form a *brand image*—a set of beliefs about a particular brand. In turn, the brand image shapes consumers' attitudes toward the product.

An **attitude** is a learned tendency to respond consistently toward a given object, such as a brand. Attitudes rest on an individual's value system, which represents personal standards of good and bad, right and wrong, and so forth; therefore, attitudes tend to be more enduring and complex than beliefs.

For an example of the nature of attitudes, consider the differing attitudes of consumers around the world toward the practice of purchasing on credit. Americans have long been enthusiastic about charging goods and services and are willing to pay high interest rates for the privilege of postponing payment. To many European consumers, doing what amounts to taking out a loan—even a small one—to pay for anything seems absurd. Germans especially are reluctant to buy on credit. Italy has a sophisticated credit and banking system well suited to handling credit cards, but Italians prefer to carry cash, often huge wads of it. Although most Japanese consumers have credit cards, card purchases amount to less than 1 percent of all consumer transactions. The Japanese have long looked down on credit purchases, but acquire cards to use while traveling abroad.

If a good or service is meeting its profit goals, positive attitudes toward the product merely need to be reinforced. If the brand is not succeeding, however, the marketing manager must strive to change target consumers' attitudes toward it. Changes in attitude tend to grow out of an individual's attempt to reconcile long-held values with a constant stream of new information. This change can be accomplished in three ways: changing beliefs about the brand's attributes, changing the relative importance of these beliefs, and adding new beliefs.

IMAGE COURTESY OF THE ADVERTISING ARCHIVES

Changing Beliefs about Attributes The first technique is to turn neutral, negative, or incorrect beliefs about product attributes into positive ones. Assume that 24 Hour Fitness does a survey among persons considering joining a health club. They find that most respondents believe that 24 Hour Fitness offers fewer classes and less variety than Shapes, Curves for Women, or Lifestyle Family Fitness. In fact, 24 Hour Fitness offers greater variety and more classes than any other health and fitness center. Thus, target consumers have incorrect beliefs and the service's attributes (number of classes and variety). So 24 Hour Fitness must advertise and do other forms of promotion, such as an open house, to correct the misimpressions.

Changing beliefs about a service can be more difficult because service attributes are usually intangible. Convincing consumers to switch hairstylists or lawyers or go to a mall dental clinic can be much more difficult than getting them to change brands of razor blades. Image, which is also largely intangible, significantly determines service patronage.

Usually changing beliefs about a product attribute is easier. For example, GE has created a new light bulb, a compact fluorescent lamp (CFL), that uses 1/3 the energy of a traditional bulb, lasts nearly 10 times longer, and can save up to $30 in energy costs over its lifetime. GE's new campaign urges the use of its new bulb by appealing to Americans' burgeoning ecological awareness, while exhibiting its own "care" for the world's resources. How could the consumer possibly resist when GE has made it so easy to participate? If every American swapped one standard bulb for a CFL, it would collectively prevent burning 30 billion pounds of coal and remove two million cars' worth of greenhouse gas emissions from the atmosphere.[41]

Changing the Importance of Beliefs The second approach to modifying attitudes is to change the relative importance of beliefs about an attribute. Cole Haan, originally a men's shoe outfitter, used boats and cars in its ads for years to associate the brand with active lifestyles, an important attribute for men. Now that it is selling women's products, such as handbags and shoes, some of its ads use models and emphasize how the products look, an important attribute for women. The company hopes the ads will change customers' perceptions and beliefs that it only sells men's products.[42]

Marketers can also emphasize the importance of some beliefs over others. For example, when consumers think of full-sized SUVs, good gas mileage doesn't often come to mind. Now, Cadillac wants to raise the importance of fuel efficiency to buyers of full-size SUVs.

REVIEW LEARNING OUTCOME

LO 8 Identify and understand the psychological factors that affect consumer buying decisions

Perception	Selective Exposure				
	Selective Retention		Selective Distortion		
Motivation	Needs				
	Physiological	Safety	Social	Esteem	Self-Actualization
Learning	Stimulus Generalization		Stimulus Discrimination		
Beliefs & Attitudes	Changing Beliefs about Attributes	Changing Importance of Beliefs	Adding New Beliefs		

The promotion for the 2009 Escalade Hybrid says, "Finally, a full-size luxury SUV confident enough to talk about fuel efficiency."[43]

Adding New Beliefs The third approach to transforming attitudes is to add new beliefs. Although changes in consumption patterns often come slowly, cereal marketers are betting that consumers will eventually warm up to the idea of cereal as a snack. A print ad for General Mills Cookie-Crisp cereal features a boy popping the sugary nuggets into his mouth while he does his homework. Koch Industries, the manufacturer of Dixie paper products, is also attempting to add new beliefs about the uses of its paper plates and cups with an advertising campaign aimed at positioning its product as a "home cleanup replacement." Commercials pitch Dixie paper plates as an alternative to washing dishes after everyday meals and not just for picnics.

U.S. companies attempting to market their goods overseas may need to help consumers add new beliefs about a product in general. Coca-Cola and PepsiCo have both found it challenging to sell their diet cola brands to consumers in India partly because diet foods of any kind are a new concept in that country where malnutrition was widespread not too many years ago. Indians also have deep-rooted attitudes that anything labeled "diet" is meant for a sick person, such as a diabetic. As a general rule, most Indians are not diet-conscious, preferring food prepared in the traditional manner that tastes good. Indians are also suspicious of the artificial sweeteners used in diet colas. India's Health Ministry has required warning labels on cans and bottles of Diet Coke and Diet Pepsi saying "Not Recommended for Children."[44]

5 ◄ number of factors determining the 3 types of consumer buying decisions

Kellogg's cereal advertising budget ► **$206 million**

4% ◄ projected growth rate for the U.S. population

projected growth rate for the population of African American women ► **8%**

73 ◄ Pecentage American Hispanics reached by Univision Radio

reported worth of Nike's endorsement deal with LeBron James ▼ **$90 million**

28 million ◄ number of registered users of the online community Piczo

number of blogs monitored by Technorati ▼ **35.3 million**

ANATOMY OF a Buying Decision: Car

For a high-involvement purchase, such as buying a car, a consumer typically practices extensive decision making. Several factors ultimately affect her buying decision.

SOCIAL FACTORS

Before deciding to buy a car, this woman may seek out others' opinions or observe what others purchase.

ADVICE FROM HER REFERENCE GROUP

EXAMPLE OF OPINION LEADER

© iStockphoto.com/ digitalskillet

© iStockphoto.com/ Palto

INDIVIDUAL FACTORS:

SELF-CONCEPT

Her buying decision will be influenced by her personality, self-concept, and lifestyle.

© iStockphoto.com/ Richard Hobson

© iStockphoto.com/Brad Killer

PSYCHOLOGICAL FACTORS:

The consumer's perception, motivation, learning, values, beliefs, and attitudes will influence her decision on which car to buy, too.

ATTITUDE

"Should I try a new brand, or stick with the familiar one?"

© iStockphoto.com/Justin Horrocks

© iStockphoto.com/ Niko Guido

REVIEW AND APPLICATIONS

LO 1 Explain why marketing managers should understand consumer behavior. Consumer behavior describes how consumers make purchase decisions and how they use and dispose of the products they buy. An understanding of consumer behavior reduces marketing managers' uncertainty when they are defining a target market and designing a marketing mix.

1.1 The type of decision making a consumer uses for a product does not necessarily remain constant. Why? Support your answer with an example from your own experience.

LO 2 Analyze the components of the consumer decision-making process. The consumer decision-making process begins with need recognition, when stimuli trigger awareness of an unfulfilled want. If additional information is required to make a purchase decision, the consumer may engage in an internal or external information search. The consumer then evaluates the additional information and establishes purchase guidelines. Finally, a purchase decision is made.

2.1 Visit Carpoint's Web site at **http://autos.msn.com/.** How does the site assist consumers in the evaluation stage of choosing a new car? Develop your own hypothetical evoked set of three or four car models and present your comparisons. Which vehicle attributes would be most important in your purchase decision?

LO 3 Explain the consumer's postpurchase evaluation process. Consumer postpurchase evaluation is influenced by prepurchase expectations, the prepurchase information search, and the consumer's general level of self-confidence. Cognitive dissonance is the inner tension that a consumer experiences after recognizing a purchased product's disadvantages. When a purchase creates cognitive dissonance, consumers tend to react by seeking positive reinforcement for the purchase decision, avoiding negative information about the purchase decision, or revoking the purchase decision by returning the product.

3.1 Recall an occasion when you experienced cognitive dissonance about a purchase. In a letter to a friend, describe the event and explain what you did about it.

LO 4 Identify the types of consumer buying decisions and discuss the significance of consumer involvement. Consumer decision making falls into three broad categories. First, consumers exhibit routine response behavior for frequently purchased, low-cost items that require very little decision effort; routine response behavior is typically characterized by brand loyalty. Second, consumers engage in limited decision making for occasional purchases or for unfamiliar brands in familiar product categories. Third, consumers practice extensive decision making when making unfamiliar, expensive, or infrequent purchases. High-involvement decisions usually include an extensive information search and a thorough evaluation of alternatives. In contrast, low-involvement decisions are characterized by brand loyalty and a lack of personal identification with the product. The main factors affecting the level of consumer involvement are previous experience, interest, perceived risk of negative consequences (financial, social, and psychological), situation, and social visibility.

4.1 Describe the three categories of consumer decision-making behavior. Name typical products for which each type of consumer behavior is used.

4.2 Describe the level of involvement and the involvement factors likely to be associated with buying a new computer. Do you think Apple's Web site at

www.apple.com simplifies or complicates the process for the average consumer? Explain.

Identify and understand the cultural factors that affect consumer buying decisions. Cultural influences on consumer buying decisions include culture and values, subculture, and social class. Culture is the essential character of a society that distinguishes it from other cultural groups. The underlying elements of every culture are the values, language, myths, customs, rituals, laws, and artifacts, or products, which are transmitted from one generation to the next. The most defining element of a culture is its values—the enduring beliefs shared by a society that a specific mode of conduct is personally or socially preferable to another mode of conduct. A culture can be divided into subcultures on the basis of demographic characteristics, geographic regions, national and ethnic background, political beliefs, and religious beliefs. Subcultures share elements of the overall culture as well as cultural elements unique to their own group. A social class is a group of people who are considered nearly equal in status or community esteem, who regularly socialize among themselves both formally and informally, and who share behavioral norms.

5.1 You are a new marketing manager for a firm that produces a line of athletic shoes to be targeted to the college student subculture. In a memo to your boss, list some product attributes that might appeal to this subculture and the steps in your customers' purchase processes, and recommend some marketing strategies that can influence their decision.

Identify and understand the social factors that affect consumer buying decisions. Social factors include such external influences as reference groups, opinion leaders, and family. Consumers seek out others' opinions for guidance on new products or services and products with image-related attributes or because attribute information is lacking or uninformative. Consumers may use products or brands to identify with or become a member of a reference group. Opinion leaders are members of reference groups who influence others' purchase decisions. Family members also influence purchase decisions; children tend to shop in similar patterns as their parents.

6.1 Family members play many different roles in the buying process: initiator, influencer, decision maker, purchaser, and consumer. Identify the person in your family who might play each of these roles in the purchase of a dinner at Pizza Hut, a summer vacation, Froot Loops breakfast cereal, an Abercrombie & Fitch sweater, golf clubs, an Internet service provider, and a new car.

Identify and understand the individual factors that affect consumer buying decisions. Individual factors that affect consumer buying decisions include gender; age and family life-cycle stage; and personality, self-concept, and lifestyle. Beyond obvious physiological differences, men and women differ in their social and economic roles, and that affects consumer buying decisions. How old a consumer is generally indicates what products he or she may be interested in purchasing. Marketers often define their target markets in terms of consumers' life-cycle stage, following changes in consumers' attitudes and behavioral tendencies as they mature. Finally, certain products and brands reflect consumers' personality, self-concept, and lifestyle.

7.1 Assume you are involved in the following consumer decision situations: (a) renting a DVD to watch with your roommates, (b) choosing a fast-food restaurant to go to with a new friend, (c) buying a popular music compact disc, (d) buying jeans to wear to class. List the individual factors that would influence your decision in each situation and explain your responses.

Identify and understand the psychological factors that affect consumer buying decisions. Psychological factors include perception, motivation, learning, values, beliefs, and attitudes. These factors allow consumers to interact with the world around them, recognize their feelings, gather and analyze information, formulate thoughts and opinions, and take action. Perception allows consumers to recognize their consumption problems. Motivation is what drives consumers to take action to satisfy specific consumption needs. Almost all consumer behavior results from learning, which is the process that creates changes in behavior through experience. Consumers with similar beliefs and attitudes tend to react alike to marketing-related inducements.

8.1 How do beliefs and attitudes influence consumer behavior? How can negative attitudes toward a product be changed? How can marketers alter beliefs about a product? Give some examples of how marketers have changed negative attitudes about a product or added or altered beliefs about a product.

KEY TERMS

Term	Page
aspirational reference group	207
attitude	220
belief	220
brand extensions	194
cognitive dissonance	195
consumer behavior	189
consumer decision-making process	189
culture	200
evoked set (consideration set)	193
extensive decision making	197
external information search	191
ideal self-image	214
internal information search	191
involvement	197
learning	219
lifestyle	214
limited decision making	197
marketing-controlled information source	192
Maslow's hierarchy of needs	218
motive	218
need recognition	190
nonaspirational reference group	208
nonmarketing-controlled information source	191
norm	207
opinion leader	208
perception	215
personality	214
primary membership group	207
real self-image	214
reference group	207
routine response behavior	197
secondary membership group	207
selective distortion	216
selective exposure	215
selective retention	216
self-concept	214
social class	204
socialization process	210
stimulus	190
stimulus discrimination	220
stimulus generalization	220
subculture	203
value	201
want	190

EXERCISES

APPLICATION EXERCISE

Principles of consumer behavior are evident in many areas of marketing. Perhaps the easiest place to see this critical foundation of marketing activity is in print ads.

Activities

1. Review the main concepts in this chapter and create a checklist that itemizes them. Then, comb through your favorite magazines and newspapers for advertisements that illustrate each concept. To get a wide variety of ads, you will need to look through several magazines. If you don't have many magazines at your disposal, go to the campus library periodical room. Photocopy the ads you select to support this chapter.
2. Because pictures can help reinforce understanding, consider doing this exercise for each chapter in the book. At the end of the semester, you will have a portfolio of ads that illustrate the concepts in the entire book, which

can help you study. Simply look through your portfolio and try to recall the concepts at work in each advertisement. This exercise can be a prelude to a longer study session for comprehensive exams.

ETHICS EXERCISE

EyeOnU operates a Web filter service for public schools and libraries to protect students from inappropriate material on the Internet. Like the industry as a whole, the company's market share has been stagnant for the past two years. Looking for new sources of revenue, the company is considering selling the data it has collected about student surfing habits to marketers trying to learn more about students' behavior on the Web. The data are anonymous, but privacy advocates are concerned about the precedent of selling information about children to marketers.

Questions

1. What should EyeOnU do? Should it protect the student's data, or should it take the opportunity to create new revenues?
2. Visit the COPPA site dedicated to distributing information about the Children's Online Privacy Protection Act at **www.coppa.org/comply.htm.** Then write a brief paragraph on the responsibilities a Web site operator has to protect children's privacy and safety online and how that relates to EyeOnU's dilemma.

MARKETING PLAN EXERCISE

The next step in preparing a marketing plan for the company you chose in Part 1 is to get a thorough understanding of the marketing opportunities in terms of marketing to customers. Once you've completed the marketing plan exercise for each chapter in Part 2 of this textbook, you can complete the Part 2 Marketing Planning Worksheet on your companion Web site at **www.cengage.com/international.** Complete the following exercises:

1. Describe the decision-making process that customers go through when purchasing your company's product or service. What are the critical factors that influence this purchase-behavior process? How will this decision-making affect your e-marketing focus and your market offering? If you have a brick-and-mortar presence, will you encourage any existing customers to shop online? Why or why not?
2. Nonmarketing periodicals can help you understand consumer behavior and apply what you've learned to your marketing plan. Research articles from such publications as the *Journal of Psychology, Journal of American Ethnic History, Psychology Today, Race and Class, Working Woman, Society*, and others. Select and read three articles that explore different topics (i.e., do not select three articles on psychology). Then, make a list of factors you think could affect consumer purchasing behavior. Include with each factor a way marketers could use this information to their benefit.

CASE STUDY: BACK TO THE FUTURE? CHOCOLATE LOUNGES TASTE SWEET SUCCESS

The chocolate house dates back to seventeenth-century London, when members of society's elite would gather in luxurious surroundings to relax and sip hot chocolate. Later, Europeans expanded on that idea and developed solid chocolate treats that sold in upscale boutiques. Lacking the resources and economy of established continentals, bootstrapping American settlers pioneered the development of cheaper chocolate bars for the masses.

Centuries have passed, however, and the American palate has tired of the taste of mass-produced chocolate. The U.S. chocolate industry has experienced growth of less than 3 percent since the turn of the millennium, and the lack of industry innovation has left a bad taste in chocolate purveyors' mouths, too. Enter Ethel's Chocolate Lounges, named in honor of the matriarch of the Mars family, who founded the candy company with her husband Frank in 1911.

Now Ethel Mars's name adorns the signs at the company's latest attempt to breathe fresh life into chocolate. Aware that chocolate sales at upscale retail outlets, like Godiva and Starbucks grew by nearly 20 percent from 2002 to 2004, Mars opened Ethel's Chocolate Lounge in the Lincoln Park neighborhood of Chicago in April 2005. More Ethel's have opened since then, and the chic chocolate houses are Mars's bet that well-heeled and sweet-toothed consumers will take to premium chocolate the same way that well-to-do coffee lovers flock to Starbucks for high-priced java. Ethel's Lounges are designed to coddle patrons in the lap of luxury, but Mars president John Haugh maintains that what makes Ethel's special is that it offers "approachable gourmet chocolate." In other words, you don't have to be a millionaire to enjoy the sweet taste of the good life.

Prices are not for everyone's wallet, however. Truffles and Tea for Two, which features all 11 of Ethel's truffles served on a silver platter, sells for $15. Chocolates and Cocoa for Two includes two cocoas and 10 pieces of chocolate for $18, and a box of 48 chocolates is $42. Five "Collections" offer over 50 individual chocolates that sell for between $.90 and $1.50.

Supporting Haugh's claim of approachability, though, the menus at Ethel's feature icons and descriptions of the chocolates' contents so that customers won't experience an unwanted surprise. A multitude of hot and cold beverages give visitors more reasons to extend their stays.

But it's not just the chocolate that makes Ethel's such a desirable destination. Advertising describes Ethel's as "a place for chocolate and chitchat." Generously stuffed pink couches with brown accents combine upscale modern and traditional looks to give the stores a hip and classy feel. For those who don't immediately get it, a sign behind the counter reads, "Chocolate is the new black." The stores' appeal is their relaxing ambience and neighborhood vibe—like a modern American coffeehouse, these shops encourage socializing and extending lounging. The effect is carefully planned. Mars's research revealed that even calorie-conscious consumers will splurge for the good stuff as long as a broader social experience comes with it.

Parallels to the Starbucks-led American coffee revival are obvious and inescapable. Confectionary industry insiders note that chocolate cafés are taking hold, and research confirms their belief. Datamonitor, a research firm specializing in trend identification, described chocolate as "the new coffee" on its list of the top ten trends to watch in 2006. The popularity of the Chocolate Bar in New York, billed as a "candy store for grown-ups," and South Bend Chocolate's ten chocolate cafés shows that the trend is for real. Even some Hershey's stores now offer seating for patrons.

Joan Steuer, president of Chocolate Marketing, claims that, for women, enjoying chocolate in a luxurious lounge is like taking a candle-lit bubble bath. She notes, too, that much of the appeal is that the experience is testimony to the person's upward mobility. It's a perfect way to cater to the American desire to have the best that money can buy.[45]

Questions

1. What type of consumer buying decision best describes the choice to indulge at Ethel's?
2. List the factors that might influence a consumer to spend money and time at Ethel's. Which factor do you think will motivate a consumer the most? Why?
3. Review the core American values in Exhibit 5.5. Which value does the Ethel's experience appeal to most? Explain.

COMPANY CLIPS

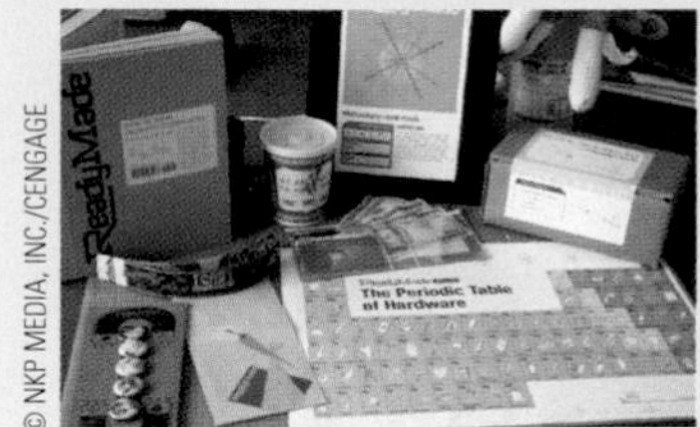

READYMADE—DO-IT-YOURSELF

In 2001 when Grace Hawthorne, CEO, and Shoshana Berger, Editor-in-Chief, came up with their idea for *ReadyMade*, there were no other publications with their unique do-it-yourself (DIY) theme. *ReadyMade* was to be a magazine about fun and creative projects for the home. Since its development, the bimonthly magazine has enjoyed a loyal subscriber base and continues to gain readership across the country. All issues include numerous DIY projects, each rated by their level of difficulty, as well as several feature articles exploring the latest in innovation and design. In this video, pay attention to *ReadyMade*'s methods as they launched their magazine. Note also how *ReadyMade* uses its knowledge of its consumer base to tailor the product.

Questions

1. While the *ReadyMade* magazine was still in the design stages, very little research was done to determine whether an interested market existed. Did this adversely affect the magazine as it moved forward to publication? Explain.
2. How does the cover of *ReadyMade* magazine reflect the principles of packaging design as influenced by the known behaviors of its consumers?
3. To what extent does *ReadyMade* rely on opinion leaders to promote the magazine? Is this a successful tactic?

Marketing & You Results

High scores suggest that you tend to shop for value, whereas lower scores indicate compulsive buying, or excessive shopping relative to your disposable income. Lower scores also suggest that you may use excessive shopping to deal with undesirable moods or negative feelings. Even though your mood might improve afterward, beware: The change is temporary, compulsive shopping behavior is very difficult to stop, and you can experience harmful consequences as a result.

© YURI ARCURS/SHUTTERSTOCK.COM

CHAPTER 7

Business Marketing

LEARNING OUTCOMES

- LO 1 Describe business marketing
- LO 2 Describe the role of the Internet in business marketing
- LO 3 Discuss the role of relationship marketing and strategic alliances in business marketing
- LO 4 Identify the four major categories of business market customers
- LO 5 Explain the North American Industry Classification System
- LO 6 Explain the major differences between business and consumer markets
- LO 7 Describe the seven types of business goods and services
- LO 8 Discuss the unique aspects of business buying behavior

WHAT IS BUSINESS MARKETING?

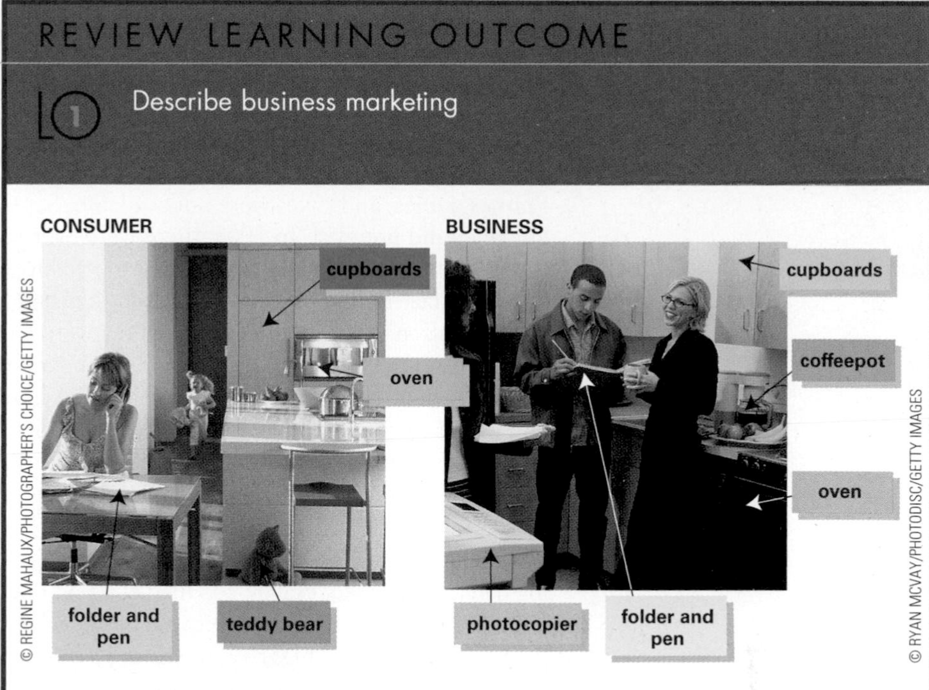

Business marketing is the marketing of goods and services to individuals and organizations for purposes other than personal consumption. The sale of a personal computer to your college or university is an example of business marketing. Business products include those that are used to manufacture other products, become part of another product, or aid the normal operations of an organization. The key characteristic distinguishing business products from consumer products is intended use, not physical characteristics. A product that is purchased for personal or family consumption or as a gift is a consumer good. If that same product, such as a personal computer or a cell phone, is bought for use in a business, it is a business product. A survey by *B to B Marketing* revealed that the three primary marketing goals of U.S. business marketers are customer acquisition (62 percent), creating brand awareness (19 percent), and customer retention (12 percent).[1]

The size of the business market in the United States and most other countries substantially exceeds that of the consumer market. In the business market, a single customer can account for a huge volume of purchases. For example, General Motors' purchasing department spends more than $125 billion per year on goods and services. General Electric, DuPont, and IBM spend over $60 million per day on business purchases.[2] The top 10 business marketing brands in 2008, according to *BtoB Magazine* are American Express, Bank of America, Cisco Systems, FedEx Corp., General Electric Co., Google, Microsoft Corp., UPS, AT&T, and IBM Corp.[3]

Marketing & You

Think about the last time you dealt with a salesperson when making a major purchase. Then, using the following scales, indicate your opinions of that salesperson.
Using the scale below, enter your answers.

1	2	3	4	5	6	7
Strongly agree						Strongly disagree

__ This salesperson was frank in dealing with me.

__ This salesperson did not make false claims.

__ I do not think this salesperson was completely open in dealing with me.*

__ This salesperson was concerned only about himself/herself.*

__ This salesperson did not seem to be concerned with my needs.*

__ I did not trust this salesperson.*

__ This salesperson was not trustworthy.*

Now, total your score, reversing your answers for the items followed by an asterisk. That is, if you put a 2, change it to a 6; if you put a 3, change it to a 5, and so forth. Read the chapter and find out what your score means at the end.

Source: From Scale #920, *Marketing Scales Handbook*, G. Bruner, K. James, H. Hensel, eds., Vol. III. © by American Marketing Association.

business marketing
The marketing of goods and services to individuals and organizations for purposes other than personal consumption.

business-to-business electronic commerce
The use of the Internet to facilitate the exchange of goods, services, and information between organizations.

BUSINESS MARKETING ON THE INTERNET

The use of the Internet to facilitate activities between organizations is called **business-to-business electronic commerce** (B-to-B or B2B e-commerce). This method of conducting business has evolved and grown rapidly throughout its short history. In 1995, the commercial Web sites that did exist were static. Only a few had data-retrieval capabilities. Frames, tables, and styles were not available. Security of any sort was rare, and streaming video did not exist. In 2005, there were over one billion Internet users worldwide. In 2008, the United States alone was expected to account for over $1 trillion of B2B e-commerce.[4] Before the Internet, customers had to call Dow Chemical and request a specification sheet for the products they were considering. The information would arrive a few days later by mail. After choosing a product, the customer could then place an order by calling Dow (during business hours, of course). Now, such information is available through **MyAccount@Dow**, which provides information tailored to the customer's requirements. For example, **MyAccount@Dow** offers secure internal monitoring of a customer's chemical tank levels. When tanks reach a predetermined level, reordering can be automatically triggered.[5]

Companies selling to business buyers face the same challenges as all marketers including determining who, exactly, the market is and how best to reach them. This is particularly difficult in business marketing because business has rapidly moved online and overseas.[6]

Each year, *BtoB Magazine* identifies 10 business marketing Web sites that are particularly good examples of how companies can use the Web to communicate with customers. Exhibit 7.1 identifies the 10 great Web sites for 2008. Many of these companies have been recognized in past years for effectively communicating with their target markets.[7]

EXHIBIT 7.1

Ten Great Web Sites

URL	Company	Target Audience
www.adobe.com	Adobe	Developers, creative professionals, knowledge workers, IT professionals
www.cisco.com/SMB	Cisco Systems	IT executives and users, and more recently small and midsize businesses
www.infocus.com	InFocus Corp.	IT professionals
www.formway.com	Formway Furniture	Architects, interior designers, business owners, facilities managers
IT.toolbox.com	Information Technologies Toolbox	IT professionals
www.specjm.com	Johns Manville	Building professionals, architects and specifiers, mechanical engineers
www.techsmith.com	TechSmith Corp.	Institutions and businesses
www.suni.com	Suni Imaging	Dental professionals
www.thomasnet.com	ThomasNet	Industrial buyers, engineers, government and military
www.usps.com	USPS	Consumers and businesses

Source: "10 Great Web Sites: Overview," *BtoB Magazine*, online, September 15, 2008.

In addition to Web sites, what Web 2.0 technologies are companies using? According to a poll taken during a webcast regarding online marketing, 64 percent reported using blogs, 61 percent use podcasts and video, 47 percent use social networks, 38 percent use RSS feeds, 22 percent use threaded discussion, and 11 percent use wikis.[8]

Measuring Online Success

Three of the most important measurements of online success are recency, frequency, and monetary value. *Recency* relates to the fact that customers who have made a purchase recently are more likely to purchase again in the near future than are customers who haven't purchased for a while. *Frequency* data help marketers identify frequent purchasers who are definitely more likely to repeat their purchasing behavior in the future. The *monetary value* of sales is important because big spenders can be the most profitable customers for a business.

NetGenesis has developed a number of equations that can help online marketers better understand their data. For example, combining frequency data with the length of time a visitor spent on the Web site (duration) and the number of site pages viewed during each visit (total site reach) can provide an analytical measure of a site's **stickiness** factor:

$$\text{Stickiness} = \text{Frequency} \times \text{Duration} \times \text{Site Reach}$$

By measuring the stickiness factor of a Web site before and after a design or function change, the marketer can quickly determine whether visitors embraced the change. By adding purchase information to determine the level of stickiness needed to provide a desired purchase volume, the marketer gains an even more precise understanding of how a site change affected business. An almost endless number of factor combinations can be created to provide a quantitative method for determining buyer behavior online. First, though, the marketer must determine what measures are required and which factors can be combined to arrive at those measurements.[9]

stickiness
A measure of a Web site's effectiveness; calculated by multiplying the frequency of visits times the duration of a visit times the number of pages viewed during each visit (site reach).

Trends in B2B Internet Marketing

According to James Soto, president of business marketing agency Industrial Strength Marketing, "the number one thing to keep in mind in terms of trends in BtoB Internet marketing is the shift of sourcing to the Net." His firm has found that 90 percent of business buyers go to the Internet at some point during the buying process, and over 50 percent start the buying process online.[10]

An Internet marketing technique that hasn't yet lived up to its potential is RSS (Real Simple Syndication) feeds. RSS feeds are used to publish frequently updated materials such as blogs, news headlines, audio, and video in a standard format. Web feeds benefit publishers by letting them syndicate content automatically. They benefit readers who want to subscribe to timely updates or aggregated information from various sources.[11]

A recent survey revealed that 7 out of 10 business marketers do not consider RSS feeds in their campaigns. However, 71 percent of technology buyers reported using feeds.[12]

W.W. Grainger Inc., a distributor of facility maintenance supplies, provides RSS feeds on its Web site **supplylink.com** to help maintenance professionals identify and solve facility issues such as security, productivity, and energy efficiency. The site features industry articles and resources as well as information on new products that Grainger has recently added.[13]

Over the last decade marketers have become more and more sophisticated in their use of the Internet. Exhibit 7.2 compares three prominent Internet business-marketing strategy

EXHIBIT 7.2

Evolution of E-Business Initiatives

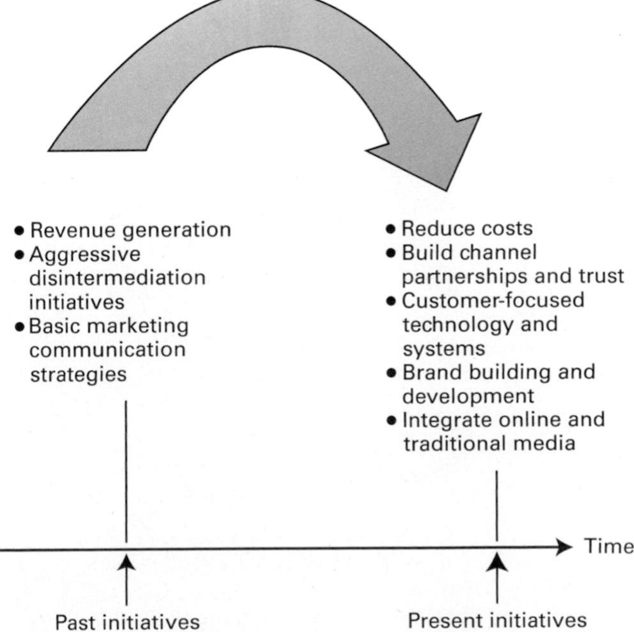

Source: Andrew J. Rohm and Fareena Sultan, "The Evolution of E-Business," *Marketing Management*, January/February, 2004, 35. Used by permission.

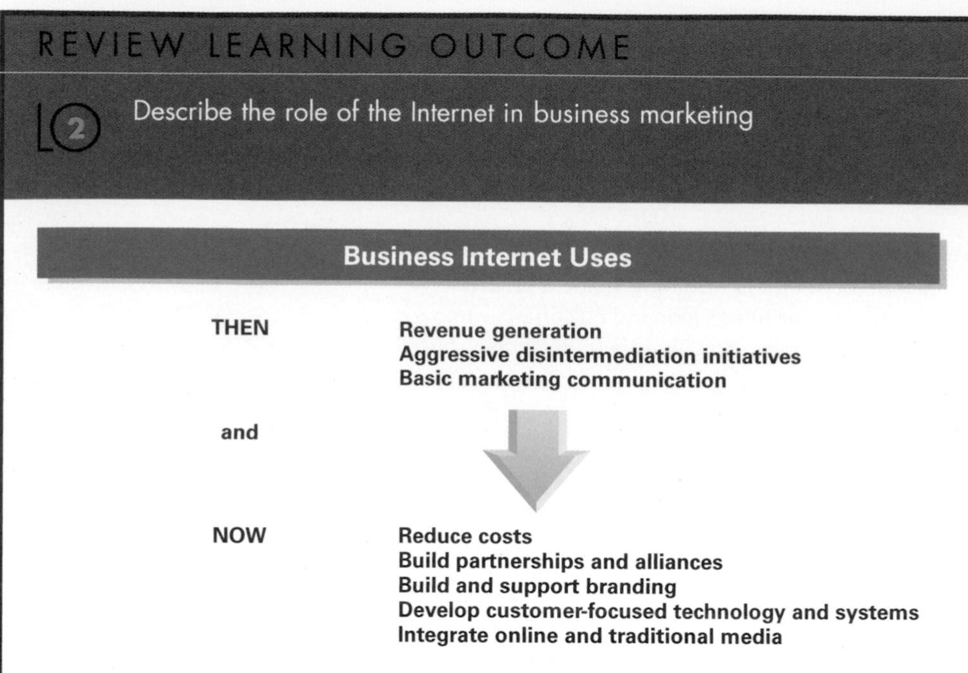

initiatives from the late 1990s to five that are currently being pursued. Companies have had to transition from "We have a Web site because our customer does" to having a store that attracts, interests, satisfies, and retains customers. New applications that provide additional information about present and potential customers, increase efficiency, lower costs, increase supply chain efficiency, or enhance customer retention, loyalty, and trust are being developed each year.

One term in Exhibit 7.2 that may be unfamiliar is **disintermediation**, which means eliminating intermediaries such as wholesalers or distributors from a marketing channel. A prime example of disintermediation is Dell, Inc., which sells directly to business buyers and consumers. Large retailers such as Wal-Mart use a disintermediation strategy to help reduce costs and prices.[14]

A few years ago, many people thought that the Internet would eliminate the need for distributors. Why would customers pay for distributor markups when they could buy directly from the manufacturers with a few mouse clicks? Yet Internet disintermediation has occurred less frequently than many expected. The reason is that distributors often perform important functions such as providing credit, aggregation of supplies from multiple sources, delivery, and processing returns. Many business customers, especially small firms, depend on knowledgeable distributors for information and advice that are not available to them online. You will notice in Exhibit 7.2 that building channel partnerships and trust has replaced aggressive disintermediation initiatives as a priority for most firms.

Some firms have followed disintermediation with **reintermediation**, the reintroduction of an intermediary between producers and users. They realized that providing direct online purchasing only was similar to having only one store in a city selling a popular brand.[15]

disintermediation
The elimination of intermediaries such as wholesalers or distributors from a marketing channel.

reintermediation
The reintroduction of an intermediary between producers and users.

Customers can use FedEx's automated shipping, tracking, and invoicing systems to save time and money. Services like these work to solidify their loyalty to FedEx.

© TERRI MILLER/E-VISUAL COMMUNICATIONS, INC.

LO3 RELATIONSHIP MARKETING AND STRATEGIC ALLIANCES

As Chapter 1 explained, relationship marketing is a strategy that entails seeking and establishing ongoing partnerships with customers. Relationship marketing has become an important business marketing strategy as customers have become more demanding and competition has become more intense. Loyal customers are also more profitable than those who are price-sensitive and perceive little or no difference among brands or suppliers. That is why firms such as online printing company Mimeo.com focus on

CUSTOMER Experience

Increasing Customer Retention

While B2B marketers are increasingly focused on improving relationships with customers, they still have a long way to go in implementing effective, consistent customer retention practices, according to a study by the Chief Marketing Officer Council. The study found that only one-third of global marketers have strategies in place to win back dormant or lost customers, and only half have strategies to further penetrate key account relationships.

"Everybody is spending money on demand-generation programs, but they are not taking their existing customer data and leveraging it," said Donovan Neale-May, executive director of the CMO Council. "Marketers should determine their most profitable customers and look at how to improve the customer experience and how to increase business with those customers."

According to the study, only 6.8 percent of marketers said they have excellent knowledge of the customer when it comes to demographic, behavioral, and psychographic data, while 51.9 percent said they have fair to little knowledge of the customer. "One of the problems is a lack of ownership of the customer relationship across the company," said Jim Hintze, senior VP-marketing at Fujitsu, which provides hardware, software, and services for the telecommunications industry. "No matter what your function, you have some relationship to the customer, whether it is direct or indirect," Hintze said. "We haven't solved it yet, but we have a game plan to do that."

Fujitsu has also implemented a customer relationship management (CRM) system and is trying to broaden its use from a sales contact tool to an enterprise-wide customer asset manager. "There are so many untapped areas for us to take advantage of [in] retaining customers. We're trying to get the systems and processes in place," Hintze said. One challenge is tracking all the interactions a customer has with the company, including the customer service experience, and including those in an overall measure of customer satisfaction. "A customer might call in to an 800-number for warranty support and get turned off because the call isn't handled properly," Hintze said. "People might not see it in total because it doesn't roll up into an overall metric." Another challenge is dealing with the sheer amount of customer data, he added. "There is so much information out there that even for a company as sophisticated as Fujitsu, managing it intelligently is really, really difficult," he said.[17]

What other ways can you think of that Fujitsu could implement to improve the quality of customer experience? What else might they do to increase customer retention?

continually improving processes for communicating with customers once they place their first order. To help retain clients, the company has developed an automated system that sends out e-mails or triggers a live contact each time a customer places an order or asks a question.[16] Building long-term relationships with customers offers companies a way to build competitive advantage that is hard for competitors to copy. For example, the FedEx Powership program includes a series of automated shipping, tracking, and invoicing systems that save customers time and money while solidifying their loyalty to FedEx. This produces a win–win situation.

The Customer Experience box in this chapter reports results of a study regarding customer retention practices, and some experiences of Fujitsu in trying to improve the customer experiences of their most valued clientele.

Strategic Alliances

A **strategic alliance**, sometimes called a *strategic partnership*, is a cooperative agreement between business firms. Strategic alliances can take the form of licensing or distribution agreements, joint ventures, research and development consortia, and partnerships. They may be between different manufacturers, manufacturers and customers, manufacturers and suppliers, and manufacturers and channel intermediaries.

Business marketers form strategic alliances to strengthen operations and better compete. Office Depot has formed an alliance with Netbizz Office Supplies, an office supplies provider in Singapore. The alliance is intended to allow customers to use the Office Depot international network for their multicountry supply needs. Singapore is

strategic alliance (strategic partnership)
A cooperative agreement between business firms.

relationship commitment
A firm's belief that an ongoing relationship with another firm is so important that the relationship warrants maximum efforts at maintaining it indefinitely.

trust
The condition that exists when one party has confidence in an exchange partner's reliability and integrity.

keiretsu
A network of interlocking corporate affiliates.

a key market for many global companies and this alliance offers a convenient procurement solution for both current and new customers.[18]

Sometimes alliance partners are also fierce competitors. For instance, in the face of rising fuel prices, the express delivery service DHL has formed an alliance with rival company UPS. Under the agreement, UPS provides all airlift services for DHL in the United States. According to one DHL executive, "the customer doesn't actually see a difference at all . . . unless they pay attention to the color of the partner's planes."[19]

Other alliances are formed between companies that operate in completely different industries. Choice Hotels and 1-800-Flowers share call-center employees because doing so is a cheaper alternative than outsourcing. When one company experiences increased demand for its products and services, it can call on its partner's employees rather than add staff or use a temporary agency. At a given time, as many as 100 call-center agents may be taking orders for the other company. Both companies report higher employee retention and better recruitment.[20]

For an alliance to succeed in the long term, it must be built on commitment and trust. **Relationship commitment** means that a firm believes that an ongoing relationship with some other firm is so important that it warrants maximum efforts at maintaining it indefinitely.[21] A perceived reduction in commitment by one of the parties often leads to a breakdown in the relationship.

Trust exists when one party has confidence in an exchange partner's reliability and integrity.[22] Some alliances fail when participants lack trust in their trading partners. For instance, General Motors, Ford, DaimlerChrysler, Nissan Motor Company, and Renault SA created an Internet automobile parts exchange, called Covisint, that they hoped would make $300 billion in sales per year. But the auto industry is characterized by mistrust between buyers and sellers. And, after being forced to accept price concessions for years, suppliers were reluctant to participate in the exchange.

Relationships in Other Cultures

Although the terms *relationship marketing* and *strategic alliances* are fairly new, and popularized mostly by American business executives and educators, the concepts have long been familiar in other cultures. Businesses in Mexico, China, Japan, Korea, and much of Europe rely heavily on personal relationships.

In Japan, for example, exchange between firms is based on personal relationships that are developed through what is called *amae*, or indulgent dependency. *Amae* is the feeling of nurturing concern for, and dependence on, another. Reciprocity and personal relationships contribute to *amae*. Relationships between companies can develop into a **keiretsu**—a network of interlocking corporate affiliates. Within a keiretsu, executives may sit on the boards of their customers or their suppliers. Members of a keiretsu trade with each other whenever possible and often engage in joint product development, finance, and marketing activity. For example, the Toyota Group keiretsu includes 14 core companies and another 170 that receive preferential treatment. Toyota holds an equity position in many of these 170 member firms and is represented on many of their boards of directors.

Many American firms have found that the best way to compete in Asian countries is to form relationships with Asian firms. For example, General Motors' joint venture with Shanghai Motors produces Buicks, Chevrolets, and Cadillacs. German automaker Volkswagen also has an alliance with Shanghai Motors to produce the Passat.[23]

Japanese keiretsu are powerful combinations of companies—manufacturers, suppliers, and finance companies—that are cemented by family ties or strong financial connections. The American version of a keiretsu is an alliance of suppliers and customers bound by the goals of mutual success. Harley-Davidson borrowed from the keiretsu model by making suppliers into partners. Those partners commit to annual cost reductions (even if materials and labor costs are rising) and participate in the company's product development program to help improve quality. In return, those partners participate in Harley's success.

REVIEW LEARNING OUTCOME

LO 3 Discuss the role of relationship marketing and strategic alliances in business marketing

Supplier (Like Intel)
Supplier
Supplier
Company (Like Dell)

Company 1 (Like Starbucks)
Company 2 (Like Jim Beam)

Company (Like UPS)
Customer/ Distributor (Like Ford)

MAJOR CATEGORIES OF BUSINESS CUSTOMERS

The business market consists of four major categories of customers: producers, resellers, governments, and institutions.

Producers

The producer segment of the business market includes profit-oriented individuals and organizations that use purchased goods and services to produce other products, to incorporate into other products, or to facilitate the daily operations of the organization. Examples of producers include construction, manufacturing, transportation, finance, real estate, and food service firms. In the United States there are over 13 million firms in the producer segment of the business market. Some of these firms are small, and others are among the world's largest businesses.

Producers are often called **original equipment manufacturers** or **OEMs**. This term includes all individuals and organizations that buy business goods and incorporate them into the products that they produce for eventual sale to other producers or to consumers. Companies such as General Motors that buy steel, paint, tires, and batteries are said to be OEMs.

original equipment manufacturers (OEMs)
Individuals and organizations that buy business goods and incorporate them into the products that they produce for eventual sale to other producers or to consumers.

Resellers

The reseller market includes retail and wholesale businesses that buy finished goods and resell them for a profit. A retailer sells mainly to final consumers; wholesalers sell

North American Industry Classification System (NAICS) A detailed numbering system developed by the United States, Canada, and Mexico to classify North American business establishments by their main production processes.

mostly to retailers and other organizational customers. There are approximately 1.5 million retailers and 500,000 wholesalers operating in the United States. Consumer-product firms like Procter & Gamble, Kraft Foods, and Coca-Cola sell directly to large retailers and retail chains and through wholesalers to smaller retail units. Retailing is explored in detail in Chapter 13.

Business product distributors are wholesalers that buy business products and resell them to business customers. They often carry thousands of items in stock and employ sales forces to call on business customers. Businesses that wish to buy a gross of pencils or a hundred pounds of fertilizer typically purchase these items from local distributors rather than directly from manufacturers such as Empire Pencil or Dow Chemical.

Governments

A third major segment of the business market is government. Government organizations include thousands of federal, state, and local buying units. They make up what may be the largest single market for goods and services in the world.

Contracts for government purchases are often put out for bid. Interested vendors submit bids (usually sealed) to provide specified products during a particular time. Sometimes the lowest bidder is awarded the contract. When the lowest bidder is not awarded the contract, strong evidence must be presented to justify the decision. Grounds for rejecting the lowest bid include lack of experience, inadequate financing, or poor past performance. Bidding allows all potential suppliers a fair chance at winning government contracts and helps ensure that public funds are spent wisely.

Federal Government Name just about any good or service and chances are that someone in the federal government uses it. The U.S. federal government buys goods and services valued at over $600 billion per year, making it the world's largest customer.

Although much of the federal government's buying is centralized, no single federal agency contracts for all the government's requirements, and no single buyer in any agency purchases all that the agency needs. We can view the federal government as a combination of several large companies with overlapping responsibilities and thousands of small independent units.

One popular source of information about government procurement is *Commerce Business Daily*. Until recently, businesses hoping to sell to the federal government found the document unorganized, and it often arrived too late to be useful. The online version (**www.cbd-net.com**) is more timely and lets contractors find leads using keyword searches.

Other examples of publications designed to

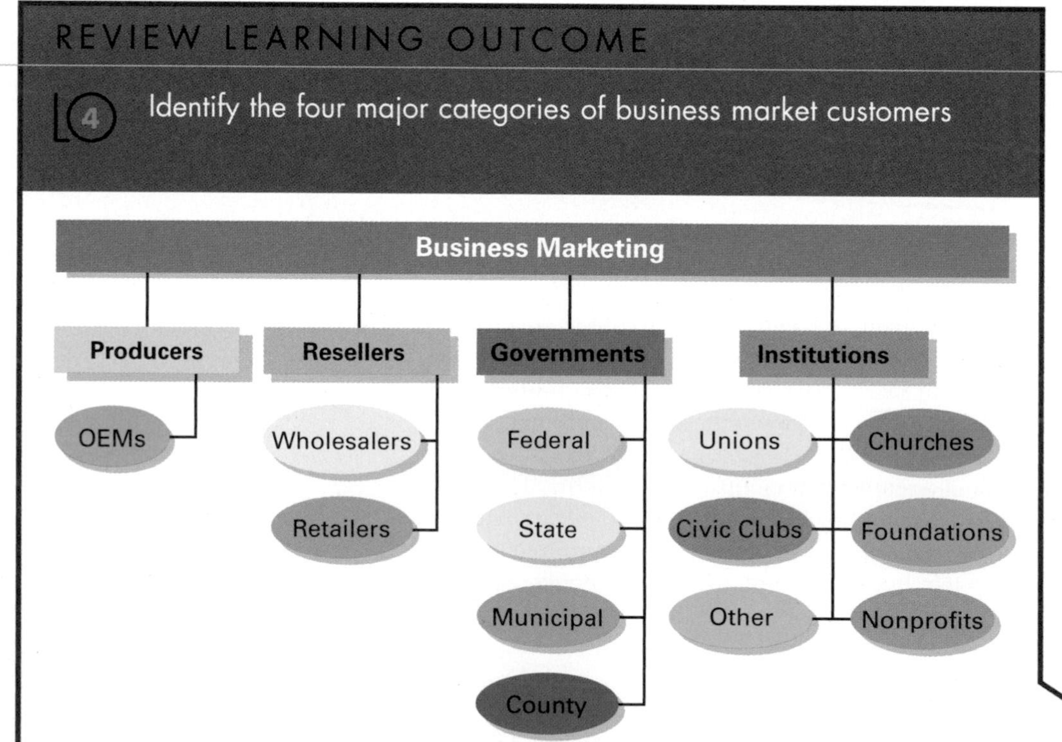

explain how to do business with the federal government include *Doing Business with the General Services Administration*, *Selling to the Military*, and *Selling to the U.S. Air Force*.

State, County, and City Government Selling to states, counties, and cities can be less frustrating for both small and large vendors than selling to the federal government. Paperwork is typically simpler and more manageable than it is at the federal level. On the other hand, vendors must decide which of the over 82,000 government units are likely to buy their wares. State and local buying agencies include school districts, highway departments, government-operated hospitals, and housing agencies.

Institutions

The fourth major segment of the business market consists of institutions that seek to achieve goals other than the standard business goals of profit, market share, and return on investment. This segment includes schools, hospitals, colleges and universities, churches, labor unions, fraternal organizations, civic clubs, foundations, and other so-called nonbusiness organizations. Xerox offers educational and medical institutions the same prices as government agencies (the lowest that Xerox offers) and has a separate sales force that calls on these customers.

THE NORTH AMERICAN INDUSTRY CLASSIFICATION SYSTEM

The **North American Industry Classification System (NAICS)** is an industry classification system introduced in 1997 to replace the standard industrial classification (SIC) system. NAICS (pronounced *nakes*) is a system for classifying North American business establishments. The system, developed jointly by the United States, Canada, and Mexico, provides a common industry classification system for the North American Free Trade Agreement (NAFTA) partners. Goods- or service-producing firms that use identical or similar production processes are grouped together.

NAICS is an extremely valuable tool for business marketers engaged in analyzing, segmenting, and targeting markets. Each classification group is relatively homogeneous in terms of raw materials required, components used, manufacturing processes employed, and problems faced. The more digits in a code, the more homogeneous the group is. Therefore, if a supplier understands the needs and requirements of a few firms within a classification, requirements can be projected for all firms in that category. The number, size, and geographic dispersion of firms can also be identified. This information can be converted to market potential estimates, market share estimates, and sales forecasts. It can also be used for identifying potential new customers. NAICS codes can help identify firms that may be prospective users of a supplier's goods and services.

Exhibit 7.3 provides an overview of NAICS. Exhibit 7.4 illustrates the six-digit classification system for two of the 20 NAICS economic sectors: manufacturing and information.

EXHIBIT 7.3

NAICS Two-Digit Codes and Corresponding Economic Sectors

NAICS Code	Economic Sector
11	Agriculture, forestry, and fishing
21	Mining
22	Utilities
23	Construction
31–33	Manufacturing
43	Wholesale trade
44–45	Retail trade
47–48	Transportation
51	Information
52	Finance and insurance
53	Real estate and rental and leasing
56	Professional and technical services
57	Management and support services
61	Education services
62	Health and social assistance
71	Arts, entertainment, and recreation
72	Food services, drinking places, and accommodations
81	Other services, except public administration
93	Public administration
98	Estates and trusts
99	Nonclassifiable

EXHIBIT 7.4

Examples of NAICS Hierarchy

NAICS Level	Example 1		Example 2	
	NAICS Code	Description	NAICS Code	Description
Sector	31–33	Manufacturing	51	Information
Subsector	334	Computer and electronic product manufacturing	513	Broadcasting and telecommunications
Industry group	3346	Manufacturing and reproduction of magnetic and optical media	5133	Telecommunications
Industry	33461	Manufacturing and reproduction of magnetic and optical media	51332	Wireless telecommunications carriers, except satellite
Industry Subdivision	334611	Reproduction of software	513321	Paging

Source: U.S. Census Bureau, "New Code System In NAICS," http://www.census.gov/epcd/www/naics.html.

The hierarchical structure of NAICS allows industry data to be summarized at several levels of detail. To illustrate,

- The first two digits designate a major economic sector such as agriculture (11) or manufacturing (31–33).
- The third digit designates an economic subsector such as crop production or apparel manufacturing.
- The fourth digit designates an industry group, such as grain and oil seed farming or fiber, yarn, and thread mills.
- The fifth digit designates the NAICS industry, such as wheat farming or broadwoven fabric mills.
- The sixth digit, when used, identifies subdivisions of NAICS industries that accommodate user needs in individual countries.[24]

For a complete listing of all NAICS codes, see **www.census.gov/epcd/www/naics.html**.

REVIEW LEARNING OUTCOME

LO 5 Explain the North American Industry Classification System

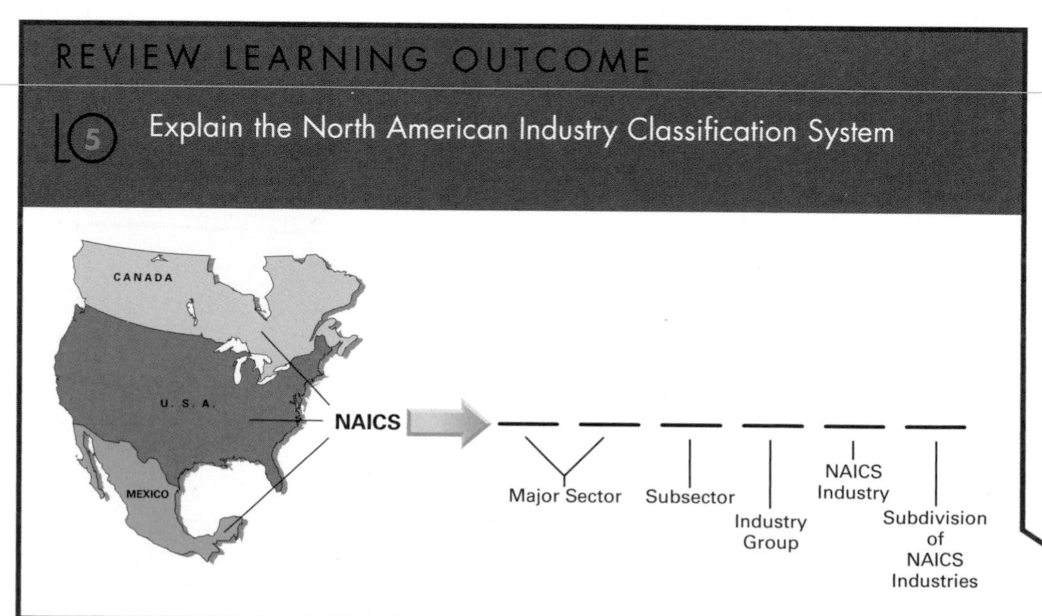

BUSINESS VERSUS CONSUMER MARKETS

The basic philosophy and practice of marketing are the same whether the customer is a business organization or a consumer. Business markets do, however, have characteristics different from consumer markets.

Demand

Consumer demand for products is quite different from demand in the business market. Unlike consumer demand, business demand is derived, inelastic, joint, and fluctuating.

Derived Demand The demand for business products is called **derived demand** because organizations buy products to be used in producing their customers' products. For instance, the number of drills or lathes that a manufacturing firm needs is "derived from," or based upon the demand for products that are produced using these machines.

> *"Unlike consumer demand, business demand is derived, inelastic, joint, and fluctuating."*

Because demand is derived, business marketers must carefully monitor demand patterns and changing preferences in final consumer markets, even though their customers are not in those markets. Moreover, business marketers must carefully monitor their customers' forecasts, because derived demand is based on expectations of future demand for those customers' products.

Some business marketers not only monitor final consumer demand and customer forecasts but also try to influence final consumer demand. Aluminum producers use television and magazine advertisements to point out the convenience and recycling opportunities that aluminum offers to consumers who can choose to purchase soft drinks in either aluminum or plastic containers.

Inelastic Demand The demand for many business products is inelastic with regard to price. *Inelastic demand* means that an increase or decrease in the price of the product will not significantly affect demand for the product. This will be discussed further in Chapter 16.

The price of a product used in the production of, or as part of, a final product is often a minor portion of the final product's total price. Therefore, demand for the final consumer product is not affected. If the price of automobile paint or spark plugs rises significantly, say, 200 percent in one year, do you think the number of new automobiles sold that year will be affected? Probably not.

Joint Demand **Joint demand** occurs when two or more items are used together in a final product. For example, a decline in the availability of memory chips will slow production of microcomputers, which will in turn reduce the demand for disk drives. Likewise, the demand for Apple operating systems exists as long as there is demand for Apple computers. Sales of the two products are directly linked.

Fluctuating Demand The demand for business products—particularly new plants and equipment—tends to be less stable than the demand for consumer products. A small increase or decrease in consumer demand can produce a much larger change in demand for the facilities and equipment needed to make the consumer product. Economists refer to this phenomenon as the **multiplier effect** (or **accelerator principle**).

Cummins Engine Company, a producer of heavy-duty diesel engines, uses sophisticated surface grinders to make parts. Suppose Cummins is using 20 surface grinders. Each machine lasts about 10 years. Purchases have been timed so 2 machines will wear out and be replaced annually. If the demand for engine parts does not change, 2 grinders will be bought this year. If the demand for parts declines slightly, only 18 grinders may be needed and Cummins won't replace the worn ones. However, suppose that next year demand returns to previous levels plus a little more. To meet the new level of demand, Cummins

derived demand
The demand for business products.

joint demand
The demand for two or more items used together in a final product.

multiplier effect (accelerator principle)
Phenomenon in which a small increase or decrease in consumer demand can produce a much larger change in demand for the facilities and equipment needed to make the consumer product.

business-to-business online exchange
An electronic trading floor that provides companies with integrated links to their customers and suppliers.

will need to replace the two machines that wore out in the first year, the two that wore out in the second year, plus one or more additional machines. The multiplier effect works this way in many industries, producing highly fluctuating demand for business products.

Purchase Volume

Business customers buy in much larger quantities than consumers. Just think how large an order Kellogg typically places for the wheat bran and raisins used to manufacture Raisin Bran. Imagine the number of tires that DaimlerChrysler buys at one time.

Number of Customers

Business marketers usually have far fewer customers than consumer marketers. The advantage is that it is a lot easier to identify prospective buyers, monitor current customers' needs and levels of satisfaction, and personally attend to existing customers. The main disadvantage is that each customer becomes crucial—especially for those manufacturers that have only one customer. In many cases, this customer is the U.S. government. The success or failure of one bid can make the difference between prosperity and bankruptcy. After 5 years of development, testing, and politicking, the Pentagon awarded Lockheed Martin a multidecade contract to build 3,000 jet fighter airplanes. Boeing Aircraft Company, the only other bidder on the $200 billion contract, immediately announced plans for substantial layoffs.

Location of Buyers

Business customers tend to be much more geographically concentrated than consumers. For instance, more than half the nation's business buyers are located in New York, California, Pennsylvania, Illinois, Ohio, Michigan, and New Jersey. The aircraft and microelectronics industries are concentrated on the West Coast, and many of the firms that supply the automobile manufacturing industry are located in and around Detroit.

Ads like this one for the Michigan Economic Development Corporation (MEDC) promote economic activity within their state by touting the benefits of locating, relocating, or expanding a business to their state.

COURTESY OF MICHIGAN ECONOMIC DEVELOPMENT CORPORATION (MEDC)

Distribution Structure

Many consumer products pass through a distribution system that includes the producer, one or more wholesalers, and a retailer. In business marketing, however, because of many of the characteristics already mentioned, channels of distribution are typically shorter. Direct channels, where manufacturers market directly to users, are much more common. The use of direct channels has increased dramatically in the past decade with the introduction of various Internet buying and selling schemes. One such technique is a **business-to-business online exchange**, which is an electronic trading floor that provides companies with integrated links to their customers and suppliers. The goal of a B2B online exchange is to simplify business purchasing and make it more efficient. For example, Exostar, the aerospace industry's online exchange, has over 12,000 participating suppliers and conducts more than 20,000 transactions each week.[25] Exchanges such as Exostar facilitate direct channel relationships between producers and their customers.

Nature of Buying

Unlike consumers, business buyers usually approach purchasing rather formally. Businesses use professionally trained purchasing agents or buyers who spend their entire career purchasing a limited number of items. They get to know the items and the sellers well. Some professional purchasers earn the designation of Certified Purchasing Manager (CPM) after participating in a rigorous certification program.

Nature of Buying Influence

Typically, more people are involved in a single business purchase decision than in a consumer purchase. Experts from fields as varied as quality control, marketing, and finance, as well as professional buyers and users, may be grouped in a buying center (discussed later in this chapter).

REVIEW LEARNING OUTCOME

LO 6 Explain the major differences between business and consumer markets

Characteristic	Business Market	Consumer Market
Demand	Organizational	Individual
Purchase volume	Larger	Smaller
Number of customers	Fewer	Many
Location of buyers	Geographically concentrated	Dispersed
Distribution structure	More direct	More indirect
Nature of buying	More professional	More personal
Nature of buying influence	Multiple	Single
Type of negotiations	More complex	Simpler
Use of reciprocity	Yes	No
Use of leasing	Greater	Lesser
Primary promotional method	Personal selling	Advertising

Type of Negotiations

Consumers are used to negotiating price on automobiles and real estate. In most cases, however, American consumers expect sellers to set the price and other conditions of sale, such as time of delivery and credit terms. In contrast, negotiating is common in business marketing. Buyers and sellers negotiate product specifications, delivery dates, payment terms, and other pricing matters. Sometimes these negotiations occur during many meetings over several months. Final contracts are often very long and detailed.

Use of Reciprocity

Business purchasers often choose to buy from their own customers, a practice known as **reciprocity**. For example, General Motors buys engines for use in its automobiles and trucks from BorgWarner, which in turn buys many of the automobiles and trucks it needs from GM. This practice is neither unethical nor illegal unless one party coerces the other and the result is unfair competition. Reciprocity is generally considered a reasonable business practice. If all possible suppliers sell a similar product for about the same price, doesn't it make sense to buy from those firms that buy from you?

Use of Leasing

Consumers normally buy products rather than lease them. But businesses commonly lease expensive equipment such as computers, construction equipment and vehicles, and automobiles. Leasing allows firms to reduce capital outflow, acquire a seller's latest products, receive better services, and gain tax advantages.

The lessor, the firm providing the product, may be either the manufacturer or an independent firm. The benefits to the lessor include greater total revenue from leasing compared to selling and an opportunity to do business with customers who cannot afford to buy.

reciprocity
The practice of business purchasers choosing to buy from their own customers.

major equipment (installations) Capital goods such as large or expensive machines, mainframe computers, blast furnaces, generators, airplanes, and buildings.

accessory equipment Goods, such as portable tools and office equipment, that are less expensive and shorter-lived than major equipment.

raw materials Unprocessed extractive or agricultural products, such as mineral ore, timber, wheat, corn, fruits, vegetables, and fish.

component parts Either finished items ready for assembly or products that need very little processing before becoming part of some other product.

Primary Promotional Method

Business marketers tend to emphasize personal selling in their promotion efforts, especially for expensive items, custom-designed products, large-volume purchases, and situations requiring negotiations. The sale of many business products requires a great deal of personal contact. Personal selling is discussed in more detail in Chapter 15.

TYPES OF BUSINESS PRODUCTS

Business products generally fall into one of the following seven categories, depending on their use: major equipment, accessory equipment, raw materials, component parts, processed materials, supplies, and business services.

Major Equipment

Major equipment includes such capital goods as large or expensive machines, mainframe computers, blast furnaces, generators, airplanes, and buildings. (These items are also commonly called **installations.**) Major equipment is depreciated over time rather than charged as an expense in the year it is purchased. In addition, major equipment is often custom-designed for each customer. Personal selling is an important part of the marketing strategy for major equipment because distribution channels are almost always direct from the producer to the business user.

Accessory Equipment

Accessory equipment is generally less expensive and shorter-lived than major equipment. Examples include portable drills, power tools, microcomputers, and fax machines. Accessory equipment is often charged as an expense in the year it is bought rather than depreciated over its useful life. In contrast to major equipment, accessories are more often standardized and are usually bought by more customers. These customers tend to be widely dispersed. For example, all types of businesses buy microcomputers.

Local industrial distributors (wholesalers) play an important role in the marketing of accessory equipment because business buyers often purchase accessories from them. Regardless of where accessories are bought, advertising is a more vital promotional tool for accessory equipment than for major equipment.

Raw Materials

Raw materials are unprocessed extractive or agricultural products—for example, mineral ore, timber, wheat, corn, fruits, vegetables, and fish. Raw materials become part of finished products. Extensive users, such as steel or lumber mills and food canners, generally buy huge quantities of raw materials. Because there is often a large number of relatively small sellers of raw materials, none can greatly influence price or supply. Thus, the market tends to set the price of raw materials, and individual producers have little pricing flexibility. Promotion is almost always via personal selling, and distribution channels are usually direct from producer to business user.

Component Parts

Component parts are either finished items ready for assembly or products that need very little processing before becoming part of some other product. Caterpillar diesel engines are component parts used in heavy-duty trucks. Other examples include spark plugs, tires, and electric motors for automobiles. A special feature of component parts is that they can retain their identity after becoming part of the final product. For example, automobile tires are clearly recognizable as part of a car. Moreover, because component parts often wear out, they may need to be replaced several times during the life of the final product. Thus, there are two important markets for many component parts: the original equipment manufacturer (OEM) market and the replacement market.

The availability of component parts is often a key factor in OEMs meeting their production deadlines. For example, Boeing Co. has had to delay final assembly of Boeing 787 Dreamliners by at least 15 months because of slower than expected completion of components prior to their arrival at the final assembly line. In addition to delayed sales and customer disappointment and dissatisfaction, Boeing will have to pay millions of dollars of penalty payments to customers.[26]

Many of the business features listed in the Review for Learning Outcome 6 characterize the OEM market. The difference between unit costs and selling prices in the OEM market is often small, but profits can be substantial because of volume buying.

Even though the Internet has greatly affected the consumption of many supplies, like envelopes, paper is still in high demand. In fact, computer technology has increased the demand for paper rather than squelching it.

The replacement market is composed of organizations and individuals buying component parts to replace worn-out parts. Because components often retain their identity in final products, users may choose to replace a component part with the same brand used by the manufacturer—for example, the same brand of automobile tires or battery. The replacement market operates differently from the OEM market, however. Whether replacement buyers are organizations or individuals, they tend to demonstrate the characteristics of consumer markets that were shown in the Review for Learning Outcome 6. Consider, for example, an automobile replacement part. Purchase volume is usually small and there are many customers, geographically dispersed, who typically buy from car dealers or parts stores. Negotiations do not occur, and neither reciprocity nor leasing is usually an issue.

Manufacturers of component parts often direct their advertising toward replacement buyers. Cooper Tire & Rubber, for example, makes and markets component parts—automobile and truck tires—for the replacement market only. General Motors and other car makers compete with independent firms in the market for replacement automobile parts.

Processed Materials

Processed materials are products used directly in manufacturing other products. Unlike raw materials, they have had some processing. Examples include sheet metal, chemicals, specialty steel, lumber, corn syrup, and plastics. Unlike component parts, processed materials do not retain their identity in final products.

Most processed materials are marketed to OEMs or to distributors servicing the OEM market. Processed materials are generally bought according to customer specifications or to some industry standard, as is the case with steel and plywood. Price and service are important factors in choosing a vendor.

Supplies

Supplies are consumable items that do not become part of the final product—for example, lubricants, detergents, paper towels, pencils, and paper. Supplies are normally standardized items that purchasing agents routinely buy. Supplies typically have relatively short lives and are inexpensive compared to other business goods. Because supplies generally fall into one of three categories—maintenance, repair, or operating supplies—this category is often referred to as MRO items.

processed materials
Products used directly in manufacturing other products.

supplies
Consumable items that do not become part of the final product.

REVIEW LEARNING OUTCOME

LO 7 Describe the seven types of business goods and services

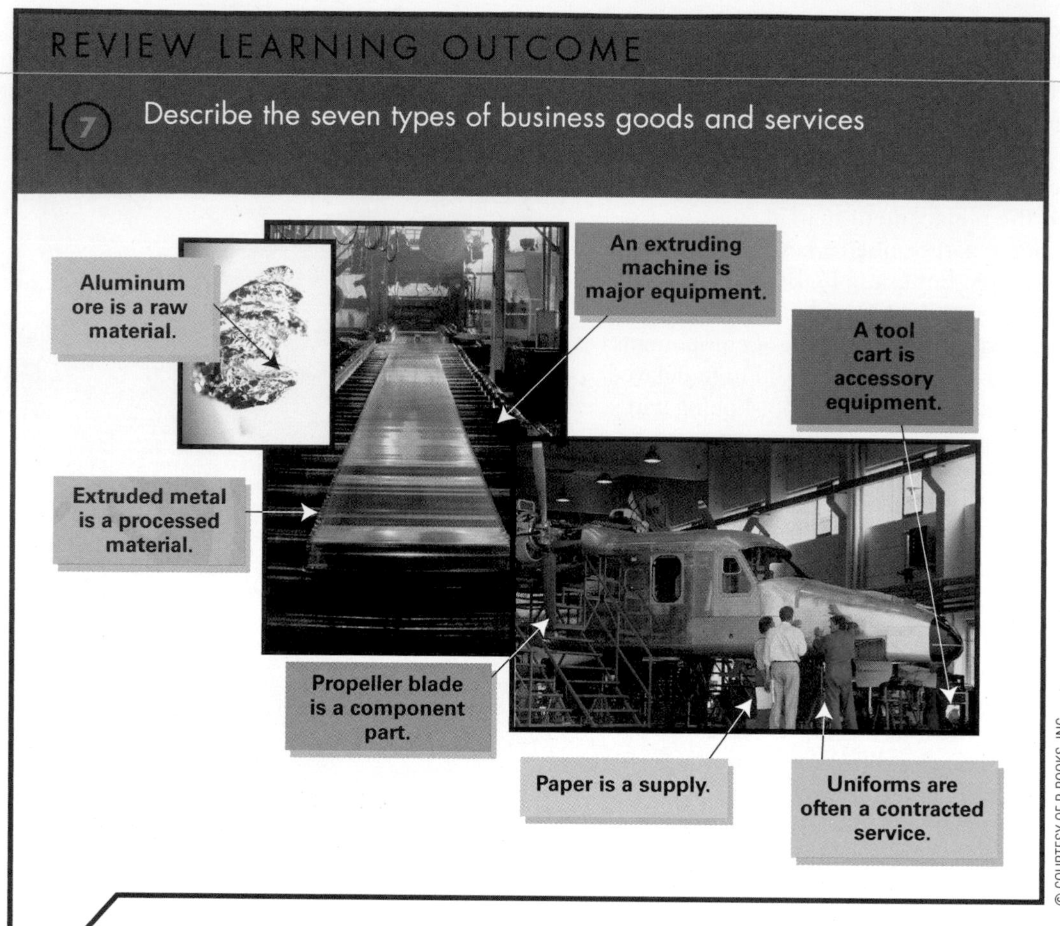

© COURTESY OF B-BOOKS, INC.

Competition in the MRO market is intense. Bic and Paper Mate, for example, battle for business purchases of inexpensive ballpoint pens.

Business Services

Business services are expense items that do not become part of a final product. Businesses often retain outside providers to perform janitorial, advertising, legal, management consulting, marketing research, maintenance, and other services. Hiring an outside provider makes sense when it costs less than hiring or assigning an employee to perform the task and when an outside provider is needed for particular expertise.

LO 8

BUSINESS BUYING BEHAVIOR

business services
Expense items that do not become part of a final product.

buying center
All those persons in an organization who become involved in the purchase decision.

As you probably have already concluded, business buyers behave differently from consumers. Understanding how purchase decisions are made in organizations is a first step in developing a business selling strategy. Business buying behavior has five important aspects: buying centers, evaluative criteria, buying situations, business ethics, and customer service.

Buying Centers

In many cases, more than one person is involved in a purchase decision. Identifying who these people are and the roles that they play greatly enhances the salesperson's chances for success.[27]

A **buying center** includes all those persons in an organization who become involved in the purchase decision. Membership and influence vary from company to company. For instance, in engineering-dominated firms like Bell Helicopter, the buying center may consist almost entirely of engineers. In marketing-oriented firms like Toyota and IBM, marketing and engineering have almost equal authority. In consumer goods firms like Procter & Gamble, product managers and other marketing decision makers may dominate the buying center. In a small manufacturing company, almost everyone may be a member.

The number of people involved in a buying center varies with the complexity and importance of a purchase decision. The composition of the buying group will usually change from one purchase to another and sometimes even during various stages of the buying process. To make matters more complicated, buying centers do not appear on formal organizational charts.

For example, even though a formal committee may have been set up to choose a new plant site, it is only part of the buying center. Other people, like the company president, often play informal yet powerful roles. In a lengthy decision-making process, such as finding a new plant location, some members may drop out of the buying center when they can no longer play a useful role. Others whose talents are needed then become part of the center. No formal announcement of "who is in" and "who is out" is ever made.

Roles in the Buying Center As in family purchasing decisions, several people may play a role in the business purchase process:

- *Initiator:* the person who first suggests making a purchase.
- *Influencers/evaluators:* people who influence the buying decision. They often help define specifications and provide information for evaluating options. Technical personnel are especially important as influencers.
- *Gatekeepers:* group members who regulate the flow of information. Frequently, the purchasing agent views the gatekeeping role as a source of his or her power. A secretary may also act as a gatekeeper by determining which vendors get an appointment with a buyer.
- *Decider:* the person who has the formal or informal power to choose or approve the selection of the supplier or brand. In complex situations, it is often difficult to determine who makes the final decision.
- *Purchaser:* the person who actually negotiates the purchase. It could be anyone from the president of the company to the purchasing agent, depending on the importance of the decision.
- *Users:* members of the organization who will actually use the product. Users often initiate the buying process and help define product specifications.

An example illustrating these basic roles is shown in Exhibit 7.5.

Implications of Buying Centers for the Marketing Manager Successful vendors realize the importance of identifying who is in the decision-making unit, each member's relative influence in the buying decision, and each member's evaluative criteria. Successful selling strategies often focus on determining the most important buying influences and tailoring sales presentations to the evaluative criteria most important to these buying-center members.

For example, Loctite Corporation, the manufacturer of Super Glue and industrial adhesives and sealants, found that engineers were the most important influencers and deciders in adhesive and sealant purchase decisions. As a result, Loctite focused its marketing efforts on production and maintenance engineers.

Marketers are often frustrated by their inability to directly reach c-level (chief) executives who play important roles in many buying centers. To circumvent gatekeepers, FedEx Corp. has initiated a marketing effort called "access," aimed at the c-suite. It includes direct mail, e-mail, and a custom magazine prepared exclusively for c-level executives. It also hosts exclusive leadership events for these senior executives.[28] Other firms, such as Motorola Corp.,

EXHIBIT 7.5

Buying-Center Roles for Computer Purchases

Role	Illustration
Initiator	Division general manager proposes to replace company's computer network.
Influencers/ evaluators	Corporate controller's office and vice president of data processing have an important say in which system and vendor the company will deal with.
Gatekeepers	Corporate departments for purchasing and data processing analyze company's needs and recommend likely matches with potential vendors.
Decider	Vice president of administration, with advice from others, selects vendor the company will deal with and system it will buy.
Purchaser	Purchasing agent negotiates terms of sale.
Users	All division employees use the computers.

new buy
A situation requiring the purchase of a product for the first time.

Intel Corp., SAS, and Xerox Corp., have developed programs utilizing a combination of print, online, and events to reach the elusive c-level audience.[29]

Evaluative Criteria

Business buyers evaluate products and suppliers against three important criteria: quality, service, and price—in that order.

Quality In this case, quality refers to technical suitability. A superior tool can do a better job in the production process, and superior packaging can increase dealer and consumer acceptance of a brand. Evaluation of quality also applies to the salesperson and the salesperson's firm. Business buyers want to deal with reputable salespeople and companies that are financially responsible. Quality improvement should be part of every organization's marketing strategy.

Service Almost as much as they want satisfactory products, business buyers want satisfactory service. A purchase offers several opportunities for service. Suppose a vendor is selling heavy equipment. Prepurchase service could include a survey of the buyer's needs. After thorough analysis of the survey findings, the vendor could prepare a report and recommendations in the form of a purchasing proposal. If a purchase results, postpurchase service might consist of installing the equipment and training those who will be using it. Postsale services may also include maintenance and repairs. Another service that business buyers seek is dependability of supply. They must be able to count on delivery of what was ordered when it is scheduled to be delivered. Buyers also welcome services that help them sell their finished products. Services of this sort are especially appropriate when the seller's product is an identifiable part of the buyer's end product.

Price Business buyers want to buy at low prices—at the lowest prices, under most circumstances. However, a buyer who pressures a supplier to cut prices to a point where the supplier loses money on the sale almost forces shortcuts on quality. The buyer also may, in effect, force the supplier to quit selling to him or her. Then a new source of supply will have to be found.

Buying Situations

Often business firms, especially manufacturers, must decide whether to make something or buy it from an outside supplier. The decision is essentially one of economics. Can an item of similar quality be bought at a lower price elsewhere? If not, is manufacturing it in-house the best use of limited company resources? For example, Briggs & Stratton Corporation, a major manufacturer of four-cycle engines, might be able to save $150,000 annually on outside purchases by spending $500,000 on the equipment needed to produce gas throttles internally. Yet Briggs & Stratton could also use that $500,000 to upgrade its carburetor assembly line, which would save $225,000 annually. If a firm does decide to buy a product instead of making it, the purchase will be a new buy, a modified rebuy, or a straight rebuy.

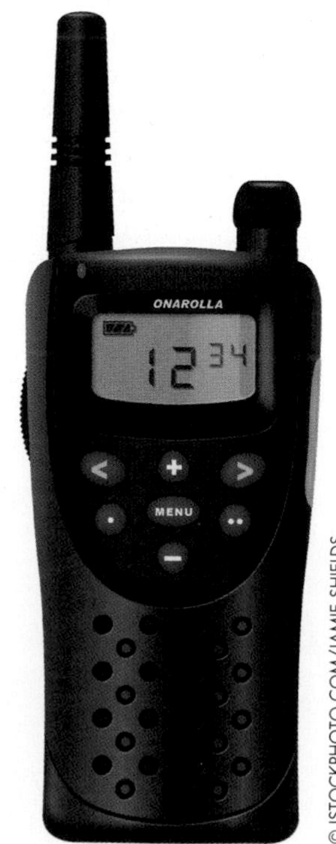

New Buy A **new buy** is a situation requiring the purchase of a product for the first time. For example, suppose a manufacturing company needs a better way to page managers while they are working on the shop floor. Currently, each of the several managers has a distinct ring, for example, two short and one long, that sounds over the plant intercom whenever he or she is being paged by anyone in the factory. The company decides to replace its buzzer system of paging with handheld wireless radio technology that will allow managers to communicate immediately with the department initiating the page. This situation represents the greatest opportunity for new vendors. No long-term relationship has been established for this product, specifications may be somewhat fluid, and buyers are generally more open to new vendors.

If the new item is a raw material or a critical component part, the buyer cannot afford to run out of supply. The seller must be able to convince the buyer that the seller's firm can consistently deliver a high-quality product on time.

Modified Rebuy A **modified rebuy** is normally less critical and less time-consuming than a new buy. In a modified-rebuy situation, the purchaser wants some change in the original good or service. It may be a new color, greater tensile strength in a component part, more respondents in a marketing research study, or additional services in a janitorial contract.

Because the two parties are familiar with each other and credibility has been established, buyer and seller can concentrate on the specifics of the modification. But in some cases, modified rebuys are open to outside bidders. The purchaser uses this strategy to ensure that the new terms are competitive. An example would be the manufacturing company buying radios with a vibrating feature for managers who have trouble hearing the ring over the factory noise. The firm may open the bidding to examine the price/quality offerings of several suppliers.

Straight Rebuy A **straight rebuy** is a situation vendors prefer. The purchaser is not looking for new information or other suppliers. An order is placed and the product is provided as in previous orders. Usually, a straight rebuy is routine because the terms of the purchase have been agreed to in earlier negotiations. An example would be the previously cited manufacturing company purchasing additional radios for new managers from the same supplier on a regular basis.

One common instrument used in straight-rebuy situations is the purchasing contract. Purchasing contracts are used with products that are bought often and in high volume. In essence, the purchasing contract makes the buyer's decision making routine and promises the salesperson a sure sale. The advantage to the buyer is a quick, confident decision and to the salesperson, reduced or eliminated competition.

Suppliers must remember not to take straight-rebuy relationships for granted. Retaining existing customers is much easier than attracting new ones.

© AP IMAGES/PRNEWSFOTO/VIRGIN AMERICA

Promoting its in-flight customer service, Virgin Airlines's ad promises "If you order it, We will come"; that is, you won't have to wait for your meal or drink to be delivered at *their* convenience, but when you want it.

Business Ethics

As we noted in Chapter 3, ethics refers to the moral principles or values that generally govern the conduct of an individual or a group. Ethics can also be viewed as the standard of behavior by which conduct is judged.

Although we have heard a lot about corporate misbehavior in recent years, most people, and most companies, follow ethical practices. To help achieve this, over half of all major corporations offer ethics training to employees. Many companies also have codes of ethics or business conduct that help guide buyers and sellers. The Ethics in Marketing box shows Lockheed Martin's Code of Ethics.

Customer Service

Business marketers are increasingly recognizing the benefits of developing a formal system to monitor customer opinions and perceptions of the quality of customer service. Companies like McDonald's, L.L. Bean, and Lexus build their strategies not only around products but also around a few highly developed service skills. These companies understand that keeping current customers satisfied is just as important as attracting new ones, if not more so. These leading-edge firms are obsessed not only with delivering high-quality customer service, but also with measuring satisfaction, loyalty, relationship quality, and other indicators of nonfinancial performance.

Most firms find it necessary to develop measures unique to their own strategy, value propositions, and target market. For example, Anderson Corporation assesses the loyalty of its trade customers by their willingness to continue carrying its windows and doors, recommend its products to colleagues and customers, increase their volume with the company, and put its products in their own homes. Basically, each firm's measures

modified rebuy
A situation where the purchaser wants some change in the original good or service.

straight rebuy
A situation in which the purchaser reorders the same goods or services without looking for new information or investigating other suppliers.

ETHICS in Marketing

Code of Ethics at Lockheed Martin

Lockheed Martin's Board of Directors has adopted the booklet, *Setting the Standard* (updated in October 2008) as the company's Code of Ethics and Business Conduct. It provides guidance on the company's expectations for all employees, contracted labor, agents, consultants, members of the Board of Directors, and others when representing or acting for the Corporation.

According to chairman, president, and chief executive officer Robert J. Stevens, "all of us have a shared responsibility to maintain the highest standard of integrity and ensure that we sustain a place where we are proud to work. If you are faced with an ethical dilemma, you have the responsibility to speak up and seek resolution. We must all be accountable for acting with integrity and upholding the values of the Corporation."[30]

The Code includes three key components: a culture of integrity, our vision, and our values.

A Culture of Integrity

Lockheed Martin is committed to dealing honestly and fairly with our employees, customers, suppliers, shareholders and the communities in which we live and work. Our success depends on maintaining a culture of integrity.

Our Vision and Our Values

Lockheed Martin holds each director, executive, leader, employee, and agent accountable for upholding Our Vision, Our Values, and Our Code. In so doing, we ensure that Lockheed Martin's business will be conducted consistent with the high ethical standards that we demand from each other, and that others have the right to demand from us.

Discuss the similarities and differences in Lockheed Martin's Code and the American Marketing Association's statement of ethics called its "Ethical Norms and Values for Marketers" at **www.marketingpower.com.**

should not only ask "What are your expectations?" and "How are we doing?" but should also reflect what the firm wants its customers to do.

Some customers are more valuable than others. They may have greater value because they spend more, buy higher-margin products, have a well-known name, or have the potential of becoming a bigger customer in the future. Some companies selectively provide different levels of service to customers based on their value to the business. By giving the most valuable customers superior service, a firm is more likely to keep them happy, hopefully increasing retention of these high-value customers and maximizing the total business value they generate over time.

To achieve this goal, the firm must be able to divide customers into two or more groups based on their value. It must also create and apply policies that govern how service will be allocated among groups. Policies might establish which customers' phone calls get "fast-tracked" and which customers are directed to use the Web and/or voice self-service, how specific e-mail questions are routed, and who is given access to online chat and who isn't.[31]

Providing different customers with different levels of service is a very sensitive matter. It must be handled very carefully and very discreetly to avoid offending lesser value, but still important customers.

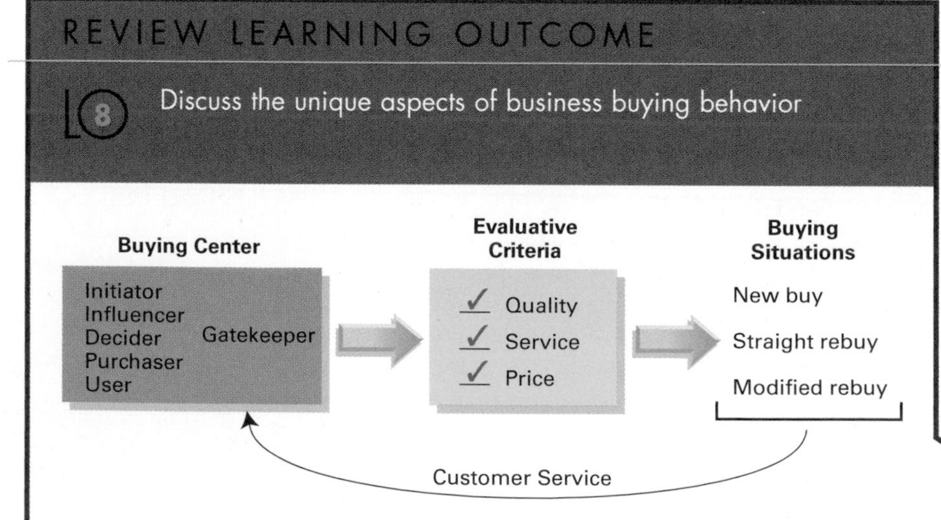

$1 trillion ◀ total U.S. B2B commerce for 2008

core companies in the Toyota Group keiretsu ▶ **14**

170 ◀ companies that receive preferential treatment from the Toyota Group keiretsu

wholesalers operating in the United States ▶ **500,000**

$600 billion ◀ amount the U.S. federal government spends each year on goods and services

NAICs economic sectors ▶ **20**

$200 billion ◀ size of the contract the Pentagon awarded to Lockheed Martin to build 3,000 jet fighter planes

20,000 ◀ transactions made each week on Exostar—the online exchange of the aerospace industry

REVIEW AND APPLICATIONS

Describe business marketing. Business marketing provides goods and services that are bought for use in business rather than for personal consumption. Intended use, not physical characteristics, distinguishes a business product from a consumer product.

1.1 As the marketing manager for Huggies diapers made by Kimberly-Clark, you are constantly going head-to-head with Pampers, produced by rival Procter & Gamble. You are considering unlocking the potential of the business market to increase your share of the disposable diaper market, but how? Write an outline of several ways you could transform this quintessentially consumer product into a successful business product as well.

Describe the role of the Internet in business marketing. The rapid expansion and adoption of the Internet have made business markets more competitive than ever before. The number of business buyers and sellers using the Internet is rapidly increasing. Firms are seeking new and better ways to expand markets and sources of supply, increase sales and decrease costs, and better serve customers. Marketers are becoming more sophisticated in their use of the Internet and are developing quantitative methods that can be used to better measure online success.

2.1 How could you use the Web site **BtoBonline.com** to help define a target market and develop a marketing plan?

2.2 Reconsider question 1.1. How could you use the Internet in your business marketing of Huggies diapers?

Discuss the role of relationship marketing and strategic alliances in business marketing. Relationship marketing entails seeking and establishing long-term alliances or partnerships with customers. A strategic alliance is a cooperative agreement between business firms. Firms form alliances to leverage what they do well by partnering with others that have complementary skills.

3.1 Why is relationship or personal selling the best way to promote in business marketing?

Identify the four major categories of business market customers. Producer markets consist of for-profit organizations and individuals that buy products to use in producing other products, as components of other products, or in facilitating business operations. Reseller markets consist of wholesalers and retailers that buy finished products to resell for profit. Government markets include federal, state, county, and city governments that buy goods and services to support their own operations and serve the needs of citizens. Institutional markets consist of very diverse nonbusiness institutions whose main goals do not include profit.

4.1 Understanding businesses is key to business marketing. Publications like *Manufacturing Automation*, *Computer Weekly*, *Power Generation Technology & Markets*, and *Biotech Equipment Update* can give you insights into many business marketing concepts. Research the industrial publications to find an article on a business marketer that interests you. Write a description of the company using as many concepts from the chapter as possible. What major category or categories of business market customers does this firm serve?

4.2 What do you have to do to get a government contract? Check out the Web sites **www.fedbizopps.gov** and **www.governmentbids.com** to find out. Does it seem worth the effort?

Explain the North American Industry Classification System. The NAICS provides a way to identify, analyze, segment, and target business and government markets. Organizations can be identified and compared by a numeric code indicating business sector, subsector, industry group, industry, and country industry. NAICS is a valuable tool for analyzing, segmenting, and targeting business markets.

5.1 Pick a product and determine its NAICS code. How easy was it to trace the groups and sectors?

Explain the major differences between business and consumer markets. In business markets, demand is derived, price-inelastic, joint, and fluctuating. Purchase volume is much larger than in consumer markets, customers are fewer in number and more geographically concentrated, and distribution channels are more direct. Buying is approached more formally using professional purchasing agents, more people are involved in the buying process, negotiation is more complex, and reciprocity and leasing are more common. And, finally, selling strategy in business markets normally focuses on personal contact rather than on advertising.

6.1 How might derived demand affect the manufacturing of an automobile?

6.2 Your boss has just asked you, the company purchasing manager, to buy new computers for an entire department. As you have just recently purchased a new home computer, you are well educated about the various products available. How will your buying process for the company differ from your recent purchase for yourself?

Describe the seven types of business goods and services. Major equipment includes capital goods, such as heavy machinery. Accessory equipment is typically less expensive and shorter-lived than major equipment. Raw materials are extractive or agricultural products that have not been processed. Component parts are finished or near-finished items to be used as parts of other products.

Processed materials are used to manufacture other products. Supplies are consumable and not used as part of a final product. Business services are intangible products that many companies use in their operations.

7.1 In small groups, brainstorm examples of companies that feature the products in different business categories. (Avoid examples already listed in the chapter.) Compile a list of ten specific business products including at least one in each category. Then match up with another group. Have each group take turns naming a product and have the other group identify its appropriate category. Try to resolve all discrepancies by discussion. Some identified products may appropriately fit into more than one category.

Discuss the unique aspects of business buying behavior. Business buying behavior is distinguished by five fundamental characteristics. First, buying is normally undertaken by a buying center consisting of many people who range widely in authority level. Second, business buyers typically evaluate alternative products and suppliers based on quality, service, and price—in that order. Third, business buying falls into three general categories: new buys, modified rebuys, and straight rebuys. Fourth, the ethics of business buyers and sellers are often scrutinized. Fifth, customer service before, during, and after the sale plays a big role in business purchase decisions.

8.1 A colleague of yours has sent you an e-mail seeking your advice as he attempts to sell a new voice-mail system to a local business. Send him a return e-mail describing the various people who might influence the customer's buying decision. Be sure to include suggestions for dealing with the needs of each of these individuals.

8.2 Intel Corporation supplies microprocessors to Hewlett-Packard for use in its computers. Describe the buying situation in this relationship, keeping in mind the rapid advance of technology in this industry.

KEY TERMS

accessory equipment 244
business marketing 231
business services 246
business-to-business electronic commerce 232
business-to-business online exchange 242
buying center 246
component parts 244
derived demand 241
disintermediation 234
joint demand 241
keiretsu 236
major equipment (installations) 244
modified rebuy 249
multiplier effect (accelerator principle) 241
new buy 248
North American Industry Classification System (NAICS) 239
original equipment manufacturers (OEMs) 237
processed materials 245
raw materials 244
reciprocity 243
reintermediation 234
relationship commitment 236
stickiness 233
straight rebuy 249
strategic alliance 235
supplies 245
trust 236

EXERCISES

APPLICATION EXERCISE

Purchasing agents are often offered gifts and gratuities. Increasingly, though, companies are restricting the amount and value of gifts that their purchasing managers can accept from vendors. The idea is that purchasing managers should consider all qualified vendors during a buying decision instead of only those who pass out great event tickets. This exercise asks you to consider whether accepting various types of gifts is ethical.[32]

Activities

1. Review the following list of common types of gifts and favors. Put a check mark next to the items that you think it would be acceptable for a purchasing manager to receive from a vendor.

   Advertising souvenirs
   Automobiles
   Clothing
   Dinners
   Discounts on personal purchases
   Food and liquor
   Golf outings
   Holiday gifts
   Large appliances
   Loans of money
   Lunches
   Small-value appliances
   Tickets (sports, theater, amusement parks, etc.)
   Trips to vendor plants
   Vacation trips

2. Now look at your list of acceptable gifts through various lenses. Would your list change if the purchasing manager's buying decision involved a low-cost item (say, pens)? Why or why not? What if the decision involved a very expensive purchase (like a major installation)?
3. Form a team and compare your lists. Discuss (or debate) any discrepancies.

ETHICS EXERCISE

Cameron Stock, purchasing manager for a sports equipment manufacturer, is responsible for buying $5 million of supplies every year. He has a preferred list of certified suppliers who are awarded a large percentage of his business. Cameron has been offered a paid weekend for two in Las Vegas as a Christmas present from a supplier with whom he has done business for a decade and built a very good relationship.

Questions

1. Would it be legal and ethical for Cameron Stock to accept this gift?
2. How is this addressed in the AMA Statement of Ethics? Go to the AMA Web site at **www.marketingpower.com/About AMA/** and reread the Statement of Ethics. Write a brief paragraph summarizing where the AMA stands on the issue of supplier gifts.

MARKETING PLAN EXERCISE

For continued general assistance in business plans and marketing plans, visit **www.bplans.com** or **www.businessplans.org.** You should also refer to the Marketing Plan Outline–Appendix I in Chapter 2 for additional checklist items. Complete the following exercises to continue the marketing plan you began in Chapter 2:

1. Identify the NAICS code for your chosen company's industry (**www.census.gov/eos/www/naics/**). Perform a brief industry analysis (from International Trade Administration, U.S. Dept. of Commerce, at **http://ita.doc.gov/td/industry/otea/**, for example) of your firm's industry, based on the NAICS code.
2. Make a list of consumer markets and business markets for your company's product or business offering. Which is the more important market for your company? Why?
3. How does the buying process differ for consumer markets and business markets for your chosen company's product or business offering?

CASE STUDY: THEY'VE GOT YOUR 'BAK

In 1989, Michael Eidson probably never imagined that his homemade, do-it-yourself fix for dehydration during long cycling races would evolve into the world's premier hydration device for outdoor enthusiasts, soldiers, and law enforcement personnel. That is exactly what happened to the CamelBak backpack, however.

The first version, which used medical tubing to flow water from an intravenous drip bag that was insulated by a sock and strapped to the back of his shirt, was born as most inventions are—out of necessity. The special pack made it possible for Eidson to take in fluids while sitting upright without having to sacrifice speed by reaching down for a water bottle during a race. The packs gained fame during the 1991 Gulf War as extreme sports enthusiasts in the U.S. Special Forces carried their personal CamelBaks into combat during Desert Storm. Thereafter, the CamelBak name would be forever associated with extreme performance and the U.S. Armed Forces.

By 1995, Eidsen sold the company for $4 million. Its buyer, Kransco, introduced the first camouflaged models, and the packs continued to gain acclaim. In 1999, two years after buying his first CamelBak pack, cyclist Chuck Hunter left Lockheed Martin to join the upstart company in hopes of growing its military business. He promptly moved the company to the Sonoma Valley, built a research and development center, and leveraged his experience in the defense industry to launch a military-specific line of packs.

Hunter partnered with DuPont to help CamelBak develop the Low Infrared Reflective (LIRR) system. LIRR applies specially developed materials to a pack's compartments, buckles, and straps to shield soldiers from enemy detection systems. As advanced identification and kill technologies are increasingly being deployed on the battlefield, individual protection applications like the LIRR will be the camouflage of tomorrow.

Other CamelBak innovations include the WaterBeast reservoir, a fluid storage system that boasts 30 percent more rigidity than other packs on the market. The WaterBeast has the ability to withstand lengthy field engagements, aided by its silver-ion reservoir and tube linings that eliminate 99.99 percent of all fungus and bacteria in the water delivery system. The WaterBeast reservoir is now a standard feature on all CamelBak packs, as is the company's proprietary drinking nozzle, or bite valve, which must withstand 10,000 compressions to guarantee it will last through three years of combat use.

Another CamelBak first is its CBR 4.0 pack system, which is specially designed to perform under chemical or biological weapons attack. The CBR 4.0 took five years to develop, and like all CamelBak military and law enforcement products, it was created to meet the specific requests and requirements of the target market. Since its introduction in 2005, the U.S. Special Forces, New York Police Department, U.S. Secret Service, Department of Health and Human Services, and a myriad of HAZMAT, law enforcement, and government agencies from around the world have adopted and deployed the CBR 4.0.

Though CamelBak specializes in offering extreme performance packs for the military, industrial, and professional markets, it also sells a variety of products for hunting, extreme sports, recreational, and "light" law enforcement applications. Having claimed more than 90 percent of the military market for hydration packs, product manager Shawn Cullen likens CamelBak to Kleenex: "Everyone calls a hydration system a CamelBak," he says. Ironically, the company's biggest customer is its biggest competitor. While it continues to use CamelBaks, the U.S. Army is working with a former supplier to develop its own version, most likely in an attempt to reduce costs.

At prices up to $200 for combat-ready systems, one thing CamelBaks aren't is cheap. But then again, neither is CamelBak itself. Its strong product lines, history of innovation, secure strategic relationships, and dominance in government and institutional markets drove its value to over $200 million when investment bank Bear Stearns Company bought the outfit from Kransco in 2003—not bad for a product that started life as an intravenous fluid bag wrapped in a sock.[33]

Questions

1. Discuss how business relationships and strategic partnerships have helped to increase the value of CamelBak's products and the business itself.
2. What type(s) of business market customers does CamelBak sell to?
3. Review the types of demand that most influence business markets. Which ones do you think are most important for CamelBak to consider in its marketing strategy? Why?
4. What type of business product is a CamelBak backpack?

COMPANY CLIPS

READYMADE—MAKING BUSINESS RELATIONSHIPS

Like most periodicals, *ReadyMade* relies on advertisers for much of its revenue. Finding companies interested in advertising in the magazine and cultivating those relationships is an important component of making the company successful. *ReadyMade* must constantly market its product to potential investors through personal contact and solicitation. *ReadyMade* also must develop relationships with distributors and other businesses that will directly or indirectly promote the magazine and help make it successful. As you watch this video, notice the strategies that Darci Andresen describes as she explains the process she goes through as head of Advertising Sales & Special Promotions when seeking new advertisers.

Questions

1. When marketing to potential advertisers, what strategies could *ReadyMade* use to promote itself without having to rely on hard statistics about its readers?
2. What sort of strategic alliances does *ReadyMade* maintain? In what ways are these partnerships beneficial to the magazine?
3. Go to *ReadyMade*'s Web site, **readymademag.com.** What evidence do you see of its business partnerships? How does it use its Web site to market itself to businesses?

Marketing & You Results

A high score indicates that you found the salesperson to be credible and concerned about your needs. Because you found the salesperson to be open and concerned, you had a higher level of trust in the salesperson than did someone with a lower score. As you read in this chapter, trust is an important element in building strategic alliances and in cultivating business clients.

© WORLDFOTO/ALAMY

CHAPTER 8

Segmenting and Targeting Markets

LEARNING OUTCOMES

- LO1 Describe the characteristics of markets and market segments
- LO2 Explain the importance of market segmentation
- LO3 Discuss criteria for successful market segmentation
- LO4 Describe the bases commonly used to segment consumer markets
- LO5 Describe the bases for segmenting business markets
- LO6 List the steps involved in segmenting markets
- LO7 Discuss alternative strategies for selecting target markets
- LO8 Explain one-to-one marketing
- LO9 Explain how and why firms implement positioning strategies and how product differentiation plays a role

MARKET SEGMENTATION

The term *market* means different things to different people. We are all familiar with the supermarket, stock market, labor market, fish market, and flea market. All these types of markets share several characteristics. First, they are composed of people (consumer markets) or organizations (business markets). Second, these people or organizations have wants and needs that can be satisfied by particular product categories. Third, they have the ability to buy the products they seek. Fourth, they are willing to exchange their resources, usually money or credit, for desired products. In sum, a **market** is (1) people or organizations with (2) needs or wants and with (3) the ability and (4) the willingness to buy. A group of people or an organization that lacks any one of these characteristics is not a market.

Within a market, a **market segment** is a subgroup of people or organizations sharing one or more characteristics that cause them to have similar product needs. At one extreme, we can define every person and every organization in the world as a market segment because each is unique. At the other extreme, we can define the entire consumer market as one large market segment and the business market as another large segment. All people have some similar characteristics and needs, as do all organizations.

From a marketing perspective, market segments can be described as somewhere between the two extremes. The process of dividing a market into meaningful, relatively similar, and identifiable segments or groups is called **market segmentation**. The purpose of market segmentation is to enable the marketer to tailor marketing mixes to meet the needs of one or more specific segments.

Exhibit 8.1 illustrates the concept of market segmentation. Each box represents a market consisting of seven persons. This market might vary as follows: one homogeneous market of seven people, a market consisting of seven individual segments, a market composed of two segments based on gender, a market composed of three age segments; or a market composed of five age and gender market segments. Age and gender and many other bases for segmenting markets are examined later in this chapter.

market
People or organizations with needs or wants and the ability and willingness to buy.

market segment
A subgroup of people or organizations sharing one or more characteristics that cause them to have similar product needs.

market segmentation
The process of dividing a market into meaningful, relatively similar, and identifiable segments or groups.

Marketing & You

Please note your opinion on each of the following questions.

Using the following scale, enter your opinion.

1	2	3	4	5	6
Strongly agree					Strongly disagree

___ I frequently have problems making ends meet.

___ My budgeting is always tight.

___ I often have to spend more money than I have available.

___ I do not consider myself financially well off.

___ I am generally on a tight budget.

___ Meeting an unexpected expense of $1,000 would be a financial hardship.

Total your score. Now, read the chapter and find out what your score means at the end.

Source: From Scale #646, *Marketing Scales Handbook*, G. Bruner, K. James, H. Hensel, eds., Vol. III. © by American Marketing Association.

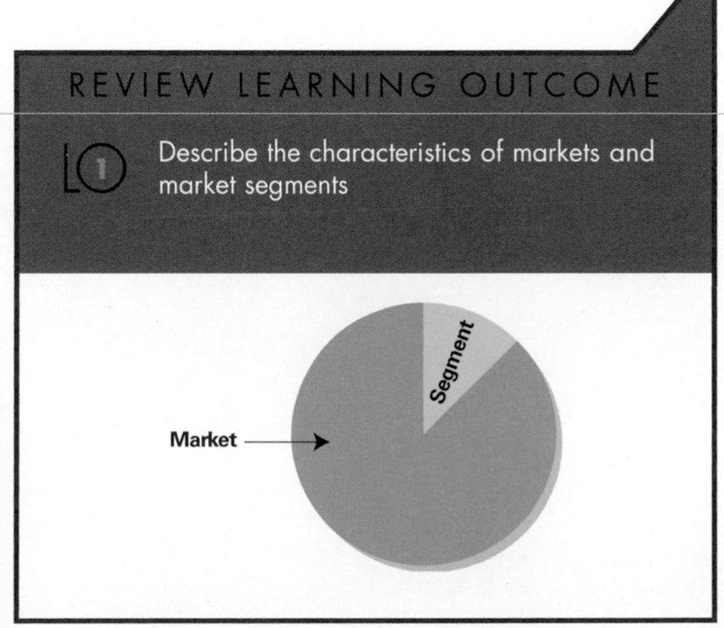

EXHIBIT 8.1

Concept of Market Segmentation

No market segmentation

Fully segmented market

Market segmentation by gender: M, F

Market segmentation by age group: 1, 2, 3

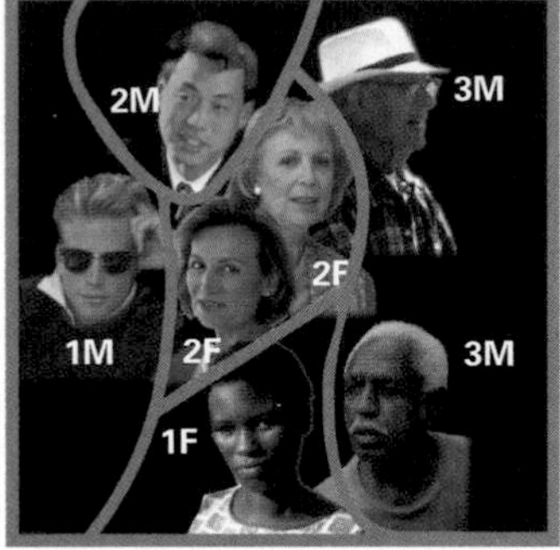

Market segmentation by gender and age group

THE IMPORTANCE OF MARKET SEGMENTATION

Until the 1960s, few firms practiced market segmentation. When they did, it was more likely a haphazard effort than a formal marketing strategy. Before 1960, for example, the Coca-Cola Company produced only one beverage and aimed it at the entire soft drink market. Today, Coca-Cola offers over a dozen different products to market segments based on diverse consumer preferences for flavors and calorie and caffeine content. Coca-Cola offers traditional soft drinks, energy drinks (such as POWERade), flavored teas, fruit drinks (Fruitopia), and water (Dasani).

© VICKI BEAVER

How many ways can you slice the market for beverages? Coca-Cola has over a dozen beverages on the market with loyal fans for each one.

Market segmentation plays a key role in the marketing strategy of almost all successful organizations and is a powerful marketing tool for several reasons. Most importantly, nearly all markets include groups of people or organizations with different product needs and preferences. Market segmentation helps marketers define customer needs and wants more precisely. Because market segments differ in size and potential, segmentation helps decision makers to more accurately define marketing objectives and better allocate resources. In turn, performance can be better evaluated when objectives are more precise.

Chico's, a successful women's fashion retailer, thrives by marketing to women aged 35 to 55 who like to wear comfortable, yet stylish, clothing. It sells private-label clothing that comes in just a few nonjudgmental sizes: zero (regular sizes 4–6), one (8–10), two (10–12), and three (14–16). Another example is Best Buy, which identifies the needs of customers depending on their geographic location. For example, the store in Baytown, Texas, caters to Eastern European workers from cargo ships or oil tankers that are temporarily docked at the city's busy port. These workers don't have a lot of time to shop, so the Baytown Best Buy moved the iPods from the back corner of the store to the front, paired them with overseas power converters, and made the signage simpler.[1]

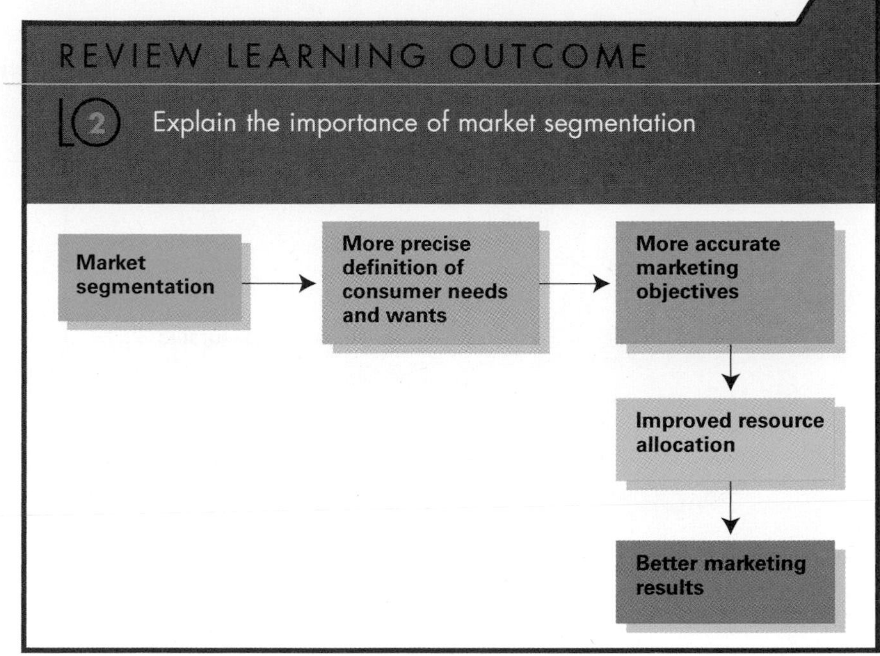

CRITERIA FOR SUCCESSFUL SEGMENTATION

Marketers segment markets for three important reasons. First, segmentation enables marketers to identify groups of customers with similar needs and to analyze the characteristics and buying behavior of these groups. Second, segmentation provides marketers with information to help them design marketing mixes specifically matched with the characteristics and desires of one or more segments. Third, segmentation is consistent with the marketing concept of satisfying customer wants and needs while meeting the organization's objectives.

To be useful, a segmentation scheme must produce segments that meet four basic criteria:

- *Substantiality:* A segment must be large enough to warrant developing and maintaining a special marketing mix. This criterion does not necessarily mean that a segment must have many potential customers. Marketers of custom-designed homes and business buildings, commercial airplanes, and large computer systems typically develop marketing programs tailored to each potential customer's needs. In most cases, however, a market segment needs many potential customers to make commercial sense. In the 1980s, home banking failed because not enough people owned personal computers. Today, a larger number of people own computers, and home banking is a thriving industry.
- *Identifiability and measurability:* Segments must be identifiable and their size measurable. Data about the population within geographic boundaries, the number of people in various age categories, and other social and demographic characteristics are often easy to get, and they provide fairly concrete measures of segment

A successful segmentation scheme must identify and measure its target customer base. GlaxoSmithKline surveyed the African American smoking population and found that, for the majority, quitting cold turkey wasn't working for them. These data justify a campaign to promote GlaxoSmithKline's product for gradually quitting smoking to that population.

REVIEW LEARNING OUTCOME

LO 3 Discuss criteria for successful market segmentation

Useful segment?

✓ Substantial

✓ Identifiable and measurable

✓ Accessible

✓ Responsive

Then, yes: Use segmentation

size. Suppose that a social service agency wants to identify segments by their readiness to participate in a drug and alcohol program or in prenatal care. Unless the agency can measure how many people are willing, indifferent, or unwilling to participate, it will have trouble gauging whether there are enough people to justify setting up the service.

- *Accessibility:* The firm must be able to reach members of targeted segments with customized marketing mixes. Some market segments are hard to reach—for example, senior citizens (especially those with reading or hearing disabilities), individuals who don't speak English, and the illiterate.
- *Responsiveness:* As Exhibit 8.1 illustrates, markets can be segmented using any criteria that seem logical. Unless one market segment responds to a marketing mix differently from other segments, however, that segment need not be treated separately. For instance, if all customers are equally price-conscious about a product, there is no need to offer high-, medium-, and low-priced versions to different segments.

segmentation bases (variables) Characteristics of individuals, groups, or organizations.

geographic segmentation Segmenting markets by region of a country or the world, market size, market density, or climate.

BASES FOR SEGMENTING CONSUMER MARKETS

Marketers use **segmentation bases**, or **variables**, which are characteristics of individuals, groups, or organizations, to divide a total market into segments. The choice of segmentation bases is crucial because an inappropriate segmentation strategy may lead to lost sales and missed profit opportunities. The key is to identify bases that will produce substantial, measurable, and accessible segments that exhibit different response patterns to marketing mixes.

Markets can be segmented using a single variable, such as age group, or several variables, such as age group, gender, and education. Although it is less precise, single-variable segmentation has the advantage of being simpler and easier to use than multiple-variable segmentation. The disadvantages of multiple-variable segmentation are that it is often harder to use than single-variable segmentation; usable secondary data are less likely to be available; and as the number of segmentation bases increases, the size of individual segments decreases. Nevertheless, the current trend is toward using more rather than fewer variables to segment most markets. Multiple-variable segmentation is clearly more precise than single-variable segmentation.

Consumer goods marketers commonly use one or more of the following characteristics to segment markets: geography, demographics, psychographics, benefits sought, and usage rate.

Geographic Segmentation

Geographic segmentation refers to segmenting markets by region of a country or the world, market size, market density, or climate. Market density means the number of people within a unit of land, such as a census tract. Climate is commonly used for geographic segmentation because of its dramatic impact on residents'

ETHICS

ETHICS in Marketing

Behavioral Targeting and Consumer Privacy[4]

Behavioral targeting segments consumers based on observed and measured online data, including pages or sites that users visit, content examined, search inquiries entered, and ads clicked. This data is then combined with the time, length, and frequency of site visits. Behavioral targeting offers many potential benefits. For marketers, effective behavioral targeting can lead to ad campaigns that are more likely to persuade their audience. The CEO of online media network Specific Media claims that compared to targeting by customer category (e.g., "sports fans"), or by only looking at click-through data, behavioral targeting has doubled marketing's efficiency. For the public, it could mean that Internet ads become more relevant to their needs. While currently behavioral targeting represents a relatively small proportion of overall Internet ad spending, eMarketer projects that spending on this technique will reach $4.4 billion by the end of 2012.

However, companies that use behavioral targeting must face the ongoing challenge of balancing online ad targeting and consumer privacy. In a recent survey, 45 percent of consumers said that they were not comfortable with policies that allow behavioral targeting. Companies have access to both customer identity (IP address) and customer personality (online behavior). Behavioral targeting relies on "cookies," small pieces of data used to track and maintain the online actions of a user, such as sites visited and items stored in an electronic shopping cart.

The U.S. Senate Commerce, Science, and Transportation Committee has held hearings on privacy issues raised by online advertising. Critics are questioning whether behavioral targeting practices violate wiretap laws, which prevent carriers from monitoring customer communications. Based on consumer privacy concerns, CenturyTel, Inc. and Charter Communications have stopped plans to use behavioral targeting. Denver-based Wide Open West has also canceled its use of behavioral targeting software.

Do you think that behavioral targeting is an ethical issue for marketers? Why or why not? What could companies using behavioral targeting do to ease consumers' privacy concerns?

needs and purchasing behavior. Snowblowers, water and snow skis, clothing, and air-conditioning and heating systems are products with varying appeal, depending on climate.

Consumer goods companies take a regional approach to marketing for four reasons. First, many firms need to find new ways to generate sales because of sluggish and intensely competitive markets. Second, computerized checkout stations with scanners give retailers an accurate assessment of which brands sell best in their region. Third, many packaged-goods manufacturers are introducing new regional brands intended to appeal to local preferences. Fourth, a more regional approach allows consumer goods companies to react more quickly to competition. For example, research showed Saks Fifth Avenue's customers differ significantly at stores around the country. At the New York store, Saks' core shopper is a mid-40s woman with a classic style. By contrast, core shoppers at its Birmingham, Alabama, store are more brand-savvy, fashion-loving, and slightly younger.[2] Macy's is another retailer that uses geographic segmentation. The company has changed the merchandise mix so that 15 percent of the merchandise in stores reflect local preferences of its customers.[3]

Demographic Segmentation

Marketers often segment markets on the basis of demographic information because it is widely available and often related to consumers' buying and consuming behavior. Some common bases of **demographic segmentation** are age, gender, income, ethnic background, and family life cycle.

demographic segmentation
Segmenting markets by age, gender, income, ethnic background, and family life cycle.

Baby boomers make up a sizable proportion of affluent households and they want attention and service. They also like to think of themselves as trailblazers, so ads appealing to their adventurous spirit are more effective than ones suggesting aging.

© COURTESY OF GEICO; © WOODBOOK STOCK/JUPITERIMAGES/GETTY IMAGES

Age Segmentation Marketers use a variety of terms to refer to different age groups. Examples include newborns, infants, young children, tweens, teens and young adults (Generation Y), adults (Generation X), baby boomers, and seniors. Age segmentation can be an important tool, as a brief exploration of the market potential of several age segments illustrates.

Through allowances, earnings, and gifts, children account for, and influence, a great deal of consumption. For example, tweens (roughly 9–14 years old) in the United States spend billions of their own dollars each year on purchases for themselves, and also have a considerable influence over major family purchase decisions. They are technology savvy and very social consumers.[5] Tweens desire to be kids, but also want some of the fun of being a teenager. Many retailers, such as Abercrombie Kids, serve this market with clothing that is similar in style to that worn by teenagers and young adults. The Generation Y market, or the Millennial Generation, spans the age groups of 14 through 29. This group also has formidable purchasing power. They like to try whatever is new and trendy, tend to change their minds quickly about things, and covet status brands.[6] The teens in this group spend most of their money on clothing, entertainment, and food. They are aware of brands and also of marketing strategies. Therefore, obvious marketing techniques won't work. Teens consider brands such as iPod, American Eagle Outfitters, Facebook, and MTV to be not only their favorites, but also as defining their generation.[7] They are environmentally conscious, and say they would shop at an environmentally friendly retailer more, and spend more money if services, products, and brands were environmentally friendly.[8] When Procter & Gamble acquired Herbal Essences, the brand was struggling to compete with other shampoos. So its marketers choose to target Gen Y and millennial women by redesigning the packaging and adding cute style names like "drama clean." The changes were successful and Herbal Essences sales began growing again.[9]

Generation X is the group that was born after the baby boomers. Members of Generation X, or Xers, tend to be disloyal to brands and skeptical of big business. Many of them are becoming parents, and they make purchasing decisions with thought for and input from their families. Xers desire an experience, not just a product. For example, Starbucks developed a market for expensive coffee by encompassing it in the coffee-drinking experience that appeals to this consumer segment.[10]

People born between 1946 and 1964 are often called "baby boomers." Boomers spend $2.1 trillion a year, and represent half of all spending in the United States. For the next 18 years, one baby boomer will turn 60 every seven seconds. They make up 49 percent of affluent households, and they want attention and service when they shop.[11] This group spends big money on products such as travel, electronics, and automobiles. Baby boomers are not particularly brand loyal, and they are a very diverse group. Some may be the parents of a baby, while others are empty nesters. The Hallmark Channel, owned and operated by Crown Media (owned by Hallmark Cards), targets those of the baby boom generation because of their wealth, and the fact that they are more engaged in TV than are members of other groups.[12] The challenges facing marketers who target boomers are great. Unlike yesterday's generation of 50-plus-year-olds, today's boomers refuse to believe they're aging, so marketers who want to appeal to this segment cannot use any kind of messaging that refers to aging. Rather, they must appeal to boomers' interests, lifestyles, and values—anything but age. Companies as diverse as Whirlpool, Gap, Moen, Fila, and OXO are doing this with great success. The president of OXO, the company that makes Good Grips cooking utensils with the thick black handles, says, "The last thing they want is the kind of patronizing, help-me-do-something kind of tools. We have almost a cult-like following among older consumers. At the same time, we have just as strong a following from people in the 20-to-40 age range because the products look cool."[13]

Consumers in their early 60s and older represent people who are part of the War Generation (ages 61 to 66), the Depression Generation (ages 67 to 76), and the G.I. Generation (age 77 and up). Collectively, they are sometimes called the "Golden Generation" (a term coined by Focalyst, a research and consultancy firm focused on older consumers). Many in this group view retirement not as a passive time, but as an active time they use to explore new knowledge, travel, volunteer, and spend time with family and friends. They are living longer and are healthier than older consumers 20 years ago. However, marketers need to be aware that physical changes in hearing, eyesight, and mobility still occur in this segment. The Hartford Financial Services Group provides auto and homeowner insurance to AARP members. The company's voice self-service system has a low-pitched male voice that is easier for their older members to hear. The Hartford trains its employees to deal with conditions such as hearing impairment and other conditions of aging, and has nine gerontologists on staff to advise on issues relating to those in their golden years.[14]

Gender Segmentation In the United States, women handle 75 percent of family finances and make or influence 80 percent of consumer purchases. They buy 51 percent of the new electronics sold, 75 percent of over-the-counter drugs, and 65 percent of new cars. That means that women are making decisions when it comes to the purchase of a huge variety of goods and services, not just the packaged goods that have traditionally been marketed to them.[15]

Women are buying and playing video games in rapidly increasing numbers. Forty percent of gamers are women, and they outnumber under-17 males by nearly two to one in the gaming world. The video game industry has been forced to respond by developing more games with female protagonists and changing its advertising strategy. A recent commercial for EA Sports featured real video gamers—some of them women—instead of actors, and presented video game playing as an interactive social activity.[16] Other marketers that traditionally focused most of their attention on males are also recognizing the potential of the female market segment. For example, the number of women shopping at hardware stores such as Home Depot and Lowe's Home Improvement Warehouse has been rising in recent years. Home Depot is testing a new store concept that is designed to attract more women shoppers. These stores will focus more on upscale home décor and organization, using showrooms that are more extravagant and carry more products.[17]

Similarly, other brands that have been targeted to men, such as Gillette razors and Rogaine baldness remedy, are increasing their efforts to attract women. For example, athletic apparel manufacturers such as Nike and Reebok have typically targeted men, and when they did target women, just copied the hard-edged, sports-marketing strategies that made them so popular with men. But these companies are now taking women's unique needs regarding athletics into consideration when they design clothing and shoes for them. The Fairmont Princess Resort in Scottsdale, Arizona, hired a cultural anthropologist when it wanted to target men in addition to its female clientele. Intrinsic differences in the way men and women approached a spa were uncovered. Research led the resort to

Many companies have profited from redesigning traditionally feminine products and marketing them towards men. Here, Lancôme advertises an anti-wrinkle cream that has been packaged to appeal to men.

IMAGE COURTESY OF THE ADVERTISING ARCHIVES

- Use darker woods and colors to create a club-like ambiance so men wouldn't feel they were entering female territory.
- Install televisions in locker rooms (to reduce awkwardness felt by males in spa wear).
- Develop customized packages, including "Keep Your Shorts On" and "Golf Performance Treatment."
- Reposition the "European Facial," as translated for men into "Barber Facial."[18]

Marketers of products such as clothing, cosmetics, personal-care items, magazines, jewelry, and gifts still commonly segment markets by gender. For instance, one Internet retailer, **CoolStuffForDads.com,** targets shoppers with a wide variety of gifts that men would enjoy.[19] Grocers market differently to men shopping alone, who make up about 18 percent of grocery shoppers. A recent study found that compared to women, men place a higher priority on location and convenience, don't like loyalty cards, and often vary from their lists, creating opportunities for grocers to encourage impulse buys.[20]

Income Segmentation Income is a popular demographic variable for segmenting markets because income level influences consumers' wants and determines their buying power. Many markets are segmented by income, including the markets for housing, clothing, automobiles, and food. Wholesale club stores such as Costco and Sam's Club appeal to many income segments. According to a Nielsen study, affluent households (those that earn more than $100,000 annually) are twice as likely to shop warehouse stores compared to households that earn $20,000 or less a year, and the affluent shopper spends an average $46 more than the lower-income shopper per trip.[21] High-income customers looking for luxury want outstanding customer service. For example, fashion companies use computer technology to customize upscale products that are designed specifically for their wealthy customers' needs.[22] Other companies try to appeal to low income customers. Casual Male has launched a big-and-tall brand of men's apparel aimed at the lower-income market. Procter & Gamble has introduced Bounty Basic paper towels and Charmin Basic bath tissue to attract more price-sensitive consumers.[23]

IMAGE COURTESY OF THE ADVERTISING ARCHIVES

Ethnic Segmentation In the past, ethnic groups in the United States were expected to conform to a homogenized, Anglo-centric ideal. This was evident both in the marketing of mass-marketed products and in the selective way that films, television, advertisements, and popular music portrayed America's diverse population. Until the 1970s, ethnic foods were rarely sold except in specialty stores. The racial barrier in entertainment lasted nearly as long, except for supporting movie and TV roles—often based on stereotypes dating back to the nineteenth century.[24] Increasing numbers of ethnic minorities in the United States, along with increased buying power, have changed this. Hispanic Americans, African Americans, and Asian Americans are the three largest ethnic groups in the United States. In 2006, these three groups accounted for 88 million people and, by 2010, are expected to represent about a third of the total U.S. population.[25] Today, companies such as Procter & Gamble, Allstate Insurance, Bank of America, and Reebok have developed multicultural marketing initiatives designed to better understand and serve the wants and preferences of U.S. minority groups. Many consumer goods companies spend 5 to 10 percent of their marketing budgets specifically targeting multicultural consumers; this proportion will likely increase in the future as ethnic groups represent larger and larger percentages of the U.S. population.

The U.S. Census Bureau estimates that the number of Hispanic Americans was 44.3 million in 2006, growing to 47.8 million by 2011. Within this segment exists a variety of nationalities (people come from nearly 24 countries), languages, degrees of acculturation, income, and education levels. The Hispanic segment also is younger than is the total U.S. population.[26] Food retailers should understand not only that Hispanic shoppers like full-flavored products, but also that Mexico has different regional variations in preferences and that menus and tastes also vary among people from Central and South

America.[27] Research shows that one-fourth of Hispanic Americans must be served in Spanish if retailers want their business. After their Spanish-speaking customers told Home Depot they prefer shopping in Spanish even if they are bilingual, the company developed a Spanish-language version of its Web site. It is one of only a few retailers offering the online option in Spanish.[28] Similarly, Amazon introduced the Software en Español Store that offers Spanish-language and bilingual software products.[29] The African American segment now makes up more than 13 percent of the U.S. population, and will continue to grow. Some characteristics of this group: (1) they are twice as likely to trust black media as they are to trust mainstream media; (2) eight in ten households watch black television at least once a week; and (3) overall, 68 percent of African Americans are online, while over 90 percent of African American teens are online.[30]

Companies that have been successful in appealing to groups within this segment include Nissan, Merrill Lynch, and AARP. Nissan found that a sense of inclusion among other ethnic groups was preferable to being singled out, so its ad campaign for the Nissan Altima incorporated people of various ethnic backgrounds. Merrill Lynch & Company sponsors community-based events such as the Lasting Foundations: The Art of Architecture in Africa in New York. A membership benefits campaign for AARP recognized that African Americans are not typically close to retirement at age 50. Thus, the organization focused on immediate benefits, such as volunteer opportunities, grandparenting programs, and discounts on travel and health care.[31] Asians in America represent a segment that has higher than average household incomes and education levels than the general population.[32] This group also makes more online purchases a year than African American and Caucasian consumers. More packaged-goods companies such as Kraft Foods and Procter & Gamble are showing interest in Asian Americans due to the growth of Asian supermarket chains. At the same time, the number of Asian media is growing rapidly. Sovereign Bank in Boston has a branch that is staffed by all Chinese Americans. Their customers are so loyal they come from around the Northeast to do business there. It's not only that the employees speak Cantonese, but also that they have the cultural sensitivity to know, for example, not to insult their customers by talking to them about saving for a vacation when they take care of their parents before they do anything else.[33]

Family Life-Cycle Segmentation The demographic factors of gender, age, and income often do not sufficiently explain why consumer buying behavior varies. Frequently, consumption patterns among people of the same age and gender differ because they are in different stages of the family life cycle. The **family life cycle (FLC)** is a series of stages determined by a combination of age, marital status, and the presence or absence of children.

The life-cycle stage consisting of the married-couple household used to be considered the traditional family in the United States. Today, however, married couples make up just about half of households, down from nearly 80 percent in the 1950s. This means that the 86 million single adults in the United States could soon define the new majority. Already, unmarried Americans make up 42 percent of the workforce, 40 percent of home buyers, and one of the most potent consumer groups on record. Exhibit 8.2 illustrates numerous FLC patterns and shows how families' needs, incomes, resources, and expenditures differ at each stage. The horizontal flow shows the traditional family life cycle. The lower part of the exhibit gives some of the characteristics and purchase patterns of families in each stage of the traditional life cycle. The exhibit also acknowledges that many first marriages end in divorce. When young marrieds move into the young divorced stage, their consumption patterns often revert to those of the young single stage of the cycle. Divorced persons frequently remarry by middle age and reenter the traditional life cycle, as indicated by the "recycled flow" in the exhibit.

Consumers are especially receptive to marketing efforts at certain points in the life cycle. Dating and engaged couples are big spenders. In the two and half years before marriage, many spend over $40,000 on vacations, jewelry, dining, and wedding expenses.[34] NBC Universal and Wal-Mart Stores have struck an advertising sales deal to target the

family life cycle (FLC)
A series of stages determined by a combination of age, marital status, and the presence or absence of children.

EXHIBIT 8.2

Family Life Cycle

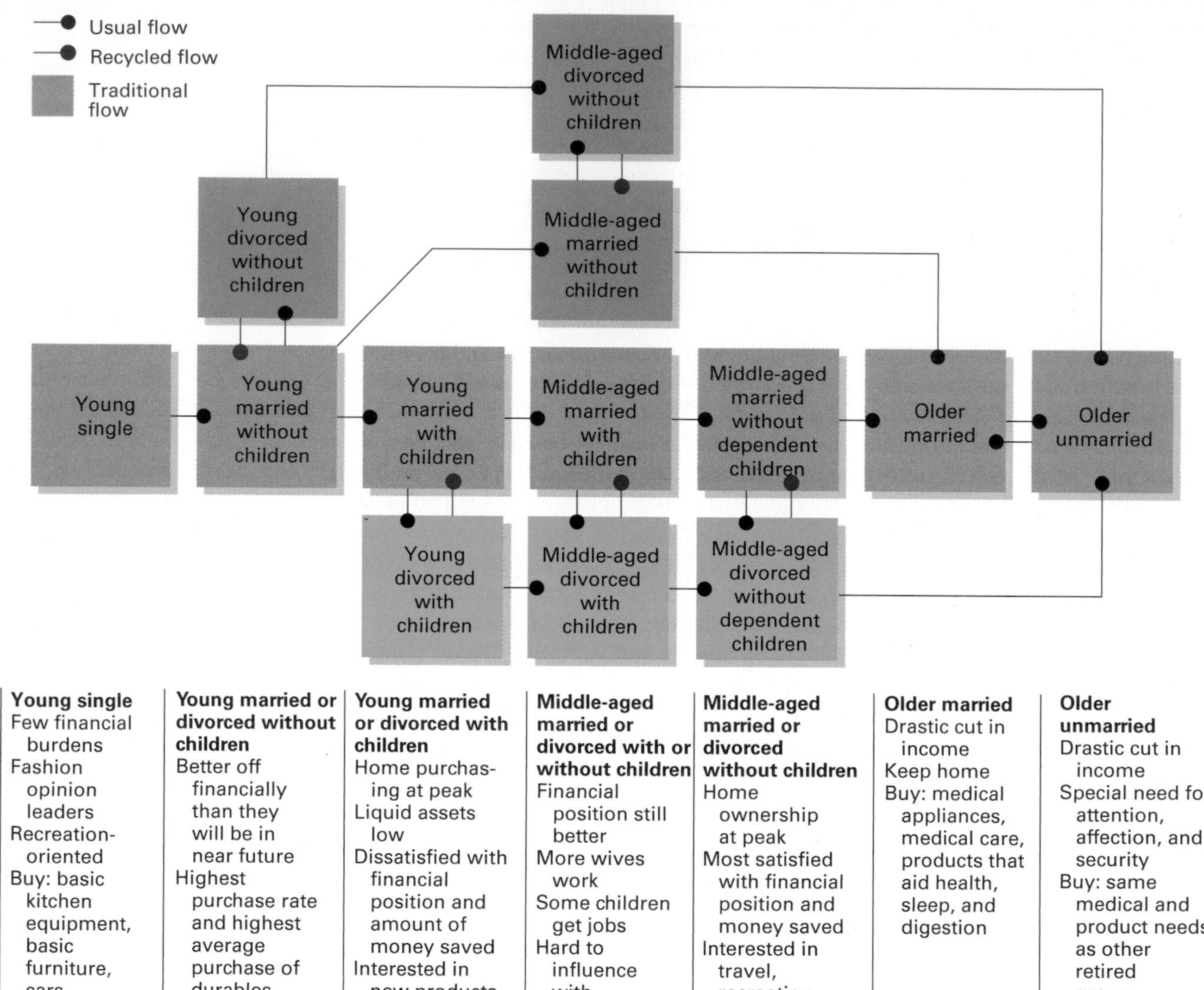

Young single	**Young married or divorced without children**	**Young married or divorced with children**	**Middle-aged married or divorced with or without children**	**Middle-aged married or divorced without children**	**Older married**	**Older unmarried**
Few financial burdens Fashion opinion leaders Recreation-oriented Buy: basic kitchen equipment, basic furniture, cars, equipment for mating game, vacations	Better off financially than they will be in near future Highest purchase rate and highest average purchase of durables Buy: cars, refrigerators, stoves, sensible and durable furniture, vacations	Home purchasing at peak Liquid assets low Dissatisfied with financial position and amount of money saved Interested in new products Like advertised products Buy: washers, dryers, televisions, baby food, chest rubs, cough medicine, vitamins, dolls, wagons, sleds, skates	Financial position still better More wives work Some children get jobs Hard to influence with advertising High average purchase of durables Buy: new and more tasteful furniture, auto travel, unnecessary appliances, boats, dental services, magazines	Home ownership at peak Most satisfied with financial position and money saved Interested in travel, recreation, self-education Make gifts and contributions Not interested in new products Buy: vacations, luxuries, home improvements	Drastic cut in income Keep home Buy: medical appliances, medical care, products that aid health, sleep, and digestion	Drastic cut in income Special need for attention, affection, and security Buy: same medical and product needs as other retired group

"momtourage"—a group of people who help mothers to be better parents, including babysitters, neighbors, teachers, and neighbors. Wal-Mart is sponsoring momtourage material that appears on two NBC outlets: the iVillage Web site and the "*Today*" show. The information featured will focus on subjects like child care and fixing family meals.[35]

Research has found that the overriding factor in describing baby boomer subsegments is the presence of children in the house. The Nielsen study discovered eight specific segments: four segments with children under 18 represented about 40 percent of the boomers, and four segments without children represented 60 percent.[36]

Psychographic Segmentation

Age, gender, income, ethnicity, family life-cycle stage, and other demographic variables are usually helpful in developing segmentation strategies, but often they don't paint the entire picture. Demographics provide the skeleton, but psychographics add meat to the bones. **Psychographic segmentation** is market segmentation on the basis of the following variables:

- *Personality:* Personality reflects a person's traits, attitudes, and habits. According to a national survey by Roper, almost half of Americans believe their cars match their personalities. For example, SUVs deliver the heady feeling of being independent and above it all. Convertibles epitomize wind-in-the-hair freedom, and off-roaders convey outdoor adventure. About 25 percent of people surveyed say that their cars make them feel powerful.[37]
- *Motives:* Marketers of baby products and life insurance appeal to consumers' emotional motives—namely, to care for their loved ones. Using appeals to economy, reliability, and dependability, carmakers like Subaru and Suzuki target customers with rational motives. Carmakers like Mercedes-Benz, Jaguar, and Cadillac appeal to customers with status-related motives.
- *Lifestyles:* Lifestyle segmentation divides people into groups according to the way they spend their time, the importance of the things around them, their beliefs, and socioeconomic characteristics such as income and education. For example, the companies behind the sport Nordic walking are targeting couch potatoes and other nonathletic types. They hope to make the activity appealing to those for whom regular exercise has been a challenge.[38] Pepsi-Cola is promoting its low-calorie, vitamin-enhanced water, Aquafina Alive, to consumers who are health conscious.[39]
- *Geodemographics:* **Geodemographic segmentation** clusters potential customers into neighborhood lifestyle categories. It combines geographic, demographic, and lifestyle segmentations. Geodemographic segmentation helps marketers develop marketing programs tailored to prospective buyers who live in small geographic regions, such as neighborhoods, or who have very specific lifestyle and demographic characteristics. H-E-B Grocery Company, a 304-store, Texas-based supermarket chain, specializes in developing its own branded products designed to meet the needs and tastes of specific communities. In the Rio Grande Valley, where summers are hot and many residents don't have air-conditioning, H-E-B markets its own brand of rubbing oil that helps cool the skin while adding moisturizers. Along the southern border, the grocer stocks *discos,* large metal disks that Mexican Americans use to cook brisket. In Detroit, Home Depot has stores in some neighborhoods that have charcoal barbecue grills, while others offer gas grills.[40]

psychographic segmentation
Market segmentation on the basis of personality, motives, lifestyles, and geodemographics.

geodemographic segmentation
Segmenting potential customers into neighborhood lifestyle categories.

Saks' marketing analysts found that the merchandise at their flagship Saks Fifth Avenue store in New York City doesn't necessarily appeal to Saks customers nationwide. To bolster sales, Saks' marketing analysts use geodemographic research to determine what merchandise will appeal to customers in each of their 54 retail stores, from Birmingham, Alabama, to Bellevue, Washington.

Psychographic variables can be used individually to segment markets or be combined with other variables to provide more detailed descriptions of market segments. One combination approach is the Claritas PRIZM Lifestyle software program that divides Americans into 66 "clusters," or consumer types, all with catchy names. The clusters combine basic demographic data such as age, ethnicity, and income with lifestyle information, such as magazine and sports preferences, taken from consumer surveys. For example,

benefit segmentation The process of grouping customers into market segments according to the benefits they seek from the product.

the "Kids and Cul-de-Sacs" group consists of upscale, married couples with children who live in recently built subdivisions. These families have a median household income of $70,233, tend to own a Honda Odyssey, and are likely to spend large sums of money for child-centered products and services such as video games and Chuck E. Cheese. The "Bohemian Mix" cluster is made up of urbanites under age 35. These young singles, couples, students, and professionals have a median income of $51,100, are early adopters in many product categories, tend to shop at Banana Republic, and are likely to read *Vanity Fair* magazine.[41] The program also predicts to which neighborhoods across the country these clusters are likely to gravitate.

Benefit Segmentation

Benefit segmentation is the process of grouping customers into market segments according to the benefits they seek from the product. Most types of market segmentation are based on the assumption that this variable and customers' needs are related. Benefit segmentation is different because it groups potential customers on the basis of their needs or wants rather than some other characteristic, such as age or gender. The snack-food market, for example, can be divided into six benefit segments, as shown in Exhibit 8.3.

Customer profiles can be developed by examining demographic information associated with people seeking certain benefits. This information can be used to match marketing strategies with selected target markets. The many different types of performance energy bars with various combinations of nutrients are aimed at consumers looking for different benefits. For example, PowerBar is designed for athletes looking for long-lasting fuel, while PowerBar Protein Plus is aimed at those who want extra protein for replenishing muscles after strength training. Carb Solutions High Protein Bars are for those on low-carb diets; Luna Bars are targeted to women who want a bar with fewer calories, soy protein, and calcium; and Clif Bars are for people who want a natural bar with ingredients like rolled oats, soybeans, and organic soy flour. Dannon introduced its Activia probiotic yogurt as a daily health booster by highlighting its benefits for the digestive tract and immune system.

EXHIBIT 8.3

Lifestyle Segmentation of the Snack-Food Market

	Nutritional Snackers	Weight Watchers	Guilty Snackers	Party Snackers	Indiscriminate Snackers	Economical Snackers
% of Snackers	22 %	14 %	9 %	15 %	15 %	18 %
Lifestyle Characteristics	Self-assured, controlled	Outdoorsy, influential, adventuresome	Highly anxious, isolated	Sociable	Hedonistic	Self-assured, price-oriented
Benefits Sought	Nutritious, without artificial ingredients, natural	Low in calories, quick energy	Low in calories, good tasting	Good to serve guests, goes well with beverages	Good tasting, satisfies hunger	Low in price, best value
Consumption Level of Snacks	Light	Light	Heavy	Average	Heavy	Average
Type of Snacks Usually Eaten	Fruits, vegetables, cheese	Yogurt, vegetables	Yogurt, cookies, crackers, candy	Nuts, potato chips, crackers, pretzels	Candy, ice cream, cookies, potato chips, pretzels, popcorn	No specific products
Demographics	Better educated, have young children	Young, single	Younger or older, female, lower socio-economic status	Middle-aged, no urban	Teenager	Have large family, better educated

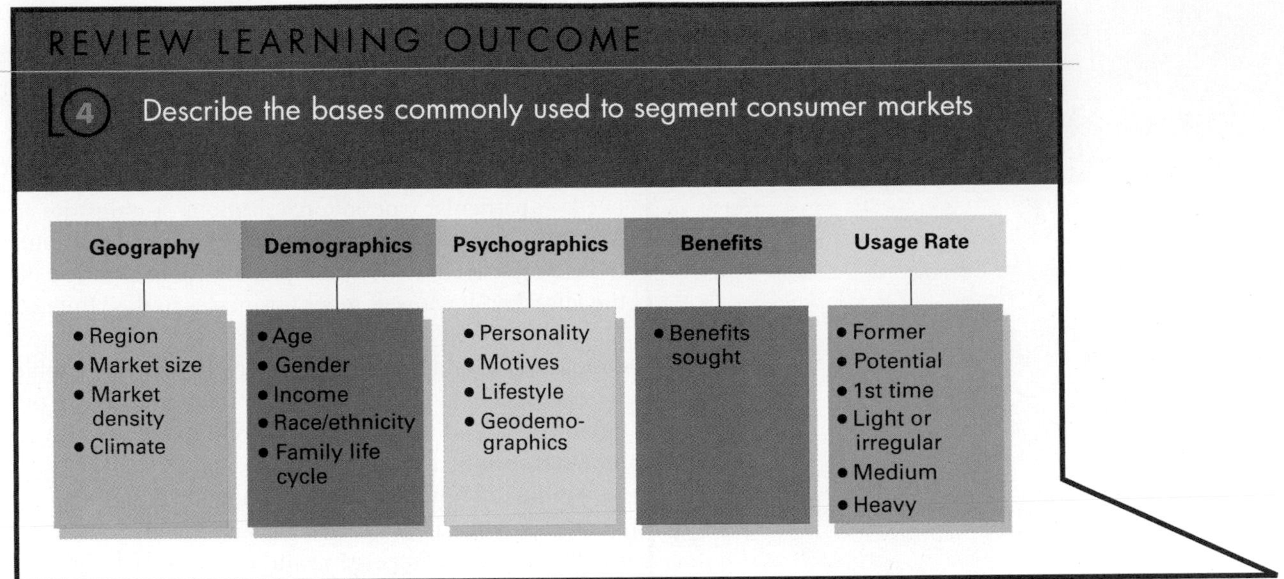

Usage-Rate Segmentation

Usage-rate segmentation divides a market by the amount of product bought or consumed. Categories vary with the product, but they are likely to include some combination of the following: former users, potential users, first-time users, light or irregular users, medium users, and heavy users. Segmenting by usage rate enables marketers to focus their efforts on heavy users or to develop multiple marketing mixes aimed at different segments. Because heavy users often account for a sizable portion of all product sales, some marketers focus on the heavy-user segment.

The **80/20 principle** holds that 20 percent of all customers generate 80 percent of the demand. Although the percentages usually are not exact, the general idea often holds true. For example, in the fast-food industry, the heavy user accounts for only one of five fast-food patrons, but makes about 60 percent of all visits to fast-food restaurants. The needs of heavy users differ from the needs of other usage-rate groups. They have intense needs for product and service selection and a variety of types of information, as well as an emotional attachment to the product category. Individuals in this group spend four to fourteen times as much in their favored product category than do light users.[42]

Developing customers into heavy users is the goal behind many frequency/loyalty programs like the airlines' frequent flyer programs. Many supermarkets and other retailers have also designed loyalty programs that reward the heavy-user segment with deals available only to them, such as in-store coupon dispensing systems, loyalty card programs, and special price deals on selected merchandise.

BASES FOR SEGMENTING BUSINESS MARKETS

The business market consists of four broad segments: producers, resellers, government, and institutions. (For a detailed discussion of the characteristics of these segments, see Chapter 7.) Whether marketers focus on only one or on all four of these segments, they are likely to find diversity among potential customers. Thus, further market segmentation offers just as many benefits to business marketers as it does to consumer-product marketers.

Company Characteristics

Company characteristics, such as geographic location, type of company, company size, and product use, can be important segmentation variables. Some markets tend to be regional because buyers prefer to purchase from local suppliers, and distant suppliers

usage-rate segmentation
Dividing a market by the amount of product bought or consumed.

80/20 principle
A principle holding that 20 percent of all customers generate 80 percent of the demand.

REVIEW LEARNING OUTCOME

LO 5 Describe the bases for segmenting business markets

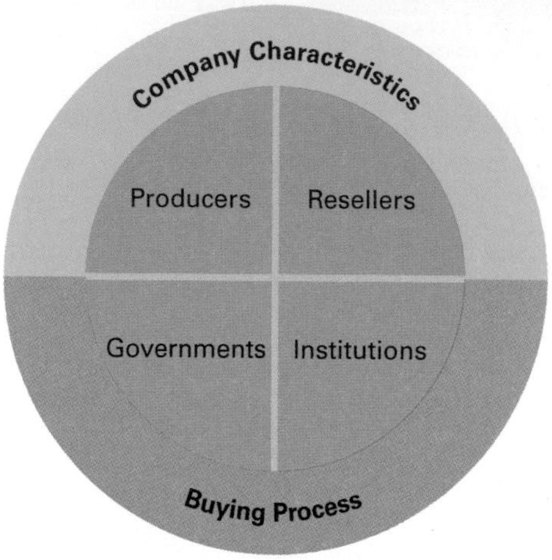

Company Characteristics
Producers
Resellers
Governments
Institutions
Buying Process

may have difficulty competing in terms of price and service. Therefore, firms that sell to geographically concentrated industries benefit by locating close to their markets.

Segmenting by customer type allows business marketers to tailor their marketing mixes to the unique needs of particular types of organizations or industries. Many companies are finding this form of segmentation to be quite effective. For example, Home Depot, one of the largest do-it-yourself retail businesses in the United States, has targeted professional repair and remodeling contractors in addition to consumers. Procter & Gamble is beginning to target business customers by focusing on janitors, fast-food workers, maids, and launderers with products specific to each group's cleaning needs.[43]

Volume of purchase (heavy, moderate, light) is a commonly used basis for business segmentation. Another is the buying organization's size, which may affect its purchasing procedures, the types and quantities of products it needs, and its responses to different marketing mixes. Banks frequently offer different services, lines of credit, and overall attention to commercial customers based on their size.

Many products, especially raw materials like steel, wood, and petroleum, have diverse applications. How customers use a product may influence the amount they buy, their buying criteria, and their selection of vendors. For example, a producer of springs may have customers that use the product in applications as diverse as making machine tools, bicycles, surgical devices, office equipment, telephones, and missile systems.

satisficers
Business customers who place an order with the first familiar supplier to satisfy product and delivery requirements.

optimizers
Business customers who consider numerous suppliers, both familiar and unfamiliar, solicit bids, and study all proposals carefully before selecting one.

Buying Processes

Many business marketers find it helpful to segment customers and prospective customers on the basis of how they buy. For example, companies can segment some business markets by ranking key purchasing criteria, such as price, quality, technical support, and service. Atlas Corporation has developed a commanding position in the industrial door market by providing customized products in just 4 weeks, which is much faster than the industry average of 12 to 15 weeks. Atlas's primary market is companies with an immediate need for customized doors.

The purchasing strategies of buyers may provide useful segments. Two purchasing profiles that have been identified are satisficers and optimizers. **Satisficers** contact familiar suppliers and place the order with the first one to satisfy product and delivery requirements. **Optimizers** consider numerous suppliers (both familiar and unfamiliar), solicit bids, and study all proposals carefully before selecting one.

The personal characteristics of the buyers themselves (their demographic characteristics, decision style, tolerance for risk, confidence level, job responsibilities, etc.) influence their buying behavior and thus offer a viable basis for segmenting some business markets. IBM computer buyers, for example, are sometimes characterized as being more risk averse than buyers of less expensive computers that perform essentially the same functions. In advertising, therefore, IBM stressed its reputation for high quality and reliability.

LO 6

STEPS IN SEGMENTING A MARKET

The purpose of market segmentation, in both consumer and business markets, is to identify marketing opportunities.

1. *Select a market or product category for study:* Define the overall market or product category to be studied. It may be a market in which the firm already competes, a new but related market or product category, or a totally new one. For instance, Anheuser-Busch closely examined the beer market before introducing Michelob Light and Bud Light. Anheuser-Busch also carefully studied the market for salty snacks before introducing the Eagle brand.
2. *Choose a basis or bases for segmenting the market:* This step requires managerial insight, creativity, and market knowledge. There are no scientific procedures for selecting segmentation variables. However, a successful segmentation scheme must produce segments that meet the four basic criteria discussed earlier in this chapter.
3. *Select segmentation descriptors:* After choosing one or more bases, the marketer must select the segmentation descriptors. Descriptors identify the specific segmentation variables to use. For example, if a company selects demographics as a basis of segmentation, it may use age, occupation, and income as descriptors. A company that selects usage segmentation needs to decide whether to go after heavy users, nonusers, or light users.
4. *Profile and analyze segments:* The profile should include the segments' size, expected growth, purchase frequency, current brand usage, brand loyalty, and long-term sales and profit potential. This information can then be used to rank potential market segments by profit opportunity, risk, consistency with organizational mission and objectives, and other factors important to the firm.
5. *Select target markets:* Selecting target markets is not a part of but a natural outcome of the segmentation process. It is a major decision that influences and often directly determines the firm's marketing mix. This topic is examined in greater detail later in this chapter.
6. *Design, implement, and maintain appropriate marketing mixes:* The marketing mix has been described as product, place (distribution), promotion, and pricing strategies intended to bring about mutually satisfying exchange relationships with target markets. Chapter 10 explores these topics in detail.

Markets are dynamic, so it is important that companies proactively monitor their segmentation strategies over time. Often, once customers or prospects have been assigned to a segment, marketers think their task is done. Once customers are assigned to an age segment, for example, they stay there until they reach the next age bracket or category, which could be ten years in the future. Thus, the segmentation classifications are static, but the customers and prospects are changing. Dynamic segmentation approaches adjust to fit the changes that occur in customers' lives. Abercrombie and Fitch, an apparel store that targets teenagers, has opened a new store called Ruehl No. 925 that

REVIEW LEARNING OUTCOME

LO 6 List the steps involved in segmenting markets

1 Select a market or product category for study. → **2** Choose a basis or bases for segmenting the market. → **3** Select segmentation descriptors. → **4** Profile and analyze segments. → **5** Select target markets. → **6** Design, implement, and maintain appropriate marketing mixes.

Note that steps 5 and 6 are actually marketing activities that follow market segmentation (steps 1 through 4).

caters to 20- to 35-year-olds, and Aeropostale owns Jimmy'Z, which stocks clothing for 18- to 25-year-olds that is higher priced than at its flagship stores for teens.

target market
A group of people or organizations for which an organization designs, implements, and maintains a marketing mix intended to meet the needs of that group, resulting in mutually satisfying exchanges.

undifferentiated targeting strategy
A marketing approach that views the market as one big market with no individual segments and thus uses a single marketing mix.

STRATEGIES FOR SELECTING TARGET MARKETS

So far this chapter has focused on the market segmentation process, which is only the first step in deciding whom to approach about buying a product. The next task is to choose one or more target markets. A **target market** is a group of people or organizations for which an organization designs, implements, and maintains a marketing mix intended to meet the needs of that group, resulting in mutually satisfying exchanges. Because most markets will include customers with different characteristics, lifestyles, backgrounds, and income levels, it is unlikely that a single marketing mix will attract all segments of the market. Thus, if a marketer wishes to appeal to more than one segment of the market, it must develop different marketing mixes. For example, Buick targets people in their 60s with the Lucerne sedan, a luxury car with a V8 engine and extras like OnStar service. The company also targets younger, Generation Y customers with the Enclave, a crossover SUV. The three general strategies for selecting target markets—undifferentiated, concentrated, and multisegment targeting—are illustrated in Exhibit 8.4. Exhibit 8.5 illustrates the advantages and disadvantages of each targeting strategy.

Undifferentiated Targeting

A firm using an **undifferentiated targeting strategy** essentially adopts a mass-market philosophy, viewing the market as one big market with no individual segments. The firm uses one marketing mix for the entire market. A firm that adopts an undifferentiated targeting strategy assumes that individual customers have similar needs that can be met with a common marketing mix.

The first firm in an industry sometimes uses an undifferentiated targeting strategy. With no competition, the firm may not need to tailor marketing mixes to the preferences of market segments. Henry Ford's famous comment about the Model T is a classic example of an undifferentiated targeting strategy: "They can have their car in any color they want, as long as it's black." At one time, Coca-Cola used this strategy with a single product and a single size of its familiar green bottle. Marketers of commodity products, such as flour and sugar, are also likely to use an undifferentiated targeting strategy.

EXHIBIT 8.4

Three Strategies for Selecting Target Markets

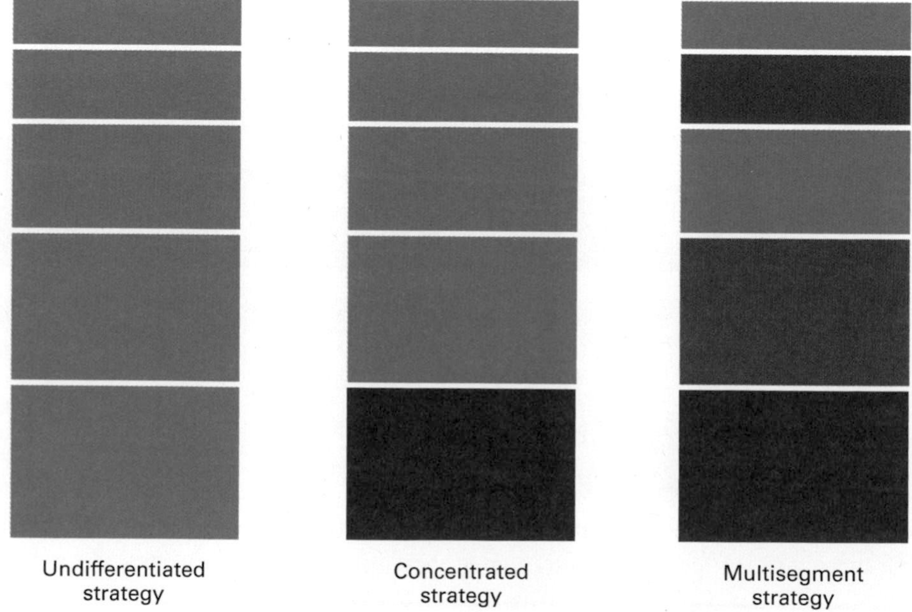

EXHIBIT 8.5

Advantages and Disadvantages of Target Marketing Strategies

Targeting Strategy	Advantages	Disadvantages
Undifferentiated Targeting	• Potential savings on production/marketing costs • Company more susceptible to competition	• Unimaginative product offerings
Concentrated Targeting	• Concentration of resources • Can better meet the needs of a narrowly defined segment • Allows some small firms to better compete with larger firms • Strong positioning	• Segments too small, or changing • Large competitors may more effectively market to niche segment
Multisegment Targeting	• Greater financial success • Economies of scale in producing/marketing	• High costs • Cannibalization

One advantage of undifferentiated marketing is the potential for saving on production and marketing. Because only one item is produced, the firm should be able to achieve economies of mass production. Also, marketing costs may be lower when there is only one product to promote and a single channel of distribution. Too often, however, an undifferentiated strategy emerges by default rather than by design, reflecting a failure to consider the advantages of a segmented approach. The result is often sterile, unimaginative product offerings that have little appeal to anyone.

Another problem associated with undifferentiated targeting is that it makes the company more susceptible to competitive inroads. Hershey lost a big share of the candy market to Mars and other candy companies before it changed to a multisegment targeting strategy. Coca-Cola forfeited its position as the leading seller of cola drinks in supermarkets to Pepsi-Cola in the late 1950s when Pepsi began offering several sizes of containers.

You might think a firm producing a standard product like toilet tissue would adopt an undifferentiated strategy. However, this market has industrial segments and consumer segments. Industrial buyers want an economical, single-ply product sold in boxes of a hundred rolls. The consumer market demands a more versatile product in smaller quantities. Within the consumer market, the product is differentiated with designer print or no print, cushioned or noncushioned, and economy priced or luxury priced. Fort Howard Corporation, the market share leader in industrial toilet paper, does not even sell to the consumer market.

Undifferentiated marketing can succeed in certain situations, though. A small grocery store in a small, isolated town may define all of the people that live in the town as its target market. It may offer one marketing mix and generally satisfy everyone in town. This strategy is not likely to be as effective if there are three or four grocery stores in the town.

Concentrated Targeting

With a **concentrated targeting strategy**, a firm selects a market **niche** (one segment of a market) for targeting its marketing efforts. Because the firm is appealing to a single segment, it can concentrate on understanding the needs, motives, and satisfactions of that segment's members and on developing and maintaining a highly specialized marketing mix. Some firms find that concentrating resources and meeting the needs of a narrowly defined market segment is more profitable than spreading resources over several different segments.

For example, Starbucks became successful by focusing on consumers who want gourmet coffee products. America Online (AOL) became one of the world's leading Internet providers by targeting Internet newcomers. By making the Internet interface easy to use, AOL was able to attract millions of people who otherwise might not have subscribed to an online service. Watchmakers Patek Philippe, Rolex, and Breguet, which sell watches priced at $200,000 or more, are definitely pursuing a concentrated targeting strategy. AARP pursues a concentrated strategy if you consider people over 50 years old to be a single market segment of the overall population.

concentrated targeting strategy
A strategy used to select one segment of a market for targeting marketing efforts.

niche
One segment of a market.

multisegment targeting strategy
A strategy that chooses two or more well-defined market segments and develops a distinct marketing mix for each.

Small firms often adopt a concentrated targeting strategy to compete effectively with much larger firms. For example, Enterprise Rent-A-Car rose to number one in the car rental industry by catering to people with cars in the shop. It has now expanded into the airport rental market. Celebrity pots and pans are a growing niche market. They now represent 10 percent of the $2 billion U.S. cookware market—an increase of 7 percent in the past decade.[44] Charming Shoppes Inc. competes with other clothing sellers by appealing to plus-size teens; it sells designer labels in sizes 14 through 32.[45] Some firms, on the other hand, use a concentrated strategy to establish a strong position in a desirable market segment. Porsche, for instance, targets an upscale automobile market through "class appeal, not mass appeal."

Concentrated targeting violates the adage, "Don't put all your eggs in one basket." If the chosen segment is too small or if it shrinks because of environmental changes, the firm may suffer negative consequences. For instance, OshKosh B'Gosh, Inc., was highly successful selling children's wear in the 1980s. It was so successful, however, that the children's line came to define OshKosh's image to the extent that the company could not sell clothes to anyone else. Attempts at marketing older children's clothing, women's casual clothes, and maternity wear were all abandoned. Recognizing it was in the children's wear business, the company expanded into products such as kids' shoes, children's eyewear, and plush toys.

A concentrated strategy can also be disastrous for a firm that is not successful in its narrowly defined target market. Before Procter & Gamble introduced Head and Shoulders shampoo, several small firms were already selling antidandruff shampoos. Head and Shoulders was introduced with a large promotional campaign, and the new brand captured over half the market immediately. Within a year, several of the firms

CUSTOMER Experience

Trader Joe's Adventure[46]

In the 1960s, Trader Joe's was a small convenience store chain called "Pronto Markets" in the Los Angeles area trying to compete with 7-Eleven. It succeeded by offering customers a unique food and beverage buying experience. The stores are decked out with cedar plank walls and nautical décor. The Captain (store manager), the First Mate (assistant store manager) and the Crew Members (employees) wear colorful Hawaiian shirts. The name Trader Joe's was chosen by the original owner because the name belonged to a trader/adventurer he had read about.

Using a niche targeting strategy, the company offers wine and stocks a limited assortment of inexpensive (mostly private label) gourmet food products in smaller stores. A trip to Trader Joe's is an adventure, and the retailer is a brand with a cultlike following. Today, Trader Joe's uses this same strategy to compete with industry giants like Wal-Mart. The company now has 250 stores in 20 states, and is still growing.

Trader Joe's mission is to bring its customers the best food and beverage values and the information to make informed purchase decisions. It carries more than 2,000 unique grocery items (compared to the approximately 30,000 items a typical supermarket carries) under its house label, and offer its products at everyday low prices. The retailer has a tasting panel that tries every product before it buys the product, and if customers don't like something, they can return it for a no-hassle refund.

Another quality aspect of the Trader Joe's experience is its superior customer service. Its Crew Members are friendly, knowledgeable, and happy to see customers. Its stores regularly cook new and interesting products for their customers to try. If a customer asks an employee about a product, he or she will find the product and join the customer in a taste test. A popular radio ad for the company features its CEO making fun of other supermarkets that have put in flat-screen TVs for customers to watch at checkout counters. At Trader Joe's, he says, customers can entertain themselves by actually talking to employees.

Would you enjoy the Trader Joe's experience? Explain your answer. Can you think of other retail formats that could use a similar niche targeting strategy to develop a unique shopping experience compared to competitors?

that had been concentrating on this market segment went out of business.

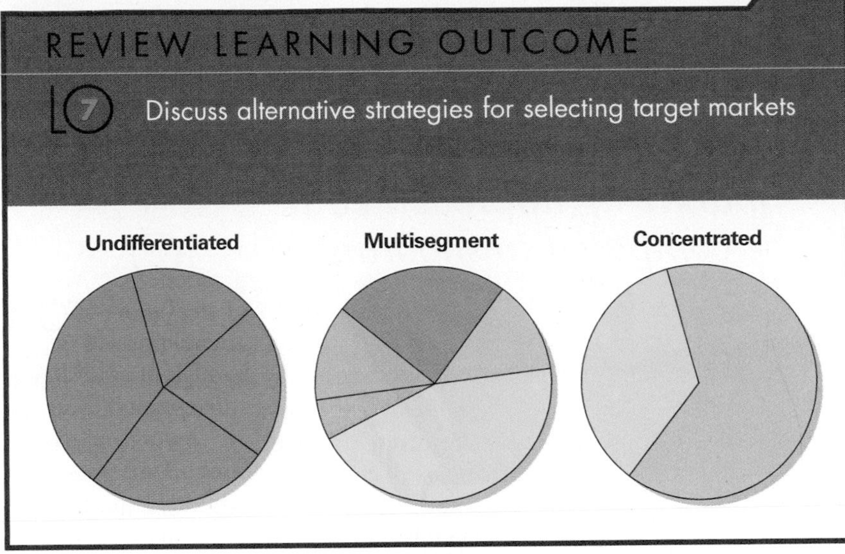

Multisegment Targeting

A firm that chooses to serve two or more well-defined market segments and develops a distinct marketing mix for each has a **multisegment targeting strategy**. Many universities offer full-time (day) MBA programs, professional (evening) programs, and executive (weekend) programs, each targeted at a distinctly different market segment. Many programs are targeting mothers returning to the workplace. Cosmetics companies seek to increase sales and market share by targeting multiple age and ethnic groups. Maybelline and CoverGirl, for example, market different lines to teenage women, young adult women, older women, and African American women. CitiCard offers its Upromise Card to those who want to earn money to save for college, its Platinum Select Card to those who want no annual fee and a competitive interest rate, its Diamond Preferred Rewards Card to customers who want to earn free rewards like travel and brand-name merchandise, and its Citi AAdvantage Card to those who want to earn American Airlines Advantage frequent-flyer miles to redeem for travel. Many credit-card companies even have programs specifically designed for tweens, teens, and college students. Wal-Mart has historically followed a concentrated strategy that targeted lower income segments. Recently, however, the company has segmented its customers into three core groups based on the type of value they seek at the stores. "Brand Aspirationals" are low income customers who like to buy brand names like KitchenAid, "Price-Sensitive Affluents" are wealthier shoppers who love deals, and "Value-Price Shoppers" who like low prices and can't afford much more.[47]

Sometimes organizations use different promotional appeals, rather than completely different marketing mixes, as the basis for a multisegment strategy. Beer marketers such as Adolph Coors and Anheuser-Busch advertise and promote special events targeted toward African American, Hispanic American, and Asian American market segments. The beverages and containers, however, do not differ by ethnic market segment.

Brands with a multisegment targeting approach develop marketing mixes for more than one distinct market segment. In this advertisement, Ralph Lauren displays the versatility of its brand by pointing out that it makes clothing for children as well as for teenagers and young adults.

IMAGE COURTESY OF THE ADVERTISING ARCHIVES

Gap, Inc., takes a different approach. It uses family and individual branding for its alternative format outlets that target different market segments. Stores operating under the family brand include Gap, Gapkids, babyGap, GapBody, and Gap Outlet. Individual brands other than Gap include Banana Republic and Old Navy. Multisegment targeting offers many potential benefits to firms, including greater sales volume, higher profits, larger market share, and economies of scale in manufacturing and marketing. Yet it may also involve greater product design, production, promotion, inventory, marketing research, and management costs. Before deciding to use this strategy, firms should compare the benefits and costs of multisegment targeting to those of undifferentiated and concentrated targeting.

Another potential cost of multisegment targeting is **cannibalization**, which occurs when sales of a new product cut into sales of a firm's existing products.

cannibalization
A situation that occurs when sales of a new product cut into sales of a firm's existing products.

> "The difference between one-to-one marketing and the traditional mass-marketing approach can be compared to shooting a rifle and a shotgun."

In many cases, however, companies prefer to steal sales from their own brands rather than lose sales to a competitor. Also, in today's fast-paced world of Internet business, some companies are willing to cannibalize existing business to build new business.

LO 8 ONE-TO-ONE MARKETING

one-to-one marketing
An individualized marketing method that utilizes customer information to build long-term, personalized, and profitable relationships with each customer.

Most businesses today use a mass-marketing approach designed to increase *market share* by selling their products to the greatest number of people. For many businesses, however, it is more efficient and profitable to use one-to-one marketing to increase *share of customer*—in other words, to sell more products to each customer. **One-to-one marketing** is an individualized marketing method that utilizes customer information to build long-term, personalized, and profitable relationships with each customer. The goal is to reduce costs through customer retention and increase revenue through customer loyalty. For example, Tesco, the British supermarket chain, sends out a mailing each quarter to 11 million households—but it produces 4 million different versions, tailored to the interests of its diverse customer base.

The difference between one-to-one marketing and the traditional mass-marketing approach can be compared to shooting a rifle and a shotgun. If you have good aim, a rifle is the more efficient weapon to use. A shotgun, on the other hand, increases your odds of hitting the target when it is more difficult to focus. Instead of scattering messages far and wide across the spectrum of mass media (the shotgun approach), one-to-one marketers look for opportunities to communicate with each individual customer (the rifle approach).

Teen retailer Karmaloop developed a system on their Web site that allows customers to preselect by brand or clothing category what types of merchandise they wanted to get e-mails about.[48] Lands' End also engages in one-to-one marketing by custom designing clothing. On Lands' End's Web site, customers provide information by answering a series of questions that takes about 20 minutes. Customer sizing information is saved, and reordering is simple. Customers who customize have been found to be more loyal.

Several factors suggest that personalized communications and product customization will continue to expand as more companies understand why and how

Carl's Jr. and Hardee's Web sites feature a 3-D bachelor-pad living room, a live-action video roommate, and a loyalty program which rewards their customers for purchasing food and for interacting with the Web site.

their customers make and execute purchase decisions. At least four trends will lead to the continuing growth of one-to-one marketing.

First, the one-size-fits-all marketing is no longer relevant. Consumers want to be treated as the individuals they are, with their own unique sets of needs and wants. By its personalized nature, one-to-one marketing can fulfill this desire.

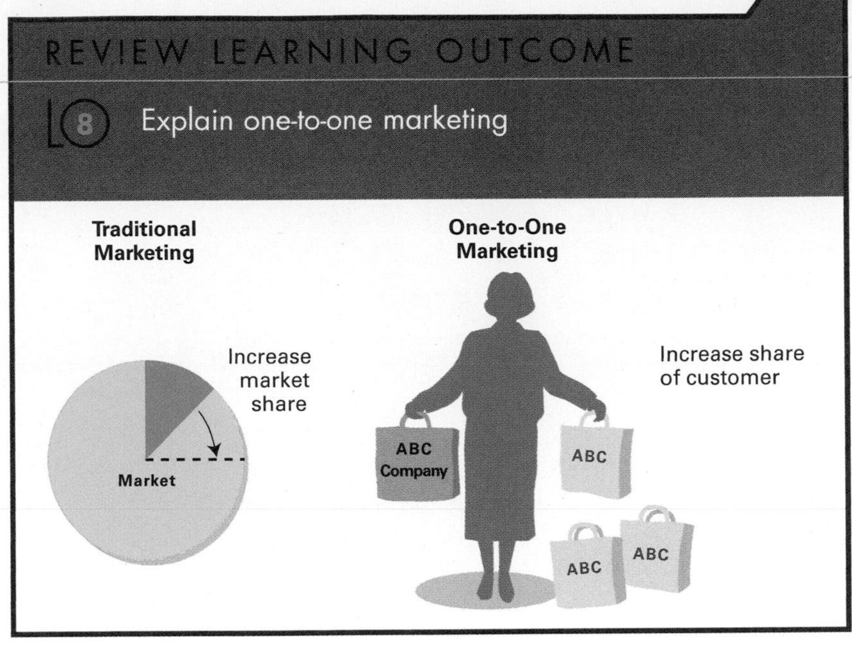

Second, direct and personal marketing efforts will continue to grow to meet the needs of consumers who no longer have the time to spend shopping and making purchase decisions. With the personal and targeted nature of one-to-one marketing, consumers can spend less time making purchase decisions and more time doing the things that are important.

Third, consumers will be loyal only to those companies and brands that have earned their loyalty and reinforced it at every purchase occasion. One-to-one marketing techniques focus on finding a firm's best customers, rewarding them for their loyalty, and thanking them for their business.

Fourth, mass-media approaches will decline in importance as advances in market research and database technology allow marketers to collect detailed information on their customers. New technology offers one-to-one marketers a more cost-effective way to reach customers and enables businesses to personalize their messages. For example, **MyYahoo.com** greets each user by name and offers information in which the user has expressed interest. Similarly, **RedEnvelope.com** helps customers keep track of special occasions and offers personalized gift recommendations. With the help of database technology, one-to-one marketers can track their customers as individuals, even if they number in the millions.

One-to-one marketing is a huge commitment and often requires a 180-degree turnaround for marketers who spent the last half of the twentieth century developing and implementing mass-marketing efforts. Although mass marketing will probably continue to be used, especially to create brand awareness or to remind consumers of a product, the advantages of one-to-one marketing cannot be ignored.

POSITIONING

The development of any marketing mix depends on **positioning**, a process that influences potential customers' overall perception of a brand, product line, or organization in general. **Position** is the place a product, brand, or group of products occupies in consumers' minds relative to competing offerings. Consumer goods marketers are particularly concerned with positioning. Procter & Gamble, for example, markets 11 different laundry detergents, each with a unique position, as illustrated in Exhibit 8.6.

Positioning assumes that consumers compare products on the basis of important features. Marketing efforts that emphasize irrelevant features are therefore likely to misfire. For example, Crystal Pepsi and a clear version of Coca-Cola's Tab failed because consumers perceived the "clear" positioning as more of a marketing gimmick than a benefit.

Effective positioning requires assessing the positions occupied by competing products, determining the important dimensions underlying these positions, and choosing a position in the market where the organization's marketing efforts will have the greatest

positioning
Developing a specific marketing mix to influence potential customers' overall perception of a brand, product line, or organization in general.

position
The place a product, brand, or group of products occupies in consumers' minds relative to competing offerings.

EXHIBIT 8.6

Positioning of Procter & Gamble Detergents

Brand	Positioning	Market Share
Tide	Tough, powerful cleaning	31.1 percent
Cheer	Tough cleaning and color protection	8.2 percent
Bold	Detergent plus fabric softener	2.9 percent
Gain	Sunshine scent and odor-removing formula	2.6 percent
Era	Stain treatment and stain removal	2.2 percent
Dash	Value brand	1.8 percent
Oxide	Bleach-boosted formula, whitening	1.4 percent
Solo	Detergent and fabric softener in liquid form	1.2 percent
Dreft	Outstanding cleaning for baby clothes, safe for tender skin	1.0 percent
Ivory Snow	Fabric and skin safety on baby clothes and fine washables	0.7 percent
Ariel	Tough cleaner, aimed at Hispanic market	0.1 percent

impact. For example, AT&T's wireless company has positioned itself as mobility-centric, offering seamless mobility for customers whose lifestyles are not tied to one place.[49] Callaway Golf positions its new line of clubs and balls as innovative and technologically superior, using the tagline "A better game by design."[50] As the previous examples illustrate, **product differentiation** is a positioning strategy that many firms use to distinguish their products from those of competitors. The distinctions can be either real or perceived. Tandem Computers designed machines with two central processing units and two memories for computer systems that can never afford to be down or lose their databases (for example, an airline reservation system). In this case, Tandem used product differentiation to create a product with very real advantages for the target market. However, many everyday products, such as bleaches, aspirin, unleaded regular gasoline, and some soaps, are differentiated by such trivial means as brand names, packaging, color, smell, or "secret" additives. The marketer attempts to convince consumers that a particular brand is distinctive and that they should demand it over competing brands.

product differentiation
A positioning strategy that some firms use to distinguish their products from those of competitors.

repositioning
Changing consumers' perceptions of a brand in relation to competing brands.

Some firms, instead of using product differentiation, position their products as being similar to competing products or brands. Two examples of this positioning include artificial sweeteners advertised as tasting like sugar or margarine tasting like butter.

EXHIBIT 8.7

Perceptual Map and Positioning Strategy for Saks Department Stores

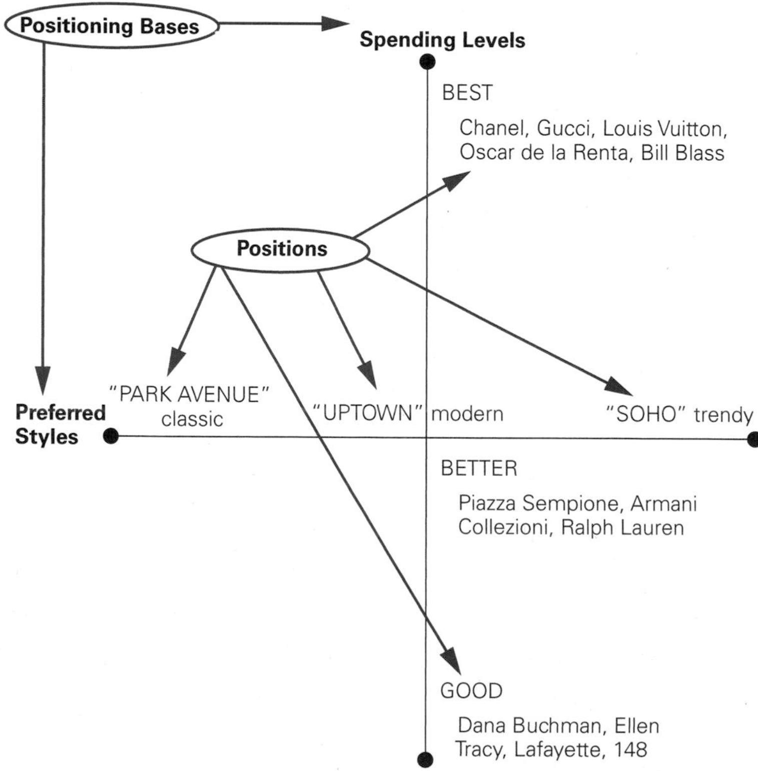

Source: Based on Vanessa O'Connell, "Park Avenue Classic or Soho Trendy?" *The Wall Street Journal*, April 20, 2007, B1.

Perceptual Mapping

Perceptual mapping is a means of displaying or graphing, in two or more dimensions, the location of products, brands, or groups of products in customers' minds. For example, Saks Inc., the tony department store chain, stumbled in sales when it tried to attract a younger core customer. To recover, Saks invested in research to determine its core customers in its 54 stores across the country. The perceptual map in Exhibit 8.7 shows how Saks Inc. uses customer demographics, such as a matrix that charts the best mix of clothes and accessories to stock in each store.

Positioning Bases

Firms use a variety of bases for positioning, including the following:

- *Attribute:* A product is associated with an attribute, product feature, or customer benefit. Kleenex has designed a tissue that contains substances to kill germs in an effort to differentiate its product from competing tissues.[51]

- *Price and quality:* This positioning base may stress high price as a signal of quality or emphasize low price as an indication of value. Neiman Marcus uses the high-price strategy; Wal-Mart has successfully followed the low-price and value strategies. The mass merchandiser Target has developed an interesting position based on price and quality. It is an "upscale discounter," sticking to low prices but offering higher quality and design than most discount chains.
- *Use or application:* Stressing uses or applications can be an effective means of positioning a product with buyers. Kahlúa liqueur used advertising to point out 228 ways to consume the product. Snapple introduced a new drink called "Snapple a Day" that is intended for use as a meal replacement.
- *Product user:* This positioning base focuses on a personality or type of user. Zale Corporation has several jewelry store concepts, each positioned to a different user. The Zales stores cater to middle-of-the-road consumers with traditional styles. Its Gordon's stores appeal to a slightly older clientele with a contemporary look. Guild is positioned for the more affluent 50-plus consumer.
- *Product class:* The objective here is to position the product as being associated with a particular category of products; for example, positioning a margarine brand with butter. Alternatively, products can be disassociated with a category. Del Monte introduced Fruit Chillers, a shelf-stable sorbet that consumers freeze themselves when they're ready to eat it. Fruit Chillers are sold next to single-serve fruit cups, positioned as fruit rather than as a frozen dessert.[52]
- *Competitor:* Positioning against competitors is part of any positioning strategy. The original Hertz rental car positioning as number two compared to Enterprise exemplifies positioning against specific competitors.
- *Emotion:* Positioning using emotion focuses on how the product makes customers feel. A number of companies use this approach. For example, Nike's "Just Do It" campaign didn't tell consumers what "it" was, but most got the emotional message of achievement and courage. Budweiser's advertising featuring talking frogs and lizards emphasized fun. Sears is drawing on the nostalgia of its brand name by remodeling a store outside Atlanta to resemble its stores of the past. The focus is on tapping into Sears' heritage and its legacy as America's store.[53]

Repositioning

Sometimes products or companies are repositioned in order to sustain growth in slow markets or to correct positioning mistakes. **Repositioning** is changing consumers' perceptions of a brand in relation to competing brands. For example, Procter & Gamble increased its baby-care business in the early 2000s when they changed Pampers' position from being about dryness to being about helping Mom with her baby's development. P&G also repositioned Olay from being a pink liquid that moisturizes to helping women look better and feel better as they age.[54] An entire industry of firms that need to think about repositioning is the supermarket industry. For over a decade, Wal-Mart has been expanding in both rural and metro areas. The result has generally been devastating to competitors, especially independent grocers. Consulting firm Retail Forward predicts that two supermarkets will go out of business for every Wal-Mart Supercenter that opens in the United States. The Strategic Resource Group adds that 27 leading national and regional supermarket operators have either gone bankrupt or have liquidated since Wal-Mart went national with Supercenters.[55] So what are competitors to do? Wal-Mart owns the low price position. Successful competitors will have to establish viable alternative positions.

H-E-B stores in Hispanic areas in Texas are tailoring their product mix to appeal to this market segment. H-E-B has also opened Asian wet markets in some stores. Its Central Market format is definitely upscale with unique products and very high-quality perishables. Research shows that over half of all families with incomes between $50,000 and $100,000 are willing to pay more for high-quality items in a more pleasant shopping environment.[56] Safeway is trying to avoid Wal-Mart by repositioning itself as upscale with about half its stores converted to "Lifestyle" markets with wood floors, on-site bakeries, and high-end private label brands.[57]

perceptual mapping
A means of displaying or graphing, in two or more dimensions, the location of products, brands, or groups of products in customers' minds.

It is too early to tell which, if any, of these repositioning strategies will be successful. Clearly, though, competing head-on with Wal-Mart is not a good idea.

REVIEW LEARNING OUTCOME

LO 9 Explain how and why firms implement positioning strategies and how product differentiation plays a role

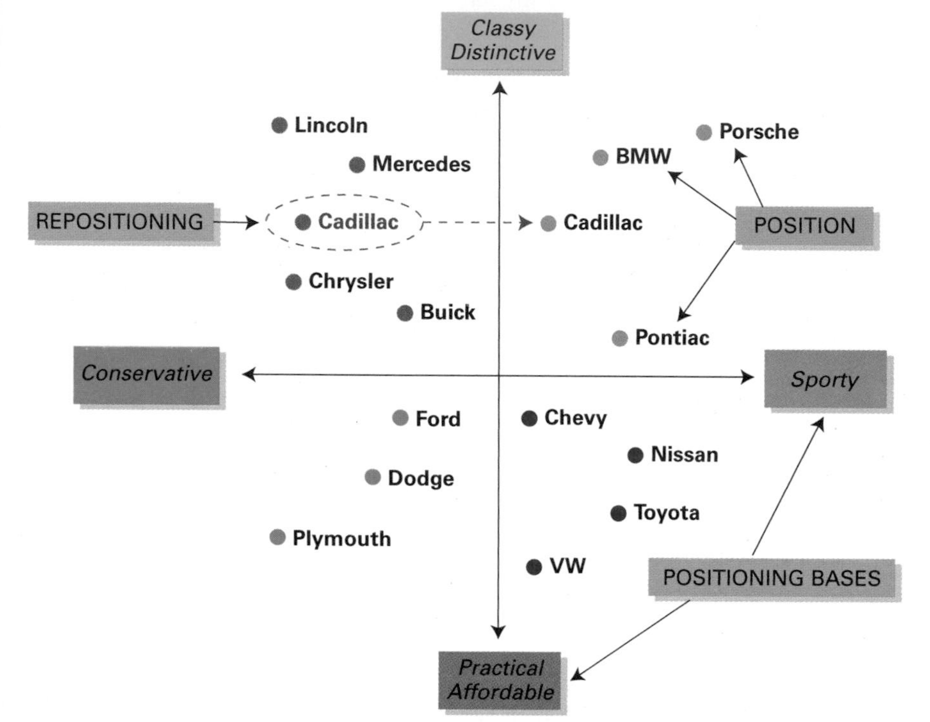

$15 billion ◄ amount marketers spend yearly advertising to young children

45 ◄ percentage of consumers who say they are uncomfortable with behavioral targeting

$2.1 trillion ◄ spent by baby boomers each year

► **75** percentage of family finances handled by women

80 ◄ percentage of consumer purchases made or influenced by women

single adults living in the U.S. ► **86 billion**

25 ◄ percentage of people who say cars make them feel powerful

$200,000 ◄ starting price of a Breguet watch

40 ◄ percentage of home purchases made by unmarried Americans

11 ◄ laundry detergents marketed by Procter & Gamble

REVIEW AND APPLICATIONS

Describe the characteristics of markets and market segments. A market is composed of individuals or organizations with the ability and willingness to make purchases to fulfill their needs or wants. A market segment is a group of individuals or organizations with similar product needs as a result of one or more common characteristics.

1.1 Mercedes-Benz is thinking about advertising its cars to college students. Do you think that college students are a viable potential market for Mercedes? Why or why not?

1.2 Go to the Web site **www.careermag.com.** How are visitors to the site segmented when seeking relevant job openings? Report your results.

Explain the importance of market segmentation. Before the 1960s, few businesses targeted specific market segments. Today, segmentation is a crucial marketing strategy for nearly all successful organizations. Market segmentation enables marketers to tailor marketing mixes to meet the needs of particular population segments. Segmentation helps marketers identify consumer needs and preferences, areas of declining demand, and new marketing opportunities.

2.1 Describe market segmentation in terms of the historical evolution of marketing.

Discuss criteria for successful market segmentation. Successful market segmentation depends on four basic criteria: (1) a market segment must be substantial and have enough potential customers to be viable, (2) a market segment must be identifiable and measurable, (3) members of a market segment must be accessible to marketing efforts, and (4) a market segment must respond to particular marketing efforts in a way that distinguishes it from other segments.

3.1 As a marketing consultant for a chain of hair salons, you have been asked to evaluate the kids' market as a potential segment for the chain to target. Write a memo to your client discussing your evaluation of the kids' segment in terms of the four criteria for successful market segmentation.

Describe the bases commonly used to segment consumer markets. Five bases are commonly used for segmenting consumer markets. Geographic segmentation is based on region, size, density, and climate characteristics. Demographic segmentation is based on age, gender, income level, ethnicity, and family life-cycle characteristics. Psychographic segmentation includes personality, motives, and lifestyle characteristics. Benefits sought is a type of segmentation that identifies customers according to the benefits they seek in a product. Finally, usage segmentation divides a market by the amount of product purchased or consumed.

4.1 Choose magazine ads for five different consumer products. For each ad, write a description of what you think the demographic characteristics of the targeted market are.

4.2 Investigate how Delta Air Lines (**www.delta.com**) uses its Web site to cater to its market segments.

4.3 Is it possible to identify a single market for two distinctly different products? For example, how substantial is the market composed of consumers who use Apple *and* who drive Volkswagens? Can you think of other product combinations that would interest a single market? (Do not use products that are complementary, like a bike and a bike helmet. Think of products, like the iPod and the car, that are very different.) Complete the following sentences and describe the market for each set of products you pair together.

Consumers of:

Propel fitness water could also be a target market for ___________.

Proactiv Solution skin care products could also be a target market for ___________.

Alienware computers could also be a target market for ___________.

Specialty luggage tags could also be a target market for ___________.

LO5 Describe the bases for segmenting business markets. Business markets can be segmented on two general bases: First, businesses segment markets based on company characteristics, such as customers' geographic location, type of company, company size, and product use. Second, companies may segment customers based on the buying processes those customers use.

WRITING

5.1 Choose five ads from business publications such as *The Wall Street Journal*, *Fortune*, and *BusinessWeek*. For each ad, write a description of how you think the company has segmented its business market.

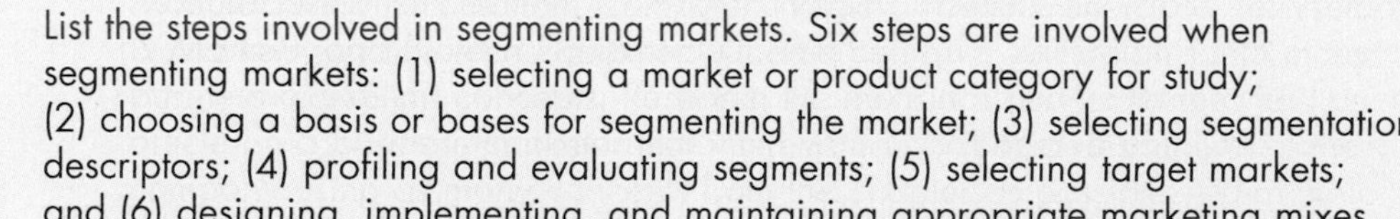

LO6 List the steps involved in segmenting markets. Six steps are involved when segmenting markets: (1) selecting a market or product category for study; (2) choosing a basis or bases for segmenting the market; (3) selecting segmentation descriptors; (4) profiling and evaluating segments; (5) selecting target markets; and (6) designing, implementing, and maintaining appropriate marketing mixes.

WRITING

6.1 Write a letter to the president of your bank suggesting ideas for increasing profits and enhancing customer service by improving segmentation and targeting strategies.

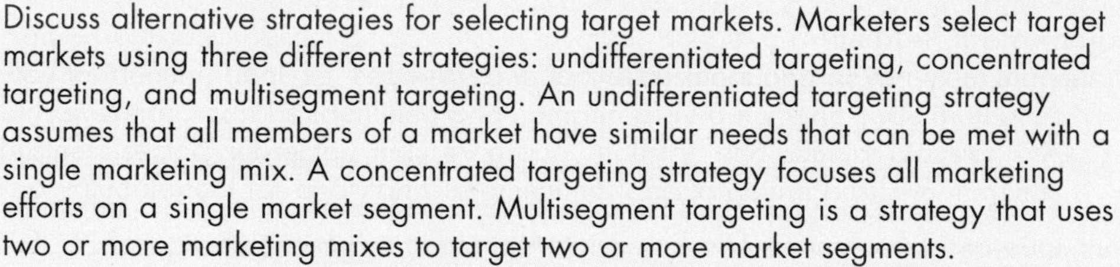

LO7 Discuss alternative strategies for selecting target markets. Marketers select target markets using three different strategies: undifferentiated targeting, concentrated targeting, and multisegment targeting. An undifferentiated targeting strategy assumes that all members of a market have similar needs that can be met with a single marketing mix. A concentrated targeting strategy focuses all marketing efforts on a single market segment. Multisegment targeting is a strategy that uses two or more marketing mixes to target two or more market segments.

7.1 Form a team with two or three other students. Create an idea for a new product. Describe the segment (or segments) you are going to target with the product and explain why you chose the targeting strategy you did.

7.2 Go to the Web sites of JCPenney, **www.jcpenney.com,** and Target, **www.target.com.** Compare the presentation of women's fashions at the Web sites. What are the major differences? Which site is more designer focused, and which is more brand focused? Which company's approach do you think will appeal more to the "Holy Grail" target market of 25- to 35-year-old women?

LO8 Explain one-to-one marketing. One-to-one marketing is an individualized marketing method that utilizes customer information to build long-term, personalized, and profitable relationships with each customer. Successful one-to-one marketing comes from understanding customers and collaborating with them rather than using them as targets for generic messages. Database technology makes it possible for companies to interact with customers on a personal, one-to-one basis.

8.1 You are the marketing manager for a specialty retailer that sells customized handbags. Write a memo to your boss describing how the company could benefit from one-to-one marketing.

LO9 Explain how and why firms implement positioning strategies and how product differentiation plays a role. Positioning is used to influence consumer perceptions of a particular brand, product line, or organization in relation to competitors. The term *position* refers to the place that the offering occupies in consumers' minds. To establish a unique position, many firms use product differentiation, emphasizing the real or perceived differences between competing offerings. Products may be differentiated on the basis of attribute, price and quality, use or application, product user, product class, or competitor.

9.1 Choose a product category (e.g., pickup trucks), and identify at least three different brands and their respective positioning strategies. How is each position communicated to the target audience?

KEY TERMS

80/20 principle	271	market segment	259	psychographic segmentation	269
benefit segmentation	270	market segmentation	259	repositioning	281
cannibalization	277	multisegment targeting strategy	276	satisficers	272
concentrated targeting strategy	275	niche	275	segmentation bases (variables)	262
demographic segmentation	263	one-to-one marketing	278	target market	274
family life cycle (FLC)	267	optimizers	272	undifferentiated targeting strategy	274
geodemographic segmentation	269	perceptual mapping	281	usage-rate segmentation	271
geographic segmentation	262	position	279		
market	259	positioning	279		
		product differentiation	280		

EXERCISES

APPLICATION EXERCISE

How tightly do you fit into a particular market segment? Do you think you can be neatly classified? If you think your purchasing habits make you an enigma to marketers, you may need to think again.[58]

Activities

1. Go to the Claritas Web site (**www.claritas.com/MyBestSegments/Default.jsp?ID=20**) and follow its "You Are Where You Live" link to find out what your ZIP code says about you. The database will generate many cluster descriptions based on your ZIP code. Depending on the functionality of the Web site at the time you access the database, you may need to reenter your ZIP code multiple times if you want to read all the cluster descriptions.
2. Now pick a product category, like automobiles, athletic shoes, beverages, or health and beauty products. Then think about which products in that category would appeal to each of the clusters generated by your ZIP code search. For example, a car that appeals to a cluster titled "Young Bohemians" may not be the car of choice for the cluster "Pools and Patios." If your search generated only one cluster type, you may wish to enter other ZIP codes for your area of town or for your region.
3. Create a perceptual map for the product you chose. Write a short statement that describes the overall position of each product with an explanation of why you located it where you did on the perceptual map.

ETHICS EXERCISE

Tobacco companies are frequently criticized for targeting potential customers below the legal age to purchase and use their products. Critics cite Joe Camel and the Marlboro Man as images meant to make smoking appealing to young people. If tobacco companies are actually following this particular demographic targeting strategy, most would agree that it is unethical if not illegal.

Questions

1. Is marketing tobacco products to younger consumers unethical?
2. Many are beginning to argue that fast-food companies, such as McDonald's and Burger King, are knowingly marketing unhealthy food to consumers. Is it unethical for fast-food companies to market kids' meals to children?
3. What does the AMA Statement of Ethics have to say about marketing unhealthy or harmful products to consumers, particularly children and young adults? Go to the AMA Web site at **www.marketingpower.com** to review the statement of ethics (**www.marketingpower.com/AboutAMA/Pages/Statement of Ethics.aspx**). Write a brief paragraph summarizing where the AMA stands on this important issue.

MARKETING PLAN EXERCISE

Once you've completed the marketing plan exercise for each chapter in Part 2 of this textbook, you can complete the Part 2 Marketing Planning Worksheet on your companion Web site at **www.cengage.com/international.** Complete the following exercises to continue the marketing plan you began in Chapter 2:

1. To whom does your company market (consumer, industrial, government, not-for-profit, or a combination of targets)? Within each market, are there specific segments or niches that your company can concentrate on? If so, which one(s) would you focus on and why? What are the factors used to create these segments? What are the Internet capabilities in those markets? If you try to encourage those segments to access your product or service via the Internet, will that change which segments are most important to your business? How? What are the factors used to create these segments? Which segments should your company focus on and why?
2. Describe your company's target market segment(s). Use demographics, psychographics, geographics, economic factors, size, growth rates, trends, NAICS codes, and any other appropriate descriptors. What role does the Internet play in your target market's life? How is the target market for your Internet business different from that of a traditional business in your market?
3. Using the list of key competitive advantages you described in Part 1 of your marketing plan, create a series of positioning grids, using two factors each as dimensions. (See grids in LO9 in your textbook, for an example.) Then plot the list of key competitors you identified earlier onto these positioning grids. Is your company too close to a key competitor? Are there spaces where the consumer needs and wants are unsatisfied? Consider how the Internet changes what factors are important to your success in your market space. Is technology the most important factor for your firm, or are there other ways for you to differentiate from and beat your competition?

CASE STUDY: VIVA LAS VEGAS

In 2003, more than 35.5 million travelers made Las Vegas their destination of choice. It was the second largest volume of visitors the city has ever entertained, lagging just slightly behind the 35.8 million recorded for the year 2000. Those numbers are remarkable given the recent slump in the travel industry, and the city has the Las Vegas Convention and Visitors Authority to thank. For almost 50 years, the LVCVA has been promoting Las Vegas in an effort to maximize occupancy for the city's hoteliers who suffer from the cyclical demand in the travel industry. The authority's marketing of the city's convention, lodging, and entertainment facilities to convention organizers, meeting planners, and leisure travelers plays an integral role in keeping hotel rooms and convention facilities occupied during off-peak times of the year.

Many types of visitors go to Las Vegas for a variety of reasons, and the LVCVA uses a multilevel promotions strategy to reach them all. The organization's promotional mix includes national television advertising, grassroots marketing, and relationship building with a variety of organizations. Each element is specifically designed to address issues within particular segments of its growing target market, such as changes in the composition of the visitor pool, shifts in visitors' travel preferences, the emergence of potentially lucrative metropolitan markets, and trends in foreign visitors.

An LVCVA study of the area's visitors for 2001, for example, found that African Americans, Hispanics, and Asian Americans accounted for 9, 5, and 4 percent, respectively, of the total visitor pool. The same study also revealed that the number of visitors from each of those groups had been steadily rising and that all U.S. visitors were beginning to prefer two- or three-day stays to weeklong vacations. With those data in hand, the LVCVA produced its award-winning "Vegas Stories" series of TV commercials. These irreverent ads poke fun at the sticky situations travelers may find themselves in as a result of too much revelry in the desert.

Using the tagline, "What happens here, stays here," the spots from the "Vegas Stories" campaign include an older Asian woman trying to alter an after-the-trip love letter while Roy Orbison's "Only the Lonely" plays in the background and a bachelorette party of African American women riding quietly in a limousine until the group is slowly overcome with sheepish laughter. Other commercials depict elderly couples, businesswomen, and young professional males. The LVCVA also produced its first-ever commercial recorded entirely in Spanish, which was written specifically to appeal to Hispanics' historical preference for family or group activities for vacations. Additionally, the authority's director of diversity began promoting Las Vegas to ethnic chambers of commerce and organizations like the International Association of Hispanic Meeting Planners and the National Coalition of Black Meeting Planners.

Other research performed by the LVCVA identified Portland, Oregon, and Atlanta as emerging regional markets based on their median household incomes, their available flights to Las Vegas, the cost of advertising in those markets, and the propensity of their citizens to gamble. The LVCVA then bought billboards in each city, cruised the towns in a specially prepared van featuring an Elvis impersonator and a traditional Vegas showgirl, and offered special travel deals to promote the entertainment options that Las Vegas offers in addition to gambling.

The authority's message carries beyond the borders of the United States, too. When it noticed significant drops in the visitor volume from Canada—Las Vegas's leading source of international travelers—the LVCVA sent an official delegation to Toronto. The group canvassed Toronto's Canadian Meeting & Incentive Travel Symposium & Trade Show to persuade convention operators to host their future productions in the desert. Representatives also met with private convention and leisure travel planners and attended events in Montreal and Vancouver to promote their cause.

Las Vegas is clearly on the rise again thanks to the tireless work of the LVCVA, and the authority has the hard data to prove it. As long as the LVCVA continues to understand its many diverse customers and communicate with them appropriately, the city of lights should continue to shine brightly for many years to come.[59]

Questions

1. What bases does the LVCVA use for segmenting its target market?
2. Does the LVCVA use an undifferentiated, a concentrated, or a multi-segment targeting strategy? Why? Should the LVCVA be concerned with cannibalization?
3. Think of the many reasons a person might want to travel to Las Vegas. Given a target market of all U.S. citizens aged 18 to 75, speculate how you might segment that market by lifestyle.
4. What do you think makes the LVCVA so successful?

COMPANY CLIPS

READYMADE—FOCUS AND SEGMENTATION

ReadyMade markets itself as a magazine catering to GenNest, the group of consumers ages 25 to 35 who are just settling down after college.

The young couples that make up this group are buying their first houses and taking on domestic and decorating roles for the first time. They are interested in being stylish, while at the same time maintaining their own unique personalities. But *ReadyMade* appeals to a wider variety of readers than just GenNest. The magazine has subscribers in all age groups, from teens looking to spruce up their rooms to retirees looking for projects to enliven their homes. This diversity offers a unique challenge to *ReadyMade* as it tries to promote itself to advertisers who need to know what sort of people will be reached through advertisements appearing in the publication.

Questions

1. How does *ReadyMade* communicate the demographics of its reader base to advertisers who want to see specific statistics that do not easily represent *ReadyMade's* target market?
2. What sort of segmentation does *ReadyMade* use when it markets to businesses and investors?
3. What ideas do you have that would help *ReadyMade* reach out to new subscribers without alienating its loyal base?

Marketing & You Results

A high score indicates that you operate within budget constraints. Living on a budget doesn't necessarily mean that you change your shopping behavior or your price comparison behavior, however. Low scores relate to financial health and a tendency to be brand loyal. After reading Chapter 8, you can see why income and financial situation can be an important segmentation variable!

CHAPTER 9

Decision Support Systems and Marketing Research

© SHEER PHOTO, INC/DIGITAL VISION/GETTY IMAGES

LEARNING OUTCOMES

LO 1 Explain the concept and purpose of a marketing decision support system

LO 2 Define marketing research and explain its importance to marketing decision making

LO 3 Describe the steps involved in conducting a marketing research project

LO 4 Discuss the profound impact of the Internet on marketing research

LO 5 Discuss the growing importance of scanner-based research

LO 6 Explain the concept of competitive intelligence

MARKETING DECISION SUPPORT SYSTEMS

Accurate and timely information is the lifeblood of marketing decision making. Good information can help an organization maximize sales and efficiently use scarce company resources. To prepare and adjust marketing plans, managers need a system for gathering everyday information about developments in the marketing environment—that is, for gathering **marketing information**. The system most commonly used these days for gathering marketing information is called a *marketing decision support system*.

A marketing **decision support system (DSS)** is an interactive, flexible computerized information system that enables managers to obtain and manipulate information as they are making decisions. A DSS bypasses the information-processing specialist and gives managers access to useful data from their own desks.

These are the characteristics of a true DSS:

- *Interactive:* Managers give simple instructions and see immediate results. The process is under their direct control; no computer programmer is needed. Managers don't have to wait for scheduled reports.
- *Flexible:* A DSS can sort, regroup, total, average, and manipulate the data in various ways. It will shift gears as the user changes topics, matching information to the problem at hand. For example, the CEO can see highly aggregated figures, and the marketing analyst can view very detailed breakouts.
- *Discovery-oriented:* Managers can probe for trends, isolate problems, and ask "what if" questions.
- *Accessible:* Managers who aren't skilled with computers can easily learn how to use a DSS. Novice users should be able to choose a standard, or default, method of using the system. They can bypass optional features so they can work with the basic system right away while gradually learning to apply its advanced features.

As a hypothetical example of how a DSS can be used, consider Renee Smith, vice president and manager of new products for Central Corporation. To evaluate sales of a recently introduced product, Renee can "call up" sales by the week, then by the month, breaking them out at her option by, say, customer segments. As she works at her desktop computer, her inquiries can go in several directions, depending on the decision at hand. If her train of thought raises questions about monthly sales last quarter compared to forecasts, she can use her DSS to analyze problems immediately. Renee might see that her new product's sales were significantly below forecasts. Were her forecasts too optimistic? She compares other products' sales to her forecasts and finds that the targets were very accurate. Was something wrong with the product? Is her sales department getting insufficient leads, or is it

Marketing & You

Please note your opinion on each of the following questions.

Using the following scale, enter your opinion.

1	2	3	4	5	6	7
Strongly disagree						Strongly agree

During a marketing project, a marketing manager should have formal or informal processes for continuously:

__ collecting information from customers.

__ collecting information about competitors' activities.

__ collecting information about relevant publics other than customers and competitors.

__ reexamining the value of information collected in previous studies.

__ collecting information from external experts, such as consultants.

Total your score. Now, read the chapter and find out what your score means at the end.

Source: From Scale #66, *Marketing Scales Handbook*, G. Bruner, James, H. Hensel, eds. Vol.III. © by American Marketing Association.

marketing information
Everyday information about developments in the marketing environment that managers use to prepare and adjust marketing plans.

decision support system (DSS)
An interactive, flexible computerized information system that enables managers to obtain and manipulate information as they are making decisions.

> Huge databases can raise a number of concerns about the safety and use of personal data.

not putting leads to good use? Thinking a minute about how to examine that question, she checks ratios of leads converted to sales, product by product. The results disturb her. Only 5 percent of the new product's leads generated orders, compared to the company's 12 percent all-product average. Why? Renee guesses that the salesforce is not supporting the new product vigorously enough. Quantitative information from the DSS could perhaps provide more evidence to back that suspicion. But already having enough quantitative knowledge to satisfy herself, the VP acts on her intuition and experience and decides to have a chat with her sales manager.

database marketing
The creation of a large computerized file of customers' and potential customers' profiles and purchase patterns.

marketing research
The process of planning, collecting, and analyzing data relevant to a marketing decision.

Perhaps the fastest-growing use of DSSs is for **database marketing,** which is the creation of a large computerized file of customers' and potential customers' profiles and purchase patterns. It is usually the key tool for successful one-to-one marketing, which relies on very specific information about a market. Huge databases can raise a number of concerns about the safety and use of personal data.

REVIEW LEARNING OUTCOME

LO1 • Explain the concept and purpose of a marketing decision support system

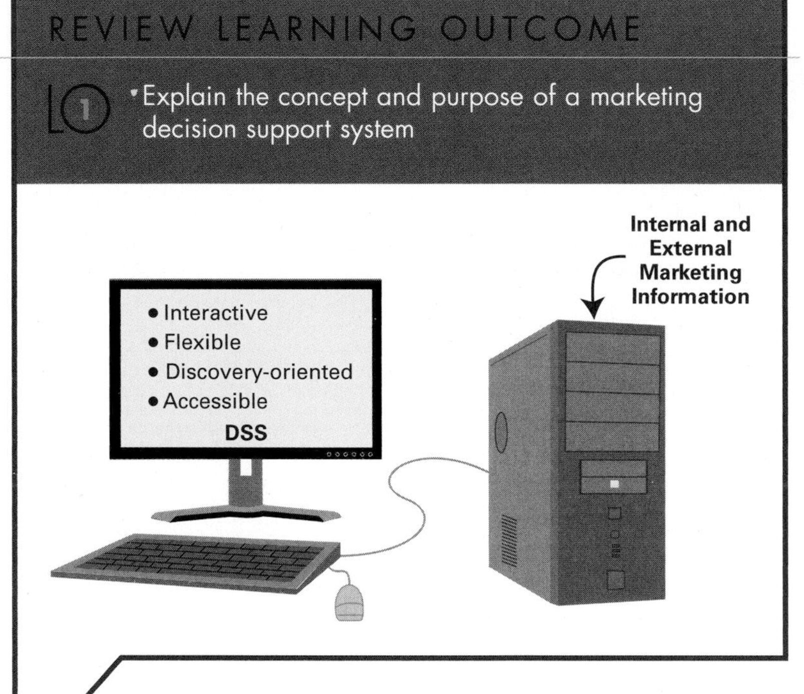

LO2

THE ROLE OF MARKETING RESEARCH

Marketing research is the process of planning, collecting, and analyzing data relevant to a marketing decision. The results of this analysis are then communicated to management. Thus, marketing research is the function that links the consumer, customer, and public to the marketer through information. Marketing research plays a key role in the marketing system. It provides decision makers with data on the effectiveness of the current marketing mix and also with insights for necessary changes. Furthermore, marketing research is a main data source for both management information systems and DSS. In other words, the findings of a marketing research project become data in a DSS.

Each year over $7 billion is spent on marketing research in the United States. That money is used to study products, advertising, prices, packages, names, logos, services, buying habits, taglines, colors, uses, awareness, familiarity, new concepts, traffic patterns, wants, needs, and politics.

Marketing research has three roles: descriptive, diagnostic, and predictive. Its *descriptive* role includes gathering and presenting factual statements. For example, what is the historic sales trend in the industry? What are consumers' attitudes toward a product and its advertising? Its *diagnostic* role includes explaining data. For instance, what was the impact on sales of a change in the design of the package? Its *predictive* function is to address "what if" questions. For example, how can the researcher use the descriptive and diagnostic research to predict the results of a planned marketing decision?

Management Uses of Marketing Research

Marketing research can help managers in several ways. It improves the quality of decision making and helps managers trace problems. Most important, sound marketing research helps managers focus on the paramount importance of keeping existing customers, aids them in better understanding the marketplace, and alerts them to marketplace trends.

Marketing research also helps managers gauge the perceived value of their goods and services as well as the level of customer satisfaction. For example, research revealed which brands of plumbing fixtures were traditional to New York City. This helped the Brooklyn Home Depot's store manager Rich Kantor to arrange his small pilot store so that it was designed to meet the needs of urban communities.

Improving the Quality of Decision Making Managers can sharpen their decision making by using marketing research to explore the desirability of various marketing alternatives. For example, on the heels of the successful launch of its Young & Tender line of bagged spinach, NewStar, a Salinas, California-based produce firm, was wondering what to do for an encore. A line of salad kits featuring spinach in combination with a dressing and/or other ingredients seemed like a natural idea. But rather than introducing a me-too product to the already-crowded salad kit market, the company wanted to add a gourmet twist.

The process began with an idea generation phase, says Christie Hoyer, vice president of product development and evaluation at the National Food Laboratory (NFL). Sessions were conducted with NFL chefs, food technologists, and other culinary arts workers. "We did a number of brainstorming sessions, game-playing, and other, more coordinated exercises. From that we came up with numerous flavor concepts for the salads and the sauté mixes."

Next came the first round of consumer testing. At this stage, Hoyer says, NFL wanted to validate the product concepts and also gauge reactions to them. A four-phase process was conducted with male and female consumers ages 21 to 64 who were their family's primary grocery shopper and were positive toward spinach salad and cooked fresh spinach.

The first phase gathered reactions to the concept of a line of gourmet salad and sauté kits and determined purchase intent for each flavor (based on descriptions of the flavors, not actual tasting). Next, the respondents tried the product prototypes, which were rotated so that half of the group tried the sautés first and half tried the salads first.

The third phase was a test of packaging. Respondents were taken to a separate area featuring a mock store display of three packaging concepts and were asked to rank their preferences for the different graphics. In the fourth phase, the consumers viewed a large copy of the nutritional information for a salad kit and a sauté kit. "Without specifically asking about it, we were interested in their reaction to things such as fat content," Hoyer says.

Since the salad and sauté mixes were introduced, they have been a hit with retailers and with consumers. Marketing research paved the way![1]

Because kids eat over 5 billion ounces of ketchup each year, Heinz decided that the heavy users (kids) should have a lot to say (via marketing research) about how to make ketchup fun. Heinz listened and watched children using ketchup, which resulted in a new bottle design, name selection, and color. The true ketchup connoisseurs helped create Heinz EZ Squirt green ketchup.

Opening a pack of bacon is a messy job. Bacon lovers have to reach into the package and if they only pull out a few slices, there's no easy way to store the remainder. Oscar Mayer marketing researchers hear plenty from consumers about what they disliked about its former bacon packaging. So marketers figured the best solution would be a packaging innovation that eliminated the chore of placing the opened packed in a resealable plastic bag or wrapping it in plastic or foil. This unwanted task was done so the last piece of bacon would be as fresh as the first.

Recently, Oscar Mayer Center Cut Bacon was introduced in a new "Stay-Fresh Reclosable Tray." The flip-top lid allows easy access

Managers can sharpen their decision making by using marketing research to explore various marketing alternatives. Heinz used the results of its marketing research—that is, listening to and watching children using ketchup—to create a new bottle design, name selection, and color for its EZ Squirt ketchup.

to the bacon inside. The top snaps closed, making it readily resealable. The flat tray makes for simplified storage in the refrigerator.[2]

Tracing Problems When Something Goes Wrong Another way managers use marketing research is to find out why a plan backfired. Was the initial decision incorrect? Did an unforeseen change in the external environment cause the plan to fail? How can the same mistake be avoided in the future?

Keebler introduced Sweet Spots, a shortbread cookie with a huge chocolate drop on it. It has had acceptable sales and is still on the market, but only after the company used marketing research to overcome several problems. Soon after the cookie's introduction, Keebler increased the box size from 10 ounces at $2.29 to 15 ounces at $3.19. Demand immediately fell. Market research showed that Sweet Spots were now considered more of a luxury than an everyday item. Keebler lowered the price and went back to the 10-ounce box. Even though Sweet Spots originally was aimed at upscale adult females, the company also tried to appeal to kids. In subsequent research, Keebler found that the package graphics appealed to mothers but not to children.

Focusing on the Paramount Importance of Keeping Existing Customers An inextricable link exists between customer satisfaction and customer loyalty. Long-term relationships don't just happen but are grounded in the delivery of service and value by the firm. Customer retention pays big dividends for organizations. Powered by repeat sales and referrals, revenues and market share grow. Costs fall because firms spend less money and energy attempting to replace defectors. Steady customers are easy to serve because they understand the modus operandi and make fewer demands on employees' time. Increased customer retention also drives job satisfaction and pride, which lead to higher employee retention. In turn, the knowledge employees acquire as they stay longer increases productivity. A Bain & Co. study estimated that a 5 percent decrease in the customer defection rate can boost profits by 25 to 95 percent.[3] Another study found that the customer retention rate has a major impact on the value of the firm.[4]

Recently, Dunkin' Donuts paid dozens of faithful customers in Phoenix, Chicago, and Charlotte, N.C., $100 a week to buy coffee at Starbucks instead. At the same time, the no-frills coffee chain paid Starbucks customers to make the opposite switch.

© AP IMAGES/PRNEWSFOTO/PROCTER & GAMBLE

When it later debriefed the two groups, Dunkin' says it found them so polarized that company researchers dubbed them "tribes"—each of whom loathed the very things that made the other tribe loyal to their coffee shop. Dunkin' fans viewed Starbucks as pretentious and trendy, while Starbucks loyalists saw Dunkin' as austere and unoriginal.

Bridging some of the divide between Starbucks and Dunkin' Donuts customers—but not too much—is key to Dunkin' Donuts' ambitious plan to expand its largely Eastern coffee chain into a national powerhouse that's as synonymous with coffee as Starbucks.

Dunkin' researchers concluded that it wasn't income that set the two tribes apart, as much as an ideal: Dunkin' tribe members wanted to be part of a crowd, while members of the Starbucks tribe had a desire to stand out as individuals. Dunkin' executives made dozens of decisions, big and small, ranging from where to put the espresso machines to how much of its signature pink and orange color scheme to retain to where to display its fresh-baked goods.

Out went the square laminate tables, to be replaced by round imitation-granite tabletops and sleek chairs. Dunkin' covered store walls in espresso brown and dialed down the pink and orange tones. Executives considered but held off on installing wireless Internet access because customers "just don't feel it's Dunkin' Donuts," says Joe Scafido, chief creative and innovation officer.[5]

One company that always goes the extra mile to provide quality service and to deliver customer satisfaction is the Ritz-Carlton hotel chain. Their training program is described in the Customer Experience box below.

CUSTOMER Experience

Ritz-Carlton Always Goes the Extra Mile

Ritz-Carlton is the only service company to have won the prestigious Malcolm Baldrige National Quality Award twice. The chain placed first in guest satisfaction among luxury hotels in the most recent J.D. Power & Associates hotel survey. Ritz-Carlton spends about $5,000 to train each new hire. First is a two-day introduction to company values (it's all about the service) and the 20 Ritz-Carlton "basics." (Basic 13 is "Never lose a guest.") Next comes a 21-day course focused on job responsibilities, such as a bellman's 28 steps to greeting a guest. Each employee carries a plastic card imprinted with the credo and the basics, as well as the "employee promise" and the three steps of service. Step 1: "A warm and sincere greeting. Use the guests' name, if and when possible."

Porters and doormen wear headsets, so when they spot your name on luggage tags, they can radio the information to the front desk. In addition, an in-house database called the Customer Loyalty Anticipation Satisfaction System stores guest preferences, such as whether an individual likes Seagram's ginger ale or Canada Dry. The software also alerts front-desk clerks when a guest who's stayed at other Ritz-Carltons has a habit of inquiring about the best sushi in town.[6]

Where does marketing research come into play at Ritz-Carlton? Is it really necessary for the Ritz-Carlton to provide such a high level of service to keep its customers?

UNDERSTANDING THE EVER-CHANGING MARKETPLACE

Marketing research also helps managers understand what is going on in the marketplace and take advantage of opportunities. Historically, marketing research has been practiced for as long as marketing has existed. The early Phoenicians carried out market demand studies as they traded in the various ports of the Mediterranean Sea. Marco Polo's diary indicates he was performing marketing research as he traveled to China. There is even evidence that the Spanish systematically conducted "market surveys" as they explored the New World, and there are examples of marketing research conducted during the Renaissance.

As the price of gasoline hit $4.00 plus per gallon, more and more manufacturers began looking at the hybrid car market. However, before committing hundreds of millions of dollars to producing hybrids, they need a better understanding of the market. Thus, the marketers turn to marketing research. When consumers were asked whether they would consider a hybrid version of their new vehicle had it been available, roughly 7 in 10 indicated they would have. In addition to their high likelihood to consider hybrid vehicles, when asked what type of alternative fuel they found most appealing, vehicle buyers most often indicate hybrid vehicles are their preferred alternative fuel type.

Also, there has been an increased interest in pure electric vehicles. The uptick likely reflects new developments in electric engines and public relations activities surrounding them. When considering purchasing a new vehicle, those who choose hybrids are motivated by a desire to obtain an environmentally friendly vehicle, but even more importantly, to achieve the greatest level of fuel economy. Those who chose hybrids are more likely than owners in general to consider issues such as style, comfort, roominess and even price to be significantly less important.

However, despite obtaining higher miles per gallon (MPG) and greater satisfaction with it, hybrid owners report their MPG falls far short of their expectations. In fact, hybrid owners are significantly more likely than vehicle purchasers in general to obtain lower-than-expected MPG.[7]

REVIEW LEARNING OUTCOME

LO2 Define marketing research and explain its importance to marketing decision making

Why marketing research?

- ☑ Improve quality of decision making
- ☑ Trace problems
- ☑ Focus on keeping existing customers
- ☑ Understand changes in marketplace

Although the material above is just a tiny piece of a nationwide study of over 100,000 vehicle owners, you can see how the insights from such a study can be extremely valuable to car manufacturers.

STEPS IN A MARKETING RESEARCH PROJECT

Virtually all firms that have adopted the marketing concept engage in some marketing research because it offers decision makers many benefits. Some companies spend millions on marketing research; others, particularly smaller firms, conduct informal, limited-scale research studies. For example, when Eurasia restaurant, serving Eurasian cuisine, first opened along Chicago's ritzy Michigan Avenue, it drew novelty seekers. But it turned off the important business lunch crowd, and sales began to decline. The owner surveyed several hundred businesspeople working within a mile of the restaurant. He found that they were confused by Eurasia's concept and wanted more traditional Asian fare at lower prices. In response, the restaurant altered its concept; it hired a Thai chef, revamped the menu, and cut prices. The dining room was soon full again.

Using marketing research helped the WD-40 Company successfully reposition its X-14 cleaning products in the marketplace. The research also identified opportunities to extend the X-14 brand.

Whether a research project costs $200 or $2 million, the same general process should be followed. The marketing research process is a scientific approach to decision making that maximizes the chance of getting accurate and meaningful results. Exhibit 9.1 traces the steps: (1) identifying and formulating the problem/opportunity, (2) planning the research design and gathering primary data, (3) specifying the sampling procedures, (4) collecting the data, (5) analyzing the data, (6) preparing and presenting the report, and (7) following up.

The research process begins with the recognition of a marketing problem or opportunity. As changes occur in the firm's external environment, marketing managers are faced with the questions, "Should we change the existing marketing mix?" and, if so, "How?" Marketing research may be used to evaluate product, promotion, distribution, or pricing alternatives.

Though famous for its well-known line of household lubricants, San Diego-based WD-40 Co. has repositioned one of its product lines as essential bathroom cleaners—the result of a research process.

Sales of the company's six household product brands (of which X-14 is one) make up a sizable percentage—more than 31 percent—of the overall portfolio. However, rival brands were more popular. Which elements in the company's marketing mix could be adjusted to gain more share of the cleaning products market?

The repositioning of WD-40's X-14 line helped the $287 million company find the brand's niche. "We previously had products that focused on the bathroom, but there wasn't a unified line in its positioning. We had a line of cleaning products that were not meeting their potential in the marketplace," says Heidi Noorany, director of marketing. The marketing research indicated that there was a need for a "bathroom expert" line of products. "We knew we had the positioning and the quality of products within the current line, but we had to communicate it," Noorany adds. That would be translated through the line's more cohesive packaging design characterized by a variety of pinks, oranges, and blues as well as several bottle designs.

Consumer research was also used to measure product effectiveness versus competitors' products, and found that the X-14 Foaming Bathroom Cleaner scored 4.5 on a scale of 1 to 5 and that its Trigger Bathroom Cleaner scored a 91 percent approval rating, placing it higher than four other competing brands. The research also found that consumers engage in two types of cleaning—weekly deep cleanings and quick daily cleanings. "We saw an opportunity for a bathroom expert line of products," says Noorany. Not only did WD-40 learn how to best reposition the X-14 line, but it also garnered enough insight from the research process that it could use the data in future product development.[8]

The WD-40 story illustrates an important point about problem/opportunity definition. The **marketing research problem** is information oriented. It involves determining what information is needed and how that information can be obtained efficiently and effectively. The **marketing research objective**, then, is to provide insightful decision-making information. This requires specific pieces of information needed to answer the marketing research problem. Managers must combine this information with their own experience and other information to make a proper decision. WD-40's marketing research problem was to gather information on how consumers clean and how they shop for cleaning products. The marketing research objective was several-fold: identify a better positioning strategy for X-14 and identify opportunities to add new items to the X-14 brand.

Whereas the marketing research problem is information-oriented, the **management decision problem** is action-oriented. Management problems tend to be much broader in scope and far more general than marketing research problems, which must be narrowly defined and specific if the research effort is to be successful. Sometimes several research studies must be conducted to solve a broad management problem. The management decision problem was: "How do we grow sales of X-14 family brand?" Management then decided to reposition X-14 as The Bathroom Expert—the centerpiece around which its new product line reenters the market. Completely redesigned, the line provides a family look for the set of products rather than a disjointed set of similar products. Yet it also includes two additions: Foaming Bathroom Cleaner and Bathroom Cleaner, which combines oxy and citrus (hydrogen peroxide with citric acid) for general bathroom cleaning. Additionally, several future products are expected to be released soon.[9]

EXHIBIT 9.1

The Marketing Research Process

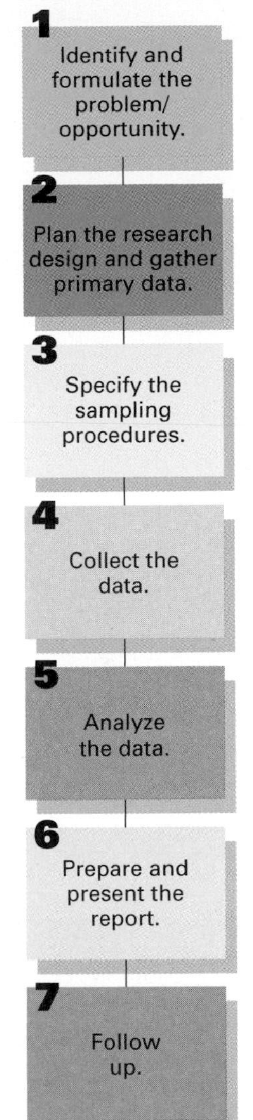

Secondary Data

A valuable tool throughout the research process, but particularly in the problem/opportunity identification stage is **secondary data**—data previously collected for any purpose other than the one at hand. Secondary information originating within the company includes documents such as annual reports, reports to stockholders, product testing results perhaps made available to the news media, and house periodicals composed by the company's personnel for communication to employees, customers, or others. Often this information is incorporated into a company's internal database.

Innumerable outside sources of secondary information also exist, principally coming from government departments and agencies (federal, state, and local) that compile and publish summaries of business data. Trade and industry associations also publish secondary data. Still more data are available in business periodicals and other news media that regularly publish studies and articles on the economy, specific industries, and even individual companies. The unpublished summarized secondary information from these sources corresponds to internal reports, memos, or special-purpose analyses with limited circulation. Economic considerations or priorities in the organization may preclude publication of these summaries. Most of the sources listed above can be found on the Internet.

Secondary data save time and money if they help solve the researcher's problem. Even if the problem is not solved, secondary data have other advantages. They can aid in formulating the problem statement and suggest research methods and other types of data needed for solving the problem. In addition, secondary data can pinpoint the kinds of people to approach and their locations and serve as a basis of comparison for other data.

marketing research problem
Determining what information is needed and how that information can be obtained efficiently and effectively.

marketing research objective
The specific information needed to solve a marketing research problem; the objective should be to provide insightful decision-making information.

management decision problem
A broad-based problem that uses marketing research in order for managers to take proper actions.

secondary data
Data previously collected for any purpose other than the one at hand.

The disadvantages of secondary data stem mainly from a mismatch between the researcher's unique problem and the purpose for which the secondary data were originally gathered, which are typically different. For example, a major consumer-products manufacturer wanted to determine the market potential for a fireplace log made of coal rather than compressed wood by-products. The researcher found plenty of secondary data about total wood consumed as fuel, quantities consumed in each state, and types of wood burned. Secondary data were also available about consumer attitudes and purchase patterns of wood by-product fireplace logs. The wealth of secondary data provided the researcher with many insights into the artificial log market. Yet, nowhere was there any information that would tell the firm whether consumers would buy artificial logs made of coal.

The quality of secondary data may also pose a problem. Often, secondary data sources do not give detailed information that would enable a researcher to assess their quality or relevance. Whenever possible, a researcher needs to address these important questions: Who gathered the data? Why were the data obtained? What methodology was used? How were classifications (such as heavy users versus light users) developed and defined? When was the information gathered?

The New Age of Secondary Information: The Internet

Gathering secondary data, though necessary in almost any research project, has traditionally been a tedious and boring job. The researcher often had to write to government agencies, trade associations, or other secondary data providers and then wait days or weeks for a reply that might never come. Often, one or more trips to the library were required, and the researcher might find that needed reports were checked out or missing. Now, however, the rapid development of the Internet has eliminated much of the drudgery associated with the collection of secondary data. A few popular sites used by marketing researchers are shown in Exhibit 9.2.

EXHIBIT 9.2

Popular Secondary Data Sites Used by Marketing Researchers

Organization	URL	Description
American Marketing Association	**www.marketingpower.com**	Enables users to search all of the AMA's publications by using keywords.
BLS Consumer Expenditure Surveys	**http://www.bls.gov/cex/**	Provides information on the buying habits of consumers, including data on their expenditures, income, and credit ratings.
U.S. Census Bureau	**www.census.gov**	Is a very useful source of virtually all census data.
U.S. Government	**www.fedstats.gov**	Source for statistics and reports for more than 100 government agencies. Also links to other sources of relevant information. Highly recommended site but you may have to dig a little.
WorldOpinion	**www.worldopinion.com**	Offers thousands of marketing research reports. This is perhaps the premier site for the marketing research industry.
Nielsen/NetRatings	**www.nielsen-netratings.com**	Is a source of Internet audience information. Researchers can find data on Internet growth and user patterns.
USADATA	**www.usadata.com**	Provides access to consumer lifestyle data on a local, regional, and national level.
FIND/SVP	**www.findsvp.com**	Offers consulting and research services. The site claims to offer access to the largest private information center for global data in the United States.

MARKETING RESEARCH AGGREGATORS

The **marketing research aggregator** industry is a $120 million business that is growing by about 6 percent a year. Companies in this field acquire, catalog, reformat, segment, and resell reports already published by large and small marketing research firms. Even Amazon.com has added a marketing research aggregation area to its high-profile e-commerce site.

The role of aggregator firms is growing because their databases of research reports are getting bigger and more comprehensive—and more useful—as marketing research firms get more comfortable using resellers as a sales channel. Meanwhile, advances in Web technology are making the databases easier to search and deliveries speedier. Research aggregators are also indirectly tapping new markets for traditional research firms. By slicing and repackaging research reports into narrower, more specialized sections for resale to small and medium-sized clients that often cannot afford to commission their own studies or buy full reports, the aggregators are nurturing a new target market for the information.

Prior to the emergence of research aggregators, a lot of marketing research was available only as premium-priced subscription services. For example, a 17-chapter $2,800 report from Wintergreen Research (based in Lexington, Massachusetts) was recently broken up and sold for $350 per chapter, significantly boosting the overall revenue generated by the report. Other major aggregators are **Mindbranch.com**, **Aarkstore.com**, and **USADATA.com.**

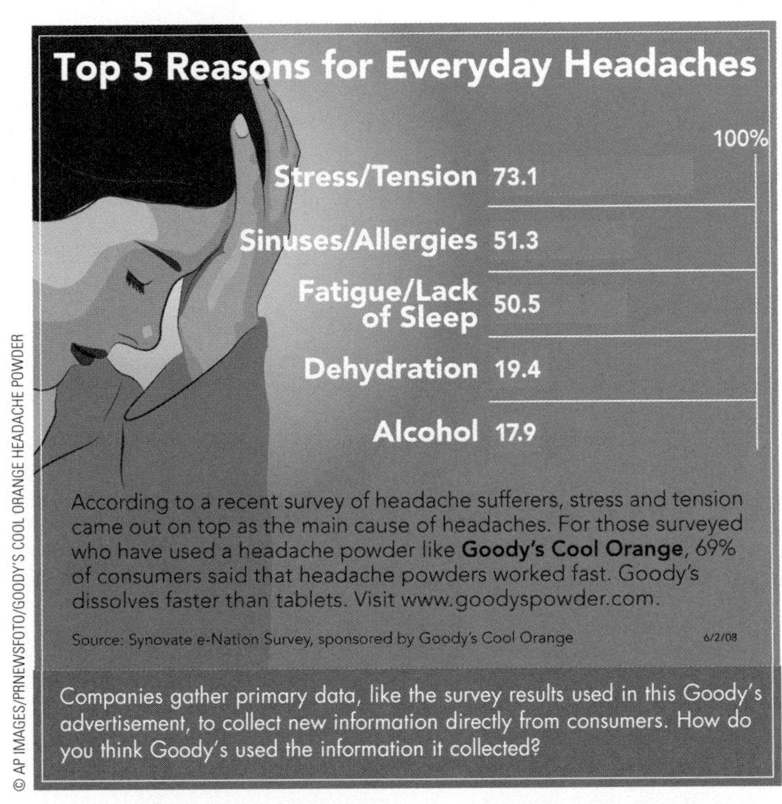

Companies gather primary data, like the survey results used in this Goody's advertisement, to collect new information directly from consumers. How do you think Goody's used the information it collected?

Planning the Research Design and Gathering Primary Data

Good secondary data can help researchers conduct a thorough situation analysis. With that information, researchers can list their unanswered questions and rank them. Researchers must then decide the exact information required to answer the questions. The **research design** specifies which research questions must be answered, how and when the data will be gathered, and how the data will be analyzed. Typically, the project budget is finalized after the research design has been approved.

Sometimes research questions can be answered by gathering more secondary data; otherwise, primary data may be needed. **Primary data**, or information collected for the first time, is used for solving the particular problem under investigation. The main advantage of primary data is that they will answer a specific research question that secondary data cannot answer. For example, suppose Pillsbury has two new recipes for refrigerated dough for sugar cookies. Which one will consumers like better? Secondary data will not help answer this question. Instead, targeted consumers must try each recipe and evaluate the taste, texture, and appearance of each cookie. Moreover, primary data are current, and researchers know the source. Sometimes researchers gather the data themselves rather than assign projects to outside companies. Researchers also specify the methodology of the research. Secrecy can be maintained because the information is proprietary. In contrast, much secondary data is available to all interested parties for relatively small fees or for free.

Gathering primary data is expensive; costs can range from a few thousand dollars for a limited survey to several million for a nationwide study. For instance, a nationwide, 15-minute telephone interview with 1,000 adult males can cost $50,000 for everything,

marketing research aggregator
A company that acquires, catalogs, reformats, segments, and resells reports already published by marketing research firms.

research design
Specifies which research questions must be answered, how and when the data will be gathered, and how the data will be analyzed.

primary data
Information that is collected for the first time; used for solving the particular problem under investigation.

survey research
The most popular technique for gathering primary data, in which a researcher interacts with people to obtain facts, opinions, and attitudes.

including a data analysis and report. Because primary data gathering in person is so expensive, many firms now use an Internet study instead. Larger companies that conduct many research projects use another cost-saving technique. They *piggyback studies*, or gather data on two different projects using one questionnaire. The drawback is that answering questions about, say, dog food and gourmet coffee may be confusing to respondents. Piggybacking also requires a longer interview (sometimes a half hour or longer), which tires respondents. The quality of the answers typically declines, with people giving curt replies and thinking, "When will this end!" A lengthy interview also makes people less likely to participate in other research surveys.

Nevertheless, the disadvantages of primary data gathering are usually offset by the advantages. It is often the only way of solving a research problem. And with a variety of techniques available for research—including surveys, observations, and experiments—primary research can address almost any marketing question.

Survey Research

The most popular technique for gathering primary data is **survey research**, in which a researcher interacts with people to obtain facts, opinions, and attitudes. Exhibit 9.3 summarizes the characteristics of traditional forms of survey research.

In-Home Personal Interviews Although in-home personal interviews often provide high-quality information, they tend to be very expensive because of the interviewers' travel time and mileage costs. Therefore, they are rapidly disappearing from the American and European marketing researcher's survey toolbox. They are, however, still popular in many countries around the globe.

EXHIBIT 9.3

Characteristics of Traditional Forms of Survey Research

Characteristic	In-Home Personal Interviews	Mall Intercept Interviews	Central Location Telephone Interviews	Self-Administered and One-Time Mail Surveys	Mail Panel Surveys	Executive Interviews	Focus Groups
Cost	High	Moderate	Moderate	Low	Moderate	High	Low
Time span	Moderate	Moderate	Fast	Slow	Relatively slow	Moderate	Fast
Use of interviewer	Yes	Yes	Yes	No	No	Yes	Yes
Ability to show concepts to respondent	Yes (also taste tests)	Yes (also taste tests)	No	Yes	Yes	Yes	Yes
Management control over interviewer	Low	Moderate	High	N/A	N/A	Moderate	High
General data quality	High	Moderate	High to moderate	Moderate to low	Moderate to low	High	Moderate
Ability to collect large amounts of data	High	Moderate	Moderate to low	Low to moderate	Moderate	Moderate	Moderate
Ability to handle complex questionnaires	High	Moderate	High, if computer-aided	Low	Low	High	N/A

Mall Intercept Interviews The **mall intercept interview** is conducted in the common area of a shopping mall or in a market research office within the mall. It is the economy version of the door-to-door interview with personal contact between interviewer and respondent, because the interviewer saves on travel time and mileage costs. To conduct this type of interview, the research firm rents office space in the mall or pays a significant daily fee. One drawback is that it is hard to get a representative sample of the population this way.

However, an interviewer can also probe when necessary—a technique used to clarify a person's response. For example, an interviewer might ask, "What did you like best about the salad dressing you just tried?" The respondent might reply, "Taste." This answer doesn't provide a lot of information, so the interviewer could probe by saying, "Can you tell me a little bit more about taste?" The respondent then elaborates: "Yes, it's not too sweet, it has the right amount of pepper, and I love that hint of garlic."

Mall intercept interviews must be brief. Only the shortest ones are conducted while respondents are standing. Usually, researchers invite respondents to their office for interviews, which are still generally less than 15 minutes long. The researchers often show respondents concepts for new products or a test commercial or have them taste a new food product. The overall quality of mall intercept interviews is about the same as telephone interviews.

Marketing researchers are applying computer technology in mall interviewing. The first technique is **computer-assisted personal interviewing**. The researcher conducts in-person interviews, reads questions to the respondent off a computer screen, and directly keys the respondent's answers into the computer. A second approach is **computer-assisted self-interviewing**. A mall interviewer intercepts and directs willing respondents to nearby computers. Each respondent reads questions off a computer screen and directly keys his or her answers into a computer. The third use of technology is fully automated self-interviewing. Respondents are guided by interviewers or independently approach a centrally located computer station or kiosk, read questions off a screen, and directly key their answers into the station's computer.

Telephone Interviews Compared to the personal interview, the telephone interview costs less, but cost is rapidly increasing due to respondent refusals to participate. Most telephone interviewing is conducted from a specially designed phone room called a **central-location telephone (CLT) facility.** A phone room has many phone lines, individual interviewing stations, sometimes monitoring equipment, and headsets. The research firm typically will interview people nationwide from a single location. The federal "Do Not Call" law does not apply to survey research.

Most CLT facilities offer computer-assisted interviewing. The interviewer reads the questions from a computer screen and enters the respondent's data directly into the computer. The researcher can stop the survey at any point and immediately print out the survey results. Thus, a researcher can get a sense of the project as it unfolds and fine-tune the research design as necessary. An online interviewing system can also save time and money because data entry occurs as the response is recorded rather than as a separate process after the interview. Hallmark Cards found that an interviewer administered a printed questionnaire for its Shoebox greeting cards in 28 minutes. The same questionnaire administered with computer assistance took only 18 minutes.

Mail Surveys Mail surveys have several benefits: relatively low cost, elimination of interviewers and field supervisors, centralized control, and actual or promised anonymity for respondents (which may draw more candid responses). Some researchers feel that mail questionnaires give the respondent a chance to reply more thoughtfully and to check records, talk to family members, and so forth. A disadvantage is that mail questionnaires usually produce low response rates.

Low response rates pose a problem because certain elements of the population tend to respond more than others. The resulting sample may therefore not represent the surveyed population. For example, the sample may have too many retired people and too few working people. In this instance, answers to a question about attitudes toward government

mall intercept interview
A survey research method that involves interviewing people in the common areas of shopping malls.

computer-assisted personal interviewing
An interviewing method in which the interviewer reads the questions from a computer screen and enters the respondent's data directly into the computer.

computer-assisted self-interviewing
An interviewing method in which a mall interviewer intercepts and directs willing respondents to nearby computers where the respondent reads questions off a computer screen and directly keys his or her answers into a computer.

central-location telephone (CLT) facility
A specially designed phone room used to conduct telephone interviewing.

executive interviews
A type of survey that involves interviewing businesspeople at their offices concerning industrial products or services.

focus group
Seven to ten people who participate in a group discussion led by a moderator.

group dynamics
Group interaction essential to the success of focus-group research.

programs to aid senior citizens might indicate a much more favorable overall view of the system than is actually the case. Another serious problem with mail surveys is that no one probes respondents to clarify or elaborate on their answers.

Mail panels like those operated by Synovate, IPSOS, and NPD Research offer an alternative to the one-shot mail survey. A mail panel consists of a sample of households recruited to participate by mail for a given period. Panel members often receive gifts in return for their participation. Essentially, the panel is a sample used several times. In contrast to onetime mail surveys, the response rates from mail panels are high. Rates of 70 percent (of those who agree to participate) are not uncommon.

Executive Interviews Marketing researchers use **executive interviews** to conduct the industrial equivalent of door-to-door interviewing. This type of survey involves interviewing businesspeople, at their offices, concerning industrial products or services. For example, if Dell wanted information regarding user preferences for different features that might be offered in a new line of computer printers, it would need to interview prospective user-purchasers of the printers. It is appropriate to locate and interview these people at their offices.

This type of interviewing is very expensive. First, individuals involved in the purchase decision for the product in question must be identified and located. Sometimes lists can be obtained from various sources, but more frequently screening must be conducted over the telephone. A particular company is likely to have individuals of the type being sought, but locating those people within a large organization can be expensive and time-consuming. Once a qualified person is located, the next step is to get that person to agree to be interviewed and to set a time for the interview. This is not as hard as it might seem because most professionals seem to enjoy talking about topics related to their work.

Finally, an interviewer must go to the particular place at the appointed time. Long waits are frequently encountered, and cancellations are not uncommon. This type of survey requires the very best interviewers because they are frequently interviewing on topics that they know very little about. Executive interviewing has essentially the same advantages and disadvantages as in-home interviewing.

Focus Groups A **focus group** is a type of personal interviewing. Often recruited by random telephone screening, seven to ten people with certain desired characteristics form a focus group. These qualified consumers are usually offered an incentive (typically \$50 to \$75) to participate in a group discussion. The meeting place (sometimes resembling a living room, sometimes featuring a conference table) has audiotaping and perhaps videotaping equipment. It also likely has a viewing room with a one-way mirror so that clients (manufacturers or retailers) may watch the session. During the session, a moderator, hired by the research company, leads the group discussion.

Focus groups can be used to gauge consumer response to a product or promotion and are occasionally used to brainstorm new product ideas.

Focus groups are much more than question-and-answer interviews. Market researchers draw a distinction between "group dynamics" and "group interviewing." The interaction provided in **group dynamics** is essential to the success of focus-group research; this interaction is the reason for conducting group rather than individual research. One of the essential postulates of group-session usage is the idea that a response from one person may become a stimulus for another, thereby generating an interplay of responses that may yield more information than if the same number of people had contributed independently.

Lewis Stone, former manager of Colgate-Palmolive's research and development division, says the following about focus groups: "If it weren't for focus groups, Colgate-Palmolive Co. might never know that some women squeeze their bottles of dishwashing soap, others squeeeeeze them, and still others squeeeeeeeeeze out the desired amount. Then there are the ones who use the soap 'neat.' That is, they put the product directly on a sponge or washcloth and wash the dishes under running water until the suds run out. Then they apply more detergent."

Stone was explaining how body language, exhibited during focus groups, provides insights into a product that are not apparent from reading questionnaires on habits and practices. Focus groups represent a most efficient way of learning how one's products are actually used in the home. By drawing out the panelists to describe in detail how they do certain tasks, you can learn a great deal about possible need-gaps that could be filled by new or improved products, and also how a new product might be received. It is estimated that over 600,000 focus groups are conducted around the world each year.[10]

A system created by FocusVision allows client companies and advertising agencies to view live focus groups in over 350 cities worldwide. For example, the private satellite network lets a Taco Bell researcher observing a San Diego focus group control two cameras in the viewing room. The researcher can get a full-group view or a close-up, zoom, or pan the participants. The researcher can also communicate directly with the moderator using an ear receiver. Ogilvy & Mather (a large New York advertising agency whose clients include StarKist Seafood, Seagram's, MasterCard, and Burger King) has installed the system.

Increasingly, focus groups are being conducted online. Online focus groups are examined in detail later in the chapter.

Questionnaire Design

All forms of survey research require a questionnaire. Questionnaires ensure that all respondents will be asked the same series of questions. Questionnaires include three basic types of questions: open-ended, closed-ended, and scaled-response (see Exhibit 9.4). An **open-ended question** encourages an answer phrased in the respondent's own words. Researchers get a rich array of information based on the respondent's frame of reference. In contrast, a **closed-ended question** asks the respondent to make a selection from a limited list of responses. Traditionally, marketing researchers separate the two-choice question (called *dichotomous*) from the many-item type (often called *multiple choice*). A **scaled-response question** is a closed-ended question designed to measure the intensity of a respondent's answer.

open-ended question
An interview question that encourages an answer phrased in the respondent's own words.

closed-ended question
An interview question that asks the respondent to make a selection from a limited list of responses.

scaled-response question
A closed-ended question designed to measure the intensity of a respondent's answer.

Closed-ended and scaled-response questions are easier to tabulate than open-ended questions because response choices are fixed. On the other hand, unless the researcher designs the closed-ended question very carefully, an important choice may be omitted.

For example, suppose a food study asked this question: "Besides meat, which of the following items do you normally add to a taco that you prepare at home?"

Avocado	1	Olives (black/green)	6
Cheese (Monterey Jack/cheddar)	2	Onions (red/white)	7
Guacamole	3	Peppers (red/green)	8
Lettuce	4	Pimento	9
Mexican hot sauce	5	Sour cream	0

© ISTOCKPHOTO.COM/C CATHLEEN CLAPPER

The list seems complete, doesn't it? However, consider the following responses: "I usually add a green, avocado-tasting hot sauce"; "I cut up a mixture of lettuce and spinach"; "I'm a vegetarian—I don't use meat at all"; or "My taco

EXHIBIT 9.4

Types of Questions Found on Questionnaires for National Market Research

<table>
<tr><th>Open-Ended Questions</th><th>Closed-Ended Questions</th><th>Scaled-Response Question</th></tr>
<tr><td>1. What advantages, if any, do you think ordering from a mail-order catalog offers compared to shopping at a local retail outlet? (Probe: What else?)

2. Why do you have one or more of your rugs or carpets professionally cleaned rather than cleaning them yourself or having someone else in the household clean them?

3. What is it about the color of the eye shadow that makes you like it the best?</td><td>Dichotomous

1. Did you heat the Danish product before serving it?
Yes 1
No 2

2. The federal government doesn't care what people like me think.
Agree 1
Disagree. 2

Multiple choice

1. I'd like you to think back to the last footwear of any kind that you bought. I'll read you a list of descriptions and would like for you to tell me which category they fall into.
(Read list and circle proper category.)
Dress and/or formal. 1
Casual 2
Canvas/trainer/gym shoes 3
Specialized athletic shoes 4
Boots. 5

2. In the last three months, have you used Noxzema skin cream . . . (Circle all that apply.)
As a facial wash 1
For moisturizing the skin 2
For treating blemishes 3
For cleansing the skin 4
For treating dry skin 5
For softening skin 6
For sunburn 7
For making the facial skin smooth . . . 8</td><td>Now that you have used the rug cleaner, would you say that you . . . (Circle one.)
Would definitely buy it 1
Would probably buy it 2
Might or might not buy it 3
Probably would not buy it 4
Definitely would not buy it. . . . . 5</td></tr>
</table>

is filled only with guacamole." How would you code these replies? As you can see, the question needs an "other" category.

A good question must also be clear and concise, and ambiguous language must be avoided. Take, for example, the question "Do you live within ten minutes of here?" The answer depends on the mode of transportation (maybe the person walks), driving speed, perceived time, and other factors. Instead, respondents should see a map with certain areas highlighted and be asked whether they live in one of those areas.

Clarity also implies using reasonable terminology. A questionnaire is not a vocabulary test. Jargon should be avoided, and language should be geared to the target audience. A question such as "What is the level of efficacy of your preponderant dishwasher powder?" would probably be greeted by a lot of blank stares. It would be much simpler to say "Are you (1) very satisfied, (2) somewhat satisfied, or (3) not satisfied with your current brand of dishwasher powder?"

Stating the survey's purpose at the beginning of the interview also improves clarity. The respondents should understand the study's intentions and the interviewer's expectations.

Sometimes, of course, to get an unbiased response, the interviewer must disguise the true purpose of the study. If an interviewer says, "We're conducting an image study for American National Bank" and then proceeds to ask a series of questions about the bank, chances are the responses will be biased. Many times respondents will try to provide answers that they believe are "correct" or that the interviewer wants to hear.

Finally, to ensure clarity, the interviewer should avoid asking two questions in one; for example, "How did you like the taste and texture of the Pepperidge Farm coffee cake?" This should be divided into two questions, one concerning taste and the other texture.

A question should also be unbiased. A question such as "Have you purchased any quality Black & Decker tools in the past six months?" biases respondents to think of the topic in a certain way (in this case, to link quality and Black & Decker tools). Questions can also be leading: "Weren't you pleased with the good service you received last night at the Holiday Inn?" (The respondent is all but instructed to say yes.) These examples are quite obvious; unfortunately, bias is usually more subtle. Even an interviewer's clothing or gestures can create bias.

Hundreds of children tested hundreds of toys at a recent Toys"R"Us opening to come up with a list of the season's favorites.

Observation Research

In contrast to survey research, **observation research** depends on watching what people do. Specifically, it can be defined as the systematic process of recording the behavioral patterns of people, objects, and occurrences without questioning them. A market researcher using the observation technique witnesses and records information as events occur or compiles evidence from records of past events. Carried a step further, observation may involve watching people or phenomena and may be conducted by human observers or machines. Examples of these various observational situations are shown in Exhibit 9.5.

Two common forms of people-watching-people research are one-way mirror observations and mystery shoppers.

At the Fisher-Price Play Laboratory, children are invited to spend 12 sessions playing with toys. Toy designers watch through one-way mirrors to see how children react to Fisher-Price's and other makers' toys. A one-way mirror allows the researchers to see the participants but they cannot see the researchers. Fisher-Price, for example, had difficulty designing a toy lawn mower that children would play with. A designer, observing behind the mirror, noticed the children's fascination with soap bubbles. He then created a lawn mower that spewed soap bubbles. It sold over a million units in the first year.

Mystery shoppers are researchers posing as customers who gather observational data about a store (e.g., are the shelves neatly stocked?) and collect data about customer/employee interactions. In the latter case, of course, there is communication between the mystery shopper and the employee. The mystery shopper may ask, "How much is

observation research
A research method that relies on four types of observation: people watching people, people watching an activity, machines watching people, and machines watching an activity.

mystery shoppers
Researchers posing as customers who gather observational data about a store.

EXHIBIT 9.5

Observational Situations

Situation	Example
People watching people	Observers stationed in supermarkets watch consumers select frozen Mexican dinners; the purpose is to see how much comparison shopping people do at the point of purchase.
People watching phenomena	Observer stationed at an intersection counts traffic moving in various directions.
Machines watching people	Movie or videotape cameras record behavior as in the people-watching-people example above.
Machines watching phenomena	Traffic-counting machines monitor traffic flow.

ethnographic research
The study of human behavior in its natural context; involves observation of behavior and physical setting.

this item?"; "Do you have this in blue?"; or "Can you deliver this by Friday?" The interaction is not an interview, and communication occurs only so that the mystery shopper can observe the actions and comments of the employee. Mystery shopping is, therefore, classified as an observational marketing research method even though communication is often involved.

Mystery shopping can provide a variety of benefits and insights, including:

- Enabling an organization to monitor compliance with product/service delivery standards and specifications (Eddie Bauer requires its sales staff to make three attempts to sell "add-ons" to each customer—would you like a tie, belt, and sunglasses to go with that shirt).
- Enabling marketers to examine the gap between promises made through advertising/sales promotion and actual service delivery.
- Helping monitor the impact of training and performance improvement initiatives.
- Identifying differences in the customer experience across different times of day, locations, product/service types, and other potential sources of variation in product/service quality.[11]

Mystery shopping typically has three different levels:

Level 1—The mystery shopper either makes a phone call or shops online. The mystery shopper follows a fixed script or set of instructions and evaluates the level of service. The scenario would involve a live online conversation with a service representative. For example, the mystery shopper claims that she is having a problem with some software that she recently purchased from the firm.

Level 2—The mystery shopper visits an establishment and makes a quick purchase with very little, if any, customer-service employee interaction. For example, buying gasoline at a Shell service station or going to a movie at a Cinemark movie theater. The shopper evaluates the purchase and the image of the facility.

Level 3—The mystery shopper visits a business and has significant interaction with the personnel. Restaurant chains such as McDonald's, Starbucks, Chipotle, T.G.I. Friday's, Sonic, IHOP, and Olive Garden strive for consistent execution of service and quality across their many stores. Results of the mystery shopping research are tied to employee incentives such as bonuses and rewards. Typical items that are evaluated include: hostess attitude and skills, food quality and presentation, condition of the restaurant (such as clean floors and walls), cleanliness of the restrooms, parking lot condition, interaction with the server (such as the introduction and suggestion selling), and the visibility of and interaction with the management staff.

Not only does management use mystery shopping as a motivator for employees but also as a coaching tool when results are not meeting standards. Thus, mystery shopping is ultimately a monitor of quality assurance.

Ethnographic Research

Ethnographic research comes to marketing from the field of anthropology. The technique is becoming increasingly popular in commercial marketing research. **Ethnographic research,** or the study of human behavior in its natural context, involves observation of behavior and physical setting. Ethnographers directly observe the population they are studying. As "participant observers," ethnographers can use their intimacy with the people they are studying to gain richer, deeper insights into culture and behavior—in short, what makes people do what they do. Ethnographers often question those being observed to gain a fuller understanding of what they are seeing.

Ethnographers can record

- what is happening, including what objects are being created or manipulated.
- where it is happening.

- flow of what is happening.
- order of what is happening.
- time spent on what is happening.
- who is doing what.
- what is being communicated verbally and nonverbally.
- reactions of the various participants (which are critical).[12]

Marriott hired IDEO Inc., an ethnographic research firm, to rethink the hotel experience for an increasingly important customer: the young, tech-savvy road warrior. "This is all about looking freshly at business travel and how people behave and what they need," explains Michael E. Jannini, Marriott's executive vice-president for brand management.[13]

To better understand Marriott's customers, IDEO dispatched a team of seven consultants, including a designer, anthropologist, writer, and architect, on a six-week trip. Covering 12 cities, the group hung out in hotel lobbies, cafes, and bars, and asked guests to graph what they were doing hour by hour. What they learned: Hotels are generally good at serving large parties but not small groups of business travelers. Researchers noted that hotel lobbies tend to be dark and better suited to killing time than conducting casual business. Marriott lacked places where guests could comfortably combine work with pleasure outside their rooms. IDEO consultant and Marriott project manager Dana Cho recalls watching a female business traveler drink wine in the lobby while trying not to spill it on papers spread out on a desk. "There are very few hotel services that address [such] problems," says Cho.[14]

Having studied IDEO's findings, Marriott announced plans to reinvent the lobbies of its Marriott and Renaissance Hotels, creating for each a social zone, with small tables, brighter lights, and wireless Web access, that is better suited to meetings. Another area will allow solo travelers to work or unwind in larger, quiet, semiprivate spaces where they won't have to worry about spilling coffee on their laptops or papers.[15]

Observation Research and Virtual Shopping

Advances in computer technology have enabled researchers to simulate an actual retail store environment on a computer screen. Depending on the type of simulation, a shopper can "pick up" a package by touching its image on the monitor and rotate it to examine all sides. Like buying on most online retailers, the shopper touches the shopping cart to add an item to the basket. During the shopping process, the computer unobtrusively records the amount of time the consumer spends shopping in each product category, the time the consumer spends examining each side of a package, the quantity of product the consumer purchases, and the order in which items are purchased.

Computer-simulated environments like this one offer a number of advantages over older research methods. First, unlike focus groups, concept tests, and other laboratory approaches, the virtual store duplicates the distracting clutter of an actual market. Consumers can shop in an environment with a realistic level of complexity and variety. Second, researchers can set up and alter the tests very quickly. Once images of the product are scanned into the computer, the researcher can make changes in the assortment of brands, product packaging, pricing, promotions, and shelf space within minutes. Data collection is also fast and error-free because the information generated by the purchase is automatically tabulated and stored by the computer. Third, production costs are low because displays are created electronically. Once the hardware and software are in place, the cost of a test is largely a function of the number of respondents, who generally are given a small incentive to participate. Fourth, the simulation has a high degree of flexibility. It can be used to test entirely new marketing concepts or to fine-tune existing programs. The simulation also makes it possible to eliminate much of the noise that exists in field experiments.[16]

experiment
A method a researcher uses to gather primary data.

sample
A subset from a larger population.

Kimberly-Clark has refined the virtual shopping experience even more. Located in Appleton, Wisconsin, the firm's virtual testing lab has a woman standing in a room surrounded by three screens showing a store aisle, a retina-tracking device recording her every glance. Asked by a Kimberly-Clark researcher to find a "big box" of Huggies Natural Fit diapers in size three, she pushed forward on a handle like that of a shopping cart, and the video simulated her progress down the aisle. Spotting Huggies' red packages, she turned the handle to the right to face a dizzying array of diapers. After pushing a button to get a kneeling view of the shelves, she reached forward and tapped the screen to put the box she wanted in her virtual cart. Kimberly-Clark hopes these virtual shopping aisles will help it better understand consumer behavior and make the testing of new products faster, more convenient, and more precise.[17]

Kimberly-Clark's lab also features a U-shaped floor-to-ceiling screen that re-creates in vivid detail interiors of the big retailers that sell the company's products—a tool that the company will use in presentations to executives in bids to win shelf space. A separate area is reserved for real replicas of store interiors, which can be customized to match the flooring, light fixtures, and shelves of retailers such as Target Corp. and Wal-Mart Stores, Inc.[18]

Kimberly-Clark says its studio allows researchers and designers to get a fast read on new product designs and displays without having to stage real-life tests in the early stages of development. Doing the research in a windowless basement, rather than an actual test market, also avoids tipping off competitors early in the development process. "We're trying to test ideas faster, cheaper, and better," says Ramin Eivaz, a vice president at Kimberly-Clark focusing on strategy. Before, new product testing typically took eight months to two years. Now, that time is cut in half, he says. Projects that test well with the virtual-reality tools will be fast-tracked to real-store trials.[19]

Virtual shopping research is growing rapidly as companies such as Frito-Lay, Goodyear, Procter & Gamble, General Mills, and Coca-Cola realize the benefits from this type of observation research. About 40,000 new consumer package goods are introduced in the United States each year.[20] All are vying for very limited retail shelf space. Any process, such as virtual shopping, that can speed product development time and lower costs is always welcomed by manufacturers.

Experiments

An **experiment** is a method a researcher can use to gather primary data. The researcher alters one or more variables—price, package design, shelf space, advertising theme, advertising expenditures—while observing the effects of those alterations on another variable (usually sales). The best experiments are those in which all factors are held constant except the ones being manipulated. The researcher can then observe that changes in sales, for example, result from changes in the amount of money spent on advertising.

Holding all other factors constant in the external environment is a monumental and costly, if not impossible, task. Such factors as competitors' actions, weather, and economic conditions are beyond the researcher's control. Yet market researchers have ways to account for the ever-changing external environment. Mars, the candy company, was losing sales to other candy companies. Traditional surveys showed that the shrinking candy bar was not perceived as a good value. Mars wondered whether a bigger bar sold at the same price would increase sales enough to offset the higher ingredient costs. The company designed an experiment in which the marketing mix stayed the same in different markets but the size of the candy bar varied. The substantial increase in sales of the bigger bar quickly proved that the additional costs would be more than covered by the additional revenue. Mars increased the bar size—and its market share and profits.

Specifying the Sampling Procedures

Once the researchers decide how they will collect primary data, their next step is to select the sampling procedures they will use. A firm can seldom take a census of all possible users of a new product, nor can they all be interviewed. Therefore, a firm must select a sample of the group to be interviewed. A **sample** is a subset from a larger population.

EXHIBIT 9.6

Types of Samples

	Probability Samples
Simple Random Sample	Every member of the population has a known and equal chance of selection.
Stratified Sample	The population is divided into mutually exclusive groups (such as gender or age); then random samples are drawn from each group.
Cluster Sample	The population is divided into mutually exclusive groups (such as geographic areas); then a random sample of clusters is selected. The researcher then collects data from all the elements in the selected clusters or from a probability sample of elements within each selected cluster.
Systematic Sample	A list of the population is obtained—e.g., all persons with a checking account at XYZ Bank—and a *skip interval* is obtained by dividing the sample size by the population size. If the sample size is 100 and the bank has 1,000 customers, then the skip interval is 10. The beginning number is randomly chosen within the skip interval. If the beginning number is 8, then the skip pattern would be 8,18, 28, ...
	Nonprobability Samples
Convenience Sample	The researcher selects the easiest population members from which to obtain information.
Judgment Sample	The researcher's selection criteria are based on personal judgment that the elements (persons) chosen will likely give accurate information.
Quota Sample	The researcher finds a prescribed number of people in several categories—e.g., owners of large dogs versus owners of small dogs. Respondents are not selected on probability sampling criteria.
Snowball Sample	Additional respondents are selected on the basis of referrals from the initial respondents. This method is used when a desired type of respondent is hard to find—e.g., persons who have taken round-the-world cruises in the last three years. This technique employs the old adage "Birds of a feather flock together."

Several questions must be answered before a sampling plan is chosen. First, the population, or **universe,** of interest must be defined. This is the group from which the sample will be drawn. It should include all the people whose opinions, behavior, preferences, attitudes, and so on are of interest to the marketer. For example, in a study whose purpose is to determine the market for a new canned dog food, the universe might be defined to include all current buyers of canned dog food.

After the universe has been defined, the next question is whether the sample must be representative of the population. If the answer is yes, a probability sample is needed. Otherwise, a nonprobability sample might be considered.

Probability Samples A **probability sample** is a sample in which every element in the population has a known statistical likelihood of being selected. Its most desirable feature is that scientific rules can be used to ensure that the sample represents the population.

One type of probability sample is a **random sample**—a sample arranged in such a way that every element of the population has an equal chance of being selected as part of the sample. For example, suppose a university is interested in getting a cross section of student opinions on a proposed sports complex to be built using student activity fees. If the university can acquire an up-to-date list of all the enrolled students, it can draw a random sample by using random numbers from a table (found in most statistics books) to select students from the list. Common forms of probability and nonprobability samples are shown in Exhibit 9.6.

Nonprobability Samples Any sample in which little or no attempt is made to get a representative cross section of the population can be considered a **nonprobability sample.** Therefore, the probability of selection of each sampling unit is not known. A common

universe
The population from which a sample will be drawn.

probability sample
A sample in which every element in the population has a known statistical likelihood of being selected.

random sample
A sample arranged in such a way that every element of the population has an equal chance of being selected as part of the sample.

nonprobability sample
Any sample in which little or no attempt is made to get a representative cross section of the population.

convenience sample
A form of nonprobability sample using respondents who are convenient or readily accessible to the researcher—for example, employees, friends, or relatives.

measurement error
An error that occurs when there is a difference between the information desired by the researcher and the information provided by the measurement process.

sampling error
An error that occurs when a sample somehow does not represent the target population.

frame error
An error that occurs when a sample drawn from a population differs from the target population.

random error
An error that occurs when the selected sample is an imperfect representation of the overall population.

field service firm
A firm that specializes in interviewing respondents on a subcontracted basis.

cross-tabulation
A method of analyzing data that lets the analyst look at the responses to one question in relation to the responses to one or more other questions.

form of a nonprobability sample is the **convenience sample,** which uses respondents who are convenient or readily accessible to the researcher—for instance, employees, friends, or relatives.

Nonprobability samples are acceptable as long as the researcher understands their nonrepresentative nature. Because of their lower cost, nonprobability samples are the basis of much marketing research.

Types of Errors Whenever a sample is used in marketing research, two major types of errors may occur: measurement error and sampling error. **Measurement error** occurs when there is a difference between the information desired by the researcher and the information provided by the measurement process. For example, people may tell an interviewer that they purchase Coors beer when they do not. Measurement error generally tends to be larger than sampling error.

Sampling error occurs when a sample somehow does not represent the target population. Sampling error can be one of several types. Nonresponse error occurs when the sample actually interviewed differs from the sample drawn. This error happens because the original people selected to be interviewed either refused to cooperate or were inaccessible. For example, people who feel embarrassed about their drinking habits may refuse to talk about them.

Frame error, another type of sampling error, arises if the sample drawn from a population differs from the target population. For instance, suppose a telephone survey is conducted to find out Chicago beer drinkers' attitudes toward Coors. If a Chicago telephone directory is used as the *frame* (the device or list from which the respondents are selected), the survey will contain a frame error. Not all Chicago beer drinkers have a phone, and many phone numbers are unlisted. An ideal sample (for example, a sample with no frame error) matches all important characteristics of the target population to be surveyed. Could you find a perfect frame for Chicago beer drinkers?

Random error occurs when the selected sample is an imperfect representation of the overall population. Random error represents how accurately the chosen sample's true average (mean) value reflects the population's true average (mean) value. For example, we might take a random sample of beer drinkers in Chicago and find that 16 percent regularly drink Coors beer. The next day we might repeat the same sampling procedure and discover that 14 percent regularly drink Coors beer. The difference is due to random error.

Error is common to all surveys, yet it is often not reported or is underreported. Typically, the only error mentioned in a written report is sampling error. When errors are ignored, misleading results can result in poor information and, perhaps, bad decisions.

Collecting the Data

Marketing research field service firms collect most primary data. A **field service firm** specializes in interviewing respondents on a subcontracted basis. Many have offices, often in malls, throughout the country. A typical marketing research study involves data collection in several cities, requiring the marketer to work with a comparable number of field service firms. Besides conducting interviews, field service firms provide focus-group facilities, mall intercept locations, test product storage, and kitchen facilities to prepare test food products.

Analyzing the Data

After collecting the data, the marketing researcher proceeds to the next step in the research process: data analysis. The purpose of this analysis is to interpret and draw conclusions from the mass of collected data. The marketing researcher tries to organize and analyze those data by using one or more techniques common to marketing research: one-way frequency counts, cross-tabulations, and more sophisticated statistical analysis. Of these three techniques, one-way frequency counts are the simplest. One-way frequency tables record the responses to a question. For example, the answers to the question "What brand of microwave popcorn do you buy most often?" would provide a one-way frequency distribution. One-way frequency tables are always done in data analysis, at least as a first step, because they provide the researcher with a general picture of the study's results.

A **cross-tabulation**, or "cross-tab," lets the analyst look at the responses to one question in relation to the responses to one or more other questions. For example, what is the association between gender and the brand of microwave popcorn bought most frequently? Hypothetical answers to this question are shown in Exhibit 9.7.

Although the Orville Reddenbacher brand was popular with both males and females, it was more popular with females. Compared with women, men strongly preferred Pop Rite, whereas women were more likely than men to buy Weight Watchers popcorn.

Researchers can use many other more powerful and sophisticated statistical techniques, such as hypothesis testing, measures of association, and regression analysis. A description of these techniques goes beyond the scope of this book, but can be found in any good marketing research textbook. The use of sophisticated statistical techniques depends on the researchers' objectives and the nature of the data gathered.

EXHIBIT 9.7

Hypothetical Cross-Tabulation between Gender and Brand of Microwave Popcorn Purchased Most Frequently

	Purchase by Gender	
Brand	Male	Female
Orville Reddenbacher	31%	48%
T.V. Time	12	6
Pop Rite	38	4
Act II	7	23
Weight Watchers	4	18
Other	8	0

GLOBAL

GLOBAL Perspectives

The Challenges of Global Marketing Research

Karl Feld, Research Manager at D3 Systems Incorporated, a Vienna, Virginia, marketing research firm, explains how global research can create unique problems not found in the United States. The story is told in his words.

Imagine you're driving a vehicle of unknown manufacture with dials you can't read down a muddy or dusty dirt track with no name to find a house with no number to make sure your contractor's employee interviewed the right respondent in a language you don't speak. You've been doing this for days, maybe even weeks. There's no running water, no electricity, no telephones, no mail service, and possibly no food other than what you've brought with you. Welcome to collecting research data from most of the world's people.

Questionnaire design in multicultural, multilingual research must use both the proper language and cultural context to elicit the desired responses. Context applies both to the language in the survey and the way it is administered, which is often more important than the questionnaire design itself. People in some cultures better relate to conversational interviewing styles than fixed questionnaire order. Some cultures require sensitive questions to be in a different order than others. In some places, people will only talk in particular settings. In research that I conducted in Bosnia-Herzegovina, for example, questionnaires had to be administered in a neutral location not affiliated with any local ethnic group.

Similarly, research in Arabic, Muslim countries which involve women generally must be conducted under the watchful eyes of the responsible male family leader, as social custom requires women not meet with outsiders without male presence. In Russia, it used to be extremely difficult to get face-to-face interviews inside people's homes. Public places were preferred. In Japan, it is only in private places like the home that face-to-face interviews will capture meaningful data.

In my experience in yesterday's Russia and Moldova, and in today's China, respondents asked questions of substance often will refuse to provide meaningful answers without approval from another authority. This is especially the case when interviewing professionals. Appropriate lag time, or preapproval, needs to be factored into timelines and interviewing environment to allow for this phenomenon.

I was also involved in a research study completed in South Africa. The study's sample frame was to draw from all adults in South Africa. Given that many South African villages lack building addresses, roads, and convenient grid layouts, sampling had to be designed using satellite maps to select dwelling units using an interval formula. A similar problem exists in Mexico, where streets are unidentified and houses unnumbered, compounded by walls and servants who keep strangers out. In Saudi Arabia, there is no officially recognized census of population and there are no elections and therefore no voter registration records or maps of population centers.[21]

Do you think that conducting research in developing countries is worth the effort? Do you think that doing marketing research in Western Europe is the same as the United States?

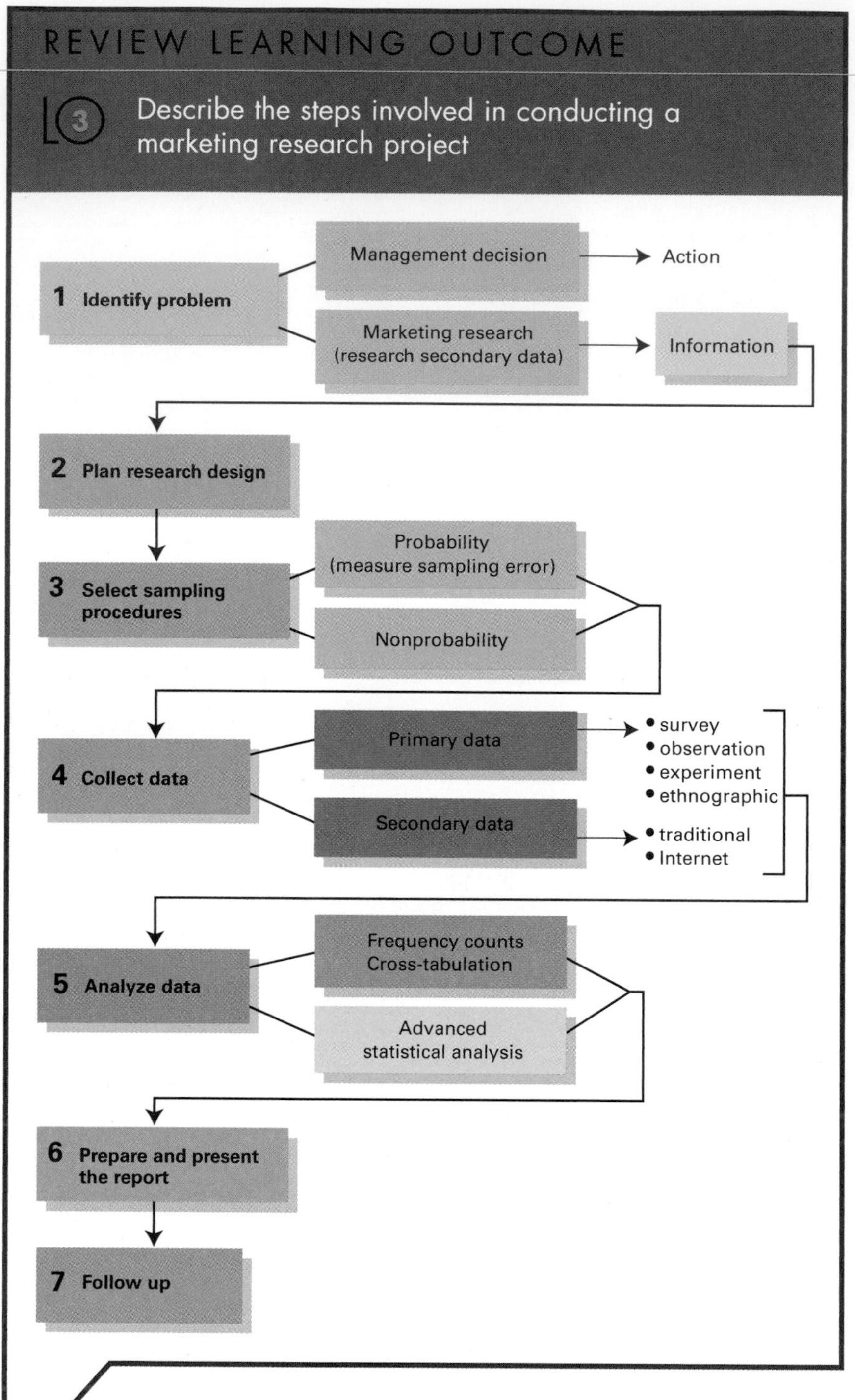

Preparing and Presenting the Report

After data analysis has been completed, the researcher must prepare the report and communicate the conclusions and recommendations to management. This is a key step in the process. If the marketing researcher wants managers to carry out the recommendations, he or she must convince them that the results are credible and justified by the data collected.

Researchers are usually required to present both written and oral reports on the project. Today, the written report is no more than a copy of the PowerPoint slides used in the oral presentation. Both reports should be tailored to the audience. They should begin with a clear, concise statement of the research objectives, followed by a complete, but brief and simple, explanation of the research design or methodology employed. A summary of major findings should come next. The conclusion of the report should also present recommendations to management.

Most people who enter marketing will become research users rather than research suppliers. Thus, they must know what to notice in a report. As with many other items we purchase, quality is not always readily apparent. Nor does a high price guarantee superior quality. The basis for measuring the quality of a marketing research report is the research proposal. Did the report meet the objectives established in the proposal? Was the methodology outlined in the proposal followed? Are the conclusions based on logical deductions from the data analysis? Do the recommendations seem prudent, given the conclusions?

Following Up

The final step in the marketing research process is to follow up. The researcher should determine why management did or did not carry out the recommendations in the report. Was sufficient decision-making information included? What could have been done to make the report more useful to management? A good rapport between the product manager, or whoever authorized the project, and the market researcher is essential. Often they must work together on many studies throughout the year.

Typically, the research process flows rather smoothly from one step to the next in the United States. However, conducting research in international markets can create a whole host of problems and challenges. These are discussed in the Global Perspectives box on page 311.

LO 4

THE PROFOUND IMPACT OF THE INTERNET ON MARKETING RESEARCH

The world's Internet population will be about 1.3 billion users by the time you read this paragraph. That's right—about one-fifth of the world's population is online. In the United States, 70 percent of the population is online spanning every ethnic, socioeconomic, and educational divide. It is no wonder then that most managers accept that online research can, under appropriate conditions, accurately represent U.S. consumers as a whole.[22] Non-adopters of the Internet tend to be older, low-income consumers (aged 65+ and with household income less than $30,000).[23] These consumers are not the target market for many companies' goods and services.

The popularity of online research continues to grow with over 90 percent of America's marketing research companies conducting some form of online research.[24] Today online survey research has replaced computer-assisted telephone interviewing (CATI) as the most popular mode of data collection.[25] Internet data collection is also rated as having the greatest potential for further growth. Having said this, we must also report that there is no sign that other types of surveys are disappearing as two-thirds of the market research companies are still relying on them.[26]

There are several reasons for the success of Internet marketing research:

- It allows for better and faster decision making through much more rapid access to business intelligence.
- It improves the ability to respond quickly to customer needs and market shifts.
- It makes follow-up studies and tracking research much easier to conduct and more fruitful.
- It slashes labor- and time-intensive research activities (and associated costs), including mailing, telephone solicitation, data entry, data tabulation, and reporting.

Advantages of Internet Surveys

The huge growth in the popularity of Internet surveys is the result of the many advantages offered by the Internet. The specific advantages of Internet surveys are related to many factors:

- *Rapid development, real-time reporting:* Internet surveys can be broadcast to thousands of potential respondents simultaneously. Respondents complete surveys simultaneously; then results are tabulated and posted for corporate clients to view as the returns arrive. The result: Survey results can be in a client's hands in significantly less time than would be required for traditional surveys.
- *Dramatically reduced costs:* The Internet can cut costs by 25 to 40 percent and provide results in half the time it takes to do traditional telephone surveys. Data collection costs account for a large proportion of any traditional market research budget. Telephone surveys are labor-intensive efforts incurring training, telecommunications, and management costs. Electronic methods eliminate these completely. While costs for traditional survey techniques rise proportionally with the number of interviews desired, electronic solicitations can grow in volume with little increase in project costs.
- *Personalized questions and data:* Internet surveys can be highly personalized for greater relevance to each respondent's own situation, thus speeding the response process. Respondents enjoy a personalized survey because they are asked to answer only pertinent questions, can pause and resume the survey as needed, and can see previous responses and correct inconsistencies.
- *Improved respondent participation:* Busy respondents may be growing increasingly intolerant of "snail mail" or telephone-based surveys. Internet surveys take half as

much time to complete as phone interviews, can be accomplished at the respondent's convenience (after work hours), and are much more stimulating and engaging. Graphics, interactivity, links to incentive sites and real-time summary reports make the interview enjoyable. The result? Much higher response rates.

- *Contact with the hard-to-reach*: Certain groups—doctors, high-income professionals, top management in Global 2000 firms—are among the most surveyed on the planet and the most difficult to reach. Many of these groups are well represented online. Internet surveys provide convenient anytime/anywhere access that makes it easy for busy professionals to participate.

Uses of the Internet by Marketing Researchers

Marketing researchers are using the Internet to administer surveys, conduct focus groups and observation research, and perform a variety of other types of marketing research.

Methods of Conducting Online Surveys

There are several basic methods for conducting online surveys: Web survey systems, survey design Web sites, and Web hosting. Each of these methods is briefly discussed.

Web Survey Systems Web survey systems are software systems specifically designed for Web questionnaire construction and delivery. They consist of an integrated questionnaire designer, Web server, database, and data delivery program, designed for use by nonprogrammers. In a typical use, the questionnaire is constructed with an easy-to-use edit feature, using a visual interface, and then automatically transmitted to the Web server system. The Web server distributes the questionnaire and files responses in a database. The user can query the server at any time via the Web for completion statistics, descriptive statistics on responses, and graphical displays of data. Several popular online survey research software packages are SPSS Quanquest, Inquisite, Sawtooth CiW, Web Survent, Infopoll, SurveyMonkey, and SurveyPro.

Survey Design and Web Hosting Sites Several Web sites allow the researcher to design a survey online without loading design software. The survey is then administered on the design site's server. Some offer tabulation and analysis packages as well. Two popular sites that offer Web hosting are WebSurveyor and Perseus. Several of the other firms mentioned in the previous paragraph also offer Web hosting.

Online Panel Providers

Designing a questionnaire is one step in the online survey process, another is procuring a sample to survey. Sometimes do-it-yourself researchers already have a sample or census of those they wish to survey, so sampling is not a problem. For example, members of a country club, persons who just purchased a new Toyota, students at a university, or customers at Best Buy. Often, however, researchers don't have a sample available, so they turn to online panel providers. The online panel providers such as Survey Sampling, Decision Analyst, Greenfield Online, Common Knowledge, and e-Rewards pre-recruit people who agree to opt-in to participate in online market research surveys.

Some online panels are created for specific industries such as construction, medical, or technology and may have a few thousand panel members, while the large commercial online panels have millions of people who have opted-in to participate in online surveys of varying topics. When people join most online panels, they answer an extensive profiling questionnaire which records demographic, lifestyle, and psychographic information, typically with hundreds of dimensions. This profiling information enables the panel provider to record detailed information on every panel member. Using this information, the panel provider can then target research efforts to panel members who meet specific criteria.

For example, a research study may require surveying avid golfers who play golf at least once a week, people who own an HDTV, or people who make decisions regarding information technology and work in companies with over 1,000 employees. Finding people who meet these criteria can be difficult, but online panel providers may be able to more easily identify these people based on their profiling information. By having millions of people pre-recruited and engaged in the research process, online panels help reduce recruitment cost and field time needed to complete a research project. For the really low-incidence groups, many of the larger panel providers, such as e-Rewards or Harris Interactive, are able to develop specialty panels for hard-to-reach audiences, such as small business owners, affluent consumers, and healthcare providers.

Online Focus Groups

A recent development in qualitative research is the online focus group. A number of organizations are currently offering this new means of conducting focus groups. The process is fairly simple.

- The research firm builds a database of respondents via a screening questionnaire on its Web site.
- When a client comes to a firm with a need for a particular focus group, the firm goes to its database and identifies individuals who appear to qualify. It sends an e-mail message to these individuals, asking them to log on to a particular site at a particular time scheduled for the group. The firm pays them an incentive for their participation.
- The firm develops a discussion guide similar to the one used for a conventional focus group.
- A moderator runs the group by typing in questions online for all to see. The group operates in an environment similar to that of a chat room so that all participants see all questions and all responses.
- The firm captures the complete text of the focus group and makes it available for review after the group has finished.

The Moderator's Role The basic way the moderator communicates with respondents in an online focus group is "freestyle" or "on the fly." That is, the moderator types in all questions, instructions, and probes into the text-entry area of the chat room in real-time (live, on-the-spot). In a variation on this method, the moderator copies and pastes questions from an electronic version of the guide into the text-entry area. Here, the moderator will toggle back and forth between the document and the chat room. An advantage of the freestyle method is that it forces the moderator to adapt to the group rather than use a series of canned questions. A disadvantage is that typing everything freestyle (or even copying and pasting from a separate document) takes time.

One way respondents can see stimuli (e.g., a concept statement, a mockup of a print ad, or a short product demonstration on video) is for the moderator to give the respondents a URL. Respondents then copy the URL from the chat stream, open another browser window, paste in the URL, and view it. An advantage of this approach is its simplicity. However, there are several disadvantages. First, if the respondents do not copy the URL correctly, they will not see it. Another disadvantage is that once respondents open another browser, they have "left the room" and the moderator has lost their attention; researchers must hope that respondents will return within the specified amount of time.

More advanced virtual focus group software reserves a frame (section) of the screen for stimuli to be shown. Here, the moderator has control over what is shown in the stimulus area. The advantage of this approach is that the respondent does not have to do any work to see the stimuli.

Types of Online Focus Groups Decision Analyst, one of America's most progressive firms in applying Internet technology to marketing research, offers two types of online focus groups:

1. *Real-time online focus groups:* These are live, interactive sessions with four to six participants and a moderator in a chat room format. The typical session does not last longer than 45 to 50 minutes. This technique is best for simple, straightforward issues that can be covered in limited time. The results tend to be superficial compared to in-person focus groups—but this is acceptable for certain types of projects. Typically, three to four groups are recommended as a minimum. Clients can view the chat room as the session unfolds and communicate with the moderator.
2. *Time-extended online focus groups:* These sessions follow a message board format and usually last five to ten days. The 15 to 20 participants must comment at least two or three times per day and spend 15 minutes a day logged in to the discussion. The moderator reviews respondents' comments several times per day (and night) and probes or redirects the discussion as needed. This technique provides three to four times as much content as the average in-person focus group. Time-extended online focus groups give participants time to reflect, talk to others, visit a store, or check the pantry. This extra time translates into richer content and deeper insights. Clients can view the online content as it is posted and may communicate with the moderator at any time.[27]

Using Channel M2 to Conduct Online Focus Groups Channel M2 provides market researchers with user-friendly virtual interview rooms, recruiting, and technical support for conducting virtual qualitative research, efficiently and effectively. By using Channel M2, the moderator and client can see and hear every respondent. You can see a demo at **www.channelM2.com.**

To recruit focus groups (from a global panel with access to over 15 million online consumers), Channel M2 uses a blend of e-mail and telephone verification and confirmation. Specifically, e-mails elicit involvement and direct participants to an online qualification questionnaire to ensure that each meets screening criteria. Telephone follow-up confirms that respondents qualify. Participants are sent a Web camera so that both verbal and nonverbal reactions can be recorded. Channel M2 tech support helps participants install the Webcam one to two days prior to the interview. Before participating, respondents must show a photo ID (their driver's license) to their Webcam so that their identity can be verified.

Participants are then provided instructions via e-mail, including a link to the Channel M2 interviewing room and a toll-free teleconference number to call. Upon clicking on the link, participants sign on and see the Channel M2 interview room, complete with live video of the other participants, text chat, screen or slide sharing, and whiteboard. (See Exhibit 9.8.)

Thus, in a Channel M2 focus group, all the participants can see and hear each other and communicate in a group setting. Once the focus group is under way, questions and answers occur in "real time" in a lively setting. Participants comment spontaneously, both verbally

EXHIBIT 9.8

An M2 Online Focus Group Under Way

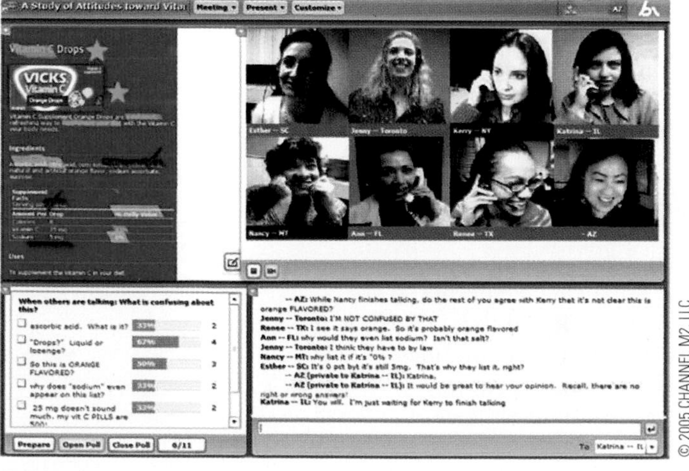

Source: From http://www.ChannelM2.com, accessed January, 2009.

and via text messaging, yet the moderator can provide direction exactly as would be done in a traditional setting.[28]

Advantages of Online Focus Groups Many advantages are claimed for cyber groups. Cyber Dialogue, a marketing research company specializing in cyber groups, lists the following benefits of online focus groups on its Web site:

- *Speed:* Typically, focus groups can be recruited and conducted, with delivery of results, within five days of client approval.
- *Cost-effectiveness:* Off-line focus groups incur costs for facility rental, airfare, hotel, and food. None of these costs is incurred with online focus groups.
- *Broad geographic scope:* In a given focus group, you can speak to people in Boise, Idaho, and Miami, Florida, at the same time.
- *Accessibility:* Online focus groups give you access to individuals who otherwise might be difficult to recruit (e.g., business travelers, doctors, mothers with infants).
- *Honesty:* From behind their screen names, respondents are anonymous to other respondents and tend to talk more freely about issues that might create inhibitions in a face-to-face group.

Web Community Research

A **Web community** is a carefully selected group of consumers who agree to participate in an ongoing dialogue with a particular corporation.[29] All community interaction takes place on a custom-designed Web site. During the life of the community—which may last anywhere from six months to a year or more—community members respond to questions posed by the corporation on a regular basis. These discussions, which typically take the form of qualitative "dialogues," are augmented by the ability of community members to talk to one another about topics that are of interest to them as well.

The popularity and power of Web communities initially came from several key benefits. They

- engage customers in a space where they are most comfortable, allowing clients to interact with them on a deeper level;
- uncover "exciters" and "eureka moments," resulting in customer-derived innovations;
- establish brand advocates who are emotionally invested in a company's success;
- offer real-time results, enabling clients to explore ideas that normal time constraints prohibit; and
- create a forum where natural dialogue allows customers to initiate topics important to them.[30]

Additionally, Web communities help companies create a customer-focused organization by putting employees into direct contact with consumers from the comfort of their own desks. Since communities provide advantages in speed, flexibility, and 24/7 access to consumers, they let the organization be agile in its research decision-making and prudent in its spending.

By adding a research focus to the Web community, it becomes a way to

- map the thinking of consumer segments;
- brainstorm new ideas;
- create and test new products; and
- observe natural consumer behavior.[31]

Web community
A carefully selected group of consumers who agree to participate in an ongoing dialogue with a particular corporation.

consumer generated media (CGM)
Media which consumers generate and share among themselves.

behavioral targeting
A form of observation marketing research that uses data mining coupled with identifying Web surfers by their IP addresses.

The Role of Consumer Generated Media in Marketing Research

Consumer generated media (CGM) is that media which consumers generate themselves and share among themselves. Because it is consumer-based, it is trusted more than traditional forms of advertising and promotion.[32] CGM originates from

- Blogs
- Message boards and forums
- Public discussions (Usenet newsgroups)
- Discussions and forums on large e-mail portals (Yahoo!, AOL, MSN)
- Online opinion/review sites and services
- Online feedback/complaint sites
- Shared videos and photos
- Podcasts

It is estimated that 2 billion CGM comments are archived on the Web today, with 83 million content creators active in 2008. Those numbers grow by about 30 percent annually.[33]

CGM can be influenced but not controlled by marketers. To influence CGM, one must first understand what is being said or shown. Nielsen BuzzMetrics is the leading marketing research firm tracking CGM. The firm uses sophisticated data mining and other technologies to help marketers understand what is being said about their company and brands on the Web. BrandPulse is BuzzMetrics' most popular product. BrandPulse can tell a company about the spread and influence of CGM. How much "buzz" exists? Where is online discussion taking place, and by whom? What issues are most important? Is the tone of discussion negative or positive?

BrandPulse enables clients to listen in on unaided consumer conversations that take place on Internet forums, boards, Usenet newsgroups, and blogs, providing timely understanding of the opinions and trends affecting a company or brand.

A second product, BrandPulse Insight reports, focuses on specific issues and concerns such as

- What's the buzz about a certain issue, trend, product, or piece of news?
- Who's active online, and what are these online consumers saying?
- Are current trends building or waning?
- Can any emerging trends be detected early, before they catch fire (or fizzle out prematurely)?
- What key motivators influence and affect consumer behavior?
- What are consumer/customer moods and emotions on a particular topic, or about a specific brand?
- Which online consumers are likely candidates for influencer panels and relationship marketing programs?[34]

A marketer wanting to know about the latest diet trend, technological gadget, automotive perceptions, or health-related concerns can tap into BrandPulse Insights to understand what's being said.

Nielsen BuzzMetrics offers a free service titled BlogPulse, **www.blogpulse.com**, which is a blog search engine and a trend tracker. You can easily create your own graphs plotting blog buzz by entering a search term. Alternatively, you can check out popular blog trends, follow a story trail between two bloggers, or see profiles of popular bloggers.

Behavioral Targeting

Behavioral targeting (BT) is fairly new with "intelligent" behavioral targeting beginning in 2000 with an online ad company called DoubleClick. BT began as a simple process by placing cookies on users' browsers to track which Web sites they visited. Researchers could determine pages visited, time at each page, and the number and type of searches made. The objective is to match the Internet user with ads for products and services that they will most likely purchase. Today, the more sophisticated forms of BT combine a consumer's online activity with psychographic and demographic profiles inferred from databases. Thus, the BT firms claim that they use IP addresses and not an individual's actual name and address. Because of the potential effectiveness of BT advertising, its popularity is skyrocketing. Over 24 percent of all online advertisers used BT in 2008.[35] That is almost double from the previous year.

The most exciting growth area of BT is in the area of social networking where users share personal information with "friends." The information that a member of MySpace, Facebook, or Friendslator shares plus marrying the information with demographic and psychographic databases becomes a very powerful tool for ad placement. Critics have called this form of BT "conversational eavesdropping analysis." Tom Kendall, a Facebook executive, counters by saying that it is simply "user-declared information targeting."[36] This is because much of it is derived from what members provide in their profile such as gender, age, political views, hobbies, college, and occupation. This type of data is much more powerful for marketers than clickstream information. For example, if a member says that they have a strong interest in kayaking, this is much more useful than knowing that someone using the same computer went to the kayaking site, Kayakonline.com. It could have been a friend using the computer.

BT has raised a number of privacy issues, particularly the latest forms of the technology that is integrated with social networking sites. Yet, according to the latest research, only 7 percent of the respondents in a nationwide survey were concerned about their ISP tracking their activity; 54 percent were worried about viruses; and 52 percent about identity theft/fraud.[37] Also, 29 percent claimed that they would rather receive appropriately targeted ads rather than random ones.

Companies using behavioral targeting include Allstate, American Express, IBM, and TDAmeritrade to name a few. When Pepsi wanted to make a splash on the Web promoting its new low-calorie vitamin-enhanced water, Aquafina Alive, the company didn't run ads just anywhere on the Internet. It placed ads only on sites it knew would be visited by people interested in healthy lifestyles. Pepsi was using behavioral targeting.

Pepsi worked with Tacoda to identify health-conscious people by looking at traffic to sites about healthy lifestyles over a month-long period. Then Pepsi arranged to place Aquafina Alive ads on some of the 4,000 Web sites affiliated with Tacoda so the ads would pop up whenever these health-conscious consumers visited. The result? Pepsi recorded a threefold increase in the number of people clicking on its Aquafina Alive ads compared with previous campaigns.[38] Pepsi's success illustrates why behavioral targeting advertising was over $1 billion in 2008.[39]

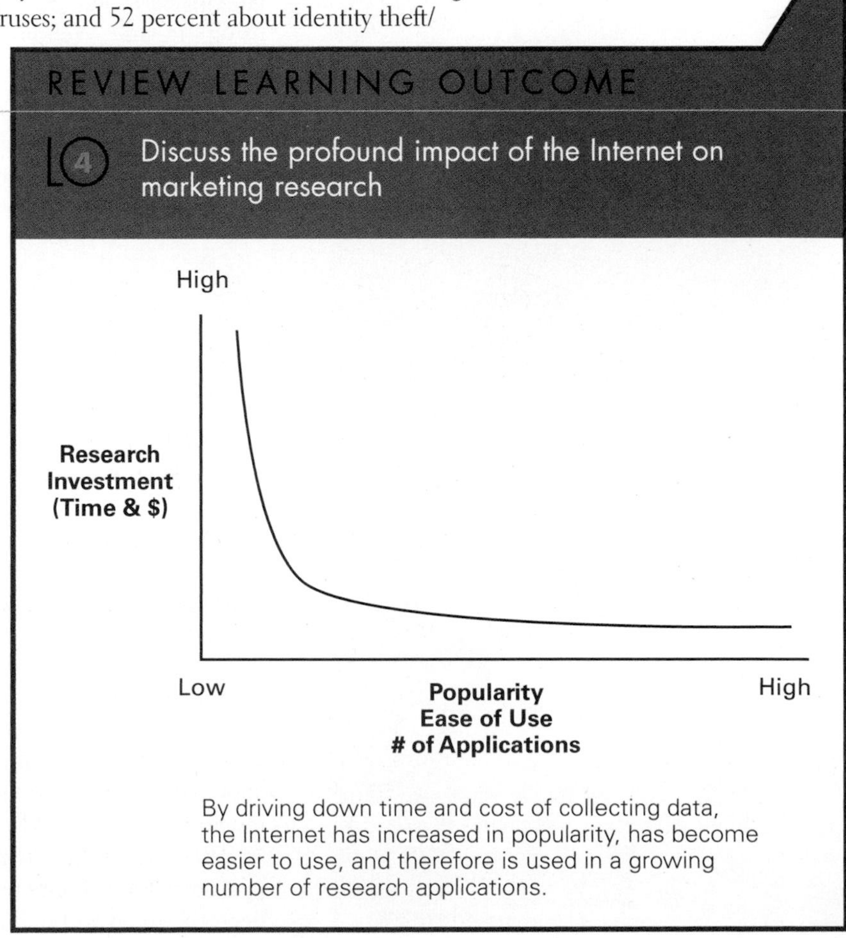

By driving down time and cost of collecting data, the Internet has increased in popularity, has become easier to use, and therefore is used in a growing number of research applications.

scanner-based research
A system for gathering information from a single group of respondents by continuously monitoring the advertising, promotion, and pricing they are exposed to and the things they buy.

BehaviorScan
A scanner-based research program that tracks the purchases of 3,000 households through store scanners in each research market.

Other Uses of the Internet by Marketing Researchers

The Internet revolution in marketing research has had an impact on more than just the way surveys and focus groups are conducted. The management of the research process and the dissemination of information have also been greatly enhanced by the Internet. Several key areas have been affected by the Internet:

- *The distribution of requests for proposals (RFPs) and proposals:* Companies can now quickly and efficiently send RFPs to a select e-mail list of research suppliers. In turn, research suppliers can develop proposals and e-mail them back to clients. A process that used to take days using snail mail now occurs in a matter of hours.
- *Collaboration between the client and the research supplier in the management of a research project:* Now a researcher and client may both be looking at a proposal, RFP, report, or some type of statistical analysis at the same time on their respective computer screens while discussing it over the telephone. This is very powerful and efficient. Changes in the sample size, quotas, and other aspects of the research plan can be discussed and made immediately.
- *Data management and online analysis:* Clients can access their survey via the research supplier's secure Web site and monitor the data gathering in real time. The client can use sophisticated tools to actually do data analysis as the survey develops. This real-time analysis may result in changes in the questionnaire, sample size, or the types of respondents being interviewed. The research supplier and the client become partners in "just-in-time" marketing research.
- *Publication and distribution of reports:* Reports can be published to the Web directly from programs such as PowerPoint and all the latest versions of leading word-processing, spreadsheet, and presentation software packages. This means that results are available to appropriate managers worldwide on an almost instantaneous basis. Reports can be searched for the content of interest using the same Web browser used to view the report.
- *Viewing of oral presentations of marketing research surveys by widely scattered audiences:* By placing oral presentations on password-protected Web sites, managers throughout the world can see and hear the actual client presentation. This saves time and money by avoiding the need for the managers to travel to a central meeting site.[40]

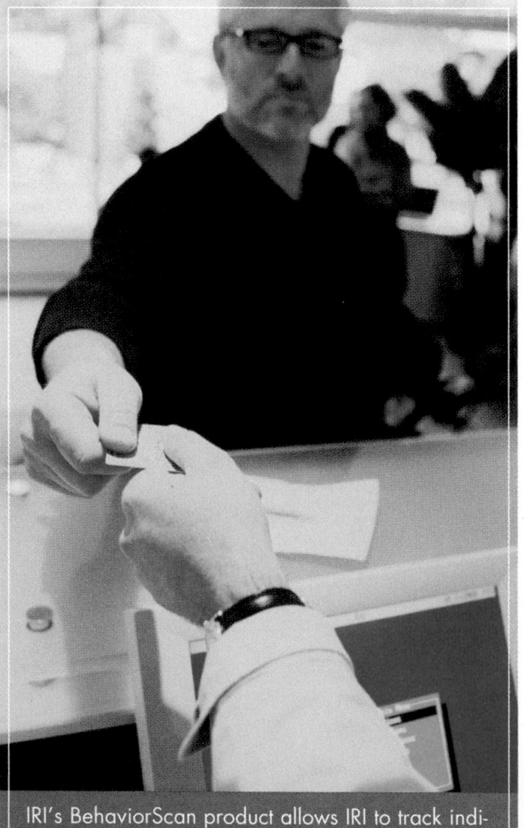
IRI's BehaviorScan product allows IRI to track individual household purchases over time. Participants in the household panel present an ID card at the checkout of a scanner-equipped grocery store.

© PHOTODISC/GETTY IMAGES

LO 5

SCANNER-BASED RESEARCH

Scanner-based research is a system for gathering information from a single group of respondents by continuously monitoring the advertising, promotion, and pricing they are exposed to and the things they buy. The variables measured are advertising campaigns, coupons, displays, and product prices. The result is a huge database of marketing efforts and consumer behavior. Scanner-based research is bringing ever closer the Holy Grail of marketing research: an accurate, objective picture of the direct causal relationship between different kinds of marketing efforts and actual sales.

The two major scanner-based suppliers are Information Resources, Inc. (IRI), and the A. C. Nielsen Company. Each has about half the market. However, IRI is the founder of scanner-based research.

IRI's first product is called **BehaviorScan.** A household panel (a group of 3,000 long-term participants in the research project) has been recruited and maintained in each BehaviorScan town. Panel members shop with an ID card, which is presented at the checkout in scanner-equipped grocery stores and drugstores, allowing IRI to track electronically each household's purchases, item by item, over time. It uses microcomputers to measure TV viewing in each panel household and can send special commercials to panel member television sets. With such a measure of household purchasing, it is possible to manipulate marketing variables, such as TV advertising or consumer promotions, or to introduce a new product and analyze real changes in consumer buying behavior.

IRI's most successful product is InfoScan Reviews—a scanner-based sales-tracking service for the consumer packaged-goods industry. Retail sales, detailed consumer purchasing information (including measurement of store loyalty and total grocery basket expenditures), and promotional activity by manufacturers and retailers are monitored and evaluated for all bar-coded products. Data are collected weekly from more than 34,000 supermarkets, drugstores, and mass merchandisers.

When Should Marketing Research Be Conducted?

When managers have several possible solutions to a problem, they should not instinctively call for marketing research. In fact, the first decision to make is whether to conduct marketing research at all.

Some companies have been conducting research in certain markets for many years. Such firms understand the characteristics of target customers and their likes and dislikes about existing products. Under these circumstances, further research would be repetitive and waste money. Procter & Gamble, for example, has extensive knowledge of the coffee market. After it conducted initial taste tests with Folgers Instant Coffee, P&G went into national distribution without further research. Consolidated Foods Kitchen of Sara Lee followed the same strategy with its frozen croissants, as did Quaker Oats with Chewy Granola Bars. This tactic, however, does not always work. P&G marketers thought they understood the pain reliever market thoroughly, so they bypassed market research for Encaprin aspirin in capsules. Because it lacked a distinct competitive advantage over existing products, however, the product failed and was withdrawn from the market.

Managers rarely have such great trust in their judgment that they would refuse more information if it were available and free. But they might have enough confidence that they would be unwilling to pay very much for the information or to wait a long time to receive it. The willingness to acquire additional decision-making information depends on managers' perceptions of its quality, price, and timing. Of course, if perfect information were available—that is, the data conclusively showed which alternative to choose—decision makers would be willing to pay more for it than for information that still left uncertainty. In summary, research should be undertaken only when the expected value of the information is greater than the cost of obtaining it.

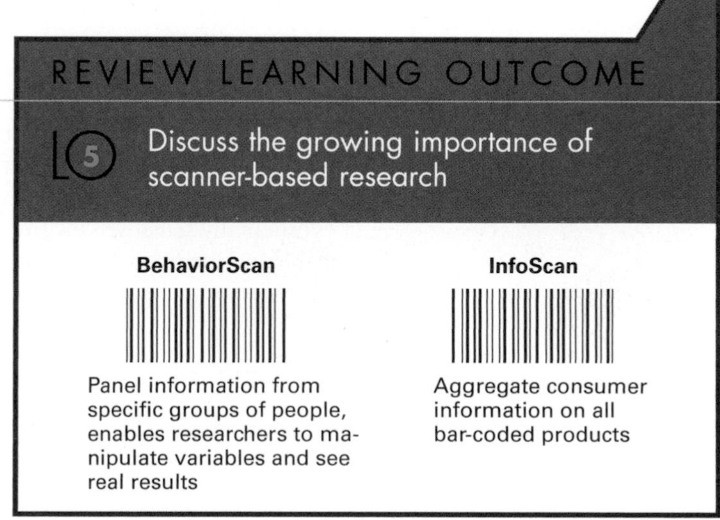

COMPETITIVE INTELLIGENCE

Derived from military intelligence, competitive intelligence is an important tool for helping a firm overcome a competitor's advantage. Specifically, competitive intelligence can help identify the advantage and play a major role in determining how it was achieved.

InfoScan
A scanner-based sales-tracking service for the consumer packaged-goods industry.

competitive intelligence (CI) An intelligence system that helps managers assess their competition and vendors in order to become more efficient and effective competitors.

Competitive intelligence (CI) helps managers assess their competitors and their vendors in order to become a more efficient and effective competitor. Intelligence is analyzed information. It becomes decision-making intelligence when it has implications for the organization. For example, one of your firm's primary competitors may have plans to introduce a product with performance standards equal to your own but with a 15 percent cost advantage. The new product will reach the market in eight months. This intelligence has important decision-making and policy consequences for management. Competitive intelligence and environmental scanning (where management gathers data about the external environment—see Chapter 4) combine to create marketing intelligence. Marketing intelligence is then used as input into a marketing decision support system. Nine out of ten large companies have employees dedicated to the CI function. Many firms spend several million dollars a year on the function.

The top corporate CI officer at a multibillion-dollar global technology company claims that competitive intelligence helped his company recover after it began losing market share to a competitor. The rival, after competing directly with the company for years, had figured out its bidding strategy. Instead of competing on price with an off-the-shelf offering, the rival was beginning to offer prospects a customized solution—and it was winning. When the CI officer's company changed to a customized approach, it won hundreds of millions of dollars in new business the following year. At Pergo, Inc., a maker of laminate flooring, CI helped win a major contract. When Pergo told a national retailer what it had learned from a mutual supplier—that the rival would not be able to launch a new product when it said it would—the retailer signed with Pergo instead.

Conferences and professional courses led by rival executives are great places to gather information. A former competitive intelligence chief at telecom-software vendor Telcordia, says his firm hit the jackpot when one of its accountants attended a professional course taught by a competitor's CFO. The CFO used his company as the case for the class, revealing all kinds of tantalizing private financial information. Listening in on competitors' presentations to analysts at investment conferences and on conference calls is another good way to get financial data.

Executives, marketers and engineers tend to enjoy talking about what's new or what is coming in the future at their companies. Talking to these people at trade shows or even watching regulatory proceedings can yield fruitful CI. When drug maker Bristol-Myers Squibb (BMS) told Congress it needed to increase its harvest of environmentally sensitive yew trees, says a former intelligence executive at SmithKline Beecham, he knew there was a good chance that BMS would soon seek Food and Drug Administration approval for a drug using yew bark.

Sources of Competitive Intelligence

The Internet and its databases are a great source of CI. CI researchers can use Internet databases to answer these and other questions:

- What articles were written about this market?
- What companies are associated with this product group?
- What patents have been filed for this technology?
- What are the major magazines or texts in this industry?
- What are the chances that I will find something in print on the target company?
- How many companies are in the same industry as the target company?
- Who are the reporters studying this industry?
- How can I be updated on industry and company events without having to constantly request the information?

- How can I compile a list of the leading experts in the industry and the key institutions they are associated with?

Non-computer-based sources of CI can be found in a variety of areas:

- A company's salespeople, who can directly observe and ask questions about the competition.
- Experts with in-depth knowledge of a subject or activity.
- CI consultants, who can use their knowledge and experience to gather needed information quickly and efficiently.
- Government agencies, a valuable source of all types of data.
- Uniform Commercial Code (UCC) filings, a system that identifies goods that are leased or pledged as collateral. This is an excellent source for learning about a company's latest additions to plant assets.
- Suppliers, a group that may offer information on products shipped to a competitor.
- Periodicals, a good source for timely articles on successes, failures, opportunities, and threats.
- The Yellow Pages, which often provide data on a number of competitors, trading areas, and special offerings.
- Trade shows, official gatherings where competitors display their latest offerings.

This list is not exhaustive, but it does provide an idea of how CI can be gathered.

REVIEW LEARNING OUTCOME

LO6 Explain the concept of competitive intelligence

CI
- Part of a sound marketing strategy
- Helps companies respond to competitive threats
- Helps reduce unnecessary costs

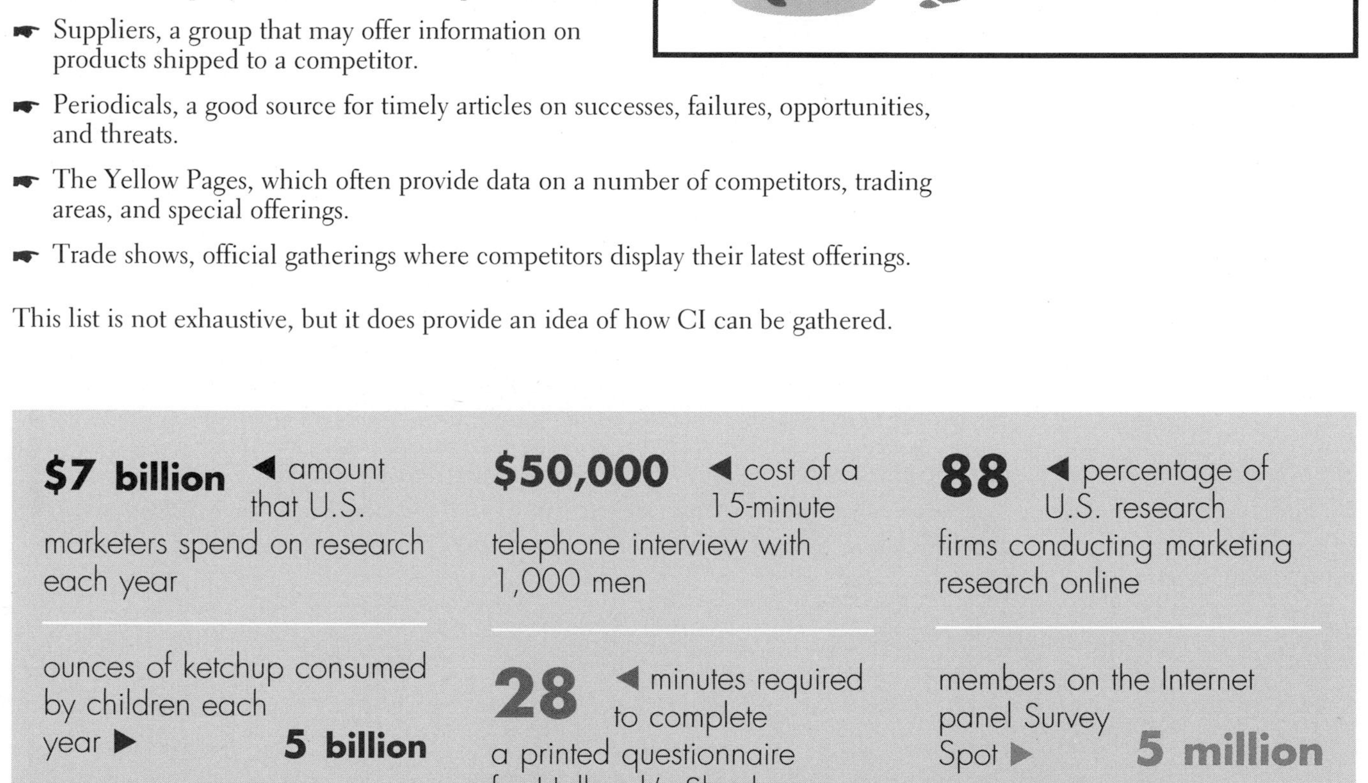

REVIEW AND APPLICATIONS

Explain the concept and purpose of a marketing decision support system. A decision support system (DSS) makes data instantly available to marketing managers and allows them to manipulate the data themselves to make marketing decisions. Four characteristics make DSSs especially useful to marketing managers: They are interactive, flexible, discovery oriented, and accessible. That is, they give managers access to information immediately and without outside assistance, they allow users to manipulate data in a variety of ways and to answer "what if" questions, and they are accessible to novice computer users.

- *Interactive:* Managers give simple instructions and see immediate results. The process is under their direct control; no computer programmer is needed. Managers don't have to wait for scheduled reports.
- *Flexible:* A DSS can sort, regroup, total, average, and manipulate the data in various ways. It will shift gears as the user changes topics, matching information to the problem at hand. For example, the CEO can see highly aggregated figures, and the marketing analyst can view very detailed breakouts.
- *Discovery-oriented:* Managers can probe for trends, isolate problems, and ask "what if" questions.
- *Accessible:* Managers who aren't skilled with computers can easily learn how to use a DSS. Novice users should be able to choose a standard, or default, method of using the system. They can bypass optional features so they can work with the basic system right away while gradually learning to apply its advanced features.

1.1 In the absence of company problems, is there any reason to develop a marketing DSS?

1.2 Explain the difference between marketing research and a DSS.

Define marketing research and explain its importance to marketing decision making. Marketing research is a process of collecting and analyzing data for the purpose of solving specific marketing problems. Marketers use marketing research to explore the profitability of marketing strategies. They can examine why particular strategies failed and analyze characteristics of specific market segments. Managers can use research findings to help keep current customers. Moreover, marketing research allows management to behave proactively, rather than reactively, by identifying newly emerging patterns in society and the economy.

2.1 The task of marketing is to create exchanges. What role might marketing research play in the facilitation of the exchange process?

2.2 Marketing research has traditionally been associated with manufacturers of consumer goods. Today, however, an increasing number of organizations, both profit and nonprofit, are using marketing research. Why do you think this trend exists? Give some examples of specific reasons why organizations might use marketing research.

2.3 Write a reply to the following statement: "I own a restaurant in the downtown area. I see customers every day who I know on a first-name basis. I understand their likes and dislikes. If I put something on the menu and it doesn't sell, I know that they didn't like it. I also read the magazine *Modern Restaurants*, so I know what the trends are in the industry. This is all of the marketing research I need to do."

2.4 Give an example of (a) the descriptive role of marketing research, (b) the diagnostic role, and (c) the predictive function of marketing research.

Describe the steps involved in conducting a marketing research project. The marketing research process involves several basic steps. First, the researcher and the decision maker must agree on a problem statement or set of research objectives. The researcher then creates an overall research design to specify how primary data will be gathered and analyzed. Before collecting data, the researcher decides whether the group to be interviewed will be a probability or nonprobability sample. Field service firms are often hired to carry out data collection. Once data have been collected, the researcher analyzes them using statistical analysis. The researcher then prepares and presents oral and written reports, with conclusions and recommendations, to management. As a final step, the researcher determines whether the recommendations were implemented and what could have been done to make the project more successful.

3.1 Critique the following methodologies and suggest more appropriate alternatives:

a. A supermarket was interested in determining its image. It dropped a short questionnaire into the grocery bag of each customer before putting in the groceries.

b. To assess the extent of its trade area, a shopping mall stationed interviewers in the parking lot every Monday and Friday evening. Interviewers walked up to people after they had parked their cars and asked them for their ZIP codes.

c. To assess the popularity of a new movie, a major studio invited people to call a 900 number and vote yes, they would see it again, or no, they would not. Each caller was billed a $2 charge.

3.2 You have been charged with determining how to attract more business majors to your school. Write an outline of the steps you would take, including the sampling procedures, to accomplish the task.

3.3 Why are secondary data sometimes preferable to primary data?

3.4 What is a marketing research aggregator? What role do these aggregators play in marketing research?

3.5 Discuss when focus groups should and should not be used.

3.6 Divide the class into teams of eight persons. Each group will conduct a focus group on the quality and number of services that your college is providing to its students. One person from each group should be chosen to act as moderator. Remember, it is the moderator's job to facilitate discussion, not to lead the discussion. These groups should last approximately 45 minutes. If possible, the groups should be videotaped or recorded. Upon completion, each group should write a brief report of its results. Consider offering to meet with the dean of students to share the results of your research.

3.7 Why do companies hire mystery shoppers?

3.8 Ethnographic research is a new (and expensive) trend in marketing research. Find an article on ethnographic research. Read and summarize the article. What is your opinion of ethnographic research? Do you think it will be the wave of the future? Explain your reasoning.

Discuss the profound impact of the Internet on marketing research. The Internet has vastly simplified the secondary data search process, placing more sources of information in front of researchers than ever before. Internet survey research is surging in popularity. Internet surveys can be created rapidly and reported in real time. They are also relatively inexpensive and can easily be personalized. Often researchers can use the Internet to contact respondents who are difficult to reach by other means. The Internet can also be used to conduct focus groups, analyze consumer-generated media, engage in behavioral targeting, distribute research proposals and reports, and to facilitate collaboration between the client and the research supplier. Clients can access real-time data and analyze the information as the collection process continues.

4.1 Go to **www.strategicbusinessinsights.com/vals/presurvey.shtml** and take the VALS Survey. Report on how marketing researchers are using this information.

4.2 Divide the class into teams. Each team should go to a different opt-in survey site on the Web and participate in an online survey. A spokesperson for each team should report the results to the class.

4.3 What are various ways to obtain respondents for online surveys?

4.4 Describe the advantages and disadvantages of online surveys.

LO5 Discuss the growing importance of scanner-based research. A scanner-based research system enables marketers to monitor a market panel's exposure and reaction to such variables as advertising, coupons, store displays, packaging, and price. By analyzing these variables in relation to the panel's subsequent buying behavior, marketers gain useful insight into sales and marketing strategies.

5.1 Why has scanner-based research been seen as "the ultimate answer" for marketing researchers? Do you see any disadvantages of this methodology?

5.2 Detractors claim that scanner-based research is like "driving a car down the road looking only in the rearview mirror." What does this mean? Do you agree?

LO6 Explain the concept of competitive intelligence. Competitive intelligence (CI) helps managers assess their competition and their vendors in order to become more efficient and effective competitors. Intelligence is analyzed information, and it becomes decision-making intelligence when it has implications for the organization.

By helping managers assess their competition and vendors, CI leads to fewer surprises. CI allows managers to predict changes in business relationships, guard against threats, forecast a competitor's strategy, and develop a successful marketing plan.

The Internet and databases accessed via the Internet offer excellent sources of CI. Company personnel, particularly sales and service representatives, are usually good sources of CI. Many companies require their salespersons to routinely fill out CI reports. Other external sources of CI include experts, CI consultants, government agencies, UCC filings, suppliers, newspapers and other publications, Yellow Pages, and trade shows.

6.1 Why do you think that CI is so hot in today's environment?

6.2 Prepare a memo to your boss at JetBlue Airlines and outline why the organization needs a CI unit.

6.3 Form a team with three other students. Each team must choose a firm in the PC manufacturing industry and then go to the Web site of the firm and acquire as much CI as possible. Each team will then prepare a five-minute oral presentation on its findings.

KEY TERMS

behavioral targeting (BT) 319
BehaviorScan 320
central-location telephone (CLT) facility 301
closed-ended question 303
competitive intelligence (CI) 322
computer-assisted personal interviewing 301
computer-assisted self-interviewing 301
consumer generated media 318
convenience sample 310
cross-tabulation 311
database marketing 292
decision support system (DSS) 291
ethnographic research 306
executive interviews 302
experiment 308
field service firm 310
focus group 302
frame error 310
group dynamics 302
InfoScan 321
mall intercept interview 301
management decision problem 297
marketing information 291
marketing research 292
marketing research aggregator 299
marketing research objective 297
marketing research problem 297
measurement error 310
mystery shoppers 305
nonprobability sample 309
observation research 305
open-ended question 303
primary data 299
probability sample 309
random error 310
random sample 309
research design 299
sample 308
sampling error 310
scaled-response question 303
scanner-based research 320
secondary data 297
survey research 300
universe 309
Web community 317

EXERCISES

APPLICATION EXERCISE

For its study, *Teens and Healthy Eating: Oxymoron or Trend?*, New York–based BuzzBack Market Research focused on snacking. Among its findings: Teens eat an average of three snacks per day; breakfast is the meal they skip most often. Though scads of snacks are stacked on store shelves, when it comes to healthier treats targeting adolescents, it's a bit of a teenage wasteland. BuzzBack asked 532 teen respondents to conjure up new foods they'd gobble up. The following are some of their ideas:

- "Travel fruit. Why can't fruit be in travel bags like chips or cookies? Canned fruit is too messy. Maybe have a dip or something sold with it, too."—Female, age 17.
- "A drink that contains five servings of fruits and vegetables."—Male, age 16, Caucasian.
- "I would invent all natural and fat-free, vitamin-enhanced cookies and chips that had great flavor."—Female, age 16.
- "I would make fruit-based cookies."—Male, age 16, Caucasian.
- "Low-carb trail mix, because trail mix is easy to eat but it has a lot of fat/carbs."—Female, age 15, Caucasian.
- "I would create some sort of microwavable spaghetti."—Male, age 16, Caucasian.
- "Something quick and easy to make that's also cheap. I'll be in college next year, and I'm trying to find things that are affordable, healthier than cafeteria food, and easy to make."—Female, age 17.
- "*Good* vegan mac 'n' cheese."—Female, age 18, Caucasian.
- "A smoothie where you could get all the nutrients you need, that tastes good, helps you stay in shape, and is good for you. Has vitamins A, B^3, B_{12}, C, ginkgo. Packaging would be bright."—Female, age 16, African American.
- "A breakfast shake for teens. Something easy that tastes good, not necessarily for dieters like Slim·Fast, etc. Something to balance you off in the morning."—Male, age 18.

Activities

1. You are a new-product development specialist at Kraft. What guidance can you get from the BuzzBack study?
2. Choose one of the suggestions from the above list of healthy snack concepts. Imagine that your company is interested in turning the idea into a new product but wants to conduct market research before investing in product development. Design a marketing research plan that will give company managers the information they need before engaging in new-product development of the idea. (Hint: Use steps 1–3 in Exhibit 9.1 as a guide.)
3. Once you have finished your plan, collect the data. Depending on the data-collection methods you have outlined in your plan, you may need to make adjustments so that you can collect actual data to analyze.
4. Analyze the data you collected, and create a report for your company either recommending that the company pursue the idea you chose or investigate another.

ETHICS EXERCISE

John Michael Smythe owns a small marketing research firm in Cleveland, Ohio, which employs 75 people. Most employees are the sole breadwinners in their families. John's firm has not fared well for the past two years and is on the verge of bankruptcy. The company recently surveyed over 2,500 people in Ohio about new-car purchase plans for the Ohio Department of Economic Development. Because the study identified many hot prospects for new cars, a car dealer has offered John $8,000 for the names and phone numbers of people saying they are "likely" or "very likely" to buy a new car within the next 12 months. John needs the money to avoid laying off a number of employees.

Questions

1. Should John Smythe sell the names?
2. Does the AMA Statement of Ethics address this issue? Go to **www.marketingpower.com/AboutAMA/Pages/Statement of Ethics.aspx.** Then write a brief paragraph on what the AMA Statement of Ethics contains that relates to John Smythe's dilemma.

MARKETING PLAN EXERCISE

For the marketing plan exercise in Chapter 6, you considered the consumer decision-making process as it applies to your marketing plan; in Chapter 7, you analyzed your potential business markets. In Chapter 8, you identified your company's target market and its various segments. Now complete the following exercises to find out more about your competitors and customers through marketing research—a key to any strategic marketing plan. Once completed, you can use your answers to complete the Marketing Plan Worksheet for Part 2, which you can find on your companion Web site at **www.cengage.com/international.**

1. Are there any critical issues that must be explored with primary marketing research before you can implement your marketing plan for your chosen company? These might include items such as customer demand, purchase intentions, customer perceptions of product quality, price perceptions, and reaction to critical promotion. List some critical research questions and decide which form of research you would use.
2. Design a brief Internet customer satisfaction survey that you could place on your company Web site. Use the "Survey Wiz" to help you with your questionnaire at **http://psych.fullerton.edu/mbirnbaum/programs/surveyWiz.HTM.**
3. What type of competitive intelligence will you need to gather in order to monitor your market space? How can analyzing the job offerings, mission or "about us" statement, products and services descriptions, or other general information on your competitors' Web sites help you figure our their strategic direction? What areas of a Web site could you scan to gather competitive information?

CASE STUDY: LOOK-LOOK

You can't always believe what you hear, particularly in the fast-moving world of youth trends. That is, unless you listen to Sharon Lee and DeeDee Gordon, founders of Look-Look, the most accurate information resource on the global youth culture. The pair founded the company in 1999, determined to find whatever makes the cultural spider-sense tingle—music, shoes, clothes, games, makeup, food, and technology. Lee and Gordon took Look-Look online in 2000, and the company has since risen to be the paragon of trend forecasting in the youth market. How?

When Sharon Lee needs to know what's cool, she taps into a network of experts the CIA would envy. It's a Web-linked weave of over 35,000 volunteers and part-timers, aged 14 to 35, recruited over several years at clubs and hangouts around the country, from New York to Los Angeles and points in between, to report on their world.

Look-Look's human database brims with youthful hipsters from all over the planet who log in to the company's Web site to answer surveys and polls, register opinions, and communicate ideas. Some of the recruits communicate through Look-Look–supplied digital or video cameras, from which they upload pictures, document reports, and post content to the firm's intranet message boards.

Some, such as Portland, Oregon's Emily Galash, receive small monthly sums—Emily's is $125 per month—for capturing and sharing the moments of their personal lives. Gordon and Lee welcome images from anything as private as underground parties to simple adornments like posters on bedroom walls.

Look-Look relies on "early adopters" and "influencers" to provide depth to information that traditional research practices only skim. For Look-Look, focus groups are strictly passé; such conventional tactics would not have raised its clients' awareness of incoming trends such as under-a-dollar stores, fold-up scooters, or over-the-shoulder bags. Strangely enough, however, Gordon and Lee and counterparts, such as Jane Buckingham's Intelligence Group, Irma Zandl's Zandl Group, and Faith Popcorn's BrainReserve, now run the risk of being out of date themselves.

Once known as "cool seekers or "cool hunters," they now prefer to refer to themselves as "futurists" and "planners." The Web-connected reality of instant digital feedback and content generation through blogs, text messages, and music, photo, and video hosting sites such as MySpace.com causes trends to flash before us and dissipate before most know they existed in the first place.

"Cool" isn't even cool anymore, and marketers to this age group must spot what's going to be "in" before or as it develops. Look-Look's success is well documented, however, and that's the reason companies like Telemundo, Procter & Gamble, Nike, Kellogg's, and Coca-Cola rely on its help to stay in the running for the $175 billion wielded by teen consumers.

Recently, Look-Look began working with Microsoft to tap into the culture of the twenty-first-century teenager. On a project designed to help the software giant's PC-gaming unit connect with the growing female presence in the video gaming market, Look-Look selected 30 teens from its database and asked them to keep blogs about their experiences with Microsoft PC games. Lisa Sikora, group product manager for Windows gaming, acknowledged Look-Look's relevance, noting that companies like hers need to "start talking to this audience in their way, not our way."

But Look-Look doesn't stop there. In addition to finding the future, Look-Look is defining it, too. Working with Virgin Mobile, an extremely youth-oriented marketer, Look-Look came up with two unique ideas. The first was to hold an art contest among members of its human database to devise cell phone covers. The top five designs, from artists aged 17 to 20 years old, are now officially sold in stores as covers for the Kyocera K10 Royale.

Remember Emily Galash? The money she earns is for the 30 to 40 pictures she sends to Look-Look every month. Instead of attempting to interpret her pictures for the sake of reporting on trends, Look-Look bolts select shots directly to the pages of Virgin Mobile's internationally viewable Web site because they *are* trends. Amateur work like Emily's and that of the artists who designed the Kyocera face plates is valued because it maintains its authenticity, individuality, and credibility with its target audience.

Clients also ask Look-Look to identify which products are the hottest in a given market. After a small army is canvassed through online polls and surveys, the results are arranged into categories. "The turnaround," says Lee, "can be as little as 48 hours." Look-Look categorizes information into ten channels: fashion, entertainment, technology, activities, eating and drinking, health and beauty, mood of culture (how kids feel about life), spirituality, city guide, and Look Out (a "best of" findings in a snapshot). The information is put through rigorous paces. "Methodology is crucial, especially with the quantity and quality of the sample," says Lee. "We can take a sample of 300 or thousands. That's up to Gallup standards."

Still, cool is as hard to pin down as a weather forecast for next week. But the real arbiters of cool are those who can afford to lead. "Ultimately," says Que Gaskins, chief marketing officer of the avant-garde, multicultural marketing Ad*itive, "the future of cool belongs to whoever has the most buying power."[41]

Questions

1. What is Look-Look offering businesses that traditional market research firms cannot offer?
2. Describe the role of the Internet in youth trend spotting. Do you think a research firm can accurately forecast youth trends without an online component to its research plan?
3. Go to Look-Look's Web site at **http://www.look-look.com** and check out some of the free information in each category. How accurate do you find the information? Have you seen any of these trends in your city or region, or among your friends and classmates?
4. Make a list of products or companies that you think could benefit from Look-Look's form of predictive market research. Next to each item, write a brief explanation of why and how you think cool seeking would benefit the company or product.

COMPANY CLIPS

READYMADE—READY RESEARCH

Having been in business for five years, *ReadyMade* now has a lot of research on the various characteristics of its readers. Its knowledge of GenNesters has made the magazine a leader in identifying and describing that segment. As a new business, *ReadyMade* found that businesses had little interest in marketing to this group. Now that businesses have become more aware of GenNester influence, however, *ReadyMade* is able to fill the need for information. *ReadyMade* has statistics on the ages at which people are marrying and the interests of couples that have just married. Because the magazine is ahead of the curve on gathering information on this segment, *ReadyMade* can help other businesses figure out how to tailor their marketing efforts to fit the needs of GenNesters.

Questions

1. How has *ReadyMade* been able to help Toyota promote its new line of cars? What benefit has *ReadyMade* seen from the partnership?
2. How does *ReadyMade* use new technology to gain information about its consumers?
3. What sorts of long-term decisions is *ReadyMade* making that could be aided by research? What would you recommend?

Marketing & You Results

Higher scores indicate that you place greater importance on collecting primary and secondary information when developing marketing campaigns or projects. A lower score means you would be less aggressive in collecting information and might plow ahead regardless of how much information you do (or don't) have. After reading Chapter 9, you can see how involved gathering and analyzing market information can be, but also how critical it is to success.

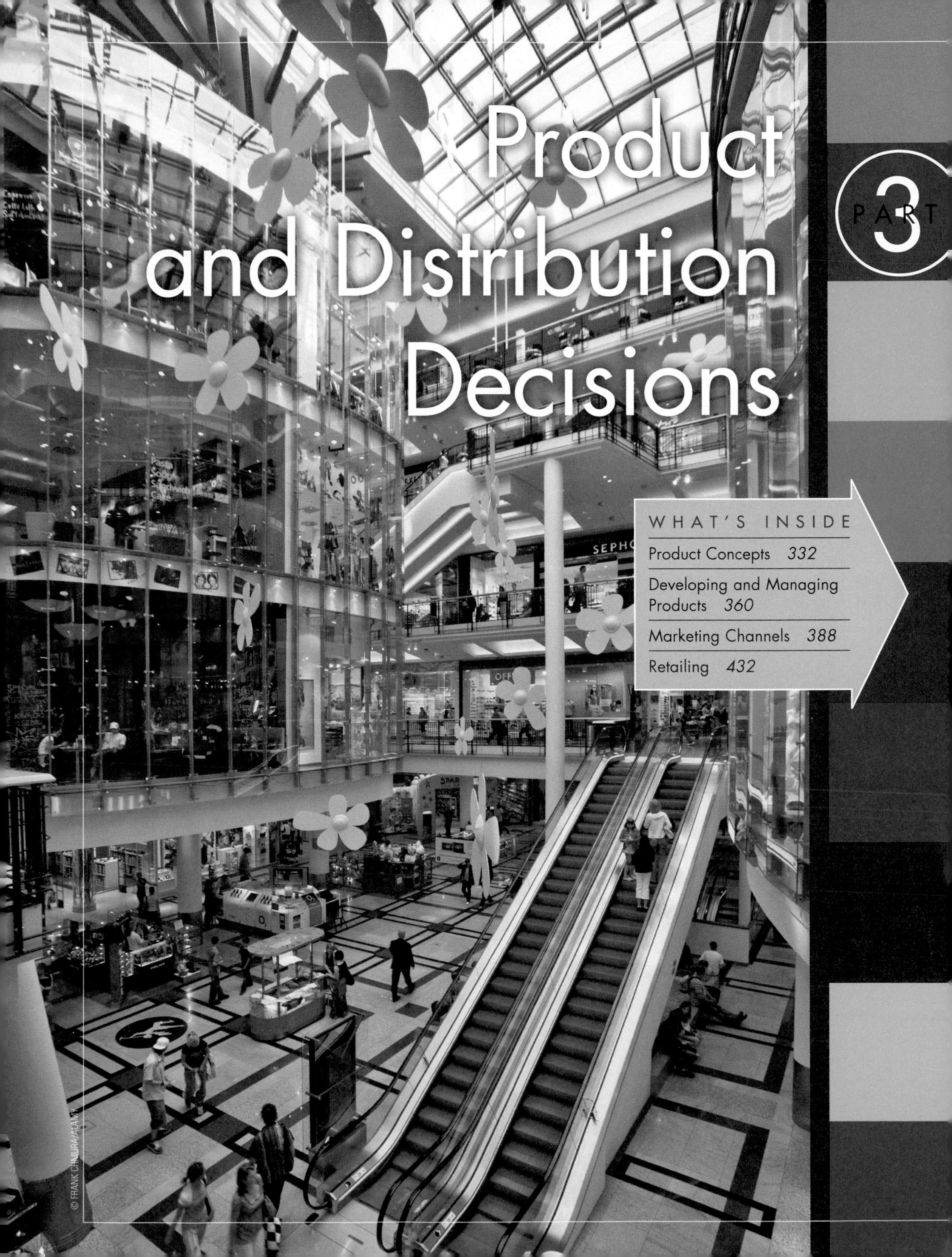

Product and Distribution Decisions

PART 3

WHAT'S INSIDE

© BRIAN SNYDER/REUTERS/LANDOV

CHAPTER 10

Product Concepts

LEARNING OUTCOMES

- LO 1 Define the term *product*
- LO 2 Classify consumer products
- LO 3 Discuss the importance of services to the economy
- LO 4 Discuss the differences between services and goods
- LO 5 Define the terms *product item, product line,* and *product mix*
- LO 6 Describe marketing uses of branding
- LO 7 Describe marketing uses of packaging and labeling
- LO 8 Discuss global issues in branding and packaging
- LO 9 Describe how and why product warranties are important marketing tools

LO 1 WHAT IS A PRODUCT?

The product offering, the heart of an organization's marketing program, is usually the starting point in creating a marketing mix. A marketing manager cannot determine a price, design a promotion strategy, or create a distribution channel until the firm has a product to sell. Moreover, an excellent distribution channel, a persuasive promotion campaign, and a fair price have no value when the product offering is poor or inadequate.

A **product** may be defined as everything, both favorable and unfavorable, that a person receives in an exchange. A product may be a tangible good such as a pair of shoes, a service such as a haircut, an idea such as "don't litter," or any combination of these three. Packaging, style, color, options, and size are some typical product features. Just as important are intangibles such as service, the seller's image, the manufacturer's reputation, and the way consumers believe others will view the product.

To most people, the term *product* means a tangible good. However, services and ideas are also products. The marketing process identified in Chapter 1 is the same whether the product marketed is a good, a service, an idea, or some combination of these.

REVIEW LEARNING OUTCOME

LO 1 Define the term *product*

Product

- Good
- Service
- Idea

Marketing & You

Using the following scale, indicate your opinion on the line before each item.

1	2	3	4	5	6
Strongly disagree	Disagree	Neutral	Agree	Strongly agree	

__ I usually purchase brand-name products.

__ Store brands are of poor quality.*

__ All brands are about the same.*

__ The well-known national brands are best for me.

__ The more expensive brands are usually my choices.

__ The higher the price of a product, the better its quality.

__ Nice department and specialty stores offer me the best products.

Total your score, reversing your scores for the items followed by an asterisk. That is, if you answered 1, change it to 5 and vice versa. Read the chapter and find out what your score means at the end.

Source: From Scale #230, *Marketing Scales Handbook*, G. Bruner, K. James, H. Hesel, eds. Vol. IIII. © by American Marketing Association.

LO 2 TYPES OF CONSUMER PRODUCTS

Products can be classified as either business (industrial) or consumer products, depending on the buyer's intentions. The key distinction between the two types of products is their intended use. If the intended use is a business purpose, the product is classified as a business or industrial product. As explained in Chapter 7, a **business product** is used to manufacture other goods or services, to facilitate an organization's operations, or to resell to other customers. A **consumer product** is bought to satisfy an individual's personal wants. Sometimes the same item can be classified as either a business or a consumer product, depending on its intended use. Examples include lightbulbs, pencils and paper, and computers.

We need to know about product classifications because business and

product
Everything, both favorable and unfavorable, that a person receives in an exchange.

business product (industrial product)
A product used to manufacture other goods or services, to facilitate an organization's operations, or to resell to other customers.

consumer product
A product bought to satisfy an individual's personal wants.

convenience product
A relatively inexpensive item that merits little shopping effort.

shopping product
A product that requires comparison shopping because it is usually more expensive than a convenience product and is found in fewer stores.

specialty product
A particular item for which consumers search extensively and are very reluctant to accept substitutes.

unsought product
A product unknown to the potential buyer, or a known product that the buyer does not actively seek.

service
The result of applying human or mechanical efforts to people or objects.

consumer products are marketed differently. They are marketed to different target markets and tend to use different distribution, promotion, and pricing strategies.

Chapter 7 examined seven categories of business products: major equipment, accessory equipment, component parts, processed materials, raw materials, supplies, and services. The current chapter examines an effective way of categorizing consumer products. Although there are several ways to classify them, the most popular approach includes these four types: convenience products, shopping products, specialty products, and unsought products (see Exhibit 10.1). This approach classifies products according to how much effort is normally used to shop for them.

Convenience Products

A **convenience product** is a relatively inexpensive item that merits little shopping effort—that is, a consumer is unwilling to shop extensively for such an item. Candy, soft drinks, combs, aspirin, small hardware items, dry cleaning, and car washes fall into the convenience product category.

Consumers buy convenience products regularly, usually without much planning. Nevertheless, consumers do know the brand names of popular convenience products, such as Coca-Cola, Bayer aspirin, and Right Guard deodorant. Convenience products normally require wide distribution in order to sell sufficient quantities to meet profit goals. For example, the gum Dentyne Ice is available everywhere, including Wal-Mart, Walgreens, gas stations, newsstands, and vending machines.

Shopping Products

A **shopping product** is usually more expensive than a convenience product and is found in fewer stores. Consumers usually buy a shopping product only after comparing several brands or stores on style, practicality, price, and lifestyle compatibility. They are willing to invest some effort into this process to get the desired benefits.

EXHIBIT 10.1

Classification of Consumer Products

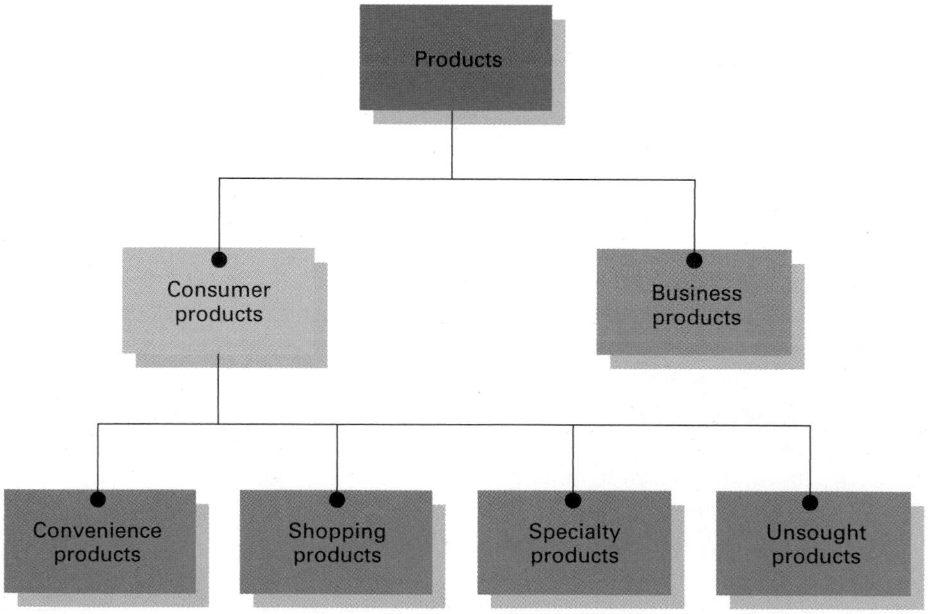

There are two types of shopping products: homogeneous and heterogeneous. Consumers perceive *homogeneous* shopping products as basically similar—for example, washers, dryers, refrigerators, and televisions. With homogeneous shopping products, consumers typically look for the lowest-priced brand that has the desired features. For example, they might compare Kenmore, Whirlpool, and General Electric refrigerators.

In contrast, consumers perceive *heterogeneous* shopping products as essentially different—for example, furniture, clothing, housing, and universities. Consumers often have trouble comparing heterogeneous shopping products because the prices, quality, and features vary so much. The benefit of comparing heterogeneous shopping products is "finding the best product or brand for me"; this decision is often highly individual. For example, it would be difficult to compare a small, private university with a large, public university.

Specialty Products

When consumers search extensively for a particular item and are very reluctant to accept substitutes, that item is a **specialty product**. Rolex watches, Rolls-Royce automobiles, Bose speakers, and highly specialized forms of medical care are generally considered specialty products.

Marketers of specialty products often use selective, status-conscious advertising to maintain their product's exclusive image. Distribution is often limited to one or a very few outlets in a geographic area. Brand names and quality of service are often very important.

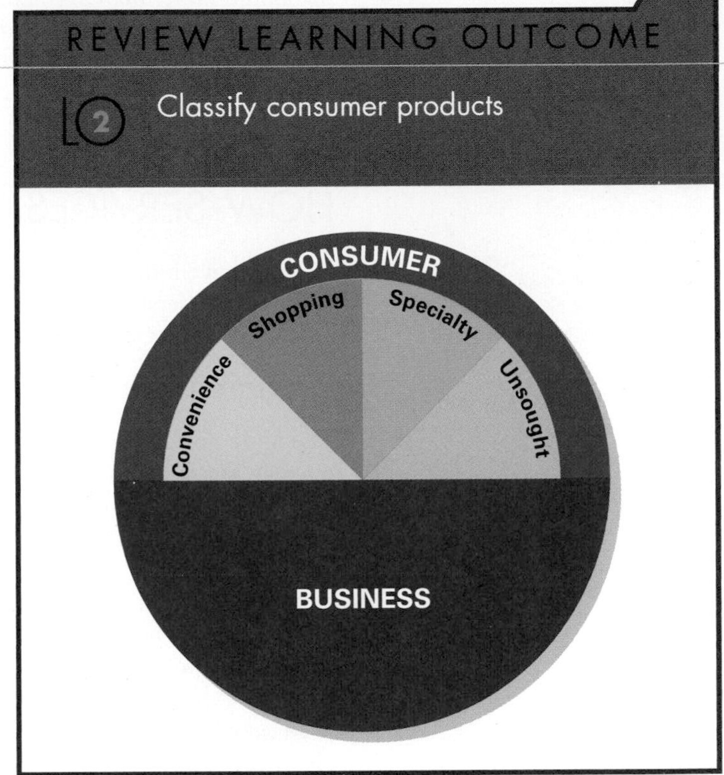

Unsought Products

A product unknown to the potential buyer or a known product that the buyer does not actively seek is referred to as an **unsought product**. New products fall into this category until advertising and distribution increase consumer awareness of them.

Some goods are always marketed as unsought items, especially needed products we do not like to think about or care to spend money on. Insurance, burial plots, and similar items require aggressive personal selling and highly persuasive advertising. Salespeople actively seek leads to potential buyers. Because consumers usually do not seek out this type of product, the company must go directly to them through a salesperson, direct mail, or direct-response advertising.

THE IMPORTANCE OF SERVICES

A **service** is the result of applying human or mechanical efforts to people or objects. Services involve a deed, a performance, or an effort that cannot be physically possessed. Today, the service sector substantially influences the U.S. economy, accounting for 81 percent of both U.S. gross domestic product and U.S. employment.[1] The demand for services is expected to continue. According to the Bureau of Labor Statistics, service occupations will be responsible for nearly all net job growth through the year 2016.[2] Much of this demand results from demographics. An aging population will need nurses, home health care, physical therapists, and social workers. Two-earner families need child-care, housecleaning, and lawn-care services. Also increasing will be the demand for information managers, such as computer engineers and systems analysts. There is also a growing market for service companies worldwide.

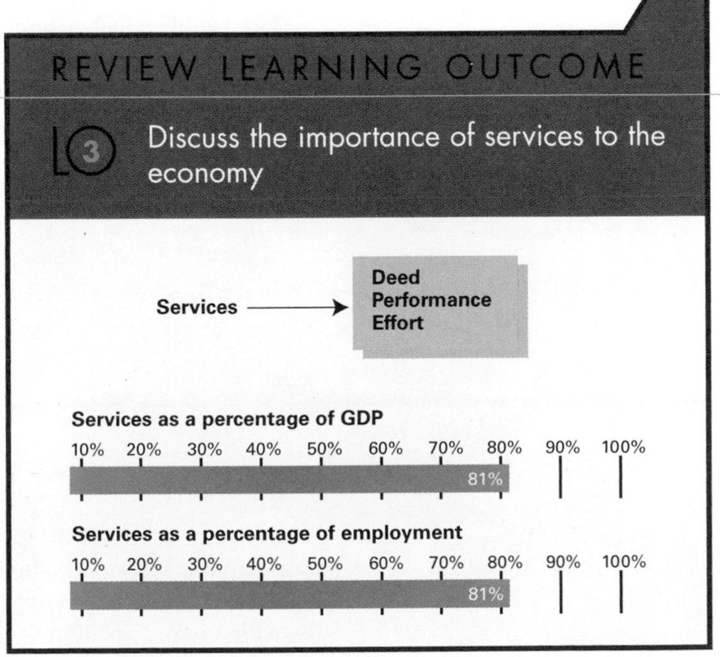

The marketing process described in Chapter 1 is the same for all types of products, whether they are goods or services. Many ideas and strategies discussed throughout this book have been illustrated with service examples. In many ways, marketing is marketing, regardless of the product's characteristics. In addition, although a comparison of goods and services marketing can be beneficial,

intangibility
The inability of services to be touched, seen, tasted, heard, or felt in the same manner that goods can be sensed.

search quality
A characteristic that can be easily assessed before purchase.

experience quality
A characteristic that can be assessed only after use.

credence quality
A characteristic that consumers may have difficulty assessing even after purchase because they do not have the necessary knowledge or experience.

inseparability
The inability of the production and consumption of a service to be separated. Consumers must be present during the production.

in reality it is hard to distinguish clearly between manufacturing and service firms. Indeed, many manufacturing firms can point to service as a major factor in their success. For example, maintenance and repair services offered by the manufacturer are important to buyers of copy machines. General Electric makes most of its revenues from finance operations rather than from products. Nevertheless, services have some unique characteristics that distinguish them from goods, and marketing strategies need to be adjusted for these characteristics.

HOW SERVICES DIFFER FROM GOODS

Services have four unique characteristics that distinguish them from goods. Services are intangible, inseparable, heterogeneous, and perishable.

Intangibility

The basic difference between services and goods is that services are intangible performances. Because of their **intangibility**, they cannot be touched, seen, tasted, heard, or felt in the same manner that goods can be sensed. Services cannot be stored and are often easy to duplicate.

Evaluating the quality of services before or even after making a purchase is harder than evaluating the quality of goods because, compared to goods, services tend to exhibit fewer search qualities. A **search quality** is a characteristic that can be easily assessed before purchase—for instance, the color of an appliance or automobile. At the same time, services tend to exhibit more experience and credence qualities. An **experience quality** is a characteristic that can be assessed only after use, such as the quality of a meal in a restaurant or the actual experience of a vacation. A **credence quality** is a characteristic that consumers may have difficulty assessing even after purchase because they do not have the necessary knowledge or experience. Medical and consulting services are examples of services that exhibit credence qualities.

These characteristics also make it harder for marketers to communicate the benefits of an intangible service than to communicate the benefits of tangible goods. Thus, marketers often rely on tangible cues to communicate a service's nature and quality. For example, Travelers Insurance Company's use of the umbrella symbol helped make tangible the benefit of protection that insurance provides.

The facilities that customers visit, or from which services are delivered, are a critical tangible part of the total service offering. Messages about the organization are communicated to customers through elements such as the décor, the clutter or neatness of service areas, and the staff's manners and dress. Reflecting this idea, the design and development team at Bass Pro Shops believes that in-store displays are not just fixtures, but marketing tools that will attract customers if designed to reflect local culture. So, for example, the Destin, Florida, store incorporates indigenous seagulls and swordfish in the chandeliers.[3]

The facilities that customers visit or from which services are delivered, such as those in a hair stylist's shop, are a critical tangible part of the total service offering.

Inseparability

Goods are produced, sold, and then consumed. In contrast, services are often sold, produced, and consumed at the same time. In other words, their production and consumption are inseparable activities. This **inseparability** means that, because consumers must be present during the production of services like haircuts or surgery, they are actually involved in the production of the services they buy. That type of consumer involvement is rare in goods manufacturing. Inseparability also means that customers have an opportunity to provide input into their service experience and outcome. For example, individuals getting a haircut can provide feedback during the process so that their hair looks the way they want it to look.

Simultaneous production and consumption also means that services normally cannot be produced in a centralized location and consumed in decentralized locations, as goods typically are. Services are also inseparable from the perspective of the service provider. Thus, the quality of service that firms are able to deliver depends on the quality of their employees.

© KATHY DEWITT/ALAMY

Heterogeneity

One great strength of McDonald's is consistency. Whether customers order a Big Mac and french fries in Fort Worth, Tokyo, or Moscow, they know exactly what they are going to get. This is not the case with many service providers. Because services have greater **heterogeneity**, or variability of inputs and outputs, they tend to be less standardized and uniform than goods. For example, physicians in a group practice or barbers in a barber shop differ from one another in their technical and interpersonal skills. A given physician's or barber's performance may even vary depending on time of day, physical health, or some other factor. Because services tend to be labor-intensive, and production and consumption are inseparable, consistency and quality control can be hard to achieve.

Standardization and training help increase consistency and reliability. Limited-menu restaurants like Pizza Hut and KFC offer customers high consistency from one visit to the next because of standardized preparation procedures. Another way to increase consistency is to mechanize the process. Banks have reduced the inconsistency of teller services by providing automated teller machines (ATMs). Automatic coin receptacles and electronic toll collection systems such as E-Z Pass have replaced human collectors on toll roads.

REVIEW LEARNING OUTCOME

LO4 Discuss the differences between services and goods

Intangible
Inseparable
Heterogeneous
Perishable

Perishability

The fourth characteristic of services is their **perishability**, which means that they cannot be stored, warehoused, or inventoried. An empty hotel room or airplane seat produces no revenue that day. The revenue is lost. Yet service organizations are often forced to turn away full-price customers during peak periods.

One of the most important challenges in many service industries is finding ways to synchronize supply and demand. The philosophy that some revenue is better than none has prompted many hotels to offer deep discounts on weekends and during the off-season and has prompted airlines to adopt similar pricing strategies during off-peak hours. Car rental agencies, movie theaters, and restaurants also use discounts to encourage demand during nonpeak periods.

PRODUCT ITEMS, LINES, AND MIXES

Rarely does a company sell a single product. More often, it sells a variety of things. A **product item** is a specific version of a product that can be designated as a distinct offering among an organization's products. Campbell's Creamy Chicken soup is an example of a product item (see Exhibit 10.2).

heterogeneity
The variability of the inputs and outputs of services, which causes services to tend to be less standardized and less uniform than goods.

perishability
The inability of services to be stored, warehoused, or inventoried.

product item
A specific version of a product that can be designated as a distinct offering among an organization's products.

EXHIBIT 10.2

Campbell's Product Lines and Product Mix

Depth of the Product Lines	Width of the Product Mix				
	Canned Soups	**Microwave Soups**	**Gravies**	**Meal Kits**	**Tomato Juice**
	Chicken Noodle	Creamy Tomato	Beef	Chicken Pasta	Regular
	Tomato	Vegetable	Turkey	Stroganoff Pasta	Low Sodium
	Vegetable Beef	Chicken Noodle	Mushroom	Chicken With Rice	Organic
	French Onion	Creamy Chicken	Chicken	Pork Chops With Stuffing	Healthy Request
	More	More	More	More	

Source: Campbell's Web site: http://www.campbellsoup.com, June 10, 2008.

product line
A group of closely related product items.

product mix
All products that an organization sells.

product mix width
The number of product lines an organization offers.

product line depth
The number of product items in a product line.

A group of closely related product items is a **product line**. For example, the column in Exhibit 10.2 titled "Canned Soups" and "Microwave Soups" represents one of Campbell's product lines. Different container sizes and shapes also distinguish items in a product line. Diet Coke, for example, is available in cans and various plastic containers. Each size and each container are separate product items.

An organization's **product mix** includes all the products it sells. Together, all of Campbell's products—canned soups, microwave soups, gravies, meal kits, and tomato juice—constitute its product mix. Each product item in the product mix may require a separate marketing strategy. In some cases, however, product lines and even entire product mixes share some marketing strategy components. Nike promotes all of its product items and lines with the theme "Just Do It."

Organizations derive several benefits from organizing related items into product lines, including the following:

- *Advertising economies:* Product lines provide economies of scale in advertising. Several products can be advertised under the umbrella of the line. Campbell's can talk about its soup being "Mm! Mm! Good!" and promote the entire line.
- *Package uniformity:* A product line can benefit from package uniformity. All packages in the line may have a common look and still keep their individual identities. Again, Campbell's soup is a good example.
- *Standardized components:* Product lines allow firms to standardize components, thus reducing manufacturing and inventory costs. For example, many of the components Samsonite uses in its folding tables and chairs are also used in its patio furniture. General Motors uses the same parts on many automobile makes and models.
- *Efficient sales and distribution:* A product line enables sales personnel for companies like Procter & Gamble to provide a full range of choices to customers. Distributors and retailers are often more inclined to stock the company's products if it offers a full line. Transportation and warehousing costs are likely to be lower for a product line than for a collection of individual items.
- *Equivalent quality:* Purchasers usually expect and believe that all products in a line are about equal in quality. Consumers expect that all Campbell's soups and all Mary Kay cosmetics will be of similar quality.

Product mix width (or breadth) refers to the number of product lines an organization offers. In Exhibit 10.2, the width of Campbell's product mix is five product lines. **Product line depth** is the number of product items in a product line. As shown in Exhibit 10.2, the Tomato Juice product line consists of four product items; the Gravies product line includes more than four product items.

Firms increase the *width* of their product mix to diversify risk. To generate sales and boost profits, firms spread risk across many product lines rather than depend on only one or two. Firms also widen their product mix to capitalize on established reputations. The Oreo Cookie brand has been extended to include items such as breakfast cereal, ice cream, Jell-O pudding, and cake mix.

Firms increase the *depth* of their product lines to attract buyers with different preferences, to increase sales and profits by further segmenting the market, to capitalize on economies of scale in production and marketing, and to even out seasonal sales patterns. Coca-Cola and PepsiCo are introducing soft drinks in the United States using the natural, plant-based sweetener stevia. These companies are targeting consumers looking for healthier sweetener alternatives.[4] As another example, Oreo Cookies now come in a variety of flavors, including Double Delight Mint Creme, Chocolate Creme, Uh-Oh Oreos (vanilla cookie, chocolate filling), Double Delight Peanut Butter, and Chocolate Fudge Sundae Creme.

Adjustments to Product Items, Lines, and Mixes

Over time, firms change product items, lines, and mixes to take advantage of new technical or product developments or to respond to changes in the environment. They may adjust by modifying products, repositioning products, or extending or contracting product lines.

Product Modification Marketing managers must decide if and when to modify existing products. **Product modification** changes one or more of a product's characteristics:

- *Quality modification:* change in a product's dependability or durability. Reducing a product's quality may let the manufacturer lower the price and appeal to target markets unable to afford the original product. Conversely, increasing quality can help the firm compete with rival firms. Increasing quality can also result in increased brand loyalty, greater ability to raise prices, or new opportunities for market segmentation. Inexpensive ink-jet printers have improved in quality to the point that they produce photo-quality images. These printers are now competing with camera film. To appeal to a more upscale market, Robert Mondavi Winery introduced a high-end wine called Twin Oaks to prestigious restaurants and hotels. This wine is positioned as a higher-quality wine than the one Mondavi sells in supermarkets.
- *Functional modification:* change in a product's versatility, effectiveness, convenience, or safety. Tide with Downy combines the functions of cleaning power and fabric softening into one product. Lea & Perrins offers its steak sauce in a value-priced squeeze bottle with a "no mess, stay clean" cap.
- *Style modification:* aesthetic product change, rather than a quality or functional change. Procter & Gamble has added Febreze scents to its Tide liquid laundry detergent, Downy liquid fabric softener, and Bounce dryer sheets. These products all promise their usual function, with a touch of scent to improve the aesthetics of each brand.[5] Clothing and auto manufacturers also commonly use style modifications to motivate customers to replace products before they are worn out. **Planned obsolescence** is a term commonly used to describe the practice of modifying products so that those that have already been sold become obsolete before they actually need replacement. For example, products such as printers and cell phones become obsolete because technology changes so quickly. Some argue that planned obsolescence is wasteful; some claim it is unethical. Marketers respond that consumers favor style modifications because they like changes in the appearance of goods such as clothing and cars. Marketers also contend that consumers, not manufacturers and marketers, decide when styles are obsolete.

Repositioning Repositioning, as Chapter 8 explained, involves changing consumers' perceptions of a brand. Kool-Aid, the soft drink brand that has stood for fun and refreshment for many years, is adding better-for-you options by introducing new and

product modification
Changing one or more of a product's characteristics.

planned obsolescence
The practice of modifying products so those that have already been sold become obsolete before they actually need replacement.

© VICKI BEAVER

reformulated products. They are repositioning the brand as supporting a healthier family lifestyle.[6]

Changing demographics, declining sales, or changes in the social environment often motivate firms to reposition established brands. The clothing retailer Banana Republic started out selling safari-style clothing, but the concept soon became outdated. Gap acquired the chain and repositioned it as a more upscale retailer offering business casual clothing. Procter & Gamble is redesigning its Dawn liquid detergent line, including adding new products, sizes and graphics. For example, its Dawn Plus line will be positioned as a tough cleaning brand, reformulated with an added enzyme to fight stuck-on foods.[7]

Product Line Extensions A **product line extension** occurs when a company's management decides to add products to an existing product line in order to compete more broadly in the industry. Procter & Gamble extended its Febreze odor freshener line with Febreze to Go aimed at travelers.[8] Kraft extended a number of its popular Nabisco brands by adding small-portioned packages. Campbell's offers its soups in cans and in microwavable containers and its sells its Swanson Broth in "chef" size cartons for serious cooks and 16 ounce packages for simple side dishes.[9]

Product Line Contraction Does the world really need 31 varieties of Head and Shoulders shampoo? Or 52 versions of Crest? Or numerous brands of apparel? When Steve Jobs took over Apple, the company sold over 40 products. He immediately simplified by cutting the product line down to four computers—two desktop and two laptops that Apple could focus on perfecting. This move helped Apple double its market share.[10] Symptoms of product line overextension include the following:

- Some products in the line do not contribute to profits because of low sales or because they cannibalize sales of other items in the line.

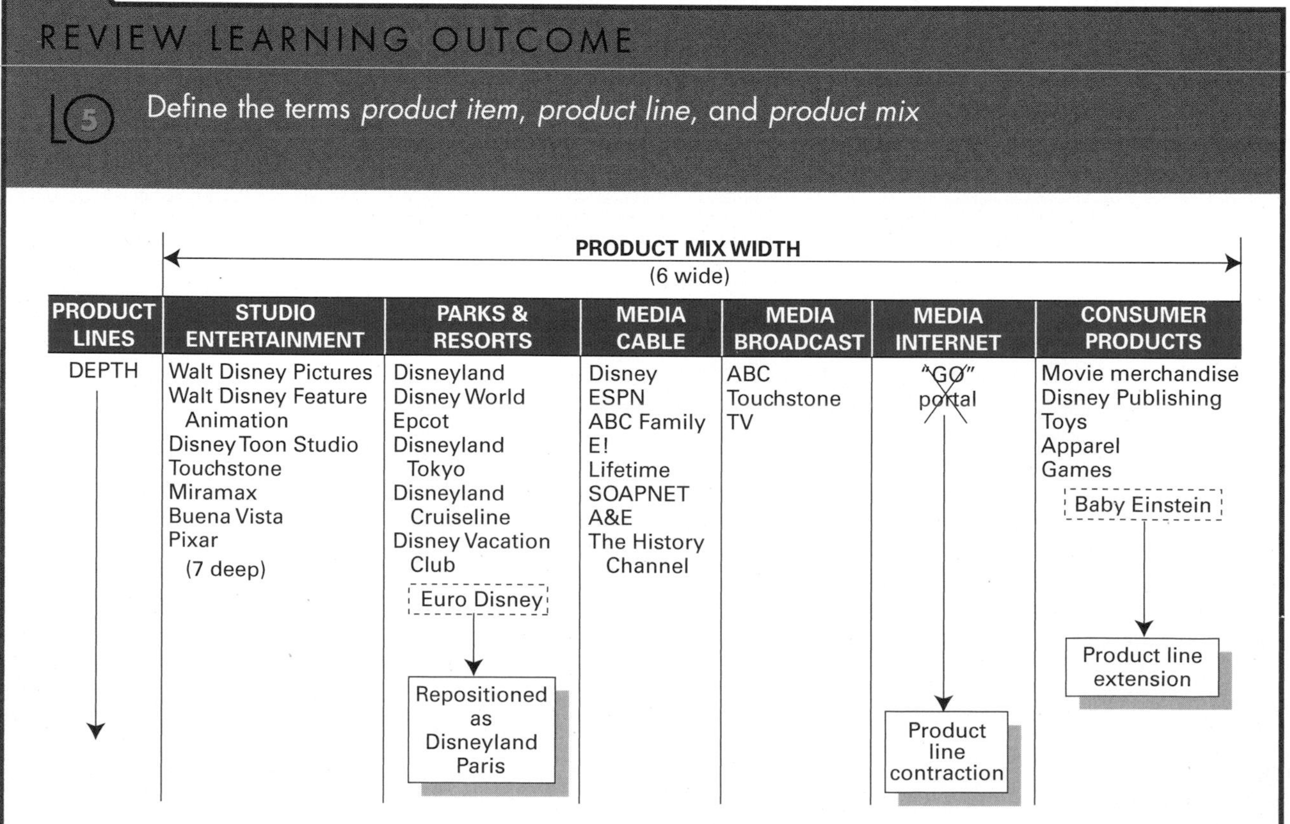

- Manufacturing or marketing resources are disproportionately allocated to slow-moving products.
- Some items in the line are obsolete because of new product entries in the line or new products offered by competitors.

Three major benefits are likely when a firm contracts its overextended product lines. First, resources become concentrated on the most important products. Second, managers no longer waste resources trying to improve the sales and profits of poorly performing products. Third, new product items have a greater chance of being successful because more financial and human resources are available to manage them.

BRANDING

The success of any business or consumer product depends in part on the target market's ability to distinguish one product from another. Branding is the main tool marketers use to distinguish their products from the competition's.

A **brand** is a name, term, symbol, design, or combination thereof that identifies a seller's products and differentiates them from competitors' products. A **brand name** is that part of a brand that can be spoken, including letters (GM, YMCA), words (Chevrolet), and numbers (WD-40, 7-Eleven). The elements of a brand that cannot be spoken are called the **brand mark**—for example, the well-known Mercedes-Benz and Delta Air Lines symbols.

> *"Brand identity is essential to developing brand loyalty."*

Benefits of Branding

Branding has three main purposes: product identification, repeat sales, and new-product sales. The most important purpose is *product identification*. Branding allows marketers to distinguish their products from all others. Many brand names are familiar to consumers and indicate quality.

The term **brand equity** refers to the value of company and brand names. A brand that has high awareness, perceived quality, and brand loyalty among customers has high brand equity. Starbucks, Volvo, and Dell are companies with high brand equity. A brand with strong brand equity is a valuable asset.

The term **global brand** refers to a brand that obtains at least a third of its earnings from outside its home country, is recognizable outside its home base of customers, and has publicly available marketing and financial data.[11] Exhibit 10.3 lists the top ten global brands. Although it's not on the top of this year's list, Yum! Brands, which owns Pizza Hut, KFC, and Taco Bell, is a good example of a company that has developed strong global brands. Yum believes that it has to adapt its restaurants to local tastes and different cultural and political climates. In Japan, for instance, KFC sells tempura crispy strips. In northern England, KFC focuses on gravy and potatoes, and in Thailand it offers rice with soy or sweet chili sauce.

The best generator of *repeat sales* is satisfied customers. Branding helps consumers identify products they wish to buy again and avoid those they do not. **Brand loyalty,** a consistent preference for one brand over all others, is quite high in some product categories. Over half the users in product categories such as cigarettes, mayonnaise, toothpaste, coffee, headache remedies, photographic film, bath soap, and ketchup are loyal to one brand. Many students come to college and purchase the same brands they used at home, rather than being "price" buyers. Brand identity is essential to developing brand loyalty.

The third main purpose of branding is to *facilitate new-product sales*. Company and brand names like those listed in Exhibit 10.3 are extremely useful when introducing new products.

The Internet provides firms with a new alternative for generating brand awareness, promoting a desired brand image, stimulating new and repeat brand sales, enhancing

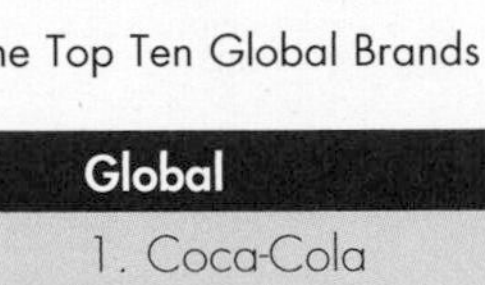

EXHIBIT 10.3

The Top Ten Global Brands

Global
1. Coca-Cola
2. IBM
3. Microsoft
4. GE
5. Nokia
6. Toyota
7. Intel
8. McDonald's
9. Disney
10. Google

Source: Reprinted from the September 29, 2008, issue of *Business Week* by special permission, copyright © 2007 by The McGraw-Hill Companies, Inc.

product line extension
Adding additional products to an existing product line in order to compete more broadly in the industry.

brand
A name, term, symbol, design, or combination thereof that identifies a seller's products and differentiates them from competitors' products.

brand name
That part of a brand that can be spoken, including letters, words, and numbers.

brand mark
The elements of a brand that cannot be spoken.

brand equity
The value of company and brand names.

global brand
A brand where at least one-third of the product is sold outside its home country or region.

brand loyalty
A consistent preference for one brand over all others.

EXHIBIT 10.4
Major Branding Decisions

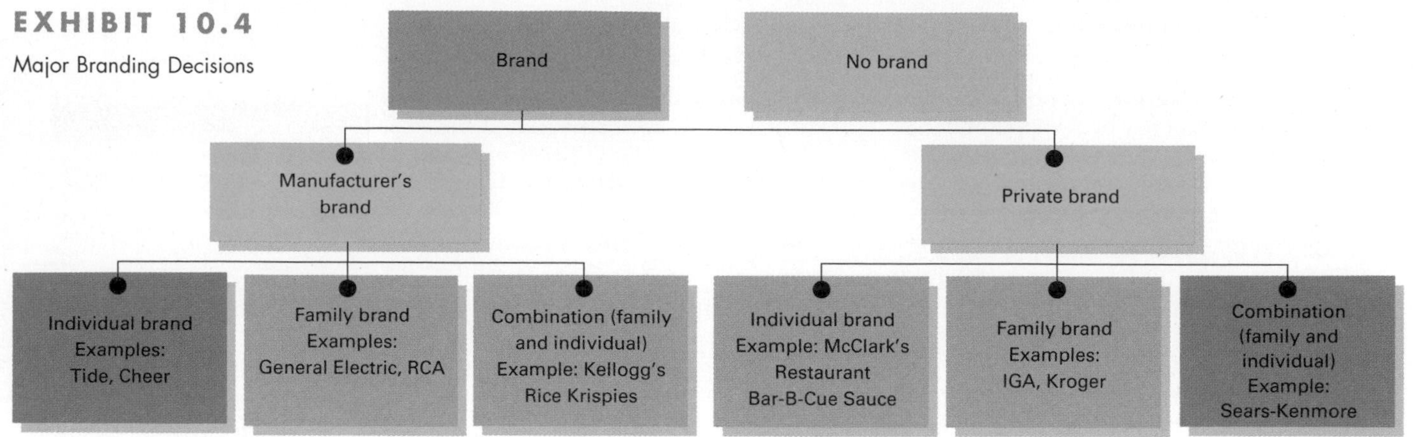

manufacturer's brand
The brand name of a manufacturer.

private brand
A brand name owned by a wholesaler or a retailer.

captive brand
A brand that carries no evidence of a retailer's affiliation, is manufactured by a third party, and is sold exclusively at the retailer.

brand loyalty, and building brand equity. Nearly all packaged-goods firms have a presence online. Tide.com offers a useful feature called Stain Detective, a digital tip sheet on how to remove almost any substance from almost any fabric.

Branding Strategies

Firms face complex branding decisions. As Exhibit 10.4 illustrates, firms may choose to follow a policy of using manufacturers' brands, private (distributor) brands, or both. In either case, they must then decide among a policy of individual branding (different brands for different products), family branding (common names for different products), or a combination of individual branding and family branding.

Manufacturers' Brands versus Private Brands The brand name of a manufacturer—such as Kodak, La-Z-Boy, and Fruit of the Loom—is called a **manufacturer's brand.** Sometimes "national brand" is used as a synonym for "manufacturer's brand." This term is not always accurate, however, because many manufacturers serve only regional markets. Using "manufacturer's brand" more precisely defines the brand's owner.

A **private brand,** also known as a private label or store brand, is a brand name owned by a wholesaler or a retailer. Private brands include Wal-Mart's Ol' Roy dog food, which has surpassed Nestlé's Purina as the world's top-selling dog food, and the George line of apparel, which has knocked Liz Claiborne's clothing out of Wal-Mart. A survey conducted for the Private Manufacturers' Label Association found that 41 percent of shoppers identify themselves as frequent buyers of store brands, and 7 out of 10 feel the private-label products they buy are as good as, if not better than, their national brand counterparts.[12]

Retailers love consumers' greater acceptance of private brands. Because overhead is low and there are no marketing costs, private-label products bring 10 percent higher margins, on average, than manufacturers' brands. More than that, a trusted store brand can differentiate a chain from its competitors. For example, many shoppers will drive the extra mile to Costco, a wholesale club, to buy the store's Kirkland brands and will also buy other goods while they are there. Costco has recently introduced a Kirkland Signature brand of wines that compete at the premium and super premium price categories.[13] Exhibit 10.5 illustrates key issues that wholesalers and retailers should consider in deciding whether to sell manufacturers' brands or private brands. Many firms offer a combination of both. Instead of marketing private brands as cheaper, and inferior to manufacturer's brands, many retailers are creating and promoting their own **captive brands.** These brands carry no evidence of the store's affiliation, are manufactured by a third party and are sold exclusively at the chains. This strategy allows the retailer to ask a price similar to manufacturer's brands, and they are typically displayed alongside marketed mainstream products. For example, bioInfusion, a line of hair-care products

EXHIBIT 10.5

Comparing Manufacturers' and Private Brands from the Reseller's Perspective

Key Advantages of Carrying Manufacturers' Brands	Key Advantages of Carrying Private Brands
• Heavy advertising to the consumer by manufacturers like Procter & Gamble helps develop strong consumer loyalties.	• A wholesaler or retailer can usually earn higher profits on its own brand. In addition, because the private brand is exclusive, there is less pressure to mark the price down to meet competition.
• Well-known manufacturers' brands, such as Kodak and Fisher-Price, can attract new customers and enhance the dealer's (wholesaler's or retailer's) prestige.	• A manufacturer can decide to drop a brand or a reseller at any time or even to become a direct competitor to its dealers.
• Many manufacturers offer rapid delivery, enabling the dealer to carry less inventory.	• A private brand ties the customer to the wholesaler or retailer. A person who wants a DieHard battery must go to Sears.
• If a dealer happens to sell a manufacturer's brand of poor quality, the customer may simply switch brands and remain loyal to the dealer.	• Wholesalers and retailers have no control over the intensity of distribution of manufacturers' brands. Wal-Mart store managers don't have to worry about competing with other sellers of Sam's American Choice products or Ol' Roy dog food. They know that these brands are sold only in Wal-Mart and Sam's Wholesale Club stores.

available only at Walgreens, has grown to become one of the top brands in the entire hair care category.[14]

This image, featuring both Nike and Apple products, illustrates an example of cobranding. Cobranding is a useful strategy when a combination of brand names enhances the prestige or perceived value of a product.

© AP IMAGES/MARY ALTAFFER

Individual Brands versus Family Brands Many companies use different brand names for different products, a practice referred to as **individual branding.** Companies use individual brands when their products vary greatly in use or performance. For instance, it would not make sense to use the same brand name for a pair of dress socks and a baseball bat. Procter & Gamble targets different segments of the laundry detergent market with Bold, Cheer, Dash, Dreft, Era, Gain, Ivory Snow, and Tide. Marriott International also targets different market segments with Courtyard by Marriott, Residence Inn, and Fairfield Inn.

In contrast, a company that markets several different products under the same brand name is using a **family brand.** Sony's family brand includes radios, television sets, stereos, and other electronic products. The Heinz brand name is attached to products such as ketchup, mustard, and pickles.

Cobranding **Cobranding** entails placing two or more brand names on a product or its package. Three common types of cobranding are ingredient branding, cooperative branding, and complementary branding. *Ingredient branding* identifies the brand of a part that makes up the product. Examples of ingredient branding are Intel (a microprocessor) in a personal computer, such as Dell, or a satellite system (OnStar) in an automobile (Cadillac). Procter & Gamble has developed Mr. Clean Disinfecting Wipes with Febreze Freshness. Febreze is also cobranded with Tide, Bounce, and Downy.[15] *Cooperative branding* occurs when two brands receiving equal treatment (in the context of an advertisement) borrow from each other's brand equity. A promotional contest jointly sponsored by Ramada Inns, American Express, and Continental Airlines is an example of cooperative branding. Guests at Ramada who paid with an American Express card were automatically entered in the contest and were eligible to win more than a hundred getaways for two at any Ramada in the continental United States and round-trip airfare from Continental. Finally, with *complementary branding*, products are advertised or marketed together to suggest usage, such as a spirits brand (Seagram's) and a compatible mixer (7-Up). A partnership between Ann Taylor Loft women's clothing stores and Procter & Gamble will promote the use of Tide Total Care and Downy Total Care to clean clothing and cut down on dry cleaning bills. The store will give free samples and

individual branding
Using different brand names for different products.

family brand
Marketing several different products under the same brand name.

cobranding
Placing two or more brand names on a product or its package.

© SUSAN VAN ETTEN

© SCOTT OLSON/GETTY IMAGES

When FedEx purchased Kinko's in 2004, it merged the company's brand names to make one brand entity in the mind of the consumer. In late 2008, having successfully cobranded a shipping business and a copy/print/data center business, the company renamed the brand "FedEx Office."

coupons to customers who buy machine washable clothes, and posters and decals placed in the stores will call attention to the product's benefits.[16]

Cobranding is a useful strategy when a combination of brand names enhances the prestige or perceived value of a product, or when it benefits brand owners and users. When Intel launched its Centrino wireless processor, it established cobranding relationships with T-Mobile and hotel chains Marriott International and Westin Hotels & Resorts because there was mutual value in establishing these relationships.

CUSTOMER Experience

World of Coca-Cola Museum

The Coca-Cola Company has created a unique venue through which consumers can experience its brands. This venue is the World of Coca-Cola Museum in Atlanta, Georgia, opened in May 2007 on a 20-acre complex called Pemberton Place (named after John Pemberton, the inventor of Coca-Cola). The attraction has 92,000 square feet, with 60,000 feet of guest areas, and attracts 1.5 million visitors a year. More than 1,200 Coca-Cola artifacts from around the world are displayed along with a number of interactive exhibits such as a 4-D movie and a gallery dedicated to Coke and pop culture. Guests pay a fee to get in the museum, and average estimated visit time is 90 minutes.

The outside of the building features a bottle sculpture with lighted streams of red and white color. Guests entering "The Lobby" see large Coca-Cola bottles manufactured from materials obtained from around the world. They then go into "The Coca-Cola Loft," which has a collection of Coca-Cola advertising artifacts from as far back as 1905. Next is the "Happiness Factory Theatre," where guests view *Inside the Happiness Factory: A Documentary,* a mock documentary that shows characters of the Happiness Factory, a central focus of the brand's current advertising campaign, "The Coke Side of Life." After the video, "The Hub" is revealed, from which guests can visit various attractions in whatever order they choose.

Attractions include posing for a picture with the Coca-Cola mascot, the Coca-Cola Polar Bear. They can listen to stories about the company's influence in the world. The "Milestones of Refreshment" attraction presents artifacts from Coca-Cola's branding efforts. For example, one item on display is a packing slip from 1888 that shows Coca-Cola U.S. sales figures. The "Bottle Works" gives visitors a tour of a fully functioning bottling line, which makes 8-ounce bottles of Coca-Cola Classic that can be received at the end of the tour. Coca-Cola's advertising campaigns are featured in three short films in the "Perfect Pauses Theater." A museum favorite is the tasting experience that provides visitors with an opportunity to sample nearly 60 different products from around the world. And the last stop is the Coca-Cola store, which offers thousands of Coca-Cola–themed products for sale. As trends and advertising campaigns change over time, the museum will update its attractions.[17]

Why do you think people visit (and pay a fee to get in) the World of Coca-Cola Museum? How does the museum support the Coca-Cola brand? Can you think of other brands that could benefit from a similar experiential attraction?

T-Mobile was able to set up global "hot spots" to reach Intel's target market of mobile professionals, while the hotel chains enabled Intel to target business professionals.

Cobranding may be used to increase a company's presence in markets where it has little or no market share. For example, Coach was able to build a presence in a whole new category when its leather upholstery with logo was used in Lexus automobiles. European firms have been slower to adopt cobranding than U.S. firms have. One reason is that European customers seem to be more skeptical than U.S. customers about trying new brands. European retailers also typically have less shelf space than their U.S. counterparts and are less willing to give new brands a try.

Trademarks

A **trademark** is the exclusive right to use a brand or part of a brand. Others are prohibited from using the brand without permission. A **service mark** performs the same function for services, such as H&R Block and Weight Watchers. Parts of a brand or other product identification may qualify for trademark protection. Some examples are

- Shapes, such as the Jeep front grille and the Coca-Cola bottle
- Ornamental color or design, such as the decoration on Nike tennis shoes, the black-and-copper color combination of a Duracell battery, Levi's tag on the left side of the rear pocket of its jeans, or the cutoff black cone on the top of Cross pens
- Catchy phrases, such as Prudential's "Own a piece of the rock," Mountain Dew's "Do the Dew," and Nike's "Just Do It"
- Abbreviations, such as Bud, Coke, or The Met
- Sounds, such as General Electric Broadcasting Company's ship's bell clock sound and the MGM lion's roar

It is important to understand that trademark rights come from use rather than registration. A company must have a genuine intention to use a trademark when it files an intent-to-use application with the U.S. Patent and Trademark Office and must actually use the mark within three years of the application being granted. Trademark protection lasts for as long as the mark is being used.

In November 1999, legislation went into effect that explicitly applies trademark law to the online world. This law includes financial penalties for those who violate trademarked products or register an otherwise trademarked term as a domain name.

Companies that fail to protect their trademarks face the possibility that their product names will become generic. A **generic product name** identifies a product by class or type and cannot be trademarked. Former brand names that were not sufficiently protected by their owners and were subsequently declared to be generic product names by U.S. courts include aspirin, cellophane, linoleum, thermos, kerosene, monopoly, cola, and shredded wheat.

Companies like Rolls-Royce, Cross, Xerox, Levi Strauss, Frigidaire, and McDonald's aggressively enforce their trademarks. Rolls-Royce, Coca-Cola, and Xerox even run newspaper and magazine ads stating that their names are trademarks and should not be used as descriptive or generic terms. Some ads threaten lawsuits against competitors that violate trademarks.

Despite severe penalties for trademark violations, trademark infringement lawsuits are not uncommon. One of the major battles is over brand names that closely resemble another brand name. The celebrity chef Wolfgang Puck filed a lawsuit against Wolfgang Zweiner when Zweiner opened Wolfgang's Steakhouse and confused fans began calling to make reservations at what they thought was the new Puck restaurant.[18]

Companies must also contend with fake or unauthorized brands, such as fake Levi's jeans, Microsoft software, Rolex watches, Reebok and Nike footwear, and Louis Vuitton handbags. Hasbro sued the makers of the online game Scrabulous, an obvious copy of Scrabble, including the rules, game pieces, and board colors, for copyright infringement on its Scrabble game.[19]

trademark
The exclusive right to use a brand or part of a brand.

service mark
A trademark for a service.

generic product name
Identifies a product by class or type and cannot be trademarked.

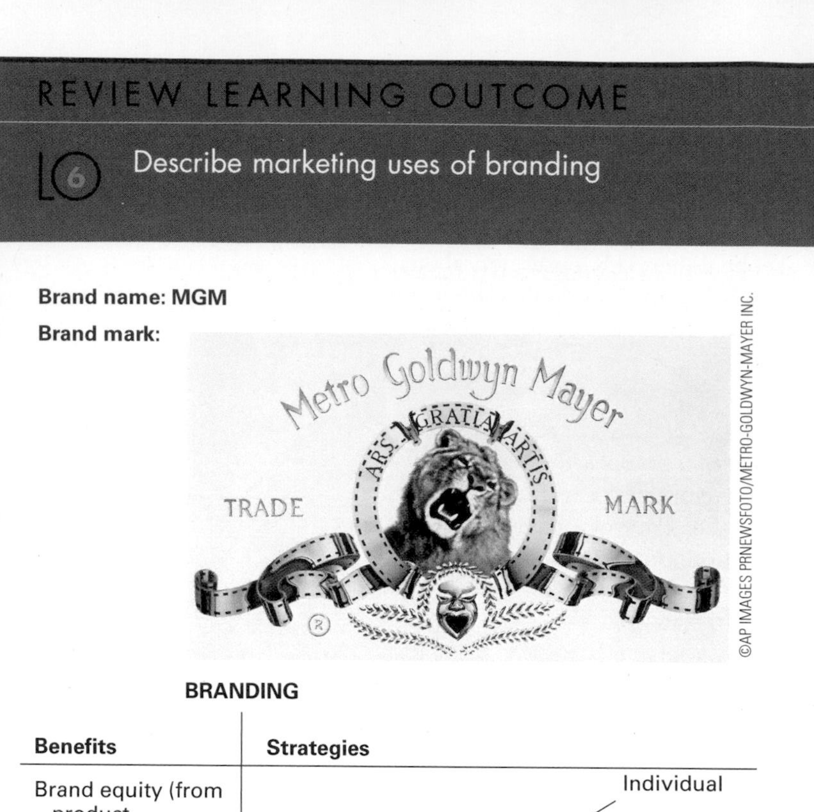

REVIEW LEARNING OUTCOME

LO 6 Describe marketing uses of branding

Brand name: MGM

Brand mark:

©AP IMAGES PRNEWSFOTO/METRO-GOLDWYN-MAYER INC.

BRANDING

Benefits	**Strategies**
Brand equity (from product identfication) Brand loyalty (from repeat sales) Brand recognition (to generate new product sales)	Generic / Brand / Trademark → Manufacturer (→ Individual, Family, Combination), Private

In Europe, you can sue counterfeiters only if your brand, logo, or trademark is formally registered. Until recently, formal registration was required in each country in which a company sought protection. A company can now register its trademark in all European Union (EU) member countries with one application.

LO 7 PACKAGING

Packages have always served a practical function—that is, they hold contents together and protect goods as they move through the distribution channel. Today, however, packaging is also a container for promoting the product and making it easier and safer to use.

Packaging Functions

The three most important functions of packaging are to contain and protect products, promote products, and facilitate the storage, use, and convenience of products. A fourth function of packaging that is becoming increasingly important is to facilitate recycling and reduce environmental damage.

Containing and Protecting Products The most obvious function of packaging is to contain products that are liquid, granular, or otherwise divisible. Packaging also enables manufacturers, wholesalers, and retailers to market products in specific quantities, such as ounces.

Physical protection is another obvious function of packaging. Most products are handled several times between the time they are manufactured, harvested, or otherwise produced and the time they are consumed or used. Many products are shipped, stored, and inspected several times between production and consumption. Some, like milk, need to be refrigerated. Others, like beer, are sensitive to light. Still others, like medicines and bandages, need to be kept sterile. Packages protect products from breakage, evaporation, spillage, spoilage, light, heat, cold, infestation, and many other conditions.

© AP IMAGES/ PRNEWSFOTO/AMERICAN DAIRY ASSOCIATION AND DAIRY COUNCIL, INC.

Promoting Products Packaging does more than identify the brand, list the ingredients, specify features, and give directions. A package differentiates a product from competing products and may associate a new product with a family of other products from the same manufacturer. Welch's repackaged its line of grape juice–based jams, jellies, and juices to unify the line and get more impact on the shelf.

Packagers use designs, colors, shapes, and materials to try to influence consumers' perceptions and buying behavior. For example, marketing research shows that health-conscious consumers are likely to think that any food is probably good for them as long as it comes in green packaging. Two top brands of low-fat foods—SnackWell's and Healthy Choice—use green packaging. Packaging can also influence consumers' perceptions of quality and/or prestige. Pennzoil redesigned its recognizable but dated package using a different color and engine part to convey a clean engine. Their focus group data told them that the only part that would be descriptive was the piston with a spot of white with shards of light coming from the part to portray cleanliness.[20] Packaging has a measurable effect on sales. Quaker Oats revised the package for Rice-A-Roni without making any other changes in marketing strategy and experienced a 44 percent increase in sales in one year.

Facilitating Storage, Use, and Convenience Wholesalers and retailers prefer packages that are easy to ship, store, and stock on shelves. They also like packages that protect products, prevent spoilage or breakage, and extend the product's shelf life.

Consumers' requirements for storage, use, and convenience cover many dimensions. Consumers are constantly seeking items that are easy to handle, open, and reclose, although some consumers want packages that are tamperproof or childproof. Research indicates that hard-to-open packages are among consumers' top complaints. Surveys conducted by *Sales & Marketing Management* magazine revealed that consumers dislike—and avoid buying—leaky ice cream boxes, overly heavy or fat vinegar bottles, immovable pry-up lids on glass bottles, key-opener sardine cans, and hard-to-pour cereal boxes. Such packaging innovations as zipper tear strips, hinged lids, tab slots, screw-on tops, and pour spouts were introduced to solve these and other problems. Nestlé improved all its packaging to make it easier for people to rip open its pouches, twist off its caps, and reseal its tubs. Easy openings are especially important for kids and aging baby boomers. The company's package designers spent nine months developing a plastic lid for ice cream that is easier to pull off when the ice cream is frozen and ribbed corners for ice cream cartons that are easier to grip when scooping.[21]

Some firms use packaging to segment markets. For example, a C&H sugar carton with an easy-to-pour, reclosable top is targeted to consumers who don't do a lot of baking and are willing to pay at least 20 cents more for the package. Different-size packages appeal to heavy, moderate, and light users. Salt is sold in package sizes ranging from single serving to picnic size to giant economy size. Campbell's soup is packaged in single-serving cans aimed at the elderly and singles market segments. Beer and soft drinks are similarly marketed in various package sizes and types. Packaging convenience can increase a product's utility and, therefore, its market share and profits. To appeal to women, Dutch Boy designed a square plastic paint container with a side handle and a spout to replace the traditional wire-handled round metal paint can. The Internet will soon give consumers more packaging options. Indeed, the Internet may significantly change the purpose and appearance of packaging. Packaging for products sold on the Internet will be more under the customer's control and will be customized by consumers to fit their needs. Some designers are already offering to personalize, for a fee, packages such as wine bottle labels.

Facilitating Recycling and Reducing Environmental Damage One of the most important packaging issues today is compatibility with the environment. In a recent study of consumers, a majority said they would give up the following conveniences if it would benefit the environment: packaging designed for easy stacking/storing, packaging that can be used for cooking, and packaging designed for easy transport.[22] Some firms use their packaging to target environmentally concerned market segments. The French winery, Boisset Family Estates, recently introduced TetraPak cartons of its French Rabbit chardonnay to offer consumers a playful and eco-friendly alternative to glass bottles. When the cartons sold well, other companies followed suit.[23] Dell has plans to cut by 10 percent the amount of materials used in its laptop and desktop packaging worldwide by 2012.[24] Groups like the Sustainable Packaging Coalition assist companies in creating perpetually recycled packaging so that materials don't ever end up in landfills, damaging the ecosystem.[25]

ETHICS in Marketing

Greenwashing

There is a strong interest today in environmental awareness. More and more, consumers are supporting companies that provide environmentally friendly, or "green," products. Consequently, more companies are engaging in green marketing, claiming that their products are manufactured in a way that does not harm the environment. Some of this green marketing, critics claim, is actually greenwash.

Greenwash is a term used to describe the practice of companies stretching the truth when they promote their products as being environmentally friendly. Often, customers are misled into thinking an aspect of the product is good for the environment when in reality it is only a cost-cutting method for the company. For example, a company may insist that people use less toilet paper in order to save trees, when in reality the company does not want to buy as much toilet paper. The term is typically used when more time and money has been spent advertising being green (i.e., operating with consideration for the environment) than has been spending resources on environmentally sound practices.

Research conducted by TerraChoice Environmental Marketing surveyed six category-leading big box stores and that included over 1,000 consumer products having 1,753 environmental claims. Their results showed that 99 percent of green claims were either not true or misleading. For example, more than half of the eco-labels on today's products promote a small eco-friendly quality, such as recycled content, without mentioning more significant environmental drawbacks such as manufacturing intensity or travel costs. The study report identified the following "Six Sins of Greenwashing":

1. Sin of the Hidden Trade-off: for example, "energy efficient" electronics that contain hazardous materials.
2. Sin of No Proof: for example, shampoos claiming to be "certified organic," but without verifiable certification.
3. Sin of Vagueness: for example, products claiming to be 100% natural when many naturally occurring substances are hazardous (e.g., arsenic or formaldehyde).
4. Sin of Irrelevance: for example, products claiming to be CFC-free, even though CFCs were banned 20 years ago.
5. Sin of Fibbing: for example, products falsely claiming to be certified by an internationally recognized environmental standard, like Energy Star.
6. Sin of Lesser of Two Evils: For example, organic cigarettes or "environmentally friendly" pesticides.

EcoLogo is a government ecolabeling program that has been accredited by the Global Ecolabelling Network, an international association of ecolabeling programs, as meeting certain environmental marketing standards. The program provides a marketing incentive to manufacturers and suppliers of environmentally preferable products and services in more than 120 product categories. EcoLogo provides an insignia that helps consumers know that an independent, credible, and expert third party has verified a product's green qualifications.[27]

Do you think greenwashing is an unethical practice? Defend your answer.

Labeling

An integral part of any package is its label. Labeling generally takes one of two forms: persuasive or informational. **Persuasive labeling** focuses on a promotional theme or logo, and consumer information is secondary. Procter & Gamble put real photography on its new Downy fabric softener labels in order to make a more personal connection with consumers. Note that the standard promotional claims—such as "new," "improved," and "super"—are no longer very persuasive. Consumers have been saturated with "newness" and thus discount these claims.

Informational labeling, in contrast, is designed to help consumers make proper product selections and lower their cognitive dissonance after the purchase. Sears attaches a "label of confidence" to all its floor coverings. This label gives such product information as durability, color, features, cleanability, care instructions, and construction standards. Most major furniture manufacturers affix labels to their wares that explain the products' construction features, such as type of frame, number of coils, and fabric characteristics. The Nutritional Labeling and Education Act of 1990 mandated detailed nutritional information be placed on most food packages and standards for health claims on food packaging. An important outcome of this legislation has been guidelines from the Food and Drug Administration for using terms like *low fat, light, reduced cholesterol, low sodium, low calorie*, and *fresh*. Getting the right information is very important to consumers—so much so that almost 75 percent said they would be willing to pay extra, for example, to have products display country of origin information.[26]

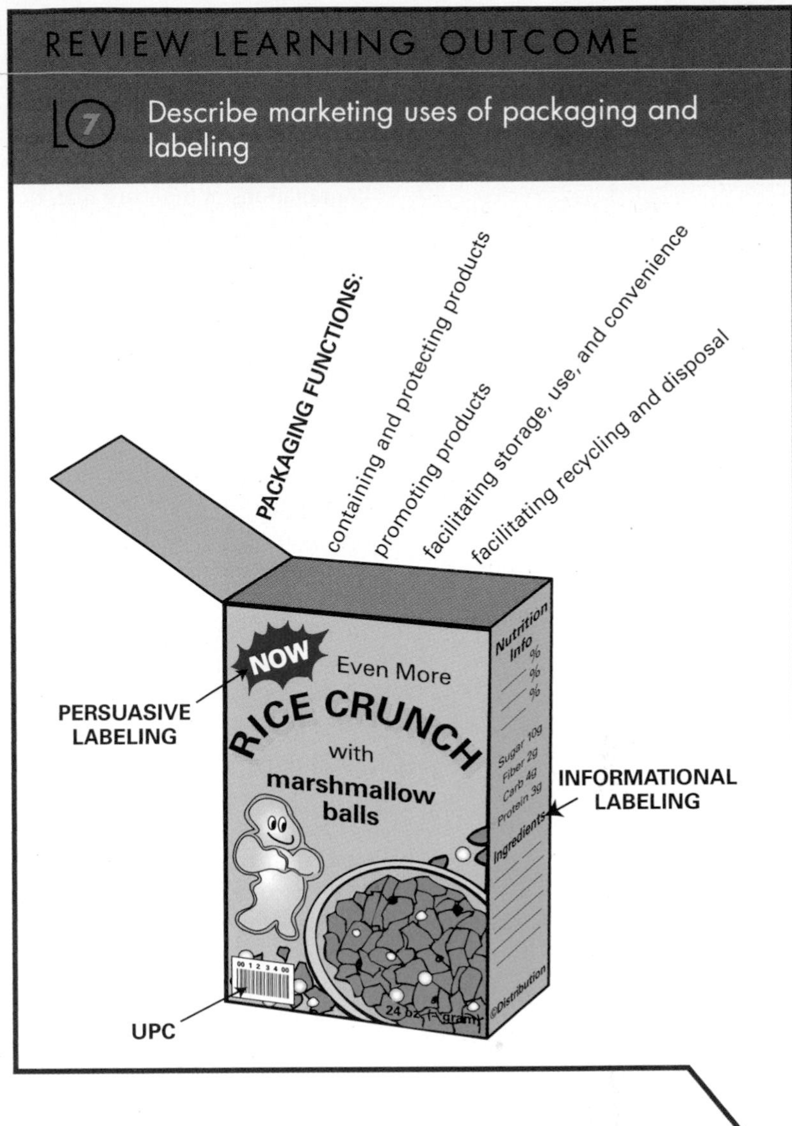

Universal Product Codes

The **universal product codes (UPCs)** that appear on most items in supermarkets and other high-volume outlets were first introduced in 1974. Because the numerical codes appear as a series of thick and thin vertical lines, they are often called *bar codes*. The lines are read by computerized optical scanners that match codes with brand names, package sizes, and prices. They also print information on cash register tapes and help retailers rapidly and accurately prepare records of customer purchases, control inventories, and track sales. The UPC (bar code) system and scanners are also used in single-source research (see Chapter 9).

GLOBAL ISSUES IN BRANDING AND PACKAGING

International marketers must address several concerns regarding branding and packaging.

Branding

When planning to enter a foreign market with an existing product, a firm has three options for handling the brand name:

- *One brand name everywhere:* This strategy is useful when the company markets mainly one product and the brand name does not have negative connotations in any local market. The Coca-Cola Company uses a one-brand-name strategy in 195 countries around the world. The advantages of a one-brand-name strategy are greater identification of the product from market to market and ease of coordinating promotion from market to market.
- *Adaptations and modifications:* A one-brand-name strategy is not possible when the name cannot be pronounced in the local language, when the brand name is owned by someone else, or when the brand name has a negative or vulgar connotation in the local language. The Iranian detergent "Barf," for example, might encounter some problems in the U.S. market.

persuasive labeling
A type of package labeling that focuses on a promotional theme or logo with consumer information being secondary.

informational labeling
A type of package labeling designed to help consumers make proper product selections and lower their cognitive dissonance after the purchase.

universal product codes (UPCs)
A series of thick and thin vertical lines (bar codes), readable by computerized optical scanners, that represent numbers used to track products.

warranty
A confirmation of the quality or performance of a good or service.

express warranty
A written guarantee.

- *Different brand names in different markets:* Local brand names are often used when translation or pronunciation problems occur, when the marketer wants the brand to appear to be a local brand, or when regulations require localization. Gillette's Silkience hair conditioner is called Soyance in France and Sientel in Italy. Coca-Cola's Sprite brand had to be renamed Kin in South Korea to satisfy a government prohibition on the unnecessary use of foreign words. Because of the feminine connotations of the word *diet*, the European version of Diet Coke is Coca-Cola Light.

Packaging

Three aspects of packaging that are especially important in international marketing are labeling, aesthetics, and climate considerations. The major *labeling* concern is properly translating ingredient, promotional, and instructional information on labels. In Eastern Europe, packages of Ariel detergent are printed in 14 languages, from Latvian to Lithuanian. Care must also be employed in meeting all local labeling requirements. Several years ago, an Italian judge ordered that all bottles of Coca-Cola be removed from retail shelves because the ingredients were not properly labeled. Labeling is also harder in countries like Belgium and Finland, which require it to be bilingual.

Package *aesthetics* may also require some attention. The key is to stay attuned to cultural traits in host countries. For example, colors may have different connotations. Red is associated with witchcraft in some countries, green may be a sign of danger, and white may be symbolic of death. Aesthetics also influence package size. Soft drinks are not sold in six-packs in countries that lack refrigeration. In some countries, products such as detergent may be bought only in small quantities because of a lack of storage space. Other products, like cigarettes, may be bought in small quantities, and even single units, because of the low purchasing power of buyers.

On the other hand, simple visual elements of the brand, such as a symbol or logo, can be a standardizing element across products and countries. For example, in Mexico, Lay's potato chips are known as Sabritas, but the packaging carries the same brand mark and graphic elements as in the United States. Extreme *climates* and long-distance shipping necessitate sturdier and more durable packages for goods sold overseas. Spillage, spoilage, and breakage are all more important concerns when products are shipped long distances or frequently handled during shipping and storage. Packages may also have to ensure a longer product life if the time between production and consumption lengthens significantly.

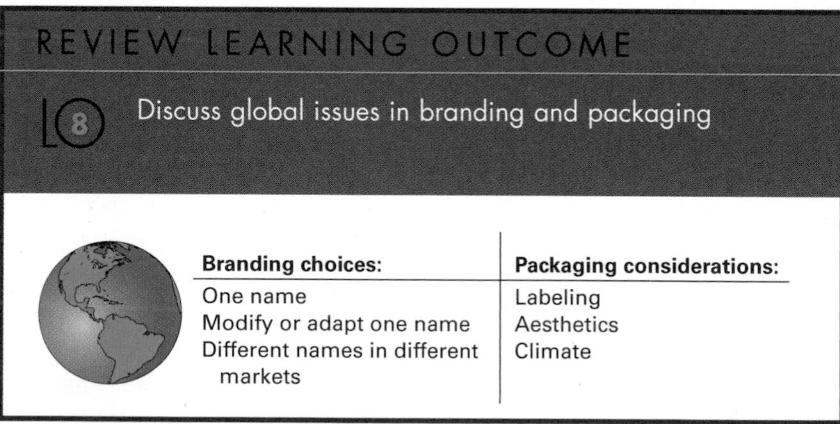

REVIEW LEARNING OUTCOME

LO 8 Discuss global issues in branding and packaging

Branding choices:	Packaging considerations:
One name	Labeling
Modify or adapt one name	Aesthetics
Different names in different markets	Climate

LO 9

PRODUCT WARRANTIES

Just as a package is designed to protect the product, a **warranty** protects the buyer and gives essential information about the product. A warranty confirms the quality or performance of a good or service. An **express warranty** is a written guarantee. Express warranties range from simple statements—such as "100 percent cotton" (a guarantee of quality) and "complete satisfaction guaranteed" (a statement of performance)—to extensive documents written in technical language. In contrast, an **implied warranty** is an unwritten guarantee that the good or service is fit for the purpose for which it was sold. All sales have an implied warranty under the Uniform Commercial Code.

Congress passed the Magnuson-Moss Warranty–Federal Trade Commission Improvement Act in 1975 to help consumers understand warranties and get action from manufacturers and dealers. A manufacturer that promises a full warranty must meet certain minimum standards, including repair "within a reasonable time and without charge" of any defects and replacement of the merchandise or a full refund if the product does not work "after a reasonable number of attempts" at repair. Any warranty that does not live up to this tough prescription must be "conspicuously" promoted as a limited warranty.

Describe how and why product warranties are important marketing tools

Express warranty = written guarantee
Implied warranty = unwritten guarantee

implied warranty
An unwritten guarantee that the good or service is fit for the purpose for which it was sold.

years within which a company must use a trademark once it has been granted ▶ **3**

categories of consumer products ▶ **4**

41 ◀ percentage of shoppers who frequently buy store brands

ANATOMY OF A Packaging Decision

Barbie

Mattel updated Barbie's packaging to keep her fresh and familiar.

1 Familiar brand mark

2 Heat- and impact-tested packaging protects Barbie from damage.

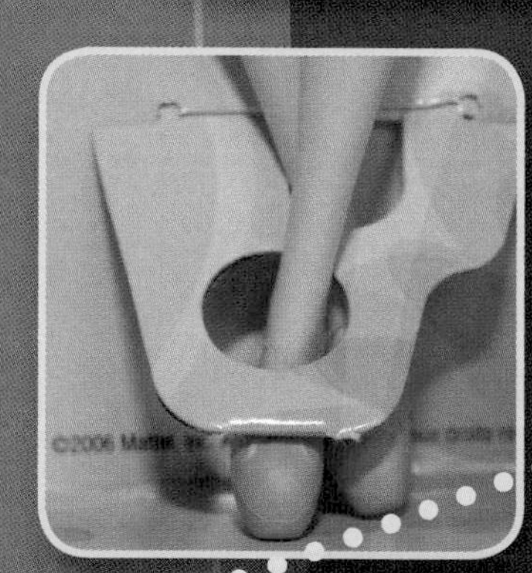

3 Die cuts keep Barbie from shifting.

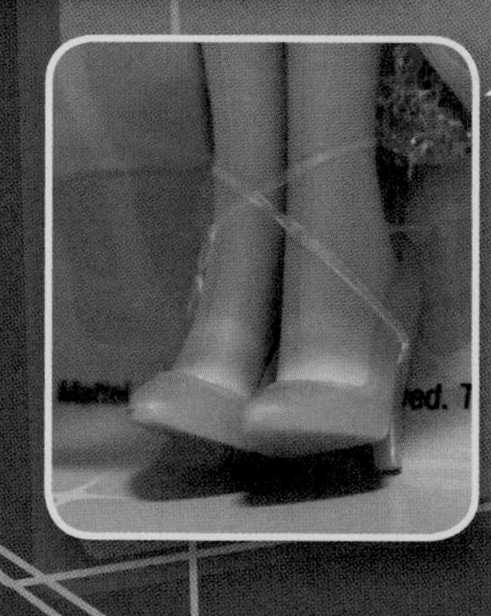

4 Plastic staples facilitate easy removal.

5 Persuasive labeling—"easy for me"—assures parents their kids can open it themselves.

REVIEW AND APPLICATIONS

Define the term product. A product is anything, desired or not, that a person or organization receives in an exchange. The basic goal of purchasing decisions is to receive the tangible and intangible benefits associated with a product. Tangible aspects include packaging, style, color, size, and features. Intangible qualities include service, the retailer's image, the manufacturer's reputation, and the social status associated with a product. An organization's product offering is the crucial element in any marketing mix.

1.1 Form a team of four or five members. Have the team determine what the tangible and intangible benefits are for a computer, a tube of toothpaste, a beauty salon, and a dentist.

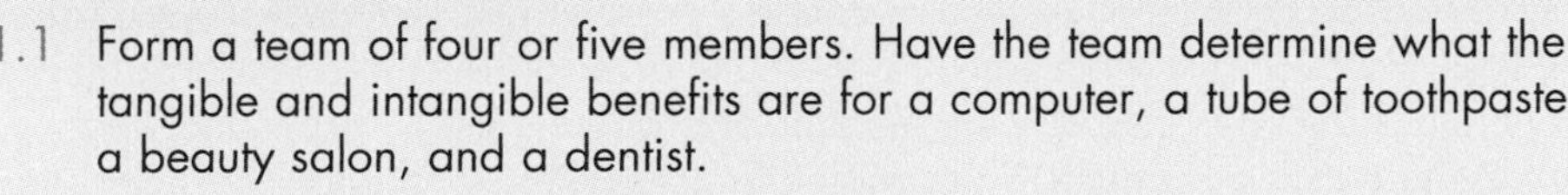

Classify consumer products. Consumer products are classified into four categories: convenience products, shopping products, specialty products, and unsought products. Convenience products are relatively inexpensive and require limited shopping effort. Shopping products are of two types: homogeneous and heterogeneous. Because of the similarity of homogeneous products, they are differentiated mainly by price and features. In contrast, heterogeneous products appeal to consumers because of their distinct characteristics. Specialty products possess unique benefits that are highly desirable to certain customers. Finally, unsought products are either new products or products that require aggressive selling because they are generally avoided or overlooked by consumers.

2.1 Break into groups of four or five. Have the members of the group classify each of the following products into the category (convenience, shopping, specialty, unsought) that they think fits best from their perspective as consumers (i.e., if they were buying the product): Coca-Cola (brand), car stereo, winter coat, pair of shoes, life insurance, blue jeans, fast-food hamburgers, shampoo, canned vegetables, curtains.

2.2 Although major appliances, like washers and dryers, are usually considered homogeneous shopping products, the high-efficiency front-loaders that boast many more features than standard machines are gaining in popularity. Do you think high-efficiency technology is enough to make washers and dryers heterogeneous shopping products? Explain.

Discuss the importance of services to the economy. The service sector plays a crucial role in the U.S. economy, employing more than 80 percent of the workforce and accounting for a similar percentage of the gross domestic product.

3.1 To keep track of how service employment is affecting the U.S. economy, go to **www.bls.gov/bdm/.** Look at the right sidebar, which gives the latest numbers for Business Employment Dynamics. What trends to you see? Do the numbers support the information from the chapter?

Discuss the differences between services and goods. Services are distinguished by four characteristics. Services are intangible performances in that they lack clearly identifiable physical characteristics, making it difficult for marketers to communicate their specific benefits to potential customers. The production and consumption of services occur simultaneously. Services are heterogeneous because their quality depends on such elements as the service provider, individual consumer, location, and so on. Finally, services are perishable in the sense that they cannot be stored or saved. As a result, synchronizing supply with demand is particularly challenging in the service industry.

4.1 Assume that you are a manager of a bank branch. Write a list of the implications of intangibility for your firm.

4.2 Over 25 years ago, Tim and Nina Zagat began publishing leisure guides containing reviews of restaurants. Today, the renowned *Zagat* guides still contain reviews of restaurants, but they also rate hotels, entertainment, nightlife, movies, shopping, and even music. Go to **www.zagat.com.** In your opinion, are *Zagat* survey guides goods or services? Explain your reasoning.

Define the terms *product item, product line,* and *product mix.* A product item is a specific version of a product that can be designated as a distinct offering among an organization's products. A product line is a group of closely related products offered by an organization. An organization's product mix includes all the products it sells. Product mix width refers to the number of product lines an organization offers. Product line depth is the number of product items in a product line. Firms modify existing products by changing their quality, functional characteristics, or style. Product line extension occurs when a firm adds new products to existing product lines.

5.1 A local civic organization has asked you to give a luncheon presentation about planned obsolescence. Rather than pursuing a negative approach by talking about how businesses exploit customers through planned obsolescence, you have decided to talk about the benefits of producing products that do not last forever. Prepare a one-page outline of your presentation.

5.2 Go to Unilever's Web site at **www.unilever.com.** Can Unilever delete anything from its product lines? Visit the company's product category pages on its "Brands" Web page to see the number of existing products and new products planned. Write a proposal for contracting one of Unilever's product lines.

Describe marketing uses of branding. A brand is a name, term, or symbol that identifies and differentiates a firm's products. Established brands encourage customer loyalty and help new products succeed. Branding strategies require decisions about individual, family, manufacturers', and private brands.

6.1 A local supermarket would like to introduce its own brand of paper goods (e.g., paper towels, facial tissue, etc.) to sell alongside its current inventory. The company has hired you to generate a report outlining the advantages and disadvantages of doing so. Write the report.

6.2 How does Hormel use its Web site (**www.hormel.com**) to promote its store brands? Is the site designed more to promote the company or its brands? Check out the Spam Web site at **www.spam.com.** How do you think Hormel is able to successfully sustain this brand that is often the punch line to a joke?

Describe marketing uses of packaging and labeling. Packaging has four functions: containing and protecting products; promoting products; facilitating product storage, use, and convenience; and facilitating recycling and reducing environmental damage. As a tool for promotion, packaging identifies the brand and its features. It also serves the critical function of differentiating a product from competing products and linking it with related products from the same manufacturer. The label is an integral part of the package, with persuasive and informational functions. In essence, the package is the marketer's last chance to influence buyers before they make a purchase decision.

7.1 Find a product at home that has a distinctive package. Write a paragraph evaluating that package based on the four functions of packaging discussed in the chapter.

Discuss global issues in branding and packaging. In addition to brand piracy, international marketers must address a variety of concerns regarding branding and packaging, including choosing a brand-name policy, translating labels and meeting host-country labeling requirements, making packages aesthetically compatible with host-country cultures, and offering the sizes of packages preferred in host countries.

8.1 List the countries to which Levi Strauss & Co. markets through the Web site **www.levi.com.** How do the product offerings differ between the U.S. and European selections?

Describe how and why product warranties are important marketing tools. Product warranties are important tools because they offer consumers protection and help them gauge product quality.

9.1 Lands' End and L.L. Bean are renowned for their product guarantees. Find and read the exact wording of their guarantees on their Web sites (**www.landsend.com** and **www.llbean.com**). Do you think a company could successfully compete against either without offering the same guarantee?

KEY TERMS

EXERCISES

APPLICATION EXERCISE

What is your favorite brand of sandwich cookie? If you're like most Americans, chances are it is Oreo. In fact, Oreos are so popular that many people think Oreo was the original sandwich cookie. But they're wrong. Sunshine first marketed its Hydrox sandwich cookie in 1908. Hydrox thrived until 1912, when Nabisco (now part of Kraft) launched Oreo. With Nabisco's superior distribution and advertising, Hydrox was soon outmatched. By 1998, Hydrox sales totaled $16 million, while Oreo's revenues were at $374 million. Hydrox has been purchased by Keebler, whose elves are trying to give the cookie a major facelift. You are part of the Keebler team deciding what to do with the Hydrox brand.

Activities

1. Can you re-create Hydrox through a name change? What kind of brand name could go head-to-head with Oreo? (Most people unfamiliar with Hydrox think it is a cleaning product.) Make a list of three to five possibilities.
2. How can you package your renewed sandwich cookie to make it more attractive on the shelf than Oreo? What about package size? Draft a brief packaging plan for the new Hydrox (or whatever name you chose).
3. Can you modify the original formula to make something new and more competitive? Will a brand extension work here? Why or why not?

ETHICS EXERCISE

A product that a potential buyer knows about but is not actively seeking is called an unsought product. Is the marketing of unsought products unethical? Discuss your answer in terms of the AMA Statement of Ethics, found at **www.marketingpower.com.**

MARKETING PLAN EXERCISE

In the first part of your strategic marketing plan, you stated your business mission and objectives, and performed a detailed SWOT analysis. In the second part of the plan, you identified and described target market segments and described their buying behaviors and decision-making processes. In addition, you identified sources of competitive intelligence and the need for any further marketing research before the marketing plan could be implemented. The next stages of the strategic planning process involve defining the elements of the marketing mix: (Part 3) product and place, (Part 4) promotion and pricing strategies.

After reading Chapter 10, you can use the following exercises to guide you through the third part of your strategic marketing plan:

1. How would you classify the offering to your customers? Is it a consumer product? A business-to-business product? A good or a service? How does this classification change the focus of your e-marketing plan? Is your product unique enough to be patented? Check with the U.S. Patent and Trademark Office at **www.uspto.gov.**
2. Place your company's offerings into a product portfolio. Consider the broader impact of marketing a product item within a line or mix. Factors to consider are those such as price, image, complementary products, distribution relationship, and so on. Are there any special product features that selling on the Internet would allow you to add or force you to take away?
3. Does your chosen company have a brand name and brand mark? If not, design both. If so, evaluate the ability of the brand name and mark to communicate effectively to the target market. Is strong branding more or less important in an Internet environment? Why? What makes branding so important?
4. What will your company Internet address be? To check and see what URLs are available, go to **www.companyname.com** and try some out. Should your URL be the same as your company name? Why or why not? What happens if a customer mistypes your name? Should you register under alternative spellings?

5. Is the product packaged and labeled? How should it be packaged and why? Does the package and label design match other communications tools? How is this an opportunity to communicate with your customers?

6. Evaluate warranties or guarantees offered by your firm, including product return policies. How will customers return products they purchased from the Web site? Design the parameters for warranties and return policies. Should your return policy be stricter online than off-line? Why or why not?

CASE STUDY: FINALLY, A GARAGEBAND THAT REALLY ROCKS

Steve Jobs's keynote address at the 2004 MacWorld conference was roundly criticized for being blasé and void of any exciting new developments. It did, however, have one major and perhaps easily overlooked bright spot—the unveiling of the latest version of Apple's iLife software. The standard suite of iLife products includes the popular and much heralded iTunes music management software, as well as a digital photograph manipulator and organizer called iPhoto, a digital video-editing program named iMovie, and a DVD mastering program called iDVD. The big news at MacWorld was that Apple has added a new program to iLife '04 called GarageBand. Complete with GarageBand, iLife '04 comes free on all new Apple computers and is available as an upgrade to owners of older systems for a mere $49.

That $49 buys more than a thousand prerecorded Apple loops (or riffs), over 50 virtual instruments, and a virtual recording engineer (which performs over 200 effects). Put simply, GarageBand helps any aspiring musician or hobbyist compose music, and all of those features turn any owner's computer into a pretty substantial home recording studio. Whether the musician needs a drumbeat to back up an external electric guitar for a jam session or a full range of orchestral instruments to provide the background to a keyboard solo, GarageBand makes sure that all selected loops come together on time and in key. The user can even manipulate loops to create an entire song without using any instruments at all. The loops are royalty-free, so new songwriters don't have to worry about paying licensing fees to loop creators if they happen to make the next Hip Hop chart topper.

The software provides a synthesizer-like keyboard that displays on the screen for those who wish to play the plethora of virtual instruments via their computer keyboards, but plugging in an external keyboard allows the aspiring or accomplished musician to seriously expand his or her range. Whether the user selects a Stratocaster guitar, a Steinway piano, a pop organ, or a big-band bass from the library of virtual instruments, the keyboard assumes its identity. Any notes or chords played on it will produce the exact sounds that would emulate from the original version of the virtual instrument. To the delight of guitar players, GarageBand also offers virtual amplifiers that allow them to extract the sounds of the British invasion, arena rock, or cool jazz from their axes.

GarageBand comes with a vast array of effects that composers can apply to their arrangements, too. Loops and any recorded pieces can be faded, reverberated, brightened, echoed, compressed, or tweaked in any number of ways to obtain just the right sound. When masterpieces are finished, GarageBand automatically exports them to iTunes where they are filed in a play list under the composer's name. The program also integrates new compositions with the rest of the iLife programs so that users can match soundtracks to their slide shows and movies. In fact, the programs are so well integrated that Apple is advertising them as "just like Microsoft Office, for the rest of your life."

GarageBand is the latest push by Jobs and Apple to make its computers the hubs of digital home entertainment centers. Unlike iTunes, GarageBand is compatible only with Apple computers. Jobs is betting that with an active musician in one of every two U.S. households, GarageBand will draw a virtually untapped market of more than a hundred million amateur musicians to Apple computers. Considering that iTunes' music store owns 70 percent of the legal music download market and that the iPod is the best- selling digital music playback device, that bet looks like a sound one.[28]

Questions

1. What type of product is GarageBand?
2. To which of Apple's product lines does GarageBand belong?
3. Is GarageBand a new product or a modification of an existing product? If it is a modification, what type of modification is it? Explain.

COMPANY CLIPS

KODAK—REINVENTING THE BRAND

Unquestionably, Kodak is one of the most recognized brands in the United States and the world. For over a century, Kodak was known as the company that brought the technology of photography into the everyday, aptly summed up in the tagline, "Celebrate the Moments of Your Life." Grocery stores, convenience stores, and camera stores contained aisles full of little yellow boxes of Kodak film in every possible speed. But after Kodak invented the digital camera, the company was faced with the challenge of leveraging the equity of its brand in a new competitive market—one that didn't include film.

Questions

1. Using Exhibit 10.1 as a guide, create a diagram that organizes the Kodak products mentioned in the video. How are changes in the company's product mix necessitating changes to the way managers market Kodak's offerings?
2. List the attributes of the Kodak brand. What benefits of branding has the company experienced over time? Have there been pitfalls to having a brand with such strong associations?
3. Describe the functions of packaging of a disposable camera.

Marketing & You Results

A higher score on this scale indicates that you are very brand conscious when you shop. You prefer to buy brands that are nationally known rather than private brands or generic brands. Conversely, a lower score suggests that you are not so brand conscious and tend to choose lower-priced, lesser-known brands.

© ISTOCKPHOTO.COM/LAURENT RENAULT

CHAPTER 11

Developing and Managing Products

LEARNING OUTCOMES

LO1 Explain the importance of developing new products and describe the six categories of new products

LO2 Explain the steps in the new-product development process

LO3 Explain why some products succeed and others fail

LO4 Discuss global issues in new-product development

LO5 Explain the diffusion process through which new products are adopted

LO6 Explain the concept of product life cycles

THE IMPORTANCE OF NEW PRODUCTS

New products are important to sustain growth, increase revenues and profits, and replace obsolete items. Research by *BusinessWeek* and the Boston Consulting Group revealed that the world's 25 most innovative companies have higher average stock returns and higher average revenue growth than companies that were not included in this group.[1] The *BusinessWeek*-Boston Consulting Group's list includes firms such as Apple Inc., Nintendo Corporation, Boeing Company, Nokia, and Microsoft Corporation.[2] These firms are known for innovative products. Other firms on the list are known for innovative business models, innovative customer experience, and/or innovative processes.[3]

In this chapter we focus on new products, processes for developing new products, and how new products spread among consumers or business users, locally, nationally, and globally.

Being first on the market has a number of advantages. These include[4]

- *Increased sales through longer sales life:* The earlier the product reaches the market, relative to the competition, the longer its life can be.
- *Increased margins:* The more innovative the product (i.e., the longer it remains unchallenged on the market), the longer consumers will accept a premium purchase price.
- *Increased product loyalty:* Early adopters are likely to upgrade, customize, or purchase companion products.
- *More resale opportunities:* For components, commodities, or products that other companies can private-label, being first to market can often help ensure sales in other channels.
- *Greater market responsiveness:* The faster that companies can bring products to market that satisfy new or changing customer needs, the greater the opportunity to capitalize on those products for margin lift and to increase brand recognition.
- A *sustained leadership position:* Being first is the market position a competitor cannot take away. And repeated firsts establish companies as innovators and leaders in the market.

In one recent year, American inventors registered about 80,000 patents in the U.S. patent system, where virtually all important technologies developed in any nation are patented. That is more patents than were registered in the rest of the world combined.[5]

Marketing & You

Using the following scale, indicate your opinion on the line before each item.

1	2	3	4	5	6
Strongly disagree					Strongly agree

___ I like introducing new brands and products to my friends.

___ I like helping people by providing them with information about many kinds of products.

___ People ask me for information about products, places to shop, or sales.

___ If someone asked where to get the best buy on several types of products, I could tell him or her where to shop.

___ My friends think of me as a good source of information when it comes to new products or sales.

___ I know a lot of different products, stores, and sales, and I like sharing this information.

Total your score. Read the chapter and find out what your score means at the end.

Source: From Scale #18, *Marketing Scales Handbook*, G. Bruner, K. James, H. Hensel, eds. Vol. III. © by American Marketing Association.

Categories of New Products

The term **new product** is somewhat confusing because its meaning varies widely. Actually, the term has several "correct" definitions. A product can be new to the world, to the market, to the producer or seller, or to some combination of these. There are six categories of new products:

new product
A product new to the world, the market, the producer, the seller, or some combination of these.

A "new product" can be new to the world, new to the market, new to the producer or seller, or new to some combination of these. For example, each time Nintendo introduces a new Wii game, it is adding to an existing product line.

- *New-to-the-world products* (also called *discontinuous innovations*): These products create an entirely new market. New-to-the-world products represent the smallest category of new products. Ten of the most important new-to-the-world products introduced in the past 100 years are[6]

   1. Penicillin
   2. Transistor radio
   3. Polio vaccine
   4. Mosaic (the first graphic Web browser)
   5. Microprocessor
   6. Black-and-white television
   7. Plain paper copier
   8. Alto personal computer (prototype of today's PCs)
   9. Microwave oven
   10. Arpanet network (the groundwork for the Internet)

Source: Reprinted from the May 14, 2007 issue of *BusinessWeek* by special permission. Copyright © 2007 by the McGraw-Hill Companies, Inc.

- *New product lines*: These products, which the firm has not previously offered, allow it to enter new or established markets. For example, Disney Consumer Products recently added a new line of fragrances targeting boys 4 to 11 in Latin communities under the brand names Pirates of the Caribbean and Buzz Lightyear.[7]
- *Additions to existing product lines*: This category includes new products that supplement a firm's established line. For example, each time Nintendo introduces a new Wii game, it is adding to an existing product line.

- *Improvements or revisions of existing products*: The "new and improved" product may be significantly or slightly changed. Procter & Gamble's Tide Coldwater is an example. The product is concentrated so that packaging materials are reduced. By not requiring hot water, Tide Coldwater requires less energy to wash a load of clothes and would reduce carbon emissions by 34 tons per year if every U.S. household used the product.[8]
- *Repositioned products*: These are existing products targeted at new markets or market segments, or repositioned to change the current market's perception of the product. Sometimes repositioning is intended to boost sales of a product with declining sales. Following a decline in sales, Diet Dr. Pepper was repositioned as an alternative to a dessert instead of comparing it to other diet drinks.
- *Lower-priced products*: This category refers to products that provide performance similar to competing brands at a lower price. Hewlett-Packard Laser Jet 3100 is a scanner, copier, printer, and fax machine combined. This product is priced lower than many conventional color copiers and much lower than the combined price of the four items purchased separately. Wal-Mart is making headway penetrating the low-price fashion market dominated by Target.

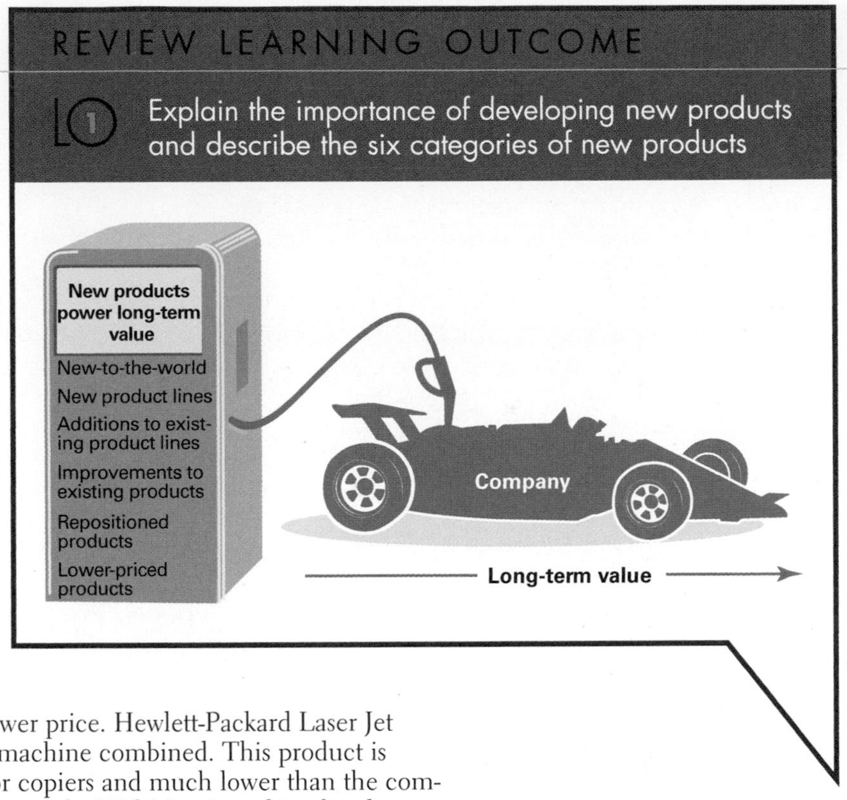

THE NEW-PRODUCT DEVELOPMENT PROCESS

The management consulting firm Booz, Allen Hamilton has studied the new-product development process for over 30 years. After analyzing five major studies undertaken during this period, the firm concluded that the companies most likely to succeed in developing and introducing new products are those that take the following actions:

- Make the long-term commitment needed to support innovation and new-product development.
- Use a company-specific approach, driven by corporate objectives and strategies, with a well-defined new-product strategy at its core.
- Capitalize on experience to achieve and maintain competitive advantage.
- Establish an environment—a management style, organizational structure, and degree of top-management support—conducive to achieving company-specific new-product and corporate objectives.

Most companies follow a formal new-product development process, usually starting with a new-product strategy. Exhibit 11.1 traces the seven-step process, which is discussed in detail in this section. The exhibit is funnel-shaped

EXHIBIT 11.1

New-Product Development Process

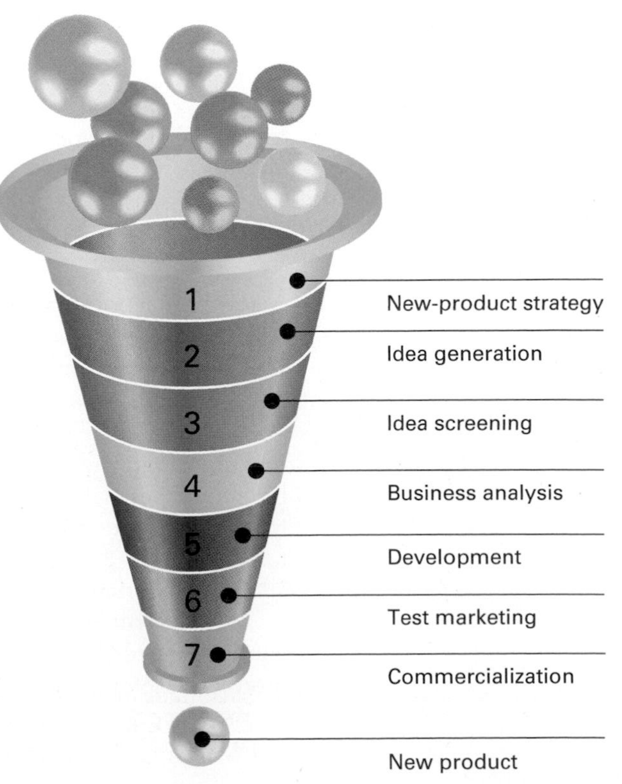

CUSTOMER Experience

New-Product Development Using Web 2.0 Tools

Web 2.0 offers marketers a great new way to engage consumers. How can companies use these new tools to build relationships and collaborate with consumers online? That was the topic of a *Wall Street Journal* article that was based on interviews with more than 30 executives and managers that are in the forefront of experimenting with Web 2.0 tools.

But first, a more basic question: What is Web 2.0, anyway? Essentially, it encompasses the set of tools that allow people to build social and business connections, share information, and collaborate on projects online. That includes blogs, wikis, social-networking sites and other online communities, and virtual worlds.

Millions of people have become familiar with these tools through sites like Facebook, Wikipedia, and Second Life, or by writing their own blogs. And a growing number of marketers are using Web 2.0 tools to collaborate with consumers on product development, service enhancement, and promotion. But most companies still don't appear to be well versed in this area.

Many marketers have been trained to bludgeon consumers with advertising—to sell, sell, sell, anytime and anywhere consumers can be found. In an online community, it pays to resist that temptation.

When consumers are invited to participate in online communities, they expect marketers to listen and to consider their ideas. They don't want to feel like they're simply a captive audience for advertising, and if they do, they're likely to abandon the community.

The head of consumer research for a leading consumer electronics organization created an online community of nearly 50,000 consumers to discuss product development and marketing issues. One of the key principles of the community, she says, was "not to do anything about marketing, because we weren't about selling; we were about conversing."

In short order, community members not only identified what it was they were looking for in the company's products, but also suggested innovations to satisfy those needs. The company quickly developed prototypes based on those suggestions, and got an enthusiastic response: Community members asked when they would be able to buy the products and if they would get the first opportunity to buy them. They didn't have to be sold on anything.[10]

Suggest other ideas that companies might use to generate and/or improve new product ideas using Web 2.0 tools. Briefly describe a positive or negative experience you have had visiting a Web 2.0 site.

new-product strategy
A plan that links the new-product development process with the objectives of the marketing department, the business unit, and the corporation.

to highlight the fact that each stage acts as a screen. The purpose is to filter out unworkable ideas.

New-Product Strategy

A **new-product strategy** links the new-product development process with the objectives of the marketing department, the business unit, and the corporation. A new-product strategy must be compatible with these objectives, and in turn, all three objectives must be consistent with one another. A new-product strategy is part of the organization's overall marketing strategy. It sharpens the focus and provides general guidelines for generating, screening, and evaluating new-product ideas. The new-product strategy specifies the roles that new products must play in the organization's overall plan and describes the characteristics of products the organization wants to offer and the markets it wants to serve.

The importance of having a well-thought-out new-product strategy is illustrated by a Dun & Bradstreet finding that for each successful new product introduced, a company needs between 50 and 60 other new-product ideas somewhere in the new-product development process.[9] Procter & Gamble has made a public commitment to introduce $20 billion worth of sustainable innovative products between 2008 and 2013.[11]

Idea Generation

New-product ideas come from many sources, including customers, employees, distributors, competitors, vendors, research and development (R&D), and consultants.

New-product ideas come from many sources, including customers, employees, distributors, competitors, vendors, R&D, and consultants.

- *Customers*: The marketing concept suggests that customers' wants and needs should be the springboard for developing new products. Many of today's most innovative and successful marketers are introducing fewer new products, but they are taking steps to ensure that these "chosen few" are truly unique and better and, above all, really do address unmet consumer needs. How do they do that? Many firms rely on "co-creation," inventing new products along with their customers.[12] At www.MyStarbucksIdea.com, customers can make suggestions, other customers can vote on and discuss them, and Starbucks can see which ideas gain support.[13] Dell Computers has a similar site, called IdeaStorm.com, that has led to a host of new offerings.[14] As the Customer Experience box in this chapter illustrates, some companies are using Web 2.0 tools to get consumers more involved in new-product development. This approach is far from an intuitive extension of previous new-product development and advertising practices.
- *Employees*: Marketing personnel—advertising and marketing research employees, as well as salespeople—often create new-product ideas because they analyze and are involved in the marketplace. The very successful introduction of Post-it Notes started with an employee's idea. In 1974, the R&D department of 3M's commercial tape division developed and patented the adhesive component of Post-it Notes. However, it was a year before an employee of the commercial tape division, who sang in a church choir, identified a use for the adhesive. He had been using paper clips and slips of paper to mark places in hymn books. But the paper clips damaged his books, and the slips of paper fell out. The solution, as we now all know, was to apply the adhesive to small pieces of paper and sell them in packages.

  Some companies have developed innovation centers to encourage and implement new ideas. For example, McDonald's has a team of 70 employees that tests new equipment ideas and procedures at its Innovation Center in Romeoville, Illinois.[15] According to the results of a survey by Prophet, a management consulting firm, 80 percent of "model innovators" encourage employees to be curious, 76 percent systematically encourage risk taking, 64 percent make it a priority to provide time and space for the development of new ideas, and 60 percent have incentive systems encouraging employees to contribute to innovation efforts.[16]
- *Distributors*: A well-trained sales force routinely asks distributors about needs that are not being met. Because they are closer to end users, distributors are often more aware of customer needs than are manufacturers. The inspiration for Rubbermaid's litter-free lunch box, named Sidekick, came from a distributor. The distributor suggested that Rubbermaid place some of its plastic containers inside a lunch box and sell the box as an alternative to plastic wrap and paper bags. The survey by Prophet mentioned in the previous paragraph found that 75 percent of model innovations actively involve their vendors and suppliers in new-product development.[17] Procter & Gamble has reported that its innovation productivity has increased 60 percent due to external collaborations.[18]
- *Competitors*: No firms rely solely on internally generated ideas for new products. A big part of any organization's marketing intelligence system should be monitoring the performance of competitors' products. One purpose of competitive monitoring is to determine which, if any, of the competitors' products should be copied. There is plenty of information about competitors on the World Wide Web. For example, AltaVista (www.altavista.com) is a powerful index tool that can be used to locate information about products and companies.

product development
A marketing strategy that entails the creation of marketable new products; the process of converting applications for new technologies into marketable products.

brainstorming
The process of getting a group to think of unlimited ways to vary a product or solve a problem.

screening
The first filter in the product development process, which eliminates ideas that are inconsistent with the organization's new-product strategy or are obviously inappropriate for some other reason.

concept test
A test to evaluate a new-product idea, usually before any prototype has been created.

Fuld & Co.'s competitive intelligence guide provides links to a variety of market intelligence sites.

- *Vendors*: 7-Eleven regularly forges partnerships with vendors to create proprietary products such as Candy Gulp (a plastic cup filled with gummies) and Blue Vanilla Laffy Taffy Rope candy developed by Nestlé's Wonka division exclusively for 7-Eleven.
- *Research and development*: R&D is carried out in four distinct ways. Basic research is scientific research aimed at discovering new technologies. Applied research takes these new technologies and tries to find useful applications for them. **Product development** goes one step further by converting applications into marketable products. *Product modification* makes cosmetic or functional changes in existing products. Many new-product breakthroughs come from R&D activities. Procter & Gamble Co., the world's largest household goods manufacturer, has 9,000 research and development employees.[19]

  Some companies are establishing innovation laboratories to complement or even replace lengthy R&D programs in which scientists spend years coming up with new-product ideas and then pass these ideas along to product developers, then to designers, and finally to marketers. Ideas labs focus on substantially increasing the speed of innovation. Motorola's Razr telephone was developed in an innovation lab called Moto City, located about 50 miles from company headquarters. Most of the development work was done by a team of engineers, designers, and marketers who worked in open spaces and waist-high cubicles. Many normal practices, such as soliciting input from regional managers around the world, were omitted to foster teamwork and speed development.[20] Innovation labs are used by a wide range of organizations including Boeing, Wrigley, Procter & Gamble, and the Mayo Clinic.
- *Consultants*: Outside consultants are always available to examine a business and recommend product ideas. Examples include the Weston Group, Booz Allen Hamilton, and Management Decisions. Traditionally, consultants determine whether a company has a balanced portfolio of products and, if not, what new-product ideas are needed to offset the imbalance. For instance, an outside consultant conceived Airwick's highly successful Carpet Fresh carpet cleaner.

Creativity is the wellspring of new-product ideas, regardless of who comes up with them. A variety of approaches and techniques have been developed to stimulate creative thinking. The two considered most useful for generating new-product ideas are brainstorming and focus-group exercises. The goal of **brainstorming** is to get a group to think of unlimited ways to vary a product or solve a problem. Group members avoid criticism of an idea, no matter how ridiculous it may seem. Objective evaluation is postponed. The sheer quantity of ideas is what matters. As noted in Chapter 9, an objective of focus-group interviews is to stimulate insightful comments through group interaction. Focus groups usually consist of seven to ten people. Sometimes consumer focus groups generate excellent new-product ideas—for example, Cycle dog food, Stick-Up room deodorizers, and DustBuster vacuum cleaners. In the industrial market, machine tools, keyboard designs, aircraft interiors, and backhoe accessories have evolved from focus groups.

Idea Screening

After new ideas have been generated, they pass through the first filter in the product development process. This stage, called **screening,** eliminates ideas that are inconsistent with the organization's new-product strategy or are obviously inappropriate for some other reason. The new-product committee, the new-product department, or some other formally appointed group performs the screening review. At General Motors, only one out of every 20 new car concepts developed will ever become a reality. That's not a bad percentage. In the pharmaceutical business, the percentage is much lower. Most new-product ideas are rejected at the screening stage.

Concept tests are often used at the screening stage to rate concept (or product) alternatives. A **concept test** evaluates a new-product idea, usually before any prototype has been created. Typically, researchers get consumer reactions to descriptions and visual representations of a proposed product.

Concept tests are considered fairly good predictors of success for line extensions. They have also been relatively precise predictors of success for new products that are not copycat items, are not easily classified into existing product categories, and do not require major changes in consumer behavior—such as Betty Crocker Tuna Helper, Cycle dog food, and Libby's Fruit Float. However, concept tests are usually inaccurate in predicting the success of new products that create new consumption patterns and require major changes in consumer behavior—such as microwave ovens, videocassette recorders, computers, and word processors.

Business Analysis

New-product ideas that survive the initial screening process move to the **business analysis** stage, where preliminary figures for demand, cost, sales, and profitability are calculated. For the first time, costs and revenues are estimated and compared. Depending on the nature of the product and the company, this process may be simple or complex.

The newness of the product, the size of the market, and the nature of the competition all affect the accuracy of revenue projections. In an established market like soft drinks, industry estimates of total market size are available. Forecasting market share for a new entry is a bigger challenge.

Analyzing overall economic trends and their impact on estimated sales is especially important in product categories that are sensitive to fluctuations in the business cycle. If consumers view the economy as uncertain and risky, they will put off buying durable goods like major home appliances, automobiles, and homes. Likewise, business buyers postpone major equipment purchases if they expect a recession.

These questions are commonly asked during the business analysis stage:

- What is the likely demand for the product?
- What impact would the new product probably have on total sales, profits, market share, and return on investment?
- How would the introduction of the product affect existing products? Would the new product cannibalize existing products?
- Would current customers benefit from the product?
- Would the product enhance the image of the company's overall product mix?
- Would the new product affect current employees in any way? Would it lead to hiring more people or reducing the size of the workforce?
- What new facilities, if any, would be needed?
- How might competitors respond?
- What is the risk of failure? Is the company willing to take the risk?

Answering these questions may require studies of markets, competition, costs, and technical capabilities. But at the end of this stage, management should have a good understanding of the product's market potential. This understanding is important as costs increase dramatically once a product idea enters the development stage.

New ideas often face resistance, especially if they are perceived as risky to the company. The ideas that survive the business analysis stage are often ones whose creators blended a careful balance of political and managerial support early in the process.

Development

In the early stage of **development**, the R&D or engineering department may develop a prototype of the product. During this stage, the firm should start sketching a marketing strategy. The marketing department should decide on the product's packaging, branding, labeling, and so forth. In addition, it should map out preliminary promotion, price, and distribution strategies. The feasibility of manufacturing the product at an acceptable cost should be thoroughly examined.

business analysis
The second stage of the screening process where preliminary figures for demand, cost, sales, and profitability are calculated.

development
The stage in the product development process in which a prototype is developed and a marketing strategy is outlined.

Specially equipped Boeing 737 will enable commercial airlines to offer passengers real-time high-speed Internet and intranet access, television, and full-featured e-mail capability.

© AP IMAGES/PR NEWSFOTO/BOEING

The development stage can last a long time and thus be very expensive. Crest toothpaste was in the development stage for 10 years. It took 18 years to develop Minute Rice, 15 years to develop the Polaroid Colorpack camera, 15 years to develop the Xerox copy machine, and 51 years to develop television. Gillette developed three shaving systems over a 27-year period (TracII, Atra, and Sensor) before introducing the Mach3 in 1998 and Fusion in 2006.[21]

The development process works best when all the involved areas (R&D, marketing, engineering, production, and even suppliers) work together rather than sequentially, a process called **simultaneous product development**. This approach allows firms to shorten the development process and reduce costs. With simultaneous product development, all relevant functional areas and outside suppliers participate in all stages of the development process. Rather than proceeding through highly structured stages, the cross-functional team operates in unison. Involving key suppliers early in the process capitalizes on their knowledge and enables them to develop critical component parts.

simultaneous product development
A team-oriented approach to new-product development.

test marketing
The limited introduction of a product and a marketing program to determine the reactions of potential customers in a market situation.

The Internet is a useful tool for implementing simultaneous product development. On the Net, multiple partners from a variety of locations can meet regularly to assess new-product ideas, analyze markets and demographics, and review cost information. Ideas judged to be feasible can quickly be converted into new products. Without the Internet it would be impossible to conduct simultaneous product development from different parts of the world. Global R&D is important for two reasons. First, large companies have become global and are no longer focused only on one market. Global R&D is necessary to connect with customers in different parts of the world. Second, companies want to tap into the world's best talent.

Some firms use online brain trusts to solve technical problems. InnoCentive, Inc., is a network of 80,000 self-selected science problem solvers in 173 countries. Its clients include Boeing, DuPont, and Procter & Gamble. Procter & Gamble has another program called the Connect-and-Develop Model. When the company selects an idea for development, it no longer tries to develop it from the ground up with its own resources and time. Instead, it issues a brief to its network of thinkers, researchers, technology entrepreneurs, and inventors around the world, hoping to generate dialog, suggestions, and solutions. Olay Regenerist Eye Derma Pods, a top-selling skin care item, was developed through Connect-and-Develop.[22]

Innovative firms are also gathering a variety of R&D input from customers online. Google polls millions of Web page creators to determine the most relevant search results. LEGO Group uses the Internet to identify its most enthusiastic customers and to help design and market products. Threadless, a T-shirt company, and Ryz, an athletic shoe manufacturer, ask consumers to vote online for their favorites. The companies use these results to determine the products they sell over the Internet.

Laboratory tests are often conducted on prototype models during the development stage. User safety is an important aspect of laboratory testing, which actually subjects products to much more severe treatment than is expected by end users. The Consumer Product Safety Act of 1972 requires manufacturers to conduct a "reasonable testing program" to ensure that their products conform to established safety standards.

Many products that test well in the laboratory are also tried out in homes or businesses. Examples of product categories well suited for such use tests include human and pet food products, household cleaning products, and industrial chemicals and supplies. These products are all relatively inexpensive, and their performance characteristics are apparent to users. For example, Procter & Gamble tests a variety of personal- and home-care products in the community around its Cincinnati, Ohio, headquarters.

Test Marketing

After products and marketing programs have been developed, they are usually tested in the marketplace. **Test marketing** is the limited introduction of a product and a marketing program to determine the reactions of potential customers in a market situation.

Test marketing allows management to evaluate alternative strategies and to assess how well the various aspects of the marketing mix fit together. Even established products are test marketed to assess new marketing strategies.

The cities chosen as test sites should reflect market conditions in the new product's projected market area. Yet no "magic city" exists that can universally represent market conditions, and a product's success in one city doesn't guarantee that it will be a nationwide hit. When selecting test market cities, researchers should therefore find locations where the demographics and purchasing habits mirror the overall market. The company should also have good distribution in test cities. Moreover, test locations should be isolated from the media. If the TV stations in a particular market reach a very large area outside that market, the advertising used for the test product may pull in many consumers from outside the market. The product may then appear more successful than it really is. Exhibit 11.2 provides a useful checklist of criteria for selecting test markets.

EXHIBIT 11.2

Checklist for Selecting Test Markets

In choosing a test market, many criteria need to be considered, especially the following:

- Similarity to planned distribution outlets
- Relative isolation from other cities
- Availability of cooperative advertising media
- Diversified cross section of ages, religions, cultural-societal preferences, etc.
- No atypical purchasing habits
- Representative population size
- Typical per capita income
- Good record as a test city, but not overly used
- Not easily "jammed" by competitors
- Stability of year-round sales
- No dominant television station; multiple newspapers, magazines, and radio stations
- Availability of research and audit services
- Availability of retailers that will cooperate
- Freedom from unusual influences, such as one industry's dominance or heavy tourism

The High Costs of Test Marketing Test marketing frequently takes one year or longer, and costs can exceed $1 million. Some products remain in test markets even longer. McDonald's spent 12 years developing and testing salads before introducing them. Despite the cost, many firms believe it is a lot better to fail in a test market than in a national introduction.

Because test marketing is so expensive, some companies do not test line extensions of well-known brands. For example, because the Folgers brand is well known, Procter & Gamble faced little risk in distributing its instant decaffeinated version nationally. Consolidated Foods Kitchen of Sara Lee followed the same approach with its frozen croissants. Other products introduced without being test marketed include General Foods' International Coffees, Quaker Oats' Chewy Granola Bars and Granola Dipps, and Pillsbury's Milk Break Bars.

The high cost of test marketing is not just financial. One unavoidable problem is that test marketing exposes the new product and its marketing mix to competitors before its introduction. Thus, the element of surprise is lost. Competitors can also sabotage or "jam" a testing program by introducing their own sales promotion, pricing, or advertising campaign. The purpose is to hide or distort the normal conditions that the testing firm might expect in the market.

Alternatives to Test Marketing Many firms are looking for cheaper, faster, and safer alternatives to traditional test marketing. Information Resources, Inc. pioneered one alternative in the 1980s: single-source research using supermarket scanner data (discussed in Chapter 9). A typical scanner test costs about $300,000. Another alternative to traditional test marketing is **simulated (laboratory) market testing**. Advertising and other promotional materials for several products, including the test product, are shown to members of the product's target market. These people are then taken to shop at a mock or real store, where their purchases are recorded. Shopper behavior, including repeat purchasing, is monitored to assess the product's likely performance under true market conditions. Research firms offer simulated

simulated (laboratory) market testing
The presentation of advertising and other promotion materials for several products, including a test product, to members of the product's target market.

> “The high price of failure simply prohibits the widespread introduction of most new products without testing.”

market tests for $25,000 to $100,000, compared to $1 million or more for full-scale test marketing.

Online Test Marketing Despite these alternatives, most firms still consider test marketing essential for most new products. The high price of failure simply prohibits the widespread introduction of most new products without testing. Many firms are finding that the Internet offers a fast, cost-effective way to conduct test marketing.

Procter & Gamble uses the Internet to assess customer demand for potential new products. Many products that are not available in grocery stores or drugstores can be sampled from P&G's corporate Web site (**www.pg.com**).

Other consumer goods firms that use online test marketing include General Mills and Quaker Oats. Other Web sites have appeared that offer consumers prototype products developed by all sizes of firms.

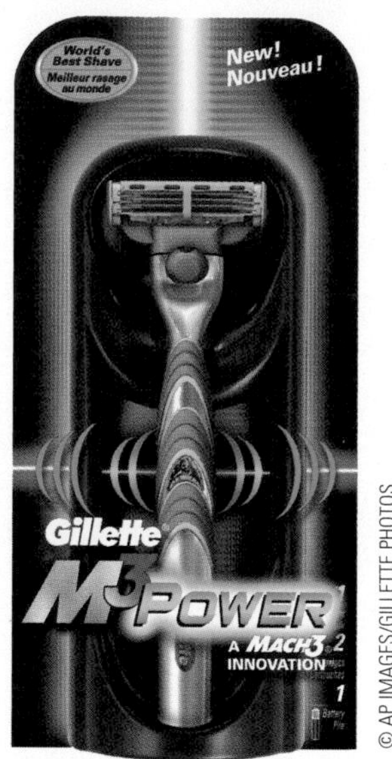

© AP IMAGES/GILLETTE PHOTOS

Commercialization

The final stage in the new-product development process is **commercialization**, the decision to market a product. The decision to commercialize the product sets several tasks in motion: ordering production materials and equipment, starting production, building inventories, shipping the product to field distribution points, training the sales force, announcing the new product to the trade, and advertising to potential customers.

The time from the initial commercialization decision to the product's actual introduction varies. It can range from a few weeks for simple products that use existing equipment to several years for technical products that require custom manufacturing equipment.

The total cost of development and initial introduction can be staggering. Gillette spent $750 million developing the Mach3, and the first-year marketing budget for the new three-bladed razor was $300 million.

For some products, a well-planned Internet campaign can provide new-product information for people who are looking for the solutions that a particular new product offers. Attempting to reach customers at the point in time when they need a product is much more cost-effective and efficient than communicating with a target market that may eventually have a need for the product.

commercialization
The decision to market a product.

REVIEW LEARNING OUTCOME

LO2 Explain the steps in the new-product development process

New-product strategy
Idea generation
Idea screening
Business analysis
Development
Test marketing
Commercialization

Number of new product ideas
0
Time

LO3 WHY SOME PRODUCTS SUCCEED AND OTHERS FAIL

Despite the amount spent on developing and testing new products, a large proportion of new-product introductions fail. Products fail for a number of reasons. One common reason is that they simply do not offer any discernible benefit compared to existing products. Another commonly cited factor in new-product failures is a poor match between product features and customer desires. For example, there are telephone systems on the market with over 700 different functions, although the average user is happy with just 10 functions. Other reasons for failure include overestimation of market size, incorrect positioning, a price too high or too low, inadequate distribution, poor promotion, or simply an inferior product compared to those of competitors.

Maybe consumers are just too preoccupied to pay much attention to commercial messages about new products. A survey reported by Schneider Associates, Mintel International, and Information Resources found that 69 percent of consumers could not name a single new product launched in 2008. The new products remembered most often were[23]

1. Nintendo Wii Fit – 22 percent recall
2. iPod Touch – 16 percent
3. Bud Light Lime – 15 percent
4. McDonald's Southern Style Chicken Biscuit and Sandwich – 14 percent
5. Kraft Mac & Cheese Crackers – 13 percent
6. KY Yours + Mine Couples Lubricant – 12 percent
7. Gatorade G2, Yoplait Fiber One – (tie) 11 percent
8. MacBook Air, Rock Band, Burger King Apple Fries,

   Neosporin Neo To Go!, Kraft Bagel-fuls – (tie) 8 percent

Interestingly, when managers are publicly committed to new products, they tend to stay committed even when new information indicates that the product will fail. This "escalation of commitment" can be disastrous for firms in today's hypercompetitive markets.[24]

Failure can be a matter of degree. Absolute failure occurs when a company cannot recoup its development, marketing, and production costs. The product actually loses money for the company. A relative product failure results when the product returns a profit but fails to achieve sales, profit, or market share goals. Some highly publicized new product failures include the Sony Betamax (1975), Apple Lisa (1983), New Coke (1985), and Kellogg's Breakfast Mates (1998).[25]

High costs and other risks of developing and testing new products do not stop many companies, such as Rubbermaid, Colgate-Palmolive, Campbell's Soup, 3M, and Procter & Gamble, from aggressively developing and introducing new products.

The most important factor in successful new-product introduction is a good match between the product and market needs—as the marketing concept would predict. Successful new products deliver a meaningful and perceivable benefit to a sizable number of people or organizations and are different in some meaningful way from their intended substitutes. Firms that routinely experience success in new-product introductions tend to share the following characteristics[26]:

- A history of carefully listening to customers
- An obsession with producing the best product possible
- A vision of what the market will be like in the future
- Strong leadership
- A commitment to new-product development
- A project-based team approach to new-product development
- Getting every aspect of the product development process right
- Willingness to fail occasionally

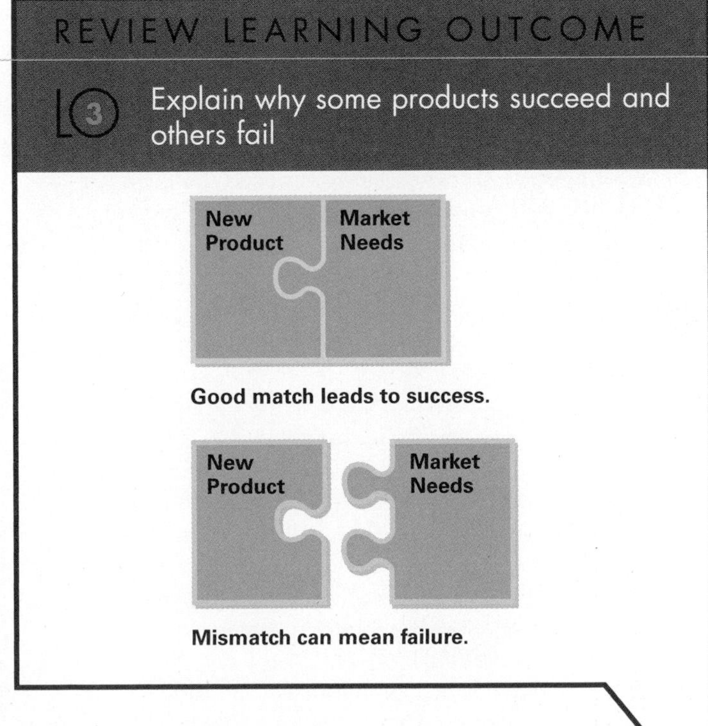

GLOBAL ISSUES IN NEW-PRODUCT DEVELOPMENT

Increasing globalization of markets and of competition provides a reason for multinational firms to consider new-product development from a worldwide perspective. That perspective includes developing countries as well as more established markets. As the Global Perspectives box in this chapter illustrates, many U.S.-based firms are highly dependent on products developed specifically for unique needs in foreign markets.

A firm that starts with a global strategy is better able to develop products that are marketable worldwide. In many multinational corporations, every product is developed for potential worldwide distribution, and unique market requirements are built in whenever possible. Procter & Gamble introduced Pampers Phases into global markets within one month of introducing the product in the United States. P&G's goal was to have the product on the shelf in 90 countries within one year. The objective was to establish brand loyalty among dealers and consumers before foreign competitors could react.

Some global marketers design their products to meet regulations in their major markets and then, if necessary, meet smaller markets' requirements country by country.

GLOBAL Perspectives

Frugal Engineering

The world is becoming one big R&D lab. Companies increasingly are finding that their international operations are coming up with ideas that resonate far beyond local markets. Case in point: Deere & Co. now is pursuing a new market in the United States—recreational farmers—thanks to innovations hatched at its research facility in Pune, India.

Deere, based in Moline, Illinois, opened the Pune center in 2001 as a way of entering the Indian market. The move was unexpected: Deere is known for its heavy-duty farm equipment and big construction gear. Many of India's 300 million-plus farmers still use oxen-pulled plows. But Deere saw potential, and its engineers in Pune responded with four no-frills models—they don't include GPS or air conditioning—that were sturdy enough to handle the rigors of commercial farming.

The tractors, which cost $8,400 to $11,600 in India, were so basic that Deere never even contemplated selling them in the United States. Then Indian tractor maker Mahindra & Mahindra began selling its wares in the United States, targeting a market Deere had largely ignored—hobbyists as well as bargain hunters. These folks didn't need advanced features, and it turns out they coveted the same qualities as Indian farmers: affordability and maneuverability. Deere, taking a cue from Mahindra, in 2002 transplanted a slightly modified version (with softer seats and higher horsepower) of the Indian line of tractors, which it markets as the 5003 series in the United States at a starting price of $14,400. Today, about half the tractors Deere manufactures in India make their way overseas.

The Indian-made Deere tractor was perfect for hobby farmer Jim Henderson, who works as a county executive in Franklin, Kentucky, and gets rid of stress by tending his 57-acre hay farm on weekends. Full-time farmer Brad Wolfe initially was more skeptical: he balked when he learned a tractor he liked was made in India. A dealer finally convinced Wolfe that the tractor was durable, and two years later he bought another Indian-made Deere. Jang Sangha is concerned about durability too. Sangha, whose family farms 5,500 acres in Jalandhar, relies on a fleet of 160 Deere tractors to operate his business, and he's been pleased so far.

Deere doesn't disclose margins for specific machines, but the company surely sees financial benefits from transplanting Indian innovations to the United States. Raj Kalathur, the managing director of Deere's Indian division, says the 5003 tractors were born out of "frugal engineering." Many of Deere's Indian employees witness poverty daily, he explains, and they took great care to minimize costs. That kind of innovation isn't just global—it's good business.[27]

What other products can you think of that might be candidates for frugal engineering? Write a memo to the director of marketing research for a U.S. manufacturer proposing and justifying your favorite idea.

Nissan develops lead-country car models that, with minor changes, can be sold in most markets. With this approach, Nissan has been able to reduce the number of its basic models from 48 to 18.

Developing countries represent huge automobile markets, but not at prevailing international prices. Renault SA introduced the Dacia Logan, an anonymous econocar with exposed screws, a coarse fabric interior, and a 90-horsepower motor. The Logan sells for about $7,300 in Eastern Europe and the Middle East, and $9,000 in Western Europe and has become more successful than predicted. Rivals such as Honda Motor Co. and Toyota Motor Corp. are preparing competitive entries priced under $10,000.[28] India's Tata Motors Ltd. has announced the launch of a new brand called the Tata Nano that will have a sticker price of $2,500.[29]

Some companies could not sell their products at affordable prices and still make an adequate profit in many countries. GE Healthcare engineers figured out a way to develop the MAC 400, a portable electrocardiograph machine selling for $1,500 in India. The MAC 400 was based upon technology developed for a U.S. ECG that sold for $5.4 million.[30] The Global Perspectives box in this chapter provides another example of adapting a product designed for developed countries to one for developing countries.

We often hear about how popular American products are in foreign countries. Recently, U.S. companies such as Levi Strauss, Coca-Cola, RJR Nabisco, and Nike have been finding that products popular in foreign markets can become hits in the United States. Häagen-Dazs's ice cream flavor *dulce de leche*, named after a caramelized milk drink that is popular in Argentina, was originally introduced in Buenos Aires. Enova, a cooking oil that helps cut body weight and fat, was the top-selling brand in Japan before it was introduced in the United States.

In other cases, former alliance partners have become competitors. For years, Shanghai Automotive Industry Corp. has worked with General Motors Corp. and Volkswagen AG to build cars for Chinese consumers. The Chinese automaker now plans to introduce its own products in global markets, competing with its partners.[31]

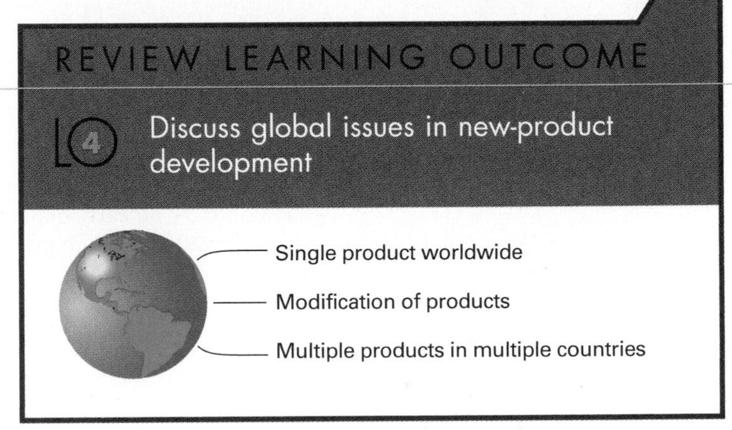

THE SPREAD OF NEW PRODUCTS

Managers have a better chance of successfully marketing products if they understand how consumers learn about and adopt products. A person who buys a new product never before tried may ultimately become an **adopter**, a consumer who was happy enough with his or her trial experience with a product to use it again.

Diffusion of Innovation

An **innovation** is a product perceived as new by a potential adopter. It really doesn't matter whether the product is "new to the world" or some other category of new product. If it is new to a potential adopter, it is an innovation in this context. **Diffusion** is the process by which the adoption of an innovation spreads.

Five categories of adopters participate in the diffusion process:

- *Innovators*: the first 2.5 percent of all those who adopt the product. Innovators are almost obsessed with trying new ideas and products. In addition to having higher incomes, they are more worldly and more active outside their community than non-innovators. They rely less on group norms and are more self-confident. Because they are well educated, they are more likely to get their information from scientific

adopter
A consumer who was happy enough with his or her trial experience with a product to use it again.

innovation
A product perceived as new by a potential adopter.

diffusion
The process by which the adoption of an innovation spreads.

The new iPhone is popular, not only for its looks but also for the fun, useful, and completely new applications (aka apps) it offers its users—something nearly irresistible to early adopters of tech gadgets.

© QI HENG/XINHUA/LANDOV

sources and experts. Innovators are characterized as being venturesome.

- *Early adopters*: the next 13.5 percent to adopt the product. Although early adopters are not the very first, they do adopt early in the product's life cycle. Compared to innovators, they rely much more on group norms and values. They are also more oriented to the local community, in contrast to the innovators' worldly outlook. Early adopters are more likely than innovators to be opinion leaders because of their closer affiliation with groups. Early adopters are a new product's best friends.[32] Apple Computer spends its entire marketing budget attempting to appeal to early adopters. Joe Bates, research director for the Consumer Electronics Association, has noted that early adopters spend up to three times more money on consumer electronics devices than other categories of adopters and are two to five times more likely to spread the word of new products than average consumers.[33] The respect of others is a dominant characteristic of early adopters. Exhibit 11.3 identifies some other characteristics of early adopters.0
- *Early majority*: the next 34 percent to adopt. The early majority weighs the pros and cons before adopting a new product. They are likely to collect more information and evaluate more brands than early adopters, therefore extending the adoption process. They rely on the group for information but are unlikely to be opinion leaders themselves. Instead, they tend to be opinion leaders' friends and neighbors. The early majority is an important link in the process of diffusing new ideas because they are positioned between earlier and later adopters. A dominant characteristic of the early majority is deliberateness.
- *Late majority*: the next 34 percent to adopt. The late majority adopts a new product because most of their friends have already adopted it. Because they also rely on group norms, their adoption stems from pressure to conform. This group tends to be older and below average in income and education. They depend mainly on word-of-mouth communication rather than on the mass media. The dominant characteristic of the late majority is skepticism.
- *Laggards*: the final 16 percent to adopt. Like innovators, laggards do not rely on group norms, but their independence is rooted in their ties to tradition. Thus, the past heavily influences their decisions. By the time laggards adopt an innovation, it has probably become outmoded and been replaced by something else. For example, they may have bought their first black-and-white TV set after color television was already widely diffused. Laggards have the longest adoption time and the lowest socioeconomic status. They tend to be suspicious of new products and alienated from a rapidly advancing society. The dominant value of laggards is tradition. Marketers typically ignore laggards, who do not seem to be motivated by advertising or personal selling and are virtually impossible to reach online.

Note that some product categories, such as monochrome televisions, may never be adopted by 100 percent of the population. The adopter categories refer to all of those who will eventually adopt a product, not the entire population.

EXHIBIT 11.3

Who are Early Adopters?

- 77 million Americans, 36 million U.S. heads of household
- About 40 percent of Gen Xers (ages 28–41) are early adopters
- 49 percent own an MP3 player
- 70 percent have broadband Internet at home
- Roughly 60 percent are "sick of advertising today"
- 1.5 times more likely than the general population to own a laptop

Source: Daniel B. Honigman, "Who's on First?" *Marketing News*, November 1, 2007, 15. Taken from Forrester Research's "The State of Consumers And Technology: Benchmark 2007" survey, September 2007. Used by permission of the American Marketing Association.

Product Characteristics and the Rate of Adoption

Five product characteristics can be used to predict and explain the rate of acceptance and diffusion of a new product:

- *Complexity*: the degree of difficulty involved in understanding and using a new product. The more complex the product, the slower is its diffusion. For instance, DVD recorders have been around for a few years, but they have been bought mostly by early adopters willing to go to the trouble of linking the gadgets to their PCs or to pay high prices for the first stand-alone machines that connect to a TV.
- *Compatibility*: the degree to which the new product is consistent with existing values and product knowledge, past experiences, and current needs. Incompatible products diffuse more slowly than compatible products. For example, the introduction of contraceptives is incompatible in countries where religious beliefs discourage the use of birth control techniques.
- *Relative advantage*: the degree to which a product is perceived as superior to existing substitutes. For example, because it reduces cooking time, the microwave oven has a clear relative advantage over a conventional oven.
- *Observability*: the degree to which the benefits or other results of using the product can be observed by others and communicated to target customers. For instance, fashion items and automobiles are highly visible and more observable than personal-care items.
- *"Trialability"*: the degree to which a product can be tried on a limited basis. It is much easier to try a new toothpaste or breakfast cereal than a new automobile or microcomputer. Demonstrations in showrooms and test-drives are different from in-home trial use. To stimulate trials, marketers use free-sampling programs, tasting displays, and small package sizes.

Exhibit 11.4 shows the time it took for various audio and video new products to reach sales of 1 million units. Note the rapid rate at which satellite radio has spread.

Marketing Implications of the Adoption Process

Two types of communication aid the diffusion process: *word-of-mouth communication* among consumers and communication from marketers to consumers. Word-of-mouth communication within and across groups speeds diffusion. Opinion leaders discuss new products with their followers and with other opinion leaders. Several studies reported in *eMarketer* revealed that word-of-mouth is the method most preferred by college students to learn about new goods and services. This includes advice from family and friends, social networks, blogs, and viral video. Television advertising ranked second followed by free samples.[34]

Marketers must therefore ensure that opinion leaders have the types of information desired in the media that they use. Suppliers of some products, such as professional and health-care services, rely almost solely on word-of-mouth communication for new business.

The Internet plays an important role in generating word-of-mouth communications. In fact, JWT Worldwide in New York estimates that over 85 percent of the country's top 1,000 marketing firms have some form of word-of-mouth communications strategy.[35] These efforts are often referred to as buzz marketing.

Often marketers recruit a core group of opinion leaders to get the buzz going. UPN recruited

EXHIBIT 11.4

Sales of New Audio Products

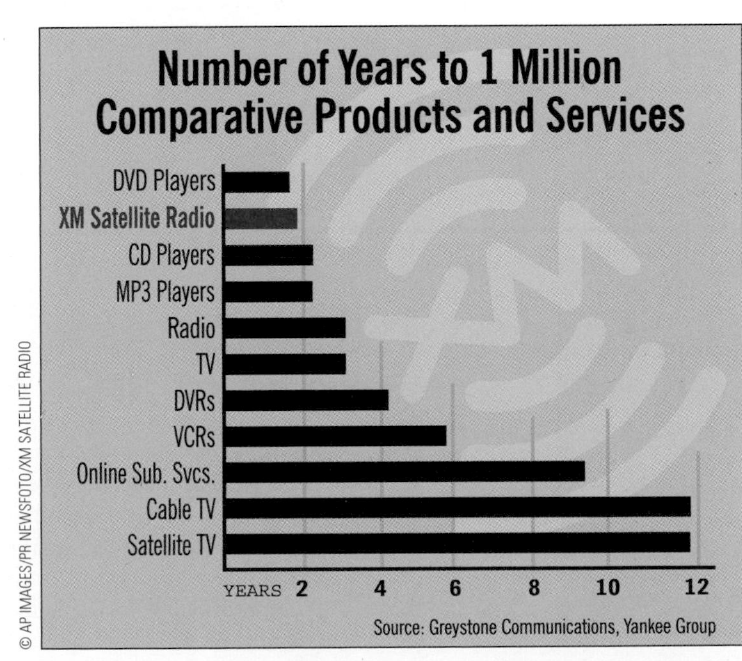

product life cycle (PLC)
A biological metaphor that traces the stages of a product's acceptance, from its introduction (birth) to its decline (death).

Alloy.com, a shopping and lifestyle site aimed at teenage girls, to develop a buzz campaign for the TV series *America's Top Model*. After analyzing the chatter on its site, Alloy identified 500 well-connected girls who had expressed interest in the show. Alloy provided the teens with *America's Top Model* party kits and encouraged them to invite an average of four friends over to their homes for gatherings themed around the TV show. According to Alloy, the results were very good.[36]

Business marketers have also developed strategies for obtaining online feedback and ideas from early adopters. Microsoft Corp. has a Most Valuable Professional (MVP) program which has 4,000 participants in 90 countries. MVPs give Microsoft user feedback for almost every new product, from Windows to Xbox. Sony's Web community of about 850 early adopters is called "Sony Frontline."[37]

The second type of communication aiding the diffusion process is communication directly from the marketer to potential adopters. Messages directed toward early adopters should normally use different appeals than messages directed toward the early majority, the late majority, or the laggards. Early adopters are more important than innovators because they make up a larger group, are more socially active, and are usually opinion leaders.

Researchers at DoubleClick found that 39 percent of early adopters reported spending five or more hours online each day, compared to 23 percent of other categories of adopters. Furthermore, 40 percent of early adopters reported using Web sites to learn about products, compared to 31 percent of other categories of adopters. Also, 19 percent of early adopters reported using online advertising as an information source, compared to 8 percent of the other respondents.[38]

As the focus of a promotional campaign shifts from early adopters to the early majority and the late majority, marketers should study the dominant characteristics, buying behavior, and media characteristics of these target markets. Then they should revise messages and media strategy to fit. The diffusion model helps guide marketers in developing and implementing promotion strategy.

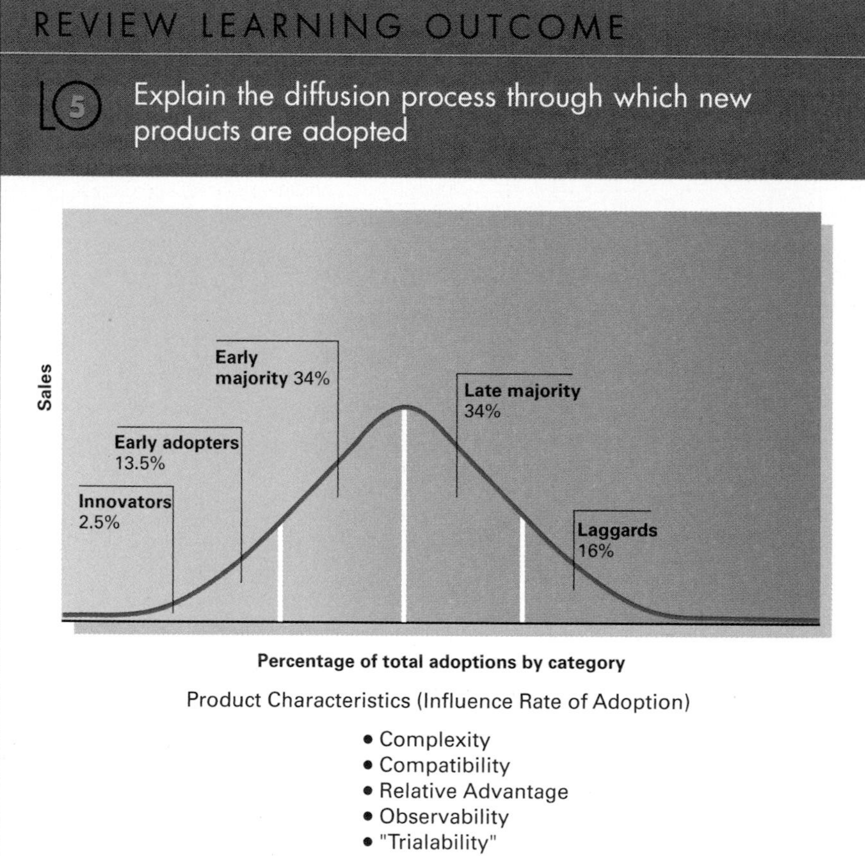

LO6

PRODUCT LIFE CYCLES

The **product life cycle (PLC)** is one of the most familiar concepts in marketing. Few other general concepts have been so widely discussed. Although some researchers and consultants have challenged the theoretical basis and managerial value of the PLC, many believe it is a useful marketing management diagnostic tool and a general guide for marketing planning in various "life-cycle" stages.

The product life cycle is a biological metaphor that traces the stages of a product's acceptance, from its introduction (birth) to its decline (death). As Exhibit 11.5 shows, a product progresses through four major stages: introduction, growth, maturity, and decline.

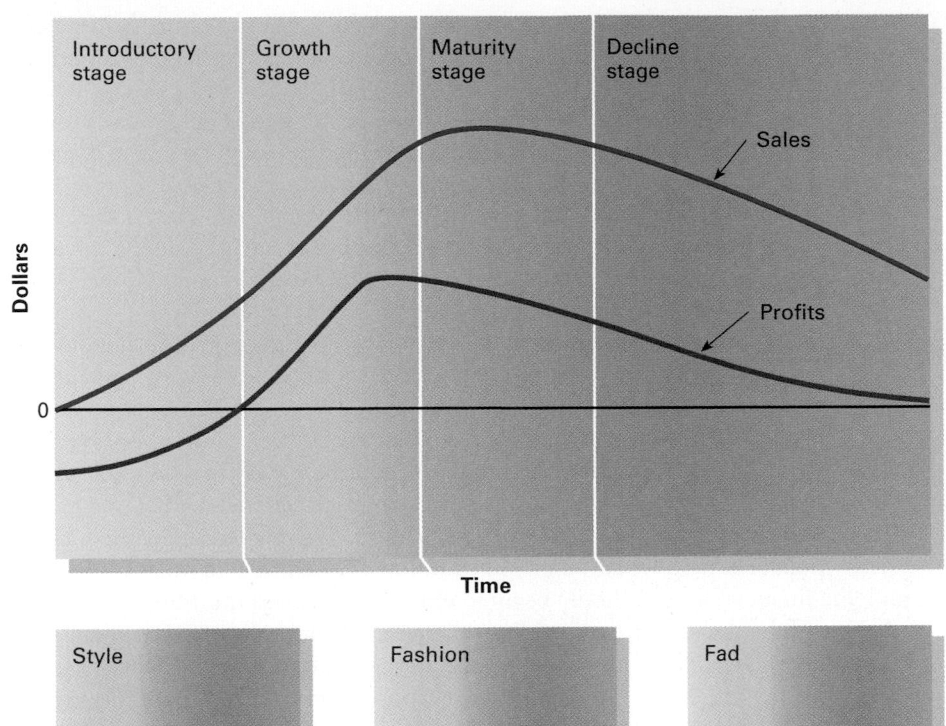

EXHIBIT 11.5

Four Stages of the Product Life Cycle

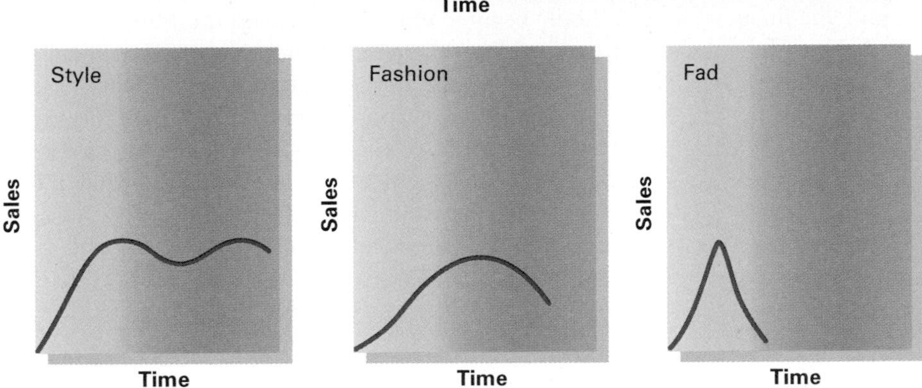

EXHIBIT 11.6

Product Life Cycles for Styles, Fashions, and Fads

The PLC concept can be used to analyze a brand, a product form, or a product category. The PLC for a product form is usually longer than the PLC for any one brand. The exception would be a brand that was the first and last competitor in a product form market. In that situation, the brand and product form life cycles would be equal in length. Product categories have the longest life cycles. A **product category** includes all brands that satisfy a particular type of need such as shaving products, passenger automobiles, or soft drinks.

The time a product spends in any one stage of the life cycle may vary dramatically. Some products, such as fad items, move through the entire cycle in weeks. Others, such as electric clothes washers and dryers, stay in the maturity stage for decades. Exhibit 11.5 illustrates the typical life cycle for a consumer durable good, such as a washer or dryer. In contrast, Exhibit 11.6 illustrates typical life cycles for styles (such as formal, business, or casual clothing), fashions (such as miniskirts or baggy jeans), and fads (such as leopard-print clothing). Changes in a product, its uses, its image, or its positioning can extend that product's life cycle.

As product life cycles continue to decrease, compressing development cycles and accelerating new-product developments are critical. The PLC concept does not tell managers the length of a product's life cycle or its duration in any stage. It does not dictate marketing strategy. It is simply a tool to help marketers forecast future events and suggest appropriate strategies. Look at Exhibit 11.7. What conclusions can you draw about the PLCs of Widgets A, B, and C over a 5-year period?

product category
All brands that satisfy a particular type of need.

introductory stage
The first stage of the product life cycle in which the full-scale launch of a new product into the marketplace occurs.

Introductory Stage

The **introductory stage** of the product life cycle represents the full-scale launch of a new product into the marketplace. Computer databases for personal use, room-deodorizing air-conditioning filters, and wind-powered home electric generators are all

EXHIBIT 11.7

U.S. Sales of "Widgets," in Billions of Dollars

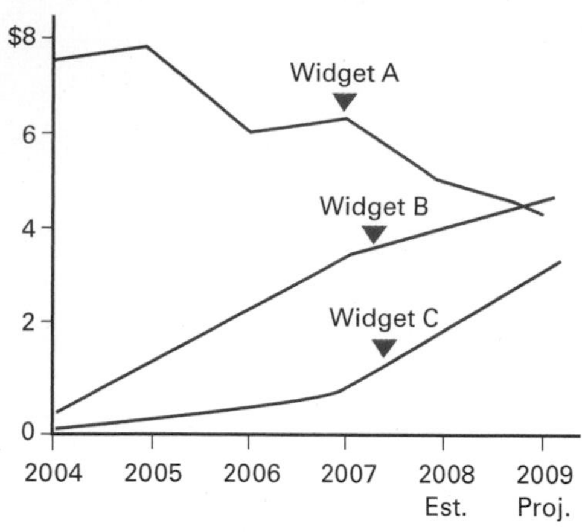

product categories that have recently entered the PLC. A high failure rate, little competition, frequent product modification, and limited distribution typify the introductory stage of the PLC.

Marketing costs in the introductory stage are normally high for several reasons. High dealer margins are often needed to obtain adequate distribution, and incentives are needed to get consumers to try the new product. Advertising expenses are high because of the need to educate consumers about the new product's benefits. Production costs are also often high in this stage, as product and manufacturing flaws are identified and corrected and efforts are undertaken to develop mass-production economies.

As Exhibit 11.5 illustrates, sales normally increase slowly during the introductory stage. Moreover, profits are usually negative because of R&D costs, factory tooling, and high introduction costs. The length of the introductory phase is largely determined by product characteristics, such as the product's advantages over substitute products, the educational effort required to make the product known, and management's commitment of resources to the new item. A short introductory period is usually preferred to help reduce the impact of negative earnings and cash flows. As soon as the product gets off the ground, the financial burden should begin to diminish. Also, a short introduction helps dispel some of the uncertainty as to whether the new product will be successful.

Promotion strategy in the introductory stage focuses on developing product awareness and informing consumers about the product category's potential benefits. At this stage, the communication challenge is to stimulate primary demand—demand for the product in general rather than for a specific brand. Intensive personal selling is often required to gain acceptance for the product among wholesalers and retailers. Promotion of convenience products often requires heavy consumer sampling and couponing. Shopping and specialty products demand educational advertising and personal selling to the final consumer.

growth stage
The second stage of the product life cycle when sales typically grow at an increasing rate, many competitors enter the market, large companies may start acquiring small pioneering firms, and profits are healthy.

maturity stage
The third stage of the product life cycle during which sales increase at a decreasing rate.

Growth Stage

If a product category survives the introductory stage, it advances to the **growth stage** of the life cycle. In this stage, sales typically grow at an increasing rate, many competitors enter the market, and large companies may start to acquire small pioneering firms. Profits rise rapidly in the growth stage, reach their peak, and begin declining as competition intensifies. Emphasis switches from primary demand promotion (for example, promoting personal digital assistants, or PDAs) to aggressive brand advertising and communication of the differences between brands (for example, promoting Casio versus Palm and Visor).

Distribution becomes a major key to success during the growth stage, as well as in later stages. Manufacturers scramble to sign up dealers and distributors and to build long-term relationships. Without adequate distribution, it is impossible to establish a strong market position.

Maturity Stage

A period during which sales increase at a decreasing rate signals the beginning of the **maturity stage** of the life cycle. New users cannot be added indefinitely, and sooner or later the market approaches saturation. Normally, this is the longest stage of the product life cycle. Many major household appliances are in the maturity stage of their life cycles.

For shopping products and many specialty products, annual models begin to appear during the maturity stage. Product lines are lengthened to appeal to additional market segments. Service and repair assume more important roles as manufacturers strive to distinguish their products from others. Product design changes tend to become stylistic (How can the product be made different?) rather than functional (How can the product be made better?).

As prices and profits continue to fall, marginal competitors start dropping out of the market. Dealer margins also shrink, resulting in less shelf space for mature items, lower dealer inventories, and a general reluctance to promote the product. Thus, promotion to dealers often intensifies during this stage in order to retain loyalty.

Heavy consumer promotion by the manufacturer is also required to maintain market share. Consider these well-known examples of competition in the maturity stage: the "cola war" featuring Coke and Pepsi, the "beer war" featuring Anheuser-Busch's Budweiser brands and Philip Morris's Miller brands, and the "burger wars" pitting leader McDonald's against challengers Burger King and Wendy's.

Another characteristic of the maturity stage is the emergence of "niche marketers" that target narrow, well-defined, underserved segments of a market. Starbucks Coffee targets its gourmet line at the only segment of the coffee market that is growing: new, young, affluent coffee drinkers.

Decline Stage

A long-run drop in sales signals the beginning of the **decline stage**. The rate of decline is governed by how rapidly consumer tastes change or substitute products are adopted. Many convenience products and fad items lose their market overnight, leaving large inventories of unsold items, such as designer jeans. Others die more slowly.

According to a report from the International Federation of the Phonographic Industry, CD sales in the United States fell by 14 percent in 2007. They have fallen 30 percent worldwide in the past three years.[39] It appears that the popularity of iTunes and other digital download options are rapidly making CDs obsolete.

Some firms have developed successful strategies for marketing products in the decline stage of the product life cycle. They eliminate all nonessential marketing expenses and let sales decline as more and more customers discontinue purchasing the products. Eventually, the product is withdrawn from the market.

Some firms practice what management sage Peter Drucker has called "organized abandonment," which is based upon a periodic audit of all goods and services that a firm markets. One key question is, if we weren't already marketing the product, would we be willing to introduce it now? If the answer is no, the product should be carefully considered as a candidate for elimination from the product mix.

Implications for Marketing Management

The product life cycle concept encourages marketing managers to plan so that they can take the initiative instead of reacting to past events. The PLC is especially useful as a predicting or forecasting tool. Because products pass through distinctive stages, it is often possible to estimate a product's location on the curve using historical data. Profits, like sales, tend to follow a predictable path over a product's life cycle.

Exhibit 11.8 shows the relationship between the adopter categories and stages of the PLC. Note that the various categories of adopters first buy products in different stages of the life cycle. Almost all sales in the maturity and decline stages represent repeat purchasing.

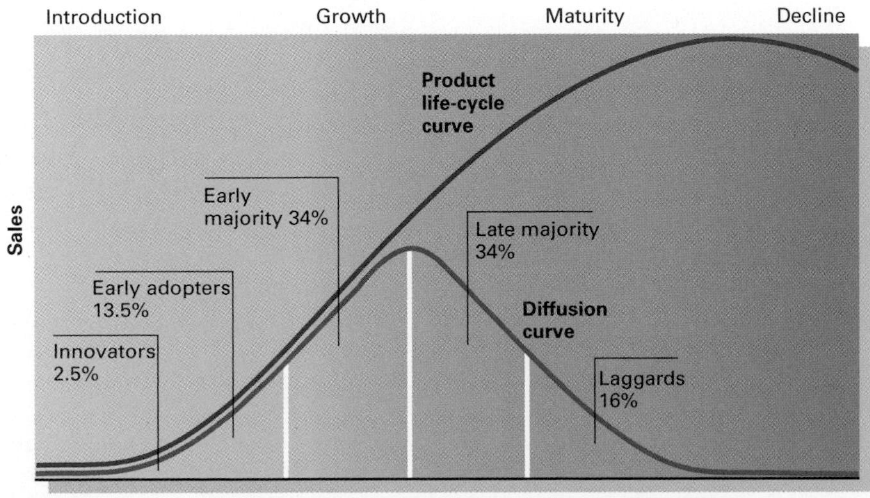

EXHIBIT 11.8

Relationship between the Diffusion Process and the Product Life Cycle

decline stage
The fourth stage of the product life cycle, characterized by a long-run drop in sales

REVIEW LEARNING OUTCOME

Explain the concept of product life cycles

Marketing Mix Strategy	Product Life Cycle Stage: Introductory	Growth	Maturity	Decline
Product Strategy	Limited number of models; frequent product modifications	Expanded number of models; frequent product modifications	Large number of models	Elimination of unprofitable models and brands
Distribution Strategy	Distribution usually limited, depending on product; intensive efforts and high margins often needed to attract wholesalers and retailers	Expanded number of dealers; intensive efforts to establish long-term relationships with wholesalers and retailers	Extensive number of dealers; margins declining; intensive efforts to retain distributors and shelf space	Unprofitable outlets phased out
Promotion Strategy	Develop product awareness; stimulate primary demand; use intensive personal selling to distributors; use sampling and couponing for consumers	Stimulate selective demand; advertise brand aggressively	Stimulate selective demand; advertise brand aggressively; promote heavily to retain dealers and customers	Phase out all promotion
Pricing Strategy	Prices are usually high to recover development costs (see Chapter 16)	Prices begin to fall toward end of growth stage as result of competitive pressure	Prices continue to fall	Prices stabilize at relatively low level; small price rises are possible if competition is negligible

Sales

Time

70 ◀ employees testing ideas at McDonald's Innovation Center

research and development employees at Procter & Gamble ▶ **9,000**

18 ◀ years spent developing Minute Rice

self-selected science problem solvers using the InnoCentive Inc. online brain trust ▶ **80,000**

$1 million ◀ cost of full-scale test marketing

amount Gillette spent to develop the Mach3 ▶ **$750 million**

percentage of the U.S. population claiming they are "not sure how to use the Internet" ▶ **8**

500 ◀ girls recruited by Alloy.com to generate buzz about the TV show *America's Top Model*

percentage drop in film camera sales in recent years ▶ **15**

850 ◀ early adopters in the Sony Frontline Web community

ANATOMY OF A Product Life Cycle

VCR

VCR sales dropped rapidly in the face of growing DVD competition.

1977
VHS first sold in the U.S.

1992
100 millionth VCR sold

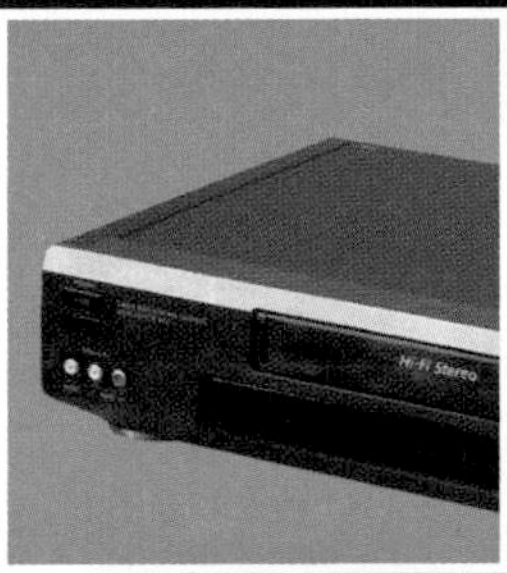

1997
First DVD titles released in the United States

2000
VCR sales peak at 23 million units

2001
DVD dollar sales surpass VHS sales

2006
More households own DVD players than VCRs

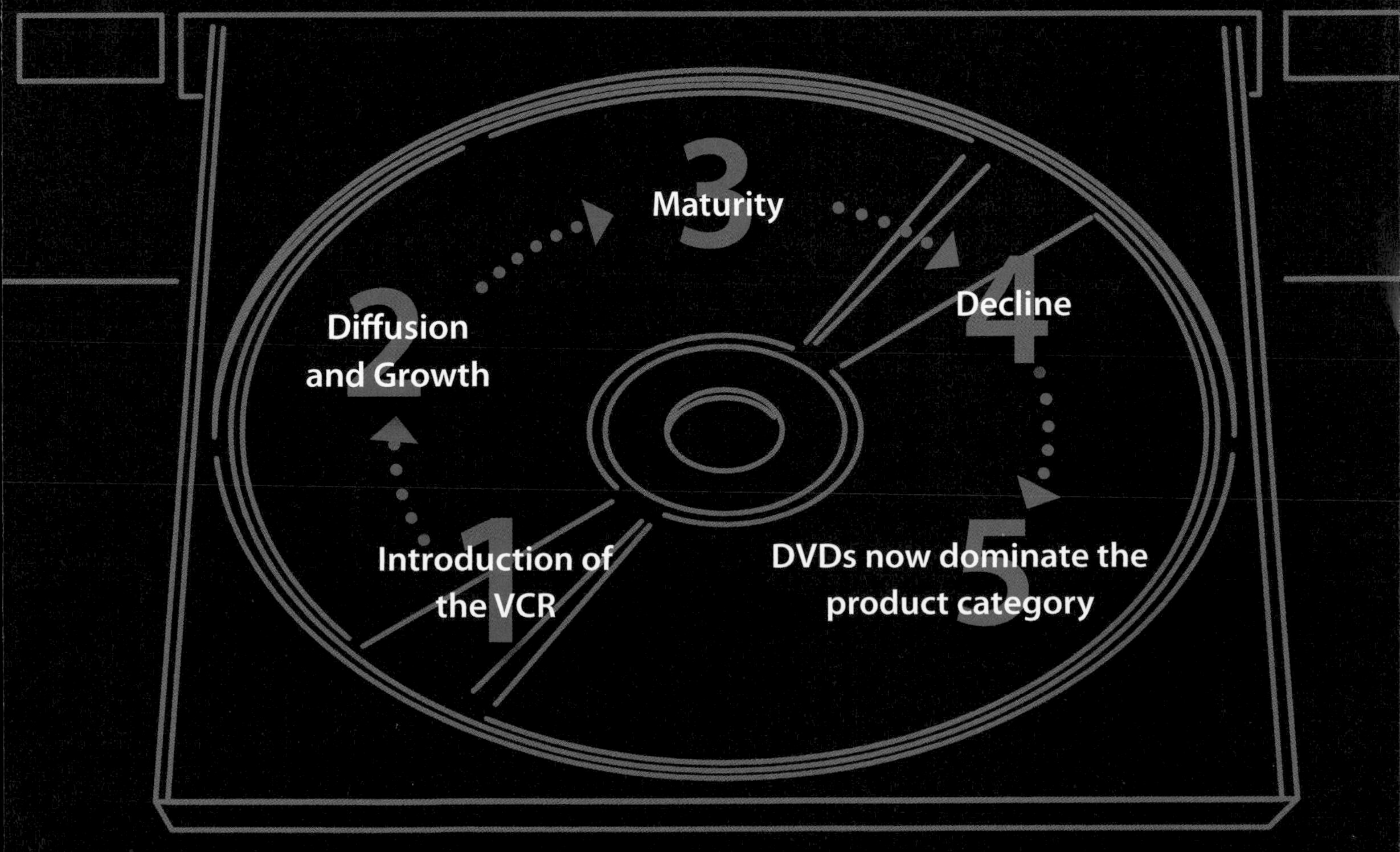

1 Introduction of the VCR

2 Diffusion and Growth

3 Maturity

4 Decline

5 DVDs now dominate the product category

REVIEW AND APPLICATIONS

Explain the importance of developing new products and describe the six categories of new products. New products are important to sustain growth and profits and to replace obsolete items. New products can be classified as new-to-the-world products (discontinuous innovations), new product lines, additions to existing product lines, improvements or revisions of existing products, repositioned products, or lower-priced products. To sustain or increase profits, a firm must innovate.

1.1 How many new products can you identify? Visit the supermarket and make a list of at least 15 items with the word "New" on the label. Include on your list anything that looks like a new product. Next to each item on your list, write the category of new product that best describes the item. Share your results with the class.

TEAM

1.2 New entertainment products aren't necessarily media products. Form a team of three or four students and brainstorm new nonmedia entertainment products. Try to identify one item for each of the categories of new products discussed in the chapter.

Explain the steps in the new-product development process. First, a firm forms a new-product strategy by outlining the characteristics and roles of future products. Then new-product ideas are generated by customers, employees, distributors, competitors, vendors, and internal R&D personnel. Once a product idea has survived initial screening by an appointed screening group, it undergoes business analysis to determine its potential profitability. If a product concept seems viable, it progresses into the development phase, in which the technical and economic feasibility of the manufacturing process is evaluated. The development phase also includes laboratory and use testing of a product for performance and safety. Following initial testing and refinement, most products are introduced in a test market to evaluate consumer response and marketing strategies. Finally, test market successes are propelled into full commercialization. The commercialization process involves starting up production, building inventories, shipping to distributors, training a sales force, announcing the product to the trade, and advertising to consumers.

2.1 List the advantages of simultaneous product development.

2.2 You are a marketing manager for Nike. Your department has come up with the idea of manufacturing a baseball bat for use in colleges around the nation. Assuming you are in the business analysis stage, write a brief analysis based on the questions in the "Business Analysis" section of the chapter.

2.3 What are the major disadvantages to test marketing, and how might they be avoided?

2.4 How could information from customer orders at **www.pizzahut.com** help the company's marketers plan new-product developments?

Explain why some products succeed and others fail. The most important factor in determining the success of a new product is the extent to which the product matches the needs of the market. Good matches are frequently successful. Poor matches are not.

3.1 In small groups, brainstorm ideas for a new wet-weather clothing line. What type of product would potential customers want and need? Prepare and deliver a brief presentation to your class.

Discuss global issues in new-product development. A marketer with global vision seeks to develop products that can easily be adapted to suit local needs. The goal is not simply to develop a standard product that can be sold worldwide. Smart global marketers also look for good product ideas worldwide.

4.1 Visit **www.pg.com** and look at the brands it offers around the world. What conclusions can you draw about Procter & Gamble's global new-product development strategy?

Explain the diffusion process through which new products are adopted. The diffusion process is the spread of a new product from its producer to ultimate adopters. Adopters in the diffusion process belong to five categories: innovators, early adopters, the early majority, the late majority, and laggards. Product characteristics that affect the rate of adoption include product complexity, compatibility with existing social values, relative advantage over existing substitutes, observability, and "trialability." The diffusion process is facilitated by word-of-mouth communication and communication from marketers to consumers.

5.1 Describe some products whose adoption rates have been affected by complexity, compatibility, relative advantage, observability, and/or "trialability."

5.2 What type of adopter behavior do you typically follow? Explain.

5.3 Review Exhibit 11.4. Analyze each product on the graph according to the characteristics that influence the rate of adoption. For example, what can you conclude from the data about the relative advantage of DVD audio? Write one to two pages explaining your analysis.

Explain the concept of product life cycles. All brands and product categories undergo a life cycle with four stages: introduction, growth, maturity, and decline. The rate at which products move through these stages varies dramatically. Marketing managers use the product life cycle concept as an analytical tool to forecast a product's future and devise effective marketing strategies.

What is Cheerios doing to compete successfully in the maturity stage? Go to its Web site (**www.cheerios.com**) to find out.

KEY TERMS

Term	Page
adopter	373
brainstorming	366
business analysis	367
commercialization	370
concept test	366
decline stage	379
development	367
diffusion	373
growth stage	378
innovation	373
introductory stage	377
maturity stage	378
new product	361
new-product strategy	364
product category	377
product development	366
product life cycle (PLC)	376
screening	366
simulated (laboratory) market testing	369
simultaneous product development	368
test marketing	368

EXERCISES

APPLICATION EXERCISE

A simple statistical analysis will help you better understand the types of new products. As in the Application Exercise in Chapter 6, you will be using print advertisements, but you will also be adding information from other sources (TV ads, trips to the store, and the like).[40]

Activities

1. Compile a list of 100 new products. If you are building a portfolio of ads (see the Application Exercise in Chapter 6), you can generate part of this list as you collect print advertisements for the topics in this chapter. Consider tabulating television ads for new products that are aired during programs you normally watch. A trip to the grocery could probably yield your entire list, but then your list would be limited to consumer products.
2. Make a table with six columns labeled as follows: new-to-the-world products, new product line, addition to existing product line, improvement/revision of existing product line, repositioned product, and lower-priced product.
3. Place each of your 100 new products into one of the six categories. Tabulate your results at the bottom of each column. What conclusions can you draw from the distribution of your products? Consider adding your results together with the rest of the class to get a larger and more random sample.

ETHICS EXERCISE

One source of new-product ideas is competitors. Steven Fischer recently joined Frankie and Alex Specialty Products as a brand manager. His new boss told him, "We don't have a budget for new-product development. We just monitor our competitors' new-product introductions and offer knockoffs of any that look like they will be successful."

Questions

1. Is this practice ethical?
2. Does the AMA Statement of Ethics address this issue? Go to **www.marketingpower.com** and review the statement. Then, write a brief paragraph on what the AMA Statement of Ethics contains that relates to knockoff products.

MARKETING PLAN EXERCISE

Complete the following exercises to continue building your strategic marketing plan for Part 3—Product Decisions. (See Marketing Planning Worksheet, Part 3, on your companion Web site at **www.cengage.com/international.**) You should also refer to Appendix I of Chapter 2 for additional marketing plan checklist items (Marketing Mix—Product).

1. Place your company's product in the appropriate stage of the product life cycle. What are the implications of being in this stage? Would the PLC be lengthened, shortened, or not affected by selling your product or service online? Would selling your offering on the Internet make it seem earlier on the PLC to your customers? Why?
2. What categories of adopters are likely to buy your company's products? Is the product diffusing slowly or quickly throughout the marketplace? Why? What elements of the diffusion process can you control to make sure your offering diffuses more quickly throughout the adopter categories and marketplace in general? Will positive word-of-mouth be easier or harder to generate online?

CASE STUDY: WELCOME TO THE KANDY KASTLE, BUT BEWARE—THINGS ARE NOT WHAT THEY SEEM

Meet Larry Jones, a former toy designer for the likes of Hasbro, Mattel and Playmates Toys. Displaced when the industry turned to electronic toys, the irrepressible Jones is hard at play designing captivating candy concepts for niche manufacturer Kandy Kastle. He is not a confectioner, nor does he aspire to be one. Instead, Jones tinkers with candy delivery mechanisms and silly, sometimes grotesque names sure to capture the eyes, imaginations, and tummies of youngsters.

His products belong to the $250 million, nonchocolate segment of the U.S. novelty candy market. It's the third largest segment of the sweets market, behind chocolate and chewy treats such as gummy candies, licorice, and taffy. The market has been flat in recent years, but several former toy designers and a slew of hobbyist designers are beginning to breathe new life into the industry.

Their creations range from the simply fun to the outright goofy, and candy makers pay handsomely in hopes of landing the next big hit. Two of Jones's latest hits include the Big Barf and the Big Burp. Repulsive though they sound, both are just mouth-shaped, sound-generating dispensers for harmless gumballs. Though items like the Big Barf reek of a style unique to Larry Jones, he is just one of a new breed of novelty candy container designers who are hoping to create the next confection legend that might someday be mentioned in the same breath as the almighty Pez.

As action figures, toy trains, and other traditional toys are increasingly overshadowed by their digital counterparts, inventors and their employers are betting that products that combine toys with candy curiosities are positioned to capture the dollars left behind by that fading market. Deirdre Gonzalez, vice president of marketing for Cap Candy, says the reinvigorated novelty candy market is "a hybrid business between the two industries." Often priced from $.99 to $1.29, candy items sold with toy novelties are now attracting dollars that used to be reserved for low-end toy purchases.

And the competition is as fierce as children's tastes are fickle. In addition to Kandy Kastle, companies like Cap Candy and Candy Planet race each other to develop new products, while the likes of Willy Wonka and Jelly Belly battle to promote their lines with tie-ins to blockbuster children's movies. Even independent entrepreneurs are getting in on the act. Two married couples quit their postal service jobs to form BAAT Enterprises (from their names: Bill, Ann, Ann, and Tom) and introduced the Spin Pop, a rotating motorized sucker. A modern take on the Ring Pop, the Spin Pop sold almost 6 million units in under two years.

What's cool with kids is fleeting, though. New products must be developed every month to keep up. Larry Jones, for example, did not rest on the laurels of his gastrointestinal gumball designs. He is also the wiz behind Ear Wax, Big Toe Goo, Tar Pits, Hose Nose, Brain Drain, and glow-in-the-dark Lightning Bugs. "What I'm after is to have the kid have a little bit of magic or a little giggle while eating his candy," Jones says. Kandy Kastle is relying on him to come up with a host of interesting fare based on the hugely popular Hello Kitty brand, too. Originality is key. The children in this market space, aged 4 to 12 years, are increasingly savvy consumers and they are gaining in influence and even buying power.

Influence with parents is crucial, of course, but sway with other kids in the peer group is more critical. Rose Downey, marketing manager at Au'Some Candy Company, puts extra emphasis on word-of-mouth endorsements for her company's novelty products. "We feel that the right way to grasp the kids' attention is word-of-mouth advertising," she says. "Kids trust other kids' judgment," she continues. "If Child A buys the product and it tastes great and looks cool and is fun, Child B is going to want the product and so on. Trust the kids. They know best when it comes to candy.[41]

Questions

1. To what category of new products does the Spin Pop belong?
2. Based on what you read in the case, what do you think Kandy Kastle's new-product development strategy is? Why do you think the development of the Hello Kitty product line is important?
3. Visit http://**www.KandyKastle.com** and review the product descriptions. Discuss the characteristics that influence their rate of adoption, and predict and explain their rates of acceptance and diffusion.
4. In what part of the product life cycle are the candy and toy categories? What kind of future do you predict for the novelty candy category?

© NKP MEDIA, INC./CENGAGE

COMPANY CLIPS

KODAK—REINVENTING PHOTOGRAPHY

Designing usable and intriguing products is an integral part of Kodak's marketing process. Paul Porter, director of corporate design and usability, focuses on creating interesting, functional, and intuitive equipment. To make sure the company is on the right track with product development, Kodak marketers interview customers and visit them in their own homes, observing how families use digital photography. The understanding gained from these interactions helps the company create a wide range of products targeted at different market segments.

Questions

1. EasyShare–One didn't sell very well, but Paul Porter claimed this wasn't the purpose of that particular product. What was the purpose of the product?
2. What kind of new product was EasyShare 1?
3. Discuss the product development process at Kodak.
4. Place Kodak's digital cameras in the product life cycle.

Marketing & You Results

If your score is high, you are most likely a "market maven." You are aware of new products earlier and talk about a variety of products to your friends. High scores also indicate a greater interest in and attentiveness to the market. Conversely, the lower your score, the less interested you are in the market and new products.

© JON FEINGERSH/RISER/GETTY IMAGES

CHAPTER 12

Marketing Channels and Supply Chain Management

LEARNING OUTCOMES

LO1 Explain what a marketing channel is and why intermediaries are needed

LO2 Define the types of channel intermediaries and describe their functions and activities

LO3 Describe the channel structures for consumer and business products and discuss alternative channel arrangements

LO4 Define the terms *supply chain* and *supply chain management*, and discuss the benefits of supply chain management

LO5 Discuss the issues that influence channel strategy

LO6 Describe the different channel relationship types and their unique costs and benefits

LO7 Describe the logistical components of the supply chain

LO8 Discuss new technology and emerging trends in supply chain management

LO9 Explain channel leadership, conflict, and partnering

LO10 Discuss channels and distribution decisions in global markets

LO11 Identify the special problems and opportunities associated with distribution in service organizations

LO 1

MARKETING CHANNELS

The term *channel* is derived from the Latin word *canalis*, which means canal. A marketing channel can be viewed as a large canal or pipeline through which products, their ownership, communication, financing and payment, and accompanying risk flow to the consumer. Formally, a **marketing channel** (also called a **channel of distribution**) is a business structure of interdependent organizations that are involved in the process of making a product or service available for use or consumption by end customers or business users. Marketing channels facilitate the physical movement of goods from location to location, thus representing "place" or "distribution" in the marketing mix (product, price, promotion, and place) and encompassing the processes involved in getting the right product to the right place at the right time.

Many different types of organizations participate in marketing channels. **Channel members** (wholesalers, distributors, and retailers, also sometimes referred to as *intermediaries, resellers,* and *middlemen*) negotiate with one another, buy and sell products, and facilitate the change of ownership between buyer and seller in the course of moving the product from the manufacturer into the hands of the final consumer. As products move through channels, channel members facilitate the distribution process by providing specialization and division of labor, overcoming discrepancies, and providing contact efficiency.

marketing channel (channel of distribution)
A set of interdependent organizations that ease the transfer of ownership as products move from producer to business user or consumer.

channel members
All parties in the marketing channel that negotiate with one another, buy and sell products, and facilitate the change of ownership between buyer and seller in the course of moving the product from the manufacturer into the hands of the final consumer.

Providing Specialization and Division of Labor

According to the concept of *specialization and division of labor,* breaking down a complex task into smaller, simpler ones and allocating them to specialists will create greater efficiency and lower average production costs. Manufacturers achieve economies of scale through the use of efficient equipment capable of producing large quantities of a single product.

Marketing channels can also attain economies of scale through specialization and division of labor by aiding producers who lack the motivation, financing, or expertise to market directly to end users or consumers. In some cases, as with most consumer convenience goods, such as soft drinks, the cost of marketing directly to millions of consumers—taking and shipping individual orders—is prohibitive. For this reason,

Using the following scale, indicate your opinions on the lines before the items.

1 2 3 4 5
Strongly disagree ... Strongly agree

__ I would prefer to be a leader.
__ I see myself as a good leader.
__ I will be a success.
__ People always seem to recognize my authority.
__ I have a natural talent for influencing people.
__ I am assertive.
__ I like to have authority over other people.
__ I am a born leader.

Now, total your score. Read the chapter and find out what your score means at the end.

Source: Scale #119, *Marketing Scales Handbook*, G. Bruner, K. James, H. Hensel, eds., Vol. III. © by American Marketing Association. Used with permission of the American Marketing Association.

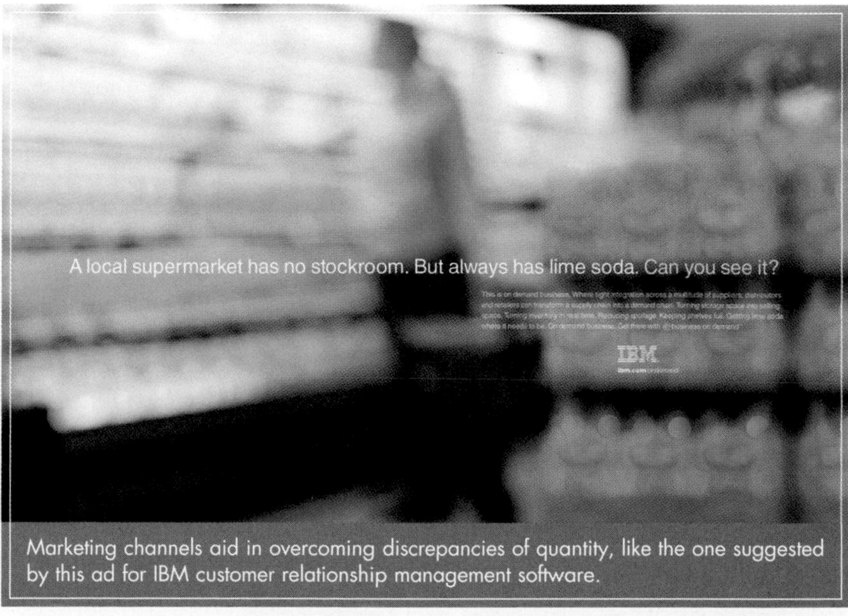

COURTESY OF IBM CORPORATION

Marketing channels aid in overcoming discrepancies of quantity, like the one suggested by this ad for IBM customer relationship management software.

CUSTOMER Experience

Capturing a Bigger Slice of the Pie

The pizza delivery business is very competitive, with both local businesses and national chains competing for a $28.5 billion U.S. consumer market annually. Many of the delivery pizzas ordered in the United States each year are purchased by young adults and teenagers. Papa John's, a 2,700-unit national pizza restaurant chain, believed it could capture more market share if it could find a way to make ordering and delivery easier and more appealing to the technologically savvy members of the younger segment. And if it could do so, it could compete more effectively with larger national companies such as Pizza Hut and Domino's.

In early 2008, Papa John's introduced a new marketing and ordering channel designed to attract younger consumers, rolling out a new service so customers could order pizza from a cell phone or PDA via text message. Once a customer first established an online account, they could at any time simply tap in their preference for one of several favorite pizzas using an abbreviated code. The meal order would be delivered to any of several preprogrammed delivery addresses, and paid for with credit or debit card information already on file in a database, and delivered within a half hour from the closest retail location.

Key additional benefits of customers' willingness to opt into this unique channel arrangement are better overall marketing and customer awareness. By keeping a database of customer purchase behavior, customized promotions flow through the channel to pizza lovers, with great deals offered on favorite crusts, meats, and other toppings according to customer's past preferences. The electronic channel can also be engaged in other ways, such as sending customers digital coupons, providing updates on new menu items, and engaging customers with reminder advertising.

The results of employing this exciting new marketing and delivery channel have been impressive, with Papa John's share rising to 6.9 percent of the marketplace despite having far fewer locations than their major competitors. The company has also recently introduced Web site ordering to great success, with 65 million unique visitors in the first year of operations. The company is optimistic that these new channels will allow it to continue to compete strongly with the "big boys" in the world of pizza delivery.[1]

producers hire channel members, such as wholesalers and retailers, to do what the producers are not equipped to do or what channel members are better prepared to do. Channel members can do some things more efficiently than producers because they have built good relationships with their customers. Therefore, their specialized expertise enhances the overall performance of the channel.

Overcoming Discrepancies

Marketing channels also aid in overcoming discrepancies of quantity, assortment, time, and space created by economies of scale in production. For example, assume that Pillsbury can efficiently produce its Hungry Jack instant pancake mix only at a rate of 5,000 units in a typical day. Not even the most ardent pancake fan could consume that amount in a year, much less in a day. The quantity produced to achieve low unit costs has created a **discrepancy of quantity**, which is the difference between the amount of product produced and the amount an end user wants to buy. By storing the product and distributing it in the appropriate amounts, marketing channels overcome quantity discrepancies by making products available in the quantities consumers desire.

© FOODPIX/JUPITER IMAGES

Mass production creates not only discrepancies of quantity but also discrepancies of assortment. A **discrepancy of assortment** occurs when a consumer does not have all of the items needed to receive full satisfaction from a product. For pancakes to provide maximum satisfaction, several other products are required to complete the assortment. At the very least, most people want a knife, fork, plate, butter, and syrup. Others might add orange juice, coffee, cream, sugar, eggs, and bacon or sausage. Even though Pillsbury is a large consumer-products company, it does not come close to providing the optimal assortment to go with its Hungry Jack pancakes. To overcome discrepancies of assortment, marketing channels assemble in one place many of the products necessary to complete a consumer's needed assortment.

A **temporal discrepancy** is created when a product is produced, but a consumer is not ready to buy it. Marketing channels overcome temporal discrepancies by maintaining inventories in anticipation of demand. For example, manufacturers of seasonal merchandise, such as Christmas or Halloween decorations, are in operation all year even though consumer demand is concentrated during certain months of the year.

Furthermore, because mass production requires many potential buyers, markets are usually scattered over large geographic regions, creating a **spatial discrepancy**. Often global, or at least nationwide, markets are needed to absorb the outputs of mass producers. Marketing channels overcome spatial discrepancies by making products available in locations convenient to consumers. For example, if all the Hungry Jack pancake mix is produced in Boise, Idaho, then Pillsbury must use an intermediary to distribute the product to other regions of the United States. Consumers elsewhere would be unwilling to drive to Boise to purchase pancake mix.

Providing Contact Efficiency

The third need fulfilled by marketing channels is they provide contact efficiency. Marketing channels provide contact efficiencies by reducing the number of stores customers must shop in to complete their purchases. Think about how much time you would spend shopping if supermarkets, department stores, and shopping malls did not exist. For example, suppose you had to buy your milk at a dairy and your meat at a stockyard. Imagine buying your eggs and chicken at a hatchery and your fruits and vegetables at various farms. You would spend a great deal of time, money, and energy just shopping for a few groceries. Channels simplify distribution by cutting the number of transactions required to get products from manufacturers to consumers and making an assortment of goods available in one location. In addition, many consumers in recent years have begun shopping using a multichannel approach whereby they view products online, in catalogues, and in the brick-and-mortar retail outlet. Savvy retailers are capitalizing on these additional customer contacts by segmenting customers according to buying versus simply shopping channels and providing consistent messages to customers regardless of channel choice.

Consider the example illustrated in Exhibit 12.1. Four consumers each want to buy a television set. Without a retail intermediary like Best Buy, television manufacturers JVC, Zenith, RCA, Sony, and Toshiba would each have to make four contacts to reach the four buyers who are in the target market, for a total of 20 transactions. However, when Best Buy acts as an intermediary between the producer and consumers, each producer has to make only one contact, reducing the number of transactions to 9. Each producer sells to one retailer rather than to four consumers. In turn, consumers buy from one retailer instead of from five producers.

Contact efficiency is being enhanced even more by information technology. Better information on product availability and pricing increasingly is reducing the need for consumers to actually shop for bargains or view ads in a traditional manner. By making information on products and services easily accessible over the Internet, Google, Yahoo! and similar information assemblers are becoming the starting points for finding and buying products and services. As they cull and organize huge digital warehouses of news, images, traffic and weather reports, and information on automobiles, real estate, and other consumer products, inefficiencies will be reduced, as will prices. These developments are revolutionizing marketing channels and benefiting consumers because

discrepancy of quantity
The difference between the amount of product produced and the amount an end user wants to buy.

discrepancy of assortment
The lack of all the items a customer needs to receive full satisfaction from a product or products.

temporal discrepancy
A situation that occurs when a product is produced but a customer is not ready to buy it.

spatial discrepancy
The difference between the location of a producer and the location of widely scattered markets.

EXHIBIT 12.1

How Marketing Channels Reduce the Number of Required Transactions

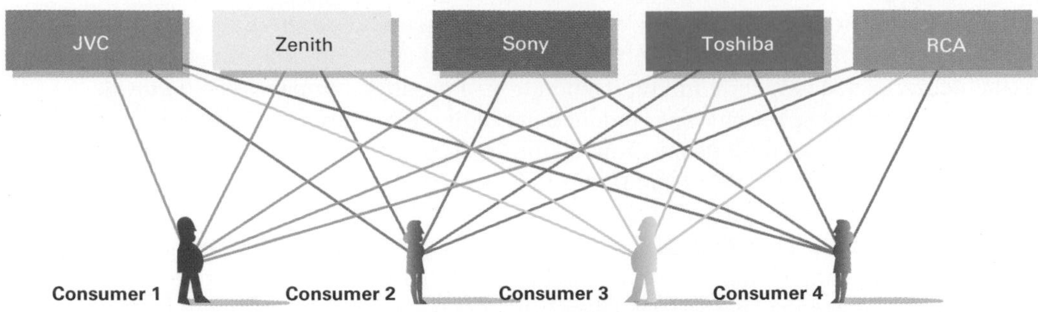

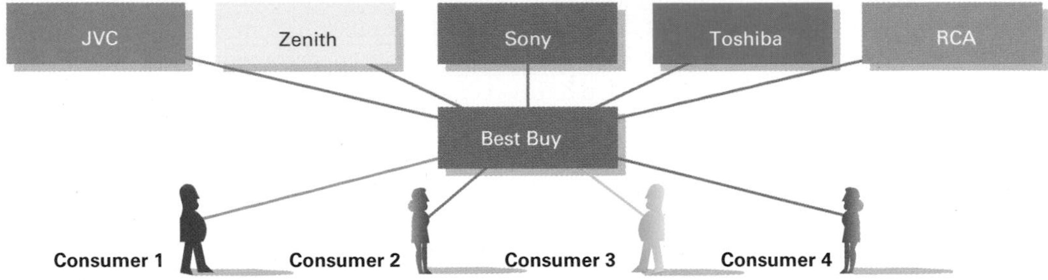

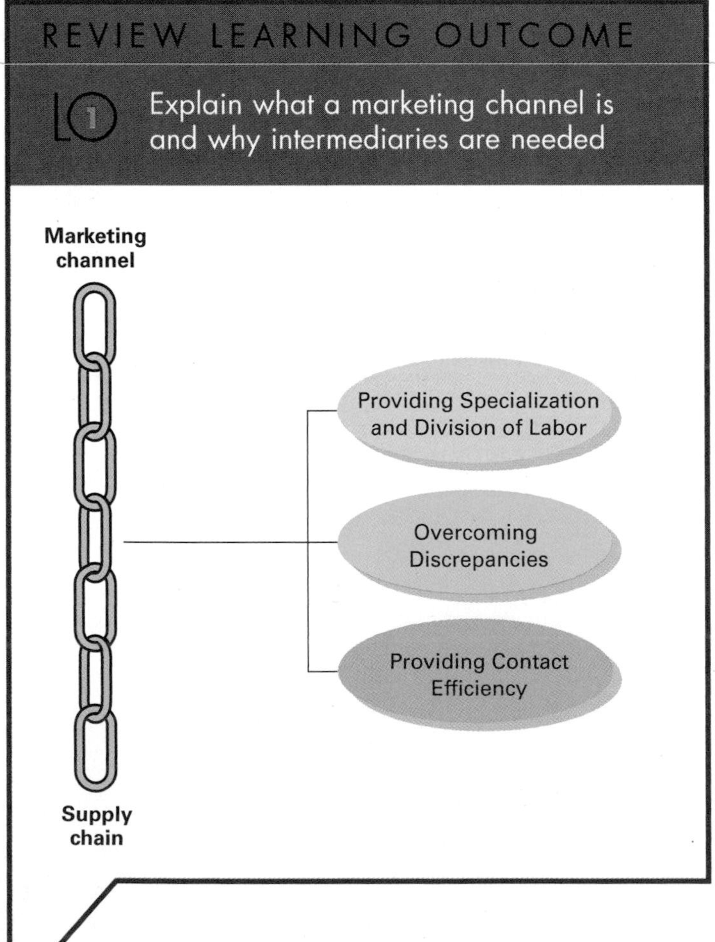

shoppers can find out where the best bargains are without having to search for them.

LO 2

CHANNEL INTERMEDIARIES AND THEIR FUNCTIONS

Intermediaries in a channel negotiate with one another, facilitate the change of ownership between buyers and sellers, and physically move products from the manufacturer to the final consumer. The most prominent difference separating intermediaries is whether they take title to the product. *Taking title* means they own the merchandise and control the terms of the sale—for example, price and delivery date. Retailers and merchant wholesalers are examples of intermediaries that take title to products in the marketing channel and resell them. **Retailers** are firms that sell mainly to consumers. Retailers will be discussed in more detail in Chapter 13.

Merchant wholesalers are organizations that facilitate the movement of products and services from the manufacturer to producers, resellers, governments, institutions, and retailers. All merchant wholesalers take title to the goods they sell, and most of them operate one or more warehouses where they receive goods, store them, and later reship them. Customers are mostly small or medium-sized retailers, but merchant wholesalers also market to manufacturers and institutional clients.

Other intermediaries do not take title to goods and services they market but do facilitate the exchange of ownership between sellers and buyers. **Agents and brokers** simply facilitate the sale of a product from producer to end user by representing retailers, wholesalers, or manufacturers. Title reflects ownership, and ownership usually implies control.

Unlike wholesalers, agents or brokers only facilitate sales and generally have little input into the terms of the sale. They do, however, get a fee or commission based on sales volume. For example, when selling a home, the owner usually hires a real estate agent who then brings potential buyers to see the house. The agent facilitates the sale by bringing the buyer and owner together, but never actually takes ownership of the home.

> "*Taking title means they own the merchandise and control the terms of the sale.*"

Variations in channel structures are due in large part to variations in the numbers and types of wholesaling intermediaries. Generally, product characteristics, buyer considerations, and market conditions determine the type of intermediary the manufacturer should use.

- *Product characteristics* that may require a certain type of wholesaling intermediary include whether the product is standardized or customized, the complexity of the product, and the gross margin of the product. For example, a customized product such as insurance is sold through an insurance agent or broker who may represent one or multiple companies. In contrast, a standardized product such as gum is sold through a merchant wholesaler that takes possession of the gum and reships it to the appropriate retailers.
- *Buyer considerations* affecting the wholesaler choice include how often the product is purchased and how long the buyer is willing to wait to receive the product. For example, at the beginning of the school term, a student may be willing to wait a few days for a textbook to get a lower price by ordering online. Thus, this type of product can be distributed directly. But, if the student waits to buy the book until the night before an exam and needs the book immediately, it will have to be purchased at the school bookstore.
- *Market characteristics* determining the wholesaler type include how many buyers are in the market and whether they are concentrated in a general location or are widely dispersed. Gum and textbooks, for example, are produced in one location and consumed in many other locations. Therefore, a merchant wholesaler is needed to distribute the products. In contrast, in a home sale, the buyer and seller are localized in one area, which facilitates the use of an agent/broker relationship.

retailer
A channel intermediary that sells mainly to consumers.

merchant wholesaler
An institution that buys goods from manufacturers and resells them to businesses, government agencies, and other wholesalers or retailers and that receives and takes title to goods, stores them in its own warehouses, and later ships them.

agents and brokers
Wholesaling intermediaries who do not take title to a product but facilitate its sale from producer to end user by representing retailers, wholesalers, or manufacturers.

Channel Functions Performed by Intermediaries

Retailing and wholesaling intermediaries in marketing channels perform several essential functions that make the flow of goods between producer and buyer possible. The three basic functions that intermediaries perform are summarized in Exhibit 12.2.

EXHIBIT 12.2

Marketing Channel Functions Performed by Intermediaries

Type of Function	Description
Transactional functions	**Contacting and promoting:** Contacting potential customers, promoting products, and soliciting orders
	Negotiating: Determining how many goods or services to buy and sell, type of transportation to use, when to deliver, and method and timing of payment
	Risk taking: Assuming the risk of owning inventory
Logistical Functions	**Physically distributing:** Transporting and sorting goods to overcome temporal and spatial discrepancies
	Storing: Maintaining inventories and protecting goods
	Sorting: Overcoming discrepancies of quantity and assortment by
	Sorting out: Breaking down a heterogeneous supply into separate homogeneous stocks
	Accumulating: Combining similar stocks into a larger homogeneous supply
	Allocating: Breaking a homogeneous supply into smaller and smaller lots ("breaking bulk")
	Assorting: Combining products into collections or assortments that buyers want available at one place
Facilitating Functions	**Researching:** Gathering information about other channel members and consumers
	Financing: Extending credit and other financial services to facilitate the flow of goods through the channel to the final consumer

logistics
The efficient and cost-effective forward and reverse flow as well as storage of goods, services, and related information, into, through, and out of channel member companies. Logistics functions typically include transportation and storage of assets, as well as their sorting, accumulation, consolidation, and/or allocation for the purpose of meeting customer requirements.

Transactional functions involve contacting and communicating with prospective buyers to make them aware of existing products and explain their features, advantages, and benefits. Intermediaries in the channel also provide *logistical* functions. **Logistics** is the efficient and cost-effective forward and reverse flow and storage of goods, services, and related information, into, through, and out of channel member companies. Logistics functions typically include transportation and storage of assets, as well as their sorting, accumulation, consolidation, and/or allocation for the purpose of conforming to customer requirements. For example, grading agricultural products typifies the sorting-out process, while consolidation of many lots of grade A eggs from different sources into one lot illustrates the accumulation process. Supermarkets or other retailers perform the sorting function by assembling thousands of different items that match their customers' desires. Similarly, while large companies typically have direct channels, many small companies depend on wholesalers to promote and distribute their products. For example, small beverage manufacturers like Jones Soda, Honest Tea, and Energy Brands depend on wholesalers to distribute their products in a marketplace dominated by large competitors like Coca-Cola and Pepsi. The management of logistics is a key component of supply chain management, which is discussed in greater detail in Learning Outcomes 4, 7, and 8.

The third basic channel function, *facilitating,* includes research and financing. Research provides information about channel members and consumers by getting answers to key questions: Who are the buyers? Where are they located? Why do they buy? Financing ensures that channel members have the money to keep products moving through the channel to the ultimate consumer.

A single company may provide one, two, or all three functions. Consider Kramer Beverage Company, a Coors beer distributor. As a beer distributor, Kramer provides transactional, logistical, and facilitating channel functions. Sales representatives contact local bars and restaurants to negotiate the terms of the sale, possibly giving the customer a discount for large purchases, and arrange for delivery of the beer. At the same time, Kramer also provides a facilitating function by extending credit to the customer. Kramer merchandising representatives, meanwhile, assist in promoting the beer on a local level by hanging Coors beer signs and posters. Kramer also provides logistical functions by accumulating the many types of Coors beer from the Coors manufacturing plant in Golden, Colorado, and storing them in its refrigerated warehouse. When an order needs to be filled, Kramer then sorts the beer into heterogeneous collections for each particular customer. For example, the local Chili's Grill & Bar may need two kegs of Coors, three kegs of Coors Light, and two cases of Killian's Red in bottles. The beer will then be loaded onto a refrigerated truck and transported to the restaurant. Upon arrival, the Kramer delivery person will transport the kegs and cases of beer into the restaurant's refrigerator and may also restock the coolers behind the bar.

Although individual members can be added to or deleted from a channel, someone must still perform these essential functions. They can be performed by producers, end users or consumers, channel intermediaries such as wholesalers and retailers, and sometimes nonmember channel participants. For example, if a manufacturer decides to eliminate its private fleet of trucks, it must still have a way to move the goods to the wholesaler. This task may be accomplished by the wholesaler, which may have its own fleet of trucks, or by a nonmember channel participant, such as an independent trucking firm. Nonmembers also provide many other essential functions that may at one time have been provided by a channel member. For example, research firms may perform the research function; advertising agencies may provide the promotion function; transportation and storage firms, the physical distribution function; and banks, the financing function.

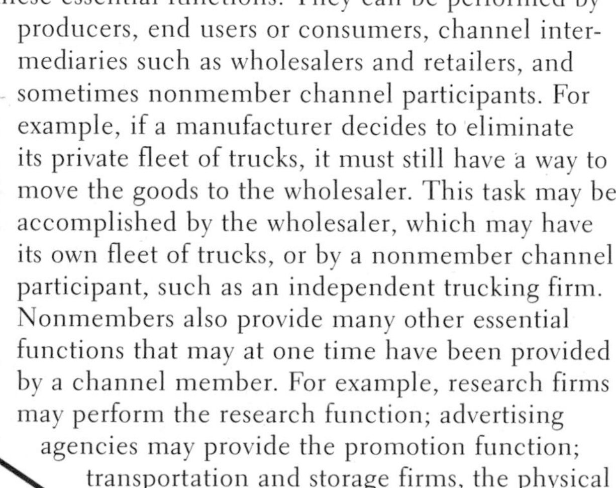

REVIEW LEARNING OUTCOME

LO 2 Define the types of channel intermediaries and describe their functions and activities

CHANNEL INTERMEDIARIES
Retailers
Wholesalers
Agents and Brokers

Perform →

CHANNEL FUNCTIONS
Transactional
Logistical
Facilitating

CHANNEL STRUCTURES

A product can take many routes to reach its final consumer. Marketers search for the most efficient channel from the many alternatives available. Marketing a consumer convenience good like gum or candy differs from marketing a specialty good like a Mercedes-Benz. The two products require very different distribution channels. Likewise, the appropriate channel for a major equipment supplier like Boeing Company would be unsuitable for an accessory equipment producer like Black & Decker. The next sections discuss the structures of typical marketing channels for consumer and business-to-business products. Alternative channel structures are also discussed.

A retailer channel is most common when the retailer is large, such as JCPenney, and can buy in large quantities directly from the manufacturer. Large retailers often bypass a wholesaler.

© AP PHOTO/MATT SLOCUM

Channels for Consumer Products

Exhibit 12.3 illustrates the four ways manufacturers can route products to consumers. Producers use the **direct channel** to sell directly to consumers. Direct marketing activities—including telemarketing, mail-order and catalog shopping, and forms of electronic retailing like online shopping and shop-at-home television networks—are a good example of this type of channel structure. For example, home computer users can purchase Dell computers directly over the telephone or from Dell's Web site. There are no intermediaries. Producer-owned stores and factory outlet stores—like Sherwin-Williams, Polo Ralph Lauren, Oneida, and West Point Pepperell—are other examples of direct channels. Farmers' markets are also direct channels. Direct marketing and factory outlets are discussed in more detail in Chapter 13.

At the other end of the spectrum, an *agent/broker channel* involves a fairly complicated process. Agent/broker channels are typically used in markets with many small manufacturers and many retailers that lack the resources to find each other. Agents or brokers bring manufacturers and wholesalers together for negotiations, but they do not take title to merchandise. Ownership passes directly to one or more

direct channel
A distribution channel in which producers sell directly to consumers.

EXHIBIT 12.3
Marketing Channels for Consumer Products

Direct channel	Retailer channel	Wholesaler channel	Agent/broker channel
Producer	Producer	Producer	Producer
			Agents or brokers
		Wholesalers	Wholesalers
	Retailers	Retailers	Retailers
Consumers	Consumers	Consumers	Consumers

wholesalers and then to retailers. Finally, retailers sell to the ultimate consumer of the product. For example, a food broker represents buyers and sellers of grocery products. The broker acts on behalf of many different producers and negotiates the sale of their products to wholesalers that specialize in foodstuffs. These wholesalers in turn sell to grocers and convenience stores.

Most consumer products are sold through distribution channels similar to the other two alternatives: the retailer channel and the wholesaler channel. A *retailer channel* is most common when the retailer is large and can buy in large quantities directly from the manufacturer. Wal-Mart, Target, JCPenney, and car dealers are examples of retailers that often bypass a wholesaler. A *wholesaler channel* is commonly used for low-cost items that are frequently purchased, such as candy, cigarettes, and magazines. For example, M&M/Mars sells candies and chocolates to wholesalers in large quantities. The wholesalers then break these quantities into smaller quantities to satisfy individual retailer orders.

Channels for Business and Industrial Products

As Exhibit 12.4 illustrates, five channel structures are common in business and industrial markets. First, direct channels are typical in business and industrial markets. For example, manufacturers buy large quantities of raw materials, major equipment, processed materials, and supplies directly from other manufacturers. Manufacturers that require suppliers to meet detailed technical specifications often prefer direct channels. The direct communication required between Ford Motor Company and its suppliers, for example, along with the tremendous size of the orders, makes anything but a direct channel impractical. The channel from producer to government buyers is also a direct channel. Because much government buying is done through bidding, a direct channel is attractive. Dell, for example, the top seller of desktop computers to federal, state, and local government agencies in the United States, sells the computers through direct channels.

Companies selling standardized items of moderate or low value often rely on *industrial distributors*. In many ways, an industrial distributor is like a supermarket for organizations. Industrial distributors are wholesalers and channel members that buy and take title to products. Moreover, they usually keep inventories of their products and sell

EXHIBIT 12.4

Channels for Business and Industrial Products

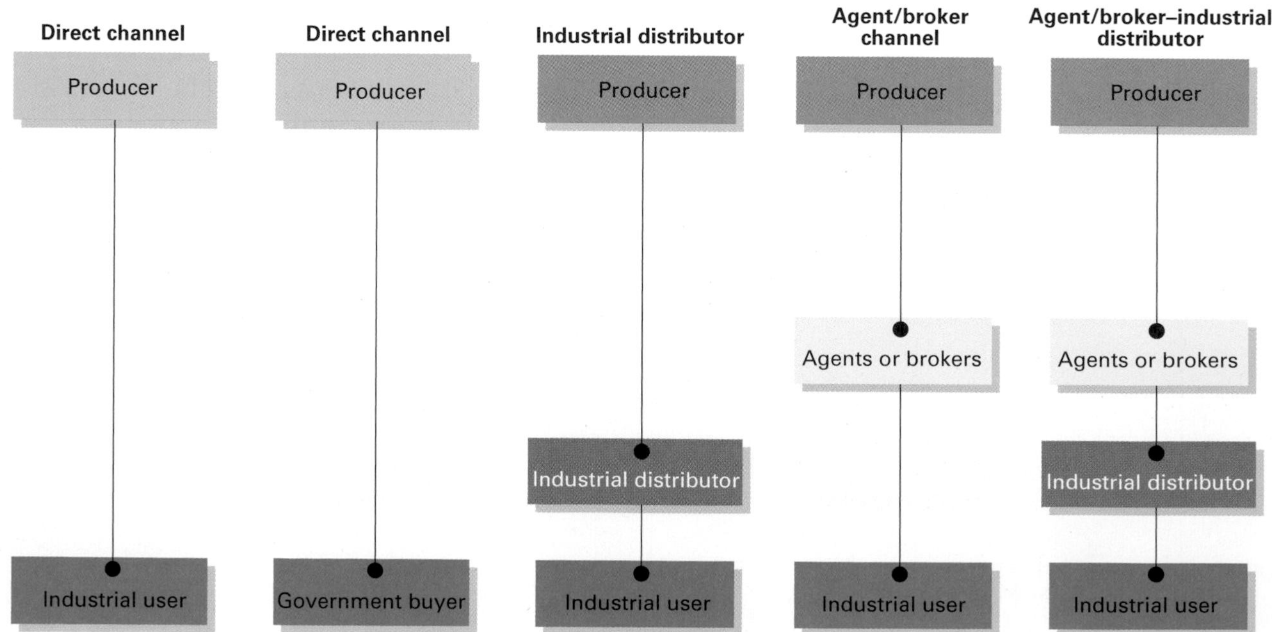

and service them. Often small manufacturers cannot afford to employ their own sales force. Instead, they rely on manufacturers' representatives or selling agents to sell to either industrial distributors or users.

Today, though, the traditional industrial distributor is facing many challenges. Manufacturers are getting bigger due to growth, mergers, and consolidation. Through technology, manufacturers and customers have access to information that in the past only the distributor had. Consequently, many manufacturers and customers are bypassing distributors and going direct, often via the Internet. The Internet has enabled virtual distributors to emerge and forced traditional industrial distributors to expand their business model. An example of how the Internet has revolutionized industrial distribution is **www.pumpbiz.com**, which sells pumps for chemicals, wastewater, sumps, water, coolants, and all other industrial process fluids. Pump types available include centrifugal, diaphragm, vertical, magnetic drive, and metering pumps. The site offers 24-7 purchasing and provides access to information on major manufacturers of pumps, including side-by-side comparisons and reviews; copies of manuals, diagrams, and other installation and repair documentation; warranted installers in the customer's local area; and instant access to past purchasing and related information on a customer's account.[2]

The Internet has also led to the emergence of three other new forms of industrial distribution. Some companies serve as agents that link buyers and sellers and charge a fee. For example, Expedia.com links business travelers to airlines, hotels, and car rental companies. A second form of marketplace has been developed by existing companies looking for a way to drop the intermediary from the channel. For example, the Worldwide Retail Exchange is a marketplace created by 17 major retailers including Target, JCPenney, and Walgreens. Retailers use the exchange to make purchases that in the past would have required telephone, fax, or face-to-face sales calls. Retailers using the exchange estimate they have saved approximately 15 percent in their purchasing costs. Finally, a third type of Internet marketplace is a "private exchange." Private exchanges allow companies to automate their channels while sharing information only with select suppliers. Ace Hardware and Hewlett-Packard, for example, use private exchanges to manage their inventory supplies. Another example is iTextiles.com which enables companies in the textile business to communicate over a secure online platform to place orders, update information, and standardize transactions.[3]

Alternative Channel Arrangements

Rarely does a producer use just one type of channel to move its product. It usually employs several different or alternative channels, which include multiple channels, nontraditional channels, and strategic channel alliances.

Multiple Channels When a producer selects two (or more) channels to distribute the same product to target markets, this arrangement is called **dual distribution** (or **multiple distribution**). As more people have access to the Internet and embrace online shopping, an increasing number of retailers are using multiple channels of distribution. For example, companies such as Limited Brands, which includes The Limited, Express, Victoria's Secret, and Bath and Body Works, sell in-store, online, and through catalogs. Other examples are Sears and Avon. Since Sears purchased Lands' End, a traditional direct business-to-consumer clothing manufacturer, Lands' End products are available in Sears's stores, and Sears credit cards are accepted on the Lands' End Web site. Avon, a direct supplier of health and beauty products for women, offers consumers four alternatives for purchasing products. They can contact a representative in person (the original business model), purchase on the Web, order direct from the company, or pick up products at an Avon Salon & Spa. The Limited, Sears/Lands' End, and Avon are each distributing identical products to existing markets using more than one channel of distribution.

dual distribution (multiple distribution)
The use of two (or more) channels to distribute the same product to target markets.

Nontraditional Channels Often nontraditional channel arrangements help differentiate a firm's product from the competition. For example, manufacturers may decide to use nontraditional channels such as the Internet, mail-order channels, or infomercials to sell

© AP IMAGES/PRNEWSFOTO/LANDS' END

An increasing number of retailers use multiple channels of distribution. For example, Sears purchased Lands' End, a traditional direct business-to-consumer clothing manufacturer. Now Lands' End products are available in Sears's stores, and Sears credit cards are accepted on the Lands' End Web site.

products instead of going through traditional retailer channels. Although nontraditional channels may limit a brand's coverage, they can give a producer serving a niche market a way to gain market access and customer attention without having to establish channel intermediaries. Nontraditional channels can also provide another avenue of sales for larger firms. For example, a London publisher sells short stories through vending machines in the London Underground. Instead of the traditional book format, the stories are printed like folded maps, making them an easy-to-read alternative for commuters.

Kiosks, long a popular method for ordering and registering for wedding gifts, dispersing cash through ATMs, and facilitating airline check-in, are finding new uses. Ethan Allen furniture stores use kiosks as a product locator tool for consumers and salespeople. Kiosks on the campuses of Cheyney University allow students to register for classes, see their class schedule and grades, check account balances, and even print transcripts. The general public, when it has access to the kiosks, can use them to gather information about the university.[4]

Strategic Channel Alliances Companies often form **strategic channel alliances**. Such an alliance enables a company to use another manufacturer's already established channel. Alliances are used most often when the creation of marketing channel relationships may be too expensive and time-consuming. Starbucks, the world's premier coffee marketer, uses strategic alliances both domestically and around the world. When Starbucks wanted to develop ready-to-drink (RTD) coffee beverages for supermarkets and other outlets, it decided not to develop a new channel from scratch. Rather, Starbucks signed an agreement with Pepsi to develop and bottle a Starbucks brand of RTD coffee, a category that had been extremely difficult to develop. The resulting Frappuccino and DoubleShot were so successful when they were launched that they were constantly sold out. Pepsi is still the sole distributor for Starbucks RTD beverages like Frappuccino and DoubleShot, and Starbucks has continued access to the thousands of outlets where Pepsi is sold.[5] Similarly, Accenture and Cisco Systems have formed an alliance to work together in the joint development, marketing, and deployment of global network solutions. The combination of Accenture's network consulting services and Cisco's advanced technology will result in cost savings in asset acquisition and service delivery for their customers.[6] Strategic channel alliances are proving to be more successful for growing businesses than mergers and acquisitions. This is especially true in global markets where cultural differences, distance, and other barriers can prove challenging. For example, Heinz has a strategic alliance with Kagome, one of Japan's largest food companies. The companies are working together to find ways to reduce operating costs while expanding both brands' market presence globally.

strategic channel alliance
A cooperative agreement between business firms to use the other's already established distribution channel.

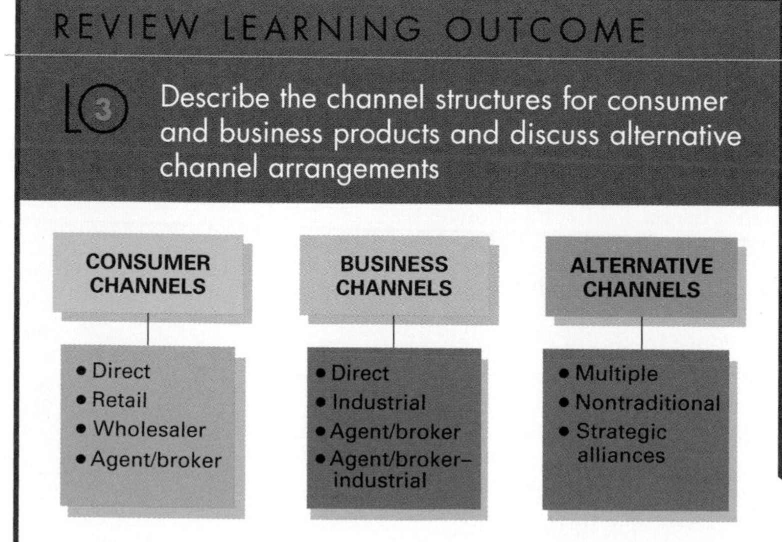

SUPPLY CHAINS AND SUPPLY CHAIN MANAGEMENT

In today's sophisticated marketplace, many companies are focusing on their supply chain and turning to supply chain management for competitive advantages. A company's **supply chain** includes all of the companies involved in all of the upstream and downstream flows of products, services, finances, and information, from initial suppliers (the point of origin) to the ultimate customer (the point of consumption). The goal of **supply chain management** is to coordinate and integrate the activities performed by supply chain members into a collection of seamless end-to-end processes, ultimately giving supply chain managers "total visibility" of the supply chain both inside and outside the firm. The philosophy behind supply chain management is that by visualizing the entire supply chain, managers can maximize strengths and efficiencies at each level of the process to create a highly competitive, customer-driven supply system that is able to respond immediately to changes in supply and demand. Companies that have a supply chain orientation are those that recognize and embrace this philosophy, and therefore see the implications of managing the flows of products, services, and so on across their direct and indirect suppliers and customers.

An important element of supply chain management is that it is completely customer driven. During the era of mass production (c. 1865–1980), manufacturers produced standardized products that were "pushed" down through the supply channel to the consumer. In contrast, products in today's marketplace are being driven by customers, who expect to receive product configurations and services matched to their unique needs. For example, Dell builds computers only according to its customers' precise specifications, such as the amount of RAM memory; type of monitor, modem, or optical drive; and amount of hard disk space. Similarly, car companies offer customers the option to customize even economy-priced cars. For about $20,000, customers can order a Ford Mustang with a V-6 engine, a six-disc CD changer, MP3 player, and eight speakers. The focus is on pulling products into the marketplace and partnering with members of the supply chain to enhance customer value. Customizing an automobile is now possible because of new supply chain relationships between the automobile manufacturers and the after-market auto-parts industry.

This reversal of the flow of demand from a "push" to a "pull" system has resulted in a radical reformulation of market expectations as well as traditional marketing, production, and distribution functions. Through the coordinated partnership of suppliers, manufacturers, wholesalers, and retailers working together along the entire supply chain, supply chain management allows companies to respond with the unique product configuration and mix of services demanded by the customer. Today, supply chain management plays a dual role: first, as a *communicator* of customer demand that extends from the point of sale all the way back to the supplier and, second, as a *physical flow process* that engineers the timely and cost-effective movement of goods through the entire source-to-consumer supply pipeline. Boeing realized the importance of these supply chain processes when it struggled to get enough titanium fasteners to assemble the new 787 Dreamliner from its supplier, Alcoa, in time to launch its widely publicized new luxury airliner.[7] Better communication with Alcoa and its titanium ore suppliers, combined with better process flow synchronization, could have reduced the stress Boeing executives felt as they scrambled to find enough fasteners to meet the publicized launch date.

Supply chain managers are responsible for making strategic decisions, such as coordinating the sourcing and procurement of raw materials, scheduling production, processing orders, managing inventory, transporting and storing supplies and finished goods, dealing with returns, and coordinating customer service activities. Supply chain managers are also responsible for the management of information that flows

supply chain
The connected chain of all of the business entities, both internal and external to the company, that perform or support the logistics function.

supply chain management
A management system that coordinates and integrates all of the activities performed by supply chain members into a seamless process, from the source to the point of consumption, resulting in enhanced customer and economic value.

through the supply chain. Coordinating the relationships between the company and its external partners, such as vendors, carriers, and third-party companies, is also a critical function of supply chain management. Because supply chain managers play such a major role in both cost control and customer satisfaction, they are more valuable than ever. In fact, demand for supply chain managers has increased substantially in recent years. According to the Council of Supply Chain Management Professionals, the supply chain career field accounts for over 9.5 percent of the U.S. gross domestic product, with thousands of new, high-paying positions becoming available yearly.

In summary, supply chain managers are responsible for directing raw materials and parts to the production department and the finished or semifinished product through warehouses and eventually to the intermediary or end user. Above all, supply chain management begins and ends with the customer. Instead of forcing a product into the market that may or may not sell quickly, supply chain managers react to actual customer demand. By doing so, they minimize the flow of raw materials, finished product, and packaging materials at every point in the supply chain, resulting in lower costs and increased customer value. Exhibit 12.5 depicts a typical supply chain model that managers attempt to optimize for firm and customer benefit.

EXHIBIT 12.5

A Typical Supply Chain Management Process

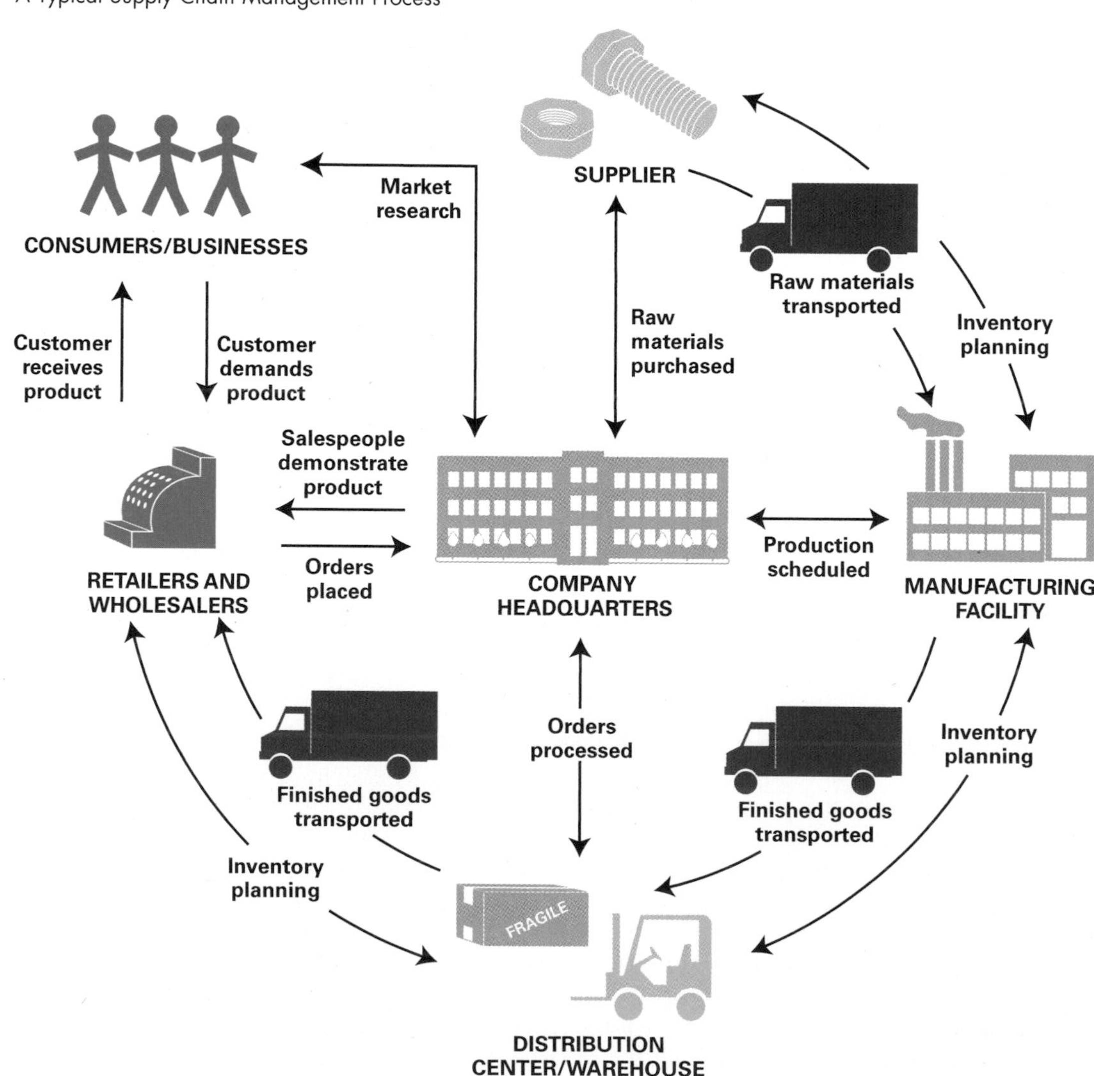

Benefits of Supply Chain Management

Supply chain management is a key means of differentiation for a firm and a critical component in marketing and corporate strategy. Supply chain–oriented companies commonly report lower inventory, transportation, warehousing, and packaging costs; greater supply chain flexibility; improved customer service; and higher revenues. Research has shown a clear relationship between supply chain performance and profitability. Specific benefits from effective implementation of supply chain procedures include an almost 20 percent increase in cash flow, a more than 50 percent increase in flexibility of supply chain activities, and a reduction of 5 to 10 percent in supply chain costs, among other potential benefits.[8]

REVIEW LEARNING OUTCOME

LO4 Define the terms *supply chain* and *supply chain management,* and discuss the benefits of supply chain management

Well-managed supply chains . . .

lead to . . .

- ✓ reduced costs
- ✓ increased flexibility
- ✓ improved customer service
- ✓ greater revenue

LO5

MAKING CHANNEL STRATEGY DECISIONS

Devising a marketing channel strategy requires several critical decisions. Managers must decide what role distribution will play in the overall marketing strategy. In addition, they must be sure that the channel strategy chosen is consistent with product, promotion, and pricing strategies. In making these decisions, marketing managers must determine what factors will influence the choice of channel and what level of distribution intensity will be appropriate.

Factors Affecting Channel Choice

Managers must answer many questions before choosing a marketing channel. The final choice depends on the analysis of several factors, which often interact. These factors can be grouped as market factors, product factors, and producer factors.

Market Factors Among the most important market factors affecting the choice of distribution channel are target customer considerations. Specifically, managers should answer the following questions: Who are the potential customers? What do they buy? Where do they buy? When do they buy? How do they buy? Additionally, the choice of channel depends on whether the producer is selling to consumers or to industrial customers. Industrial customers' buying habits are very different from those of consumers. Industrial customers tend to buy in larger quantities and require more customer service. For example, Toyota Industrial Equipment manufactures the leading lift truck used to move materials in and out of warehouses and other industrial facilities. Its business customers buy large numbers of trucks at one time and require additional services such as data tracking on how the lift truck is used. In contrast, consumers usually buy in very small quantities and sometimes do not mind if they get little or no service, such as in a discount store like Wal-Mart or Target.

The geographic location and size of the market are also important to channel selection. As a rule, if the target market is concentrated in one or more specific areas, then direct selling through a sales force is appropriate. When markets are more widely dispersed, intermediaries would be less expensive. The size of the market also influences channel choice. Generally, larger markets require more intermediaries. For instance, Procter & Gamble has to reach millions of consumers with its many brands of household goods. It needs many intermediaries, including wholesalers and retailers.

Product Factors Products that are more complex, customized, and expensive tend to benefit from shorter and more direct marketing channels. These types of products sell better through a direct sales force. Examples include pharmaceuticals, scientific instruments, airplanes, and mainframe computer systems. On the other hand, the more standardized a product is, the longer its distribution channel can be and the greater the number of intermediaries that can be involved. For example, with the exception of flavor and shape, the formula for chewing gum is about the same from producer to producer. Chewing gum is also very inexpensive. As a result, the distribution channel for gum tends to involve many wholesalers and retailers.

The product's life cycle is also an important factor in choosing a marketing channel. In fact, the choice of channel may change over the life of the product. For example, when photocopiers were first available, they were typically sold by a direct sales force. Now, however, photocopiers can be found in several places, including warehouse clubs, electronics superstores, and mail-order catalogs. As products become more common and less intimidating to potential users, producers tend to look for alternative channels. Gatorade was originally sold to sports teams, gyms, and fitness clubs. As the drink became more popular, mainstream supermarket channels were added, followed by convenience stores and drugstores. Now Gatorade can be found in vending machines and even in some fast-food restaurants.

Another factor is the delicacy of the product. Perishable products like vegetables and milk have a relatively short life span. Fragile products like china and crystal require a minimum amount of handling. Therefore, both require fairly short marketing channels. Online retailers such as eBay facilitate the sale of unusual or difficult-to-find products that benefit from a direct channel.

Producer Factors Several factors pertaining to the producer itself are important to the selection of a marketing channel. In general, producers with large financial, managerial, and marketing resources are better able to use more direct channels. These producers have the ability to hire and train their own sales force, warehouse their own goods, and extend credit to their customers. For example, variety store Dollar Tree distributes products through retail locations at low prices. To increase cost-efficiency, Dollar Tree has a coast-to-coast logistics network of nine distribution centers to service its almost 3,000 stores.[9] Smaller or weaker firms, on the other hand, must rely on intermediaries to provide these services for them. Compared to producers with only one or two product lines, producers that sell several products in a related area are able to choose channels that are more direct. Sales expenses then can be spread over more products.

A producer's desire to control pricing, positioning, brand image, and customer support also tends to influence channel selection. For instance, firms that sell products with exclusive brand images, such as designer perfumes and clothing, usually avoid channels in which discount retailers are present. Manufacturers of upscale products, such as Gucci (handbags) and Godiva (chocolates), may sell their wares only in expensive stores in order to maintain an image of exclusivity. Many producers have opted to risk their image, however, and test sales in discount channels. Levi Strauss expanded its distribution to include JCPenney, Sears, and Wal-Mart.

Intensive distribution is susceptible to errors when intermediaries are expected to handle products in a prespecified manner detailed in buyer–seller agreements. For example, Scholastic executives were alarmed when copies of the final book in the Harry Potter series were mistakenly released a day earlier than the widely publicized release date.

© AP IMAGES/MARK BAKER

Levels of Distribution Intensity

Organizations have three options for intensity of distribution: intensive distribution, selective distribution, or exclusive distribution (see Exhibit 12.6).

EXHIBIT 12.6

Intensity of Distribution Levels

Intensity Level	Distribution Intensity Objective	Number of Intermediaries in Each Market	Examples
Intensive	Achieve mass-market selling; popular with health and beauty aids and convenience goods that must be available everywhere	Many	Pepsi-Cola, Frito-Lay potato chips, Huggies diapers, Alpo dog food, Crayola crayons
Selective	Work closely with selected intermediaries who meet certain criteria; typically used for shopping goods and some specialty goods	Several	Donna Karan clothing, Hewlett-Packard printers, Burton snowboards, Aveda aromatherapy products
Exclusive	Work with a single intermediary for products that require special resources or positioning; typically used for specialty goods and major industrial equipment	One	BMW cars, Rolex watches

Intensive Distribution **Intensive distribution** is a form of distribution aimed at maximum market coverage. The manufacturer tries to have the product available in every outlet where potential customers might want to buy it. If buyers are unwilling to search for a product (as is true of convenience goods and operating supplies), the product must be very accessible to buyers. A low-value product that is purchased frequently may require a lengthy channel. For example, candy, chips, and other snack foods are found in almost every type of retail store imaginable. These foods typically are sold to retailers in small quantities by food or candy wholesalers. The Wrigley Company could not afford to sell its gum directly to every service station, drugstore, supermarket, and discount store. The cost would be too high. Sysco delivers food and related products to restaurants and other food service companies that prepare meals for customers dining out. It is not economically feasible for restaurants to go to individual vendors for each product. Therefore, Sysco serves as an intermediary by delivering all products necessary to fulfill restaurants' needs.[10]

Most manufacturers pursuing an intensive distribution strategy sell to a large percentage of the wholesalers willing to stock their products. Retailers' willingness (or unwillingness) to handle items tends to control the manufacturer's ability to achieve intensive distribution. For example, a retailer already carrying ten brands of gum may show little enthusiasm for one more brand. Intensive distribution is also susceptible to errors when intermediaries who are shipped products are expected to handle them in a prespecified manner detailed in buyer–seller agreements. For example, executives at Scholastic Books were quite alarmed when some 1,200 of the 12 million copies of the final book in the Harry Potter series, *Harry Potter and the Deathly Hallows*, were mistakenly released through an Internet retailing Web site a day earlier than the widely publicized release date.[11]

Selective Distribution **Selective distribution** is achieved by screening dealers and retailers to eliminate all but a few in any single area. Because only a few are chosen, the consumer must seek out the product. For example, when Heeling Sports Ltd. launched Heelys, thick-soled sneakers with a wheel embedded in each heel, the company hired a group of 40 teens to perform Heelys exhibitions in targeted malls, skate parks, and college campuses across the country to create demand. Then the company made the decision to avoid large stores like Target and to distribute the shoes only through selected mall retailers and skate and surf shops in order to position the product as "cool and kind of irreverent." Selective distribution strategies often hinge on a manufacturer's desire to maintain a superior product image so as to be able to charge a premium price. DKNY clothing, for instance, is sold only in select retail outlets, mainly full-price department

intensive distribution
A form of distribution aimed at having a product available in every outlet where target customers might want to buy it.

selective distribution
A form of distribution achieved by screening dealers to eliminate all but a few in any single area.

exclusive distribution
A form of distribution that establishes one or a few dealers within a given area.

stores. Likewise, premium pet food brands such as Hill's Pet Nutrition and Nestlé Purina's Pro Plan are distributed chiefly through specialty pet food stores and veterinarians, rather than mass retailers like Wal-Mart, so that a premium price can be charged. Manufacturers sometimes expand selective distribution strategies, believing that doing so will enhance revenues without diminishing their product's image. For example, when Procter & Gamble purchased premium pet food brand Iams, it expanded the brand's selective distribution strategy and began selling Iams food in mass retailer Target. Even though the new strategy created channel conflict with breeders and veterinarians who had supported the product, sales increased.[12] Similarly, Playboy Energy, a new energy drink manufactured and bottled by the media enterprise of the same name, uses selective distribution to position itself as a higher-end option versus more intensively distributed competitor Red Bull.[13] The drink has been introduced in luxurious nightclubs and upscale bars only in Boston, Miami, Las Vegas, and Los Angeles in order to draw the attention of "elite" customers prior to its broader release in grocery and convenience stores in the future.

Recently, a high-tech form of selective distribution has emerged whereby products are pushed through to the membership of exclusive virtual social networks. Scion Speak was developed as a social network Internet portal where Toyota Scion owners could design and share their own unique graffiti-type artwork which then could be airbrushed onto the body of their cars. Members of the network, which is managed by a quirky marketing firm called StrawberryFrog, have the exclusive rights to the car customization services, as well as to some available custom designs made by a professional artist contracted by the company. This type of service is among the first to leverage the power of social network Web sites as a product distribution medium.[14]

Exclusive Distribution The most restrictive form of market coverage is **exclusive distribution**, which entails only one or a few dealers within a given area. Because buyers may have to search or travel extensively to buy the product, exclusive distribution is usually confined to consumer specialty goods, a few shopping goods, and major industrial equipment. Products such as Rolls-Royce automobiles, Chris-Craft powerboats, and Pettibone tower cranes are distributed under exclusive arrangements. Sometimes exclusive territories are granted by new companies (such as franchisors) to obtain market coverage in a particular area. Limited distribution may also serve to project an exclusive image for the product.

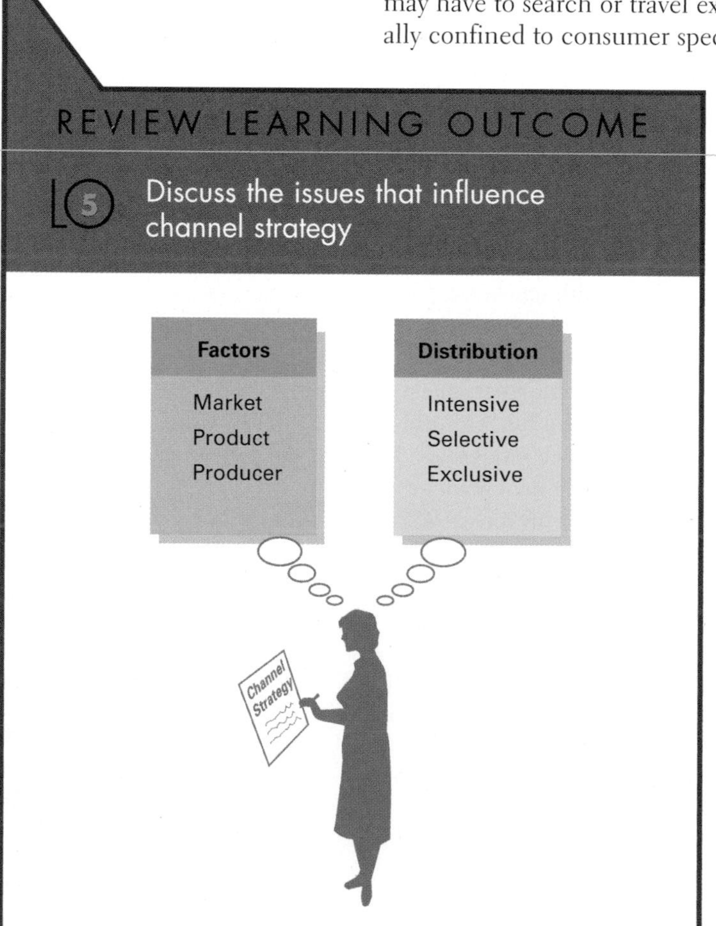

Retailers and wholesalers may be unwilling to commit the time and money necessary to promote and service a product unless the manufacturer guarantees them an exclusive territory. This arrangement shields the dealer from direct competition and enables it to be the main beneficiary of the manufacturer's promotion efforts in that geographic area. With exclusive distribution, channels of communication are usually well established because the manufacturer works with a limited number of dealers rather than many accounts.

Exclusive distribution also takes place within a retailer's store rather than a geographic area—for example, when a retailer agrees not to sell a manufacturer's competing brands. Mossimo, traditionally an apparel wholesaler, developed an agreement with Target to design clothing and related items sold exclusively at Target stores. Other exclusive distributors involved in this successful model include Thomas O'Brien domestics, Sonia Kashuk makeup, Isaac Mizrahi domestics and apparel, and Todd Oldham home furnishings for college students.

TYPES OF CHANNEL RELATIONSHIPS

A marketing channel is more than a set of institutions linked by economic ties. Social relationships play an important role in building unity among channel members. A critical aspect of channel management, therefore, is managing the social relationships among channel members to achieve synergy. Marketing managers should carefully consider the types of relationships they choose to foster between their company and other companies, and in doing so, pay close attention to the benefits and hazards associated with each relationship type.

Channel Relationship Types

Channel members must create and manage multiple relationships with other members in order to create an efficient environment for exchange. Relationships among channel members range from "loose" to "tight," taking the form of a continuum stretching from single transactions to complex interdependent relationships such as partnerships or alliances. The choice of relationship type is important for channel management because each relationship type carries with it different levels of time, financial, and resource investment. Three basic types of relationships, organized by degree of closeness, are commonly considered: Arm's-Length, integrated relationships, and cooperative.

Arm's-Length Relationships At one end of the relationship continuum are relationships considered by channel members to be temporary or one-time-only. These relationships are often referred to as **"Arm's-Length" relationships** due to the companies' unwillingness or lack of ability to develop a closer type of relationship. In Arm's-Length relationships, both parties retain their independence and pursue only their own interests while attempting to benefit from the goods or services provided by the other. This type of relationship is often used when a company has a sudden and/or unique need for a product or service and does not anticipate this need will arise again in the near future. For example, what might happen if Chevrolet were suddenly faced with an unusual situation where Bridgestone, its usual tire producer for the Chevy Tahoe, were unable to provide shipment of tires in reasonable time for a planned production run? One solution might be to engage in a temporary, Arm's-Length relationship with an alternate provider such as Michelin, who might be able to supply substitute tires on a temporary basis and thus save Chevrolet the costs associated with delaying the production run.

This sort of channel arrangement, however, involves a number of downsides. Because Chevrolet needs the tires on short notice, Michelin might decide to charge a somewhat higher price then usual, and furthermore, because the order placed was a onetime-only order and contained a fixed number of units, it is unlikely that Chevrolet would be able to take advantage of discounts available for customers buying in large quantities. In addition, because the relationship between Chevrolet and Michelin is new, there is no history or friendship to draw on in cases where disagreements or conflicts arise related to the terms of the agreement. In closer relationships, channel members might easily resolve their differences through communication, future promises, or bargaining. But in Arm's-Length relationships it is sometimes necessary to resolve Arm's-Length disputes through more formal and costly means such as arbitration or lawsuits. For all of these reasons, companies often find it appealing to develop more concrete, long-term relationships with other channel members.

Integrated Relationships At the opposite end of the relationship continuum from Arm's-Length relationships is a situation where one company (vertical integration) or several companies acting as one (a supply chain), perform all channel functions. These closely bonded types of relationships are collectively referred to as **integrated relationships**. Integrated relationships are characterized by formal arrangements that explicitly define the relationships to the involved channel members. For example, with vertical integration,

Arm's-Length relationships
A relationship between companies that is loose, characterized by low relational investment and trust, and usually taking the form of a series of discrete transactions with no/low expectation of future interaction or service.

integrated relationships
A relationship between companies that is tightly connected, with linked processes across and between firm boundaries, and high levels of trust and interfirm commitment.

cooperative relationships
A relationship between companies that takes the form of informal partnership with moderate levels of trust and information sharing as needed to further each company's goals.

all of the related channel members are collectively owned by a single legal entity (which may be one of the channel members, or may be a third party), with ownership established through formal legal titles and/or agreements. This sort of relational arrangement has often been employed by McDonald's Corporation, whose subsidiary companies have owned dairy and potato farms and processing plants that grow and process components of the products served by the chain's fast-food restaurants. A supply chain consists of several companies acting together in a highly organized and efficient manner, while employing the same or similar techniques as a single vertically integrated company.

Based on these descriptions, it seems that integrated relationships would be the preferred relationship type in almost all company-to-company channel settings. However, highly integrated relationships also come with some significant costs and/or hazards. For example, the single-owner model is somewhat risky because a large amount of capital assets must be purchased or leased (requiring a potentially huge initial cash outlay), and the failure of any portion of the business may result in not only the economic loss of that portion, but may also reduce the value of the other business units (or render them totally worthless). Because these trade-offs are sometimes hard to justify, companies often look for a sort of "happy medium" between Arm's-Length and integrated relationships that enables them to maximize the advantages of both relationship types while limiting their potential risks.

REVIEW LEARNING OUTCOME

LO 6 Discuss the different channel relationship types and their unique costs and benefits

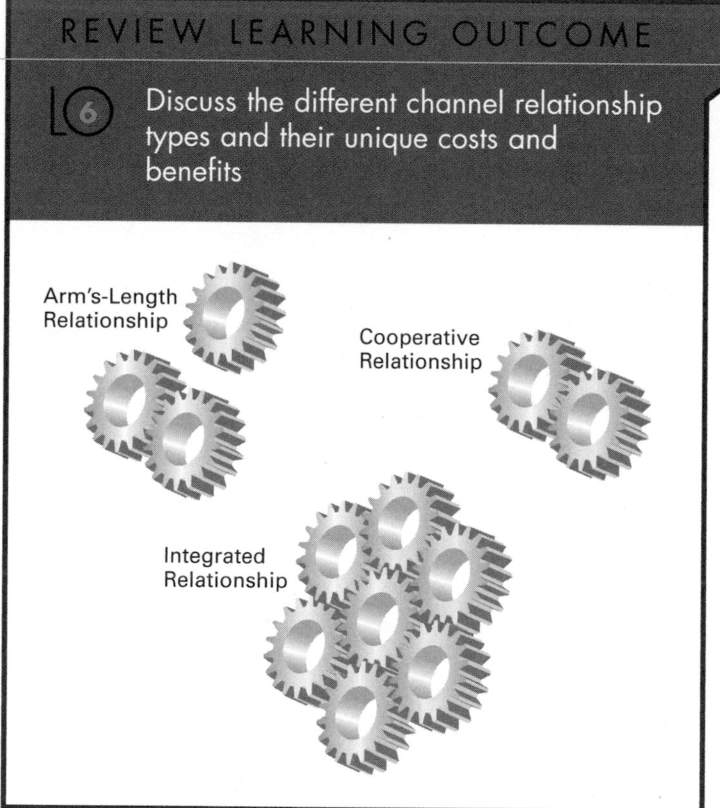

Cooperative Relationships Cooperative relationships, which exist between Arm's-Length and integrated relationships in terms of their connectedness, take many different forms. Cooperative relationships include non-equity agreements such as franchising and licensing, as well as equity-based joint ventures and strategic alliances (see Chapter 5 for a review). In general, cooperative relationships are administered using some sort of formal contract. This is in contrast to Arm's-Length relationships, which are enforced through legal action (or the implied threat thereof), and integrated relationships that rely on informal social enforcement to secure the agreement based on trust, commitment, and loyalty. Cooperative relationships thus tend to be more flexible than integrated relationships, but are also structured with greater detail and depth than Arm's-Length relationships. They tend to be used when a company wants less ambiguity in the channel relationship than the Arm's-Length relationship can provide, but without the long-term and/or capital investment required to achieve full integration.

LO 7

THE LOGISTICS FUNCTION IN THE SUPPLY CHAIN

Now that you are familiar with the structure and strategy of supply chain management, it is important to also understand the physical means through which products move through the supply chain. As mentioned earlier, supply chain management coordinates and integrates all of the activities performed by supply chain members into a seamless process. The logistics function of the supply chain is responsible for the movement and delivery of goods and services into, through, and out of each firm in the supply chain network. The logistics function consists of several interrelated and integrated logistical components: (1) sourcing and procurement of raw materials and supplies,

(2) production scheduling, (3) order processing, (4) inventory management and control, (5) warehousing and materials-handling, and (6) transportation.

A **logistics information system** provides the technological link connecting all of the logistics components of the supply chain. The components of the system include, for example, software for materials acquisition and handling, warehouse-management and enterprise-wide solutions, data storage and integration in data warehouses, mobile communications, electronic data interchange, RFID chips, and the Internet. Working together, the components of the logistics information system are the fundamental enablers of successful supply chain management.

The **supply chain team,** leveraging the capabilities of the logistics information system, orchestrates the movement of goods, services, and information from the source to the consumer. Supply chain teams typically cut across organizational boundaries, embracing all parties who participate in moving the product to market. The best supply chain teams also move beyond the organization to include the external participants in the chain, such as suppliers, transportation carriers, and third-party logistics suppliers. Members of the supply chain communicate, coordinate, and cooperate extensively to make the logistics function as efficient and effective as possible.

Today's corporate supply chain logisticians have become so efficient that the U.S. Marine Corps is now consulting with companies like Wal-Mart, UPS, and Unilever to improve its own supply chain efficiency. The Marine Corps's goal is to reduce the time it takes to deliver supplies to the front lines from one week to 24 hours and lower costs by cutting inventories in half.

Sourcing and Procurement

One of the most important links in the supply chain is the one between the manufacturer and the supplier. Purchasing professionals are on the front lines of supply chain management. Purchasing departments plan purchasing strategies, develop specifications, select suppliers, and negotiate price and service levels. Often, goods are procured for use in local manufacturing processes from suppliers halfway around the world. This is especially true for the United States, which is the world's top importer with nearly $2 trillion worth of purchased merchandise entering the nation annually through its international ports.[15]

The goal of most sourcing and procurement activities is to reduce the costs of raw materials and supplies. Purchasing professionals have traditionally relied on tough negotiations to get the lowest price possible from suppliers of raw materials, supplies, and components. Perhaps the biggest contribution purchasing can make to supply chain management, however, is in the area of vendor relations. Companies can use the purchasing function to strategically manage suppliers in order to reduce the total cost of materials and services. Through enhanced vendor relations, buyers and sellers can develop cooperative relationships that reduce costs and improve efficiency with the aim of lowering prices and enriching profits. By integrating suppliers into their companies' businesses, purchasing managers have become better able to streamline purchasing processes, manage inventory levels, and reduce overall costs of the sourcing and procurement operations.

Order Processing

The order is often the catalyst that sets the supply chain in motion, especially in the build-to-order environments of leading computer manufacturers such as Dell. The **order processing system** processes the requirements of the customer and sends the information into the supply chain via the logistics information system. The order goes to the manufacturer's warehouse. If the product is in stock, the order is filled and arrangements are made to ship it. If the product is not in stock, it triggers a replenishment request that finds its way to the factory floor.

The role of proper order processing in providing good service cannot be overemphasized. As an order enters the system, management must monitor two flows: the flow of goods and the flow of information. Often marketers' best-laid plans get entangled in the order processing system. Obviously, good communication among sales representatives, office personnel, and warehouse and shipping personnel is essential to correct order

logistics information system
The link that connects all of the logistics components of the supply chain.

supply chain team
An entire group of individuals who orchestrate the movement of goods, services, and information from the source to the consumer.

order processing system
A system whereby orders are entered into the supply chain and filled.

electronic data interchange (EDI)
Information technology that replaces the paper documents that usually accompany business transactions, such as purchase orders and invoices, with electronic transmission of the needed information to reduce inventory levels, improve cash flow, streamline operations, and increase the speed and accuracy of information transmission.

inventory control system
A method of developing and maintaining an adequate assortment of materials or products to meet a manufacturer's or a customer's demand.

materials requirement planning (MRP) (materials management)
An inventory control system that manages the replenishment of raw materials, supplies, and components from the supplier to the manufacturer.

distribution resource planning (DRP)
An inventory control system that manages the replenishment of goods from the manufacturer to the final consumer.

processing. Shipping incorrect merchandise or partially filled orders can create just as much dissatisfaction as stockouts or slow deliveries. The flow of goods and information must be continually monitored so that mistakes can be corrected before an invoice is prepared and the merchandise shipped.

Order processing is becoming more automated through the use of computer technology known as **electronic data interchange (EDI)**. The basic idea of EDI is to replace the paper documents that usually accompany business transactions, such as purchase orders and invoices, with electronic transmission of the needed information. A typical EDI message includes all the information that would traditionally be included on a paper invoice such as product code, quantity, and transportation details. The information is usually sent via private networks, which are more secure and reliable than the networks used for standard e-mail messages. Most importantly, the information can be read and processed by computers, significantly reducing costs and increasing efficiency. Companies that use EDI can reduce inventory levels, improve cash flow, streamline operations, and increase the speed and accuracy of information transmission. EDI also creates a closer relationship between buyers and sellers.

It should not be surprising that retailers have become major users of EDI. For Wal-Mart, Target, and the like, logistics speed and accuracy are crucial competitive tools in an overcrowded retail environment. Many big retailers are helping their suppliers acquire EDI technology so that they can be linked into the system. EDI works hand in hand with retailers' *efficient consumer response* programs, which are designed to have the right products on the shelf, in the right styles and colors, at the right time, through improved inventory, ordering, and distribution techniques.

Inventory Management and Control

Closely interrelated with the procurement, manufacturing, and ordering processes is the **inventory control system**—a method that develops and maintains an adequate assortment of materials or products to meet a manufacturer's or a customer's demands.

Inventory decisions, for both raw materials and finished goods, have a big impact on supply chain costs and the level of service provided. If too many products are kept in inventory, costs increase—as do risks of obsolescence, theft, and damage. If too few products are kept on hand, then the company risks product shortages and angry customers, and ultimately lost sales. For example, negative sales forecasts for the Christmas buying season in the past few years caused many retailers to cut back on orders because they were afraid of having to discount large end-of-the-year inventories. As a result, many companies, including Panasonic and Lands' End, lost sales due to inventory shortages on popular items. The goal of inventory management, therefore, is to keep inventory levels as low as possible while maintaining an adequate supply of goods to meet customer demand.

Managing inventory from the supplier to the manufacturer is called **materials requirement planning (MRP)**, or **materials management**. This system also encompasses the sourcing and procurement operations, signaling purchasing when raw materials, supplies, or components will need to be replenished for the production of more goods. The system that manages the finished goods inventory from manufacturer to end user is commonly referred to as **distribution resource planning (DRP)**. Both inventory systems use various inputs, such as sales forecasts, available inventory, outstanding orders, lead times, and

Most trading partners that adopt EDI do so for increased efficiencies and cost savings. Sometimes pressures from larger trading partners force smaller trading partners to use EDI. For instance, Wal-Mart will not do business with a supplier that doesn't agree to use its preferred EDI processes.

EXHIBIT 12.7

Inventory Replenishment Example

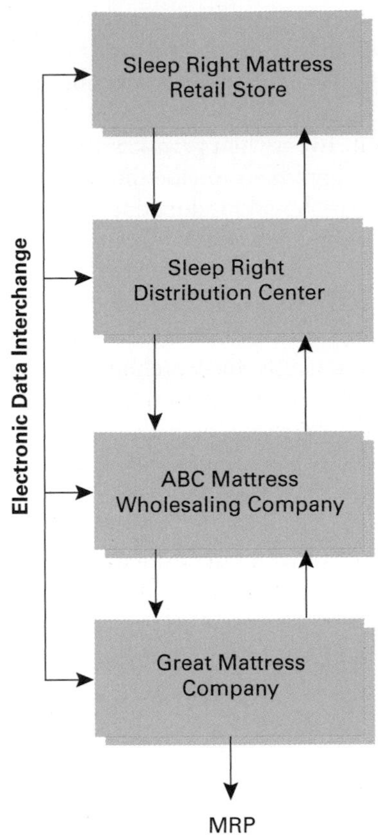

Sleep Right is planning a promotion on the Great Mattress Company's Gentle Rest mattress. Sales forecast is for 50 units to be sold. Sleep Right has 10 open Gentle Rest orders with its distribution center. New mattresses must be delivered in two weeks in time for the promotion.

Sleep Right's Distribution Center is electronically notified of the order of 50 new Gentle Rest mattresses. It currently has 20 Gentle Rest mattresses in inventory and begins putting together the transportation plans to deliver these to the Sleep Right Store. Delivery takes one day. It orders 40 new mattresses from its mattress wholesaler to make up the difference.

ABC Mattress Wholesaling Company is electronically notified of Sleep Right DC's order of 40 new Gentle Rest mattresses. It currently does not have any of these in stock but electronically orders 40 from the Great Mattress Company's factory. Once it receives the new mattresses, it can have them delivered to the Sleep Right DC in two days.

The Great Mattress Company electronically receives ABC's order and forwards it to the factory floor. Production of a new mattress takes 20 minutes. The total order of 40 mattresses can be ready to be shipped to ABC in two days. Delivery takes one day. Raw material supplies for this order are electronically requested from Great Mattress's supply partners, who deliver the needed materials just-in-time to its stitching machines.

mode of transportation to be used, to determine what actions must be taken to replenish goods at all points in the supply chain. Demand in the system is collected at each level in the supply chain, from the retailer back up the chain to the manufacturer. With the use of electronic data interchange, the information can be transmitted much faster to meet the quick-response needs of today's competitive marketplace. Exhibit 12.7 provides an example of inventory replenishment using DRP from the retailer to the manufacturer.

Other inventory management systems that have gained in popularity in recent years, however, use few or no forecasts at all during the scheduling of shipments. Known as **automatic replenishment programs**, these systems trigger shipments only once a good (usually something with a relatively predictable demand pattern) is sold to the customer. Using an EDI linkage connected with barcode scanners at the point of purchase, the supplier can view the inventory being held at the next tier of the supply chain in real time. When stock of a good at the customer location falls below preestablished safety levels, orders are automatically packed and shipped from the supplier location. Thus, in this type of system, the supplier takes responsibility for keeping inventory on the shelves or in the customer's warehouse; this usually results in reduced stockouts and lowers overall inventory levels.

Warehousing and Materials-Handling

Supply chain logisticians oversee the constant flow of raw materials from suppliers to manufacturer and finished goods from the manufacturer to the ultimate consumer. Although build-to-order manufacturing processes may eliminate the need to warehouse many raw materials, manufacturers may often keep some safety stock on hand in the event of an emergency, such as a strike at a supplier's plant or a catastrophic event that temporarily stops the flow of raw materials to the production line. Likewise, the final user may not need or want the goods at the same time the manufacturer produces and wants to sell them. Products like grain and corn are produced seasonally, but consumers demand them year-round. Other products, such as Christmas ornaments and turkeys, are produced

automatic replenishment program
An inventory management system that triggers shipments only once a good is sold to the customer; the program uses EDI linkage connected with barcode scanners at the point of purchase, so the supplier can view the inventory being held at the next tier of the supply chain in real time.

materials-handling system
A method of moving inventory into, within, and out of the warehouse.

year-round, but consumers do not want them until autumn or winter. Therefore, management must have a storage system to hold these products until they are shipped.

Storage is what helps manufacturers manage supply and demand, or production and consumption. It provides time utility to buyers and sellers, which means that the seller stores the product until the buyer wants or needs it. Even when products are used regularly, not seasonally, many manufacturers store excess products in case the demand surpasses the amount produced at a given time. Storing additional product does have disadvantages, however, including the costs of insurance on the stored product, taxes, obsolescence or spoilage, theft, and warehouse operating costs. Another drawback is opportunity costs—that is, the opportunities lost because money is tied up in stored product instead of being used for something else.

Because businesses are focusing on cutting supply chain costs, the warehousing industry is also changing to better serve its customers. For example, many warehouses are putting greater emphasis on more efficient unloading and reloading layouts and customized services that move merchandise through the warehouse faster, often in the same day. They also are investing in services using sophisticated tracking technology such as materials-handling systems.

A **materials-handling system** moves inventory into, within, and out of the warehouse. Materials-handling includes these functions:

- Receiving goods into the warehouse or distribution center
- Identifying, sorting, and labeling the goods
- Dispatching the goods to a temporary storage area
- Recalling, selecting, or picking the goods for shipment (may include packaging the product in a protective container for shipping)

The goal of the materials-handling system is to move items quickly with minimal handling. With a manual, nonautomated materials-handling system, a product may be handled more than a dozen times. Each time it is handled, the cost and risk of damage increase; each lifting of a product stresses its package. Consequently, most manufacturers today have switched to automated systems. Scanners quickly identify goods entering and leaving a warehouse through bar-coded labels affixed to the packaging. Electronic storage and retrieval systems automatically store and pick goods in the warehouse or distribution center. Automated materials-handling systems decrease product handling, ensure accurate placement of product, and improve the accuracy of order picking and the rates of on-time shipment. In fact, many firms are relying on materials handling systems operated either partially, or in rare cases fully, by robots. For example, at office supply giant Staples, over 150 robots collect materials, process, and pack up to 8,000 orders daily.[16]

At Dell, the OptiPlex system runs the factory. The computer software receives orders, sends requests for parts to suppliers, orders components, organizes assembly of the product, and even arranges for it to be shipped. Thus, instead of hundreds of workers, often fewer than six are working at one time. An order for a few hundred computers can be filled in less than eight hours using the automated system. With the OptiPlex system, productivity has increased dramatically.

Transportation

Transportation typically accounts for 5 to 10 percent of the price of goods. Supply chain logisticians must decide which mode of transportation to use to move products from supplier to producer and from producer to buyer. These decisions are, of course, related to all other logistics decisions. The five major modes of transportation are railroads, motor carriers, pipelines, water transportation, and airways. Supply chain managers generally choose a mode of transportation on the basis of several criteria:

- *Cost:* The total amount a specific carrier charges to move the product from the point of origin to the destination

- *Transit time:* The total time a carrier has possession of goods, including the time required for pickup and delivery, handling, and movement between the point of origin and the destination
- *Reliability:* The consistency with which the carrier delivers goods on time and in acceptable condition
- *Capability:* The ability of the carrier to provide the appropriate equipment and conditions for moving specific kinds of goods, such as those that must be transported in a controlled environment (for example, under refrigeration)
- *Accessibility:* A carrier's ability to move goods over a specific route or network
- *Traceability:* The relative ease with which a shipment can be located and transferred

EXHIBIT 12.8

Criteria for Ranking Transportation Modes

	Highest				Lowest
Relative Cost	Air	Truck	Rail	Pipe	Water
Transit Time	Water	Rail	Pipe	Truck	Air
Reliability	Pipe	Truck	Rail	Air	Water
Capability	Water	Rail	Truck	Air	Pipe
Accessibility	Truck	Rail	Air	Water	Pipe
Traceability	Air	Truck	Rail	Water	Pipe

The mode of transportation used depends on the needs of the shipper, as they relate to these six criteria. Exhibit 12.8 compares the basic modes of transportation on these criteria.

The importance of transportation to modern companies is difficult to overstate. Many industry experts regard on-time delivery and shipment of products as the single most important supply chain management criteria leading to customer satisfaction. This perspective is reflected in companies' investment in transportation management systems—software applications designed to optimize transportation modes' routing, loading, unloading, and other functions. U.S. firms are expected to spend between $500 and $800 million annually on specialized transportation management software by 2011.[17]

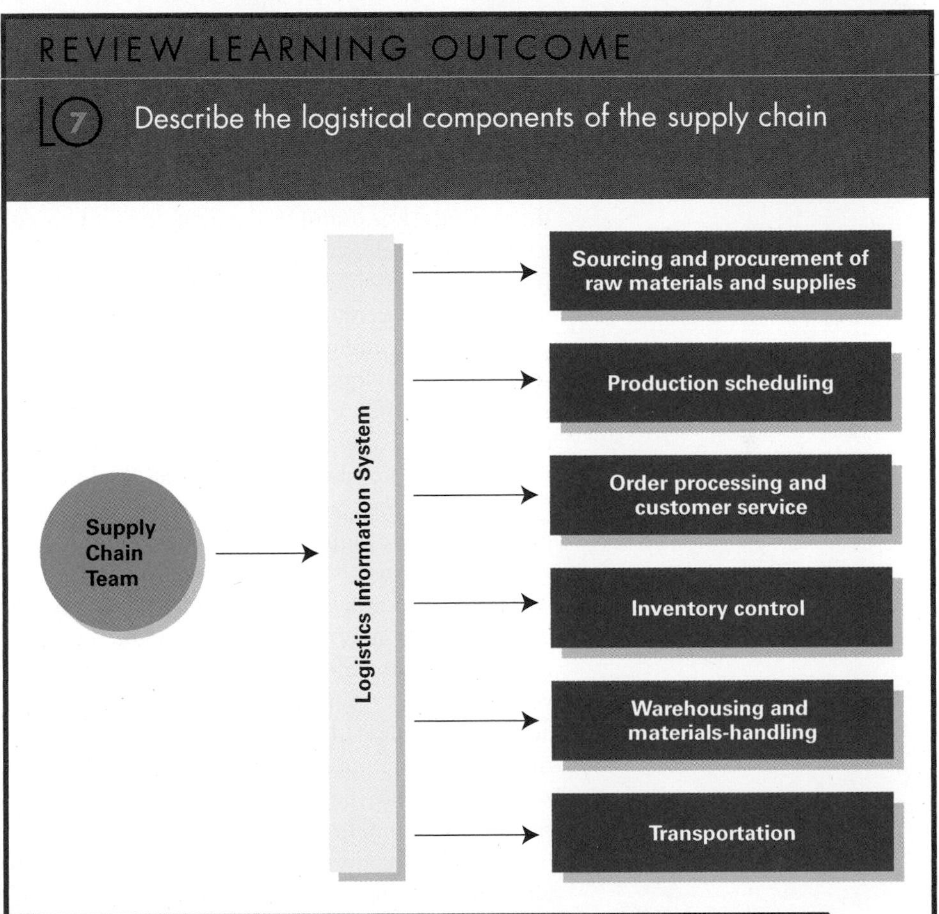

TRENDS IN SUPPLY CHAIN MANAGEMENT

Several technological advances and business trends are affecting the job of the supply chain manager today. Four of the most important trends are the globalization of supply chain management, advanced computer technology, outsourcing of logistics functions, and electronic distribution.

The multitude of global trade rules is why multinational companies like Eastman Kodak are so committed to working through the World Trade Organization to develop a global set of rules and to encourage countries to participate.

© VICKI BEAVER

Global Supply Chain Management

As global trade becomes a more decisive factor in success or failure for firms of all sizes, global supply chain management increases in importance. For example, one supply chain management consultant reported cost savings of 20 to 40 percent on finished goods imported from China versus their American counterparts.[18] In addition to savings, another supply chain research team estimated the output of the global economy will grow at a rate of 3 percent or more until the year 2030, with much of the growth occurring outside the United States, and thereby increasing the U.S. import base.[19] Thus, one of the most critical global supply chain issues for importers of any size is coping with the legalities of trade in other countries. Companies must be aware of the permits, licenses, and registrations they may need to acquire and, depending on the type of product they are importing, the tariffs, quotas, and other regulations that apply in each country. This multitude of different rules is why multinational companies like Eastman Kodak are so committed to working through the World Trade Organization to develop a global set of rules and to encourage countries to participate. Other goals for these companies include reducing trade barriers, such as tariffs. As these barriers fall, the flow of merchandise across borders is increasing due to more companies sourcing from multiple countries. For instance, a Kodak camera sold in France may have been assembled there, but the camera mechanism probably came from China and the film from the United States.

The presence of different rules hasn't slowed the spread of supply chain globalization, however. In spite of the added costs associated with importing and exporting goods, many companies are looking to other countries for their sourcing and procurement needs. For example, Applica, Inc., a U.S. maker of small appliances, is committed to using technology to improve its relationships with suppliers in Mexico. The company has linked its suppliers directly to sales data from Wal-Mart stores to help manage production and inventory costs. In another case, U.S. soap producers faced with increased prices for a key ingredient due to new government legislation were forced to look for substitutes in Indonesia and Malaysia in order to remain profitable.[20]

Transportation can also be a major issue for companies dealing with global supply chains. Uncertainty regarding shipping usually tops the list of reasons why companies, especially smaller ones, resist international markets. Even companies that have scored overseas successes often are vulnerable to logistical problems. Large companies have the capital to create global logistics systems, but smaller companies often must rely on the services of carriers and freight forwarders to get their products to overseas markets.

In some instances, poor infrastructure makes transportation dangerous and unreliable. And the process of moving goods across the borders of even the most industrialized nations can still be complicated by government regulations. For example, NAFTA was supposed to improve the flow of goods across the continent, but moving goods across the border still requires approvals from dozens of government agencies, broker intervention, and hours spent at border checks. Shipping companies like Ryder are working to make the process easier. Currently, Ryder operates a cross-border facility in San Antonio to help clients like General Motors and Xerox with customs and logistics costs. The company also is part of a pilot project to automate border crossings with technology similar to that of an E-Zpass. The new system sends and receives short-range radio signals containing information on the load to tollbooths, weigh stations, and border crossings. If the cargo meets requirements, the truck or train receives a green light to go ahead. Questionable cargo is set aside for further inspection. Transportation industry experts say the system can reduce delivery times by hours.

Advanced Computer Technology

Advanced computer technology has boosted the efficiency of logistics dramatically with tools such as automatic identification systems (auto ID) using bar coding and radio-frequency technology, communications technology, and supply chain software systems that help synchronize the flow of goods and information with customer demand. Amazon.com's state-of-the-art distribution centers, for instance, use sophisticated order picking systems that utilize computer terminals to guide workers through the picking and packing process. Radio-frequency technology, which uses radio signals that work with scanned bar codes to identify products, directs Amazon's workers to the exact locations in the warehouse where the product is stored. Warehouse management software examines pick rates, location, and picking and storage patterns, and builds combinations of customer orders for shipping. After installing these supply chain technology tools, Amazon saw a 70 percent improvement in operational efficiency.

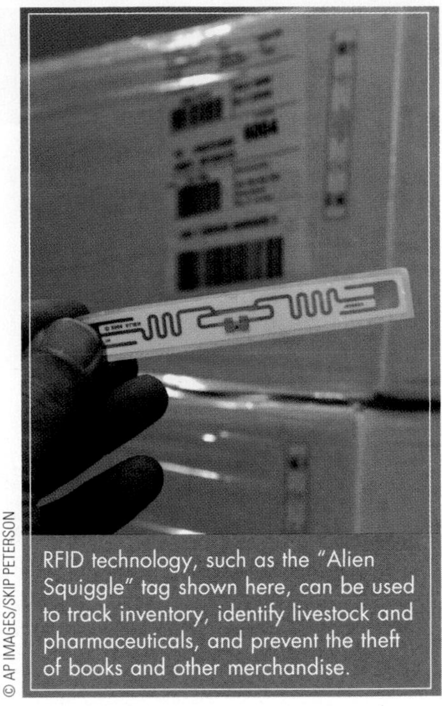
© AP IMAGES/SKIP PETERSON

RFID technology, such as the "Alien Squiggle" tag shown here, can be used to track inventory, identify livestock and pharmaceuticals, and prevent the theft of books and other merchandise.

Procter & Gamble and many other companies use RFID tags in shipments to Wal-Mart stores. RFID tags are chips attached to a pallet of goods that allow the goods to be tracked from the time they are packed at the manufacturing plant until the consumer purchases them. Benefits include increased revenue for Wal-Mart (because the shelves are always full) and reduced inventory management costs (because overstocking and time spent counting items is minimized). Best Buy is currently planning to use an RFID-enabled payment system to reduce and eventually eliminate checkout lines at the front of the store—customers with a personalized Best Buy RFID shopping card could simply load up their carts and walk out the front door, with their checking or credit card account debited for the price of their merchandise before they even unlock their car.[21] However, RFID has been slower than expected in penetrating the retail sector. While 44 percent of manufacturers have adopted RFID at some level, only about 10 percent of retailers have done so.[22] Though some experts attribute the slowness of retail adoption of RFID to its complexity of implementation, many others suggest that retailers are scared away because of difficulty in determining their return on RFID-related investment.

One of the other major goals of technology is to bring up-to-date information to the supply chain manager's desk. The transportation system has long been referred to as an informational "black hole," where products and materials fall out of sight until they reappear some time later in a plant, store, or warehouse. Now carriers have systems that track freight, monitor the speed and location of carriers, and make routing decisions on the spur of the moment. Roadway Express, named one of the "Top 100 U.S. Motor Carriers" by Inbound Logistics, handles more than 70,000 shipments a day, many for large retailers like Wal-Mart, Target, and Home Depot. Information technology systems enable each package to be tracked from the minute it is received at one of Roadway's terminals until it is delivered. Customers can check on the progress of their shipment anytime by logging on to Roadway's Web site and entering the tracking number. Companies needing trucking services can go to the Inbound Logistics Web site and use their Trucking Decision Support Tool to identify motor carriers that can meet their service needs.[23] Swedish-based communications giant Ericsson, whose operations span the globe, uses specialized supply chain software to gain visibility over the 50,000 outbound shipments it makes a year. As products leave its manufacturing facilities, transportation providers transmit status information at specified intervals to Ericsson's information system, which is accessible to management using a standard Web browser. The company has benefited greatly from the increased visibility of shipments the system has provided. Ericsson's management is now in a position to identify bottlenecks and respond before a crisis occurs, as well as measure the performance of its supply chain at different checkpoints.

Outsourcing Logistics Functions

External partners are becoming increasingly important in the efficient deployment of supply chain management. **Outsourcing, or contract logistics,** is a rapidly growing segment of the distribution industry in which a manufacturer or supplier turns over an entire function of the logistics system, such as buying and managing transportation or warehousing, to an independent third party. Many manufacturers are turning to outside

outsourcing (contract logistics)
A manufacturer's or supplier's use of an independent third party to manage an entire function of the logistics system, such as transportation, warehousing, or order processing.

UPS offers more services than its hallmark package delivery. In fact, UPS helps companies open new global supply chains, manage raw material, and add distribution channels. To find out more, visit www.ups.com/supplychain.

partners for their logistics expertise in an effort to focus on the core competencies that they do best. Partners create and manage entire solutions for getting products where they need to be, when they need to be there. Logistics partners offer staff, an infrastructure, and services that reach consumers virtually anywhere in the world. Because a logistics provider is focused, clients receive service in a timely, efficient manner, thereby increasing customers' level of satisfaction and boosting their perception of added value to a company's offerings.

Third-party contract logistics allows companies to cut inventories, locate stock at fewer plants and distribution centers, and still provide the same or increased level of service. The companies then can refocus investment on their core business. Ford Motor Company uses third-party logistics provider UPS Worldwide Logistics Group to manage the delivery of Ford and Lincoln cars and trucks in the United States, Canada, and Mexico. The alliance between Ford and UPS has substantially reduced the time it takes to move vehicles from Ford's assembly plants to dealers and customers. Moreover, the Web-based system enables Ford and its dealers to track an individual vehicle's location from production through delivery to the final destination. Similarly, in the hospitality industry, procurement services company Avendra enables Fairmont Hotels & Resorts, Hyatt Hotels, Intercontinental Hotels Group, Marriott International, and others to enjoy significant savings and value-added supply chain services.[24] Avendra negotiates with suppliers to obtain virtually everything a hotel might need, from food and beverages to golf course maintenance. By relying on Avendra to manage many aspects of the supply chain, the hotels are able to concentrate on their core function—providing hospitality.

electronic distribution
A distribution technique that includes any kind of product or service that can be distributed electronically, whether over traditional forms such as fiber-optic cable or through satellite transmission of electronic signals.

Many firms are taking outsourcing one step further by allowing business partners to take over the final assembly of their product or its packaging in an effort to reduce inventory costs, speed up delivery, or better meet customer requirements. Ryder Truck Lines assembles and packages 22 different combinations of shrink-wrapped boxes that contain the ice trays, drawers, shelves, doors, and other accessories for the various refrigerator models Whirlpool sells. Similarly, outsourcing firm StarTek, Inc. packages and ships products for Microsoft, provides technical support to customers of America Online, and maintains AT&T communication systems.

Electronic Distribution

Electronic distribution is the most recent development in the logistics arena. Broadly defined, **electronic distribution** includes any kind of product or service that can be distributed electronically, whether over traditional forms such as fiber-optic cable or through satellite transmission of electronic signals. For instance, instead of buying and installing software from stores, computer users purchase and download software over the Internet or rent the same software from Internet services that have the program available for use on their servers. For example, Intuit, Inc., allows people to fill out their tax returns on its Web site for a fee rather than buying its TurboTax software. Consumers can purchase tickets to sporting events, concerts, and movies over the Internet and print the tickets at home. And music, television shows, and movies have long been delivered to consumers through electronic pipelines. Apple sells over 20 million songs and TV shows annually through iTunes.[25]

One of the most innovative electronic distribution ventures of late has come from ESPN. The sports broadcaster offers free access on the iPhone to the most comprehensive sports coverage available in a mobile format. Using an iPhone App, ESPN Mobile Web broadcasts a multimedia-rich sports information package unlike anything else, including breaking news and analysis, up-to-the-minute scores, ESPN Fantasy teams, ESPN columnists, the ESPN Podcenter, and more. There's also a special section where users can select to receive news and stats about their favorite players and teams.[26]

Supply Chain Security

Firms are expending more effort on securing their supply chains from external threats than at any time in recent memory. Natural disasters, widespread technology failures, political instability, terrorism, disease pandemics, and worker strikes are but a few of the major events that can cause a supply chain to shut down temporarily or for an extended amount of time. The supply chain must be guarded from end to end because it is only as strong as its weakest link.

Managing supply chain disruptions begins with identifying the risks potentially affecting each node and link in the supply chain network.[27] This is especially true when the supply chain is global, with nodes and links located in or across international boundaries. Global supply chains are particularly at risk because members in faraway places often fail to completely understand the political, legal, and technological culture of the local area. Once risks are identified and assessed, the firm should put controls in place to monitor dangerous or volatile situations, and buy insurance when it appears that things could go wrong in the supply chain. The very best supply chains with respect to security also build contingency plans that are able to address situations quickly in the event of an emergency and get the supply chain back online. In fact, some businesses have completely replicated their systems and facilities in different geographic locations and, in the event of a disaster, can activate these backups within 24 hours.

Green Supply Chain Management

In response to the need for firms to both gain cost savings and act as leaders in protecting the natural environment, many are adopting green supply chain management principles as a key part of their supply chain strategy. Green supply chain management involves the integration of environmentally conscious thinking into all phases of key supply chain management processes. Such activities include green materials sourcing, the design of products with consideration given to their environmental impact based on packaging, shipment and use, as well as end-of-life management for products including easy recycling and/or clean disposal. By enacting green supply chain management principles, firms hope to simultaneously generate cost savings and protect our natural resources from excess pollution, damage, and/or wastefulness.

A number of relatively simple changes to typical supply chain management processes can achieve significant positive environmental impacts.

REVIEW LEARNING OUTCOME

LO 8 Discuss the new and emerging trends in supply chain management

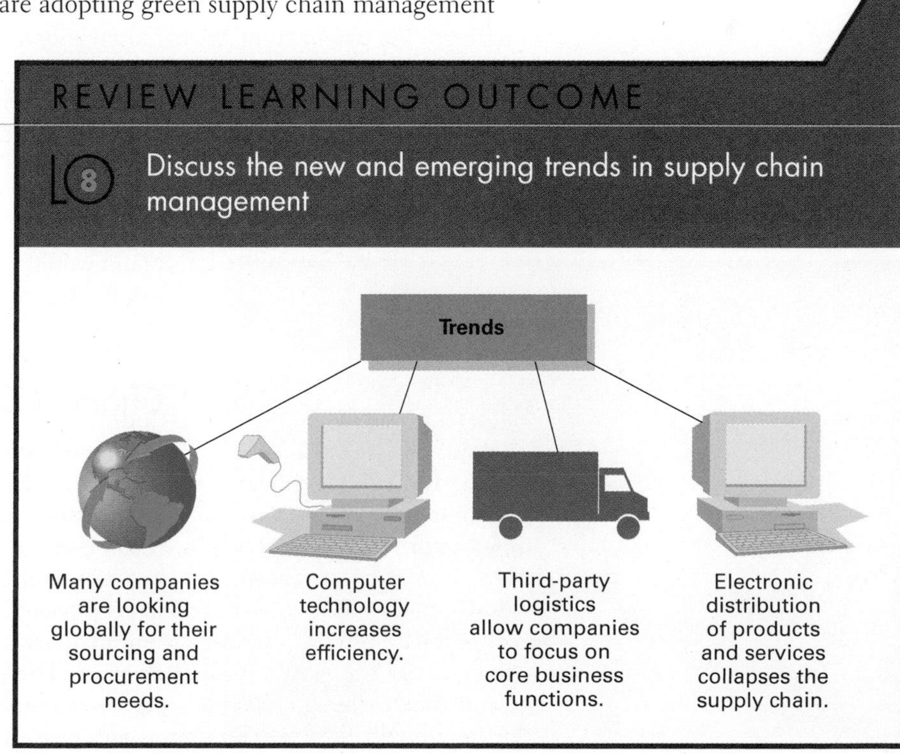

channel power
The capacity of a particular marketing channel member to control or influence the behavior of other channel members.

channel control
A situation that occurs when one marketing channel member intentionally affects another member's behavior.

channel leader (channel captain)
A member of a marketing channel that exercises authority and power over the activities of other channel members.

channel conflict
A clash of goals and methods between distribution channel members.

Trucks can switch to alternative fuels on long routes; drivers can be retrained and routes revised to limit the amount of time trucks sit idling; excess materials from manufacturing and staff processes can be recycled, composted, or avoided altogether; and reusable shipping containers and pallets introduced into the supply chain.[28] Though these activities may seem costly at first, many firms are recognizing the long term benefits. Whereas the common assumption among supply chain managers used to be that greening the supply chain would increase costs, many companies are realizing that environmentally conscious supply chain management can increase profits. General Motors, for example, increased profitability by over $12 million annually by switching to reusable containers when receiving shipments from their suppliers.[29]

LO 9

MANAGING CHANNEL RELATIONSHIPS

In addition to considering the multiple different types of channel relationships and their costs and benefits, managers must also be aware of the social dimensions that are constantly impacting their relationships. The basic social dimensions of channels are power, control, leadership, conflict, and partnering.

Channel Power, Control, and Leadership

Channel power is a channel member's ability to control or influence the behavior of other channel members. **Channel control** occurs when one channel member's power affects another member's behavior. To achieve control, a channel member assumes channel leadership and exercises authority and power. This member is termed the **channel leader**, or **channel captain**. In one marketing channel, a manufacturer may be the leader because it controls new-product designs and product availability. In another, a retailer may be the channel leader because it wields power and control over the retail price, inventory levels, and postsale service.

The exercise of channel power is a routine element of many business activities in which the outcome is often greater control over a company's brands. For example, the Sheraton Hotel chain operates hundreds of hotels across North America and worldwide, most of which are owned by franchisees. As with many franchises, it is in the best interest of the parent company to closely monitor and control operations to prevent the brand name from being devalued. However, when the chain asked its franchisees to invest nearly $4 billion of their own money to make improvements (such as redesigned lobbies and bathrooms) to keep the brand name from weakening, many owners balked and a power struggle ensued. Eventually, the parent company and ownership group came to an agreement detailing the hotel features Sheraton would control, such as lobby design, room layout, and even which coffee brand would be provided in the rooms, and which would be controlled by the owners (including the number of sheets provided on each bed).[30]

© SUSAN VAN ETTEN

Channel Conflict

Inequitable channel relationships often lead to **channel conflict**, which is a clash of goals and methods among the members of a distribution channel. In a broad context, conflict may not be bad. Often it arises because staid, traditional channel members refuse to keep pace with the times. Removing an outdated intermediary may result in reduced costs for the entire channel. The Internet has forced many intermediaries to offer services such as merchandise tracking and inventory availability online.

Conflicts among channel members can be due to many different situations and factors. Oftentimes, conflict arises because channel members have conflicting goals. For instance, athletic footwear retailers want to sell as many shoes as possible in order to maximize profits, regardless of whether the shoe is manufactured by Nike, Adidas, or Saucony, but the Nike manufacturer wants a certain sales volume and market share in each market.

Conflict can also arise when channel members fail to fulfill expectations of other channel members—for example, when a franchisee does not follow the rules set down by the franchisor or when communications channels break down between channel members. As another example, if a manufacturer shortens the period of warranty coverage and fails to inform dealers of this change, conflict may occur when dealers make repairs expecting that they will be reimbursed by the manufacturer. Further, ideological differences and different perceptions of reality can also cause conflict among channel members. For instance, retailers may believe "the customer is always right" and offer a very liberal return policy. Wholesalers and manufacturers may feel that people "try to get something for nothing" or don't follow product instructions carefully. Their differing views of allowable returns will undoubtedly conflict with those of retailers.

Conflict within a channel can be either horizontal or vertical. **Horizontal conflict** occurs among channel members on the same level, such as two or more different wholesalers or two or more different retailers that handle the same manufacturer's brands. This type of channel conflict is found most often when manufacturers practice dual or multiple distribution strategies. When Apple changed its distribution strategy and began opening its own stores, it angered Apple's traditional retail partners, some of whom ultimately filed lawsuits against the company. The primary allegation was that Apple stores were competing unfairly with them and that Apple favored its own stores when allocating desirable inventory (like iPods). Horizontal conflict can also occur when some channel members feel that other members on the same level are being treated differently by the manufacturer. For example, the American Booksellers Association, a group representing small independent booksellers, filed a lawsuit against bookstore giants Barnes & Noble and Borders, claiming they had violated antitrust laws by using their buying power to demand "illegal and secret" discounts from publishers. These deals, the association contended, put independent booksellers at a serious competitive disadvantage.

Many marketers and customers regard horizontal conflict as healthy competition. Much more serious is **vertical conflict**, which occurs between different levels in a marketing channel, most typically between the manufacturer and wholesaler or the manufacturer and retailer. Producer-versus-wholesaler conflict occurs when the producer chooses to bypass the wholesaler and deal directly with the consumer or retailer.

Dual distribution strategies can also cause vertical conflict in the channel. For example, high-end fashion designers traditionally sold their products through luxury retailers such as Neiman Marcus and Saks Fifth Avenue. Interested in increasing sales and gaining additional control over presentation, many designers such as Giorgio Armani, Donna Karan, and Louis Vuitton opened their own boutiques in the same shopping centers anchored by the luxury retailers. As a result, the retailers lost substantial revenues on the designers' items. Similarly, manufacturers experimenting with selling to customers directly over the Internet create conflict with their traditional retailing intermediaries. For example, Walgreens sells about 2 billion photo prints a year, all of which once were printed on Kodak paper using Kodak chemicals. When Kodak launched **KodakGallery.com**, a site where customers could upload digital prints to the Internet, view them, and order prints directly from Kodak, Walgreens took exception. It installed 2,300 traditional and digital photo kiosks made by Fuji, Kodak's main competitor.[31] The channel conflict cost Kodak an estimated $500 million a year in sales. In another case, Hollywood Studios petitioned federal regulators to allow them to release first-run movies over special cable and satellite channels in order to reduce the negative effects of movie piracy. Though the government has not yet ruled whether Hollywood's strategy will be allowed, the measure is being strongly opposed by DVD rental companies currently holding agreements with Hollywood, who would likely

horizontal conflict
A channel conflict that occurs among channel members on the same level.

vertical conflict
A channel conflict that occurs between different levels in a marketing channel, most typically between the manufacturer and wholesaler or between the manufacturer and retailer.

channel partnering (channel cooperation)
The joint effort of all channel members to create a channel that serves customers and creates a competitive advantage.

experience major sales losses if such first-run movies could be broadcast directly into homes rather than rented from their retail outlets.[32]

Producers and retailers may also disagree over the terms of the sale or other aspects of the business relationship. When Procter & Gamble introduced "everyday low pricing" to its retail channel members, a strategy designed to standardize wholesale prices and eliminate most trade promotions, many retailers retaliated. Some cut the variety of P&G sizes they carried or eliminated marginal brands. Others moved P&G brands from prime shelf space to less visible shelves.

Channel Partnering

Regardless of the locus of power, channel members rely heavily on one another. Even the most powerful manufacturers depend on dealers to sell their products; even the most powerful retailers require the products provided by suppliers. In sharp contrast to the adversarial relationships of the past between buyers and sellers, contemporary management thought emphasizes the development of close working partnerships among channel members. **Channel partnering**, or **channel cooperation**, is the joint effort of all channel members to create a channel that serves customers and creates a competitive advantage. Channel partnering is vital if each member is to gain something from other members. By cooperating, retailers, wholesalers, manufacturers, and suppliers can speed up inventory replenishment, improve customer service, and reduce the total costs of the marketing channel.

ETHICS in Marketing

Willbros Petroleum's Bribery Problem in Nigeria

As national economies become increasingly globalized, Western businesspeople are struggling with how to deal with local business corruption. Bribes, kickbacks, and under-the-table payments to both local channel partners and government officials are considered to be just "part of the cost of doing business" in many emerging nations. Though American law clearly makes such practices illegal, U.S. firms wanting to do business in places such as China, Russia, and Eastern Europe are increasingly finding they must develop tactics to address corrupt practices if they expect to succeed when developing these marketplaces.

Though many different types of corrupt activities are taking place, bribery is particularly problematic for American businesses doing business in foreign markets. For example, though Houston-based company Willbros had been working in Nigeria for nearly a half century, it was recently caught up in a bribery scandal that resulted in government allegations the firm had violated the Foreign Corrupt Practices Act (FCPA). The FCPA is a U.S. law that prohibits engaging in illicit business dealings both at home and abroad. In order to win more business, Willbros officials paid over $6 million to members of a government-run supplier consortium, with the result being their selection to build a $387 million natural gas pipeline, using those suppliers as partners throughout the project. The Willbros top management team was later blackmailed for an additional $1.5 million in payments in order to maintain the contract.

Willbros acknowledged as part of a plea for reduced punishment that members of its leadership team owned portions of some of Willbros' Nigerian customers and suppliers, and may have received illegal payments related to deals made with these companies and government officials. The results were predictable: The company was prosecuted by the U.S. Securities and Exchange Commission, and its leaders scrambled to cooperate with investigators in an attempt to avoid jail time. Yet, while Willbros was made an example of what can happen to U.S. businesses that participate in shady deals overseas, the problem of bribery remains one that continues to vex American companies wanting to expand their operations to new markets.

When attempting to increase business by entering emerging markets, how should U.S. companies handle local corruption by suppliers or governments? Should they "do as the Romans do" and risk prosecution at home, or attempt to impose Western values on foreign business cultures, and risk failure in entering the new marketplace? Payments to suppliers, bribes, money laundering, and kickback schemes are commonplace in many nations; how should a U.S. firm cope?[33]

Channel alliances and partnerships help managers create the parallel flow of materials and information required to leverage the channel's intellectual, material, and marketing resources. The rapid growth in channel partnering is due to new enabling technology and the need to lower costs. A comparison between companies that approach the marketplace unilaterally and those that engage in channel cooperation and form partnerships is detailed in Exhibit 12.9.

Collaborating channel partners meet the needs of consumers more effectively by ensuring that the right products are available at the right time and for a lower cost, thus boosting sales and profits. Forced to become more efficient, many companies are turning formerly adversarial relationships into partnerships. For example, Kraft is the largest coffee purchaser in the world. Rather than clash with coffee bean growers, Kraft partners with them to help build customer demand and develop "sustainable" coffee production (growing coffee in a way that reduces the impact on the environment, provides higher-quality ingredients for manufacturers to meet consumer needs, and is more valuable to the farmer).

EXHIBIT 12.9

Transaction-Based versus Partnership-Based Firms

Intensity Level	Transaction-Based	Partnership-Based
Relationships between Manufacturer and Supplier	• Short-term • Adversarial • Independent • Price more important	• Long-term • Cooperative • Dependent • Value-added services more important
Number of Suppliers	Many	Few
Level of Information Sharing	Minimal	High
Investment Required	Minimal	High

Source: David Frederick Ross, *Competing Through Supply Chain Management: Creating Market-Winning Strategies through Supply Chain Partnerships* (New York: Chapman & Hall, 1998), 61. Reprinted with kind permission from Springer Science and Business Media.

CHANNELS AND DISTRIBUTION DECISIONS FOR GLOBAL MARKETS

With the spread of free-trade agreements and treaties in recent decades, such as the European Union and the North American Free Trade Agreement (NAFTA), global marketing channels and management of the channels have become increasingly important to U.S. companies that export their products or manufacture abroad.

Developing Global Marketing Channels

Executives should recognize the unique cultural, economic, institutional, and legal aspects of each market before trying to design marketing channels in foreign countries. Manufacturers introducing products in global markets face a tough decision: what type of channel structure to use. Specifically, should the product be marketed directly, mostly by company salespeople, or through independent foreign intermediaries, such as agents and distributors? Using company salespeople generally provides more control and is less risky than using foreign intermediaries. However, setting up a sales force in a foreign country also entails a greater commitment, both financially and organizationally.

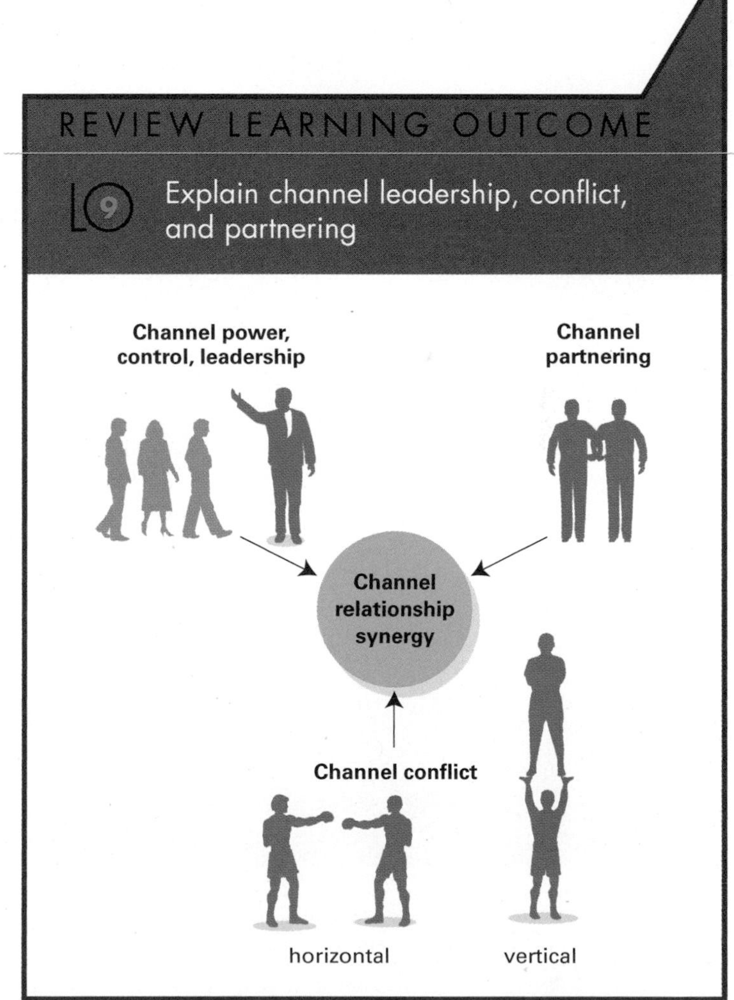

© AP IMAGES/NG HAN GUAN

Marketers should be aware that channel structures and types abroad may differ from those in the United States. For instance, the more highly developed a nation is economically, the more specialized its channel types. Therefore, a marketer wishing to sell in Germany or Japan will have several channel types to choose from. Conversely, developing countries such as India, Ethiopia, and Venezuela have limited channel types available—there are typically few mail-order channels, vending machines, or specialized retailers and wholesalers. Some countries also regulate channel choices. Until 2004, Chinese regulations required foreign retailers to have a local partner. So when IKEA, the Swedish home furnishings retailer, opened its first two stores in China, it used joint ventures. When the regulations were lifted, however, IKEA opened its first wholly owned store in Guangzhou and then a Beijing store that is almost as big as eight football fields, second in size only to the company's flagship store in Stockholm.[34]

Developing effective marketing channels in emerging nations is further complicated due to different retail format preferences and differences in the ways locals shop. In many emerging nations, consumers shun large-scale formats popularized in the United States and Western Europe such as supercenter and other big-box retailers, in favor of tiny, independently owned street-side retailers that may be no larger than a closet. These small retailers (known at Procter & Gamble as "high frequency shops") provide small packages of goods that are intended to fulfill customer needs only for a day or two. Procter & Gamble estimates that over 620,000 such stores exist in Mexico alone, and that 80 percent of emerging nation citizens shop high-frequency stores multiple times per week. New channel strategies are currently being developed by firms like P&G in order to maximize sales and penetration into high-frequency shops, including reliance on local sales agents who are paid to ensure that popular products are placed as close as possible to the street and/or cash register.[35]

Marketers must also be aware that many countries have "gray" marketing channels in which products are distributed through unauthorized channel intermediaries. It is estimated that sales of counterfeit luxury items like Prada handbags and Big Bertha golf clubs have reached almost $2 billion a year. The new fakes are harder to detect and hit the market almost instantly. For instance, a fake Christian Dior saddlebag was available just weeks after the original arrived on retailers' shelves. Similarly, Chinese companies are producing so many knockoffs of Yamaha, Honda, and Suzuki motorcycles that the Japanese companies are seeing a drop in sales. What's more, many companies are getting so good at design piracy that they are beginning to launch their own new products.

The Internet has also proved to be a way for pirates to circumvent authorized distribution channels, especially in the case of popular prescription drugs. In recent years, the U.S. Customs Service has seized millions of dollars worth of prescription drugs, most of which were purchased from foreign Internet sites. Some were seized because they had not been approved for use in the United States, others because they did not comply with U.S. labeling laws. Most sites offer just a handful of the most popular drugs, such as Viagra. Consumers can get the drugs after obtaining the approval of a doctor, affiliated with the site, who never sees the patient.

REVIEW LEARNING OUTCOME

LO 10 Discuss channels and distribution decisions in global markets

- Distribute directly or through foreign partners
- Different channel structures than in domestic markets
- Illegitimate "gray" marketing channels
- Legal and infrastructure differences

CHANNELS AND DISTRIBUTION DECISIONS FOR SERVICES

The fastest-growing part of our economy is the service sector. Although distribution in the service sector is difficult to visualize, the same skills, techniques, and strategies used to manage inventory can also be used to manage service inventory—for instance, hospital beds, bank accounts, or airline seats. The quality of the planning and execution of distribution can have a major impact on costs and customer satisfaction.

One thing that sets service distribution apart from traditional manufacturing distribution is that, in a service environment, production and consumption are simultaneous. In manufacturing, a production setback can often be remedied by using safety stock or a faster mode of transportation. Such substitution is not possible with a service. The benefits of a service are also relatively intangible—that is, a consumer normally can't see the benefits of a service, such as a doctor's physical exam, but normally can see the benefits provided by a product—for example, cold medicine relieving a stuffy nose.

Because service industries are so customer-oriented, customer service is a priority. To manage customer relationships, many service providers, such as insurance carriers, physicians, hair salons, and financial services, use technology to schedule appointments, manage accounts, and disburse information. Service distribution focuses on three main areas:

- *Minimizing wait times:* Minimizing the amount of time customers wait in line to deposit a check, wait for their food at a restaurant, or wait in a doctor's office for an appointment is a key factor in maintaining the quality of service. People tend to overestimate the amount of time they spend waiting in line, researchers report, and unexplained waiting seems longer than explained waits. To reduce anxiety among waiting customers, some restaurants give patrons pagers that allow them to roam around or go to the bar. Banks sometimes install electronic boards displaying stock quotes or sports scores. Car rental companies reward repeat customers by eliminating their waits altogether. Airports have designed comfortable sitting areas with televisions and children's play areas for those waiting to board planes. Some service companies are using sophisticated technology to further ease their customers' waiting time. For example, many hotels and airlines are using electronic check-in kiosks. Travelers can insert their credit cards to check in upon arrival, receive their room key, get directions, print maps to area restaurants and attractions, and print out their hotel bills.
- *Managing service capacity:* For product manufacturers, inventory acts as a buffer, enabling them to provide the product during periods of peak demand without extraordinary efforts. Service firms don't have this luxury. If they don't have the capacity to meet demand, they must either turn down some prospective customers, let service levels slip, or expand capacity. For instance, at tax time a tax preparation firm may have so many customers desiring its services that it has to either turn business away or add temporary offices or preparers. Popular restaurants risk losing business when seating is unavailable or the wait is too long. To manage their capacity, travel Web sites allow users to find last-minute deals to fill up empty airline seats and hotel rooms.
- *Improving service delivery:* Like manufacturers, service firms are now experimenting with different distribution channels for their services. Choosing the right distribution channel can increase the times that services are available (such as using the Internet to disseminate information and services 24-7) or add to customer

GEICO's early business model—a first in the insurance industry—involved direct marketing to targeted customers without the use of agents. In its early years, GEICO contacted its customers by mail and telephone, but now it offers online service 24 hours a day, seven days a week.

REVIEW LEARNING OUTCOME

LO 11 Identify the special problems and opportunities associated with distribution in service organizations

Minimizing wait times is a key factor in maintaining service quality.

Managing service capability is critical to successful service distribution.

Improving service delivery makes it easier and more convenient for consumers to use the service.

convenience (like pizza delivery, walk-in medical clinics, or a dry cleaner located in a supermarket). The airline industry has found that using the Internet for ticket sales both reduces distribution costs and raises the level of customer service by making it easier for customers to plan their own travel. Cruise lines, on the other hand, have found that travel agents add value by helping customers sort through the abundance of information and complicated options available when booking a cruise. In the real estate industry, realtors are placing kiosks in local malls that enable consumers to directly access listings.

The Internet is quickly becoming an alternative channel for delivering services. Consumers can now purchase plane tickets, reserve a hotel room, pay bills, purchase mutual funds, and receive electronic newspapers in cyberspace. Insurance giant Allstate, for instance, now sells auto and home insurance directly to consumers in some states through the Internet in addition to its traditional network of agents. The effort reduces costs so that Allstate can stay competitive with rival insurance companies Progressive and GEICO that already target customers directly. Similarly, several real estate Web sites are making it easier for customers to shop for a new home on the Web. Traditionally, the only way for customers to gain access to realtors' listings was to work through a real estate agent, who would search the listings and then show customers' homes that met their requirements. The new companies offer direct access to the listings, enabling customers to review properties for sale on their own and choose which ones they would like to visit.

17 ◀ major retailers in the Worldwide Retail Exchange

percentage of purchasing costs saved by using the exchange ▶ **15**

3,000 ◀ Dollar Tree Stores

Dollar Tree distribution centers ▶ **9**

copies of *Harry Potter and the Deathly Hallows* mistakenly released early ▶ **1,200**

2 billion ◀ photo prints sold by Walgreens each year

yearly profits Kodak lost to channel conflict with Walgreens ▶ **$500 million**

small "high frequency" stores in Mexico ▶ **620,000**

percentages of emerging nation citizens who shop in such stores multiple times each week ▶ **80**

ANATOMY OF A Marketing Channel

Electronics

Channel members facilitate the distribution process by providing specialization and division of labor, overcoming discrepancies, and providing contact efficiency.

Producer

© iStockphoto.com/Andreas Reh

Au GOLD | Sn TIN | Li LITHIUM

Materials used to make the components of electronic devices come from around the globe, for example, South America provides tin (solder), lithium (batteries), and gold (a/v cables).

Customers have the option of buying their computer supplies online through a direct channel with the manufacturer.

Distributor

COURTESY CHAPEL HOUSE PHOTOGRAPHY

Dual distribution: Consumers can buy directly from producers or through a retailer.

Wholesaler

© iStockphoto.com/tomczybartek

Wholesalers may transport and distribute products.

Electronics retailers (such as Best Buy) bridge the gap between companies and consumers.

Retailer

© COURTESY CHAPEL HOUSE PHOTOGRAPHY

Customer

© Image Source

REVIEW AND APPLICATIONS

Explain what a marketing channel is and why intermediaries are needed. A marketing channel is a business structure of interdependent organizations that reach from the point of product origin to the consumer with the purpose of physically moving products to their final consumption destination, representing "place" or "distribution" in the marketing mix, and encompassing the processes involved in getting the right product to the right place at the right time. Members of a marketing channel create a continuous and seamless system that performs or supports the marketing channel functions. Channel members provide economies to the distribution process in the form of specialization and division of labor; overcoming discrepancies in quantity, assortment, time, and space; and providing contact efficiency.

1.1 Your family runs a specialty ice cream parlor called Scoops. It manufactures its own ice cream in small batches and sells it only in pint-sized containers. After someone not affiliated with the company sent six pints of its ice cream to a popular talk-show host, she proclaimed on her national TV show that it was the best ice cream she had ever eaten. Immediately after the broadcast, orders came flooding in, overwhelming your small-batch production schedule and your limited distribution system. The company's shipping manager thinks she can handle it, but you disagree. List the reasons why you need to restructure your channel of distribution.

Define the types of channel intermediaries and describe their functions and activities. The most prominent difference separating intermediaries is whether they take title to the product. Retailers and merchant wholesalers take title, but agents and brokers do not. Retailers are firms that sell mainly to consumers. Merchant wholesalers are organizations that facilitate the movement of products and services from the manufacturer to producers, resellers, governments, institutions, and retailers. Agents and brokers do not take title to the goods and services they market, but they do facilitate the exchange of ownership between sellers and buyers. Channel intermediaries perform three basic types of functions. Transactional functions include contacting and promoting, negotiating, and risk taking. Logistical functions performed by channel members include physical distribution, storing, and sorting functions. Finally, channel members may perform facilitating functions, such as researching and financing.

2.1 What kind of marketing channel functions can be performed over the Internet? Why do you think so?

Describe the channel structures for consumer and business products and discuss alternative channel arrangements. Marketing channels for consumer and business products vary in degree of complexity. The simplest consumer-product channel involves direct selling from producers to consumers. Businesses may sell directly to business or government buyers. Marketing channels grow more complex as intermediaries become involved. Consumer-product channel intermediaries include agents, brokers, wholesalers, and retailers. Business-product channel intermediaries include agents, brokers, and industrial distributors. Marketers often use alternative channel arrangements to move their products to the consumer. With dual distribution or multiple distribution, they choose two or more different channels to distribute the same product. Nontraditional channels help differentiate a firm's product from the competitor's or provide a manufacturer with another avenue for sales. Finally, strategic channel alliances are arrangements that use another manufacturer's already established channel.

3.1 Describe the most likely marketing channel structure for each of these consumer products: candy bars, Tupperware products, nonfiction books, new automobiles, farmers' market produce, and stereo equipment. Now, construct alternative channels for these same products.

3.2 You have been hired to design an alternative marketing channel for a firm specializing in the manufacturing and marketing of novelties for college student organizations. In a memo to the president of the firm, describe how the channel operates.

3.3 Building on question 1.1 determine a new channel structure for Scoops. Write a proposal to present to your key managers.

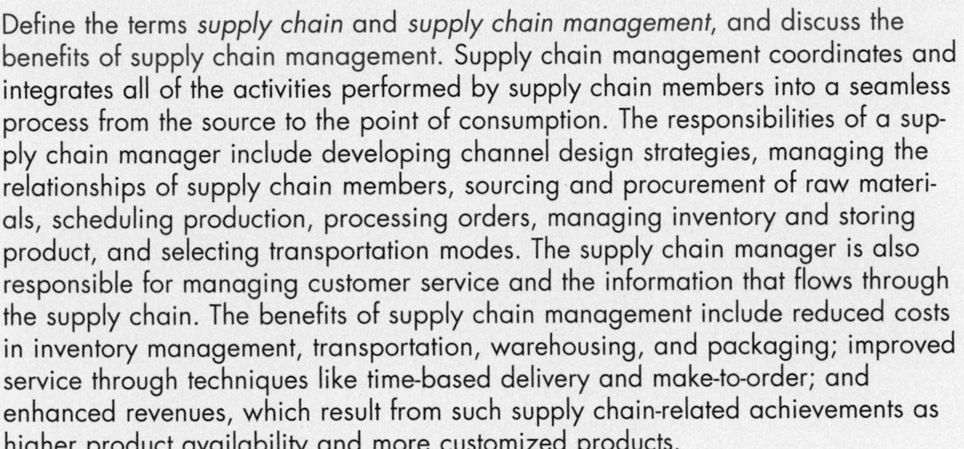

Define the terms *supply chain* and *supply chain management*, and discuss the benefits of supply chain management. Supply chain management coordinates and integrates all of the activities performed by supply chain members into a seamless process from the source to the point of consumption. The responsibilities of a supply chain manager include developing channel design strategies, managing the relationships of supply chain members, sourcing and procurement of raw materials, scheduling production, processing orders, managing inventory and storing product, and selecting transportation modes. The supply chain manager is also responsible for managing customer service and the information that flows through the supply chain. The benefits of supply chain management include reduced costs in inventory management, transportation, warehousing, and packaging; improved service through techniques like time-based delivery and make-to-order; and enhanced revenues, which result from such supply chain-related achievements as higher product availability and more customized products.

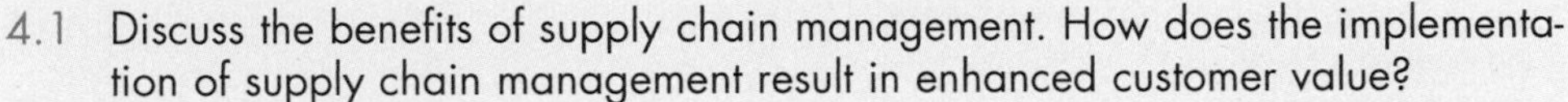

4.1 Discuss the benefits of supply chain management. How does the implementation of supply chain management result in enhanced customer value?

Discuss the issues that influence channel strategy. When determining marketing channel strategy, the channel manager must determine what market, product, and producer factors will influence the choice of channel. The manager must also determine the appropriate level of distribution intensity. Intensive distribution is distribution aimed at maximum market coverage. Selective distribution is achieved by screening dealers to eliminate all but a few in any single area. The most restrictive form of market coverage is exclusive distribution, which entails only one or a few dealers within a given area.

5.1 Decide which distribution intensity level—intensive, selective, or exclusive—is used for each of the following products, and explain why: Piaget watches, Land Rover sport-utility vehicles, M&Ms, special edition Barbie dolls, Crest toothpaste.

5.2 Now that you have a basic channel structure for Scoops (from question 3.3), form a team of three to four students and list the market, product, and producer factors that will affect your final channel structure.

Describe the different channel relationship types and their unique costs and benefits. Channel relationships can be plotted on a continuum ranging from Arm's-Length to integrated, with cooperative relationships somewhere in between. Arm's-Length relationships generally consist of unique transactions that are intended to occur once or very infrequently, and are pursued when closer relationships are undesirable or impractical. Although Arm's-Length relationships are low risk, they also provide few benefits in terms of favorable conditions for the agreement, and disputes are often resolved in court. Integrated relationships, on the opposite end of the spectrum, are very close relationships that are backed by formal agreements and can result in great efficiency and effectiveness. However, given that integrated relationships tend either to involve high levels of expense (in the case of vertical integration) or require enormous amounts of trust in the partner company (as in the case of supply chains), many companies prefer cooperative relationships in some settings. Cooperative relationships are a hybrid form of relationship that is governed by formal contract, are temporary, and are enforced by the agreement itself.

6.1 Working with another student in the class, decide when it would be most advantageous for large companies like Procter & Gamble, IBM, and/or Ford Motor Company to develop integrated relationships with smaller suppliers. Would the same rules for integrated relationship development also apply to customers? Why or why not?

Describe the logistical components of the supply chain. The logistics supply chain consists of several interrelated and integrated logistical components: (1) sourcing and procurement of raw materials and supplies, (2) production scheduling, (3) order processing, (4) inventory control, (5) warehousing and materials-handling, and (6) transportation. The logistics information system is the link connecting all of the logistics components of the supply chain. Information technology connects the various components and partners of the supply chain into an integrated whole. The supply chain team, in concert with the logistics information system, orchestrates the movement of goods, services, and information from the source to the consumer. Supply chain teams typically cut across organizational boundaries, embracing all parties who participate in moving product to market. Procurement deals with the purchase of raw materials, supplies, and components according to production scheduling. Order processing monitors the flow of goods and information (order entry and order handling). Inventory control systems regulate when and how much to buy (order timing and order quantity). Warehousing provides storage of goods until needed by the customer while the materials-handling system moves inventory into, within, and out of the warehouse. Finally, the major modes of transportation are railroads, motor carriers, pipelines, waterways, and airways.

7.1 Assume that you are the supply chain manager for a producer of expensive, high-tech computer components. Identify the most suitable method(s) of transporting your product in terms of cost, transit time, reliability, capability, accessibility, and traceability. Now, assume you are the supply chain manager for a producer of milk. How does this change your choice of transportation?

Discuss new technology and emerging trends in supply chain management. Several emerging trends are changing the job of today's supply chain manager. Technology and automation are bringing up-to-date distribution information to the decision maker's desk. Technology is also linking suppliers, buyers, and carriers for joint decision making, and it has created a new electronic distribution channel. Many companies are saving money and time by outsourcing third-party carriers to handle some or all aspects of the distribution process. Firms are taking major steps toward the goal of securing their supply chains from external threats.

8.1 Visit the Web site of Menlo Logistics at **www.menlolog.com.** What logistics functions can this third-party logistics supplier provide? How does its mission fit in with the supply chain management philosophy?

Explain channel leadership, conflict, power, and partnering. Power, control, leadership, conflict, and partnering are the main social dimensions of marketing channel relationships. Channel power refers to the capacity of one channel member to control or influence other channel members. Channel control occurs when one channel member intentionally affects another member's behavior. Channel leadership is the exercise of authority and power. Channel conflict occurs when there is a clash of goals and methods among the members of a distribution channel. Channel conflict can be either horizontal, between channel members at the same level, or vertical, between channel members at different levels of the channel. Channel partnering is the joint effort of all channel members to create an integrated system that serves customers and creates a competitive advantage. Collaborating channel partners meet the needs of consumers more effectively by ensuring that the right products reach shelves at the right time and at a lower cost, boosting sales and profits.

9.1 Procter & Gamble and Wal-Mart are key partners in a shared channel. P&G is one of Wal-Mart's biggest suppliers, and Wal-Mart provides extremely detailed scanner data about customer purchases of P&G products. Wal-Mart has begun selling its own brand of Sam's Choice laundry detergent in bright orange bottles alongside P&G's Tide, but for a greatly reduced price. What do you think will be the impact of this new product on what has been a stable channel relationship?

Discuss channels and distribution decisions in global markets. Global marketing channels are becoming more important to U.S. companies seeking growth abroad. Manufacturers introducing products in foreign countries must decide what type of channel structure to use—in particular, whether the product should be marketed through direct channels or through foreign intermediaries. Marketers should be aware that channel structures in foreign markets may be very different from those they are accustomed to in the United States. Global distribution expertise is also emerging as an important skill for channel managers as many countries are removing trade barriers.

10.1 Go to the World Trade Organization's Web site at **www.wto.org.** What can you learn at the site about how globalization affects channel management and other aspects of business?

Identify the special problems and opportunities associated with distribution in service organizations. Managers in service industries use the same skills, techniques, and strategies to manage logistics functions as managers in goods-producing industries. The distribution of services focuses on three main areas: minimizing wait times, managing service capacity, and improving service delivery.

11.1 Assume that you are the marketing manager of a hospital. Write a report indicating the distribution functions that concern you. Discuss the similarities and dissimilarities of distribution for services and for goods.

KEY TERMS

Term	Page
agents and brokers	392
Arm's-Length relationships	405
automatic replenishment program	409
channel conflict	416
channel control	416
channel leader (channel captain)	416
channel members	389
channel partnering (channel cooperation)	418
channel power	416
cooperative relationships	406
direct channel	395
discrepancy of assortment	391
discrepancy of quantity	390
distribution resource planning (DRP)	408
dual distribution (multiple distribution)	397
electronic data interchange (EDI)	408
electronic distribution	414
exclusive distribution	404
horizontal conflict	417
integrated relationships	405
intensive distribution	403

inventory control system	408
logistics	394
logistics information system	407
marketing channel (channel of distribution)	389
materials-handling system	410
materials requirement planning (MRP) (materials management)	408
merchant wholesaler	392
order processing system	407
outsourcing (contract logistics)	413
retailer	392
selective distribution	403
spatial discrepancy	391
strategic channel alliance	398
supply chain	399
supply chain management	399
supply chain team	407
temporal discrepancy	391
vertical conflict	417

EXERCISES

APPLICATION EXERCISE

It may be easy to understand how distribution channels work just from reading, but you may still not appreciate their broad scope. This exercise will help you see for yourself how complex a single distribution channel is. Then, when you think of the number of products and services available on the market at any one time, you will understand how tremendous the national (and international) distribution network actually is.[36]

Activities

1. Create a list of approximately 20 products that you often purchase for personal use and/or that are present in your home.
2. For each of the products you listed, speculate whether the product was routed through the marketing channel using (a) exclusive, (b) selective, or (c) intensive distribution.
3. Now, for each product/distribution strategy combination, speculate as to the product, market, or producer factors that lead to this distribution strategy.
4. Finally, identify any potential alternative distribution channel options through which you might have purchased this product. Would the alternative channel choice have changed the way (location, timing, price) you purchased this good? Why or why not?

ETHICS EXERCISE

Wholesome Snacks, Inc., the maker of a variety of cookies and crackers, has just created a new vitamin-packed cookie. The new cookie has the potential to combat many of the health problems caused by malnutrition in children throughout poverty-stricken areas of the world. To date, however, many of the larger developing markets have resisted opening distribution channels to Wholesome's products. Wholesome realizes that its new cookie could also help open the door for the company to sell its less nutritious products in these markets. Therefore, the company is offering the new cookie at a low cost to government relief programs in exchange for the long-sought distribution channels. The company feels the deal is good for business, but the countries feel it is corporate bullying.

Questions

1. What do you think about Wholesome's idea for opening a new distribution channel?
2. Does the AMA Statement of Ethics address this issue? Go to **www.marketingpower.com** and review the code. Then, write a brief paragraph stating what the AMA Statement of Ethics contains that relates to distribution channels in developing nations.

MARKETING PLAN EXERCISE

In Part 1 of your strategic marketing plan, you stated your business mission and objectives and performed a detailed SWOT analysis. In Part 2 of the plan, you identified and described target market segments, identified sources of competitive intelligence and the need for further marketing research. In Part 3, you began the process of defining the marketing mix, starting with the first component: product. The next stage of the strategic planning process continues defining the elements of the marketing mix, and this section focuses on place, or distribution. Use the following exercises to guide you through the distribution part of your strategic marketing plan.

1. Discuss the implications of dual/multiple distribution. If your chosen company sells through a major department store and its own catalog and then decides to have an online site or open its own store in a factory outlet, what will happen to channel relationships? To the final price offered to consumers? To promotional vehicles? Most e-marketers assume that a direct distribution channel, with no intermediaries, is the most efficient and least costly method for getting product offerings to customers. However, if you decide on a different distribution channel, you will also have to identify warehouses, fulfillment services, transportation firms, packing companies, and many other facilitating agencies. Does your company have the capabilities to handle this, or should your company invest in channel members to take over these tasks and functions?
2. Decide what channel(s) your company should be using. Describe the intermediaries involved and their likely behavior. What are the implications of these channels? Describe the conflict that might arise from having both an e-marketing offering as well as a brick-and-mortar offering. If distribution costs are different, will your company set the same or different prices for end customers?
3. Which distribution intensity level would be best for your company's product? Justify your decision.

CASE STUDY: CURRENT TV PLUGS INTO THE 'NET GENERATION

Ten years ago, the Internet began a revolution that has forever changed the way consumers shop for goods, send and receive mail, find and read news, and acquire and listen to music. A relatively new electronic distribution channel, the Web enables billions of near-instantaneous commercial, consumer, and information exchanges each day. And with the widespread dispersion of increasingly powerful and portable digital technologies, marketers are witnessing a new phenomenon—consumers devoting considerable time to archiving and sharing the personal events of their lives.

Tech-savvy members of Generations X and Y are photographing, recording, cataloging, uploading, blogging, hyperlinking, downloading, and sharing peer-to-peer files at an accelerating pace. Moreover, the independent Web sites where those opinions, files, and reports are located are becoming an increasingly valid means of staying connected with the world. Quite simply, this phenomenon is turning traditional media channels on their collective ear.

Few companies really comprehend that the digital technologies driving homemade reporting and entertainment productions are simultaneously increasing demand for them. One company that understands, and even anticipated, this trend is start-up cable channel Current TV. Cofounded, chaired, and shaped by the vision of former vice president Al Gore, and Joel Hyatt, Current predicted the relevance of do-it-yourself (DIY) media some time ago. Gore's objective, as stated on Current TV's Web site, is to democratize the production, distribution, and consumption of television.

Years ago Gore recognized that the proliferation of affordable digital technology would make it possible to create "a powerful new brand of television that doesn't treat audiences as merely viewers, but as collaborators." And those collaborations, fueled by viewer-created content (VCC), are powering the DIY media boom. Shari Anne Brill, vice president and director of programming at the Carat Group, an independent media agency, predicts that "Current will appeal to a much younger-skewing and very unique audience. It opens up tremendous avenues between Internet and television, and it's a very interesting way to reach out to viewers who want to participate in the viewing experience."

Current TV's Web site already hosts a menu of more than 50 "pods" containing program lists chosen for their appeal to independent spirits who have grown disenchanted with the staid format of mainstream television. Recent feature programs on Current TV have included a piece on a man who spends his free time jumping from cliffs and bridges, a first-person perspective on the rescue efforts in the aftermath of Hurricane Katrina, and an in-depth report on a San Francisco rock band produced by a local college student.

Most programs relate to current affairs, but other topics routinely covered include lifestyle themes such as art, fashion, culture, the environment, music, language, relationships, careers, travel, movies, and more. Regardless of subject, all Current TV programming has an intimate and unpretentious feel. Ever mindful of past pitfalls, Current is adamant that it will not devolve into a twenty-first century version of the public access fiascoes that gave VCC a bad name many years ago.

One third of Current's programming is viewer created. The company doesn't believe that will dissuade viewers as long as its professionally produced work has credibility, relevance, and appeal.The viewer-submitted content that is aired is also paid for, though it is repeated quite a bit, and watchers have the ability to vote for shows at Current TV's Web site.

What would enable Current to run more VCC? The answer, in a word, is access. At this time, Current distributes its programming to 40 million US homes in select metropolitan areas via Comcast, DirecTV, Time Warner, and Dish Network. It lacks support from the major cable and satellite companies that, together, feed popular stations to around 80 million homes. Current needs access to viewers in order to appeal to their creative alter egos and fuel the DIY cycle.

In an age when countless business models have seen explosive growth followed by a dramatic collapse, Current's approach and situation look promising. Its concept has recently been validated by MTV's purchase of independent, Web-based VCC site iFilm.com. MTV Networks Music Group president, Brian Graden, says that VCC "is obviously the next wave, and the purchase by Viacom of iFilm is probably the strongest statement that we're very much on to that. The more control you put of everything into the viewers' hands in this sort of multiplatform, on-demand age, that's the only way you're going to win."[37]

Questions

1. Explain Current TV's channel strategy. What factors influence it the most? Why?
2. Describe Current TV's channel arrangement. What role do the intermediaries play? What potential conflicts would you predict for Current?
3. Who are Current's channel partners? What do you think will be needed to sustain those relationships?

COMPANY CLIPS

©NKP MEDIA, INC./CENGAGE

SEPHORA—BUSINESS IS BEAUTIFUL

The beauty-retail store Sephora was founded in 1969 in France, and since then has become a leader in sales of heath and beauty-aid products. It opened its first store in the United States in 1998 on Fifth Avenue in New York City and prides itself on being ahead of the market in skin care trends. Its luxurious environment is the selling point for over 250 brands. On its shelves, Sephora maintains a balance of big brand names with lesser-known, up-and-coming brands. Sephora also carries its own private brand that it promotes independently in the store. Each sales representative in a Sephora store is trained to best help customers find the products that best fit their skin types and lifestyles. Watch the video to learn what techniques Sephora uses to keep its shelves stocked and customers happy.

Questions

1. Why is important to customers that Sephora keep detailed information about their inventory? What does Sephora do to insure their numbers are accurate?
2. How does Sephora manage its marketing channel? What information goes into deciding which suppliers become incorporated?

Marketing & You Results

A higher score indicates that you like to be a leader and use authority. Studies have linked authority to vanity, so a high score also suggests a high level of vanity. In particular, you have "achievement view vanity," which is strongly linked to authority. That means that you have very high opinions of your accomplishments and think that others consider you successful as well.

CHAPTER

13 Retailing

© SPENCER PLATT/GETTY IMAGES

- LO 1 Discuss the importance of retailing in the U.S. economy
- LO 2 Explain the dimensions by which retailers can be classified
- LO 3 Describe the major types of retail operations
- LO 4 Discuss nonstore retailing techniques
- LO 5 Define *franchising* and describe its two basic forms
- LO 6 List the major tasks involved in developing a retail marketing strategy
- LO 7 Describe new developments in retailing

LO 1

THE ROLE OF RETAILING

Retailing—all the activities directly related to the sale of goods and services to the ultimate consumer for personal, nonbusiness use—has enhanced the quality of our daily lives. When we shop for groceries, hairstyling, clothes, books, and many other products and services, we are involved in retailing. The millions of goods and services provided by retailers mirror the needs and styles of U.S. society.

Retailing affects all of us directly or indirectly. The retailing industry is one of the largest employers; over 1.6 million U.S. retailers employ more than 24 million people—about one in five American workers.[1] Retail trade accounts for 11.6 percent of all U.S. employment, and almost 13 percent of all businesses are considered retail under NAICS.[2] At the store level, retailing is still largely a mom-and-pop business. Almost nine out of ten retail companies employ fewer than 20 employees, and, according to the National Retail Federation, over 90 percent of all retailers operate just one store.[3]

The U.S. economy depends heavily on retailing. Retailers ring up over $4 trillion in sales annually, about 40 percent of the gross domestic product (GDP).[4] Although most retailers are quite small, a few giant organizations dominate the industry, most notably Wal-Mart, whose annual U.S. sales alone are greater than the next five U.S. retail giants' sales combined. Who are these giants? Exhibit 13.1 lists the ten largest U.S. retailers.

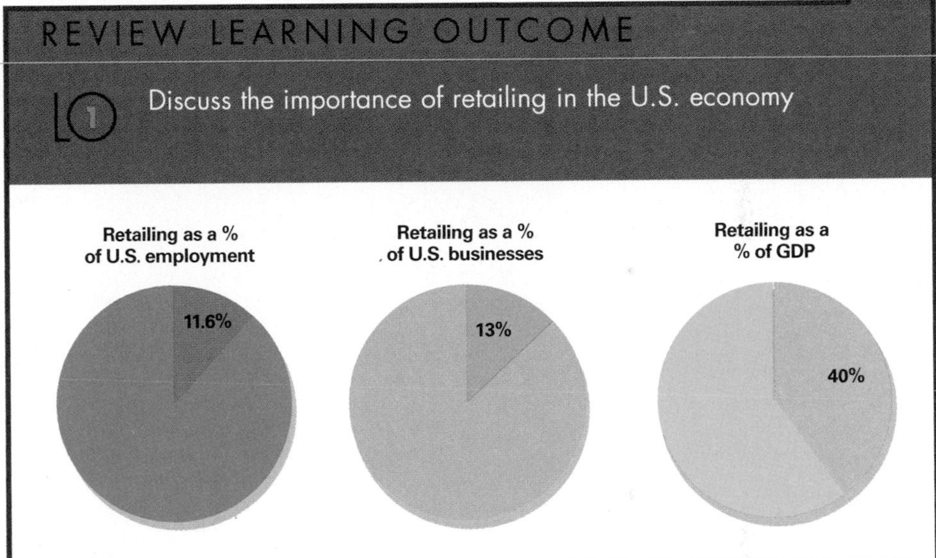

Marketing & You

How much do you enjoy shopping? Enter your answers on the lines provided.

1	2	3	4	5	6
Strongly disagree	Disagree	Neutral	Agree	Strongly agree	

__ I shop because buying things makes me happy.

__ Shopping is fun.

__ I get a real "high" from shopping.

__ I enjoy talking with salespeople and other shoppers who are interested in the same things I am.

__ I like having a salesperson bring merchandise out for me to choose from.

__ I enjoy seeing mall exhibits while shopping.

Total your score, and find out what it means after you read the chapter.

LO 2

CLASSIFICATION OF RETAIL OPERATIONS

A retail establishment can be classified according to its ownership, level of service, product assortment, and price. Specifically, retailers use the latter three variables to position themselves in the competitive marketplace. (As noted in Chapter 7, *positioning* is the strategy used to influence how consumers perceive one product in relation to all competing products.) These three variables can be combined in several ways to create distinctly different retail operations. Exhibit 13.2 lists the major types of retail stores discussed in this chapter and classifies

retailing
All the activities directly related to the sale of goods and services to the ultimate consumer for personal, nonbusiness use.

EXHIBIT 13.1

Ten Largest U.S. Retailers

2007 Rank	Company	Retailing Format	Revenue (billions $)	Number of Stores
1	**Wal-Mart** Bentonville, AR	Discount stores, supercenters, and warehouse clubs	378.8	7,262
2	**Home Depot** Atlanta, GA	Home improvement center	77.3	2,234
3	**CVS Caremark** Woonsocket, RI	Drugstores	76.3	6,301
4	**Kroger** Cincinnati, OH	Supermarkets, drugstores, specialty, and convenience stores	70.2	3,662
5	**Costco** Issaquah, WA	Warehouse clubs	64.4	520
6	**Target** Minneapolis, MN	Discount stores and supercenters	63.4	1,591
7	**Walgreens** Deerfield, IL	Drugstores	53.8	5,997
8	**Sears Holding** Hoffman Estates, IL	Department stores, catalogs, home centers, specialty	50.7	3,800
9	**Lowe's** Mooresville, NC	Home improvement center	48.3	1,525
10	**SUPERVALU** Eden Prarie, MN	Supermarkets, drugstores	44.1	2,474

Source: "The Nation's Retail Power Players," www.stores.org, accessed February 11, 2009.

them by level of service, product assortment, price, and gross margin.

Ownership

Retailers can be broadly classified by form of ownership: independent, part of a chain, or franchise outlet. Retailers owned by a single person or partnership and not operated as part of a larger retail institution are **independent retailers**. Around the world, most retailers are independent, operating one or a few stores in their community. Local florists, shoe stores, and ethnic food markets typically fit this classification.

Chain stores are owned and operated as a group by a single organization. Under this form of ownership, many administrative tasks are handled by the home office for the entire chain. The home office also buys most of the merchandise sold in the stores. Gap and Starbucks are examples of chains.

Franchises are owned and operated by individuals but are licensed by a larger supporting organization, such as Subway or Quiznos. The franchising approach combines the advantages of independent ownership with those of the chain store organization. Franchising is discussed in more detail later in the chapter.

EXHIBIT 13.2

Types of Stores and Their Characteristics

Type of Retailer	Level of Service	Product Assortment	Price	Gross Margin
Department store	Moderately high to high	Broad	Moderate to high	Moderately high
Specialty store	High	Narrow	Moderate to high	High
Supermarket	Low	Broad	Moderate	Low
Convenience store	Low	Medium to narrow	Moderately high	Moderately high
Drugstore	Low to moderate	Medium	Moderate	Low
Full-line discount store	Moderate to low	Medium to broad	Moderately low	Moderately low
Discount specialty store	Moderate to low	Medium to broad	Moderately low to low	Moderately low
Warehouse clubs	Low	Broad	Low to very low	Low
Off-price retailer	Low	Medium to narrow	Low	Low
Restaurant	Low to high	Narrow	Low to high	Low to high

Level of Service

The level of service that retailers provide can be classified along a continuum, from full service to self-service. Some retailers, such as exclusive clothing stores, offer high levels of service. They provide alterations, credit, delivery, consulting, liberal return policies, layaway, gift wrapping, and personal shopping. Discount stores usually offer fewer services. Retailers such as factory outlets and warehouse clubs offer virtually no services.

Product Assortment

The third basis for positioning or classifying stores is by the breadth and depth of their product line. Specialty stores—for example, Best Buy, Toys"R"Us, or GameStop—have the most concentrated product assortments, usually carrying single or narrow product lines but in considerable depth. On the other end of the spectrum, full-line discounters typically carry broad assortments of merchandise with limited depth. For example, Target carries automotive supplies, household cleaning products, and pet food. Typically, though, it carries only 4 or 5 brands of dog food. In contrast, a specialty pet store, such as PetSmart, may carry as many as 20 brands in a large variety of flavors, shapes, and sizes.

Other retailers, such as factory outlet stores, may carry only part of a single line. Nike stores sell only certain items of its own brand. Discount specialty stores such as Home Depot and Rack Room Shoes carry a broad assortment in concentrated product lines, such as building and home supplies or shoes.

Price

Price is a fourth way to position retail stores. Traditional department stores and specialty stores typically charge the full "suggested retail price." In contrast, discounters, factory outlets, and off-price retailers use low prices as a major lure for shoppers.

The last column in Exhibit 13.2 shows the typical **gross margin**—how much the retailer makes as a percentage of sales after the cost of goods sold is subtracted. The level of gross margin and the price level generally match. For example, a traditional jewelry store has high prices and high gross margins. A factory outlet has low prices and low gross margins. Markdowns on merchandise during sale periods and price wars among competitors, in which stores lower prices on certain items in an effort to win customers, cause gross margins to decline. When Wal-Mart entered the grocery business in a small Arkansas community, a fierce price war ensued. By the time the price war was in full swing, the price of a quart of milk had plummeted by more than 50 percent (below the price of a pint) and a loaf of bread sold for only 9 cents—prices at which no retailer could make a profit.

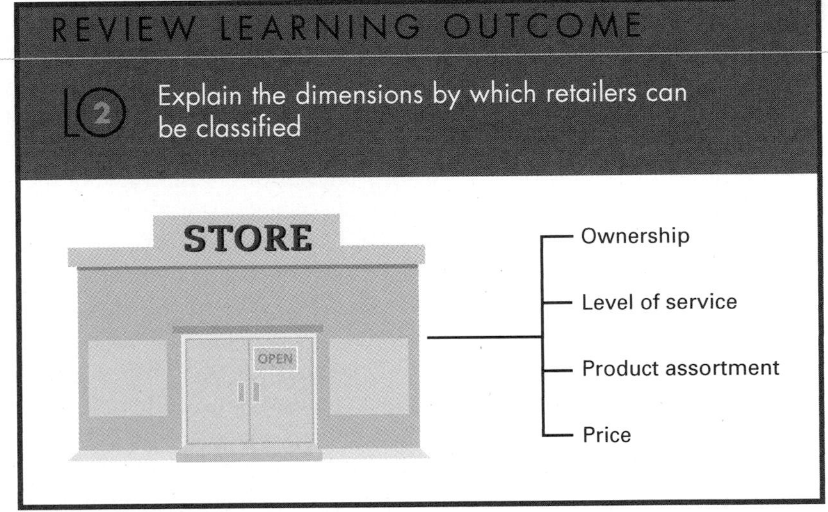

MAJOR TYPES OF RETAIL OPERATIONS

Traditionally, there have been several distinct types of retail stores, each offering a different product assortment, type of service, and price level, according to its customers' shopping preferences.

In a recent trend, however, retailers are experimenting with alternative formats that make it harder to classify them. For instance, supermarkets are expanding their nonfood items and services; discounters are adding groceries; drugstores are becoming more

independent retailers
Retailers owned by a single person or partnership and not operated as part of a larger retail institution.

chain stores
Stores owned and operated as a group by a single organization.

franchises
The right to operate a business or to sell a product.

gross margin
The amount of money the retailer makes as a percentage of sales after the cost of goods sold is subtracted.

department store
A store housing several departments under one roof.

buyer
A department head who selects the merchandise for his or her department and may also be responsible for promotion and personnel.

specialty store
A retail store specializing in a given type of merchandise.

supermarket
A large, departmentalized, self-service retailer that specializes in food and some nonfood items.

like convenience stores; and department stores are experimenting with smaller stores. Nevertheless, many stores still fall into the basic types.

Department Stores

A **department store** carries a wide variety of shopping and specialty goods, including apparel, cosmetics, housewares, electronics, and sometimes furniture. Purchases are generally made within each department rather than at one central checkout area. Each department is treated as a separate buying center to achieve economies in promotion, buying, service, and control. Each department is usually headed by a **buyer**, a department head who not only selects the merchandise for his or her department, but may also be responsible for promotion and personnel. For a consistent, uniform store image, central management sets broad policies about the types of merchandise carried and price ranges. Central management is also responsible for the overall advertising program, credit policies, store expansion, customer service, and so on.

Large independent department stores are rare today. Most are owned by national chains. Among the largest U.S. department store chains are Macy's, Inc. (formerly known as Federated Department Stores, Inc.), JCPenney, Sears, Dillard's, and Nordstrom. Dillard's is known for its distribution expertise. Nordstrom offers innovative customer service.

Specialty Stores

Specialty store formats allow retailers to refine their segmentation strategies and tailor their merchandise to specific target markets. A **specialty store** is not only a type of store but also a method of retail operations—namely, specializing in a given type of merchandise. Examples include children's clothing, men's clothing, candy, baked goods, gourmet coffee, sporting goods, and pet supplies. A typical specialty store carries a deeper but narrower assortment of specialty merchandise than does a department store. Generally, specialty stores' knowledgeable sales clerks offer more attentive customer service. The format has become very powerful in the apparel market and other areas. In fact, consumers buy more clothing from specialty stores than from any other type of retailer. The Children's Place, Gadzooks, Williams-Sonoma, and Foot Locker are examples of successful chain specialty retailers.

Consumers usually consider price to be secondary in specialty outlets. Instead, the distinctive merchandise, the store's physical appearance, and the caliber of the staff determine its popularity. For example, industry experts found that consumers are mostly confused by the wide array of new high-tech products available these days. One study found that only about 10 percent of the capability of new gadgetry is ever utilized.[5] Customers who shop for high-end electronics often find that specialty stores cannot compete on price with big-box stores. Instead, consumer electronics specialty stores compete by offering better-trained sales staff, more expertise, and better customer service than the big-box retailers. For instance, Tweeter, a regional electronics chain in New England, specializes in helping its customers overcome confusion and become comfortable with their purchases. Tweeter's customers can try out the latest technology by accompanying "hyperinformed" salespeople through replica kitchens, dens, and bedrooms loaded with complicated gadgets.[6] Because of specialty stores' attention to the customer and limited product line, manufacturers often favor introducing new products in them before moving on to larger retail and department stores.

Supermarkets

According to the U.S. Department of Agriculture, U.S. consumers spend about 10 percent of their disposable income on food, and roughly half of those expenditures occur in **supermarkets** on food for at-home consumption. Supermarkets are large, departmentalized, self-service retailers that specialize in food and some nonfood items.

Supermarkets have experienced declining sales in recent years. Some of this decline has been the result of increased competition from discounter Wal-Mart and Sam's Clubs. But demographic and lifestyle changes have also affected the supermarket industry.

One major change has been the increase in dual-income and single-parent families that eat out more or are just too busy to prepare meals at home. According to the U.S. Department of Agriculture, Americans spend about 50 percent of their food money in retail grocery stores and nearly 50 percent on food away from home. In comparison, Americans spent over three-fourths of their food money in grocery stores in 1950.[7]

For supercenter operators, food is a customer magnet that sharply increases the store's overall volume while taking customers away from traditional supermarkets.

As stores seek to meet consumer demand for one-stop shopping, conventional supermarkets are being replaced by bigger *superstores*, which are usually twice the size of supermarkets. Superstores meet the needs of today's customers for convenience, variety, and service. Superstores offer one-stop shopping for many food and nonfood needs, as well as many services—including pharmacies, flower shops, salad bars, in-store bakeries, takeout food sections, sit-down restaurants, health food sections, video rentals, dry-cleaning services, shoe repair, photo processing, and banking. Some even offer family dentistry or optical shops. This tendency to offer a wide variety of nontraditional goods and services under one roof is called **scrambled merchandising**. Safeway supermarkets are a good example of scrambled merchandising. In addition to including a liquor store, floral department, and pharmacy, they also lease space to Starbucks and local banks. Another trend in supermarket diversification is the addition of store-owned gas stations. The gas stations are not only a revenue source for the supermarkets and a convenience for customers, but they also attract customers to the location by offering lower prices than can usually be found at a traditional gas station. Store-owned stations are expected to account for as much as 20 percent of overall gasoline sales in the near future.

To stand out in an increasingly competitive marketplace, many supermarket chains are tailoring marketing strategies to appeal to specific consumer segments. Most notable is the shift toward *loyalty marketing programs* that reward loyal customers carrying frequent shopper cards with discounts or gifts. Once scanned at the checkout, frequent shopper cards help supermarket retailers electronically track shoppers' buying habits. More than half of the customers who shop at the over 600 Piggly Wiggly stores carry the Pig's Favorite loyalty card. Customers use their card each time they shop to get special discounts on items. The supermarket chain was also one of the first grocers to implement biometrics. Instead of carrying a loyalty card, the customer simply places a fingertip on a biometric finger-scan reader at a kiosk positioned near the front of the store. The shopper then receives a printout of personalized offers, which change weekly.[8] Piggly Wiggly also uses consumer purchase data stored in its database to determine customer preferences. If management sees that a customer buys flowers regularly, then it sends that customer a coupon redeemable in its floral department.[9]

Drugstores

Drugstores stock pharmacy-related products and services as their main draw. Consumers are most often attracted to a drugstore by its pharmacy or pharmacist, its convenience, or because it honors their third-party prescription drug plan. Drugstores also carry an extensive selection of over-the-counter (OTC) medications, cosmetics, health and beauty aids, seasonal merchandise, specialty items such as greeting cards and a limited

scrambled merchandising
The tendency to offer a wide variety of nontraditional goods and services under one roof.

drugstore
A retail store that stocks pharmacy-related products and services as its main draw.

convenience store
A miniature supermarket, carrying only a limited line of high-turnover convenience goods.

discount store
A retailer that competes on the basis of low prices, high turnover, and high volume.

full-line discount stores
A retailer that offers consumers very limited service and carries a broad assortment of well-known, nationally branded "hard goods."

mass merchandising
A retailing strategy using moderate to low prices on large quantities of merchandise and lower service to stimulate high turnover of products.

selection of toys, and some nonrefrigerated convenience foods. As competition has increased from mass merchandisers and supermarkets with their own pharmacies, as well as from direct-mail prescription services, drugstores have added value-added services such as 24-hour operations, drive-through pharmacies, and low-cost health clinics staffed by nurse practitioners.

Demographic trends in the United States look favorable for the drugstore industry. As the baby boom population continues to age, they will spend an increasing percentage of their disposable income on health care and wellness. In fact, the average 60-year-old purchases 15 prescriptions per year, nearly twice as many as the average 30-year-old. Because baby boomers are attentive to their health and keenly sensitive about their looks, the increased traffic at the pharmacy counter in the future should also spur sales in other traditionally strong drugstore merchandise categories, most notably OTC drugs, vitamins, and health and beauty aids.

Convenience Stores

A **convenience store** can be defined as a miniature supermarket, carrying only a limited line of high-turnover convenience goods. These self-service stores are typically located near residential areas and are open 24 hours, seven days a week. Convenience stores offer exactly what their name implies: convenient location, long hours, and fast service. However, prices are almost always higher at a convenience store than at a supermarket. Thus, the customer pays for the convenience.

When the original convenience stores added self-service gas pumps, full-service gas stations fought back by closing service bays and opening miniature stores of their own, selling convenience items like cigarettes, sodas, and snacks. Supermarkets and discount stores also wooed customers with one-stop shopping and quick checkout. To combat the gas stations' and supermarkets' competition, convenience store operators have changed their strategy. They have expanded their offerings of nonfood items with video rentals and health and beauty aids and added upscale sandwich and salad lines and more fresh produce. Some convenience stores are even selling Pizza Hut, Subway, and Taco Bell products prepared in the store. For example, Exxon On the Run features Green Mountain Coffee Roasters, Blimpie subs and salads, and an On the Run Café that offers everything from fresh sandwiches and fresh fruits to a grilled hamburger and french fries.[10]

Discount Stores

A **discount store** is a retailer that competes on the basis of low prices, high turnover, and high volume. Discounters can be classified into four major categories: full-line discount stores, specialty discount stores, warehouse clubs, and off-price discount retailers.

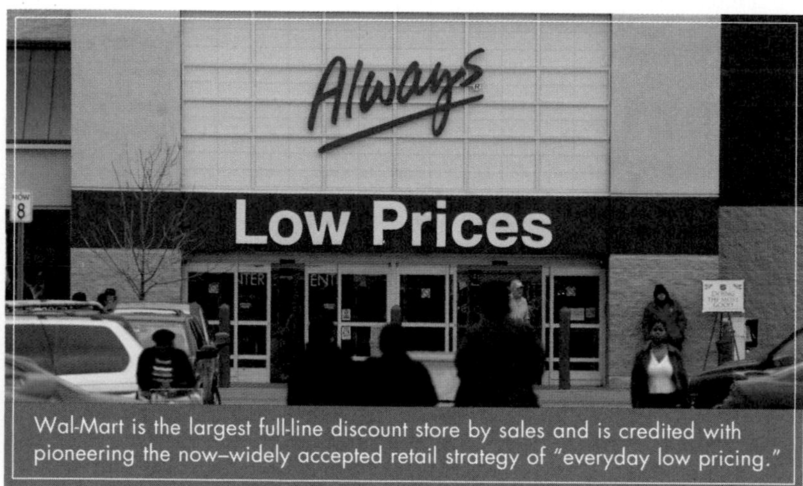

© AP IMAGES/KIICHIRO SATO

Wal-Mart is the largest full-line discount store by sales and is credited with pioneering the now–widely accepted retail strategy of "everyday low pricing."

Full-Line Discount Stores Compared to traditional department stores, **full-line discount stores** offer consumers very limited service and carry a much broader assortment of well-known, nationally branded "hard goods," including housewares, toys, automotive parts, hardware, sporting goods, and garden items, as well as clothing, bedding, and linens. Some even carry limited nonperishable food items, such as soft drinks, canned goods, and potato chips. As with department stores, national chains dominate the discounters. Full-line discounters are often called mass merchandisers. **Mass merchandising** is the retailing strategy whereby retailers use moderate to low prices on large quantities of merchandise and lower service to stimulate high turnover of products.

Wal-Mart is the largest full-line discount store in terms of sales. Wal-Mart initially expanded rapidly by locating on the outskirts of small towns and absorbing business for miles around. In recent years, most of its growth has come in larger cites. Today, it has over 6,000 stores on four continents. Much of Wal-Mart's success has been attributed to its merchandising foresight, cost consciousness, efficient communication and distribution systems, and involved, motivated employees. Wal-Mart is credited with pioneering the retail strategy of "everyday low pricing," a strategy now widely copied by retailers the world over. Besides expanding throughout all 50 states and Puerto Rico, Wal-Mart has expanded globally into Argentina, Brazil, Canada, China, Costa Rica, El Salvador, Guatemala, Honduras, Japan, Mexico, Nicaragua, South Korea, and the United Kingdom. Wal-Mart has also become a formidable retailing giant in online shopping, concentrating on toys and electronics. With tie-ins to its stores across the country, Wal-Mart offers online shopping with in-store kiosks linking to the site and the ability to handle returns and exchanges from Internet sales at its physical stores.[11]

Supercenters combine a full line of groceries and general merchandise with a wide range of services, including pharmacy, dry cleaning, portrait studios, photo finishing, hair salons, optical shops, and restaurants—all in one location. For supercenter operators like Wal-Mart, food is a customer magnet that sharply increases the store's overall volume, while taking customers away from traditional supermarkets. Wal-Mart opened its first supercenter in 1988 and now operates over 2,000 supercenters worldwide. Target was the last major discounter to embrace the supercenter concept. The chain currently has 177 SuperTarget locations and plans to open 200 more over the next 10 years.[12]

Supercenters are also threatening to push Europe's traditional small and medium-sized food stores into extinction. Old-fashioned corner stores and family businesses are giving way to larger chains that offer food, drugs, services, and general merchandise all in one place. Today, the largest British food retailer is Tesco, a chain operator that has over 30 percent of the grocery market in the United Kingdom. Tesco is expanding rapidly and now has over 1,800 stores in the UK and almost 2,500 stores globally, including a joint venture with Safeway in the United States.[13]

Many European countries, however, are passing legislation to make it more difficult for supercenters to open. In France, for example, laws ban authorizations for new supercenters over 1,000 square meters (10,800 square feet). Belgium and Portugal have passed similar bans. In Britain and the Netherlands, areas outside towns and cities are off limits to superstores. By imposing planning and building restrictions for large stores, these countries are trying to accommodate environmental concerns, movements to revive city centers, and the worries of small shopkeepers.

An increasingly popular variation of full-line discount stores is *extreme-value retailing*, the most notable examples being Dollar General and Family Dollar. Extreme-value retailers have grown in popularity as major discounters continue to shift toward the supercenter format, broadening their customer base and increasing their offerings of higher-priced goods aimed at higher-income consumers. This has created an opening for extreme-value retailers to entice shoppers from the low-income segment. Low- and fixed-income customers are drawn to extreme-value retailers, whose stores are located within their communities. Extreme-value retailers also build smaller stores (a typical store is about the size of one department in a Wal-Mart superstore) with a narrower selection of merchandise emphasizing day-to-day necessities. Rock-bottom prices are also key to their success. With the average transaction under $10, extreme-value retailers have found low prices to be far more critical to building traffic and loyalty than any other retailing format.[14]

Specialty Discount Stores Another discount niche includes the single-line **specialty discount stores**—for example, stores selling sporting goods, electronics, auto parts, office supplies, housewares, or toys. These stores offer a nearly complete selection of single-line merchandise and use self-service, discount prices, high volume, and high

supercenters
A retail store that combines groceries and general merchandise goods with a wide range of services.

specialty discount stores
A retail store that offers a nearly complete selection of single-line merchandise and uses self-service, discount prices, high volume, and high turnover.

category killers
Specialty discount stores that heavily dominate their narrow merchandise segment.

warehouse membership clubs
Limited-service merchant wholesalers that sell a limited selection of brand-name appliances, household items, and groceries on a cash-and-carry basis to members, usually small businesses and groups.

off-price retailer
A retailer that sells at prices 25 percent or more below traditional department store prices because it pays cash for its stock and usually doesn't ask for return privileges.

factory outlet
An off-price retailer that is owned and operated by a manufacturer.

turnover to their advantage. Specialty discount stores are often termed **category killers** because they so heavily dominate their narrow merchandise segment. Examples include Toys"R"Us in toys (the first category killer in the market) and Best Buy in electronics, Staples and Office Depot in office supplies, Home Depot and Lowe's in home improvement supplies, IKEA in home furnishings, Bed Bath & Beyond in kitchen and bath accessories, and Dick's in sporting goods.

Category killers have emerged in other specialty segments as well, creating retailing empires in highly fragmented mom-and-pop markets. For instance, the home improvement industry, which for years was served by professional builders and small hardware stores, is now dominated by Home Depot and Lowe's. Category-dominant retailers like these serve their customers by offering a large selection of merchandise, stores that make shopping easy, and low prices every day—which eliminates the need for time-consuming comparison shopping.

Warehouse Membership Clubs **Warehouse membership clubs** sell a limited selection of brand-name appliances, household items, and groceries. These are usually sold in bulk from warehouse outlets on a cash-and-carry basis to members only. Individual members of warehouse clubs are charged low or no membership fees. Currently, the leading stores in this category are Wal-Mart's Sam's Club, Costco, and BJ's Wholesale Club.

Warehouse clubs have had a major impact on supermarkets. With 90,000 square feet or more, warehouse clubs offer 60 to 70 percent general merchandise and health- and beauty-care products, with grocery-related items making up the difference. Warehouse club members tend to be more educated and more affluent and have a larger household than regular supermarket shoppers. These core customers use warehouse clubs to stock up on staples; then they go to specialty outlets or food stores for perishables. Warehouse clubs are also expanding into luxury items. Sam's Club recently had a $347,000 diamond solitaire ring on sale before Christmas and Costco sells Dom Pérignon champagne.

A new trend in supermarket diversification—or scrambled merchandising—is the addition of store-owned gas stations. The gas stations are not only a revenue source for the supermarkets, but they also attract customers to the location by offering lower prices than can usually be found at a traditional gas station.

Off-Price Retailers An **off-price retailer** sells at prices 25 percent or more below traditional department store prices because it pays cash for its stock and usually doesn't ask for return privileges. Off-price retailers buy manufacturers' overruns at cost or even less. They also absorb goods from bankrupt stores, irregular merchandise, and unsold end-of-season output. Nevertheless, much off-price retailer merchandise is first-quality, current goods. Because buyers for off-price retailers purchase only what is available or what they can get a good deal on, merchandise styles and brands often change monthly. Today, there are hundreds of off-price retailers, including T.J. Maxx, Ross Stores, Marshalls, HomeGoods, and Tuesday Morning.

Factory outlets are an interesting variation on the off-price concept. A **factory outlet** is an off-price retailer that is owned and operated by a manufacturer. Thus, it carries one line of merchandise—its own. Each season, from 5 to 10 percent of a manufacturer's output does not sell through regular distribution channels because it consists of closeouts (merchandise being discontinued), factory seconds, and canceled orders. With factory outlets, manufacturers can regulate where their surplus is sold, and they can realize higher profit margins than they would by disposing of the goods through independent wholesalers and retailers. Factory outlet malls are typically located in out-of-the-way rural areas or near vacation destinations. Most are situated 10 to 15 miles from urban or suburban shopping areas so that manufacturers don't alienate their department store accounts by selling the same goods virtually next door at a discount.

Manufacturers reaping the benefits of outlet mall popularity include Gap, J.Crew, and Calvin Klein clothiers; West Point Pepperel textiles; Pottery Barn and Crate & Barrel home products; Oneida silversmiths; and Dansk kitchenwares. Top-drawer department stores have also opened outlet stores to sell hard-to-move merchandise. Dillard's has opened a series of clearance centers to make final attempts to move merchandise that failed to sell in the department store. To move their clearance items, Nordstrom operates Nordstrom Rack, Saks Fifth Avenue has Off Fifth, and Neiman Marcus has Last Call.

Restaurants

Restaurants straddle the line between retailing establishments and service establishments. Restaurants do sell tangible products—food and drink—but they also provide a valuable service for consumers in the form of food preparation and food service. As a retailing institution, restaurants must deal with many of the same issues as a more traditional retailer, such as personnel, distribution, inventory management, promotion, pricing, and location.

Eating out is an important part of Americans' daily activities and is growing in strength. According to the National Restaurant Association, more than 70 billion meals are eaten in restaurants or cafeterias annually. This means that Americans consume an average of 5.8 commercially prepared meals per week. Food away from home accounts for about 48 percent, or $1,078 per person, of the annual household food budget. The trend toward eating out has been fueled by the increase in working mothers and dual-income families who have more money to eat out and less time to prepare meals at home. The restaurant industry provides work for more than 9 percent of the American workforce and is expected to add 2 million jobs in the next few years, for total employment of 14.8 million people in 2017.[15]

The restaurant industry is one of the most entrepreneurial of businesses and one of the most competitive. Because barriers to entering the restaurant industry are low, the opportunity appeals to many people. The risks, however, are great. About 50 percent of all new restaurants fail within the first year of operation. Restaurants face competition not only from other restaurants but also from the consumer who can easily choose to cook at home. Competition has fostered innovation and ever-changing menus in most segments of the restaurant industry. Many restaurants are now competing directly with supermarkets by offering take-out and delivery in an effort to capture more of the home meal replacement market.

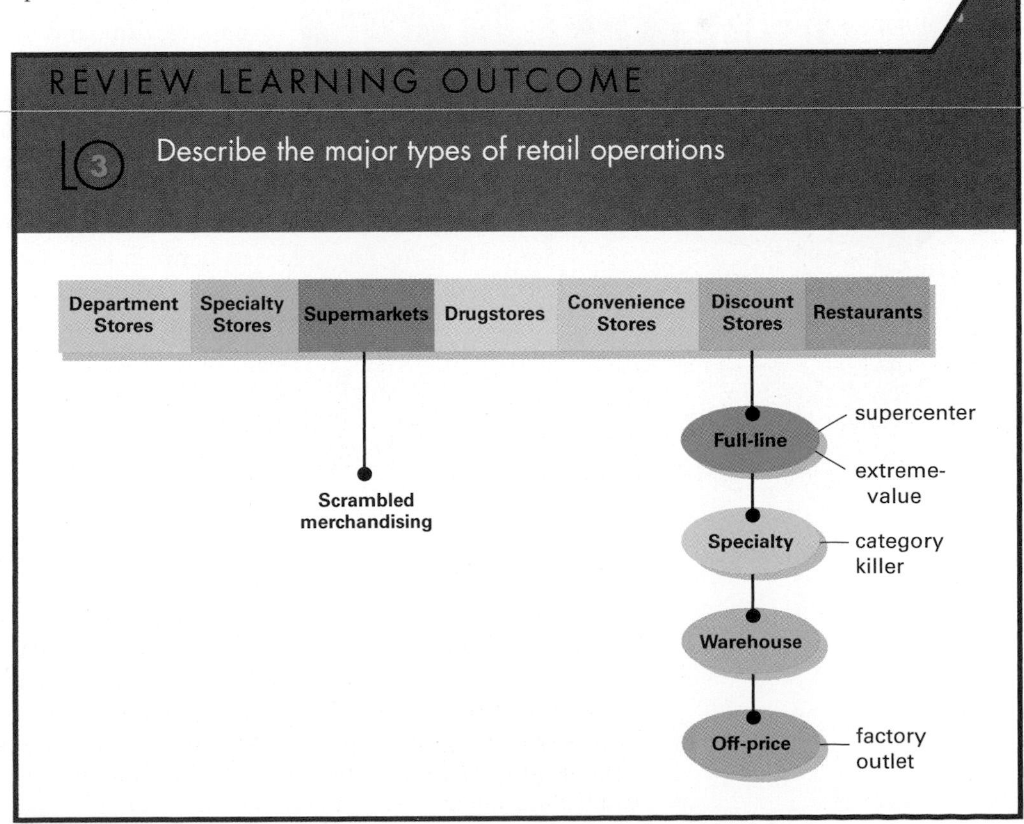

nonstore retailing
Selling to consumers through other means than by visiting a store.

automatic vending
The use of machines to offer goods for sale.

direct retailing
The selling of products by representatives who work door-to-door, office-to-office, or at home parties.

NONSTORE RETAILING

The retailing methods discussed so far have been in-store methods, in which customers must physically shop at stores. In contrast, **nonstore retailing** is shopping without visiting a store. Because consumers demand convenience, nonstore retailing is currently growing faster than in-store retailing. The major forms of nonstore retailing are automatic vending, direct retailing, direct marketing, and electronic retailing.

Automatic Vending

A low-profile yet important form of retailing is **automatic vending**, the use of machines to offer goods for sale—for example, the soft drink, candy, or snack vending machines found in college cafeterias and office buildings. Vending is the most pervasive retail business in the United States, with about six million vending machines selling $40 billion annually. Food and beverages account for about 85 percent of all sales from vending machines. Due to the convenience, consumers are willing to pay higher prices for products from a vending machine than for the same products in traditional retail settings.

© AP IMAGES/PRNEWSFOTO/MOTOROLA INSTANTMOTO

Retailers are constantly seeking new opportunities to sell via vending. For example, United Artists Theaters offer moviegoers the option of purchasing hot popcorn, Tombstone pizza, Kraft Macaroni & Cheese, and chicken fingers from a vending machine instead of waiting in line at the concession stand. Many vending machines today also sell nontraditional kinds of merchandise, such as videos, toys, stickers, sports cards, office-type supplies, film, and disposable cameras. In a sign of the times, shoppers can purchase iPod music players and accessories from specially designed Zoom Store vending machines located in select stores, airports, supermarkets, and other high foot-traffic areas.[16]

Of course, vending machines are also an important tool in the ongoing cola wars between Coca-Cola and Pepsi. Both companies are constantly looking for new ways to improve vending machine sales. For example, Coca-Cola is implementing Intelligent Vending, a "cashless" payment system. Vending machines with this system accept credit cards, RFID devices, and hotel room keys and can be accessed via cell phone (mobile e-commerce, or m-commerce, as discussed later in this chapter).[17] Recent estimates suggested that credit card technology will be available in over 11.5 million vending machines of different types by 2009.[18]

Direct Retailing

In **direct retailing**, representatives sell products door-to-door, office-to-office, or at home sales parties. Companies like Avon, Mary Kay Cosmetics, The Pampered Chef, Usborne Books, and World Book Encyclopedia have used this approach for years. But recently direct retailers' sales have suffered as women have entered the workforce. Working women are not home during the day and have little time to attend selling parties. Although most direct sellers like Avon and Silpada still advocate the party plan method, the realities of the marketplace have forced them to be more creative in reaching their target customer. Direct sales representatives now hold parties in offices, parks, and even parking lots. Others hold informal gatherings where shoppers can drop in at their convenience or offer self-improvement classes. Many direct retailers are also turning to direct mail, telephone, or more traditional retailing venues to find new avenues to their customers and increase sales. Avon, for instance, has begun opening cosmetic kiosk counters, called Avon Beauty Centers, in malls and strip centers. Avon has also launched a new brand—mark, a beauty "experience" for young women. Most mark representatives are largely college students who typically sell the product as an after-school, part-time job. Prospective representatives and consumers can buy products or register to be a representative in person, online, or over the phone.[19] Direct retailers are also using the Internet as a channel to reach more customers and increase sales. At Avon's site, individual reps have their own home pages that link from Avon's home page so that sales are credited to them.

direct marketing (direct-response marketing)
Techniques used to get consumers to make a purchase from their home, office, or another nonretail setting.

In response to the decline in U.S. sales, many longtime direct retailers are exploring opportunities in other countries. For example, Mary Kay, Avon, and Amway have started successful operations in China by adapting their business models to China's laws. Mary Kay agents in China do not purchase and resell the products but are paid a sales commission instead. The company also changed its slogan from "God First, Family Second, Career Third," to "Faith First, Family Second, Career Third."

Direct Marketing

According to the Direct Marketing Association, companies spend more than $167 billion annually on direct marketing in the United States and generate about $1.93 trillion in sales.[20] **Direct marketing**, sometimes called **direct-response marketing**, refers to the techniques used to get consumers to make a purchase from their home, office, or other nonretail setting. These techniques include direct mail, catalogs and mail order, telemarketing, and electronic retailing. Shoppers using these methods are less bound by traditional shopping situations. Time-strapped consumers and those who live in rural or suburban areas are most likely to be direct-response shoppers because they value the convenience and flexibility that direct marketing provides.

Direct Mail Direct mail can be the most efficient or the least efficient retailing method, depending on the quality of the mailing list and the effectiveness of the mailing piece. With direct mail, marketers can precisely target their customers according to demographics, geographics, and even psychographics. Good mailing lists come from an internal database or from list brokers for about $35 to $150 per thousand names.

Direct mailers are becoming more sophisticated in targeting the "right" customers. Using statistical methods to analyze census data, lifestyle and financial information, and past-purchase and credit history, direct mailers can pick out those most likely to buy their products. So, despite increases in postal rates and raw material and logistics costs, U.S. direct mail services were almost $61 billion in 2006, an increase of more than 7 percent over the previous year.[21]

Direct mailers, such as L.L. Bean's successful catalogs, are created and designed for highly segmented markets. Direct mailers target customers most likely to buy their products by analyzing census data, lifestyle and financial information, and past-purchase and credit history.

telemarketing
The use of the telephone to sell directly to consumers.

Catalogs and Mail Order Consumers can now buy just about anything through the mail, from the mundane, like books, music, and polo shirts, to the outlandish, such as the $5 million diamond-and-ruby-studded bra available through the Victoria's Secret catalog. Although women make up the bulk of catalog shoppers, the percentage of male catalog shoppers has recently soared. As changing demographics have shifted more of the shopping responsibility to men, they are viewing shopping via catalog, mail order, and the Internet as more sensible than a trip to the mall.

Successful catalogs usually are created and designed for highly segmented markets. For example, Schwan Food Company recently launched Impromptu Gourmet, which offers convenient gourmet and fine dining frozen foods. Certain types of retailers are using mail order successfully. For example, computer manufacturers have discovered that mail order is a lucrative way to sell personal computers to home and small-business users, evidenced by Dell's tremendous success. Dell has used its direct business model to become a $60 billion company and one of the largest PC sellers worldwide. With a global market share of about 20 percent, it sells over $50 million in computers and equipment online every day.[22]

Telemarketing **Telemarketing** is the use of the telephone to sell directly to consumers. It consists of outbound sales calls, usually unsolicited, and inbound calls—that is, orders through toll-free 800 numbers or fee-based 900 numbers.

Rising postage rates and decreasing long-distance phone rates have made *outbound* telemarketing an attractive direct-marketing technique. Skyrocketing field sales costs have also led marketing managers to use outbound telemarketing. Searching for ways to keep costs under control, marketing managers have learned how to pinpoint prospects quickly, zero in on serious buyers, and keep in close touch with regular customers. Meanwhile, they are reserving expensive, time-consuming, in-person calls for closing sales. So many consumers complained about outbound telemarketing calls, however, that Congress passed legislation establishing a national "do not call" list of consumers who do not want to receive unsolicited telephone calls. In addition, Congress passed laws requiring e-mail marketers to allow recipients to opt out of mass e-mails (spam). The laws also prohibit marketers from camouflaging their identity through false return addresses and misleading subject lines. A problem with the telemarketing law, however, is that it exempts nonprofits, so some companies have set up nonprofit subsidiaries to continue their calling activities. Some industry experts say the lists help them by eliminating nonbuyers, but others believe this legislation could have a long-term negative effect on telemarketing sales.

Inbound telemarketing programs, which use 800 and 900 numbers, are mainly used to take orders, generate leads, and provide customer service. Inbound 800 telemarketing has successfully supplemented direct-response TV, radio, and print advertising for more than 25 years.

Electronic Retailing

Electronic retailing includes the 24-hour, shop-at-home television networks and online retailing.

Shop-at-Home Networks The shop-at-home television networks are specialized forms of direct-response marketing. Shows display merchandise, with the retail price, to home viewers. Viewers can phone in their orders directly on a toll-free line and shop with a credit card. The shop-at-home industry has quickly grown into a multibillion-dollar business with a loyal customer following. Shop-at-home networks have the capability of reaching nearly every home that has a television set.

The best-known shop-at-home networks are the Home Shopping Network and the QVC (Quality, Value, Convenience) Network. Home shopping networks attract a broad audience through diverse programming and product offerings and are now adding new products to appeal to more affluent audiences. For instance, on QVC, cooking programs attract both men and women, fashion programs attract mostly women, and the NFL Team Shop attracts primarily men. Since it began broadcasting, the channel has sold everything from Sony electronics to Bugs Bunny to Gucci. With annual sales of almost $6 billion, QVC ships more than 150 million packages worldwide to about 10 million customers every year. The company owes its success in part to its customer files of more than 20 million people in 40 countries and to the fact that it introduces as many as 250 new products each week.[23]

As the popularity of online retailing grows, it is becoming critical that retailers, like L.L. Bean, be online and that their stores, Web sites, and catalogs be integrated. Customers expect to find the same brands, products, and prices whether they purchase online, on the phone, or in a store.

Online Retailing For years, shopping at home meant looking through catalogs and then placing an order over the telephone. For many people today, however, it now means turning on a computer, surfing retail Web sites, and selecting and ordering products online with the click of a mouse. **Online retailing**, or *e-tailing*, is a type of shopping available to consumers with access to the Internet. Over 70 percent of Americans have Internet access either at home or at work.

Online retailing has exploded in the last several years as consumers have found this type of shopping convenient and, in many instances, less costly. Consumers can shop without leaving home, choose from a wide selection of merchants, use shopping comparison services to search the Web for the best price, and then have the items delivered to their doorsteps. As a result, online shopping continues to grow, with online sales accounting for about 8 percent of total retail sales. As an example of the growing enthusiasm for online retailing, a recent survey indicated that 31 percent of consumers prefer to make their purchases online, versus 27 percent who preferred physical stores.[24] Online retail sales recently topped $160 billion and are projected to reach almost $275 billion, or 9 percent of retail sales, by 2011.[25]

Broadcast and cable television networks are cultivating a new source of income by selling products online that are featured in their TV shows. Delivery Agent, a San Francisco company that calls itself the leader in shopping-enabled entertainment, manages e-commerce for NBC, Bravo, and Martha Stewart Omnimedia, among others. The producers of Bravo's *Project Runway* contracted with Delivery Agent to sell the clothing designed on the reality fashion competition show. After the challenge to create an outfit for My Scene Barbie, the Bravo.com site sold out of the 3,300 dolls wearing the winning design creation.[26]

As the popularity of online retailing grows, it is becoming critical that retailers be online and that their stores, Web sites, and catalogs be integrated. Customers expect to find the same brands, products, and prices whether they purchase online, on the phone, or in a store. Therefore, retailers are increasingly using in-store kiosks to help tie the channels together for greater customer service. Retailer and cataloger

online retailing
A type of shopping available to consumers with access to the Internet.

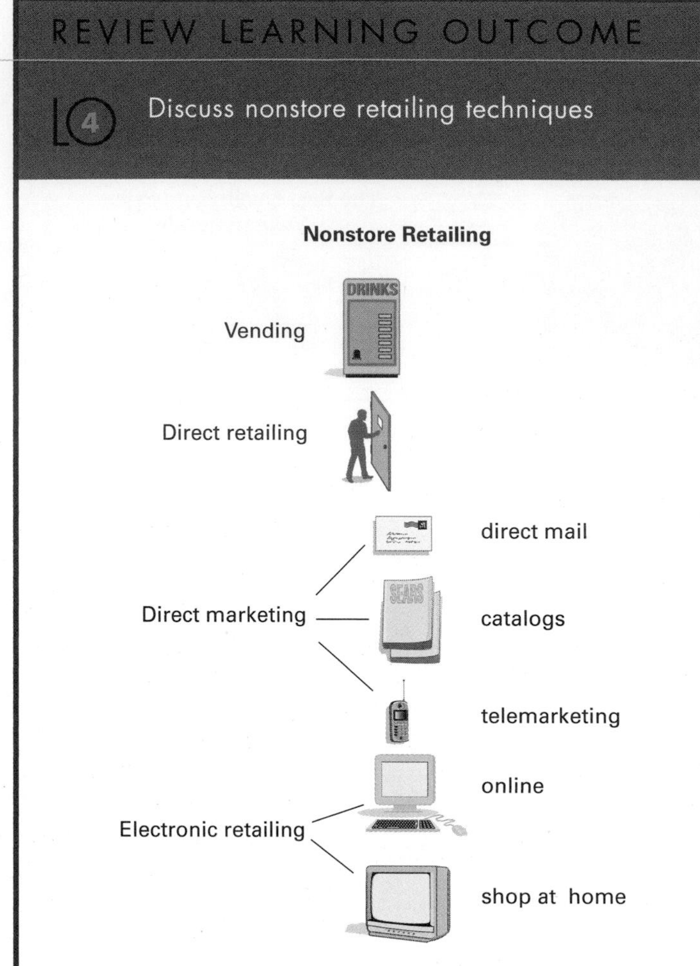

Williams-Sonoma, for example, has linked its store gift registry to its Web site, allowing brides to see who has bought what in real time. Banana Republic stores in New York and Santa Monica, California, have kiosks so customers can order items that aren't on the shelves. Kiosks are even more popular among retailers that target younger, more computer-oriented customers. For example, Van's (**www.vans.com**) sells alternative sportswear online as well as in 160 retail stores. Each of its eight skate parks is a combination retail store, entertainment venue, and alternative sports arena. In addition to the skating rink, each park has a lounge area where customers can hang out, watch customized videos, and surf Van's Web site at a bank of kiosks. Each kiosk not only offers a complete selection of Van's footwear, apparel, and accessories, but also includes a full-service pro shop that sells over 500 skateboards, bicycles, helmets, and other equipment and an information center with the latest tour, special event, and contest information.[27]

Online auctions run by Internet companies such as eBay and Amazon.com have enjoyed phenomenal success in recent years. With more than two million items for sale each day, ranging from antique clocks to car stereos, eBay is the leader in cyberspace auctions. Internet auction services like eBay run the Web service and collect a listing fee, plus a commission of 1 to 5 percent when a sale is completed. They also host auctions for other companies. For example, eBay and Sotheby's have a joint venture that offers fine art, rare coins, sports collectibles, jewelry, and antiques online. Each item carries a stamp of authenticity from Sotheby's or one of the 2,800 art and antiques dealers worldwide who have signed exclusive agreements with Sotheby's. The joint venture supports eBay's fine arts and antiques division and enables Sotheby's to offer online sales without the overhead expense of managing its own site.[28]

franchisor
The originator of a trade name, product, methods of operation, and so on, that grants operating rights to another party to sell its product.

franchisee
An individual or business that is granted the right to sell another party's product.

LO5

FRANCHISING

A *franchise* is a continuing relationship in which a franchisor grants to a franchisee the business rights to operate or to sell a product. The **franchisor** originates the trade name, product, methods of operation, and so on. The **franchisee**, in return, pays the franchisor for the right to use its name, product, or business methods. A franchise agreement between the two parties usually lasts for 10 to 20 years, at which time it can be renewed if both parties are agreeable.

To be granted the rights to a franchise, a franchisee usually pays an initial, one-time franchise fee. The amount of this fee depends solely on the individual franchisor, but it generally ranges from $50,000 to $250,000 or higher. In addition to this initial franchise fee, the franchisee is expected to pay royalty fees, usually in the range of 3 to 7 percent of gross revenues. The franchisee may also be expected to pay advertising fees, which usually cover the cost of promotional materials and, if the franchise organization is large enough, regional or national advertising. A McDonald's franchise, for example, costs an initial $45,000 franchise fee. The franchisee must make a down payment of 40 percent of the total cost of a new restaurant or 25 percent of the total cost of an existing restaurant plus a monthly fee based on the restaurant's sales performance and base rent. In addition, a new McDonald's franchisee can expect start-up costs for equipment and preopening expenses to range from $506,000 to $1.6 million.[29] The size of the restaurant facility, area of the country, inventory, selection of kitchen equipment, signage, and style of décor and landscaping affect new restaurant costs. Though the dollar amount will vary depending on the type of franchise, fees such as these are typical for all major franchisors, including Burger King, Jani-King, Athlete's Foot, Sonic, and Subway.

Franchising is not new. General Motors has used this approach since 1898, and Rexall drugstores, since 1901. Today, there are over half a million franchised establishments in the United States, with combined sales approaching $1.5 trillion, or about 40 percent of all retail trade. Although franchised restaurants attract most of those dollars, hundreds of retail and service franchises, such as Alphagraphics Printshops, Supercuts, and Sylvan Learning Systems, also are thriving. Indeed, there are over 320,000 franchises in 75 industries.[30] Industries expected to see real growth in franchising include home repair, business support services, automotive repairs, hair salons, children's services, and telecommunications. Exhibit 13.3 lists some facts about some of the largest and best-known U.S. franchisors. Exhibit 13.4 lists some Web sites that provide information about franchises.

Two basic forms of franchises are used today: product and trade name franchising and business format franchising. In *product and trade name franchising*, a dealer agrees to sell certain products provided by a manufacturer or a wholesaler. This approach has been used most widely in the auto and truck, soft-drink bottling, tire, and gasoline service industries. For example, a local tire retailer may hold a franchise to sell Michelin tires. Likewise, the Coca-Cola bottler in a particular area is a product and trade name franchisee licensed to bottle and sell Coca-Cola's soft drinks.

Business format franchising is an ongoing business relationship between a franchisor and a franchisee. Typically, a franchisor "sells" a franchisee the rights to use the franchisor's format or approach to doing business. This form of franchising has rapidly expanded through retailing, restaurant, food-service, hotel and motel, printing, and real estate franchises. Fast-food restaurants like McDonald's, Wendy's, and Burger King use this kind of franchising, as do other companies such as Hyatt Corporation, Unocal Corporation, and ExxonMobil Corporation. To be eligible to be a Domino's Pizza franchisee, you must have worked in a Domino's pizza store for at least one year. The company believes that after working in an existing location, you will have a better understanding of the company and its values and standards. Then potential franchisees must participate in a series of career development, franchise orientation, presentation skills, and franchise development programs.

Like other retailers, franchisors are seeking new growth abroad. Hundreds of U.S. franchisors have begun international expansion and are actively looking for foreign franchisees to open new locations. KFC serves nearly 8 million customers daily at its more than 11,000 restaurants in over 80 countries and territories around the world, including Australia, China, Indonesia, Japan, and Saudi Arabia. KFC's parent company, Yum! Brands, Inc., the world's largest restaurant system, attributes the franchise's success to its ability to adapt to local cultures and tastes without losing control of quality and brand image.[31] The International Franchise Association includes over 100 franchise organizations in countries from Argentina to Zimbabwe.

Franchisors usually allow franchisees to alter their business format slightly in foreign markets. For example, some McDonald's franchisees in Germany sell beer, and in Japan they offer food items that appeal to Japanese tastes, such as steamed dumplings, curry with rice, and roast pork cutlet burgers with melted cheese. McDonald's franchisees in India serve mutton instead of beef because most Indians are Hindu, a religion whose followers believe cows are a sacred symbol of the source of life. The menu also features rice-based Vegetable Burgers made with peas, carrots, red pepper, beans, and Indian spices as well as Vegetable McNuggets. But, in spite of menu

EXHIBIT 13.3

Largest U.S. Franchisors

Rank	Franchise	Type of Business	Initial Investment
1	Subway	Submarine Sandwiches & Salads	$78,600–238,300
2	McDonald's	Hamburgers, Chicken, Salads	$950,200–1,800,000
3	Liberty Tax Service	Income-Tax Preparation	$53,800–66,900
4	Sonic Drive-In Restaurants	Drive-In Restaurant	$1,200,000–3,200,000
5	InterContinental Hotels Group	Hotels	Varies
6	Ace Hardware Corp.	Hardware & Home Improvement Store	$243,500–1,000,000
7	Pizza Hut	Pizza	$638,000–2,970,000
8	The UPS Store, Mail Boxes Etc.	Postal, Business & Communications Services	$171,200–280,000
9	Circle K	Convenience Store	$161,000–1,400,000
10	Papa John's Int'l. Inc.	Pizza	$135,800–491,600
11	Jiffy Lube Int'l. Inc.	Fast Oil Change	$214,000–273,000
12	Instant Tax Service	Retail Tax Preparation & Electronic Filing	$39,000–89,000
13	Baskin-Robbins USA Co.	Ice Cream, Frozen Yogurt, Frozen Beverages	$121,300–419,600
14	KFC Corp.	Chicken	$1,200,000–1,800,000
15	Jani-King	Commercial Cleaning	$11,300–34,100+
16	Dairy Queen	Soft-Serve Dairy Products & Sandwiches	$70,000–1,300,000
17	Super 8	Economy Motels	$274,960–3,100,000
18	Arby's	Sandwiches, Chicken, Salads	$336,500–2,400,000
19	Jan-Pro Franchising Int'l. Inc.	Commercial Cleaning	$3,300–54,300
20	Taco Bell Corp.	Quick-Service Mexican Restaurant	$1,300,000–2,500,000
21	Hampton Inn/Hampton Inn & Suites	Mid-Price Hotels	$3,600,000–10,900,000
22	Days Inn Worldwide	Hotels & Inns	$392,100–6,400,000
23	GNC Franchising Inc.	Vitamin & Nutrition Store	$130,200–232,700
24	Snap Fitness Inc.	24-Hour Fitness Center	$71,100–241,900
25	Denny's Inc.	Full-Service Family Restaurant	$1,200,000–2,600,000
26	Hardee's	Burgers, Chicken, Biscuits	$1,100,000–1,500,000
27	Kumon Math & Reading Centers	Supplemental Education	$30,960–129,400
28	Servpro	Insurance/Disaster Restoration & Cleaning	$100,300–159,200
29	Supercuts	Hair Salon	$95,600–219,200
30	7-Eleven Inc.	Convenience Store	Varies

Source: "2009 Franchise 500 Rankings," www.entrepreneur.com, accessed February 11, 2009.

Some Web sites Where People with Franchising-related Questions Can Find Answers:
• **Federal Trade Commission (http://www.ftc.gov)** Has a host of information consumers looking to buy a franchise might need. Click on the "Franchise & Business Opportunities" link. Contains information on FTC regulation as well as contact information for state regulators.
• **North American Securities Administrators Association (http://www.nasaa.org)** The umbrella group for state securities regulators offers links to find regulators and also has links to other governmental agencies.
• **International Franchise Association (http://www.franchise.org)** Contains information on such topics as buying a franchise and government relations. The site's FAQ section deals with some issues of franchise regulation.
• **American Franchisee Association (http://www.franchisee.org)** Represents franchisees and has information on legal resources, FTC regulations, and state law.
• **American Association of Franchisees & Dealers (http://www.aafd.org)** Offers legal and financial information.

EXHIBIT 13.4

Sources of Franchise Information

differences, McDonald's foreign franchisees still maintain the company's standards of service and cleanliness.

REVIEW LEARNING OUTCOME

LO5 Define *franchising* and describe its two basic forms

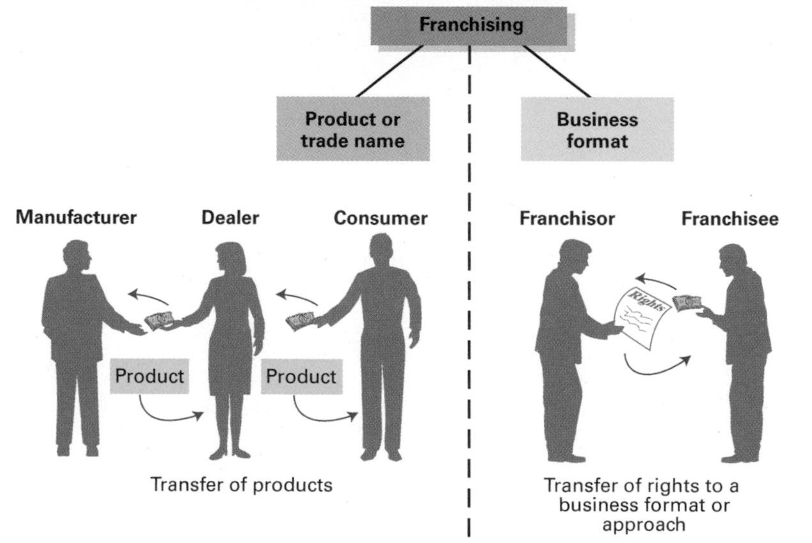

Franchising

Product or trade name — Manufacturer, Dealer, Consumer; Product, Product. Transfer of products

Business format — Franchisor, Franchisee; Rights. Transfer of rights to a business format or approach

LO6

RETAIL MARKETING STRATEGY

Retailers must develop marketing strategies based on overall goals and strategic plans. Retailing goals might include more traffic, higher sales of a specific item, a more upscale image, or heightened public awareness of the retail operation. The strategies that retailers use to obtain their goals might include a sale, an updated décor, or a new advertisement. The key tasks in strategic retailing are defining and selecting a target market and developing the retailing mix to successfully meet the needs of the chosen target market.

Defining a Target Market

The first and foremost task in developing a retail strategy is to define the target market. This process begins with market segmentation, the topic of Chapter 8. Successful retailing has always been based on knowing the customer. Sometimes retailing chains flounder when management loses sight of the customers the stores should be serving.

Target markets in retailing are often defined by demographics, geographics, and psychographics. For instance, Bluefly.com, a discount fashion e-tailer, targets both men and women in their thirties, who have a higher-than-average income, read fashion magazines, and favor high-end designers. By understanding who its customers are, the company has been able to tailor its Web site to appeal specifically to its audience. The result is a higher sales rate than most clothing e-tailers, rating number 131 in the Internet Retailer Top 500 Guide.[32]

Determining a target market is a prerequisite to creating the retailing mix. For example, Target's merchandising approach for sporting goods is to match its product assortment to the demographics of the local store and region. The amount of space devoted to sporting goods, as well as in-store promotions, also varies according to each store's target market.

EXHIBIT 13.5

The Retailing Mix

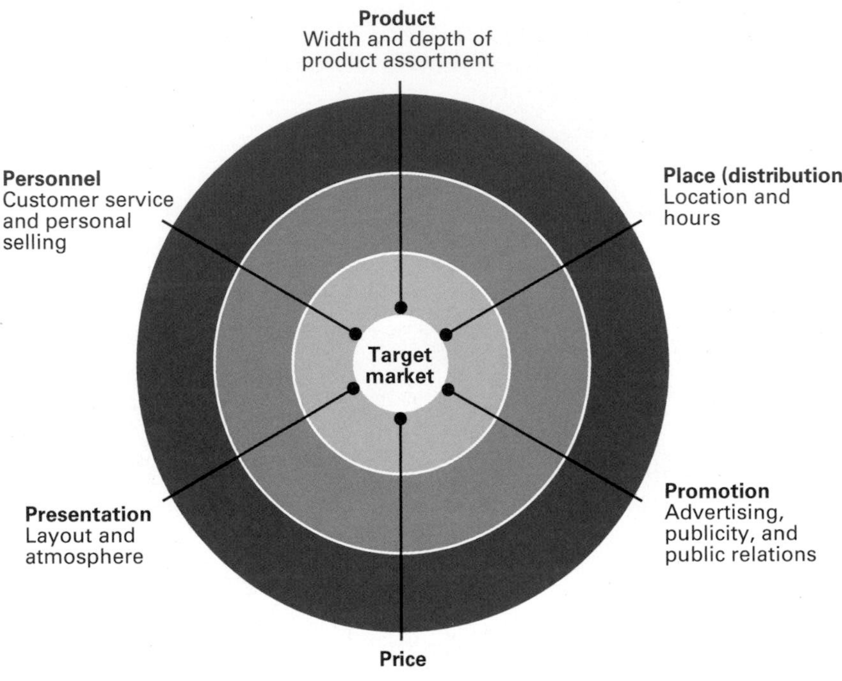

Choosing the Retailing Mix

Retailers combine the elements of the retailing mix to come up with a single retailing method to attract the target market. The **retailing mix** consists of six Ps: the four Ps of the marketing mix (product, place, promotion, and price) plus presentation and personnel. (See Exhibit 13.5.)

The combination of the six Ps projects a store's image, which influences consumers' perceptions. Using these impressions of stores, shoppers position one store against another. A retail marketing manager must make sure that the store's positioning is compatible with the target customers' expectations. As discussed at the beginning of the chapter, retail stores can be positioned on three broad dimensions: service provided by store personnel, product assortment, and price. Management should use everything else—place, presentation, and promotion—to fine-tune the basic positioning of the store.

The Product Offering The first element in the retailing mix is the **product offering**, also called the *product assortment* or *merchandise mix*. Retailers decide what to sell on the basis of what their target market wants to buy. They can base their decision on market research, past sales, fashion trends, customer requests, and other sources. A recent approach, called data mining, uses complex mathematical models to help retailers make better product mix decisions. Early users of the approach, such as Dillard's, Target, and Wal-Mart, use data mining to determine which products to stock at what price, how to manage markdowns, and how to advertise to draw target customers.

Prices for private-label goods are typically lower than prices for national brands, giving customers greater value. Sears has been using private-label branding for decades, and its Kenmore, Craftsman, and DieHard brands have grown into household names.

Developing a product offering is essentially a question of the width and depth of the product assortment. *Width* refers to the assortment of products offered; *depth* refers to the number of different brands offered within each assortment. Price, store design, displays, and service are important to consumers in determining where to shop, but the most critical factor is merchandise selection. For example, Target recently expanded its width by introducing a new line of eco-friendly women's clothing, with the fabrics used made of 100 percent certified organic fiber.[33] This reasoning also holds true for online retailers. Amazon.com, for instance, is building the world's biggest online department store so that shoppers can get whatever they want with one click on their Web browsers. Like a traditional department store or mass merchandiser, Amazon offers considerable width in its product assortment with millions of different items, including books, music, toys, videos, tools and hardware, health and beauty aids, electronics, and software. Conversely, online specialty retailers, such as 1-800-Flowers.com, gloss.com (makeup), and polo.com (clothing), focus on a single category of merchandise, hoping to attract loyal customers with a larger depth of products at lower prices and better customer service. Many online retailers purposely focus on single product line niches that could never garner enough foot traffic to support a traditional brick-and-mortar store.

After determining what products will satisfy target customers' desires, retailers must find sources of supply and evaluate the products. When the right products are found, the retail buyer negotiates a purchase contract. The buying function can either be performed in-house or be delegated to an outside firm. The goods must then be moved from the seller to the retailer, which means shipping, storing, and stocking the inventory. The trick is to manage the inventory by cutting prices to move slow goods and by keeping adequate supplies of hot-selling items in stock. As in all good systems, the final step is to evaluate the entire process to seek more efficient methods and eliminate problems and bottlenecks.

As margins drop and competition intensifies, retailers are becoming ever more aware of the advantages of *private brands*, or those brands that are designed and developed using the retailer's name. Because the cost of goods typically makes up between 60 and 75 percent of a retailer's expenses, eliminating intermediaries can shave costs. As a result, prices of private-label goods are typically lower than for national brands, giving customers greater value. Private-label branding is not new. For decades, Sears has fashioned its Kenmore, Craftsman, and DieHard brands into household names. Wal-Mart has several successful private-label brands such as White Cloud paper products, Spring Valley nutritional supplements, Sam's American Choice laundry detergent, EverActive alkaline batteries, and EverStart auto batteries. Its Ol' Roy dog food and Sam's American Choice garden fertilizer are now the best-selling brands in their categories.

Promotion Strategy Retail promotion strategy includes advertising, public relations and publicity, and sales promotion. The goal is to help position the store in consumers' minds. Retailers design intriguing ads, stage special events, and develop promotions aimed at their target markets. Today's grand openings are a carefully orchestrated blend of advertising, merchandising, goodwill, and glitter. All the elements of an opening—press coverage, special events, media advertising, and store displays—are carefully planned. For example, when Victoria's Secret opened its megastore in Dallas, the opening featured a $150 gift with a $50 purchase, free makeovers from a Victoria's Secret Fashion Show makeup artist, $10 gift cards that could be redeemed in the store, and an appearance by supermodel Heidi Klum.

Retailers' advertising is carried out mostly at the local level. Local advertising by retailers usually provides specific information about their stores, such as location, merchandise, hours, prices, and special sales. In contrast, national retail advertising generally focuses on image. For example, Target has used its "sign of the times" advertising campaign to effectively position itself as the "chic place to buy cheap."

Target's advertising campaign also takes advantage of cooperative advertising, another popular retail advertising practice. Traditionally, marketers would pay retailers to feature their products in store mailers, or a marketer would develop a TV campaign for the product and simply tack on several retailers' names at the end. But Target's advertising makes use of a more collaborative trend by integrating products such as Tide

retailing mix
A combination of the six Ps—product, place, promotion, price, presentation, and personnel—to sell goods and services to the ultimate consumer.

product offering
The mix of products offered to the consumer by the retailer; also called the product assortment or merchandise mix.

laundry detergent, Tums antacids, or Coca-Cola into the actual campaign. Another common form of cooperative advertising involves promotion of exclusive products. For example, Target hires famous designers to develop reasonably priced product lines available exclusively at Target stores.

Many retailers are forgoing media advertising these days in favor of direct-mail or frequent shopper programs. Direct-mail and catalog programs are luring many retailers, which hope they will prove to be a cost-effective means of increasing brand loyalty and spending by core customers. Nordstrom, for example, mails catalogs featuring brand-name and private-brand clothing, shoes, and accessories to target the shop-at-home crowd. Restaurants and small retailers have successfully used frequent diner or frequent shopper programs for years. For example, customers with a Victoria's Secret Angel credit card are offered monthly specials on store merchandise, including items that generally are not put on sale to the public.

The Proper Location The retailing axiom "location, location, location" has long emphasized the importance of place to the retail mix. The location decision is important first because the retailer is making a large, semipermanent commitment of resources that can reduce its future flexibility. Second, the location will affect the store's future growth and profitability.

Site location begins by choosing a community. Important factors to consider are the area's economic growth potential, the amount of competition, and geography. For instance, retailers like T.J. Maxx, Wal-Mart, and Target build stores in areas where the

GLOBAL Perspectives

Adding Insult to Injury? Retail Price Gouging in the Wake of Disaster[34]

No one likes to pay more than they have to for goods and services when shopping at a retail location. At the same time, retailers are in business to make money, and in general, are free to charge whatever price they want for their offerings—opting to let the free marketplace decide whether or not to buy is a longstanding American value. However, some retailers were accused of taking their usual profit motives too far in charging much higher-than-normal prices in the days and weeks following the 9/11 tragedy, Hurricanes Katrina and Ike, and other similarly unfortunate events.

Price gouging, otherwise known as profiteering, has significant ethical implications for retail business practice. As examples of price gouging behavior (i.e., the arbitrary raising of prices beyond what would normally be considered to be reasonable or fair, often to take advantage of a seemingly unrelated situation), one needs only to envision the aftermath of Hurricane Katrina. Following the storm, low-quality motels in eastern and southern Texas were reported as charging over $300 per night, a sixfold increase over normal prices. Gas stations across the southern U.S.—even some far from the reaches of the storm, raised prices per gallon to over $6. Other needed commodities such as food, ice, and plywood needed to cover windows were widely reported as being similarly marked up prior to the time the storm hit land.

A Gallup opinion poll taken afterward found that 79 percent of respondents believed sellers were exploiting the hurricane in order to charge unfair prices. Feelings were so strong about the unfairness of the situation that the U.S. Congress considered bills prohibiting unfair pricing practices in the wake of national disasters and other similar events. Yet an alternative school of thought suggests that the retailers in question were doing nothing wrong—they were simply acting in the best interests of their business mission. After all, retailers are in the business of making money, and why should external and uncontrollable conditions impede them from serving their stakeholders as much as possible?

Furthermore, many retailers believe the prices they charged following the numerous disastrous events of recent years are somewhat out of their control. In the petroleum industry specifically, many retailers suggested that the prices charged by their suppliers, who were predicting the impact of the event on commodity futures markets, made it necessary for them to raise prices in order to remain profitable.

What do you think? Should retailers be held accountable in a court of law when they raise prices in response to weather, earthquakes, or terrorism-related events? Should Congress pass laws prohibiting such behavior? Or is there some reasonable middle ground to be identified?

population is growing. Often these large retailers will build stores in new communities that are still under development. On the other hand, while population growth is an important consideration for fast-food restaurants, most also look for an area with other fast-food restaurants because being located in clusters helps to draw customers for each restaurant. However, even after careful research the perfect position can be elusive in the face of changing markets. For example, Wendy's found when attempting to enter the competitive breakfast business that its locations weren't positioned on the right side of the road to attract the bulk of commuters looking for breakfast.[35] Finally, for many retailers geography remains the most important factor in choosing a community. For example, Starbucks coffee looks for densely populated urban communities for its stores, Talbots looks for locations near upper-class neighborhoods, and Buckle stores look for locations in small, underserved cities.

After settling on a geographic region or community, retailers must choose a specific site. In addition to growth potential, the important factors are neighborhood socioeconomic characteristics, traffic flows, land costs, zoning regulations, and public transportation. A particular site's visibility, parking, entrance and exit locations, accessibility, and safety and security are also considered. Additionally, a retailer should consider how its store would fit into the surrounding environment. Retail decision makers probably would not locate a Dollar General store next door to a Neiman Marcus department store.

Retailers face one final decision about location: whether to have a freestanding unit or to become a tenant in a shopping center or mall.

Freestanding Stores An isolated, freestanding location can be used by large retailers like Wal-Mart or Target and sellers of shopping goods like furniture and cars because they are "destination" stores. **Destination stores** are stores consumers seek out and purposely plan to visit. An isolated store location may have the advantages of low site cost or rent and no nearby competitors. On the other hand, it may be hard to attract customers to a freestanding location, and no other retailers are around to share costs.

Freestanding units are increasing in popularity as retailers strive to make their stores more convenient to access, more enticing to shop, and more profitable. Freestanding sites now account for more than half of all retail construction in the United States as more and more retailers are deciding not to locate in pedestrian malls. Perhaps the greatest reason for developing a freestanding site is greater visibility. Retailers often feel they get lost in huge centers and malls, but freestanding units can help stores develop an identity with shoppers. The ability to grow at faster rates through freestanding buildings has also propelled the surge toward stand-alone units. Retailers like The Sports Authority, Best Buy, and Bed Bath & Beyond choose to be freestanding to achieve their expansion objectives. An aggressive expansion plan may not allow time to wait for shopping centers to be built. Similarly, drugstore chains like Walgreens and Rite Aid have been aggressively relocating their existing mall and shopping center stores to freestanding sites, especially street corner sites for drive-through accessibility.

Shopping Centers Shopping centers began in the 1950s when the U.S. population started migrating to the suburbs. The first shopping centers were *strip centers*, typically located along busy streets. They usually included a supermarket, a variety store, and perhaps a few specialty stores. Then *community shopping centers* emerged, with one or two small department stores, more specialty stores, a couple of restaurants, and several apparel stores. These community shopping centers provided off-street parking and a broader variety of merchandise.

Regional malls offering a much wider variety of merchandise started appearing in the mid-1970s. Regional malls are either entirely enclosed or roofed to allow shopping in any weather. Most are landscaped with trees, fountains, sculptures, and the like to enhance the shopping environment. They have acres of free parking. The *anchor stores* or *generator stores* (JCPenney, Sears, or major department stores) are usually located at opposite ends of the mall to create heavy foot traffic. Las Vegas's Fashion Show Mall takes the concept to the extreme. The mall has 2 million square feet of retail space and boasts over 250 stores, 8 of which are anchor stores, including Neiman Marcus, Saks

destination stores
Stores that consumers purposely plan to visit.

Fifth Avenue, Macy's, Bloomingdale Home, and Nordstrom. Mall of America goes even further, with 2.5 million square feet of retail space and over 520 stores.

According to shopping center developers, the newest generation of shopping centers are *lifestyle centers*. These new open-air shopping centers are targeted to upper-income shoppers with an aversion for "the mall" and seek to create an atmosphere that is part neighborhood park and part urban shopping center. Lifestyle centers typically combine outdoor shopping areas composed of upscale retailers and restaurants, with plazas, fountains, and pedestrian streets. Newer centers like the Easton Town Center in Columbus, Ohio, and the Legacy Town Center in Plano, Texas, also include luxury apartments and condominiums. Lifestyle centers are appealing to retail developers looking for an alternative to the traditional shopping mall, a concept rapidly losing favor among shoppers. Consumers have also become more pressed for time in recent years and are choosing more convenient stand-alone stores and neighborhood centers instead of malls. And recently, outlet malls are enjoying a sort of resurgence, with many retailers stepping up their outlet offerings in order to capture a greater share of retail dollars. This is true even for upscale retailers such as Neiman Marcus, whose NM Last Call is planning on adding two new locations in the near future.[36] Faced with this trend, mall developers have improved the layout of many malls to make it more convenient for customers to shop. For instance, the RiverTown Crossings center in Grandville, Michigan, clusters competing stores, like Abercrombie Kids, GapKids, Gymboree, and other kids' clothing stores in one section of the mall to accommodate time-strapped parents.[37] Locating in a community shopping center or regional mall offers several advantages and disadvantages, as shown in Exhibit 13.6.

EXHIBIT 13.6

Advantages and Disadvantages of Locating in a Community Shopping Center or Regional Mall

Advantages	Disadvantages
facilities present a unified image and are designed to attract shoppers	expensive leases
tenants share the expenses of the mall's common area and promotions for the whole mall	common promotion efforts might not attract customers to a particular store
the shopping environment, anchor stores, and "village square" activities draw customers	anchor stores dominate the tenants' association
malls can target different demographic groups, such as upscale or bargain shoppers	possibility of having direct competitors within the same facility
ample parking is available	lease restrictions on merchandise carried and hours of operation

Retail Prices Another important element in the retailing mix is price. Retailing's ultimate goal is to sell products to consumers, and the right price is critical in ensuring sales. Because retail prices are usually based on the cost of the merchandise, an essential part of pricing is efficient and timely buying.

Price is also a key element in a retail store's positioning strategy. Higher prices often indicate a level of quality and help reinforce the prestigious image of retailers, such as Tiffany, Saks Fifth Avenue, Gucci, Cartier, and Neiman Marcus. On the other hand, discounters and off-price retailers, such as Target and T.J. Maxx, offer good value for the money. There are even stores, such as Dollar Tree, where everything costs one dollar. Dollar Tree's single-price-point strategy is aimed at getting customers to make impulse purchases through what analysts call the "wow factor"—the excitement of discovering that an item costs only a dollar.

A pricing trend among American retailers that seems to be here to stay is *everyday low pricing*, or EDLP. Introduced to the retail industry by Wal-Mart, EDLP offers consumers a low price all the time rather than holding periodic sales on merchandise. Even large retail giants, like Macy's, Inc., have phased out deep discounts and sales in favor of lower prices every day. Similarly, Gap reduced prices on denim jeans, denim shirts, socks, and other items to protect and broaden the company's share of the casual clothes market. Supermarkets such as Albertsons and Winn-Dixie have also found success in EDLP.

Presentation of the Retail Store The presentation of a retail store helps determine the store's image and positions the retail store in consumers' minds. For instance, a retailer that wants to position itself as an upscale store would use a lavish or sophisticated presentation.

The main element of a store's presentation is its **atmosphere**, the overall impression conveyed by a store's physical layout, décor, and surroundings. The atmosphere might create a relaxed or busy feeling, a sense of luxury or of efficiency, a friendly or cold attitude, a sense of organization or of clutter, or a fun or serious mood. For example, Wolfgang Puck restaurants feature tiles in the shape of a pizza on the floors, walls, and countertops. Urban Outfitters stores, targeted to Generation Y consumers, use raw concrete, original brick, rusted steel, and unfinished wood to convey an urban feel. Likewise, REI sporting-goods stores feature indoor rock-climbing walls, bike test trails, and rain rooms for testing outdoor gear.

When not actually browsing or buying, people enjoy a comfortable and memorable experience in a shopping environment. Shopping malls and lifestyle centers now provide shoppers with kids' play towns and parents' rooms for retreating with babies and toddlers.

The layout of retail stores is a key factor in their success. The goal is to use all space in the store effectively, including aisles, fixtures, merchandise displays, and nonselling areas. In addition to making shopping easy and convenient for the customer, an effective layout has a powerful influence on customer traffic patterns and purchasing behavior. For instance, Kohl's unique circular layout encourages customers to pass all of a store's departments to reach the checkout lanes. The stores are smaller than most department stores but have a wide aisle with plenty of room for customers and shopping carts. Each department is limited to five display racks on the main aisle. Displays are spaced widely and are set at varying heights so that customers can see everything in the department, including wall displays, from the main aisle. To further enhance the store's clean crisp presentation, merchandise is displayed from light to dark, which research suggests is most pleasing to the eye. Finally, to encourage last-minute, impulse purchases, Kohl's displays low-cost items at the checkout register. Together with other merchandising strategies, the store layout generates an average of over $300 in sales per square foot (a standard industry measure) in Kohl's almost 750 stores in 41 states and typical annual sales increases of more than 10 percent.[38]

Layout also includes where products are placed in the store. Many technologically advanced retailers are using a technique called *market-basket analysis* to analyze the huge amounts of data collected through their point-of-purchase scanning equipment. The analysis looks for products that are commonly purchased together to help retailers place products in the right places. Wal-Mart uses market-basket analysis to determine where in the store to stock products for customer convenience.[39] In a typical Wal-Mart Supercenter, bananas are placed not only in the produce section but also in the cereal aisle. Kleenex tissues are in the paper-goods aisle and also mixed in with the cold medicines. Measuring spoons are in the housewares and also hanging next to Crisco shortening. During October, flashlights are with the Halloween costumes as well as in the hardware aisle.

These are the most influential factors in creating a store's atmosphere:

- *Employee type and density*: Employee type refers to an employee's general characteristics—for instance, neat, friendly, knowledgeable, or service-oriented. Density is the number of employees per thousand square feet of selling space. A discounter like Kmart has a low employee density that creates a "do-it-yourself,"

atmosphere
The overall impression conveyed by a store's physical layout, décor, and surroundings.

casual atmosphere. In contrast, Neiman Marcus's density is much higher, denoting readiness to serve the customer's every whim. Too many employees and not enough customers, however, can convey an air of desperation and intimidate customers.

- *Merchandise type and density:* The type of merchandise carried and how it is displayed add to the atmosphere the retailer is trying to create. A prestigious retailer like Saks or Bloomingdale's carries the best brand names and displays them in a neat, uncluttered arrangement. Discounters and off-price retailers, such as Marshalls and T.J. Maxx, may sell some well-known brands, but many carry seconds or out-of-season goods. Their merchandise is crowded into small spaces and hung on long racks by category—tops, pants, skirts, and so on—to create the impression that "We've got so much stuff, we're practically giving it away."
- *Fixture type and density:* Fixtures can be elegant (rich woods), trendy (chrome and smoked glass), or consist of old, beat-up tables, as in an antiques store. The fixtures should be consistent with the general atmosphere the store is trying to create. Apple has let its focus on design inform the look of its retail stores. Many Apple stores contain a signature glass staircase designed in part by CEO Steve Jobs, and all use large open tables to display company products. Because products are not cluttered on store shelves, it is easier for store visitors to play with them.[40]
- *Sound:* Sound can be pleasant or unpleasant for a customer. Classical music at a nice Italian restaurant helps create ambience, just as country-and-western music does at a truck stop. Music can also entice customers to stay in the store longer and buy more or eat quickly and leave a table for others. For instance, rapid music tends to make people eat more, chew less, and take bigger bites, whereas slow music prompts people to dine more leisurely and eat less. Retailers can tailor their musical atmosphere to their shoppers' demographics and the merchandise they're selling. Music can control the pace of the store traffic, create an image, and attract or direct the shopper's attention. Starbucks has parlayed its unique in-store music selections into a new business with its Hear Music Cafés and kiosks selling featured Hear Music artists in most Starbucks locations.
- *Odors:* Smell can either stimulate or detract from sales. The wonderful smell of pastries and breads entices bakery customers. Conversely, customers can be repulsed by bad odors such as cigarette smoke, musty smells, antiseptic odors, and overly powerful room deodorizers. If a grocery store pumps in the smell of baked goods, sales in that department increase threefold. Department stores have pumped in fragrances that are pleasing to their target market, and the response has been favorable. Not surprisingly, retailers are increasingly using fragrance as a key design element, as important as layout, lighting, and background music. Research suggests that people evaluate merchandise more positively, spend more time shopping, and are generally in a better mood when an agreeable odor is present. Retailers use fragrances as an extension of their retail strategy.
- *Visual factors:* Colors can create a mood or focus attention and therefore are an important factor in atmosphere. Red, yellow, and orange are considered warm colors and are used when a feeling of warmth and closeness is desired. Cool colors like blue, green, and violet are used to open up closed-in places and create an air of elegance and cleanliness. For example, Starbucks uses an eggplant, golden yellow, and dark olive color combination so that customers will feel comfortable yet sophisticated. Some colors are better for display. For instance, diamonds appear most striking against black or dark blue velvet. Lighting can also have an important effect on store atmosphere. Jewelry is best displayed under high-intensity spotlights and cosmetics under more natural lighting. Many retailers have found that natural lighting, either from windows or skylights, can lead to increased sales. Outdoor lighting can also affect consumer patronage. Consumers often are afraid to shop after dark in many areas and prefer strong lighting for safety. The outdoor facade of the store also adds to its ambience and helps create favorable first impressions.

Personnel and Customer Service People are a unique aspect of retailing. Most retail sales involve a customer–salesperson relationship, if only briefly. When customers shop at a grocery store, the cashiers check and bag their groceries. When customers shop at a prestigious clothier, the salesclerks may help select the styles, sizes, and colors. They may also assist in the fitting process, offer alteration services, wrap purchases, and even offer a glass of champagne. Sales personnel provide their customers with the amount of service prescribed in the retail strategy of the store.

Retail salespeople serve another important selling function: They persuade shoppers to buy. They must therefore be able to persuade customers that what they are selling is what the customer needs. Salespeople are trained in two common selling techniques: trading up and suggestion selling. Trading up means persuading customers to buy a higher-priced item than they originally intended to buy. To avoid selling customers something they do not need or want, however, salespeople should take care when practicing trading-up techniques. Suggestion selling, a common practice among most retailers, seeks to broaden customers' original purchases with related items. For example, if you buy a new printer at Office Depot, the sales representative will ask if you would like to purchase paper, a USB cable, and/or extra ink cartridges. Similarly, McDonald's cashiers are trained to ask customers if they would like a hot apple pie with their hamburger and fries. Suggestion selling and trading up should always help shoppers recognize true needs rather than sell them unwanted merchandise.

> *"Trading up means persuading customers to buy a higher-priced item than they originally intended to buy."*

Providing great customer service is one of the most challenging elements in the retail mix because customer expectations change. In the 1990s shoppers wanted personal one-on-one attention. Today, many customers are happy to help themselves as long as they can easily find what they need. To respond to this new perspective, some retailers are adding retail sales technologies that maximize salesperson helpfulness while minimizing intrusion. New handheld devices marketed by Motorola enable sales associates to look up product information on the spot and to communicate with other associates in order to facilitate the quick response needed for customer questions.[41] In addition, customer expectations for service vary considerably. What customers expect in a department store is very different from their expectations for a discount store. Luxury retailers, for whom extreme customer service has always been a hallmark, are beginning to add a new level of service personnel to their high-profile locations: the store concierge. Concierges routinely fulfill customer requests that have nothing to do with shopping. Gary Jackson is the concierge for the Dallas store of luxury retailer Barneys New York. He has called a new private club to get a customer on the guest list and has squired another customer's college-age daughter and her out-of-town guests around to Dallas's newest nightspots. When one customer ripped a pair of pants and needed replacements that matched his suit jacket before an important meeting the next morning, Jackson delivered a selection of pants to the customer's hotel room at 11 P.M. the night before.[42]

Customer service is also critical for online retailers. Online shoppers expect a retailer's Web site to be easy to use, products to be available, and returns to be simple. Therefore, customer-friendly retailers like Bluefly .com design their sites to give their customers the information they need such as what's new and what's on sale. Other companies, such as Amazon.com and LandsEnd.com, offer product recommendations and

REVIEW LEARNING OUTCOME

LO 6 List the major tasks involved in developing a retail marketing strategy

personal shoppers. Some retailers that have online, catalog, and traditional brick-and-mortar stores, such as Lands' End, Gap, and Williams-Sonoma, now allow customers to return goods bought through the catalog or online to their traditional store to make returns easier.

LO 7

NEW DEVELOPMENTS IN RETAILING

In an effort to better serve their customers and attract new ones, retailers are constantly adopting new strategies. Two recent developments are interactivity and m-commerce.

Interactivity

Adding interactivity to the retail environment is one of the most popular strategies in retailing in the past few years. Small retailers as well as national chains are using interactivity in stores to differentiate themselves from the competition. For some time, retailers have used "entertainment" retailing in the form of playing music, showing videos, hosting special events, and sponsoring guest appearances, but the new interactive trend gets customers involved rather than just catching their eye. For example, at the American Girl store in Chicago, customers can purchase a doll made to look like them, take their dolls to the in-store American Girl café, go to the American Girl Theater, and even have their birthday parties. Similarly, Build-A-Bear enables customers to make their own stuffed animal by choosing which animal to stuff and then dressing and naming it. You can hold birthday parties there, too.

Involvement isn't just for children, either. For Your Entertainment, one of the country's leading specialty retailers of movies, music, and games, regularly invites artists to perform in its stores. Performers may be local favorites or national superstars. FYE even has a MySpace site that features a state-by-state touring schedule and allows local performers to sign up to play at its stores. Fans can request to see a local group perform at an FYE store or ask the stores to stock recordings by their local favorites.[43]

M-Commerce

M-commerce (mobile e-commerce) enables consumers using wireless mobile devices to connect to the Internet and shop. Essentially, m-commerce goes beyond text message advertisements to allow consumers to purchase goods and services by using wireless mobile devices, such as mobile telephones, pagers, personal digital assistants (PDAs), and handheld computers. For example, both PepsiCo and Coca-Cola have developed smart vending technologies that utilize a "cashless" payment system that accepts credit cards, RFID devices, and even hotel room keys. Offices across the country are installing self-serve coffee machines where office workers can buy freshly brewed single-cup gourmet coffee and conveniently pay with their traditional magnetic stripe credit or debit cards. The company AIR-serv plans to install thousands of cashless transaction terminals in its coin-operated tire inflation and vacuuming machines at gas stations and convenience stores. Cashless services are also available for the vending industry, laundry facilities, parking and toll booths, photo and video kiosks, hotel business centers, and a variety of other commercial markets.[44] M-commerce enjoyed early success overseas, but has been slower in gaining acceptance and popularity in the United States. For instance, Japan has over 95 million wireless subscribers, and there are more than 200 million in the United States. But only about $480 million in revenue was generated by about 7 million U.S. m-commerce users compared to Japan's 27 million m-commerce users generating $10 billion in sales. One research company in the UK, Juniper Research, predicts the global m-commerce market will reach $88 billion in 2009.[45]

M-commerce users adopt the new technology because it saves time and offers more convenience in a greater number of locations. Vending machines have become an important venue for m-commerce. More than 75 million Americans subscribe to mobile Internet providers to search, e-mail, and check weather and sports. Even so, the U.S. is an immature market compared to Japan and Western Europe.

Pop-Up Shops

Companies of all sizes are experimenting with **pop-up shops**. As the name implies, pop-up shops are temporary retail establishments that allow companies flexible locations without the long-term commitment of a more expensive retail lease. Italian coffee maker illy opened a pop-up shop at Time Warner Center in New York for ten days. In addition to selling coffee, the illy shop, created from a shipping container, offered free samples from the company's soon-to-be-released Hyper Espresso System machine.[46] Pop-up shops aren't always sized like kiosks, however. Toys"R"Us opened a 25,000-square-foot temporary store in the former Tower Records building during the Christmas shopping season.[47]

Wired magazine incorporated interactivity in its holiday pop-up shop. Customers could try out over 100 of the latest techie toys and participate in a SoHo scavenger hunt (contestants used a Palm Centro to navigate through the game) for a chance at winning a Nintendo Wii.[48]

pop-up shops
Temporary retail establishments that allow flexible locations without the long-term commitment of a more expensive retail lease.

CUSTOMER Experience

What's in Store for Customers? In Some Cases, Another Store.

Modern retailers are constantly on the lookout for ways to differentiate themselves from the competition, whether it be offering different products, providing unique services, or simply through lower pricing or superior service. Such activities are particularly important in challenging economic times, and in locations where competition is potent. In response to these conditions, some retailers are using an innovative new venture designed to extend their brands into previously uncharted market territory—pop-up stores. Pop-up stores are smaller retail spaces housed entirely within larger retailers that offer related goods to the host retailer, but of a slightly different level of quality or prestige. When retail traffic is lagging at malls or shopping centers, pop-up stores are one more reason for potential customers to come inside.

Though the store-within-a-store concept is not entirely new—Apple, for example, opened such formats in CompUSA locations several years ago—their emergence as a method for exploring new markets appears to have reached a tipping point in recent years. In general, pop-up stores carry merchandise intended to appeal to a slightly different market segment than the host. For example, JCPenney has implemented upscale Sephora cosmetic shops in many of its locations in an attempt to appeal to younger shoppers. One alternative goal is that as the younger women age, they will "graduate" to the regular brands carried by the retailer that cater to older women. Similarly, FAO Schwarz toy boutiques are popping up in the nearly 700 Macy's department stores that retail children's clothing, providing Macy's with a more upscale brand of children's products while at the same time combating the perception that all Schwarz toys are expensive. In this case, Schwarz is hoping to gain share from parents who would otherwise be hesitant to spend time shopping for toys at a specialty retailer.

In the case of both Schwarz and Sephora, the host retailer is lent a little extra brand image by allowing the pop-up to operate for a fixed time period within its advantageous retail space. In some other cases, however, the pop-up store gains in brand image by becoming associated with the host. For instance, Levi Strauss & Company recently completed a 60-day stint in the more exclusive American Rag Cie Denim Bar on Los Angeles's La Brea Avenue, a premier shopping area. To accommodate the tastes of the store's usual patrons, Levi's stocked the pop-up with a limited edition model of jeans and used live celebrity spokespeople such as Mary-Kate Olsen in an in-store fashion show format to get the point across that the brand was worth owning even for more discerning customers.

Through the creative use of store-in-store techniques, retailers are able to branch out into different customer groups, and potentially convert customers toward new and different product types and brands. Though the war for retail dollars is always fierce, at least in the short run, some retailers are winning the battle for customer attention.[49]

REVIEW LEARNING OUTCOME

Describe new developments in retailing

Interactivity gets consumers involved in retail experience.

M-commerce is purchasing goods through mobile devices.

Pop-up shops provide flexible locations without long-term commitment.

Small stores within larger stores—a store-in-a-store—provide shopping convenience.

Another trend in pop-up retailing is the store-in-a-store model. Companies as diverse as Levenger (whose tagline is "Tools for Serious Readers"), Apple, Kolo (an international photo album company), Procter & Gamble, and more have used the store-in-a-store concept. Levenger has small stores inside two Chicago Macy's locations; Apple has stores in various Best Buy stores in the United States and FNAC stores in France; Kolo opened a 450-square-foot Kolo Boutique inside Kate's Paperie, a famous stationery store in Soho; and Procter & Gamble has dedicated shops for health and beauty inside certain Royal Ahold grocery stores.[50]

90 ◀ percentage of retailers operating just one store

10 ◀ percentage of the capability of new electronic gear actually used by consumers

15 ◀ prescriptions purchased by the average 60-year-old each year

SuperTarget ▶ **177** locations in the U.S.

$347,000 ◀ cost of the diamond solitaire ring offered by Sam's Club at Christmastime

meals Americans eat in restaurants and cafeterias each year ▶ **70 billion**

Dell's daily online sales of computers and equipment ▶ **$50 million**

250 ◀ new products introduced on QVC each week

percentage of Americans with Internet access at home or work ▶ **70**

80 ◀ countries with KFC franchises

ANATOMY OF A Store Layout

Grocery

1 If a store wants to project a "service" image as well as "fresh food" image, services are placed near the entrance.

© iStockphoto.com/Sean Locke

© iStockphoto.com/Sean Locke

© iStockphoto.com/Catherine Yeulet

2 Vegetables and fruits are placed near beginning of the store's traffic pattern for their inviting, "fresh food" image.

3 Pharmacy + floral shop + restaurant = scrambled merchandizing.

© iStockphoto.com/Edward Bock

4 "Race track" arrangement keeps customers moving through the store and making purchases.

© iStockphoto.com/Willie B. Thomas

© iStockphoto.com/Derek Dafoe

5 Staples such as meat, eggs, milk, and bakery items are placed farthest from the entrance because the more products a shopper passes by, the more he or she is likely to purchase.

7 Reduced service (self bagging and self checkout) saves time and reduces costs.

© iStockphoto.com/Derek Dafoe

6 Food manufacturers pay "slotting" fees to get aisle end caps and eye-level shelf space. Upper- and lower-level shelf space is reserved for low-margin/low-profit items.

REVIEW AND APPLICATIONS

Discuss the importance of retailing in the U.S. economy. Retailing plays a vital role in the U.S. economy for two main reasons. First, retail businesses contribute to our high standard of living by providing a vast number and diversity of goods and services. Second, retailing employs a large part of the U.S. working population—over 15 million people.

1.1 To fully appreciate the role retailing plays in the U.S. economy, it may be helpful to review a selection of press articles related to the retailing industry. Search for articles pertaining to retailing. Read a selection of articles, and report your findings to the class.

1.2 Keep a shopping journal that details all the retail establishments you visit in a week, how long you spent in each store, how much money you spent, and the reason for your visit. At the end of the week, review your journal and analyze your relationship to retail. As a class, compile your results to get a picture of shopping habits and consumer behavior.

Explain the dimensions by which retailers can be classified. Many different kinds of retailers exist. A retail establishment can be classified according to its ownership, level of service, product assortment, and price. On the basis of ownership, retailers can be broadly differentiated as independent retailers, chain stores, or franchise outlets. The level of service retailers provide can be classified along a continuum of high to low. Retailers also classify themselves by the breadth and depth of their product assortments; some retailers have concentrated product assortments, whereas others have extensive product assortments. Last, general price levels also classify a store, from discounters offering low prices to exclusive specialty stores where high prices are the norm. Retailers use these latter three variables to position themselves in the marketplace.

2.1 Form a team of three classmates to identify different retail stores in your city where pet supplies are sold. Include nonstore forms of retailing, such as catalogs, the Internet, or the local veterinarian. Team members should divide up and visit all the different retailing outlets for pet supplies. Prepare a report describing the differences in brands and products sold at each of the retailing formats and the differences in store characteristics and service levels. For example, which brands are sold via mass merchandiser, independent specialty store, or other venue? Suggest why different products and brands are distributed through different types of stores.

Describe the major types of retail operations. The major types of retail stores are department stores, specialty retailers, supermarkets, drugstores, convenience stores, discount stores, and restaurants. Department stores carry a wide assortment of shopping and specialty goods, are organized into relatively independent departments, and offset higher prices by emphasizing customer service and décor. Specialty retailers typically carry a narrower but deeper assortment of merchandise, emphasizing distinctive products and a high level of customer service. Supermarkets are large self-service retailers that offer a wide variety of food products and some nonfood items. Drugstores are retail formats that sell mostly prescription and over-the-counter medications, health and beauty aids, cosmetics, and specialty items. Convenience stores carry a limited line of high-turnover convenience goods. Discount stores offer low-priced general merchandise and consist of four types: full-line discounters, specialty discount retailers, warehouse clubs, and off-price retailers. Finally, restaurants straddle the line between the retailing and services industries; although restaurants sell a product, food and drink, to final consumers, they can also be considered service marketers because they provide consumers with the service of preparing food and sometimes table service.

3.1 Discuss the possible marketing implications of the recent trend toward supercenters, which combine a supermarket and a full-line discount store.

3.2 Explain the function of warehouse clubs. Why are they classified as both wholesalers and retailers?

3.3 Would you be interested in buying luxury items, like expensive jewelry, at a warehouse club? Wal-Mart offered a $350,000 diamond solitaire ring during a recent Christmas shopping season. If you could afford such a ring, would you consider buying it at Wal-Mart? Why or why not?

Discuss nonstore retailing techniques. Nonstore retailing, which is shopping outside a store setting, has three major categories. Automatic vending uses machines to offer products for sale. In direct retailing, the sales transaction occurs in a home setting, typically through door-to-door sales or party plan selling. Direct marketing refers to the techniques used to get consumers to buy from their homes or place of business. Those techniques include direct mail, catalogs and mail order, telemarketing, and electronic retailing, such as home shopping channels and online retailing.

4.1 Go to the Gift Center at the online wine retailer's Web site at **www.wine.com.** How does this site help shoppers select gifts?

4.2 How much does the most powerful computer with the fastest modem, most memory, largest monitor, biggest hard drive, and all the available peripherals cost at **www.dell.com**? Then visit a store like Best Buy or CompUSA and price a comparable computer. How can you explain any price differences between the two retail operations? Explain any differences in features that you encountered. What conclusions can you draw from your research?

4.3 Most catalog companies also offer online shopping. Visit the Web site of one of your favorite catalogs to see if you can buy online. If so, surf the online catalog for a few minutes. Then compare the two retailing methods (paper and Internet) for prices, products, and so forth. Which do you prefer—the paper catalog or online shopping? Why?

4.4 To what can you attribute the renewed interest in the party format of retailing? Go to the library and research direct sales parties. Write a paragraph describing the target market for these parties and the shifts in the external environment that contribute to their resurgent popularity.

Define *franchising* and describe its two basic forms. Franchising is a continuing relationship in which a franchisor grants to a franchisee the business rights to operate or to sell a product. Modern franchising takes two basic forms. In product and trade name franchising, a dealer agrees to buy or sell certain products or product lines from a particular manufacturer or wholesaler. Business format franchising is an ongoing business relationship in which a franchisee uses a franchisor's name, format, or method of business in return for several types of fees.

5.1 What advantages does franchising provide to franchisors as well as franchisees?

5.2 Curves is the world's largest fitness franchise and was recently the fastest-growing franchise of any kind. What do you need to do to become a Curves franchisee? Visit the Web page **www.curves.com** to find out. Does anything surprise you?

LO6 List the major tasks involved in developing a retail marketing strategy. Retail management begins with defining the target market, typically on the basis of demographic, geographic, or psychographic characteristics. After determining the target market, retail managers must develop the six variables of the retailing mix: product, promotion, place, price, presentation, and personnel.

6.1 Identify a successful retail business in your community. What marketing strategies have led to its success?

6.2 How can a company create an atmosphere on its Web site? Visit the pages of some of your favorite retailers to see if they have been able to re-create the store atmosphere on the Internet.

Describe new developments in retailing. Three major trends are evident in retailing today. First, adding interactivity to the retail environment is one of the most popular strategies in retailing in recent years. Small retailers as well as national chains are using interactivity to involve customers and set themselves apart from the competition. Second, m-commerce (mobile e-commerce) is gaining in popularity. M-commerce enables consumers to purchase goods and services using wireless mobile devices, such as mobile telephones, pagers, PDAs, and handheld computers. Pop-up shops give companies flexible locations without the expense of a long-term lease.

7.1 Make a list of stores that actively incorporate some kind of interactivity or entertainment into their retailing strategy. Now, make a list of stores that do not, such as office supply stores. Compare your two lists. Select a company from your second list and draft a strategy to help it become more interactive.

7.2 What kind of retailers or brands do you think would most benefit from a pop-up shop? Why?

KEY TERMS

atmosphere	455	drugstore	437	pop-up shops	459
automatic vending	442	factory outlet	440	product offering	450
buyer	436	franchises	434	retailing	433
category killers	440	franchisee	446	retailing mix	450
chain stores	434	franchisor	446	scrambled merchandising	437
convenience store	438	full-line discount stores	438	specialty discount store	439
department store	436	gross margin	435	specialty store	436
destination stores	453	independent retailers	434	supercenter	439
direct marketing (direct-response marketing)	443	mass merchandising	438	supermarket	436
direct retailing	442	nonstore retailing	442	telemarketing	444
discount store	438	off-price retailer	440	warehouse membership clubs	440
		online retailing	445		

EXERCISES

APPLICATION EXERCISE

After reading the chapter, you can see that differences in retailing are the result of strategy. To better understand the relationship between strategic retailing factors and consumer perceptions, you can conduct a simple observation exercise. First, pick a product to shop for, and then identify two stores where you have *never* shopped as places to look for your product. The two stores must be different types of retailers. For example, you can shop for a new HDTV at Best Buy (category killer) and at Hollywood Video (specialty retailer). Once you have identified what you are looking for and where you're going to look, visit each store and record your observations of specific strategic retailing factors.[51]

Activities

1. Go through each store and make careful observations of the following:
   - *Location:* Where is each store? How congested is the area of town where each store is located? What influence does the neighborhood have on your impression of the store? Would you travel to this store under normal circumstances? Write a detailed paragraph on the location of each store.
   - *Exterior atmosphere:* Is there parking? If so, is it convenient? Is it adequate? Observe other parking issues (cleanliness and size of the lot, size of spaces, well lit, etc.). What kinds of stores are around the store you are visiting? Do you think being located next to them increases traffic at your store? Are direct competitors nearby? Is the building modern or historic? Is it attractive, clean, and appealing? Is the entrance inviting to shoppers?
   - *Interior atmosphere:* Compare the following attributes at each store: aisle width; lighting; number of customers; noise (background music, loudspeakers, etc.); store layout; signage; accessibility of the cashier; number of products available (depth and width of assortment); ability to inspect the product before purchase; quality of the fixtures (shelves, lights, etc.); availability of salespeople and their knowledge about the product; willingness of salespeople to help.
   - *Product:* Is your product available? If not, is there a satisfactory substitute? What is your perception of the quality of goods offered? Why do you think as you do?
   - *Price:* What is the price of the product/brand at this store? Is the price prominently marked? How do the prices at the two stores compare? How does the price compare to your expectations?
2. From which of these two stores would you actually purchase the item? Why, specifically? List the factors that played a role in your decision. Which factor is most important to you? If you would not purchase the item at either store, why not?
3. What are the three most important differences you observed between the stores?
4. Using the results of your research, write a short paper that outlines your observations. Conclude your paper with your answers to questions 2 and 3.

ETHICS EXERCISE

A–Z Grocery Company is well known for offering quality grocery products at the lowest prices in the market. When the company applied for a zoning change to build a new store in a middle-class neighborhood, several members of the city council objected because the company has no stores in low-income neighborhoods, where they argue the low prices are needed most. The company contends that it cannot operate profitably in these neighborhoods because of higher security and operating costs.

Questions

1. Should low-cost retailers be required to locate near low-income customers? Why or why not?
2. Does the AMA Statement of Ethics address this issue? Go to **www.marketingpower.com** and review the code. Then, write a brief paragraph on how the AMA Statement of Ethics relates to retailing locations.

MARKETING PLAN EXERCISE

Chapter 13 is the final chapter in Part 3, Product and Distribution Decisions. Once you've completed this exercise, you can complete the Marketing Plan Worksheet for Part 3 on your companion Web site at **www.cengage.com/international.** Distribution is a key component of any business. For the e-business, distribution seems "invisible" to the consumer, because the consumer may not care where your firm is located but wants product delivery quickly and inexpensively. Creating a worldwide distribution system is an additional challenge to the marketer. Use the following exercises to guide you through the retail distribution part of your strategic marketing plan:

1. What types of retail establishments might be used for your firm's product? Are they in locations convenient to the target customers? What is the atmosphere of the facility for each type? How can you get the atmosphere of the brick-and-mortar offering to match the offering of your Web site?
2. If you have developed a service, to what other Web sites might you "distribute" your Internet-based service? How will working with these other Web sites help you reach your target audience? Are there other Web sites from which you might accept distribution deals in order to make your product or service offering stronger? Explain how strategic distribution with other Web sites or services can give you a competitive advantage.

CASE STUDY: BEST BUY GIVES A WHOLE NEW MEANING TO "THOUSANDS OF POSSIBILITIES. GET YOURS."

The promise of the long-awaited digital revolution has finally been fulfilled. Flat-panel televisions, MP3 players, wireless laptops, cell phones with Internet browsing capability, wirelessly networked computing devices for the home, digitally controlled home appliances, and more are no longer the toys of a future generation. They are here today, and Best Buy wants to sell them—all of them—to anyone with the money to burn on such luxury items. In addition to all the gee-whiz electronic merchandise, the company still sells coffee makers, vacuum cleaners, and washing machines, albeit slightly more expensive ones than before.

The new digital gadgets, however, are fast crossing the threshold from expensive luxury items to affordable common electronics. The upside is that more customers are able to buy such products; the downside is the negative pressure put on prices and revenues. If any retailer can find a way to survive and turn a profit in the fiercely competitive electronics and home appliance industry, it's Best Buy. Twenty years ago, when it operated under the name Sound of Music, a tornado ripped through its flagship store, and the company held a "best buy" sale to liquidate its merchandise and cover the costs of repairs. The success of the sale was the impetus for the name change to Best Buy, and the opening of its first superstore in 1984 marked the beginning of "big box" retailing as it is known today. Nine years later, the new-look national chain surpassed Circuit City as the number one retailer in the segment.

Best Buy's stores offer a dizzying array of products (its stores have nearly 25,000 separate items) at affordable prices. Usually located in small- or medium-sized outdoor shopping centers with other "big box" retailers, an average 40,000-square-foot Best Buy store is large enough to hold ample stock of all available items while still comfortably accommodating customers. Bright lights, concrete floors, wide and easily navigated aisles, oversize shopping carts, and a helpful but unobtrusive staff dressed in blue shirts and khaki pants have put Best Buy at the head of the retail class when it comes to customer satisfaction surveys. Best Buy's television commercials, which feature the tagline, "Thousands of Possibilities. Get Yours," communicate an accurate picture of the customer experience. Inside every Best Buy store, a canned deejay plays the latest popular music over the public address system; recently released DVDs play on big-screen TVs; and personal computers, video game modules, home stereo systems, and more are turned on and available for customers to tinker with.

The ability to connect with its customers has brought Best Buy a 16 percent share of the $130 billion North American market for electronics and related devices. It now operates 600 stores in the United States and plans to open 60 or so new stores each year for the near future. Competition, however, is stiffening. Best Buy's main threat now comes from discount superstore Wal-Mart, whose share of the market has climbed rapidly to just 5 percentage points behind Best Buy's. That development, combined with a downward pressure on prices for electronic devices similar to the pressures in the PC industry, has forced Best Buy to explore new and more profitable ways of meeting the needs of the market.

The firm's latest initiatives include selling more upscale and higher-margin merchandise, hiring highly trained sales "consultants" to assist with more complex and expensive purchases, staying open for longer hours on weekends, outsourcing lower-end items to China, and selling installation and connection services for its products. Those who prefer to shop in their pajamas can check out the possibilities online at BestBuy.com. Best Buy is also selling home entertainment packages direct to upscale homebuilders in cities such as Minneapolis, Dallas, and Las Vegas. For a nominal surcharge as low as $1,000, Best Buy will install, connect, and integrate the system while the house is being constructed, leaving the home's new owner to sit back and enjoy the show.[52]

Questions

1. What type of retailer is Best Buy?
2. Describe the six components of Best Buy's retailing mix. Is there anything you would change? Explain.
3. Do you agree with the strategy Best Buy has adopted to respond to its competition? Why or why not?

COMPANY CLIPS

© NKP MEDIA, INC./CENGAGE

SEPHORA—RETAILING FOR SUCCESS

From the beginning, Sephora has carried quality skincare products. Excellent retailing techniques, however, are the real driving force behinds Sephora's success. The company's open-sale environment allows consumers to try any product, or even take home a free sample, before they buy. A great location in the heart of the New York City retail district makes it easy for Sephora to attract potential buyers. Sephora also invests a lot of time and money into training their sales staff so that when customers enter the store, they gain a total shopping experience in which their every need is met. The salespeople are not paid on commission, so they are free to give honest recommendations of products that would be best for their customers. As you watch the video, notice what other retailing methods Sephora uses to promote sales.

Questions

1. Visit **www.Sephora.com** and browse the online store. How does Sephora use the online environment to promote its products without the advantage of letting customers try before they buy?
2. Sephora is working out the details of a new loyalty program, and they have asked you to give your input and advice. What do you tell them? How should they integrate this new program with the retailing mix they have already adopted?

Marketing & You Results

If your score was on the low side, it means you don't find shopping in stores to be enjoyable. The higher your score, the more likely you are to think shopping is a fun activity. But beware: a high score can also indicate a tendency toward being a compulsive buyer!

Promotion and Pricing Decisions

PART 4

WHAT'S INSIDE

CHAPTER 14

Marketing Communications and Advertising

LEARNING OUTCOMES

- LO 1 Discuss the role of promotion in the marketing mix
- LO 2 Describe the communication process
- LO 3 Explain the goals of promotion
- LO 4 Discuss the elements of the promotional mix
- LO 5 Discuss the AIDA concept and its relationship to the promotional mix
- LO 6 Discuss the concept of integrated marketing communications
- LO 7 Describe the factors that affect the promotional mix
- LO 8 Discuss the effects of advertising on market shares and consumers
- LO 9 Identify the major types of advertising
- LO 10 Discuss the creative decisions in developing an advertising campaign
- LO 11 Describe media evaluation and selection techniques

THE ROLE OF PROMOTION IN THE MARKETING MIX

Few goods or services, no matter how well developed, priced, or distributed, can survive in the marketplace without effective **promotion**—communication by marketers that informs, persuades, and reminds potential buyers of a product in order to influence their opinion or elicit a response.

Promotional strategy is a plan for the optimal use of the promotional mix elements: advertising, public relations, personal selling, and sales promotion. As Exhibit 14.1 shows, the marketing manager determines the goals of the company's promotional strategy in light of the firm's overall goals for the marketing mix—product, place (distribution), promotion, and price.

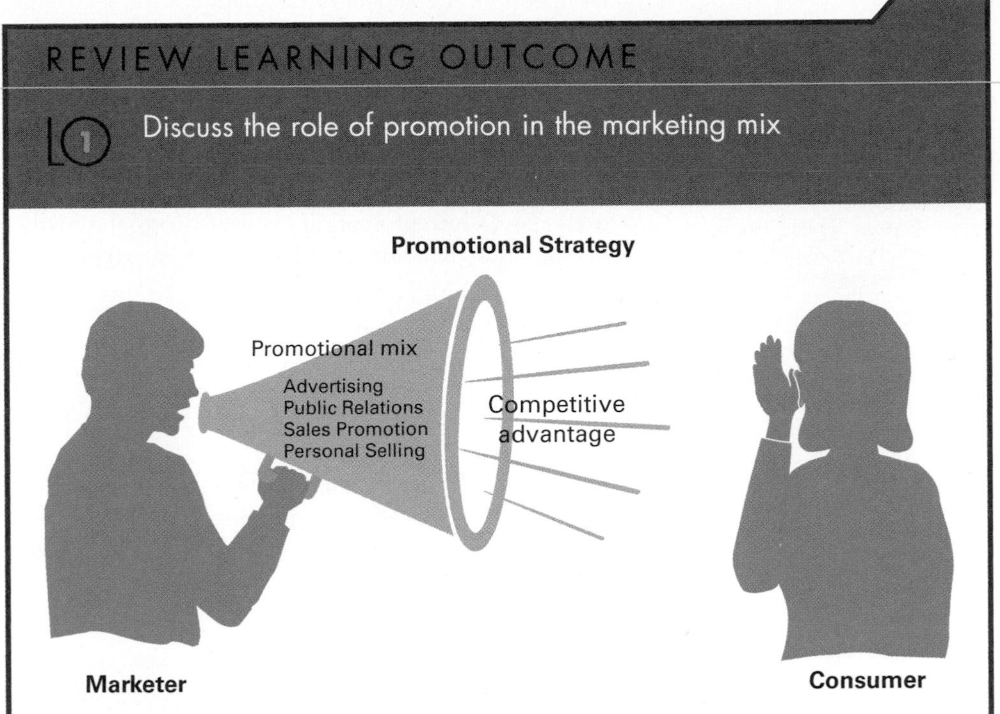

Marketing & You

Using the following scale, enter your opinions on the lines provided.

1 2 3 4 5 6

Strongly disagree — Strongly agree

— People frequently tell me about themselves.
__ I've been told that I'm a good listener.
__ I'm very accepting of others.
__ People trust me with their secrets.
__ I easily get people to "open up."
__ People feel relaxed around me.
__ I enjoy listening to people.
__ I'm sympathetic to people's problems.
__ I encourage people to tell me how they are feeling.
__ I can keep people talking about themselves.

Total your score, and see what it means after you read the chapter.

Source: Scale #455, *Marketing Scales Handbook*, G. Bruner, K. James, H. Hensel, eds., Vol. III. © by American Marketing Association. Used with permission of the American Marketing Association.

EXHIBIT 14.1

Role of Promotion in the Marketing Mix

promotion
Communication by marketers that informs, persuades, and reminds potential buyers of a product in order to influence an opinion or elicit a response.

promotional strategy
A plan for the optimal use of the elements of promotion: advertising, public relations, personal selling, and sales promotion.

competitive advantage
One or more unique aspects of an organization that cause target consumers to patronize that firm rather than competitors.

communication
The process by which we exchange or share meanings through a common set of symbols.

Using these overall goals, marketers combine the elements of the promotional mix into a coordinated plan. This promotional plan defines the promotional strategy, which then becomes an integral part of the overall marketing strategy for reaching the target market.

The main function of a marketer's promotional strategy is to convince target customers that the goods and services offered provide a competitive advantage over the competition. A **competitive advantage** is the set of unique features of a company and its products that are perceived by the target market as significant and superior to the competition. Such features can include high product quality, rapid delivery, low prices, excellent service, or a feature not offered by the competition. For example, fast-food restaurant Subway promises fresh sandwiches that are better for you than a hamburger or pizza. Subway effectively communicates its competitive advantage through advertising featuring longtime "spokes-eater" Jared Fogle, who lost weight by eating at Subway every day.[1] Thus, promotion is a vital part of the marketing mix, informing consumers of a product's benefits and thereby positioning the product in the marketplace.

LO2

MARKETING COMMUNICATION

Promotional strategy is closely related to the process of communication. As humans, we assign meaning to feelings, ideas, facts, attitudes, and emotions. **Communication** is the process by which we exchange or share meanings through a common set of symbols. When a company develops a new product, changes an old one, or simply tries to increase sales

CUSTOMER Experience

Obama for President: The Ultimate IMC Campaign

Start with a young, relatively unknown black man with a Muslim-sounding name. His first opponent was the best-known woman in America married to one of the most successful politicians in history. His second competitor was a well-known and respected war hero with 40 years as a senator. But President Barack Obama had a better marketing strategy than either one of them: Change.

Obama's presidential campaign, launched in February 2007, began with the message of "change" and did not deviate from it. Ever. The message resonated with American voters and would-be voters. He kept the message simple and consistent through endless repetition. Obama also effectively defined the message so that all of the other candidates were also forced to talk about change. This follows classic marketing positioning principles.

But Team Obama went further. They used behavioral targeting to segment their voter audience so that each message was tailored specifically to the individual voter. Traditional media were used in untraditional ways—specifically by purchasing viewing time on big events, such as the Summer Olympics, and by airing a 30-minute infomercial on seven networks just days before the election. Team Obama raised the use of digital media to a completely new level and created content for online distribution. They used text messaging and e-mail effectively by using the list sparingly through most of the campaign and then sending a flurry of e-mails during the last few weeks of the campaign urging supporters to make calls and visits, host parties, and volunteer. Obama had more than double John McCain's online traffic. The campaign even created their own social network of 2 million users, MyBarackObama.com, and leveraged other social networks such as Facebook and MySpace as well as specialized networks such as Eon and BlackPlanet. Search engine optimization was used to dispel negative information and Internet rumors. The campaign demonstrated not only knowledge of basic marketing principles, but also an understanding of ground-level tactics on everything from segmentation and database management to analytics, social networking, and online communities.

And consider the results. First there was the obvious landslide victory—even in states that Democrats have not captured in years. Second, the campaign set fund-raising records of more than half a billion dollars, specifically from everyday voters who donated less than an average of $100. Third, they have a database of more than 13 million engaged voters and 5 million supporters on social networks. With all of this momentum, the real question is how Obama will use his marketing skills to run the country.[2]

of an existing good or service, it must communicate its selling message to potential customers. Marketers communicate information about the firm and its products to the target market and various publics through its promotion programs. When Sara Lee Corp. decided to reinvigorate its legacy brand, Kiwi shoe polish, it began with communication: It asked people about their shoe care needs. After interviewing 3,500 people across eight countries, it found out that people cared more about fresh, comfortable shoes than whether those shoes were polished. Sara Lee's new CEO welcomes innovation. She found out which innovations would be welcome by communicating with Kiwi's consumers, marketers, and retailers; then she pushed the employees to "think outside the box—or inside the shoe." And it paid off. Kiwi's new products—including thin insoles with built-in fresheners and single-use polishes—pushed Kiwi's sales up by 4.4 percent (for the first time in a long time). Now Sara Lee is using that same innovation-driven-by-communication model and holding focus groups with its employees and customers to find out which new products will revive Sara Lee's other brands (**www.kiwicare.com**).[3]

The Obama presidential campaign demonstrated not only knowledge of basic marketing principles, but also an understanding of ground-level tactics on everything from segmentation and database management to analytics, social networking, and online communities.

Communication can be divided into two major categories: interpersonal communication and mass communication. **Interpersonal communication** is direct, face-to-face communication between two or more people. When communicating face-to-face, people see the other person's reaction and can respond almost immediately. A salesperson speaking directly with a client is an example of an interpersonal marketing communication. **Mass communication** involves communicating a concept or message to large audiences. A great deal of marketing communication is directed to consumers as a whole, usually through a mass medium such as television, newspapers, or the Internet. When a company advertises, it generally does not personally know the people with whom it is trying to communicate. Furthermore, the company is unable to respond immediately to consumers' reactions to its message. Instead, the marketing manager must wait to see whether people are reacting positively or negatively to the mass-communicated promotion. Any clutter from competitors' messages or other distractions in the environment can reduce the effectiveness of the mass-communication effort.

The Communication Process

Marketers are both senders, and receivers of messages. As *senders*, marketers attempt to inform, persuade, and remind the target market to adopt courses of action compatible with the need to promote the purchase of goods and services. As *receivers*, marketers attune themselves to the target market in order to develop the appropriate messages, adapt existing messages, and spot new communication opportunities. In this way, marketing communication is a two-way, rather than one-way, process. The two-way nature of the communication process is shown in Exhibit 14.2.

The Sender and Encoding The **sender** is the originator of the message in the communication process. In an interpersonal conversation, the sender may be a parent, a friend, or a salesperson. For an advertisement or press release, the sender is the company or organization itself. For example, the Swedish brand Absolut Vodka launched a marketing campaign using the theme "In an Absolut World." At the outset, the objective of the campaign was to increase Absolut's market share in the crowded and increasingly competitive U.S. vodka market. To appeal to this market, Absolut had to differentiate its message from the "rational benefits" (such as best taste or smooth feel) being claimed by so many of the upstarts in the vodka category. Absolut changed its near-legendary super-premium brand strategy—a print campaign pairing the iconic shape of its bottle with equally iconic art figures—to a campaign that would appeal to the "emotional benefits" of the brand.[4] Thus, Absolut launched a new campaign using

interpersonal communication
Direct, face-to-face communication between two or more people.

mass communication
The communication of a concept or message to large audiences.

sender
The originator of the message in the communication process.

EXHIBIT 14.2

Communication Process

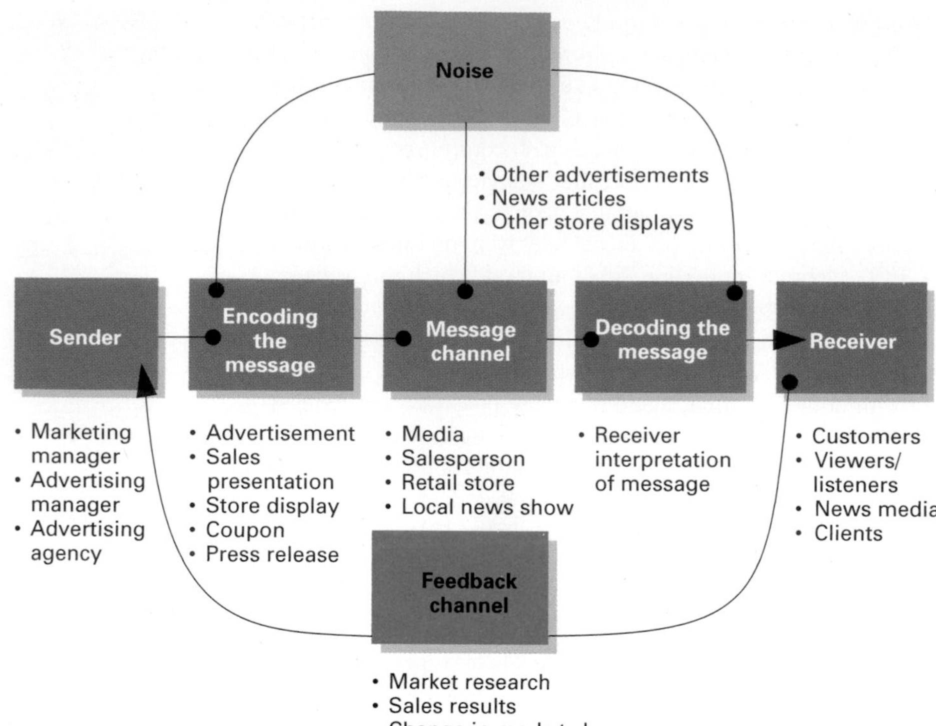

encoding
The conversion of a sender's ideas and thoughts into a message, usually in the form of words or signs.

channel
A medium of communication—such as a voice, radio, or newspaper—for transmitting a message.

noise
Anything that interferes with, distorts, or slows down the transmission of information.

the phrase "Absolut World" to promote the message that its vodka was the brand to choose if the customer was intelligent, savvy, and wanted to challenge the status quo by taking on bold and optimistic new world views. The new ads assert that Absolut vodka is in a class by itself—indeed, in a world of its own, an "Absolut World." The ad campaign also invites Absolut's consumers to visualize a world that appeals to them—even a world that may be idealized or "fantastic."[5]

Encoding is the conversion of the sender's ideas and thoughts into a message, usually in the form of words or signs. A basic principle of encoding is that what matters is not what the source says but what the receiver hears. One way of conveying a message that the receiver will hear properly is to use concrete words and pictures. For example, Absolut's marketers encoded the message by a creating a series of life-size outdoor ads, wrapped buildings, and other media that imagined an "Absolut World" where factories emit harmless bubbles instead of smoke, ATMs dispense "free" money, politicians' noses grow if they lie, and people in bars wear buttons labeling their dating status and mind-set.[6]

Message Transmission Transmission of a message requires a **channel**—a voice, radio, newspaper, computer, or other communication medium. A facial expression or gesture can also serve as a channel.

Reception occurs when the message is detected by the receiver and enters his or her frame of reference. In a two-way conversation such as a sales pitch given by a sales representative to a potential client, reception is normally high. In contrast, the desired receivers may or may not detect the message when it is mass communicated because most media are cluttered by **noise**—anything that interferes with, distorts, or slows down the transmission of information. In some media overcrowded with advertisers, such as newspapers and television,

the noise level is high and the reception level is low. For example, competing network advertisements, other entertainment option advertisements, or other programming on the network itself might hamper reception of the "Absolut World" advertising campaign message. Transmission can also be hindered by situational factors: physical surroundings such as light, sound, location, and weather; the presence of other people; or the temporary moods consumers might bring to the situation. Mass communication may not even reach all the right consumers. Some members of the target audience were likely watching television when Absolut's commercials were shown, but others probably were not.

The Receiver and Decoding Marketers communicate their message through a channel to customers, or **receivers**, who will decode the message. **Decoding** is the interpretation of the language and symbols sent by the source through a channel. Common understanding between two communicators, or a common frame of reference, is required for effective communication. Therefore, marketing managers must ensure a proper match between the message to be conveyed and the target market's attitudes and ideas.

Even though a message has been received, it will not necessarily be properly decoded—or even seen, viewed, or heard—because of selective exposure, distortion, and retention (see Chapter 6). Even when people receive a message, they tend to manipulate, alter, and modify it to reflect their own biases, needs, knowledge, and culture. Differences in age, social class, education, culture, and ethnicity can lead to miscommunication, for example. Further, because people don't always listen or read carefully, they can easily misinterpret what is said or written. In fact, researchers have found that consumers misunderstand a large proportion of both printed and televised communications. Bright colors and bold graphics have been shown to increase consumers' comprehension of marketing communication. Even these techniques are not foolproof, however. A classic example of miscommunication occurred when Lever Brothers mailed out samples of its then new dishwashing liquid, Sunlight, which contains real lemon juice. The package clearly stated that Sunlight was a household cleaning product. Nevertheless, many people saw the word *sunlight*, the large picture of lemons, and the phrase "with real lemon juice" and thought the product was lemon juice.

Marketers targeting consumers in foreign countries must also worry about the translation and possible miscommunication of their promotional messages by other cultures. An important issue for global marketers is whether to standardize or customize the message for each global market in which they sell. While Absolut's marketers used the "World" message globally, they tailored the ads to reflect how people in various regions might envision an "Absolut World." For example, a bus shelter on Second Avenue in New York City was wrapped to look like a subway entrance—a dream of many New York commuters.[7] In Germany, consumers were given a firsthand experience of the "Absolut World." For one week, a fleet of Porsche taxis chauffeured passengers quickly—and for free—around Hamburg, Munich, and Berlin. By the end of that week, the taxis had generated over 15 million media contacts through TV, print, and online news coverage.[8]

Feedback In interpersonal communication, the receiver's response to a message is direct **feedback** to the source. Feedback may be verbal, as in saying "I agree," or nonverbal, as in nodding, smiling, frowning, or gesturing.

Because mass communicators like Absolut's are often cut off from direct feedback, they must rely on market research or analysis of viewer responses from indirect feedback. Absolut might use such measurements as the percentage of television viewers who recognized, recalled, or stated they were exposed to Absolut's messages. Indirect feedback enables mass communicators to decide whether to continue, modify, or drop a message. Web sites also facilitate feedback. For example, Absolut could capture consumer feedback in e-mails, discussion boards, blogs, and other tools from its Web site.

receiver
The person who decodes a message.

decoding
Interpretation of the language and symbols sent by the source through a channel.

feedback
The receiver's response to a message.

The Impact of Web 2.0 on Marketing Communication

The Internet and related technologies are having a profound impact on marketing communication. When companies initially developed Web sites the primary formats

corporate blogs
Blogs that are sponsored by a company or one of its brands and maintained by one or more of the company's employees.

noncorporate blogs
Independent blogs that are not associated with the marketing efforts of any particular company or brand.

were either online brochures, where essentially the corporate brochure or catalog was put online, or e-commerce sites, where the companies could facilitate online sales of products. The next generation of the Internet, Web 2.0, facilitated consumer empowerment. For the first time, consumers were able to directly speak to other consumers, the company, and Web communities.

Web 2.0 tools include blogs (online journals), podcasting (online radio shows), vodcasts (online videos and newscasts), and social networks such as MySpace and Facebook. In the beginning, these tools were primarily used by individuals to express themselves. For example, a lawyer may develop a blog to talk about politics because that is a hobby. Or a college freshman may develop a profile on Facebook to stay in touch with high school friends. But soon, businesses began to see that these tools can be used to engage with consumers as well. The rise of blogging, for example, has created a completely new way for marketers to manage their image, connect with consumers, and generate interest in and desire for their companies' products.

Despite what could be considered a national obsession with blogs, measuring blogging activity remains challenging. According to Technorati, the first blog search engine, there were more than 28 million blogs online in 2006. But by early 2008, there were so many blogs that there was not a consistent number. While research companies agree that there are millions of blogs, comScore Media Metrix says that as of August 2008, there were 189 million blogs (counting Facebook) and Universal McCann reports there were 184 million blogs.[9] As part of its annual *State of the Blogosphere*, Technorati says the real trend is with the active blogosphere that tends to influence the mainstream media. Brands also permeate the blogosphere. Four of five bloggers post brand or product reviews, so even if a company does not have a formal social media strategy, chances are the brand is still out in the blogosphere thanks to the millions of bloggers. As such, companies are now reaching out to the most influential bloggers. Indeed, more than one-third of those with a blog have been approached to be a brand advocate.

The question then is whether blogging is a passing fad, representing at best an unreliable means of communicating, or an emerging trend. If it is a fad, why are marketers so interested in blogging as a promotional tool? The answer in part is that blogging alters the marketing communication process for the promotional elements that rely on mass communication—advertising, public relations, and sales promotion—by moving them away from impersonal, indirect communication toward a personalized, direct communication model.

Blogs can be divided into broad categories: corporate blogs and professional blogs versus noncorporate blogs (such as personal blogs). **Corporate blogs** are sponsored by a company or one of its brands and maintained by one or more of the company's employees. Corporate blogs disseminate marketing-controlled information. (Recall from Chapter 6 that marketing-controlled information is a source of product information that originates with marketers promoting the product.) Because blogs are designed to change daily, corporate blogs are dynamic and highly flexible, giving marketers the opportunity to adapt their messages more frequently than with any other communication channel. Initially, blogs were maintained by only the most technology-savvy companies. But today companies as diverse as Coca-Cola, Starwood Hotels, Honda, Nokia, Benetton, Ducati, Guinness, and HSBC have all launched corporate blogs. Undoubtedly, many more will appear in the near future.

In contrast, **noncorporate blogs** are independent and not associated with the marketing efforts of any particular company or brand. As such, noncorporate blogs function much like nonmarketing-controlled information: They provide a source of information and opinion perceived to be independent and more authentic than a corporate blog.[10] Michael Marx loves Barq's root beer. He wears Barq's T-shirts, brings the beverage to parties, and calls it his "beer." He established a blog dedicated to Barq's, **www.thebarqsman.com**, where he posted news about the brand, Barq's commercials he likes, and musings on why Barq's is superior to other root beers. Thebarqsman.com is not affiliated with Coca-Cola, the owner of the Barq's brand, which had no idea of the blog's existence until a *New York Times* reporter writing a story on brand blogs mentioned it. Even though thebarqsman.com is dedicated to a single brand, Marx's blog is an example of a noncorporate blog.[11]

Both corporate and noncorporate blogs have had an impact on the communication model depicted in Exhibit 14.2. That model shows the feedback channel as primarily impersonal and numbers-driven. In the traditional communication process, marketers can see the results of consumer behavior (e.g., a drop in sales), but are only able to explain them using their judgment. Even the information generated by market research is not as natural as that gleaned from bloggers. Corporate blogs allow marketers to personalize the feedback channel by opening the door for direct conversation with consumers. However, because there is no control over noncorporate blogs, there is a chance that comments and postings will be negative. Thus, many companies have a crisis communication strategy to deal with negative information in the blogosphere.

When marketers launch a corporate blog, they create an unfiltered feedback channel. For example, Enrico Minoli, CEO of Ducati, the Italian motorcycle brand, launched **blog.ducati.com.** He vowed to write "openly about what's going on at Ducati." Within three days, his postings had generated 99 responses, from motorcycle enthusiasts from Greece to Daytona Beach who all seemed most pleased that the CEO himself was a motorbike enthusiast. They began peppering him with questions about when new models would hit production and chatted with each other about their own bikes and biking experiences. Minoli's blog put a face on the impersonal nature of a large corporation.[12]

Noncorporate blogs have also personalized the feedback channel. But while corporate blogs create a *direct*, personalized feedback channel for masses of consumers, noncorporate blogs represent an *indirect*, personalized feedback channel. Because noncorporate blogs are independent, they are often perceived as more authentic. Blogging experts offer marketers some solid advice for giving their blogs the honest quality many bloggers associate with noncorporate blogs: open the feedback channel. Todd Copilevitz, a consultant specializing in digital marketing, says, "Blogs are not an environment where you just hold forth opinion and don't accept feedback. You have to have your wits about you to understand it's not the same old PR machine."[13]

REVIEW LEARNING OUTCOME

LO2 Describe the communication process

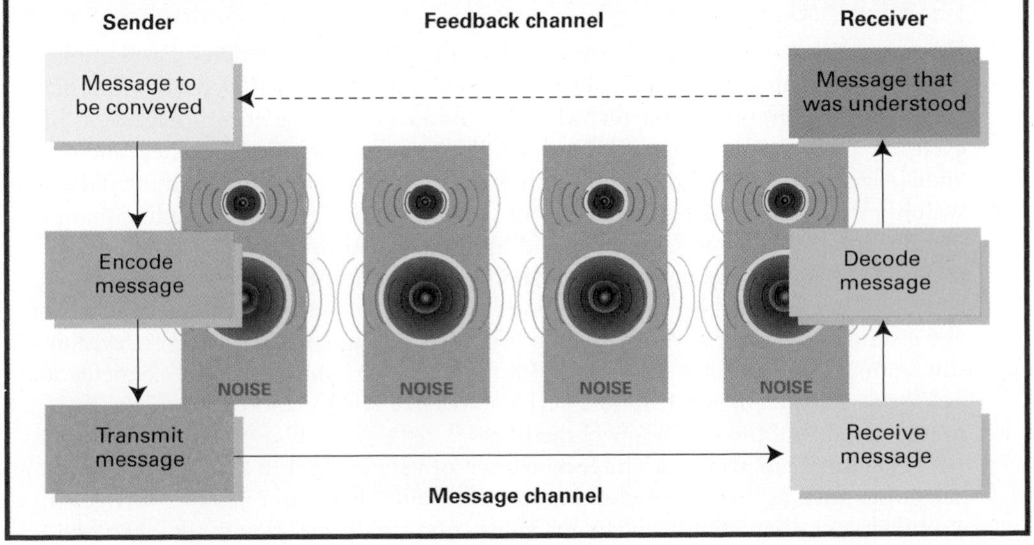

promotional mix
The combination of promotional tools—including advertising, public relations, personal selling, and sales promotion—used to reach the target market and fulfill the organization's overall goals.

THE GOALS OF PROMOTION

People communicate with one another for many reasons. They seek amusement, ask for help, give assistance or instructions, provide information, and express ideas and thoughts. Promotion, on the other hand, seeks to modify behavior and thoughts in some way. For example, promoters may try to persuade consumers to drink Pepsi rather than Coke, or to eat at Burger King instead of McDonald's. Promotion also strives to reinforce existing behavior—for instance, getting consumers to continue dining at Burger King once they have switched. The source (the seller) hopes to project a favorable image or to motivate purchase of the company's goods and services.

Effective promotion will achieve one or more of three goals: It will *inform* the target audience, *persuade* the target audience, or *remind* the target audience. Often a marketer will try to achieve two or more of these goals at the same time.

Informing

Informative promotion seeks to convert an existing need into a want or to stimulate interest in a new product. It is generally more prevalent during the early stages of the product life cycle. People typically will not buy a product or service or support a nonprofit organization until they know its purpose and its benefits to them. Informative messages are important for promoting complex and technical products such as automobiles, computers, and investment services. For example, Philips's original advertisement for the Magnavox flat-screen television showed young, urban consumers trying the flat-screen TV all over the house, including the ceiling. The ad focused on "how to" use the flat-screen TV rather than the Philips Magnavox brand or the technological capabilities.[14] Informative promotion is also important for a "new" brand being introduced into an "old" product class—for example, a new brand of frozen pizza (such as Kashi Frozen Pizza) entering the frozen pizza industry, which is dominated by well-known brands like Kraft's DiGiorno and Schwan's Grocery Products' Red Baron. Kashi Frozen Pizza cannot establish itself against more mature products unless potential buyers are aware of it, value its benefits, and understand its positioning in the marketplace.

© VICKI BEAVER

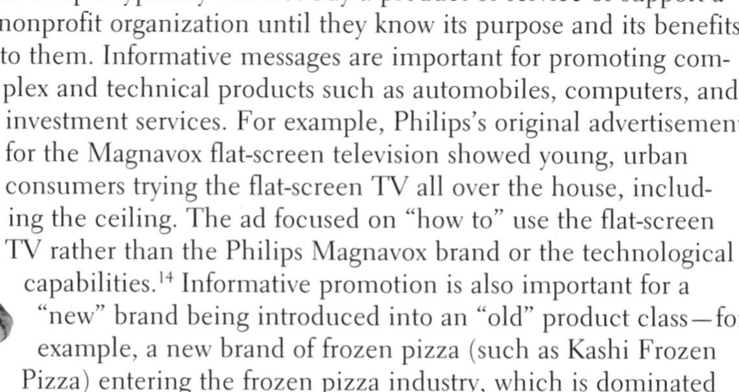

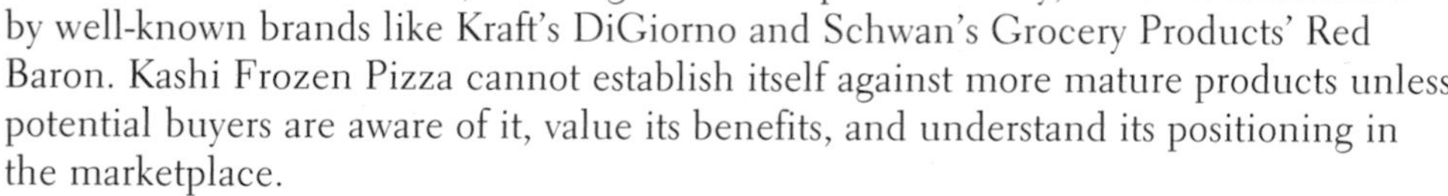

Persuading

Persuasive promotion is designed to stimulate a purchase or an action—for example, to eat more Doritos or use Verizon wireless mobile phone service. Persuasion normally becomes the main promotion goal when the product enters the growth stage of its life cycle. By this time, the target market should have general product awareness and some knowledge of how the product can fulfill their wants. Therefore, the promotional goal switches from informing consumers about the product category to persuading them to buy the company's brand rather than the competitor's. At this time, the promotional message emphasizes the product's real and perceived competitive advantages, often appealing to emotional needs such as love, belonging, self-esteem, and ego satisfaction. For example, the latest advertisement for the Philips Magnavox flat-screen television still features young, urban consumers. But the ad focuses on the product's benefits such as lifestyle enhancements, technological features like HDTV and Dolby digital surround sound, and the superiority of the brand.[15]

Persuasion can also be an important goal for very competitive mature product categories such as many household items, soft drinks, beer, and banking services. In a marketplace characterized by many competitors, the promotional message often encourages brand switching and aims to convert some buyers into loyal users. For example, to persuade new customers to switch their checking accounts, a bank's marketing manager may offer a year's worth of free checks with no fees.

Critics believe some promotional messages and techniques can be too persuasive, causing consumers to buy products and services they really don't need.

Reminding

Reminder promotion is used to keep the product and brand name in the public's mind. This type of promotion prevails during the maturity stage of the life cycle. It assumes that the target market has already been persuaded of the good's or service's merits. Its purpose is simply to trigger a memory. Crest toothpaste, Tide laundry detergent, Miller beer, and many other consumer products often use reminder promotion. Similarly, Philips Magnavox could advertise just the brand rather than the benefits of the product.

REVIEW LEARNING OUTCOME

Explain the goals of promotion

- **Informative promotion**
  Increasing the awareness of a new brand, product class, or product attribute
  Explaining how the product works
  Suggesting new uses for a product
  Building a company image
- **Persuasive promotion**
  Encouraging brand switching
  Changing customers' perceptions of product attributes
  Influencing customers to buy now
  Persuading customers to call
- **Reminder promotion**
  Reminding consumers that the product may be needed in the near future
  Reminding consumers where to buy the product
  Maintaining consumer awareness

THE PROMOTIONAL MIX

As you read earlier, most promotional strategies use several elements or tools—which may include advertising, public relations, sales promotion, and personal selling—to reach a target market. That combination is called the **promotional mix**. The proper promotional mix is the one that management believes will meet the needs of the target market and fulfill the organization's overall goals. The more funds allocated to each promotional element and the more managerial emphasis placed on each technique, the more important that element is thought to be in the overall mix.

Advertising

Almost all companies selling a good or a service use some advertising, whether in the form of a multimillion-dollar campaign or a simple classified ad in a newspaper. *Advertising* is any form of impersonal (one-way) paid communication in which the sponsor or company is identified. One of the primary benefits of advertising is its ability to communicate to a large number of people at one time. Traditional media—such as television, radio, newspapers, magazines, books, direct mail, billboards, and transit cards (advertisements on buses and taxis and at bus stops)—are most commonly used to transmit advertisements to consumers. With the increasing fragmentation of traditional media choices, marketers are using other methods to send their advertisements to consumers, such as Web sites, e-mail, and interactive video kiosks located in department stores and supermarkets. However, as the Internet becomes a more vital component of many companies' promotion and marketing mix, consumers and lawmakers are increasingly concerned about possible violations of consumers' privacy. Read more about this issue in the Ethics in Marketing box about how social networking sites are using all the information that is freely collected.

ETHICS in Marketing

Who's Peeping at your Facebook? Privacy Concerns and Social Networks

Millions of people have embraced social networking sites such as Facebook (70 million U.S. users) and MySpace (110 million users) and increasingly specialized sites such as LinkedIn. While social networks are easy ways to keep in touch with friends and family, there are privacy concerns. A study at Carnegie Mellon found that a large portion of the Facebook users the researchers studied generously supplied plenty of personal data and limited privacy settings. Does this mean the users were oblivious to several privacy concerns? A simple viewing of personal information can make it easier for stalking and identify theft. More insidiously, Facebook and MySpace allow outside developers to create widgets or apps for the sites. Since 2007, 24,000 applications have been created by more than 400,000 developers and more than 95 percent of Facebook users have downloaded at least one application.

No big deal, right? Well, all of those developers are allowed to see your personal information to develop their applications. That's right. Twenty guys you don't know could be looking at your personal information and that of your friends. When a user installs an app, the developer can see everything but contact information. The data is available for only 24 hours, but once that data gets onto a third-party server, there is little Facebook or MySpace can do. Facebook states that developers are not allowed to share data with advertisers, but they can use the information to tailor features to users—in essence, they can use it during new product development. Developers interviewed for this case have not ruled out the prospect of using the data for targeted advertising; some think that leveraging this data does make sense for some marketing applications.

There are several things you can do to protect your privacy, such as not using friend lists; removing yourself from Facebook results; removing yourself from Google; avoiding photo tags; and others. Currently, there is no policy addressing concerns about privacy and social networks. Consumer advocates and the Center for Digital Democracy are urging the Federal Trade Commission to develop a policy surrounding third-party applications.[16] Do you think this gold mine of information should be leveraged as marketing research or should there be limits? And if limits are necessary, what should they be?

Public Relations

Concerned about how they are perceived by their target markets, organizations often spend large sums to build a positive public image. *Public relations* is the marketing function that evaluates public attitudes, identifies areas within the organization the public may be interested in, and executes a program of action to earn public understanding and acceptance. Public relations helps an organization communicate with its customers, suppliers, stockholders, government officials, employees, and the community in which it operates. Marketers use public relations not only to maintain a positive image but also to educate the public about the company's goals and objectives, introduce new products, and help support the sales effort. Public relations will be covered in more depth in Chapter 15.

Personal Selling

Personal selling is a purchase situation involving a personal, paid-for communication between two people in an attempt to influence each other. Traditional methods of personal selling include a planned presentation to one or more prospective buyers for the purpose of making a sale. More current notions on personal selling emphasize the relationship that develops between a salesperson and a buyer. Recently, both business-to-business and business-to-consumer selling focus on building long-term relationships rather than on making a onetime sale.

Personal selling, like other promotional mix elements, increasingly depends on the Internet. Most companies use their Web sites to attract potential buyers seeking information on products and services. While some companies sell products direct to consumers online, many do not. Instead, they rely on the Web site to drive customers to their physical locations where personal selling can close the sale. Whether it takes place face-to-face, over the phone, or online, personal selling attempts to persuade the buyer to accept a point of view or take some action. Personal selling is discussed further in Chapter 15.

Sales Promotion

Sales promotion consists of all marketing activities—other than personal selling, advertising, and public relations—that stimulate consumer purchasing and dealer effectiveness. Sales promotion is generally a short-run tool used to stimulate immediate increases in demand. In fact, marketers often use sales promotion to improve the effectiveness of other ingredients in the promotional mix, especially advertising and personal selling. Research shows that sales promotion complements advertising by yielding faster sales responses. Sales promotion can be aimed at end consumers, trade customers, or a company's employees. Sales promotions include free samples, contests, premiums, trade shows, giveaways, and coupons. A major promotional campaign might use several of these sales promotion tools. Sales promotion is discussed in more detail in Chapter 15.

"Sales promotion is generally a short-run tool used to stimulate immediate increases in demand."

The Communication Process and the Promotional Mix

The four elements of the promotional mix differ in their ability to affect the target audience. For instance, promotional mix elements may communicate with the consumer directly or indirectly. The message may flow one way or two ways. Feedback may be fast or slow, a little or a lot. Likewise, the communicator may have varying degrees of control over message delivery, content, and flexibility. Exhibit 14.3 outlines differences among the promotional mix elements with respect to mode of communication, marketer's control over the communication process, amount and speed of feedback, direction of message flow, marketer's control over the message, identification of the sender, speed in reaching large audiences, and message flexibility.

EXHIBIT 14.3

Characteristics of the Elements in the Promotional Mix

	Advertising	Public Relations	Sales Promotion	Personal Selling
Mode of Communication	Indirect and impersonal	Usually indirect and impersonal	Usually indirect and impersonal	Direct and face-to-face
Communicator Control over Situation	Low	Moderate to low	Moderate to low	High
Amount of Feedback	Little	Little	Little to moderate	Much
Speed of Feedback	Delayed	Delayed	Varies	Immediate
Direction of Message Flow	One-way	One-way	Mostly one-way	Two-way
Control over Message Content	Yes	No	Yes	Yes
Identification of Sponsor	Yes	No	Yes	Yes
Speed in Reaching Large Audience	Fast	Usually fast	Fast	Slow
Message Flexibility	Same message to all audiences	Usually no direct control over message	Same message to varied target audiences	Tailored to prospective buyer

REVIEW LEARNING OUTCOME

LO 4 Discuss the elements of the promotional mix

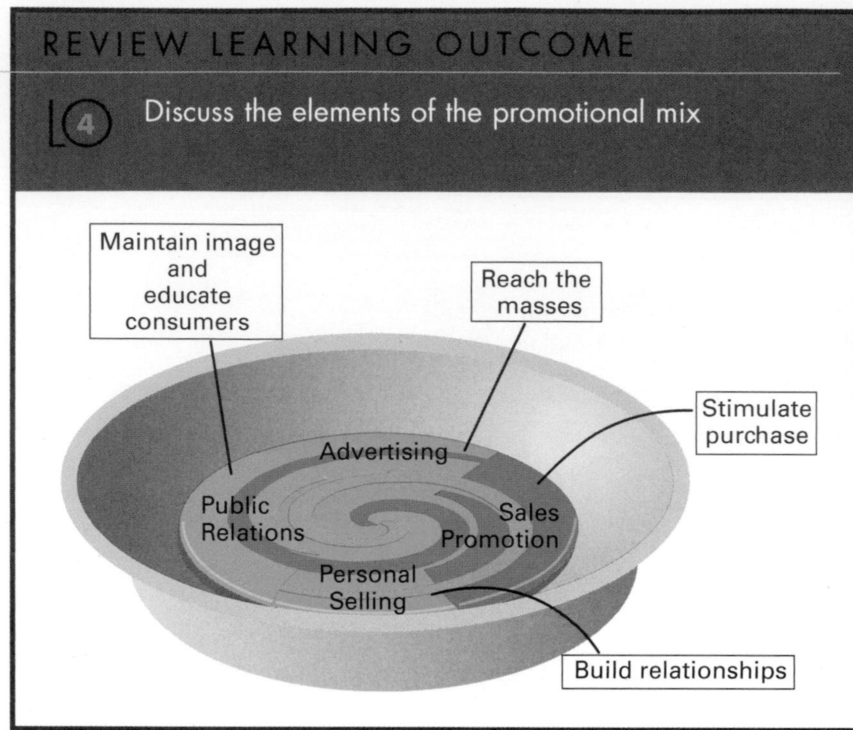

Exhibit 14.3 illustrates that most elements of the promotional mix are indirect and impersonal when used to communicate with a target market, providing only one direction of message flow. For example, advertising, public relations, and sales promotion are generally impersonal, one-way means of mass communication. Because they provide little opportunity for direct feedback, it can be more difficult to adapt these promotional elements to changing consumer preferences, individual differences, and personal goals. One exception is how a company uses its Web site, which can provide a forum for some types of feedback.

Personal selling, on the other hand, is personal, two-way communication. The salesperson receives immediate feedback from the consumer and can adjust the message in response. Personal selling, however, is very slow in dispersing the marketer's message to large audiences. Because a salesperson can communicate to only one person or a small group of persons at one time, it is a poor choice if the marketer wants to send a message to many potential buyers.

© AP IMAGES/PR NEWSFOTO/JOHANSEN KRAUSE/APPLE COMPUTER, INC.

LO 5

PROMOTIONAL GOALS AND THE AIDA CONCEPT

The ultimate goal of any promotion is to get someone to buy a good or service or, in the case of nonprofit organizations, to take some action (for instance, donate money or volunteer time). A classic model for reaching promotional goals is called the **AIDA concept**.[17] The acronym stands for *attention, interest, desire,* and *action*—the stages of consumer involvement with a promotional message.

This model proposes that consumers respond to marketing messages in a cognitive (thinking), affective (feeling), and conative (doing) sequence. First, a promotion manager may focus on attracting a person's *attention* by training a salesperson to use a friendly greeting and approach, or by using loud volume, unusual color contrasts, bold headlines, movement, bright colors, and the like in an advertisement. Next, a good sales presentation, demonstration, or advertisement creates *interest* in the product and then, by illustrating how the product's features will satisfy the consumer's needs, arouses *desire*. Finally, a special offer or a strong closing sales pitch may be used to obtain purchase *action*.

The AIDA concept assumes that promotion propels consumers along the following four steps in the purchase-decision process:

1. *Attention:* The advertiser must first gain the attention of the target market. A firm cannot sell something if the market does not know that the good or service exists. When Apple introduced the iPod, it was a new product for the company. To create awareness and gain attention for the new product, Apple had to advertise and promote it extensively through ads on TV, in magazines, and on the Internet. Because the iPod was a brand extension of the Apple computer, it required less effort than if it had been an entirely new brand. At the same

time, because the iPod was an innovative new product line, the promotion had to get customers' attention and create awareness of a new idea from an established company.

2. *Interest:* Simple awareness of a brand seldom leads to a sale. The next step is to create interest in the product. A print ad or TV commercial cannot tell potential customers all the features and benefits of the iPod. Thus, Apple had to arrange iPod demonstrations and target messages to innovators and early adopters to create interest in the new portable music players.
3. *Desire:* Potential customers for the Apple iPod may like the concept of a portable music player, but they may not feel it is necessarily better than a Sony Walkman portable radio or a portable music player with fewer features. Therefore, Apple had to create brand preference with its iTunes Music Store, extended-life battery, clock and alarm, calendar and to-do list, photo storage, and other features. Specifically, Apple had to convince potential customers that the iPod was the best solution to meet their desire for a portable digital music player.
4. *Action:* Some potential target market customers may have been convinced to buy an iPod but had not yet made the actual purchase. To motivate them to take action, Apple continued advertising to more effectively communicate the features and benefits and also used promotions and price discounts.

Following the initial success of the iPod, to continue its market dominance of the portable digital music player market, Apple introduced new models such as the Nano and Shuffle that were smaller and lighter and yet had longer battery life and more storage. Then podcasting and video were added with access to thousands of network and cable shows and interfaces with auto, boat, and home equipment—and the iPod became a "portable media player."

With each product innovation, the cycle of attention, interest, desire, and action began again. But with the familiarity and success of earlier models, the time frame became shorter. In fact, during one Christmas season, Apple was selling more than 100 iPods per minute; by early 2009 it had sold over 150 million iPods. Moreover, Apple's iTunes Store now sells more music than any other retailer in the United States except for Wal-Mart—more than 4 billion songs to over 50 million customers.[18]

AIDA concept
A model that outlines the process for achieving promotional goals in terms of stages of consumer involvement with the message; the acronym stands for attention, interest, desire, and action.

REVIEW LEARNING OUTCOME

LO 5 Discuss the AIDA concept and its relationship to the promotional mix

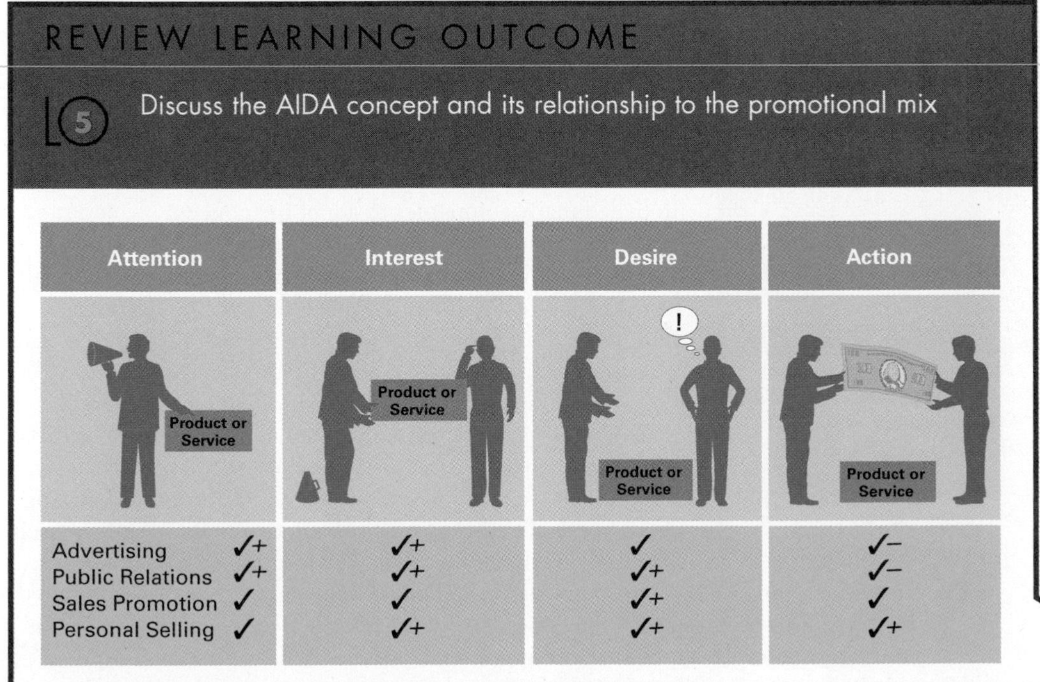

integrated marketing communications (IMC) The careful coordination of all promotional messages for a product or a service to assure the consistency of messages at every contact point where a company meets the consumer.

Most buyers involved in high-involvement purchase situations pass through the four stages of the AIDA model on the way to making a purchase. The promoter's task is to determine where on the purchase ladder most of the target consumers are located and design a promotion plan to meet their needs. For instance, if Apple learned from its market research that many potential customers were in the desire stage but had not bought an iPod for some reason, then Apple could place advertising on Yahoo! or Google, and in video games as well, to target younger individuals who are the primary target market with specific messages to motivate them to take immediate action and buy an iPod.

The AIDA concept does not explain how all promotions influence purchase decisions. The model suggests that promotional effectiveness can be measured in terms of consumers progressing from one stage to the next. However, the order of stages in the model, as well as whether consumers go through all steps, has been much debated. For example, a purchase can occur without interest or desire, perhaps when a low-involvement product is bought on impulse. Regardless of the order of the stages or consumers' progression through these stages, the AIDA concept helps marketers by suggesting which promotional strategy—that is, which plan for using the promotional mix—will be most effective.[19]

LO6

INTEGRATED MARKETING COMMUNICATIONS

Ideally, marketing communications from each promotional mix element (personal selling, advertising, sales promotion, and public relations) should be integrated—the message reaching the consumer should be the same regardless of whether it is from an advertisement, a salesperson in the field, a magazine article, or a coupon in a newspaper insert.

Moviemakers frequently use integrated marketing techniques to promote their films. Internet contests on Google, guide books from key cities in the story, and controversy over the movie's religious themes all contributed to the box-office success of *The Da Vinci Code*.

© AP IMAGES

From the consumer's standpoint, a company's communications are already integrated. Consumers do not think in terms of the four elements of promotion: advertising, sales promotion, public relations, and personal selling. Instead, everything is an "ad." In general, the only people who recognize the distinctions among these elements are the marketers themselves. Unfortunately, many marketers neglect this fact when planning promotional messages and fail to integrate their communication efforts from one element to the next. The most common rift typically occurs between personal selling and the other elements of the promotional mix.

This unintegrated, disjointed approach to promotion has propelled many companies to adopt the concept of **integrated marketing communications (IMC)**. IMC is the careful coordination of all promotional messages—traditional advertising, direct marketing, interactive, public relations, sales promotion, personal selling, event marketing, and other communications—for a product or service to ensure the consistency of messages at every contact point where a company meets the consumer. Following the concept of IMC, marketing managers carefully work out the roles that various promotional elements will play in the marketing mix. Timing of promotional activities is coordinated, and the results of each campaign are carefully monitored to improve future use of the promotional mix tools. Typically, a marketing communications director is appointed who has overall responsibility for integrating the company's marketing communications.

Movie marketing campaigns benefit greatly from an IMC approach. Those campaigns that are most integrated generally have more impact and make a deeper impression on potential moviegoers, leading to higher box-office sales. An integrated marketing approach was used to introduce *The Da Vinci Code*. Excitement about the release of the film gathered momentum months in advance as the trailer was shown on the Internet and television. Along with the release of the trailer, the movie was supported by numerous merchandising efforts. Bookstores and gift shops stocked hardback, paperback, and special illustrated editions, as well as *Da Vinci Code* walking tours of key cities in the story, playing cards, calligraphy sets, music CDs, video games, podcasts, and more. Google and Sony launched a game called "The Sony Ericsson Da Vinci Code Trail" in 22 languages. Players competed against each other online and then in a real-life challenge in Paris. The winner was awarded a two-week trip to Rome, Paris, London, and New York. The game did more than promote the movie, however. "Da Vinci Code Trail" familiarized people with Google's services beyond search and drove traffic to Sony's Web site, which rose 30 percent as a result of the promotion. Finally, before the movie's release, there were over 500,000 English language posts on blogs like Technorati, Google, IceRocket, and BlogPulse. The integrated marketing campaign (plus the religious controversy surrounding the story) helped the film generate over $77 million at the box office on opening weekend.[20]

The IMC concept has been growing in popularity for several reasons. First, the proliferation of thousands of media choices beyond traditional television has made promotion a more complicated task. Instead of promoting a product just through mass-media options, like television and magazines, promotional messages today can appear in many varied sources. Furthermore, the mass market has also fragmented—more selectively segmented markets and an increase in niche marketing have replaced the traditional broad market groups that marketers promoted to in years past. For instance, many popular magazines now have Spanish-language editions targeted toward America's growing Hispanic population. Finally, marketers have slashed their advertising spending in favor of promotional techniques that generate immediate sales responses and those whose effects are more easily measured, such as direct marketing. Thus, the interest in IMC is largely a reaction to the scrutiny that marketing communications has come under and, particularly, to suggestions that uncoordinated promotional activity leads to a strategy that is wasteful and inefficient.

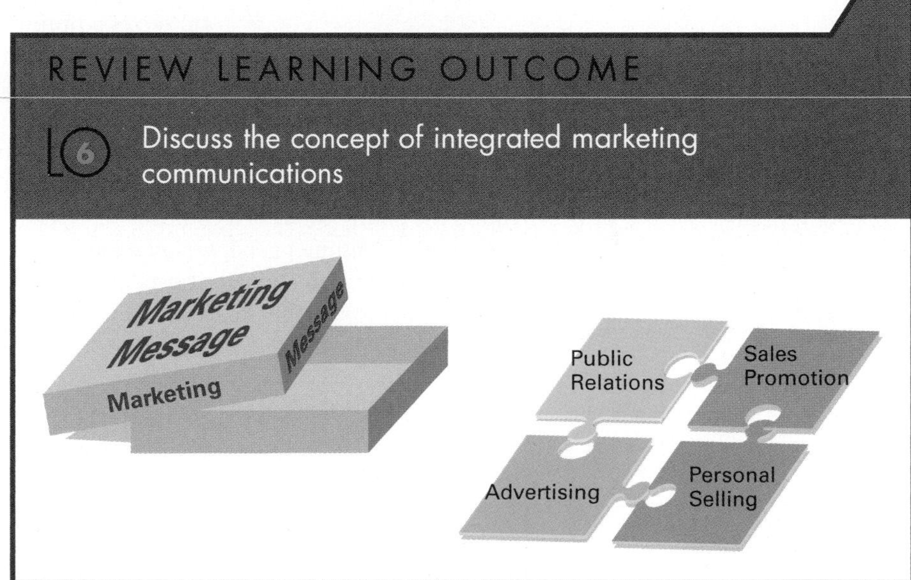

LO 7 FACTORS AFFECTING THE PROMOTIONAL MIX

Promotional mixes vary a great deal from one product and one industry to the next. Normally, advertising and personal selling are used to promote goods and services, and are supported and supplemented by sales promotion. Public relations helps develop a positive image for the organization and the product line. However, a firm may choose not to use all four promotional elements in its promotional mix, or it may choose to use them in varying degrees. The particular promotional mix chosen by a firm for a product or service depends on several factors: the nature of

Buying specialty products such as jewelry and clothing often involves a social risk. Many consumers depend on sales personnel for guidance and advice in making the "proper" choice.

the product, the stage in the product life cycle, target market characteristics, the type of buying decision, funds available for promotion, and whether a push or a pull strategy will be used.

Nature of the Product

Characteristics of the product itself can influence the promotional mix. For instance, a product can be classified as either a business product or a consumer product (refer to Chapters 7 and 10). As business products are often custom-tailored to the buyer's exact specifications, they are often not well suited to mass promotion. Therefore, producers of most business goods, such as computer systems or industrial machinery, rely more heavily on personal selling than on advertising. Informative personal selling is common for industrial installations, accessories, and component parts and materials. Advertising, however, still serves a purpose in promoting business goods. Advertisements in trade media may be used to create general buyer awareness and interest. Moreover, advertising can help locate potential customers for the sales force. For example, print media advertising often includes coupons soliciting the potential customer to "fill this out for more detailed information."

In contrast, because consumer products generally are not custom-made, they do not require the selling efforts of a company representative who can tailor them to the user's needs. Thus, consumer goods are promoted mainly through advertising to create brand familiarity. Television and radio advertising, consumer-oriented magazines, and the Internet and other highly targeted media are used extensively to promote consumer goods, especially nondurables. Sales promotion, the brand name, and the product's packaging are about twice as important for consumer goods as for business products. Persuasive personal selling is important at the retail level for shopping goods such as automobiles and appliances.

The costs and risks associated with a product also influence the promotional mix. As a general rule, when the costs or risks of using a product increase, personal selling becomes more important. Items that are a small part of a firm's budget (supply items) or of a consumer's budget (convenience products) do not require a salesperson to close the sale. In fact, inexpensive items cannot support the cost of a salesperson's time and effort unless the potential volume is high. On the other hand, expensive and complex machinery, new buildings, cars, and new homes represent a considerable investment. A salesperson must assure buyers that they are spending their money wisely and not taking an undue financial risk.

Social risk is an issue as well. Many consumer goods are not products of great social importance because they do not reflect social position. People do not experience much social risk in buying a loaf of bread or a candy bar. However, buying some shopping products and many specialty products such as jewelry and clothing does involve a social risk. Many consumers depend on sales personnel for guidance and advice in making the "proper" choice.

Stages in the Product Life Cycle

The product's stage in its life cycle is a big factor in designing a promotional mix. (See Exhibit 14.4.) During the *introduction stage*, the basic goal of promotion is to inform the target audience that the product is available. Initially, the emphasis is on the general product class—for example, mobile phones. The emphasis gradually changes to gaining attention for a particular brand, such as Nokia, Samsung, Sony Ericsson, or Motorola. Typically, both extensive advertising and public relations inform the target audience of the product class or brand and heighten awareness

EXHIBIT 14.4

Product Life Cycle and the Promotional Mix

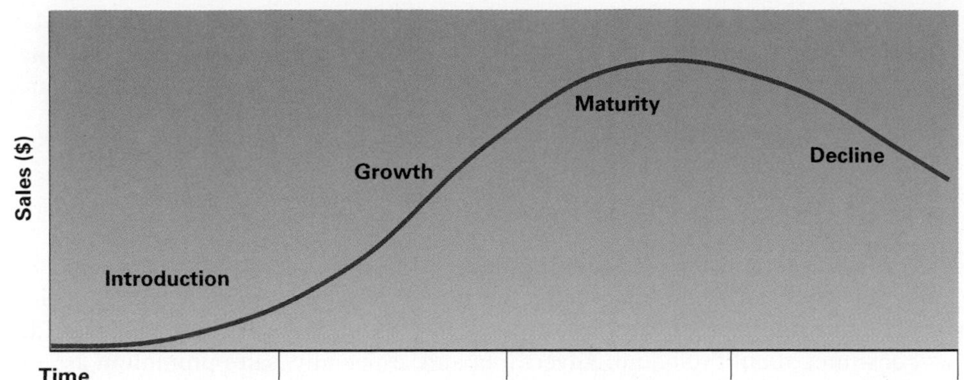

Preintroduction publicity; small amounts of advertising near introduction	Heavy advertising and public relations to build awareness; sales promotion to induce trial; personal selling to obtain distribution	Heavy advertising and public relations to build brand loyalty; decreasing use of sales promotion; personal selling to maintain distribution	Advertising slightly decreased — more persuasive and reminder in nature; increased use of sales promotion to build market share; personal selling to maintain distribution	Advertising and public relations drastically decreased; sales promotion and personal selling maintained at low levels

levels. Sales promotion encourages early trial of the product, and personal selling gets retailers to carry the product.

When the product reaches the *growth stage* of the life cycle, the promotion blend may shift. Often a change is necessary because different types of potential buyers are targeted. Although advertising and public relations continue to be major elements of the promotional mix, sales promotion can be reduced because consumers need fewer incentives to purchase. The promotional strategy is to emphasize the product's differential advantage over the competition. Persuasive promotion is used to build and maintain brand loyalty to support the product during the growth stage. By this stage, personal selling has usually succeeded in getting adequate distribution for the product.

As the product reaches the *maturity stage* of its life cycle, competition becomes much stronger, and thus persuasive and reminder advertising are more strongly emphasized. Sales promotion comes back into focus as product sellers try to increase their market share.

All promotion, especially advertising, is reduced as the product enters the *decline stage*. Nevertheless, personal selling and sales promotion efforts may be maintained, particularly at the retail level.

Target Market Characteristics

A target market characterized by widely scattered potential customers, highly informed buyers, and brand-loyal repeat purchasers generally requires a promotional mix with more advertising and sales promotion and less personal selling. Sometimes, however, personal selling is required even when buyers are well informed and geographically dispersed. Although industrial installations and component parts may be sold to extremely competent people with extensive education and work experience, salespeople must still be present to explain the product and work out the details of the purchase agreement.

pull strategy
A marketing strategy that stimulates consumer demand to obtain product distribution.

push strategy
A marketing strategy that uses aggressive personal selling and trade advertising to convince a wholesaler or a retailer to carry and sell particular merchandise.

Often firms sell goods and services in markets where potential customers are hard to locate. Print advertising can be used to find them. The reader is invited to go online, call, or mail in a reply card for more information. As the online inquiries, calls, or cards are received, salespeople are sent to visit the potential customers.

Type of Buying Decision

The promotional mix also depends on the type of buying decision (routine or complex). For example, the most effective promotion for routine consumer decisions, like buying toothpaste or soft drinks, calls attention to the brand or reminds the consumer about the brand. Advertising and, especially, sales promotion are the most productive promotion tools to use for routine decisions.

If the decision is neither routine nor complex, advertising and public relations help establish awareness for the good or service. Suppose a man is looking for a bottle of wine to serve to his dinner guests. As a beer drinker, he is not familiar with wines, yet he has seen advertising for Robert Mondavi wine and has also read an article in a popular magazine about the Robert Mondavi winery. He may be more likely to buy this brand because he is already aware of it. Indeed, online reviews can be important tools in this type of buying decision.

In contrast, consumers making complex buying decisions are more extensively involved. They rely on large amounts of information to help them reach a purchase decision. Personal selling is most effective in helping these consumers decide. For example, consumers thinking about buying a car typically research the car online using corporate and third party Web sites. However, few people buy a car without visiting the dealership. They depend on a salesperson to provide the information they need to reach a decision. In addition to online resources, print advertising and brochures may also be used for high-involvement purchase decisions because they can often provide a large amount of information to the consumer.

© VICKI BEAVER

Available Funds

Money, or the lack of it, may easily be the most important factor in determining the promotional mix. A small, undercapitalized manufacturer may rely heavily on free publicity if its product is unique. If the situation warrants a sales force, a financially strained firm may turn to manufacturers' agents, who work on a commission basis with no advances or expense accounts. Even well-capitalized organizations may not be able to afford the advertising rates of publications like *Time Magazine*, *Reader's Digest*, and *The Wall Street Journal*, or the cost of running television commercials on *Desperate Housewives*, *American Idol*, or the Super Bowl. The price of a high-profile advertisement in these media could support several salespeople for an entire year.

When funds are available to permit a mix of promotional elements, a firm will generally try to optimize its return on promotion dollars while minimizing the *cost per contact*, or the cost of reaching one member of the target market. In general, the cost per contact is very high for personal selling, public relations, and sales promotions like sampling and demonstrations. On the other hand, given the number of people national advertising reaches, it has a very low cost per contact.

Usually, there is a trade-off among the funds available, the number of people in the target market, the quality of communication needed, and the relative costs of the promotional elements. A company may have to forgo a full-page, color advertisement in *People* magazine in order to pay for a personal selling effort. Although the magazine ad will reach more people than personal selling, the high cost of the magazine space is a problem. There are plenty of low cost options available to companies without a huge budget. Many of these include online strategies and public relations efforts, where the company relies on free publicity.

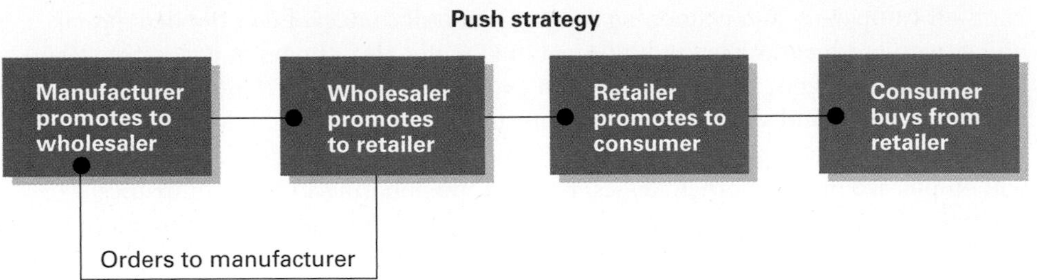

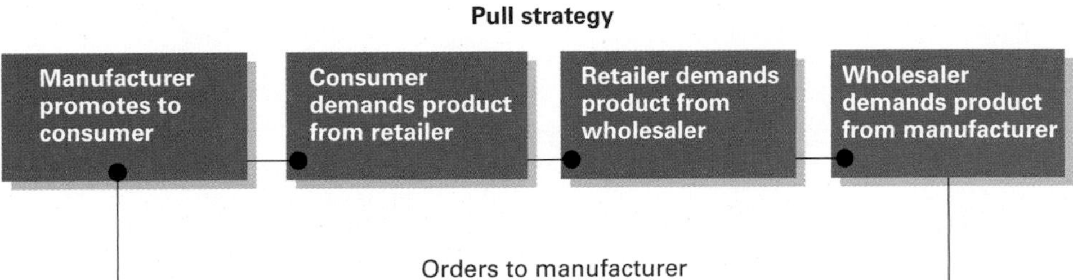

EXHIBIT 14.5

Push Strategy versus Pull Strategy

Push and Pull Strategies

The last factor that affects the promotional mix is whether to use a push or a pull promotional strategy. Manufacturers may use aggressive personal selling and trade advertising to convince a wholesaler or a retailer to carry and sell their merchandise. This approach is known as a **push strategy**. (See Exhibit 14.5.) The wholesaler, in turn, must often push the merchandise forward by persuading the retailer to handle the goods. The retailer then uses advertising, displays, and other forms of promotion to convince the consumer to buy the "pushed" products. This concept also applies to services. For example, the Jamaican Tourism Board targets promotions to travel agencies, which, in turn, tell their customers about the benefits of vacationing in Jamaica.

At the other extreme is a **pull strategy**, which stimulates consumer demand to obtain product distribution. Rather than trying to sell to the wholesaler, the manufacturer using a pull strategy focuses its promotional efforts on end consumers or opinion leaders. For example, Procter & Gamble recently spent $100 million on an advertising campaign to promote its new toothpaste. P&G's new Crest Pro-Health claims to deliver everything a consumer could want in one tube—it supposedly protects against gingivitis, plaque, cavities, sensitivity, and stains, and it freshens breath. The theme of the campaign, targeted to the information-seeking customer, is "Healthy, beautiful smiles for life."[21] Consumers responded positively to the campaign and began demanding the product from their retailer. The retailer ordered the merchandise from the wholesaler. The wholesaler, confronted with rising demand, then placed an order for the "pulled" merchandise from the manufacturer. Consumer demand pulled the product through the channel of distribution, (See Exhibit 14.5.) Heavy sampling, introductory consumer advertising,

REVIEW LEARNING OUTCOME

LO7 Describe the factors that affect the promotional mix

advertising
Impersonal, one-way mass communication about a product or organization that is paid for by a marketer.

cents-off campaigns, and couponing are part of a pull strategy. P&G flooded dental offices with product samples and informational materials in hopes of generating favorable testimonials from users. Similarly, Splenda No Calorie Sweetener offered free samples, recipes, and a coupon to potential consumers who tried Splenda.[22]

Rarely does a company use a pull or a push strategy exclusively. Instead, the mix will emphasize one of these strategies. For example, pharmaceutical companies generally use a push strategy, through personal selling and trade advertising, to promote their drugs and therapies to physicians. Sales presentations and advertisements in medical journals give physicians the detailed information they need to prescribe medication to their patients. Most pharmaceutical companies supplement their push promotional strategy with a pull strategy targeted directly to potential patients through advertisements in consumer magazines and on television.

THE EFFECTS OF ADVERTISING

Advertising is defined as any form of impersonal, paid communication in which the sponsor or company is identified. It is a popular form of promotion, especially for consumer packaged goods and services. Advertising expenditures typically increase annually but were expected to decline in 2009, due to economic conditions. In recent years 30 companies spent over $1 billion each, with the top 100 global marketers spending more than $108 billion overall on measured media. Among the top brands advertised by these companies were Procter & Gamble ($9.4 billion), Unilever ($5.3 billion), L'Oreal ($3.4 billion), and General Motors Company ($3.3 billion).[23]

Advertising and marketing services agencies and other firms that provide marketing and communications services to marketers employ an estimated 750,000 people. About another 850,000 people work in media advertising, such as newspapers, broadcast and cable TV, radio, magazines, and Internet media companies.[24] This represents a decrease in both areas primarily due to economic conditions and much lower newspaper employment.

The money budgeted for advertising by some firms is staggering. (See Exhibit 14.6.) Procter & Gamble, Verizon, AT&T, General Motors, and Johnson & Johnson each spend anywhere from $2.5 billion to nearly $5 billion annually in the United States on national advertising alone. That's about $10 million a day on national advertising. If local advertising, sales promotion, and public relations are included, this figure rises much higher. Over 100 companies spend more than $300 million each on advertising every year.[25]

Spending on advertising varies by industry. For example, book publishers have one of the highest ratios of advertising dollars to sales. They spend roughly 27 cents on advertising for every dollar of book revenue. Similarly, for every dollar of merchandise sold in

EXHIBIT 14.6

Top Ten Leaders by U.S. Advertising Spending

Rank	Advertiser	Total U.S. Ad Spending In 2008 (in millions)
1	Procter & Gamble	$4,838
2	Verizon Communications	$3,700
3	AT&T	$3,073
4	General Motors Corporation	$2,901
5	Johnson & Johnson	$2,529
6	Unilever	$2,423
7	Walt Disney Co.	$2,218
8	Time Warner	$2,208
9	General Electric Co.	$2,019
10	Sears Holdings Corp.	$1,865

0 500 1000 1500 2000 2500 3000 3500 4000 4500 5000

Source: Reprinted with permission from the June 23, 2009, issue of *Advertising Age*.

the game and toy industry, about 12 to 15 cents is spent on advertising these products to consumers. Other consumer goods manufacturers that spend heavily on advertising in relation to total sales include sugar and confectionery products manufacturers, leather manufacturers, watchmakers, perfume and cosmetic manufacturers, detergent makers, and wine and liquor companies.[26]

Advertising and Market Share

Today's most successful brands of consumer goods, like Ivory soap and Coca-Cola, were built by heavy advertising and marketing investments long ago. Today's advertising dollars for successful consumer brands are spent on maintaining brand awareness and market share.

New brands with a small market share tend to spend proportionately more for advertising and sales promotion than those with a large market share, typically for two reasons. First, beyond a certain level of spending for advertising and sales promotion, diminishing returns set in. That is, sales or market share begins to decrease no matter how much is spent on advertising and sales promotion. This phenomenon is called the **advertising response function**. Understanding the advertising response function helps marketers use budgets wisely. A market leader like Johnson & Johnson's Neutrogena typically spends proportionately less on advertising than a newcomer like Jergens Natural Glow Daily Moisturizer brand. Jergens spends more on its brand to gain attention and increase market share. Neutrogena, on the other hand, spends only as much as is needed to maintain market share—anything more would produce diminishing benefits. Neutrogena has already captured the attention of the majority of its target market. It needs only to remind customers of its product.

The second reason new brands tend to require higher spending for advertising and sales promotion is that a certain minimum level of exposure is needed to measurably affect purchase habits. If Jergens advertised Natural Glow Daily Moisturizer in only one or two publications and bought only one or two television spots, it certainly would not achieve the exposure needed to penetrate consumers' perceptual defenses, gain attention, and ultimately affect purchase intentions. Instead, Natural Glow Daily Moisturizer was advertised in many different media for a sustained time.

The Effects of Advertising on Consumers

Advertising affects consumers' daily lives, informing them about products and services and influencing their attitudes, beliefs, and ultimately their purchases. The average U.S. citizen is exposed to hundreds of advertisements a day from all types of advertising media. In the television medium alone, researchers estimate that the average viewer watches at least six hours of commercial television messages a week. In addition, that person is exposed to countless print ads and promotional messages seen in other places. Advertising affects the TV programs people watch, the content of the newspapers they read, the politicians they elect, the medicines they take, and the toys their children play with. Consequently, the influence of advertising on the U.S. socioeconomic system has been the subject of extensive debate among economists, marketers, sociologists, psychologists, politicians, consumerists, and many others.

Though advertising cannot change consumers' deeply rooted values and attitudes, it may succeed in transforming a person's negative attitude toward a product into a positive one. For instance, serious or dramatic advertisements are more effective at changing consumers' negative attitudes. Humorous ads, on the other hand, have been shown to be more effective at shaping attitudes when consumers already have a positive image of the advertised brand.[27] However, as much as humor in advertising tends to improve brand recognition, it does not necessarily improve product recall, message credibility, or buying intentions. Consumers who find the ad funny may have good feelings about the product, but their purchasing decisions will not be affected unless they can actually recall the brand. The best results with humorous ads are achieved by making the message relevant

advertising response function
A phenomenon in which spending for advertising and sales promotion increases sales or market share up to a certain level but then produces diminishing returns.

to the product. For example, Taco Bell saw a substantial rise in sales after promoting a tiny talking Chihuahua who was crazy about their product, constantly demanding to be fed by saying, "Yo quiero Taco Bell." The phrase caught on and got people repeating—and remembering—the company's name across the country. The actual content of the commercial reinforced the company's message in a relevant manner.[28]

Advertising can also affect the way consumers rank a brand's attributes, such as color, taste, smell, and texture. For example, in years past, car ads emphasized brand attributes such as roominess, speed, and low maintenance. Today, however, car marketers have added safety, versatility, and customization to the list. Safety features such as antilock brakes, power door locks, and front and side air bags are now a standard part of the message in many carmakers' ads. Toyota Scion appeals to consumers' sense of individuality by allowing purchasers to custom-design their cars by selecting features such as the steering wheel color, multi-shade illuminated cup holders, and "sport" pedals.[29]

CUSTOMER Experience

CUSTOMER

Pepsi's New Look

How much does a brand logo makeover cost these days? Well more than one million dollars and five months if you are Pepsi-Cola. Pepsi recently revealed its new logo—only the 11th change since 1898, five changes coming in the last 21 years. According to Pepsi's top executives, part of the strategy was to move the brand from the traditional mass marketing and mass distribution era into the current culture of personalization. "By making the logo more dynamic and more alive . . . it is absolutely a huge step in the right direction," said Pepsi VP portfolio brands, Frank Cooper. While the $1 million dollars spent on design could be considered hefty, the real costs come in the other changes—from the trucks, vending machines, stadium signage, point of sale materials, and more. This could easily reach into the hundreds of millions of dollars.

So just what does the new logo signify? According to Pepsi, the new logo has a white band in the middle of the Pepsi circle that represents a series of smiles . . . a smile for Pepsi, a grin for Diet Pepsi, and a laugh for Pepsi Max. Branding experts are mixed: Some think the new look will make the logo less durable and classic while others feel that it is more adventurous and youthful. Indeed, Pepsi has succeeded in the past by targeting the "new generation."

There are also mixed consumer reviews. Some think the new logo looks like the old Diet Pepsi logo with the identical sans-serif typeface and the red and blue Pepsi wave in a diagonal slope. Others feel the new logo looks similar to the campaign for President Barack Obama. Regardless, there is a minimalist feel that has captured the attention of the iPod generation—that idea of simple elegance.

Interestingly, Pepsi's new advertising campaign also comes with a dose of optimism "every generation refreshes the world." However, arch rival Coca-Cola is also dosing out the optimism with its new advertising tagline "Open happiness."[30] While both companies have embraced this message at various times, never has this happened simultaneously. So the question is whether this helps or hurts the differentiation of each brand.

REVIEW LEARNING OUTCOME

LO 8 Discuss the effects of advertising on market share and consumers

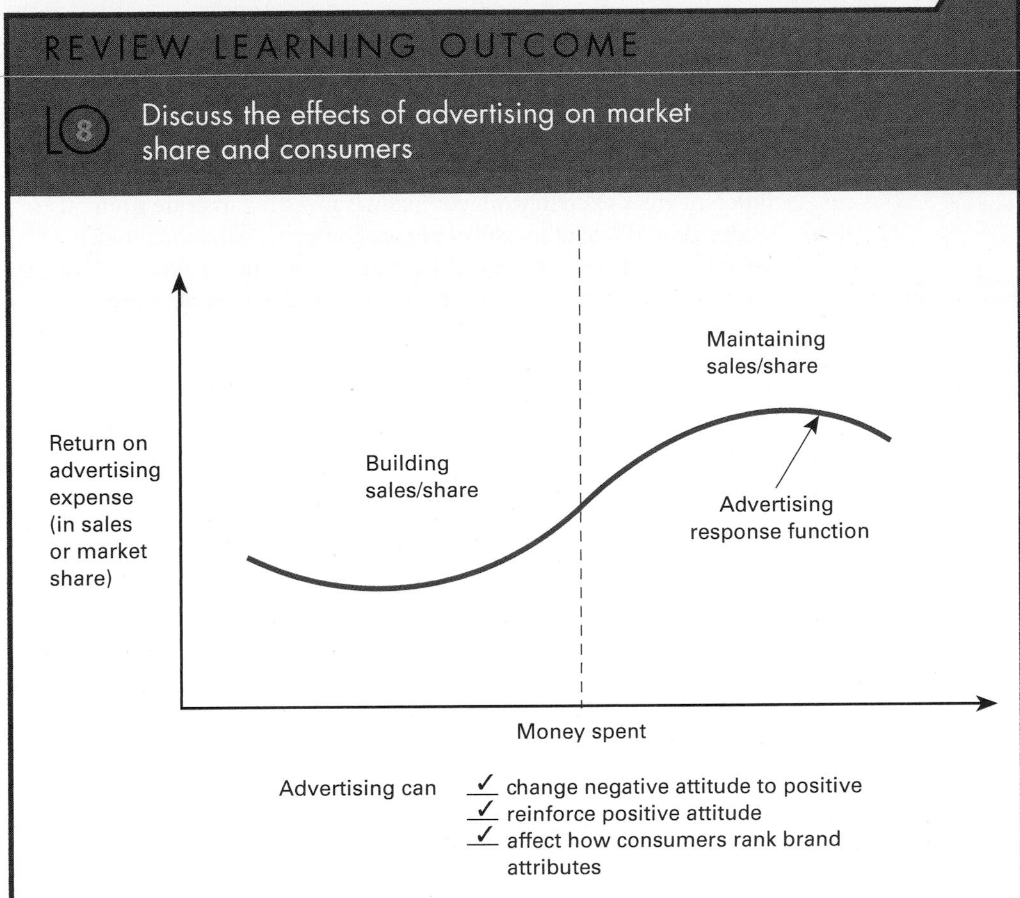

LO 9

MAJOR TYPES OF ADVERTISING

The firm's promotional objectives determine the type of advertising it uses. If the goal of the promotion plan is to build up the image of the company or the industry, **institutional advertising** may be used. In contrast, if the advertiser wants to enhance the sales of a specific good or service, **product advertising** is used.

Institutional Advertising

Historically, advertising in the United States has been product oriented. Today, however, companies market multiple products and need a different type of advertising. Institutional advertising, or corporate advertising, promotes the corporation as a whole and is designed to establish, change, or maintain the corporation's identity. It usually does not ask the audience to do anything but maintain a favorable attitude toward the advertiser and its goods and services. For example, when Time Warner dropped AOL from the company's corporate brand name, it hired a branding agency to develop institutional advertising to reposition the brand without the Internet unit and refocus the image on Time Warner as a media giant. In designing the "rebranding," executives did not want a radical change. Rather, they wanted to "freshen" the previous image and maintain its favorable status. The logo itself changed in texture, color, and typeface. In addition to changing the logo on buildings, business cards, and stationery, the company changed its stock ticker symbol to reflect the new image.[31]

A form of institutional advertising called **advocacy advertising** is typically used to safeguard against negative consumer attitudes and to enhance the company's credibility

institutional advertising
A form of advertising designed to enhance a company's image rather than promote a particular product.

product advertising
A form of advertising that touts the benefits of a specific good or service.

advocacy advertising
A form of advertising in which an organization expresses its views on controversial issues or responds to media attacks.

© AP IMAGES/PRNEWSFOTO/PEABODY ENERGY

Institutional advertising is designed to promote, establish, change, or maintain a corporation's positive identity. Usually the audience isn't asked to do anything except maintain a favorable attitude toward the institution.

among consumers who already favor its position. Often corporations use advocacy advertising to express their views on controversial issues. At other times, firms' advocacy campaigns react to criticism or blame, some in direct response to criticism by the media. For example, oil and gas companies typically get blamed for high gas prices and high profits. One of the largest in the world, Chevron Texaco, recently launched a campaign called "The Power of Human Energy" to highlight the different areas of energy the company is investing in aside from oil exploration. BP, another global energy company, rebranded itself BP—Beyond Petroleum to highlight its investments in alternative energy sources.[32] Other advocacy campaigns may try to ward off increased regulation, damaging legislation, or an unfavorable outcome in a lawsuit. The tobacco companies have utilized "good citizen campaigns" in the United States and around the world in an effort to create a positive public image for themselves after losing several class-action suits and being accused of targeting children with their marketing campaigns. In an effort to improve its corporate image, Philip Morris has been spending more than $120 million a year promoting its environmental and community development programs, such as building homes for Habitat for Humanity, making donations to food banks, and supporting meal programs for seniors and shelters for battered women.[33]

Product Advertising

Unlike institutional advertising, product advertising promotes the benefits of a specific good or service. The product's stage in its life cycle often determines which type of product advertising is used: pioneering advertising, competitive advertising, or comparative advertising.

pioneering advertising
A form of advertising designed to stimulate primary demand for a new product or product category.

competitive advertising
A form of advertising designed to influence demand for a specific brand.

Pioneering Advertising Pioneering advertising is intended to stimulate primary demand for a new product or product category. Heavily used during the introductory stage of the product life cycle, pioneering advertising offers consumers in-depth information about the benefits of the product class. Pioneering advertising also seeks to create interest. Pharmaceutical companies are the latest big players in pioneering advertising. For instance, one pharma giant, Pfizer, has steadily ramped up consumer advertising of a new drug, Lyrica—first approved by the FDA to treat pain caused by diabetic nerve damage. Then Pfizer found a broader market for Lyrica when it was approved for treatment of the disputed pain condition fibromyalgia. In just six months Pfizer spent $46 million on a new ad campaign for Lyrica as a treatment for fibromyalgia, compared with $33 million the previous year, in spite of the protest by many doctors who do not believe fibromyalgia is a real medical condition. There are no biological tests to diagnose fibromyalgia, and the condition has not been linked to any environmental or biological causes. But worldwide sales of Lyrica reached $1.8 billion in 2007. Analysts predicted sales would rise an additional 30 percent in 2008, helped by consumer advertising and the interest from other drug companies who see the potential for a major new market in aggressively pursuing fibromyalgia treatments.[34]

Competitive Advertising Firms use competitive or brand advertising when a product enters the growth phase of the product life cycle and other companies begin to enter the marketplace. Instead of building demand for the product category, the goal of **competitive advertising** is to influence demand for a specific brand. Often promotion becomes less informative and appeals more to emotions during this phase. Advertisements may emphasize subtle differences between brands, focusing on building recall of a brand name and creating a favorable brand attitude. Automobile advertising has long used very competitive messages, drawing distinctions based on factors such as quality, performance, and image. Similarly, in an effort to obtain market share from

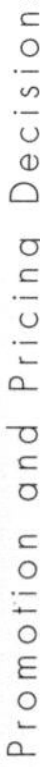
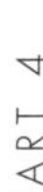

competitors and to build brand awareness in the wireless industry, Nextel Communications signed a ten-year title sponsorship agreement with NASCAR. NASCAR executives, interested in building a younger fan base, consider the telecom industry one of the best ways to reach younger consumers because they always have a cell phone "stuck" to their ear.[35]

The Mac vs. PC ads for Apple use comparative advertising by portraying the PC (and everything and everyone associated with it) as "stodgy" and constantly losing to a hip, cool Mac.

Comparative Advertising Comparative advertising directly or indirectly compares two or more competing brands on one or more specific attributes. Some advertisers even use comparative advertising against their own brands. Products experiencing slow growth or entering the marketplace against strong competitors are more likely to employ comparative claims in their advertising. For instance, the Mac versus PC ads for Apple have been masterful. The ads create an image of a stodgy PC battling with a hip, cool Mac. The campaign's success has escalated the battle between the two computer icons with each creating new ads aimed at the other. Other recent campaigns include Hoover versus Dyson vacuum cleaners, Miller Lite versus Bud Light, and Pampers versus Huggies. In addition to comparative advertising, some companies have brought back the "taste test." These include Progresso soups versus Campbell's Select Harvest soups and Dunkin' Donuts versus Starbucks (which is even supported by a microsite **www.dunkinbeatstarbucks.com**).[36]

REVIEW LEARNING OUTCOME

LO 9 Identify the major types of advertising

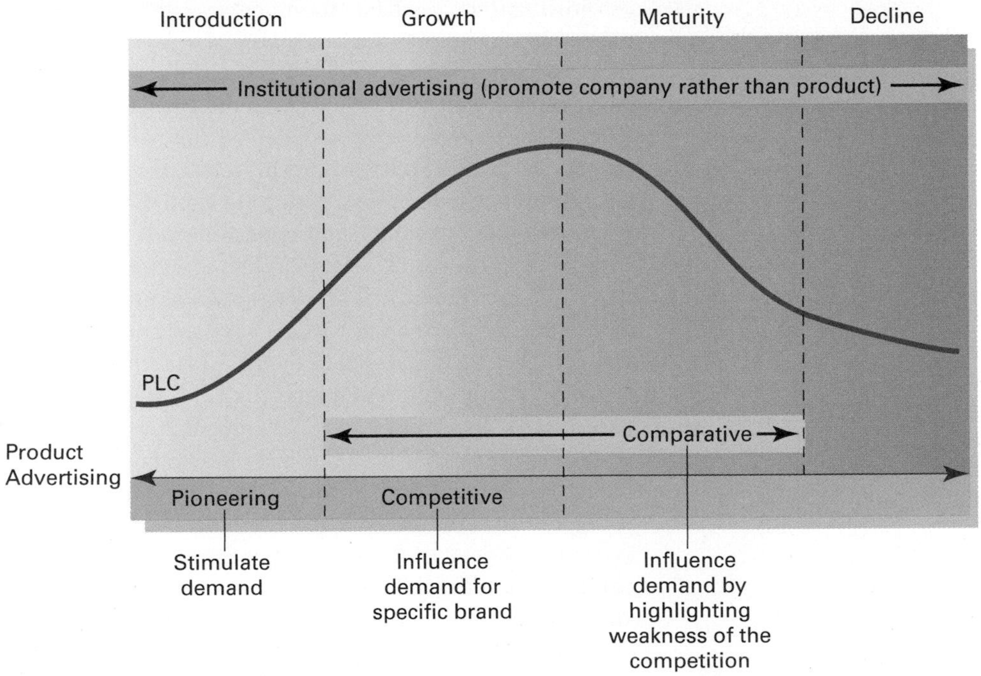

Before the 1970s, comparative advertising was allowed only if the competing brand was veiled and unidentified. In 1971, however, the Federal Trade Commission (FTC) fostered the growth of comparative advertising by saying that it provided information to the customer and that advertisers were more skillful than the government in communicating this information. Federal rulings prohibit advertisers from falsely describing competitors' products and allow competitors to sue if ads show their products or mention their brand names in an incorrect or false manner.

FTC rules also apply to advertisers making false claims about their own products. For example, the FTC recently filed a false-advertising suit against a company that

comparative advertising
A form of advertising that compares two or more specifically named or shown competing brands on one or more specific attributes.

advertising campaign
A series of related advertisements focusing on a common theme, slogan, and set of advertising appeals.

advertising objective
A specific communication task that a campaign should accomplish for a specified target audience during a specified period.

marketed a weight-loss product, claiming that its users could lose substantial amounts of weight rapidly, including as much as 18 pounds per week and as much as 50 percent of all excess weight in just 14 days, without dieting or exercise. The company also included (false) assurances that clinical studies prove those claims.[37]

Companies must be careful with comparative advertising approaches in other countries as well. Germany, Italy, Belgium, and France, for example, do not permit advertisers to claim that their products are the best or better than competitors' products, both of which are common claims in the United States. In the Netherlands, car manufacturers cannot make claims in their advertising about the fuel consumption or environmental aspects of the car. Similarly, Lands' End ran afoul of a German law prohibiting lifetime guarantee claims, which happen to be one of Lands' End's guiding principles. The law has made it difficult for the direct retailer to sell its products and advertise its lifetime guarantee through the Internet and direct mail in Germany.

In other countries, hard-hitting comparative advertising will not be effective because it offends cultural values. For example, Arabic culture generally encourages people not to compete with one another, and the sharing of wealth is common practice. Therefore, comparative advertising is not consistent with social values in Arabic countries. Japanese advertisers have also been reluctant to use comparative advertising because it is considered confrontational and doesn't promote the respectful treatment of consumers or portray a company in a respectful light. Nevertheless, although the Japanese have traditionally favored soft-sell advertising approaches, consumers are witnessing a trend toward comparative ads.

CREATIVE DECISIONS IN ADVERTISING

Advertising strategies typically are organized around an advertising campaign. An **advertising campaign** is a series of related advertisements focusing on a common theme, slogan, and set of advertising appeals. It is a specific advertising effort for a particular product that extends for a defined period of time. For example, Hewlett-Packard's celebrity-drenched global ad campaign, "The computer is personal again," helped HP gain the lead in worldwide market share for personal computers, and also imbued a once-faded brand with some cool. The glossy campaign, featuring print, video, and television ads, showcased achievers such as "CEO of Hip-Hop" Jay-Z, "Master of Snowboards" Shaun White, designer Vera Wang, and Brazilian author Paulo Coelho. Each celebrity was shown manipulating images that seemingly revolved around their laptop to show what's on their computer, what they do in their spare time, and why the PC is personal to them. A concurrent online campaign included a virtual motorcycle tour with the Orange County Choppers team, who were also the celebrity stars of HP's Super Bowl ad. That campaign was designed to create demand among 18- to 34-year-olds for the HP Pavilion entertainment notebook and specially designed Orange County Choppers "skins," or computer covers.[38]

Before any creative work can begin on an advertising campaign, it is important to determine what goals or objectives the advertising should achieve. An **advertising objective** identifies the specific communication task that a campaign should accomplish for a specified target audience during a specified period. The objectives of a specific advertising campaign often depend on the overall corporate objectives and the product being advertised. For example, McIlhenny Company's Tabasco Hot Sauce launched a print advertising campaign with the objective of educating consumers about how to use the product and the variety of flavors offered. The ads featured product information embedded in the label, which was blown up to cover the entire page. The ad copy for the Garlic Pepper Sauce read: "The only one potent enough to ward off both hypothermia and vampires at once." The original Tabasco Pepper Sauce ad copy read: "It's like love, you always want more no matter how badly you got burned last time." The ad campaign increased sales by over 11 percent in the first four weeks. The print medium was also supported by participation in special events, such as the National Collegiate Tailgate Tour.[39]

The DAGMAR approach (Defining Advertising Goals for Measured Advertising Results) is one method of setting objectives. According to this method, all advertising objectives should precisely define the target audience, the desired percentage change in some specified measure of effectiveness, and the time frame in which that change is to occur. For example, the objectives for an advertising campaign for Coca-Cola's revamped POWERade brand might be to achieve a 15 percent increase in its share of the sports-drink market within eight months.

Once objectives are defined, creative work can begin on the advertising campaign. Advertising campaigns often follow the AIDA model, which was discussed in Chapter 14. Depending on where consumers are in the AIDA process, the creative development of an advertising campaign might focus on creating attention, arousing interest, stimulating desire, or ultimately leading to the action of buying the product. Specifically, creative decisions include identifying product benefits, developing and evaluating advertising appeals, executing the message, and evaluating the effectiveness of the campaign.

Identifying Product Benefits

A well-known rule of thumb in the advertising industry is "Sell the sizzle, not the steak"—that is, in advertising the goal is to sell the benefits of the product, not its attributes. An attribute is simply a feature of the product such as its easy-open package or special formulation. A benefit is what consumers will receive or achieve by using the product. A benefit should answer the consumer's question, "What's in it for me?" Benefits might be such things as convenience, pleasure, savings, or relief. A quick test to determine whether you are offering attributes or benefits in your advertising is to ask, "So?" Consider this example:

© AP IMAGES/PR NEWSFOTO/PEPSI CO.

- *Attribute*: "SoBe Life Water has reformulated five delicious, low-calorie flavors—Blackberry Grape, Pomegranate Cherry, Orange Tangerine, Strawberry Kiwi and Passionfruit Citrus—each infused with a unique mix of antioxidant vitamins C & E, essential B vitamins and healthy herbal ingredients . . ." "So . . . ?"
- *Benefit*: "So . . . SoBe Life Water is not only an enhanced water; it is a lifestyle unto itself . . . providing consumers the healthiest, most fun and refreshing products, delivering the incredibly positive benefits of hydration and unmatched brand experiences."[40]

Marketing research and intuition are usually used to unearth the perceived benefits of a product and to rank consumers' preferences for these benefits. Coke's rival, PepsiCo, has its own sports drink, Gatorade. Already positioned as *the* thirst-quencher, Gatorade's advertising touts its refueling benefits to serious athletes of mainstream sports. Similarly, Kellogg's ad campaign for its latest cereal, Frosted Flakes Gold, has partnered with ESPN to promote the new frosted flake as a product that provides longer-lasting energy because it's a whole grain cereal. The ads underscore the message of increased, longer-lasting energy by featuring adolescent athletes being cheered on by Tony the Tiger.[41]

Developing and Evaluating Advertising Appeals

An **advertising appeal** identifies a reason for a person to buy a product. Developing advertising appeals, a challenging task, is typically the responsibility of the creative people in the advertising agency. Advertising appeals typically play off of consumers' emotions, such as fear or love, or address some need or want the consumer has, such as a need for convenience or the desire to save money.

advertising appeal
A reason for a person to buy a product.

Advertising campaigns can focus on one or more advertising appeals. Often the appeals are quite general, thus allowing the firm to develop a number of subthemes or

EXHIBIT 14.7

Common Advertising Appeals

Profit	Lets consumers know whether the product will save them money, make them money, or keep them from losing money
Health	Appeals to those who are body-conscious or who want to be healthy
Love or Romance	Is used often in selling cosmetics and perfumes
Fear	Can center around social embarrassment, growing old, or losing one's health; because of its power, requires advertiser to exercise care in execution
Admiration	Is the reason that celebrity spokespeople are used so often in advertising
Convenience	Is often used for fast-food restaurants and microwave foods
Fun and Pleasure	Are the key to advertising vacations, beer, amusement parks, and more
Vanity and Egotism	Are used most often for expensive or conspicuous items such as cars and clothing
Environmental Consciousness	Centers around protecting the environment and being considerate of others in the community

minicampaigns using both advertising and sales promotion. Several possible advertising appeals are listed in Exhibit 14.7.

Choosing the best appeal from those developed normally requires market research. Criteria for evaluation include desirability, exclusiveness, and believability. The appeal first must make a positive impression on and be desirable to the target market. It must also be exclusive or unique; consumers must be able to distinguish the advertiser's message from competitors' messages. Most importantly, the appeal should be believable. An appeal that makes extravagant claims not only wastes promotional dollars but also creates ill will for the advertiser.

The advertising appeal selected for the campaign becomes what advertisers call its **unique selling proposition**. The unique selling proposition usually becomes the campaign's slogan. For example, Red Bull's "Red Bull has wings" touts its benefits including improved concentration and reaction time, improved performance, and increased endurance (**www.redbullusa.com**). Similarly, POWERade's advertising campaign aimed at the sports enthusiast carries the slogan "Sport Is What You Make It." This is POWERade's unique selling proposition, implying that you can push yourself to the limit if you are motivated and use POWERade.[42]

unique selling proposition
A desirable, exclusive, and believable advertising appeal selected as the theme for a campaign.

Effective slogans often become so ingrained that consumers hearing the slogan immediately conjure up images of the product. For example, many consumers can easily name the companies and products behind these memorable slogans or even hum the jingle that goes along with them: "Have it your way," "Tastes great, less filling," "Ring around the collar," and "Tum te Tum Tum." Advertisers often revive old slogans or jingles in the hope that the nostalgia will create good feelings with consumers. Burger King brought back the King in its advertising. Maytag refreshed its campaign featuring its appliance pitchman by changing the actor who plays him and giving him a helper—the third change since the ads originated in 1967. And Hershey's Kit Kat bar's jingle "Gimme a Break" is so etched in consumers' minds that recently the agency hired a film crew to ask people on the street to sing the jingle for use on the Internet, in future ad campaigns, and in its Kit Kat "Gimme a Break" Café.[43]

Executing the Message

Message execution is the way an advertisement portrays its information. In general, the AIDA plan (see Chapter 14) is a good blueprint for executing an advertising message. Any ad should immediately draw the reader's, viewer's, or listener's attention. The advertiser must then use the message to hold interest, create desire for the good or service, and ultimately motivate action—a purchase.

The style in which the message is executed is one of the most creative elements of an advertisement. Exhibit 14.8 lists some examples of executional styles used by advertisers. Executional styles often dictate what type of media is to be employed to convey the message. Scientific executional styles lend themselves well to print advertising where more information can be conveyed. On the other hand, demonstration and musical styles are more likely found in broadcast advertising.

Testimonials by athletes are one of the more popular executional styles. Tiger Woods and Shaquille O'Neal are two of the most successful athlete spokespersons.

Read Shaq's own words about the power of marketing and advertising in Exhibit 14.9.

Injecting humor into an advertisement is a popular and effective executional style. Selection of a humorous approach is based on the communications goal. Humorous executional styles are more often used in radio and television advertising than in print or magazine advertising where humor is less easily communicated. Regardless of the advertising medium, however, humor can be tricky to use because not all people find the same things funny and marketers have to be sure the humor won't be misconstrued. For instance, a print and e-mail ad campaign for Timbuk2's limited-edition messenger bags caused an uproar even while the ad's creators protested it was supposed to be funny. The ad featured a photo of a crying girl in a prom dress next to a

This "talk-of-the-world, spectacular" outdoor ad welcoming visitors to the 2006 FIFA World Cup soccer match is an example of an aesthetically imaginative executional style.

© VALERY HACHE/AFP/GETTY IMAGES

EXHIBIT 14.8

Ten Common Executional Styles for Advertising

Slice-of-Life	Depicts people in normal settings, such as at the dinner table or in their car. McDonald's often uses slice-of-life styles showing youngsters munching french fries and Happy Meals on family outings.
Lifestyle	Shows how well the product will fit in with the consumer's lifestyle. As their Volkswagen Jetta moves through the streets of the French Quarter, the Gen X drivers plug in a techno music CD and marvel at how the rhythms of the world mimic the ambient vibe inside their vehicle.
Spokesperson/ Testimonial	Can feature a celebrity, company official, or typical consumer making a testimonial or endorsing a product. Sarah Michelle Gellar, star of *Buffy the Vampire Slayer*, endorses Maybelline cosmetics while country singer Shania Twain introduced Revlon's ColorStay Liquid Lip. Dell, Inc. founder Michael Dell touts his vision of the customer experience via Dell in television ads.
Fantasy	Creates a fantasy for the viewer built around use of the product. Carmakers often use this style to let viewers fantasize about how they would feel speeding around tight corners or down long country roads in their cars.
Humorous	Advertisers often use humor in their ads, such as Snickers' "Not Going Anywhere for a While" campaign featuring hundreds of souls waiting, sometimes impatiently, to get into heaven.
Real/Animated Product Symbols	Creates a character that represents the product in advertisements, such as the Energizer bunny, Starkist's Charlie the Tuna, or General Mills' longtime icon, Betty Crocker, redesigned for the new millennium.
Mood or Image	Builds a mood or image around the product, such as peace, love, or beauty. De Beers ads depicting shadowy silhouettes wearing diamond engagement rings and diamond necklaces portrayed passion and intimacy while extolling that a "diamond is forever."
Demonstration	Shows consumers the expected benefit. Many consumer products use this technique. Laundry-detergent spots are famous for demonstrating how their product will clean clothes whiter and brighter. Fort James Corporation demonstrated in television commercials how its Dixie Rinse & ReUse disposable stoneware product line can stand up to the heat of a blowtorch and survive a cycle in a clothes washer.
Musical	Conveys the message of the advertisement through song. For example, Nike's ads depicting a marathoner's tortured feet, skier Picabo Street's surgery-scarred knee, and a surfer's thigh scarred by a shark attack while strains of Joe Cocker's "You Are So Beautiful" are heard in the background.
Scientific	Uses research or scientific evidence to give a brand superiority over competitors. Pain relievers like Advil, Bayer, and Excedrin use scientific evidence in their ads.

EXHIBIT 14.9

Dreamful Attraction: Shaquille O'Neal's Thoughts on Marketing and Advertising

While on the outside looking in, I did not realize that marketing was so complicated. I never knew that a person, such as an athlete, could have such a powerful effect on people's thought processes and purchasing behavior. The use of a well-known athlete in marketing a product or service can have a great impact on the sales of that product or service. Look at Michael Jordan. Almost overnight most every kid either was wearing or wanted to wear Air Jordan shoes.

Why does this happen? Is it the appeal of a great athlete or is it great marketing? The answer is "none of the above." It's both. In my years as a professional basketball player, I have seen firsthand the dramatic appeal that athletes have for the fans and public in general. Top-name athletes are like E. F. Hutton—when they talk, people listen. But why do they listen? I believe they listen to us, the athletes, because we have credibility. The effectiveness of celebrity endorsements depends largely on how credible and attractive the spokesperson is and how familiar people are with him or her. Companies sometimes use sports figures and other celebrities to promote products hoping they are appropriate opinion leaders.

Because of an athlete's fame and fortune, or attraction, the athlete can often have the right credibility to be a successful spokesperson. The best definition of credibility that I could find was by James Gordon in his book, *Rhetoric of Western Thought*. He said that attraction "can come from a person's observable talents, achievements, occupational position or status, personality and appearance, and style."* That may be why a famous athlete's personality and position can help him or her communicate more effectively than a not-so-famous athlete.

Credibility is a positive force in the persuasive promotion used predominantly by cola marketers like Pepsi because of what I like to call "dreamful attraction." For example, when I was young, I dreamed that I was like Dr. J., the famous basketball player for the Philadelphia 76ers. I would take his head off a poster and put my head on it. I wanted to be Dr. J. That is dreamful attraction. The youth of today are no different. Just the other day a kid stopped me and told me that he wanted to be like me. He had a dreamful attraction. This dreamful attraction can help sell products. In my case, Pepsi, Spalding, Kenner, and Reebok are hoping that they are able to package properly and market whatever dreamful attraction I might have for their target audience—kids.

There are many ways to communicate to my target audience. I find that the most effective way for me is through television commercials. This avenue gives me a chance to express myself and show my real feelings about a message we are trying to communicate—either visually or vocally. I feel that I have what Clint Eastwood has—"Sudden Impaq." My impact is revealed through my sense of humor and my nonverbal communication.

Why does Shaq sell? Communication. Although the verbal communication in many of my commercials is slim, the impact is still there. This makes me believe even more in the quote that who you are can almost be as important as what you say. But if you can blend the two together—who you are and what you have to say—then imagine how much more successful the communication message can be in the marketing process. Andre Agassi's favorite quote from his Canon commercial is "Image is everything." If it is not everything, it is almost everything. If you have the right image, match it with the right product, and market it properly, then success should follow.

I have been involved in commercials and the marketing of products for only a short time, but I have learned a great deal. If there is one formula for success in selling products, it would be this: Marketing plus credibility and image plus effective communications equals increase in sales—hopefully.

Now, you can call me Dr. Shaq, M.E. (Marketing Expert).

*James Gordon, *Rhetoric of Western Thought* (Dubuque, Iowa: Kendall-Hunt Publishing Co., 1976), 207.

photo of a tough-looking guy across whom was written: "Here today. Gone tomorrow. Just like that jerk who stole your virginity, these bags are only around for a short time." Timbuk2 finally pulled the ad in response to a storm of negative blog postings and e-mail protests against the ad saying that trying to be funny using a reference to date-rape was offensive.[44] Used appropriately, humor can be effective in attracting and holding audience attention. For example, Altoids used humor to create and reinforce its quirky yet strong persona. With a significantly lower budget than key competitors, the Altoids campaign helped the product grow from a sleepy brand to the number one mint in America based on flavor.[45]

Executional styles for foreign advertising are often quite different from those we are accustomed to in the United States. Sometimes they are sexually oriented or aesthetically imaginative. For example, Adidas commissioned a German ad company to come up with a "talk-of-the-world, spectacular" outdoor ad to welcome visitors to the FIFA World Cup soccer match. They designed a 65-meter, front-and-back billboard of soccer star Oliver Kahn diving to catch a soccer ball, which stretched across a four-lane highway near the airport in Munich, Germany. Four million cars drove under the installation, and it became the visual that accompanied almost every foreign news coverage of the World Cup event.[46] European advertising avoids the direct-sell approaches common in U.S. ads and instead is more indirect, more symbolic, and, above all, more visual. Nike, known in the United States for "in-your-face" advertising and irreverent slogans such as "Just Do It," discovered that its brash advertising did not appeal to Europeans.

Sometimes a company will modify its executional styles to make its advertising more effective. For decades, Procter & Gamble has advertised shampoo in China using a demonstrational executional style. Television ads demonstrated how the science of shampoo worked and then showed a woman with nice, shiny hair. Because today's urban Chinese customers are more financially secure, they no longer make solely utilitarian purchases. To reflect that shift, Procter & Gamble has begun incorporating more of an emotional appeal into its advertisements. A new set of TV ads shows a woman emerging from an animated cocoon as a sophisticated butterfly. A voice-over says, "Head & Shoulders metamorphosis—new life for hair."[47]

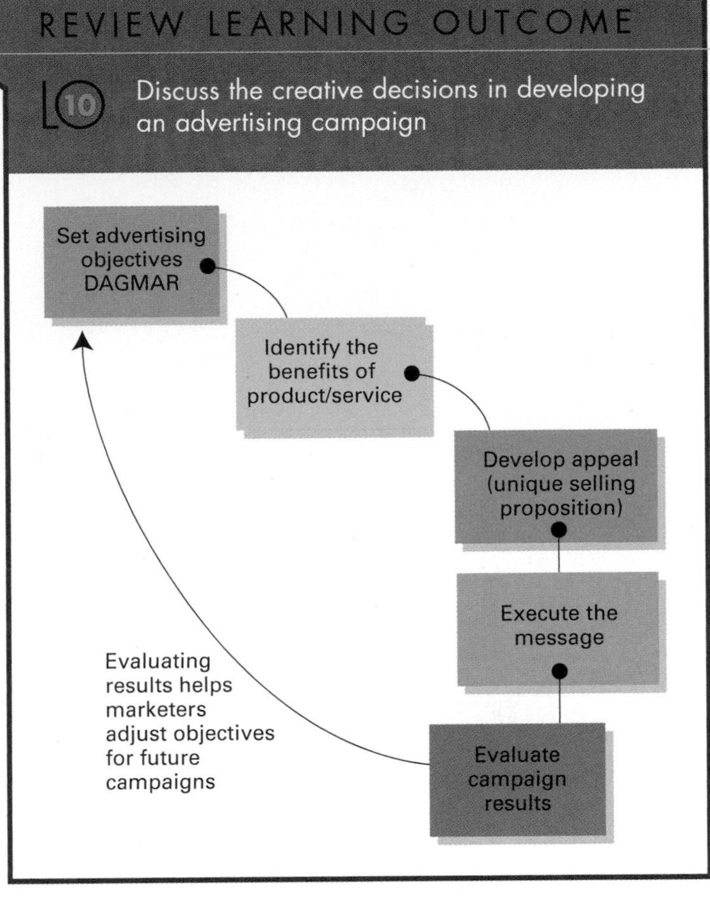

Post-Campaign Evaluation

Evaluating an advertising campaign can be the most demanding task facing advertisers. How do advertisers know whether the campaign led to an increase in sales or market share or elevated awareness of the product? Most advertising campaigns aim to create an image for the good or service instead of asking for action, so their real effect is unknown. So many variables shape the effectiveness of an ad that, in many cases, advertisers must guess whether their money has been well spent. Despite this gray area, marketers spend a considerable amount of time studying advertising effectiveness and its probable impact on sales, market share, or awareness.

Testing ad effectiveness can be done either before or after the campaign. Before a campaign is released, marketing managers use pretests to determine the best advertising appeal, layout, and media vehicle. After advertisers implement a campaign, they often conduct tests to measure its effectiveness. Several monitoring techniques can be used to determine whether the campaign has met its original goals. Even if a campaign has been highly successful, advertisers still typically do a post-campaign analysis. They assess how the campaign might have been more efficient and what factors contributed to its success. For example, Hallmark's market researchers wanted to capitalize on aging baby boomers. Research indicated that baby boomers do not want to age, but since that is inevitable, boomers want to see the positive side of aging. Therefore, Hallmark created the "Time of Your Life" series that flattered their egos. The cards were not successful, however, because they were placed in the "over 50" section of the store and baby boomers do not want to shop in that section.[48]

LO 11

MEDIA DECISIONS IN ADVERTISING

A major decision for advertisers is the choice of **medium**—the channel used to convey a message to a target market. **Media planning**, therefore, is the series of decisions advertisers make regarding the selection and use of media, allowing the marketer to optimally and cost-effectively communicate the message to the target audience. Specifically, advertisers must determine which types of media will best communicate the benefits of their product or service to the target audience and when and for how long the advertisement will run.

Promotional objectives and the appeal and executional style of the advertising strongly affect the selection of media. It is important to understand that both creative and media decisions are made at the same time. Creative work cannot be completed without knowing which medium will be used to convey the message to the target

medium
The channel used to convey a message to a target market.

media planning
The series of decisions advertisers make regarding the selection and use of media, allowing the marketer to optimally and cost-effectively communicate the message to the target audience.

EXHIBIT 14.10

Domestic Advertising Spending by Media Type, in billions

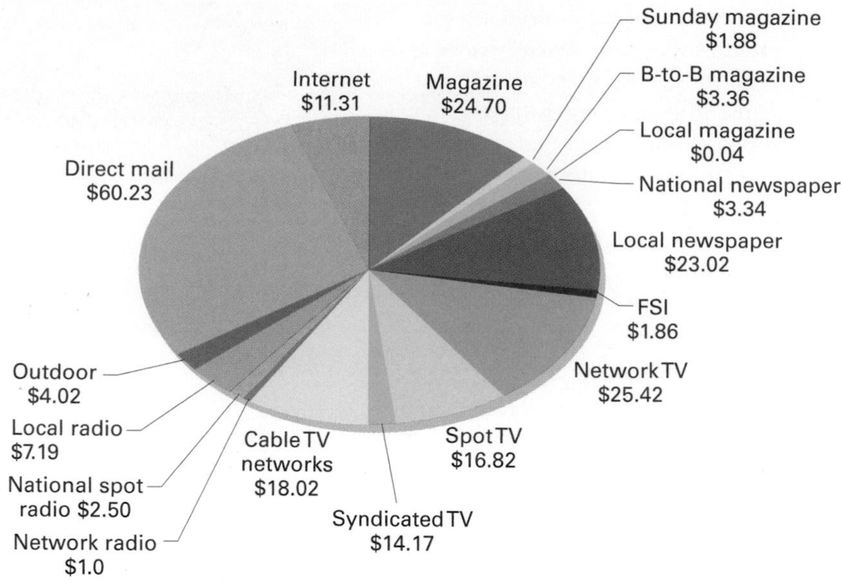

Source: Adapted from "Total U.S. Advertising Spending by Medium," *Advertising Age*, June 23, 2008.

cooperative advertising
An arrangement in which the manufacturer and the retailer split the costs of advertising the manufacturer's brand.

market. For instance, creative planning will likely differ for an ad to be displayed on a Web site versus one placed in a print medium, such as a newspaper or magazine. In many cases, the advertising objectives dictate the medium and the creative approach to be used. For example, if the objective is to demonstrate how fast a product operates, a TV commercial that shows this action may be the best choice.

U.S. advertisers spend about $300 billion on media advertising annually. Almost half of that is spent on media monitored by national reporting services—newspapers, magazines, Internet, radio, television, and outdoor media. The remainder is spent on unmonitored media, such as direct mail, trade exhibits, cooperative advertising, brochures, coupons, catalogs, and special events. Exhibit 14.10 shows advertising spending by media type. About 44 percent of every media dollar goes toward TV ads, 20 percent toward direct mail, and about 18 percent for newspaper ads.[49] But these traditional mass-market media are declining in usage and more targeted media are growing.[50]

Media Types

Advertising media are channels that advertisers use in mass communication. The six major advertising media are newspapers, magazines, radio, television, outdoor media, and the Internet. Exhibit 14.11 summarizes the advantages and disadvantages of these major channels. In recent years, however, alternative media vehicles have emerged that give advertisers innovative ways to reach their target audience and avoid advertising clutter.

Newspapers The advantages of newspaper advertising include geographic flexibility and timeliness. Because copywriters can usually prepare newspaper ads quickly and at a reasonable cost, local merchants can reach their target market almost daily. Because newspapers are generally a mass-market medium, however, they may not be the best vehicle for marketers trying to reach a very narrow market. For example, local newspapers are not the best media vehicles for reaching purchasers of specialty steel products or even tropical fish. These target consumers make up very small, specialized markets. Newspaper advertising also encounters a lot of distractions from competing ads and news stories; thus, one company's ad may not be particularly visible.

The main sources of newspaper ad revenue are local retailers, classified ads, and cooperative advertising. In **cooperative advertising**, the manufacturer and the retailer

EXHIBIT 14.11

Advantages and Disadvantages of Major Advertising Media

Medium	Advantages	Disadvantages
Newspapers	Geographic selectivity and flexibility; short-term advertiser commitments; news value and immediacy; year-round readership; high individual market coverage; co-op and local tie-in availability; short lead time	Little demographic selectivity; limited color capabilities; low pass-along rate; may be expensive
Magazines	Good reproduction, especially for color; demographic selectivity; regional selectivity; local market selectivity; relatively long advertising life; high pass-along rate	Long-term advertiser commitments; slow audience buildup; limited demonstration capabilities; lack of urgency; long lead time
Radio	Low cost; immediacy of message; can be scheduled on short notice; relatively no seasonal change in audience; highly portable; short-term advertiser commitments; entertainment carryover	No visual treatment; short advertising life of message; high frequency required to generate comprehension and retention; distractions from background sound; commercial clutter
Television	Ability to reach a wide, diverse audience; low cost per thousand; creative opportunities for demonstration; immediacy of messages; entertainment carryover; demographic selectivity with cable stations	Short life of message; some consumer skepticism about claims; high campaign cost; little demographic selectivity with network stations; long-term advertiser commitments; long lead times required for production; commercial clutter
Outdoor Media	Repetition; moderate cost; flexibility; geographic selectivity	Short message; lack of demographic selectivity; high "noise" level distracting audience
Internet	Fastest-growing medium; ability to reach a narrow target audience; relatively short lead time required for creating Web-based advertising; moderate cost	Difficult to measure ad effectiveness and return on investment; ad exposure relies on "click-through" from banner ads; not all consumers have access to the Internet

split the costs of advertising the manufacturer's brand. One reason that manufacturers use cooperative advertising is the impracticality of listing all their dealers in national advertising. Also, co-op advertising encourages retailers to devote more effort to the manufacturer's lines.

Magazines Compared to the cost of other media, the cost per contact in magazine advertising is usually high. The cost per potential customer may be much lower, however, because magazines are often targeted to specialized audiences and thus reach more potential customers. The types of products most frequently advertised in magazines include automobiles, apparel, computers, and cigarettes.

One of the main advantages of magazine advertising is its market selectivity. Magazines are published for virtually every market segment. For instance, *Lucky* "The Magazine about Shopping and Style" is a leading fashion magazine; *ESPN the Magazine* is a successful sports magazine; *Essence* is targeted toward African American women; *Marketing News* is a trade magazine for the marketing professional; and *The Source* is a niche publication geared to young urbanites with a passion for hip-hop music.

Philips Electronics used an innovative magazine advertising campaign by sponsoring the magazines' contents page. Issues of four Time Warner magazines (*Time, Fortune, People,* and *Business 2.0*) featured the table of contents on the first page rather than several pages later. The inside front cover featured a Philips ad with the following copy: "Philips Electronics is bringing the table of contents to the front of selected Time, Inc. magazines to make things easier for readers." In general, the placement of the contents page varies from magazine to magazine, but it is not uncommon for the contents to appear after numerous advertisements; as many as 24 pages of ads can appear before a magazine's contents page. Philips paid Time, Inc., $5 million to sponsor the contents pages in the four magazines for only one issue each.[51]

Radio Radio has several strengths as an advertising medium: selectivity and audience segmentation, a large out-of-home audience, low unit and production costs, timeliness, and geographic flexibility. Local advertisers are the most frequent users of radio advertising, contributing over three-quarters of all radio ad revenues. Like newspapers, radio also lends itself well to cooperative advertising.

Radio advertising is enjoying a resurgence in popularity. As Americans become more mobile and pressed for time, media such as network television and newspapers have lost viewers and readers, particularly in the youth market. Radio listening, however, has grown in step with population increases mainly because its immediate, portable nature meshes so well with a fast-paced lifestyle. The ability to target specific demographic groups is a major selling point for radio stations, attracting advertisers pursuing narrowly defined audiences that are more likely to respond to certain kinds of ads and products. Radio listeners also tend to listen habitually and at predictable times, especially during "drive time," when commuters form a vast captive audience. Finally, satellite radio has attracted new audiences that are exposed to ads when allowed on that format.

The ad-skipping functionality offered by TiVo and other digital video recorders has been the most significant recent trend to affect TV advertising.

Television Because television is an audiovisual medium, it provides advertisers with many creative opportunities. Television broadcasters include network television, independent stations, cable television, and a relative newcomer, direct broadcast satellite television. ABC, CBS, NBC, and the Fox Network dominate network television, which reaches a wide and diverse market. Conversely, cable television and direct broadcast satellite systems, such as DirecTV and Dish Network, offer consumers a multitude of channels devoted exclusively to particular audiences—for example, women, children, African Americans, nature lovers, senior citizens, Christians, Hispanics, sports fans, and fitness enthusiasts. Recent niche market entries include CSTV Network (college sports) and the NFL Network—focused exclusively on the sports enthusiast—and the casino and gambling channel. Because of its targeted channels, cable television is often characterized as "narrowcasting" by media buyers.

Advertising time on television can be very expensive, especially for network and popular cable channels. The top-ranked TV programs in recent years are aired on networks ABC, CBS, and Fox. The biggest draws are Fox's *American Idol* and *House;* ABC's *Dancing with the Stars, Lost,* and *Grey's Anatomy;* NBC's *Sunday Night Football* and *The Office;* and CBS's crime series *CSI.*[52] First-run prime-time shows and special events command the highest rates for a typical 30-second spot, with the least expensive ads costing about $300,000 and the more expensive costing $500,000. Super Bowl spots are the most expensive—a 30-second spot during the 2009 Super Bowl telecast cost advertisers an average of $3 million.[53] The two dozen or so marketers paying such a premium price include typical big ad spenders such as Procter & Gamble, Anheuser-Busch, Pepsi, and E-Trade. Most marketers consider the Super Bowl the "last bastion" of mass marketing available, with about 100 million viewers tuning in.[54]

infomercial
A 30-minute or longer advertisement that looks more like a TV talk show than a sales pitch.

One of the more successful recent television formats to emerge is the **infomercial**, a 30-minute or longer advertisement. Infomercials are an attractive advertising vehicle for many marketers because of the relatively inexpensive airtime and the lower production costs. Advertisers say the infomercial is an ideal way to present complicated information to potential customers, which other advertising vehicles typically don't allow time to do. Now a $200 billion-dollar industry, infomercials are increasingly being used by some mainstream marketers. Once relegated to late-night TV, infomercials are showing up in early evening time slots, such as Fox's *The O'Reilly Factor*, CBS's *60 Minutes*, CNBC's *Mad Money*. Consumers who might have been skeptical of an ad's veracity on shopping networks, are less likely to suspect an ad shown during prime-time television programs. A shorter direct-retail infomercial is more common in daytime programming, running an average of 120 seconds.[55]

Probably the most significant trend to affect television advertising is the rise in popularity of digital video recorders (DVRs) such as TiVo. For every hour of television programming, an average of 15 minutes is dedicated to nonprogram material (ads, public service announcements, and network promotions), so it's hardly surprising that viewers weary of ad breaks have embraced ad-skipping DVR technology as the solution to interruptions during their favorite shows. Marketers of the products featured in those advertisements are not the only ones trying to figure out ways to keep consumers from avoiding them; networks are also concerned about ad skipping. If consumers are not watching advertisements, then marketers will spend a greater proportion of their advertising budgets on alternative media, and a critical revenue stream for networks will disappear. While NBC ran a test to measure the effectiveness of running shorter blocks of advertising, the company also said that it has no intention of changing its business model relative to advertising sales. TiVo then began offering interactive banner ads to advertisers, making those sponsors' names visible as their ads are being fast-forwarded. The full impact of DVR technology on television as an advertising medium has yet to be determined, but research companies such as Nielsen have started to measure the number of people who time shift—that is, record a show and watch at their convenience.[56]

Outdoor Media Outdoor or out-of-home advertising is a flexible, low-cost medium that may take a variety of forms. Examples include billboards, skywriting, giant inflatables, mini-billboards in malls and on bus stop shelters, signs in sports arenas, lighted moving signs in bus terminals and airports, and ads painted on cars, trucks, buses, water towers, manhole covers, drinking glass coasters, and even people, called "living advertising." Students in London "rented" their foreheads for temporary tattoos of brands and then walked around specified areas of the city.[57] The plywood scaffolding that rings downtown construction sites can also carry ads. Manhattan's Times Square, with an estimated 1.5 million daily pedestrians, has been a popular area for outdoor advertising using scaffolding.

Outdoor advertising reaches a broad and diverse market and is, therefore, ideal for promoting convenience products and services as well as directing consumers to local businesses. One of outdoor's main advantages over other media is that its exposure frequency is very high, yet the amount of clutter from competing ads is very low. Outdoor advertising also has the ability to be customized to local marketing needs. For these reasons, local business establishments, such as local services and amusements, retailers, public transportation, and hotels and restaurants, are the leading outdoor advertisers. Outdoor advertising categories on the rise include telecommunications with a heavy emphasis on wireless services, financial services, and packaged goods.

Outdoor advertising is becoming more innovative. New technology is enabling outdoor ads to become interactive and to be more like online ads. For example, Nike commissioned a 23-story interactive, digital billboard on New York's Times Square. People passing the display on the sidewalk could use their cell phones to temporarily control

New technology is enabling outdoor ads to become more interactive. For example, Virgin Atlantic Airways projected ads onto skyscrapers inviting passersby to send a text message. That drove traffic to its Web site, which was accessible by Web-enabled mobile devices.

advergaming
Placing advertising messages in Web-based or video games to advertise or promote a product, service, organization, or issue.

the billboard and design their own shoes.[58] Virgin Atlantic Airways projected ads onto New York's and Chicago's skyscrapers, inviting passersby to access the airline's "Love From Above" campaign rewards.[59]

Unusual outdoor advertising campaigns are not limited to the United States. Adidas Japan created a "living billboard" in the form of a vertical soccer field on the side of a skyscraper. The billboard featured live players and a ball attached by ropes to the side of the building.[60] Virgin Atlantic painted an ad on the grass next to the runway at South Africa's Johannesburg International Airport to greet arriving and departing passengers. A world's first, the ad required 1,000 liters of paint and nine separate permits from different regulatory authorities due to the sensitive nature of the site.[61]

The Internet and Alternative Media Marketing The Internet has dramatically changed the advertising industry. With ad revenues exceeding $26 billion annually, the Internet has become a solid advertising medium. Online advertising continues to grow at double-digit rates—well ahead of other advertising media.[62] In fact, online ad spending is expected to exceed $60 billion annually by 2012 and account for 18 percent of all marketing expenditures.[63] Internet advertising provides an interactive and versatile platform that offers rich data on consumer usage, enabling advertisers to improve their ad targetability and achieve measurable results.[64]

Popular Internet sites and search engines, such as Google and Yahoo!, as well as online service providers such as America Online, generally sell advertising space to marketers to promote their goods and services. Internet surfers click on these ads to be linked to more information about the advertised product or service. Established brands such as General Motors, Anheuser-Busch, Procter & Gamble, and Verizon have been adjusting their budgets to include Internet advertising, and other firms are not far behind. For example, Vonage, Circuit City, Ameritrade Brokerage, Amazon.com, Overstock.com, Netflix.com, and Monster.com have been among the top 50 advertisers on the Internet in recent years.

> *"Marketers' primary objective in using search engine ads is to enhance brand awareness."*

The effectiveness of Internet advertising has been hotly debated, however. Early research on banner ads found response rates as high as 30 percent, but more recent studies indicate much lower response rates. With high-speed broadband spreading rapidly in the United States, advertisers increasingly are switching to other online approaches. For example, marketers are using ads that float, sing, or dance; video commercials similar to traditional TV spots; and ads that pop up in another window, use larger, hard-to-miss shapes, and include both online and offline cross-promotions. These new formats are often large enough for marketers to include their entire message so that users don't have to click through to another site.

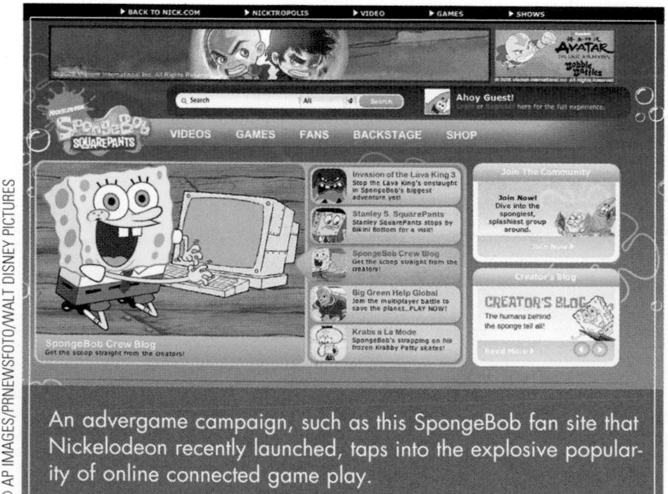

An advergame campaign, such as this SpongeBob fan site that Nickelodeon recently launched, taps into the explosive popularity of online connected game play.

Search Engine Ads One of the most popular approaches for Internet advertising is search engine ads. More than 120 billion searches are conducted annually in the United States with Google getting the lion's share—nearly 65 billion.[65] In second place is Yahoo! with more than two billion searches, followed by Microsoft's MSN with 940 million.[66] Google's market share of Internet search grew from 43 percent in 2005 to over 56 percent in 2008.[67] Marketers' primary objective in using search engine ads is to enhance brand awareness. Search engine optimization (SEO) accounted for the largest portion of online advertising expenditure with 41 percent of online marketing dollars going to SEO.

Advergaming Another popular Internet advertising format is advergaming. In **advergaming**, companies put ad messages in Web-based or video games to advertise or promote a product, service, organization, or issue. Sometimes the entire game amounts to a virtual commercial, other times advertisers sponsor games or buy ad space for product placement in them. Organizations using advergaming include Disney, Viacom's Nickelodeon, and even the U.S. Army.[68] The format encourages users to register for sweepstakes and other promotions and play the game. For example, a company with a heritage of aligning their products with gamers, Pepsi developed a multiplayer online game in which players get a chance to choose the next flavor of Mt. Dew. The site, dewmocracy.com, drew 700,000 unique visitors and 200,000 registered users who spent an average of 28 minutes per gaming session. Pepsi's "dewmocracy" advergame campaign taps into the explosive popularity of online connected game play, such as "World of Warcraft" with more than 10 million paying subscribers.[69]

An increasingly popular Internet advertising medium is social media marketing. Social media marketing is the collaboration and sharing of online content between the sender and the receiver—the brand and the consumer. The social media network, as one media pundit put it, "is where word-of-mouth meets word-of-mouse . . . where authentic brands are rewarded and fake brands (and their empty promises) are punished."[70] Social media is sometimes referred to as user-generated content, or consumer-generated media, and includes blogs, podcasts, forums, interactive video tours, social networks, and virtual worlds.[71] This new way of using the Internet is possible in part because of Internet-driven technology such as RSS (Really Simple Syndication)—a data exchange format that provides Internet users with quick access to frequently updated online content such as blogs and news headlines.[72]

Blogging Initially, blogs had no advertising. But the popularity of some blogs has made them an attractive medium for marketing messages. Budget Rent-A-Car recently bought ads on 177 blogs, Audi of America paid for advertising on 286 blogs, and MSNBC bought ads on more than 800 blogs.[73] Seed Media, which produces science publications in print and online, sells advertising on its network of more than 15 blogs just as it does in its magazine *Seed*. Seed Media contends that by advertising on its blog network, marketers will gain access to a group of bright, curious consumers who buy all kinds of products.[74]

Podcasts Podcasts are audio or video shows on computers, portable MP3 players, or other Web-connected devices. All that is needed to produce a podcast is a microphone connected to a computer and audio software. Most consumer-users promote their "show" on a Web site or a blog and submit their podcast to podcast directories. Many major broadcasters now participate in podcasting. Apple's iTunes directory, for instance, offers NPR, ABC News, CNN, Comedy Central, MTV, *The New York Times*, and PBS podcasts.[75]

Advertainment To cut through the clutter of traditional advertising media, advertisers are creating even more new media vehicles to advertise their products, some ordinary and others quite innovative. Alternative media vehicles can include shopping carts in grocery stores, computer screen savers, DVDs, interactive kiosks in department stores, advertisements run before movies at the cinema, and "advertainments"—"mini movies" that promote a product and are shown via the Internet.[76] For example, BMW shows films by recognized directors that run six to eight minutes and feature the cars in extreme situations.[77] Likewise, Coca-Cola sponsored a 25-minute advertainment program called "Sound Check" that was available only on TiVo. The program featured exclusive interviews, music videos, live shows, behind-the-scenes filming, and recordings by artists such as Ashanti, Sting, and Mary J. Blige.[78]

Indeed, almost anything can become a vehicle for displaying advertising. For instance, supermarkets have begun using "Flooranimation"—ads that are animated with graphics and sounds and installed on supermarket floors. Unanimated floor ads have been in use for some time, and research shows they increase sales 15 to 30 percent. Marketers are hoping that with animation and sound, sales will increase even more.[79] Billboards now include motion graphics, and sound, and as an additional advertising media, are an excellent way to communicate with consumers in the evenings in metro markets such as New York City, Chicago, Los Angeles, and San Francisco.[80] Marketers are also looking for more innovative ways to reach captive and often bored commuters. For instance, subway systems now show ads via lighted boxes installed along tunnel walls. As a train passes through the tunnel, the passengers view the illuminated boxes,

media mix
The combination of media to be used for a promotional campaign.

cost per contact
The cost of reaching one member of the target market.

reach
The number of target consumers exposed to a commercial at least once during a specific period, usually four weeks.

which create the same kind of illusion as a child's flip book, in which the images appear to move as the pages are flipped rapidly.

Video Game Advertising When trying to reach males aged 18 to 34, video game advertising is emerging as an excellent medium, second only to prime-time *Monday Night Football.* The medium first attracted attention when Massive, Inc., (**http://www.massiveincorporated.com**) started a videogame advertising network and later established a partnership with Nielsen Entertainment, Inc., to provide ad ratings. Massive provides the capability to have ads with full motion and sound inserted into games played on Internet-connected computers. This is a big improvement over previous ads, which had to be inserted when the games were made and therefore quickly became obsolete. In 2006, Microsoft acquired Massive, a move that the company says will help it "deliver dynamic, relevant ads" across its online services including Xbox Live and MSN Games.[81]

Cell phones Cell phones are among the newest advertising media and are particularly useful for reaching the youth market. Mobile advertising has substantial upside potential when you consider there are more than four billion cell phone users in the world. In 2008, cell phone advertising sales was almost $1.6 billion in the United States and nearly $4.4 billion worldwide.[82] Mobile ad spending is expected to grow dramatically in the next few years. Today's data- and video-oriented phones can deliver advertisements and also have GPS capability, so they can receive "location-based" advertising; for example, a nearby restaurant can alert potential customers about specials. McDonald's enjoyed success doing this at locations in California where it gave away free McFlurry desserts. Marketers also are using text and video messages to notify customers of special deals, such as ring tone downloads. Cell phone advertising is less popular in the United States than in Europe and Asia, where cell phone owners use text messaging much more heavily. Although there is concern that cell phone spam will become as much of a problem as Internet spam, cell phone advertisers are targeting their ads to users who agree to receive the ads in exchange for premium services or who sign up on opt-in lists to learn about items that interest them, such as a particular band's next album or concert.[83]

Stealth Marketing The term "stealth" might conjure images of undercover operations, possibly even sneakiness. In marketing, however, stealth has come to mean a campaign of outsmarting the competition, rather than outspending them. Stealth marketing, also known as guerrilla marketing, or buzz, is usually just any unconventional way of performing marketing promotions on a low budget. Stealth marketing is often designed to leave the target audience unaware they have been marketed to, but that they have simply participated in something fun, or sometimes shocking. For instance, in a recent guerilla campaign to promote the film *The Water Horse: Legend of the Deep*, a 50-foot dragon (think Loch Ness monster) was created by way of hologram projection on the water surface of Tokyo Bay, in Japan. Conjuring a huge monster practically out of thin air created marketing "buzz" online, on the street, and in the media.[84]

Media Selection Considerations

An important element in any advertising campaign is the **media mix**, the combination of media to be used. Media mix decisions are typically based on several factors: cost per contact, reach, frequency, target audience considerations, flexibility of the medium, noise level, and the life span of the medium.

Cost per contact is the cost of reaching one member of the target market. Naturally, as the size of the audience increases, so does the total cost. Cost per contact enables an advertiser to compare media vehicles, such as television versus radio or magazine versus newspaper, or even the same media, such as *Newsweek* versus *Time*. An advertiser debating whether to spend local advertising dollars for TV spots or radio spots could consider the cost per contact of each. The advertiser might then pick the vehicle with the lowest cost per contact to maximize advertising punch for the money spent.

Reach is the number of different target consumers exposed to a commercial at least once during a specific period, usually four weeks. Media plans for product introductions and attempts at increasing brand awareness usually emphasize reach. For example, an advertiser might try to reach 70 percent of the target audience during the first three months of the campaign. Reach is related to a medium's ratings, generally referred to in the industry as *gross ratings points*, or GRP. A television program with a higher GRP means that more people are tuning in to the show and the reach is higher. Accordingly, as GRP increases for a particular medium, so does cost per contact.

Because the typical ad is short-lived and because often only a small portion of an ad may be perceived at one time, advertisers repeat their ads so that consumers will remember the message. **Frequency** is the number of times an individual is exposed to a message during a specific period. Advertisers use average frequency to measure the intensity of a specific medium's coverage. For example, Coca-Cola might want an average exposure frequency of five for its POWERade television ads. That means each of the television viewers who saw the ad saw it an average of five times.

Media selection is also a matter of matching the advertising medium with the product's target market. If marketers are trying to reach teenage females, they might select *Seventeen* magazine. If they are trying to reach consumers over 50 years old, they may choose *Modern Maturity* magazine. A medium's ability to reach a precisely defined market is its **audience selectivity**. Some media vehicles, like general newspapers and network television, appeal to a wide cross section of the population. Others—such as *Brides*, *Popular Mechanics*, *Architectural Digest*, *Lucky*, MTV, ESPN, and Christian radio stations—appeal to very specific groups.

Noise level, or the level of distraction to the target audience, is high in an ad-jammed city street such as this one.

The *flexibility* of a medium can be extremely important to an advertiser. In the past, because of printing timetables, production requirements, and so on, some magazines required final ad copy several months before publication. Therefore, magazine advertising traditionally could not adapt as rapidly to changing market conditions. While this is changing quickly due to computer technology that creates electronic ad images and layouts, the lead time for magazine advertising is still considerably longer. Radio and Internet advertising, on the other hand, provide maximum flexibility. Usually, the advertiser can change a radio ad on the day it is aired, if necessary. Similarly, advertisements on the Internet can be changed in minutes with the click of a few buttons.

Noise level is the level of distraction associated with a medium. For example, to understand a televised promotional message, viewers must watch and listen carefully. But they often watch television with others, who may well provide distractions. Noise can also be created by competing ads, as when a street is lined with billboards or when a television program is cluttered with competing ads. About two-thirds of a newspaper's pages are now filled with advertising. A recent Sunday issue of the *Los Angeles Times* contained over one thousand ads, not counting the small classifieds. Even more space is dedicated to ads in magazines. For example, 85 percent of the space in *Brides* magazine is typically devoted to advertisements. In contrast, direct mail is a private medium with a low noise level. Typically, no other advertising media or news stories compete for direct-mail readers' attention.

Media have either a short or a long life span. *Life span* means that messages can either quickly fade or persist as tangible copy to be carefully studied. For example, a radio commercial may last less than a minute. Listeners can't replay the commercial unless they have recorded the program. One way advertisers overcome this problem is by repeating radio ads often. In contrast, a magazine has a relatively long life span. A person may read several articles, put the magazine down, and pick it up a week later to

frequency
The number of times an individual is exposed to a given message during a specific period.

audience selectivity
The ability of an advertising medium to reach a precisely defined market.

media schedule
Designation of the media, the specific publications or programs, and the insertion dates of advertising.

continuous media schedule
A media scheduling strategy in which advertising is run steadily throughout the advertising period; used for products in the latter stages of the product life cycle.

continue reading. In addition, magazines often have a high pass-along rate. That is, one person will read the publication and then give it to someone else to read.

Media planners have traditionally relied on the above factors in selecting an effective media mix, with reach, frequency, and cost often the overriding criteria. But some experts question the reliance media planners have traditionally placed on reach and frequency. For instance, well-established brands with familiar messages probably need fewer exposures to be effective, while newer brands or brands with unfamiliar messages likely need more exposures to become familiar.

Additionally, media planners have hundreds more media options today than they had when network television reigned. For instance, there are over 1,600 television stations across the country. Similarly, in the Los Angeles market alone there are more than 80 radio stations, with 7 offering an "adult contemporary" format. The number of unique magazine titles has more than doubled over the last decade, with publications now targeting every possible market segment. Satellite television brings hundreds of channels into viewers' homes. The Internet provides media planners with even more targeted choices in which to send their messages. And alternative media choices are popping up in some very unlikely places. *Media fragmentation* is forcing media planners to pay as much attention to where they place their advertising, as to how often the advertisement is repeated. Indeed, experts recommend evaluating reach along with frequency in assessing the effectiveness of advertising. That is, in certain situations it may be important to reach potential consumers through as many media vehicles as possible. When this approach is considered, however, the budget must be large enough to achieve sufficient levels of frequency to have an impact. In evaluating reach versus frequency, therefore, the media planner ultimately must select an approach that is most likely to result in the ad being understood and remembered when a purchase decision is being made.

Advertisers also evaluate the qualitative factors involved in media selection. These qualitative factors include such things as attention to the commercial and the program, involvement, lack of distractions, how well the viewer likes the program, and other audience behaviors that affect the likelihood a commercial message is being seen and, hopefully, absorbed. While advertisers can advertise their product in as many media as possible and repeat the ad as many times as they like, the ad still may not be effective if the audience is not paying attention. Research on audience attentiveness for television, for example, shows that the longer viewers stay tuned to a particular program, the more memorable they find the commercials. Holding power, therefore, can be more important than ratings (the number of people tuning in to any part of the program) when selecting media vehicles, challenging the long-held assumption that the higher the rating of a program, the more effective the advertising run during the program, even though it is more costly. For instance, *ER*, once one of the top-rated shows among 25- to 54-year-olds, cost about $400,000 for a 30-second spot but ranked relatively low for holding power. In contrast, the low-rated *Candid Camera*, which ranked high in holding power, used to cost only about $55,000 for a 30-second spot.[85]

See the Global Perspectives box and consider what kind of media campaign would be most effective in promoting Bollywood movies.

Media Scheduling

After choosing the media for the advertising campaign, advertisers must schedule the ads. A **media schedule** designates the medium or media to be used (such as magazines, television, or radio), the specific vehicles (such as *People* magazine, the TV show *CSI*, or the American Top 40 national radio program), and the insertion dates of the advertising.

There are three basic types of media schedules:

- Products in the latter stages of the product life cycle, which are advertised on a reminder basis, use a **continuous media schedule**. A continuous schedule allows

GLOBAL Perspectives

Welcome to Bollywood

With the smashing success of the low budget film *Slumdog Millionaire* (which grossed more than $69 million in the United States and won countless awards around the globe), Hollywood is starting to take notice of Bollywood. Bollywood, shorthand for the Indian movie industry in Mumbai, pumps out more movies than Hollywood (1,200 in 2007 compared to 600 in the United States.). The budgets are much smaller as well—a big budget film runs about $15 million compared to Hollywood's $100 million blockbuster films. With the success of *Slumdog Millionaire*, as well as the size of the Indian market, Hollywood is starting to investigate partnerships with Indian film companies.

While the Indian movie industry has been around for almost 100 years, its appeal has been limited. The traditional Indian movie can be considered kitschy, with song and dance scenes and melodramatic plots. While that may not go over well in the United States, the partnership is more of a collaboration between India and the West. Many of the new movies blend Indian themes and storylines with American cinematic styles. Collaborations abound between movie companies, producers, directors, screenwriters, and actors. Some of the top actors in both countries are considering projects. This new blend of entertainment could have huge marketing and advertising implications in the United States.

This is especially true for the Desis. The Desis are Americans of Indian, Pakistani, Bangladeshi, Sri Lankan, Bhutanese, and Nepalese descent. They make up 2.5 million people in the United States—small by the standards represented by other groups such as Hispanics—and most of them are Indian. But unlike their other minority counterparts, Desis come to the United States with knowledge of English and an appreciation of the culture, even if it is primarily British influenced. Their median income is 50 percent higher than the U.S. national average and they represent $76 billion of disposable income. And they are educated; 64 percent hold a bachelor's degree compared to 24 percent of the U.S. population.

With the increasing influence of Indian culture in the United States, it will be interesting to see what happens with marketing and advertising campaigns. Already some companies have targeted the Desi subculture mostly by focusing on the community as opposed to traditional advertising. Community is an important characteristic in this large immigrant group. It will also be interesting to see what influence the United States has on Bollywood. Already some of the most popular actors are attractive and light skinned, as opposed to the dark skinned actors of earlier films.[86] The question remains how much will each culture influence the other? What kind of campaign would you use to promote Bollywood movies? How successful do you think Bollywood movies will be in the United States?

the advertising to run steadily throughout the advertising period. Examples include Ivory soap, Tide detergent, Bounty paper towels, and Charmin toilet tissue, which may have an ad in the newspaper every Sunday and a TV commercial on NBC every Wednesday at 7:30 P.M. over a three-month period.

- With a **flighted media schedule**, the advertiser may schedule the ads heavily every other month or every two weeks to achieve a greater impact with an increased frequency and reach at those times. Movie studios might schedule television advertising on Wednesday and Thursday nights, when moviegoers are deciding which films to see that weekend. A variation is the **pulsing media schedule**, which combines continuous scheduling with flighting. Continuous advertising is simply heavier during the best sale periods. A retail department store may advertise on a year-round basis but place more advertising during certain sale periods such as Thanksgiving, Christmas, and back-to-school.
- Certain times of the year call for a **seasonal media schedule**. Products like Contac cold tablets and Coppertone sunscreen lotion, which are used more during certain times of the year, tend to follow a seasonal strategy. Advertising for

flighted media schedule
A media scheduling strategy in which ads are run heavily every other month or every two weeks, to achieve a greater impact with an increased frequency and reach at those times.

pulsing media schedule
A media scheduling strategy that uses continuous scheduling throughout the year coupled with a flighted schedule during the best sales periods.

seasonal media schedule
A media scheduling strategy that runs advertising only during times of the year when the product is most likely to be used.

REVIEW LEARNING OUTCOME

LO 11 Describe media evaluation and selection techniques

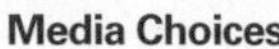

Type:

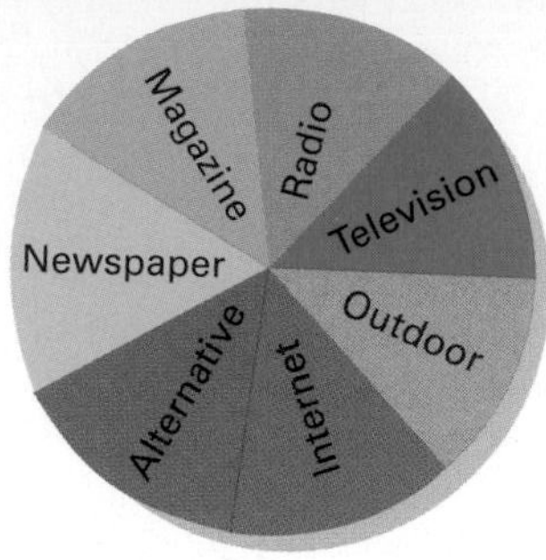

Considerations:

Mix	**(How much of each?)**
Cost per contact	**(How much per person?)**
Reach	**(How many people?)**
Frequency	**(How often?)**
Audience selectivity	**(How targeted is audience?)**

flexibility
noise
life span
fragmentation

Scheduling:

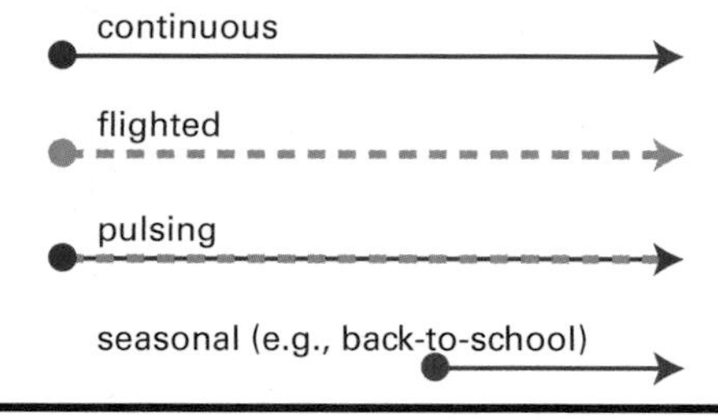

champagne is concentrated during the weeks of Christmas and New Year's, whereas health clubs concentrate their advertising in January to take advantage of New Year's resolutions.

New research comparing continuous media schedules and flighted ones finds that continuous schedules for television advertisements are more effective than flighting in driving sales. The research suggests that it may be more important to get exposure as close as possible to the time when someone is going to make a purchase. For example, if a consumer shops on a weekly basis, the best time to reach that person is right before he or she shops. Therefore, the advertiser should maintain a continuous schedule over as long a time as possible. Often called *recency planning*, this theory of scheduling is now commonly used for scheduling television advertising for frequently purchased products, such as Coca-Cola or Tide detergent. Recency planning's main premise is that advertising works by influencing the brand choice of people who are ready to buy.

3,500 ◄ people interviewed by Sara Lee Corp. before it innovated Kiwi shoe polish

media ► **15 million** contacts generated by Absolut's Porsche taxis in Germany

112.8 ◄ **million** blogs tracked by Technorati

10 ◄ percentage of blogs updated weekly

70 ◄ percentage of e-mail messages that are spam

100 ◄ iPods sold per minute during the 2005 Christmas season

$100 million ◄ cost of Procter & Gamble's recent advertising campaign for Crest Pro-Health

22 ◄ languages in which Google and Sony offered "The Sony Ericsson Da Vinci Code Trail"

30 ◄ percentage of increased traffic at Sony's Web site during the promotion

$77 million ◄ ticket sales for *The DaVinci Code*'s opening weekend

ANATOMY OF AN

Indiana Jones movie

Lucasfilm Ltd. used integrated marketing communications to ensure that *Indiana Jones and the Kingdom of the Crystal Skull* was widely and consistently promoted before its release.

NASCAR cars increase publicity.

Hallmark greeting cards and Scholastic books hold kids' interest even after the movie leaves theaters.

Legos and Kellogg's cereal attract kids.

Burger King's "Indy Double Whopper" and Mar's M&M's tie the movie to summer fun.

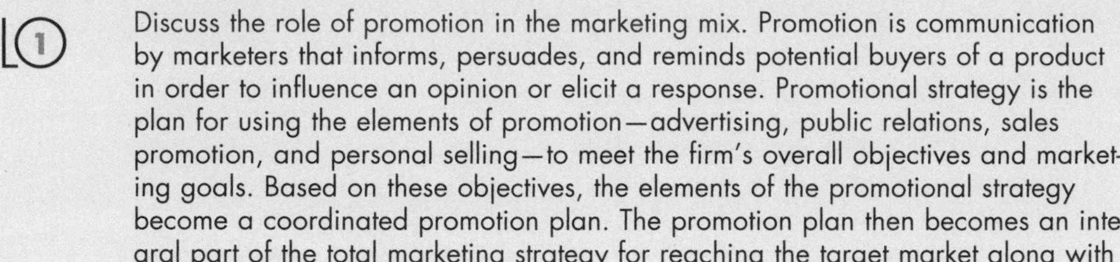

REVIEW AND APPLICATIONS

LO 1

Discuss the role of promotion in the marketing mix. Promotion is communication by marketers that informs, persuades, and reminds potential buyers of a product in order to influence an opinion or elicit a response. Promotional strategy is the plan for using the elements of promotion—advertising, public relations, sales promotion, and personal selling—to meet the firm's overall objectives and marketing goals. Based on these objectives, the elements of the promotional strategy become a coordinated promotion plan. The promotion plan then becomes an integral part of the total marketing strategy for reaching the target market along with product, distribution, and price.

1.1 What is a promotional strategy? Explain the concept of a competitive advantage in relation to promotional strategy.

LO 2

Describe the communication process. The communication process has several steps. When an individual or organization has a message it wishes to convey to a target audience, it encodes that message using language and symbols familiar to the intended receiver and sends the message through a channel of communication. Noise in the transmission channel distorts the source's intended message. Reception occurs if the message falls within the receiver's frame of reference. The receiver decodes the message and usually provides feedback to the source. Normally, feedback is direct for interpersonal communication and indirect for mass communication.

2.1 Why is understanding the target market a crucial aspect of the communication process?

LO 3

Explain the goals of promotion. The fundamental goals of promotion are to induce, modify, or reinforce behavior by informing, persuading, and reminding. Informative promotion explains a good's or service's purpose and benefits. Promotion that informs the consumer is typically used to increase demand for a general product category or to introduce a new good or service. Persuasive promotion is designed to stimulate a purchase or an action. Promotion that persuades the consumer to buy is essential during the growth stage of the product life cycle, when competition becomes fierce. Reminder promotion is used to keep the product and brand name in the public's mind. Promotions that remind are generally used during the maturity stage of the product life cycle.

3.1 Why might a marketing manager choose to promote his or her product using persuasion? Give some current examples of persuasive promotion.

3.2 Choose a partner from class and go together to interview the owners or managers of several small businesses in your city. Ask them what their promotional objectives are and why. Are they trying to inform, persuade, or remind customers to do business with them? Also determine whether they believe they have an awareness problem or whether they need to persuade customers to come to them instead of to competitors. Ask them to list the characteristics of their primary market, the strengths and weaknesses of their direct competitors, and how they are positioning their store to compete. Prepare a report to present in class summarizing your findings.

Discuss the elements of the promotional mix. The elements of the promotional mix include advertising, public relations, sales promotion, and personal selling.

Advertising is a form of impersonal, one-way mass communication paid for by the source. Public relations is the function of promotion concerned with a firm's public image. Sales promotion is typically used to back up other components of the promotional mix by stimulating immediate demand. Finally, personal selling typically involves direct communication, in person or by telephone; the seller tries to initiate a purchase by informing and persuading one or more potential buyers.

4.1 As the promotional manager for a new line of cosmetics targeted to preteen girls, you have been assigned the task of deciding which promotional mix elements—advertising, public relations, sales promotion, and personal selling—should be used in promoting it. Your budget for promoting the preteen cosmetics line is limited. Write a promotional plan explaining your choice of promotional mix elements given the nature of the product, the stage in the product life cycle, the target market characteristics, the type of buying decision, available funds, and the use of a pull or push strategy.

Discuss the AIDA concept and its relationship to the promotional mix. The AIDA model outlines the four basic stages in the purchase decision-making process, which are initiated and propelled by promotional activities: (1) attention, (2) interest, (3) desire, and (4) action. The components of the promotional mix have varying levels of influence at each stage of the AIDA model. Advertising is a good tool for increasing awareness and knowledge of a good or service. Sales promotion is effective when consumers are at the purchase stage of the decision-making process. Personal selling is most effective in developing customer interest and desire.

5.1 Discuss the AIDA concept. How do these different stages of consumer involvement affect the promotional mix?

5.2 How does a Web site's ease of use affect its ability to create attention, interest, desire, and action? Visit the kitchen and bath pages of Kohler's Web site (**www.kohler.com**), and determine how successful the company is at moving consumers through the AIDA process.

Discuss the concept of integrated marketing communications. Integrated marketing communications is the careful coordination of all promotional messages for a product or service to ensure the consistency of messages at every contact point where a company meets the consumer—advertising, sales promotion, personal selling, public relations, as well as direct marketing, packaging, and other forms of communication. Marketing managers carefully coordinate all promotional activities to ensure that consumers see and hear one message. Integrated marketing communications has received more attention in recent years due to the proliferation of media choices, the fragmentation of mass markets into more segmented niches, and the decrease in advertising spending in favor of promotional techniques that generate an immediate sales response.

6.1 Discuss the importance of integrated marketing communications. Give some current examples of companies that are and are not practicing IMC.

6.2 What do you think is the role of Hallmark's Web site (**www.hallmark.com**) in the company's integrated marketing communications plan? What seems to be the marketing function of the site? Do you think the site is effective?

Describe the factors that affect the promotional mix. Promotion managers consider many factors when creating promotional mixes. These factors include the nature of the product, product life-cycle stage, target market characteristics, the type of buying decision involved, availability of funds, and feasibility of push or pull strategies. Because most business products tend to be custom-tailored to the buyer's exact specifications, the marketing manager may choose a promotional mix that relies more heavily on personal selling. On the other hand, consumer products are generally mass produced and lend themselves more to mass promotional efforts such as advertising and sales promotion. As products move through different stages of the product life cycle, marketers will choose to use different promotional elements. For example, advertising is emphasized more in the introductory stage of the product life cycle than in the decline stage. Characteristics of the target market, such as geographic location of potential buyers and brand loyalty, influence the promotional mix as does whether the buying decision is complex or routine. The amount of funds a firm has to allocate to promotion may also help determine the promotional mix. Small firms with limited funds may rely more heavily on public relations, whereas larger firms may be able to afford broadcast or print advertising. Last, if a firm uses a push strategy to promote the product or service, the marketing manager may choose to use aggressive advertising and personal selling to wholesalers and retailers. If a pull strategy is chosen, then the manager often relies on aggressive mass promotion, such as advertising and sales promotion, to stimulate consumer demand.

7.1 Explain the difference between a "pull" and a "push" promotional strategy. Under what conditions should each strategy be used?

ONLINE @

7.2 Use Radioguide (**www.radioguide.fm**) to find a listing of radio Web sites in your area. View several of the stations' sites and compare the promotions featured. What conclusions can you draw about the target market of each station based on the types of promotions they are currently running? Would any of the promotions entice you to tune to a station that you normally don't listen to?

7.3 Visit **www.teenresearch.com**. What research can this company offer about the size and growth of the teen market, the buying power of teenagers, and their buying habits? Why might these statistics be important to a company targeting teenagers in terms of marketing communications and promotion strategy?

Discuss the effects of advertising on market share and consumers. Advertising helps marketers increase or maintain brand awareness as well as market share. Typically, more is spent to advertise new brands with a small market share than to advertise older brands. Brands with a large market share use advertising mainly to maintain their share of the market. Advertising affects consumers' daily lives as well as their purchases. Although advertising can seldom change strongly held consumer attitudes and values, it may transform a consumer's negative attitude toward a product into a positive one. Additionally, when consumers are highly loyal to a brand, they may buy more of that brand when advertising is increased. Lastly, advertising can also change the importance of a brand's attributes to consumers. By emphasizing different brand attributes, advertisers can change their appeal in response to consumers' changing needs or try to achieve an advantage over competing brands.

8.1 Discuss the reasons why new brands with a smaller market share spend proportionately more on advertising than brands with a larger market share.

8.2 Form a three-person team. Divide the responsibility for getting newspaper advertisements and menus for several local restaurants. While you are at the restaurants to obtain copies of their menus, observe the atmosphere and interview the manager to determine what he or she believes are the primary reasons people choose to dine there. Pool your information and develop a table comparing the restaurants in terms of convenience of location, value for the money, food variety and quality, atmosphere, and so on. Rank the restaurants in terms of their appeal to college students. Explain the basis of your rankings. What other market segment would be attracted to the restaurants and why? Do the newspaper advertisements emphasize the most effective appeal for a particular restaurant? Explain.

Identify the major types of advertising. Advertising is any form of impersonal, paid communication in which the sponsor or company is identified. The two major types of advertising are institutional advertising and product advertising. Institutional advertising is not product oriented; rather, its purpose is to foster a positive company image among the general public, investment community, customers, and employees. Product advertising is designed mainly to promote goods and services, and it is classified into three main categories: pioneering, competitive, and comparative. A product's place in the product life cycle is a major determinant of the type of advertising used to promote it.

9.1 At what stage in a product's life cycle are pioneering, competitive, and comparative advertising most likely to occur? Give a current example of each type of advertising.

Discuss the creative decisions in developing an advertising campaign. Before any creative work can begin on an advertising campaign, it is important to determine what goals or objectives the advertising should achieve. The objectives of a specific advertising campaign often depend on the overall corporate objectives and the product being advertised. Once objectives have been defined, creative work can begin on the advertising campaign. Creative decisions include identifying the product's benefits, developing possible advertising appeals, evaluating and selecting the advertising appeals, executing the advertising message, and evaluating the effectiveness of the campaign.

10.1 What is an advertising appeal? Give some examples of advertising appeals you have observed recently in the media.

10.2 Design a full-page magazine advertisement for a new brand of soft drink. The name of the new drink and its package design are at your discretion. On a separate sheet, specify the benefits stressed or appeals made in the advertisement.

Describe media evaluation and selection techniques. Media evaluation and selection make up a crucial step in the advertising campaign process. Major types of advertising media include newspapers, magazines, radio, television, outdoor advertising such as billboards and bus panels, and the Internet. Recent trends in advertising media include video shopping carts, computer screen savers, cinema and DVD advertising, cell phones, and videogames. Promotion managers choose the advertising campaign's media mix on the basis of the following variables: cost per contact, reach, frequency, characteristics of the target audience, flexibility of the medium, noise level, and the life span of the medium. After choosing the media mix, a media schedule designates when the advertisement will appear and the specific vehicles it will appear in.

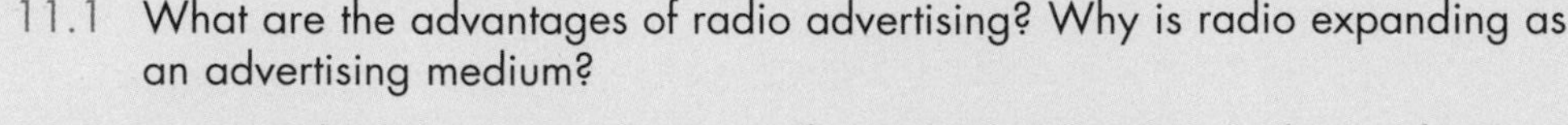

11.1 What are the advantages of radio advertising? Why is radio expanding as an advertising medium?

11.2 You are the advertising manager of a sailing magazine, and one of your biggest potential advertisers has questioned your rates. Write the firm a letter explaining why you believe your audience selectivity is worth the extra expense for advertisers.

11.3 Identify an appropriate media mix for the following products:

a. Chewing tobacco

b. *People* magazine

c. Weed-Eaters

d. Foot odor killers

e. "Drink responsibly" campaigns by beer brewers

11.4 How easy is it to find out about advertising options on the Internet? Go to LookSmart's and Yahoo!'s advertiser pages (**www.looksmart.com/aboutus/media** and **www.yahoo.com/info/advertising**). What kind of information do they require from you? Send an e-mail requesting information and compare what you receive.

KEY TERMS

EXERCISES

APPLICATION EXERCISE 1

Many people are not aware of the rationale behind certain advertising messages. "Why do Infiniti ads show rocks and trees instead of automobiles?" "If car safety is so important, why do automobile ads often show cars skidding on wet, shiny surfaces?" "Target's ads are funky, with all the bright colors and product packaging, but what's the message?"

One way to understand the vagaries of the encoding process is to think of the popular board game *Taboo* by Hasbro. In this game, each team tries to get its members to guess a word without using obvious word clues. For example, to get the team to guess "apple," you may not say such words as *red, fruit, pie, cider,* or *core*. Sometimes advertising is like *Taboo* in that advertisers are not allowed to use certain words or descriptions. For example, pharmaceutical companies are not permitted to make certain claims or to say what a drug treats unless the ad also mentions the potential side effects. Language choices are also limited in advertising. To appreciate this, you can apply the *Taboo* game rules in an advertising format.[87]

Activities

1. Select a product from the list below, and then create a print advertisement or a television storyboard for that product. As part of the exercise, give your product a brand name. Taboo words, visuals, and concepts are given for each product type. *Taboo* items cannot be present in your work.

Product	Taboo Words, Visuals, and Concepts
Deodorant	Odor, underarm, perspiration, smell, sweat
Pain reliever	Pain, aches, fever, child-proof cap, gel
Soft drinks	Sugar-free, refreshing, thirst, swimwear, any celebrity

2. Now create a second ad or storyboard for your product. This time, however, you must use all the words, visuals, and concepts that are listed in the right column.

Product	Must-Use Words, Visuals, and Concepts
Deodorant	A romantic couple, monster trucks
Pain reliever	A mother and child, oatmeal, homework
Soft drinks	A cup of coffee, cookies, birthday cake, wine

APPLICATION EXERCISE 2

An important concept in promotion is semiotics, or the study of meaning and meaning-producing events. An understanding of semiotics can help you not only to identify objects (denotation) but also to grasp the utility of images and associations (connotation). By manipulating connotations of objects in advertising, you can create, change, or reinforce images for products. Thus, semiotics is a powerful tool for brand management and promotion.[86]

Activities

1. Make a list of ten images and associations that come to mind for each of the following items: baseball, vinyl record album, spoon, rubber band.
2. Look through magazines and see if you can find print advertisements that include each of the items (baseball, vinyl record album, spoon, rubber band) in a supporting role. What seems to be the message of each ad? How does the item help create or reinforce an image for the product being sold in the ad?

3. Think of an everyday object of your own. What are its likely connotations? For example, a dog in a car might signal a family vehicle, but a dog also connotes loyalty, "man's best friend," and dependability. What images and associations are likely with your item? Make a list of as many as you can.

4. Now use your object and list of associations to create an image for another product. Think of the likely connotations your object will have for a certain target market and how such connotations can support a brand image. For example, if your everyday object is a candle, you might choose lingerie for your product, based on a candle's romantic connotations.

ETHICS EXERCISE

Integrated Marketing Solutions is a consumer-products marketing services firm. Currently, the firm is handling the launch of a new book for one of its publishing clients. The campaign includes advance review copies for key book reviewers, "Coming Soon" posters for booksellers, an author book-signing tour, and several television interviews. Everything has been produced and scheduled for release next week. Today, Jane Kershaw, the account executive, has learned that although the book received numerous favorable reviews, the review quoted on all of the promotional materials is fabricated.

Questions

1. What should Jane do? Why?
2. What does the AMA Code of Ethics say about accuracy in promotional materials? Go to **www.marketingpower.com** and review the code. Then, write a brief paragraph describing how the AMA Code of Ethics relates to this issue.

MARKETING PLAN EXERCISE

In Part 3, you began the process of defining the marketing mix, starting with the components of product and distribution. The next stage of the strategic planning process continues defining the elements of the marketing mix, and this section—Part 4—focuses on promotion and communication decisions for the promotion mix, including advertising, public relations, sales promotion, and personal selling. Use the following exercises to guide you through the promotions part of your strategic marketing plan:

1. Define your promotional objectives. What specific results do you hope to accomplish, and which promotional tools will be responsible? How will you use promotions to differentiate yourself from your competition? Remember that promotions cannot be directly tied with sales because there are too many other factors (competition, environment, price, distribution, product, customer service, company reputation, and so on) that affect sales. State specific objectives that can be tied directly to the result of promotional activities—for example, number of people redeeming a coupon, share of audience during a commercial, percent attitude change before and after a telemarketing campaign, or number of people calling a toll-free information hotline. Remember to have offline promotions drive online traffic.

2. Design a promotional message or theme. Does this message inform, remind, persuade, or educate the target market? Make sure this message will work across both traditional and electronic media. How is your promotional message consistent with your branding? Is this message or slogan unique and important enough to be copyrighted? Check with the U.S. Copyright Office at **http://lcweb.loc.gov/copyright.**

3. Will you be designing and producing all your promotion tools in-house, or do you need to find an agency? What are the advantages of designing promotional tools in-house? Disadvantages? Try **http://www.agencyfinder.com** to assist in your decision.

CASE STUDY: WICKED AWESOME! MUSICAL ENCHANTS RECORD CROWDS AFTER ROCKY START

When the curtains first lifted on the Broadway musical *Wicked,* it appeared that audiences had been scared away from the box office. The Gershwin Theater was rarely full, and a production that had cost over $14 million posted advance ticket sales of only $9 million. Crippled by cost overruns, cast changes, song rewrites, and a 2003 start date that was much later than projected, excitement and enthusiasm waned for what was once a much-anticipated show.

Based on Gregory Maguire's best-selling 1995 novel of the same name, the story is a prequel to Frank Baum's 1939 classic, *The Wizard of Oz.* The musical examines the lives of two teenage witches, Glinda and Elphaba, and wonders which one is truly evil. Glinda, a beautiful, ambitious, and popular blond, grows up to become the Good Witch; Elphaba, a green-skinned, intelligent, free-spirited rebel, develops into the nefarious Wicked Witch of the West. Elaborate sets, lighting, and costumes and a score by Academy Award–winning songwriter Stephen Schwartz did not impress the *New York Times,* however. Its scathing review claimed, "There's trouble in Emerald City . . . [it's] a sermon of a musical."

Unfazed, *Wicked* producer Marc Platt, a former Universal Pictures executive, never lost faith in his production. He remained convinced that if he could just get people in the door, they would leave completely captivated by what he considered a truly exceptional experience. So he cut ticket prices by 30 percent and watched as patrons began to make repeat ticket purchases during intermission. After the shows, swarms of enthralled teenage girls began to gather outside the stage door in hopes of meeting the cast.

As the target market emerged before his eyes, Platt leveraged his Hollywood experience to turn *Wicked* into a musical marketing machine. The hot ticket sales during show intermissions indicated that the show's success would hinge on word-of-mouth referrals from the show's core audience—teenage girls. To get more of them talking, Platt and the marketing team published feature articles on the show's Web site and seeded Internet chat rooms with *Wicked*-related topics. An all-out promotions blitz ensued.

Wicked lined up character endorsement deals with makeup manufacturer, Stila, and sent hot new stars Kristin Chenoweth and Idina Menzel to Sephora stores to give makeovers to teen fans with Glinda facial glitter and Elphaba lipstick. In an interesting twist on *American Idol, Wicked* karaoke contests at malls served as fake auditions that awarded real tickets to the most passionate fans. Radio promos in New York and Chicago were supported by advertising at Macy's and in *Elle Girl* magazine for a Halloween campaign that lasted a month.

As the show became profitable, two U.S. tours were launched. The shows routinely sell out, and yearly revenues are now close to $200 million. Tickets to the show on Broadway now command a record-tying $110, and the show's take is about $1.3 million a week in New York alone. Mike Isaacson, vice president of the Fox Theatre in St. Louis, sold an amazing $1.5 million worth of tickets a mere 48 hours after they went on sale. "This show is a rocket because it's attracting people from teenagers to grandparents," he mused.

Day-of-show raffles for tickets at sold-out venues give a few lucky patrons a chance to buy $25 tickets. Those raffles generally appeal to younger theatergoers, but those witch-wannabes bring mom and dad out for the night of mischief too. And their dollars help fund purchases of merchandise at the traveling OzDust Boutiques. Items like *Wicked*-branded golf balls, T-shirts, necklaces, and CDs of the show's musical numbers sell at the stands and at **http://www.wickedthemusical.com.** Sales generate weekly merchandise receipts of more than $300,000. But that doesn't surprise Marc Platt. Reflecting on the show's universal premise, he quips, "There's a little green girl inside all of us."[89]

Questions

1. Identify and describe the elements of *Wicked*'s promotional mix.
2. Describe how the AIDA process worked for various Wicked promotions. Which one do you think was most effective?
3. Did *Wicked* use a push or a pull promotional strategy? Explain.
4. As *Wicked* progresses through its life cycle, what changes would you recommend making to the current promotional mix? Why?

COMPANY CLIPS

VANS—OFF THE WALL AND ON TARGET

You have undoubtedly heard of Vans. The company has sold footwear, apparel, and extreme sports equipment for over 40 years using the distinct tagline, "Off the Wall." The company's founder wanted to control his own retail channel, so he transformed his manufacturing company into a marketing company. Always carefully protecting its unique brand image, Vans has crafted successful marketing messages and promotions that resonate with the youth culture that represents the company's target market. This video examines the carefully planned strategy that Vans developed to create loyalty in a fickle niche market.

Questions

1. Does Vans use a push or pull strategy to market its apparel? How does Steve feel about the two strategies?
2. What does Steve mean when he refers to tours and events as "planting seeds?"
3. Describe Vans' pyramid strategy. How does it protect the brand?
4. How does Steve's hands-on approach to events and promotion benefit the company?

Marketing & You Results

Higher scores on this scale indicate that others perceive you to be responsive, warm, and a good listener. A high score also corresponds to a willingness to mentor others. If your score is low, it indicates that you don't actively encourage other people to share information about themselves with you. That doesn't mean you are a poor listener, however. Rather, you prefer not to take the initiative in the interaction.

© iSTOCKPHOTO.COM/STEVE SNYDER

CHAPTER

15

Public Relations, Sales Promotion, and Personal Selling

LEARNING OUTCOMES

- LO1 Discuss the role of public relations in the promotional mix
- LO2 Define and state the objectives of sales promotion
- LO3 Discuss the most common forms of consumer sales promotion
- LO4 List the most common forms of trade sales promotion
- LO5 Describe personal selling
- LO6 Discuss the key differences between relationship selling and traditional selling
- LO7 List the steps in the selling process

PUBLIC RELATIONS

Public relations is the element in the promotional mix that evaluates public attitudes, identifies issues that may elicit public concern, and executes programs to gain public understanding and acceptance. Like advertising and sales promotion, public relations is a vital link in a company's marketing communication mix. Marketing managers plan solid public relations campaigns that fit into overall marketing plans and focus on targeted audiences. These campaigns strive to maintain a positive image of the corporation in the eyes of the public. Before launching public relations programs, managers evaluate public attitudes and company actions. Then they create programs to capitalize on factors that enhance the firm's image and minimize the factors that could generate a negative image.

In recent years, fast-food companies like McDonald's and soft drink companies like Coca-Cola have been criticized for contributing to childhood obesity, particularly in the United States. In response, the companies have undertaken public relations campaigns to try to minimize the impact on their reputations and ultimately sales. For example, Coca-Cola created the Beverage Institute for Health and Wellness to support nutrition research, education, and outreach. The company also spent $4 million to develop the "Live It" children's fitness campaign in schools across the country. Coke's nutrition communication manager says the campaign will not address childhood obesity or encourage students to drink Coke and that the company's logo will not appear on "Live It" materials. In addition to promoting the campaign, Coke is paying for campaign posters, pedometers, and nutrition education materials and offering prizes to children who meet the program's exercise goal of walking 10,000 steps a day. Such efforts are designed to offset a push by the Center for Science in the Public Interest to persuade the Food and Drug Administration to require labels on sodas warning about obesity, tooth decay, and diabetes.[1]

A public relations program can generate favorable **publicity**—public information about a company, product, service, or issue appearing in the mass media as a new item. Organizations generally do not pay for the publicity and are not identified as the source of the information, but they can benefit tremendously from it. For example, the rapid growth of the satellite radio industry is partly due to publicity. Subscribers were expected to top 20 million in 2009. Satellite radio's profile received a huge boost from the storm of publicity surrounding the decision by the country's most notorious and popular radio host, "shock jock" Howard Stern, to quit CBS radio and join censor-free Sirius satellite radio. Stern's first satellite broadcast was a major event, with the national media breathlessly reporting on the number of times he swore and looking for acceptable ways to report the more graphic—usually sexual—content of the show. Satellite radio, now called Sirius XM after the merger, benefited from the publicity

Marketing & You

What do you think of coupons? Enter your answers on the lines provided.

1	2	3	4	5
Strongly disagree				Strongly agree

__ Coupons can save a person a lot of money.

__ The money I can save by using coupons does not amount to much.*

__ I believe that people can help their families financially by using coupons.

__ Overall, I like using coupons.

__ Personally for me, using coupons for supermarket products is or would be useless.*

__ Taking everything into account, using coupons for supermarket shopping is wise.

Now, total your score, reversing your answers for the items followed by an asterisk (for example, if you answered 4, change it to 2). Find out what your score means after you read the chapter.

Source: Scale #115, *Marketing Scales Handbook*, G. Bruner, K. James, H. Hensel, eds., Vol. III. © by American Marketing Association.

public relations
The marketing function that evaluates public attitudes, identifies areas within the organization the public may be interested in, and executes a program of action to earn public understanding and acceptance.

publicity
Public information about a company, product, service, or issue appearing in the mass media as a news item.

product placement
A public relations strategy that involves getting a product, service, or company name to appear in a movie, television show, radio program, magazine, newspaper, video game, video or audio clip, book, or commercial for another product; on the Internet; or at special events.

Stern generated for the whole satellite broadcast medium as well as by signing up both Oprah Winfrey and reclusive music legend Bob Dylan to host shows.[2]

Again, although organizations do not directly pay for publicity, it should not be viewed as free. Preparing news releases, staging special events, and persuading media personnel to broadcast or print publicity messages costs money. Public relations departments may perform any or all of the following functions:

- *Press relations:* Placing positive, newsworthy information in the news media to attract attention to a product, a service, or a person associated with the firm or institution
- *Product publicity:* Publicizing specific products or services
- *Corporate communication:* Creating internal and external messages to promote a positive image of the firm or institution
- *Public affairs:* Building and maintaining national or local community relations
- *Lobbying:* Influencing legislators and government officials to promote or defeat legislation and regulation
- *Employee and investor relations:* Maintaining positive relationships with employees, shareholders, and others in the financial community
- *Crisis management:* Responding to unfavorable publicity or a negative event

Major Public Relations Tools

Public relations professionals commonly use several tools, including new-product publicity, product placement, consumer education, sponsorship, and Web sites. Although many of these tools require an active role on the part of the public relations professional, such as writing press releases and engaging in proactive media relations, some techniques create their own publicity.

New-Product Publicity Publicity is instrumental in introducing new products and services. Publicity can help advertisers explain what's different about their new product by prompting free news stories or positive word of mouth about it. During the introductory period, an especially innovative new product often needs more exposure than conventional, paid advertising affords. Public relations professionals write press releases or develop videos in an effort to generate news about their new product. They also jockey for exposure of their product or service at major events, on popular television and news shows, or in the hands of influential people.

Product Placement Marketers are increasingly using product placement to reinforce brand awareness and create favorable attitudes. **Product placement** is a strategy that involves getting one's product, service, or name to appear in a movie, television show, radio program, magazine, newspaper, video game, video or audio clip, book, or commercial for another product; on the Internet; or at special events. Including an actual product such as a can of Pepsi adds a sense of realism to a movie, TV show, video game, book, or similar vehicle that a can simply marked "soda" cannot. Product placements are arranged through barter (trade of product for placement), through paid placements, or at no charge when the product is viewed as enhancing the vehicle where it is placed.

Product placement expenditures amount to about $5 billion annually. Though this amount is small relative to other marketing expenditures, it is growing about 30 percent annually due to increasing audience fragmentation and the spread of ad-skipping technology.[3] More than two-thirds of product placements are in movies and TV shows, but placements in alternative media are growing, particularly on the Internet and in video games. Most product placements are for transportation, clothing, food, beverages, home furnishings, travel, and leisure time activities. Companies like BMW, Lexus, Coca-Cola, Pepsi, Procter & Gamble, and Hershey have frequently used product placement as a public relations strategy. Indeed, Pepsi appeared in seven top-ranked films in one year. Digital technology now enables companies to "virtually" place their products in any audio or video production. Virtual placement not only reduces the cost of product placement for new productions, but also enables companies to place products in previously produced programs, such as reruns of television shows and movies.

Companies obtain valuable product exposure, brand reinforcement, and increased sales through product placement, often at a much lower cost than in mass media like television ads. For example, Burger King products were woven into *The Apprentice* when contestants wore Burger King uniforms and flipped burgers as part of a challenge; Ford sponsored the show *24*, with the main character, Jack Bauer, driving a Ford Expedition; and S.C. Johnson placed the ant killer RAID in an episode of the popular HBO series *The Sopranos*. When Red Stripe, a Jamaican-brewed beer, appeared in the movie *The Firm*, its U.S. sales increased more than 50 percent in the first month after the movie was released.[4]

Consumer Education Some major firms believe that educated consumers are better, more loyal customers. BMW of North America, for example, sponsored an instructional driving school for teenagers in major cities across the United States. Teens received a special four-hour training session that included driving techniques, accident avoidance skills, and traction aid tricks from a professional driver. Financial planning firms often sponsor free educational seminars on money management, retirement planning, and investing in the hope that the seminar participants will choose the sponsoring organization for their future financial needs. Likewise, computer hardware and software firms, realizing that many consumers are intimidated by new technology and recognizing the strong relationship between learning and purchasing patterns, sponsor computer seminars and free in-store demonstrations.

Sponsorships Sponsorships are increasing both in number and as a proportion of companies' marketing budgets, with spending reaching $17 billion annually in the United States and Canada. Overall, global spending on sponsorships including North America was expected to exceed $44 billion in 2008. Probably the biggest reason for the increasing use of sponsorships is the difficulty of reaching audiences and differentiating a product from competing brands through the mass media. With a **sponsorship**, a company spends money to support an issue, cause, or event that is consistent with corporate objectives, such as improving brand awareness or enhancing corporate image. The biggest category is sports, which accounts for almost 70 percent of spending in sponsorships. Nonsports categories include entertainment tours and attractions, causes, arts, festivals, fairs and annual events, and association and membership organizations.[5] Typical examples of sponsorships include Jose Cuervo Tequila's sponsorship of the Pro Beach Volleyball Tour, Domino's Pizza's sponsorship of Michael Waltrip for NASCAR, Hilton Hotels' sponsorship of the Hilton Family Skating & Gymnastics Spectacular on NBC, Levi Strauss & Co.'s partnership with the San Francisco Giants to sponsor the right field section of the park to be named "Levi's Landing," and Anheuser-Busch's Bud Bowl that featured hip-hop star Snoop Dogg and rock band 3 Doors Down.[6] In addition, multiple companies sponsored the 2008 summer Olympics in Beijing.

sponsorship
A public relations strategy in which a company spends money to support an issue, cause, or event that is consistent with corporate objectives, such as improving brand awareness or enhancing corporate image.

Although companies have recently been turning to specialized events such as tie-ins with schools, charities, and other community service organizations, the most popular sponsorship events are still those involving sports, music, or the arts. McDonald's expanded its "I'm lovin' it" campaign to include sponsorships of NASCAR, the Pro Beach Volleyball Tour, and the Big Mac Challenge—a 20-stop lifestyle-oriented car

cause-related marketing
A type of sponsorship involving the association of a for-profit company and a nonprofit organization; through the sponsorship, the company's product or service is promoted, and money is raised for the nonprofit.

show including DJs and other youth-focused activities. And, Yahoo! sponsored a video game tour to promote Yahoo! Music Unlimited, Napster forged a deal with the Dew Action Sports Tour, and MSN Music hosted Milwaukee's Summerfest and Manchester, Tennessee's Bonnaroo Music and Arts Festival.[7]

Marketers sometimes create their own events tied around their products. The state of Hawaii organized its own mall touring event, titled "Experience Aloha: Hawaii on Tour," to promote the islands as a tourist destination. The tour traveled to 22 U.S. cities for weekend mall visits that included hula dancers, chefs cooking Hawaiian cuisine, lei-making demonstrations, and a virtual reality film simulating a helicopter ride over Hawaii's islands. Many other states also sponsor events promoting tourism.

Corporations sponsor issues as well as events. Sponsorship issues are quite diverse, but the three most popular are education, health care, and social programs. Firms often donate a percentage of sales or profits to a worthy cause favored by their target market.

A special type of sponsorship, **cause-related marketing**, involves the association of a for-profit company with a nonprofit organization. Through the sponsorship, the company's product or service is promoted, and money is raised for the nonprofit. In a common type of cause-related sponsorship, a company agrees to donate a percentage of the purchase price of a particular item to a charity, but some arrangements are more complex. In the United Kingdom, for example, Blockbuster Entertainment Ltd. works with Starlight Children's Foundation to raise money, and Tesco supermarkets raise money for computers in schools. Similarly, in the United States Avon, Yoplait Yogurt, and BMW support the Susan G. Komen Breast Cancer Foundation, and J. P. Morgan Chase & Co. Bank works with St. Jude Children's Research Hospital.[8] Recently, companies are partnering with nonprofit organizations to create new "cause brands." For example, the American Heart Association and several corporations have developed the "Go Red for Women" campaign to increase the awareness of heart disease for women (**www.goredforwomen.org**).[9] Findings from several studies suggest that some consumers consider a company's reputation when making purchasing decisions and that a company's community involvement boosts employee morale and loyalty.[10]

Internet Web Sites Companies increasingly are using the Internet in their public relations strategies. Company Web sites are used to introduce new products, promote existing products, obtain consumer feedback, post news releases, communicate legislative and regulatory information, showcase upcoming events, provide links to related sites, release financial information, interact with customers and potential customers, and perform many more marketing activities. Online reviews from opinion leaders and other consumers help marketers sway purchasing decisions in their favor. On its Web site for PlayStation 3 (**www.playstation.com**), Sony has online support, events and promotions, game trailers, and new and updated product releases such as *Killzone 2*, *Street Fighter IV*, *F.E.A.R. 2: Project Origin*, and *MLB 09*. The site also includes message boards where the gaming community posts notes and chats, exchanges tips on games, votes on lifestyle issues like music and videos, and learns about promotional events.[11]

Web sites are also being incorporated into integrated marketing communications strategies. For example, CBS integrated broadcast advertising with product placement by placing a bonus scene from *CSI: Miami* on its Web site featuring a plot twist that was not revealed to television viewers until later in the season. The bonus scene page was sponsored by General Motors' Hummer brand, which also appeared in the bonus scene itself.[12]

More and more often, companies are also using blogs—both corporate and noncorporate—as a tool to manage their public images. Noncorporate blogs cannot be controlled, but marketers must monitor them to be aware of and respond to negative information and encourage positive content. Wal-Mart has been especially active in cultivating bloggers to get the company's message out. Mona Williams, Wal-Mart's spokeswoman, says, "We reach out to bloggers in the same way we reach out to reporters. A lot of people are looking to bloggers for their news source, and this is a good way to get our message out."[13] The company hired a public relations firm to combat negative publicity. The publicist assigned to the Wal-Mart account, Marshall Manson, contacts bloggers who write pro-Wal-Mart content and asks if he can send them materials to use in their commentaries. Those who agree become champions for the giant retailer.[14]

In addition to "getting the message out," companies are using blogs to create communities of consumers who feel positively about the brand. The hope is that the positive attitude toward the brand will build into strong word-of-mouth marketing. Companies must exercise caution when diving into corporate blogging, however. Coca-Cola launched a blog authored by a fictional character that did little except parrot the company line. Consumers immediately saw the blog for what it was (a transparent public relations platform) and lambasted Coca-Cola for its insincerity.[15]

Managing Unfavorable Publicity

Although marketers try to avoid unpleasant situations, crises do happen. In our free-press environment, publicity is not easily controlled, especially in a crisis. **Crisis management** is the coordinated effort to handle the effects of unfavorable publicity, ensuring fast and accurate communication in times of emergency.

A good public relations staff is as important in bad times as in good. Companies must have a communication policy firmly in hand before a disaster occurs, because timing is uncontrollable. For example, McDonald's was caught off-guard by the wave of negative publicity that followed the release of *Super Size Me,* a documentary film which chronicled the deterioration of filmmaker Morgan Spurlock's health while he experimented with an all-McDonald's diet. In anticipation of a similar response to the movie version of Eric Schlosser's best seller *Fast Food Nation,* McDonald's contemplated dispatching a "truth squad" and a team of "ambassadors of the brand" to remind consumers that the restaurant offers a healthy menu and provides good

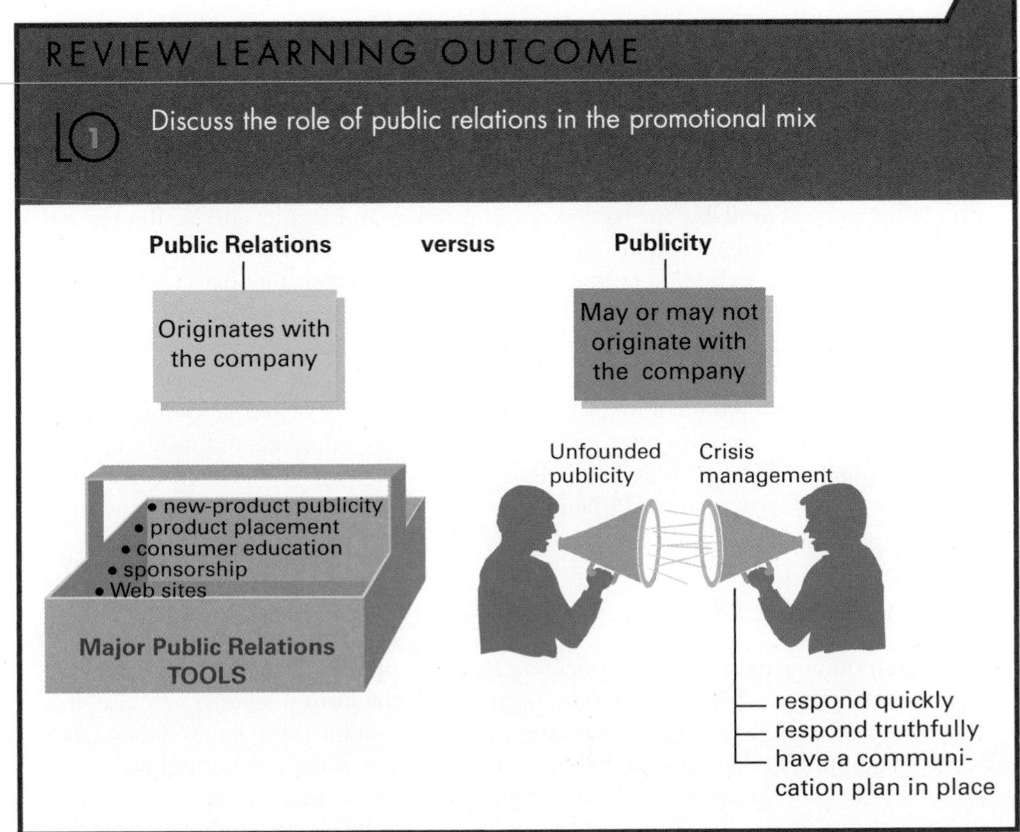

crisis management
A coordinated effort to handle all the effects of unfavorable publicity or of another unexpected unfavorable event.

sales promotion
Marketing activities—other than personal selling, advertising, and public relations—that stimulate consumer buying and dealer effectiveness.

consumer sales promotion
Sales promotion activities targeting the ultimate consumer.

trade sales promotion
Sales promotion activities targeting a channel member, such as a wholesaler or retailer.

jobs. The company also modified its menu to include more salads and apple dippers. McDonald's new marketing communication focused on the importance of a balanced lifestyle appears to have offset potential negative publicity resulting from the documentary.[16]

When Wal-Mart became the target of negative publicity regarding its low wages and sparse benefits, publicist Marshall Manson sent a special missive to his network of bloggers. It revealed that unions were hiring homeless and day laborers to protest at nonunion businesses, including Wal-Mart. The unions paid the picketers minimum wage and gave them no benefits. Manson's release was used by numerous bloggers and represented a counterattack in the publicity war over Wal-Mart's employment practices.[17]

LO 2

SALES PROMOTION

In addition to using advertising, public relations, and personal selling, marketing managers can use sales promotion to increase the effectiveness of their promotional efforts. **Sales promotion** is marketing communication activities, other than advertising, personal selling, and public relations, in which a short-term incentive motivates consumers or members of the distribution channel to purchase a good or service immediately, either by lowering the price or by adding value.

Advertising offers the consumer a reason to buy. Sales promotion offers an incentive to buy. Both are important, but sales promotion is usually cheaper than advertising and easier to measure. A major national TV advertising campaign often costs over $5 million or more to create, produce, and place. In contrast, promotional campaigns using the Internet or direct marketing methods can cost less than half that amount. It is also very difficult to determine how many people buy a product or service as a result of radio or TV ads. But with sales promotion, marketers know the precise number of coupons redeemed or the number of contest entries.

Sales promotion is usually targeted toward either of two distinctly different markets. **Consumer sales promotion** is targeted to the ultimate consumer market. **Trade sales promotion** is directed to members of the marketing channel, such as wholesalers and retailers. Sales promotion has become an important element in a marketer's integrated marketing communications program. Sales promotion expenditures have been steadily increasing over the last several years as a result of increased competition, the ever-expanding array of available media choices, consumers and retailers demanding more deals from manufacturers, and the continued reliance on accountable and measurable marketing strategies. In addition, product and service marketers that have traditionally ignored sales promotion activities, such as power companies and restaurants, have discovered the marketing power of sales promotion. In fact, annual expenditures on promotion marketing in the United States now exceed $400 billion. Direct mail is the most widely used promotional medium, accounting for 50 percent of annual promotional expenditures.[18] The next two most widely used media are sampling and in-store promotions. Examples of these include point-of-purchase promotions (17 percent of expenditures), events and sponsorships (14 percent), and promotions via Internet and mobile devices (7 percent).[19]

The Objectives of Sales Promotion

Sales promotion usually has more effect on behavior than on attitudes. Immediate purchase is the goal of sales promotion, regardless of the form it takes. Therefore, it seems to make more sense when planning a sales promotion campaign to target customers according to their general behavior. For instance, is the consumer loyal to your product or to your competitor's? Does the consumer switch brands readily in favor of the best deal? Does the consumer buy only the least expensive product, no matter what? Does the consumer buy any products in your category at all?

The objectives of a promotion depend on the general behavior of target consumers. (See Exhibit 15.1.) For example, marketers targeting loyal users of their product do not want to change behavior. Instead, they need to reinforce existing behavior or increase product usage. An effective tool for strengthening brand loyalty is the *frequent buyer program* that rewards consumers for repeat purchases. Other types of promotions are more effective with customers prone to brand switching or with those who are loyal to a competitor's product. A cents-off coupon, free sample, or eye-catching display in a store will often entice shoppers to try a different brand. Consumers who do not use the product may be enticed to try it through the distribution of free samples.

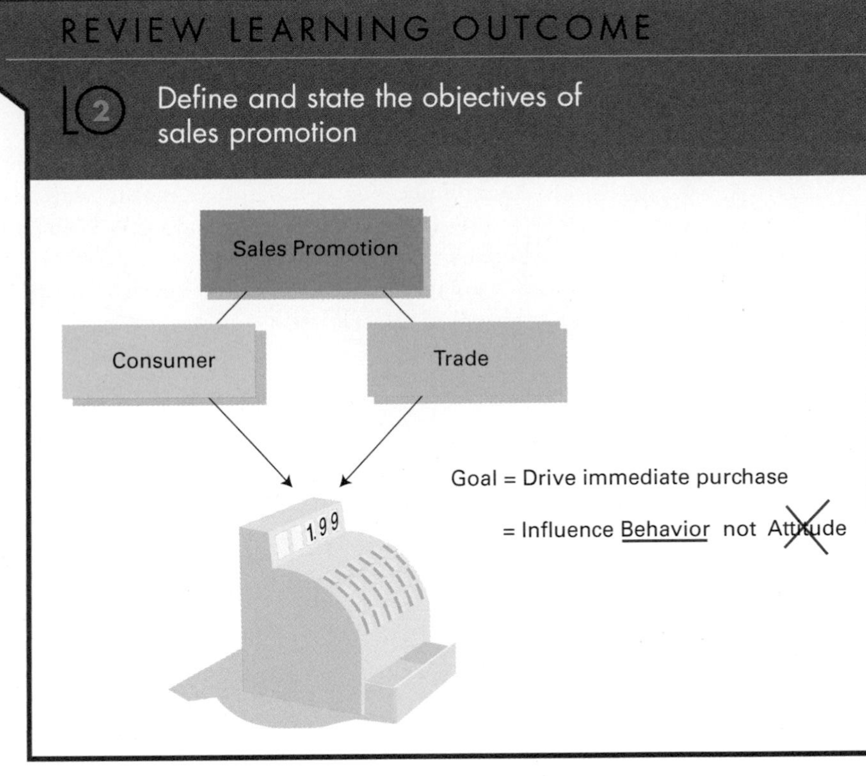

Once marketers understand the dynamics occurring within their product category and have determined the particular consumers and consumer behaviors they want to influence, they can then go about selecting promotional tools to achieve these goals.

EXHIBIT 15.1

Types of Consumers and Sales Promotion Goals

Type of Buyer	Desired Results	Sales Promotion Examples
Loyal customers People who buy your product most or all of the time	Reinforce behavior, increase consumption, change purchase timing	• Loyalty marketing programs, such as frequent buyer cards or frequent shopper clubs • Bonus packs that give loyal consumers an incentive to stock up or premiums offered in return for proofs of purchase
Competitor's customers People who buy a competitor's product most or all of the time	Break loyalty, persuade to switch to your brand	• Sampling to introduce your product's superior qualities compared to their brand • Sweepstakes, contests, or premiums that create interest in the product
Brand switchers People who buy a variety of products in the category	Persuade to buy your brand more often	• Any promotion that lowers the price of the product, such as coupons, price-off packages, and bonus packs • Trade deals that help make the product more readily available than competing products
Price buyers People who consistently buy the least expensive brand	Appeal with low prices or supply added value that makes price less important	• Coupons, price-off packages, refunds, or trade deals that reduce the price of the brand to match that of the brand that would have been purchased

Source: From *Sales Promotion Essentials*, 2nd ed., by Don E. Schultz, William A. Robinson, and Lisa A. Petrison. Reprinted by permission of NTC Publishing Group, 4255 Touhy Ave., Lincolnwood, IL 60048.

CUSTOMER Experience

Has Starbucks Lost Its Mojo with Average Joes?

Once considered a master at branding and one of the most admired companies in the world, the company that taught America about coffee and provided a "third place" to enjoy it has lost its luster. At one point, Starbucks was opening a new store a day. It still has more than 15,000 stores in 44 countries and Starbucks represents more than half (2.9 billion servings) of total coffee consumption (4.6 billion servings) according to NPD Group/Crest. But sales of specialty coffee were down in 2008 (the first decline in 5 years), and many people have traded down to other new (and less expensive) competitors, such as Dunkin' Donuts and McDonald's. However, Starbucks' slide started long before the economy took a downturn.

The real reason behind Starbucks' trouble is that management began to ignore the customer. While trying to solve some customer complaints, Starbucks degraded the overall customer experience, becoming less passionate about customer relationships and their coffee experience. For example, when some customers complained about the length of the lines and the pace of the service, Starbucks elected to take out some of the sofas and comfortable chairs that made Starbucks unique. This made space for more people in line, but not much room for people to relax. And in order to speed up the service, Starbucks got rid of the coffee bean grinders, which took a lot of time. Hand-pulled shots also took up time and were shuttered. But once the couches and coffee bean smells were gone, so was much of the Starbucks experience. Soon customers began to realize the price they paid for their lattes was pretty expensive relative to the experience.

When Starbucks stock prices and sales began to tumble, management attempted to recover; founder Howard Schultz returned as CEO after 8 years away from the role. Starbucks planned to reignite the customer connection, slow store growth, shut down underperforming stores, increase global expansion, and improve the state of the U.S. business. New coffee blends, new products (particularly hot food), and even coupons were introduced. So far, Starbucks has not had much luck. In 2008, 600 stores were closed and more are expected to be shut down in light of the economic downturn.

Starbucks created and profited from the specialty coffee category, but customer preferences and loyalties changed. Indeed, in the 2006 Customer Loyalty Engagement Index Starbucks dominated its competitors; by the end of 2007 Starbucks had surrendered its dominance to Dunkin' Donuts. A Lightspeed Research study revealed that more than 60 percent of Americans scaled back on expensive coffee in the past six months. This is good news for "low rung" coffee companies like McDonald's; it has plans to open coffee bars in 14,000 U.S. restaurants.[20] So, how can Starbucks return to the "Starbucks Experience"?

TOOLS FOR CONSUMER SALES PROMOTION

Marketing managers must decide which consumer sales promotion devices to use in a specific campaign. The methods chosen must match the objectives to ensure success of the overall promotion plan. Popular tools for consumer sales promotion are coupons and rebates, premiums, loyalty marketing programs, contests and sweepstakes, sampling, and point-of-purchase promotion. Consumer sales promotion tools have also been easily transferred to online versions to entice Internet users to visit sites, purchase products, or use services on the Web.

Coupons and Rebates

A **coupon** is a certificate that entitles consumers to an immediate price reduction when they buy the product. Coupons are a particularly good way to encourage product trial and repurchase. They are also likely to increase the amount of a product bought.

Traditional types of coupon distribution, such as newspapers, direct mail, and magazines, had been declining but began increasing in recent years. For example, consumer packaged goods marketers issued over 300 billion coupons valued at almost $400 billion in 2008. To make coupons more attractive, the average value was increased, and the result was the first increase in redemption rates (from about 1.5 percent to 2.6 percent) in 25 years.[21] Online and in-store distribution of coupons also has been increasing. These trends are the result of intense competition in the consumer packaged goods category and the introduction of over 1,200 new products each year, as well as the economic downturn. Though coupons are often criticized for reaching customers who have no interest in the product or service, or for encouraging repeat purchase by regular users, studies indicate coupons promote new-product use and are likely to stimulate purchases. The use of colorful free-standing inserts (FSIs), mostly in Sunday newspapers, continues to grow despite declines in newspaper readership. FSIs are the most frequent way marketers distribute coupons (88.1 percent) followed by handouts (4.7 percent), direct mail (2.2 percent), magazines (2.1 percent), newspapers (1.2 percent), in/on pack (1.2 percent), and Internet (0.4 percent). But online coupon distribution sites such as **www.coolsavings.com** and **www.valpak.com** are emerging as major coupon distribution outlets. Unfortunately, redemption rates for coupons often are 2 percent or lower.[22]

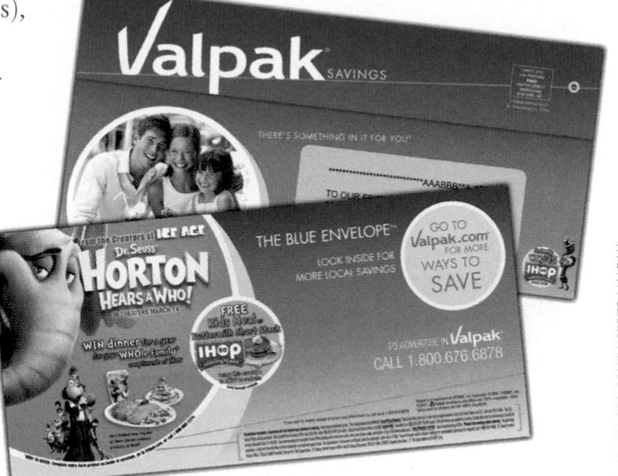

© AP IMAGES/PRNEWSFOTO/VALPAK

To overcome the low redemption rates for coupons, marketers are using new strategies. For example, by shortening the time in which coupons can be redeemed or reducing the requirement for multiple purchases, some marketers have increased the redemption rate by creating a greater sense of urgency to redeem the coupon. Some marketers are de-emphasizing their use of coupons in favor of everyday low pricing, while others are distributing single, all-purpose coupons that can be redeemed for several brands.

In-store coupons have become popular because they are more likely to influence customers' buying decisions. Instant coupons on product packages, coupons distributed from on-shelf coupon-dispensing machines, and electronic coupons issued at the checkout counter are achieving much higher redemption rates. Indeed, instant coupons are redeemed more than 15 times more frequently than traditional newspaper coupons, indicating that consumers are making more in-store purchase decisions.

Starbucks has taken in-store coupons to a new level by installing interactive units on grocery store shelves. Each unit provides consumers with product information related to brewing, coffee education, and a taste matcher. In one test the units resulted in a 200 percent increase in sales. Internet coupons are also gaining in popularity. For example, Kroger has launched "Coupons that you click. Not clip." on Kroger.com. Registered Kroger Plus Shopper card members just log on to the Web site and click on the coupons they want. Coupons are automatically loaded on to the Kroger Plus card and redeemed at checkout when the shopper's Kroger Plus card is scanned.[23]

As marketing tactics grow more sophisticated, coupons are no longer viewed as a stand-alone tactic, but as an integral component of a larger promotional campaign. For example, Papa John's Pizza teamed up with Warner Bros. Home Entertainment and DC Comics to offer an instantly redeemable $3 coupon for online purchases as well as a limited edition "Dark Knight" gift card that could be redeemed for Papa John's products in store or online. Exclusive content and trailers from the movie are available on the restaurant's Web site. Subway restaurants in Buffalo, New York, developed a campaign that offers consumer alerts and discount coupons via customers' mobile phones. This was a major breakthrough in marketing to the 18- to 34-year-old customer. Other firms are experimenting with mobile phone coupons as well while working out the technical issues such as using the coupons at the cashier.[24]

Rebates are similar to coupons in that they offer the purchaser a price reduction; however, because the purchaser must mail in a rebate form and usually some proof of purchase, the reward is not as immediate. Traditionally used by food and cigarette

coupon
A certificate that entitles consumers to an immediate price reduction when they buy the product.

rebate
A cash refund given for the purchase of a product during a specific period.

premium
An extra item offered to the consumer, usually in exchange for some proof of purchase of the promoted product.

loyalty marketing program
A promotional program designed to build long-term, mutually beneficial relationships between a company and its key customers.

frequent buyer program
A loyalty program in which loyal consumers are rewarded for making multiple purchases of a particular good or service.

manufacturers, rebates now appear on all types of products, from computers and software to film and cell phones. In the run-up to Super Bowl XL, Pepsi-Cola offered consumers a $10 dollar rebate as an incentive to stock up on the company's soda products and Frito-Lay brand chips in time for the big game.[25]

Manufacturers prefer rebates for several reasons. Rebates enable manufacturers to offer price cuts directly to consumers. Manufacturers have more control over rebate promotions because they can be rolled out and shut off quickly. Further, because buyers must fill out forms with their names, addresses, and other data, manufacturers use rebate programs to build customer databases. Perhaps the best reason of all to offer rebates is that although rebates are particularly good at enticing purchase, most consumers never bother to redeem them. Studies show only about one-half of customers eligible for rebates actually collect them.[26]

Premiums

A **premium** is an extra item offered to the consumer, usually in exchange for some proof that the promoted product has been purchased. Premiums reinforce the consumer's purchase decision, increase consumption, and persuade nonusers to switch brands. Premiums like telephones, tote bags, and umbrellas are given away when consumers buy cosmetics, magazines, bank services, rental cars, and so on. Probably the best example of the use of premiums is the McDonald's Happy Meal, which rewards children with a small toy. Many companies have been built around furnishing clients with customized premiums. Because of the widespread use of premiums, especially in trade relationships, it is getting harder to capture someone's attention with a premium. Kellogg's decided to use the animated character Shrek in a mix of premium-based promotions to get kids to eat healthy. Three games aimed at healthy lifestyles were created and appeared on 100 million cereal boxes. And for the first time, a bilingual promotional insert was included in Spanish using Puss 'n' Boots, Shrek's Latin sidekick. As a result, 125,000 cereal bowls, 85,000 boogie boards, 43,000 helmet covers, 37,000 talking key chains, and 16,000 soccer balls were redeemed. Kellogg's also saw major sales increases for Rice Krispies (21.5 percent), Froot Loops (16.7 percent), and Corn Pops (5.6 percent).[27]

Premiums can also include more product for the regular price, such as two-for-the-price-of-one bonus packs or packages that include more of the product. Kellogg's, for instance, added two more pastries and waffles to its Pop-Tarts and Eggo packages without increasing the price in an effort to boost market share lost to private-label brands and new competitors. The promotion was so successful the company decided to keep the additional product in its regular packaging. Another possibility is to attach a premium to the product's package. For example, when research showed that consumers who drink tequila are often trendsetters who entertain at home, 1-800-Tequila launched a holiday promotion that included an instant camera and entertainment guide attached to the bottle.[28]

Loyalty Marketing Programs

Loyalty marketing programs and **frequent buyer programs** reward loyal consumers for making multiple purchases. Promotional spending related to loyalty programs has increased almost 4 percent to $2.1 billion. Popularized by the airline industry through frequent-flyer programs, loyalty marketing enables companies to strategically invest sales promotion dollars in activities designed to capture greater profits from customers already loyal to the product or company. This is critical, as studies show that consumer loyalty is on the decline. Forrester Research showed the percentage of consumers ranking price as more important than brand rose from 41 to 47 percent over 3 years. According to research conducted by Gartner, more than 75 percent of consumers have more than one loyalty card that rewards them with redeemable points. Furthermore, there are almost 1.5 billion loyalty program memberships in the United States, with the average household participating in 12 programs.[29]

The objective of loyalty marketing programs is to build long-term, mutually beneficial relationships between a company and its key customers. In the retail sector, programs such as My Coke Rewards and Nike Plus are enabling these brands to learn more about what customers buy and their choice of rewards. Frequent shopper card programs offered by many supermarkets and other retailers have exploded in popularity. Research from Forrester shows that 54 percent of primary grocery shoppers belong to two or more supermarket loyalty programs. Although this speaks to the popularity of loyalty cards, it also shows that customers are pledging "loyalty" to more than one store: 15 percent of primary grocery shoppers are cardholders in at least three programs, and 4 percent participate in four or five programs.[30] Combined with the statistics on the growing importance of price over brands, frequent shopper programs need to offer something more than just discounts to build customer loyalty. One of the more successful recent premium promotions is Starbucks' Duetto Card, which combines a Visa credit card with a reloadable Starbucks card. The card allows members to collect "Duetto Dollars" that can be redeemed for anything they want to purchase at a Starbucks location. Starbucks also sends members quarterly opportunities based on usage, such as product samples and previews. One study reported that over 60 percent of Duetto cardholders said they were more likely to purchase Starbucks products as a result of the program.[31]

Cobranded credit cards are an increasingly popular loyalty marketing tool. Annually over 6 billion direct marketing appeals for a cobranded credit card are sent to potential customers in the United States. Gap, Sony, and American Airlines are only a few examples of companies sponsoring cobranded Visa, MasterCard, or American Express cards. Target has a card (Take Charge of Education) that enables consumers to identify the school they would like to give money to (**www.target.com**). In addition, many nonprofit organizations participate in these cobranded affinity programs. American Express has a program with Space Adventures, a company that offers simulated space flight experiences.[32]

Through loyalty programs, shoppers receive discounts, alerts on new products, and other enticing offers. In exchange, retailers are able to build customer databases that help them better understand customer preferences. Verizon Wireless builds loyalty with its "New Every Two" program. Consumers who have been Verizon customers for 2 years are eligible for a $100 credit toward a new digital phone.[33]

Companies increasingly are using the Internet to build customer loyalty through e-mail and blogs. Over 80 percent of supermarket chains are using e-mail to register customers for their loyalty programs and to entice them with coupons, flyers, and promotional campaigns.[34] Blogs are becoming a critical component of some companies' loyalty marketing programs. Blogging technology enables marketers to create a community of consumers who feel positively about the company's brand and to build deeper relationships with them. Starwood Hotels launched a corporate blog called TheLobby.com. Although the blog is open to the public, the company is aiming the content specifically at members of the Starwood Preferred Guest loyalty program. Features include postings about special events at specific Starwood properties and how travelers can earn loyalty points through special promotions. The company's goal is to combine advertising with useful information to create a Web destination for its guests—and divert them away from other travel blogs that might contain negative postings about Starwood hotels.[35]

Companies like McDonald's and Cannondale are also using blogging technology to create communities around their brands. Robin Hopper, CEO of iUpload, the company that hosts the blogs for these two companies, says that companies publish blogs to build

sampling
A promotional program that allows the consumer the opportunity to try a product or service for free.

social networks around their brands. "It's a whole new way to market," he says. "People willingly provide all sorts of demographic information on blogs" that companies can use to target them more effectively.[36]

Contests and Sweepstakes

Contests and sweepstakes are generally designed to create interest in a good or service, often to encourage brand switching. *Contests* are promotions in which participants use some skill or ability to compete for prizes. A consumer contest usually requires entrants to answer questions, complete sentences, or write a paragraph about the product and submit proof of purchase. Winning a *sweepstakes*, on the other hand, depends on chance or luck, and participation is free. Sweepstakes usually draw about ten times more entries than contests do. Marketers were expected to spend almost $2 billion in 2009 building games, contests, and sweepstakes. Contests and sweepstakes calling for consumer-generated content remain the favorite. For example, Dole launched its Sweet Retreat contest using blogs and parfait parties. In order to enter, people have to submit photos of themselves enjoying Dole's parfaits and include a caption about their "indulgent moment." Consumers then vote on the winners who then receive a variety of prizes. Bloggers that focus on moms, health, and wellness were asked to talk about the Dole parfait parties. Last, specific groups like book clubs, scrapbooking groups, and others were identified in several cities to participate in the parfait parties.[37]

Red Baron, Freschetta, and Tony's pizzas' mega event "Fuel-Up The Family" gives consumers an opportunity to win a Toyota Prius. To participate, consumers enter the UPC code from specially marked packages and play an Instant Win game on an interactive Web site.

While contests and sweepstakes may draw considerable interest and publicity, generally they are not effective tools for generating long-term sales. To increase their effectiveness, sales promotion managers must make certain the award will appeal to the target market. For example, Home & Garden Television Network's annual "Dream Home Giveaway" sweepstakes awards a fully furnished, custom-built home to one lucky viewer. The promotion is cosponsored by General Motors, which fills the garage with a new sport-utility vehicle, and other home-related companies such as Sherwin-Williams paint, Lumber Liquidators flooring, California Closets, and Jeld-Wen windows and doors. The annual sweepstakes typically draws over four million entries.[38] Offering several smaller prizes to many winners instead of one huge prize to just one person often will increase the effectiveness of the promotion, but there's no denying the attractiveness of a jackpot-type prize.

Sampling

Consumers generally perceive a certain amount of risk in trying new products. Many are afraid of trying something they will not like (such as a new food item) or spending too much money and getting little reward. **Sampling** enables customers to try a product risk-free. Sampling can increase retail sales by more than 40 percent. It is no surprise, therefore, that product sampling is the dominant in-store marketing method when it comes to influencing consumer purchase decisions.[39]

Spending on sampling increased by 5 percent in 2008, to $2.3 billion.[40] Sampling can be accomplished by directly mailing the sample to the customer, delivering the sample door-to-door, packaging the sample with another product, or demonstrating or sampling the product at a retail store or service outlet. Coca-Cola partnered with Domino's Pizza to sample its Coca-Cola Zero beverage. Every Domino's customer placing an order got a complimentary 20-ounce bottle of Coca-Cola Zero.[41] Kleenex launched its broadest sampling program ever for the new enhanced tissue with lotion product. The campaign put 60 million samples in places consumers would not typically find tissues, such as free-standing dispensers so consumers could try it. Kleenex supported the effort with magazine advertising and a sampling van tour. Similarly, when Masterfoods wanted to increase sales of its Dove "Promises" product line of dark and milk chocolates, it used both print media and sampling. To reach the upscale target market, samples were handed out at high-end hotels, spas, and gourmet cooking shows.[42]

Sampling at special events is a popular, effective, and high-profile distribution method that permits marketers to piggyback onto fun-based consumer activities—including sporting events, college fests, fairs and festivals, beach events, and chili cook-offs. General Mills used 500 "meal assembly kitchens" to provide samples of its Chocolate Turtle Chex Mix where busy moms could prepare ready-to-eat food. Companies like Tabasco, Juicy Juice, and Lipton Iced Tea are also sampling in these kitchens. Product sampling during tailgating at college and professional football stadiums enables marketers to reach from 10,000 to 100,000 consumers in a single afternoon. H.J. Heinz tests products such as new barbecue sauces and ketchups to get immediate feedback about what consumers like and dislike about the products.[43]

Distributing samples to specific location types where consumers regularly meet for a common objective or interest, such as health clubs, churches, or doctors' offices, is one of the most efficient methods of sampling. What better way to get consumers to try a product than to offer a sample exactly when it is needed most? If someone visits a health club regularly, chances are he or she is a good prospect for a health-food product or vitamin supplement. Health club instructors are also handing out body wash, deodorant, and face cloths to sweating participants at the end of class, and, more surprisingly, hot drinks! Dunkin' Donuts used a sampling program in more than 200 health clubs to promote its new Latte Lite drink, a zero percent fat product that gives health-conscious consumers a lighter alternative.[44] Meanwhile, makers of stain removers and hand cleansers are giving away samples in mall food courts and petting zoos. Likewise, pharmaceutical companies offer free samples of new and expensive drugs as a tactic to entice doctors and consumers to become loyal to a product. Online sampling is gaining momentum as Web communities bring people together with common interests in trying new products, often using blogs to spread the word. Nail polish company OPI used SheSpeaks.com to encourage trials of new lacquer nail polish pens. Consumers had to register and then order one of five color pens and coupons. Consumers also blogged about the new pens and passed along the coupons to friends.[45]

Point-of-Purchase Promotion

Point-of-purchase (P-O-P) promotion includes any promotional display set up at the retailer's location to build traffic, advertise the product, or induce impulse buying. Point-of-purchase promotions include shelf "talkers" (signs attached to store shelves), shelf extenders (attachments that extend shelves so products stand out), ads on grocery carts and bags, end-aisle and floor-stand displays, television monitors at supermarket checkout counters, in-store audio messages, and audiovisual displays. One big advantage of P-O-P promotion is that it offers manufacturers a captive audience in retail stores. Another advantage is between 70 and 80 percent of all retail purchase decisions are made in-store, so P-O-P promotions can be very effective. P-O-P promotions can increase sales by as much as 65 percent. Strategies to increase sales include adding header or riser cards, changing messages on base or case wraps, adding inflatable or mobile displays, and using signs that advertise the brand's sports, movie, or charity tie-in.[46] When Hershey launched its new Swoops, a "chip" version of popular candy bars such as Almond Joy, Reese's, and Hershey Bars, it successfully used in-store displays to stimulate in-store, impulse purchases of the new candy.[47]

point-of-purchase display (P-O-P)
A promotional display set up at the retailer's location to build traffic, advertise the product, or induce impulse buying.

Online Sales Promotion

Online sales promotions have expanded dramatically in recent years. Marketers are now spending billions of dollars annually on such promotions. Sales promotions

trade allowance
A price reduction offered by manufacturers to intermediaries, such as wholesalers and retailers.

push money
Money offered to channel intermediaries to encourage them to "push" products—that is, to encourage other members of the channel to sell the products.

online have proved effective and cost-efficient, generating response rates three to five times higher than off-line promotions. The most effective types of online sales promotions are free merchandise, sweepstakes, free shipping with purchases, and coupons.

Eager to boost traffic, Internet retailers are busy giving away free services or equipment, such as personal computers and travel, to lure consumers not only to their own Web sites, but to the Internet in general. Another goal is to add potential customers to their databases. For example, Heineken USA, Inc. launched the "Headline Hoax" online promotional campaign in which consumers (hoaxers) trick a friend (victim). The hoax is a fake headline with a photograph that looks as though it is on the front page of a major magazine's Web page such as *Maxim* or *The Sporting News*. The hoaxer can choose from a selection of pictures and headlines. One photo shows two football players attacking one another and the tackler has one hand inside the other's shirt and another hand pulling on his shorts; the headline reads "[Person's Name] is too touchy at touch football game." Once the victim opens this e-mail, other friends on the hoaxer's list are alerted to the joke. At the start of the campaign, Heineken had only 5,000 e-mail addresses in its database. Within six months, it had collected an additional 95,000 e-mail addresses. The program has been so successful that it has been updated and expanded to the "Heineken Holiday Headline Hoax" and similar programs.[48]

Marketers have discovered that online coupon distribution provides another vehicle for promoting their products. Online coupons often have a redemption rate of more than 20 percent, as much as 10 times higher than for traditional coupons.[49] In fact, nearly 50 percent of consumers who purchase something online use a coupon or discount promotional code. According to CMS, a coupon-management company, over 2.6 billion coupons are redeemed annually, representing $331 billion in potential consumer savings. Moreover, almost 142 million U.S. consumers use coupons each year, with substantial usage across ethnic and demographic lines.[50] In addition, e-coupons can help marketers lure new customers. Lucky Brand Jeans created a program in which users controlled a green-nosed reindeer that tried to "buck off" various holiday characters for discounts in store and online. The discounts could go up to 30 percent off. The Lucky Buck Off was also augmented with street teams in various cities. Similarly, Staples.com jumped from 23rd to 14th among retail Web sites with the most buyers through an e-coupon promotion that offered $25 off on purchases of $75 or more.[51]

Online versions of loyalty programs are also popping up, and although many types of companies have these programs, the most successful are those run by hotel and airline companies. But other programs such as the Starbucks "I'm In" program, that promoted volunteerism by getting consumers to go online and pledge five hours in return for a free coffee, have also been successful at engaging consumers (**www.starbucks.com**).

TOOLS FOR TRADE SALES PROMOTION

Whereas consumer promotions *pull* a product through the channel by creating demand, trade promotions *push* a product through the distribution channel. (See Chapter 14.) When selling to members of the distribution channel, manufacturers use many of the same sales promotion tools used in consumer promotions—such as sales contests, premiums, and point-of-purchase displays. Several tools, however, are unique to manufacturers and intermediaries:

- *Trade allowances:* A **trade allowance** is a price reduction offered by manufacturers to intermediaries such as wholesalers and retailers. The price reduction or rebate is given in exchange for doing something specific, such as allocating space for a new product or buying something during special periods. For example, a local Best Buy outlet could receive a special discount for running its own promotion on Sony Surround Sound Systems.
- *Push money:* Intermediaries receive **push money** as a bonus for pushing the manufacturer's brand through the distribution channel. Often the push money is directed toward a retailer's salespeople. LinoColor, the leading high-end scanner company, produces a Picture Perfect Rewards catalog filled with merchandise retailers can purchase with points accrued for every LinoColor scanner they sell. The cover of the catalog features a wave runner that was brought to three industry trade shows and given away in a sweepstakes to one of the dealers who had visited all the product displays and passed a quiz. The program resulted in a 26 percent increase in LinoColor sales, and the manufacturer recruited 32 new dealers to carry the product line.[52]
- *Training:* Sometimes a manufacturer will train an intermediary's personnel if the product is rather complex—as frequently occurs in the computer and telecommunication industries. For example, representatives of a TV manufacturer like Toshiba may train salespeople in how to demonstrate the new features of the latest models of TVs to consumers. This is particularly helpful when salespeople must explain the features to older consumers who are less technology oriented.
- *Free merchandise:* Often a manufacturer offers retailers free merchandise in lieu of quantity discounts. For example, a breakfast cereal manufacturer may throw in one case of free cereal for every 20 cases ordered by the retailer. Occasionally, free merchandise is used as payment for trade allowances normally provided through other sales promotions. Instead of giving a retailer a price reduction for buying a certain quantity of merchandise, the manufacturer may throw in extra merchandise "free" (that is, at a cost that would equal the price reduction).
- *Store demonstrations:* Manufacturers can also arrange with retailers to perform an in-store demonstration. Food manufacturers often send representatives to grocery stores and supermarkets to let customers sample a product while shopping. Cosmetic companies also send their representatives to department stores to promote their beauty aids by performing facials and makeovers for customers.
- *Business meetings, conventions, and trade shows:* Trade association meetings, conferences, and conventions are an important aspect of sales promotion and a growing, multibillion-dollar market. At these shows, manufacturers, distributors, and other vendors have the chance to display their goods or describe their services to customers and potential customers. Moreover, the cost of closing leads generated at trade shows is often less than 50 percent of those developed in the field.[53] Trade shows have been uniquely effective in introducing new

In a multisensory sampling campaign, Stove Top stuffing workers handed out samples to commuters and shoppers in Chicago. The campaign also included heated bus shelters and bus shelter print ads.

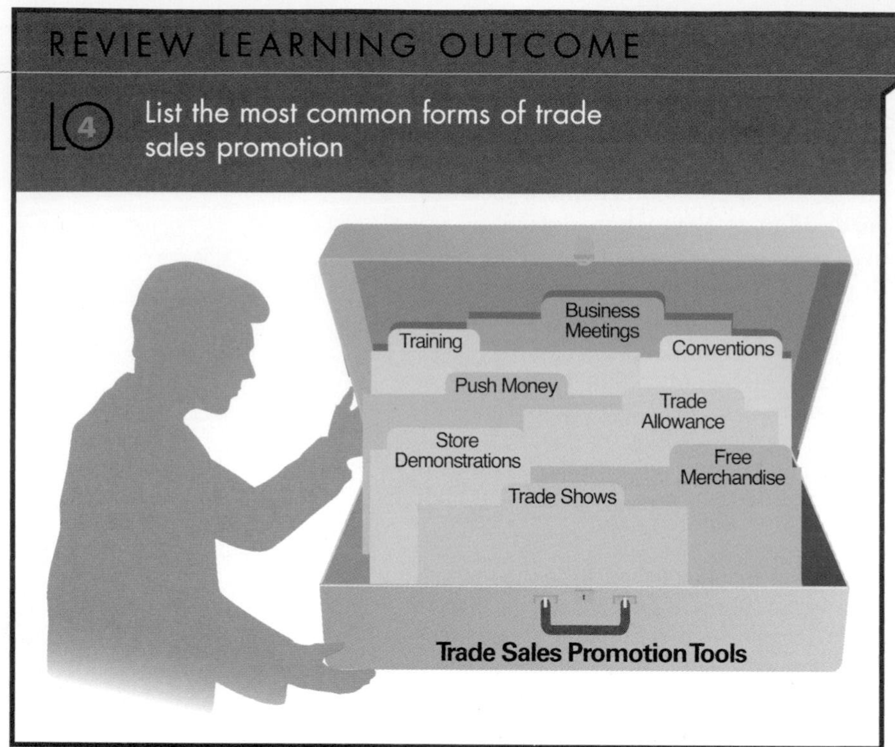

products; they can establish products in the marketplace more quickly than advertising, direct marketing, or sales calls can. Companies participate in trade shows to attract and identify new prospects, serve current customers, introduce new products, enhance corporate image, test the market response to new products, enhance corporate morale, and gather competitive product information.

Trade promotions are popular among manufacturers for many reasons. Trade sales promotion tools help manufacturers gain new distributors for their products, obtain wholesaler and retailer support for consumer sales promotions, build or reduce dealer inventories, and improve trade relations. Car manufacturers annually sponsor dozens of auto shows for consumers. Many of the displays feature interactive computer stations where consumers enter vehicle specifications and get a printout of prices and local dealer names. In return, the local car dealers get the names of good prospects. The shows attract millions of consumers, providing dealers with increased store traffic as well as good leads.

personal selling
A purchase situation involving a personal, paid-for communication between two people in an attempt to influence each other.

LO 5 PERSONAL SELLING

As mentioned in Chapter 14, **personal selling** is direct communication between a sales representative and one or more prospective buyers in an attempt to influence each other in a purchase situation.

In a sense, all businesspeople are sales people. An individual may become a plant manager, a chemist, an engineer, or a member of any profession and yet still have to sell. During a job search, applicants must "sell" themselves to prospective employers in an interview. To reach the top in most organizations, individuals need to sell ideas to peers, superiors, and subordinates. Most important, people must sell themselves and their ideas to just about everyone with whom they have a continuing relationship and to many other people they see only once or twice. Chances are that students majoring in business or marketing will start their professional careers in sales. Even students in nonbusiness majors may pursue a sales career.

Personal selling offers several advantages over other forms of promotion:

- Personal selling provides a detailed explanation or demonstration of the product. This capability is especially needed for complex or new goods and services.
- The sales message can be varied according to the motivations and interests of each prospective customer. Moreover, when the prospect has questions or raises objections, the salesperson is there to provide explanations. In contrast, advertising and sales promotion can respond only to the objections the copywriter thinks are important to customers.
- Personal selling can be directed only to qualified prospects. Other forms of promotion include some unavoidable waste because many people in the audience are not prospective customers.

EXHIBIT 15.2

Comparison of Personal Selling and Advertising/Sales Promotion

Personal selling is more important if . . .	Advertising and sales promotion are more important if . . .
The product has a high value. It is a custom-made product. There are few customers. The product is technically complex. Customers are concentrated.	The product has a low value. It is a standardized product. There are many customers. The product is easy to understand. Customers are geographically dispersed.
Examples: insurance policies, custom windows, airplane engines	**Examples:** soap, magazine subscriptions, cotton T-shirts

- Personal selling costs can be controlled by adjusting the size of the sales force (and resulting expenses) in one-person increments. On the other hand, advertising and sales promotion must often be purchased in fairly large amounts.
- Perhaps the most important advantage is that personal selling is considerably more effective than other forms of promotion in obtaining a sale and gaining a satisfied customer.

Personal selling may work better than other forms of promotion given certain customer and product characteristics. Generally speaking, personal selling becomes more important as the number of potential customers decreases, as the complexity of the product increases, and as the value of the product grows. (See Exhibit 15.2.) When there are relatively few potential customers and the value of the good or service is relatively high, the time and travel costs of personally visiting each prospect are justifiable. For highly complex goods, such as business jets or private communication systems, a salesperson is needed to determine the prospective customer's needs, explain the product's basic advantages, and propose the exact features and accessories that will meet the client's needs.

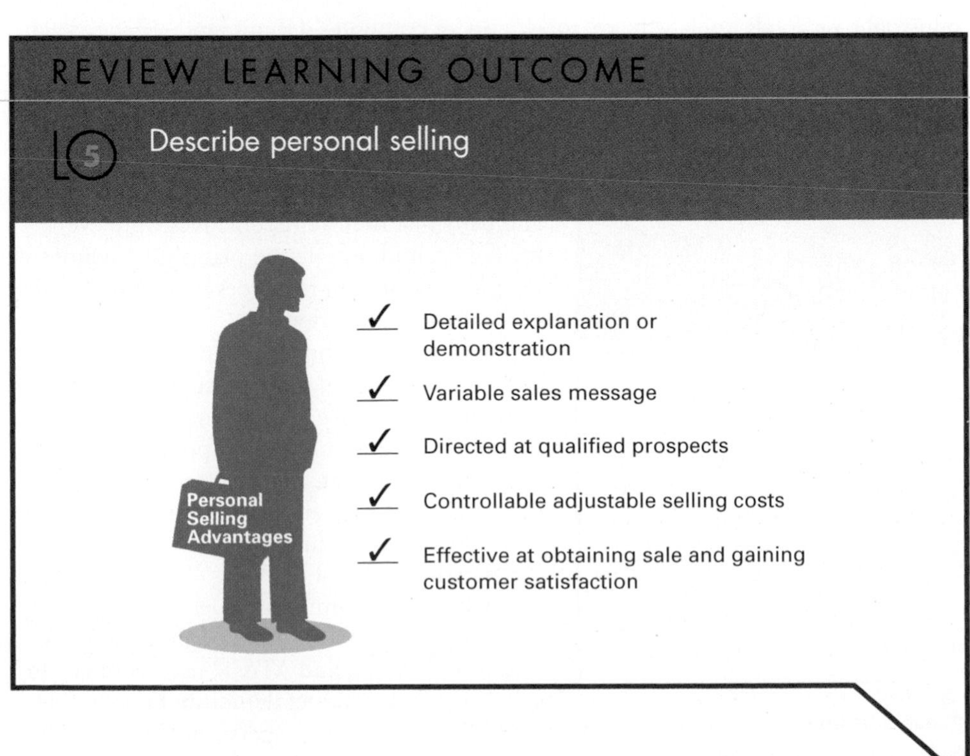

relationship selling (consultative selling) A sales practice that involves building, maintaining, and enhancing interactions with customers in order to develop long-term satisfaction through mutually beneficial partnerships.

LO6

RELATIONSHIP SELLING

Until recently, marketing theory and practice concerning personal selling focused almost entirely on a planned presentation to prospective customers for the sole purpose of making the sale. In contrast, modern views of personal selling emphasize the relationship that develops between a salesperson and a buyer. **Relationship selling**, or **consultative selling**, is a multistage process that emphasizes personalization and empathy as key ingredients in identifying prospects and developing them as long-term, satisfied customers. The old way was to sell a product, but with relationship selling, the objective is to build long-term branded relationships with consumers/buyers. Thus, the focus is on building mutual trust between the buyer and seller through the delivery of anticipated, long-term, value-added benefits to the buyer.

Relationship or consultative salespeople, therefore, become consultants, partners, and problem solvers for their customers. They strive to build long-term relationships with key accounts by developing trust over time. The emphasis shifts from a one-time sale to a long-term relationship in which the salesperson works with the customer to develop solutions for enhancing the customer's bottom line. Moreover, research has shown that positive customer-salesperson relationships contribute to trust, increased customer loyalty, and the intent to continue the relationship with the salesperson.[54] Thus, relationship selling promotes a win–win situation for both buyer and seller.

"It typically costs businesses six times more to gain a new customer than to retain a current one."

The result of relationship selling tends to be loyal customers who purchase from the company time after time. A relationship selling strategy focused on retaining customers costs a company less than constantly prospecting and selling to new customers. Companies that focus on customer retention through high customer service gain 6 percent market share per year, while companies that offer low customer service lose 2 percent market share per year.[55] In fact, it typically costs businesses six times more to gain a new customer than to retain a current one.[56]

Relationship selling is more typical with selling situations for industrial-type goods, such as heavy machinery or computer systems, and services, such as airlines and insurance, than for consumer goods. For example, FedEx Kinko's has built a long-term business relationship with PeopleSoft. The software maker now gives many of its training and educational materials printing jobs to FedEx Kinko's—a deal worth close to $5 million in revenues. FedEx Kinko's forged such a close relationship with the company that their representatives were even invited to sit in on internal planning meetings in PeopleSoft's human resources department at the company's headquarters.

"Webinars" (online seminars lasting about an hour) are a popular way to support relationship selling tasks like lead generation, client support, sales training, and corporate meetings. For example, 3Com, a computer data networking system, held a webinar that was attended by 1,300 executives in 80 countries; the session generated 60 percent of 3Com's five-month lead generation goals. Similarly, SpectraLink, a provider of wireless phone and text messaging systems to Verizon and AT&T, uses webinars to give new-product demonstrations so that channel managers can focus on other tasks. DMReview, a Web-based

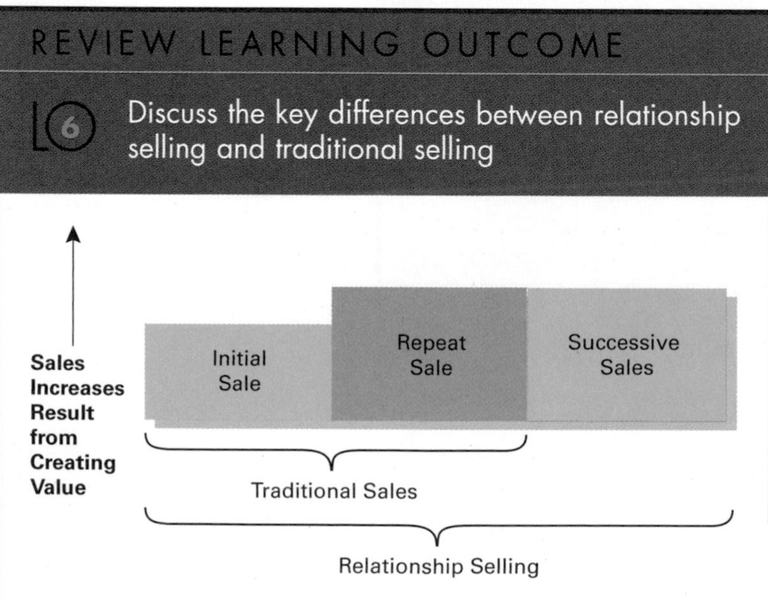

EXHIBIT 15.3

Key Differences between Traditional Selling and Relationship Selling

Traditional Personal Selling	Relationship or Consultative Selling
Sell products (goods and services)	Sell advice, assistance, and counsel
Focus on closing sales	Focus on improving the customer's bottom line
Limited sales planning	Consider sales planning as top priority
Spend most contact time telling customers about product	Spend most contact time attempting to build a problem-solving environment with the customer
Conduct "product-specific" needs assessment	Conduct discovery in the full scope of the customer's operations
"Lone wolf" approach to the account	Team approach to the account
Proposals and presentations based on pricing and product features	Proposals and presentations based on profit impact and strategic benefits to the customer
Sales follow-up is short term, focused on product delivery	Sales follow-up is long term, focused on long-term relationship enhancement

Source: Robert M. Peterson, Patrick L. Schul, and George H. Lucas, Jr., "Consultative Selling: Walking the Walk in the New Selling Environment," National Conference on Sales Management, *Proceedings*, March 1996.

portal on technology, has found webinars to be so successful that it offers them continuously "on demand" on business intelligence and data mining topics. The webinars are cosponsored by major firms in insurance, banking, health care, and related fields. To maximize the opportunities provided by webcasting, marketers are using technology that effectively delivers content to other audiences using devices such as mobile phones, TiVo-type digital video recorders, and game consoles.[57]

Exhibit 15.3 lists the key differences between traditional personal selling and relationship or consultative selling. These differences will become more apparent as we explore the personal selling process later in the chapter.

STEPS IN THE SELLING PROCESS

Although personal selling may sound like a relatively simple task, completing a sale actually requires several steps. The **sales process**, or **sales cycle**, is simply the set of steps a salesperson goes through to sell a particular product or service. The sales process or cycle can be unique for each product or service, depending on the features of the product or service, characteristics of customer segments, and internal processes in place within the firm, such as how leads are gathered.

Some sales take only a few minutes, but others may take much longer to complete. Sales of technical products, such as a Boeing or Airbus airplane, and customized goods and services typically take many months, perhaps even years, to complete. On the other end of the spectrum, sales of less technical products such as copy machines or office supplies are generally more routine and may take only a few days. Whether a salesperson spends a few minutes or a few years on a sale, these are the seven basic steps in the personal selling process:

1. Generating leads
2. Qualifying leads
3. Approaching the customer and probing needs
4. Developing and proposing solutions

sales process (sales cycle)
The set of steps a salesperson goes through in a particular organization to sell a particular product or service.

lead generation (prospecting) Identification of those firms and people most likely to buy the seller's offerings.

5. Handling objections
6. Closing the sale
7. Following up

Like other forms of promotion, these steps of selling follow the AIDA concept discussed in Chapter 14. Once a salesperson has located a prospect with the authority to buy, he or she tries to get the prospect's attention. A thorough needs assessment turned into an effective sales proposal and presentation should generate interest. After developing the customer's initial desire (preferably during the presentation of the sales proposal), the salesperson seeks action in the close by trying to get an agreement to buy. Follow-up after the sale, the final step in the selling process, not only lowers cognitive dissonance (refer to Chapter 6) but also may open up opportunities to discuss future sales. Effective follow-up will also lead to repeat business in which the process may start all over again at the needs assessment step.

Traditional selling and relationship selling follow the same basic steps. They differ in the relative importance placed on key steps in the process. (See Exhibit 15.4.) Traditional selling efforts are transaction oriented, focusing on generating as many leads as possible, making as many presentations as possible, and closing as many sales as possible. Minimal effort is placed on asking questions to identify customer needs and wants or matching these needs and wants to the benefits of the product or service. In contrast, salespeople practicing relationship selling emphasize an up-front investment in the time and effort needed to uncover each customer's specific needs and wants and match the product or service offering to them as closely as possible. By doing their homework up front, relationship salespeople create the conditions necessary for a relatively straightforward close. Let's look at each step of the selling process individually.

Generating Leads

Initial groundwork must precede communication between the potential buyer and the salesperson. **Lead generation**, or **prospecting**, is the identification of the firms and people most likely to buy the seller's offerings. These firms or people become "sales leads" or "prospects."

Sales leads can be obtained in several different ways, most notably through advertising, trade shows and conventions, or direct-mail and telemarketing programs. One accounting firm used direct mail, telephone, sales visits, and seminars in a four-step process aimed at generating business-to-business leads. The initial step was a direct-mail piece, in the form of an introductory letter from a firm partner. The second piece, sent one month later, was a black-and-white direct-mail circular with company contact information. The third step was a follow-up call from a firm partner to arrange a meeting. In the last stage, partners contacted prospects who had initially declined appointments and invited them to attend a free tax seminar the following month. Of the 1,100 businesses targeted, 200 prospects set up meetings. Favorable publicity also helps to create leads. Company records of past client purchases are another excellent source of leads. Many sales professionals are also securing valuable leads from their firm's Internet Web site. For example, Chrysler's use of interactive media to create ongoing interaction with online consumers is paying off. The company recently sponsored 42 online video

EXHIBIT 15.4

Relative Amount of Time Spent in Key Steps of the Selling Process

Key Selling Steps	Traditional Selling	Relationship/ Consultative Selling
Generating leads	High	Low
Qualifying leads	Low	High
Approaching the customer and probing needs	Low	High
Developing and proposing solutions	Low	High
Handling objections	High	Low
Closing the sale	High	Low
Following up	Low	High

games featuring Chrysler, Jeep, and Dodge vehicles, generating more than 10,000 sales leads among the estimated 3.5 million consumers who downloaded the games. The company generates an estimated 40,000 sales leads monthly through its Web site and other online venues.[58]

Another way to gather a lead is through a **referral**—a recommendation from a customer or business associate. The advantages of referrals over other forms of prospecting include highly qualified leads, higher closing rates, larger initial transactions, and shorter sales cycles. Simply put, the salesperson and the company can earn more money in less time when prospecting using referrals. Referrals typically are as much as ten times more productive in generating sales than are cold calls. Unfortunately, although most clients are willing to give referrals, many salespeople do not ask for them. Effective sales training can help to overcome this reluctance to ask for referrals. To increase the number of referrals, some companies even pay or send small gifts to customers or suppliers that provide referrals.

Networking is being transformed by the Internet. Sites like LinkedIn connect the contact lists of thousands of users, creating easily navigable networks composed of millions of people working in nearly every industry.

Networking is using friends, business contacts, coworkers, acquaintances, and fellow members in professional and civic organizations to identify potential clients. Indeed, a number of national networking clubs have been started for the sole purpose of generating leads and providing valuable business advice. The networking clubs usually have between 15 and 30 members in noncompeting business categories. During weekly breakfast or lunch meetings, each member is allowed to talk about the company he or she represents for an allotted period of time. Then members exchange lead cards. Research suggests that, on average, chapter members see an increase in business volume of between 16 and 25 percent after they've been with their group for three to six months. Increasingly, sales professionals are also using online networking sites such as Ryze, LinkedIn, and The Ladders to connect with targeted leads and clients around the world 24 hours a day. Some of LinkedIn's estimated 4.8 million users have reported response rates between 50 and 60 percent, versus 3 percent from direct marketing efforts.[59]

Qualifying Leads

When a prospect shows interest in learning more about a product, the salesperson has the opportunity to follow up, or qualify, the lead. Personally visiting unqualified prospects wastes valuable salesperson time and company resources. Often many leads go unanswered because salespeople are given no indication as to how qualified the leads are in terms of interest and ability to purchase. Unqualified prospects give vague or incomplete answers to a salesperson's specific questions, try to evade questions on budgets, and request changes in standard procedures like prices or terms of sale. In contrast, qualified leads are real prospects that answer questions, value your time, and are realistic about money and when they are prepared to buy. Salespersons given accurate information on qualified leads are more than twice as likely to follow up.[60]

Lead qualification involves determining whether the prospect has three things: a recognized need, willingness to see a salesperson, and buying power. Lead qualification is often handled by a telemarketing group or a sales support person who prequalifies the lead for the salesperson. But companies are increasingly using Web sites to qualify leads. When leads are qualified online, companies want visitors to register, indicate the products and services they are interested in, and provide information on their time frame and resources. Leads from the Internet can then be prioritized

referral
A recommendation to a salesperson from a customer or business associate.

networking
A process of finding out about potential clients from friends, business contacts, coworkers, acquaintances, and fellow members in professional and civic organizations.

lead qualification
Determination of a sales prospect's (1) recognized need, (2) buying power, and (3) receptivity and accessibility.

preapproach
A process that describes the "homework" that must be done by a salesperson before he or she contacts a prospect.

needs assessment
A determination of the customer's specific needs and wants, and the range of options the customer has for satisfying them.

sales proposal
A formal written document or professional presentation that outlines how the salesperson's product or service will meet or exceed the prospect's needs.

(those indicating a short time frame, for instance, given a higher priority) and then transferred to salespeople. Often Web site visitors can be enticed to answer questions with offers of free merchandise or information. Enticing visitors to register also enables companies to customize future electronic interactions—for example, by giving prospects who visit the Web site their choice from a menu of products tailored specifically to their needs.

Approaching the Customer and Probing Needs

Before approaching customers, the salesperson should learn as much as possible about the prospect's organization and its buyers. This process, called the **preapproach**, describes the "homework" that must be done by the salesperson before contacting the prospect. This may include visiting company Web sites, consulting standard reference sources such as Moody's, Standard & Poor's, or Dun & Bradstreet, or contacting acquaintances or others who may have information about the prospect. Another preapproach task is to determine whether the actual approach should be a personal visit, a phone call, a letter, or some other form of communication.

During the sales approach, the salesperson either talks to the prospect or secures an appointment for a future time in which to probe the prospect further as to his or her needs. Relationship selling theorists suggest that salespeople should begin developing mutual trust with their prospect during the approach. Salespeople should use the approach as a way of introducing themselves and their company and products. They must sell themselves before they can sell the product. Small talk that projects sincerity and some suggestion of friendship is encouraged because it builds rapport with the prospect, but remarks that could be construed as insincere should be avoided.

The salesperson's ultimate goal during the approach is to conduct a **needs assessment** to find out as much as possible about the prospect's situation. This involves interviewing the customer to determine his or her specific needs and wants and the range of options the customer has for satisfying them. The salesperson should be determining how to maximize the fit between what he or she can offer and what the prospective customer wants. In conducting a needs assessment, consultative salespeople must learn about the product or service, the customers and their needs, the competition, and the industry. Using this information, a customer profile is created.

Creating a *customer profile* during the approach helps salespeople optimize their time and resources. This profile is then used to help develop an intelligent analysis of the prospect's needs in preparation for the next step, developing and proposing solutions. Customer profile information is typically stored and manipulated using sales force automation software packages designed for use on laptop computers. Sales force automation software provides sales reps with a computerized and efficient method of collecting customer information for use during the entire sales process. Further, customer and sales data stored in a computer database can be easily shared among sales team members. The information can also be appended with industry statistics, sales or meeting notes, billing data, and other information that may be pertinent to the prospect or the prospect's company. The more salespeople know about their prospects, the better they can meet their prospects' needs.

Developing and Proposing Solutions

Once the salesperson has gathered the appropriate information about the client's needs and wants, the next step is to determine whether his or her company's products or services match the needs of the prospective customer. The salesperson then develops a solution, or possibly several solutions, in which the salesperson's product or service solves the client's problems or meets a specific need.

These solutions are typically offered to the client in the form of a sales proposal delivered during a sales presentation. A **sales proposal** is a written document or professional presentation that outlines how the company's product or service will meet or exceed the client's needs. The **sales presentation** is the formal meeting in which the salesperson has the opportunity to present the sales proposal. The presentation should be explicitly tied to the prospect's expressed needs. Further, the prospect should be involved in the presentation by being encouraged to participate in demonstrations or by exposure to computer exercises, slides, video or audio, flip charts, photographs, and the like.

Technology has become an important part of presenting solutions for many salespeople. Pen manufacturer BIC uses the Internet to connect with its wholesale and convenience store customers. Before launching BIClink.com, BIC received 80 percent of its order volume by fax. Processing these orders was time-consuming, and the orders often were filled with errors. BIClink.com has eliminated the potential for errors and made it easier and faster to validate purchase order numbers, ship dates, case quantities, and pricing. When customers sign on (through a secure, password-protected system), the welcome screen is personalized with their company's name and the name of their BIC rep. On placing an order, customers receive both a hard copy and e-mail confirmation statement with the salesperson's name and contact information including e-mail, voice mail, phone, and fax numbers. Virtually all of BIC's customers now order online.[61]

Because the salesperson often has only one opportunity to present solutions, the quality of both the sales proposal and presentation can make or break the sale. Salespeople must be able to present the proposal and handle any customer objections confidently and professionally. For a powerful presentation, salespeople must be well prepared, use direct eye contact, ask open-ended questions, be poised, use hand gestures and voice inflection, focus on the customer's needs, incorporate visual elements that impart valuable information, know how to operate the audio/visual or computer equipment being used for the presentation, make sure the equipment works, and practice, practice, practice.[62] Nothing dies faster than a boring presentation. If the salesperson doesn't have a convincing and confident manner, then the prospect will very often forget the information. Prospects take in body language, voice patterns, dress, and body type. Customers are more likely to remember how salespeople present themselves than what they say.

Handling Objections

Rarely does a prospect say "I'll buy it" right after a presentation. Instead, the prospect often raises objections or asks questions about the proposal and the product. The potential buyer may insist that the price is too high, that he or she does not have enough information to make a decision, or that the good or service will not satisfy the present need. The buyer may also lack confidence in the seller's organization or product.

One of the first lessons every salesperson learns is that objections to the product should not be taken personally as confrontations or insults. Rather, salespeople should view objections as requests for information. A good salesperson considers objections a legitimate part of the purchase decision. To handle objections effectively, the salesperson should anticipate specific objections, such as concerns about price, fully investigate the objection with the customer, be aware of what the competition is offering, and, above all, stay calm. When Dell introduced its direct selling model, salespeople anticipated that customers would worry that they would not receive the same level of service and dedication as they would get from a reseller. As a result, the salespeople included assurances about service and support following the sale in their sales presentations.

sales presentation
A formal meeting in which the salesperson presents a sales proposal to a prospective buyer.

Zig Ziglar, a renowned sales trainer, created a popular method for handling objections: "When an objection occurs, always use the fundamentals of FEEL, FELT, FOUND. It gives you an extra cushion of time and allows the prospect to identify with others." For example: "I see how

© PETER LILJA/GETTY IMAGES

negotiation
The process during which both the salesperson and the prospect offer special concessions in an attempt to arrive at a sales agreement.

follow-up
The final step of the selling process, in which the salesperson ensures that delivery schedules are met, that the goods or services perform as promised, and that the buyers' employees are properly trained to use the products.

you FEEL! Others have FELT the same way too until they FOUND. . . ." Imagine a copy machine salesperson pitching his machine to a doctor. The doctor might say, "The copy machine seems to be very expensive." Using the Zig Ziglar method the salesperson would respond, "I see how you *feel*. Other doctors have *felt* the same way until they *found* out how much money they were saving after the first year."[63]

Often salespeople can use objections to close the sale. If the customer tries to pit suppliers against each other to drive down the price, the salesperson should be prepared to point out weaknesses in the competitor's offer and stand by the quality in his or her own proposal.

Closing the Sale

At the end of the presentation, the salesperson should ask the customer how he or she would like to proceed. If the customer exhibits signs that he or she is ready to purchase and all questions have been answered and objections have been met, then the salesperson can try to close the sale. Customers often give signals during or after the presentation that they are ready to buy or are not interested. Examples include changes in facial expressions, gestures, and questions asked. The salesperson should look for these signals and respond appropriately.

© ISTOCKPHOTO.COM/DMITRIY SHIRONOSOV

Closing requires courage and skill. Naturally, the salesperson wants to avoid rejection, and asking for a sale carries with it the risk of a negative answer. A salesperson should keep an open mind when asking for the sale and be prepared for either a yes or a no. Rarely is a sale closed on the first call. In fact, the typical salesperson makes several hundred sales calls a year, many of which are repeat calls to the same client in an attempt to make a sale. Some salespeople may negotiate with large accounts for several years before closing a sale. As you can see, building a good relationship with the customer is very important. Often, if the salesperson has developed a strong relationship with the customer, only minimal efforts are needed to close a sale.

Negotiation often plays a key role in the closing of the sale. **Negotiation** is the process during which both the salesperson and the prospect offer special concessions in an attempt to arrive at a sales agreement. For example, the salesperson may offer a price cut, free installation, free service, or a trial order. Effective negotiators, however, avoid using price as a negotiation tool because cutting price directly affects a company's profitability. Because companies spend millions on advertising and product development to create value, when salespeople give in to price negotiations too quickly, it decreases the value of the product. Instead, effective salespeople should emphasize value to the customer, rendering price a nonissue. Salespeople should also be prepared to ask for trade-offs and try to avoid giving unilateral concessions. If you're making only a 30 percent margin on a product, and you need at least a 40 percent margin, raise your prices or drop the product. Moreover, if the customer asks for a 5 percent discount, the salesperson should ask for something in return, such as higher volume or more flexibility in delivery schedules.

Following Up

Unfortunately, many salespeople have the attitude that making the sale is all that's important. Once the sale is made, they can forget about their customers. They are wrong. Salespeople's responsibilities do not end with making the sales and placing the orders. One of the most important aspects of their jobs is **follow-up**—the final step in the selling process, in which they must ensure that delivery schedules are met, that the goods or services perform as promised, and that the buyers' employees are properly trained to use the products.

In the traditional sales approach, follow-up with the customer is generally limited to successful product delivery and performance. A basic goal of relationship selling is to motivate customers to come back, again and again, by developing and nurturing long-term relationships. Most businesses depend on repeat sales, and repeat sales depend on thorough and continued follow-up by the salesperson. Finding a new customer is far more expensive than retaining an existing customer. When customers feel abandoned, cognitive dissonance arises and repeat sales decline. Today, this issue is more pertinent than ever because customers are far less loyal to brands and vendors. Buyers are more inclined to look for the best deal, especially in the case of poor after-the-sale follow-up. More and more buyers favor building a relationship with sellers. One Farmers Insurance agent suggests following up on insurance claims with a question to determine the customer's level of satisfaction. For example, he may ask, "Were you happy with the way your claim was handled?" Depending on the response, the agent can either get a referral from the customer or try to fix any problems so that the customer does not choose another agency in the future. This agent also makes telephone and personal follow-up visits after a marriage, death, birth, or birthday in the customer's family. These visits are used as sales opportunities to cross-sell products such as life insurance.[64]

Automated e-mail follow-up marketing—a combination of sales automation and Internet technology—is enhancing customer satisfaction as well as bringing in more business for some marketers. Here's how it works: After the initial contact with a prospect, a software program automatically sends a series of personalized e-mails over a period. CollegeRecruiter.com is one company taking advantage of this technology. The company posts ads for businesses recruiting recent college graduates on its Web site and has seen phenomenal results from auto-response marketing. Prospects start receiving a series of e-mails once they have visited the site and requested advertising rates. The first message goes out immediately. The next two go out in 4 to 11 days. From there, e-mails go out monthly. Using the automated follow-up e-mail system has helped CollegeRecruiter.com become the highest traffic career site used by job-hunting students and recent graduates. Its Web site regularly posts more than 100,000 job openings.[65]

REVIEW LEARNING OUTCOME

LO 7 List the steps in the selling process

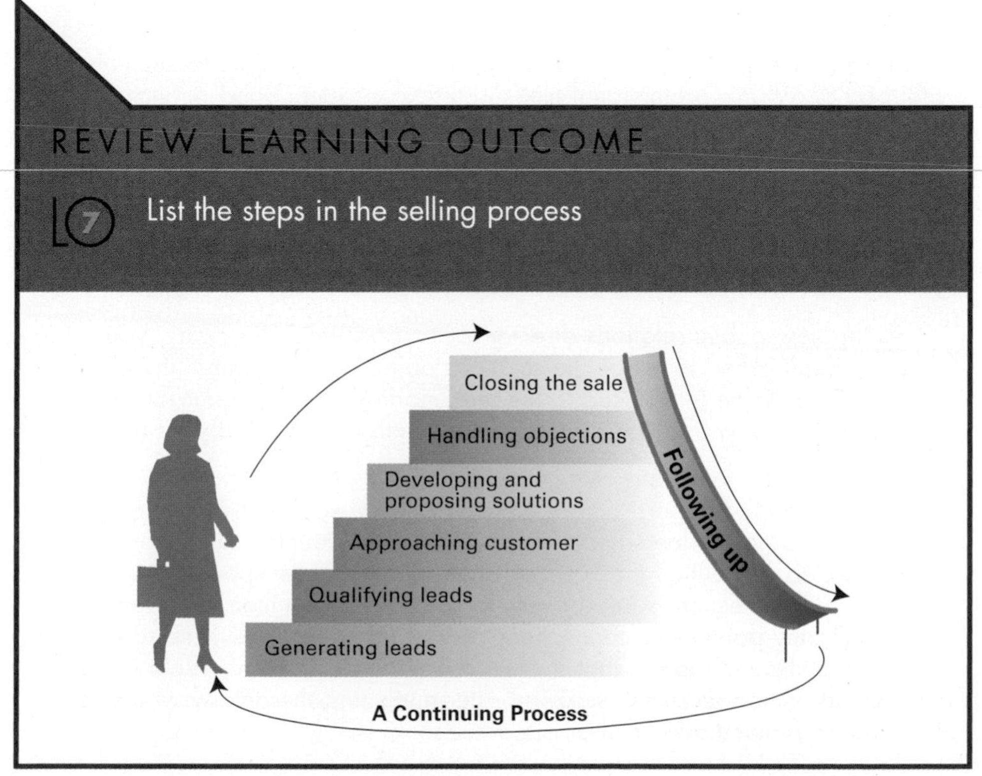

$5 million
▲ cost of creating, producing, and placing a national TV advertising campaign

new products introduced ▶ **1,200**

2 ◀ percentage of coupons that are redeemed

20 ◀ percentage of online coupons that are redeemed

loyalty program memberships in the U.S.
1.5 billion ◀

health clubs in which Dunkin' Donuts distributed samples of its Latte Lite drink ▶ **200**

percentage of market share gained each by companies with high customer service ▶ **6**

percentage of market share lost by companies with low customer service ▶ **2**

online video games sponsored by Chrysler and featuring their vehicles ▶ **42**

job openings on CollegeRecruiter.com ▼
100,000

REVIEW AND APPLICATIONS

Discuss the role of public relations in the promotional mix. Public relations is a vital part of a firm's promotional mix. A company fosters good publicity to enhance its image and promote its products. Popular public relations tools include new-product publicity, product placements, consumer education, sponsorships, and Web sites. An equally important aspect of public relations is managing unfavorable publicity to minimize damage to a firm's image.

1.1 How can advertising and publicity work together? Give an example.

1.2 As the new public relations director for a sportswear company, you have been asked to set public relations objectives for a new line of athletic shoes to be introduced to the teen market. Draft a memo outlining the objectives you propose for the shoe's introduction and your reasons for them.

1.3 Review the newspapers in your area for one week. Try to review several and varied newspapers (local, campus, cultural, countercultural, etc.) During this period, cut out all the event advertisements that list sponsors. Once you have your collection, spread them out so you can see them all at once. Identify any patterns or connections between the type of event and its sponsors. Identify companies that sponsor more than one event. What do sponsors tell you about target markets? After analyzing the ads, write a brief paragraph summarizing your discoveries.

Define and state the objectives of sales promotion. Sales promotion consists of those marketing communication activities, other than advertising, personal selling, and public relations, in which a short-term incentive motivates consumers or members of the distribution channel to purchase a good or service immediately, either by lowering the price or by adding value. The main objectives of sales promotion are to increase trial purchases, consumer inventories, and repeat purchases. Sales promotion is also used to encourage brand switching and to build brand loyalty. Sales promotion supports advertising activities.

2.1 What is the primary factor that determines sales promotion objectives? Name some different types of sales promotion techniques, and explain the type of customer they are intended to influence.

2.2 You have recently been assigned the task of developing promotional techniques to introduce your company's new product, a Cajun chicken sandwich. Advertising spending is limited, so the introduction will include only some low-budget sales promotion techniques. Write a sales promotion plan that will increase awareness of your new sandwich and allow your customer base to try it risk-free.

Discuss the most common forms of consumer sales promotion. Consumer forms of sales promotion include coupons and rebates, premiums, loyalty marketing programs, contests and sweepstakes, sampling, and point-of-purchase displays. Coupons are certificates entitling consumers to an immediate price reduction when they purchase a product or service. Coupons are a particularly good way to encourage product trial and brand switching. Similar to coupons, rebates provide purchasers with a price reduction, although it is not immediate. To receive a rebate, consumers generally must mail in a rebate form with a proof of purchase. Premiums offer an extra item or incentive to the consumer for buying a product or service. Premiums reinforce the consumer's purchase decision, increase consumption, and persuade nonusers to switch brands. Rewarding loyal customers is the basis of loyalty marketing programs. Loyalty programs are extremely effective at building long-term, mutually beneficial relationships between a company and its key customers. Contests and sweepstakes are generally designed to create interest, often to encourage brand switching. Because consumers perceive risk in trying new products, sampling is an effective method for gaining new customers. Finally, point-of-purchase displays set up at the retailer's location build traffic, advertise the product, and induce impulse buying.

3.1 Discuss how different forms of sales promotion can erode or build brand loyalty. If a company's objective is to enhance customer loyalty to its products, what sales promotion techniques will be most appropriate?

3.2 What forms of consumer sales promotion might induce impulse purchases? What forms of sales promotion are more effective at persuading consumers to switch brands?

3.3 Consider the different consumer sales promotion tools. Give an example of how each type of tool has influenced you to purchase—or purchase more of—a product or service.

3.4 Not everyone thinks supermarket shopper cards are a bargain. Go to **www.nocards.org** and read several pages. Is the information on the site compelling? What do you think of shopper cards? You may want to use the Internet to research shopper cards in more detail before forming an opinion.

3.5 Contests and sweepstakes are very common in the entertainment industry. Radio stations have contests almost weekly (some daily); local television morning shows quiz viewers on trivia; even movies offer sweepstakes in conjunction with film previews and premiere nights. Think of a television or radio program unlikely to have contests or sweepstakes (things like *Cops, The View, Scooby Doo,* or your local classical music radio station, for example). Once you have chosen your program, design a contest or sweepstake to promote the show or the channel on which it airs. List the objectives, and describe the rationale behind each part of your promotion.

3.6 How can uPromote.com help you with your sales promotions efforts (visit **www.upromote.com**)? What kind of marketing budget would you need to take advantage of its services? What kind of company would be best served by uPromote.com?

List the most common forms of trade sales promotion. Manufacturers use many of the same sales promotion tools used in consumer promotions, such as sales contests, premiums, and point-of-purchase displays. In addition, manufacturers and channel intermediaries use several unique promotional strategies: trade allowances, push money, training programs, free merchandise, store demonstrations, and meetings, conventions, and trade shows.

4.1 How does trade sales promotion differ from consumer sales promotion? How is it the same?

4.2 What are the main forms of trade sales promotion? Which type might be most enticing to a grocery store manager? To a buyer for a major electronics chain?

4.3 Form a team of three to five students. As marketing managers, you are in charge of selling Dixie cups. Design a consumer sales promotion plan and trade sales promotion plan for your product. Incorporate at least three different promotion tools into each plan. Share your results with the other teams in the class.

Describe personal selling. Personal selling is direct communication between a sales representative and one or more prospective buyers in an attempt to influence each other in a purchase situation. Broadly speaking, all businesspeople use personal selling to promote themselves and their ideas. Personal selling offers several advantages over other forms of promotion. Personal selling allows salespeople to thoroughly explain and demonstrate a product. Salespeople have the flexibility to tailor a sales proposal to the needs and preferences of individual customers. Personal selling is more efficient than other forms of promotion because salespeople target qualified prospects and avoid wasting efforts on unlikely buyers. Personal selling affords greater managerial control over promotion costs. Finally, personal selling is the most effective method of closing a sale and producing satisfied customers.

5.1 Discuss the role of personal selling in promoting products. What advantages does personal selling offer over other forms of promotion?

5.2 What are the major advantages of personal selling to the company selling a product? What are the advantages to the person or company buying the product?

Discuss the key differences between relationship selling and traditional selling. Relationship selling is the practice of building, maintaining, and enhancing interactions with customers in order to develop long-term satisfaction through mutually beneficial partnerships. Traditional selling, on the other hand, is transaction focused. That is, the salesperson is most concerned with making onetime sales and moving on to the next prospect. Salespeople practicing relationship selling spend more time understanding a prospect's needs and developing solutions to meet those needs.

6.1 What are the key differences between relationship selling and traditional methods of selling? What types of products or services do you think would be conducive to relationship selling?

6.2 Based on the key differences between traditional and relationship selling, which type of sales approach would you use as a salesperson? Do the different approaches require different personal strengths or attributes?

List the steps in the selling process. The selling process is composed of seven basic steps: (1) generating leads, (2) qualifying leads, (3) approaching the customer and probing needs, (4) developing and proposing solutions, (5) handling objections, (6) closing the sale, and (7) following up.

7.1 You are a new salesperson for a well-known medical software company, and one of your clients is a large group of physicians. You have just arranged an initial meeting with the office manager. Develop a list of questions you might ask at this meeting to uncover the group's specific needs.

7.2 What does sales follow-up entail? Why is it an essential step in the selling process, particularly from the perspective of relationship selling? How does it relate to cognitive dissonance?

7.3 How many ways can zapdata (**www.zapdata.com**) benefit salespeople? Which of its services would be most useful to marketing managers? Other businesspeople?

7.4 Consider each step in the selling process. Which steps could be conducted through technology (Internet, webinars, etc.)? Which are most important to handle "face-to-face"?

KEY TERMS

EXERCISES

APPLICATION EXERCISE

Have you ever waited forever to get a fast-food hamburger? Have you even been left to languish in a dressing room by a salesperson who left for a coffee break? If so, you already know that sales and customer service are integral parts of marketing. While you are working on this chapter, keep a journal of your personal sales and/or customer service experiences with local merchants. Don't ignore the details. Even such things as how crowded a store or restaurant is when you visit may affect your perceptions of the service you received.[66]

Activities

1. Keep your journal for a week, recording all sales and service transactions, if possible, on the day they occur.
2. At the end of the week, examine your journal, and pick the most noteworthy entry. Provide the basic information about the transaction: company where it occurred, type of transaction (purchase, return, complaint, etc.), type of good or service involved, and so forth.
3. Once you have the outlined the situation, evaluate the experience. Use the information about selling in this chapter as support for your evaluation. For example, did the salesperson seem to treat the situation as an individual, discrete transaction, or did he or she seem interested in building a relationship?
4. Finally, make recommendations as to how the company can improve its sales and/or service. Suggestions should be logical and achievable (meaning you have to consider the cost of implementing your suggestion).

ETHICS EXERCISE

Sally Burke works for Hi-Tech Electronics. Her responsibilities include selecting items to advertise in her company's Sunday newspaper FSIs. One hot item is a 50-inch flat-panel plasma TV. The list price is $4,999, but her manager tells her to advertise it at $3,999, since customers can apply for a $1,000 mail-in rebate. The advertised price has attracted many people to buy the TV; however, Sally has heard several complaints from customers who found the rebate process unusually complex and were denied a rebate because the manufacturer claimed they hadn't provided the required information. She would prefer to advertise the "real" list price, knowing that customers are not guaranteed to receive a rebate.

Questions

1. Is it unethical to advertise products at their post-rebate price in order to increase sales? Why or why not? What is another sales promotion method Hi-Tech Electronics could use to persuade customers to buy their plasma TV at the store?
2. Rebate programs are commonly used by electronics manufacturers because the rebates arouse consumers' interest in buying products; yet only half of purchasers ultimately claim their rebates. Is a rebate program itself unethical if the manufacturer knows consumers are unlikely to receive their money?
3. Visit a local electronics store—or Web site—and find a product being sold with a mail-in rebate offer. Are the rebate instructions clear? Would you take the time to complete the process?

MARKETING PLAN EXERCISE

For the next stage of the strategic planning process you'll focus on your chosen company's sales promotion and personal selling decisions. Use the following exercises to guide you through the final elements of Part 4 of your strategic marketing plan:

1. Evaluate or create printed materials for you chosen company (such as data sheets, brochures, stationery, or rate cards). Does the literature sufficiently answer questions? Provide enough information for further contact? Effectively promote product features and customer service? Note a differential or competitive advantage?
2. Think about ways your promotions could turn a first-time customer or deal-hunter into a repeat, loyal customer. Which sales promotion tools should your company use? What trade shows could your firm attend? Search the Eventline database for trade shows appropriate to your firm. Order media kits and explore the feasibility and costs of attending those trade shows. For a listing of tradeshows, go to **www.exhibitornet.com** and look for the directory of shows, or the Trade Show News Network at **www.tsnn.com**.
3. What other sales promotion tools could your firm use? What are the costs? What is the impact of using these methods on pricing?
4. Will you need a sales force? Identify and justify the best type (internal or external) and structure (product, customer, geographic, etc.) for your firm's sales force. You may find that in e-marketing, a sales force is more of a customer service and customer relations management tool. True selling activities may be limited to selling and buying online media space and links. In many circumstances, forming strategic partnerships and distribution deals have replaced traditional sales in the Internet space. What types of alliances and partnerships will you pursue? Will you work with other online firms, offline firms, or both?

CASE STUDY: RON POPEIL WHEELS, DEALS, HAS MASS APPEAL

At age 71, Ron "Ronco" Popeil is an avid inventor, tireless entrepreneur, clever marketer, and master salesman all in one. He just happens to be an American icon, too. The godfather of the infomercial, Popeil even has his famous Veg-O-Matic on display in the Smithsonian Institution as an American cultural artifact. His other famous products include the food dehydrator, the Ronco spray gun, and the Popeil Pocket Fisherman.

As a teenager, Popeil helped his father sell his kitchen gadgets at local Woolworth's and later, in the 1950s, on the Chicago fair circuit. That is probably why his famous shtick, which included such memorable catch phrases as "But wait, there's more," "Price so low," and "Operators are standing by," always seemed like a blend between sincere eccentric inventor and excitable carnival barker. The combination suited him well and brought him enough financial success that he could afford to take his act to television. In the 1960s, he incorporated Ronco, and its name became synonymous with gadgets like the smokeless ashtray and Mr. Microphone.

Regardless of the product he is selling or the catchy pitch phrases he invents on the fly to sell them, Popeil is always sincere. "The easiest thing to do in the world is to sell a product I believe in," he has said. "If I spent two years creating a product, conceiving it, tinkering with it, I can get up and sell it. Who can sell it better than the guy who invented it?" Len Green, a professor in entrepreneurship at Babson University, says, "Ron is one of a kind. He is different from the rest because he not only invents, he sells. Most entrepreneurs come up with a concept and then give it to others to manufacture or sell. He's his own best salesman."

Though Popeil has suffered his fair share of flops, like spray-on hair and a brief bankruptcy in 1987, he has always managed to bounce back. Returning from bankruptcy, he relaunched the popular food dehydrator in 1990, and eight years later he designed and sold his most successful product ever, the Showtime rotisserie BBQ. Having sold over seven million units for four installments of $39.95 each, the rotisserie alone has grossed over $1 billion in sales. During the taping of the infomercial for that product, the live studio audience was treated to yet another of Popeil's catch phrases that has become part of the fabric of American speech. "Just set it and forget it!" is now used to sell all kinds of non-Popeil products from VCRs and digital video recorders to ovens and coffee makers.

Through the medium of television, Popeil was able to reach tens of millions of people. With an innate ability to invent or improve on everyday household products, his live product demonstrations captured the imaginations and dollars of generations of consumers. In 1976, he was even the subject of what was probably Dan Aykroyd's most famous bit on *Saturday Night Live*. Parodying Popeil, Aykroyd hawked "Rovco's Super Bass-O-Matic '76," which was capable of turning a bass or any other "small aquatic creature" into liquid without any "scaling, cutting or gutting."

Having recently sold Ronco to an investment group for over $55 million and accumulated a personal net worth of over $100 million, Popeil has had the last laugh. He will continue to serve as a product developer, pitchman, and consultant for the new company and already promises an even bigger hit than the Showtime rotisserie. Having identified a market of over 20 million Americans who fry turkeys every year, Popeil says he has a new fryer on the way that will make it possible to safely fry a 20-pound turkey in 70 minutes—indoors. Given that he has created over 150 products and invented personal selling via the mass marketing medium, there is little reason to doubt him.

As Barbara Gross, professor of marketing at California State University, Northridge, states, "His success speaks for itself; probably that has more to do with his personality. He's comfortable and sincere. He comes across like he really believes in it. When you hear him talk, you never feel like he's lying to you.[67]

Questions

1. What does Ron Popeil bring to personal selling that makes him so effective?
2. What trade sales promotion tools does he use? Why does he use sales promotion tools when he is selling direct to consumers?
3. Explain how Popeil's selling tactics allow him to achieve the desired objectives of sales promotions.
4. Do you think it is likely that America will ever see someone like Ron Popeil in the future? Why or why not?

COMPANY CLIPS

© NKP MEDIA, INC./CENGAGE

VANS—OFF THE WALL PROMOTIONS

Steve Van Doren, son of Vans founder, is the self-proclaimed "ambassador of fun" at Vans. Because the company doesn't want to discount its products or lower its prices, it has to find other ways to create value for consumers. So, to keep the brand energized, the company is constantly developing promotions that can only be described as fun, an important element for attracting trendsetting customers. The core of Vans's strategy revolves around unique and authentic contests and giveaways. The company relies on word-of-mouth advertising and credible personal selling. In this video segment, Vans marketers explain how they use Web sites, contests, giveaways, and athletic events to attract and keep customers.

Questions

1. How does Vans use giveaways and contests to market its products? Why do these strategies work so well for Vans?
2. How does Vans approach recruiting and training its sales force?
3. How have trade shows changed in recent years? What is Vans's main goal at trade shows today?

Marketing & You Results

High scores on this poll indicate a preference for using coupons, which may indicate that you are a comparison shopper. If your score was low, you probably don't see any economic benefits to using coupons, and you're likely not a comparison shopper. Instead, you probably prefer to buy what you want regardless of any coupon promotion.

CHAPTER

16

Pricing Concepts

LEARNING OUTCOMES

LO1 Discuss the importance of pricing decisions to the economy and to the individual firm

LO2 List and explain a variety of pricing objectives

LO3 Explain the role of demand in price determination

LO4 Understand the concept of yield management systems

LO5 Describe cost-oriented pricing strategies

LO6 Demonstrate how the product life cycle, competition, distribution and promotion strategies, guaranteed price matching, customer demands, the Internet, and perceptions of quality can affect price

LO7 Describe the procedure for setting the right price

LO8 Identify the legal and ethical constraints on pricing decisions

THE IMPORTANCE OF PRICE

Price means one thing to the consumer and something else to the seller. To the consumer, it is the cost of something. To the seller, price is revenue, the primary source of profits. In the broadest sense, price allocates resources in a free-market economy. With so many ways of looking at price, it's no wonder that marketing managers find the task of setting prices a challenge.

What is Price?

Price is that which is given up in an exchange to acquire a good or service. Price plays two roles in the evaluation of product alternatives: as a measure of sacrifice and as an information cue. To some degree, these are two opposing effects.[1]

The Sacrifice Effect of Price Price is, again, "that which is given up," which means what is sacrificed to get a good or service. In the United States, the sacrifice is usually money, but it can be other things as well. It may also be time lost while waiting to acquire the good or service. Standing in long lines at the airport first to check in and then to get through the security checkpoint procedures is a cost. In fact, these delays are one reason more people are selecting alternative modes of transportation for relatively short trips. Price might also include "lost dignity" for individuals who lose their jobs and must rely on charity to obtain food and clothing.

The Information Effect of Price Consumers do not always choose the lowest-priced product in a category, such as shoes, cars, or wine, even when the products are otherwise similar. One explanation of this, based upon research, is that we infer quality information from price.[2] That is, higher quality equals higher price. The information effect of price may also extend to favorable price perceptions by others because higher prices can convey the prominence and status of the purchaser to other people. Thus, a Swatch and a Rolex both can accurately tell time but convey different meanings. Similarly, a Buick Enclave and the Lexus 450LX are both SUVs, and both can take you from point A to B. However, the two vehicles convey different meanings. We will return to the price-quality relationship later in the chapter.

Value Is Based upon Perceived Satisfaction Consumers are interested in obtaining a "reasonable price." "Reasonable price" really means "perceived reasonable value" at the time of the transaction. One of the authors of this textbook bought a fancy European-designed toaster for about $45. The toaster's wide mouth made it possible to toast a bagel, warm a muffin, and, with a special $15 attachment, make a grilled sandwich. The author felt that a toaster with all these features surely must be worth the total price of $60. But after three months of using the device, toast that burned around the

Marketing & You

Using the following scale, enter your opinion of the following items on the lines provided.

1 2 3 4 5 6 7

Strongly disagree — Strongly agree

__ People notice when you buy the most expensive brand of a product.

__ Buying the most expensive brand of a product makes me feel classy.

__ I enjoy the prestige of buying a high-priced brand.

__ It says something to people when you buy the high-priced version of a product.

__ I have purchased the most expensive brand of a product just because I knew other people would notice.

__ Even for a relatively inexpensive product, I think that buying a costly brand is impressive.

Total your score, and find out what it means after you read the chapter.

Source: Scale #265, *Marketing Scales Handbook*, G. Bruner, K. James, H. Hensel, eds., Vol. III. © by American Marketing Association.

price
That which is given up in an exchange to acquire a good or service.

revenue
The price charged to customers multiplied by the number of units sold.

profit
Revenue minus expenses.

edges and remained raw in the middle lost its appeal. The disappointed buyer put the toaster in the attic. Why didn't he return it to the retailer? Because the boutique had gone out of business, and no other local retailer carried the brand. Also, there was no U.S. service center. Remember, the price paid is based on the satisfaction consumers *expect* to receive from a product and not necessarily the satisfaction they actually receive.

Price can relate to anything with perceived value, not just money. When goods and services are exchanged, the trade is called *barter*. For example, if you exchange this book for a chemistry book at the end of the term, you have engaged in barter. The price you paid for the chemistry book was this textbook.

REVIEW LEARNING OUTCOME

LO 1 Discuss the importance of pricing decisions to the economy and to the individual firm

Price × Sales Unit = Revenue

Revenue − Costs = Profit

Profit drives growth, salary increases, and corporate investment.

The Importance of Price to Marketing Managers

Prices are the key to revenues, which in turn are the key to profits for an organization. **Revenue** is the price charged to customers multiplied by the number of units sold. Revenue is what pays for every activity of the company: production, finance, sales, distribution, and so on. What's left over (if anything) is **profit**. Managers usually strive to charge a price that will earn a fair profit.

To earn a profit, managers must choose a price that is not too high or too low, a price that equals the perceived value to target consumers. If, in consumers' minds, a price is set too high, the perceived value will be less than the cost, and sales opportunities will be lost. Many mainstream purchasers of cars, sporting goods, CDs, tools, wedding gowns, and computers are buying "used or preowned" items to get a better deal. Pricing a new product too high may give some shoppers an incentive to go to a "preowned" or consignment retailer. Lost sales mean lost revenue. Conversely, if a price is too low, the consumer may perceive it as a great value, but the firm loses revenue it could have earned.

Trying to set the right price is one of the most stressful and pressure-filled tasks of the marketing manager, as trends in the consumer market attest:

- Confronting a flood of new products, potential buyers carefully evaluate the price of each one against the value of existing products.
- The increased availability of bargain-priced private and generic brands has put downward pressure on overall prices.
- Many firms are trying to maintain or regain their market share by cutting prices. For example, IKEA has gained market share in the furniture industry by aggressively cutting prices.
- The Internet has made comparison shopping easier.
- The United States was in a recession from late 2007 until late 2009.

In the organizational market, where customers include both governments and businesses, buyers are also becoming more price sensitive and better informed. Computerized information systems enable the organizational buyer to compare price and performance with great ease and accuracy. Improved communication and the increased use of direct marketing and computer-aided selling have also opened up many markets to new competitors. Finally, competition in general is increasing, so some installations, accessories, and component parts are being marketed like indistinguishable commodities.

LO 2

PRICING OBJECTIVES

To survive in today's highly competitive marketplace, companies need pricing objectives that are specific, attainable, and measurable. Realistic pricing goals then require periodic monitoring to determine the effectiveness of the company's strategy. For convenience, pricing objectives can be divided into three categories: profit oriented, sales oriented, and status quo.

Profit-Oriented Pricing Objectives

Profit-oriented objectives include profit maximization, satisfactory profits, and target return on investment. A brief discussion of each of these objectives follows.

Profit Maximization Profit maximization means setting prices so that total revenue is as large as possible relative to total costs. (A more theoretically precise definition and explanation of profit maximization appears later in the chapter.) Profit maximization does not always signify unreasonably high prices, however. Both price and profits depend on the type of competitive environment a firm faces, such as whether it is in a monopoly position (being the only seller) or in a much more competitive situation. Also, remember that a firm cannot charge a price higher than the product's perceived value. Many firms do not have the accounting data they need for maximizing profits. It is easy to say that a company should keep producing and selling goods or services as long as revenues exceed costs. Yet it is often hard to set up an accounting system that can accurately determine the point of profit maximization.

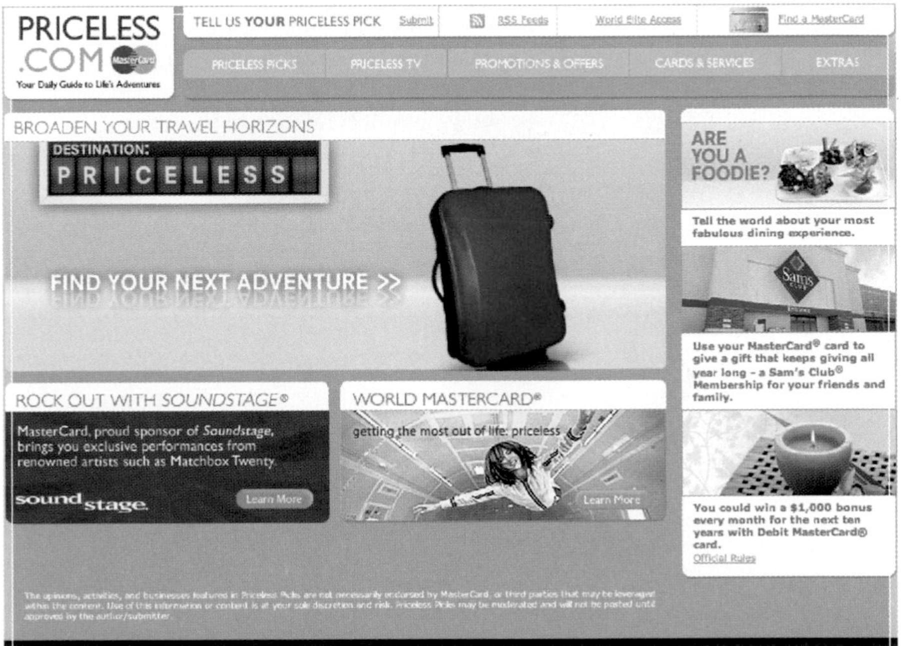

Facing heavy competition from Visa and American Express, MasterCard's "priceless" campaign was meant to position it as the credit card company that was in a relationship with its customer. The ads suggested that MasterCard understood what its customers wanted—the intangibles and experiences that make life "priceless" *and* the tangible things that they could purchase.

COURTESY, MASTERCARD

Sometimes managers say that their company is trying to maximize profits—in other words, trying to make as much money as possible. Although this goal may sound impressive to stockholders, it is not good enough for planning. The statement "We want to make all the money we can" is vague and lacks focus. It gives management license to do just about anything it wants to do.

In attempting to maximize profits, managers can try to expand revenue by increasing customer satisfaction, or they can attempt to reduce costs by operating more efficiently. A third possibility is to attempt to do both. Recent research has shown that striving to enhance customer satisfaction leads to greater profitability (and customer satisfaction) than following a cost reduction strategy or attempting to do both.[3] This means that companies should consider allocating more resources to customer service initiatives, loyalty programs, and customer relationship management programs and allocating fewer resources to programs that are designed to improve efficiency and reduce costs. Both types of programs, of course, are critical to the success of the firm.

return on investment (ROI) Net profit after taxes divided by total assets.

market share A company's product sales as a percentage of total sales for that industry.

Satisfactory Profits Satisfactory profits are a reasonable level of profits. Rather than maximizing profits, many organizations strive for profits that are satisfactory to the stockholders and management—in other words, a level of profits consistent with the level of risk an organization faces. In a risky industry, a satisfactory profit may be 35 percent. In a low-risk industry, it might be 7 percent. To maximize profits, a small-business owner might have to keep his or her store open seven days a week. However, the owner might not want to work that hard and might be satisfied with less profit.

Target Return on Investment The most common profit objective is a target **return on investment (ROI)**, sometimes called the firm's *return on total assets*. ROI measures management's overall effectiveness in generating profits with the available assets. The higher the firm's ROI, the better off the firm is. Many companies—including DuPont, General Motors, Navistar, ExxonMobil, and Union Carbide—use a target ROI as their main pricing goal. In summary, ROI is a percentage that puts a firm's profits into perspective by showing profits relative to investment.

Return on investment is calculated as follows:

$$\text{Return on investment} = \frac{\text{Net profits after taxes}}{\text{Total assets}}$$

Assume that in 2010 Johnson Controls had assets of $4.5 million, net profits of $550,000, and a target ROI of 10 percent. This was the actual ROI:

$$\text{ROI} = \frac{\$550{,}000}{\$4{,}500{,}000}$$

$$= 12.2 \text{ percent}$$

As you can see, the ROI for Johnson Controls exceeded its target, which indicates that the company prospered in 2010.

Comparing the 12.2 percent ROI with the industry average provides a more meaningful picture, however. Any ROI needs to be evaluated in terms of the competitive environment, risks in the industry, and economic conditions. Generally speaking, firms seek ROIs in the 10 to 30 percent range. For example, General Electric seeks a 25 percent ROI, whereas Alcoa, Rubbermaid, and most major pharmaceutical companies strive for a 20 percent ROI. In some industries such as the grocery industry, however, a return of under 5 percent is common and acceptable.

A company with a target ROI can predetermine its desired level of profitability. The marketing manager can use the standard, such as 10 percent ROI, to determine whether a particular price and marketing mix are feasible. In addition, however, the manager must weigh the risk of a given strategy even if the return is in the acceptable range.

Sales-Oriented Pricing Objectives

Sales-oriented pricing objectives are based either on market share or on dollar or unit sales. The effective marketing manager should be familiar with these pricing objectives.

Market Share Market share is a company's product sales as a percentage of total sales for that industry. Sales can be reported in dollars or in units of product. It is very important to know whether market share is expressed in revenue or units because the results may be different. Consider four companies competing in an industry with 2,000 total unit sales and total industry revenue of $4 million. (See Exhibit 16.1.) Company A has the largest unit market share at 50 percent, but it has only 25 percent of the revenue market share. In contrast, company D has only a 15 percent unit share but the largest revenue share: 30 percent. Usually, market share is expressed in terms of revenue and not units.

Many companies believe that maintaining or increasing market share is an indicator of the effectiveness of their marketing mix. Larger market shares have

EXHIBIT 16.1

Two Ways to Measure Market Share (Units and Revenue)

Company	Units Sold	Unit Price	Total Revenue	Unit Market Share	Revenue Market Share
A	1,000	$1.00	$1,000,000	50%	25%
B	200	4.00	800,000	10	20
C	500	2.00	1,000,000	25	25
D	300	4.00	1,200,000	15	30
Total	2,000		$4,000,000		

indeed often meant higher profits, thanks to greater economies of scale, market power, and ability to compensate top-quality management. Conventional wisdom also says that market share and return on investment are strongly related. For the most part they are; however, many companies with low market share survive and even prosper. To succeed with a low market share, companies need to compete in industries with slow growth and few product changes—for instance, industrial component parts and supplies. Otherwise, they must vie in an industry that makes frequently bought items, such as consumer convenience goods.

The conventional wisdom about market share and profitability isn't always reliable, however. Because of extreme competition in some industries, many market share leaders either do not reach their target ROI or actually lose money. Freightliner, a manufacturer of heavy trucks, aggressively fought for market share gains during the past decade. Though Freightliner grew to become the market leader with a 36 percent market share, its profits suffered. It lost hundreds of millions of dollars and slashed 8,000 jobs in an effort to cut costs.[4] The personal computer and food industries have also had this problem. Procter & Gamble switched from market share to ROI objectives after realizing that profits don't automatically follow from a large market share. PepsiCo says its new Pepsi challenge is to be number one in share of industry profit, not in share of sales volume.

Still, the struggle for market share can be all-consuming for some companies. For years, Intel Corporation has had a "monopoly grip" on the chip market. Advanced Micro Devices (AMD) has had a singular focus of breaking that grip. Through acquisitions, advanced technology, and aggressive pricing, AMD attained 23 percent market share in 2008. Together, the two companies account for 99 percent of the chip market for the X86 processor. AMD's objective is to grow its total chip market share to 30 percent over the next several years.[5]

Research organizations like A. C. Nielsen and Information Resources, Inc. provide excellent market share reports for many different industries. These reports enable companies to track their performance in various product categories over time.

Sales Maximization Rather than strive for market share, sometimes companies try to maximize sales. A firm with the objective of maximizing sales ignores profits, competition, and the marketing environment as long as sales are rising.

If a company is strapped for funds or faces an uncertain future, it may try to generate a maximum amount

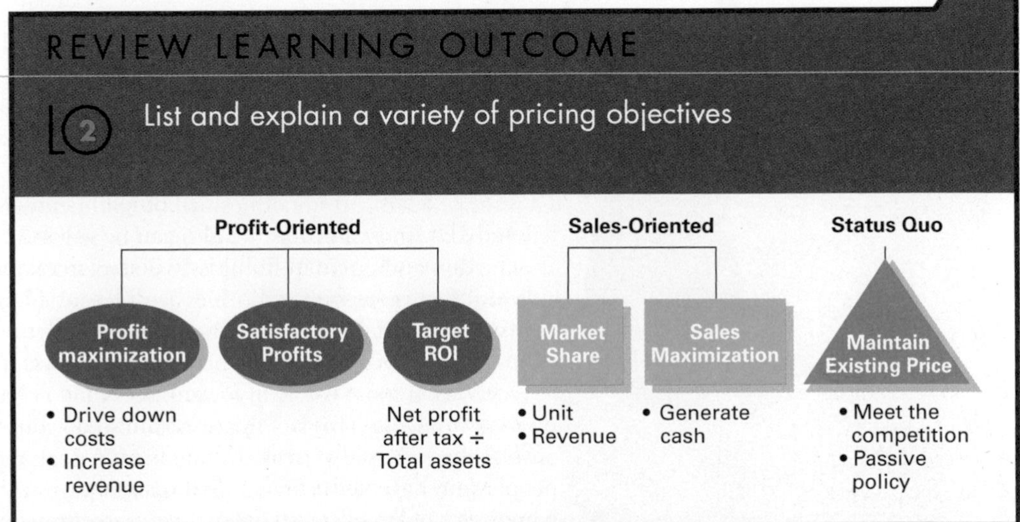

status quo pricing
A pricing objective that maintains existing prices or meets the competition's prices.

demand
The quantity of a product that will be sold in the market at various prices for a specified period.

supply
The quantity of a product that will be offered to the market by a supplier at various prices for a specified period.

price equilibrium
The price at which demand and supply are equal.

of cash in the short run. Management's task when using this objective is to calculate which price-quantity relationship generates the greatest cash revenue. Sales maximization can also be effectively used on a temporary basis to sell off excess inventory. It is not uncommon to find Christmas cards, ornaments, and other seasonal items discounted at 50 to 70 percent off retail prices after the holiday season. In addition, management can use sales maximization for year-end sales to clear out old models before introducing the new ones.

Maximization of cash should never be a long-run objective because cash maximization may mean little or no profitability. Without profits, a company cannot survive.

Status Quo Pricing Objectives

Status quo pricing seeks to maintain existing prices or to meet the competition's prices. This third category of pricing objectives has the major advantage of requiring little planning. It is essentially a passive policy.

Often firms competing in an industry with an established price leader simply meet the competition's prices. These industries typically have fewer price wars than those with direct price competition. In other cases, managers regularly shop competitors' stores to ensure that their prices are comparable. Target's middle managers may visit competing Wal-Mart stores to compare prices and then make adjustments.

THE DEMAND DETERMINANT OF PRICE

After marketing managers establish pricing goals, they must set specific prices to reach those goals. The price they set for each product depends mostly on two factors: the demand for the good or service and the cost to the seller for that good or service. When pricing goals are mainly sales oriented, demand considerations usually dominate. Other factors, such as distribution and promotion strategies, perceived quality, demands of large customers, the Internet, and stage of the product life cycle, can also influence price.

The Nature of Demand

Demand is the quantity of a product that will be sold in the market at various prices for ified period. The quantity of a product that people will buy depends on its price. igher the price, the fewer goods or services consumers will demand. Conversely, ‚ver the price, the more goods or services they will demand.

This trend is illustrated in Exhibit 16.2(a), which graphs the demand per week for fruit smoothies at a local retailer at various prices. This graph is called a *demand curve*. The vertical axis of the graph shows different prices of fruit smoothes, measured in dollars per package. The horizontal axis measures the quantity f fruit smoothies that will be demanded per week at each price. For example, t a price of $2.50, 50 smoothies will be sold per week; at $1.00, consumers will lemand 120 smoothies—as the demand schedule in Exhibit 16.2(b) shows.

The demand curve in Exhibit 16.2 slopes downward and to the right, which indicates that more fruit smoothies are demanded as the price is lowered. In other words, if smoothie makers put a greater quantity on the market, then their hope of selling all of it will be realized only by selling it at a lower price.

One reason more is sold at lower prices than at higher prices is that lower prices ng in new buyers. This fact might not be so obvious with fruit smoothies, but onsider the example of steak. As the price of steak drops lower and lower, some people who have not been eating steak will probably start buying it rather than hamburger. With each reduction in price, existing customers may also buy extra

© VICKI BEAVER

amounts. Similarly, if the price of smoothies falls low enough, some people will buy more than they have bought in the past.

Supply is the quantity of a product that will be offered to the market by a supplier or suppliers at various prices for a specified period. Exhibit 16.3(a) illustrates the resulting supply curve for fruit smoothies. Unlike the falling demand curve, the supply curve for smoothies slopes upward and to the right. At higher prices, smoothie makers will obtain more resources (apples, peaches, strawberries) and make more smoothies. If the price consumers are willing to pay for smoothies increases, producers can afford to buy more ingredients.

Output tends to increase at higher prices because a smoothie shop can sell more smoothies and earn greater profits. The supply schedule in Exhibit 16.3(b) shows that at $2 suppliers are willing to place 110 smoothies on the market, but that they will offer 140 drinks at a price of $3.

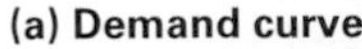

EXHIBIT 16.2

Demand Curve and Demand Schedule for Fruit Smoothies

(a) Demand curve

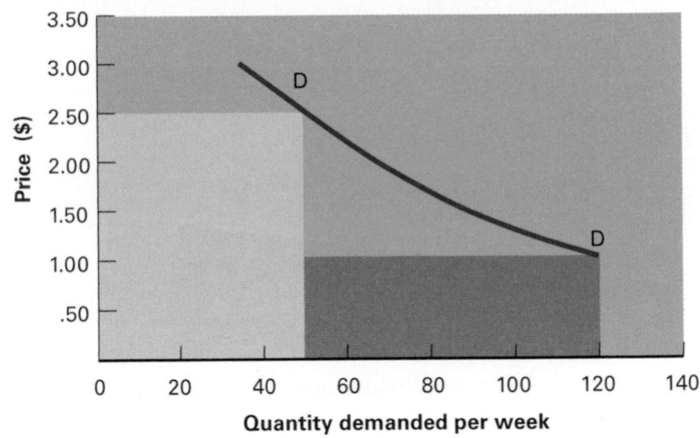

(b) Demand schedule

Price per package of fruit smoothies ($)	Packages of fruit smoothies demanded per week
3.00	35
2.50	50
2.00	65
1.50	85
1.00	120

How Demand and Supply Establish Prices

At this point, let's combine the concepts of demand and supply to see how competitive market prices are determined. So far, the premise is that if the price is X, then consumers will purchase Y amount of smoothie. How high or low will prices actually go? How many drinks will be produced? How many will be consumed? The demand curve cannot predict consumption, nor can the supply curve alone forecast production. Instead, we need to look at what happens when supply and demand interact—as shown in Exhibit 16.4.

At a price of $3, the public would demand only 35 smoothies. However, suppliers stand ready to place 140 smoothies on the market at this price (data from the demand and supply schedules). If they do, they would create a surplus of 105 smoothies. How does a merchant eliminate a surplus? It lowers the price.

At a price of $1, 120 smoothies would be demanded, but only 25 would be placed on the market. A shortage of 95 units would be created. If a product is in short supply and consumers want it, how do they entice the seller to part with one unit? They offer more money—that is, pay a higher price.

Now let's examine a price of $1.50. At this price, 85 smoothies are demanded and 85 are supplied. When demand and supply are equal, a state called **price equilibrium** is achieved. A temporary price below equilibrium—say, $1.00—results in a shortage because at that price the demand for fruit smoothies is greater than the available supply. Shortages put upward pressure on price. As long as demand and supply remain the same, however, temporary price increases or decreases tend to return

EXHIBIT 16.3

Supply Curve and Supply Schedule for Fruit Smoothies

(a) Supply curve

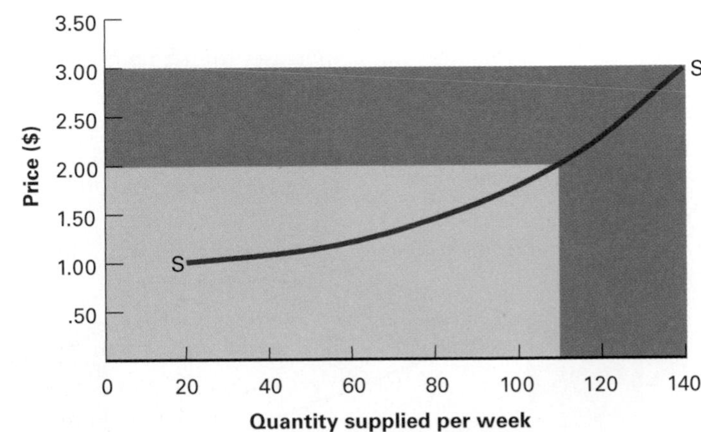

(b) Supply schedule

Price per package of fruit smoothies ($)	Packages of fruit smoothies supplied per week
3.00	140
2.50	130
2.00	110
1.50	85
1.00	25

EXHIBIT 16.4

Equilibrium Price for Fruit Smoothies

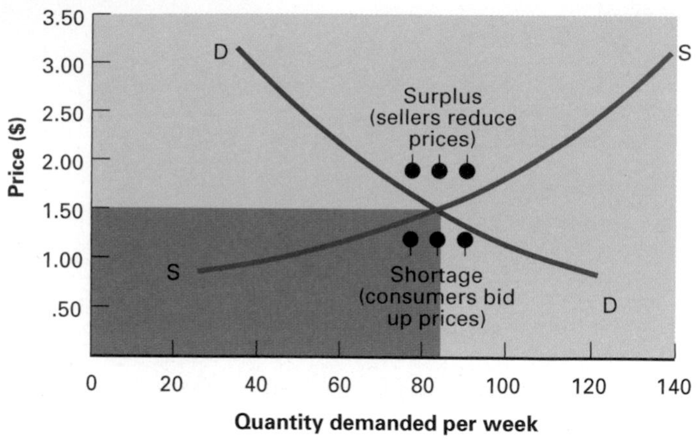

to equilibrium. At equilibrium, there is no inclination for prices to rise or fall.

An equilibrium price may not be reached all at once. Prices may fluctuate during a trial-and-error period as the market for a good or service moves toward equilibrium. Sooner or later, however, demand and supply will settle into proper balance.

Elasticity of Demand

To appreciate demand analysis, you should understand the concept of elasticity. **Elasticity of demand** refers to consumers' responsiveness or sensitivity to changes in price. **Elastic demand** occurs when consumers buy more or less of a product when the price changes. Conversely, **inelastic demand** means that an increase or a decrease in price will not significantly affect demand for the product.

elasticity of demand
Consumers' responsiveness or sensitivity to changes in price.

elastic demand
A situation in which consumer demand is sensitive to changes in price.

inelastic demand
A situation in which an increase or a decrease in price will not significantly affect demand for the product.

unitary elasticity
A situation in which total revenue remains the same when prices change.

Elasticity over the range of a demand curve can be measured by using this formula:

$$\text{Elasticity (E)} = \frac{\text{Percentage change in quantity demanded of good A}}{\text{Percentage change in price of good A}}$$

If E is greater than 1, demand is elastic.
If E is less than 1, demand is inelastic.
If E is equal to 1, demand is unitary.

Unitary elasticity means that an increase in sales exactly offsets a decrease in prices, so total revenue remains the same.

Elasticity can be measured by observing these changes in total revenue:

If price goes down and revenue goes up, demand is elastic.
If price goes down and revenue goes down, demand is inelastic.
If price goes up and revenue goes up, demand is inelastic.
If price goes up and revenue goes down, demand is elastic.
If price goes up or down and revenue stays the same, elasticity is unitary.

Exhibit 16.5(a) shows a very elastic demand curve. Decreasing the price of Apple iPhones from $300 to $200 increases sales from 18,000 units to 59,000 units. Revenue increases from $5.4 million ($300 x 18,000) to $11.8 million ($200 x 59,000). The price decrease results in a large increase in sales and revenue.

Exhibit 16.5(b) shows a completely inelastic demand curve. The state of Nevada dropped its used-car vehicle inspection fee from $20 to $10. The state continued to inspect about 400,000 used cars annually. Decreasing the price (inspection fee) 50 percent did not cause people to buy more used cars. Demand is completely inelastic for inspection fees, which are required by law. Thus, it also follows that Nevada could double the original fee to $40 and double the state's inspection revenues. People won't stop buying used cars if the inspection fee increases—within a reasonable range.

EXHIBIT 16.5

Elasticity of Demand for Apple iPhones and Auto Inspection Stickers

(a) Apple iPhones

Price ($): 300, 200, 100 — D, D — Quantity: 0, 18,000, 59,000

(b) Auto inspection stickers

Price ($): 20, 10 — D, D — Quantity: 0, 400,000

Exhibit 16.6 presents the demand curve and demand schedule for three-ounce bottles of

Spring Break suntan lotion. Let's follow the demand curve from the highest price to the lowest and examine what happens to elasticity as the price decreases.

Inelastic Demand The initial decrease in the price of Spring Break suntan lotion, from \$5.00 to \$2.25, results in a decrease in total revenue of \$969 (\$5,075–\$4,106). When price and total revenue fall, demand is inelastic. The decrease in price is much greater than the increase in suntan lotion sales (810 bottles). Demand is therefore not very flexible in the price range \$5.00 to \$2.25.

When demand is inelastic, sellers can raise prices and increase total revenue. Often items that are relatively inexpensive but convenient tend to have inelastic demand.

Elastic Demand In the example of Spring Break suntan lotion, shown in Exhibit 16.6, when the price is dropped from \$2.25 to \$1.00, total revenue increases by \$679 (\$4,785–\$4,106). An increase in total revenue when price falls indicates that demand is elastic. Let's measure Spring Break's elasticity of demand when the price drops from \$2.25 to \$1.00 by applying the formula presented earlier:

$$E = \frac{\text{Change in quantity/(Sum of quantities/2)}}{\text{Change in price/(Sum of prices/2)}}$$

$$= \frac{(4{,}785 - 1{,}825/[(1{,}825 + 4{,}785)/2]}{(2.25 - 1.00)/[(2.25 + 1.00)/2]}$$

$$= \frac{2{,}960/3{,}305}{1.25/1.63}$$

$$= \frac{.896}{.769}$$

$$= 51.17$$

Because E is greater than 1, demand is elastic.

EXHIBIT 16.6

Demand for Three-Ounce Bottles of Spring Break Suntan Lotion

(a) Demand curve

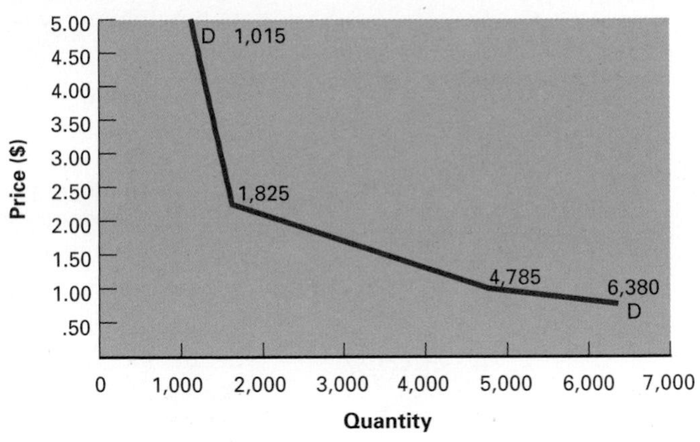

(b) Demand schedule

Price (\$)	Quantity demanded	Total revenue (price × quantity)	Elasticity
5.00	1,015	\$5,075	Inelastic
2.25	1,825	4,106	
1.00	4,785	4,785	Elastic
0.75	6,380	4,785	Unitary

Factors That Affect Elasticity Several factors affect elasticity of demand, including the following:

- *Availability of substitutes:* When many substitute products are available, the consumer can easily switch from one product to another, making demand elastic. The same is true in reverse: A person with complete renal failure will pay whatever is charged for a kidney transplant because there is no substitute. Interestingly, Bose stereo equipment is priced 300 to 500 percent higher than other stereo brands. Yet consumers are willing to pay the price because they perceive the equipment as being so superior to other brands that there is no acceptable substitute.
- *Price relative to purchasing power:* If a price is so low that it is an inconsequential part of an individual's budget, demand will be inelastic. For example, if the price of salt doubles, consumers will not stop putting salt and pepper on their eggs because salt is cheap anyway.

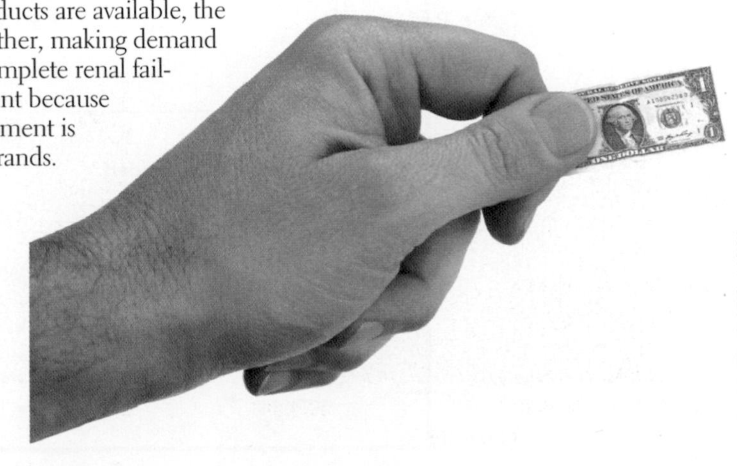

© ISTOCKPHOTO.COM/RICH YASICK

- *Product durability:* Consumers often have the option of repairing durable products rather than replacing them, thus prolonging their useful life. If a person plans to buy a new car and prices suddenly begin to rise, he or she may elect to fix the old car and drive it for another year. In other words, people are sensitive to the price increase, and demand is elastic.
- *A product's other uses:* The greater the number of different uses for a product, the more elastic demand tends to be. If a product has only one use, as may be true of a new medicine, the quantity purchased probably will not vary as price varies. A person will consume only the prescribed quantity, regardless of price. On the other hand, a product like steel has many possible applications. As its price falls, steel becomes more economically feasible in a wider variety of applications, thereby making demand relatively elastic.
- *Rate of inflation:* Recent research has found that when a country's inflation rate (the rate at which the price level is rising) is high, demand becomes more elastic. In other words, rising price levels make consumers more price sensitive. The research also found that during inflationary periods consumers base their timing (when to buy) and quantity decisions on price promotions. This suggests that a brand gains additional sales or market share if the product is effectively promoted or if the marketing manager keeps the brand's price increases low relative to the inflation rate.[6]

Examples of both elastic and inelastic demand abound in everyday life. Recently, fans balked at high prices for concerts. Promoters lost money, and some shows including some by artists Christina Aguilera and Marc Anthony were canceled. This is price elasticity in action. On the other hand, demand for some tickets was highly inelastic. The Rolling Stones are still selling out concerts with tickets priced at up to $400.[7]

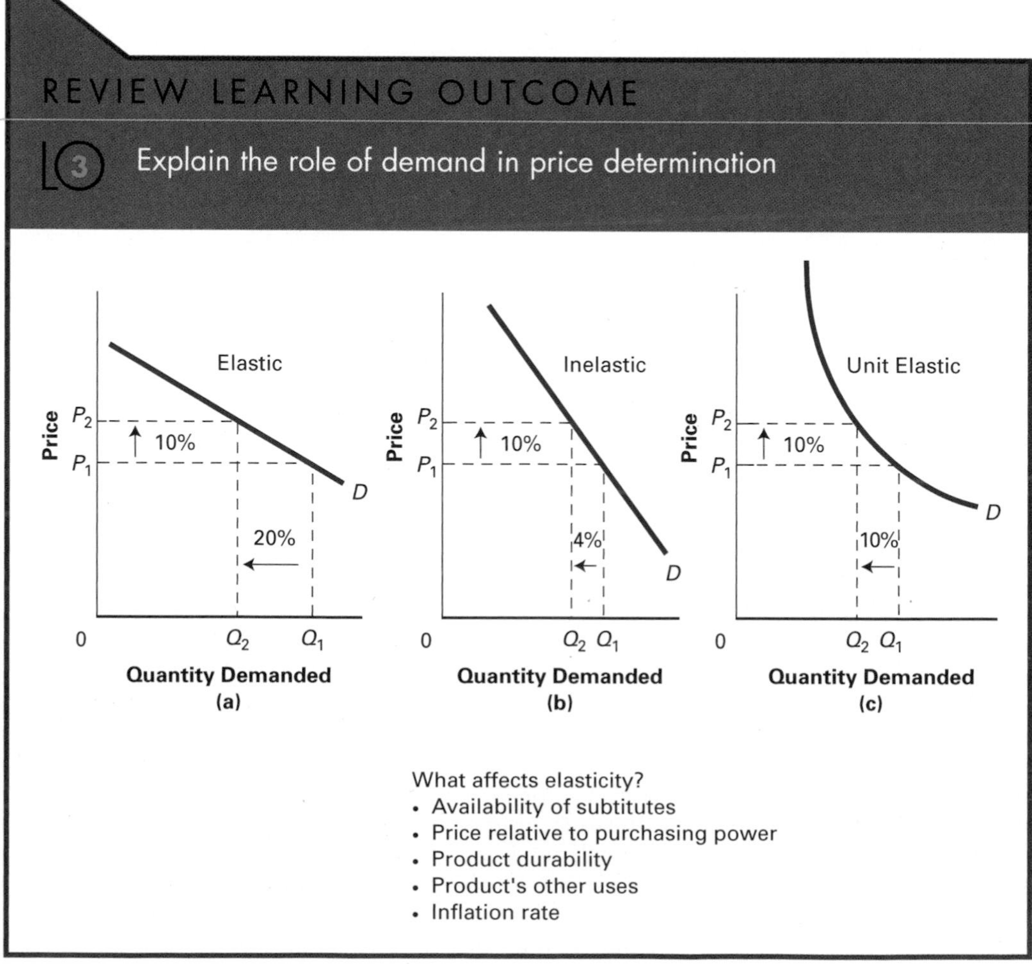

Pricing Power For many companies most pricing power vanished long ago. A lack of pricing power means that when a company tries to raise its prices, it loses sales volume as customers shift to low cost competitors or find a substitute product. Ultimately, many of these companies have had to lower prices again—sometimes dropping them even further than they were before the attempted price increase—in an effort to recapture lost share.

In contrast, pricing power means making a price increase stick. It means that demand is relatively inelastic for the product. How does a firm gain pricing power? One strategy is to produce something radically new, and most importantly, better than the competition. Eric Soule had been waiting 15 months for this moment. The semiconductor engineer was about to launch a new chip, and he needed his pricing approved. In a conference room at Linear Technology Corp., Mr. Soule anxiously explained why his amplifier chip is so advanced that it should sell for $1.68, a third more than its rivals. His bosses' reaction: Charge even more. The chip is 20 times better than the competition, they asserted, and high-end customers will crave it on any terms. Why not boost the $1.68 list price by 10 cents? Mr. Soule was nervous. "I can live with that," he guardedly replied, "but what does that accomplish?"

"It's a dime!" declared Linear's chairman and founder, Robert Swanson. "And those dimes add up."[8] The moral of the story: If you have pricing power, use it because it doesn't last forever.

yield management systems (YMS)
A technique for adjusting prices that uses complex mathematical software to profitably fill unused capacity by discounting early purchases, limiting early sales at these discounted prices, and overbooking capacity.

Parker Hannifin Corporation, a manufacturer of over 800,000 different parts—from heat resistant seals for jet engines to steel valves for hoist buckets—took a different approach to find pricing power. Initially, no matter how much a product improved, the company ended up charging the same markup it would for a more standard product. And if the company found a way to make a product less expensively, it ultimately cut the product's price as well. Hannifin's President, Donald Washkiewicz, knew that there must be a better way. He analyzed the product line searching for items that would offer pricing power. The new strategy is outlined in Exhibit 16.7. It has boosted revenue by $200 million.[9] The items identified as having greater inelasticity of demand have greater profit margins.

EXHIBIT 16.7

Parker Hannifin's Strategy to Create Pricing Power

Product Categories	Pricing Strategy Rationale	Price Increase (%)
Core products	Basic commodity in high volume with market competition	−3–5
Partially differentiated products (A)	Some differentiation to core product that meets wider market's needs in competitive market	0–5
Partially differentiated products (B)	Some differentiation to product or niche product with little or no market competition	0–9
System or differentiated products	Custom engineering to customer specifications that improves customer's productivity and profitability; some market competition	0–25
Classic or Special products	Custom-designed or unique product with no market competition	>25

Source: Adapted from Timothy Aeppel's *Wall Street Journal* article, "Seeking Perfect Prices, CEO Tears Up the Rules," March 27, 2007, James Sagar's article "Pricing Strategy: Capture More Revenue," Marketing M.O. Consulting, online at **http://www.marketingmo.com**, March 27, 2007, and Parker Hannifin Corporation, online at **http://www.parker.com**, accessed June 30, 2007.

LO4

THE POWER OF YIELD MANAGEMENT SYSTEMS AND TARGETING TECHNOLOGY

Another important tool for gaining pricing power is the yield management system. More and more companies are turning to yield management systems to help fine-tune prices. First developed in the airline industry, **yield management systems (YMS)** use complex mathematical software to profitably fill unused capacity. The software employs techniques such as discounting early purchases, limiting early sales at these discounted prices, and overbooking capacity. YMS now are appearing in other services such as lodging, other transportation forms, rental firms, retailers, and even hospitals.

Yield management systems are spreading beyond service industries as their popularity increases. The lessons of airlines and hotels aren't entirely applicable to other industries, however, because plane seats and hotel beds are perishable—if they go empty, the revenue opportunity is lost forever. So it makes sense to slash prices to move toward capacity if it's possible to do so without reducing the prices that other customers pay. Cars and steel aren't so perishable. Still, the capacity to make these goods is perishable. An underused factory or mill is a lost revenue opportunity. So it makes sense to cut prices to use up capacity if it's possible to do so while getting other customers to pay full price.

By using a type of yield management system, Allstate has gotten smarter about what to charge which drivers. In the past, customers were divided into three categories for car insurance. Now Allstate has more than 1,500 price levels. Agents used to simply refer to a manual to give customers a price; now they log on to a computer that uses complex algorithms to analyze 16 credit report variables, such as late payments and card balances, as well as data such as claims history for specific car models. Thus, safe drivers are rewarded, saving up to 20 percent over the old system, and high-risk drivers are penalized, paying up to 20 percent more. The system has worked so well that Allstate now applies it to other lines, such as homeowners insurance.[10]

Yield management software is the reason that consumers now find prices at the 390 Longs Drug Stores in amounts like $2.07 or $5.84 instead of the traditional price-ending digits of .95 or .99. The company says the software has triggered a "category-by-category increase in sales and profit margins."[11] That's the main reason that DemandTec's YMS algorithms, and not manufacturers' suggested retail prices, now govern pricing in all Longs' stores in the continental United States. Similarly, Duane Reade, the drug chain that blankets New York City, was struggling to boost sales of its merchandise. With diapers, for example, competitors were outselling the chain and discounts and coupons failed to move the diapers faster. Duane Reade called DemandTec. The consulting firm's software suggested that the markup on the diapers be a function of the child's age. For example, make the newborn sizes more expensive, and the big-kid pull-ups cheaper. After a year an increase in diaper sales helped boost baby care revenue by 27 percent even as the category's gross margin rose 2 percentage points. Why? Parents of newborns are far less price-sensitive than parents of toddlers. "It was a eureka moment," says Gary Charboneau, Duane Reade's head of sales and marketing and a 37-year retail veteran. "There's no way we could've spotted that."[12]

Duane Reade now has DemandTec's algorithms determining prices for two-thirds of the items it sells. The prices of some cough medicines are up. (Sick people don't shop around.) The per-pill price of the 50-pill bottles of certain pain relievers used to be lower than on the 24-pill bottle. Now it's higher. The kind of people who buy jugs of pills are a bit less sensitive to a higher unit price.[13]

Behavioral Targeting Technology

Internet retailers are now offering different prices and promotional offers to different customers based upon their Internet shopping and browsing habits. Using Internet cookies and new targeting software, Internet retailers can identify you each time you visit, and e-stores can gather reams of preferences as you shop. "It's as if we had a little camera that can watch you flip through a catalog. We can see where you stopped, what pages you dog-eared, what pages you ripped out and what made you pick up the phone to buy," says John Squire, vice president of product strategy at Coremetrics, a San Mateo, California, software company that helps online retailers analyze and act on consumer behavior.[14]

At Overstock.com, the company watches how long you linger on the site and how much you spend. That alone could determine whether you'll see an ad for a liquidation sale on last year's sweatshirts or a notice about a new shipment of pricey freshwater pearls. Watchmaker Fossil sometimes offers discounts and deals to first-time site visitors that it hides from repeat customers. Folks who abandon a virtual shopping cart at flower-delivery sites are sometimes e-mailed a 10 percent coupon to lure them back. Targeted offers can also boost the effectiveness of e-mail campaigns. Consumers typically open one out of five e-mail offers from retailers, and only 20 percent of those views lead to a site visit. When e-mail is customized with anything from the customer's name to a discount for something they've bought before, conversion rates double.[15]

No wonder, then, that high-profile e-commerce sites like **RedEnvelope.com**, **Travelocity.com**, and **eBay.com**, along with the online arms of big retailers like Best Buy, Petco, and JCPenney, are pouring resources into targeting technology. In 2008, approximately $775 million was spent on behavioral targeting. That number is expected to jump to $4.4 billion by 2012.[16] Advertisers are getting their ads to the "right audiences" and consumers are seeing more relevant ads.

There is a potential downside to behavioral targeting which is consumer privacy. In a recent survey conducted by TNS for TRUSTe, a San Francisco–based consumer privacy organization, 71 percent of consumers said they're aware that their online browsing might be tracked for advertising purposes. Of the 1,105 consumers polled, 72 percent find ads that are not relevant to their wants and needs to be intrusive or annoying, but only 24 percent said they're comfortable with advertisers using their browsing history to deliver more relevant ads, even if that data contains no personally identifiable information—and 91 percent of respondents said they're willing to take steps to ensure their online privacy is protected.[17] Many activists are encouraging the Federal Trade Commission to set up a federally regulated "Do No Track" list to make consumer opt-outs easier.

REVIEW LEARNING OUTCOME

LO 4 Understand the concept of yield management systems

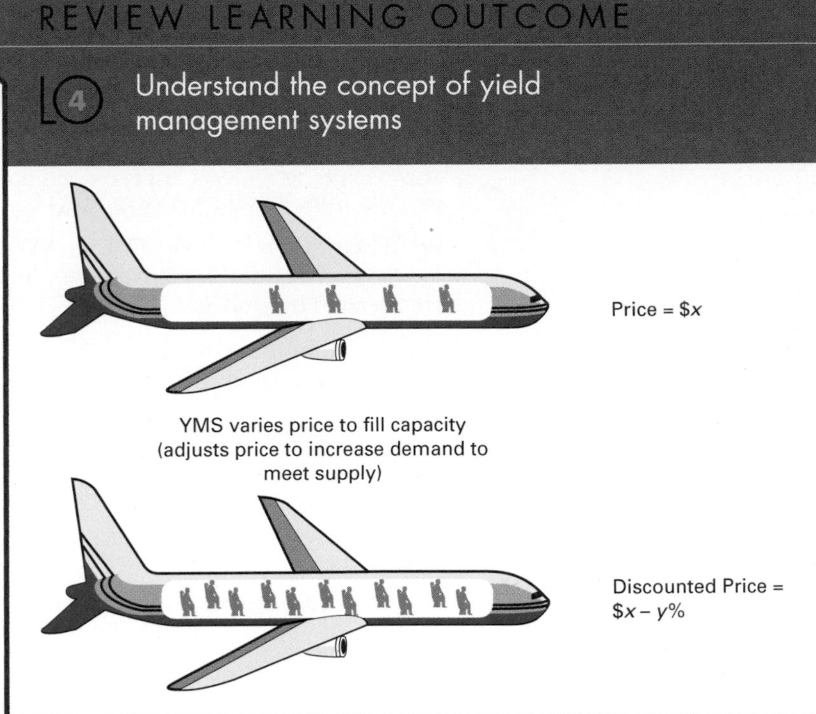

THE COST DETERMINANT OF PRICE

Sometimes companies minimize or ignore the importance of demand and decide to price their products largely or solely on the basis of costs. Prices determined strictly on the basis of costs may be too high for the target market, thereby reducing or eliminating sales. On the other hand, cost-based prices may be too low, causing the firm to earn a lower return than it should. Nevertheless, costs should generally be part of any price determination, if only as a floor below which a good or service must not be priced in the long run.

The idea of cost may seem simple, but it is actually a multifaceted concept, especially for producers of goods and services. A **variable cost** is a cost that varies with changes in the level of output; an example of a variable cost is the cost of materials. In contrast, a **fixed cost** does not change as output is increased or decreased. Examples include rent and executives' salaries.

To compare the cost of production to the selling price of a product, it is helpful to calculate costs per unit, or average costs. **Average variable cost (AVC)** equals total variable costs divided by quantity of output. **Average total cost (ATC)** equals total costs divided by output. As the graph in Exhibit 16.8(a) shows, AVC and ATC are basically U-shaped curves. In contrast, average fixed cost (AFC) declines continually as output increases because total fixed costs are constant.

Marginal cost (MC) is the change in total costs associated with a one-unit change in output. Exhibit 16.8(b) shows that when output rises from seven to eight units, the change in total cost is from $640 to $750; therefore, marginal cost is $110.

variable cost
A cost that varies with changes in the level of output.

fixed cost
A cost that does not change as output is increased or decreased.

average variable cost (AVC)
Total variable costs divided by quantity of output.

average total cost (ATC)
Total costs divided by quantity of output.

marginal cost (MC)
The change in total costs associated with a one-unit change in output.

All the curves illustrated in Exhibit 16.8(a) have definite relationships:

- AVC plus AFC equals ATC.
- MC falls for a while and then turns upward, in this case with the fourth unit. At that point diminishing returns set in, meaning that less output is produced for every additional dollar spent on variable input.
- MC intersects both AVC and ATC at their lowest possible points.
- When MC is less than AVC or ATC, the incremental cost will continue to pull the averages down. Conversely, when MC is greater than AVC or ATC, it pulls the averages up, and ATC and AVC begin to rise.
- The minimum point on the ATC curve is the least cost point for a fixed-capacity firm, although it is not necessarily the most profitable point.

Costs can be used to set prices in a variety of ways. For example, markup pricing is relatively simple. Profit maximization pricing and break-even pricing make use of the more complicated concepts of cost.

EXHIBIT 16.8

Hypothetical Set of Cost Curves and a Cost Schedule

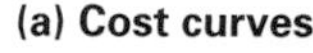

(a) Cost curves

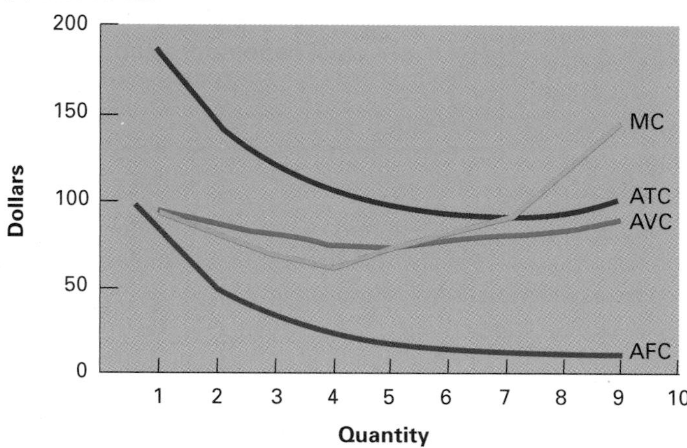

(b) Cost schedule

Total-cost data, per week				Average-cost data, per week			
(1) Total product (Q)	(2) Total fixed cost (TFC)	(3) Total variable cost (TVC)	(4) Total cost (TC)	(5) Average fixed cost (AFC)	(6) Average variable cost (AVC)	(7) Average total cost (ATC)	(8) Marginal cost (MC)
			TC = TFC + TVC	$AFC = \frac{TFC}{Q}$	$AVC = \frac{TVC}{Q}$	$ATC = \frac{TC}{Q}$	$(MC) = \frac{\text{change in TC}}{\text{change in Q}}$
0	$100	$ 0	$ 100	—	—	—	—
1	100	90	190	$100.00	$90.00	$190.00	$ 90
2	100	170	270	50.00	85.00	135.00	80
3	100	240	340	33.33	80.00	113.33	70
4	100	300	400	25.00	75.00	100.00	60
5	100	370	470	20.00	74.00	94.00	70
6	100	450	550	16.67	75.00	91.67	80
7	100	540	640	14.29	77.14	91.43	90
8	100	650	750	12.50	81.25	93.75	110
9	100	780	880	11.11	86.67	97.78	130
10	100	930	1,030	10.00	93.00	103.00	150

Markup Pricing

Markup pricing, the most popular method used by wholesalers and retailers to establish a selling price, does not directly analyze the costs of production. Instead, **markup pricing** uses the cost of buying the product from the producer, plus amounts for profit and for expenses not otherwise accounted for. The total determines the selling price.

A retailer, for example, adds a certain percentage to the cost of the merchandise received to arrive at the retail price. An item that costs the retailer \$1.80 and is sold for \$2.20 carries a markup of 40 cents, which is a markup of 22 percent of the cost (\$.40 ÷ \$1.80). Retailers tend to discuss markup in terms of its percentage of the retail price—in this example, 18 percent (\$.40 ÷ \$2.20). The difference between the retailer's cost and the selling price (40 cents) is the gross margin, as Chapter 13 explained.

$$\text{Retail price} = \frac{\text{Cost}}{\text{I} - \text{Desired return on sales}}$$

$$= \frac{\$1.80}{1.00 - .18}$$

$$= \$2.20$$

If the retailer wants a 30 percent return, then

$$\text{Retail price} = \frac{\$1.80}{1.00 - .30}$$

$$= \$2.57$$

The reason that retailers and others speak of markups on selling price is that many important figures in financial reports, such as gross sales and revenues, are sales figures, not cost figures.

To use markup based on cost or selling price effectively, the marketing manager must calculate an adequate gross margin—the amount added to cost to determine price. The margin must ultimately provide adequate funds to cover selling expenses and profit. Once an appropriate margin has been determined, the markup technique has the major advantage of being easy to employ. Wal-Mart, for example, strives for a gross margin of around 16 percent. Because supermarket chains, such as Safeway and Kroger, have typically had gross margins of 24 percent, they are now finding it extremely difficult to compete with Wal-Mart supermarkets. Wal-Mart is now the nation's largest grocery chain.

Markups are often based on experience. For example, many small retailers mark up merchandise 100 percent over cost. (In other words, they double the cost.) This tactic is called **keystoning**. Some other factors that influence markups are the merchandise's appeal to customers, past response to the markup (an implicit demand consideration), the item's promotional value, the seasonality of the goods, their fashion appeal, the product's traditional selling price, and competition. Most retailers avoid any set markup because of such considerations as promotional value and seasonality.

What if a firm charged zero markup? The Customer Experience box explains this unusual phenomenon.

Profit Maximization Pricing

Producers tend to use more complicated methods of setting prices than distributors use. One is **profit maximization**, which occurs when marginal revenue equals marginal cost. You learned earlier that marginal cost is the change in total costs associated with a one-unit change in output. Similarly, **marginal revenue (MR)** is the extra revenue associated with selling an extra unit of output. As long as the revenue of the last unit produced and sold is greater than the cost of the last unit produced and sold, the firm should continue manufacturing and selling the product.

Exhibit 16.9 shows the marginal revenues and marginal costs for a hypothetical firm, using the cost data from Exhibit 16.8(b). The profit-maximizing quantity, where MR = MC, is six units. You might say, "If profit is zero, why produce the sixth unit?

markup pricing
The cost of buying the product from the producer plus amounts for profit and for expenses not otherwise accounted for.

keystoning
The practice of marking up prices by 100 percent, or doubling the cost.

profit maximization
A method of setting prices that occurs when marginal revenue equals marginal cost.

marginal revenue (MR)
The extra revenue associated with selling an extra unit of output or the change in total revenue with a one-unit change in output.

CUSTOMER Experience

Pay What It's Worth

Terra Bite Lounge has no prices listed on its wall menu. The Kirkland, Washington, coffee shop's customers pay what and whenever they like and leave the money in a locked box on the counter. Ervin Peretz, one of the café's founders, figures that generous patrons cover the tabs of those who pay less than what's fair. And the business saves money by not having to pay for workers or services to handle financial transactions. The approach has allowed Terra Bite to both make money and help out those who can't always afford a good meal. "We're not nearly as selfless as a soup kitchen," says the 38-year-old Mr. Peretz, who also works as a lead software-development engineer for Google, Inc. "We're able to operate without charity."

Such a business model contradicts the basic concept of running a business: the exchange of goods for a set amount of money. But a crop of eateries and shops in Utah, Colorado, Washington, and other places are finding that doing away with set prices and making payment voluntary can be both a profitable and charitable way of doing business. And the marketing buzz such a scheme generates can help a business stand out from the pack.

But can the good-karma model be a smart long-term business strategy? It's worked for One World Café in Salt Lake City, which has been serving an ever-changing menu of organic fare. The business has been profitable since 2005, with about a 5 percent profit margin. Customer payments average about $10. Denise Cerreta, a former acupuncturist and founder of the café, says the business helps in her mission to end hunger. But the café is a "hand-up, not a hand out," she says, meaning that people down in their luck may not be able to pay now, but they'll eventually pay later.[18]

Would this concept work in an upscale restaurant? Why or why not? Could this model be applied to other types of businesses? Give an example.

Why not stop at five?" In fact, you would be right. The firm, however, would not know that the fifth unit would produce zero profits until it determined that profits were no longer increasing. Economists suggest producing up to the point where MR = MC. If marginal revenue is just one penny greater than marginal costs, it will still increase total profits.

EXHIBIT 16.9

Point of Profit Maximization

Quantity	Marginal Revenue (MR)	Marginal Cost (MC)	Cumulative Total Profit
0	—	—	—
1	$140	$90	$50
2	130	80	100
3	105	70	135
4	95	60	170
5	85	70	185
6	80	80	185
7	75	90	170
8	60	110	120
9	50	130	40
10	40	150	(70)

Break-Even Pricing

Now let's take a closer look at the relationship between sales and cost. **Break-even analysis** determines what sales volume must be reached before the company breaks even (its total costs equal total revenue) and no profits are earned.

The typical break-even model assumes a given fixed cost and a constant average variable cost. Suppose that Universal Sportswear, a hypothetical firm, has fixed costs of $2,000 and that the cost of labor and materials for each unit produced is 50 cents. Assume that it can sell up to 6,000 units of its product at $1 without having to lower its price.

Exhibit 16.10(a) illustrates Universal Sportswear's break-even point. As Exhibit 16.10(b) indicates, Universal Sportswear's total variable costs increase by 50 cents every time a new unit is produced, and total fixed costs remain constant at $2,000 regardless of the level of output. Therefore, for 4,000 units of output, Universal Sportswear has $2,000 in fixed costs and $2,000 in total variable costs (4,000 units × $.50), or $4,000 in total costs.

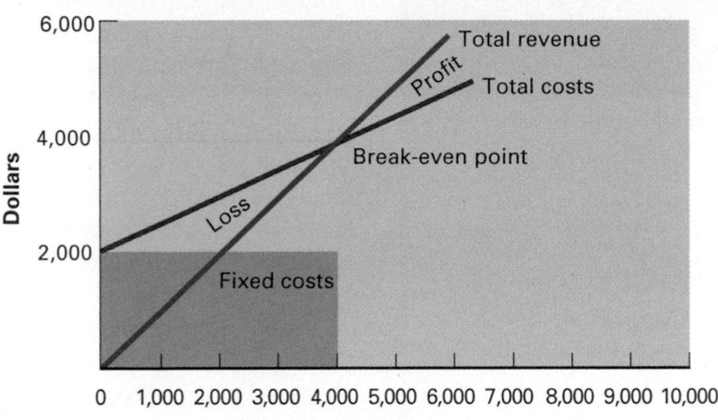

EXHIBIT 16.10

Costs, Revenues, and Break-Even Point for Universal Sportswear

(b) Costs and revenues

Output	Total fixed costs	Average variable costs	Total variable costs	Average total costs	Average revenue (price)	Total revenue	Total costs	Profit or loss
500	$2,000	$0.50	$ 250	$4.50	$1.00	$ 500	$2,250	($1,750)
1,000	2,000	0.50	500	2.50	1.00	1,000	2,500	(1,500)
1,500	2,000	0.50	750	1.83	1.00	1,500	2,750	(1,250)
2,000	2,000	0.50	1,000	1.50	1.00	2,000	3,000	(1,000)
2,500	2,000	0.50	1,250	1.30	1.00	2,500	3,250	(750)
3,000	2,000	0.50	1,500	1.17	1.00	3,000	3,500	(500)
3,500	2,000	0.50	1,750	1.07	1.00	3,500	3,750	(250)
*4,000	2,000	0.50	2,000	1.00	1.00	4,000	4,000	0
4,500	2,000	0.50	2,250	.94	1.00	4,500	4,250	250
5,000	2,000	0.50	2,500	.90	1.00	5,000	4,500	500
5,500	2,000	0.50	2,750	.86	1.00	5,500	4,750	750
6,000	2,000	0.50	3,000	.83	1.00	6,000	5,000	1,000

*Break-even point

Revenue is also $4,000 (4,000 units × $1), giving a net profit of zero dollars at the break-even point of 4,000 units. Notice that once the firm gets past the break-even point, the gap between total revenue and total costs gets wider and wider because both functions are assumed to be linear.

break-even analysis
A method of determining what sales volume must be reached before total revenue equals total costs.

The formula for calculating break-even quantities is simple:

$$\text{Break-even quantity} = \frac{\text{Total fixed costs}}{\text{Fixed cost contribution}}$$

Fixed cost contribution is the price minus the average variable cost. Therefore, for Universal Sportswear,

$$\text{Break-even quantity} = \frac{\$2{,}000}{(\$1.00 - \$.50)}$$

$$= \frac{\$2{,}000}{\$.50}$$

$$= 4{,}000 \text{ units}$$

The advantage of break-even analysis is that it provides a quick estimate of how much the firm must sell to break even and how much profit can be earned if a higher sales volume is obtained. If a firm is operating close to the break-even point,

REVIEW LEARNING OUTCOME

LO 5 Describe cost-oriented pricing strategies

Markup: Cost + x% = Price

Profit Maximization: Price set at point where MR = MC

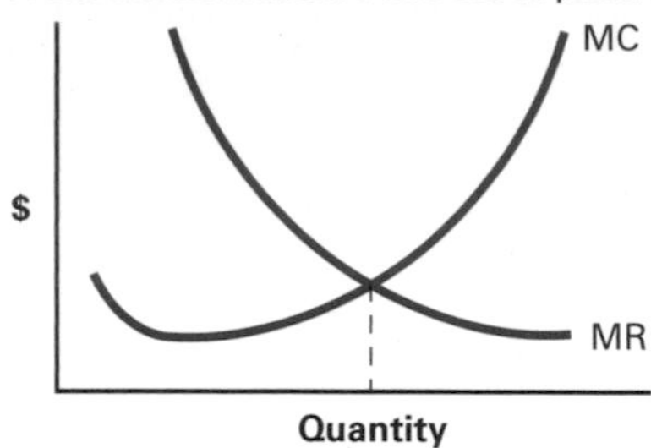

Break-even: Price set at point where total cost = total revenue

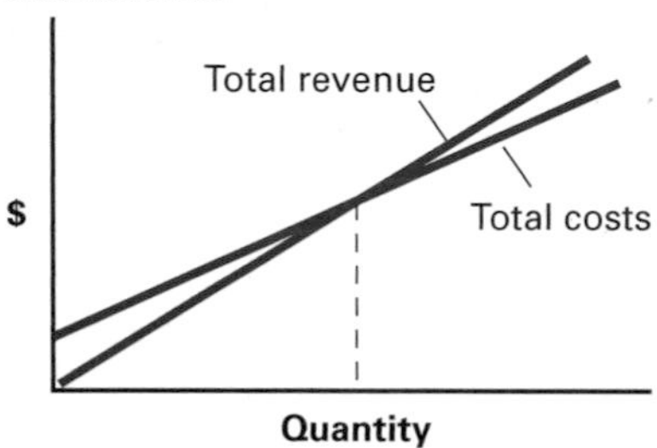

it may want to see what can be done to reduce costs or increase sales. Moreover, in a simple break-even analysis, it is not necessary to compute marginal costs and marginal revenues because price and average cost per unit are assumed to be constant. Also, because accounting data for marginal cost and revenue are frequently unavailable, it is convenient not to have to depend on that information.

Break-even analysis is not without several important limitations. Sometimes it is hard to know whether a cost is fixed or variable. If labor wins a tough guaranteed-employment contract, are the resulting expenses a fixed cost? Are middle-level executives' salaries fixed costs? More important than cost determination is the fact that simple break-even analysis ignores demand. How does Universal Sportswear know it can sell 4,000 units at $1? Could it sell the same 4,000 units at $2 or even $5? Obviously, this information would profoundly affect the firm's pricing decisions.

LO 6

OTHER DETERMINANTS OF PRICE

Other factors besides demand and costs can influence price. For example, the stages in the product life cycle, the competition, the product distribution strategy, the promotion strategy, and perceived quality can all affect pricing.

Stages in the Product Life Cycle

As a product moves through its life cycle (see Chapter 11), the demand for the product and the competitive conditions tend to change:

- *Introductory stage:* Management usually sets prices high during the introductory stage. One reason is that it hopes to recover its development costs quickly. In addition, demand originates in the core of the market (the customers whose needs ideally match the product's attributes) and thus is relatively inelastic. On the other hand, if the target market is highly price sensitive, management often finds it better to price the product at the market level or lower. For example, when Kraft Foods brought out Country Time lemonade, it was priced like similar products in the highly competitive beverage market because the market was price sensitive.
- *Growth stage:* As the product enters the growth stage, prices generally begin to stabilize for several reasons. First, competitors have entered the market, increasing the available supply. Second, the product has begun to appeal to a broader market, often lower-income groups. Finally, economies of scale are lowering costs, and the savings can be passed on to the consumer in the form of lower prices.
- *Maturity stage:* Maturity usually brings further price decreases as competition increases and inefficient, high-cost firms are eliminated. Distribution channels become a significant cost factor, however, because of the need to offer wide product lines for highly segmented markets, extensive service requirements, and the sheer number of dealers necessary to absorb high-volume production. The manufacturers

that remain in the market toward the end of the maturity stage typically offer similar prices. Usually, only the most efficient remain, and they have comparable costs. At this stage, price increases are usually cost initiated, not demand initiated. Nor do price reductions in the late phase of maturity stimulate much demand. Because demand is limited and producers have similar cost structures, the remaining competitors will probably match price reductions.

- *Decline stage*: The final stage of the life cycle may see further price decreases as the few remaining competitors try to salvage the last vestiges of demand. When only one firm is left in the market, prices begin to stabilize. In fact, prices may eventually rise dramatically if the product survives and moves into the specialty goods category, as horse-drawn carriages and vinyl records have.

Is Wal-Mart unbeatable? In its marketing and in its dealings with its suppliers, the retail giant sends a clear message to competitors that it will not be undersold. What would you do if you were in competition with Wal-Mart?

The Competition

Competition varies during the product life cycle, of course, and so at times it may strongly affect pricing decisions. Although a firm may not have any competition at first, the high prices it charges may eventually induce another firm to enter the market. A number of Internet auto sellers, such as Autobytel.com, have sprung up in response to the perceived high profit margins earned by car dealers.

On the other hand, intense competition can sometimes lead to price wars. One company recently took action to avoid a calamitous price war by outsmarting its competition. A company (call it Acme) heard that its competitor was trying to steal some business by offering a low price to one of its best customers. Instead of immediately cutting prices, Acme reps visited three of its competitor's best clients and said they figured the client was paying *x*, the same price that the competitor had quoted to Acme's own customer. Within days, the competitor had retracted its low-price offer to Acme's client. Presumably, the competitor had received calls from three angry clients asking for the same special deal.

Often, in hotly competitive markets, price wars break out. For Christmas 2008, Wal-Mart, which accounts for more than a fourth of all toy sales, sent a clear message to competitors that it would not be undersold. It announced that 10 well-known toys, including some Barbie dolls and Hot Wheels car sets, would retail for $10. This price was 25 to 40 percent below the prices of Toys"R"Us and Amazon.com. Target began quickly matching Wal-Mart's prices.[19]

> *"Target began quickly matching Wal-Mart's prices."*

Distribution Strategy

An effective distribution network can often overcome other minor flaws in the marketing mix.[20] For example, although consumers may perceive a price as being slightly higher than normal, they may buy the product anyway if it is being sold at a convenient retail outlet.

Adequate distribution for a new product can often be attained by offering a larger-than-usual profit margin to distributors. A variation on this strategy is to give dealers a large trade allowance to help offset the costs of promotion and further stimulate demand at the retail level.

Manufacturers have gradually been losing control within the distribution channel to wholesalers and retailers, which often adopt pricing strategies that serve their own

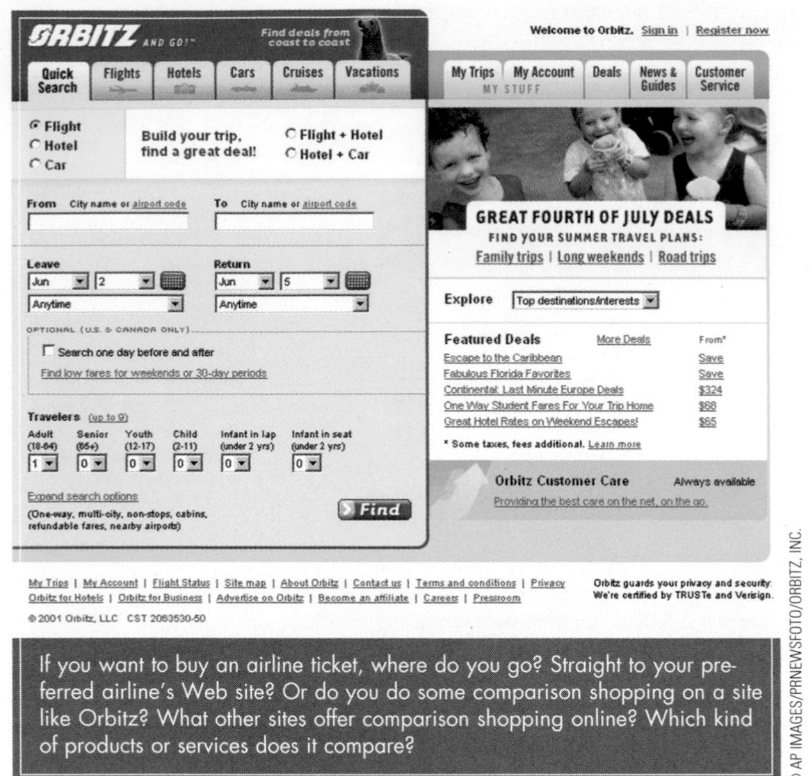

If you want to buy an airline ticket, where do you go? Straight to your preferred airline's Web site? Or do you do some comparison shopping on a site like Orbitz? What other sites offer comparison shopping online? Which kind of products or services does it compare?

purposes. For instance, some distributors are **selling against the brand**: They place well-known brands on the shelves at high prices while offering other brands—typically, their private-label brands, such as Craftsman tools, Kroger canned pears, or Cost Cutter paper towels—at lower prices. Of course, sales of the higher-priced brands decline.

Wholesalers and retailers may also go outside traditional distribution channels to buy gray-market goods. As explained previously, distributors obtain the goods through unauthorized channels for less than they would normally pay, so they can sell the goods with a bigger-than-normal markup or at a reduced price. Imports seem to be particularly susceptible to gray marketing. Porsches, JVC stereos, and Seiko watches are among the brand-name products that have experienced this problem. Although consumers may pay less for gray-market goods, they often find that the manufacturer won't honor the warranty.

Manufacturers can regain some control over price by using an exclusive distribution system, by franchising, or by avoiding doing business with price-cutting discounters. Manufacturers can also package merchandise with the selling price marked on it or place goods on consignment. The best way for manufacturers to control prices, however, is to develop brand loyalty in consumers by delivering quality and value.

selling against the brand
Stocking well-known branded items at high prices in order to sell store brands at discounted prices.

The Impact of the Internet

The Internet, corporate networks, and wireless setups are linking people, machines, and companies around the globe—and connecting sellers and buyers as never before. This link is enabling buyers to quickly and easily compare products and prices, putting them in a better bargaining position. At the same time, the technology allows sellers to collect detailed data about customers' buying habits, preferences, and even spending limits so that the sellers can tailor their products and prices.

Picking a Product to Buy Online The online shopping process begins with selecting a product. If you want a pet, camera, electronics product, or computer but don't know which brand, try **www.activebuyersguide.com**, which will help you narrow your choice. If you want help with outdoor gear, try **http://outside.away.com.** Once you select a brand, you can always get a second opinion at **www.consumersearch.com**. This is an expert site that aggregates reviews from many sources such as *Consumer Digest*, *Consumer Reports*, and *PC World*. For example, a quick click on sleeping bags led to reviews from *Backpacker* and *Outside* magazines. The problem with expert reviews is that each judgment reflects the views of a few people at most. Many shoppers find **www.consumerreview.com** or **www.epinions.com** helpful. These sites provide user opinions of hundreds of different products. Unfortunately, consumer reviews vary widely in quality. Some are quite terse whereas others tend to ramble on and on.

Using Shopping Bots A shopping bot is a program that searches the Web for the best price for a particular item that you wish to purchase. *Bot* is short for *robot*. Shopping bots theoretically give pricing power to the consumer. The more information that the shopper has, the more efficient his or her purchase decision will be. When consumers use their money wisely, they can raise their standard of living by approximately one-third. This applies not only to purchasing but to the wise use of credit as well.

There are two general types of shopping bots. The first is the broad-based type that searches a wide range of product categories such as mySimon.com, DealTime.com, Bizmate.com, pricegrabber.com, and PriceSCAN.com. These sites operate using a Yellow Pages type of model, in that they list every retailer they can find. The second is the niche-oriented type that searches for only one type of product such as computer equipment (CNET.com), books (BookFinder.com), or CDs (CDPriceShop.com).

Most shopping bots give preferential listings to those e-retailers that pay for the privilege. These so-called merchant partners receive about 60 percent of the click-throughs.[21] Typically, the bot lists its merchant partners first, not the retailer that offers the lowest price.

If a bot steers you to really low prices, be careful, as Internet fraud is huge. If you are considering buying from a site that you don't know, check out customer feedback at **www.resellerratings.com** or **http://ratingwonders.com.** Also, if a merchant's site doesn't answer questions about the product, call for details before giving out your credit-card information. Sometimes a really low price is for a reconditioned or refurbished item, or, in the case of clothing and similar items, it may be a "second." Also, ask about in-stock status, pricing breakdowns such as taxes and shipping, and return policies including restocking charges.

In summary, recent research on 1,500 car purchases found that consumers who used the Internet received about a 2 percent lower price. The Internet lowers prices for two distinct reasons: First, the Internet informs consumers. The information that seems to be most valuable to consumers in the auto study was the invoice price of the dealer; it enables them to negotiate a low price at a given dealership. Internet information seems not to help consumers find low-price dealerships. In particular, the Internet does not substitute for searching at multiple dealers, and searching at multiple dealers does not substitute for being better informed.

Second, the incentives provided by online buying services' contracts with dealerships help consumers obtain lower prices through a referral process. Referrals from manufacturer Web sites do not lower prices. Online buying services, such as Autobytel.com or edmunds.com, are more effective because unlike manufacturers, they can exert pressure on dealers by directing incremental business to affiliated (and away from unaffiliated) dealerships.[22]

Internet Auctions The Internet auction business is huge. Part of the lure of buying online is that shoppers don't have to go to a flea market or use up a coveted weekend day or worry about the weather. Plus, bidding itself can be fun and exciting. Among the most popular consumer auction sites are the following:

- **www.auctions.amazon.com:** Links to Sotheby's for qualified sellers of high-end items.
- **www.ebay.com:** The most popular auction site.
- **http://bidz.com/:** Bidz.com buys closeout deals in very large lots and offers them online in their no-reserve auctions.

Even though consumers are spending billions on Internet auctions, business-to-business (B2B) auctions are likely to be the dominant form in the

Americans report millions of online fraud losses each year to the FBI. The average dollar loss per complaint is nearly $700. Don't today's Internet shoppers know that online auction fraud, nondelivery of goods and services, and credit card fraud can happen to anyone? Why do eBay.com users worldwide trade $2,000 worth of goods on the site every second? What does an auction site like eBay have to do to protect consumers and keep them coming back?

future. Recently, Whirlpool began holding online auctions. Participants bid on the price of the items that they would supply to Whirlpool, but with a twist: They had to include the date when Whirlpool would have to pay for the items. The company wanted to see which suppliers would offer the longest grace period before requiring payment. Five auctions held over five months helped Whirlpool uncover savings of close to $2 million and more than doubled the grace period.

Whirlpool's success is a sign that the B2B auction world is shifting from haggling over prices to niggling over parameters of the deal. Warranties, delivery dates, transportation methods, customer support, financing options, and quality have all become bargaining chips.

There is also a dark side to Internet auctions, however, especially those where most participants are consumers. Every day crooks lure hundreds of unsuspecting users with auctions that appear legitimate but are really a hollow shell. They hop from user ID to user ID, feeding the system with fake information and stolen credit cards so that the auction site can't tell who they are. In response to a dramatic increase in auction-fraud complaints, the Federal Trade Commission banded together with the National Association of Attorneys General to conduct Operation Bidder Beware, a nationwide crackdown and consumer-education campaign.

Americans reported $240 million in online fraud losses in 2007 to the FBI. This was an increase of $40 million over the previous year. The Internet Crime Complaint Center received over 207,000 complaints in 2007. The average dollar loss per complaint referred to various law enforcement agencies was $680. Online auction fraud was the most reported crime followed by nondelivery of goods and services, confidence scams, and credit card fraud.[23]

Promotion Strategy

Price is often used as a promotional tool to increase consumer interest. The weekly flyers sent out by grocery stores in the Sunday newspaper, for instance, advertise many products with special low prices. Crested Butte Ski Resort in Colorado tried a unique twist on price promotions. It made the unusual offer of free skiing between Thanksgiving and Christmas. Its only revenues were voluntary contributions from lodging and restaurant owners who benefited from the droves of skiers taking advantage of the promotion. Lodging during the slack period is now booked solid, and on the busiest days 9,000 skiers jam slopes designed for about 6,500. Crested Butte Resort no longer loses money during this time of the year.

Pricing can be a tool for trade promotions as well. For example, Levi's Dockers (casual men's pants) are very popular with white-collar men ages 25 to 45, a growing and lucrative market. Sensing an opportunity, rival pants-maker Bugle Boy began offering similar pants at cheaper wholesale prices, which gave retailers a bigger gross margin than they were getting with Dockers. Levi Strauss had to either lower prices or risk its $400 million annual Dockers sales. Although Levi Strauss intended its cheapest Dockers to retail for $35, it started selling Dockers to retailers for $18 a pair. Retailers could then advertise Dockers at a very attractive retail price of $25.

Guaranteed Price Matching

Closely related to promotion pricing is the price guarantee. In its most basic form, a firm promotes the fact that it will match any competitor's price. Others, such as Hotwire.com, claim that they will refund double the difference if you find a lower airfare or hotel price. One of your authors recently booked a hotel on Hotwire.com and subsequently found a lower rate through Mobissimo.com. Mobissimo is a Web crawler that searches over 175 sites and then passes you directly to the site that you select. After finding the cheaper rate, Hotwire credited his account for $160—double the difference in prices! On the downside, the same author booked a car on Hotwire for a week for $265. He had to cancel the trip and Hotwire kept his $265 because of its "no cancellation" policy.

Research shows that when a retailer offers a price-matching guarantee, it is signaling to the target market that it is positioned as a low-price dealer. Conversely, a lack of a price-matching guarantee signals a high-service positioning.[24] A second study found different reactions to price matching depending upon whether the consumer was price conscious or not. Nonprice conscious consumers perceived a deep refund (to match a competitor's price) as a signal of low prices. Yet for the price conscious consumer, the same deep refund was perceived as the retailer having increased prices.[25] Certainly not a desired outcome for the retailer.

Demands of Large Customers

Manufacturers find that their large customers such as Wal-Mart, JCPenney, and other department stores often make specific pricing demands that the suppliers must agree to. Department stores are making greater-than-ever demands on their suppliers to cover the heavy discounts and markdowns on their own selling floors. They want suppliers to guarantee their stores' profit margins, and they insist on cash rebates if the guarantee isn't met. They are also exacting fines for violations of ticketing, packing, and shipping rules. Cumulatively, the demands are nearly wiping out profits for all but the very biggest suppliers, according to fashion designers and garment makers.

In 2008, with gas, grain, and dairy prices exploding, you'd think the biggest seller of corn flakes and Cocoa Puffs would be getting hit by rising food costs. But Wal-Mart temporarily rolled back prices on hundreds of food items by as much as 30 percent. How? By pressuring vendors to take costs out of the supply chain. "When our grocery suppliers bring price increases, we don't just accept them," says Pamela Kohn, Wal-Mart's general merchandise manager for perishables.[26] To be sure, Wal-Mart isn't the only retailer working to cut fat from the food chain, but as the largest grocer—Wal-Mart's food and consumables revenue is nearly $100 billion—it has a disproportionate amount of leverage. Here's how the retailer is throwing its weight around.

Shrink the Goods Ever wonder why that cereal box is only two-thirds full? Foodmakers love big boxes because they serve as billboards on store shelves. Wal-Mart has been working to change that by promising suppliers that their shelf space won't shrink even if their boxes do. As a result, some of its vendors have reengineered their packaging. General Mills' Hamburger Helper is now made with denser pasta shapes, allowing the same amount of food to fit into a 20 percent smaller box at the same price. The change has saved 890,000 pounds of paper fiber and eliminated 500 trucks from the road, giving General Mills a cushion to absorb some of the rising costs.[27]

Cut Out the Middleman Wal-Mart typically buys its brand-name coffee from a supplier, which buys from a cooperative of growers, which works with a roaster—which means "there are a whole bunch of people muddled in the middle," says Wal-Mart spokeswoman Tara Raddohl.[28] In April of 2008 the chain began buying directly from a cooperative of Brazilian coffee farmers for its Sam's Choice brand, cutting three or four steps out of the supply chain.

Go Local Wal-Mart has been going green, but not entirely for the reasons you might think. By sourcing more product locally—it now sells Wisconsin-grown yellow corn in 56 stores in or near Wisconsin—it is able to cut shipping costs.

The Relationship of Price to Quality

As mentioned at the beginning of the chapter, when a purchase decision involves uncertainty, consumers tend to rely on a high price as a predictor of good quality. Reliance on price as an indicator of quality seems to occur for all products, but it

prestige pricing
Charging a high price to help promote a high-quality image.

reveals itself more strongly for some items than for others.[29] Among the products that benefit from this phenomenon are coffee, stockings, aspirin, salt, floor wax, shampoo, clothing, furniture, perfume, whiskey, and many services. In the absence of other information, people typically assume that prices are higher because the products contain better materials, because they are made more carefully, or, in the case of professional services, because the provider has more expertise. In other words, consumers assume that "You get what you pay for."

Research has found that products that are perceived to be of high quality tend to benefit more from price promotions than products perceived to be of lower quality.[30] However, when perceived high- and lower-quality products are offered in settings where consumers have difficulty making comparisons, then price promotions have an equal effect on sales. Comparisons are more difficult in end-of-aisle displays, feature advertising, and the like.

Knowledgeable merchants take these consumer attitudes into account when devising their pricing strategies. **Prestige pricing** is charging a high price to help promote a high-quality image. A successful prestige pricing strategy requires a retail price that is reasonably consistent with consumers' expectations. No one goes shopping at a Gucci's shop in New York and expects to pay $9.95 for a pair of loafers. In fact, demand would fall drastically at such a low price. Bayer aspirin would probably lose market share over the long run if it lowered its prices. A new mustard packaged in a crockery jar was not successful until its price was doubled.

Some of the latest research on price-quality relationships has focused on consumer durable goods. The researchers first conducted a study to ascertain the dimensions of quality. These are (1) ease of use; (2) versatility (the ability of a product to perform more functions, special stitch types on sewing machines, or be more flexible, continuous temperature controls on microwave ovens); (3) durability; (4) serviceability (ease of obtaining quality repairs); (5) performance; and (6) prestige. The researchers found that when consumers focused on prestige and/or durability to assess quality, price was a strong indicator of perceived overall quality. Price was less important as an indicator of quality if the consumer was focusing on one of the other four dimensions of quality.[31]

Other research has found three basic effects associated with the price quality relationship. These are prestige, hedonistic, and allocative effects.[32] As noted earlier, the purchase, use, display, and consumption of goods and services that bear high prices may provide a means to gain social status. Therefore, consumers also may perceive price as an indicator of prestige. For example, some consumers purchase an expensive car not because of their quality perceptions per se but because of their perception that the purchase will signal prestige and wealth to others.

High purchase prices may also create feelings of pleasure and excitement associated with consuming higher-priced products. This is the hedonistic effect. Hedonistic consumption refers to pursuing emotional responses associated with using a product, such as pleasure, excitement, arousal, good feelings, and fun. Hedonistic consumers may prefer high prices as a means of affirming their own self-worth and to satisfy their egos.

The allocative effect refers to the notion that consumers must allocate their budgets across alternative goods and services. The more you spend on one product the less you have to spend on all others. Consumers sensitive to the allocative effects likely prefer low prices. However, managers must be aware that setting low prices or lowering prices with a discount offer not only attracts buyers but also threatens to lower perceptions of product quality, prestige value, and hedonistic value. This is because of the negative cues associated with lower selling prices.[33]

As incomes rise in less developed countries, the prestige and hedonistic effects of price can begin to come into play. The Global Perspectives box below explains how one multinational firm handles this opportunity.

GLOBAL Perspectives

L'Oreal Plays the Price-Quality Card in India

In India, most beauty products sell for less than a dollar. L'Oreal SA is betting its future there on products costing three to 20 times as much. The French cosmetics giant has embarked on a strategy that sharply differs from that of its rivals. Having failed to turn a profit selling low-priced shampoo in India, it now hopes to capture the growing ranks of middle-class Indian women by luring them upscale. In shops across the country, L'Oreal's offerings include a $5.60 Garnier Nutrisse hair dye, a $17 L'Oreal Paris face powder and a $25 Vichy sunscreen. Jaya Sethi says she's willing to splurge. The office assistant in New Delhi recently bought two bottles of the Garnier hair dye. Ms. Sethi used to buy cheaper dyes made of henna plant extract, but says the foreign brand is "good quality" and "fun."

Racing to expand in a competitive global marketplace, L'Oreal is tapping into a powerful demographic force: India's emerging middle class, estimated at 200 million people. Over the past decade, foreign brands, from Tommy Hilfiger jeans to Absolut vodka, have moved in to capture a slice of the market. At the heart of the transformation in consumer spending is a cultural shift among Indian women. Decades of poverty instilled a strong sense of price-consciousness in women, which was passed on from mothers to daughters. But the generation that came of age during the market liberalization of the early 1990s is more willing to splurge on luxuries, from bottled water to lipstick and eating out. "For these people, consumption is a way of life," says Neelesh Hundekari, principal at AT Kearney Inc., a management consulting firm in Mumbai.

L'Oreal's strategy stands out as particularly aggressive compared with its competitors. Most Western cosmetics companies stock grocery stores in India with low-priced basic shampoo and cold creams that compete with an array of local brands. For example, market leader Hindustan Unilever Ltd. sells 70-cent bottles of body lotion and 90-cent shampoo. Its target audience includes the more than 800 million people in India who live on less than $2 a day. In contrast, L'Oreal's biggest seller in India is its Excellence Crème hair color—priced at $11 a bottle. Teeing off its success at the high end of the market, L'Oreal recently accelerated its rollout of mass-market products, too, including a $2.70 hair dye and small packets of shampoo costing less than $1. But many L'Oreal products are still relatively pricey by Indian standards. "We don't do poor products for poor people," says Alain Evrard, managing director for L'Oreal's Africa, Orient, and Pacific zone.

Mr. Evrard says his first step was to understand what products would best resonate with middle-class working women. He spent months speaking with advertising executives and editors of fashion magazines including *Elle*, which had launched in India in 1996. He quizzed L'Oreal's local employees on their families' consumer habits, focusing on hair care. He says the breakthrough came when some of these employees complained that they and their peers were getting gray hairs—and they were still only in their twenties. At the time, Western-style, do-it-yourself hair-coloring kits barely existed in India; women used henna and other ammonia-based liquids and powders to cover their gray. But these women said ammonia dried out their hair, while henna faded quickly. Moreover, hair dye was one of the few items Hindustan did not make.

So in late 1996, Mr. Evrard introduced L'Oreal Excellence Crème into India. Excellence Crème was one of the French company's most innovative and pricey mass-market products in Europe. In cream form, dye is considered more gentle on hair than liquid products. In India, it cost $9 at the time, or about the same as in France. L'Oreal set out to market it as a luxury purchase. The company signed on Diana Hayden, winner of the Miss World contest in 1997, as L'Oreal's first Indian advertising face. "For me, beauty starts with beautiful hair," Ms Hayden cooed in one television commercial. Two years later, Ms. Hayden attended the Cannes film festival on behalf of L'Oreal, along with other top models such as Claudia Schiffer.[34]

What pricing effects is L'Oreal appealing to with Indian women? Do you think that L'Oreal can use the same strategy in China? Why or why not?

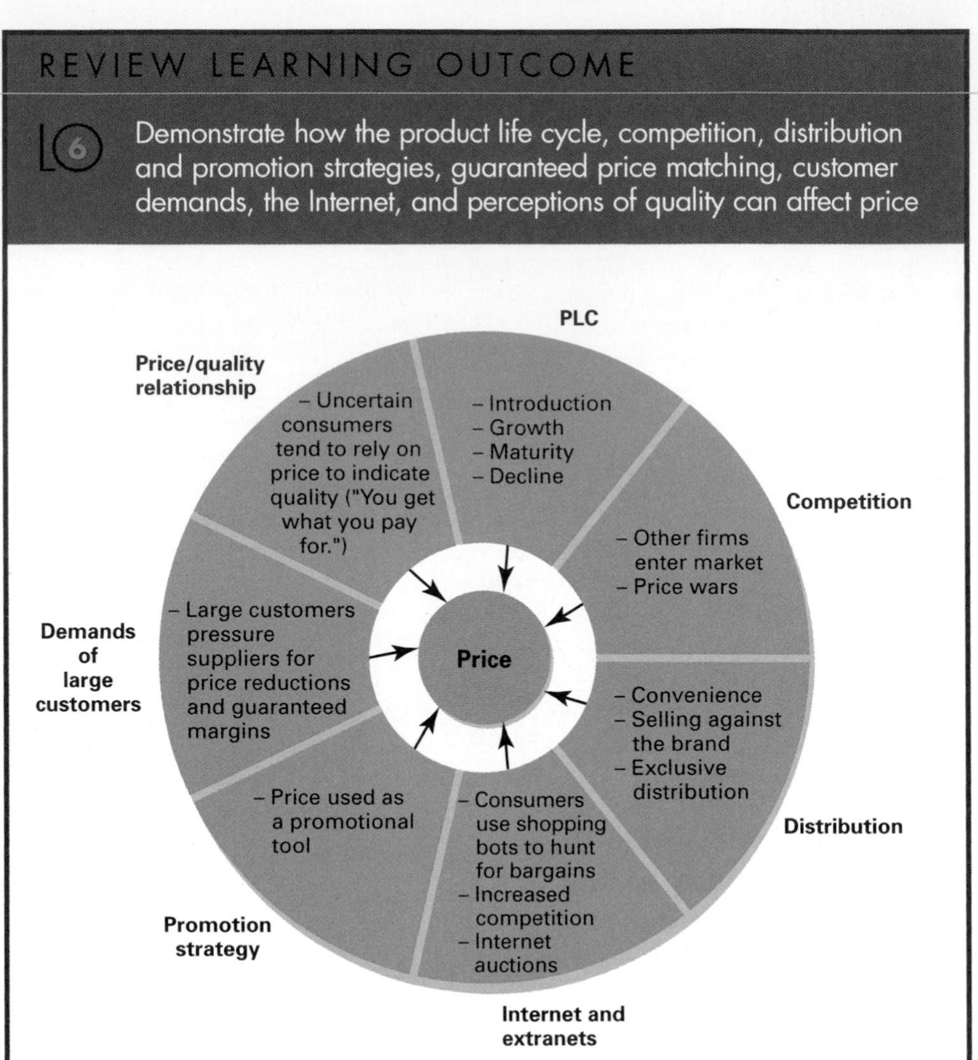

HOW TO SET A PRICE ON A PRODUCT OR SERVICE

Setting the right price on a product is a four-step process (see Exhibit 16.11):

1. Establish pricing goals.
2. Estimate demand, costs, and profits.
3. Choose a price strategy to help determine a base price.
4. Fine-tune the base price with pricing tactics.

The first three steps are discussed next; the fourth step is discussed later in the chapter.

Establish Pricing Goals

The first step in setting the right price is to establish pricing goals. Recall that pricing objectives fall into three categories: profit oriented, sales oriented, and status quo. These goals are derived from the firm's overall objectives. If, for example, a company's objective is to be the dominant sales leader in an industry, then it will pursue a sales-oriented market share pricing goal. A conservative organization that is attempting to lower risks by being a follower, rather than attempting to be a market leader, may establish a status quo goal. This company is simply trying to preserve its position in the marketplace. Finally, a company committed to maximizing shareholder value will establish aggressive profit-oriented pricing goals.

A good understanding of the marketplace and of the consumer can sometimes tell a manager very quickly whether a goal is realistic. For example, if firm A's objective is a 20 percent target return on investment (ROI), and its product development and implementation costs are \$5 million, the market must be rather large or must support the price required to earn a 20 percent ROI. Assume that company B has a pricing objective that all new products must reach at least 15 percent market share within 3 years after their introduction. A thorough study of the environment may convince the marketing manager that the competition is too strong and the market share goal can't be met.

All pricing objectives have trade-offs that managers must weigh. A profit maximization objective may require a bigger initial investment than the firm can commit or wants to commit. Reaching the desired market share often means sacrificing short-term profit because without careful management, long-term profit goals may not be met. Meeting the competition is the easiest pricing goal to implement. But can managers really afford to ignore demand and costs, the life-cycle stage, and other considerations? When creating pricing objectives, managers must consider these trade-offs in light of the target customer, the environment, and the company's overall objectives.

EXHIBIT 16.11

Steps in Setting the Right Price on a Product

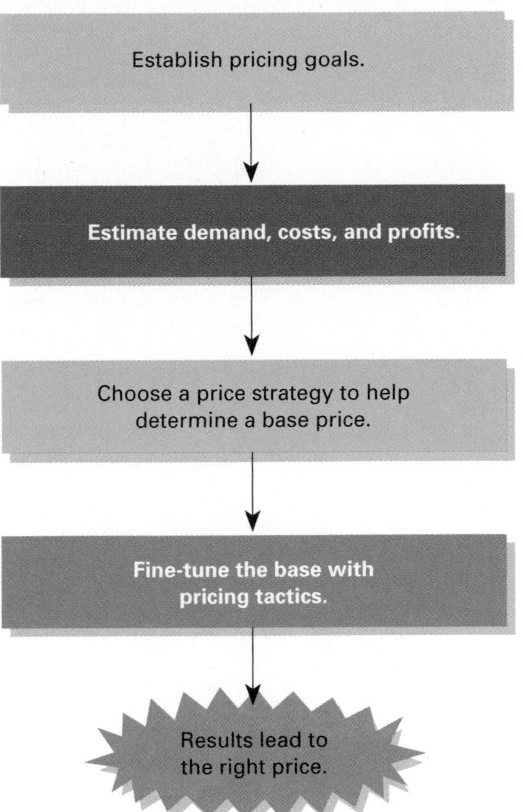

Estimate Demand, Costs, and Profits

You've learned that total revenue is a function of price and quantity demanded and that quantity demanded depends on elasticity. Some key questions that a manager might consider when conducting marketing research on demand and elasticity are

- What price is so low they would question its quality?
- What is the highest price at which the product would still be a bargain?
- What is the price at which the product is starting to get expensive?
- What is the price at which the product becomes too expensive to consider buying?[35]

After establishing pricing goals, managers should estimate total revenue at a variety of prices. Next, they should determine corresponding costs for each price. They are then ready to estimate how much profit, if any, and how much market share can be earned at each possible price. These data become the heart of the developing price policy. Managers can study the options in light of revenues, costs, and profits. In turn, this information can help determine which price can best meet the firm's pricing goals.

Choose a Price Strategy

The basic, long-term pricing framework for a good or service should be a logical extension of the pricing objectives. The marketing manager's chosen **price strategy** defines the initial price and gives direction for price movements over the product life cycle.

price strategy
A basic, long-term pricing framework, which establishes the initial price for a product and the intended direction for price movements over the product life cycle.

The price strategy sets a competitive price in a specific market segment, based on a well-defined positioning strategy. Changing a price level from premium to superpremium may require a change in the product itself, the target customers served, the promotional strategy, or the distribution channels. Thus, changing a price strategy can require

price skimming
A pricing policy whereby a firm charges a high introductory price, often coupled with heavy promotion.

dramatic alterations in the marketing mix. A carmaker cannot successfully compete in the superpremium category if the car looks and drives like an economy car.

A company's freedom in pricing a new product and devising a price strategy depends on the market conditions and the other elements of the marketing mix. If a firm launches a new item resembling several others already on the market, its pricing freedom will be restricted. To succeed, the company will probably have to charge a price close to the average market price. In contrast, a firm that introduces a totally new product with no close substitutes will have considerable pricing freedom.

Most companies do not do a good job of doing research to create a price strategy. A recent study found that only about 8 percent of the companies surveyed conducted serious pricing research to support the development of an effective pricing strategy. In fact, 88 percent of them did little or no serious pricing research. McKinsey & Co.'s Pricing Benchmark Survey estimated that only about 15 percent of companies do serious pricing research. A Coopers & Lybrand study found that 87 percent of the surveyed companies had changed prices in the previous year. Only 13 percent of the price changes, however, came after a scheduled review of pricing strategy.[36]

These numbers indicate that strategic pricing decisions tend to be made without an understanding of the likely buyer or the competitive response. Further, the research shows that managers often make tactical pricing decisions without reviewing how they may fit into the firm's overall pricing or marketing strategy. The data suggest that many companies make pricing decisions and changes without an existing process for managing the pricing activity. As a result, many of them do not have a serious pricing strategy and do not conduct pricing research to develop their strategy.[37]

Often companies will abandon a skimming strategy over time, but at Chanel that is not the case. Managers destroy unsold inventory as a way to maintain higher prices and avoid any suggestion of putting product on the market at a discount.

Companies that do serious planning for creating a price strategy can select from three basic approaches: price skimming, penetration pricing, and status quo pricing. A discussion of each type follows.

Price Skimming Price skimming is sometimes called a "market-plus" approach to pricing because it denotes a high price relative to the prices of competing products. The term **price skimming** is derived from the phrase "skimming the cream off the top." Companies often use this strategy for new products when the product is perceived by the target market as having unique advantages. For example, Caterpillar sets premium prices on its construction equipment to support and capture its high perceived value. Genzyme Corporation introduced Ceredase as the first effective treatment for Gaucher's disease. The pill allows patients to avoid years of painful physical deterioration and lead normal lives. The cost of a year's supply for one patient can exceed $300,000.

Often companies will use skimming initially and then lower prices over time. This is called "sliding down the demand curve." Hardcover book publishers, such as HarperCollins and Random House, lower the price when the books are re-released in paperback. Calloway lowers the price of its old model golf clubs as new models hit the sales floor. Yet some manufacturers such as Porsche and Cuisinart, the maker of kitchen appliances, maintain skimming prices throughout a product's life cycle. A manager of the factory that produces Chanel purses (retailing for over $2,000 each) told one of your authors that the company takes back unsold inventory and destroys it rather than selling it at a discount. Retailers such as Tiffany and Neiman Marcus maintain skimming policies. Though both retailers occasionally have sales, their basic price strategy is price skimming.

Price skimming works best when the market is willing to buy the product even though it carries an above-average price. If, for example, some purchasing agents feel that Caterpillar equipment is far superior to competitors' products, then Caterpillar can charge premium prices successfully. Firms can also effectively use price skimming when a product is well protected legally, when it represents a technological breakthrough, or when it has in some other way blocked the entry of competitors. Managers may follow a skimming strategy when production cannot be expanded rapidly because of technological difficulties, shortages, or constraints imposed by the skill and time required to produce a product. As long as demand is greater than supply, skimming is an attainable strategy.

A successful skimming strategy enables management to recover its product development or "educational" costs quickly. (Often consumers must be "taught" the advantages of a radically new item, such as Viking's new combination steam/convection oven that lists for $4,440. Even if the market perceives an introductory price as too high, managers can easily correct the problem by lowering the price. Firms often feel it is better to test the market at a high price and then lower the price if sales are too slow. They are tacitly saying, "If there are any premium-price buyers in the market, let's reach them first and maximize our revenue per unit." Successful skimming strategies are not limited to products. Well-known athletes, entertainers, lawyers, and hairstylists are experts at price skimming. Naturally, a skimming strategy will encourage competitors to enter the market.

Above all, if price skimming is to be successful, customers must perceive a high value for the product or service. Otherwise, failure can come at a high price. Iridium phones are an example of a technology-driven, feature-loaded, high-cost, high-price innovation. The phones were billed as a "use anywhere" mobile phone system. The original developers of the system poured $5 billion into a 66-satellite system. But phones and needed accessories took up so much space that they required a special briefcase. The purchase price for a phone system was $3,000, and airtime fees were $7 per minute. At the same time, cellular phones—with more limited coverage but adequate for many customers—were selling for less than $100 and were much more "user-friendly." Though the Iridium system was technologically brilliant, it was clear from its inception that customers would neither pay the high purchase price nor accept the high user fees. Approximately 50,000 customers purchased phone systems, but this was well below the volume required to sustain the business. The original owners sold the system for $25 million.[38]

penetration pricing
A pricing policy whereby a firm charges a relatively low price for a product initially as a way to reach the mass market.

Penetration Pricing Penetration pricing is at the opposite end of the spectrum from skimming. **Penetration pricing** means charging a relatively low price for a product in order to reach the mass market. The low price is designed to capture a large share of a substantial market, resulting in lower production costs. If a marketing manager has made obtaining a large market share the firm's pricing objective, penetration pricing is a logical choice.

Penetration pricing does mean lower profit per unit, however. Therefore, to reach the break-even point, it requires a higher volume of sales than would a skimming policy. If reaching a high volume of sales takes a long time, then the recovery of product development costs will also be slow. As you might expect, penetration pricing tends to discourage competition.

Procter & Gamble examined the electric toothbrush market and noted that most electric brushes cost over $50. The company brought out the Crest SpinBrush that works on batteries and sells for just $5. It is now the nation's

Dollar General, like most dollar stores, sells staple products at cut-rate prices. Dollar stores are now one of the fastest-growing retailers in America. The chains can put their much smaller stores right in downtown neighborhoods, closer to where people live.

best-selling toothbrush, manual or electric, and has helped the Crest brand of products become P&G's twelfth billion-dollar brand.[39]

A penetration strategy tends to be effective in a price-sensitive market. Price should decline more rapidly when demand is elastic because the market can be expanded through a lower price. Also, price sensitivity and greater competitive pressure should lead to a lower initial price and a relatively slow decline in the price later or to a stable low price.

Although Wal-Mart is associated with penetration pricing, other chains have done an excellent job of following this strategy as well. Dollar stores, those bare-bones, strip-mall chains that sell staples at cut-rate prices, are now the fastest-growing retailers in America. They've become an alternative for a growing legion of shoppers who find Wal-Mart a bit too pricey or a bit too hard to get to. Led by Dollar General, Family Dollar, and Dollar Tree, the sector adds about 1,500 stores per year. Wal-Mart usually opens its huge stores on the edge of town. Dollar chains can put their much smaller stores right in downtown neighborhoods, closer to where people live. Parking is usually a snap, and shoppers can be in and out in less time than it takes to hike across a jumbo Wal-Mart lot. And as their name implies, the dollar stores offer low prices, sometimes even beating Wal-Mart. "Wal-Mart competes on price and assortment," says David A. Perdue, Dollar General's chief executive. "We compete on price and convenience."[40]

Another form of extreme penetration pricing that has dramatically increased sales during the recent economic downturn is salvage or surplus grocers. Salvage grocers sell "close-outs" which include products that manufacturers have discontinued, seasonal items that are outdated, and goods that are near the date when manufacturers expect freshness to wane. Many such grocers also sell products that were damaged in transit but remain edible, such as a dented box of Cheerios. Prices tend to be significantly lower than those at conventional stores and big discounters like Wal-Mart Stores Inc.[41]

If a firm has a low fixed cost structure and each sale provides a large contribution to those fixed costs, penetration pricing can boost sales and provide large increases in profits—but only if the market size grows or if competitors choose not to respond. Low prices can attract additional buyers to the market. The increased sales can justify production expansion or the adoption of new technologies, both of which can reduce costs. And, if firms have excess capacity, even low-priced business can provide incremental dollars toward fixed costs.

Penetration pricing can also be effective if an experience curve will cause costs per unit to drop significantly. The experience curve proposes that per-unit costs will go down as a firm's production experience increases. On average, for each doubling of production, a firm can expect per-unit costs to decline by roughly 20 percent. Cost declines can be significant in the early stages of production. Manufacturers that fail to take advantage of these effects will find themselves at a competitive cost disadvantage relative to others that are further along the curve.

The big advantage of penetration pricing is that it typically discourages or blocks competition from entering a market. The disadvantage is that penetration means gearing up for mass production to sell a large volume at a low price. What if the volume fails to materialize? The company will face huge losses from building or converting a factory to produce the failed product. Skimming, in contrast, lets a firm "stick its toe in the water" and see if limited demand exists at the high price. If not, the firm can simply lower the price. Skimming lets a company start out with a small production facility and expand it gradually as price falls and demand increases.

Penetration pricing can also prove disastrous for a prestige brand that adopts the strategy in an effort to gain market share and fails. When Omega—once a more prestigious brand than Rolex—was trying to improve the market share of its watches, it adopted a penetration pricing strategy that flooded the market with lower-priced products and destroyed the brand's image. Omega never gained sufficient share on its lower-priced/lower-image competitors to justify destroying its brand image and high-priced position with upscale buyers. Lacoste clothing experienced a similar outcome from a penetration pricing strategy.

Status Quo Pricing The third basic price strategy a firm may choose is status quo pricing, also called *meeting the competition* or *going rate pricing*. It means charging a price identical to or very close to the competition's price. JCPenney, for example, makes sure it is charging comparable prices by sending representatives to shop at similar retailers.

Although status quo pricing has the advantage of simplicity, its disadvantage is that the strategy may ignore demand or cost or both. If the firm is comparatively small, however, meeting the competition may be the safest route to long-term survival.

CUSTOMER Experience

Are Consumers Rational about Prices?

Dan Ariely is a professor at Duke University's Fuqua School of Business and a leading expert in behavioral economics, which explores the inner processes we all rely on to make decisions. Dr. Ariely is also the author of *Predictably Irrational: The Hidden Forces That Shape Our Decisions.* He spoke with Alden M. Hayashi, senior editor of *MIT Sloan Management Review*, for the Business Insight Journal Report.

Business Insight: Your research suggests that, when selling a new product, companies should always compare it with something that the customer is already familiar with, even if the product is so novel that there really isn't something similar on the market.

Dr. Ariely: Absolutely, for two reasons. One is because the "space" for a new product in people's minds is ill-defined, and it's very hard for people to figure out how to place a value on something in isolation. The second thing is that we are mainly creatures of habit and decisions are actually quite tough. How many times a day do we really want to contemplate buying something by analyzing everything, thinking about the opportunity cost, and so on? So we rely on our old past decisions, including comparisons to other products.

Take, for example, TiVo. What's the value of TiVo? How do you compute that? Do you take into account how many minutes of commercials you're saving, multiply that by your income per hour, deduct from it the breaks you get to go to the bathroom and take a snack, and so on? That would be very, very hard to do. So instead, you rely on your past impressions and use that to infer value. If companies want to understand how people make decisions about their products, they have to take the decision process into account.

Business Insight: So the trick for companies is to figure out what to compare their new product to.

Dr. Ariely: Imagine two universes. In the first, TiVo is compared to a VCR and is introduced at $200. In the second, it's compared to a computer and is introduced at $1,000. Then imagine that in both worlds the price goes to $500. In the first universe, people will presumably be outraged and nobody will buy it. In the second, people will think it's a great deal. And that's why the principle of relativity is so important, especially for new products, because we just have such a hard time computing the real value of things.

Business Insight: And in the comparison you can define the product.

Dr. Arielly: Yes, and the thing you need to understand is that that definition will last for a long, long time. We can speculate, for example, about the iPhone. Apple put this iPhone out at $600 and immediately reduced it to $400. Now, it could have been a mistake but it also could have been a smart trick because the question to the consumer at that time was, what is the comparison price? All of a sudden, something can look like a great deal at $400 when it was $600 just a few weeks earlier.

If Apple had introduced the iPhone at $400, it would have been a different story. But the initial $600 price and then the $400 helped, I think, create a very high price point in people's minds. And now that the iPhone is being offered at $200, it looks like a fantastic deal because we still have these very high prices sticking in our minds.

Business Insight: Many outsiders have assumed that Apple made a mistake in initially offering the iPhone at $600 because there were so many outraged customers who had paid $600 only to see the price drop to $400.

Dr. Ariely: But still the high price point is stuck in people's minds; everybody remembers it was $600.[42]

Can you always determine the value of something after you have used it? You probably use e-mail for free. What if all providers started charging $30 per month? Would you pay? How about $75? Do you think that most people make irrational pricing decisions about big ticket items?

Source: Reprinted with permission of *The Wall Street Journal* from "The Irrationalities of Product Pricing", *Wall Street Journal*, September 22, 2008, R2.

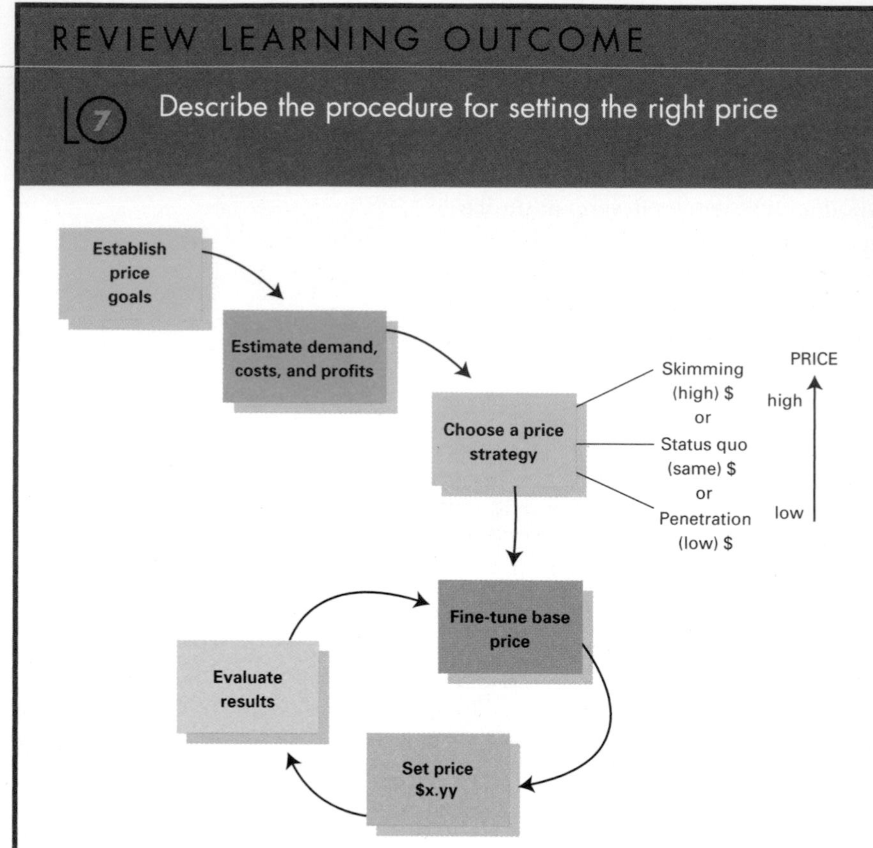

Consumers have rather complex reactions to prices of new products whether the firm uses skimming, penetration, or status quo. The Customer Experience box features an interview with a well-known behavioral economist that sheds light on consumers' price perceptions.

LO 8

THE LEGALITY AND ETHICS OF PRICE STRATEGY

As we mentioned in Chapter 4, some pricing decisions are subject to government regulation. Before marketing managers establish any price strategy, they should know the laws that limit their decision making. Among the issues that fall into this category are unfair trade practices, price fixing, price discrimination, and predatory pricing.

unfair trade practice acts
Laws that prohibit wholesalers and retailers from selling below cost.

price fixing
An agreement between two or more firms on the price they will charge for a product.

Unfair Trade Practices

In over half the states, **unfair trade practice acts** put a floor under wholesale and retail prices. Selling below cost in these states is illegal. Wholesalers and retailers must usually take a certain minimum percentage markup on their combined merchandise cost and transportation cost. The most common markup figures are 6 percent at the retail level and 2 percent at the wholesale level. If a specific wholesaler or retailer can provide "conclusive proof" that operating costs are lower than the minimum required figure, lower prices may be allowed.

The intent of unfair trade practice acts is to protect small local firms from giants like Wal-Mart and Target, which operate very efficiently on razor-thin profit margins. State enforcement of unfair trade practice laws has generally been lax, however, partly because low prices benefit local consumers.

Price Fixing

Price fixing is an agreement between two or more firms on the price they will charge for a product. For instance, two or more executives from competing firms might meet to decide how much to charge for a product or to decide which of them will submit the lowest bid on a certain contract. Such practices are illegal under the Sherman Act and the Federal Trade Commission Act. Offenders have received fines and sometimes prison terms. Price fixing is one area where the law is quite clear, and the Justice Department's enforcement is vigorous.

Chinese manufacturers currently supply more than 85 percent of the vitamin C used in the United States. Just like the oil cartel, they can heavily influence world prices. After an agreement among China's four largest producers, spot prices for vitamin C rose to as high as $9 a kilogram from lows of less than $3. Chinese companies deny breaking U.S. law and have hired U.S. law firms to mount a defense. The companies are expected to argue they are acting as agents of the Chinese government and therefore aren't subject to American laws against price fixing.[43]

In 2006, several major air-cargo carriers were raided by U.S. and European antitrust enforcers as part of a trans-Atlantic investigation into possible price-fixing and collusion in air cargo. Federal Bureau of Investigation agents raided British Airways facilities at New York's Kennedy Airport. In August 2007, British Airways pleaded guilty and was sentenced to pay a $300-million fine for conspiring to fix cargo rates for international air shipments and conspiring to fix passenger fuel surcharges for long-haul flights. At least two senior British Airways executives resigned amid the probe.

The price-fixing probe, which has been carried out by regulators from the European Union and the United Kingdom along with the U.S. Justice Department, has enveloped a range of other carriers. Other airlines that have pleaded guilty to price-fixing charges to include Air France, Cathay Pacific Airways, Japan Airlines, Korean Air Lines, Martinair, KLM Royal Dutch Airlines, Scandinavian group SAS, and Australia's Quantas. Fines assessed by the Justice Department have totaled more than $1.2 billion.[44]

In a recent year the Supreme Court abandoned the "per se" rule. Instead, the court ruled, resale price maintenance agreements should be judged by a "rule of reason" analysis that balances pro-competitive justifications and anticompetitive harms.

In October 2008, the Justice Department announced that a former British Airways executive will serve eight months in jail and pay a $20,000 criminal fine for conspiracy to fix rates on international air cargo shipments.[45]

Similarly, Fresh Del Monte Produce paid $3 million on fixing the price of bananas. In a little over a year, the price of bananas jumped from $5.40 a box to more than $10 a box. Settlements of $2.5 million were also reached with Chiquita Brands and Dole Food.[46]

Price-fixing prosecution is not limited to huge, global competitors. In San Diego, two groups of anesthesiologists recently settled federal charges that they conspired to set prices for Sharp Grossmont Hospital.[47]

Most price-fixing cases focus on high prices charged to customers. A reverse form of price fixing occurs when powerful buyers force their suppliers' prices down. Recently, Maine blueberry growers alleged that four big processors conspired to push down the price they would pay for fresh wild berries. A state court jury agreed and awarded millions in damages. In South Carolina, International Paper Company faces a lawsuit alleging that it conspired with its timber buyers to depress softwood prices in several states. In Alabama and Pennsylvania, federal antitrust enforcers targeted insurance companies that imposed contracts forcing down fees charged by doctors and hospitals. The insurers abandoned the practice.[48]

Resale Price Maintenance **Resale price maintenance** is the practice whereby a manufacturer and its distributors agree that the retailers will sell the producer's product at a certain price (resale price maintenance), at or above a price floor. These rules prevent retailers from competing too fiercely on price and thus driving down profits. Some argue that the manufacturer may do this because it wishes to keep retailers profitable, and thus keep the manufacturer profitable. Others contend that minimum resale price maintenance, for instance, ensures that distributors who invest in promoting the manufacturer's product are able to recoup the additional costs of the promotion in the price they charge consumers. Some manufacturers also defend resale price maintenance by saying it ensures fair returns for all. The primary negative argument is that resale price maintenance results in higher consumer prices because efficient retailers, such as Wal-Mart, Costco, or Best Buy must sell at a higher price than they would normally charge.

resale price maintenance
Retailers must sell a manufacturer's product at or above a specific price.

For almost 100 years, resale price maintenance has been illegal under the Sherman Antitrust Act because it was viewed as *horizontal price fixing* (price fixing at the same level—such as two or more retailers). The Supreme Court said that it was illegal per se, meaning that resale price maintenance was illegal without regard to its impact on the

predatory pricing
The practice of charging a very low price for a product with the intent of driving competitors out of business or out of a market.

marketplace or consumers. Then, in July 2007, the Supreme Court abandoned the "per se" rule and said that, instead, resale price maintenance agreements should be judged by a "rule of reason" analysis. That is, a balancing of procompetitive justifications and anticompetitive harms. Critics say that the ruling gives manufacturers the ability to raise prices and this will hurt consumers. It is estimated that it could add $300 billion to consumer costs.[49]

Retailers say an array of manufacturers now require them to abide by minimum-pricing pacts, or risk having their supplies cut off. Jacob Weiss of BabyAge.com, which specializes in maternity and children's gear, says nearly 100 of his 465 suppliers now dictate minimum prices, and nearly a dozen have cut off shipments to him. "If this continues, it's going to put us out of the baby business," he says.[50]

Consumer advocates say they are seeing the impact particularly in baby goods, consumer electronics, home furnishings, and pet food. Recently, Old Mother Hubbard Dog Food Company wrote a letter to Morris Sussex Pet Supply, a New Jersey pet shop, that complained about Morris Sussex selling 30-pound bags of its dog-food brand, Wellness Chicken Super5Mix, at 20 cents below the minimum $39.99 price. The director of Old Mother Hubbard said he would stop shipping the brand to the store for as long as six months if price-cutting continued.

The pet-supply shop fought back. It placed a billboard in front of its store urging customers to "Boycott Wellness Pet Food for Price Fixing," and aggressively steered customers to other types of dog food. "Our suppliers can set pricing policies all they want—but it's their loss, not ours," says Nancy Ruiz, the store's manager. Morris Sussex persuaded 85 percent of its Wellness customers to switch to another brand, Ms. Ruiz says. It now sells only a handful of Old Mother Hubbard products.[51]

Makers of books, toiletries, and towels also could find it difficult to flex their new pricing muscle with retailers such as Wal-Mart or Target Corp., for fear of losing their business. Just as Wal-Mart bargains hard for what it pays for merchandise, it will be able to bargain with manufacturers to keep its discounts.

Price Discrimination

The Robinson-Patman Act of 1936 prohibits any firm from selling to two or more different buyers, within a reasonably short time, commodities (not services) of like grade and quality at different prices where the result would be to substantially lessen competition. The act also makes it illegal for a seller to offer two buyers different supplementary services and for buyers to use their purchasing power to force sellers into granting discriminatory prices or services.

Six elements are therefore needed for a violation of the Robinson-Patman Act to occur:

- There must be price discrimination; that is, the seller must charge different prices to different customers for the same product.
- The transaction must occur in interstate commerce.
- The seller must discriminate by price among two or more purchasers; that is, the seller must make two or more actual sales within a reasonably short time.
- The products sold must be commodities or other tangible goods.
- The products sold must be of like grade and quality, not necessarily identical. If the goods are truly interchangeable and substitutable, then they are of like grade and quality.
- There must be significant competitive injury.

The Robinson-Patman Act provides three defenses for the seller charged with price discrimination (in each case the burden is on the defendant to prove the defense):

- *Cost:* A firm can charge different prices to different customers if the prices represent manufacturing or quantity discount savings.

- *Market conditions:* Price variations are justified if designed to meet fluid product or market conditions. Examples include the deterioration of perishable goods, the obsolescence of seasonal products, a distress sale under court order, and a legitimate going-out-of-business sale.
- *Competition:* A reduction in price may be necessary to stay even with the competition. Specifically, if a competitor undercuts the price quoted by a seller to a buyer, the law authorizes the seller to lower the price charged to the buyer for the product in question.

Predatory Pricing

Predatory pricing is the practice of charging a very low price for a product with the intent of driving competitors out of business or out of a market. Once competitors have been

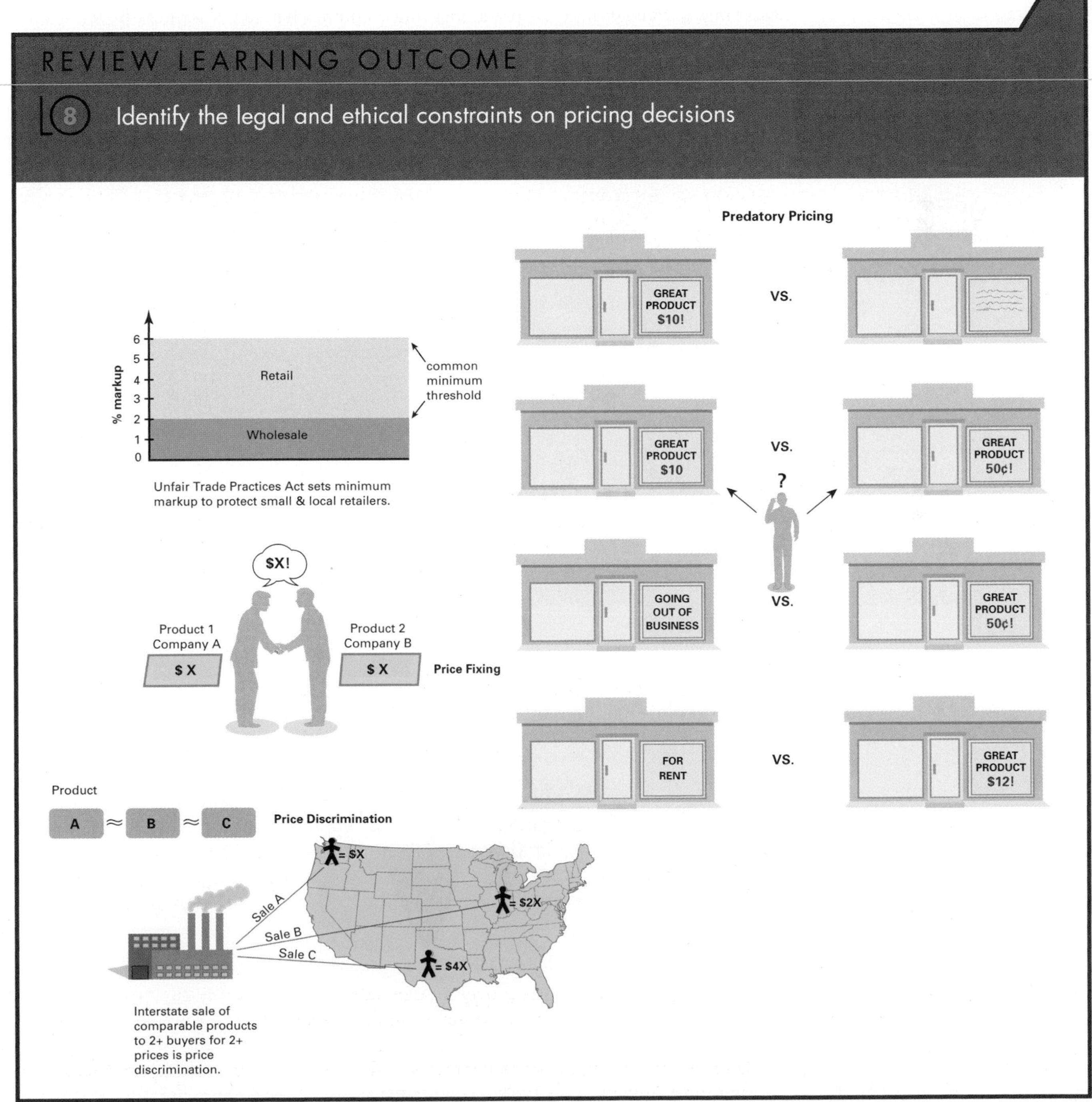

driven out, the firm raises its prices. This practice is illegal under the Sherman Act and the Federal Trade Commission Act. Proving predatory pricing is difficult and expensive, however. The Justice Department must demonstrate that the predator, the destructive company, explicitly tried to ruin a competitor and that the predator's intent was to raise prices to recover its losses once competitors had been driven out of business. The U.S. Supreme Court recently noted, "Predatory pricing is rarely tried and even more rarely successful."[52] The Court also said that lowering prices typically signals legitimate competition.

Predatory bidding is similar to predatory pricing and is held to the same legal standards. In a recent case of Weyerhaeuser versus Ross-Simmons Hardwood Lumber Company, Ross-Simmons claimed that Weyerhaeuser had driven them out of business. Ross-Simmons had operated a single sawmill in the Pacific Northwest since 1962. The mill purchased alder logs and processed them into finished lumber. Logs can account for up to 75 percent of a mill's cost. Weyerhaeuser entered the Pacific Northwest in 1980 and opened six mills. Ross-Simmons claimed that Weyerhaeuser deliberately overpaid for raw alder logs in order to raise the prices that Ross-Simmons had to pay for logs. By artificially "bidding up" log costs, Ross-Simmons declared bankruptcy. The Court held in favor of Weyerhaeuser noting that there are many reasons why the company may have bid up the price of alder logs. It could have been miscalculation, part of a risk strategy, or in response to increased consumer demand for the final product.[53]

a satisfactory profit in a high-risk industry ▶ **35%**

8,000 ◀ jobs slashed by Freightliner to cut costs

used cars inspected annually in Nevada ▶ **400,000**

price of a Rolling Stones concert ticket ▶ **$400**

1,500 ◀ price levels at Allstate

price decrease for safe drivers and increase for unsafe drivers ▶ **20%**

Ryanair's profit margin ▶ **22%**

100% ◀ price markup used by small-retailers

REVIEW AND APPLICATIONS

LO1 **Discuss the importance of pricing decisions to the economy and to the individual firm.** Pricing plays an integral role in the U.S. economy by allocating goods and services among consumers, governments, and businesses. Pricing is essential in business because it creates revenue, which is the basis of all business activity. In setting prices, marketing managers strive to find a level high enough to produce a satisfactory profit.

1.1 Why is pricing so important to the marketing manager?

1.2 How does price allocate goods and services?

LO2 **List and explain a variety of pricing objectives.** Establishing realistic and measurable pricing objectives is a critical part of any firm's marketing strategy. Pricing objectives are commonly classified into three categories: profit oriented, sales oriented, and status quo. Profit-oriented pricing is based on profit maximization, a satisfactory level of profit, or a target return on investment. The goal of profit maximization is to generate as much revenue as possible in relation to cost. Often, a more practical approach than profit maximization is setting prices to produce profits that will satisfy management and stockholders. The most common profit-oriented strategy is pricing for a specific return on investment relative to a firm's assets. The second type of pricing objective is sales oriented, and it focuses on either maintaining a percentage share of the market or maximizing dollar or unit sales. The third type of pricing objective aims to maintain the status quo by matching competitors' prices.

2.1 Give an example of each major type of pricing objective.

2.2 Why do many firms not maximize profits?

Explain the role of demand in price determination. Demand is a key determinant of price. When establishing prices, a firm must first determine demand for its product. A typical demand schedule shows an inverse relationship between quantity demanded and price: When price is lowered, sales increase; and when price is increased, the quantity demanded falls. For prestige products, however, there may be a direct relationship between demand and price: The quantity demanded will increase as price increases.

Marketing managers must also consider demand elasticity when setting prices. Elasticity of demand is the degree to which the quantity demanded fluctuates with changes in price. If consumers are sensitive to changes in price, demand is elastic; if they are insensitive to price changes, demand is inelastic. Thus, an increase in price will result in lower sales for an elastic product and little or no loss in sales for an inelastic product. Inelastic demand creates pricing power.

3.1 Explain the role of supply and demand in determining price.

3.2 If a firm can increase its total revenue by raising its price, shouldn't it do so?

3.3 Explain the concepts of elastic and inelastic demand. Why should managers understand these concepts?

Understand the concept of yield management systems. Yield management systems use complex mathematical software to profitably fill unused capacity. The software uses techniques such as discounting early purchases, limiting early sales at these discounted prices, and overbooking capacity. These systems are used in service and retail businesses and are substantially raising revenues. The use of Internet cookies and targeting software enables online retailers to offer different pricing and promotional offers to online buyers based upon their online shopping and browsing habits.

4.1 Why are so many companies adopting yield management systems?

4.2 Explain the relationship between supply and demand and yield management systems.

4.3 Why is targeting technology so effective?

Describe cost-oriented pricing strategies. The other major determinant of price is cost. Marketers use several cost-oriented pricing strategies. To cover their own expenses and obtain a profit, wholesalers and retailers commonly use markup pricing: They tack an extra amount onto the manufacturer's original price. Another pricing technique is to maximize profits by setting price where marginal revenue equals marginal cost. Still another pricing strategy determines how much a firm must sell to break even and uses this amount as a reference point for adjusting price.

5.1 Your firm has based its pricing strictly on cost in the past. As the newly hired marketing manager, you believe this policy should change. Write the president a memo explaining your reasons.

5.2 Why is it important for managers to understand the concept of break-even points? Are there any drawbacks?

Demonstrate how the product life cycle, competition, distribution and promotion strategies, guaranteed price matching, customer demands, the Internet, and perceptions of quality can affect price. The price of a product normally changes as it moves through the life cycle and as demand for the product and competitive conditions change. Management often sets a high price at the introductory stage, and the high price tends to attract competition. The competition usually drives prices down because individual competitors lower prices to gain market share.

Adequate distribution for a new product can sometimes be obtained by offering a larger-than-usual profit margin to wholesalers and retailers. The Internet enables consumers to compare products and prices quickly and efficiently. Price is also used as a promotional tool to attract customers. Special low prices often attract new customers and entice existing customers to buy more. Price matching positions the retailer as a low-price vendor. Firms that don't match prices are perceived as offering a higher level of service. Large buyers can extract price concessions from vendors. Such demands can squeeze the profit margins of suppliers.

Perceptions of quality can also influence pricing strategies. A firm trying to project a prestigious image often charges a premium price for a product. Consumers tend to equate high prices with high quality.

6.1 Divide the class into teams of five. Each team will be assigned a different grocery store from a different chain. (An independent is fine.) Appoint a group leader. The group leaders should meet as a group and pick 15 nationally branded grocery items. Each item should be specifically described as to brand name and size of the package. Each team will then proceed to its assigned store and collect price data on the 15 items. The team should also gather price data on 15 similar store brands and 15 generics, if possible.

Each team should present its results to the class and discuss why there are price variations between stores, national brands, store brands, and generics.

As a next step, go back to your assigned store and share the overall results with the store manager. Bring back the manager's comments and share them with the class.

6.2 How does the stage of a product's life cycle affect price? Give some examples.

6.3 Go to **Priceline.com.** Can you research a ticket's price before purchasing it? What products and services are available for purchasing? How comfortable are you with naming your own price? Relate the supply and demand curves to customer-determined pricing.

Describe the procedure for setting the right price. The process of setting the right price on a product involves four major steps: (1) establishing pricing goals; (2) estimating demand, costs, and profits; (3) choosing a price policy to help determine a base price; and (4) fine-tuning the base price with pricing tactics.

A price strategy establishes a long-term pricing framework for a good or service. The three main types of price policies are price skimming, penetration pricing, and status quo pricing. A price-skimming policy charges a high introductory price, often followed by a gradual reduction. Penetration pricing offers a low introductory price to capture a large market share and attain economies of scale. Finally, status quo pricing strives to match competitors' price.

7.1 A manufacturer of office furniture decides to produce antique-style rolltop desks reconfigured to accommodate personal computers. The desks will have built-in surge protectors, a platform for raising or lowering the monitor, and a number of other features. The high-quality, solid-oak desks will be priced far below comparable products. The marketing manager says, "We'll charge a low price and plan on a high volume to reduce our risks." Comment.

7.2 Janet Oliver, owner of a mid-priced dress shop, notes, "My pricing objectives are simple: I just charge what my competitors charge. I'm happy because I'm making money." React to Janet's statement.

7.3 What is the difference between a price policy and a price tactic? Give an example.

Identify the legal and ethical constraints on pricing decisions. Government regulation helps monitor five major areas of pricing: unfair trade practices, price fixing, resales price maintenance, predatory pricing and predatory bidding, and price discrimination. Many states have enacted unfair trade practice acts that protect small businesses from large firms that operate efficiently on extremely thin profit margins; the acts prohibit charging below-cost prices. The Sherman Act and the Federal Trade Commission Act prohibit both price fixing, which is an agreement between two or more firms on a particular price, and predatory pricing, in which a firm undercuts its competitors with extremely low prices to drive them out of business. Finally, the Robinson-Patman Act makes it illegal for firms to discriminate between two or more buyers in terms of price.

8.1 What are the three basic defenses that a seller can use if accused under the Robinson-Patman Act?

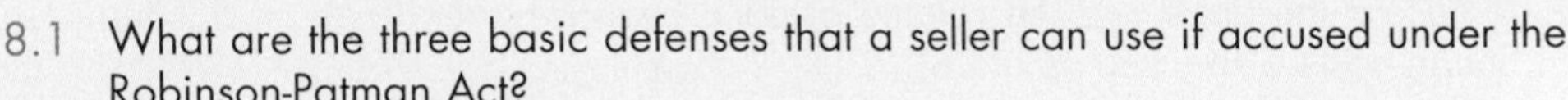

KEY TERMS

- average total cost (ATC) 571
- average variable cost (AVC) 571
- break-even analysis 574
- demand 564
- elastic demand 566
- elasticity of demand 566
- fixed cost 571
- inelastic demand 566
- keystoning 573
- marginal cost (MC) 571
- marginal revenue (MR) 573
- market share 562
- markup pricing 573
- penetration pricing 587
- predatory pricing 593
- prestige pricing 582
- price 559
- price equilibrium 565
- price fixing 590
- price skimming 586
- price strategy 585
- profit 560
- resale price maintenance 591
- profit maximization 573
- return on investment (ROI) 562
- revenue 560
- selling against the brand 578
- status quo pricing 564
- supply 565
- unfair trade practice acts 590
- unitary elasticity 566
- variable cost 571
- yield management systems (YMS) 569

EXERCISES

APPLICATION EXERCISE

Reliance on price as a predictor of quality seems to occur for all products. Does this mean that high-priced products are superior? Well, sometimes. Price can be a good predictor of quality for some products, but for others, price is not always the best way to determine the quality of a product or service before buying it. This exercise (and worksheet) will help you examine the price-quality relationship for a simple product: canned goods.[54]

Activities

1. Take a trip to a local supermarket where you are certain to find multiple brands of canned fruits and vegetables. Pick a single type of vegetable or fruit you like, such as cream corn or peach halves, and list five or six brands in the following worksheet.

		Price				
(1) Brand	(2) Quality/Rank (*y*)	(3) Price/Weight	(4) Price per Ounce	(5) Price Rank (*x*)	(6) $d(y - x)$	(7) d^2
Total						

2. Before going any further, rank the brands according to which you think is the highest quality (1) to the lowest quality (5 or 6, depending on how many brands you find). This ranking will be *y*.
3. Record the price and the volume of each brand. For example, if a 14-ounce can costs $.89, you would list $.89/14 oz.
4. Translate the price per volume into price per ounce. Our 14-ounce can costs $.064 per ounce.
5. Now rank the price per ounce (we'll call it *x*) from the highest (1) to the lowest (5 or 6, again depending on how many brands you have).
6. We'll now begin calculating the coefficient of correlation between the price and quality rankings. The first step is to subtract *x* from *y*. Enter the result, *d*, in column 6.
7. Now calculate d^2 and enter the value in column 7. Write the sum of all the entries in column 7 in the final row.
8. The formula for calculating a price-quality coefficient *r* is as follows:

   In the formula, r_s is the coefficient of correlation, 6 is a constant, and *n* is the number of items ranked.
9. What does the result of your calculation tell you about the correlation between the price and the quality of the canned vegetable or fruit you selected? Now that you know this, will it change your buying habits?

ETHICS EXERCISE

Advanced Bio Medics (ABM) has invented a new stem-cell-based drug that will arrest even advanced forms of lung cancer. Development costs were actually quite low because the drug was an accidental discovery by scientists working on a different project. To stop the disease requires a regimen of one pill per week for 20 weeks. There is no substitute offered by competitors. ABM is thinking that it could maximize its profits by charging $10,000 per pill. Of course, many people will die because they can't afford the medicine at this price.

Questions

1. Should ABM maximize its profits?
2. Does the AMA Statement of Ethics address this issue? Go to **www.marketing power.com** and review the code. Then, write a brief paragraph on what the AMA Statement of Ethics contains that relates to ABM's dilemma.

MARKETING PLAN EXERCISE

In the last part of your strategic marketing plan you began the process of defining the marketing mix, starting with the components of product, distribution, and promotion. The next stage of the strategic planning process—pricing—completes the elements of the marketing mix.

In recent years, pricing has become a special challenge to the marketer because prices can be quickly and easily compared on the Internet. In any case, your goal should be to make pricing competitive and value-driven, as well as cover costs. Other features and benefits of your offering are likely to be more important than price. Use the following exercises to guide you through the pricing part of your strategic marketing plan:

1. List possible pricing objectives for your chosen firm. How might adopting different pricing objectives change the behavior of the firm and its marketing plans?
2. Gather information on tactics you decided on for the first parts of your marketing plan. What costs are associated with those decisions? Will you incur more or fewer costs by selling online? Will your marketing costs increase or decrease? Why? Calculate the break-even point for selling your offering. Can you sell enough to cover your costs? Try the break-even calculator at **http://connection.cwru.edu/mbac424/breakeven/BreakEven.html.**
3. Pricing is an integral component of marketing strategy. Discuss how your firm's pricing can affect or be affected by competition, the economic environment, political regulations, product features, extra customer service, changes in distribution, or changes in promotion.
4. Is demand elastic or inelastic for your company's product or service? Why? What is the demand elasticity for your offering in an off-line world? Whatever the level, it is likely to be *more* elastic online. What tactics can you use to soften or reduce this online price sensitivity?

CASE STUDY: HDNET AIMS TO REDEFINE TELEVISION

If billionaire entrepreneur Mark Cuban had his way, the future would be today. The Web broadcasting pioneer earned nearly $2 billion when he and his partner sold their Broadcast.com business to Yahoo! for the princely sum of $5.7 billion at the height of the Internet frenzy in 2000. While looking to spend some of his newly found wealth on the latest and greatest in home entertainment systems, Cuban had his first experience with high-definition television. High-definition TV is a digital format that produces a picture resolution that can be up to ten times sharper than that of standard TVs (depending on screen pixel count), and it is typically presented in a wide-screen format along with digital surround sound. Cuban was so captivated by the amazing resolution on his new 100-inch projection set that he decided to start his own high-definition television network.

With a $100 million investment from Cuban, HDNet—the first-ever all-high-definition network—was off and running less than a year later. Three years later,

HDNet boasts over 1,200 hours of original programming. In addition to the shows it produces, it has licensing contracts that double its programming inventory. HDNet also has broadcasting agreements that allow it to carry live sporting events from the National Hockey League, Major League soccer, and the NCAA. The company also operates HDNetMovies, which has scored deals with several major movie studios to convert their 35-millimeter films to a high-definition format.

Though HDNet's current subscriber base is estimated at around 1 million, industry statistics suggest that 60 million U.S. homes have television sets capable of delivering high-definition programming. With prices that started near $5,000 a couple of years ago, the prohibitive cost of the special television sets required to transmit high-definition programming was one of the company's major early hurdles. The other was the lack of available programming. High-definition shows must be produced on special equipment, and only a few major networks, such as NBC, CBS, ABC, HBO, Showtime, and the Discovery channel, have made the investment to do so.

Cuban has stayed the course, patiently waiting for prices of high-definition TV sets to drop to where they would have mass-market appeal. As with his Internet business, his timing appears to be perfect. Electronics retailer Best Buy now sells 27-inch high-definition TV sets for as low as $500. Of course, the discerning customer can spend as much as $9,000 in the same store for a top-of-the-line 60-inch model; but now that the television sets are affordable, adoption rates could be on the verge of exploding. Cuban, therefore, has turned his attention to securing distribution deals with major cable operators and satellite programmers.

His company has already locked in deals with all but three of the nation's largest cable television providers and with satellite broadcasters DirecTV and DISHNET. Both satellite programmers and the heavyweight cable-operating trio of Time Warner, Charter Communications, and Adelphia have begun to sell subscriptions to HDNet, which comes packaged with HDNetMovies. Those companies pay an as yet undisclosed amount of money back to Cuban for the rights to carry the channel and license HDNet's exclusive content. To reduce some of the technical confusion for customers, the satellite companies offer subscribers package deals. DirecTV's includes a dish, a high-definition receiver (required to transmit the signal to the high-definition TV), professional installation, and a year's worth of high-definition programming for $399. DISHNET offers a similar package, but throws in a TV for a total start-up cost of $1,000. Its subscriptions are priced separately and start at $110 per year. Cable operators charge a premium for HDNet and include it only with their high-end digital offerings, which generally cost around $100 per month. To entice skeptical consumers into signing up, some cable companies are offering 30-day free trials.

Mark Cuban truly believes that the story of high-definition television services will someday mirror that of FM radio or basic cable television. Of course, only time will tell if he is right, but one thing is for sure—with high-definition television, the future certainly appears brighter.[55]

Questions

1. Based on how resellers are pricing HDNet for their subscribers, how would you characterize HDNet's pricing objectives?
2. How will demand and supply trends in the high-definition industry affect the price for HDNet's programming?
3. From what you can discern about HDNet's stage in the product life cycle, competition, distribution, resellers' sales promotion strategies, customer demands, and perception of quality, submit a projection of what you think HDNet should charge carriers for access to its channels and original programming. Defend your answer.

COMPANY CLIPS

© NKP MEDIA, INC./CENGAGE

ACID+ALL = SERIOUS PRICING

As long as people have stomach aches, companies will sell remedies. Acid+All is banking that America will continue its love affair with bad food and has made an interesting move into the antacid market. The tiny pills come packaged in a tin priced at $3.89, which clearly sets the product apart from competitors like Rolaids, Tums, and others. The gambit of staking out a position as a prestige product is high. Watch the video to see what issues helped forge the $3.89 unit price and if the company has been successful at this price point.

Questions

1. How do the product, place, and promotion elements of Acid+All's marketing mix influence the pricing strategy the company has chosen?
2. Would you expect demand for Acid+All to be elastic? Why or why not?
3. What role do the product life cycle, competition, and perceptions of quality play in Acid+All's suggested retail price?
4. Would you buy Acid+All for the $3.89 retail price? Why or why not?

Marketing & You Results

High scores on this poll relate to a belief that you'll get more enjoyment and make better impressions if you buy high-priced brands. That is, you have a higher prestige sensitivity than someone with a lower score. If your score was low, compare it with your score for the Chapter 15 poll, which was probably high. That's because people with lower prestige sensitivities are more likely to use coupons!

GLOSSARY

80/20 principle A principle holding that 20 percent of all customers generate 80 percent of the demand.

A

accelerator principle See *multiplier effect.*

accessory equipment Goods, such as portable tools and office equipment, that are less expensive and shorter-lived than major equipment.

adopter A consumer who was happy enough with his or her trial experience with a product to use it again.

advergaming Placing advertising messages in Web-based or video games to advertise or promote a product, service, organization, or issue.

advertising Impersonal, one-way mass communication about a product or organization that is paid for by a marketer.

advertising appeal A reason for a person to buy a product.

advertising campaign A series of related advertisements focusing on a common theme, slogan, and set of advertising appeals.

advertising objective A specific communication task that a campaign should accomplish for a specified target audience during a specified period.

advertising response function A phenomenon in which spending for advertising and sales promotion increases sales or market share up to a certain level but then produces diminishing returns.

advocacy advertising A form of advertising in which an organization expresses its views on controversial issues or responds to media attacks.

agents and brokers Wholesaling intermediaries who do not take title to a product but facilitate its sale from producer to end user by representing retailers, wholesalers, or manufacturers.

AIDA concept A model that outlines the process for achieving promotional goals in terms of stages of consumer involvement with the message; the acronym stands for attention, interest, desire, and action.

applied research An attempt to develop new or improved products.

Arm's-Length relationship A relationship between companies that is loose, characterized by low relational investment and trust, and usually taking the form of a series of discrete transactions with no/low expectation of future interaction or service.

aspirational reference group A group that someone would like to join.

ATC See *average total cost.*

atmosphere The overall impression conveyed by a store's physical layout, décor, and surroundings.

attitude A learned tendency to respond consistently toward a given object.

audience selectivity The ability of an advertising medium to reach a precisely defined market.

automatic replenishment program An inventory management system that triggers shipments only once a good is sold to the customer; the program uses EDI linkage connected with barcode scanners at the point of purchase, so the supplier can view the inventory being held at the next tier of the supply chain in real time.

automatic vending The use of machines to offer goods for sale.

AVC See *average variable cost.*

average total cost (ATC) Total costs divided by quantity of output.

average variable cost (AVC) Total variable costs divided by quantity of output.

B

baby boomers People born between 1946 and 1964.

bar codes See *universal product codes.*

basic research Pure research that aims to confirm an existing theory or to learn more about a concept or phenomenon.

behavioral targeting A form of observation marketing research that uses data mining coupled with identifying Web surfers by their IP addresses plus demographic/psychographic profiles.

BehaviorScan A scanner-based research program that tracks the purchases of 3,000 households through store scanners in each research market.

belief An organized pattern of knowledge that an individual holds as true about his or her world.

benefit segmentation The process of grouping customers into market segments according to the benefits they seek from the product.

brainstorming The process of getting a group to think of unlimited ways to vary a product or solve a problem.

brand A name, term, symbol, design, or combination thereof that identifies a seller's products and differentiates them from competitors' products.

brand equity The value of company and brand names.

brand loyalty A consistent preference for one brand over all others.

brand mark The elements of a brand that cannot be spoken.

brand name That part of a brand that can be spoken, including letters, words, and numbers.

brand extensions A well-known and respected brand name from one product category is extended into other product categories.

break-even analysis A method of determining what sales volume must be reached before total revenue equals total costs.

business analysis The second stage of the screening process where preliminary figures for demand, cost, sales, and profitability are calculated.

business marketing The marketing of goods and services to individuals and organizations for purposes other than personal consumption.

business product (industrial product) A product used to manufacture other goods or services, to facilitate an organization's operations, or to resell to other customers.

business services Expense items that do not become part of a final product.

business-to-business electronic commerce The use of the Internet to facilitate the exchange of goods, services, and information between organizations.

business-to-business online exchange An electronic trading floor that provides companies with integrated links to their customers and suppliers.

buyer A department head who selects the merchandise for his or her department and may be responsible for promotion and personnel.

buyer for export An intermediary in the global market that assumes all ownership risks and sells globally for its own account.

buying center All those persons in an organization who become involved in the purchase decision.

C

CAFTA See *Central America Free Trade Agreement.*

cannibalization A situation that occurs when sales of a new product cut into sales of a firm's existing products.

capital-intensive Using more capital than labor in the production process.

captive brand A brand that carries no evidence of a retailer's affiliation, is manufactured by a third party, and is sold exclusively at the retailers.

cash cow In the portfolio matrix, a business unit that usually generates more cash than it needs to maintain its market share.

casuist ethical theory A theory that compares a current ethical dilemma with examples of similar ethical dilemmas and their outcomes.

category killers Specialty discount stores that heavily dominate their narrow merchandise segment.

cause-related marketing The cooperative marketing efforts between a "for-profit" firm and a "nonprofit organization."

Central America Free Trade Agreement (CAFTA) A trade agreement, instituted in 2005, that includes Costa Rica, the Dominican Republic, El Salvador, Guatemala, Honduras, Nicaragua, and the United States.

central-location telephone (CLT) facility A specially designed phone room used to conduct telephone interviewing.

CGM See *consumer generated media.*

chain stores Stores owned and operated as a group by a single organization.

channel A medium of communication—such as a voice, radio, or newspaper—for transmitting a message.

channel captain See *channel leader.*

channel conflict A clash of goals and methods between distribution channel members.

channel control A situation that occurs when one marketing channel member intentionally affects another member's behavior.

channel cooperation See *channel partnering.*

channel leader (channel captain) A member of a marketing channel that exercises authority and power over the activities of other channel members.

channel members All parties in the marketing channel that negotiate with one another, buy and sell products, and facilitate the change of ownership between buyer and seller in the course of moving the product from the manufacturer into the hands of the final consumer.

channel of distribution See *marketing channel.*

channel partnering (channel cooperation) The joint effort of all channel members to create a channel that serves customers and creates a competitive advantage.

channel power The capacity of a particular marketing channel member to control or influence the behavior of other channel members.

CI See *competitive intelligence.*

closed-ended question An interview question that asks the respondent to make a selection from a limited list of responses.

CLT See *central-location telephone facility.*

cobranding Placing two or more brand names on a product or its package.

code of ethics A guideline to help marketing managers and other employees make better decisions.

cognitive dissonance Inner tension that a consumer experiences after recognizing an inconsistency between behavior and values or opinions.

commercialization The decision to market a product.

communication The process by which we exchange or share meanings through a common set of symbols.

comparative advertising A form of advertising that compares two or more specifically named or shown competing brands on one or more specific attributes.

competitive advantage The set of unique features of a company and its products that are perceived by the target market as significant and superior to the competition.

competitive advertising A form of advertising designed to influence demand for a specific brand.

competitive intelligence (CI) An intelligence system that helps managers assess their competition and vendors in order to become more efficient and effective competitors.

component lifestyles The practice of choosing goods and services that meet one's diverse needs and interests rather than conforming to a single, traditional lifestyle.

component parts Either finished items ready for assembly or products that need very little processing before becoming part of some other product.

computer-assisted personal interviewing An interviewing method in which the interviewer reads the questions from a computer screen and enters the respondent's data directly into the computer.

computer-assisted self-interviewing An interviewing method in which a mall interviewer intercepts and directs willing respondents to nearby computers where the respondent reads questions off a computer screen and directly keys his or her answers into a computer.

concentrated targeting strategy A strategy used to select one segment of a market for targeting marketing efforts.

concept test A test to evaluate a new-product idea, usually before any prototype has been created.

consideration set See *evoked set.*

consultative selling See *relationship selling.*

consumer behavior Processes a consumer uses to make purchase decisions, as well as to use and dispose of purchased goods or services; also includes factors that influence purchase decisions and product use.

consumer decision-making process A five-step process used by consumers when buying goods or services.

consumer generated media (CGM) Media which is consumer generated and shared with other consumers.

consumer product A product bought to satisfy an individual's personal wants.

Consumer Product Safety Commission (CPSC) A federal agency established to protect the health and safety of consumers in and around their homes.

consumer sales promotion Sales promotion activities targeting the ultimate consumer.

continuous media schedule A media scheduling strategy in which advertising is run steadily throughout the advertising period; used for products in the latter stages of the product life cycle.

contract logistics See *outsourcing.*

contract manufacturing Private-label manufacturing by a foreign company.

control Provides the mechanisms for evaluating marketing results in light of the plan's objectives and for correcting actions that do not help the organization reach those objectives within budget guidelines.

convenience product A relatively inexpensive item that merits little shopping effort.

convenience sample A form of nonprobability sample using respondents who are convenient or readily accessible to the researcher—for example, employees, friends, or relatives.

convenience store A miniature supermarket, carrying only a limited line of high-turnover convenience goods.

cooperative advertising An arrangement in which the manufacturer and the retailer split the costs of advertising the manufacturer's brand.

cooperative relationship A relationship between companies that takes the form of informal partnership with moderate levels of trust and information sharing as needed to further each company's goals.

corporate blogs Blogs that are sponsored by a company or one of its brands and maintained by one or more of the company's employees.

corporate social responsibility Business's concern for society's welfare.

cost competitive advantage Being the low-cost competitor in an industry while maintaining satisfactory profit margins.

cost per contact The cost of reaching one member of the target market.

countertrade A form of trade in which all or part of the payment for goods or services is in the form of other goods or services.

coupon A certificate that entitles consumers to an immediate price reduction when they buy the product.

CPSC See *Consumer Product Safety Commission.*

credence quality A characteristic that consumers may have difficulty assessing even after purchase because they do not have the necessary knowledge or experience.

crisis management A coordinated effort to handle all the effects of unfavorable publicity or of another unexpected unfavorable event.

cross-tabulation A method of analyzing data that lets the analyst look at the responses to one question in relation to the responses to one or more other questions.

culture The set of values, norms, attitudes, and other meaningful symbols that shape human behavior, and the artifacts, or products, of that behavior as they are transmitted from one generation to the next.

customer satisfaction Customers' evaluation of a good or service in terms of whether it has met their needs and expectations.

customer value The relationship between benefits and the sacrifice necessary to obtain those benefits.

D

database marketing The creation of a large computerized file of customers' and potential customers' profiles and purchase patterns.

decision support system (DSS) An interactive, flexible computerized information system that enables managers to obtain and manipulate information as they are making decisions.

decline stage The fourth stage of the product life cycle, characterized by a long-run drop in sales.

decoding Interpretation of the language and symbols sent by the source through a channel.

demand The quantity of a product that will be sold in the market at various prices for a specified period.

demographic segmentation Segmenting markets by age, gender, income, ethnic background, and family life cycle.

demography The study of people's vital statistics, such as their age, race and ethnicity, and location.

deontological ethical theory A theory that states that people should adhere to their obligations and duties when analyzing an ethical dilemma.

department store A store housing several departments under one roof.

derived demand The demand for business products.

destination stores Stores that consumers purposefully plan to visit.

development The stage in the product development process in which a prototype is developed and a marketing strategy is outlined.

diffusion The process by which the adoption of an innovation spreads.

direct channel A distribution channel in which producers sell directly to consumers.

direct foreign investment Active ownership of a foreign company or of overseas manufacturing or marketing facilities.

direct marketing (direct-response marketing) Techniques used to get consumers to make a purchase from their home, office, or another nonretail setting.

direct retailing The selling of products by representatives who work door-to-door, office-to-office, or at-home parties.

direct-response marketing See *direct marketing.*

discount store A retailer that competes on the basis of low prices, high turnover, and high volume.

discrepancy of assortment The lack of all the items a customer needs to receive full satisfaction from a product or products.

discrepancy of quantity The difference between the amount of product produced and the amount an end user wants to buy.

disintermediation The elimination of intermediaries such as wholesalers or distributors from a marketing channel.

distribution resource planning (DRP) An inventory control system that manages the replenishment of goods from the manufacturer to the final consumer.

diversification A strategy of increasing sales by introducing new products into new markets.

dog In the portfolio matrix, a business unit that has low growth potential and a small market share.

DRP See *distribution resource planning.*

drugstore A retail store that stocks pharmacy-related products and services as its main draw.

DSS See *decision support system.*

dual distribution (multiple distribution) The use of two (or more) channels to distribute the same product to target markets.

dumping The sale of an exported product at a price lower than that charged for the same or a like product in the "home" market of the exporter.

E

EDI See *electronic data interchange.*

elastic demand A situation in which consumer demand is sensitive to changes in price.

elasticity of demand Consumers' responsiveness or sensitivity to changes in price.

electronic data interchange (EDI) Information technology that replaces the paper documents that usually accompany business transactions, such as purchase orders and invoices, with electronic transmission of the needed information to reduce inventory levels, improve cash flow, streamline operations, and increase the speed and accuracy of information transmission.

electronic distribution A distribution technique that includes any kind of product or service that can be distributed electronically, whether over traditional forms such as fiber-optic cable or through satellite transmission of electronic signals.

empowerment Delegation of authority to solve customers' problems quickly–usually by the first person that the customer notifies regarding a problem.

encoding The conversion of a sender's ideas and thoughts into a message, usually in the form of words or signs.

environmental management When a company implements strategies that attempt to shape the external environment within which it operates.

environmental scanning Collection and interpretation of information about forces, events, and relationships in the external environment that may affect the future of the organization or the implementation of the marketing plan.

ethics The moral principles or values that generally govern the conduct of an individual.

ethnographic research The study of human behavior in its natural context; involves observation of behavior and physical setting.

EU See *European Union.*

European Union (EU) A free trade zone encompassing 27 European countries.

evaluation Gauging the extent to which the marketing objectives have been achieved during the specified time.

evoked set (consideration set) A group of brands, resulting from an information search, from which a buyer can choose.

exchange People giving up something to receive something they would rather have.

exclusive distribution A form of distribution that establishes one or a few dealers within a given area.

executive interviews A type of survey that involves interviewing businesspeople at their offices concerning industrial products or services.

experience curves Curves that show costs declining at a predictable rate as experience with a product increases.

experience quality A characteristic that can be assessed only after use.

experiment A method a researcher uses to gather primary data.
export agent An intermediary who acts like a manufacturer's agent for the exporter. The export agent lives in the foreign market.
export broker An intermediary who plays the traditional broker's role by bringing buyer and seller together.
exporting Selling domestically produced products to buyers in another country.
express warranty A written guarantee.
extensive decision making The most complex type of consumer decision making, used when buying an unfamiliar, expensive product or an infrequently bought item; requires use of several criteria for evaluating options and much time for seeking information.
external information search The process of seeking information in the outside environment.

F

factory outlet An off-price retailer that is owned and operated by a manufacturer.
family brand Marketing several different products under the same brand name.
family life cycle (FLC) A series of stages determined by a combination of age, marital status, and the presence or absence of children.
FDA See *Food and Drug Administration.*
Federal Trade Commission (FTC) A federal agency empowered to prevent persons or corporations from using unfair methods of competition in commerce.
feedback The receiver's response to a message.
field service firm A firm that specializes in interviewing respondents on a subcontracted basis.
fixed cost A cost that does not change as output is increased or decreased.
FLC See *family life cycle.*
flighted media schedule A media scheduling strategy in which ads are run heavily every other month or every two weeks, to achieve a greater impact with an increased frequency and reach at those times.
floating exchange rates Prices of different currencies move up and down based on the demand for and the supply of each currency.
focus group Seven to ten people who participate in a group discussion led by a moderator.
follow-up The final step of the selling process, in which the salesperson ensures that delivery schedules are met, that the goods or services perform as promised, and that the buyers' employees are properly trained to use the products.
Food and Drug Administration (FDA) A federal agency charged with enforcing regulations against selling and distributing adulterated, misbranded, or hazardous food and drug products.
Foreign Corrupt Practices Act A law that prohibits U.S. corporations from making illegal payments to public officials of foreign governments to obtain business rights or to enhance their business dealings in those countries.
four Ps Product, place, promotion, and price, which together make up the marketing mix.
frame error An error that occurs when a sample drawn from a population differs from the target population.
franchise The right to operate a business or to sell a product.
franchisee An individual or business that is granted the right to sell another party's product.
franchisor The originator of a trade name, product, methods of operation, and so on that grants operating rights to another party to sell its product.
frequency The number of times an individual is exposed to a given message during a specific period.
frequent buyer program A loyalty program in which loyal consumers are rewarded for making multiple purchases of a particular good or service.
FTC See *Federal Trade Commission.*
full-line discount stores A retailer that offers consumers very limited service and carries a broad assortment of well-known, nationally branded "hard goods."

G

GATT See *General Agreement on Tariffs and Trade.*
General Agreement on Tariffs and Trade (GATT) A trade agreement that contained loopholes that enabled countries to avoid trade-barrier reduction agreements.
Generation X People born between 1965 and 1978.
Generation Y People born between 1979 and 1994.
generic product name Identifies a product by class or type and cannot be trademarked.
geodemographic segmentation Segmenting potential customers into neighborhood lifestyle categories.
geographic segmentation Segmenting markets by region of a country or the world, market size, market density, or climate.
global brand A brand where at least one-third of the product is sold outside its home country or region.
global marketing Marketing that targets markets throughout the world.
global marketing standardization Production of uniform products that can be sold the same way all over the world.
global vision Recognizing and reacting to international marketing opportunities, using effective global marketing strategies, and being aware of threats from foreign competitors in all markets.
gross margin The amount of money the retailer makes as a percentage of sales after the cost of goods sold is subtracted.
group dynamics Group interaction essential to the success of focus-group research.
growth stage The second stage of the product life cycle when sales typically grow at an increasing rate, many competitors enter the market, large companies may start acquiring small pioneering firms, and profits are healthy.

H

heterogeneity The variability of the inputs and outputs of services, which causes services to tend to be less standardized and less uniform than goods.
horizontal conflict A channel conflict that occurs among channel members on the same level.

I

ideal self-image The way an individual would like to be.
IMC See *integrated marketing communications.*
IMF See *International Monetary Fund.*
implementation The process that turns a marketing plan into action assignments and ensures that these assignments are executed in a way that accomplishes the plan's objectives.
implied warranty An unwritten guarantee that the good or service is fit for the purpose for which it was sold.
independent retailers Retailers owned by a single person or partnership and not operated as part of a larger retail institution.
individual branding Using different brand names for different products.
industrial product See *business product.*
inelastic demand A situation in which an increase or a decrease in price will not significantly affect demand for the product.
inflation A measure of the decrease in the value of money, expressed as the percentage reduction in value since the previous year.
infomercial A 30-minute or longer advertisement that looks more like a TV talk show than a sales pitch.
informational labeling A type of package labeling designed to help consumers make proper product selections and lower their cognitive dissonance after the purchase.
InfoScan A scanner-based sales-tracking service for the consumer packaged-goods industry.

innovation A product perceived as new by a potential adopter.

inseparability The inability of the production and consumption of a service to be separated. Consumers must be present during the production.

installations See *major equipment.*

institutional advertising A form of advertising designed to enhance a company's image rather than promote a particular product.

intangibility The inability of services to be touched, seen, tasted, heard, or felt in the same manner that goods can be sensed.

integrated marketing communications (IMC) The careful coordination of all promotional messages for a product or a service to assure the consistency of messages at every contact point where a company meets the consumer.

integrated relationship A relationship between companies that is tightly connected, with linked processes across and between firm boundaries, and high levels of trust and interfirm commitment.

intensive distribution A form of distribution aimed at having a product available in every outlet where target customers might want to buy it.

internal information search The process of recalling past information stored in the memory.

International Monetary Fund (IMF) An international organization that acts as a lender of last resort, providing loans to troubled nations, and works to promote trade through financial cooperation.

interpersonal communication Direct, face-to-face communication between two or more people.

introductory stage The first stage of the product life cycle in which the full-scale launch of a new product into the marketplace occurs.

inventory control system A method of developing and maintaining an adequate assortment of materials or products to meet a manufacturer's or a customer's demand.

involvement The amount of time and effort a buyer invests in the search, evaluation, and decision processes of consumer behavior.

J

joint demand The demand for two or more items used together in a final product.

joint venture When a domestic firm buys part of a foreign company or joins with a foreign company to create a new entity.

K

keiretsu A network of interlocking corporate affiliates.

keystoning The practice of marking up prices by 100 percent, or doubling the cost.

L

laboratory market testing See *simulated market testing.*

lead generation (prospecting) Identification of those firms and people most likely to buy the seller's offerings.

lead qualification Determination of a sales prospect's (1) recognized need, (2) buying power, and (3) receptivity and accessibility.

learning A process that creates changes in behavior, immediate or expected, through experience and practice.

licensing The legal process whereby a licensor agrees to let another firm use its manufacturing process, trademarks, patents, trade secrets, or other proprietary knowledge.

lifestyle A mode of living as identified by a person's activities, interests, and opinions.

limited decision making The type of decision making that requires a moderate amount of time for gathering information and deliberating about an unfamiliar brand in a familiar product category.

logistics The efficient and cost-effective forward and reverse flow as well as storage of goods, services, and related information, into, through, and out of channel member companies. Logistics functions typically include transportation and storage of assets, as well as their sorting, accumulation, consolidation, and/or allocation for the purpose of meeting customer requirements.

logistics information system The link that connects all of the logistics components of the supply chain.

loss-leader pricing See *leader pricing.*

loyalty marketing program A promotional program designed to build long-term, mutually beneficial relationships between a company and its key customers.

M

major equipment (installations) Capital goods such as large or expensive machines, mainframe computers, blast furnaces, generators, airplanes, and buildings.

mall intercept interview A survey research method that involves interviewing people in the common areas of shopping malls.

management decision problem A broad-based problem that uses marketing research in order for managers to take proper actions.

manufacturer's brand The brand name of a manufacturer.

marginal cost (MC) The change in total costs associated with a one-unit change in output.

marginal revenue (MR) The extra revenue associated with selling an extra unit of output or the change in total revenue with a one-unit change in output.

market People or organizations with needs or wants and the ability and willingness to buy.

market development A marketing strategy that entails attracting new customers to existing products.

market opportunity analysis (MOA) The description and estimation of the size and sales potential of market segments that are of interest to the firm and the assessment of key competitors in these market segments.

market orientation A philosophy that assumes that a sale does not depend on an aggressive sales force but rather on a customer's decision to purchase a product. It is synonymous with the marketing concept.

market penetration A marketing strategy that tries to increase market share among existing customers.

market segment A subgroup of people or organizations sharing one or more characteristics that cause them to have similar product needs.

market segmentation The process of dividing a market into meaningful, relatively similar, and identifiable segments or groups.

market share A company's product sales as a percentage of total sales for that industry.

marketing The activity, set of institutions, and processes for creating, communicating, delivering, and exchanging offerings that have value for customers, clients, partners, and society at large.

marketing audit A thorough, systematic, periodic evaluation of the objectives, strategies, structure, and performance of the marketing organization.

marketing channel (channel of distribution) A set of interdependent organizations that ease the transfer of ownership as products move from producer to business user or consumer.

marketing concept The idea that the social and economic justification for an organization's existence is the satisfaction of customer wants and needs while meeting organizational objectives.

marketing information Everyday information about developments in the marketing environment that managers use to prepare and adjust marketing plans.

marketing mix A unique blend of product, place, promotion, and pricing strategies designed to produce mutually satisfying exchanges with a target market.

marketing myopia Defining a business in terms of goods and services rather than in terms of the benefits that customers seek.

marketing objective A statement of what is to be accomplished through marketing activities.

marketing plan A written document that acts as a guidebook of marketing activities for the marketing manager.

marketing planning Designing activities relating to marketing objectives and the changing marketing environment.

marketing research The process of planning, collecting, and analyzing data relevant to a marketing decision.

marketing research aggregator A company that acquires, catalogs, reformats, segments, and resells reports already published by marketing research firms.

marketing research objective The specific information needed to solve a marketing research problem; the objective should be to provide insightful decision-making information.

marketing research problem Determining what information is needed and how that information can be obtained efficiently and effectively.

marketing strategy The activities of selecting and describing one or more target markets and of developing and maintaining a marketing mix that will produce mutually satisfying exchanges with target markets.

marketing-controlled information source A product information source that originates with marketers promoting the product.

markup pricing The cost of buying the product from the producer plus amounts for profit and for expenses not otherwise accounted for.

Maslow's hierarchy of needs A method of classifying human needs and motivations into five categories in ascending order of importance: physiological, safety, social, esteem, and self-actualization.

mass communication The communication of a concept or message to large audiences.

mass merchandising A retailing strategy using moderate to low prices on large quantities of merchandise and lower service to stimulate high turnover of products.

materials management See *materials requirement planning.*

materials requirement planning (MRP) (materials management) An inventory control system that manages the replenishment of raw materials, supplies, and components from the supplier to the manufacturer.

materials-handling system A method of moving inventory into, within, and out of the warehouse.

maturity stage The third stage of the product life cycle during which sales increase at a decreasing rate.

MC See *marginal cost.*

measurement error An error that occurs when there is a difference between the information desired by the researcher and the information provided by the measurement process.

media mix The combination of media to be used for a promotional campaign.

media planning The series of decisions advertisers make regarding the selection and use of media, allowing the marketer to optimally and cost-effectively communicate the message to the target audience.

media schedule Designation of the media, the specific publications or programs, and the insertion dates of advertising.

medium The channel used to convey a message to a target market.

merchant wholesaler An institution that buys goods from manufacturers and resells them to businesses, government agencies, and other wholesalers or retailers and that receives and takes title to goods, stores them in its own warehouses, and later ships them.

Mercosur The largest Latin American trade agreement; includes Argentina, Bolivia, Brazil, Chile, Colombia, Ecuador, Paraguay, Peru, Venezuela, and Uruguay.

mission statement A statement of the firm's business based on a careful analysis of benefits sought by present and potential customers and an analysis of existing and anticipated environmental conditions.

MOA See *market opportunity analysis.*

modified rebuy A situation where the purchaser wants some change in the original good or service.

moral relativists Persons who believe that ethical truths depend on the individuals and groups holding them.

morals The rules people develop as a result of cultural values and norms.

motive A driving force that causes a person to take action to satisfy specific needs.

MR See *marginal revenue.*

MRP See *materials requirement planning.*

multiculturalism When all major ethnic groups in an area—such as a city, county, or census tract—are roughly equally represented.

multinational corporation A company that is heavily engaged in international trade, beyond exporting and importing.

multiple distribution See *dual distribution.*

multiplier effect (accelerator principle) Phenomenon in which a small increase or decrease in consumer demand can produce a much larger change in demand for the facilities and equipment needed to make the consumer product.

multisegment targeting strategy A strategy that chooses two or more well-defined market segments and develops a distinct marketing mix for each.

mystery shoppers Researchers posing as customers who gather observational data about a store.

N

NAFTA See *North American Free Trade Agreement.*

NAICS See *North American Industry Classification System.*

need recognition Result of an imbalance between actual and desired states.

needs assessment A determination of the customer's specific needs and wants, and the range of options the customer has for satisfying them.

negotiation The process during which both the salesperson and the prospect offer special concessions in an attempt to arrive at a sales agreement.

networking A process of finding out about potential clients from friends, business contacts, coworkers, acquaintances, and fellow members in professional and civic organizations.

new buy A situation requiring the purchase of a product for the first time.

new product A product new to the world, the market, the producer, the seller, or some combination of these.

new-product strategy A plan that links the new-product development process with the objectives of the marketing department, the business unit, and the corporation.

niche One segment of a market.

niche competitive advantage The advantage achieved when a firm seeks to target and effectively serve a small segment of the market.

noise Anything that interferes with, distorts, or slows down the transmission of information.

nonaspirational reference group A group with which an individual does not want to associate.

noncorporate blogs Independent blogs that are not associated with the marketing efforts of any particular company or brand.

nonmarketing-controlled information source A product information source that is not associated with advertising or promotion.

nonprobability sample Any sample in which little or no attempt is made to get a representative cross section of the population.

nonstore retailing Selling to customers through other means than by visiting a store.

norm A value or attitude deemed acceptable by a group.

North American Free Trade Agreement (NAFTA) An agreement between Canada, the United States, and Mexico to reduce trade barriers between the countries.

North American Industry Classification System (NAICS) A detailed numbering system developed by the United States, Canada, and Mexico to classify North American business establishments by their main production processes.

O

observation research A research method that relies on four types of observation: people watching people, people watching an activity, machines watching people, and machines watching an activity.

OEMs See *original equipment manufacturers.*

off-price retailer A retailer that sells at prices 25 percent or more below traditional department store prices because it pays cash for its stock and usually doesn't ask for return privileges.

one-to-one marketing An individualized marketing method that utilizes customer information to build long-term, personalized, and profitable relationships with each customer.

online retailing A type of shopping available to consumers with access to the Internet.

open-ended question An interview question that encourages an answer phrased in the respondent's own words.

opinion leader An individual who influences the opinions of others.

optimizers Business customers who consider numerous suppliers, both familiar and unfamiliar, solicit bids, and study all proposals carefully before selecting one.

order processing system A system whereby orders are entered into the supply chain and filled.

original equipment manufacturers (OEMs) Individuals and organizations that buy business goods and incorporate them into the products that they produce for eventual sale to other producers or to consumers.

outsourcing (contract logistics) A manufacturer's or supplier's use of an independent third party to manage an entire function of the logistics system, such as transportation, warehousing, or order processing.

P

penetration pricing A pricing policy whereby a firm charges a relatively low price for a product initially as a way to reach the mass market.

perception The process by which people select, organize, and interpret stimuli into a meaningful and coherent picture.

perceptual mapping A means of displaying or graphing, in two or more dimensions, the location of products, brands, or groups of products in customers' minds.

perishability The inability of services to be stored, warehoused, or inventoried.

personal selling A purchase situation involving a personal, paid-for communication between two people in an attempt to influence each other.

personality A way of organizing and grouping the consistencies of an individual's reactions to situations.

persuasive labeling A type of package labeling that focuses on a promotional theme or logo with consumer information being secondary.

pioneer advertising A form of advertising designed to stimulate primary demand for a new product or product category.

planned obsolescence The practice of modifying products so those that have already been sold become obsolete before they actually need replacement.

planning The process of anticipating future events and determining strategies to achieve organizational objectives in the future.

PLC See *product life cycle.*

point-of-purchase display (POP) A promotional display set up at the retailer's location to build traffic, advertise the product, or induce impulse buying.

pop-up shops Temporary retail establishments that provide flexible locations without a long-term commitment.

portfolio matrix A tool for allocating resources among products or strategic business units on the basis of relative market share and market growth rate.

position The place a product, brand, or group of products occupies in consumers' minds relative to competing offerings.

positioning Developing a specific marketing mix to influence potential customers' overall perception of a brand, product line, or organization in general.

preapproach A process that describes the "homework" that must be done by a salesperson before he or she contacts a prospect.

predatory pricing The practice of charging a very low price for a product with the intent of driving competitors out of business or out of a market.

premium An extra item offered to the consumer, usually in exchange for some proof of purchase of the promoted product.

prestige pricing Charging a high price to help promote a high-quality image.

price That which is given up in an exchange to acquire a good or service.

price equilibrium The price at which demand and supply are equal.

price fixing An agreement between two or more firms on the price they will charge for a product.

price skimming A pricing policy whereby a firm charges a high introductory price, often coupled with heavy promotion.

price strategy A basic, long-term pricing framework, which establishes the initial price for a product and the intended direction for price movements over the product life cycle.

primary data Information that is collected for the first time; used for solving the particular problem under investigation.

primary membership group A reference group with which people interact regularly in an informal, face-to-face manner, such as family, friends, or fellow employees.

private brand A brand name owned by a wholesaler or a retailer.

probability sample A sample in which every element in the population has a known statistical likelihood of being selected.

problem child (question mark) In the portfolio matrix, a business unit that shows rapid growth but poor profit margins.

processed materials Products used directly in manufacturing other products.

product Everything, both favorable and unfavorable, that a person receives in an exchange.

product advertising A form of advertising that touts the benefits of a specific good or service.

product category All brands that satisfy a particular type of need.

product development A marketing strategy that entails the creation of new products for current customers.

product differentiation A positioning strategy that some firms use to distinguish their products from those of competitors.

product item A specific version of a product that can be designated as a distinct offering among an organization's products.

product life cycle (PLC) A biological metaphor that traces the stages of a product's acceptance, from its introduction (birth) to its decline (death).

product line A group of closely related product items.

product line depth The number of product items in a product line.

product line extension Adding additional products to an existing product line in order to compete more broadly in the industry.

product mix All products that an organization sells.

product mix width The number of product lines an organization offers.

product modification Changing one or more of a product's characteristics.

product offering The mix of products offered to the consumer by the retailer; also called the *product assortment* or *merchandise mix.*

product orientation A philosophy that focuses on the internal capabilities of the firm rather than on the desires and needs of the marketplace.

product placement A public relations strategy that involves getting a product, service, or company name to appear in a movie, television show, radio program, magazine, newspaper, video game, video or audio clip, book, or commercial for another product; on the Internet; or at special events.

product/service differentiation competitive advantage The provision of something that is unique and valuable to buyers beyond simply offering a lower price than the competition's.

production orientation A philosophy that focuses on the internal capabilities of the firm rather than on the desires and needs of the marketplace.

profit Revenue minus expenses.

profit maximization A method of setting prices that occurs when marginal revenue equals marginal cost.

promotion Communication by marketers that informs, persuades, and reminds potential buyers of a product in order to influence an opinion or elicit a response.

promotional mix The combination of promotional tools—including advertising, public relations, personal selling, and sales promotion—used to reach the target market and fulfill the organization's overall goals.

promotional strategy A plan for the optimal use of the elements of promotion: advertising, public relations, personal selling, and sales promotion.

prospecting See *lead generation.*

psychographic segmentation Market segmentation on the basis of personality, motives, lifestyles, and geodemographics.

public relations The marketing function that evaluates public attitudes, identifies areas within the organization the public may be interested in, and executes a program of action to earn public understanding and acceptance.

publicity Public information about a company, product, service, or issue appearing in the mass media as a news item.

pull strategy A marketing strategy that stimulates consumer demand to obtain product distribution.

pulsing media schedule A media scheduling strategy that uses continuous scheduling throughout the year coupled with a flighted schedule during the best sales periods.

purchasing power A comparison of income versus the relative cost of a set standard of goods and services in different geographic areas.

push money Money offered to channel intermediaries to encourage them to "push" products—that is, to encourage other members of the channel to sell the products.

push strategy A marketing strategy that uses aggressive personal selling and trade advertising to convince a wholesaler or a retailer to carry and sell particular merchandise.

pyramid of corporate social responsibility A model that suggests corporate social responsibility is composed of economic, legal, ethical, and philanthropic responsibilities and that the firm's economic performance supports the entire structure.

Q

question mark See *problem child.*

R

random error An error that occurs when the selected sample is an imperfect representation of the overall population.

random sample A sample arranged in such a way that every element of the population has an equal chance of being selected as part of the sample.

raw materials Unprocessed extractive or agricultural products, such as mineral ore, timber, wheat, corn, fruits, vegetables, and fish.

reach The number of target consumers exposed to a commercial at least once during a specific period, usually four weeks.

real self-image The way an individual actually perceives himself or herself.

rebate A cash refund given for the purchase of a product during a specific period.

receiver The person who decodes a message.

recession A period of economic activity characterized by negative growth, which reduces demand for goods and services.

reciprocity The practice of business purchasers choosing to buy from their own customers.

reference group A group in society that influences an individual's purchasing behavior.

referral A recommendation to a salesperson from a customer or business associate.

reintermediation The reintroduction of an intermediary between producers and users.

relationship commitment A firm's belief that an ongoing relationship with another firm is so important that the relationship warrants maximum efforts at maintaining it indefinitely.

relationship marketing A strategy that focuses on keeping and improving relationships with current customers.

relationship selling (consultative selling) A sales practice that involves building, maintaining, and enhancing interactions with customers in order to develop long-term satisfaction through mutually beneficial partnerships.

repositioning Changing consumers' perceptions of a brand in relation to competing brands.

resale price maintenance A manufacturer, and its distributors, agree that retailers will sell products at a certain price floor.

research design Specifies which research questions must be answered, how and when the data will be gathered, and how the data will be analyzed.

retailer A channel intermediary that sells mainly to consumers.

retailing All the activities directly related to the sale of goods and services to the ultimate consumer for personal, nonbusiness use.

retailing mix A combination of the six Ps—product, place, promotion, price, presentation, and personnel—to sell goods and services to the ultimate consumer.

return on investment (ROI) Net profit after taxes divided by total assets.

revenue The price charged to customers multiplied by the number of units sold.

routine response behavior The type of decision making exhibited by consumers buying frequently purchased, low-cost goods and services; requires little search and decision time.

S

sales cycle See *sales process.*

sales orientation The idea that people will buy more goods and services if aggressive sales techniques are used and that high sales result in high profits.

sales presentation A formal meeting in which the salesperson presents a sales proposal to a prospective buyer.

sales process (sales cycle) The set of steps a salesperson goes through in a particular organization to sell a particular product or service.

sales promotion Marketing activities—other than personal selling, advertising, and public relations—that stimulate consumer buying and dealer effectiveness.

sales proposal A formal written document or professional presentation that outlines how the salesperson's product or service will meet or exceed the prospect's needs.

sample A subset from a larger population.

sampling A promotional program that allows the consumer the opportunity to try a product or service for free.

sampling error An error that occurs when a sample somehow does not represent the target population.

satisficers Business customers who place an order with the first familiar supplier to satisfy product and delivery requirements.

SBU See *strategic business unit.*

scaled-response question A closed-ended question designed to measure the intensity of a respondent's answer.

scanner-based research A system for gathering information from a single group of respondents by continuously monitoring the advertising, promotion, and pricing they are exposed to and the things they buy.

scrambled merchandising The tendency to offer a wide variety of nontraditional goods and services under one roof.

screening The first filter in the product development process, which eliminates ideas that are inconsistent with the organization's new-product strategy or are obviously inappropriate for some other reason.

search quality A characteristic that can be easily assessed before purchase.

seasonal media schedule A media scheduling strategy that runs advertising only during times of the year when the product is most likely to be used.

secondary data Data previously collected for any purpose other than the one at hand.

secondary membership group A reference group with which people associate less consistently and more formally than a primary membership group, such as a club, professional group, or religious group.

segmentation bases (variables) Characteristics of individuals, groups, or organizations.

selective distortion A process whereby a consumer changes or distorts information that conflicts with his or her feelings or beliefs.

selective distribution A form of distribution achieved by screening dealers to eliminate all but a few in any single area.

selective exposure The process whereby a consumer notices certain stimuli and ignores others.

selective retention A process whereby a consumer remembers only that information that supports his or her personal beliefs.

self-concept How consumers perceive themselves in terms of attitudes, perceptions, beliefs, and self-evaluations.

selling against the brand Stocking well-known branded items at high prices in order to sell store brands at discounted prices.

sender The originator of the message in the communication process.

service The result of applying human or mechanical efforts to people or objects.

service mark A trademark for a service.

shopping product A product that requires comparison shopping because it is usually more expensive than a convenience product and is found in fewer stores.

simulated (laboratory) market testing The presentation of advertising and other promotion materials for several products, including a test product, to members of the product's target market.

simultaneous product development A team-oriented approach to new-product development.

site reach See *stickiness*.

social class A group of people in a society who are considered nearly equal in status or community esteem, who regularly socialize among themselves both formally and informally, and who share behavioral norms.

socialization process How cultural values and norms are passed down to children.

societal marketing orientation The idea that an organization exists not only to satisfy customer wants and needs and to meet organizational objectives, but also to preserve or enhance individuals' and society's long-term best interests.

spatial discrepancy The difference between the location of a producer and the location of widely scattered markets.

specialty discount store A retail store that offers a nearly complete selection of single-line merchandise and uses self-service, discount prices, high volume, and high turnover.

specialty product A particular item for which consumers search extensively and are very reluctant to accept substitutes.

specialty store A retail store specializing in a given type of merchandise.

sponsorship A public relations strategy in which a company spends money to support an issue, cause, or event that is consistent with corporate objectives, such as improving brand awareness or enhancing corporate image.

stakeholder theory A theory that holds that social responsibility is paying attention to the interest of every affected stakeholder in every aspect of a firm's operation.

star In the portfolio matrix, a business unit that is a fast-growing market leader.

status quo pricing A pricing objective that maintains existing prices or meets the competition's prices.

stickiness (site reach) A measure of a Web site's effectiveness; calculated by multiplying the frequency of visits times the duration of a visit times the number of pages viewed during each visit.

stimulus Any unit of input affecting one or more of the five senses: sight, smell, taste, touch, hearing.

stimulus discrimination A learned ability to differentiate among similar products.

stimulus generalization A form of learning that occurs when one response is extended to a second stimulus similar to the first.

straight rebuy A situation in which the purchaser reorders the same goods or services without looking for new information or investigating other suppliers.

strategic alliance (strategic partnership) A cooperative agreement between business firms.

strategic business unit (SBU) A subgroup of a single business or a collection of related businesses within the larger organization.

strategic channel alliance A cooperative agreement between business firms to use the other's already established distribution channel.

strategic partnership See *strategic alliance*.

strategic planning The managerial process of creating and maintaining a fit between the organization's objectives and resources and evolving market opportunities.

subculture A homogeneous group of people who share elements of the overall culture as well as unique elements of their own group.

supercenter A retail store that combines groceries and general merchandise goods with a wide range of services.

supermarket A large, departmentalized, self-service retailer that specializes in food and some nonfood items.

supplies Consumable items that do not become part of the final product.

supply The quantity of a product that will be offered to the market by suppliers at various prices for a specified period.

supply chain The connected chain of all of the business entities, both internal and external to the company, that perform or support the logistics function.

supply chain management A management system that coordinates and integrates all of the activities performed by supply chain members into a seamless process, from the source to the point of consumption, resulting in enhanced customer and economic value.

supply chain orientation The connected chain of all of the business entities, both internal and external to the company, that perform or support the logistics function.

supply chain team An entire group of individuals who orchestrate the movement of goods, services, and information from the source to the consumer.

survey research The most popular technique for gathering primary data, in which a researcher interacts with people to obtain facts, opinions, and attitudes.

sustainability The idea that socially responsible companies will outperform their peers by focusing on the world's social problems and viewing them as opportunities to build profits and help the world at the same time.

sustainable competitive advantage An advantage that cannot be copied by the competition.

SWOT analysis Identifying internal strengths (S) and weaknesses (W) and examining external opportunities (O) and threats (T).

T

target market A defined group most likely to buy a firm's product.

target market A group of people or organizations for which an organization designs, implements, and maintains a marketing mix intended to meet the needs of that group, resulting in mutually satisfying exchanges.

teamwork Collaborative efforts of people to accomplish common objectives.

telemarketing The use of the telephone to sell directly to consumers.

temporal discrepancy A situation that occurs when a product is produced but a customer is not ready to buy it.
test marketing The limited introduction of a product and a marketing program to determine the reactions of potential customers in a market situation.
trade allowance A price reduction offered by manufacturers to intermediaries, such as wholesalers and retailers. See *promotional allowance.*
trade discount See functional discount.
trade sales promotion Sales promotion activities targeting a channel member, such as a wholesaler or retailer.
trademark The exclusive right to use a brand or part of a brand.
trust The condition that exists when one party has confidence in an exchange partner's reliability and integrity.

U

undifferentiated targeting strategy A marketing approach that views the market as one big market with no individual segments and thus uses a single marketing mix.
unfair trade practice acts Laws that prohibit wholesalers and retailers from selling below cost.
unique selling proposition A desirable, exclusive, and believable advertising appeal selected as the theme for a campaign.
unitary elasticity A situation in which total revenue remains the same when prices change.
universal product codes (UPCs) A series of thick and thin vertical lines (bar codes), readable by computerized optical scanners, that represent numbers used to track products.
universe The population from which a sample will be drawn.
unsought product A product unknown to the potential buyer, or a known product that the buyer does not actively seek.
UPCs See *universal product codes.*
Uruguay Round An agreement to dramatically lower trade barriers worldwide; created the World Trade Organization.
usage-rate segmentation Dividing a market by the amount of product bought or consumed.
utilitarian ethical theory A theory that holds that the choice that yields the greatest benefit to the most people is the choice that is ethically correct.

V

value The enduring belief that a specific mode of conduct is personally or socially preferable to another mode of conduct.
variable cost A cost that varies with changes in the level of output.
variable pricing See *flexible pricing.*
variables See *segmentation bases.*
vertical conflict A channel conflict that occurs between different levels in a marketing channel, most typically between the manufacturer and wholesaler or between the manufacturer and retailer.
virtue A character trait valued as being good.

W

want The way a consumer goes about addressing a need.
warehouse membership clubs Limited-service merchant wholesalers that sell a limited selection of brand-name appliances, household items, and groceries on a cash-and-carry basis to members, usually small businesses and groups.
warranty A confirmation of the quality or performance of a good or service.
Web community A carefully selected group of consumers who agree to participate in an ongoing dialogue with a particular corporation.
World Bank An international bank that offers low-interest loans, advice, and information to developing nations.
World Trade Organization (WTO) A trade organization that replaced the old General Agreement on Tariffs and Trade (GATT).
WTO See *World Trade Organization.*

Y

yield management systems (YMS) A technique for adjusting prices that uses complex mathematical software to profitably fill unused capacity by discounting early purchases, limiting early sales at these discounted prices, and overbooking capacity.
YMS See *yield management systems.*

ENDNOTES

CHAPTER 1

1. Announcement to the AMA Academic Council from Patricia K. Goodrich, Senior Director, Professional Development, American Marketing Association, October 25, 2007.
2. George Anderson, "Satisfied Workers Generate Greater Returns," *Retailwire*, online, January 16, 2008.
3. Ann Zimmerman, "Home Depot Chief Renovates," *The Wall Street Journal*, June 5, 2008, B1, B2.
4. Robert Levering and Milton Moskowitz, "The 100 Best Companies to Work For," *Fortune*, January 25, 2005, 73.
5. Philip Kotler and Kevin Lane Keller, "*A Framework for Marketing Management*, 3rd ed. (Upper Saddle River, NJ: Prentice-Hall, 2007), 3.
6. Woody Driggs, "Serving Up Customer Delight," *Customer Relationship Management*, April 2008, 14.
7. Ibid.
8. George Anderson, "Customer Service Tops NRF Agenda," *Retailwire*, January 16, 2008, online; "The Bean Delivers," *Marketing News*, February 15, 2008, 5.
9. Jena McGregor, "Customer Service Champs," *BusinessWeek*, March 3, 2008, 37–42.
10. Anya Kamenetz, "Cleaning Solution," *Fast Company*, September 2008, 121–124.
11. Ibid.
12. Todd Wasserman, "P&G's Green Guru Tells Us Why There's No Green Tide," *Brandweek*, May 26, 2008, 15, 17.
13. Elena Malykhina, "Purex Detergent Joins the 'Green' Movement," **Brandweek.com**, online, July 15, 2008.
14. Becky Ebenkamp, "Study: 'Green' Products Leave Consumers Puzzled," **Brandweek.com**, online, July 15, 2008.
15. Marc Gunther, "Coca-Cola's Green Crusader," *Fortune*, April 28, 2008, 150.
16. Rachel Tobin Ramos, "UPS, Coke, Home Depot Push Green Strategies," **ajc.com**, online, April 23, 2008.
17. Ibid.; "Wal-Mart Says More Consumers Looking For 'Green' Products," **homeworld business.com**, online, April 22, 2008.
18. Todd Wasserman, "Mintel: 'Green' Products Top 5,933 in 2007," **Brandweek.com**, online, May 21, 2008.
19 Nora Isaccs, "Crash and Burn," **upsidetoday.com**, online.
20. A. G. Lafley and Rom Charan, "The Consumer is Boss," *Fortune*, March 17, 2008, 121–126.
21. Ibid., used by permission.
22. "The Importance of Great Customer Experiences and the Best Ways to Deliver Them," *Insight*, November 2007, 32.
23. Ibid.
24. Phred Dvorak, "Next in Line for Reinvention: The Art of Selling," *The Wall Street Journal*, January 28, 2008, B3.
25. Christopher Musico, "7 Essential Consumer Service Processes," **destinationcrm.com**, online, January 16, 2008.
26. Brian Hindo, "Satisfaction Not Guaranteed," *BusinessWeek*, June 19, 2006, 32–36.
27. Jena McGregor, "Customer Service Champs," *BusinessWeek*, March 5, 2007, 52–64.
28. "Many Companies Not Working to Earn Loyalty," *Quirk's Marketing Research Review*, October 2008, 80.
29. Jena McGregor, "Customer Service Champs."
30. Jeffrey M. O'Brien, "A Perfect Season," *Fortune*, February 4, 2008, 61–66.
31. Julie Barker, "Power to the People: Reducing Turnover With Empowerment," *Incentive*, online, February 8, 2008.
32. Samuel Fromartz, "Good Enough to Eat," *Fast Company*, September 2008, 29.
33. Lafley and Charan, "The Consumer is Boss," 122.
34. **http://en.wikipedia.org/wiki/demographics_of_the_United_States**
35. The application exercises throughout the book are based on the winning entries in the "Best of the Great Ideas in Teaching Marketing" contest held in conjunction with the publication of the Eighth Edition of *Marketing*. Ideas came from marketing professors all across the country who teach many different sizes and types of marketing courses. Information on ways to implement these great ideas in the classroom can be found in the Instructor Manual that accompanies this text.
36. Jena McGregor, "At Netflix, the Secret Sauce is Software," *Fast Company*, December 2005, 48–51; Jennifer Netherby, "Netflix Delivers Big Earnings Increase: Sets 5.9 Million Subs as Modest 2006 Goal," *Video Business*, January 30, 2006, 1; Steven Zeitchnik, "Download Dreams: Netflix Eager to Expand Online Efforts," *Daily Variety*, January 25, 2006, 5; Jennifer Moeller, "You've Got (Movies in the) Mail," *The Christian Science Monitor*, December 2, 2005, 15; Ben Fritz, "Freaky Disc Biz: Netflix Grows at Blockbuster's Expense," *Daily Variety*, October 20, 2005, 1; "All Queued Up: How the Netflix Distribution Network Supports the Company's Business Model," *Material Handling Management*, November 2005, 9.

CHAPTER 2

1. Kate Maddox, "Marketer of the Year: Dan Henson, VP-CMO, General Electric, Co.," *BtoB's Best*, October 22, 2007.
2. Joseph Pereira, "Toys 'R' Us Unwraps Plans for Expansion," *The Wall Street Journal*, May 22, 2008, B1.
3. Melanie Warner, "McDonald's' Push a Boon for Produce," *The Star Telegram*, February 26, 2005, C1.
4. Ben & Jerry's, online, **www.benjerry.com**, (accessed December 1, 2008).
5. Mark Gongloff, "Golden Arches Offer Shelter in Storm," *The Wall Street Journal*, July 23, 2008, C1; Suzanne Vranica, "Marketers Find Ways to Exploit Gas Prices," *The Wall Street Journal*, July 7, 2008, B5.
6. Nike's site at **www.nike.com**, December 5, 2007.
7. Sarah Butrymowitz and Jayne O'Donnell, "Malls Get Creative to Draw More Shoppers in Tough Economy," **usatoday.com**, July 17, 2008; Store Review: Bass Pro Shops, **flyfishingabout.com**, December 1, 2008.
8. Julie Jargon, "New Leaf for Sara Lee, Kraft: Salads," *The Wall Street Journal*, March 26, 2007, A9.
9. John Brodie, "The Many Faces of Ralph Lauren," **money.cnn.com**, September 5, 2007.
10. Niraj Sherth, "India Liquor, Tobacco Firms Shift Tack," *The Wall Street Journal*, May 6, 2008, B8; Kounteya Sinha, "Surrogate Ads Luring Kids to Smoking: Study," **epaper.timesofindia.com**, December 1, 2008; "Surrogate Ads Will be Stopped, Assures I&B," **timesofindia.indiatimes.com**, December 1, 2008.
11. Geoff Keighly, "The Phantasmagoria Factory," *Business 2.0*, January/February 2004, 103; Christopher J. Chipello, "Cirque du Soleil Seeks Partnerships to Create Entertainment Centers," *WSJ.com*, July 18, 2001; Steve Friess, "Cirque Dreams Big," *Newsweek*, July 14, 2003, 42; "Bravo Announces Programming Alliance with Cirque du Soleil; Original Series, Specials, and Documentaries to Air on Bravo, 'The Official U.S. Network of Cirque du Soleil,'" *Business Wire*, June 19, 2000; "Inhibitions Take the Night Off for International Gala Premiere of ZUMANITY ™; Another Side of Cirque du Soleil™ at New York–New York Hotel and Casino," *PR Newswire*, September 21, 2003; Laura Del Rosso, "'O' Dazzles with Air, Underground Acrobatics," *Travel Weekly*, August 5, 2002; Gigi Berardi, "Circus Dance Cirque du Soleil," *Dance Magazine*, September 2002.

MARKETING PLAN APPENDIX

The authors would like to thank e-motion software for allowing us to include its marketing plan in the Eleventh Edition of *Marketing*. We greatly appreciate Mr. Keohane's contribution of a real plan used by his growing company, which demonstrates to students the level of detail and the elements required to build an effective plan.

CHAPTER 3

1. "Report to the Principal, Big Shot," *BusinessWeek*, July 30, 2007, 9.
2. Partially adapted from: Edwin M. Epstein, "The Good Company: Rhetoric or Reality? Corporate Social Responsibility and Business Ethics Redux," *American Business Law Journal*, July 1, 2007, 207.
3. Neil Parmer, "Taking Care of Business," *SmartMoney*, October 2008, 77–82.
4. Ibid.
5. Marianne M. Jennings, *Business Ethics, 5th Ed.* (Mason, Ohio: Thomson Higher Education), 2006, 5–6.
6. These ethical theories are from: Catherine Rainbow, "Descriptions of Ethical Theories and Principles," **www.bio.davidson.edu/people/Kabernd/Indep/carainbow.htm** (June 22, 2005).
7. Jennings, 7.
8. Ibid.
9. Based on Edward Stevens, *Business Ethics* (New York: Paulist Press, 1979). Reprinted with permission. Used with permission of Paulist Press.
10. Anusorn Singhapakdi, Skott Vitell, and Kenneth Kraft, "Moral Intensity and Ethical Decision-making of Marketing Professionals," *Journal of Business Research* 36, March 1996, 245–255; Ishmael Akaah and Edward Riordan, "Judgments of Marketing Professionals about Ethical Issues in Marketing Research: A Replication and Extension," *Journal of Marketing Research*, February 1989, 112–120. See also Shelby Hunt, Lawrence Chonko, and James Wilcox, "Ethical Problems of Marketing Researchers," *Journal of Marketing Research*, August 1984, 309–324; Kenneth Andrews, "Ethics in Practice," *Harvard Business Review*, September/October 1989, 99–104; Thomas Dunfee, Craig Smith, and William T. Ross, Jr., "Social Contracts and Marketing Ethics," *Journal of Marketing*, July 1999, 14–32; Jan Handleman and Stephen Arnold, "The Role of Marketing Actions with a Social Dimension: Appeals to the Institutional Environment," *Journal of Marketing*, July 1999, 33–48; David Turnipseed, "Are Good Soldiers Good? Exploring the Link between Organizational Citizenship Behavior and Personal Ethics," *Journal of Business Research*, January 2002, 1–16; Tim Barnett and Sean Valentine, "Issue Contingencies and Marketers' Recognition of Ethical Issues, Ethical Judgments and Behavioral Intentions," *Journal of Business Research*, April 2004, 338–346.
11. "The Stat," *BusinessWeek*, September 12, 2005, 16.
12. Ibid.
13. "Actions Contributing Most to Ethical Behavior and Compliance Identified," *Workspan*, February 1, 2007, 1.
14. "Taser Settled 10 of 52 Cases It Said Were Dismissed," **Bloomberg.com**, August 28, 2007.
15. Ibid.
16. Erin White, "'What Would You Do?' Ethics Courses Get Context," *The Wall Street Journal*, June 12, 2006, B3.
17. Ibid.
18. Angelina MacKewn and K. W. VanVuren, "Business Training, Reasoning Skills, and Philosophical Orientation: Correlates of Ethical Decision-Making," *International Journal of Management and Marketing Research* 1, no. 1 (2008): 111–121; and Deloise Frisque and Judith Kolb, "The Effects of Ethics Training Programs On Attitude, Knowledge, and Transfer of Training of Office Professionals: A Treatment and Control Design," *Human Resource Development Quarterly*, March 2008, 35–53.
19. Kellye Whitney, "Ernst & Young Ethics Training: Part of the Company Fabric," **clomedia.com** (July 2007).
20. "Wal-Mart Raises Bar on Toy-Safety Standards," *The Wall Street Journal*, May 14, 2008, B1–B2.
21. "Wal-Mart Suppliers Face Energy, Other Mandates," *The Wall Street Journal*, October 22, 2008, B1, B4.
22. Remi Trudel and June Cotte, "Does Being Ethical Pay?" *The Wall Street Journal*, May 12, 2008, R4.
23. "Study Links Ethics and Profits," *Quality Progress*, March 2008, 26.
24. **www.cdc.gov/tobacco**, August 29, 2007.
25. This section is partially adapted from Jennings, *Business Ethics*, 72–75.
26. Milton Friedman, "The Social Responsibility of Business Is to Increase Its Profits," *The New York Times*, September 1962, 126.
27. "Valero To Pay Pollution Fines," *Oil Daily*, August 30, 2007.
28. John Carey, "Big Strides to Become the Jolly Green Giant," *BusinessWeek*, January 29, 57.
29. Xueming Luo and C. B. Bhattacharya, "Corporate Social Responsibility, Customer Satisfaction, and Market Value," *Journal of Marketing*, October 2006, 1–18.
30. "Globally, Companies are Giving Back," *HR Magazine*, June 1, 2007, 30.
31. "Americans Seek More Responsibility from Companies," *Daytona Beach News Journal*, May 26, 2007, 3B.
32. **www.unglobalcompact.org/participantsandstakeholders/index/htm** (October 27, 2008).
33. "Secretary-General Opens Global Compact Leaders Summit as Business, Government, Civil Society Leaders Rally for Corporate Citizenship," *UNESCAP Press Release*, July 5, 2007, Press Release No. L/38/2007.
34. The Heinz story is from "A Clear Mission," *PR Week*, July 16, 2007, 12.
35. Jennifer Alsever, "Chiquita Cleans Up Its Act," *Fortune*, November 27, 2007, 73.
36. Joe Nocera, "The Promise and Limits of Good Works," *International Herald Tribune*, August 9–10, 2008, 11–12.
37. Michael Liedtke, "AOL Enters Settlement Over Cancellation Process," *Marketing News*, August 15, 2007, 14.
38. **www.marketingpower.com** (accessed October 28, 2008).
39. "Marketing a Green Product," *BusinessWeek Online*, March 5, 2007, 13.
40. Ibid.
41. "It's Not Easy Being Green," **www.usbusiness-review.com** (July–August 2008), 14–15.
42. "Easy but Green, Rider," *Marketing Magazine*, July 14, 2008, 29.
43. **www.wm.com** (accessed October 21, 2008).
44. "Shopping Can Boost Donations to Charity," *Augusta Chronicle*, May 29, 2007, C7.
45. "Shoppers Without A Cause," *BusinessWeek*, July 9, 2007, 14.
46. Larry Chiagouris and Ipshita Ray, "Saving the World With Cause-Related Marketing," *Marketing Management*, July/August 2007, 48–51.
47. "Cause-tied Marketing Not Perfect," *The Toronto Star*, July 16, 2007, AA02.
48. "Op-Ed: Cause Efforts Go Deeper Than Dollars," *PR Week*, April 16, 2007, 8.
49. "Susan G. Komen Breast Cancer Foundation Creates Five Questions to Ask Before Participating in a Cause-Related Marketing Program," *PR Newswire*, September 28, 2005; also see Michael Barone, Andrew Norman, and Anthony Miyazakij, "Consumer Response to Retailer Use of Cause-Related Marketing: Is More Better?" *Journal of Retailing*, December 2007, 437–445.
50. **http://www.rockstargames.com; http://www.take2games.com;** Logan Hill, "Why Rockstar Games Rock," *Wired.com*, July 2002; Michael Serazio, "Vice City Confidential: The 'Atari' Generation Grows Up," *Columbia.edu*, March 7, 2003; "The Games Kids Play: Are Mature Video Games Too Violent for Teens?" *Current Events*, February 7, 2003; "Deadly Inspiration? Teens Say Video Game Inspired Them in Deadly Highway Shooting," *ABCnews.com*, September 5, 2003; "Florida Officials Take Aim at Violent Games," *Reuters*, February 6, 2004; Andrew Bushell, "Popular Video Game Instructs Players to 'Shoot the Haitians'—New York AG Takes on Grand Theft Auto," *VillageVoice.com*, January 30, 2004; Christopher Byron, "Give Back Take-Two," *New York Post*, December 29, 2003.

CHAPTER 4

1. "A Shift in Dining Scene: Nicks, a Once-Hot Chain," *The Wall Street Journal*, June 29, 2007, A1, A13.
2. "Get in the Loop," *Marketing News*, May 1, 2008, 5.
3. Kerry Capell, "Thinking Simple at Philips," *BusinessWeek*, December 11, 2006, 50.
4. Calvin P. Duncan, Constance O'Hare, and John M. Mathews, "Raising Your Market IQ," *The Wall Street Journal*, December 102, 2007, R4.
5. "TJX: Dressed to Kill for the Downturn," *BusinessWeek*, October 27, 2008, 60.
6. The material on personality and geography is adapted from: Stephanie Simon, "The United States of Mind," *The Wall Street Journal*, September 23, 2008, A26.
7. "Stats on Women in Business," **www.score.org** (September 4, 2007).
8. "Women Want Home Improvement Retailers to Boost Service; National Survey Reveals Gaps in Service, Product Knowledge," *PR Newswire*, February 27, 2006.
9. "Single Women in U.S. Buying More Homes," *New York Times*, May 25, 2007, G6.
10. "Young Women Earn More than Men in Big U.S. Cities," *Renters News*, August 3, 2007.
11. Author's projection based upon J. Walker Smith, "Make Time Worth It," *Marketing Management*, July/August 2005, 56.
12. "Another Casualty Emerges From the Crises: Family Time," *The Wall Street Journal*, October 15, 2008, B1.
13. Michael Mandel, "The Real Reasons You're Working So Hard," *BusinessWeek*, October 3, 2005, 60.
14. Smith, "Make Time Worth It."
15. Elisabeth A. Sullivan, "HOG—Harley-Davidson Shows Brand Strength As It Navigates Down New Roads—And Picks Up More Female Riders Along the Way," *Marketing News*, November 1, 2008, 8.

16. "Changing Consumer Lifestyles Create New American Neighborhood," *Marketing Matters Newsletter*, **www.marketingpower.com**; (accessed October 28, 2008).
17. "American Time Use Survey—2007 Results," (Washington: Bureau of Labor Statistics) June 25, 2008.
18. "Changing Consumer Lifestyles…."
19. June Kronholz, "The Coming Crunch," *The Wall Street Journal*, October 13, 2006, B1, B8; U.S. Census Press Release, **www.census.gov/Press-Release/www/releases/archives/population/012496.html,** August 14, 2008.
20. "Fewer Americans Are Relocating Within the U.S.," *The Wall Street Journal*, July 10, 2008, A3.
21. "Targeting Tweens," *Chain Store Age*, July 1, 2007.
22. "Filling a Niche for Tweens," *Houston Chronicle*, August 23, 2007, 5.
23. "Celling to Tweens," *New York Post*, June 10, 2007, 32.
24. "Coming of Age in Consumerdom," *American Demographics*, April 2004, 14.
25. "Literal Fitness for Kids," *Brandweek*, September 24, 2007, 16.
26. "Spas for the Pre-Tween Set: More Businesses Are Offering Pampered-Treatment Packages for Kids," *Vancouver Sun*, October 30, 2006, C3.
27. "Tween Trend Report Investigates the World of Generation Y," *Harrison Group/VNU* (2006).
28. "Teens Prefer Real Friends to Online Ones," *Quirk's Marketing Research Review*, August 2008, 6.
29. "Retailers Sell to Teens in Virtual Worlds," *The Wall Street Journal*, August 19, 2008, B8.
30. "Understanding Tweens and Teens," *Youth Markets Alert*, August 1, 2007, 7; and "EPM Offers Advice for Marketing to Tweens and Teens," *Research Alert*, June 1, 1007, 5.
31. Karen Akers, "Generation Y: Marketing to the Young and the Restless," *Successful Promotions*, January/February 2005, 33–38.
32. "Young, Rich, and Famous," *USA Today*, January 10, 2007, 6B, 7B.
33. "Gen Y's Fave: Whole Foods," *Brandweek*, July 28, 2008, 13.
34. "Gen X More Involved Than Boomers," *USA Today*, April 4, 2007, D5.
35. "Gen Xers and Their Concerns Are Reshaping the Retail Landscape: Be True to Your Word, When Marketing to Them, Researcher Advises," *Montreal Gazette*, June 13, 2007, B1
36. "Gen X Wants No-Debt," *American Demographics*, April 2004, 43.
37. "Gen X Slackers Get Serious," *Brandweek*, June 30, 2008, 8.
38. "The Changing Face of the U.S. Consumer," *Advertising Age*, July 7, 2008, 1–10.
39. Ibid.
40. Louise Lee, "Love Those Boomers," *BusinessWeek*, October 24, 2005, 94–101.
41. "Boomer Bust," *The Wall Street Journal*, October 21, 2008, A13.
42. "Baby Boomers Delay Retirement," *The Wall Street Journal*, September 22, 2008, A4.
43. Lee, "Love Those…."
44. Dick Chay, "New Segments of Boomers Reveal New Marketing Implications," *Marketing News*, March 14, 2005, 24.
45. "Marketers Rethink Retail; Boomers Get Fresh Look," *Brandweek*, May 21, 2007, 10.
46. "Personal Touch," *Marketing Management*, May/June 2007, 4.
47. Robert J. Morais, "It's Time to Connect With Baby Boomers," *Brandweek*, March 6, 2006, 20.
48. "Minority Population Tops 100 Million," *US Fed News*, May 17, 2007.
49. "Nonwhites to Be Majority in U.S. by 2042," *The Wall Street Journal*, August 14, 2008, A4.
50. Ibid.
51. Ibid.
52. "Minority Population…."
53. Projections by the authors.
54. "Pepsi, Vowing Diversity Isn't Just Image Polish, Seeks Inclusive Culture," *The Wall Street Journal*, April 19, 2005, B1.
55. "Give Me Your Tired, Your Poor, Your Beloved Products," *Business 2.0*, October 2005, 29–30.
56. "Wal-Mart's Hispanic Outreach," *The Wall Street Journal*, May 31, 2005, B9.
57. "Claim That Tune," *Adweek Media*, January 14, 2008, 1.
58. "Online Shopping By Minorities Up Sharply," *Quirk's Marketing Research Review*, June 2008, 80.
59. "To Woo Gen Y, Marketers Push Culture, Not Language," *Brandweek*, January 1, 2007, 5.
60. "Has This Group Been Left Behind?" *Brandweek*, March 14, 2005, 35.
61. "African-American TV Usage and Buying Power Highlighted," **www.marketingcharts.com,** accessed November 12, 2008.
62. "Affluent African Americans Making Impact on Consumer Economy," **www.marketingcharts.com,** accessed November 12, 2008.
63. Ibid.
64. "Coca Cola Kicks Off 2007 With New Advertising and 'American Idol' Integration in the U.S.," *PR Newswire*, January 17, 2007; also see Sonya Grier, Anne Brumbaugh, and Corliss Thornton, "Crossover Dreams: Consumer Responses to Ethnic-Oriented Products," *Journal of Marketing*, April 2006, 35–51.
65. "Affluent African Americans Wield $29.8 Billion in Spending Power," **www.marketingcharts.com**, accessed November 12, 2008.
66. Ibid.
67. "The Asian-American Market," *delivermagazine*, September 2008, 8.
68. Ibid.
69. "The Asian-American Market Is a Diverse Group, and There Are Cultural Nuances Particular to Each," *National Jeweler*, September 1, 2006.
70. Jerry Goodbody, "Taking the Pulse of Asian Americans," *Adweek's Marketing Week*, August 12, 2001, 32.
71. "The Invisible Market," *Brandweek*, January 30, 2006, 22–26.
72. U.S. Census Bureau, data with projections by the authors.
73. **http://earnmydegree.com**, accessed November 9, 2008.
74. U.S. Income gap widens, richest share hits record," **www.reuters.com/article/domesticNews/idUSN1241503820071012**, accessed November 9, 2008.
75. Christopher Conkey, "Snapshot of America: Who's Richest, Poorest, Where the Single Men Are," *The Wall Street Journal*, August 30, 2006, D1, D3.
76. "At the Supermarket Checkout, Frugality Trumps Brand Loyalty," *The Wall Street Journal*, November 6, 2008, D1.
77. "The Recession Could Be Mild But Long," *BusinessWeek*, October 20, 2008, 12.
78. "At the Supermarket Checkout…."
79. "Why Some Brands Cheer a Sour Economy," *Brandweek*, October 13, 2008, 5.
80. "Looking for Cost Cuts in Lots of New Places," *The Wall Street Journal*, October 16, 2008, B5.
81. "Costco's Artful Discounts," *BusinessWeek*, October 20, 2008, 58–60.
82. "How Technology Delivers for UPS," *BusinessWeek*, March 5, 2007, 60.
83. Diane Brady, "Reaping the Wind," *BusinessWeek*, October 11, 2004, 201.
84. "Creativity Pays. Here's How Much," *BusinessWeek*, April 24, 2006, 45.
85. "Yes, Innovations Do Pay Off, Study Finds," *International Herald Tribune*, August 30–31, 2008, 15.
86. Cornelia Dean, "Maybe Science Can Save the Planet: But Should It?" *International Herald Tribune*, August 13, 2008, 2.
87. "More Paper Tiger Than Watchdog?" *BusinessWeek*, September 3, 2007, 45.
88. "Spamalot No More," *Marketing Management*, October 2008, 47–50.
89. "Editorial: Shop With Cash," *The Providence Journal*, February 9, 2007, B4.
90. "Identity Theft Protection Bill Clears Hurdle," *Associates Press Newswires*, May 4, 2007.
91. "K-C, P&G's Lotion Tissue War Is Nothing to Sneeze At," *Brandweek*, September 18, 2008, 12–13.
92. Ibid.
93. "Home Economics," *BusinessWeek*, March 14, 2005, 12.
94. "DHL Beats a Retreat from the U.S.," *The Wall Street Journal*, November 11, 2008, B1.

CHAPTER 5

1. William Wrigley Jr. Company, news release, July 2, 2007.
2. *Trade and American Jobs: The Impact of Trade on U.S. and State-Level Employment* (Washington: Business Roundtable), February 2007.
3. Ibid.
4. Ibid.
5. "Top U.S. Trade Partners," U.S. Department of Commerce, Census Bureau, Foreign Trade Division, International Trade Administration, October 2008.
6. David Wessel and Bod Davis, "Pain from Free Trade Spurs Second Thoughts," *The Wall Street Journal*, March 28, 2007, A1, A14. Reprinted with permission of *The Wall Street Journal*, © 2007 Dow Jones & Company, Inc. All Rights Reserved Worldwide.
7. Ibid.
8. Ibid.
9. "Can the U.S. Bring Jobs Back from China?" *BusinessWeek*, June 30, 2008, 39–43.
10. Ibid.
11. "Globalization's Gains Come with a Price," *The Wall Street Journal*, May 24, 2007, A1, A12.
12. "Multinationals: Are They Good for America?" *BusinessWeek*, March 10, 2008, 41–45.
13. Ibid.
14. Ibid.
15. "Foreign Investors Face New Hurdles Across the Globe," *The Wall Street Journal*, July 6, 2007, A1, A7.
16. Theodore Levitt, "The Globalization of Markets," *Harvard Business Review*, May/June 1983, 92–100.

17. "Levi's Marketers Hope One Size Fits All," *The Wall Street Journal*, July 18, 2008, B7.
18. Ibid.
19. The Italian cleaning products stories are from "Convenience Is a Dirty Word to These Italian Consumers," *Quirk's Marketing Research Review*, October 2006, 6.
20. "Slacker Nation? Young Japanese Shun Promotions," *The Wall Street Journal*, November 1–2, 2008, A1, A6.
21. "French Protestors Wage War on Billboards," *The Wall Street Journal*, September 26, 2008, B5.
22. Ibid.
23. "Indian Farmers Threaten to Renew Nano Protests," *International Herald Tribune*, September 12, 2008, 17.
24. **www.finfacts.com**, November 22, 2005.
25. "World's Most Expensive Cities," **CNNMoney.com**, June 18, 2007.
26. The China/India story is from Anil K. Gupta and Haiyan Wang, "How to Get China and India Right," *The Wall Street Journal*, April 28–29, 2007, R9. Reprinted with permission of *The Wall Street Journal* © 2007 Dow Jones & Company, Inc. All Rights Reserved Worldwide.
27. "China Pushes Foreign Companies to Unionize," *The Global Edition of the New York Times*, September 12, 2008, 14.
28. Ibid.
29. "Doing Business 2008," The World Bank.
30. Ibid.
31. "Global Ties Under Stress As Nations Grab Power," *The Wall Street Journal*, April 28, 2008, A1, A16.
32. Ibid.
33. "China Says It Is Free to Set High Tariffs," *The Wall Street Journal*, July 30, 2008, A9; and "China Sides With Developing Nations in Trade Talks," *The Wall Street Journal*, July 30, 2008, A10.
34. "The End of Free Trade?" *The Wall Street Journal*, July 31, 2008, A14.
35. "South Korea Looks to the West," *Fortune*, October 31, 2008, 52; and "Liberalizing Trans-Atlantic Trade," *The Wall Street Journal*, September 5, 2008, 5.
36. "The Trade Stimulus," *International Trade Administrator*, October 27, 2008, 1.
37. "Most Canadians, Americans Support NAFTA: Poll," *Xinhua News Agency*, October 1, 2007.
38. "5 Myths About NAFTA," *The Fort Worth Star Telegram*, April 14, 2008, 9B.
39. "Top U.S. Trading Partners," *Top U.S. Export Markets*, Washington: International Trade Association, Summer 2008, 4.
40. Jack Welch, "A Punching Bag Named NAFTA," *BusinessWeek*, April 28, 2008, 138.
41. "Refighting NAFTA," *BusinessWeek*, March 31, 2008, 56–59; also see: "Make the World Go Away," *Fortune*, February 4, 2008, 105–107.
42. "U.S. Central America-Dominican Republic Free Trade Agreement (CAFTA-DR) Analysis," (Washington: International Trade Association), Summer 2008, 12.
43. **www.eurunion.org**, accessed November 5, 2008.
44. Ibid.
45. Ibid.
46. "European Union's Kroes Says U.S. Criticism of Microsoft Ruling Is Unacceptable," *Associated Press Newswires*, September 19, 2007.
47. Jonathan Bensky, "World's Biggest Market: European Union Offers Great Opportunities for U.S. Companies, But There Are Also Plenty of Challenges," *Shipping Digest*, July 30, 2007.
48. Ibid.
49. "World Bank Group 2008 Global Poll: Overcoming Poverty Remains Biggest Challenge to Developing Countries," press release, The World Bank, October 31, 2008.
50. **www.sba.gov**, accessed November 4, 2008.
51. **www.exim.gov**, October 3, 2007.
52. "$187 Billion Global Licensing Industry Comes to Life," **www.reuters.com** (press release), June 6, 2008.
53. "Entertainment/Character Licenses Generated Largest Share of Worldwide Sales," *Licensing Letter*, June 6, 2005.
54. **www.franchise.org**, December 5, 2005.
55. "Foreign Flavors," *The Wall Street Journal*, September 25, 2006, R8.
56. Roger Parloff, "Not Exactly Counterfeit," *Fortune*, May 1, 2006, 109–116.
57. "Dangerous Fakes," *BusinessWeek*, October 13, 2008, 34–44.
58. Andrew R. Thomas, Timothy J. Wilkinson, and Jon M. Hawes, "Making It in China," *The Wall Street Journal*, May 12, 2008, R11.
59. "GM's China Partner Looms as a New Rival," *The Wall Street Journal*, April 20, 2007, A1, A8.
60. "Partners Fight over Wahaha in China," *The Wall Street Journal*, July 28, 2008, B1.
61. "Danone's China Strategy in Set Back," *The Wall Street Journal*, June 15, 2007, A10.
62. **www.walmartstores.com/FactsNews**, accessed November 8, 2008.
63. "Investment Will Favor International Markets," *The Toronto Star*, October 29, 2008, BO2.
64. "Toyota Eyes India Market, Builds School to Get Edge," *The Wall Street Journal*, November 3, 2008, B1–B2.
65. "Starbucks Expansion Plan in China Unchanged," *China Knowledge Press*, August 7, 2008.
66. Kenneth Hein, "Emerging Markets Still Like U.S. Brands," *BrandWeek*, April 16, 2007, 4. Used by permission of Aegis Group, plc.; also see "Best Global Brands," September 29, 2008, 52–57.
67. "Fad Marketing's Balancing Act," *BusinessWeek*, August 6, 2007, 42.
68. "Machines for the Masses," *The Wall Street Journal*, December 9, 2005, A4.
69. Peter Gumbel, "Big Mac's Local Flavor," *Fortune*, May 5, 2008, 115–121.
70. "Kraft Reformulates Oreo, Scores in China," *The Wall Street Journal*, May 1, 2008, B1, B7.
71. "If Only 'Krispy Kreme' Meant 'Makes You Smarter,'" *Business 2.0*, August 2005, 108.
72. Amy Chozick, "The Samurai Sell: Lexus Dealers Bow to Move Swank Cars," *The Wall Street Journal*, July 9, 2007, A1, A12.
73. Jane Lanhee Lee, "China Hurdle: Lack of Refrigeration," *The Wall Street Journal*, August 30, 2007, A7.
74. Eric Bellmann and Cecilie Rohwedder, "Western Grocer Modernizes Passage to India's Markets," *The Wall Street Journal*, November 28, 2007, B1.
75. "UPS Battles Traffic to Gain Ground in India," *The Wall Street Journal*, January 25, 2008, B1, B2.
76. Michael Arndt, "Knock, Knock, It's Your Big Mac," *BusinessWeek*, July 23, 2007, 36.
77. "Vietnam Denies Garment Dumping in U.S. Market," Thai News Service, October 1, 2007.
78. Martin Lindstrom, "One Voice?" *Clickz.com*, February 26, 2002; Steve McClure, "New MTV Post in OZ, Japan: MTV Asia President to Assume Responsibility," *Billboard*, March 8, 2003, 59; "MTV Announces International Expansion Plans for Europe, Asia, and Latin America: Company to Add New Services in Regional Growth Markets Worldwide," *Business Wire*, March 9, 1996; Kerry Cappel, Catherine Belton, Tom Lowry, Manjeet Kripalani, Brian Bremner, and Dexter Roberts, "MTV's World," *BusinessWeek.com*, February 18, 2002.

CHAPTER 6

1. **www.persil.com/persil_products/pfam_home/**, February 2006; **www.eu.pg.com/ourbrands/ariel.html**, February 2006.
2. "Virtually Satisfied," *Marketing News*, October 15, 2008, 26.
3. Allen Weiss, Nicholas Lurie, and Deborah MacInnis, "Listening to Strangers: Whose Responses Are Valuable, How Valuable Are They, and Why?" *Journal of Marketing Research*, August 2008, 450–461.
4. Jonah Berger and Grainne Fitzsimons, "Dogs on the Street, Pumas on Your Feet: How Cues in the Environment Influence Product Evaluation and Choice," *Journal of Marketing Research*, February 2008, 1–14.
5. The section on categorization is adapted from: Roger Blackwell, Paul Miniard, and James Engel, *Consumer Behavior, 10th Edition* (Mason, Ohio: Cengage Learning), 2006, 132–133.
6. Jeffrey Inman and Russell Winer, "Impulse Buys," *The Wall Street Journal*, April 15, 1999, A1; and David Silvera, Anne Lavack, and Fredric Kropp, "Impulse Buying: The Role of Affect, Social Influence, and Subjective Well-Being," *Journal of Consumer Research*, 25, no. 1 (2008), 23–33.
7. Paula Andruss, "Delivering Wow Through Service," *Marketing News*, October 15, 2008, 10.
8. Toyota ad, *Wired*, March, 2007, 72–73.
9. Ira Teinowitz, "Kellogg Move Bodes Ill for Ads to Kids," *Advertising Age*, June 18, 2007.
10. Sandra Yin, "Color Bind," *American Demographics*, September 2003, 24, 26.
11. Geoff Colvin, "Selling P&G," *Fortune*, September 17, 2007, 156, 6, 163.
12. "Thank God for the Chinese Consumer," *The Wall Street Journal*, August 8, 2008, A15; and Nicholas Casey, "Fisher-Price Game Plan: Pursue Toy Sales in Developing Markets," *The Wall Street Journal*, May 29, 2008, B1, B2.
13. Lorenza Muñoz," Selling Spanish TV to Ad Buyers," *Los Angeles Times*, May 15, 2007.
14. "Rise of the Have-Nots," *Adweek*, October 1, 2007, 29.
15. Bradley Johnson, "Mo' Money, Mo' Buyin'," *Advertising Age*, January 15, 2007, 78, 3, 29.
16. "TJX: Dressed to Kill for the Downturn," *BusinessWeek*, October 27, 2008, 60.
17. Ulrich Orth and Lynn Kahle, "Intrapersonal Variation in Consumer Susceptibility to Normative Influence: Toward a Better Understanding of Brand Choice Decisions," *Journal of Social Psychology*, August 8, 2008, 423–448.
18. Ibid.

19. Ronald Clark, James Zboja, and Ronald Goldsmith, "Status Consumption and Role-Relaxed Consumption: A Tale of Two Retail Consumers," *Journal of Retailing and Consumer Services*, January 2007, 45–59.
20. Neil E. Boudette and Gina Ghon, "Brawny BMW Seeks 'the Idea Class'," *The Wall Street Journal*, August 2, 2006, B1.
21. Katie Delahaye Paine, "How Do Blogs Measure Up? Forget Reach and Frequency. Success in Today's Marketplace is Measured Not by How Broad Your Reach is But by How Deep Your Network Is," *Communication World*, Sept–Oct 2007, 24, 5, 30.
22. Rachel Dodes, "Bloggers Get Under the Tent," *The Wall Street Journal, September* 12, 2006, B1, B2.
23. Chenting See, Kevin Zheng Zhou, Nan Zhou, and Julie Juan Li, "Harmonizing Conflict in Husband-Wife Purchase Decision-Making: Perceived Fairness and Spousal Influence Dynamics," *Journal of the Academy of Marketing Science* (Fall 2008), 378–394; also see: Michel Laroche, Zhiyong Yang, Kim Chankon, and Marie-Odile Richard, "How Culture Matters in Children's Purchase Influence: A Multi-level Investigation," *Journal of the Academy of Marketing Science* (Spring 2007), 113–116.
24. Ibid.
25. Derek Gale, "Who's the Boss?" *Restaurants & Institutions*, February 1, 2007, 117, 2, 50.
26. Jeanine Poggi, "Teen Queens; The Age Group's Spending Is on the Rise, Making It a Coveted—Albeit Fickle—Market," *WWD*, June 28, 2007, 85.
27. Karin Ekstrom, "Parental Consumer Learning or 'Keeping Up With Their Children'," *Journal of Consumer Behavior* (July/August 2007), 203–217.
28. Bureau of Labor Statistics, Consumer Expenditures Annual Reports: 2005, Census Bureau, **www.bls.gov/ces/**.
29. Stephanie Rosenbloom, "My Dad, American Inventor," *The New York Times*, August 16, 2007.
30. Nanette Byrnes, "Secrets Of the Male Shopper," *BusinessWeek*, online, **www.businessweek.com/magazine/content/06_36/b3999001.htm**, accessed August 17, 2007; also see: Xin He, Jeffrey Inman, and Vikas Mittal, "Gender Jeopardy in Financial Risk-Taking," *Journal of Marketing Research*, August 2008, 414–424.
31. Anil Mathur, George Moschis, and Euehun Lee, "A Longitudinal Study of the Effects of Life Style Status Changes on Changes in Consumer Preferences," *Journal of the Academy of Marketing Sciences*, Summer 2008, 234–246.
32. "Study: Snacking Has Become the Fourth Meal of the Day," *Brandweek*, September 29, 2008, 8.
33. Ibid.
34. Loretta Chao and Betsy McKay, "Pepsi Steps into Coke Realm," *The Wall Street Journal*, September 12, 2007.
35. **www.ampacet.com**, December 28, 2007.
36. Laura Petrecca, "Axe Ads Turn Up the Promise of Sex Appeal," *USA Today*, April 17, 2007.
37. Joshua Rosenbaum, "Guitar Maker Looks for a New Key," *The Wall Street Journal*, February 11, 1998, B1, B5.
38. Elizabeth J. Wilson, "Using the Dollar-metric Scale to Establish the Just Meaningful Difference in Price," in 1987 AMA *Educators' Proceedings*, ed. Susan Douglas et al. (Chicago: American Marketing Association, 1987), 107.
39. Kenneth Hein, "Teens Schizophrenic About Their Brands: Millennials Have Complex Feelings About Brands Unless, of Course, It's Apple," *Brandweek*, June 18, 2007.
40. International Chamber of Commerce's new initiative: BASCAP—Business Action to Stop Counterfeiting and Piracy **www.icc-ccs.co.uk/bascap/digest/Cases.htm**, September 11, 2007; Global Brand Protection Directory: **www.iccwbo.org/bascap/id12418/index.html**, September 11, 2007.
41. Press release: "GE Announces Advancement in Incandescent Technology; New High-Efficiency Lamps Targeted for Market by 2010," February 23, 2007; Lloyd Alter, "GE Announces High Efficiency Incandescent Light Bulbs. Why?" *Design & Architecture*, February 24, 2007, accessed online at **www.treehugger.com/files/2007/02/ge_announces_hi.php**, May 29, 2008.
42. Stephanie Thompson, "Cole Haan Fashions an Effort for Women," *Advertising Age*, August 25, 2003, 6.
43. **www.Cadillac.com**, accessed October 25, 2008.
44. Jyothi Datta, "Aspartame: Bitter Truth in Artificial Sweeteners?" Mumbai, Oct. 3, **www.thehindubusinessline.com/2005/10/04/stories/2005100404220300.htm**, accessed September 14, 2007.
45. Amy Chozick and Timothy Martin, "A Place for Cocoa Nuts?"*Wall Street Journal*, July 15, 2005, B1, B3; **http://www.ethelschocolate.com**; "Ethel's Launches First-Ever Approachable, Everyday Gourmet Chocolate and Chocolate Lounges; Opens First Two Stores in Chicago, Expected to Expand to Six by End of Summer," *PR Newswire*, June 6, 2005; Karen Hawkins, "Chocolate Lounges' Present Themselves as Sweet Alternatives to Coffee Shops, Bars," *Associated Press*, February 13, 2006; Melinda Murphy, "Trend Report: Chocolate Is Hot," *CBS News Online*, **http://www.cbsnews.com/stories/2006/02/07/earlyshow/contributors/melindamurphy/main1289922.shtml**.

CHAPTER 7

1. "2008 Marketing Priorities and Plans," *BtoB Magazine*, July 15, 2008, 25.
2. Michael D. Hutt and Thomas W. Speh, *Business Marketing Management: B2B, 9e*. (Cincinnati: Thomson, 2007), 4.
3. Patricia Riedman, "BtoB's Best Brands," *BtoB Magazine*, Special Issue, 2008, 21–25.
4. Hutt and Speh, 315.
5. Ibid.
6. Mary E. Morrison, "Industrial Buyers Shopping Online," *BtoB Magazine*, October 13, 2008, 19.
7. Karen J. Bannan, "10 Great Web Sites: Overview," *BtoB Magazine*, online, September 15, 2008.
8. "Survey Says! Recent BtoB Webcast Audience Poll Results," *BtoB Magazine*, November 10, 2008, 8.
9. NetGenesis, E-Metrics: Business Metrics for the New Economy, **www.spss.com**.
10. Morrison, 19.
11. "RSS," Wikipedia, the Free Encyclopedia, accessed online at **http://en.wikipedia.org/wiki/**.
12. "B2B Marketers Missing Out on Influencing Buyers Online," *Marketing Matters Newsletter*, Chicago: American Marketing Association, online, October 28, 2008.
13. "Grainger Introduces SupplyLink Site," *BtoB Magazine*, online, July 24, 2008.
14. "Disintermediation," Wikipedia, the Free Encyclopedia, accessed online at **http://en.wikipedia.org/wiki/**.
15. Ibid.
16. Kate Maddox, "Marketers Look to Boost Customer Retention," *BtoB Magazine*, online, May 5, 2008.
17. Ibid. Reprinted with permission of Crane Communications.
18. "Office Depot Forms Alliance With Netbizz in Singapore," *BtoB Magazine*, online, August 13, 2008.
19. Steven Reinberg, "The Issue: DHL Turns to Rival UPS," *BusinessWeek*, June 11, 2008, online.
20. Erin White, "A Cheaper Alternative to Outsourcing: Choice Hotels and 1-800-Flowers Swap Call-Center Employees," *The Wall Street Journal*, April 10, 2006, B3.
21. Robert M. Morgan and Shelby D. Hunt, "The Commitment-Trust Theory of Relationship Marketing," *Journal of Marketing*, 58, no. 3 (1994): 23.
22. Ibid.
23. Gordon Fairclough, "GM's Chinese Partner Looms as a New Rival," *The Wall Street Journal*, April 20, 2007, A1.
24. U.S. Census Bureau, "North American Industry Classification System (NAICS) – United States," accessed online at **www.census.gov/epcd/www/naics.html**, January 12, 2009.
25. Steve Butler, "B2B Exchanges Transaction Activity," *eMarketer*, online.
26. J. Lynn Lunsford, "Boeing Delays Dreamliner Delivery Again," *The Wall Street Journal*, April 10, 2008, B3.
27. Marshall Lager, "Listen Up," *Customer Relationship Management*, March 2007, 24–27.
28. Kate Maddox, "Relevant Content Connects with C-suite," *BtoB Magazine*, October 13, 2008, 37–38.
29. Ibid.
30. Setting the Standard: Code of Ethics and Business Conduct. Office of Ethics and Business Conduct, Lockheed Martin Corporation, Bethesda, MD, October 2008.
31. "Right Channeling: Making Sure Your Best Customers Get Your Best Service," Right Now Technologies, online at **www.rightnow.com**, June 3, 2008.
32. This application exercise is based on the contribution of Gregory B. Turner (College of Charleston) to *Great Ideas in Teaching Marketing*, a teaching supplement that accompanies Lamb, Hair, and McDaniel's *Marketing*. Professor Turner's entry titled "Student Ethics versus Practitioner Ethics" received an Honorable Mention in the "Best of the Great Ideas in Teaching Marketing" contest held in conjunction with the publication of the eighth edition of *Marketing*.
33. 22. Jonathan Karp, "How Bikers' Water Backpack Became Soldiers' Essential,"*Wall Street Journal*, July 19, 2005, B1, B2; "CamelBak Introduces New Line of Strength/Stealth Technology Responding to Law Enforcement and Military Needs; R&D Innovations Protect against Infrared Detection, Provide Strongest Hydration Reservoir Available," *PR Newswire*, January 27, 2005; Mark Riedy, "The Birth of CamelBak," *Mountain Bike*,

Summer 2004, 104; "CamelBak Announces Chem-Bio Hydration Reservoir for Military, Law Enforcement and First Responders; New Reservoir Is World's Only Hands-Free Hydration System That Withstands Exposure to Chemical and Biological Agents to Provide Safe Drinking Water in All Combat Environments 24/7/365," *PR Newswire*, August 26, 2004.

CHAPTER 8

1. Jena McGregor, "At Best Buy, Marketing Goes Micro," *BusinessWeek*, May 26, 2008, 52, 53.
2. Vanessa O'Connell, "Park Avenue Classic or Soho Trendy?" *The Wall Street Journal*, April 20, 2007, B1, B2.
3. Vanessa O'Connell, "Reversing Field, Macy's Goes Local," *The Wall Street Journal*, April 21, 2008, B1, B8.
4. Evan Bailyn, "Keeping It Simple: Marketing to Tweens on a Shoestring," **www.mediapost.com**, December 2, 2008.
5. Emily Steel and Vishesh Kumar, "Targeted Ads Raise Privacy Concerns," *The Wall Street Journal*, July 8, 2008, B1; Jessica Tsai, "Oh, Behave!," *Customer Relationship Management*, January 2008, 25–29; "The Aim of Behavioral Targeting," **www.eMarketer.com**, August 5, 2008; "Behavioral Targeting and Privacy," **www.eMarketer.com**, July 29, 2008.
6. Khanh T. L. Tran, "Retailing's Sweet Spot: Stores Look to Lure Millennial Generation," **www.wwd.com**, July 2, 2008.
7. Kenneth Hein, "How to Reach Teens? It's All about the Brand," online, **www.brandweek.com**, June 18, 2007.
8. Sarah Mahoney, "Study: Gen Y Shoppers Drawn to Greener Marketers," online, **www.mediapostpublications.com**, September 21, 2007.
9. "The Issue: How P&G Brought Back Herbal Essences," *BusinessWeek*, June 17, 2008, online.
10. Jessica Sebor, "Y me," *Customer Relationship Management*, November 2006, 24–35.
11. Toni Whitt, "Boomers Rewrite Rules for Marketing," **www.heraldtribune.com**, June 25, 2007.
12. Jennifer Mann, "Advertising and Marketing: 50-year-olds Not Dead Yet," **star-telegram.com**, August 10, 2008.
13. Ylan Q. Mui, "Retailers Redesign as Boomers Hit 60," **www.washingtonpost.com**, January 17, 2006, D01.
14. Sebor, "Y me."
15. Emily Fromm, "Marketing to Women," *Brandweek*, October 4, 2004, 21–28.
16. Ross Kenneth Urken, "EA Sports' Ads Feature New Stars: John (and Jane) Q. Public," *The Wall Street Journal*, July 25, 2008, online.
17. Jennifer Waters, "Home Depot Woos Women With Concept Store Exuding 'Romance'," *The Wall Street Journal*, October 9, 2007, online.
18. Rupa Ranganathan, "Resort Spa Uncovers Cultural Anthropology to Cultivate Male Clients," *RetailWire*, June 30, 2005, online.
19. "CoolStuffForDads.com, an Online Store Dedicated to Gifts for Dads, Continues to Add Great Products for Men," **www.biz.yahoo.com**, September 22, 2008.
20. Tom Ryan, "Targeting Male Grocery Shoppers," **www.retailwire.com**, June 4, 2007.
21. Francine Kizner, "Where the Rich Shop," **www.entrepreneur.com**, February 16, 2007.
22. "Luxury Brands: Marketing the Upscale during a Downturn," **http://knowledge.wharton.upenn.edu**, November 13, 2008.
23. Constantine von Hoffman, "For Some Marketers, Low Income Is Hot," *Brandweek*, September 11, 2006, 6.
24. "The New Mainstream: How the Buying Habits of Ethnic Groups Are Creating a New American Identity," **http://knowledge.wharton.upenn.edu/article.cfm?articleid=1270**, November 15, 2005; accessed June 9, 2008.
25. Laura Klepacki, "Ethnic Products Now Front and Center," **www.retailwire.com**, June 11, 2007.
26. "What's 'Online Marketing' in Spanish?" *RetailWire*, November 5, 2007.
27. Dan Raftery, "R&FF Retailer: Hispanic Foods Move Beyond Hot & Spicy," **www.retailwire.com**, June 4, 2007.
28. Ann Zimmerman and Miguel Bustillo, "Home Depot's New Web Site Opens Door to Hispanics," *The Wall Street Journal*, November 17, 2008, B1, B9.
29. "Amazon Launches New Software en Español Store as the Software Shopping Destination for Hispanic Consumers," **www.biz.yahoo.com**, August 12, 2008.
30 David Morse, "Brain Trust Query: Do African Americans Require a Targeted Marketing Approach?" **www.retailwire.com**, July 30, 2008.
31. Deborah L. Vence, "Mix It Up—Segmentation, Unique Events Key to Targeting Blacks," *Marketing News*, October 15, 2006, 19, 22.
32. Andrew Pierce, "Multiculti Markets Demand Multilayered Marketing," *Marketing News*, May 1, 2008, 21.
33. Ibid.
34. Alison Damast, "Love Can Hurt—Your Bank Account," *BusinessWeek*, February 7, 2008, online.
35. Stuart Elliott, "To Reach Mothers, Wal-Mart Signs Deal with an NBC Unit," **www.nytimes.com**, July 14, 2008.
36. "Baby Boomer Segmentation: Kids/No Kids," **www.retailwire.com**, February 2, 2007, online.
37. Dianne Hales, "What Your Car Says About You," *Parade*, May 15, 2005, 8.
38. Joseph Pereira, "New Exercise Targets Less-Than-Fit," *The Wall Street Journal*, February 1, 2007, B1, B9.
39. Deborah L. Vence, "Divide and Conquer," *Marketing News*, July 15, 2007, 15, 18.
40. Ann Zimmerman, "Home Depot Learns to Go Local," *The Wall Street Journal*, October 7, 2008, B1.
41. **www.claritas.com**, December 15, 2008.
42. George Stalk, Jr., "In Praise of the Heavy Spender," **www.reportonbusiness.com**, May 21, 2007, online.
43. Ellen Byron, "Aiming to Clean Up, P&G Courts Business Customers," *The Wall Street Journal*, January 26, 2007, B1, B2.
44. Juliet Chung, "Cooking Like the Stars?" *The Wall Street Journal*, June 20, 2008.
45. Jennifer Saranow and Vanessa O'Connell, "Concierge Services and Mismatched Socks," *The Wall Street Journal*, June 5, 2008.
46. Barry Silverstein, "Trader Joe's: Quirky Mart," **www.brandchannel.com**, December 13, 2008; Christopher Palmeri, "Trader Joe's Recipe for Success," *BusinessWeek* February 21, 2008, online; "A Unique Grocery Store," **http://eastontowncenter.com**, December 13, 2008.
47. "Targeting Wal-Mart's Core Customer Segments," **www.retailwire.com**, April 2, 2008.
48. "How Teen E-retailer Tripled Revenue by Allowing Consumers to Select What Email Content They Really Want," **www.marketingsherpa.com**, June 28, 2007.
49. Dianna Dilworth, "AT&T's New Multichannel Work Targets Young, On-the-Go Crowd," **www.dmnews.com**, September 18, 2007.
50. Chuck Stogel, "Callaway Gets 'Personal' With $30M Campaign," *Brandweek*, February 12, 2007, 14.
51. Ellen Byron, "Can a Re-Engineered Kleenex Cure a Brand's Sniffles?" *The Wall Street Journal*, January 22, 2007, B1.
52. Sonia Reyes, "Can Frozen Treats Sell Outside the Freezer Aisle?" *Brandweek*, March 26, 2007, 16.
53. Sandra Jones, "Sears Steps Back in Time to Go Forward," **www.chicagotribune.com**, March 12, 2007.
54. Geoff Colvin, "Selling P&G," *Fortune*, September 17, 2007, 163–169.
55. Jenny McTaggart, "Taking a Bite Out of Baggers," *Brandweek*, June 27, 2005, 42–45.
56. Ibid.
57. Gary McWilliams, "Not Copying Wal-Mart Pays Off for Grocers," *The Wall Street Journal*, June 6, 2007, B1, B5.
58. This application exercise is based on the contribution of Kim McKeage (University of Maine) to *Great Ideas in Teaching Marketing*, a teaching supplement that accompanies Lamb, Hair, and McDaniel's *Marketing*. Professor McKeage's entry, titled "Students Practice Making Market/Product Grids on Themselves," received an Honorable Mention in the "Best of the Great Ideas in Teaching Marketing" contest held in conjunction with the publication of the eighth edition of *Marketing*.
59. "Las Vegas Tourism Agency Announces 1.3 Percent Rise in Visitor Totals for 2003," *Las Vegas Review-Journal*, February 14, 2004; Jennifer Bjorhus, "Las Vegas Tourism Authorities Campaign in Portland, Ore," *Knight Ridder/Tribune Business News*, June 4, 1999; Chris Jones, "Las Vegas Tourism Agency Executive Says Research, Marketing Are Key to Success," *Las Vegas Review-Journal*, April 6, 2003; Chris Jones, "Las Vegas Tourism Chief Opposes Ads; Board Members Object to 'Sin City' Phrase," *Las Vegas Review-Journal*, December 16, 2003; Chris Jones, "Las Vegas Tourism Officials Plan Marketing Blitz to Attract Canadian Tourists," *Travel Weekly*, March 3, 2003; Chris Jones, "New Las Vegas Tourism Ads Target Hispanics with Tradition-Focused Messages," *Las Vegas Review-Journal*, July 17, 2003; Chris Jones, "Las Vegas Tourism Authority Unveils Culturally Diverse Television Ads," *Las Vegas Review-Journal*, February 11, 2004.

CHAPTER 9

1. Joseph Rydholdm, "A Natural Extension," *Quirk's Marketing Research Review*, May 2002, 22–23, 69–70.
2. "Oscar Mayer Prepares a Better Bacon Package," *Brandweek*, June 11, 2007, 11.
3. "Why Some Customers Are More Equal Than Others," *Fortune*, September 19, 1994, 215–224.
4. Sunil Gupta, Donald Lehmann, and Jennifer Ames Stuart, "Valuing Customers," *Journal of Marketing Research*, February 2004, 7–18.
5. Janet Adamy, "Dunkin Donuts Tries to Go Upscale, But Not Too Far," *The Wall Street Journal*, April 8–9, 2006, A1, A7.

6. "Roll Out the Blue Carpet," *Business 2.0*, May 2007, 53–54.
7. Scott Pimley, "Looking to Increase Their (s) Miles Per Gallon," *Quirk's Marketing Research Review*, August 2008, 32–38.
8. Michael Fielding, "A Clean Slate," *Marketing News*, May 1, 2007, 9–10.
9. Ibid.
10. "Respondents Lie and Good Ideas Die," *Quirk's Marketing Research Review*, May 2007, 48–54.
11. D. Randall Brandt, "Improve the Customer Service," *Quirk's Marketing Research Review*, January 2006, 68.
12. "Watch and Learn," *Marketing News*, February 1, 2006, 60.
13. "The Science of Desire," *BusinessWeek*, June 5, 2006, 104.
14. Ibid.
15. Ibid.
16. Raymond R. Burke, "Virtual Shopping: Breakthrough in Marketing Research," *Harvard Business Review*, March/April 1996, 120–131.
17. Ellen Byron, "A Virtual View of the Store Aisle," *The Wall Street Journal*, October 3, 2007, B1, B12.
18. Ibid.
19. Ibid.
20. Ibid.
21. Karl Feld, "Do You Know Where Your Data Came From?" *Quirk's Marketing Research Review*, November 2007, 24–31.
22. Kira Signer and Andy Korman, "One Billion and Growing," *Quirk's Marketing Research Review*, July/August 2006, 62–67.
23. Ibid.
24. Conversation with Craig Stevens, Senior VP E-Rewards, based upon company research (November 2, 2007); also see "Market Research," *Marketing News*, September 15, 2007, 16.
25. Ibid.
26. Tim Macer and Sheila Wilson, "Online Makes More Inroads," *Quirk's Marketing Research Review*, February 2007, 50–58.
27. Based on the author's conversation with Jerry Thomas, CEO Decision Analyst, Inc. This firm has one of the largest Internet panels in the world.
28. **www.ChannelM2.com**, (accessed October 31, 2008).
29. Gregory S. Heist, "Beyond Brand Building," *Quirk's Marketing Research Review*, July/August 2007, 62–67.
30. Ibid.
31. Ibid.
32. "CGM Overview, **www.nielsenbuzzmetrics.com**, August 27, 2007.
33. Pete Blackshaw, "The Pocket Guide to Consumer Generated Media," **www.clickz.com**, August 28, 2005; Paul Verna, "User-Generated Content: More Popular than Profitable," **www.emarketer.com**, January 2009, accessed February 13, 2009.
34. "BrandPulse Insights," **www.nielsenbuzzmetrics.com**, August 28, 2007.
35. "Behavioral Issues," *Brandweek*, October 20, 2008, 21–25.
36. Ibid.
37. Ibid.
38. Emily Steel, "How Marketers Hone Their Aim," *The Wall Street Journal*, June 19, 2007, B6.
39. "Online Ads Mature," *Marketing Management*, July/August 2007, 5.
40. Carl McDaniel and Roger Gates, *Marketing Research*, 7th ed. (Hoboken: John Wiley & Sons, 2007).
41. Gina Piccalo, "Fads Are So Yesterday," *Los Angeles Times*, October 9, 2005; Stephanie Kang, "Trying to Connect with a Hip Crowd," *Wall Street Journal*, October 13, 2005, B1.

CHAPTER 10

1. Valarie A. Zeithaml, Mary Jo Bitner, and Dwayne Gremler, *Services Marketing* (New York: McGraw-Hill, 2009).
2. "Employment Outlook: 2006–2016," November 2007, **www.bls.gov.**
3. Bridget Finn, "Luring 'Em In," *Business 2.0*, March 2005, 44–46.
4. "Coke, Pepsi to Sell Drinks with Stevia," *The Atlantic Journal-Constitution*, online, December 18, 2008.
5. Todd Wasserman, "P&G Seeks Right Ingredient to Wash Out Laundry Woes," *Brandweek*, August 8, 2005, 5.
6. "Kool-Aid Announces New Products and Better-For-You Brand Direction," *Yahoo! Finance*, May 27, 2008.
7. Vanessa L. Facenda, "Procter Dishes Out 3-Tiered Dawn Attack," *Brandweek*, September 24, 2007, 4.
8. Vanessa L. Facenda, "In Search of More Growth, P&G's Febreze Hits the Road," *Brandweek*, August 6, 2007, 6.
9. Julie Jargon, "Campbell's Chief Looks for Splash of Innovation," *The Wall Street Journal*, May 30, 2008, B8.
10. Al Ries, "The Pitfalls of Megabranding," *Advertising Age Online*, August 4, 2008.
11. David Kiley, "Best Global Brands," *BusinessWeek*, August 6, 2007, 56–64.
12. Nirmalya Kumar and Jan-Benedict E. M. Steenkamp, "Premium Store Brands: The Hottest Trend in Retailing," **www.marketingprofs.com**, March 20, 2007.
13. "Costco Buying Power Makes Dent in Private-Label Wine Market," **http://seattle.bizjournals.com**, April 2, 2007.
14. Elaine Wong, "Retailers Rally Behind Their 'Captive Brands'," **www.Brandweek.com**, September 29, 2008.
15. Elaine Wong, "Mr. Clean Finds Fresh Smell by Teaming with Febreze," *Brandweek*, August 11, 2008, 14.
16. Douglas Quenqua, "A Way to Save and Still Have Crisp Clothes," *The New York Times*, online, October 10, 2008.
17. "World of Coca-Cola," **www.worldofcoca-cola.com** (accessed January 11, 2009); "World of Coca-Cola," **http://en.wikipedia.org/wiki/World_of_Coca-Cola** (accessed February 21, 2009).
18. Jim Edwards, "Brand Defense," *Brandweek*, August 25–September 1, 2008, S1, S2.
19. Ibid.
20. Steve Miller, "Pennzoil Fires on all Cylinders for Overhaul," *Brandweek*, February 18, 2008, 13.
21. Deborah Ball, "The Perils of Packaging: Nestlé Aims for Easier Openings," *The Wall Street Journal*, November 17, 2005, B1.
22. "Environmentally Responsible Packaging: Convenience vs. Conscience," **www.retailwire.com**, April 30, 2008.
23. Alissa Walker, "Spin the Bottle," *Fast Company*, June 2008, 54.
24. "Dell Expands 'Green' Packaging Initiative," *Austin American Statesman*, online, December 16, 2008.
25. Ted Mininni, "Packaging That Works For the Planet," *Brandweek*, April 23, 2007, 20.
26. George Anderson, "Consumers Want More/Different Info on Labels," **www.retailwire.com**, July 17, 2008.
27. "Greenwash," **http://en.wikipedia.org/wiki/Greenwash**, January 11, 2009; David Roberts, "Another Inconvenient Truth," *Fast Company*, March 2008, 70; "The Six Sins of Greenwashing," TerraChoice Environmental Marketing Inc., November 2007.
28. **http://www.apple.com**; Riva Richmond, "Apple's New GarageBand Makes Making Music Easy," *Dow Jones Newswires*, January 27, 2004; Walter Mossberg, "How to Become a Rock Star: Apple's Latest Music Offering Lets Closet Crooners Record and Mix Their Own Tunes," *WSJ.com*, February 4, 2004; Bob Massey, "Music-Making Made Slick," *Washington Post*, January 25, 2004, F07; Jonathan Seff, "Center of Attention—iPod Mini, iLife '04 Expand Apple's Digital Hub," **http://www.macworld.com**, March 2004.

CHAPTER 11

1. Reena Jana, "In Data," *BusinessWeek*, September 22, 2008, 48.
2. Jana McGregor, "In Focus," *BusinessWeek*, April 28, 2008, 61–72.
3. Reena Jana, "In Data."
4. "The Value of New Product Time to Market," **www.retailwire.com**, November 21, 2006.
5. Michael E. Porter, "Why America Needs an Economic Strategy," *BusinessWeek*, November 10, 2008, 39–42.
6. "Changing the World," *Entrepreneur*, October 2003, 30.
7. Vanessa L. Facenda, "Oh Boy! Disney Sees Market for Pre-Teen Fragrances," *Brandweek*, July 23, 2007, 5.
8. Melanie Warner, "P&G's Chemistry Test," *Fast Company*, July/August 2008, 71.
9. Renee Hopkins Callahan, Gwen Ishmael, and Leyla Nomiranian, "The Case for In-the-Box Innovation," Innovation Brochure (Arlington, TX: Decision Analysts, 2005.)
10. Melanie Warner, "P&G's Chemistry Test."
11. Geoff Colvin, "Here It Is. Now, You Design It!" *Fortune*, May 26, 2008, 34.
12. Jeff Jarvis, "The Buzz From Starbucks Customers," *BusinessWeek*, April 28, 2008, 42, 44.
13. Ibid.
14. Salvatore Parise, Patricia J. Guinan, and Bruce Weinberg, "The Secrets of Marketing In a Web 2.0 World," *The Wall Street Journal*, December 15, 2008, R4, 11. Used by permission.
15. Chris Pentilla, "Big Ideas," *Entrepreneur*, March 2007, 62.
16. Allison Enright, "P&G Looks Outside for Innovative Solutions," *Marketing News*, March 1, 2007, 20–21.
17. Tom Ryan, "Finding Sources of Innovation," *RetailWire*, July 18, 2008, online.
18. Ibid.

19. John Karolefski, "CPG Matters: P&G Changes Rules for Product Development," *RetailWire*, February 19, 2008, online.
20. Joseph L. Weber, Stanley Holmes, and Christopher Palmeri, "Mosh Pits of Creativity," *BusinessWeek*, November 7, 2005, 98–100.
21. Andrew Marton, "2006: A Face Odyssey," *Fort Worth Star-Telegram*, February 16, 2006, E1, E8.
22. Chuck Salter, "The Faces and Voices of the World's Most Innovative Company," *Fast Company*, March 2008, 74–96.
23. George Anderson, "New Products Fail to Make Impression," *RetailWire*, November 20, 2008, online.
24. Eyal Biyalogorsky, William Boulding, and Richard Staelin, "Stuck in the Past: Why Managers Persist with New Product Failures," *Journal of Marketing*, 70 (April 2006), 108–121.
25. Ibid.
26. Jena McGregor, "How Failure Breeds Success," *BusinessWeek*, July 10, 2006, 42–52.
27. Jenny Mero, "John Deere's Farm Team," *Fortune*, April 14, 2008, 121, 126. Reprinted with permission.
28. Norihiko Shirouzu and Stephen Power, "Unthrilling but Inexpensive, the Logan Boosts Renault in Emerging Markets," *The Wall Street Journal*, October 9, 2006, B1.
29. Michael Fielding, "Driving Into the Global Market," *Marketing News*, November 1, 2008, 14–17.
30. Jena McGregor, "GE Reinventing Tech For The Emerging World," *BusinessWeek*, April 28, 2008, 68.
31. Gordon Fairclough, "GM's Partner in China Plans Competing Car," *The Wall Street Journal*, April 5, 2006, B1.
32. Robert Scoble, "PassionPlay," *Fast Company*, November 2008, 90.
33. Daniel B. Honigman, "Who's on First?" *Marketing News*, November 1, 2007, 16.
34. "Colleges Perfect for Word of Mouth," *eMarketer*, August 23, 2007, online.
35. Todd Wasserman, "Word Games," *Brandweek*, April 14, 2006, 24–28.
36. Ibid.
37. Daniel B. Honigman, "Who's on First?"
38. "Internet Key to Influencing the Influencers," *Marketing Matters Newsletter*, January 12, 2007, 1.
39. "Looking for Ways to Replace CD Sales in a Flash," *Retailing Today*, February 11, 2008, online.
40. This application exercise is based on the contribution of Karen Stewart (Richard Stockton College of New Jersey) to *Great Ideas in Teaching Marketing*, a teaching supplement that accompanies Lamb, Hair, and McDaniel's *Marketing*. Professor Stewart's entry titled "New-product Development" was a winner in the "Best of the Great Ideas in Teaching Marketing" contest held in conjunction with the publication of the eighth edition of *Marketing*.
41. Neil Parmar, "Idled Toy Inventors Find a Sweet Niche: 'Novelty' Candy," *Wall Street Journal*, July 21, 2005, B1, B3; "Novelties Engender Avid Fans," *MMR*, June 13, 2005, 64; "Timing Is Everything with Licensed Novelty Candy," *Confectioner*, March 2005, 32; "Securing Play Value: Novelty/Interactive Candy Isn't Just Playing Around; It's Aiming for a More Stable Shelf Spot," *Confectioner*, February 2005, 38.

CHAPTER 12

1. **www.papajohns.com**, January 2009; Mike Sachoff, "Papa John's Launches Text-Message Ordering," **www.webpronews.com** feature article, November 15, 2007; Emily Steel and Suzanne Vranica, "Papa John's Gets Finger Friendlier," *The Wall Street Journal*, November 13, 2007, B4; **www.qsrmagazine.com**, January 2009, "Papa John's Introduces Text Ordering."
2. **www.pumpbiz.com**, January 2006.
3. **www.l-textile.com**, August 2009.
4. **www.meridiankiosks.com**, January 2006.
5. "Pepsi, Supermarkets Teaming Up," *Supermarket News*, October 31, 1994, 31; included in Starbucks Annual Report 2006.
6. **www.cisco.com**, January 2006.
7. J. Lynn Lunsford and Paul Glader, "Boeing's Nuts and Bolts Problem," *The Wall Street Journal*, June 19, 2007, A8.
8. **www.dod.mil** and **www.cmcusa.org** (accessed February 2006).
9. **www.dollartree.com**, January 2006.
10. **www.sysco.com**, January 2006.
11. Dean Foust, "Harry Potter and the Logistical Nightmare," *BusinessWeek*, August 6, 2007, 9.
12. Shelly Branch, "P&G Buys Iams: Will Pet Food Fight Follow?" *The Wall Street Journal*, August 12, 1999. Reprinted at **www.pg.com**, January 2006.
13. Eric Newman, "Red Bull, Meet Black Bunny," *Brandweek*, February 25, 2008 (accessed online July 22, 2008).
14. Lynnley Browning, "Do-it-Yourself Logos for Proud Scion Owners," *The New York Times*, March 24, 2008 (accessed online March 24, 2008).
15. Brian Nadel, "Supply and Global Demand," *Fortune*, July 9, 2007, S1–S6.
16. Evan West, "These Robots Play Fetch," *Fast Company*, July/August 2007, 49–50.
17. Ben Worthen, "Weak Links in the (Supply) Chain," *The Wall Street Journal*, June 24, 2008, B5.
18. **knowledge.wharton.upenn.edu** (accessed June 2, 2008).
19. Monica Isbell and Chris Norek, "How Global Trade and Transportation Trends Impact America's Transportation Infrastructure," *CSCMP Explores*, Spring 2008, 3.
20. John J. Fialka, "Fuel Rules Soak Soap Makers," *The Wall Street Journal*, July 10, 2007, A6.
21. George Anderson, "Best Buy Focusing RFID Efforts at Front of Store," **www.retailwire.com** (accessed June 6, 2006).
22. Faye Brookman, "RFID and Retailers: Will It Ever Be Perfect Together?" **www.retailwire.com** (accessed April 2, 2007).
23. **www.yrc.com**; **http://www.inboundlogistics.com** (accessed August 2006).
24. Anonymous, "Leveraged Procurement," **www.outsourcing-supply-chain-management.com** and **www.avendra.com** and **www.ford.com** (accessed August 2009).
25. **www.appleinsider.com** (accessed February 2006).
26. **www.iphonetoolbox.com** (accessed August 14, 2009).
27. Russ Banham, "Keeping the Links Together," *The Wall Street Journal*, June 5, 2007, A17.
28. **www.greenbiz.com/news/2008/09/25/green-supply-chain-thinking-outside-cardboardbox** (accessed January 14, 2009).
29. **http://logistics.about.com** (accessed January 14, 2009).
30. Tamara Audi, "Ailing Sheraton Shoots for a Room Upgrade," *The Wall Street Journal*, March 25, 2008, A1.
31. J. Bander, "Losing Focus: As Kodak Eyes Digital Future, a Big Partner Starts to Fade," *The Wall Street Journal*, January 23, 2004, p. A1.
32. Amy Schatz and Sarah McBride, "Hollywood Studios Seek Control over Deliveries," *The Wall Street Journal*, June 12, 2008, B6.
33. Michael Freedman, "Out of Africa," *Forbes*, November 27, 2006, 45.
34. Mei Fong, "IKEA Hits Home in China," *The Wall Street Journal*, March 3, 2006, B1.
35. Ellen Byron, "P&G's Global Target: Shelves of Tiny Stores," *The Wall Street Journal*, July 16, 2007, A1.
36. This application exercise is based on the contribution of John Beisel (University of Pittsburgh) to Great Ideas in Teaching Marketing, a teaching supplement that accompanies Lamb, Hair, and McDaniel's Marketing. The entry by Professor Beisel was a runner-up in the "Best of the Great Ideas in Teaching Marketing" contest held in conjunction with the publication of the 8th Edition of Marketing.
37. Christopher Lawton, "Made-by-Viewers TV," *Wall Street Journal*, December 13, 2005, B1, B2; Steve Tomich, "Current TV: Think Outside, Get Inside the Box—Taking the Leap with a 'New TV' Network," *Digital Video Magazine*, January 1, 2006, 38; James Hibberd, "Progress Report: The New Nets; Three Rookies, All with Major Backers, Devise Strategies That Help Them Overcome the Odds and Find Their Place." *Television Week*, November 14, 2005, 26; Paul Gogh, "Gore: Current TV Aims for the Masses." *Hollywood Reporter*, October 10, 2005, 6.

CHAPTER 13

1. *Retail Industry Indicators 2007*, National Retail Federation, online at **www.nrf.com** (accessed December 27, 2007).
2. Bureau of Labor Statistics, "Industry at a Glance: NAICS 42–45, Wholesale and Retail Trade," online at **www.bls.gov**, May 4, 2007.
3. Ibid.
4. U.S. Census Bureau, *Monthly Retail Trade Report*, 2006, online at **www.census.gov/mrts/www/mrts.html** (accessed December 28, 2007).
5. Alan Breznick, "Specialty Shops: What's Your Value Proposition?" *Consumer Electronics Vision Magazine*, online at **www.ce.org**, January/February 2007.
6. "Tweeter CE Playground Store," Best of Boston 2007 Electronics, *Boston Magazine*, online at **www.bostonmagazine.com**.
7. *Food CPI, Prices and Expenditures: Food Expenditure Tables*, U.S. Dept of Agriculture, **www.ers.usda.gov** (accessed December 28, 2007).
8. **www.pigglywiggly.com**; Michael Garry, "Loyalty Program Cuts Defections," *Supermarket News*, January 22, 2007.
9. Ibid.
10. **www.exxonmobil.com** (accessed June 19, 2008).
11. "Wal-Mart to Open its 3,000th International Store," online at **www.walmartfacts.com**, November 14, 2007.
12. "Supercenter Industry," HHC Publishing, online at **www.warehouseclubfocus.com** (accessed December 28, 2007).

13. **www.tescopoly.org** (accessed June 19, 2008).
14. **www.familydollar.com** and **www .dollargeneral.com**.
15. "Restaurant Industry Facts," National Restaurant Association, online at **www.restaurant.org/research/ind_glance.cfm**, December 31, 2007.
16. Gene Marcial, "Vending Machines are Learning to Love Plastic," *BusinessWeek*, August 13, 2007.
17. Alli McConnon, "The Va Va Vooming of Vending Machines," BusinessWeek, January 3, 2008.
18. **www.usatech.com** (accessed June 19, 2008).
19. **www.meetmark.com** (accessed June 19, 2008).
20. **www.the-dma.org** accessed October 30, 2007.
21. "Overall Spending on Direct Mail to Reach $73.6 Billion by 2009," a white paper presented by the Winterberry Group, online at **www .winterberrygroup.com** (accessed October 30, 2007).
22. **www.dell.com**, December 2007.
23. **www.qvc.com**, February 2006.
24. **www.emarketer.com**, September 2008.
25. Ken Magill, "Great Expectations," *Multichannel Merchant*, December 1, 2007.
26. Abbey Klaassen, "Buy It from Radio Ads at the Push of a Button," *Advertising Age*, February 21, 2006, online.
27. **www.vans.com**, January 2006.
28. Alexander Peers and Nick Wingfield, "Sotheby's, eBay Team Up to Sell Fine Art Online," *The Wall Street Journal*, January 31, 2002, B8; **http://search.sothebys.com**, **www .ebay.com**, January 2006.
29. McDonald's Corporation, Inside the U.S. Franchising Fact Sheet, **www.mcdonalds.com/corp/franchise**; **www.entrepreneur.com/franchises/mcdonalds/282570-0.html** (accessed December 27, 2007).
30. International Franchise Association Web site, **www.franchise.org**, December 2007.
31. Kentucky Fried Chicken corporate Web site, **www.kfc.com/about**, December 2007.
32. **www.bluefly.com**; **www.internetretailer .com/top500/**. Vince Veneziani, "Top Online Clothing Stores," *Digital Trends*, online at **http://reviews.digitaltrends.com/guide49.html** (accessed December 28, 2007).
33. Ann Zimmerman, "Target's New Eco-Apparel Line to Debut at Barneys New York," *The Wall Street Journal*, January 2008.
34. Dean Foust, "Just Making an Honest Buck?" *BusinessWeek*, September 19, 2005; Matt Zwolinski, "The Ethics of Price Gouging," *Business Ethics Quarterly*, 18, no. 3 (2008), 347–378.
35. Janet Adamy, "Why Wendy's Finds Vanilla So Exciting," *The Wall Street Journal*, April 6, 2007, B1, B2.
36. David Moin, "High-End Opportunity for Outlets," *Women's Wear Daily*, April 14, 2008.
37. **www.rivertowncrossings.com/html/index4.asp**, February 2006.
38. Calmetta Y. Coleman, "Kohl's Retail Racetrack," *The Wall Street Journal*, March 13, 2001, B1; **www.kohls.com**.
39. "Highland Village: A Supercenter with a View," *Retailing Today*, December 10, 2007.
40. Nick Wingfield, "How Apple's Store Strategy Beat the Odds," *The Wall Street Journal*, May 17, 2006, B1.
41. Sara Silver, "Motorola's New Devices Target Retailers," *The Wall Street Journal*, January 14, 2008, B4.
42. Ann Zimmerman, "Latest Luxury: The Store Concierge," *The Wall Street Journal*, December 20, 2007, B1.
43. **www.fye.com**; **www.myspace.com/fyeevents** (accessed June 19, 2008).
44. "USA Technologies Expands into $4B Office Coffee Industry," **www.usatech.com**, February 18, 2009; **www.verisign.com/verisign-inc/news-and-events/news-archive/us-news-2006/page_039937.html** (accessed October 30, 2007).
45. Samantha Murphy, "Getting iReady: M-Commerce to Pick-Up Steam in United States," *Chain Store Age*, August 2007.
46. Leslie Price, "'Tis the Season for Holiday Pop-Up Shops," **www.racked.com**, November 14, 2007.
47. "New Pop-Up Stores: Wired, illy, Mishka, Toys 'R' Us," **www.newyorkology.com**, November 14, 2007.
48. Ibid.
49. Vanessa O'Connell, "Macy's Plans to Open FAO Schwarz Toy Boutiques in its Stores," *The Wall Street Journal*, May 16, 2008, B1; Khanh T.L. Tran, "Levi's Pops Up at American Rag," *Women's Wear Daily*, April 22, 2008, 18; Bryan Chaffin, "HP to Open Store-Within-a-Store, and It's Good For Apple," **www.themacobserver.com**, August 2003; Sharon Edelson, "Bloomingdale's, Chef Charlie Palmer Join Forces," *Women's Wear Daily*, May 27, 2008.
50. **www.levenger.com**; Peter Sayer, "Apple Opens Largest European Store-in-Store in Paris," *PC World*, June 29, 2007, **http://pcworld.about.com/od/companynews/Apple-opens-largest-European-s.htm**; "Kolo Opens First Manhattan Store-Within-a-Store at Kate's Paperie in Soho," *PRNewswire*, May 30, 2007; Paul Nunes and Brian Johnson, *Mass Affluence: Seven New Rules of Marketing to Today's Consumer* (Cambridge: Harvard Business School Press, 2004) 182.
51. This application exercise is based on the contribution of Amy Hubbert (University of Nebraska at Omaha) to *Great Ideas in Teaching Marketing*, a teaching supplement that accompanies Lamb, Hair, and McDaniel's *Marketing*. Professor Hubbert's entry titled "Discovery of Strategic Retailing Factors" was a winner in the "Best of the Great Ideas in Teaching Marketing" contest conducted in conjunction with the publication of the eighth edition of *Marketing*.
52. **http://www.bestbuy.com**; Mark Tatge, "Fun and Games," *Forbes*, January 12, 2004, 138; Scott Carlson, "Best Buy Extends Weekend Store Hours," *Saint Paul Pioneer Press*, February 17, 2004; Scott Carlson, "Best Buy, Target Stores Score High in Consumer-Approval Survey," *Saint Paul Pioneer Press*, January 30, 2004; Laura Heller, "Connected Life Blooms in the Desert," *DSN Retailing News*, February 9, 2004, 188.

CHAPTER 14

1. Stuart Elliot, "Subway's New Campaign," *New York Times*, February 22, 2003, online; Emily Bryson York, "Subway Can't Stop Jonesing for Jared," **www.adage.com**, February 18, 2008.
2. Matthew Creamer, "Barack Obama and the Audacity of Marketing," *Advertising Age*, November 10, 2008, **www.adage .com** (accessed February 2009); Chris Dannen, "How Obama Won It on the Web," *Fast Company*, November 4, 2008, **www.fastcompany.com** (accessed February 2009); Michael Learmonth, "One Way Media Lost the Election as Cable, Interactive Dominated," *Advertising Age*, November 10, 2008, **www.adage .com** (accessed February 2009); Daniel Lyons and Daniel Stone "President 2.0," *Newsweek*, December 1, 2008, **www.newsweek.com** (accessed February 2009); Al Ries, "What Marketers Can Learn from Obama's Campaign," *Advertising Age*, November 5, 2008, **www .adage.com** (accessed February 2009); Jose Antonio Vargas, "Obama Raised Half a Billion Online," *The Washington Post*, November 20, 2008, **www.washingtonpost.com** (accessed February 2009).
3. Julie Jargon, "Kiwi Goes Beyond Shine in Effort to Step up Sales," *The Wall Street Journal*, December 20, 2007, pB1.
4. Andrew McMains, "'Absolut World' Debuts," ADWEEK, April 27, 2007, pNA, **www.adweek .com**; Jeremy Mullman, "Breaking with Bottle Fires up Absolut Sales," *Advertising Age*, February 18, 2008.
5. Ibid.
6. **www.absolut.com/iaaw/** (accessed June 23, 2008).
7. Mullman, "Breaking with Bottle Fires up Absolut Sales."
8. Stuart Elliott, "In an 'Absolut World,' a Vodka Could Use the Same Ads for More Than 25 Years," *The New York Times*, April 27, 2007.
9. State of the Blogosphere 2008, **http://technorati.com** (accessed February 2009).
10. Jason Fry, "Blog Epitaphs? Get Me Rewrite!" *The Wall Street Journal*, February 27, 2006, online, **www.technorati.com/weblog/2006/02/81.html**.
11. Tania Ralli, "Brand Blogs Capture the Attention of Some Companies," *New York Times*, October 24, 2005, C6.
12. "Blogs Can Offer a Big Advantage to Brands—If They're Honest," *New Age Media*, March 23, 2006,
13. Peter Sanders, "Starwood's Web Log Caters to Loyalty," *The Wall Street Journal*, April 12, 2006, B3.
14. **www.philips.com**.
15. Ibid.
16. Kim Hart, "A Flashy Facebook Page at a Cost to Privacy," *The Washington Post*, June 12, 2008, **www.washingtonpost.com** (accessed February 2008); **www.allfacebook .com/2009/facebook-privacy** (accessed February 2009); Ralph Gross and Alessandro Acquisti, "Information Revelation and Privacy in Online Social Networks (The Facebook Case)," *ACM Workshop on Privacy in the Electronic Society*, November 7, 2007.
17. The AIDA concept is based on the classic research of E. K. Strong, Jr., as theorized in *The Psychology of Selling and Advertising* (New York: McGraw-Hill, 1925) and "Theories of Selling," *Journal of Applied Psychology* 9 (1925), 75–86.

18. Apple Quarterly Sales, **www.apple.com**; Bob Keefe, "During the Holiday Quarter, Apple Sold 14 Million iPods, Which Equates to More Than 100 a Minute," *Atlanta Journal Constitution*, January 11 2006, C-1, and **www .appleinsider. com** (accessed January 2006); **www.apple.com/ pr/library/2008/02/26itunes.html** (accessed February 26, 2008).
19. Thomas E. Barry and Daniel J. Howard, "A Review and Critique of the Hierarchy of Effects in Advertising," *International Journal of Advertising* 9 (1990), 121–135.
20. **http://www.imdb.com/title/tt0382625/**.
21. Louise Kramer, "In a Battle of Toothpastes, It's Information vs. Emotion," *The New York Times*, January 17, 2007, C6.
22. **www.freestuffonline.com**.
23. Bradley Johnson, "Global Marketers," Datacenter: **www.adage.com**, December 8, 2008.
24. Industry Series Reports, Professional, Scientific, and Technical Services, Advertising and Related Services, NAICS code 5184, **www.census.gov.**
25. Bradley Johnson, "Global Marketers," Ad Industry Jobs: Advertising Age Data Center **www.adage.com** (accessed February 2009); Bradley Johnson, "New Source: Media Work Force Sinks to 15-Year Low," **www.adage.com** February 18, 2008.
26. Bradley Johnson, "Global Marketers."
27. Michael R. Solomon, *Consumer Behavior*, 6th ed. (Upper Saddle River, NJ: Prentice Hall, 2004), 275.
28. Mark Levit, "Humor in Advertising," **www.xomreviews.com/marketingsource.com** (accessed March 3, 2008).
29. **www.scion.com**.
30. Natalie Zmuda, "What Went into the Updated Pepsi Logo" *Advertising Age*, October 27, 2008, **www.adage.com** (accessed February 2009); Natalie Zmuda, "Pepsi, Coke Try to Outdo Each Other with Rays of Sunshine," *Advertising Age*, January 19, 2009, **www .adage.com** (accessed February 2009); Jim Edwards, "Pepsi's New $1 Million Logo Looks Like Old Diet Pepsi Logo," *BNET Industries*, October 27, 2008, **http:// industry.bnet.com/advertising/1000270**.
31. Saul Hansell, "The Loneliness of Being AOL," *The New York Times*, February 11, 2008, C8.
32. **www.bp.com**; **www.chevron.com** (accessed February 2009).
33. **www.philipmorrisusa.com** and **www.altria.com** (accessed January 2006).
34. Alex Berenson, "Drug Approved. Is Disease Real?" *The New York Times*, January 14, 2008, A1.
35. Sean Callahan, "Nextel Wins the Race to Sponsor NASCAR," *BtoB* online, July 14, 2003; Rich Thomaselli, "Nextel Link Takes Nascar to New Level," *Advertising Age*, October 27, 2003, S-7.
36. Emily Bryson York, "Brand vs. Brand: Attacks Ads on the Rise" *Advertising Age* October 27, 2008, **www.adage.com** (accessed February 2009).
37. Press release, "FTC Sues Sellers of Weight-Loss Pills for False Advertising," online at **www.ftc.gov/opa/2008/02/zyladex.shtm**, February 8, 2008.
38. Press release, "HP Gets Personal with Super Bowl Ad, Extends PC Marketing Campaign," **www.hp.com**, February 2, 2007; Neal Leavitt, "HP Goes Wide to Get Personal," *iMedia Connection*, June 2006, **www.imediaconnection .com/content/10070.asp**.
39. Tabasco advertisement, *Advertising Age*, October 13, 2003, 8.
40. "SoBe Lizards Take Manhattan by Storm: Unleashing SoBe Life Water Thrillicious Movement in Times Square," *PR Newswire*, February 27, 2008.
41. Vanessa L. Facenda, "Kellogg Injects Some New Energy into Frosted Flakes," **www.brandweek.com**, February 4, 2008.
42. **www.us.powerade.com**.
43. Laura Q. Hughes and Wendy Davis, "Revival of the Fittest," *Advertising Age*, March 12, 2001, 18–19; **www.hersheys.com/chocolateworld/** (accessed January 2006).
44. "What the Heck Were These People Thinking?" **www.tribe.net**, May 17, 2007.
45. **www.adweek.com/aw/national/ article_display.jsp?vnu_content_id=1000475212** and **www.leoburnett.com/ideas/altoids.asp** (accessed January 2006).
46. Press release, Clio Awards, **http://www .clioawards.com/winners/image_pop .cfm?medium_id=4&media_ directory=billboard&website_entry_ id=200729270&is_c=0&image_no=1**
47. Geoffrey A. Fowler, "For P&G in China, It's Wash, Rinse, Don't Repeat," *The Wall Street Journal*, April 7, 2006.
48. Pamela Paul, "Sell It to the Psyche," *Time*, September 29, 2003.
49. Press release, "TNS Media Intelligence Forecasts 4.2 percent Increase in U.S. Advertising Spending for 2008," **www.tns-mi .com/ news/01072008** (accessed February 20, 2008); **http://www.adage.com**.
50. Ibid.
51. Brian Steinberg, "Philips and Time Agree to Keep It Simple," *The Wall Street Journal*, April 21, 2006, B3.
52. Steven Levingston, "Spots on Traditional TV Still the Biggest Show on Super Bowl Sunday," *Washington Post*, Saturday, January 14, 2006.
53. **www.neilsen.com** (accessed February 2009).
54. Matthew Boyle, "Superbucks," *Fortune*, February 4, 2008.
55. Gergana Koleva, "Don't Buy It," *MarketWatch*, January 24, 2008, online.
56. Suzanne Vranica, "TV-Ad Test to Show If Less Is More; NBC Universal's Trial Run Will Measure Effectiveness of Fewer Commercials," *The Wall Street Journal*, April 5, 2006, B3; Maria Aspan, "TiVo Shifts to Help Companies It Once Threatened," *The New York Times*, December 10, 2007.
57. Erin White, "In-Your-Face Marketing: Ad Agency Rents Foreheads," *The Wall Street Journal*, February 11, 2003, B2; **www.commercialalert.org**.
58. Mike Esterl, "Going Outside, Beyond the Billboard," *The Wall Street Journal*, July 21, 2005, B3.
59. Press release, "Virgin Atlantic Airways Takes Off with New Marketing Campaign," *PR Newswire*, February 11, 2008.
60. Ryan Woo, "Adidas Wows Japan with Vertical Soccer Field," *The Wall Street Journal*, September 22, 2003, B1.
61. Virgin Atlantic Airways, **www.theloerieawards.co.za/winners/ search/?show=1** (accessed January 2006).
62. TNS Media Intelligence Forecast, January 7, 2008, online at **www.tns-mi.com/ news/01072008.htm#**; Internet Advertising Bureau, **www.iab.com** (accessed February 2009).
63. Brian Morrissey, "Web Ad Spend to Diversify," **www.adweek.com**, October 11, 2007.
64. David Ho, "Advertisers Ditch Pop-Ups for New Tricks," *Atlanta Journal-Constitution*, December 4, 2005, C-3.
65. Carol Krol, "ComScore: Yellow Book, Google, Facebook are Internet winners of '07," *BtoB* magazine, January 31, 2008.
66. Ibid.
67. Mike Shields, "Google Leads Search Party," **www.adweek.com**, February 18, 2008.
68. Michael McCarthy, "Disney Plans to Mix Ads, Video Games to Target Kids, Teens," *USA Today*, January 15, 2005, B-1.
69. John Gaudiosi, "Mountain Dew Makes MMO More Than Just a Game," *Advertising Age*, January 28, 2008, 21.
70. Social Media Marketing Hits & Misses, **www.oneupweb.com/search-marketing-library/ Oneupweb.07HolidayStudy.Followup.pdf**.
71. Ibid.
72. **www.rss-specifications.com/what-is-rss.htm**.
73. Stuart Elliott, "Science Blogs as a Vehicle for Upscale Ads," *New York Times*, January 10, 2006, C2.
74. Ibid.
75. Mark Glaser, "MediaShift: Your Guide to Podcasts," **www.pbs.org/mediashift/2007/02/ digging_deeperyour_guide_to_po.html**.
76. Press release, "Microsoft Bringing Ads to Shopping Carts," **www.cnn.com/2008/ TECH/01/14/microsoft.shoppingcart.ap/index .html**.
77. **www.bmwusa.com/Standard/Content/ Uniquely/TVAndNewMedia/BMWFilms.aspx** (accessed March 6, 2008).
78. Tobi Elkin, "Coca-Cola's First TiVo Advertainment Airs Today," **www.adage.com**, October 9, 2003.
79. Jack Neff, "Floors in Stores Start Moving," *Advertising Age*, August 20, 2001, 15.
80. **www.altterrain.com/light_projection_ advertising.htm**; "BroadSign Works with Zoom Media & Marketing Digital Signage Network to Manage Advertainment Screens in Popular Nightlife Venues Nationwide," *Internet Wire*, January 22, 2008.
81. Christopher Lawton, "Videogame Ads Attempt Next Level," *The Wall Street Journal*, July 25, 2005, B6; "Video Game Advertising Gets a Boost," *USA Today*, December 16, 2004, B-1; Derek Sooman, "World's First Video Game Advertising Network," October 20, 2004, **www.techspot.com**; **www.massiveincorporated. com** (accessed January 2006); **www.microsoft. com/presspass/press/2006/ may06/05-04-MassiveIncPR.mspx** (accessed May 20, 2006).
82. Digital Fact Pact 2007, *Advertising Age*, **www.adage.com** (accessed February 2009).
83. Paul Korzeniowski, "Cell Phones Emerge as New Advertising Medium," *TechNewsWorld*, November 16, 2005, online at **www.tech-newsworld.com/story/46630.html** (accessed June 23, 2008); Philip John, "Going Mobile: Cell Phone Advertising Leaps Forward by Moving Sideways," *Mediaweek, September 17, 2007*, **www.mediaweek.com** (accessed June 23, 2008).
84. Juan Sanchez, "The Water Horse: Legend of the Deep" *CultureBuzz*, **www.culturebuzz.com/ a_live_advertising_monster_japan_article_1566. html** (accessed February 12, 2008).

85. Sally Beatty, "Ogilvy's TV-Ad Study Stresses 'Holding Power' Instead of Ratings," *The Wall Street Journal*, June 4, 1999, B2, **www.ogilvy.com/viewpoint** (accessed January 2006).
86. Barbara Kiviat, "Chasing the Desi Dollars" *Time*, July 6, 2005, **www.time.com** (accessed February 2009); Coeli Carr, "Ring, Ring, Bollywood Calling", *Time*, February 5, 2009, **www.time.com** (accessed February 2009); Alexandra Alter, "A Passage to Hollywood," *Wall Street Journal*, February 6, 2009, **www.online.wsj.com** accessed February 2009.
87. This application exercise is based on the contribution of Lyn R. Godwin (University of St. Thomas) to *Great Ideas in Teaching Marketing*, a teaching supplement that accompanies Lamb, Hair, and McDaniel's *Marketing*. Professor Godwin's entry titled "Taboo or Not Taboo: That Is the Question" was a runner-up in the "Best of the Great Ideas in Teaching Marketing" contest held in conjunction with the publication of the eighth edition of *Marketing*.
88. This application exercise is based on the contribution of David M. Blanchette (Rhode Island College) to *Great Ideas in Teaching Marketing*, a teaching supplement that accompanies Lamb, Hair, and McDaniel's *Marketing*. Professor Blanchette's entry titled "Applying Semiotics in Promotion" was a runner-up in the "Best of the Great Ideas in Teaching Marketing" contest held in conjunction with the publication of the eighth edition of *Marketing*.
89. Brooks Barnes, "How 'Wicked' Cast Its Spell,"*Wall Street Journal*, October 22, 2005, A1, A4; **http://www.wickedthemusical.com; http://broadwayworld.com**.

CHAPTER 15

1. **http://prweek.com/news/news_story.cfm?ID=239635&site=3** (accessed January 2006).
2. "Satellite Cured Radio Star," **http://news.yahoo.com/**, and "Oprah Signs Three-Year Deal with XM Satellite Radio," **www.philly.com/mld/belleville/business/13837515.htm?source=rss&channel=belleville_ business** (accessed February 2006).
3. Adam Bluestein, "Prime-Time Exposure: How Companies Can Make a Splash in the Big-Money World of TV Product Placement—Without Spending a Dime," *Inc.*, March 2008, 66 (accessed online on June 23, 2008); **www.sourcewatch.org/index.php?title= Product_placement**; Kris Oser, "How a Product Placement Strategy Worked for Yahoo," *AdAge.com*, January 31, 2005, **http://adage.com/latestnews; http:// money.howstuffworks.com/product-placement.htm**; "Product Placement Spending in Media 2005," **www.pqmedia.com** (accessed January 2006).
4. Ibid.
5. Sponsorship Spending, IEG sponsorship, **www.sponsorship.com** (accessed February 2009).
6. **www.sponsorship.com, www.dominos.com, www.hiltonworldwide.com**, and **www.anheuser-busch.com** (accessed January 2006).
7. IEG sponsorship, **www.sponsorship.com**.
8. **www.stjude.org/corporate/0,2516,410_2034_16782,00.html**, **www.thinkbeforeyoupink.org/Pages/InfoMktgCampaigns.html**, and **www.bitc.org.uk/resources/research/research_publications/corp_survey_3.html** (accessed January 2006).
9. **www.goredforwomen.org/our_partners.aspx** (accessed February 17, 2009).
10. **www.stjude.org/corporate/0,2516,410_2034_16782,00.html**, **www.thinkbeforeyoupink.org/Pages/InfoMktgCampaigns.html**, and **www.bitc.org.uk/resources/research/research_publications/corp_survey_3.html** (accessed January 2006).
11. **www.playstation.com** (accessed February 2009).
12. Gavin O'Malley, "CBS Puts *CSI Miami* Twist Online," November 16, 2005, **publications.mediapost.com,** and **www.adverblog.com/archives/cat_integrated_marketing.htm** (accessed January 2006).
13. Ann Zimmerman, "Wal-Mart Enlists Bloggers to Combat Negative News," *The Wall Street Journal*, March 7, 2006, D7.
14. Ibid.
15. "Blogs Can Offer a Big Advantage to Brands—If They're Honest," *New Age Media*, March 23, 2006, 15.
16. Janet Adamy and Richard Gibson, "McDonald's Isn't Slow to React to 'Fast-Food Nation' this Time," *The Wall Street Journal*, April 12, 2006, B3.
17. Zimmerman, "Wal-Mart Enlists Bloggers to Combat Negative News."
18. Annual Report: Industry Report, October 2008, *PROMO Magazine*, **promomagazine.com** (accessed February 2009).
19. Ibid.
20. Robert Passikoff, "Why Starbucks Has Ground to a Halt," *Brandweek*, November 10, 2008, **www.brandweek.com** (accessed February 2009); Andy Serwer, "Howard Schultz Spills the Beans on His Plans to Save the Company He Founded," **www.cnnmoney.com** (accessed February 2009); Emily Bryson York, "Consumers Skip Starbucks for Plain Ole Joe," *Advertising Age*, January 19, 2009 (accessed February 2009); Howard Schultz Transformation Agenda #1, **www.starbucks.com** (accessed February 2009).
21. **www.cms.inmar.com/newsandevents**; Find/SVP, "Cut It Out: Coupons Are on an Upswing," **www.forbes.com** (accessed January 2006).
22. Annual Report: Industry Report October 2008, *PROMO Magazine*, **www.promomagazine.com** (accessed February 2009).
23. **www.kroger.com**; Internet Coupons link at **gs2.coolsavings.com/kroger/index.aspx.**
24. "Papa John's Pushes Dark Knight with Pizza," *PROMO Magazine*, **www.promomagazine.com** (accessed February 2009).
25. Suzanne Vita Palazzo, "Countdown to Kickoff," *Grocery Headquarters*, December 2005, 43.
26. **www.businessweek.com/bwdaily/dnflash/nov2005/nf20051123_4158_db016.htm** (accessed February 2008).
27. Patricia Odell, "Shrek Premiums Drive Big Sales for Kellogg's," *PROMO Magazine*, November 1, 2008, **www.promomgazine.com** (accessed February 2009).
28. **www.tequilaaficionado.com/article.php?sid=336** (accessed February 2008).
29. **www.ecommercetimes.com** accessed January 2008; Industry Report, *PROMO Magazine*, **www.promomagazine.com** (accessed January 2009).
30. **www.crmtrends.com/loyalty.html**, (accessed February 200)8; Matthew Haeberle, "Loyalty Is Dead: Great Experiences, Not Price, Will Create Loyal Customers," *Chain Store Age*, January 2004, 17.
31. **www.creditcards.com/New-Starbucks-Duetto-Visa-Credit-Card.php; www.askmrcreditcard.com/starbucksduettovisa.html** (accessed February 2008).
32. **www.crmtrends.com/loyalty.html** (accessed February 2009).
33. **www.verizonwireless.com** (accessed June 25, 2008).
34. "Grocers' Use of E-Mail Growing," *Promo P&I*, August 2005, **www.promomagazine.com** (accessed February 2009).
35. Peter Sanders, "Starwood's Web Log Caters to Loyalty," *The Wall Street Journal*, April 12, 2006, B3; **www.starwoodhotels.com/corporate/company_info.html** (accessed February 2009).
36. "The Inside Story on Company Blogs: Corporate America May Fear Critical Comments in Public Blogs, but It Isn't Ignoring the Medium's Potential for Improving Internal Communications," *BusinessWeek Online*, February 15, 2006.
37. Patricia Odell, "Dole Uses Blogs and Parties to Promote Fruit Parfaits, January 1, 2009, *PROMO Magazine*, **www.promomagazine.com** (accessed February 2009).
38. **www.hgtv.com/hgtv/pac_ctnt_988/text/0,,HGTV_22056_38648,00.html** (accessed February 2009).
39. **www.marketresearch.com/product/display.asp?productid=1278351&g=1, bloggybiz.com/business-news/use-product-samples-to-boost-your-business-in-2008/** (accessed February 2009). Tim Parry, "Sampling—Teaching Tools," *PROMO Magazine*, **www.promomagazine.com** (accessed January 2008).
40. Industry Report October 2008, PROMO Magazine, **www.promomagazine.com** (accessed February 2009).
41. "Domino's Customers Get Free Coca-Cola Zero," *PROMO Xtra*, December 22, 2005, **www.promomagazine.com** (accessed January 2008).
42. Stephanie Thompson, "Dove Targets the Chocoholic," *Advertising Age*, September 15, 2003, 45.
43. Patricia Odell, "Brands Test Sampling at Meal Assembly Kitchens," *PROMO Magazine*, December 1, 2008, **www.promomagazine.com** (accessed February 2009).
44. Patricia Odell, "Sampling Reigns as Key Method to Drive In-Store Sales," *PROMO Magazine*, online at **www. promomagazine.com** (accessed December 2008); "Dunkin' Donuts Targets Health Clubs with Sampling Program," *PROMO Xtra*, December 28, 2005, **www.promomagazine.com** (accessed February 2009).
45. "Industry report October 2008 *PROMO Magazine*, **www.promomagazine.com** (accessed February 2009).
46. "Point-of-Purchase: $17 Billion," *PROMO Magazine*, October 29, 2001, 3; "In Praise of Promotion," *PROMO Xtra*, **www.promomagazine.com** (accessed January 2009).
47. Stephanie Thompson, "Hershey Sets $30M Push," *Advertising Age*, September 15, 2003, 3, 45.
48. Mickey Khan, "Heinekin Hoaxes Are Real Deal for Building E-mail Names," *DM News Online*, October 7, 2003, **www.heineken.com** (accessed February 2009).

49. **www.marketingsherpa.com/article.html?ident=29788** (accessed February 2009).
50. **www.couponinfonow.com/Couponing/2007trendsoverview.cfm** (accessed February 2009).
51. Patricia Odell, "Lucky Brand Debuts Consumer-Generated Coupon," *PROMO Magazine*, December 10, 2008, **www.promomagazine.com** (accessed February 2009).
52. Roger O. Crocket, "Penny-Pinchers' Paradise," *BusinessWeek*, January 22, 2001, EB12.
53. **www.trade-show-advisor.com/trade-show-survey.html** (accessed February 2008).
54. Michael Beverland, "Contextual Influences and the Adoption and Practice of Relationship Selling in a Business-to-Business Setting: An Exploratory Study," *Journal of Personal Selling & Sales Management*, Summer 2001, 207.
55. Richard Morrison, "The Business Process of Customer Retention and Loyalty," *Customer Interaction Solutions*, October 2001, 4.
56. "The Right Questions and Attitudes Can Beef Up Your Sales, Improve Customer Retention," *Selling*, June 2001, 3.
57. Larry Rigs, "Hit 'Em Where They Work," *Direct*, October 15, 2003, **www.directmag.com**; **www.dmreview.com** (accessed January 2008); "Webcast Essentials," supplement to *CRM Magazine*, 2005.
58. Jean Halliday, "Chrysler Web Offerings Draw Sales Leads," *Automotive News*, December 5, 2005, 22.
59. Alf Nucifora, "Need Leads? Try a Networking Group," *Business News New Jersey*, November 14, 2000, 22; Catherine Seda, "The Meet Market," *Entrepreneur*, August 2004, 68; Jim Dickie, "Is Social Networking an Overhyped Fad or a Useful Tool?" *Destination CRM*, January 21, 2005; Kristina Dell, "What Are Friends For?" *Time*, September 21, 2004.
60. B. Weitz, S. Castleberry, and J. Tanner, *Selling* (Burr Ridge, IL: McGraw-Hill/Irwin, 2007), 196–197.
61. **www.bicworld.com**; **www.BIClink.com**.
62. **www.presentations.com**.
63. **www.chanimal.com**, "Chatrooms" link at the "Overcoming Objections" Web page (link to **www.chanimal.com/html/objections.html**).
64. Troy Korsgaden, "Fine-Tuning Your Agency's Office Systems," **www.roughnotes.com/rnmagazine/2000/june00/06p116.htm**.
65. **www.collegerecruiter.com** (accessed January 2009).
66. This application exercise is based on the contribution of John Ronchetto (University of San Diego) to *Great Ideas in Teaching Marketing*, a teaching supplement that accompanies Lamb, Hair, and McDaniel's *Marketing*. Professor Ronchetto's entry titled "Sales and Customer Service Experiential Journal and Paper" was a winner in the "Best of the Great Ideas in Teaching Marketing" contest held in conjunction with the publication of the eighth edition of *Marketing*.
67. "Ron Popeil, He of the Pocket Fisherman and Spray-On Hair, Has Perfected His Formula for Success: Invent, Market, and Sell with a Passion," *BusinessWeek Online*, October 3, 2005; Brent Hopkins, "How Ron Popeil Invented Himself," *Knight-Ridder/Tribune Business News*, August 31, 2005; Matt Myerhoff, "Infomercial King Sells Company, Ronco Goes Public for Expansion," *Los Angeles Business Journal*, July 29, 2005, 1; **http://snltranscripts.jt.org/75/75qbassamatic.phtml**.

CHAPTER 16

1. Franziska Volckner, "The Dual Role of Price: Decomposing Consumers' Reactions to Price," *Journal of the Academy of Marketing Science*, Fall 2008, 359–377.
2. Ibid.
3. Roland Rust, Christine Moorman, and Peter R. Dickson, "Getting Return on Quality: Revenue Expansion, Cost Reduction, or Both?" *Journal of Marketing*, October 2002, 7–24.
4. "DaimlerChrysler's Freightliner Puts New Chief at the Wheel," *The Wall Street Journal*, May 29, 2001, B4.
5. "AMD Once Again Hits the Roaring 20s," **www.clnetnews.com**, January 24, 2006; Tom Krazit, "Intel Gained Back Some Chip Market Share on the Heels of Advanced Micro Devices' Abysmal First Quarter," ZDNet News (accessed online April 24, 2007).
6. Tammo H. A. Bijmolt, Harald J. van-Heerde, and Rik G. M. Pieters, "New Empirical Generalizations on the Determinants of Price Elasticity," *Journal of Marketing Research*, May 2005, 141–156; Christian Homburg, Wayne Hoyer, and Nicole Koschate, "Customers' Reactions to Price Increases: Do Customer Satisfaction and Perceived Motive Fairness Matter?" *Journal of the Academy of Marketing Science*, Winter 2005, 35–49; Gadi Fibich, Arieh Gavious, and Oded Lowengart, "The Dynamics of Price Elasticity of Demand in the Presence of Reference Price Effects," *Journal of the Academy of Marketing Science*, Winter 2005, 66–78.
7. "Summer Concerts Try New Tactics to Fill Seats," *The Wall Street Journal*, May 19, 2005, D1.
8. "In a Tech Backwater, a Profit Fortress Rises," *The Wall Street Journal*, July 10, 2007, A1. Reprinted with permission of *The Wall Street Journal*, © Dow Jones & Company, Inc. All Rights Reserved Worldwide.
9. "Seeking Perfect Prices, CEO Tears up the Rules," *The Wall Street Journal*, March 27, 2007, A1, A16.
10. Michael Mendano, "Priced to Perfection," **www.business2.com**, March 6, 2001, 40–41.
11. "The Power of Optimal Pricing," *Business 2.0*, September 2002, 68–70.
12. "What the Traffic Will Bear," *Forbes*, July 3, 2008, 69.
13. Ibid.
14. Anne Kadet, "Buyer Beware," *Smart Money*, May 2006, 90–95.
15. Ibid.
16. "Behave," *Marketing News*, September 15, 2008, 13–15.
17. Ibid.
18. Raymund Flandez, "Voluntary Pricing Lets Small Eateries Give—and Get Back," *The Wall Street Journal*, August 28, 2007, B8.
19. "Wal-Mart Launches Toy Price War," *The Wall Street Journal*, October 9, 2008, B1; also see: Harald J. VanHeerde, Els Gijsbrechts, and Koen Pauwels, "Winners and Losers in a Major Price War," *Journal of Marketing Research*, October 2008, 499–518.
20. See Joseph Cannon and Christian Homburg, "Buyer-Supplier Relationships and Customer Firm Costs," *Journal of Marketing*, January 2001, 29–43.
21. "How Shopping Bots Really Work," *MSN-Money*, July 11, 2005, **http://moneycentral.msn.com**.
22. Florian Zettelmeyer, Fiona Scott Morton, and Jorge Silva-Risso, "How the Internet Lowers Prices: Evidence from Matched Survey and Auto Transaction Data," *Journal of Marketing Research*, May 2006, 168–181.
23. *2007 Internet Crime Report* (Washington, DC: FBI) 1–17.
24. Sridhar Moorthy and Xubing Zhang, "Price Matching by Vertically Differentiated Retailers: Theory and Evidence," *Journal of Marketing Research*, May 2006, 156–167.
25. Monika Kukar-Kinney, Rockney Walters, and Scott MacKenzie, "Consumer Responses to Characteristics of Price-Matching Guarantees: The Moderating Role of Price Consciousness," *Journal of Retailing*, April 2007, 211–221.
26. "Wal-Mart Puts the Squeeze on Food Costs," *Fortune*, June 9, 2008, 16.
27. Ibid.
28. Ibid.
29. R. Chandrashekaran, "The Implications of Individual Differences in Reference to Price Utilization for Designing Effective Price Communications," *Journal of Business Research*, August 2001, 85–92.
30. Katherine Lemon and Stephen Nowlis, "Developing Synergies between Promotions and Brands in Different Price-Quality Tiers," *Journal of Marketing Research*, May 2002, 171–185. Also see Valerie Taylor and William Bearden, "The Effects of Price on Brand Extension Evaluations: The Moderating Role of Extension Similarity," *Journal of the Academy of Marketing Science*, Spring 2002, 131–140; and Raj Sethuraman and V. Srinivasan, "The Asymmetric Share Effect: An Empirical Generalization on Cross-Price Effects," *Journal of Marketing Research*, August 2002, 379–386.
31. Merrie Brucks, Valarie Zeithaml, and Gillian Naylor, "Price and Brand Name as Indicators of Quality Dimensions for Consumer Durables," *Journal of the Academy of Marketing Science*, Summer 2000, 359–374; Wilford Amaldoss and Sanjay Jain, "Pricing of Conspicuous Goods: A Competitive Analysis of Social Effects," *Journal of Marketing Research*, February 2005, 30–42; and also see Margaret Campbell, "Says Who?! How the Source of Price Information and Affect Influence Perceived Price (UN)fairness," *Journal of Marketing Research*, May 2007, 261–271.
32. Volckner, "The Dual Role of Price."
33. Ibid.
34. Christina Passariello, "Beauty Fix: Behind L'Oreal's Makeover in India: Going Upscale . . . When Cheap Shampoo Didn't Sell, Company Tapped the Rising Class," *The Wall Street Journal*, July 13, 2007, A1, A8.
35. Keith Chrzan, "An Overview of Pricing Research," *Quirk's Marketing Research Review*, July/August 2006, 24–29.
36. Kent Monroe and Jennifer Cox, "Pricing Practices That Endanger Profits," *Marketing Management*, September/October 2001, 42–46.
37. Thomas T. Nagle and George Cressman, "Don't Just Set Prices, Manage Them," *Marketing Management*, November/December 2002, 29–33; Jay Klompmaker, William H. Rogers, and Anthony Nygren, "Value, Not Volume," *Marketing Management*, June 2003, 45–48; Alison Wellner,

"Boost Your Bottom Line by Taking the Guesswork Out of Pricing," *Inc.*, June 2005, 72–82.
38. George Cressman, "Reaping What You Sow," *Marketing Management*, March/April 2004, 34–40.
39. "Why P&G's Smile Is So Bright," *BusinessWeek*, August 12, 2002, 58–60.
40. "Out-Discounting the Discounter," *BusinessWeek*, May 10, 2004, 78–79. An interesting article on shoppers who use penetration pricing to their advantage is Edward J. Fox and Stephen J. Hoch, "Cherry-Picking," *Journal of Marketing*, January 2005, 46–62.
41. "One Store's Old Food Is Other's Bread and Butter," *The Wall Street Journal*, February 22, 2008, B1–B2.
42. "The Irrationalities of Product Pricing," *The Wall Street Journal*, September 22, 2008, R2.
43. "As China's Trade Clout Grows, So Do Price-Fixing Accusations," *The Wall Street Journal*, February 10, 2006, A1, A16.
44. "Ex-British Air Manager Sentenced to Jail," *The Wall Street Journal*, October 1, 2008, B2.
45. Ibid.
46. "Fresh Del Monte Settles Banana Price-Fixing Suits for More than $3 Million," *Palm Beach Daily Business Review*, June 28, 2007.
47. "Doctor Group Settle Charges," *San Diego Union-Tribune*, May 31, 2003, C-3.
48. "How Driving Prices Lower Can Violate Antitrust Statutes," *The Wall Street Journal*, January 24, 2004, A1, A11.
49. "Price-Fixing Makes Comeback After Supreme Court Ruling," *The Wall Street Journal*, August 18, 2008, A1, A12.
50. Ibid.
51. Ibid.
52. "Antitrust Trade and Practice; Predatory Bidding Mirrors Predatory Pricing," *New York Law Journal*, March 20, 2007, 3.
53. Ibid.; Alison Lo, John Lynch, and Richard Staelin, "How to Attract Consumers by Giving Them the Short End of the Stick," *Journal of Marketing Research*, February 2007, 128–141.
54. This application exercise is based on the contribution of Vaughn C. Judd (Auburn University, Montgomery) to Great Ideas in Teaching Marketing, a teaching supplement and accompanies Lamb, Hair, and McDaniel's *Marketing*. Professor Judd's entry, titled "Analyzing the Price-Quality Relationship," was a winner in the "Best of the Great Ideas in Teaching Marketing" contest held in conjunction with the publication of the eighth edition of *Marketing*.
55. **http://www.hd.net/; http://www.DirectTV.com; http://www.Adelphia.com; http://www.timewarner.com**; Leigh Gallagher, "The Big Picture," *Forbes*, March 1, 2004, 78; Allison Roman, "All HD All the Time: Mark Cuban's HDNet Is Typically Offered on Operators' Premium Tier," *Broadcasting & Cable*, January 26, 2004, 20; Meredith Amdur, "New Definition at TW; Cuban's HDNet Lands Carriage with Cabler," *Daily Variety*, December 18, 2003, 6.

I NAME, COMPANY, AND BRAND INDEX

Note: Locators followed by "ex" indicate exhibits.

F

G

SUBJECT INDEX

F

G